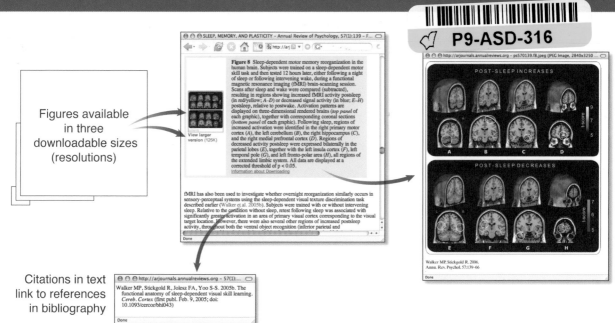

Figures available in three downloadable sizes (resolutions)

Citations in text link to references in bibliography

References in Annual Reviews article bibliography link out to sources of cited articles online

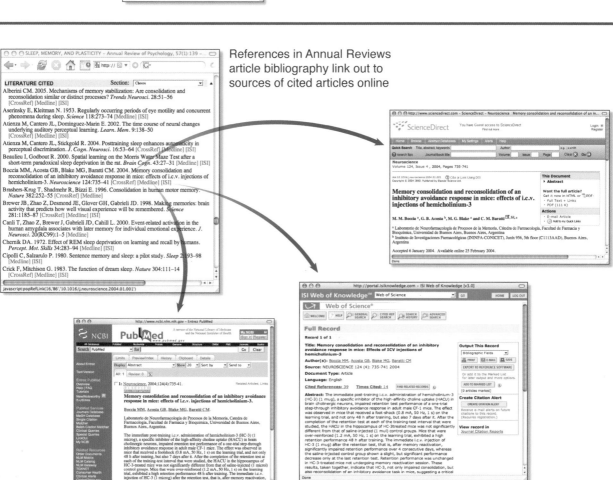

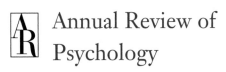

Annual Review of
Psychology

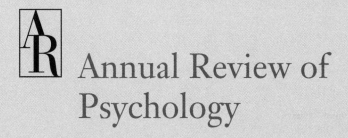

Annual Review of Psychology

Volume 61, 2010

Susan T. Fiske, *Editor*

Princeton University

Daniel L. Schacter, *Associate Editor*

Harvard University

Robert J. Sternberg, *Associate Editor*

Tufts University

www.annualreviews.org • science@annualreviews.org • 650-493-4400

Annual Reviews

4139 El Camino Way • P.O. Box 10139 • Palo Alto, California 94303-0139

Annual Reviews
Palo Alto, California, USA

International Standard Serial Number: 0066-4308
International Standard Book Number: 978-0-8243-0261-0
Library of Congress Catalog Card Number: 50-13143

TYPESET BY APTARA
PRINTED AND BOUND BY MALLOY INCORPORATED, ANN ARBOR, MICHIGAN

Preface

Psychology is a hub science. Our enviable position is brought home to us every year, when our top-notch Production Editor, Lisa Dean, requests lists of related Annual Review articles from neighboring Annual Review journals, such as *Neuroscience*, *Clinical Psychology*, *Sociology*, *Public Health*, *Political Science*, and *Anthropology*. (These "Other Reviews of Interest" appear in the print and online versions of each volume.) Annual Review editors are wannabe polymaths, so our first instinct is to list every review in our neighboring journals as an article related to our field. But by this premise, one would have to read almost an entire Annual Review volume every week—or several reviews daily—just to keep up. Theoretically appealing, but still. We all have day jobs.

Just in time, we have scientific maps to guide our attention. In the consensus of knowledge networks, psychological sciences sit between neurosciences and social sciences (Klavans & Boyack 2009, figure 4), with links to medicine and health sciences (figure 5). Some maps include a weak link to humanities, but Annual Reviews and other media do not often count them as sciences. Otherwise, we mediate between our neighbor disciplines.

To be sure, all sciences link to other sciences, especially in these interdisciplinary times. Psychological sciences qualify as a hub for two reasons (Boyack et al. 2005). One is the sheer density of journals, making our field one of a dozen or so qualifying as major disciplines in a bibliometric analysis. Another reason is the rich linkage of our field to adjoining fields and subfields; many major fields are more isolated than we are. Keep up with the psychology hub, and link to the wide world of science.

> Susan T. Fiske, Princeton
> Daniel L. Schacter, Cambridge
> Robert J. Sternberg, Medford

LITERATURE CITED

Boyack KW, Klavans R, Börner K. 2005. Mapping the backbone of science. *Scientometrics* 64:351–74

Klavans R, Boyack KW. 2009. Toward a consensus map of science. *J. Am. Soc. Inf. Sci. Technol.* 60:455–76

**Annual Review of
Psychology**

Volume 61, 2010

Contents

Errata

An online log of corrections to *Annual Review of Psychology* articles may be found at http://psych.annualreviews.org/errata.shtml

Related Articles

Love in the Fourth Dimension

Ellen Berscheid

Department of Psychology, University of Minnesota, Minneapolis, Minnesota 55455;
email: bersc001@umn.edu

Annu. Rev. Psychol. 2010. 61:1–25

The *Annual Review of Psychology* is online at
psych.annualreviews.org

This article's doi:
10.1146/annurev.psych.093008.100318

Key Words

companionate love, romantic love, compassionate love, adult
attachment, temporal course, interpersonal relationships

Abstract

Psychologists' efforts to understand love began in the mid-twentieth
century. The fact that they continue apace in the twenty-first century
reflects increased awareness of the importance of love to understanding
relationship phenomena and acknowledgment that an understanding of
love has yet to be achieved. This article (*a*) describes one source of increased recognition that the present confusions surrounding love must
be transcended if progress is to be made in understanding many relationship phenomena; (*b*) discusses the failure to explicate the love construct,
which constitutes the major obstacle to the study of love phenomena;
(*c*) discusses the need for a temporal model of love in relationships; and
(*d*) suggests that it is important to consider the presence or absence of
four types of love, each of which appears to be associated with different
causal conditions and thus is likely to have a different temporal course
as an adult relationship moves through time.

Contents

INTRODUCTION

Some anthropologists and social psychologists maintain that love is a cultural universal. They believe that at least one variety of love, romantic love, is likely to have appeared in all human groups at all times in human history (see Hatfield & Rapson 2002). As evidenced by ancient human artifacts, it is clear that love, in one form or another, has always been on people's minds. It also has been on some of the finest scholarly minds of every age, with Plato's Symposium, circa 400 BC (Waterfield 2001), being one of the earliest and most often cited examples. Until the second half of the twentieth century, however, and excepting Freud's scant remarks about "normal" as opposed to "neurotic" adult love (1912/1963), psychologists were not among those minds.

The absence of any serious psychological treatment of love had become obvious to many by the mid-twentieth century, and psychologists were scolded by one of their own for neglecting the discipline's "particular obligation" to further its understanding (Maslow 1954, p. 235). At the time Maslow was castigating psychologists for their neglect of a phenomenon central to people's lives, two of psychology's most talented theoreticians and empirical researchers, Harry Harlow (e.g., 1958) and John Bowlby (e.g., 1969), were, independently, endeavoring to fill the void. At that time, too, the subdiscipline of social psychology was coming into its own. Fritz Heider, whose classic work, *The Psychology of Interpersonal Relations* (1958), was highly influential in shaping the developing field, observed that "Sentiments are such an integral part of interpersonal relations that one hardly need explain why they are to be discussed in a book such as this" (p. 174). By the late 1960s, sufficient social psychological theory and research on the conditions that "attract" one person to another (e.g., as evidenced by an expression of "liking" for that person or a desire to interact with him or her) had been conducted to permit their compilation in the first edition of the *Handbook of Social Psychology* (Lindzey & Byrne 1968) and also in a thin book titled *Interpersonal Attraction* (Berscheid & Walster 1969). The former had nothing to say about love and the latter very little.

Reflecting the prevailing theoretical approach to attraction—social exchange theory, which posits that people exchange rewards and punishments in their interactions—each chapter of *Interpersonal Attraction* focused on a kind of reward shown to generate attraction. The last chapter departed from the pattern. Titled "Courtship and Love" and a mere nine pages in length, it began by saying that "little experimental research exists to tell us about the antecedents of a strong form of interpersonal attraction—romantic love" (p. 105). This apologia was telling in at least three respects: First, it reflected the emphasis on experimentation—as opposed to survey, interview, observational, and other data collection methods—at a time when fledgling social psychology was eager to be accepted by "real" psychologists who wore white coats and experimented with rats. Second, it reflected the fact that of the many varieties of love, it was romantic love that was, and still is, of primary interest. And, third, it reflected the belief of most attraction researchers that romantic love was "a strong form of attraction."

Underlying the belief that romantic love was a strong form of attraction was the assumption that such mild forms of attraction as liking and such strong forms as romantic love were simply different points along the same quantitative continuum of positive sentiment and, therefore, the causal determinants of liking and love were the same, differing only in their magnitude. The causal forces that could be generated only weakly in the laboratory to produce liking were believed to be amplified sufficiently in the "real world" to sometimes produce romantic love.

The assumption that the same causes that produce liking also produce romantic love soon came under attack. Rubin (1970) published a romantic Love Scale, partially validating that scale by showing that responses to it and to his Liking Scale were only moderately correlated. Berscheid & Walster (1974), too, had been having their doubts that more and more liking led to anything but a whole lot of liking. They itemized several apparent differences between liking and romantic love that suggested they had qualitatively different determinants and presented their own theoretical stab at causally differentiating the two. The first edition's nine-page chapter grew to two chapters in the second edition of *Interpersonal Attraction* (1978), one titled "Companionate Love" and the other "Romantic Love." The only difference between companionate love and liking was said to be the intensity of the liking (more in the case of companionate love) and whom the liking was for (someone with whom one's life was "deeply intertwined" as opposed to a "casual acquaintance" in the case of liking). Thus it was proposed that liking and companionate love were on the same causal continuum but that romantic love was a causally different animal.

Efforts by psychologists and other social scientists to understand love steadily increased in sophistication and intensity throughout the remainder of the twentieth century as theory and research directed toward an understanding of close relationships blossomed (e.g., Kelley et al. 1983/2002). Psychology is a major contributor to the multidisciplinary field of relationship science (Berscheid 1999), for psychologists have increasingly recognized that virtually all human behavior takes place in the context of relationships with others (Reis et al. 2000). The overriding theme of the omnipresent interpersonal relationship context is, as Heider declared, sentiment, positive and negative, just as it is toward all in the human's environment (Osgood 1969).

LOVE AND MARRIAGE

The interpersonal relationship that has historically captured the lion's share of social scientists' attention is the marital relationship, the nucleus of the family, widely believed to be the fundamental unit of society. Sociologists, the first to systematically attack questions concerning the marital relationship, focused primarily on issues concerning the *stability* of marriages. Because the spouses' *satisfaction* with their relationship was assumed to be the prime determinant of marital stability, identification of the factors that influence marital satisfaction became the aim of myriad investigations. From the beginning, spouses' sentiments toward each other were viewed as important in predicting marital satisfaction and stability—but the prediction was not what we might now imagine.

Early on, sociologist Ernest Burgess (1926) fingered romantic love as the likely culprit for much marital unhappiness in his influential article "The Romantic Impulse and Family Disorganization." The first few decades of the twentieth century had seen a gradual shift in the social definition and basis for marriage—from what has become known as "traditional" marriage as a practical social and economic alliance to "companionate" marriage in which the sentiments aroused by the partner are of prime importance (see Amato & Irving 2006). Many sociologists subsequently followed Burgess's lead. For example, in 1938 and again in its mid-century second edition, a classic marriage and family text declared that:

> …romantic love has been a disturbing, upsetting source of change in the marriage relation, incompatible with the settled, ordered living ultimately required of a family. Wherever romantic love is valued highly, marriages are generically unstable. (Waller & Hill 1951, p. 362)

Shortly thereafter, and at the same time Maslow, Harlow, and Bowlby were decrying the neglect of love in psychology, sociologist William Goode (1959) argued that there existed a "romantic love complex" in the United States—"an ideological prescription that falling in love is a highly desirable basis of courtship and marriage" (p. 42)—and that it deserved serious sociological attention. His contention that romantic love had become strongly institutionalized was subsequently substantiated by another sociologist, William Kephart (1967), who asked a large sample of young men and women if they would marry a person who possessed all the qualities they desired in a spouse if they were not "in love" with that person. "No," said twothirds of the men and about one-quarter of the women. By the mid-1980s, at least 80% of both men and women said that they would not marry a person with whom they were not in love even if he or she had all the other qualities they desired in a mate (Simpson et al. 1986). These figures continued to increase, and the importance of romantic love in the contraction of marriage is now found in many other cultures and countries as well (e.g., Levine et al. 1995).

Burgess's speculation that there was a link between the "romantic impulse" and "family disorganization" had the appearance of being confirmed in the concurrent rise of romantic love as the *sine qua non* for marriage and the divorce rate, the latter beginning in the late 1950s and continuing to increase through the next several decades. As more and more marriages tottered on the brink of dissolution, people cried out for help, but many practicing psychologists, as well as others in the helping professions, were not prepared to assist. Complaints that practice in marital therapy had outstripped its theoretical and research base were frequently heard, both inside and outside the field. Reviewing research, theory, and clinical practice in marital and family therapy over the decade of the 1960s, Olson (1970) concluded that "The professional gaps between therapists, theorists and researchers have not been effectively bridged so there is a dearth of research or empirical facts to build upon" (p. 270).

Research psychologists then began to enter the picture in earnest, joining their sociological colleagues and those in the developing hybrid field of marital and family studies. Over the next several decades, research on marital satisfaction and stability steadily increased in both quantity and in methodological and analytical sophistication (see Karney & Bradbury 1995). Much of this research focused on the disturbing results of a longitudinal study begun by Burgess and Wallin, in the last phase of which couples were interviewed up to 20 years after their initial interviews (see Pineo 1961). Over their two decades of marriage, spouses' satisfaction had declined, their intimacy had lessened (e.g., kissing, confiding), and shared activities, including sexual intercourse, had diminished.

Many cross-sectional studies subsequently corroborated the decline in satisfaction over time with the exception that a slight increase was sometimes seen in long-duration marriages. The so-called U-curve of marital satisfaction became a staple in textbooks, holding out hope for those who persevered. However, longitudinal studies, which have grown in number (see Bradbury 1998), have revealed that the slight but significant increase in happiness in long-term marriages was a mirage produced by cross-sectional methodology; that is, highly dissatisfied couples do not appear in the long-term marriage cohort because they have already divorced or separated, leaving those who were more satisfied all along to produce the appearance of an "increase" in satisfaction. It now appears that as a marriage moves through time, spouses' satisfaction with it continues to decline as far as the eye can see and researchers can measure (e.g., VanLaningham et al. 2001), although most spouses who remain married still exhibit moderate satisfaction.

Rogge & Bradbury (2002) observe that because the causes of the decline are not yet clear, "...a large proportion of current marital research seeks to explain how couples can begin their marriages with high levels of satisfaction and then, with surprising regularity, grow to become unhappy in a relatively short period of time" (p. 228). Until recently, explanations for the decline focused almost exclusively on the inevitability of conflict and the negative sentiments that accompany it. Accordingly, therapies for distressed marriages have concentrated heavily on increasing the couple's conflict resolution and communication skills.

The assumption that conflict is the sole, or even the prime, cause of marital dissatisfaction has begun to be questioned. Huston and his associates (2001), who followed couples longitudinally from the time they were newlyweds up to 14 years later, found that whereas changes in the marriage over the first two years did indeed foreshadow the marriage's fate, little support was found for the claim that increasing negativity early in the marriage forecasts later failure; rather, what appeared to distinguish couples headed for divorce from those whose marriages remained intact appeared to be disillusionment, "as reflected in an abatement of love, a decline in overt affection, a lessening of the conviction that one's spouse is responsive, and an increase in ambivalence" (p. 237). Recognition is increasing among marital relationship researchers "...that enduringly happy relationships involve more than just the absence of antagonism and strife—affectionate and supportive behaviors are also important" (Caughlin & Huston 2006, p. 132).

How Love Became Forgotten

The almost exclusive focus on conflict as the source of couple distress and marital failure led at least one practitioner to complain that love had become a "forgotten variable" in marital therapy (Roberts 1992) and researchers

Gable & Reis (2001) to ask "Why has relationship research emphasized the causal antecedents and consequences of negative processes such as conflict...to the exclusion of more positive processes?" (p. 189). One answer is that it simply seemed eminently reasonable that the negative sentiments associated with conflict—widely viewed as inevitable in any close, interdependent relationship—should be the principal cause of dissatisfaction, thus obviating the need to look further afield.

Other, less obvious, factors have contributed to the relative neglect of the role of love and other positive sentiments in studies of relationship satisfaction and stability. For example, few investigators have assessed positive and negative sentiment separately in couples' relationships, thereby rendering it impossible to determine the extent to which each independently influences the relationship. Bipolar self-report scales (e.g., the anchor "dislike" or "dissatisfied" at one pole and "like" or "satisfied" at the other) are the usual method of assessing sentiment in attraction and marital satisfaction research despite ample evidence that positive affect and negative affect are relatively independent, not bipolar opposites (e.g., Watson et al. 1999) and thus require two unipolar scales for assessment, as a study by Ellis & Malamuth (2000) illustrates. These investigators found that the "love" and "anger/upset" systems in dating couples were largely independent in the classes of information partners tracked. Differences across relationships in love covaried with differences in facilitation of the partner but not in interference, and differences in anger/upset during conflict covaried with differences in interference but not facilitation.

That positive and negative sentiment may sit side by side in a relationship, each taking center stage at different times and in different degrees and sometimes interacting (see Huston & Chorost 1994), was clear in an early study conducted by Braiker & Kelley (1979). Surprised that when young married couples recounted their courtships they "often referred to feelings of love and belonging while simultaneously describing instances of conflict and ambivalence"

(p. 148), Braiker and Kelley subsequently found that love and conflict were orthogonal characteristics of the couples' growth toward marriage: "There appears to be no relation between the amount of interdependence and love in a relationship, on the one hand, and the amount of negative affect and open conflict, on the other hand" (p. 152). This appears to be true of other close relationships as well. For example, Collins & Laursen (2000) conclude from their review of parent-adolescent and adolescent peer relationships that "conflicts are neither inimical to closeness nor inevitably harmful to either the relationships or the partners in it" (p. 65).

An exception to the use of self-report bipolar assessments of sentiment are studies in which the couples are observed as they interact, often as they discuss a conflict, for it is customary for the partners' oral and nonverbal interaction behaviors to be coded for both positive and negative sentiment. This practice allowed Gottman & Levenson (2000) to conclude that although negativity was predictive of earlier divorces, "The absence of positive affect and not the presence of negative affect. . . was most predictive of later divorcing" (p. 743). In addition, it allowed Gottman (1999) to conclude that a ratio of 5 positive behaviors to 1 negative behavior seems to be characteristic of stable marriages and that "Most marital conflict is about 'perpetual problems' that never get resolved; what matters most is the *affect* around which the problems don't get resolved" (p. 110, emphasis added).

Another contributing factor to the neglect of the role of positive sentiment in marital relationships is that little attention has been paid to ex-spouses' retrospective reports of the reasons for the demise of their marriages—or even practitioners' reports of the problems they confront in attempting to repair marriages. Ex-spouses often mention the "death of love" as the principal cause of their divorces and separations (e.g., Gigy & Kelly 1992, Kayser 1993), and marital therapists, when asked to name the factors most damaging to the relationship, cite "lack of loving feelings" (Whisman et al. 1997). Therapists also name "lack of loving feelings" as one of the

two most difficult problems to treat (alcoholism being the other).

Yet another source of the neglect of the role of positive sentiment in long-term close relationships concerns the subject of this article. Marital researchers Caughlin & Huston (2006) express dismay that despite the fact that most people today contract marriage on the basis of love, "there are shockingly few studies that have assessed constructs such as affectionate behavior and love over time in a marriage" (p. 139). At least part of the neglect must be attributed to the confusing love literature that has not lent itself to the task of tracing the temporal course of love in an ongoing relationship.

THE PROBLEM WITH LOVE

When it comes to the word "love," we all have much in common with Humpty Dumpty (Carroll 1865/1965). When Alice stepped through the looking glass and encountered Humpty, she complained that she didn't know what he meant when he used a word because he used it in so many different ways. Humpty's scornful reply was that each time he used the word it meant just exactly what he chose it to mean, neither more nor less. But, Alice protested, "'The question is whether you *can* make words mean so many different things'" (p. 94). If the word is "love," we can. And we do.

The Polysemous Nature of the Word "Love"

Linguists recognize that it is rare that any word has only one meaning; all human language is polysemous (D'Andrade 1989). That the word "love" is polysemous in the extreme is often lamented by love scholars. Murstein (1988), for example, complained that "Love is an Austro-Hungarian Empire uniting all sorts of feelings, behaviors, and attitudes, sometimes having little in common, under the rubric 'love'" (p. 33). One word, "love," must serve many different purposes and carry many different meanings. "'When I make a word do a lot of work like that,' Humpty told Alice, 'I always pay it extra'" (Carroll 1965, p. 95). Because there isn't enough gold in Fort Knox to pay "love" what it deserves, it gets its revenge in myriad misunderstandings in our daily lives and in frustrating love scholars.

How many meanings does the word "love" have? Legion. For example, Fehr & Russell (1991) asked college students to list as many types of love as came to mind. After collapsing syntactic variants, 216 kinds of love were named and, of those, 93 were mentioned by more than one person. Love always has a target, and the targets of many types of love named were objects (e.g., love of money). Love for a person usually occurs within a relationship, and several types of love named simply referred to the type of relationship in which the respondents believed a certain kind of love typically appears (e.g., "maternal love").

Love scholars have been as zealous as students in listing types of love—or, perhaps more accurately, creating different names for kinds of love that may or may not be different in any way that matters. The array is daunting, as illustrated in Sternberg & Barnes's (1988) anthology of contemporary theories of love, in which many of the authors presented their own love taxonomies. Rubin's (1988) preface and critique of the volume said what needed to be said then and which, regrettably, remains true now:

> . . .the science of love is still in its infancy. One sign of this immaturity is the fact that investigators represented in this volume share so little of a common vocabulary. Love researchers are saddled with the problem that "love" means different things to different people. . . . Because of this problem, many of the contributors to this volume have developed their own taxonomies of love. Each categorizing scheme differs from the next, and there are no ready translation rules from one chapter's formulation to another's. Just as partners with different views of love may find themselves talking past each other. . .I suspect that some of the contributors to this volume may find it difficult to relate to others' perspectives. (pp. viii–ix)

Rubin went on to advise that "Love researchers might do well to move toward a more commonvocabulary" (p. ix), but the new edition of this volume (Sternberg & Weis 2006) reveals that this is a feat easier said than done. The vocabulary of love is as diverse as ever, perhaps even more so, as several biologically tinged theories influenced by the evolutionary perspective in psychology have appeared. Whereas most evolutionary theories of love focus on mate selection and sex differences in desired attributes of a mate, some now address love directly and emphasize the presumed evolutionary function of certain varieties of love in furthering species survival (e.g., Kenrick 2006).

EXPLICATING LOVE

Some suspect that the polyglot nature of the love domain reflects the "softness" of psychological science in general and relationship science in particular. However, the problem of explicating—or making more exact—a word often used in a vague way in everyday language or in an early stage of scientific language often is an important stage in the development of a science and of mathematics, as philosopherof-science Carnap (1953) discusses and illustrates with the word "probability": "The history of the theory of probability is the history of attempts to find an explication for the prescientific concept of probability" (p. 441). Carnap's description of the "bewildering multiplicity" of meanings, of definitional attempts, and of classificatory solutions associated with the word "probability" resembles the history of the study of "love." Carnap conducted a painstaking conceptual analysis of the meanings in use, concluded that "probability" was used to refer to two fundamentally different concepts, and demonstrated that this was the source of many heated controversies in probability theory.

Love in the Abstract

Some researchers have tried to transcend the messy particulars and define love on an abstract level, allying love with constructs associated with established bodies of knowledge in the hope they would shed their light on love. Because most theory and research on love has been conducted by social psychologists and because *attitude* is the social psychologists' construct of choice, it is not surprising that many love scholars define love as an attitude—or a predisposition to think, feel, and behave in positive ways toward another (e.g., Hendrick & Hendrick 1986). Much attraction theory and research has usefully applied attitude theory and research to the predisposition to like another (e.g., see Berscheid & Reis 1998), but the application has not been as successful with love, perhaps because some forms of love do not seem to always follow the reward-punishment principles on which attitude theory and research rest.

As opposed to an attitude, most laypersons and some love scholars prefer to think of love as an *emotion*. After surveying over 200 emotion words, Shaver et al. (1987) found that the single word that students were most confident represented an emotion was "love"—even more confident than that "terror" or "elation" are emotions. Whether love qualifies as an emotion depends on how one defines emotion and, unfortunately for love scholars, the emotion literature, like the love literature, is littered with definitions. Emotion theorists Russell & Barrett (1999) observe that "The emotion experts do not agree on what is an emotion and what is not" (p. 805) and conclude, as have several other emotion theorists, that "Emotion is too broad a class of events to be a single scientific category" (p. 805). They observe that theorizing about emotion centers on what they call "prototypical emotional episodes," which are usually thought of as discrete categories (e.g., fear, anger, love). Because prototypical emotion episodes "are complex packages of components, it is possible to organize them in different ways with each component of the episode providing a separate basis for a taxonomic structure" (p. 807). The numerous taxonomic structures associated with love may be an illustration. In short, emotion theorists have their own problems and are not yet in a position to help love scholars.

The Psychometric Approach

In the 1980s, social psychologists began to use psychometric techniques (e.g., principal components analysis) to develop taxonomies of love by identifying the dimensions that underlie people's descriptions of their experiences in romantic relationships. It should be noted that the term "romantic relationship" is used loosely (see Berscheid & Regan 2005). In addition to marital relationships, the term usually includes current or past dating relationships despite the fact that most college students, who are the respondents in most psychometric studies of love, would be hesitant to describe all of their present and past dating relationships as "romantic" or "loving" (e.g., as opposed to "something to do on a Saturday night"). Thus, the term generally refers to any opposite-sex (or same-sex) relationship in which there is at least some *potential* for strong positive sentiment and sexual attraction although such feelings may not *presently* characterize the relationship and may *never* characterize the relationship. In other words, there may be no romantic love, or any other kind of love, in a "romantic relationship," as the term is used as the instructed referent for responding to items on a love scale.

Robert Sternberg and his colleagues were among the first to use the psychometric approach to love (e.g., Sternberg & Grajek 1984). Consideration of previous theory and research on love and the results of analyses of people's experiences in romantic relationships led Sternberg to develop the Triangular Theory of Love (e.g., Sternberg 1986). This theory proposes that love has three components—intimacy, passion, and commitment—that, when combined in different proportions, result in eight types of love, including romantic love and companionate love.

Another ambitious attempt to construct a love taxonomy through psychometric means was Clyde and Susan Hendrick's (1986) development of the Love Attitudes Scale (LAS) to measure six types of love. Their subsequent factor analysis of data obtained from administration of the LAS and a number of other love scales—including Sternberg's scales and Hatfield & Sprecher's (1986) Passionate Love Scale—found several factors underlying students' responses, but these did not correspond well to the six proposed love types, nor did they support Sternberg's triangular theory (Hendrick & Hendrick 1989). The first two factors extracted seemed roughly to correspond to the romantic-companionate love distinction, but the investigators believed it premature to accept this taxonomy.

In another psychometric study, Fehr (1994) conducted a cluster analysis of many types of love that students had named in the Fehr & Russell (1991) study and found two primary groupings: a companionate love grouping that included friendship, affection, and familial love, and a passionate love grouping that included romantic love and sexual love.

The psychometric approach has several limitations, some a consequence of the way it has been used in the study of love. One of these pertains to the romantic relationship with reference to which participants are instructed to respond to the scales. Hendrick & Hendrick (1989) report that in their study, only "approximately half the present sample reported themselves to be in love" (p. 785), a figure comparable to that found in their previous research and presumably that of others. The remainder, then, were responding with reference to a "former partner" (perhaps "former" because no love developed) or, for those who had never been in love, "in terms of what they thought their response would be."

Another limitation, especially for those who hope to track the temporal course of love, pertains to the young college student samples used in psychometric and most other studies of love. Hendrick & Hendrick (1989) comment that "Whether it is love by an older adult definition or not, it is love by the respondents' definition" and "many of the love relationships of today are the marriages of tomorrow" (p. 793). Nevertheless, those who wish to examine love in older relationships, or the temporal course of love as a young relationship ages, need to take a leap of faith that the results of studies conducted with young adults (mostly women, for men are notoriously hard to recruit for relationship studies) in young relationships are generalizable to older people in older relationships.

Other limitations concern the love scales themselves. A frequent concern has been that scale items often include general relationship statements in addition to items directed toward a specific relationship. For example, the LAS instructions tell respondents that "Some of the items refer to a specific love relationship, while others refer to general attitudes and beliefs about love" (Hendrick & Hendrick 1986, p. 394). A relationship-specific version of the scale was constructed (Hendrick & Hendrick 1990) but it is rarely used.

Yet another limitation concerns the scales available to be included in psychometric studies. The LAS includes subscales for six types of love whereas many other scales are focused on a single type of love and scales for some putative types of love have been constructed too recently for inclusion. Because the nature of the scales one puts into a psychometric analysis determines what one gets out, perhaps it is not surprising that romantic and companionate love often emerge from these studies.

Other limitations of the inductive psychometric approach to psychological phenomena are inherent in the method. Kelley (1992) observes that most sciences begin with commonsense observations and commonsense language to describe those observations. From these, scientists typically try to bootstrap themselves to a more precise descriptive language that allows them to measure the phenomenon of interest and then test hypotheses about its causes and consequences. Because the initial scales to measure the phenomenon usually have their roots in commonsense psychology, these scales not only include items useful in measuring the phenomenon (e.g., relationship satisfaction) but they also unwittingly include elements that refer to the causal conditions and consequences associated with it (e.g., frequency of disagreement). As a result, the measuring instrument constructed to investigate the causes and consequences of the phenomenon becomes confounded with the very causes and consequences whose investigation the instrument was designed to facilitate. Kelley argues that the psychometric approach to a phenomenon, although useful initially, cannot achieve what a theory that specifies the antecedents and consequences of a specific set of behaviors associated with the phenomenon can.

The Theoretical Approach

Few love taxonomists have constructed fully developed theories for each type of love named in their classification scheme. Kelley (1983/2002) observes that theories of love should include ideas concerning (*a*) certain observable phenomena theorized to be its characteristic manifestations, (*b*) the current causes responsible for the observed phenomena, (*c*) the historical antecedents of the current causes, and (*d*) the future course of the phenomenon. All of these components must be addressed for each type of love the theorist is focusing on because:

> The single word *love* refers to different phenomena.... Consequently in both common lore and scientific thought, there are a number of different models of love. It is important to recognize that these models are *not* alternative, competing views of a single phenomenon, each of which historically has been termed *love*. The different models are addressed to the major forms or types of love. They imply that one person's "love" for another should always be qualified as to the type or combination of types it involves (p. 280).

Love scholars have often ignored the imperative that when love is discussed, a descriptor of the type of love addressed must be stated. As Sternberg (1987) concluded in his review of theories of liking and love: "If there has been a problem in theory about love, it has been that theories of part of the phenomenon have tended to be labeled as theories of the phenomenon as a whole" (p. 344).

The Neuropsychological Approach

Social neuroscience, particularly efforts to identify the neuropsychological correlates of love, has captivated the American public, perhaps because it has absorbed the deep-veined biological reductionism of American science and the suspicion that neither the mind nor any other entity can be considered "real"—and therefore subject to scientific analysis—unless it can be shown to have a material, physical basis. Again, romantic love has been the principal focus (see Hatfield & Rapson 2009 for a review). For example, Bartels & Zeki (2000) compared people's cortical activity as they looked at a picture of the person with whom they were "deeply in love" with their brain activity as they looked at pictures of their friends and concluded that "underlying one of the richest experiences of mankind is a functionally specialized system of the brain" (p. 3833), one that seemed to them to have a neural link with euphoric states.

In their critique of brain-imaging research in cognitive and social neuroscience, Cacioppo and his colleagues (2003) observe that interpretation of the psychological significance of fMRI data depends on the nature of the psychological differences between the comparison conditions. Noting, for example, that Bartels and Zeki constructed their contrasts with the belief that the psychological difference between their two conditions was romantic love, they ask: "Is romantic love a single process or a unified construct? Might there be other differences between these conditions? . . . might the participants have had more knowledge about, interest in, sexual attraction to, perceived similarity to, personal investments in, commitment to, and conflicted feelings or anxieties about a romantic partner than a friend?" (pp. 657–58). In other words, brain imaging is not a magic wand that obviates the need for adequate conceptualization and measurement of the psychological constructs whose underlying neurological structure and process is sought.

For these and more technical reasons, Cacioppo and his associates conclude that "the fact that romantic love is associated with changes in brain activation is not theoretically informative to neuroscientists or social scientists" (p. 658). Nevertheless, the neuropsychological approach to love currently represents an important promissory note for the future—one that apparently can't come too soon for those who envision sticking their partner's head under a magnet to verify that they are "really, truly" loved.

LOVE IN RELATIONSHIPS

Relationships are temporal in nature. Like rivers, they flow through time and space and change as the properties of the environment in which they are embedded change. The significance of this fact for love and other relationship phenomena is, to paraphrase ancient sage Heraclitus: "One never steps in the same river twice." Because relationships are not static, neither are the phenomena that occur within them. The social and physical environments that encase the relationship change, biological changes associated with human aging occur, and so the individual changes, the partner changes, their interactions change, and love, a product of those interactions, also changes.

Many regard the inevitability of changes in the quality, if not also the quantity, of love in a relationship as anathema. People who vow their love will be "forever" usually are not only vowing that their love will be everlasting but also that the *kind* of love they feel today will be the kind of love they will feel tomorrow. Despite the ubiquity of the "forever" vow, people are becoming skeptical. Books that treat the question, such as *Can Love Last?* (Mitchell 2002), sell like hotcakes in college bookstores. The kind of love that people hope will last, and that such books address, is romantic love. For the fortunate, love in a relationship may be everlasting, but it is likely that its quality will change over time. But how it changes, when it changes, and why it changes are questions that relationship scholars, marital or otherwise, need to examine, most effectively through longitudinal studies.

The Need for a Temporal Model of Love

Interest in relationship change in general is growing (e.g., see Vangelisti et al. 2002). For example, Rogge & Bradbury (2002) state that "one central question has begun to guide the course of marital research: How do marriages change?" (p. 228). A developmental view of the relationship not only requires asking "who, what, and when" of changes but also, they argue, an expansion of the range of process and outcome variables examined and movement beyond static theories of marriage that fail to distinguish newlyweds from established couples. Reminiscent of Gertrude Stein's "A rose is a rose is a rose," many researchers assume that "A marriage is a marriage is a marriage." But assuming that young and old relationships have the same dynamics is even worse than the proverbial mistake of comparing apples and oranges, both of which at least belong to the fruit family.

To track the course of love over time in a relationship, researchers must first hack through the love vocabulary thicket and identify which of the many types of love that have been posited it would be useful to track. What is needed a model that specifies a limited range of varieties of love that are likely to be important in assessing both quantitative and qualitative changes in love as the relationship moves through time. To construct such a model, it may be instructive for love scholars to consider the manner in which personality scholars managed to cut their problem down to size—the problem being hundreds, if not thousands, of personality traits and scales offered over the years— with development of the "Big Five" model of personality.

The five-factor model, according to Costa & McCrae (1992), evolved from (*a*) consideration of the pervasiveness of certain terms in lay vocabularies of personality, (*b*) their frequency of appearance in theories of personality, (*c*) consideration of their similarity in substance if not in name, and (*d*) their emergence in factor analytic studies of responses to various personality scales. Given the many types of love posited, any such model of love will not satisfy everyone, for it can neither aspire to include all of the varieties of love that have been posited nor can it capture all the permutations and nuances associated even with those it does include. Similarly, Costa & McCrae (1992) acknowledge that critics of the five-factor model who argue that the five factors cannot account for the full range of personality traits are correct. They point out, however, that the usefulness of the model is that it "helps us specify the range of traits that a comprehensive personality instrument should measure" (p. 653).

FOUR CANDIDATES FOR A TEMPORAL MODEL OF LOVE

At least three varieties of love appear to satisfy the criteria outlined by Costa and McCrae and thus might profitably be assessed in investigations of the course of love within a relationship: (*a*) Companionate Love, (*b*) Romantic Love, and (*c*) Compassionate Love. Although each of these types of love has been given several different names, the many labels associated with each seem to refer to substantially the same variety of love (an attempt will be made to refer to each by only one name here). The fourth candidate, for which the evidence is diaphanous but provocative, is Adult Attachment Love. Each of these types of love appears to be associated with different causal conditions and, thus, over time is likely to be vulnerable to different changes in the relationship's social and physical environments and, as a consequence, changes in the partners' sentiments (e.g., Berscheid 2006). Whether none, one, or some combination of the four is experienced at one time or at different times over the span of a relationship is an empirical question that cannot be answered unless each is assessed separately over time in the relationship. As this implies, asking people if they "love" their partner is likely to be minimally informative of the sentiment existing in the relationship and its future course.

Companionate Love

Companionate Love has been called "strong liking," "friendship love," "philias," "conjugal love," and "storge." It appears in virtually all taxonomies of love and has often emerged in psychometric analyses of love scales, as previously noted. It also is prominent in lay vocabularies of love. For example, when the several types of love named by students (Fehr & Russell 1991, Study 1) were subsequently rated for prototypicality (Study 2), companionate types of love received the highest ratings as the best examples of love. From subsequent investigations, Fehr (1994) concluded that "for laypeople, companionate varieties of love, such as friendship love or familial kinds of love capture the meaning of the concept" (p. 329). Grote & Frieze (1994), who developed a friendship-based love (FBL) scale applicable to both young and old adults, define friendship-based love as "a comfortable, affectionate, trusting love for a likable partner, based on a deep sense of friendship and involving companionship and the enjoyment of common activities, mutual interests, and shared laughter" (p. 275).

Theory and research on adult friendship development is sparse. Nevertheless, and as early sociologists believed, Companionate Love may be the "staff of life" for many relationships and a better basis for a satisfying marriage than romantic love. For example, Gottman's (1999) research and marital therapy experience led him to conclude that the foundation of what he calls "a sound marital house" is friendship laced with fondness and admiration. Orbuch et al. (1993), who asked newlyweds to talk about their relationship history up to the time of their marriage and then assessed their marital satisfaction two years later, were surprised that "having a highly romantic reconstruction of one's courtship does not predict marital well-being ... Instead, only a generally positive tone without romanticism seems to be important" (p. 824).

Grote & Frieze (1994) administered their FBL scale to a large sample of older married adults and found that Companionate Love was more highly correlated with relationship satisfaction, perceived importance of the relationship, and respect for and feelings of closeness to the partner than was Romantic Love (although the latter also independently contributed to relationship satisfaction). When the FBL was administered to college students, Companionate Love was again significantly more related than Romantic Love to relationship satisfaction—and also to courtship progress.

Causal conditions. Companionate Love follows the pleasure-pain principle; we like those who reward us and dislike those who punish us. Although the universe of rewards one person may confer upon another is vast, the interpersonal attraction literature has identified those especially potent in generating liking (see Berscheid & Reis 1998). These include *similarity* along virtually every dimension, including attitudes, values, and educational and socioeconomic background. We also tend to like people who are *familiar* (and, therefore, unlikely to do us harm). Similarity, of course, contributes to feelings of familiarity, as does increased exposure to the other, usually through physical proximity. *Expressions of esteem* and validation of one's worth are valuable to others (again signaling likelihood of help, not harm) and they generally inspire liking in return. We also tend to like *physically attractive* people for several reasons, including our inference that they possess other favorable but less visible characteristics.

Friendships, and the intimacy they entail, usually grow through the process of mutual self-disclosures that meet with positive and validating responses from the partner, as Reis & Shaver's (1988) theory of intimacy predicts. Some friendship investigators have concluded that friendships serve mostly socioemotional functions and that joint participation in leisure and recreational activities is particularly important in fostering friendship.

Temporal hypotheses. From his review of the friendship literature, Hays (1988) concluded that friendships are relatively slow to develop. Once developed, it is often assumed that Companionate Love is stable. For example, after stating that the Storge subscale of the LAS measures an individual's love style of merging friendship and love, Hendrick & Hendrick (1986) comment: "There is no fire in storgic love; it is solid, down-to-earth, and presumably enduring" (p. 400). However, a rare longitudinal study that measured Companionate Love in newlywed couples shortly after marriage and one year later found that it had declined for both husbands and wives in the same degree that their Romantic Love had declined (Hatfield et al. 2008). The presumed endurance of Companionate Love deserves further test, for the causal conditions conducive to liking and friendship are not impervious to changes in the partners as a result of changes in their social and physical environments.

Another popular temporal hypothesis is that in romantic relationships, such as marriage, Romantic Love eventually is replaced by Companionate Love. This hypothesis was advanced early by Walster [Hatfield] & Walster (1978) and even earlier by Reik (1944/1972), who declared that, as time passes, all that people can expect from the fire of romantic love is the "afterglow" of dying embers. Evidence is accumulating, however, that Companionate Love may be important from the beginning and, in fact, may be vital to the development of Romantic Love.

Romantic Love

Romantic Love also has many aliases, including "passionate love," "erotic love" (or "Eros"), "addictive love," "obsessive love," "deficiencylove," and being "in love." Like Companionate Love, it is prominent in lay vocabularies, appears in virtually all love taxonomies, and often emerges from psychometric analyses of love scales.

Causal conditions. On the word of no less an authority than Albert Einstein, scholars can eliminate gravitation as a cause of romantic love. Commenting on an Englishman's theory that as the earth rotated, gravity caused people to be upside-down or horizontal at times and to do foolish things like falling in love, Einstein declared that "Falling in love is not the most stupid thing people do but gravitation cannot be held responsible for it" (Isaacson 2007, p. 423).

Freud (1912/1963) believed that this form of love had two components. Contrasting "neurotic love" with "normal love" in adults, he stated simply and without further elaboration, "To ensure a fully normal attitude in love, two currents of feeling have to unite—we may describe them as the tender affectionate feelings and the sensual feelings. . . ." (p. 49). Virtually all theories of Romantic Love do link it to the sensual feelings, specifically, the experience of sexual desire (see Berscheid & Regan 2005, p. 334–35, for a listing), and most laypersons believe that an individual cannot be "in love" with another unless sexual desire for that person is experienced (Regan 1998).

As for Freud's other component, love researchers have been slow to recognize the role that "affectionate feelings," such as those associated with Companionate Love, play in Romantic Love, perhaps because the early Companionate Love-Romantic Love distinction was often translated as Companionate versus Romantic Love. In the early 1990s, however, Hendrick & Hendrick (1993) noticed that the most frequent theme of college students' freeform accounts of their romantic love relationships was Companionate Love and that almost half of the students named their romantic partner as their closest friend. It should be parenthetically noted that this may be an illustration of cultural shifts making love a moving target (Hatfield & Rapson 2002), for it seems doubtful that a strong association between Companionate and Romantic Love would have been found before women shared similar educational and occupational backgrounds and aspirations with men, thereby providing the fertile soil of similarity in which friendships develop.

Evidence that both sexual desire and friendship may be jointly necessary and sufficient for today's college students to conclude they are "in love" with another was obtained by Meyers & Berscheid (1997), who asked young adults to list all persons in their social network whom they "loved," were "in love," were "friends," and all for whom they felt "sexual desire." The person named in the "in love" category (usually only one person, perhaps reflecting the cultural belief that one can be in love with only one person at a time) was almost always also named in the "friend" category and in the "sexual desire" category; that is, unless a person was named in *both* of these categories, each of which usually contained several other people, it was unlikely that respondents would report that they were "in love" with that person.

Temporal hypotheses. If Romantic Love is a felicitous combination of Companionate Love and sexual desire, then any weakening of the causal conditions associated with Companionate Love or those associated with sexual desire for the partner should weaken Romantic Love. Whereas many of the causal conditions associated with Companionate Love are known, those associated with sexual desire are not. A healthy body and a physically attractive partner figure prominently as causal conditions (see Regan & Berscheid 1999), and Freud (1912/1963) proposed another: "It is easy to show that the value the mind sets on erotic needs instantly sinks as soon as satisfaction becomes readily obtainable. Some obstacle is needed to swell the tide of the libido to its height. . . ." (p. 57). Obstacles frequently generate emotion and passion.

"Passionate love" and "romantic love" appear to be synonymous in laypersons' conceptions of love (see Fehr 1994). Most scholars also use the terms interchangeably, but Hatfield (e.g., 1988) prefers the former phrase, perhaps because she emphasizes the emotional quality of romantic love. The word "passion" denotes excitement and physiological arousal, known to be causally associated with the experience of the intense emotions that are often observed in people experiencing the thrall of Romantic Love. Excitement and arousal, in turn, usually are generated by surprise and uncertainty.

Surprise and uncertainty tend to be characteristic of any new relationship. Because the partner is not well known, expectancies about the partner's attributes and behaviors are often violated. Berscheid's (1983/2002) emotion-in-relationships model posits that violations of expectancies about the partner usually have implications for the individual's well-being and, as a consequence, are likely to occasion an emotional experience, which may be either positive or negative depending on whether the individual believes the violation has enhanced or diminished his or her well-being. When partners surprisingly facilitate personally valued activities and the achievement of desired goals, well-being is enhanced and positive emotion is likely to be experienced. If happy facilitative surprises occur in a new relationship, positive emotions are likely to be experienced, the relationship will be perceived to promote well-being, and the partners will try to maintain it. When, however, partners unexpectedly interfere with the pursuit of valued activities and goals, well-being is jeopardized, negative emotion is likely to result, and, if the relationship is new, it may be terminated.

As the relationship ages, the partners' mutual interdependencies are likely to grow in number and complexity, with the associated expectancies having become so deeply entrenched that they have fallen from awareness. In most established relationships, the partner's facilitative behaviors are taken for granted and, because they no longer surprise, they no longer have the power to arouse strong positive emotion. Now it is the partner's violation of those facilitation expectancies that have the power to surprise; failures to facilitate as expected are likely to be perceived as threatening to well-being and negative emotion is likely to result. Partners in established relationships who do not behave as expected once again become strangers, as is reflected in the word "estrangement," often used to describe a disintegrating relationship. Most partners in long-term relationships do behave as expected, however, and, as a consequence, the partners seldom arouse each others' intense emotional passions—either positive or negative.

Baumeister & Bratslavsky (1999) propose that degree of passion is a function of a rapid change in intimacy, where "intimacy" is defined similarly to Companionate Love and to Reis & Shaver's (1988) definition of intimacy (i.e., knowledge and understanding of the other combined with communication of a strong positive attitude toward the other). These theorists endorse the generally accepted view that intimacy usually grows gradually, but in those instances in which it rises rapidly, passion should result; in addition, citing Berscheid's model, they predict that when intimacy stabilizes, the relationship should become passionless. Aron & Aron (1986), too, believe that certain rapid changes in a new relationship, namely, the rapid "expansion of the self" or incorporation into the self-concept of the qualities of the other, produce the euphoria often associated with falling in love.

As the relationship ages, then, uncertainty and facilitative surprises wane, predictability grows, erotic satisfaction becomes readily available, and thus the emotional experiences that are associated with Romantic Love should wane. With respect to sexual activity, if not desire, national studies are consistent in showing that sexual intercourse in married couples declines with the partners' age and length of marriage. Among the factors claimed to be responsible is "a reduction in novelty associated with being with the same person for a long period of time," a conclusion based on evidence that older partners in young relationships show higher sexual activity than do their cohorts in older relationships (Sprecher et al. 2006, p. 467).

Although Companionate Love is believed to be relatively slow to develop, sexual desire may sometimes provide the motivational spark that initiates the relationship and sustains it until friendship combines with sexual desire to produce Romantic Love. Gillath et al. (2008, Study 1) found that when sex-related representations (e.g., an erotic photo) were subliminally primed, relationship-related motives were activated, "causing people to become more interested in, or inclined, to engage in behaviors that would foster initiation and maintenance of a more extended couple relationship" (p. 1067).

Several investigators have attempted to plot the course of Romantic Love through crosssectional studies that examine self-reports of love in marital relationships of varying length. For example, Montgomery & Sorrell (1997) administered the LAS to four groups whose marriages were of varying durations and found that neither LAS Eros subscale scores nor Storge subscale scores differed across groups. As in similar cross-sectional studies of the temporal course of romantic love, the older marriages were intact, and it is not known how many marriages in the older cohort had failed, possibly for lack of either Romantic Love or Companionate Love, nor were the initial levels on the two dimensions of the older couples known. Knowledge of the temporal fate of love requires longitudinal methodology.

In their longitudinal study, Hatfield and her associates (2008) found that a year's time had significantly eroded Romantic Love, as previously noted. In another rare, albeit short-term, longitudinal study, Tucker & Aron (1993) measured passionate love and marital satisfaction two months before and eight months after three transitions (e.g., engagement to marriage). Passionate love declined over all three transitions (but a moderate level remained). The passionate love pattern remained mostly unchanged when marital satisfaction was controlled, but the similar pattern found for satisfaction disappeared when passionate love was controlled, leading these investigators to conclude, "This asymmetry suggests that passionate love, and not marital satisfaction, may be the key variable associated with any differences over the stage of family life cycle" (p. 142).

Compassionate Love

Compassionate Love has several aliases, including "agape," "caregiving love," "selfless love," "being-love" (love for another's being), "sacrificial love," "pure love," "true love," "unconditional love," "altruistic love," and, more recently, "communal responsiveness." Although featured in religious and many love literatures for thousands of years and despite it being the first factor extracted in the construction of the LAS scale with college students (Hendrick & Hendrick 1986), systematic examination of Compassionate Love is relatively recent.

Interest in caregiving in ongoing relationships has grown for several reasons, including its role in relationship satisfaction and stability (e.g., Pasch & Bradbury 1998). Because reciprocity of negative behavior is the hallmark of unhappy relationships, several researchers have highlighted the importance of the partners' ability to restrain the tendency to respond to negativity with more negativity (e.g., Gottman 1999, Rusbult et al. 1998) and to overlook the partner's negative behavior or otherwise respond with Compassionate Love to the partner's shortcomings.

In addition to the LAS Agape subscale, at least two other scales are available to measure Compassionate Love in ongoing relationships: Kunce & Shaver's (1994) Caregiving Scale and, more recently, Sprecher & Fehr's (2005) Compassionate Love Scale, based on their definition of Compassionate Love as "an attitude toward other(s)...containing feelings, cognitions, and behaviors that are focused on caring, concern, tenderness, and an orientation toward supporting, helping, and understanding the other(s), particularly when the other(s) is (are) perceived to be suffering or in need" (p. 630).

The term "communal responsiveness," coined by Clark and her associates (e.g., Clark & Monin 2006), reflects growing interest in the interactional dynamics of Compassionate Love in ongoing adult relationships (e.g., Cutrona 1996, Feeney & Collins 2004). As opposed to "exchange" relationships in which benefits are given to another on a quid pro quo basis (e.g., see Clark & Mills 1979), mutual communally responsive relationships are defined as those in which the partners attend to one another's needs and welfare and are confident that the other will do the same when their own needs arise. Repeated acts of mutual "communal responsiveness" that are noncontingent (i.e., given without demanding or expecting future benefits in return) are theorized to contribute to a sense of love in all types of relationships—friendship, family, and romantic.

Causal conditions. Bowlby (e.g., 1973) theorized that humans possess an innate caregiving system along with its complement, an attachment system. Despite the flood of research on adult attachment, the caregiving system, especially as it may be manifested in adult relationships, has been relatively neglected. This lacuna is surprising given that Bowlby theorized that people become attached to an individual who provides care in times of need and generates feelings of safety and security, a "safe haven" and a "secure base" from which to explore the environment.

Like Bowlby, Clark & Monin (2006) believe that acts of communal responsiveness provide the partner with an ongoing sense of security, which, they hypothesize, increases the likelihood that he or she will be communally responsive in turn. Consistent with this hypothesis, Mikulincer et al. (2005) have shown experimentally that increasing an individual's felt security increases the likelihood of compassionate behavior toward another.

Reis et al. (2004) hypothesize that what will be perceived as "responsive," and presumably what kinds of caregiving acts are likely to increase felt security, depends on the type of relationship and its place in a triangularly shaped hierarchy of communal relationships—spouses and children at the peak, followed in descending order by parents, close friends, casual friends, acquaintances, and strangers at the broad base. It is the broad stranger base that heretofore has been the primary focus of the vast social support literature, which primarily addresses questions about when people will aid strangers in need and the effects of support on the recipient. Sprecher & Fehr (2005) found that scores on their Compassionate Love Scale were lowest for strangers, higher for close friend relationships, and highest for dating and marital relationships, consistent with Reis et al.'s (2004) communal relationship hierarchy and also with Gillath et al.'s (2008, Study 2) finding that a subliminal sexual prime increased the willingness of people in relationships of varying length (3 months to 40 years) to sacrifice for their romantic partner's benefit.

Clark & Monin (2006) believe that for a relationship to be communally responsive, responses to the partner's needs not only must be noncontingent but both partners must be willing to receive care. Not all partners are. Not only is support sometimes unwelcome but it also may exacerbate rather than ameliorate distress. Some of the conditions under which such negative outcomes of care can be avoided have been identified (e.g., Bolger et al. 2000, Gleason et al. 2003), but the dynamics of caregiving in ongoing relationships are likely to be complex. Iida et al.'s (2008) examination of couples' daily reports of giving and receiving support found that whether support was given in times of need and how it was received was a function of many factors, including characteristics of the providers (e.g., positive mood), the recipients (e.g., requests for support), and their relationship (e.g., their support history).

Temporal hypotheses. Clark & Monin (2006) note that research indicates that "most people are quite adept at immediately behaving communally when they desire a new friendship or romantic relationship" (p. 212) and that most spouses endorse communal norms and try to abide by them, at least initially. However, conflict and stress often cause partners to start calculating fairness and equity, which has been shown to lower marital satisfaction (e.g., Grote & Clark 2001). They believe that whether a communal orientation continues in a relationship depends importantly on each individual's trust that the partner truly cares about the individual's welfare and, also, the partner's acceptance of care.

More research needs to be conducted on Compassionate Love, especially in older relationships with older partners, who often are experiencing the infirmities and frustrations of biological aging, as well as in relationships, both young and old, in which malevolent fate plunges one of the partners from "better" to a permanent "worse." It is one thing to exercise Compassionate Love when it is rarely required and/or when it requires small and temporary sacrifice and quite another when Compassionate Love must be sustained at great personal cost for long periods of time and selfpreservation needs arise (see Bolger et al. 1996). Investigation of when sacrifice is harmful, both to the caregiver and the relationship, is needed (e.g., see Whitton et al. 2002).

Adult Attachment Love

Both Harlow (e.g., 1958) and Bowlby (e.g., 1979) believed that humans possess an innate behavioral system that is activated by threat and leads them to form an attachment to a familiar person who provides comfort and protection. Harlow believed attachment to be a form of love, and Bowlby defined attachment as a "strong affectional bond" to a specific person, whom he termed an "attachment figure." Attachment to a specific person is revealed when the individual seeks proximity to that person when threatened. It also is revealed when the individual experiences distress when involuntarily separated from that person and grief when the loss is permanent, for the individual views that person as unique and irreplaceable.

Bowlby's theory of attachment and his belief that "attachment behavior is a normal and healthy part of human nature from the cradle to the grave" (1973, p. 46) spawned a great deal of research, mostly by developmental psychologists on humans recently emerged from the cradle and lately by social psychologists on those closer to the grave. The latter has focused on individual differences in "adult attachment style," or differences in adults' orientations to close relationships, inspired by classification systems of differences in the quality of children's attachments to their caregivers. The normative implications of attachment theory for adults have been relatively neglected (see Simpson & Rholes 1998), despite the fact that attachment theory is "first and foremost a normative theory" (Hazan & Shaver 1994, p. 17).

Most normative adult attachment research has been influenced by Ainsworth's (1985) hypothesis that some of the affectional bonds people form after childhood "may be characterized either as having attachment components or at least meeting some of the criteria that distinguish attachments from other bonds" (p. 792). She noted that although parents remain attachment figures for many adults, certain others may become attachment figures as well, including close friends, mentors, and partners in a long-term sexual relationship such as marriage. With respect to this last, Ainsworth (1985) speculated that over the course of a long-term sexual relationship, "an attachment relationship tends also to be built up, the attachment and caregiving components interacting to make for a reciprocal give-and-take relationship" (p. 804). She cautioned, however, that the caregiving and attachment components may not be symmetrical and reciprocal in all relationships.

The conjecture that partners in long-term sexual relationships may alternate between giving care and receiving care, which may result in each partner becoming an attachment figure for the other, captured the attention of Shaver and his associates (e.g., 1988), who view Romantic Love as an integration of the attachment, caregiving, and sexual behavioral systems originally posited by Bowlby. Normative adult attachment research has continued to focus on romantic relationships. Hazan & Zeifman (1999) state, in fact, that "The importance of the question—whether romantic bonds are attachments in the technical sense—can hardly be overestimated" because "The entire field of adult attachment research has been constructed on the premise that they are" (p. 336).

Such a premise might have startled Bowlby (1979), for he warned that "by no means all affectional bonding between adults is accompanied by sexual relations; whereas, conversely, sexual relations often occur independently of any persisting affectional bonds" (p. 70). Ainsworth (1985), too, cautioned that "a relationship or a class of relationships may be important to an individual without implying either an affectional bond in general or an attachment in particular" (p. 800).

Nevertheless, many have enthusiastically embraced the assumption that romantic partners, including those in dating relationships of short duration, are each other's "attachment figures." This assumption is in dire need of empirical scrutiny.

Causal conditions. It is not known how usual it is for adults to display in any relationship, romantic or otherwise, the defining features of attachment to their partners—proximity maintenance, safe haven, secure base, and separation distress. It also is not known how adult attachments form. The provision of care from another in time of need—that is, Compassionate Love consistently received from another over a long enough time-span that the individual feels confident of the availability of that love, as Clark & Monin (2006) describe, may be the primary process. Fraley & Davis (1997), for example, found that associated with young adults naming another as an attachment figure were "factors that generally promote the development of attachment formation in infancy (such as caregiving, trust, and intimate contact)" (p. 131).

The sustained receipt of Compassionate Love from another in times of need usually is accompanied by a growth of familiarity with the caregiver. Bowlby (e.g., 1979, p. 115) believed that familiarity was of immense importance in the lives of animals and humans because familiarity signals safety and security, particularly important to people who are sick, tired, threatened, or otherwise experiencing stressful circumstances, and for this reason he emphasized the importance of familiarity in attachment formation. Indeed, what distinguished Bowlby's theory from the reinforcement theories prevalent at the time was his insistence that not all affectional bonds follow reinforcement principles—that on the basis of familiarity even abused children and battered adults may form attachments to their abusers and vigorously resist separation from them, an observation well documented by social workers. The role of familiarity in adult attachment formation is not clear. It seems likely, however, that the frequent receipt of care from another and the growth of familiarity with that person over time may be jointly necessary and sufficient for an attachment to develop.

Temporal hypotheses. If Attachment Love grows at all in a relationship, it appears to do so slowly and stealthily, under the radar of consciousness. In his studies of separated and recently divorced marital partners, Weiss (1975) observed what he called "the erosion of love and the persistence of attachment" (p. 36). Some of the separated, many of whom instigated the separation themselves and currently felt strong negative sentiment for the partner, nevertheless periodically, and inexplicably to them, felt a compelling urge to re-establish proximity to their now disliked, even hated, partner. Weiss concluded, "Even when marriages turn bad and the other components of love fade or turn into their opposites, attachment is likely to remain" (p. 44) because the attachment figure represents feelings of "at-homeness and ease"— a safe haven—much needed under the stress of divorce. Moreover, and as Bowlby theorized, Weiss (1988) observed that adult attachments do not seem responsive to the absence of reinforcement—they persist "even when the attachment figure is neglecting, disparaging, or abusive" (p. 40).

It was Weiss's impression that attempts to restore proximity to the now disliked partner generally were experienced by individuals who had been with their partner for at least two years. The temporal hypothesis that attachment takes time to develop, possibly two years in most relationships, was investigated by Hazan & Zeifman (1999), who questioned young adults about their secure base (e.g., "Whom do you feel you can always count on?") and separation distress (e.g., "Whom do you hate to be away from?"). Those involved in romantic relationships of at least two years duration tended to name their romantic partners in answer to both questions, but those in shorter-term romantic relationships and those without partners mostly named a parent.

The identity of the persons named as attachment figures has been addressed by several researchers. Fraley & Davis (1997), for example, found parents to be the primary attachment figures of most in their college student sample, but the students seemed to be in the process of transferring some attachmentrelated functions to their best friends and romantic partners, as Hazan and her colleagues have hypothesized (see Hazan & Shaver 1994). However, Trinke & Bartholomew (1997) found that, on average, young adults named over five attachment figures, and concluded that "a focus on romantic partners is limited: almost everyone in the current sample had more than one attachment figure, and [romantic] partners were primary figures for only one-third of the individuals" (p. 622).

To determine if Compassionate Love is essential to the development of Attachment Love in an adult relationship and, if so, its frequency of receipt over differing time periods requires separate measurement of Compassionate Love and Attachment Love. Ainsworth's (1985) warning that the caregiving and attachment components may not be symmetrical and reciprocal in relationships—or, of course, may not be present at all—also demands their separate measurement. Vormbrock (1993), who studied spouses repeatedly separated in wartime or because of job demands, found that spouses left at home typically showed attachment activation whereas leavers showed caregiving activation. She concluded, "The differential separation reactions of home-based and traveling spouses suggest that these systems are indeed distinct, and feelings related to the attachment system and those related to the caregiving system need to be assessed separately" (p. 140). It also suggests that tests of Hazan & Shaver's (1994) hypothesis that "prototypical" romantic relationships involve "the integration of three behavioral systems—attachment, caregiving, and sexual mating" requires measuring each of the associated types of love separately (and perhaps adding Companionate Love, absent from the hypothesized prototype), for separate measurement over time would permit observation of the integration processes presumed to occur.

Given the volatility of young romantic relationships and the rapidity with which old partners are discarded and new ones found, it seems improbable that all, or even many, short-term romantic partners truly are attachment figures as Bowlby and Ainsworth defined an attachment figure—a person regarded as unique and irreplaceable. It also is questionable whether all long-term romantic partners are attachment figures. These are empirical questions, but their investigation is not likely as long as it is assumed that romantic partners are attachment figures and as long as the most likely process to result in Attachment Love—the receipt of Compassionate Love over time—is not assessed over time and independently of the other forms of love that may be present in the relationship.

SUMMARY COMMENTS

Many psychologists have responded to Harlow, Bowlby, and Maslow's passionate and persuasive pleas for a scientific understanding of love, for it is a prepotent force in human affairs, as is its antithesis, hatred. The latter, in its many forms, including aggression, conflict, and hostility, has received far more attention from psychologists than love has, even in the study of close relationships, perhaps because its harmful effects are more visible and seemingly in more urgent need of understanding and control than are the presumed salutary effects of love. Indeed, love, which is truly all around us in the small groups in which people live, tends to be taken for granted—until it inexplicably evaporates, changes form, or metamorphoses into enmity.

The question, then, is not "why" but rather "how" to advance the systematic study of love. The impoverished vocabulary people have to describe their strong positive sentiments for another has made the conceptualization and measurement of love difficult. Although a constructionist view of love probably is the correct one—no one loves another exactly the same at two different points in time and no two people love in exactly the same way (or, it should be noted, as the recipient wishes to be loved)—overlapping love taxonomies as well as psychometric studies sketch sufficient commonalities to postulate several major forms of love, each of which appears to be associated with different causal conditions and behavioral manifestations that remain mostly the subject of anecdotal comment, isolated hypotheses, and speculative conjecture, unbound and unarticulated by formal, empirically testable theory.

It seems likely that the cataloging of putative types of love and inductive psychometric studies have reached their points of diminishing return. New approaches to the study of love are needed. The scientific dictum that the dynamics of a phenomenon are best understood when it is in the process of change and the fact that relationships are temporal, and thus the phenomena within them change over time, suggest that a temporal approach to the study of love would be profitable. The fruits of previous taxonomic and psychometric efforts are sufficient to specify a limited number of types of love for the development of a comprehensive instrument to measure love over time in a relationship. Because conceptualization and theory have been sparse, it should be noted that few of the available love scales are "pure"; each often contains items clearly more relevant to types of love other than that reflected in the scale's label. An early example is Hatfield's (1988) comment that Rubin's (1970) Love Scale, still often used to measure Romantic Love, seemed to her, as it subsequently has to others, to be a Companionate Love scale!

The development of a comprehensive instrument, in concert with adequate conceptualization of each type of love within an encompassing theory, would facilitate the test of causal hypotheses about each, knowledge of its likely temporal course, and the differential vulnerability of each to negative sentiment, which arises in any close interdependent relationship. It also would provide information about if and how the types of love become integrated, as Hazan & Shaver (1994) posit.

Four candidates for such an instrument, and the need for a theory that incorporates all of them, have been suggested here with no expectation that such an instrument will fully describe any one individual's sentiment for another. It should, however, facilitate the identification of normative trends in the patterns of "marbling" of the four types of love over time in a relationship and their correspondence to the causal conditions theorized to be associated with each. Empirical tests of a temporal theory of love will require longitudinal methodology and, because love is not the exclusive province of romantic relationships, the investigative terrain must be expanded to include the other types of relationships that play a significant role in people's lives, especially long-term family relationships and friendships. It is in these that one can expect the preeminent role of Compassionate Love in enduring relationships, long overlooked by love scholars in their focus on Romantic Love and short-term relationships, to be revealed.

DISCLOSURE STATEMENT

The author is not aware of any biases that might be perceived as affecting the objectivity of this review.

ACKNOWLEDGMENTS

The author wishes to express her appreciation to Elaine Hatfield, who has inspired many to study love, for her comments on this article, as well as for the helpful advice of Harry Reis, John Holmes, Jeff Simpson, Beverly Fehr, and Pamela Regan.

LITERATURE CITED

Ainsworth MDS. 1985. Attachments across the life span. *Bull. N. Y. Acad. Med.* 61:792–812

Amato PR, Irving S. 2006. Historical trends in divorce in the United States. In *Handbook of Divorce and Relationship Dissolution*, ed. MA Fine, JH Harvey, pp. 41–58. Mahwah, NJ: Erlbaum

Aron A, Aron EN. 1986. *Love and the Expansion of Self: Understanding Attraction and Satisfaction*. New York: Hemisphere

Bartels A, Zeki S. 2000. The neural basis of romantic love. *Neuro Rep.* 11(3829):29–34

Baumeister RF, Bratslavsky E. 1999. Passion, intimacy, and time: passionate love as a function of change in intimacy. *Personal. Soc. Psychol. Rev.* 3:49–67

Berscheid E. 1983/2002. Emotion. See Kelley et al. 1983/2002, pp. 110–68

Berscheid E. 1999. The greening of relationship science. *Am. Psychol.* 54:260–66

Berscheid E. 2006. Searching for the meaning of "love." See Sternberg & Weis 2006, pp. 171–83

Berscheid E, Regan P. 2005. *The Psychology of Interpersonal Relationships*. New York: Prentice-Hall

Berscheid E, Reis HT. 1998. Interpersonal attraction and close relationships. In *Handbook of Social Psychology, Vol. 2*, ed. S Fiske, D Gilbert, G Lindzey, pp. 193–281. New York: Random House

Berscheid E, Walster [Hatfield] EH. 1969. *Interpersonal Attraction*. Reading, MA: Addison-Wesley

Berscheid E, Walster [Hatfield] EH. 1974. A little bit about love. In *Foundations of Interpersonal Attraction*, ed. TL Huston, pp. 157–215. New York: Academic

Berscheid E, Walster [Hatfield] EH. 1978. *Interpersonal Attraction*. Reading, MA: Addison-Wesley. 2nd ed.

Bolger N, Foster M, Vinokur AD, Ng R. 1996. Close relationships and adjustment to a life crisis: the case of breast cancer. *J. Personal. Soc. Psychol.* 70:283–94

Bolger N, Zuckerman A, Kessler RC. 2000. Invisible support and adjustment to stress. *J. Personal. Soc. Psychol.* 69:890–902

Bowlby J. 1969. *Attachment and Loss. Volume 1: Attachment*. New York: Basic Books

Bowlby J. 1973. Affectional bonds: their nature and origin. In *Loneliness: The Experience of Emotional and Social Isolation*, ed. RS Weiss, pp. 38–52. Cambridge, MA: MIT Press

Bowlby J. 1979. *The Making and Breaking of Affectional Bonds*. London: Tavistock

Bradbury TN, ed. 1998. *The Developmental Course of Marital Dysfunction*. New York: Cambridge Univ. Press

Braiker HB, Kelley HH. 1979. Conflict in the development of close relationships. In *Social Exchange in Developing Relationships*, ed. RL Burgess, TL Huston, pp. 135–68. New York: Academic

Burgess EW. 1926. The romantic impulse and family disorganization. *Survey* 57:290–95

Cacioppo JT, Berntson GG, Lorig TS, Norris CJ, Rickett E, Nusbaum H. 2003. Just because you're imaging the brain doesn't mean you can stop using your head: a primer and set of first principles. *J. Personal. Soc. Psychol.* 85:650–61

Carnap R. 1953. The two concepts of probability. In *Readings in the Philosophy of Science*, ed. H Feigl, M Brodbeck, pp. 438–55. New York: Appleton-Century-Crofts

Carroll L. 1965. *Through the Looking-Glass*. New York: Random House [Original work published 1865]

Caughlin JP, Huston TL. 2006. The affective structure of marriage. In *The Cambridge Handbook of Personal Relationships*, ed. D Perlman, A Vangelisti, pp. 131–55. New York: Cambridge Univ. Press

Clark MS, Mills J. 1979. Interpersonal attraction in exchange and communal relationships. *J. Personal. Soc. Psychol.* 37:12–24

Clark MS, Monin JK. 2006. Giving and receiving communal responsiveness as love. See Sternberg & Weis 2006, pp. 200–21

Collins WA, Laursen B. 2000. Adolescent relationships: the art of fugue. In *Close Relationships: A Sourcebook*, ed. C Hendrick, SS Hendrick, pp. 59–69. Thousand Oaks, CA: Sage

Costa PT, McCrae RR. 1992. Four ways five factors are basic. *Personal. Individ. Differ.* 13:653–65

Cutrona CE. 1996. *Social Support in Couples*. Thousand Oaks, CA: Sage

D'Andrade RG. 1989. Cultural cognition. In *Foundations of Cognitive Science*, ed. MI Posner, pp. 795–830. Cambridge, MA: MIT Press

Ellis B, Malamuth NM. 2000. Love and anger in romantic relationships: a discrete systems model. *J. Personal.* 68:525–56

Feeney BC, Collins NL. 2004. Interpersonal safe haven and secure base caregiving processes in adulthood. In *Adult Attachment: Theory, Research, and Clinical Interventions*, ed. WS Rholes, JA Simpson, pp. 300–38. New York: Guilford

Fehr B. 1994. Prototype-based assessments of laypeople's views of love. *Pers. Relat.* 1:309–31

Fehr B, Russell JA. 1991. The concept of love viewed from a prototype perspective. *J. Personal. Soc. Psychol.* 60:425–38

Fraley RC, Davis KE. 1997. Attachment formation and transfer in young adults' close friendships and romantic relationships. *Pers. Relat.* 4:131–44

Freud S. 1912/1963. *Sexuality and the Psychology of Love.* New York: Touchstone

Gable S, Reis HT. 2001. Appetitive and aversive social interaction. In *Close Romantic Relationships: Maintenance and Enhancement,* ed. J Harvey, A Wenzel, pp. 169–94. Mahwah, NJ: Erlbaum

Gigy L, Kelly JB. 1992. Reasons for divorce: perspectives of divorcing men and women. *J. Divorce Remarriage* 18:169–87

Gillath O, Mikulincer M, Birnbaum GE, Shaver PR. 2008. When sex primes love: subliminal sexual priming motivates relationship goal pursuit. *Personal. Soc. Psychol. Bull.* 34:1057–69

Gleason MEJ, Iida M, Bolger N, Shrout PE. 2003. Daily supportive equity in close relationships. *Personal. Soc. Psychol. Bull.* 29:1036–45

Goode WJ. 1959. The theoretical importance of love. *Am. Sociol. Rev.* 24:38–47

Gottman JM. 1999. *The Marriage Clinic.* New York: Norton

Gottman JM, Levenson RW. 2000. The timing of divorce: predicting when a couple will divorce over a 14-year period. *J. Marriage Fam.* 62:737–45

Grote NK, Clark MS. 2001. Perceiving unfairness in the family: cause or consequence of marital distress? *J. Personal. Soc. Psychol.* 80:281–93

Grote NK, Frieze IH. 1994. The measurement of friendship-based love in intimate relationships. *Pers. Relat.* 1:275–300

Harlow HF. 1958. The nature of love. *Am. Psychol.* 13:673–85

Hatfield E. 1988. Passionate and companionate love. See Sternberg & Barnes 1988, pp. 191–217

Hatfield E, Pillemer JT, O'Brien MU, Le YL. 2008. The endurance of love: passionate and companionate love in newlywed and long-term marriages. *Interpersona: Int. J. Pers. Relationships* 2:35–64

Hatfield E, Rapson RL. 2002. Passionate love and sexual desire: cultural and historical perspectives. See Vangelisti et al. 2002, pp. 306–24

Hatfield E, Rapson RL. 2009. The neuropsychology of passionate love. In *Neuropsychology of Social Relationships,* ed. D Marazziti. Hauppauge, NY: Nova Sci. In press

Hatfield E, Sprecher S. 1986. Measuring passionate love in intimate relations. *J. Adolesc.* 9:383–410

Hays RB. 1988. Friendship. In *Handbook of Personal Relationships: Theory, Research, and Interventions,* ed. S Duck, pp. 391–408. Chichester, UK: Wiley

Hazan C, Shaver PR. 1994. Attachment as an organizational framework for research on close relationships. *Psychol. Inq.* 5:1–22

Hazan C, Zeifman D. 1999. Pair bonds as attachments: evaluating the evidence. In *Handbook of Attachment: Theory, Research, and Clinical Applications,* ed. J Cassidy, PR Shaver, pp. 336–54. New York: Guilford

Heider F. 1958. *The Psychology of Interpersonal Relations.* New York: Wiley

Hendrick C, Hendrick SS. 1986. A theory and method of love. *J. Personal. Soc. Psychol.* 50:392–402

Hendrick C, Hendrick SS. 1989. Research on love: Does it measure up? *J. Personal. Soc. Psychol.* 56:784–94

Hendrick C, Hendrick SS. 1990. A relationship-specific version of the Love Attitudes Scale. *J. Soc. Behav. Personal.* 5:239–54

Hendrick SS, Hendrick C. 1993. Lovers as friends. *J. Soc. Personal. Relat.* 10:459–66

Huston TL, Caughlin JP, Houts RM, Smith SE, George LJ. 2001. The connubial crucible: newlywed years as predictors of marital delight, distress, and divorce. *J. Personal. Soc. Psychol.* 80:237–52

Huston TL, Chorost A. 1994. Behavioral buffers on the effect of negativity on marital satisfaction: a longitudinal study. *Pers. Relat.* 1:223–39

Iida M, Seidman G, Shrout PE, Fujita K. 2008. Modeling support provision in intimate relationships. *J. Personal. Soc. Psychol.* 94:460–78

Isaacson W. 2007. *Einstein: His Life and Universe.* New York: Simon & Schuster

Karney BR, Bradbury TN. 1995. The longitudinal course of marital quality and stability: a review of theory, method, and research. *Psychol. Bull.* 118:3–34

Kayser K. 1993. *When Love Dies: The Process of Marital Disaffection.* New York: Guilford

Kelley HH. 1983/2002. Love and commitment. See Kelley et al. 1983/2002, pp. 265–314

Kelley HH. 1992. Common-sense psychology and scientific psychology. *Annu. Rev. Psychol.* 43:1–23

Kelley HH, Berscheid E, Christensen A, Harvey JH, Huston TL, et al. 1983/2002. *Close Relationships*. Clinton Corners, NY: Percheron (Original work published 1983)

Kenrick DT. 2006. A dynamical evolutionary view of love. See Sternberg & Weis 2006, pp. 15–34

Kephart WM. 1967. Some correlates of romantic love. *J. Marriage Fam.*, August, 470–74

Kunce LJ, Shaver PR. 1994. An attachment-theoretical approach to caregiving in romantic relationships. In *Attachment Processes in Adulthood. Advances in Personal Relationships, Vol. 5*, ed. K Bartholomew, D Perlman. pp. 205–37. London: Jessica Kingsley

Levine R, Sato S, Hashimoto T, Verna J. 1995. Love and marriage in eleven cultures. *J. Cross-Cult. Psychol.* 26:554–71

Lindzey G, Byrne D. 1968. Measurement of social choice and interpersonal attractiveness. In *The Handbook of Social Psychology, Vol. 2*, ed. G Lindzey, E Aronson, pp. 452–525. Reading, MA: Addison-Wesley

Maslow AH. 1954. *Motivation and Personality*. New York: Harper

Meyers SA, Berscheid E. 1997. The language of love: the difference a preposition makes. *Personal. Soc. Psychol. Bull.* 23:347–62

Mikulincer M, Shaver PR, Gillath O, Nitzberg RE. 2005. Attachment, caregiving, and altruism: augmentation of attachment security increases compassion and helping. *J. Personal. Soc. Psychol.* 85:817–39

Mitchell S. 2002. *Can Love Last? The Fate of Romance Over Time*. New York: Norton

Montgomery MJ, Sorrell GT. 1997. Differences in love attitudes across family life stages. *Fam. Relat.* 46:55–61

Murstein BI. 1988. A taxonomy of love. See Sternberg & Barnes 1988, pp. 13–37

Olson DH. 1970. Marital and family therapy: Integrative review and critique. In *A Decade of Family Research and Action*, ed. CB Broderick, pp. 241–78. Minneapolis, MN: Natl. Counc. Family Relat.

Orbuch TL, Veroff J, Holmberg D. 1993. Becoming a married couple: the emergence of meaning in the first years of marriage. *J. Marriage Fam.* 55:815–26

Osgood CE. 1969. On the whys and wherefores of E, P, and A. *J. Personal. Soc. Psychol.* 12:194–99

Pasch LA, Bradbury TN. 1998. Social support, conflict, and the development of marital dysfunction. *J. Consult. Clin. Psychol.* 66:219–30

Pineo PC. 1961. Disenchantment in the later years of marriage. *Marriage Fam. Living* 23:3–11

Regan PC. 1998. Of lust and love: Beliefs about the role of sexual desire in romantic relationships. *Pers. Relat.* 5:139–57

Regan PC, Berscheid E. 1999. *Lust: What We Know about Human Sexual Desire*. Thousand Oaks, CA: Sage

Reik T. 1944/1972. *A Psychologist Looks at Love*. New York: Lancer Books (original work published 1944 by Farrar & Rinehart)

Reis HT, Clark MS, Holmes JG. 2004. Perceived partner responsiveness as an organizing construct in the study of intimacy and closeness. In *Handbook of Closeness and Intimacy*, ed. DJ Mashek, A Aron, pp. 201–25. Mahwah, NJ: Erlbaum

Reis HT, Collins WA, Berscheid E. 2000. The relationship context of human behavior and development. *Psychol. Bull.* 126:844–72

Reis HT, Shaver P. 1988. Intimacy as an interpersonal process. In *Handbook of Personal Relationships: Theory, Research, and Interventions*, ed. S Duck, pp. 367–89. Chichester, UK: Wiley

Roberts TW. 1992. Sexual attraction and romantic love: forgotten variables in marital therapy. *J. Marital Fam. Therapy* 18:357–64

Rogge RD, Bradbury TN. 2002. Developing a multifaceted view of change in relationships. See Vangelisti et al. 2002, pp. 228–53

Rubin Z. 1970. Measurement of romantic love. *J. Personal. Soc. Psychol.* 16:265–73

Rubin Z. 1988. Preface. See Sternberg & Barnes 1988, pp. vii–xii

Rusbult CE, Bissonnette VL, Arriaga XB, Cox CL. 1998. Accommodation processes during the early years of marriage. See Bradbury 1998, pp. 74–113

Russell JA, Barrett LF. 1999. Core affect, prototypical emotional episodes, and other things called *emotion*: dissecting the elephant. *J. Personal. Soc. Psychol.* 76:805–19

Shaver PR, Hazan C, Bradshaw D. 1988. Love as attachment: the integration of three behavioral systems. See Sternberg & Barnes 1988, pp. 68–99

Shaver PR, Schwartz J, Kirson D, O'Connor C. 1987. Emotion knowledge: further exploration of a prototype approach. *J. Personal. Soc. Psychol.* 52:1061–86

Simpson JA, Campbell B, Berscheid E. 1986. The association between romantic love and marriage: Kephart (1967) twice revisited. *Personal. Soc. Psychol. Bull.* 12:363–72

Simpson JA, Rholes WS. 1998. Attachment in adulthood. In *Attachment Theory and Close Relationships*, ed. JA Simpson, WS Rholes, pp. 3–21. New York: Guilford

Sprecher S, Christopher FS, Cate R. 2006. Sexuality in close relationships. In *The Cambridge Handbook of Personal Relationships*, ed. D Perlman, A Vangelisti, pp. 463–82. New York: Cambridge Univ. Press

Sprecher S, Fehr B. 2005. Compassionate love for close others and humanity. *J. Soc. Personal. Relat.* 22:629–51

Sternberg RJ. 1986. A triangular theory of love. *Psychol. Rev.* 93:119–35

Sternberg RJ. 1987. Liking versus loving: a comparative evaluation of theories. *Psychol. Bull.* 102:331–45

Sternberg RJ, Barnes ML, eds. 1988. *The Psychology of Love*. New Haven, CT: Yale Univ. Press

Sternberg RJ, Grajek A. 1984. The nature of love. *J. Personal. Soc. Psychol.* 47:312–29

Sternberg RJ, Weis K, eds. 2006. *The New Psychology of Love*. New Haven, CT: Yale Univ. Press

Trinke SJ, Bartholomew K. 1997. Hierarchies of attachment relationships in young adulthood. *J. Soc. Personal. Relat.* 14:603–25

Tucker P, Aron A. 1993. Passionate love and marital satisfaction at key transition points in the family life cycle. *J. Soc. Clin. Psychol.* 12:135–47

Vangelisti AL, Reis HT, Fitzpatrick MA, eds. 2002. *Stability and Change in Relationships*. Cambridge, UK: Cambridge Univ. Press

VanLaningham J, Johnson DR, Amato P. 2001. Marital happiness, marital duration, and the U-shaped curve: evidence from a five-wave panel study. *Soc. Forces* 79:1313–41

Vormbrock JK. 1993. Attachment theory as applied to war-time and job-related marital separation. *Psychol. Bull.* 114:122–44

Waller WW, Hill R. 1951. *The Family: A Dynamic Interpretation*. New York: Dryden. Rev. ed. (original published 1938, New York: Dryden)

Walster [Hatfield] E, Walster GW. 1978. *A New Look at Love*. Reading, MA: Addison-Wesley

Waterfield R. 2001. *Plato Symposium*. New York: Oxford Univ. Press (original ca. 400 BC)

Watson D, Wiese D, Vaidya J, Tellegen A. 1999. The two general activation systems of affect: structural findings, evolutionary considerations, and psychobiological evidence. *J. Personal. Soc. Psychol.* 76:820–38

Weiss RS. 1975. *Marital Separation*. New York: Basic Books

Weiss RS. 1988. Loss and recovery. *J. Soc. Issues* 44:37–52

Whisman MA, Dixon AE, Johnson B. 1997. Therapists' perspectives of couple problems and treatment issues in couple therapy. *J. Fam. Psychol.* 11:361–66

Whitton S, Stanley S, Markman H. 2002. Sacrifice in romantic relationships. See Vangelisti et al. 2002, pp. 156–81

The Role of the Hippocampus in Prediction and Imagination

Randy L. Buckner

Howard Hughes Medical Institute at Harvard University, Cambridge, Massachusetts 02138;
email: Randy_Buckner@Harvard.edu

Annu. Rev. Psychol. 2010. 61:27–48

First published online as a Review in Advance on
October 19, 2009

The *Annual Review of Psychology* is online at
psych.annualreviews.org

This article's doi:
10.1146/annurev.psych.60.110707.163508

0066-4308/10/0110-0027$20.00

Key Words

preplay, replay, memory, amnesia, prospection

Abstract

Traditionally, the hippocampal system has been studied in relation to the goal of retrieving memories about the past. Recent work in humans and rodents suggests that the hippocampal system may be better understood as a system that facilitates predictions about upcoming events. The hippocampus and associated cortical structures are active when people envision future events, and damage that includes the hippocampal region impairs this ability. In rats, hippocampal ensembles preplay and replay event sequences in the absence of overt behavior. If strung together in novel combinations, these sequences could provide the neural building blocks for simulating upcoming events during decision-making, planning, and when imagining novel scenarios. Moreover, in both humans and rodents, the hippocampal system is spontaneously active during task-free epochs and sleep, further suggesting that the system may use idle moments to derive new representations that set the context for future behaviors.

Contents

INTRODUCTION

Patients with memory impairment often also have difficulties in imagining upcoming events and novel scenarios (Hassabis et al. 2007, Klein et al. 2002b, Korsakoff 1889/1996, Talland 1965, Tulving 1985). This observation in amnesia provides an important clue about the adaptive function of memory systems. Remnants of past events may serve as the building blocks for prediction and imagination. Here emerging findings are reviewed that suggest an essential role of the hippocampal-cortical system is to facilitate predictions about the future. At the center of this perspective is the idea that the capture of associations that define event sequences is adaptive because these sequences can be reassembled into novel combinations that anticipate and simulate future events. Traditional memory tests tap into hippocampal mechanisms because stored associations are necessary for veridical recall, but the functional role of the hippocampus is nonetheless best understood from an adaptive, forward-oriented perspective.

The idea that the hippocampal-cortical system is important to prediction is receiving growing attention. Cohen & Eichenbaum (1993) end their book by noting that the representational flexibility of the hippocampal system permits the ability to "manipulate" stored representations in the service of problem-solving behaviors. Such ideas are echoed in cognitive theories. Johnson & Sherman (1990) proposed that expectations about the future are an amalgamation of all past events that one has experienced and stored. Klein and colleagues (2002b; see also Klein et al. 2002a) poignantly noted, "a case can be made that information storage is intrinsically prospective, used to support future decisions and judgments that cannot be known in advance with certainty." Attance & O'Neill (2001), Ingvar (1985), Suddendorf & Corballis (1997), and Tulving (2005) have all thoughtfully discussed the role of memory in thinking about the future. Several recent reviews specifically elaborate on the possibility that the hippocampus plays a role in prediction or imagination (e.g., Bar 2007; Bird & Burgess 2008; Buckner & Carroll 2007; Buckner et al. 2008; Hassabis & Maguire 2007; Johnson et al. 2007; Lisman & Redish 2009; Schacter & Addis 2007, 2009; Schacter et al. 2007, 2008). These past ideas and papers serve as an important basis for the present review.

The review begins with a brief historical orientation to the problem by drawing from the seminal work of Edward Tolman, who showed that learning can be flexibly expressed in novel contexts. Next, imaging and neuropsychological data in humans are reviewed that suggest the hippocampal-cortical system plays a critical role in envisioning the future. Following the description of findings in humans, recent electrophysiological studies in rodents are described that reveal the presence of preplay and replay sequences that might provide the building blocks for representation of upcoming events. These combined observations are then integrated into a mechanistic model of how the hippocampus might contribute to prediction and imagination.

TOLMAN'S THEORY OF EXPECTANCY

A classic series of studies by Tolman and colleagues provides a good beginning point for discussion. Confronted with the prevailing view that all learning results from direct reinforcement of specific behaviors, Tolman developed an alternative formulation that he called "theory of expectancy." He was motivated by the observation that purposeful behaviors often follow a route for which the animal has no direct prior experience. How could a system that only has access to reinforced responses act in such a flexible manner? Tolman constructed several ingenious experiments to show that rats combine remnants of past experiences to guide de novo behaviors. These studies were instrumental in his development of the concept of a "cognitive map" (Tolman 1948) and its later link to the hippocampus (O'Keefe & Nadel 1978).

As one illustrative example, Tolman et al. (1946) trained rats to go down a path making several turns away from, and then back toward, an eventual food reward (**Figure 1**, see color insert). After several training sessions, the apparatus was modified for a single critical trial to test the flexibility of the rats' use of memory. Specifically, they blocked the learned route and observed whether the rats would take a correct alternative path or remain stereotyped in their response and choose the path closest to the

original (reinforced) route. They hypothesized that rats can flexibly express their prior experience to navigate novel situations, and found that many rats correctly chose the direct path to the food reward even though they had no experience with the route and it was positioned distant from the original path.

A second study by Tolman & Gleitman (1949) illustrated that rats can combine information across temporally distinct events. In this later study, they had rats explore a standard T-maze (**Figure 2**, see color insert). Across sequential trials, the rats foraged for food equally in both arms, sometimes receiving a reward after turning right and at other times after turning left. Following initial training, the rats were removed from the maze and placed directly in one arm of the box, where they received a series of foot shocks. On a single critical test trial, the rats were placed back in the original maze and allowed to forage. Eighty-eight percent of the rats chose the safe arm even though they had never previously chosen the to-be-shocked corner in the T-maze and received an aversive outcome. Sequences experienced across prior episodes must have been combined to make the adaptive response.

Tolman's elegant studies illustrate that the use of memory extends beyond the exact retrieval of reinforced sequences. Behavior requires the novel recombination of remnants of past experiences to make predictions. In this review, I explore the possibility that the hippocampal-cortical system contributes to the construction of de novo predictions such as tapped into by Tolman's paradigms and presumably relied upon, in elaborated form, to support the human capacity to think about the future.

THE HIPPOCAMPAL-CORTICAL SYSTEM

The hippocampal-cortical system includes the hippocampal region as well as its widespread cortical targets. Within the hippocampal region is a set of interconnected structures (the CA fields, the dentate gyrus, and the subicular complex) that are positioned as a loop

Hippocampal-cortical system: includes the hippocampal region, the immediately adjacent cortex (e.g., entorhinal cortex), and widespread cortical targets

Preplay: an activity sequence that anticipates an upcoming event sequence (sequence A-B-C is preplayed in anticipation of experiencing A-B-C)

Replay: activity sequences that repeat past events (experience of A-B-C leads to replay sequence A-B-C)

Hippocampal region: the CA fields, the dentate gyrus, and the subicular complex of the hippocampus receiving and projecting information to neocortex (for a recent review, see Squire et al. 2004). The hippocampal region is connected to cortical areas through the adjacent entorhinal cortex that then projects to the perirhinal and parahippocampal cortices. In turn, the perirhinal and parahippocampal cortices project to widespread cortical regions. Much of the electrophysiology in rodents has focused on the CA fields within the hippocampus itself or the immediately adjacent entorhinal cortex. In this review, we refer to the hippocampal region and its broad cortical targets collectively as the hippocampal-cortical system.

Across rat, monkey, and human, the hippocampal region interacts with neocortex through parallel pathways. Anatomical convergence from multiple processing pathways allows the hippocampus to integrate both spatial and nonspatial information. In the monkey, the perirhinal and parahippocampal cortices are distinguished by separate connections with temporal and parietal pathways, respectively (Suzuki & Amaral 1994). Functional connectivity analysis in humans reveals a similar distinction (Kahn et al. 2008). The rat hippocampal system is divided between two major input pathways that converge on perirhinal and postrhinal cortex (the equivalent of primate parahippocampal cortex) (Burwell 2000). Thus, although there are differences across species, the general architecture of the hippocampal-cortical system is similar and includes parallel pathways that convey multiple sources of information to the hippocampus.

Figure 3 (see color insert) shows the cortical areas that are connected to the hippocampal region across the three species. The estimated cortical targets in the rat and macaque monkey come from studies of connectional anatomy (e.g., Burwell 2000, Insausti et al. 1997, Kobayashi & Amaral 2003, Lavenex & Amaral 2000, Suzuki & Amaral 1994). In humans, direct assessment of connectional anatomy is not possible; however, functional connectivity based on functional magnetic resonance imaging (fMRI) provides an approximation (Biswal et al. 1995; see Fox & Raichle

2007 for review). The estimated cortical targets of the human hippocampal region bear a strong resemblance to expectations from monkey anatomy (Kahn et al. 2008, Vincent et al. 2006), with the caveat that several of the regions include areas disproportionately expanded in hominid evolution (e.g., inferior parietal lobule, medial prefrontal cortex; Öngür & Price 2000, Van Essen & Dierker 2007). The specific topography of the cortical targets illustrated in **Figure 3** are especially relevant to the review of findings from human neuroimaging studies in the next section.

THE HIPPOCAMPAL-CORTICAL SYSTEM IS ACTIVE WHEN PEOPLE ENVISION THE FUTURE

Traditional tests of memory ask subjects to retrieve information about their past. Was this or that item presented on the earlier study list? Or, recall what happened at your college graduation. The central thesis of this review is that brain systems involved in memory are best understood in terms of their adaptive, future-oriented functions.

"Memory" systems are hypothesized to provide the building blocks that are used to construct predictions about upcoming events. Consistent with this possibility, accumulating evidence suggests that thinking about the future shares similar behavioral properties and uses the same hippocampal-cortical system as remembering the past.

Cognitive Observations

Behavioral studies have explored whether self-reported descriptions about possible upcoming events demonstrate properties that are shared in common with answers on typical memory tests. For example, recent memories are recalled with greater detail than distant memories (Johnson et al. 1988). Do projections about the future show a similar property? Several studies have adopted this approach (D'Argembeau & Van der Linden 2004, 2006; Spreng & Levine 2006; Szpunar & McDermott 2008). In one

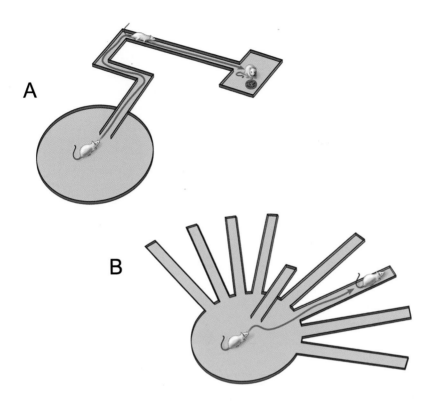

Figure 1

Edward Tolman's classic paradigms demonstrate that rats can use past experience to make de novo predictions. When confronted with a barrier that prevents a learned route, rats will often take a novel direct path—a shortcut—to the food reward. Tolman illustrated this behavior by first training the animals on a circuitous route to a food reward (*A*). Then, following training during a single critical trial, the learned path was blocked. The animals tended to take the angled path that could lead directly to the food reward. Adapted from Tolman et al. (1946).

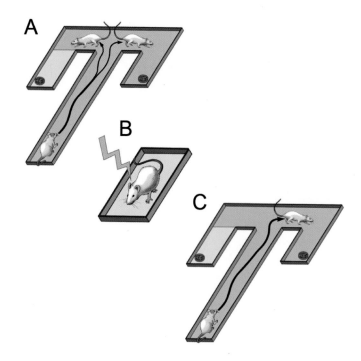

Figure 2

Rats were trained to forage freely in an environment (*A*). After being foot shocked in a chamber that was associated with one of the chamber's endpoints (*B*), rats avoided the path in the maze that led to the chamber (*C*) even though they had never actually experienced the aversive chamber when foraging. Adapted from Tolman & Gleitman (1949).

Rat   Monkey   Human

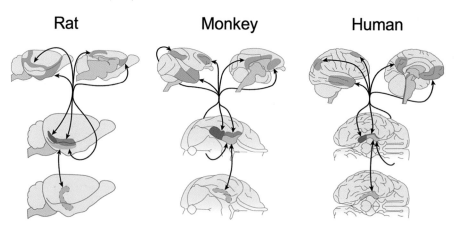

Figure 3

The hippocampal-cortical system in rat, monkey, and human. In each species, the hippocampus proper (*blue*) projects to the entorhinal cortex (*pink*). The entorhinal cortex projects to the perirhinal (*red*) and parahippocampal (postrhinal in rat) (*orange*) cortices that, in turn, project to widespread regions of cortex that include the posterior midline, lateral parietal cortex, and medial prefrontal cortex in monkey and human. The general architecture of the hippocampal region is preserved across species. Estimates of rat and monkey cortical projections redrawn from Eichenbaum (2000). Estimates of human cortical projects are based on Vincent et al. (2006) and Kahn et al. (2008).

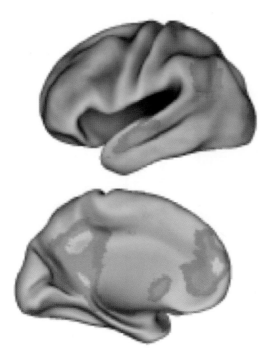

Figure 4

Autobiographical memory retrieval and envisioning the future both activate the hippocampal-cortical system. Cortical activation during a functional MRI task that targets imagining the future is shown for a group of subjects from Addis et al. (2007). Note the overlap between the regions active and the hippocampal-cortical system as diagrammed in **Figure 3**. The representation is a left hemisphere surface based on the Population-Average, Landmark- and Surface-based (PALS) atlas of Van Essen (2005).

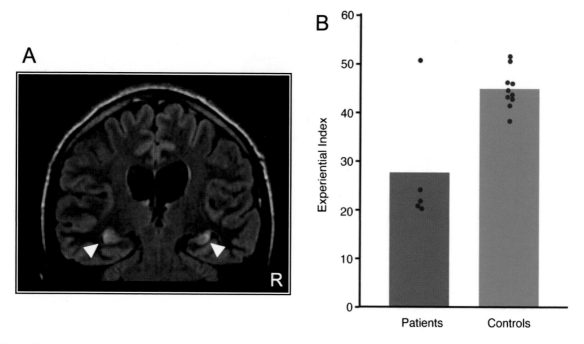

Figure 5

Patients with brain lesions that include the hippocampus are impaired at envisioning novel scenarios. (*A*) An example of a 24-year-old male patient (P03) studied by Hassabis et al. (2007). The patient's MRI scan showed bilateral hippocampal damage following limbic encephalitis (*arrows*), and he had significant autobiographical memory deficits. (*B*) Data plotted for five amnesic patients, including P03, on a test of their ability to imagine novel scenarios (e.g., "Imagine you are standing in the main hall of a museum containing many exhibits"). The plotted index, referred to as the experiential index, reflects the overall richness of the imagined experience. Note that the patients provide relatively sparse descriptions of imagined scenarios that are devoid of the elaborate and detailed content typical of normal subjects. Adapted from data reported by Hassabis et al. (2007).

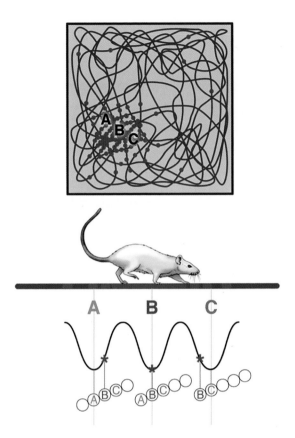

Figure 6

Place fields and theta phase precession provide insight into hippocampal function. (*Top*) A schematic diagram of a rat's path through a square environment. The view is from above, and the black path reflects the path of a freely foraging rat. Each time the rat transverses the bottom left, the place cell fires (*red dots*). The preferential firing in the specific location is the place field. (*Bottom*) Theta phase precession is illustrated for the rat running through the place field. The place field is represented by the red area under the rat's position, and locations A, B, and C are demarcated. The red dots reflect the firing of a single cell labeled B, and the oscillating line schematically illustrates theta. As the rat approaches the place field, the B cell fires relatively late in theta. As the rat moves through the field, the cell fires earlier and earlier in relation to theta. This property, known as theta phase precession, can be explained if the cell is embedded within firing sequences among multiple cells, some of which anticipate the upcoming location. The cell sequences are illustrated at the bottom of the panel as chains of circles with the A, B, and C cells labeled.

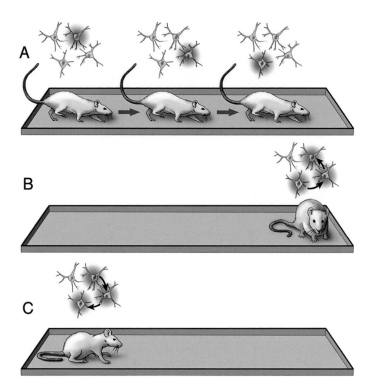

Figure 7

Replay and preplay sequences in the hippocampus. (*A*) As rats navigate, multiple place cells fire in sequence, reflecting the changing location of the animal. When multiple units are recorded, the place of the rat can be accurately estimated based on the firing pattern among the cells. (*B*) When rats stop following reward delivery, place fields sometimes spontaneously fire in reverse order to their original sequence. These firing events are referred to as "reverse replay" sequences and occur during sharp-wave ripple events at the ends of reinforced journeys (Foster & Wilson 2006). (*C*) Anticipatory activity sequences are also observed during sharp-wave ripple events. "Preplay" sequences occur almost exclusively at the beginning of journeys and anticipate the upcoming sequential positions of the animal (Diba & Buzsáki 2007).

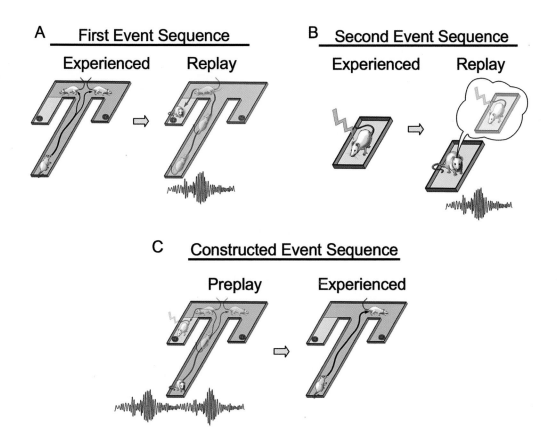

Figure 8

The hippocampal prediction model. Diagrams show how replay and preplay activity within hippocampal cell assemblies might allow for construction of de novo predictions. The model is applied to the paradigm studied by Tolman and Gleitman (1949) for illustrative purposes, but the framework is meant to be quite general and extend to humans in an elaborated form. (*A*) Activity sequences associated with experienced events are captured and can be replayed. The sequences are consolidated through replay that occurs at the end of journeys during sharp-wave ripple events or perhaps at other times. (*B*) Sequences are consolidated for distinct, isolated events using similar mechanisms. Presumably as exploration is undertaken, numerous sequences associated with experienced events are captured and available to future needs. (*C*) By chaining together multiple past event sequences in constructed combinations, complex event sequences that represent novel predictions emerge. In this instance, by chaining together the past experience of traveling down the left arm and the distinct experience of being shocked, the rat presumably predicts the aversive event and turns right to avoid it. Note that this is a de novo prediction because the rat never experienced turning left and receiving a shock.

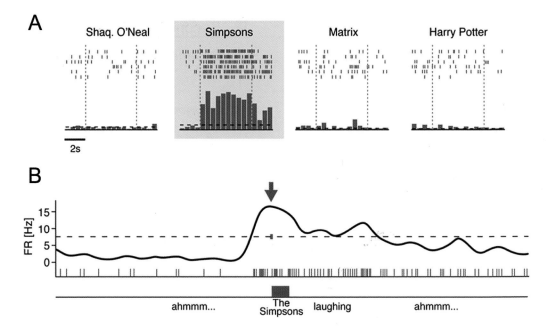

Figure 9

Human hippocampal cells exhibit spontaneous activity when episodes are imagined. (*A*) Single-unit recordings from an entorhinal cortex cell while the patient viewed video episodes of Shaquille O'Neal, *The Simpsons* cartoon, and movie scenes from *The Matrix* and *Harry Potter*. The small dash marks represent an action potential, with each line representing a different epoch of stimulus viewing. The histogram below represents the summed action potentials across the viewing epochs. Note that this particular cell is selectively responsive when the Simpsons cartoon is viewed. (*B*) Single-unit recordings from the same cell while the participant freely recalled the viewed epochs from memory. The words below represent the utterances of the patient as he reported what he was recalling. The spontaneous activity increase in the cell corresponded to the report of the patient imagining the episode of *The Simpsons*, which suggests that the hippocampal-cortical system is involved in replay. Adapted from Gelbard-Sagiv et al. (2008).

of the first explorations, D'Argembeau & Van der Linden (2004) noted that temporally close events, both in the past and in the future, are experienced with more sensory and contextual details than are distant events. They had subjects re-experience memories or pre-experience possible future events. After each event, subjects rated the vividness of the experience for visual details, clarity of the spatial arrangements of objects and people, and several other features. For most features, temporally close future episodes were experienced with rich details, whereas distant events were relatively impoverished. This pattern is the same as that observed for past events. Psychiatric patients (D'Argembeau et al. 2008a) and older adults (Addis et al. 2008) show impoverished episodic details similarly for both recollection of the past and imagination of the future. These collective results demonstrate that people imagine future event scenarios in ways that parallel remembering the past.

Szpunar & McDermott (2008) recently expanded upon this procedure and provide evidence that future event constructions actively rely on past experience. In addition to probing content, they also manipulated the degree to which the future event could be based on past experience. In one study, subjects imagined future events in previously experienced environments (e.g., a friend's apartment) as compared to never-experienced environments (e.g., the jungle). In a second study, subjects imagined events in recently experienced environments (e.g., their university campus) as compared to environments lacking recent experience (e.g., their high school). In both studies, envisioned future events contained significantly more sensory and contextual details if they were built upon familiar environments. Although alternative explanations are possible, these findings suggest that acts of envisioning the future rely upon sampling memories from the past.

Evidence from Functional Brain Imaging

Direct evidence that the hippocampal-cortical system is used during future episodic thought emerges from functional brain imaging studies. Traditional retrieval tasks that encourage recollection, in particular from autobiographical memory, have reliably activated components of the hippocampal-cortical system or the system in its entirety (Cabeza & St. Jacques 2007, Maguire 2001, Svoboda et al. 2006, Vilberg & Rugg 2008, Wagner et al. 2005). In a particularly thorough analysis, Svoboda et al. (2006) aggregated data from 24 positron emission tomography and fMRI studies that examined autobiographical memory retrieval. The network of regions consistently activated across studies included the hippocampal region as well as the distributed cortical regions that comprise the hippocampal-cortical system. Critical to the present review, studies that examine tasks where subjects imagine future scenarios demonstrate that the same hippocampal-cortical system is active. Schacter et al. (2007, 2008) discuss in detail findings from such paradigms, so they are only briefly mentioned here.

In the prototypical paradigm, participants are given a cue and instructed to imagine a future situation related to that cue. For example, cued with the word "dress," a student tested by Addis et al. (2007) responded with the following imagined scene: "My sister will be finishing her undergraduate education... And I can see myself sitting in some kind of sundress, like yellow, and under some trees." Several such studies have been reported using positron emission tomography and fMRI (Addis et al. 2007, Botzung et al. 2008, D'Argembeau et al. 2008b, Okuda et al. 2003, Partiot et al. 1995, Sharot et al. 2007, Szpunar et al. 2007). Example data from Addis et al. (2007) are displayed in **Figure 4** (see color insert). The network active for episodic future thought is strikingly similar to that for autobiographical recall.

Analyses that combine data across studies suggest there is convergent activation in the hippocampal-cortical system including the hippocampal region, the posterior cingulate extending into precuneus, the inferior parietal lobule, and the medial frontal cortex (Schacter et al. 2008, Spreng et al. 2009). Correspondence is not perfect. Medial frontal regions implicated as components of the hippocampal-cortical system include ventral regions, while the studies of future thought converge on a region that is more dorsal (see Buckner et al. 2008 for anatomical review). Predictions are also likely dependent on more than just episodic processes (see Szpunar 2009). Addis and colleagues further provide evidence that activity within the hippocampal region tracks the amount of detail recollected or projected to an imagined future event (Addis & Schacter 2008) and also that the region (particularly the anterior hippocampal formation) is most active when imagined events about the future must combine details across episodes (Addis et al. 2009, Schacter & Addis 2009). Taken collectively, the functional imaging results suggest that (*a*) the same regions are active during envisioning the future as remembering the past, and (*b*) these regions include the hippocampus and cortical targets that (largely) overlap the hippocampal-cortical system.

MEMORY IMPAIRMENT DISRUPTS THE ABILITY TO IMAGINE FUTURE EVENT SCENARIOS

Neuropsychological studies of amnesia have long emphasized the profound memory loss that results from damage to the medial temporal lobe (MTL) and associated structures. Following bilateral MTL damage, the ability to recount recent events and learn new episodes is significantly impaired while global cognitive functions and procedural memory remain intact. Several prior reviews have discussed these classic neuropsychological findings (Milner et al. 1998, Squire et al. 2004). Here attention will be drawn to a lesser-studied aspect of amnesia that surrounds deficits in the ability to envision future events and imagination. Such deficits, which have been anecdotally reported since the earliest descriptions of amnesia, are emerging as an often-observed feature of memory impairment and have important implications for how we conceptualize the function of the hippocampal-cortical system.

Korsakoff (1889/1996) discussed the absence of imagination and flexible thinking in his memory-impaired patients, as reflected in his description below:

> This is why, after conversing at length with one of the patients, his initially striking perceptiveness and presence of mind seem somewhat deficient. We realize that: (1) the patient reasons by making use of old material, accumulated during a long period of time. Recent impressions have almost no role in his reasoning; (2) even with this old material, the patient makes only routine combinations and repeats phrases learned long ago; (3) the circle of ideas in which the patient's intelligence moves becomes very restricted, and even this narrow frame, he always makes the same connections.

Talland (1965) noted a similar loss of imagination in his case studies of amnesia. When asked about their future plans, his patients could only state generalities such as that they would return to work; their answers lacked details about possible future interactions with other people and events. Although the brain lesions in these patients confound medial temporal and frontal damage (e.g., Shimamura et al. 1990),[1] it is nonetheless intriguing that deficits in memory were intertwined with parallel deficits in imagining the future.

More recently, observations of patients H.M. and K.C. also revealed similar deficits. H.M., who became densely amnesic following bilateral resection of the hippocampus and adjacent structures in the MTL (Corkin 2002, Scoville & Milner 1957), did not make predictions about future autobiographical events. When pushed to do so, he responded with

---

[1] The contribution of frontal systems to deficits in future thought, including foresight and planning, have been reviewed previously (e.g., Fuster 1989, Mesulam 2002, Shallice 1982). Interactions between frontal and hippocampal systems will undoubtedly be important to understanding how predictions are constructed and used to guide decisions. The emphasis on the hippocampal system in this review is a matter of focus and is not meant to minimize the importance of frontal systems (e.g., see Buckner & Carroll 2007).

a happening from the distant past or simply did not respond (S. Steinvorth and S. Corkin, personal communication). K.C., another well-studied individual with amnesia (Rosenbaum et al. 2005), also failed to respond in similar situations (Tulving 1985). In a recent test of K.C.'s deficits, Rosenbaum et al. (2009) observed that he could not imagine fictitious events with the same richness in detail as that of controls.

Deficits of envisioning the future were systematically studied in patient D.B., who developed amnesia following anoxia (Klein et al. 2002b). Motivated by the possibility that memory systems are intrinsically prospectively focused, Klein and colleagues probed D.B.'s deficits by asking him a series of questions about the future. They observed that D.B. either confabulated or did not know what he would be doing on most questions about his personal future, although he retained general knowledge. For example, he remarked that a future issue facing the environment was a "threat that weather and rainfall patterns are going to change because of industrial pollution." It is unknown the exact anatomy of D.B.'s lesion, which resulted from an anoxic episode during cardiac arrest. The hippocampus is affected during anoxia because it is among the structures most sensitive to damage and cell loss due to ischemia, although such damage is not typically limited to the hippocampus (Squire & Zola 1996).

The studies described above make a strong case that brain systems important to memory are also critical to imagining the future; impairments in one domain appear linked to the other. However, the findings do not allow a strong statement to be made about the exact anatomic structures damaged, especially in relation to determining whether lesions restricted to the hippocampus are sufficient to cause deficits. Among the above patients, the lesions sustained by H.M. have been the best characterized, but his behavioral deficits in this domain were insufficiently documented. Animal models and considerably more information than is available today will be required to resolve this issue.

Hassabis et al. (2007) recently tested patients with documented hippocampal amnesia providing some initial insight. Their study is important for two reasons. First, the anatomic analysis of the lesions and clinical description suggested that the hippocampus was specifically damaged in four patients showing the greatest functional impairments. As an example, **Figure 5** (see color figure) shows the MRI scan of patient P03, a 24-year-old male with a rare form of limbic encephalitis. His MRI revealed hyperintense signals in the bilateral hippocampus, and electroencephalogram (EEG) analysis showed bilateral epileptic discharges in the medial temporal regions (Samarasekera et al. 2007). Generalized atrophy was also present (note the enlarged ventricles), so it is not possible to conclude that his impairments result from focal hippocampal damage. However, in aggregate, the convergence of damage to the hippocampal region across patients supports the possibility that the hippocampus and interconnected structures are intimate to the origin of the deficits.

Second, Hassabis et al. (2007) explored the nature of the patient's impairment in considerable detail, including analysis of which components of imagination are disrupted. The paradigm involved asking patients and matched controls to imagine experiences in response to short verbal cues. For example, the participants were asked to describe scenes involving "lying on a white sandy beach in a beautiful tropical bay" and "a possible event over the next weekend." A composite index measuring the overall richness of the imagined experiences was markedly reduced in four of five patients compared to controls (**Figure 5**). The patients' own narratives also revealed these deficits. For example, when patient P03 was asked to imagine lying on a white sandy beach, he provided a vague description of objects that are typically associated with a beach but did not describe a coherent visual scene. As a final analysis, the patients were asked to judge the appropriateness of statements that described their internal mental experience. Some of the statements asked whether the imagined scenes were integrated (e.g., "I could see the whole scene in my mind's eye"), while others probed whether the scenes were fragmented (e.g., "It was a collection of separate images"). Results again confirmed that the patients' imagined scenes were fragmentary and lacked an integrated spatial context.

Taken together, these findings suggest that amnesia is associated with deficits in the ability to envision the future and other forms of events that depend on an imagined scene. A possibility is that such deficits result because of the loss of mechanisms to store and flexibly recombine the remnants of past events into novel, prospectively useful forms. In the section below, I review physiological studies of rats navigating environments that suggest mechanisms by which cell assemblies in the hippocampus might support such prospective functions.

HIPPOCAMPAL CELL ASSEMBLIES PROVIDE THE BUILDING BLOCKS FOR PREDICTION

The question addressed in this section is whether activity patterns exhibited by hippocampal cell assemblies are consistent with a role in prediction. That is, do hippocampal neurons fire in a manner that could contribute to expectations about the future? The most basic expected property is that activity should represent upcoming actions and events. Under appropriate conditions, prospective activity correlates should be detached from the stimuli in the immediate environment and current behaviors of the animal. A second property is that the activity should predict future behavior. Error trials are particularly informative for testing this property. Finally, manipulation or disruption of the activity should influence later behaviors. Ultimately, a prediction mechanism would be most convincingly demonstrated by showing experimental control over an animal's decision-making.

The vast majority of information about neuronal activity patterns in the hippocampus comes from studies in rodents navigating spatial environments. To foreshadow the observations that will be discussed, hippocampal cell assemblies exhibit firing patterns during navigation

that (*a*) reflect past and upcoming locations, (*b*) are spontaneously emitted, and (*c*) correlate with the future behavior of the animal under specific conditions. As is discussed, caveats and open questions remain concerning the functions of these activity patterns because causal manipulations have yet to be demonstrated.

Two important discoveries provide the backdrop for understanding the potential role of hippocampal neurons in prediction. The first is the phenomenon of place fields (O'Keefe & Dostrovsky 1971; for recent review, see Moser et al. 2008) and the second is of theta phase precession (O'Keefe & Recce 1993, Skaggs et al. 1996; for recent reviews see Buzsáki 2005 and Maurer & McNaughton 2007). These two phenomena are discussed first, followed by a more extensive description of recent studies that provide evidence for prospective coding.

Place Fields

Place fields are spatial receptive fields that are present in hippocampal pyramidal cells in CA1 and CA3. As a rat moves through the environment, neurons exhibiting place fields will preferentially respond when the rodent transverses a specific location (**Figure 6**, see color insert). The observation of place fields led O'Keefe & Nadel (1978) to propose that cells exhibiting such fields—place cells—are the building blocks of an internal map-like representation of the environment. Numerous studies have confirmed and extended these observations, including the remarkable discovery of neurons in the medial entorhinal cortex—grid cells—that map multiple locations of the environment in a grid-like pattern (Fyhn et al. 2004). A great deal of recent focus has been on unraveling the network properties that enable the computation of place fields and how the population signals are used for spatial navigation and memory (e.g., Burgess et al. 2007, Hasselmo & Eichenbaum 2005, Lisman 2005, McNaughton et al. 2006, Moser et al. 2008).

For the present purpose of exploring the role of the hippocampus in prediction, place fields provide a powerful way to measure what hippocampal cell assemblies are representing at any given moment in time. Once the receptive fields of multiple units have been mapped, it becomes possible to measure the ensemble activity to determine whether the neuronal population is representing the current position of the animal or a past or future position. That is, one can obtain a readout of what the animal's brain is representing. This is a major breakthrough because measurement of ensemble activity provides a direct way to peer into the rat's brain during navigation to determine what the hippocampus is representing without the need to infer what the animal is thinking.

Three further aspects of hippocampal response properties are relevant. First, spatial signals do not necessarily arise within the circuitry of the CA fields of the hippocampus. Inputs from the medial entorhinal cortex, as demonstrated by grid cells, are a likely source of spatial information relevant to navigation (Fyhn et al. 2004; see Moser et al. 2008 for review). The representational properties of hippocampal neurons should be considered as byproducts of larger circuit properties including interactions with cortex. Second, in paradigms where associations between nonspatial sources of information are demanded, hippocampal neurons respond in ways that suggest they also code aspects of the environment beyond location (Eichenbaum 2000). Consistent with this, the anatomic input streams to the hippocampus provide multiple sources of information with afferents from the lateral, in contrast to medial, entorhinal cortex, providing nonspatial information (Hargreaves et al. 2005; see also Lisman 2007). In this regard, while studies of rat navigation provide the richest source of information about hippocampal function, it is likely that the properties discussed here will generalize to other informational domains beyond spatial information conveyed to the hippocampus via external inputs (Eichenbaum 2004). Finally, place fields are not solely determined by the location of the animal but can respond to higher-order features such as where the animal has come from and where it will go to (Ferbinteanu & Shapiro 2003, Frank et al. 2000, Ji & Wilson

2008, Smith & Mizumori 2006, Wood et al. 2000; see Shapiro et al. 2006 for review). These properties suggest that there is substantial representational flexibility within hippocampal circuits.

Theta Phase Precession and Theta Sequences

In addition to exhibiting place-specific response firing at the level of individual neurons, hippocampal neurons as a population manifest remarkably regular oscillations during active navigation, referred to as theta oscillations. Six to eight times a second, the aggregate synaptic activity—measured by the local field potential—increases to a peak and then decreases. O'Keefe & Recce (1993) and Skaggs et al. (1996) observed a timing relationship between place cell firing and theta oscillations that provides an essential insight into the activity of hippocampal cell assemblies. They noted that as a rat approaches the location of a place field, the place cell fires late in relation to theta; as the animal leaves the critical location, the place cell fires early. Given that it typically takes 8 to 12 theta cycles for a rat to move through a place field, the timing of place cell firing appears to progress along the full phase of the theta oscillation—a process called theta phase precession.

What does the phenomenon of theta phase precession tell us about the structure of hippocampal cell assemblies? Recognizing that there are alternative possibilities (e.g., see Maurer & McNaughton 2007 for discussion), theta phase precession may be revealing the presence of firing sequences or chains across multiple neurons within a network. Using a computational model, Tsodyks and colleagues (1996) elegantly demonstrated how activity sequences could give rise to timing shifts observed in individual neurons. To conceptually illustrate how this possibility follows, consider the simple case where there exists only three neurons and only three locations that a rat transverses (**Figure 6**). Let's label the neurons A, B, and C. If the neurons were independent and the animal ran through the three locations, one would observe sequential firing of neurons A, B, and C as the animal entered each location. Now consider the alternative, where A-B-C are linked in a chain such that when an animal enters the location coded by neuron A, it will fire, followed by B and C in succession. In this latter case, one would observe a more complex behavior when recording activity from the neurons. As an animal enters the location represented by A, neuron B will fire but will do so with a very brief delay (late from the relative perspective of neuron B firing). As the animal enters the location represented by B, neuron B will fire without delay (early from the relative perspective of neuron B firing). Thus, as the animal runs through the sequence of locations, recording from a single neuron will reveal a firing precession from late to early as the animal moves through the receptive field. An observer with access only to a single neuron sees theta phase precession.

Foster & Wilson (2007) recently demonstrated directly the presence of neuronal activity sequences time-locked to theta, appropriately calling them "theta sequences" (see also Dragoi & Buzsáki 2006, Itskov et al. 2008). In their experiment, they had rats run back and forth on a linear track; the investigators simultaneously recorded the place fields of many neurons. Typical of such paradigms, CA1 neurons exhibited place fields that temporally precessed in relation to theta. Critically, when activity patterns across multiple neurons were examined, Foster & Wilson (2007) observed sequences of firing that rapidly (<100 ms) recapitulated the sequential patterns of place cell firing experienced by the animal during navigation. Neurons that sequentially fired during multisecond navigation fired in rapid, sequential bursts as the animal moved through the place fields. The theta-phase precession observed at the level of individual cells could be accounted for by the sequences of activity across multiple neurons.

The functions of hippocampal theta-phase precession and theta sequences are presently unknown. The kind of rapid temporal prediction afforded by theta sequences might be useful to bridge processing events that unfold over hundreds of milliseconds or to compress the timescale of experiences to optimize plasticity (e.g., Buzsáki 2002, Itskov et al. 2008). They are almost certainly not, in isolation, responsible for the forms of prediction that span multiple event contingencies or anticipate distant upcoming events. Perhaps the lesson most relevant for our present purposes is to raise the possibility that networks of hippocampal neurons code predictive event sequences. That is, neurons within the cell assemblies do not simply fire based on inputs that specify a single location but rather are triggered by inputs to earlier locations that anticipate them (see also Lisman & Redish 2009 for discussion).

Evidence for Prospective Coding

The preceding sections review observations that suggest hippocampal circuits have the capacity to encode sequential associations. However, they do not necessarily reveal activity patterns used as prospective codes for planning or decision-making. All of the results concerned generation of spiking sequences triggered by entry or exit of a specific location, so the simplest interpretation is that they are stimulus bound. It is in this context that one can appreciate the importance of recent demonstrations that nonlocal activity sequences are spontaneously emitted independent of immediate cues arising from the environment (Csicsvari et al. 2007, Davidson et al. 2009, Diba & Buzsáki 2007, Foster & Wilson 2006, Johnson & Redish 2007, Karlsson & Frank 2009, Pastalkova et al. 2008).

The first example of such a phenomenon was reported during sharp-wave ripple events. Ripple events occur when theta oscillations are minimal, such as during resting moments and slow-wave sleep (Buzsáki 1989). At a circuit level, ripple events reflect the coordinated discharge of large numbers of pyramidal cells. Foster & Wilson (2006) recorded multiunit activity while rats ran back and forth on a linear track as described earlier for their documentation of theta sequences. However, unlike the typical analysis of activity sequences that emerge during active navigation, they focused on the time periods after the rat had completed its lap and received a food reward. During these stop periods, structured activity sequences were observed that mimicked the navigation path, but in reverse order. These reverse replay events were common and preferentially occurred during sharp-wave ripple events.

Diba & Buzsáki (2007) observed a similar phenomenon but, critically, also observed ripple-linked sequences that evolved in forward order—"preplay" events. Taking advantage of the high percentage of place fields that were directionally selective, they were further able to quantify the number of forward preplay and reverse replay events that occurred at the beginning versus the end of the journey. Consistent with an anticipatory role in upcoming behavior, the vast majority (95%) of preplay events took place before the journey was initiated. Thus, hippocampal cell assemblies can emit prospectively oriented firing patterns prior to an event journey. These firing patterns anticipate upcoming work toward a reward as distinct from what just happened following reward delivery (**Figure 7**, see color insert).

An unresolved question concerning the relation of preplay (and replay) events to prospective behavior surrounds their brevity. The activity sequences observed during ripple events, which last upwards of about 100 milliseconds, represent track positions spanning only 1–2 meters in length. Navigation in the wild rodent spans large environments with many distantly encountered choice points. There are likely other mechanisms at work, as it is difficult to imagine how an extended trajectory could be represented.

Davidson et al. (2009) provide evidence that brief activity sequences can be chained together to represent extended epochs. Their study deviated from the earlier work by using a longer track (~10 meters) that included angled and hairpin turns. Despite the added complexity, there were no choice points; the activity sequences could be analyzed in reference to a linear path. Under such conditions, extended

sequences were observed that spanned the full 10-m length of the path. Detailed analysis of the ripple events showed that the extended sequences were played back across chains of discrete ripple events possibly mediated by re-entrant processes between the hippocampus and entorhinal cortex (Davidson et al. 2009). This result reinforces the growing consensus that the hippocampus can represent nonlocal positions in the environment and further documents mechanisms that string together chains of sequences representing distant locations and extended paths.

How do such activity sequences relate to decision processes? This is perhaps the most critical open question as well as the most difficult to resolve. There are two challenges. The first challenge is that decision paradigms are inherently more complicated than those amenable to linear paths where cues and cue-sequences can be held constant. Second, decisions presumably occur during active navigation, when theta oscillations are dominant, making it difficult to link the preplay sequences observed during ripple events to choice behaviors. Providing a clue that decision processes are being engaged, rodents move slower during novel trajectories (Ji & Wilson 2008) and engage exploratory behaviors at choice junctions (Johnson & Redish 2007, Lisman & Redish 2009). Nonetheless, there are many unresolved questions about how activity sequences spanning theta oscillations and sharp-wave ripple events might contribute to choice decisions.

Important initial observations are provided by two recent studies that explored paradigms with choice points. The first study, reported by Johnson & Redish (2007), had rats navigate a maze with multiple T-junctions. A sophisticated behavioral paradigm allowed multiple choice-point locations to be probed for nonlocal activity patterns. The investigators recorded from the dorsal CA3 region and observed prospective activity sequences that aligned to theta oscillations, although the sweeps showed evidence for spanning multiple theta cycles. Most interestingly, there was a tendency for the activity sequences to sweep forward down the

Reverse replay: activity sequences that repeat past events but in reverse order (experience of A-B-C leads to replay sequence C-B-A)

alternative paths at the choice points. Although these nonlocal sweeps of activity have yet to be linked to the animal's behavioral decision, they provide intriguing evidence that hippocampal cell assemblies can represent alternative paths during navigation, including entry into routes ultimately not taken by the animal.

Pastalkova et al. (2008) provide the most compelling link to date between spontaneous hippocampal activity and choice behavior. In their study, rats alternated arms through a figure-eight maze. Prior to initiating each journey, the rats ran on a wheel, creating an extended delay. Alternation under these delay conditions was dependent on intact hippocampal function as demonstrated using bilateral lidocaine injections. Multiunit activity recorded from the intact hippocampus during the delay period revealed remarkably robust spontaneous firing patterns. In aggregate, the cells showing place fields were more active during wheel running than during actual navigation. Such an observation reinforces the point that spontaneous emission of nonlocal activity reflects a prominent component of hippocampal physiology. Second, the activity of several units correlated with the eventual choice of the animal (left versus right turn) and also predicted error trials. Predictive firing patterns were most prevalent during the earliest periods of wheel running, ten seconds or more before the decisions were made. An open question is to what extent the wheel running contributed to the observation of activity sequences. It remains possible that the predictive signals observed by Pastalkova et al. (2008) are an illusion of active navigation induced by wheel running. These results are compelling because they reveal that spontaneous hippocampal activity predicts future behavior on a task demonstrated to be dependent on intact hippocampal function.

A HIPPOCAMPAL PREDICTION MODEL

Findings reviewed above suggest that (*a*) the hippocampal-cortical system is active when people envision the future, (*b*) human amnesia

is often accompanied by deficits in imagining the future, and (*c*) activity patterns in the rat hippocampus reflect both preplay and replay of event sequences. In the following section, a provisional model is provided that suggests how the observed prospective coding sequences in the hippocampus might contribute to future-oriented thinking. The proposal is in the spirit of Buzsáki (2005), who outlines a possible relationship between hippocampal theta sequences observed in rats and the human capacity for memory recall. The present model explores the question of what relationship, if any, exists between the behavior of the hippocampal cell assemblies described above and the ability in humans to think flexibly about the future. The model can be summarized as follows:

1. Experiences are characterized by repeated and novel sequences. Through some form of Hebbian plasticity, short spans of novel event sequences are linked together through modification of synaptic strengths.

2. Hippocampal cell assemblies have the capacity to replay and preplay event sequences when appropriately cued (such as when triggered by a related input).

3. Extended event sequences can be produced by chaining together multiple, shorter sequences. In its most basic form, the terminating event of one sequence might serve as the beginning trigger for another. The mechanisms of this chaining are presently unclear and may involve reentrant processes between the hippocampus and cortex. As a result of this process, temporally extended complex event sequences will be produced that span many theta oscillations or ripple events.

4. Sequences may also be triggered by extremely weak cues or through purely spontaneous processes. Constraints from the environment via cortical inputs and the current state of the hippocampal cell assemblies presumably bias which sequences are produced. Yet, the process is expected to be somewhat stochastic, and

thus novel combinations of sequences will chain together to yield de novo extended sequences that represent novel events.

Figure 8 (see color insert) diagrams the main properties of the model in the context of Tolman's classic study of shock avoidance (Tolman & Gleitman 1949). The model proposes that sequences of learned associations can be replayed in novel combinations. This model illustrates an important difference between the current proposal and traditional models of memory. The hippocampal-cortical system is postulated to generate activity sequences that, while constrained by past events, fundamentally reflect novel predictions. This property, in an elaborated form, may have allowed our distant ancestors to evolve from primarily trial-and-error learners to mental explorers who solve problems by imagining the alternatives.

The Importance of Randomness

A central feature of the model is that a certain level of randomness is explicitly required for the process to unfold properly and flexibly. Given weak inputs, there should be a tendency for the circuits to chain together similar sequences, but the exact chains will vary from moment-to-moment and trial-to-trial. That is, the activity patterns emitted by the circuit should be constrained, but not dictated, by the past. Intrinsic properties or small differences in cortical inputs might contribute to the emergence of chaotic activity fluctuations (see Levy et al. 2005 for relevant discussion). As a result, rare complex event sequences should periodically emerge that allow internal exploration of radically different routes than have actually been experienced. It is this hypothesized feature of the circuit that may have allowed Tolman's rats to navigate using a shortcut (Tolman et al. 1946). In their expanded forms, such internal explorations may also contribute to human creativity and imagination (see Campbell 1960).

The notion that variability can be a critical feature of a neural circuit has precedent. A striking example is found in songbird learn-

ing, where young finches produce randomly patterned songs akin to human babbling (Aronov et al. 2008). Recent ablation studies have demonstrated that a specific structure within the fiche forebrain—lateral magnocellular nucleus of the nidopallium (LMAN)—is required to produce variability. Adult, stereotypic behaviors do not require LMAN. Although it is presently unexplored, the model predicts that the architecture of the hippocampal-cortical system will be shown to have similar properties that promote some level of stochastic behavior. All sequence alternatives and chains are surely not equiprobable. Nonetheless, uncommon chains linked by weak associations or even jumps between previously linked sequences are expected to emerge with some frequency.

Linking Rodent Navigation to Flexible Human Cognition

The model outlined above is based largely on physiological properties observed during rodent navigation. A critical question is whether the response properties observed in the rodent generalize to the human, and if so, how they are expanded to support cognitive abilities that are elaborated in the human. Human hippocampal recordings obtained during surgical cases show response properties that parallel rodent recordings, which suggests that the basic circuitry is more similar than different. For example, single-unit recordings in people reveal place fields similar to those observed in rodent (Ekstrom et al. 2003). Also similar to rodents, theta oscillations are observed in the human temporal lobe including the hippocampus during navigation of virtual environments (Ekstrom et al. 2005, Kahana et al. 1999). Finally, physiological response properties in the hippocampus and surrounding cortex identify distinct populations of neurons that likely reflect the differences between pyramidal and interneurons described in animals models (Viskontas et al. 2007).

The presence of characteristically similar firing patterns in the rat and human hippocampus supports the possibility that our ability to think about the future may extend from the same circuit properties that have been studied in the rodent. This does not mean that rats and humans have similar capacities—the question at hand is whether preplay and replay observed in the rodent provide insight into mechanisms that are co-opted to support more complex cognitive abilities in people.

Relevant to this question, Gelbard-Sagiv et al. (2008) provide evidence that human hippocampal neurons show spontaneous replay events (**Figure 9**, see color insert). In their study, they focused on neurons exhibiting stimulus-preferential responses in the hippocampus and entorhinal cortex. Subjects first viewed video clips that depicted short episodes of famous people and characters. For example, one clip was of the actor Tom Cruise being interviewed by the talk-show host Oprah Winfrey; another clip depicted a scene from the popular television show *The Simpsons*. Many neurons responded strongly to only one or a few of the episodes. Subjects were then asked to freely recall the video clips with no stimulus cues provided. Remarkably, units that selectively fired while watching the videos were again selectively active when the clips were recalled. These results demonstrate that hippocampal neurons encoding episodes are active during the mental representation of those episodes. Going beyond what is possible to probe in the rodent, Gelbard-Sagiv et al. (2008) were further able to link the hippocampal activity to conscious perception. During neural replay, subjects reported vivid re-experiences of the originally encoded events. These findings add weight to the possibility that the hippocampal-cortical circuitry observed in the rodent is preserved in the human and put toward considerably more elaborated use.

Relationship to Prior Frameworks

The idea that the hippocampal-cortical system is important to future-oriented thinking and imagination has received growing interest over the past decade. Many contemporary proposals have their antecedents in the seminal work of Edward Tolman, David Ingvar, and Endel Tulving discussed above. Among recent proposals, Suddendorf & Corballis (1997, 2007) thoughtfully considered the possibility that memory systems evolved to aid constructive aspects of representing the future. They noted that "the real importance of mental time travel applies to travel into the future rather than the past; that is, we predominantly stand in the present facing the future rather than looking back to the past." They further suggested that "the constructive element in episodic recall is adaptive in that it underlies our ability to imagine possible scenarios rather than the actual ones." Schacter & Addis (2007) echo a similar perspective: "Since the future is not an exact replica of the past, simulation of future episodes may require a system that can draw on the past in a manner that flexibly extracts and recombines elements of previous experiences—a constructive rather than a reproductive system."

The model proposed above is consistent with these earlier themes and suggests specific circuit mechanisms linked to the hippocampus that may contribute to these functions. At the center of this model is the idea that the adaptive function of the hippocampal-cortical system is the capture of sequential associations and relations that define events because these sequences can be reassembled into novel combinations that anticipate and simulate future events. The intent of the model is to provide a framework to link the findings in rodent studies of hippocampal physiology with the growing body of data on the homologous system in humans.

Lisman & Redish (2009) previously discussed the possibility of a relation between rodent hippocampal physiology and constructive processes, but also noted that no result to date has provided direct evidence that the hippocampus emits activity sequences that are functional recombinations of past events. They further noted that traditional memory tasks relying on simple expectations do not require hippocampal integrity. Rather, an intact hippocampus becomes necessary as more complex changes in contingencies are added, which suggests that flexible forms of sequence generation are likely present even though empirical data are so far lacking. Cohen & Eichenbaum (e.g., 1993) have long emphasized the particular role of the hippocampus in establishing novel associations that allow for the flexible expression of memory, referring to them as relational associations. Thus, there are many reasons to postulate that the two sets of observations—those from rat physiology and those from humans—may be linked.

A BRIEF COMMENT ON THE ROLE OF SLEEP AND IDLE MOMENTS

To this point, activity sequences that occur just prior to upcoming events have been the focus of discussion. However, it is also possible that constructed event sequences are adaptive independent of a targeted decision. That is, even without a specific task goal, spontaneous event sequences may result in adaptive, novel representations that are stored for later use (Bar 2007). It is difficult to speculate on the specific nature of these derived representations, but some possibilities seem more likely than others. For example, derived sequences that link temporally distinct episodes may be adaptive because they create new relations that are not present at the time of encoding.

Paradigms requiring judgments about stimuli that are encoded across separate presentations provide a nice illustration of the value of recoding. One such example is the transitive inference paradigm. During training, a subject learns that A is better than B, B is better than C, C is better than D, and D is better than E. Then, during the critical probe trial, the subject is asked if B is better than D. The relations across the stimuli suggest the answer is yes even though B itself was never simultaneously presented with D. Of interest, lesions to the hippocampal region in rat (Dusek & Eichenbaum 1997), monkey (Buckmaster et al. 2004), and human (Smith & Squire 2005)

impair performance on transitive inference tests.[2] It is also interesting to note the similarities between this form of inference task and the original paradigm studied by Tolman (**Figures 2** and **7**). Both require decisions that are based on novel relations drawn from multiple past events. Although it is possible that transitive inferences rely on the retrieval of the exact encoded events and then a secondary process of comparison, it is also possible that the needed relations are derived spontaneously in advance of their use.

Ellenbogen and colleagues (2007) provide evidence that such relations emerge spontaneously. In their study, subjects studied a series of abstract picture pairs, one of which was arbitrarily designated the correct item within the pair. The pairs followed a hierarchy as described above but were presented in random order so that the hierarchy was difficult to discern. The task was further made challenging by training the initial pairs to a high, but not ceiling, level of performance. Under these conditions,[2] they observed that subjects performed poorly on transitive judgments shortly after studying the pairs (20-minute delay). However, the subjects were significantly better following 12- and 24-hour intervals. And, if sleep intervened, they were particularly adept at succeeding on the most difficult judgments that spanned multiple event pairs (e.g., B versus E). Although further study will be required to extend this observation, the findings suggest that certain relational links emerge gradually following learning.

Spontaneous activity events during idle moments may function to build a repository of derived information that is considerably richer

---

[2]Studies of transitive inference in amnesic participants also show impairment on the acquisition of the initial premise pairs (B-C, C-D, etc.), suggesting that people use hippocampal-dependent processes even for simple learning situations (Smith & Squire 2005). Performance of normal participants in transitive inference paradigms is influenced by differences in the awareness level of the participants during training, whether premise pairs are learned to ceiling and whether premise pairs are presented hierarchically or in random order.

than that captured at the time of encoding. This process can be called "prospective consolidation" to make clear that the stored representations are recoded, chunked, or otherwise derived forms of the original experiences. The stored representations are not expected to be replicas of the original experiences but rather derived representations that extract relations among past events in prospectively useful forms. Relevant to this possibility, hippocampal replay events have been repeatedly documented during sleep, in particular slow-wave sleep when sharp-wave ripple events are prominent. Pavlides & Winson (1989) first noted that if a rat spends extended awake time exploring a particular location, the firing rates of the associated place cells increase during the next period of sleep. In a compelling extension of this observation, Wilson & McNaughton (1994) demonstrated that cell pairs showing correlated firing during awake navigation replay their correlated firing patterns during sleep and further that the correlated events occur preferentially during sharp-wave ripple events. Sleep replay involves coordinated reactivation across the cortex and hippocampus (Euston et al. 2007, Ji & Wilson 2007) and preserves the temporal order of the original firing patterns (Lee & Wilson 2002, Skaggs & McNaughton 1996). In a recent analysis, O'Neill et al. (2008) observed that correlated replay during sleep mimics the frequency of the rat's awake experiences.

Such findings provide strong evidence that activity sequences experienced during awake behavior are replayed during sleep. The leading hypothesis about the functional role of sleep replay is that it participates in consolidating long-lasting representations of the day's events (for relevant reviews see Maquet 2001, Walker & Stickgold 2006). An implication of the hippocampal prediction model presented above is that spontaneous activity events during sleep may be important to prospective consolidation. That is, although methods to date have identified replay sequences that replicate earlier events, it may also be the case that novel sequences that emerge spontaneously during sleep form new links between episodes.

Evolution may have co-opted periods of sleep and idle moments to precompute adaptive information. An interesting topic for future investigation will be to reexamine spontaneous activity events occurring during sleep and rest states to determine if novel sequences are emitted that can be shown to be adaptive and predict upcoming decisions.

In its most elaborated form, offline processing in humans has been proposed to facilitate problem solving (Stickgold 2005). Support comes from insight learning, where an unexpected, novel relationship must be discovered to solve a problem. In an elegant study, Wagner et al. (2004) presented subjects with an arithmetic puzzle that required a series of digits to be sequentially transformed into a new pattern. Unbeknownst to the subjects, there was a hidden rule that would allow them to complete the transformation rapidly. The majority of subjects never discovered the rule. However, allowing the subjects to sleep on the problem more than doubled their chances of gaining insight into the shortcut. Control studies established that it was not sleep per se that facilitated insight, but rather specifically sleep following training exposure to the task. Replay of hippocampal cell assemblies during the intervening sleep may have facilitated a qualitative restructuring of the memory representation into a prospectively adaptive form.

CONCLUSIONS

The hippocampus and associated cortical structures are active when people envision future events, and studies of amnesic patients suggest that damage to the hippocampal region impairs this ability. As rodents navigate, the hippocampus spontaneously emits forward-oriented activity sequences that predict future choices under certain conditions. These findings collectively raise the possibility that a core function of the hippocampal-cortical system is to use remnants of past experiences to make predictions about upcoming events.

Eichenbaum, Cohen, and colleagues have previously emphasized the importance of the hippocampus for establishing novel associations that allow for the flexible expression of memory, referred to as relational associations (e.g., Cohen & Eichenbaum 1993). As one example, Eichenbaum et al. (1990) demonstrated that rats fail to navigate novel paths following hippocampal lesions, consistent with an important role for the hippocampus in solving Tolman-type paradigms (also Dusek & Eichenbaum 1997, Eichenbaum & Fortin 2009).

In this review, the idea of flexible expression of memory was extended to the possibility that a fundamental role of the hippocampal-cortical system is to provide building blocks, based on past experiences, that can be strung together in novel combinations to predict and mentally explore upcoming events (e.g., Buckner & Carroll 2007, Lisman & Redish 2009, Schacter & Addis 2007). The shift from a retrospectively oriented model of hippocampal function to a prospectively oriented model pushes the field to consider novel paradigms and theoretical orientations, including those that can link observations in rodents, monkeys, and humans. It will be interesting to develop human testing paradigms, perhaps based on navigation and interactions in virtual environments, that create situations where moments of prediction can be isolated and manipulated.

To paraphrase Aspinwall (2005), future-oriented thinking—our plans, goals, daydreams, worries, predictions, and the various scenarios through which these potential outcomes may or may not be realized—is the stuff of mental life. Humans can imagine far into the future and spend a great deal of time engaged in such thoughts. To gain insight into underlying mechanisms of such abilities, it will be necessary to rely heavily on animal models where the neural circuitry of human-like processes, or their proto-forms, can be explored. The present review provides a beginning framework to integrate recent observations from rodent physiology and the human abilities to predict and imagine the future.

DISCLOSURE STATEMENT

The author is not aware of any biases that might be perceived as affecting the objectivity of this review.

ACKNOWLEDGMENTS

I thank Dan Schacter and Matt Wilson for valuable discussion and Katie Powers for assistance in preparing the manuscript. Haderer & Muller Biomedical Art assisted with the illustrations. Funding was provided by the NIA (AG-021910) and the Howard Hughes Medical Institute.

LITERATURE CITED

Addis DR, Pan L, Vu MA, Laiser N, Schacter DL. 2009. Constructive episodic simulation of the future and past: distinct subsystems of a core brain network mediate imagining and remembering. *Neuropsychologia* 47:2222–38

Addis DR, Schacter DL. 2008. Constructive episodic simulation: temporal distance and detail of past and future events modulate hippocampal engagement. *Hippocampus* 18:227–37

Addis DR, Wong AT, Schacter DL. 2007. Remembering the past and imagining the future: common and distinct neural substrates during event construction and elaboration. *Neuropsychologia* 45:1363–77

Addis DR, Wong AT, Schacter DL. 2008. Age-related changes in the episodic simulation of future events. *Psychol. Sci.* 19:33–41

Aronov D, Andalman S, Fee MS. 2008. A specialized forebrain circuit for vocal babbling in the juvenile songbird. *Science* 320:630–34

Aspinwall LG. 2005. The psychology of future-oriented thinking: from achievement to proactive coping, adaptation, and aging. *Motiv. Emot.* 29:203–35

Attance CM, O'Neill DK. 2001. Episodic future thinking. *Trends Cogn. Sci.* 5:533–39

Bar M. 2007. The proactive brain: using analogies and associations to generate predictions. *Trends Cogn. Sci.* 11:280–89

Bird CM, Burgess N. 2008. The hippocampus and memory: insights from spatial processing. *Nat. Rev. Neurosci.* 9:182–94

Biswal B, Yetkin FZ, Haughton VM, Hyde JS. 1995. Functional connectivity in the motor cortex of resting human brain using echo-planar MRI. *Magn. Reson. Med.* 34:537–41

Botzung A, Denkova E, Manning L. 2008. Experiencing past and future personal events: functional neuroimaging evidence on the neural bases of mental time travel. *Brain Cogn.* 66:202–12

Buckmaster CA, Eichenbaum H, Amaral DG, Suzuki WA, Rapp PR. 2004. Entorhinal cortex lesions disrupt the relational organization of memory in monkeys. *J. Neurosci.* 24:9811–25

Buckner RL, Andrews-Hanna JR, Schacter DL. 2008. The brain's default network: anatomy, function, and relevance to disease. *Ann. N. Y. Acad. Sci.* 1124:1–38

Buckner RL, Carroll DC. 2007. Self-projection and the brain. *Trends Cogn. Sci.* 11:49–57

Burgess N, Barry C, O'Keefe J. 2007. An oscillatory interference model of grid cell firing. *Hippocampus* 17:801–12

Burwell RD. 2000. The parahippocampal region: corticocortical connectivity. *Ann. N. Y. Acad. Sci.* 911:25–42

Buzsáki G. 1989. Two-stage model of memory trace formation: a role for "noisy" brain states. *Neuroscience* 31:551–70

Buzsáki G. 2002. Theta oscillations in the hippocampus. *Neuron* 33:325–40

Buzsáki G. 2005. Theta rhythm of navigation: link between path integration and landmark navigation, episodic and semantic memory. *Hippocampus* 15:827–40

Cabeza R, St Jacques P. 2007. Functional neuroimaging of autobiographical memory. *Trends Cogn. Sci.* 11:219–27

Campbell D. 1960. Blind variation and selective retentions in creative thought as in other knowledge processes. *Psychol. Rev.* 67:380–400

Cohen NJ, Eichenbaum H. 1993. *Memory, Amnesia, and the Hippocampal System.* Cambridge, MA: MIT Press

Corkin S. 2002. What's new with the amnesic patient H.M.? *Nat. Rev. Neurosci.* 3:153–60

Csicsvari J, O'Neill J, Allen K, Senior T. 2007. Place-selective firing contributes to the reverse-order reactivation of CA1 pyramidal cells during sharp waves in open-field exploration. *Eur. J. Neurosci.* 26:704–16

D'Argembeau A, Van Der Linden M. 2004. Phenomenal characteristics associated with projecting oneself back into the past and forward into the future: influence of valence and temporal distance. *Conscious. Cogn.* 13:844–58

D'Argembeau A, Van Der Linden M. 2006. Individual differences in the phenomenology of mental time travel: the effect of vivid visual imagery and emotion regulation strategies. *Conscious. Cogn.* 15:342–50

D'Argembeau A, Raffard S, Van Der Linden M. 2008a. Remembering the past and imagining the future in schizophrenia. *J. Abnorm. Psychol.* 117:247–51

D'Argembeau A, Xue G, Lu Z, Van Der Linden M, Bechara A. 2008b. Neural correlates of envisioning emotional events in the near and far future. *Neuroimage* 40:398–407

Davidson TJ, Kloosterman F, Wilson MA. 2009. Hippocampal replay of extended experience. *Neuron* 63:497–507

Diba K, Buzsáki G. 2007. Forward and reverse hippocampal place-cell sequences during ripples. *Nat. Neurosci.* 10:1241–42

Dragoi G, Buzsáki G. 2006. Temporal encoding of place sequences by hippocampal cell assemblies. *Neuron* 50:145–57

Dusek JA, Eichenbaum H. 1997. The hippocampus and memory for orderly stimulus relations. *Proc. Natl. Acad. Sci. USA* 94:7109–14

Eichenbaum H. 2000. A cortical-hippocampal system for declarative memory. *Nat. Rev. Neurosci.* 1:42–50

Eichenbaum H. 2004. Hippocampus: cognitive processes and neural representations that underlie declarative memory. *Neuron* 44:109–20

Eichenbaum H, Fortin NJ. 2009. The neurobiology of memory-based predictions. *Philos. Trans. R. Soc. Lond. B Biol. Sci.* 364:1183–91

Eichenbaum H, Stewart C, Morris RG. 1990. Hippocampal representation in place learning. *J. Neurosci.* 10:3531–42

Ekstrom AD, Kahana MJ, Caplan JB, Fields TA, Isham EA, et al. 2003. Cellular networks underlying human spatial navigation. *Nature* 425:184–88

Ekstrom AD, Caplan JB, Ho E, Shattuck K, Fried I, Kahana MJ. 2005. Human hippocampal theta activity during virtual navigation. *Hippocampus* 15:881–89

Ellenbogen JM, Hu PT, Payne JD, Titone D, Walker MP. 2007. Human relational memory requires time and sleep. *Proc. Natl. Acad. Sci. USA* 104:7723–28

Euston DR, Tatsuno M, McNaughton BL. 2007. Fast-forward playback of recent memory sequences in prefrontal cortex during sleep. *Science* 318:1147–50

Ferbinteanu J, Shapiro ML. 2003. Prospective and retrospective memory coding in the hippocampus. *Neuron* 40:1227–39

Foster DJ, Wilson MA. 2006. Reverse replay of behavioural sequences in hippocampal place cells during the awake state. *Nature* 440:680–83

Foster DJ, Wilson MA. 2007. Hippocampal theta sequences. *Hippocampus* 17:1093–99

Fox MD, Raichle ME. 2007. Spontaneous fluctuations in brain activity observed with functional magnetic resonance imaging. *Nat. Rev. Neurosci.* 8:700–11

Frank LM, Brown EN, Wilson M. 2000. Trajectory encoding in the hippocampus and entorhinal cortex. *Neuron* 27:169–78

Fuster JM. 1989. *The Prefrontal Cortex: Anatomy, Physiology, and Neuropsychology of the Frontal Lobe.* New York: Raven

Fyhn M, Molden S, Witter MP, Moser EI, Moser MB. 2004. Spatial representation in the entorhinal cortex. *Science* 305:1258–64

Gelbard-Sagiv H, Mukamel R, Harel M, Malah R, Fried I. 2008. Internally generated reactivation of single neurons in human hippocampus during free recall. *Science* 322:96–101

Hargreaves EL, Rao G, Lee I, Knierim JJ. 2005. Major dissociation between medial and lateral entorhinal input to dorsal hippocampus. *Science* 308:1792–94

Hasselmo ME, Eichenbaum H. 2005. Hippocampal mechanisms for the context-dependent retrieval of episodes. *Neural. Netw.* 18:1172–90

Hassabis D, Kumaran D, Vann SD, Maguire EA. 2007. Patients with hippocampal amnesia cannot imagine new experiences. *Proc. Natl. Acad. Sci. USA* 104:1726–31

Hassabis D, Maguire EA. 2007. Deconstructing episodic memory with construction. *Trends Cogn. Sci.* 11:299–306

Ingvar DH. 1985. "Memory of the Future": an essay on the temporal organization of conscious awareness. *Hum. Neurobiol.* 4:127–36

Insausti R, Trinidad Herrero M, Witter MP. 1997. Entorhinal cortex of the rat; cytoarchitectronic subdivisions and the origin and distribution of cortical efferents. *Hippocampus* 7:146–83

Itskov V, Pastalkova E, Mizuseki K, Buzsáki G, Harris KD. 2008. Theta-mediated dynamics of spatial information in hippocampus. *J. Neurosci.* 28:5959–64

Ji D, Wilson MA. 2007. Coordinated memory replay in the visual cortex and hippocampus during sleep. *Nat. Neurosci.* 10:100–7

Ji D, Wilson MA. 2008. Firing rate dynamics in the hippocampus induced by trajectory learning. *J. Neurosci.* 28:4679–89

Johnson A, Redish AD. 2007. Neural ensembles in CA3 transiently encode paths forward of the animal at a decision point. *J. Neurosci.* 27:12176–89

Johnson A, Van Der Meer MA, Redish AD. 2007. Integrating hippocampus and striatum in decision-making. *Curr. Opin. Neurobiol.* 17:692–97

Johnson MK, Foley MA, Suengas AG, Raye CL. 1988. Phenomenal characteristics of memories for perceived and imagined autobiographical events. *J. Exp. Psychol.: Gen.* 117:371–76

Johnson MK, Sherman SJ. 1990. Constructing and Reconstructing the Past and the Future in the Present. In *Handbook of Motivation and Cognition*, ed. ET Higgins, RM Sorrentino, pp. 482–526. New York: Guilford

Kahana MJ, Sekuler R, Caplan JB, Kirschen M, Madsen JR. 1999. Human theta oscillations exhibit task dependence during virtual maze navigation. *Nature* 399:781–84

Kahn I, Andrews-Hanna JR, Vincent JL, Snyder AZ, Buckner RL. 2008. Distinct cortical anatomy linked to subregions of the medial temporal lobe revealed by intrinsic functional connectivity. *J. Neurophysiol.* 100:129–39

Karlsson MP, Frank LM. 2009. Awake replay of remote experiences in the hippocampus. *Nat. Neurosci.* 12:913–18

Klein SB, Cosmides, L, Tooby J, Chance S. 2002a. Decisions and the evolution of memory: multiple systems, multiple functions. *Psychol. Rev.* 109:306–29

Klein SB, Loftus J, Kihlstrom JF. 2002b. Memory and temporal experience: the effects of episodic memory loss on an amnesic patient's ability to remember the past and imagine the future. *Soc. Cogn.* 20:353–79

Kobayashi Y, Amaral DG. 2003. Macaque monkey retrosplenial cortex: II. Cortical afferents. *J. Comp. Neurol.* 466:48–79

Korsakoff SS. 1889 /1996. Medico-psychological study of a memory disorder. *Conscious. Cogn.* 5:2–21

Lavenex P, Amaral DG. 2000. Hippocampal-neocortical interactions: a hierarchy of associativity. *Hippocampus* 10:420–30

Lee AK, Wilson MA. 2002. Memory of sequential experience in the hippocampus during slow wave sleep. *Neuron* 36:1183–94

Levy WB, Hocking AB, Wu X. 2005. Interpreting hippocampal function as recoding and forecasting. *Neural Netw.* 18:1242–64

Lisman JE. 2005. The theta/gamma discrete phase code occurring during the hippocampal phase precession may be a more general brain coding scheme. *Hippocampus* 15:913–22

Lisman JE. 2007. Role of the dual entorhinal inputs to hippocampus: a hypothesis based on cue/action (non-self/self) couplets. *Prog. Brain Res.* 163:615–25

Lisman J, Redish AD. 2009. Prediction, sequences, and the hippocampus. *Philos. Trans. R. Soc. Lond. B Biol. Sci.* 364:1191–201

Maguire EA. 2001. Neuroimaging studies of autobiographical event memory. *Philos. Trans. R. Soc. Lond. B Biol. Sci.* 356:1441–51

Maquet P. 2001. The role of sleep in learning and memory. *Science* 294:1048–52

Maurer AP, McNaughton BL. 2007. Network and instrinsic cellular mechanisms underlying theta phase precession of hippocampal neurons. *Trends Neurosci.* 30:325–33

McNaughton BL, Battaglia FP, Jensen O, Moser EI, Moser MB. 2006. Path integration and the neural basis of the "cognitive map." *Nat. Rev. Neurosci.* 7:663–78

Mesulam MM. 2002. The human frontal lobes: transcending the default mode through contingent encoding. In *Principles of Frontal Lobe Function*, ed. DT Stuss, RT Knight, pp. 8–30. New York: Oxford Univ. Press

Milner B, Squire LR, Kandel ER. 1998. Cognitive neuroscience and the study of memory. *Neuron* 20:445–68

Moser EI, Kropff E, Moser MB. 2008. Place cells, grid cells, and the brain's spatial representation system. *Annu. Rev. Neurosci.* 31:69–89

O'Keefe J, Dostrovsky J. 1971. The hippocampus as a spatial map. Preliminary evidence from unit activity in the freely-moving rat. *Brain Res.* 34:171–75

O'Keefe J, Nadel L. 1978. *The Hippocampus as a Cognitive Map*. London: Clarendon

O'Keefe J, Recce ML. 1993. Phase relationship between hippocampal place units and the EEG theta rhythm. *Hippocampus* 3:317–30

Okuda J, Fujii T, Ohtake H, Tsukiura T, Tanji K, et al. 2003. Thinking of the future and past: the roles of the frontal pole and the medial temporal lobes. *Neuroimage* 19:1369–80

O'Neill J, Senior TJ, Allen K, Huxter JR, Csicsvari J. 2008. Reactivation of experience-dependent cell assembly patterns in the hippocampus. *Nat. Neurosci.* 11:209–15

Öngür D, Price JL. 2000. The organization of networks within the orbital and medial prefrontal cortex of rats, monkeys and humans. *Cereb. Cortex* 10:206–19

Partiot A, Grafman J, Sadato N, Wachs J, Hallett M. 1995. Brain activation during the generation of nonemotional and emotional plans. *Neuroreport* 6:1397–400

Pastalkova E, Itskov V, Amarasingham A, Buzsáki G. 2008. Internally generated cell assembly sequences in the rat hippocampus. *Science* 321:1322–27

Pavlides C, Winson J. 1989. Influences of hippocampal place cell firing in the awake state on the activity of these cells during subsequent sleep episodes. *J. Neurosci.* 9:2907–18

Rosenbaum RS, Gilboa A, Levine B, Winocur G, Moscovitch M. 2009. Amnesia as an impairment of detail generation and binding: evidence from personal, fictional, and semantic narratives in K.C. *Neuropsychologia* 47:2181–87

Rosenbaum RS, Köhler S, Schacter DL, Moscovitch M, Westmacott R, et al. 2005. The case of K.C.: contributions of a memory-impaired person to memory theory. *Neuropsychologia* 43:989–1021

Samarasekera S, Vincent A, Welch JL, Jackson M, Nichols P, Griffiths TD. 2007. Course and outcome of acute limbic encephalitis with negative voltage-gated potassium channel antibodies. *J. Neurol. Neurosurg. Psychiatry* 78:391–94

Schacter DL, Addis DR. 2007. The cognitive neuroscience of constructive memory: remembering the past and imagining the future. *Philos. Trans. R. Soc. Lond. B Biol. Sci.* 362:773–86

Schacter DL, Addis DR. 2009. On the nature of medial temporal lobe contributions to the constructive simulation of future events. *Philos. Trans. R. Soc. Lond. B Biol. Sci.* 364:1245–53

Schacter DL, Addis DR, Buckner RL. 2007. Remembering the past to imagine the future: the prospective brain. *Nat. Rev. Neurosci.* 8:657–61

Schacter DL, Addis DR, Buckner RL. 2008. Episodic simulation of future events: concepts, data, and applications. *Ann. N. Y. Acad. Sci.* 1124:39–60

Scoville WB, Milner B. 1957. Loss of recent memory after bilateral hippocampal lesions. *J. Neurol. Neurosurg. Psychiatry* 20:11–21

Shapiro ML, Kennedy PJ, Ferbinteanu J. 2006. Representing episodes in the mammalian brain. *Curr. Opin. Neurobiol.* 16:701–9

Shallice T. 1982. Specific impairments of planning. *Philos. Trans. R. Soc. Lond. B Biol. Sci.* 298:199–209

Sharot T, Riccardi AM, Raio CM, Phelps EA. 2007. Neural mechanisms mediating optimism bias. *Nature* 450:102–5

Shimamura AP, Janowsky JS, Squire LR. 1990. Memory for the temporal order of events in patients with frontal lobe lesions and amnesic patients. *Neuropsychologia* 28:803–13

Skaggs WE, McNaughton BL. 1996. Replay of neuronal firing sequences in rat hippocampus during sleep following spatial experience. *Science* 271:1870–73

Skaggs WE, McNaughton BL, Wilson MA, Barnes CA. 1996. Theta phase precession in hippocampal neuronal populations and the compression of temporal sequences. *Hippocampus* 6:149–72

Smith C, Squire LR. 2005. Declarative memory, awareness, and transitive inference. *J. Neurosci.* 25:10138–46

Smith DM, Mizumori SJ. 2006. Hippocampal place cells, context, and episodic memory. *Hippocampus* 16:716–29

Spreng RN, Levine B. 2006. The temporal distribution of past and future autobiographical events across the lifespan. *Mem. Cogn.* 34:1644–51

Spreng RN, Mar RA, Kim AS. 2009. The common neural basis of autobiographical memory, prospection, navigation, theory of mind and the default mode: a quantitative meta-analysis. *J. Cogn. Neurosci.* 21:489–510

Squire LR, Stark CE, Clark RE. 2004. The medial temporal lobe. *Annu. Rev. Neurosci.* 27:279–306

Squire LR, Zola SM. 1996. Ischemic brain damage and memory impairment: a commentary. *Hippocampus* 6:546–52

Stickgold R. 2005. Sleep-dependent memory consolidation. *Nature* 437:1272–78

Suddendorf T, Corballis MC. 1997. Mental time travel and the evolution of the human mind. *Genet. Soc. Gen. Psychol. Monogr.* 123:133–67

Suddendorf T, Corballis MC. 2007. The evolution of foresight: What is mental time travel, and is it unique to humans? *Behav. Brain Sci.* 30:299–313

Suzuki WA, Amaral DG. 1994. Perirhinal and parahippocampal cortices of the macaque monkey: cortical afferents. *J. Comp. Neurol.* 350:497–533

Svoboda E, McKinnon MC, Levine B. 2006. The functional neuroanatomy of autobiographical memory: a meta-analysis. *Neuropsychologia* 44:2189–208

Szpunar KK. 2009. Episodic future thought: an emerging concept. *Perspect. Psychol. Sci.* In press

Szpunar KK, McDermott KB. 2008. Episodic future thought and its relation to remembering: evidence from ratings of subjective experience. *Conscious. Cogn.* 17:330–34

Szpunar KK, Watson JM, McDermott KB. 2007. Neural substrates of envisioning the future. *Proc. Natl. Acad. Sci. USA* 104:642–47

Talland GA. 1965. *Deranged Memory: A Psychonomic Study of the Amnesic Syndrome*. New York: Academic

Tolman EC. 1948. Cognitive maps in rats and men. *Psychol. Rev.* 55:189–208

Tolman EC, Gleitman H. 1949. Studies in learning and motivation: I. Equal reinforcements in both end-boxes, followed by shock in one end-box. *J. Exp. Psychol.* 39:810–19

Tolman EC, Ritchie BF, Kalish D. 1946. Studies in spatial learning. I. Orientation and the short-cut. *J. Exp. Psychol.* 36:13–24

Tsodyks M, Skaggs WE, Sejnowski TJ, McNaughton BL. 1996. Population dynamics and theta rhythm phase precession of hippocampal place cell firing: a spiking neuron model. *Hippocampus* 6:271–80

Tulving E. 1985. Memory and consciousness. *Can. Psych.* 26:1–12

Tulving E. 2005. Episodic memory and autonoesis: uniquely human? In *The Missing Link in Cognition: Origins of Self-Reflective Consciousness*, ed. HS Terrace, J Metcalfe, pp. 3–56. New York: Oxford Univ. Press

Van Essen DC. 2005. A Population-Average, Landmark- and Surface-based (PALS) atlas of the human cerebral cortex. *Neuroimage* 28:635–62

Van Essen DC, Deirker DL. 2007. Surface-based and probabilistic atlases of primate cerebral cortex. *Neuron* 56:209–25

Vilberg KL, Rugg MD. 2008. Memory retrieval and the parietal cortex: a review of evidence from a dual-process perspective. *Neuropsychologia* 46:1787–99

Vincent JL, Snyder AZ, Fox MD, Shannon BJ, Andrews JR, et al. 2006. Coherent spontaneous activity identifies a hippocampal-parietal memory network. *J. Neurophysiol.* 96:3517–31

Viskontas IV, Ekstrom AD, Wilson CL, Fried I. 2007. Characterizing interneuron and pyramidal cells in the human medial temporal lobe in vivo using extracellular recordings. *Hippocampus* 17:49–57

Wagner AD, Shannon BJ, Kahn I, Buckner RL. 2005. Parietal lobe contributions to episodic memory retrieval. *Trends Cogn. Sci.* 9:445–53

Wagner U, Gais S, Haider H, Verlegar R, Born J. 2004. Sleep inspires insight. *Nature* 427:352–55

Walker MP, Stickgold R. 2006. Sleep, memory, and plasticity. *Annu. Rev. Psychol.* 57:139–66

Wilson MA, McNaughton BL. 1994. Reactivation of hippocampal ensemble memories during sleep. *Science* 265:676–79

Wood ER, Dudchenk PA, Robitsek JR, Eichenbaum H. 2000. Hippocampal neurons encode information about different types of memory episodes occurring in the same location. *Neuron* 27:623–33

Hippocampal-Neocortical Interactions in Memory Formation, Consolidation, and Reconsolidation

Szu-Han Wang and Richard G.M. Morris

Center for Cognitive and Neural Systems, Neuroscience, The University of Edinburgh, Edinburgh EH8 9JZ, Scotland; email: S.Wang@ed.ac.uk; R.G.M.Morris@ed.ac.uk

Annu. Rev. Psychol. 2010. 61:49–79

First published online as a Review in Advance on September 28, 2009

The *Annual Review of Psychology* is online at psych.annualreviews.org

This article's doi:
10.1146/annurev.psych.093008.100523

Key Words

episodic-memory, paired-associate memory, long-term potentiation, NMDA receptor, spatial memory

Abstract

This review, focusing on work using animals, updates a theoretical approach whose aim is to translate neuropsychological ideas about the psychological and anatomical organization of memory into the neurobiological domain. It is suggested that episodic-like memory consists of both automatic and controlled components, with the medial temporal mediation of memory encoding including neurobiological mechanisms that are primarily automatic or incidental. These ideas, in the cognitive and behavioral domain, are linked to neurophysiological ideas about cellular consolidation concerning synaptic potentiation, particularly the relationship between protein synthesis-dependent long-term changes and shorter-lasting post-translational mechanisms. Ideas from psychology about mental schemas are considered in relation to the phenomenon of systems consolidation and, specifically, about how prior knowledge can alter the rate at which consolidation occurs. Finally, the hippocampal-neocortical interactions theory is updated in relation to reconsolidation, a process that enables updating of stored memory traces in response to novelty.

Contents

BACKGROUND

Memory is fundamental to human life. Qualitatively distinct types of memory enable us to acquire and use a repository of knowledge, to change our behavior in response to experience, to recollect events from the past, and to plan for the future. The use of memory is changing, with a great deal of human knowledge now externalized and then sought on-demand through the use of search engines on the Web. Nonetheless, the loss of memory remains greatly feared. The inability to recollect the events of our life can develop from a minor irritation to a condition that undermines normal existence and even aspects of personal identity. Given its central role in cognition, a grand challenge for neuroscience is to understand the neural mechanisms of the capacity to encode, store, consolidate,

and retrieve information. Over recent years, there has been an explosion of research that is gradually revealing the underlying psychological processes and neural mechanisms of memory, such as consolidation and reconsolidation, now thought to depend on an interaction of cellular and systems-level mechanisms.

Different forms of memory include the fundamental dissociation between short-term and long-term (Baddeley 2001) memory and the qualitatively distinct systems of long-term memory (LTM). Different theoretical frameworks of LTM distinguish perceptual representations, semantic and episodic memory (Schachter & Tulving 1994), declarative memory (Squire 1992), spatial memory (O'Keefe & Nadel 1978), emotional memory (LeDoux 2007), and the learning of actions and habits

(Everitt & Robbins 2005, Schultz & Dickinson 2000). Cutting across these distinctions is the issue of whether memory expression is explicit or implicit—a distinction easier to make in humans than in animals (Graf & Schacter 1985, Griffiths et al. 1999). These memory systems operate semi-independently, involving distinct but overlapping brain networks that interact to realize the apparently seamless control of cognition and behavior.

This review is largely built around a specific neurobiological hypothesis about memory encoding, consolidation, and memory schemas (Morris 2006), emphasizing the importance of interactions between the hippocampal formation and cortical regions in which associative memory traces are stored. We relate our experimental work to other recent studies and develop the hypothesis further with reference to reconsolidation. We restrict our focus to animal work because it is only in animals that we can perform prospective interventions that can definitively reveal causal mechanisms.

THEORETICAL OVERVIEW: HIPPOCAMPAL-NEOCORTICAL INTERACTIONS THEORY

From its clinical origins (such as the phenomenon of amnesia), a diverse field of memory research has developed. Much of this has been concerned with the role of the hippocampus (HPC) and adjacent structures in the formation and consolidation of explicit memory. The mammalian hippocampal formation (HF) is a set of brain structures including the entorhinal cortex (EC), the dentate gyrus (DG), the individual CA fields of the HPC proper, and the subicular complex (SUB). Importantly, the HF does not work in isolation but rather together with subcortical networks (such as neuromodulatory systems involving cholinergic and catacholaminergic afferents) and with cortical networks where it is widely believed that long-term memory traces are stored (Osada et al. 2008). A comprehensive review of the various neurophysiological, neuropsychological, and computational models of

the mechanisms and functions of the HF in memory, together with a detailed description of its extrinsic and intrinsic anatomy (human, monkey and rat), has recently been presented in *The Hippocampus Book* (Andersen et al. 2007).

This review builds upon neuropsychological foundations with the aim of extending to anatomical and physiological levels of analysis. These foundations include Tulving's serial, parallel, independent (SPI) framework (Schachter & Tulving 1994) and the idea that hippocampal memory includes the ability to remember events and episodes (Aggleton & Brown 1999, de Haan et al. 2006, Eichenbaum 2004). It recognizes that other brain structures also contribute to episodic memory via their role in executive function and working memory (Fletcher & Henson 2001), but this aspect of episodic-like memory processing is not discussed in detail.

Four key ideas of this theory (**Table 1**) on which we focus are (*a*) the automaticity of aspects of episodic encoding in the HF (Miyashita 2004), (*b*) the role of synaptic tagging and capture in the neural mechanisms of cellular consolidation (Frey & Morris 1997), (*c*) the critical role of mental schemas in systems consolidation (Tse et al. 2007), and (*d*) memory updating as a key factor for memory reconsolidation in the HF. We refer to the theory as the hippocampal-neocortical interactions theory, as it attempts to map existing neuropsychological ideas about the determinants of episodic-like memory onto the neural circuits and synaptic processes in both hippocampus and neocortex that have been identified as relevant to memory formation.

If events are encoded automatically on-line (Marr 1971), there must exist physiological mechanisms for capturing information about them as they happen (**Table 1**, Proposition #1). For context/event associations that are critical for episodic memory, area CA1 is critical. Anatomically, CA1 receives (*a*) an excitatory input from layer III of EC, which could carry information pertaining to familiar spatial locations at which new events are occurring (Morris 2006, Witter & Moser 2006);

Hippocampus (HPC): a brain area in the medial temporal lobe that is involved in memory encoding and retrieval

HF: hippocampal formation

Neuromodulatory: describes a class of neurotransmitter systems with diffuse projections in areas of the forebrain that modulate the actions of excitatory and inhibitory neurotransmission

Episodic-like memory: a term used to describe episodic memory as studied in animals, in which it is not possible to examine the sense of the self as revealed in verbal reports by humans

Synaptic tagging and capture: a physiological process by which local changes at synapses can, through tagging in association with potentiation or depression, capture diffusely transported gene products that stabilize synaptic change

Table 1 Elements of the hippocampal/neocortical interactions theory of memory formation (updated from Morris 2006)

Proposition #1. Encoding and storage: Activity-dependent hippocampal synaptic potentiation is critical for the automatic recording of attended events (a component of episodic-like memory formation). The memory traces in hippocampal formation (HF) are likely indices of locations in the neocortex where more detailed sensory/perceptual features of information are stored and normally activated during recall.

Proposition #2. Cellular consolidation: The flipside of automaticity is the rapid decay of HF memory traces to avoid the saturation of distributed associative storage. However, index traces in HF can persist for longer if encoding happens around the time of the synthesis, distribution, and synaptic capture of plasticity-related proteins at tagged synapses.

Proposition #3. Systems consolidation: These HF traces enable, through indirect association, a systems consolidation process that builds connections between relevant modules in cortex. Importantly, this can be very rapid when consolidation involves an interaction with activated associative schemas previously stored in the neocortical networks.

Proposition #4. Retrieval and reconsolidation: Retrieval activates the index traces in HF that in turn reactivate cortically stored memory traces. This will re-engage cellular mechanisms responsible for trace stabilization in circumstances in which there is new information occurring at the time of retrieval that is to be assimilated into existing memory traces (memory updating).

Cellular consolidation: intracellular mechanisms, such as signal-transduction and transcriptional activation, by which cell-biological mechanisms give rise to lasting changes in the structure or function of a neuron with respect to information storage

Mental schemas: frameworks of knowledge, built up through paired-associations and the establishment of transitive and other relationships

Systems consolidation: intercellular and interregional mechanisms by which the activity in one brain area can influence that of another in relation to information storage

(*b*) separate excitatory inputs via the Schaffer collaterals from CA3, which could involve index representations of events; (*c*) neuromodulatory inputs from subcortical regions, such as the dopaminergic input from the ventral tegmental area (VTA); and (*d*) numerous inhibitory inputs (projection and intrinsic) that regulate the timing of neural events and the opportunity for plasticity (Dudai 2004). The paired-association of spatial information and event information could be realized automatically by hippocampal N-methyl-D-aspartate (NMDA) receptor–dependent synaptic plasticity at CA1 synapses, subject to modulation via other afferents. Assessed via the phenomenon of long-term potentiation (LTP), this plasticity exhibits many physiological properties that are suitable for memory, provided it is embedded into appropriate distributed-associative anatomical circuitry such as that of areas CA3 and CA1. A growing body of evidence supports this aspect of the synaptic plasticity and memory (SPM) hypothesis (Bliss et al. 2007, Martin et al. 2000).

Propositions #2 and #3 relate to the persistence of encoded traces. Most automatically encoded traces will fade and be lost. It is vital that only some memory traces persist, the flipside of automaticity being the need to guard against saturation of distributed associative memory. The psychological determinants of trace selection include information content, the novelty or emotional significance of an event (linked to VTA dopamine upregulation), and that of others happening in the same spatio-temporal context. The relevance of ongoing events to the existing knowledge structures is also critical for consolidation.

Mediating these psychological processes of persistence are two neural mechanisms of memory consolidation (Dudai & Morris 2000): (*a*) cellular consolidation mechanisms that include the synthesis and synaptic capture of plasticity-proteins that stabilize memory traces within neurons at the level of the individual synapse, perhaps involving calcium-calmodulin kinases, such as calcium-calmodulin-dependent protein kinase (CaMKII), together with the products of mRNA activation at the soma or locally in the dendrites; and (*b*) systems consolidation mechanisms that reflect a dynamic interaction between populations of interconnected neurons within hippocampus and neocortex. The products of cellular consolidation are stable memory indices in HPC that last long enough for the slower systems consolidation process to work selectively. Cellular consolidation provides an initial filter on what could potentially be retained at the systems level. The synaptic tagging and capture (STC) hypothesis of cellular consolidation makes a number of behavioral predictions, which we discuss here.

We outline a new approach to systems consolidation. The standard theory holds that it is a process that involves a dynamic interaction between the HPC and cortex that gradually—over weeks or months—enables a stable associative network of traces that are later used for memory retrieval (Squire 1992). Multiple trace theory asserts, in contrast, that some long-lasting traces remain in HPC, e.g., for spatial memory (Nadel & Moscovitch 1997). However, our recent data suggest that the cortex can be both a fast learning system and a fast consolidating system (Tse et al. 2007). For associative memory, the cortex makes immediate but transient changes in connectivity that decay rapidly unless the new hippocampally processed information is interleaved within existing, activated cortical frameworks (schema). HF index traces, retained by cellular consolidation mechanisms, guide the process by which new information is subject to systems consolidation, possibly by altering the synaptic weights of initially "silent" connections to allow for rapid incorporation of new information in schema. Such intercortical connections may take time to develop (Chklovskii et al. 2004). However, once built, relevant new information can be assimilated into schema very rapidly. Put simply: we rapidly remember what interests us, but what interests us takes time to develop.

Although novelty-detection in HPC followed by the activation of dopaminergic neurons in the VTA—which, in turn, provides a reward signal for new learning that is projected to various networks (Lisman & Grace 2005)— and/or a temporary shutdown of certain inhibitory interneurons (Paulsen & Moser 1998) may together aid new memory encoding and trace persistence, we need to consider circumstances in which new memories supplant, interact, or assimilate with earlier consolidated memories. Thus, Proposition #4 provides a way to incorporate the new concept of reconsolidation—the idea that the act of retrieving previously consolidated memories can, in certain situations, put those memory traces back into a labile state such that they are again sensitive to the inhibition of protein synthesis and that they might be strengthened, over-ridden, or incorporated with new information. This is what Dudai (2004) and others (Alberini

2005, Sara 2000) have referred to as memory updating.

AUTOMATIC ASPECTS OF EPISODIC-LIKE MEMORY ENCODING IN ANIMALS

The Concept of Automatic Memory Encoding

A longstanding concept in human cognition is the distinction between automatic and controlled processes (Schneider & Shiffrin 1977). Is this distinction relevant to episodic-like memory formation in animals? And, if so, how and in what neural circuits do these ostensibly distinct processes operate?

With respect to episodic-like memory, unexpected neural events happen and it may be important for an animal to encode what, where, and perhaps when they have occurred—and to do so irrespective of whether episodic-like memory is engaged in some other purposeful activity. Attention will be momentarily diverted and, even though the animal had no intention of remembering this unexpected information nor was motivated to do so, it nonetheless encodes something about it. This is automatic or incidental encoding. Conversely, the animal may be engaged in some very specific goal-seeking activity when novel stimuli arise that are directly relevant to the task underway. This would engage intentional or controlled processing that is both task- and goal-related. The automatic versus controlled distinction does not map easily onto classical animal learning concepts, such as those of classical and instrumental conditioning, primarily because there is no obvious role for reinforcement in automatic processing. However, the idea does have echoes in classical phenomena such as latent learning, in which laboratory animals are shown to learn about the layout of a maze during exploration that occurs prior to being made hungry and the availability of food at the goal. It recently has been shown that the EC and HPC are engaged in different aspects of latent learning and goal-place associations, respectively (Gaskin & White 2007).

Memory reconsolidation: the process by which the act of memory retrieval appears to destabilize previously stored memory traces and thereby enable them to be strengthened or to incorporate new information

CA1: one subregion (the others are CA3, DG, EC, SUB) of the hippocampal formation containing different cell types and local circuits and interconnected by largely unidirectional circuitry

VTA: ventral tegmental area; a small brain area containing dopaminergic neurons

NMDA: N-methyl-D-aspartate

LTP: long-term potentiation

CaMKII: calcium-calmodulin-dependent protein kinase; an enzyme located at synapses widely believed to play a critical role in early stages of synaptic change at the time of memory formation

VPC: visual paired comparison task; an incidental memory task as used in human and nonhuman primate studies

SOR: spontaneous object recognition task, which does not involve food reward or other apparent reinforcer; the equivalent task to VPC for work with rodents

Various lines of evidence in nonhuman primates (Miyashita 2004) and rodents (Floresco et al. 1997, Seamans et al. 1998) are consistent with the automatic/controlled distinction, although it is not always expressed in such terms. Moreover, with respect to automatic and controlled aspects of encoding and retrieving experience, the supposition is that the medial temporal lobe is involved primarily in automatic encoding. This is not to deny that the prefrontal lobe can play a critical role in episodic memory encoding as well—it is only to assert that it does so when subjects engage in a more deliberate or prospective attempt to remember events.

Relevant Data

It is unclear what constitutes an incidental episodic-like learning paradigm for animals, as we cannot directly ask to what stimulus information they are consciously attending. The basic requirements are that encoding should be fast (e.g., one trial), lack explicit motivation or incentive for learning (e.g., explicit reward), and not require elaborate task planning of a prospective nature.

One example is the diverse family of visual paired comparison (VPC) and visual object recognition (VOR) tasks. In a spontaneous object recognition (SOR) task, introduced by Ennaceur & Delacour (1988), animals are first habituated to a test arena and then are merely exposed to toy objects placed within it for a short period of time and given the opportunity to investigate them. Rats and mice typically do this by cautiously approaching the objects and then engaging in sniffing and tactile behavior. After a memory delay, the animals are placed back into the arena containing duplicates of some of these objects, with one or more of the originals replaced by one or more novel objects. The animals typically explore the novel object(s) more than the familiar one(s). There is no apparent reinforcement for this exploration—it just happens. The differential sensitivity of various versions of VPC/VOR to hippocampal, perirhinal, and parahippocampal lesions (and other interventions) has been

debated extensively in recent years (Aggleton & Brown 1999, Eichenbaum et al. 2007, Mumby 2001, Squire et al. 2007), with a number of studies revealing conflicting results (contrast Ainge et al. 2006 with Broadbent et al. 2004). A key idea is that the episodic-like character of some of these recognition tasks derives from protocols in which there is more than mere object recognition at stake—namely memory for object-place, object-context, and object-context-place associations—with impairments after localized HF lesions seen in these variations of the VPC/SOR task. A familiar object may be moved to a new location in the arena, or the arena context in which testing takes place may be changed, but the location of the objects within it remain the same—and other permutations. Eichenbaum et al. (2007) suggest that the HPC is essential for those variants of the task that require associations between objects and places, the parahippocampal cortex is important for place memory, while the perirhinal cortex subserves object familiarity.

In a new development in this field, reversible manipulations such as drugs that inactivate neural activity offer an opportunity to dissociate the contributions that the HF or perirhinal/parahippocampal cortex make to object recognition by giving the drugs at the time of encoding, the start of the consolidation period, or the time of retrieval (Barker & Warburton 2008, Winters et al. 2008). The use of such procedures is a conceptual improvement on classical lesion approaches that cannot easily dissociate distinct memory processes such as encoding and retrieval, but there are disadvantages. The spread of a drug may be incomplete within a target brain area, or it may pass beyond a cytochemical boundary and affect a different region. Histological data is rarely available to detect such imprecision. The use of drug manipulations with the VOR family of tasks is also less successful for studying consolidation because long-term memory traces are either not formed or relatively weak.

A related strand to thinking about episodic-like memory has been interest in the distinction between a hippocampal-independent familiarity component of memory retrieval and a hippocampal-dependent recollection component—with signal-detection theory and receiver operating characteristic (ROC) procedures developed to help make this distinction (Haskins et al. 2008). The curvilinear component of the ROC curve is held to reflect familiarity, whereas a step-function at the origin is thought to reflect recollection. In animal experiments in which experimental lesions of the hippocampus (Fortin et al. 2004) or medial prefrontal cortex (Farovik et al. 2008) have been examined, a partial dissociation of familiarity and recollection is observed, supporting the two-process models of recognition memory (Eichenbaum et al. 2007). This work could, subject to the caveats raised above, be developed further through drug manipulations to establish whether the familiarity/recollection distinction operates at the time of encoding or retrieval (or both). For example, the claim that the hippocampus mediates recollection is really a claim about the phenomenological experience at the time of memory retrieval. Does this experience only require the HPC to be active at the time of retrieval? Or does it also require hippocampal-mediated encoding as well?

Although the ROC approach to distinguishing familiarity and recollection is intriguing, the analytic adequacy of this approach has been questioned (Wixted & Squire 2008) and, with it, the possibility that the ostensibly qualitative distinction between recall and familiarity actually reflects a distinction between strong and weak memories. Might there be other ways of making the distinction in animals that are qualitative rather than quantitative? In a new development, it has been suggested that VOR paradigms be supplemented by procedures that require recall rather than recognition of object-place associations (Eacott & Easton 2007). For example, in a study that used an E-shaped maze in which rats have to make a choice of which way to turn at a choice point without being able to see the target objects, fornix lesions were observed to disrupt choice behavior without affecting the relative time investigating novel and familiar objects found at the ends

of the maze (Easton et al. 2009). This suggests that such lesions disrupt recollection without affecting familiarity, consistent with the work of the Eichenbaum group and the theoretical distinctions developed by Aggleton & Brown (1999).

Other tasks have been introduced as models of episodic-like memory in avian species (Clayton & Dickinson 1998). The idea was that the what-where-when triad of episodic memory might be addressed by specific behavioral protocols in animals. Initial attempts to show the same in rodents were unsuccessful, but recent work has established that rats can show integrated what-where-when in food-finding, replenishment, and degrade paradigms when appropriately trained in the radial maze (Babb & Crystal 2006, Naqshbandi et al. 2007). The sensitivity of these tasks to hippocampal dysfunction is unknown.

Paired-Associate Learning in an Event Arena

The event-arena protocols are a new set of procedures for rats that enable multiple, within-subject object-place associations to be encoded and stored across varying time periods (Day et al. 2003). In these procedures, the object is a flavored reward that can then be used as a cue for associative retrieval of place information. In addition, encoding is incidental in the sense that, on sample trials, the animal is engaged in securing a food reward with no imposed discrimination necessity for it to encode the location where the food was found (**Figure 1A**). After a short delay, the animal is placed in a different start box and a second sample trial is run, now to a different sandwell containing a different flavor of food (**Figure 1B**). An unexpected memory retrieval trial follows after a delay, ranging from minutes to hours, in which both sandwells are now available (**Figure 1C**). The question is, what do the animals then do when the door opens? In practice, the animals display a tendency to revisit the location in the arena from which they earlier secured that food. In effect, the rat brings to mind the specific

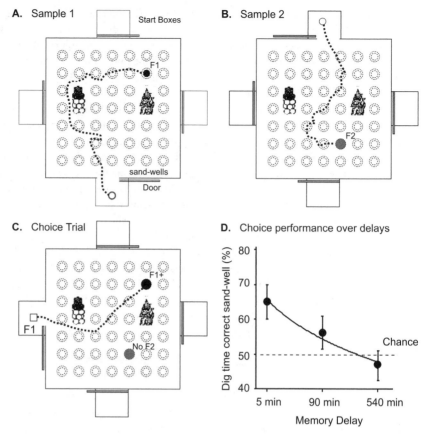

A. Sample 1

Start Boxes

F1

sand-wells

Door

B. Sample 2

F2

C. Choice Trial

F1+

F1

No F2

D. Choice performance over delays

Dig time correct sand-well (%)

Chance

5 min   90 min   540 min

Memory Delay

Figure 1

The event arena. (*A*) Schematic drawing of arena showing 7–7 array of possible sandwell locations, the two intra-arena landmarks, and the path of a rat from the south start-box to the single open sandwell containing food 1. (*B*) Path taken on the sample trial 2. (*C*) In the cued-recall choice trial, both sandwells used earlier are available, but the animal is cued with only one of the flavors (in this case, F1). The animal correctly takes a path to the sandwell that had previously contained this food. (*d*) Memory performance in the nonrewarded choice probe trials decays over a period of around 90 min.

location of the associated cue flavor and goes there. A contingency is arranged such that, if it goes there, it is rewarded by more of the same taste of food. Thus, it seems that the animals have automatically encoded the places where the food flavors had been located and, at retrieval, preferentially revisit the cued location. On the next day, a different pair of sandwell locations and flavors of food are used and the procedure is repeated, a process that can continue indefinitely across months of training. The task is thus an object-place task with one-trial automatic encoding, albeit supported by a

contingency at the point of retrieval. Memory decays relatively rapidly (**Figure 1D**).

The primary function of food in this unusual task is to act as a retrieval cue, although it also has the secondary role of acting as an incentive to the food-motivated animal. This renders performance less variable than is typical for VPC/SOR, but it creates an ambiguity regarding the automatic versus controlled dimension. Nonetheless, the results reveal effective single-trial information encoding, with rapid forgetting over a delay of around 90 min, that is sensitive to intrahippocampal infusions of NMDA and α-amino-3-hydroxy-5-methyl-4-isoxazolepropionic acid (AMPA) receptor antagonists (Day et al. 2003). Infusions of the NMDA antagonist D-AP5 prior to sample encoding block later memory, whereas infusions given before memory retrieval are without effect. Conversely, the AMPA antagonist CNQX blocks both encoding and retrieval. A spatial memory control task has also been developed with similar pharmacological sensitivity (Bast et al. 2005).

A potential weakness of the single-trial paired-associate encoding task is that, like VPC tasks, performance is never very good. We suspect this is typical of much automatic encoding, yet we can clearly remember some single events for long periods. These may occur in circumstances of surprise or emotional significance, as in "flashbulb" memories (Brown & Kulick 1977) or, more commonly, when new information is directly relevant to a person's existing knowledge base. In a new protocol, aimed at producing long-term reference memories lasting over days (Tse et al. 2007), six paired associates were trained concurrently (one trial/day for each pair), with repeated training across days (**Figure 2A**, see color insert). After 15 sessions, the animals develop an associative schema denoting the locations of these six foods (inset in **Figure 2B**) such that the rats could be cued with any of the foods to revisit the correct location and so secure more of the same food. It turns out that once the schema is learned, new paired-associates could then be trained in a single trial (session 21 in **Figure 2B**), and the level of memory retrieval was very high (**Figure 2C**).

Implications

Part of the difficulty of discussing incidental and intentional encoding in animals is that the distinction involves a feature of information processing by humans that is not easily captured by specific protocols. The differential effects of HF lesions on incidental tasks, such as visual paired comparison, and deliberate tasks, such as delayed nonmatching to sample (Nemanic et al. 2004), have been noted before (Eichenbaum

et al. 2007). The idea that episodic-like memory can be subdivided into automatic and controlled aspects is not new, but the supposition that the automatic component is captured by local synaptic learning mechanisms, such as hippocampal LTP, brings a neurobiological dimension to the debate. And with this comes the possibility of using regionally specific genetically modified animals (Nakazawa et al. 2003) to attribute the relative contribution of NMDA and other receptor mechanisms in different circuits of the hippocampus and cortex to automatic versus controlled processing.

Single-unit recording techniques, coupled to tasks that distinguish retrospective and prospective memory encoding (Ferbinteanu & Shapiro 2003), are also likely to be helpful because they will provide a neural signature, over and beyond place or reward-related information, of the content of information processing on any trial (Kametani & Kesner 1989). Additionally, the mere absence of reward in a task is no grounds on which to classify it as incidental—what matters is the relevance or novelty of the information in relation to the task in which an animal is engaged. Moreover, incidental encoding can still occur during a deliberate task. Given these complexities, it seems clear that there is still a huge task before us of designing appropriate behavioral protocols for animals to study the ever more subtle aspects of memory processing that are revealed by taking a neurobiological perspective.

During the course of a day, it is to be expected that a great deal of information that is automatically encoded should be forgotten rapidly, with only a subset retained—an insight about memory originally proposed by Marr (1971). This raises the possibility of there being a window of time in which separate processes intervene to determine information retention. That is, there is no need for all the neurobiological events that determine persistence to occur or be set in train when an event occurs. This is not to deny that on-line cognitive processes will influence the electrophysiological or hemodynamic signature of a stimulus and so contribute to its eventual memorability (Brewer et al. 1998,

AMPA: α-amino-3-hydroxy-5-methyl-4-isoxazolepropionic acid

D-AP5: aminophosphono-pentanoic acid

Wagner et al. 1998). Rather, it is to recognize that various memory-related neural events take time—such as signal-transduction, gene transcription, and the transport of molecules to synaptic targets. A key novel feature of our neurobiological framework of memory persistence builds upon the neural concept of synaptic tagging and capture (see below).

SYNAPTIC TAGGING AND CAPTURE: COGNITIVE AND BEHAVIORAL IMPLICATIONS

Memory Consolidation and the Concept of Synaptic Tagging and Capture

The idea that memory traces might gradually stabilize over time is an old one. That a time period is required for a memory to be maintained for any length of time was first proposed by Müller and Pilzecker (see Lechner et al. 1999 for a summary in English). They called this the consolidation period—a time during which interfering material could impair the recall of the target memory at a later time. Retroactive inhibition paradigms have since provided evidence that new traces are subject to consolidation (Heinemann et al. 1981, McGeoch 1932).

The understanding of how the brain contributes to consolidation in humans drew upon seminal reports of amnesic patients. One of the earliest reports of memory loss came from the study of Korsakoff syndrome, first described in 1887, which characterizes the memory loss associated with chronic alcoholism (Shimamura et al. 1988). However, this syndrome involves a wide range of abnormalities in the brain, offering less precision about the link between a specific brain area and a particular memory function. One well-characterized amnesic patient, H.M., was reported by Scoville & Milner (1957). H.M. had selective surgical damage to the medial temporal lobe for the relief of epilepsy and is reported to have had a remote memory gradient of around 3+ years (Corkin 1984). This temporal graded retrograde amnesia was later demonstrated in animal models

using experimental lesions (Kim & Fanselow 1992, Zola-Morgan & Squire 1990).

Parallel to human studies, early animal studies offered different evidence for causal links between brain and memory consolidation. Duncan (1949) applied electroconvulsive shock (ECS) to rodents after training to induce experimental amnesia, a procedure that was later shown not to be dependent on the punishment effect of ECS (Gold et al. 1973). Experimental amnesia was also demonstrated by using protein synthesis inhibition, validating the role of protein synthesis in memory consolidation (Squire & Barondes 1972). This was an important advance because it suggested that cerebral protein synthesis was more than mere housekeeping—rather, it was a vital biological process necessary for new memories to be stabilized. The idea that such manipulations, when applied within a certain time window after training, impair the long-term maintenance of the memory was theorized within a consolidation framework (Matthies 1989, McGaugh 2000). A distinction between systems consolidation (suggested by the human studies) and cellular consolidation (suggested by the ECS and protein synthesis-inhibition work with animals) is now widely used (Dudai & Morris 2000). Cellular consolidation reflects processes happening at the single-cell level involving signal-transduction pathways and gene activation, whereas systems consolidation involves an interaction between distinct brain areas.

The theoretical framework developed by Morris (2006) capitalizes on these earlier ideas by relating mechanisms of cellular consolidation to the physiological phenomenon of LTP. Specifically, it was proposed that memory traces in the mammalian brain are encoded as distributed patterns of synaptic weights that persist over time. LTP is a physiological model of such changes, but lasting for variable durations of time (Bliss & Lømo 1973). A protein synthesis–independent form of LTP, often called early LTP (E-LTP), is perhaps akin to the rapidly decaying memories seen in the event arena (**Figure 1**). Protein synthesis–dependent late LTP (L-LTP) lasts longer, both in vivo

(Krug et al. 1984) and in vitro (Frey et al. 1988). The difference between E-LTP and L-LTP also reflects a key difference between STM and LTM—that de novo protein synthesis is required for a short-lasting trace to be converted into a long-lasting one. It draws upon experimental work in *Drosophila* (Belvin & Yin 1997), *Aplysia* (Montarolo et al. 1986), early learning in birds (Rose 1995), and mammalian memory (Davis & Squire 1984, Dudai & Morris 2000, Goelet et al. 1986, Kelleher et al. 2004).

The new perspective, now embedded within the hippocampal-neocortical interactions theory, is the synaptic tagging and capture (STC) hypothesis of memory trace formation (Frey & Morris 1997). This hypothesis accepts that plasticity-related proteins (PRPs) are critical for the persistence of synaptic memory traces, but argues against the standard model that their de novo synthesis is necessarily triggered by neural activity associated with the actual events to be remembered. New PRPs are still required, but their synthesis may be regulated in other ways and over a longer time window. According to this idea, the creation of long-term memory traces is a dual process. In one step, the potential for a long-term memory is established locally at synapses in the form of rapidly decaying E-LTP accompanied by the setting of a synaptic tag and triggered by glutamatergic activation of NMDA and AMPA receptors. In the other step, a series of biochemical interactions, including activation of various signal transduction pathways and protein-protein interactions, converts this synaptic potentiation into a stabilized trace at those synapses at which tags have been set. The events that lead to these interactions can be set in motion shortly before the event to be remembered, at the same time, or shortly afterward. This leads to the interesting psychological idea that the persistence of memory does not have to be determined at the exact moment of initial memory trace formation.

Relevant Data

In the original tagging experiment (hippocampal CA1 brain slices in vitro), Frey & Morris (1997) arranged for one afferent stimulus pathway (S2) to be strongly tetanized in the presence of anisomycin (an antibiotic drug with a number of actions including the inhibition of protein synthesis). Ordinarily, this protocol leads to a short-lasting potentiation lasting 2–3 hr. However, when S2 tetanization occurs 1 hr after equally strong stimulation to an independent S1 pathway to the same population of neurons given in the absence of anisomycin, long-lasting LTP (>8 hr) occurs on both pathways. This is paradoxical, as LTP lasting 8 hr is known to depend on protein synthesis, yet is here induced on S2 during the inhibition of such synthesis. It was argued that synaptic tags on the S2 pathway (that are set by a post-translational mechanism) sequester PRPs induced in response to stimulation of the S1 pathway.

Follow-up studies have included weak-before-strong experiments showing that weak tetanization, which ordinarily results only in STP, can lead to L-LTP after strong stimulation of S1 (Frey & Morris 1998); competitive maintenance under circumstances of competition for PRPs (Fonseca et al. 2004); priming experiments (Young & Nguyen 2005); tag-resetting investigations (Sajikumar & Frey 2004b); and intriguing cross-tagging and capture experiments revealing that E-LTP can be transformed in L-LTP by prior L-LTD on an independent pathway, and vice versa, i.e., E-LTD to L-LTD by L-LTP on the other pathway (Sajikumar & Frey 2004a). The latter finding strongly suggests that the PRPs upregulated by L-LTP and L-LTD are overlapping. Using a transgenic mouse overexpressing a constitutive CREB, Barco et al. (2002) have shown the relatively immediate induction of L-LTP (identified in this case by its insensitivity to depotentiation). These findings are complemented by earlier experiments in *Aplysia* neurons in culture (Bailey et al. 2000, Martin et al. 1997), suggesting the phenomenon might be widespread in diverse neural circuits. In conclusion, STC points to dual regulation of potentiation (strength) and persistence (stability) via interacting synaptic and cytosolic processes and suggests a powerful framework for enriching the repertoire of long-term memory mechanisms (**Figure 3A**, see color insert). Further physiological and molecular aspects of STC, beyond the scope of this review, are discussed in Kelleher et al. (2004) and Reymann & Frey (2007).

Cognitive and Behavioral Implications

Various behavioral paradigms have been developed to explore the relevance of these physiological ideas to memory formation. Frey's group has examined the persistence of LTP in vivo as a function of reinforcing behavioral events happening shortly after LTP induction. For example, Seidenbecher et al. (1997) observed that allowing thirsty rats to drink water within a discrete interval after induction of an LTP that normally decayed to baseline could result in this LTP in vivo lasting much longer. They argued and presented evidence that this was due to engaging reward-associated dopaminergic neurons whose activation of the hippocampus triggered signal-transduction mechanisms that upregulate the availability of PRPs. The idea that a dopaminergic input to the hippocampus might modulate the persistence of memory has also been successfully tested using a water-maze paradigm.

In a particularly interesting test of the STC framework, recent experiments have shown that the memory for weakly trained inhibitory avoidance, which is normally forgotten over 24 hr, can persist if the trained animals are given the opportunity to explore a separate novel environment (Moncada & Viola 2007). This exposure has few stimulus attributes in common with the inhibitory avoidance paradigm itself and would not be expected to interfere or enhance performance in a direct stimulus-specific manner. Instead, exploration is known to upregulate plasticity-related mRNAs (such as Arc and zif-268), raising the possibility that they or other similarly upregulated genes synthesize PRPs that are captured at task-relevant synapses in the hippocampal network and so stabilize the learning-associated synaptic changes responsible for inhibitory avoidance memory.

Moncada & Viola (2007) established that the ability of exploration to enhance memory for inhibitory avoidance was sensitive to both intrahippocampal infusions of anisomycin and the D1/D5 antagonist SCH23390 given shortly before exploration—indicating a clear compatibility with the STC framework. Parallel and independent work by our own group indicates that novelty exploration can increase appetitive one-trial spatial memory, which is normally rapidly forgotten within 24 hr (S-H Wang, R Redondo, and RGM Morris, manuscript in preparation).

It has also been shown, using a conditioned taste-aversion task, that weak aversive conditioning of a taste can be made more persistent by prior strong conditioning of a different novel taste. The novelty of the facilitating, strong taste is critical; a well-familiarized taste did not enhance the subsequent learning. The facilitating taste conditioning is, however, unable to rescue the learning impairment seen when strong taste conditioning is induced during protein synthesis inhibition (Merhav & Rosenblum 2008). This pattern of results fits aspects of STC. Moncada & Viola's (2007) finding suggests that PRP upregulation by novelty exploration can be used by later learning. This implies that the exploration has a neurobiological impact on a hippocampal cell population that at least partially overlaps with or encompasses the cell population activated by a contiguous learning event. It is possible that box exploration drives a dopamine input from the VTA to HPC, while learning may trigger a specific cell assembly within HPC (Lisman & Grace 2005). Frey & Morris (1998) also predict a substantial overlap of the population of cells affected by both events—something more difficult to achieve in behavioral studies than in in vitro slice work. On the other hand, Merhav & Rosenblum's (2008) finding implies that although the facilitating taste helps with subsequent learning, the upregulation of PRPs either is not sufficient to rescue the impairment induced by protein synthesis inhibition in the insular cortex or is not in the same pool of cells that are recruited to represent the learning event (**Figure 3B,C**).

Implications

There are a number of outstanding issues concerning the possible role of STC in cellular consolidation. First, the phenomenon, widely studied in vitro, has not yet been shown neurophysiologically in vivo. Such experiments are not easy but are underway in several labs. Second, STC is a cellular phenomenon, but activation of PRPs may be triggered by neural events such as novelty detection and consequent upregulation of neuromodulatory transmitters that involve diverse neural circuits. It is therefore a phenomenon that links cellular and systems aspects of consolidation. This is important because, as noted in the Theoretical Overview: Hippocampal-Neocortical Interactions Theory section above, STC acts as a kind of filter that selects a subset of automatically captured events and thus allows only them to be subject to the longer time scale of systems consolidation. The dovetailing of time scales is intriguing and merits further examination. Third, the phenomenon of behavioral tagging, as first shown by Moncada & Viola (2007), deserves more investigation—not least because it forces us to think more about behavior as a stream of events and actions over time, whose underlying neurobiological mediation interacts, than as the discrete events we isolate and study in laboratory experiments.

HIPPOCAMPAL-NEOCORTICAL INTERACTIONS IN SYSTEMS CONSOLIDATION AND THE ROLE OF SCHEMAS

The Concept of Systems Consolidation and Mental Schemas

The question of whether the HF is always required for explicit memory formation or has a time-limited role has long been studied and debated. We have already noted that patients with medial temporal lobe damage can show temporal-graded amnesia, impairing recent but not remote memory (Scoville & Milner 1957, Zola-Morgan et al. 1986). This upward temporal gradient—paradoxically better memory for older information—suggested that the HF is required for consolidating memory over time, with long-term memory traces gradually consolidated in relevant cortical areas (Squire 1992). Systems consolidation theory has been developed, hypothesizing that the HF is required to strengthen the initially weak connections among cortical modules/areas that are encoded in parallel with the potential index sites in the hippocampus (Teyler & DiScenna 1986). Complementary to work on patients, recent functional brain imaging data in humans suggest that during the recall of semantic memories (i.e., facts), hemodynamic activity in the HF is highest for recent news events (3 years) but decreases with the age of the events (over a 30-year span) (Smith & Squire 2009). Takashima et al. (2006) have also shown that for confident memory recall, there is reduced hippocampal activity for 90-day memories compared to 1-day information.

However, flat gradients of remote memory are also seen in amnesic patients, notably in Korsakoff cases (McCarthy & Warrington 1990), leading initially to the idea that amnesia may be a problem of memory retrieval. While Korsakoff cases are complicated by damage and metabolic abnormalities in more widespread brain areas (Kopelman 1995), several studies have shown flat gradients of retrograde amnesia in more focused MTL-damaged patients (e.g., Cipolotti et al. 2001). Some functional brain imagining studies also reveal HF to be equally activated for recent or remote memories in the retrieval of autobiographical memories (Ryan et al. 2001).

Accordingly, proponents of multiple-trace theory have challenged the standard model (Moscovitch et al. 2006, Nadel & Moscovitch 1997). This theory proposes that, upon each occasion of memory retrieval, a new trace may be created by the HPC—regardless of memory age. Although the gist of a memory may be intact after HF damage, the theory asserts that the detail and vividness of memory requires the HPC (Nadel et al. 2000). Specifically, it suggests that HPC is always required for storage and retrieval of allocentric and spatial memories (Rosenbaum et al. 2001), whereas semantic memory is mediated by neocortex alone, subject to the completion of a systems consolidation process after learning.

Our alternative perspective considers the place of prior knowledge or mental schemas in determining the speed with which systems consolidation takes place. According to the standard model, it is widely thought that it takes a long time before intercortical connections become strong enough to support unaided memory retrieval. From a theoretical perspective, it has sometimes been argued that the HF is a fast learning system, whereas the cortex is a slow learning system (McClelland et al. 1995). Supporting evidence comes from recent immediate early gene (IEG) studies in animals, which show that a dynamic shift in maximal IEG expression after learning—from HF to cortex—takes place over weeks (Frankland & Bontempi 2005). However, the animals in which these observations are made are typically experimentally naïve at the time of initial training. This is not only unlike the situation in human amnesics, who have a lifetime of experience behind them, but is also unnatural in that adult learning by animals in their normal habitat will generally take place against a background of prior knowledge.

The question we considered is whether new information processed by the HF can be consolidated into the cortex more easily, or in a different way, if this new information is relevant to prior knowledge. An extensive body of human literature suggests that it should (Bartlett 1932, Bransford 1979). Associative frameworks of knowledge are stored in the cortex, with growing evidence that the dynamic changes in circuitry required involve activity-dependent synaptic plasticity, with dendritic and synaptic growth mediated by BDNF and other growth-associated signal-transduction pathways (Osada et al. 2008). Like the standard model of consolidation, it is reasonable to suppose that such growth processes take time. However, once a framework or schema is created, it may then be possible to assimilate relevant new information relatively easily. We therefore created a paradigm in which animals first learned

multiple paired-associates involving spatial locations over several weeks—and so became task experienced—and were then required to learn two new paired-associates, each in a single trial. As described in the Automatic Aspects of Episodic Memory-Like Encoding in Animals section above, a single trial of training proved sufficient to create a memory of the new paired-associates lasting at least 24 hr (Tse et al. 2007). We turn below to the issue of what happens when lesions of the HF are made shortly after such training.

Relevant Data

Because the site and extent of brain damage varies across human amnesic patients, complicating comparisons across studies (Rosenbaum et al. 2001), we focus here on animal studies. These offer greater precision of lesion size and location and the opportunity of using other techniques, such as IEG expression, to study consolidation (Frankland et al. 2007).

Several animal studies suggest that the HF plays a time-limited role in the stabilization of certain memories, such as contextual fear conditioning (Kim & Fanselow 1992; see review in Morris 2007). Brain imaging approaches, using immediate early-gene activation, also support similar ideas that recent, contextual fear memory triggers more IEG expression in the hippocampus and less expression in the neocortex (e.g., anterior cingulate cortex, infralimbic and prelimbic cortex), whereas the opposite pattern is observed for remote memory (Frankland et al. 2004). A similar finding was reported using a spatial radial-maze task (Maviel et al. 2004).

However, whereas a temporal gradient of amnesia or IEG expression is seen for context fear conditioning and certain radial-maze paradigms, such a gradient does not occur with spatial learning in the water maze. Several studies have now shown that HF lesions made remotely after training still impair memory that might have been expected to have been consolidated in neocortex over such an interval (Broadbent et al. 2006, Clark et al. 2005, Martin et al. 2005). On the face of it, these data support

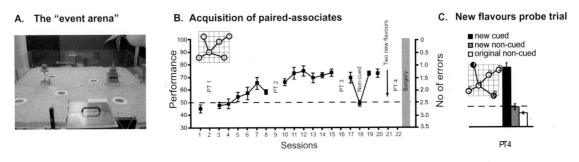

Figure 2

Paired-associate learning in rats. (*A*) Arena with multiple sandwells for the concurrent task of Tse et al. (2007). (*B*) Gradual acquisition of a schema (*inset*) over 15 sessions, a noncued control task (S17–S19), and the learning of two new associates (S21). (*C*) Effective cued recall of new flavors in a probe test (S22) after only one training trial (S21).

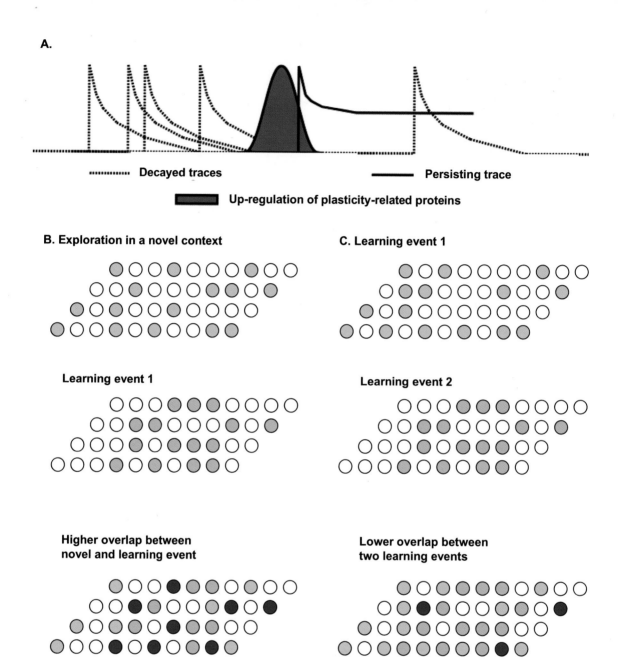

A.

•••••••••••• **Decayed traces**   ——— **Persisting trace**

▬ **Up-regulation of plasticity-related proteins**

B. Exploration in a novel context

C. Learning event 1

Learning event 1

Learning event 2

**Higher overlap between
novel and learning event**

**Lower overlap between
two learning events**

Figure 3

Synaptic tagging and capture. (*A*) The LTP traces that are induced by a weak tetanus and the memory traces that are formed after weak training normally decay with time (*dashed curves*). However, if there is a temporary upregulation of plasticity-related proteins (PRPs) that can be captured by neurons encoding these events (either tetanus or training), LTP or memory occurring around the same time can persist longer (*solid curve*). (*B*) A hypothetical example shows when the event that upregulates PRP (e.g., exploration in a novel context) has a higher overlap with the learning event (event 1) at the neuronal level. It is likely that event 1 can capture the PRP induced by novelty exploration. (*C*) A hypothetical example shows when two learning events encourage representations by separate neurons. The PRPs upregulated by event 1 are less likely to be captured by the tags associated with event 2.

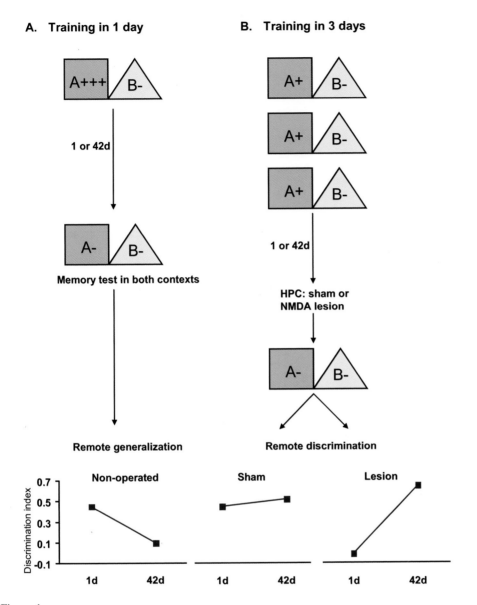

A. Training in 1 day

A+++ / B-

1 or 42d

A- / B-

Memory test in both contexts

Remote generalization

B. Training in 3 days

A+ / B-

A+ / B-

A+ / B-

1 or 42d

HPC: sham or NMDA lesion

A- / B-

Remote discrimination

Non-operated

Sham

Lesion

Discrimination index

0.7
0.5
0.3
0.1
-0.1

1d   42d   1d   42d   1d   42d

Figure 4

Memory persists or changes with time. (*A*) A training protocol of contextual fear conditioning that encourages memory generalization between contexts at a remote time point. Context A was paired with three footshocks; context B was never paired with footshocks. When tested one day after training, animals showed more freezing in context A than context B, hence better discrimination. When tested 42 days after training, animals froze similarly in context A and B, hence near zero discrimination. (*B*) A contextual fear-conditioning protocol that encourages memory discrimination between contexts across time. Training was spread out over three days; within each day, context A was paired with one footshock while context B was never paired with footshocks. Animals that received sham lesions showed good discrimination at both recent and remote time points (contrasting the poor discrimination at remote time points in **Figure 4*A***). Hippocampus (HPC)-damaged animals showed poor discrimination at recent time points, suggesting a critical role of HPC in consolidating this learning. However, animals could discriminate between contexts when the lesion was made much later, suggesting a time-limited role of HPC.

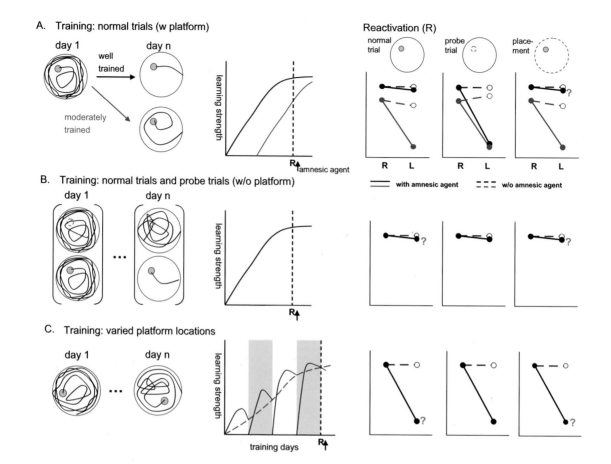

Figure 6

Reconsolidation of spatial memory in the water maze. (*A*) In a standard reference memory task, the escape platform is fixed at one location in the water maze. After moderate training (*middle panel, blue curve*), reactivation (R) with another training trial, a probe trial [i.e., omission of platform (*small dashed gray circle*)], or simple placement on the platform without (w/o) precedent swimming in the water maze (*large dashed gray circle*) is likely to trigger memory updating and subsequent reconsolidation in the hippocampus (HPC) (*right panel*). This is revealed by post-reactivation long-tem memory (L) impairment by amnesia agents applied after reactivation (*middle panel, short arrow*). However, after performance reaches a plateau (*middle panel, black curve*), memory updating/reconsolidation in the HPC is unlikely to occur after a training trial. (*B*) If the training mixes nonreinforced probe trials with normal reinforced trials, another trial with or without reinforcement or simple placement is unlikely to trigger memory updating and reconsolidation in the HPC. (*C*) If the training involves changing platform locations across days (e.g., delayed-matching-to-place task), the animals are encouraged to update this information every day. Hence, reactivation with any one of the three scenarios is likely to induce reconsolidation. The symbol "?" refers to the lack of empirical data. *Black irregular curves* in the *large blue circle* (water maze) represent the swimming traces.

multiple trace theory. Moreover, using both causal and correlational approaches, Teixeira et al. (2006) showed that hippocampus inactivation by lidocaine at retrieval disrupted both 1-day and 30-day spatial memory in the water maze. In addition, memory recall at 1 day or 30 days after training was equally good at triggering IEG expression in subfields of HF. These studies suggest the HF plays a special lasting role in supporting spatial navigation that relies on the use of allocentric information.

Thus, the debate between standard systems consolidation theory (Squire & Bayley 2007) and multiple trace theory (Moscovitch et al. 2006) also exists for animal work and is unresolved for several reasons. Each theory has abundant supporting evidence. In addition, multiple trace theory can accommodate negative findings that do not seem to fit the theory (e.g., the lack of remote memory impairment could be because the level of detail of the memory is not tested); likewise, standard systems consolidation theory can also explain findings that appear at first to be in conflict. Although new findings will continue to inform this debate, new issues are also emerging: (*a*) whether the qualitative nature of memory traces changes over time; and (*b*) whether systems consolidation can occur in a much shorter time scale, challenging the concept of "fast" and "slow" learning systems.

Regarding the first issue, recent studies using context fear conditioning suggest remote memory can generalize across contexts, whereas recent memory tends to be more discriminative. For example, Winocur et al. (2007) showed that, when tested a few days after learning, animals discriminated a dangerous context that was previously paired with footshock and a safe context that had never been paired with footshock. In contrast, their remote memory tested weeks later of the dangerous context remained generalized to the safe context. When HF lesions were made one day after training, the generalization remained, although the overall performance was also reduced. Wiltgen & Silva (2007) made similar findings and indicated that a deficit in retrieval may contribute to poor

performance of an old context memory because brief re-exposure to the training context was sufficient to enhance discrimination on the next day. Biedenkapp & Rudy (2007) also found that context memory can become less precise with time. Interestingly, pre-exposure to the to-be-reinforced context, but not to an irrelevant context, helped to maintain the discrimination for longer.

These changes in the performance of normal animals when memories are tested at varying intervals after training must be born in mind when making comparisons between control and lesioned animals. For example, when remote memories generalize across contexts in normal animals and if generalization is also observed in lesioned animals, it cannot be unambiguously claimed that the brain area targeted plays an equally important role in recent and remote memory. To address this, a paradigm that allows for similarly precise recent and remote memory becomes crucial. Wang et al. (2009b) showed that context discrimination can remain as good when tested 42 days later as when tested after 1 day later when a training protocol is used that encourages discrimination between reinforced context and nonreinforced context. Control experiments showed that this is not an effect of memory strength, as equivalent training compressed into one session did not encourage discrimination over time (**Figure 4A**, see color insert). Critically, HF lesioned mice discriminated similarly to sham-lesion controls when lesions were made 42 days but not 1 day after training (**Figure 4B**). The 42-day lesioned animals also discriminated well in reinforced versus novel contexts or versus hybrid contexts that contained some elements of reinforced and nonreinforced context. This study suggests that the ability to differentiate between contexts can be preserved without the hippocampus, provided sufficient time has been allowed for systems consolidation.

Training protocols not only influence whether memory retains its precision over time; training can also determine if the HF is persistently required for representing memory. For example, extensive familiarity with the environment where the memory is going to be built can enable the memory to become hippocampus independent. Winocur et al. (2005) showed that if rats were substantially habituated to a complex training village containing multiple pathways for accessing water and food in various compartments, post-training hippocampus lesions did not impair performance in searching around the village—suggesting that extensive experience of an enriched environment can enable animals to maintain at least some aspects of spatial memory without the hippocampus. However, it is unclear whether rearing in an enriched environment promotes hippocampal-independent spatial memory, or whether the extensive experience of the training and testing environment is critical for the observation of a lack of effect of the lesions.

Rapid Systems Consolidation

Our new schema idea about consolidation has emerged from our work with the concurrent paired-associate task following an astonishing but predicted observation—cortical consolidation can occur very rapidly. Having previously learned six paired-associates and developed a schema, rats trained for a single trial on each of two new paired-associates 48 hr prior to being given bilateral HF lesions could successfully recall the correct location at which to dig for more food when given a recall trial two weeks later (Tse et al. 2007; **Figure 5A**). Moreover, upon returning the control and HF lesioned animals to the old test environment many weeks later, the HF animals were immediately (trial 1) above chance in remembering the correct locations to visit in the cued-recall paradigm that they had learned prior to being given the lesions (**Figure 5C**). A within-subjects design was used in which one testing environment made sense with associations between flavors and locations remaining stable over days and weeks. In the other environment, they remained stable for only two days before being changed, such that a given flavor now had no stable spatial paired-associate. When the animals were given the opportunity to learn two new paired-

associates in two trials in each environment (one trial per associate), without re-exposure to the old flavors, learning was successful in the stable environment but unsuccessful in the inconsistent environment, when memory was tested 24 hr later (**Figure 5D**). Thus, prior knowledge plays a causal role in encoding and/or consolidation. Last, and most critical, an investigation of the time interval after learning new paired-associates before hippocampal lesions were made revealed that lesions made 3 hr after training blocked consolidation completely, whereas those made 48 hr after training did not (**Figure 5E**). This finding confirmed the observation of rapid systems consolidation and set a boundary condition, requiring further investigation, of the time over which it may take place. This short interval also points to the potential importance of sleep in consolidation, in keeping with much current theorizing in humans (Stickgold & Walker 2007) and in animals (Buzsaki 1989, Sutherland & McNaughton 2000).

Implications and Related Issues

Since the idea was first proposed that hippocampus processes information for memory automatically and rapidly (Marr 1971), computational models have been developed to account for how memory traces may or may not become hippocampus independent (McClelland et al. 1995, Meeter & Murre 2004). At the neuronal level, one early suggestion is that a replay of neuron assembly activity that represents a memory can be the mechanism for strengthening intercortical connections that may eventually become strong enough to support memory without the hippocampus—possibly via sharp waves (Buzsaki 1989). During sleep, replay of a neural firing pattern that was previously recorded during training in the awake period is observed in the rat hippocampus (Skaggs & McNaughton 1996) and prefrontal cortex (Euston et al. 2007). Takehara-Nishiuchi & McNaughton (2008) further showed that prefrontal cortical neurons maintain increased activity for up to six weeks

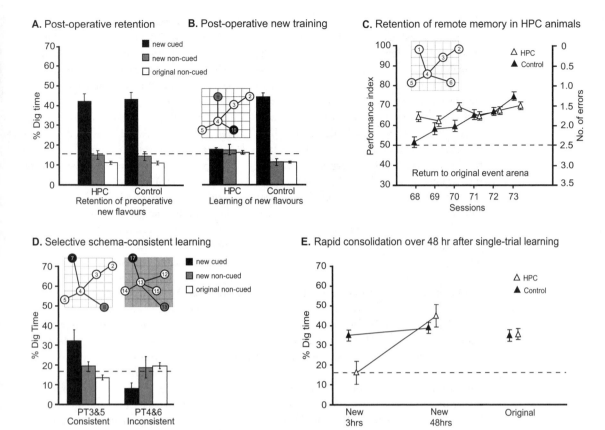

A. Post-operative retention

% Dig time

HPC — Control
Retention of preoperative
new flavours

■ new cued
■ new non-cued
□ original non-cued

B. Post-operative new training

HPC — Control
Learning of new flavours

C. Retention of remote memory in HPC animals

Performance index

△ HPC
▲ Control

No. of errors

Return to original event arena

68 69 70 71 72 73
Sessions

D. Selective schema-consistent learning

% Dig Time

PT3&5   PT4&6
Consistent   Inconsistent

■ new cued
■ new non-cued
□ original non-cued

E. Rapid consolidation over 48 hr after single-trial learning

% Dig time

△ HPC
▲ Control

New   New   Original
3hrs   48hrs

Figure 5

Rapid consolidation in association with schemas. (*A*) Normal retention by HPC-lesioned rats when a retention test was given two weeks after lesions made 48 hr after a single trial of training to each of two new paired-associates, after extensive training on a schema of six paired-associates. (*B*) The same HPC-lesioned rats are unable to learn new paired-associates in the event arena. (*C*) After extensive training in a new context over many weeks, return of the control and lesioned animals to the original training context reveals effective memory by the HPC-lesioned animals on the first trial of training. Poorer memory by controls, which rapidly catch up, probably reflects interference that they, but not the HPC-lesioned rats, have from the other context of learning. (*d*) Extensive training with a consistent schema or an inconsistent schema in separate contexts enables new paired-associate learning and retention over 24 hr only in the consistent environment. (*E*) Varying the time when HPC lesions are made after introducing two new paired-associates against the background of a prior schema reveals a rapid upward gradient of systems memory consolidation.

after training. Evidence for hippocampus-neocortical interaction comes from a study showing that signatures of neural activity in the hippocampus coincide with neocortical activity (Battaglia et al. 2004), suggesting an orchestration of activity between hippocampus and neocortex. A recent study showed that at the time of memory recall, neuronal activation that resembles firing patterns that occurred during encoding may be replayed (Gelbard-Sagiv et al. 2008). Although these observations point to a

correlational biological mechanism, the causal role of this mechanism in supporting systems consolidation needs future studies.

What is the distinction between a memory that permanently requires the hippocampus and a memory that can become hippocampus independent? A temporal gradient of retrograde amnesia is observed in context fear conditioning (Kim & Fanselow 1992) but not water-maze learning (Martin et al. 2005); thus, it has been proposed that the HPC is necessary for the latter, as it plays a critical role in spatial navigation in which the constant use of allocentric information is required to guide the animals' sense of location, direction, and destination. However, the HPC may also play a role in other components of spatial learning, such as distance estimation by using visible beacons (Clark et al. 2007). Of note here is Teixeira et al.'s (2006) observation that HPC inactivation can trigger more thigmotaxic behavior (i.e., swimming near the walls) whether given under recent or remote conditions. It is unclear whether HPC inactivation encourages animals to use different swimming strategies (swimming near the wall) compared to control animals (preferentially swimming in the center zone).

One discrepancy between the schema version of the event arena and reference memory in the water maze is that performance can be eventually independent of HPC in the event arena but always requires it in the water maze. One possibility is that in the event arena, the cued-recall nature of the memory test (where a particular flavor is given to cue the corresponding location), and that only a limited number of target locations are used (e.g., six open sandwells), is easier or does not require recollection. For the water maze, on the other hand, the free-recall nature of the memory test is harder and may require recollection.

RECONSOLIDATION AND THE UPDATING OF MEMORY

The Concept of Reconsolidation

One outstanding question about consolidation theory is whether memory traces are permanently stabilized once they are consolidated. Some early studies suggest this may not always be the case. For example, the loss of an apparently consolidated fear memory was demonstrated when ECS was applied immediately after memory recall (Misanin et al. 1968, Schneider & Sherman 1968). This cue-induced amnesia suggested that a once-consolidated memory could still be plastic, leading to the concept of a reconsolidation process. Lewis (1979) proposed the idea of active and inactive states of memory to describe the lability of the memory. Two decades later, interest in this concept has been reawakened (Nader et al. 2000, Sara 2000).

At first sight, reconsolidation appears paradoxical. The framework we have discussed so far supposes that when an animal is confronted by unexpected new events, it engages an automatic encoding process, which may then trigger the successive steps of cellular and systems consolidation. As time goes by, a stable long-term memory trace is established that would be accessed at the time of memory retrieval. Why and when might it be appropriate for that access to reinstate lability of the trace? We suggest below that the "why" component of reconsolidation differs across distinct types of memory (particularly in amygdala versus hippocampus). However, for hippocampus-dependent memory, we concur with others in proposing that reconsolidation occurs when there is new information at the time of memory retrieval—information that might potentially require an established long-term memory trace to be altered. Hence, the function of re-engaging lability is to change or strengthen the ostensibly consolidated trace. These ways of thinking about reconsolidation have been called memory updating (Dudai 2004), as the new information at reactivation updates information acquired during earlier experiences. There are two major sources of updating: training-induced updating, and updating induced by a discrepancy between training and reactivation.

Memory updating, as a particular form of reconsolidation, may be involved in the recall-triggered modification of existing long-term memories. Memory updating during retrieval mirrors the novelty detection proposed in Morris (2006) and bears the automaticity property of Proposition #1. Novelty detection is evident in studies showing increased exploration of objects in new contexts (Good et al. 2007, Save et al. 1992), in studies showing increased immediate early-gene expression in the hippocampus after exploration in a novel environment

(Guzowski et al. 2006), and in studies exploiting exploration in a novel place with respect to its impact on other learning (Moncada & Viola 2007). In the context of memory reconsolidation, novelty is likely derived from mismatch between consolidated and current information, which then re-engages the encoding process.

Relevant Data

The past decade has seen the publication of new evidence for the memory reconsolidation phenomenon. For example, Nader et al. (2000) showed that auditory fear memory can be weakened by protein synthesis inhibition in the amygdala after memory reactivation. In this study, several important control conditions were performed: No memory impairment was observed when protein synthesis inhibition was given without memory reactivation; a time window was identified, as no memory impairment was seen when the protein synthesis inhibition was long delayed after reactivation; and an intact post-reactivation short-term memory test was used to rule out nonspecific side effects of the drug. Diverse studies have shown memory reconsolidation in a wide spectrum of animals and various types of memory (Nader & Hardt 2009).

In an examination of reconsolidation in context-related learning using systemic drug application, it has been shown that context-associated memory, such as contextual fear conditioning (Eisenberg et al. 2003) and inhibitory avoidance (Przybyslawski et al. 1999), undergoes reconsolidation. Despite the ubiquitous nature of the phenomenon, reconsolidation does not always occur after memory reactivation. Several factors have been described to determine when memory reconsolidation happens.

The first of these factors is memory strength. For a stronger training protocol, a longer reactivation session is required to trigger reactivation and a reconsolidation process that is susceptible to protein synthesis inhibition (Suzuki et al. 2004). A second factor is memory age.

Inhibitory avoidance memory undergoes reconsolidation if reactivation occurs within seven days but not when scheduled two to four weeks after training (Milekic & Alberini 2002). Similar data, but over a different time scale, have been reported for context fear memory in mice (Suzuki et al. 2004). Third, there is evidence that reactivation should be nonrewarded. This was first suggested many years ago in the era of cue-induced amnesia (DeVietti & Holliday 1972), and was recently shown in context-visual danger-association learning in crabs (Pedreira et al. 2004). Paradoxically, although a nonreinforced trial at reactivation may be necessary for observing reconsolidation, multiple nonreinforced trials may give rise to extinction—and with it, new learning. Thus, fourth, when reactivation is a prolonged nonreinforced session that triggers extinction, the extinction process can dominate, and reconsolidation will fail to occur (Suzuki et al. 2004). On the other hand, if the training is so weak that a nonreinforced trial is sufficient to trigger extinction, then the impairment of extinction, instead of a reconsolidation impairment, is observed (Eisenberg et al. 2003).

Although these factors have been discussed and called boundary conditions (Nader & Hardt 2009, Tronson & Taylor 2007), the same set of conditions, based on studies with systemic treatments that affect the entire brain, may not apply to reconsolidation in specific brain areas. For example, memory age may not be a boundary condition in hippocampal reconsolidation based on current studies. It was shown in rats that old (45 days after training) context fear memory still undergoes reconsolidation in the hippocampus (Debiec et al. 2002). Although in mice it might not be the case (Frankland et al. 2006), the discrepancy could be due to the differential potency of intervention (i.e., impairment of recent memory is only partial in the mice studies but more substantial in rat studies (Debiec et al. 2002, Lee 2008). On the other hand, memory strength (Mamiya et al. 2009) and reactivation procedures (Fischer et al. 2004) are critical in the hippocampus reconsolidation.

Memory Updating and Spatial Memory

We now focus on an aspect of reconsolidation most relevant to a theme of this review—the circumstances in which it occurs in association with spatial memory. Morris et al. (2006) trained animals in a reference memory water-maze task in which the submerged escape platform remained at a fixed location across days. When the memory of the platform location was reactivated by one nonreinforced probe trial, post-reactivation protein synthesis inhibition in the dorsal hippocampus did not impair the memory. A positive control for the effectiveness of the anisomycin established separately that overnight consolidation of this reference memory task requires protein synthesis. However, when the animals were trained to search for new platform locations on each day, in the episodic-like delayed-matching-to-place task (Steele & Morris 1999), protein synthesis inhibition immediately after a nonreinforced probe trial was sufficient to impair memory tested on the following day. A control with the omission of memory reactivation showed that this impairment was seen only if anisomycin was contingent on memory reactivation. Taken together, the findings from this study suggest that reconsolidation is only observed when the reactivation involves new memory encoding.

On the other hand, other studies have suggested that spatial reference memory in a water maze can undergo reconsolidation. For example, Rossato et al. (2006) showed that reactivation with one nonreinforced probe trial rendered memory labile if coupled to anisomycin infusion into area CA1 of the dorsal hippocampus. Further experiments indicated that this spatial memory did not undergo protein synthesis-dependent reconsolidation when memory reactivation was omitted, anisomycin infusion delayed, and most importantly, when reactivation was a reinforced, relearning trial. The same lab later used a similar paradigm to confirm the same conclusions by using intra-CA1 PKC inhibition (Bonini et al. 2007) and

intra-CA1 mRNA inhibition (Da Silva et al. 2008).

The idea that the reference memory in the water maze can undergo reconsolidation was also demonstrated in mice. Artinian et al. (2007) used intra-CA3 anisomycin infusion and different reactivation protocols and found impaired reconsolidation when the reactivation involved (*a*) a swimming/relearning trial, (*b*) a placement on the submerged platform without swimming, or (*c*) a placement on the emerged platform without swimming. Thus, mere exposure to the platform in the water maze may be sufficient to reactivate spatial reference memory, which then becomes labile and sensitive to protein synthesis inhibition (Artinian et al. 2008).

It might seem puzzling that water-maze spatial memory sometimes undergoes reconsolidation, but sometimes does not. Its occurrence could reflect when the hippocampus engages memory updating during reactivation. One occasion is when updating occurs in the course of training of the delayed-matching-to-place task. In this task, animals are explicitly trained to find a new platform location on each day. Hence, at every first trial on a training day, the animals encode new information and retain it to guide later swimming trials on the same day. In this case, the reactivation trial of a memory reconsolidation experiment would trigger the retrieval of the previous day's platform location at the same time as an updating process is engaged for the expected new learning of the day. This may render the memory trace of the retrieved memory labile such that, when protein synthesis in the hippocampus is inhibited, information about this platform location is lost (Morris et al. 2006; **Figure 6**, see color insert).

Another scenario is that updating is triggered by some feature of testing that is different from the usual events of training. Most reconsolidation studies use a short, nonreinforced trial to reactivate the memory that had previously been acquired through consistent reinforcement. This procedural difference may itself trigger hippocampal protein synthesis to register the new nonreinforced experience along with the memory. In other words, the short, nonreinforced reactivation may be insufficient to cause behavior change or induce extinction, but the experience is nonetheless linked to the memory by the hippocampus. The hippocampal protein synthesis then acts to restabilize the memory network with links to the new nonreinforced experience. It is possible that the negative finding in reference memory by Morris et al. (2006) was due to familiarization with the nonreinforced probe trials that were used daily throughout the course of training. This frequent use of probe trials during training may have greatly reduced the necessity of registering the lack of reinforcement with memory reactivation and/or may have introduced a partial-reinforcement condition (Prados et al. 2008) that resulted in persistent nonlabile memory traces. Memory trace strength may then reach an asymptote that greatly reduces the possibility of observing an updating process in the HPC at reactivation (**Figure 6**).

A variation of memory reactivation in the water-maze task is to provide reinforcement without the swimming (Artinian et al. 2007). In this case, the updating process could be associated with incremental learning. Although learning curves can be very sharp in some cases (e.g., context fear conditioning), it can be more gradual in others (e.g., spatial learning in the radial-arm maze). The build-up of learning strength can be a more incremental process (Rescorla & Wagner 1972). During each additional learning trial, the previous learning experience is reactivated with more information added from the subsequent trial. It is possible that when incremental learning occurs during memory reactivation, hippocampal protein synthesis is also engaged (e.g., in Artinian et al. 2007, but not in Bonini et al. 2007). Lee (2008) showed that a second learning trial followed by a previously consolidated weak learning trial can strengthen context fear memory, supporting the idea of updating through incremental learning. Because the incremental part and the original part of the memory were both impaired by interference of reconsolidation, it suggests

that additional learning indeed triggers the representation of the previous learning.

Extinction Differs from Memory Updating

After animals have acquired a learned task, the omission of reinforcement generally causes a decline in performance, which is called extinction (Pavlov 1927). Extinction is not a simple process of erasing the previously acquired memory, but rather is a form of new learning that inhibits the expression of a still present long-term memory (Bouton 2004). Evidence supporting this comes from the observation that once a memory is extinguished, it can reappear if the animal is provided with appropriate cues (Miller & Kraus 1977). The relevance of this to reconsolidation is that a memory reactivation trial in the absence of further reinforcement is—operationally speaking—an extinction trial. Accordingly, the question arises of when memory reactivation triggers reconsolidation and when it contributes to extinction.

Studies of taste aversion show that inhibition of protein synthesis in the insular cortex disrupts the extinction memory trace when nonreinforced reactivation extinguishes performance after a weak training, but it interrupts reconsolidation if reactivation is not sufficient to cause extinction after a strong training (Eisenberg et al. 2003). It is proposed that the dominant trace during reactivation requires protein synthesis for stabilization (new learning during extinction) or restabilization (old memory subject to reconsolidation). The concept of trace dominance is also supported by experiments using systemic anisomycin treatment in context fear conditioning and reference water-maze learning in mice (Suzuki et al. 2004).

Does trace dominance also occur in the hippocampus? That is, can one see differential effects of intrahippocampal anisomycin as a function of whether memory retrieval is or is not activating an extinction process? Morris et al. (2006) showed that reactivation with eight nonreinforced probe trials caused extinction of spatial memory that persisted for one week. Immediate postextinction infusion of anisomycin in the hippocampus did not disrupt extinction, suggesting that the extinction memory trace associated with removal of the escape platform over several trials is not consolidated in the hippocampus in a protein-synthesis manner. New data by Mamiya et al. (2009) point to a role for the medial prefrontal cortex in this process. One exception showing extinction in the water maze requiring the hippocampus is likely due to side effects of altered performance by prereactivation drug treatment (Rodriguez-Ortiz et al. 2008).

Rossato et al. (2006) also supported the idea that extinction of spatial learning is not consolidated in the hippocampus when extinction involved as many as 16 nonreinforced probe trials. Interestingly, when extinction involved fewer trials (4 or 8), spatial memory showed spontaneous recovery on the next day. This recovery was blocked by intrahippocampus anisomycin infusion immediately after the extinction trials. The authors suggest that the role of reconsolidation here is to recover or update retrieval-weakened memory from incomplete extinction. When inhibitory learning in other brain areas (potentially in frontal cortex; Quirk & Beer 2006) is not fully established and decays overnight, the interference in water-maze performance seen after a small number of extinction trials will dissipate and so lead to spontaneous recovery.

Implications and Related Issues

Current literature so far points to a set of factors that create an automatic updating process that requires the hippocampus. To summarize, these include updating driven by training protocols, updating triggered by mismatch between training and reactivation, and updating triggered by incremental learning. Future studies are needed to determine whether this model, mainly based on spatial water-maze and context fear learning, extends to other types of memories.

Importantly, the same set of factors does not apply to amygdala-based learning. Evidence from auditory fear conditioning suggests that reconsolidation always occurs in the amygdala, whether the reactivation is a brief nonreinforced session (Duvarci & Nader 2004, Nader et al. 2000), a reinforcer (Wang & Nader 2003), an extinction session (Duvarci et al. 2006), or even a relearning session (Duvarci & Nader 2004). Other factors such as direct or indirect memory reconsolidation in second-order conditioning (Debiec et al. 2006, using auditory fear conditioning; but see Tronel et al. 2005, using inhibitory avoidance) and overtraining (Wang et al. 2009a) seem to be critical to influence reconsolidation in the amygdala.

The distinction between hippocampus-based reconsolidation and amygdala-based reconsolidation may reflect very different psychological functions. This brings us back to the "why" of reconsolidation that was touched on earlier. First, hippocampus is hypothesized to process associations and to serve as an index to access memory traces represented in the cortex (Teyler & DiScenna 1986, Teyler & Rudy 2007). On the other hand, the tone-fear traces of emotional conditioning are believed to be stored within the intrinsic circuitry of amygdala (Fanselow & LeDoux 1999, Han et al. 2009, LeDoux 2007). Second, in the hippocampus-neocortical system, the associations are arbitrary—e.g., factual associations. It is not beneficial to change the content of knowledge about such facts, or personal events, each time we retrieve them unless there is conflicting or new information that requires updating. In contrast, in amygdala, the associations learned are about the value (e.g., fearfulness) of initially neutral stimuli. Having learned that a stimulus is fearful, there may be good reasons to re-evaluate whether it continues to be fearful every time we experience it. The amygdala might have it both ways—be very slow about extinction and yet always open to change. Slow because having learned that a stimulus is fearful, it would be in the survival interests of the animal to be conservative about changing its appraisal of the stimulus. At the same time, it would not be in the interests of an animal to retain unaltered the memory that every stimulus that had been associated with a negative outcome in the past would remain fearful forever. So, in the case of value learning, it could be that retrieval constitutes an opportunity for changing prior learned association—a change is distinct from the new learning associated with extinction.

Recent studies also suggest that reconsolidation in cortex is different from reconsolidation in hippocampus or the amygdala. For example, Mamiya et al. (2009) used both a brain-imaging approach and local protein synthesis inhibition to show that in context fear memory, reconsolidation requires the hippocampus as well as amygdala, whereas extinction requires the prefrontal cortex and amygdala. It therefore seems that different brain areas are performing different functions during memory reconsolidation.

Finally, memory reactivation is critical to trigger reconsolidation, as many studies show normal memory after the application of amnesic agents when reactivation is omitted (Tronson & Taylor 2007). What mechanism in the hippocampus is responsible for the retrieval of the memory and hence the requirement of protein synthesis for reconsolidation? Several recent studies have been trying to approach this by looking at the molecular mechanisms needed to destabilize memory traces (Alberini et al. 2006). Lee (2008) suggests that some existing proteins associated with memory retrieval need to be degraded to allow for the new protein synthesis to restabilize the trace. If protein degradation is subject to interference, memory traces may stay in a locked state. Similar ideas have emerged in relation to NMDA receptor activation during the retrieval of auditory fear memory in the amygdala (Ben Mamou et al. 2006) and voltage-gated calcium channels (Suzuki et al. 2008).

CONCLUSION

This review updates a neurobiological theory of hippocampus function in memory (Morris 2006) with reference to recent findings related to automatic encoding and to synaptic and behavior tagging/capture. It also discusses hippocampal-neocortical interactions at the systems level, particularly in relation to schemas and reconsolidation.

First, we reassert that hippocampus has the property of automatic encoding of relational events (Eichenbaum 2004), objects-in-places (Eacott & Easton 2007), and goals-in-places (Day et al. 2003), and hence leads to rapid associative memory. Linking this rapid learning to synaptic plasticity, studies have shown that hippocampal NMDA receptors are required for the encoding of one-trial place information, and AMPA receptor activation is required for memory retrieval both in the event arena (Bast et al. 2005, Day et al. 2003) and in the water maze (Steele & Morris 1999).

Second, the encoding of events in HPC engages signal transduction cascades that contribute to cellular consolidation, enabling the memory of selected events to persist. The idea of synaptic tagging and capture has been widely demonstrated in brain-slice recoding and recently in behavior learning (Moncada & Viola 2007). This offers a biological mechanism by which distinct prior experiences that are temporally (and anatomically) close to subsequent learning can influence the persistence of memory of other events. One potential advantage of this is to allow for the modulation of memory through events that are contiguous to each other. One potential drawback of this might be interference between events. This disadvantage may be avoided by distinct representations at the anatomical level.

Third, the memory of events may persist (Wang et al. 2009b) or change (Winocur et al. 2007) with time. Memory traces can reorganize in the brain in a time-dependent manner. Complimentary to the role of HPC in automatic encoding, selective systems consolidation occurs in cortical areas. One benefit from this is to reduce information processing load on the HPC when facing new information flooding in. This systems consolidation process typically takes days to weeks but can be facilitated when new information is assimilated into a prebuilt mental framework (Tse et al. 2007). We suggest that once the knowledge of the environmental context, or a mental schema of paired-associates, is represented in cortical areas, the HPC is only required for rapidly updating any new event in relation to these frameworks. To associate the updating component within these frameworks takes fewer links or biological modifications (and hence less time) relative to their initial acquisition.

Finally, reactivation and reconsolidation of an encoded event is functionally related to information updating, whereas automatic encoding is triggered by novelty detection (Lisman & Grace 2005, Nyberg 2005). This issue, extensively studied in animals, recently received attention in human work (Kumaran & Maguire 2009). To study learning and memory, novel tasks are typically used to allow for comparisons between control and experimental conditions and so avoid confounding interference from previous experiences. In this case, the activation of the HPC is likely to correlate with how novel an event may be and to follow a repetition-suppression rule (Grill-Spector et al. 2006). However, during memory retrieval or reactivation, subjects may refer to previous learning experiences to compare with a current situation, and the hippocampus will follow an updating/mismatch rule as suggested by both animal studies (Fyhn et al. 2002) and human literature (Kumaran & Maguire 2007).

DISCLOSURE STATEMENT

The authors are not aware of any biases that might be perceived as affecting the objectivity of this review.

ACKNOWLEDGMENTS

Supported by a U.K. Medical Research Council Program Grant held by R.G.M.M. and grants from the Human Frontiers Science Program and the Volkswagen Foundation. We thank Yadin Dudai, Emma Wood, and Stephen Martin for their comments.

LITERATURE CITED

Aggleton JP, Brown MW. 1999. Episodic memory, amnesia, and the hippocampal-anterior thalamic axis. *Behav. Brain Sci.* 22:425–89

Ainge JA, Heron-Maxwell C, Theofilas P, Wright P, de Hoz L, Wood ER. 2006. The role of the hippocampus in object recognition in rats: examination of the influence of task parameters and lesion size. *Behav. Brain Res.* 167:183–95

Alberini CM. 2005. Mechanisms of memory stabilization: Are consolidation and reconsolidation similar or distinct processes? *Trends Neurosci.* 28:51–56

Alberini CM, Milekic MH, Tronel S. 2006. Mechanisms of memory stabilization and destabilization. *Cell Mol. Life Sci.* 63:999–1008

Andersen P, Morris RGM, Amaral DG, Bliss TVP, O'Keefe J. 2007. *The Hippocampus Book*. London: Oxford Univ. Press. 832 pp.

Artinian J, De Jaeger X, Fellini L, de Saint Blanquat P, Roullet P. 2007. Reactivation with a simple exposure to the experimental environment is sufficient to induce reconsolidation requiring protein synthesis in the hippocampal CA3 region in mice. *Hippocampus* 17:181–91

Artinian J, McGauran AM, De Jaeger X, Mouledous L, Frances B, Roullet P. 2008. Protein degradation, as with protein synthesis, is required during not only long-term spatial memory consolidation but also reconsolidation. *Eur. J. Neurosci.* 27:3009–19

Babb SJ, Crystal JD. 2006. Discrimination of what, when, and where is not based on time of day. *Learn. Behav.* 34:124–30

Baddeley A. 2001. The concept of episodic memory. *Philos. Trans. R. Soc. Lond. B Biol. Sci.* 356:1345–50

Bailey CH, Giusetto M, Huang YY, Hawkins RD, Kandel ER. 2000. Is heterosynaptic modulation essential for stabilizing Hebbian synaptic plasticity and memory? *Nat. Neurosci.* 1:11–20

Barco A, Alarcon JM, Kandel ER. 2002. Expression of constitutively active CREB protein facilitates the late phase of long-term potentiation by enhancing synaptic capture. *Cell* 108:689–703

Barker GR, Warburton EC. 2008. NMDA receptor plasticity in the perirhinal and prefrontal cortices is crucial for the acquisition of long-term object-in-place associative memory. *J. Neurosci.* 28:2837–44

Bartlett FC. 1932. *Remembering: A Study in Experimental and Social Psychology.* London: Cambridge Univ. Press

Bast T, da Silva BM, Morris RGM. 2005. Distinct contributions of hippocampal NMDA and AMPA receptors to encoding and retrieval of one-trial place memory. *J. Neurosci.* 25:5845–56

Battaglia FP, Sutherland GR, McNaughton BL. 2004. Hippocampal sharp wave bursts coincide with neocortical "up-state" transitions. *Learn. Mem.* 11:697–704

Belvin MP, Yin JC. 1997. *Drosophila* learning and memory: recent progress and new approaches. *Bioessays* 19:1083–89

Ben Mamou C, Gamache K, Nader K. 2006. NMDA receptors are critical for unleashing consolidated auditory fear memories. *Nat. Neurosci.* 9:1237–39

Biedenkapp JC, Rudy JW. 2007. Context preexposure prevents forgetting of a contextual fear memory: implication for regional changes in brain activation patterns associated with recent and remote memory tests. *Learn. Mem.* 14:200–3

Bliss T, Collingridge G, Morris R. 2007. Synaptic plasticity in the hippocampus. In *The Hippocampus Book*, ed. P Andersen, R Morris, D Amaral, T Bliss, J O'Keefe, pp. 343–474. London: Oxford Univ. Press

Bliss TVP, Lømo T. 1973. Long-lasting potentiation of synaptic transmission in the dentate area of the anaesthetized rabbit following stimulation of the perforant path. *J. Physiol. (Lond.)* 232:331–56

Bonini JS, Da Silva WC, Bevilaqua LR, Medina JH, Izquierdo I, Cammarota M. 2007. On the participation of hippocampal PKC in acquisition, consolidation and reconsolidation of spatial memory. *Neuroscience* 147:37–45

Bouton ME. 2004. Context and behavioral processes in extinction. *Learn. Mem.* 11:485–94

Bransford JD. 1979. *Human Cognition: Learning, Understanding and Remembering.* Belmont, CA: Wadsworth

Brewer JB, Zhao Z, Desmond JE, Glover GH, Gabrieli JD. 1998. Making memories: brain activity that predicts how well visual experience will be remembered. *Science* 281:1185–87

Broadbent NJ, Squire LR, Clark RE. 2004. Spatial memory, recognition memory, and the hippocampus. *Proc. Natl. Acad. Sci. USA* 101:14515–20

Broadbent NJ, Squire LR, Clark RE. 2006. Reversible hippocampal lesions disrupt water maze performance during both recent and remote memory tests. *Learn. Mem.* 13:187–91

Brown R, Kulick J. 1977. Flashbulb memories. *Cognition* 5:73–99

Buzsaki G. 1989. Two-stage model of memory trace formation: a role for "noisy" brain states. *Neuroscience* 31:551–70

Chklovskii DB, Mel BW, Svoboda K. 2004. Cortical rewiring and information storage. *Nature* 431:782–88

Cipolotti L, Shallice T, Chan D, Fox N, Scahill R, et al. 2001. Long-term retrograde amnesia... the crucial role of the hippocampus. *Neuropsychologia* 39:151–72

Clark RE, Broadbent NJ, Squire LR. 2005. Impaired remote spatial memory after hippocampal lesions despite extensive training beginning early in life. *Hippocampus* 15:340–46

Clark RE, Broadbent NJ, Squire LR. 2007. The hippocampus and spatial memory: findings with a novel modification of the water maze. *J. Neurosci.* 27:6647–54

Clayton NS, Dickinson A. 1998. Episodic-like memory during cache recovery by scrub jays. *Nature* 395:272–74

Corkin S. 1984. Lasting consequences of bilateral medial temporal lobectomy: clinical course and experimental findings in H.M. *Semin. Neurol.* 4:249–59

Da Silva WC, Bonini JS, Bevilaqua LR, Medina JH, Izquierdo I, Cammarota M. 2008. Inhibition of mRNA synthesis in the hippocampus impairs consolidation and reconsolidation of spatial memory. *Hippocampus* 18:29–39

Davis HP, Squire LR. 1984. Protein synthesis and memory: a review. *Psychol. Bull.* 96:518–59

Day M, Langston R, Morris RGM. 2003. Glutamate-receptor-mediated encoding and retrieval of paired-associate learning. *Nature* 424:205–9

Debiec J, Doyere V, Nader K, Ledoux JE. 2006. Directly reactivated, but not indirectly reactivated, memories undergo reconsolidation in the amygdala. *Proc. Natl. Acad. Sci. USA* 103:3428–33

Debiec J, LeDoux JE, Nader K. 2002. Cellular and systems reconsolidation in the hippocampus. *Neuron* 36:527–38

de Haan M, Mishkin M, Baldeweg T, Vargha-Khadem F. 2006. Human memory development and its dysfunction after early hippocampal injury. *Trends Neurosci.* 29:374–81

DeVietti TL, Holliday JH. 1972. Retrograde amnesia produced by electroconvulsive shock after reactivation of a consolidated memory trace: a replication. *Psychon. Sci.* 29:137–38

Dudai Y. 2004. The neurobiology of consolidations, or, how stable is the engram? *Annu. Rev. Psychol.* 55:51–86

Dudai Y, Morris RGM. 2000. To consolidate or not to consolidate: What are the questions? In *Brain, Perception, Memory: Advances in Cognitive Sciences*, ed. JJ Bolhuis, pp. 149–62. London: Oxford Univ. Press

Duncan CP. 1949. The retroactive effect of electroconvulsive shock. *J. Comp. Physiol. Psychol.* 42:32–44

Duvarci S, Mamou CB, Nader K. 2006. Extinction is not a sufficient condition to prevent fear memories from undergoing reconsolidation in the basolateral amygdala. *Eur. J. Neurosci.* 24:249–60

Duvarci S, Nader K. 2004. Characterization of fear memory reconsolidation. *J. Neurosci.* 24:9269–75

Eacott MJ, Easton A. 2007. On familiarity and recall of events by rats. *Hippocampus* 17:890–97

Easton A, Zinkivskay A, Eacott MJ. 2009. Recollection is impaired, but familiarity remains intact in rats with lesions of the fornix. *Hippocampus.* Epub ahead of print

Eichenbaum H. 2004. Hippocampus: cognitive processes and neural representations that underlie declarative memory. *Neuron* 44:109–20

Eichenbaum H, Yonelinas AP, Ranganath C. 2007. The medial temporal lobe and recognition memory. *Annu. Rev. Neurosci.* 30:123–52

Eisenberg M, Kobilo T, Berman DE, Dudai Y. 2003. Stability of retrieved memory: inverse correlation with trace dominance. *Science* 301:1102–4

Ennaceur A, Delacour J. 1988. A new one-trial test for neurobiological studies of memory in rats. I: Behavioral data. *Behav. Brain Res.* 31:47–59

Euston DR, Tatsuno M, McNaughton BL. 2007. Fast-forward playback of recent memory sequences in prefrontal cortex during sleep. *Science* 318:1147–50

Everitt BJ, Robbins TW. 2005. Neural systems of reinforcement for drug addiction: from actions to habits to compulsion. *Nat. Neurosci.* 8:1481–89

Fanselow MS, LeDoux JE. 1999. Why we think plasticity underlying Pavlovian fear conditioning occurs in the basolateral amygdala. *Neuron* 23:229–32

Farovik A, Dupont LM, Arce M, Eichenbaum H. 2008. Medial prefrontal cortex supports recollection, but not familiarity, in the rat. *J. Neurosci.* 28:13428–34

Ferbinteanu J, Shapiro ML. 2003. Prospective and retrospective memory coding in the hippocampus. *Neuron* 40:1227–39

Fischer A, Sananbenesi F, Schrick C, Spiess J, Radulovic J. 2004. Distinct roles of hippocampal de novo protein synthesis and actin rearrangement in extinction of contextual fear. *J. Neurosci.* 24:1962–66

Fletcher PC, Henson RN. 2001. Frontal lobes and human memory: insights from functional neuroimaging. *Brain* 124:849–81

Floresco SB, Seamans JK, Phillips AG. 1997. Selective roles for hippocampal, prefrontal cortical, and ventral striatal circuits in radial-arm maze tasks with or without a delay. *J. Neurosci.* 17:1880–90

Fonseca R, Nagerl UV, Morris RG, Bonhoeffer T. 2004. Competing for memory: hippocampal LTP under regimes of reduced protein synthesis. *Neuron* 44:1011–20

Fortin NJ, Wright SP, Eichenbaum H. 2004. Recollection-like memory retrieval in rats is dependent on the hippocampus. *Nature* 431:188–91

Frankland PW, Bontempi B. 2005. The organization of recent and remote memories. *Nat. Rev. Neurosci.* 6:119–30

Frankland PW, Bontempi B, Talton LE, Kaczmarek L, Silva AJ. 2004. The involvement of the anterior cingulate cortex in remote contextual fear memory. *Science* 304:881–83

Frankland PW, Ding HK, Takahashi E, Suzuki A, Kida S, Silva AJ. 2006. Stability of recent and remote contextual fear memory. *Learn. Mem.* 13:451–57

Frankland PW, Teixeira CM, Wang SH. 2007. Grading the gradient: evidence for time-dependent memory reorganization in experimental animals. *Debates Neurosci.* 1:67–78

Frey U, Krug M, Reymann KG, Matthies H. 1988. Anisomycin, an inhibitor of protein synthesis, blocks late phases of LTP phenomena in the hippocampal CA1 region in vitro. *Brain Res.* 452:57–65

Frey U, Morris RG. 1997. Synaptic tagging and long-term potentiation. *Nature* 385:533–36

Frey U, Morris RGM. 1998. Synaptic tagging: implications for late maintenance of hippocampal long-term potentiation. *Trends Neurosci.* 21:181–88

Fyhn M, Molden S, Hollup S, Moser MB, Moser E. 2002. Hippocampal neurons responding to first-time dislocation of a target object. *Neuron* 35:555–66

Gaskin S, White NM. 2007. Unreinforced spatial (latent) learning is mediated by a circuit that includes dorsal entorhinal cortex and fimbria fornix. *Hippocampus* 17:586–94

Gelbard-Sagiv H, Mukamel R, Harel M, Malach R, Fried I. 2008. Internally generated reactivation of single neurons in human hippocampus during free recall. *Science* 322:96–101

Goelet P, Castellucci VF, Schacher S, Kandel ER. 1986. The long and the short of long-term memory—a molecular framework. *Nature* 322:419–22

Gold PE, Haycock JW, Marri J, McGaugh JL. 1973. Retrograde amnesia and the "reminder effect": an alternative interpretation. *Science* 180:1199–201

Good MA, Barnes P, Staal V, McGregor A, Honey RC. 2007. Context- but not familiarity-dependent forms of object recognition are impaired following excitotoxic hippocampal lesions in rats. *Behav. Neurosci.* 121:218–23

Graf P, Schacter DL. 1985. Implicit and explicit memory for new associations in normal and amnesic subjects. *J. Exp. Psychol.: Learn. Mem. Cogn.* 11:501–18

Griffiths D, Dickinson A, Clayton N. 1999. Episodic memory: What can animals remember about their past? *Trends Cogn. Sci.* 3:74–80

Grill-Spector K, Henson R, Martin A. 2006. Repetition and the brain: neural models of stimulus-specific effects. *Trends Cogn. Sci.* 10:14–23

Guzowski JF, Miyashita T, Chawla MK, Sanderson J, Maes LI, et al. 2006. Recent behavioral history modifies coupling between cell activity and Arc gene transcription in hippocampal CA1 neurons. *Proc. Natl. Acad. Sci. USA* 103:1077–82

Han JH, Kushner SA, Yiu AP, Hsiang HL, Buch T, et al. 2009. Selective erasure of a fear memory. *Science* 323:1492–96

Haskins AL, Yonelinas AP, Quamme JR, Ranganath C. 2008. Perirhinal cortex supports encoding and familiarity-based recognition of novel associations. *Neuron* 59:554–60

Heinemann EG, Sage-Day J, Brenner N. 1981. Retroactive interference in discrimination learning. *Science* 214:1254–57

Kametani H, Kesner RP. 1989. Retrospective and prospective coding of information: dissociation of parietal cortex and hippocampal formation. *Behav. Neurosci.* 103:84–89

Kelleher RJ 3rd, Govindarajan A, Tonegawa S. 2004. Translational regulatory mechanisms in persistent forms of synaptic plasticity. *Neuron* 44:59–73

Kim JJ, Fanselow MS. 1992. Modality-specific retrograde amnesia of fear. *Science* 256:675–77

Kopelman MD. 1995. The Korsakoff syndrome. *Br. J. Psychiatry* 166:154–73

Krug M, Lossner B, Ott T. 1984. Anisomycin blocks the late phase of long-term potentiation in the dentate gyrus of freely moving rats. *Brain Res. Bull.* 13:39–42

Kumaran D, Maguire EA. 2007. Match mismatch processes underlie human hippocampal responses to associative novelty. *J. Neurosci.* 27:8517–24

Kumaran D, Maguire EA. 2009. Novelty signals: a window into hippocampal information processing. *Trends Cogn. Sci.* 13:47–54

Lechner HA, Squire LR, Byrne JH. 1999. 100 years of consolidation—remembering Muller and Pilzecker. *Learn. Mem.* 6:77–87

LeDoux J. 2007. The amygdala. *Curr. Biol.* 17:R868–74

Lee JL. 2008. Memory reconsolidation mediates the strengthening of memories by additional learning. *Nat. Neurosci.* 11:1264–66

Lewis DJ. 1979. Psychobiology of active and inactive memory. *Psychol. Bull.* 86:1054–83

Lisman JE, Grace AA. 2005. The hippocampal-VTA loop: controlling the entry of information into long-term memory. *Neuron* 46:703–13

Mamiya N, Fukushima H, Suzuki A, Matsuyama Z, Homma S, et al. 2009. Brain region-specific gene expression activation required for reconsolidation and extinction of contextual fear memory. *J. Neurosci.* 29:402–13

Marr D. 1971. Simple memory: a theory for archicortex. *Philos. Trans. R. Soc. Lond. B Biol. Sci.* 262:23–81

Martin KC, Casadio A, Zhu HEY, Rose JC, Chen M, et al. 1997. Synapse-specific, long-term facilitation of aplysia sensory to motor synapses: a function for local protein synthesis in memory storage. *Cell* 91:927–38

Martin SJ, de Hoz L, Morris RG. 2005. Retrograde amnesia: neither partial nor complete hippocampal lesions in rats result in preferential sparing of remote spatial memory, even after reminding. *Neuropsychologia* 43:609–24

Martin SJ, Grimwood PD, Morris RGM. 2000. Synaptic plasticity and memory: an evaluation of the hypothesis. *Annu. Rev. Neurosci.* 23:649–711

Matthies H. 1989. Neurobiological aspects of learning and memory. *Annu. Rev. Psychol.* 40:381–404

Maviel T, Durkin TP, Menzaghi F, Bontempi B. 2004. Sites of neocortical reorganization critical for remote spatial memory. *Science* 305:96–99

McCarthy RA, Warrington EK. 1990. *Cognitive Neuropsychology: A Clinical Introduction.* New York: Academic

McClelland JL, McNaughton BL, O'Reilly RC. 1995. Why there are complementary learning systems in the hippocampus and neocortex: insights from the successes and failures of connectionist models of learning and memory. *Psychol. Rev.* 102:419–57

McGaugh JL. 2000. Memory—a century of consolidation. *Science* 287:248–51

McGeoch JA. 1932. Forgetting and the law of disuse. *Psychol. Rev.* 39:352–70

Meeter M, Murre JM. 2004. Consolidation of long-term memory: evidence and alternatives. *Psychol. Bull.* 130:843–57

Merhav M, Rosenblum K. 2008. Facilitation of taste memory acquisition by experiencing previous novel taste is protein-synthesis dependent. *Learn. Mem.* 15:501–7

Milekic MH, Alberini CM. 2002. Temporally graded requirement for protein synthesis following memory reactivation. *Neuron* 36:521–25

Miller RR, Kraus JN. 1977. Somatic and autonomic indexes of recovery from electroconvulsive shock-induced amnesia in rats. *J. Comp. Physiol. Psychol.* 91:434–42

Misanin JR, Miller RR, Lewis DJ. 1968. Retrograde amnesia produced by electroconvulsive shock after reactivation of a consolidated memory trace. *Science* 160:554–55

Miyashita Y. 2004. Cognitive memory: cellular and network machineries and their top-down control. *Science* 306:435–40

Moncada D, Viola H. 2007. Induction of long-term memory by exposure to novelty requires protein synthesis: evidence for a behavioral tagging. *J. Neurosci.* 27:7476–81

Montarolo PG, Goelet P, Castellucci VF, Morgan J, Kandel ER, Schacher S. 1986. A critical period for macromolecular synthesis in long-term heterosynaptic facilitation in *Aplysia. Science* 234:1249–54

Morris RGM. 2006. Elements of a neurobiological theory of hippocampal function: the role of synaptic plasticity, synaptic tagging and schemas. *Eur. J. Neurosci.* 23:2829–46

Morris RGM. 2007. Theories of hippocampal function. In *The Hippocampus Book*, ed. P Andersen, R Morris, D Amaral, T Bliss, J O'Keefe, pp. 581–714. London: Oxford Univ. Press

Morris RGM, Inglis J, Ainge JA, Olverman HJ, Tulloch J, et al. 2006. Memory reconsolidation: sensitivity of spatial memory to inhibition of protein synthesis in dorsal hippocampus during encoding and retrieval. *Neuron* 50:479–89

Moscovitch M, Nadel L, Winocur G, Gilboa A, Rosenbaum RS. 2006. The cognitive neuroscience of remote episodic, semantic and spatial memory. *Curr. Opin. Neurobiol.* 16:179–90

Mumby DG. 2001. Perspectives on object-recognition memory following hippocampal damage: lessons from studies in rats. *Behav. Brain Res.* 127:159–81

Nadel L, Moscovitch M. 1997. Memory consolidation, retrograde amnesia and the hippocampal complex. *Curr. Opin. Neurobiol.* 7:217–27

Nadel L, Samsonovich A, Ryan L, Moscovitch M. 2000. Multiple trace theory of human memory: computational, neuroimaging, and neuropsychological results. *Hippocampus* 10:352–68

Nader K, Hardt O. 2009. A single standard for memory: the case for reconsolidation. *Nat. Rev. Neurosci.* 10:224–34

Nader K, Schafe GE, Le Doux JE. 2000. Fear memories require protein synthesis in the amygdala for reconsolidation after retrieval. *Nature* 406:722–26

Nakazawa K, Sun LD, Quirk MC, Rondi-Reig L, Wilson MA, Tonegawa S. 2003. Hippocampal CA3 NMDA receptors are crucial for memory acquisition of one-time experience. *Neuron* 38:305–15

Naqshbandi M, Feeney MC, McKenzie TL, Roberts WA. 2007. Testing for episodic-like memory in rats in the absence of time of day cues: replication of Babb and Crystal. *Behav. Process.* 74:217–25

Nemanic S, Alvarado MC, Bachevalier J. 2004. The hippocampal/parahippocampal regions and recognition memory: insights from visual paired comparison versus object-delayed nonmatching in monkeys. *J. Neurosci.* 24:2013–26

Nyberg L. 2005. Any novelty in hippocampal formation and memory? *Curr. Opin. Neurol.* 18:424–28

O'Keefe J, Nadel L. 1978. *The Hippocampus as a Cognitive Map.* Oxford, UK: Clarendon. 570 pp.

Osada T, Adachi Y, Kimura HM, Miyashita Y. 2008. Towards understanding of the cortical network underlying associative memory. *Philos. Trans. R. Soc. Lond. B Biol. Sci.* 363:2187–99

Paulsen O, Moser EI. 1998. A model of hippocampal memory encoding and retrieval: GABAergic control of synaptic plasticity. *Trends Neurosci.* 21:273–78

Pavlov IP. 1927. *Conditioned Reflexes.* New York: Dover

Pedreira ME, Perez-Cuesta LM, Maldonado H. 2004. Mismatch between what is expected and what actually occurs triggers memory reconsolidation or extinction. *Learn. Mem.* 11:579–85

Prados J, Sansa J, Artigas AA. 2008. Partial reinforcement effects on learning and extinction of place preferences in the water maze. *Learn. Behav.* 36:311–18

Przybyslawski J, Roullet P, Sara SJ. 1999. Attenuation of emotional and nonemotional memories after their reactivation: role of beta adrenergic receptors. *J. Neurosci.* 19:6623–28

Quirk GJ, Beer JS. 2006. Prefrontal involvement in the regulation of emotion: convergence of rat and human studies. *Curr. Opin. Neurobiol.* 16:723–27

Rescorla R, Wagner A. 1972. A theory of Pavlovian conditioning: variations in the effectiveness of reinforcement and nonreinforcement. In *Classical Conditioning II*, ed. A Black, W Prokasy, pp. 64–99. East Norwalk, CT: Appleton-Century-Crofts

Reymann KG, Frey JU. 2007. The late maintenance of hippocampal LTP: requirements, phases, "synaptic tagging," "late-associativity" and implications. *Neuropharmacology* 52:24–40

Rodriguez-Ortiz CJ, Garcia-DeLaTorre P, Benavidez E, Ballesteros MA, Bermudez-Rattoni F. 2008. Intrahippocampal anisomycin infusions disrupt previously consolidated spatial memory only when memory is updated. *Neurobiol. Learn. Mem.* 89:352–59

Rose SPR. 1995. Glycoproteins and memory formation. *Behav. Brain Res.* 66:73–78

Rosenbaum RS, Winocur G, Moscovitch M. 2001. New views on old memories: re-evaluating the role of the hippocampal complex. *Behav. Brain Res.* 127:183–97

Rossato JI, Bevilaqua LR, Medina JH, Izquierdo I, Cammarota M. 2006. Retrieval induces hippocampal-dependent reconsolidation of spatial memory. *Learn. Mem.* 13:431–40

Ryan L, Nadel L, Keil K, Putnam K, Schnyer D, et al. 2001. Hippocampal complex and retrieval of recent and very remote autobiographical memories: evidence from functional magnetic resonance imaging in neurologically intact people. *Hippocampus* 11:707–14

Sajikumar S, Frey JU. 2004a. Late-associativity, synaptic tagging, and the role of dopamine during LTP and LTD. *Neurobiol. Learn. Mem.* 82:12–25

Sajikumar S, Frey JU. 2004b. Resetting of "synaptic tags" is time- and activity-dependent in rat hippocampal CA1 in vitro. *Neuroscience* 129:503–7

Sara SJ. 2000. Retrieval and reconsolidation: toward a neurobiology of remembering. *Learn. Mem.* 7:73–84

Save E, Poucet B, Foreman N, Buhot MC. 1992. Object exploration and reactions to spatial and nonspatial changes in hooded rats following damage to parietal cortex or hippocampal formation. *Behav. Neurosci.* 106:447–56

Schachter D, Tulving E, eds. 1994. *Memory Systems.* Cambridge, MA: MIT Press

Schneider AM, Sherman W. 1968. Amnesia: a function of the temporal relation of footshock to electroconvulsive shock. *Science* 159:219–21

Schneider W, Shiffrin R. 1977. Controlled and automatic human information processing: I. Detection, search, and attention. *Psychol. Rev.* 84:1–66

Schultz W, Dickinson A. 2000. Neuronal coding of prediction errors. *Annu. Rev. Neurosci.* 23:473–500

Scoville WB, Milner B. 1957. Loss of recent memory after bilateral hippocampal lesions. *J. Neurol. Neurosurg. Psychiatry* 20:11–21

Seamans JK, Floresco SB, Phillips AG. 1998. D1 receptor modulation of hippocampal-prefrontal cortical circuits integrating spatial memory with executive functions in the rat. *J. Neurosci.* 18:1613–21

Seidenbecher T, Reymann KG, Balschun D. 1997. A post-tetanic time-window for the reinforcement of long-term potentiation by appetitive and aversive stimuli. *Proc. Natl. Acad. Sci. USA* 94:1494–99

Shimamura AP, Jernigan TL, Squire LR. 1988. Korsakoff's syndrome: radiological (CT) findings and neuropsychological correlates. *J. Neurosci.* 8:4400–10

Skaggs WE, McNaughton BL. 1996. Replay of neuronal firing sequences in rat hippocampus during sleep following spatial experience. *Science* 271:1870–73

Smith CN, Squire LR. 2009. Medial temporal lobe activity during retrieval of semantic memory is related to the age of the memory. *J. Neurosci.* 29:930–38

Squire LR. 1992. Memory and the hippocampus: a synthesis from findings with rats, monkeys, and humans. *Psychol. Rev.* 99:195–231

Squire LR, Barondes SH. 1972. Variable decay of memory and its recovery in cycloheximide-treated mice. *Proc. Natl. Acad. Sci. USA* 69:1416–20

Squire LR, Bayley PJ. 2007. The neuroscience of remote memory. *Curr. Opin. Neurobiol.* 17:185–96

Squire LR, Wixted JT, Clark RE. 2007. Recognition memory and the medial temporal lobe: a new perspective. *Nat. Rev. Neurosci.* 8:872–83

Steele RJ, Morris RGM. 1999. Delay-dependent impairment of a matching-to-place task with chronic and intrahippocampal infusion of the NMDA-antagonist D-AP5. *Hippocampus* 9:118–36

Stickgold R, Walker MP. 2007. Sleep-dependent memory consolidation and reconsolidation. *Sleep Med.* 8:331–43

Sutherland GR, McNaughton B. 2000. Memory trace reactivation in hippocampal and neocortical neuronal ensembles. *Curr. Opin. Neurobiol.* 10:180–86

Suzuki A, Josselyn SA, Frankland PW, Masushige S, Silva AJ, Kida S. 2004. Memory reconsolidation and extinction have distinct temporal and biochemical signatures. *J. Neurosci.* 24:4787–95

Suzuki A, Mukawa T, Tsukagoshi A, Frankland PW, Kida S. 2008. Activation of LVGCCs and CB1 receptors required for destabilization of reactivated contextual fear memories. *Learn. Mem.* 15:426–33

Takashima A, Petersson KM, Rutters F, Tendolkar I, Jensen O, et al. 2006. Declarative memory consolidation in humans: a prospective functional magnetic resonance imaging study. *Proc. Natl. Acad. Sci. USA* 103:756–61

Takehara-Nishiuchi K, McNaughton BL. 2008. Spontaneous changes of neocortical code for associative memory during consolidation. *Science* 322:960–63

Teixeira CM, Pomedli SR, Maei HR, Kee N, Frankland PW. 2006. Involvement of the anterior cingulate cortex in the expression of remote spatial memory. *J. Neurosci.* 26:7555–64

Teyler TJ, DiScenna P. 1986. The hippocampal memory indexing theory. *Behav. Neurosci.* 100:147–54

Teyler TJ, Rudy JW. 2007. The hippocampal indexing theory and episodic memory: updating the index. *Hippocampus* 17:1158–69

Tronel S, Milekic MH, Alberini CM. 2005. Linking new information to a reactivated memory requires consolidation and not reconsolidation mechanisms. *PLoS Biol.* 3:e293

Tronson NC, Taylor JR. 2007. Molecular mechanisms of memory reconsolidation. *Nat. Rev. Neurosci.* 8:262–75

Tse D, Langston RF, Kakeyama M, Bethus I, Spooner PA, et al. 2007. Schemas and memory consolidation. *Science* 316:76–82

Wagner A, Schacter D, Rotte M, Koutstaal W, Maril A, et al. 1998. Building memories: remembering and forgetting of verbal experiences as predicted by brain activity. *Science* 281:1188–91

Wang SH, de Oliveira Alvares L, Nader K. 2009a. Cellular and systems mechanisms of memory strength as a constraint on auditory fear reconsolidation. *Nat. Neurosci.* 12:905–12

Wang SH, Nader K. 2003. Consolidated auditory fear memories return to a labile state by reinforcer-induced memory reactivation. *Soc. Neurosci. Conf. Abstr.*

Wang SH, Teixeira CM, Wheeler AL, Frankland PW. 2009b. The precision of remote context memories does not require the hippocampus. *Nat. Neurosci.* 12:253–55

Wiltgen BJ, Silva AJ. 2007. Memory for context becomes less specific with time. *Learn. Mem.* 14:313–17

Winocur G, Moscovitch M, Fogel S, Rosenbaum RS, Sekeres M. 2005. Preserved spatial memory after hippocampal lesions: effects of extensive experience in a complex environment. *Nat. Neurosci.* 8:273–75

Winocur G, Moscovitch M, Sekeres M. 2007. Memory consolidation or transformation: context manipulation and hippocampal representations of memory. *Nat. Neurosci.* 10:555–57

Winters BD, Saksida LM, Bussey TJ. 2008. Object recognition memory: neurobiological mechanisms of encoding, consolidation and retrieval. *Neurosci. Biobehav. Rev.* 32:1055–70

Witter MP, Moser EI. 2006. Spatial representation and the architecture of the entorhinal cortex. *Trends Neurosci.* 29:671–78

Wixted JT, Squire LR. 2008. Constructing receiver operating characteristics (ROCs) with experimental animals: cautionary notes. *Learn. Mem.* 15:687–90; discussion 691–93

Young JZ, Nguyen PV. 2005. Homosynaptic and heterosynaptic inhibition of synaptic tagging and capture of long-term potentiation by previous synaptic activity. *J. Neurosci.* 25:7221–31

Zola-Morgan S, Squire LR. 1990. The primate hippocampal formation: evidence for a time-limited role in memory storage. *Science* 250:288–90

Zola-Morgan S, Squire LR, Amaral DG. 1986. Human amnesia and the medial temporal region: enduring memory impairment following a bilateral lesion limited to field CA1 of the hippocampus. *J. Neurosci.* 6:2950–67

Stress Hormone Regulation: Biological Role and Translation into Therapy

Florian Holsboer and Marcus Ising

Max Planck Institute of Psychiatry, Kraepelinstr. 2-10, 80804 Munich, Germany;
email: holsboer@mpipsykl.mpg.de; ising@mpipsykl.mpg.de

Annu. Rev. Psychol. 2010. 61:81–109

First published online as a Review in Advance on
September 28, 2009

The *Annual Review of Psychology* is online at
psych.annualreviews.org

This article's doi:
10.1146/annurev.psych.093008.100321

0066-4308/10/0110-0081$20.00

Key Words

corticosteroids, corticotrophin-releasing hormone, arginine
vasopressin, depression, anxiety

Abstract

Stress is defined as a state of perturbed homeostasis following endangerment that evokes manifold adaptive reactions, which are summarized as
the stress response. In the case of mental stress, the adaptive response
follows the perception of endangerment. Different peptides, steroids,
and biogenic amines operate the stress response within the brain and
also after they have been released into circulation. We focus in this review on the biological roles of corticosteroids, corticotrophin-releasing
hormone (CRH), and arginine vasopressin (AVP), and we evaluate the
effects of treatments directed against the actions of these hormones.
CRH and AVP are the central drivers of the stress hormone system,
but they also act as neuromodulators in the brain, affecting higher
mental functions including emotion, cognition, and behavior. When
released toward the pituitary, these central neuropeptides elicit corticotrophin into the periphery, which activates corticosteroid release from
the adrenal cortex. These stress hormones are essential for the adequate
adaptation to stress, but they can also evoke severe clinical conditions
once persistently hypersecreted. Depression and anxiety disorders are
prominent examples of stress-related disorders associated with an impaired regulation of stress hormones. We summarize the effects of drugs
acting at specific targets of the stress hormone axis, and we discuss their
potential use as next-generation antidepressant medications. Such treatments require the identification of patients that will optimally benefit
from such specific interventions. These could be a first step into personalized medicine using treatments tailored to the specific pathology
of the patients.

Contents

INTRODUCTION

"It is not the strongest of the species that survives, nor the most intelligent, but rather the one most responsive to change." Hardly any other physiological system in mammals matches as precisely with this quote attributed to the British naturalist Charles Darwin (1809–1882) as what we term stress. Originally used in the field of engineering to describe a force that exerts physical strain on a structure, stress has eluded precise definition for life sciences ever since the term was coined.

Hans Selye was the first to demonstrate empirically the profound physiological consequences of stress in his seminal paper of 1936, "A Syndrome Produced by Diverse Nocuous Agents" (Selye 1936). The difficulty of finding a universal definition of the stress syndrome is best reflected by Selye's own conclusion when he—after nearly 40 years of excessively productive research—stated, "Everybody knows what stress is and nobody knows what it is" (Selye 1973). Pragmatic approaches define stress as a state of perturbed homeostasis following perception of endangerment. Stress-elicited changes range from behavioral to molecular

adaptations, and the molecules conveying these messages throughout the body's humoral system are called stress hormones. In this treatise, we confine ourselves to those hormones, whose roles in adaptation to stress are well elaborated and whose signaling cascades are amenable to drug intervention. The latter aspect is of paramount clinical importance because in contrast to the response of acute stressors, where homeostatic adaptations to an aversive situation can be health saving, persistent uncontrollable stress can cause stress-related diseases. Depression is just one, albeit the most prominent, example. Other clinical conditions of high socioeconomic importance, such as age-related cognitive decline, neurodegenerative diseases, cardiovascular disorders, diabetes, and abdominal obesity, are exacerbated once stress-elicited hormonal changes fail to normalize.

The extent of the stress response depends on an individual's experience. For example, a mouse observing a rat predator in the wild would experience serious stress, but the response would be different if the animals had grown up in neighboring cages. Even the level of stress-evoked hormones cannot be used as a quantitative measure because enjoyable activities not perceived as stressful are frequently associated with elevated plasma stress-hormone concentrations. The hormonal or, more precisely, neuroendocrine mechanisms of the stress response are illustrated in **Figure 1** (see color insert) and may serve as a simplified navigation chart.

Real or perceived stress involves a large number of neuronal circuits, including the prefrontal cortex, hippocampus, amygdala, septum, and hypothalamus, ultimately resulting in an activation of the hypothalamic-pituitary-adrenocortical (HPA) axis by stimulating the production of corticotrophin-releasing hormone (CRH) and arginine vasopressin (AVP) in the paraventricular nuclei (PVN) of the hypothalamus. From there, both neuropeptides reach the pituitary gland through small blood vessels (CRH) or neural projections (AVP), which results in secretion and release of corticotrophin (adrenocorticotrophic

Depression: stress-related mental disorder characterized by a broad spectrum of emotional, cognitive, and behavioral symptoms accompanied by impaired stress hormone regulation and sleep disturbance

HPA: hypothalamic-pituitary adrenocortical

CRH: corticotrophin-releasing hormone

AVP: arginine vasopressin

hormone, ACTH) into the circulation, which in turn stimulates the cortex of the adrenal gland located atop the kidneys to synthesize and release glucocorticoids, in particular cortisol (in humans) or corticosterone (in rodents). CRH- and AVP-containing fibers project into many brain areas implicated in the neuroanatomy of behavioral adaptation to stress, but also in stress-related disorders including depression. Notably, CRH- and AVP-containing fibers are intertwined with monoaminergic fibers, projecting to brainstem structures, including the norepinephrinergic locus coeruleus and the serotonergic raphe nuclei. These neuroanatomic connections reflect how closely monoaminergic and stress hormone systems are connected when regulating stress response. Such interactions result in concomitant stress-induced activation of both the HPA-axis and the sympathetic nervous system, which had been among other clinical conditions demonstrated in depression (Wong et al. 2000). Once ACTH is binding to specialized receptors at the adrenal gland, a number of corticosteroids are released, which serve to adapt to stress-induced demands, e.g., to provide increased glucose—an important support when coping with stress—and to maintain electrolyte balance, mainly achieved by the mineralocorticosteroid aldosterone, also released from the adrenal cortex.

The release of corticosteroids occurs in pulses, and the amplitude and frequency of secretory bursts are heightened under stressful conditions. These hormones readily pass cell membranes and bind to two types of nuclear receptors: mineralocorticoid receptors (MRs) and glucocorticoid receptors (GRs), which are ligand-activated transcription factors functioning directly by deoxyribonucleic acid (DNA) binding or indirectly by protein-protein interactions controlling genomic activity (de Kloet et al. 2005). DNA binding occurs at specific response elements within the promoter region of a gene, and the nucleotide sequence of these binding sites modulates the activity of the corticosteroid receptor toward the target gene (Meijsing et al. 2009).

One of the key mechanisms involved in stress response is limiting the extent of behavioral and humoral adaptation to the acute need. Curtailing overshooting response is achieved by negative feedback, where ligand-activated GRs play a particularly important role because in contrast to MRs, they have a fairly low affinity to cortisol in humans (or corticosterone in rodents), allowing them to be responsive even at high stress-evoked hormone levels. Activated GRs help to bring the HPA axis back to baseline by direct or indirect genomic actions promoting consolidation of the system, which is pertinent for dealing with subsequent stressors. This applies not only to the negative feedback regulation of ACTH synthesis and release, but also to a myriad of other activities of the central nervous system (CNS). Among the effects of activated GRs is the suppression of both CRH and AVP, although it is not entirely clear under which conditions some nuclei in the amygdala complex may produce increased CRH in the presence of high corticosterone concentrations. The low-affinity GRs act as dimers when binding to DNA, modulating gene activity. Also, the MRs in the brain, mainly located in the limbic structures, are dimerized, but their functions were only recently revealed (Joels et al. 2008). Despite their full ligand occupation at all times, MRs serve an important function of setting the threshold at the onset of the stress response. If both receptors are in the same cell, they can also heterodimerize, i.e., form MRGR that when ligand-activated is binding to DNA with high affinity (Trapp et al. 1994). It seems plausible that three different dimers— MRMR, GRGR, and MRGR—with varying affinities for corticosteroids are needed to facilitate the cellular responsivity to the wide concentration range of corticosteroids as it occurs throughout the circadian rhythm and following stress exposure (Trapp & Holsboer 1996). Another level of complexity was introduced by Karst et al. (2005), who showed that MRs also reside in the cell membrane, having much lower affinity to corticosterone and exerting fast nongenomic actions. The authors postulated

ACTH: adrenocorticotrophic hormone, corticotrophin

Hypothalamic-pituitary-adrenocortical (HPA) axis: the primary stress hormone system including CRH and AVP release from the hypothalamus, ACTH release from the pituitary, and corticosteroid secretion from the adrenal cortex

Corticosteroids: stress hormones that are synthesized by and released from the adrenal cortex, exerting their effects after binding to two types of receptors, GRs and MRs

MRs: mineralocorticoid receptors

GRs: glucocorticoid receptors

Deoxyribonucleic acid (DNA): a chain of 3 billion nucleotide molecules containing all genetic instructions stored in the nucleus of every cell of an organism

that low-affinity MRs convey stress hormone signals amplifying with other mediators, e.g., CRH, AVP, and monoamines, to fine-tune the initial stress reaction (Joels et al. 2008).

CORTICOSTEROIDS

Sorting out individual behavioral effects of single corticosteroids is not possible. Any attempt to substitute corticosteroids in adrenalectomized rodents, or to treat rodents or primates including humans with varying dosages of corticosteroids, allows only to a very limited extent reasoning as to what behavioral effect this steroid is specifically exerting. Whenever a corticosteroid is administered, it readily enters the pituitary and brain tissue, modulating the expression of a host of known and unknown genes, which all are potentially influencing brain function and subsequently behavior. A recent study by Sato et al. (2008) used a comprehensive gene expression profile technique and identified 22 genes that responded to short-term treatment with the synthetic selective GR agonist dexamethasone. Most of these genes were not yet identified as coding for behaviorally relevant molecules. However, the regulation of prime candidates such as CRH, AVP, brain-derived neurotrophic factor (BDNF), and enzymes involved in monoamine biosynthesis by corticosteroid-activated GRs is also well established (de Kloet et al. 2005). Each of these peptides is known to exert behavioral effects; thus, any manipulation of plasma corticosteroid concentration can only deliver a readout averaging over a huge number of diverse effects induced by corticosteroids and other mediators of behavior.

Neuropsychological research has firmly established the effects of corticosteroids on cognition. Subjects in these studies included patients with Cushing's disease (where an autonomous ACTH-secreting pituitary tumor results in hypercortisolemia), patients with Cushing's syndrome following high-dosed corticosteroid treatment for medical reasons (e.g., rheumatoid arthritis), or healthy volunteers to whom corticosteroids were administered. These investiga-

tions found that hypercortisolemia is associated with declarative memory impairment (Brunner et al. 2005, Leon-Carrion et al. 2009, Rubinow et al. 1984) and submitted that this change in cognitive performance is caused by detrimental influences on hippocampal functions. These actions induced by long-lasting corticosteroid overexposure are contrasted by acute effects, which are known to enhance memory consolidation (Roozendaal 2000). These acute effects fit well into Selye's adaptation concept, where stress-evoked cortisol enhancement is one feature of stress-response aiming to enhance memory consolidation (Buchanan & Lovallo 2001). The endogenous cannabinoid system seems to play an important role in moderating acute glucocorticoid effects on memory consolidation and extinction. Infusion of a cannabinoid receptor 1 (CB1) antagonist into the basolateral amygdala in rats blocked the memory-enhancing effect of a systemic corticosterone administration (Campolongo et al. 2009), whereas mice lacking CB1 showed impaired extinction of stress-related aversive memories (Marsicano et al. 2002). These findings support the existence of a host of nongenomic pathways that are modulated by glucocorticoids. Specifically, stress-evoked release of corticosteroids induces endocannabinoid synthesis and release, which via activation of CB1 receptors inhibit γ-aminobutyric acid (GABA)–secreting neurons. This reduction of GABA activity disinhibits noradrenergic neurons, which evokes norepinephrine release into the basolateral nucleus of the amygdala postulated to increase memory consolidation (Roozendaal et al. 2006). These findings highlight that specialized brain cells carry membrane-bound GR and MR, which regulate corticosteroid-mediated rapid responses to stress.

It is also well established that elevated corticosteroid levels at the time of retention testing decrease the retrieval of previously acquired information (Buchanan et al. 2006, de Quervain et al. 1998, 2000). A recent study by Coluccia et al. (2008) compared acute and chronic glucocorticoid treatment with regard to memory retrieval and associated changes in hippocampal volume. They found that acute effects of prednisone (a synthetic specific GR agonist) when given before retention testing impaired word recall and concluded that memory deficits observed under long-term elevation of plasma glucocorticoid concentrations result from glucocorticoid effects on memory retrieval but not from hippocampal volume changes. Although these studies are intriguing, they are burdened with the open question of whether the effects of steroid treatment are specific for GR-mediated effects or are sequelae of the many brain gene expression and activity changes in neural circuitries that are triggered by high corticosteroid exposure (Datson et al. 2008).

Beside its impact on cognition, hypercortisolemia induced by autonomously secreting adrenal or pituitary glands or by medication inducing Cushing's syndrome also has repercussions upon mood and anxiety. The majority of these patients suffer from depression (Newell-Price et al. 2006). In fact, most of these patients seek medical care primarily because of their depressive state. Likewise, patients having suffered from depression previously are prone to relapse into subsequent depressive episodes when treated with corticosteroids for medical reasons such as inflammation, e.g., arthritis or asthma. Here again, it remains elusive whether or not corticosteroids have a specific effect on mood and anxiety or whether manifold effects upon cellular function and signaling cascades accumulate to modify these clinical endpoints.

A widely used experimental paradigm to quantify anxiety-like behavior in rodents employs the elevated plus maze, which consists of two opposing open arms and two enclosed arms, surrounded by a black wall, that are elevated from the ground. When animals are placed at the center of the maze, they choose between entering the open as opposed to the enclosed arm, depending on their anxiety-like state, and the number of entries and the time spent either in open arms or in enclosed arms is measured. From these figures, the level of anxiety is derived as a function of decreased open-arm exploration (Korte & de Boer 2003). When rats were treated either with a single dose of corticosterone (the main corticosteroid in rats) or chronically for 10 days, increased levels of anxiety-like behavior are measured (Mitra & Sapolsky 2008). Also, this phenomenon is plausibly an indispensable component of the stress response because it is prudent to be anxious when exposed to a stressful situation. Much more important, however, are long-term consequences of heightened corticosteroids. Here again we fail to find a clear picture: Exposure to a phobic stimulus induces plasma cortisol increase in humans via a central mechanism as described above, but it remains unresolved whether corticosteroid elevations feed back to elicit fear. A study by Soravia and colleagues (2006) attempted to clarify this issue in humans. Volunteers fulfilling the formal diagnostic criteria for social phobia were exposed to the Trier Social Stress Test (TSST), a well-validated test to quantify an individual's stress reactivity (Kirschbaum et al. 1993). In this test, an unprepared speech must be given and a mental arithmetic task must be performed in front of an audience consisting of peers. This task is perceived as a stressful stimulus by everyone, but it is a particularly strong phobic stimulus for shy people, who fear the embarrassment of underperforming while under the scrutiny by others, as is the case in social phobia. This experiment found that cortisone-pretreated individuals with social phobia have reduced self-reported fears before, during, and after TSST exposure (Soravia et al. 2006), supporting the notion of stress-related behavior fine-tuned by corticosteroids.

From the standpoint of clinical psychology, disentangling the long-term sequelae of aversive experiences is a particularly challenging task because a link between early childhood trauma and the risk to develop depression has been firmly established (Heim et al. 2008b). In aggregate, studies exploring the long-term implications of childhood trauma (or early-life stress) convincingly associated exaggerated stress reactivity and excessive HPA responsivity with increased vulnerability to develop an affective disorder. Disturbed HPA axis regulation can be evaluated with a neuroendocrine test

Neurogenesis:
creation of new
neurons mostly
occurring in the
hippocampal dentate
gyrus and
hypothesized to be
involved in
antidepressant action

that combines dexamethasone-induced HPA-axis suppression with HPA stimulation by an intravenous bolus of CRH (Heuser et al. 1994). The cortisol release following this combined dexamethasone (dex)/CRH test is considered to sensitively gauge HPA regulation and can be used as a biomarker to monitor the clinical course of depression, as normalization of subsequent test results predicts beneficial clinical outcome (Appelhof et al. 2006; Binder et al. 2009; Hatzinger et al. 2002; Hennings et al. 2009; Heuser et al. 1994; Holsboer-Trachsler et al. 1991; Ising et al. 2005, 2007a; Schüle et al. 2009; Zobel et al. 1999). Among asymptomatic first-degree relatives of depressed patients, higher stress-hormone release was detected following dex/CRH-test administration (Holsboer et al. 1995). In addition, individuals with childhood trauma have an increased plasma cortisol response to the dex/CRH test under both conditions, with or without current major depression (Heim et al. 2008a). These findings agree with many other studies in animals and humans (Coplan et al. 1996, Nicolson 2004, Pryce et al. 2005, Tyrka et al. 2008) and trace back to pioneering studies by the late Seymour Levine, who showed that prolonged early maternal separation of rat pups produces a life-long increased stress sensitivity on neuroendocrine and behavioral characteristics (Levine 1967, Levine & Mody 2003). Using the dex/CRH-test allows the identification of both genetic and acquired liability for developing a stress-related disease (**Figure 2**, see color insert).

How the early trauma imprints onto intra- and intercellular functions in brain circuits became only recently amenable to investigation. Following a series of studies showing decreased hippocampal volumes in individuals exposed to chronic stress or stress-related clinical conditions, a hypothesis was generated postulating that stress can cause (*a*) retraction of dendritic processes in hippocampal neurons (McEwen 2000); (*b*) inhibition of neurogenesis in the adult hippocampus (Gould et al. 1998, Sapolsky 2000); and (*c*) loss of preexisting hippocampal neurons (Sapolsky 2003). Although the latter

aspect, i.e., neurotoxicity of stress hormones, is not likely to be central to the corticosteroid-induced neuromorphological changes, the majority of reported volumetric findings agree with reduced hippocampal (Campbell & MacQueen 2004), amygdalae (Hajek et al. 2008), and subgenual cingulate volumes (Hajek et al. 2008). These studies generated much excitement, although it remains yet to be clarified whether these volume changes in neuroanatomical brain areas implicated in mood and cognition are related to morphological changes in neurons. On a microscopic level, enduring stress indeed suppresses hippocampal neurogenesis and dendritic arborization. Considering the preponderance of glial cells, which outnumber neurons tenfold, and the possibility of local shifts of other brain constituents, e.g., water, it would be premature to attribute the neuroradiological finding entirely to changes in neuronal morphology (Müller et al. 2001). On the neurochemical level, it was suggested that stress-induced suppression of BDNF accounts for these changes (Malberg et al. 2000). The link between stress-evoked hypercortisolism and BDNF suppression is obvious, as the gene encoding BDNF is negatively regulated by activated corticosteroid receptors (Schaaf et al. 1997). A series of studies hypothesized that some of the behavioral changes following enduring stress exposure are caused by morphological changes of neurons in the limbic system. In support of this assumption, it was found that antidepressants normalizing these behavioral changes in mice also increase BDNF levels and reverse the stress-induced decrease of hippocampal neurogenesis (Malberg et al. 2000). As one of the antidepressant modes of action is improving MR- and GR-mediated signaling, these drugs decrease plasma cortisol levels via optimizing negative feedback (Holsboer 2000) and therefore may reverse stress-evoked BDNF suppression. In addition, a recent study by Kronenberg et al. (2009) provided evidence for a direct involvement of GRs in the stress-dependent suppression of hippocampal neurogenesis. In this study, heterozygous GR knockout mice were used—a

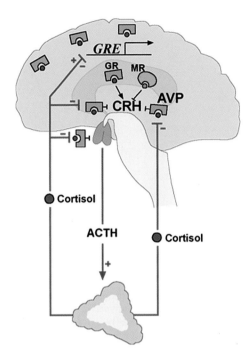

Figure 1

Hypothalamic-pituitary-adrenocortical (HPA) axis. In response to stress, hypothalamic neurons release the neuropeptides corticotrophin-releasing hormone (CRH) and arginine vasopressin (AVP), which act synergistically at corticotrophic cells in the pituitary to synthesize proopiomelanocortin (POMC), which is enzymatically cleaved into corticotrophin (adrenocorticotrophic hormone, ACTH) and other peptides. ACTH released from the anterior pituitary stimulates the adrenal cortex, which synthesizes and releases cortisol in humans and corticosterone in rodents. This physiological system, where stress hormones serve as signaling molecules, is the HPA axis. The primary regulatory elements of the HPA axis are glucocorticoid receptors (GRs) and mineralocorticoid receptors (MRs) located in the hypothalamus and the pituitary. The GR is ubiquitously distributed throughout the brain while the MR is predominantly expressed in the hippocampus, but it is also present at much lower concentrations in the prefrontal cortex, limbic system, hypothalamus, and brain stem. When a glucocorticoid binds to the GR or MR, the receptors are activated to translocate into the nucleus, where they directly or indirectly interact with glucocorticoid response elements (GREs) in the nuclear DNA, affecting the expression of the target genes.

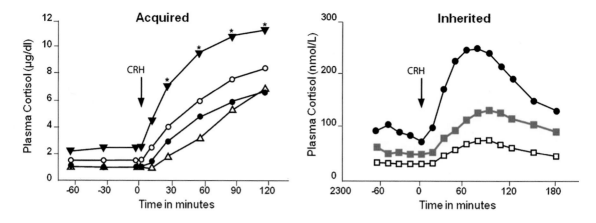

Plasma cortisol concentrations (mean) in the dex/CRH-test in men

▼ with early life trauma and major depression
○ with early life trauma without major depression
● without early life trauma and without current or previous psychiatric disorder
△ without early life trauma, but with current major depression

Plasma cortisol concentrations (mean) in the dex/CRH-test in

● patients with depression
■ healthy controls with first degree relatives having major depression
□ healthy controls without family history of psychiatric disorder

Figure 2

Impaired hypothalamic-pituitary-adrenocortical (HPA) axis regulation, as evaluated with the combined dexamethasone/corticotrophin-releasing hormone (dex/CRH) test, can be acquired from early childhood trauma (*left*; Heim et al. 2008a) or can be genetically transmitted within families with a high genetic load for depression (*right*; Holsboer et al. 1995).

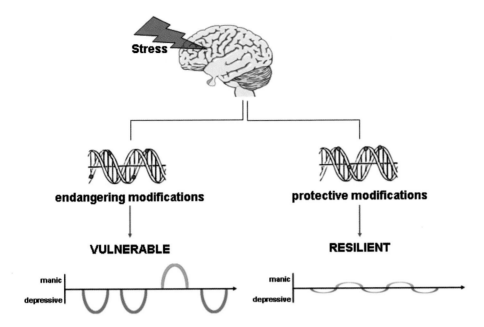

Figure 3

Stress induces depression in individuals with enhanced risk. Stressful life events may trigger the development of depression or bipolar disorder in vulnerable individuals, whereas the same stressors do not affect psychopathology in resilient subjects. Vulnerability and resilience can be genetically inherited or acquired by past experience.

A

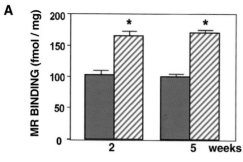

Antidepressant induced MR

B

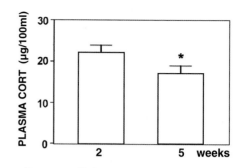

Stress-elicited corticosterone

C

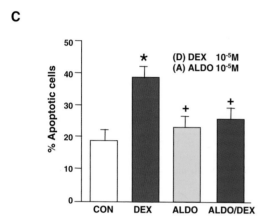

ALDO counteracts DEX actions
on neurons

D

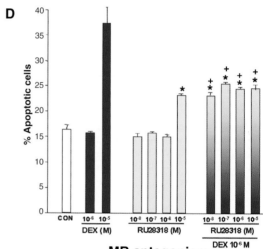

MR antagonism
accentuates DEX actions

E

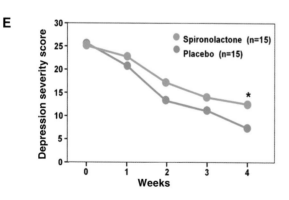

MR antagonist co-administration
decreases antidepressant effect

F

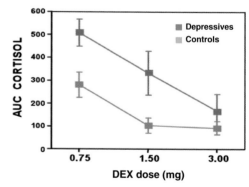

Depressives have a lowered
sensitivity to DEX in the
dex/CRH test

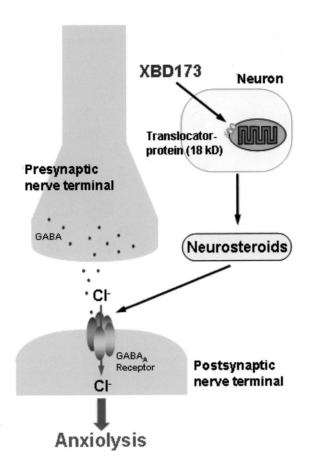

Figure 5

Mechanism of action of XBD173. XBD173, a ligand of the translocator protein (18 kD), enhances the synthesis of neurosteroids, which moderate the activity of gamma-aminobutyric acid (GABA)$_A$ receptors. This compound was demonstrated to act as an anxiolytic compound in a rodent model of panic disorders and also showed anxiolytic effects in human volunteers similar to those of benzodiazepines, but with fewer side effects (Rupprecht et al. 2009).

Figure 4

Effects of glucocorticoid receptor (GR) and mineralocorticoid receptor (MR) ligands upon hypothalamic-pituitary-adrenocortical (HPA) axis function, cell survival, and efficacy of antidepressant treatment. (*A*) After two weeks of antidepressant treatment, hippocampal MR capacity increases in rats (*hatched bars*), while (*B*) stress-induced plasma corticosterone concentrations decrease (Reul et al. 1993); (*C*) the synthetic GR agonist dexamethasone (DEX) induces apoptosis, an effect that is counteracted by the MR agonist aldosterone (ALDO). (*D*) GR agonistic effects amplify with the MR antagonist RU28318 to increased apoptosis (Crochemore et al. 2005). (*E*) Antidepressant efficacy is decreased if the MR antagonist spironolactone is coadministered (Holsboer 1999). (*F*) Increasing dosages of DEX decrease corticotrophin-releasing hormone (CRH)-induced plasma adrenocorticotrophic hormone (ACTH) and cortisol concentrations (area under the curve, AUC) (Modell et al. 1997), and patients with depression have higher mean stress hormone secretion (Heuser et al. 1994, Ising et al. 2005).

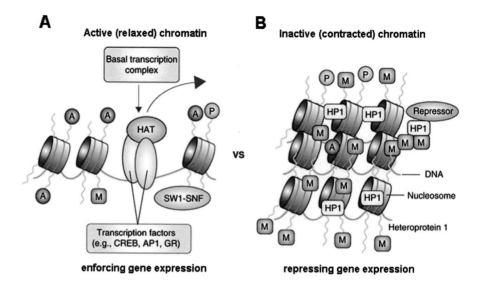

A Active (relaxed) chromatin

Basal transcription complex

HAT

A A A P

VS

A M SW1-SNF

Transcription factors
(e.g., CREB, AP1, GR)

enforcing gene expression

B Inactive (contracted) chromatin

P M P M

HP1 HP1 Repressor

M HP1

A M M M M

DNA

M M

Nucleosome

HP1 HP1

M

Heteroprotein 1

M M M

repressing gene expression

Figure 6

Differential states of chromatin transcription activity. (*A*) Histone acetylation is associated with chromatin relaxation facilitating binding of transcription factors and coactivators (e.g., histone acetyl transferase, or HAT) that mediate movement of nucleosomes along a strand of DNA; as a result, gene expression is enforced. (*B*) In contrast, methylation at genomic regions rich in CpG islands results in DNA contraction, decreasing transcription factor access and thus repressing gene activity (modified from McClung & Nestler 2008).

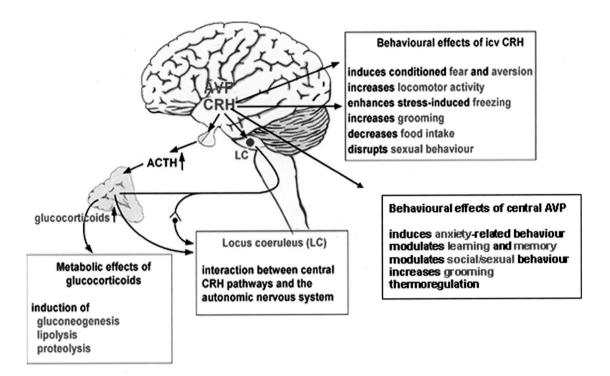

Figure 7

The dual actions of corticotrophin-releasing hormone (CRH) and arginine vasopressin (AVP): activator of the hypothalamic-pituitary-adrenocortical (HPA) axis and neurotransmitter. Increased levels of CRH and AVP induce many features common in depression and anxiety disorder, including behavioral alterations, cognitive impairment, motivational deficits, and metabolic disturbances. ACTH, adrenocorticotrophic hormone. (From Holsboer 1999.)

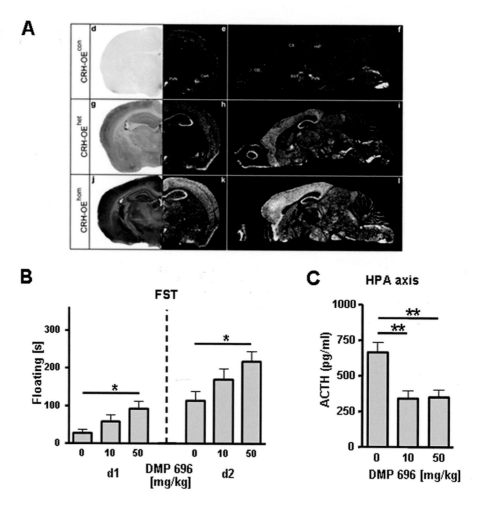

Figure 8

Corticotrophin-releasing hormone (CRH) overexpression in the mouse brain. (*A*) Use of a refined knock-in technique allows confining CRH overexpression to the central nervous system (CNS). (*B*) Stress-elicited hyperarousal in these CRH-overexpressing mice is manifested by decreased floating behavior in the forced swim test (FST). Hyperarousal is reversed by i.p. injection of the CRHR1 antagonist DMP696 in a dose-dependent mode and (*C*) accompanied by suppression of adrenocorticotrophic hormone (ACTH) (Lu et al. 2008).

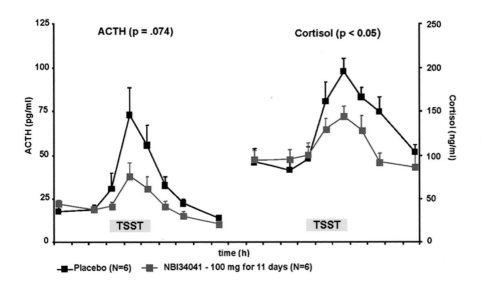

Figure 9

The corticotrophin-releasing hormone receptor 1 (CRHR1) antagonist NBI-34041 improves resilience to psychosocial stress. Adrenocorticotrophic hormone (ACTH) (*left*) and cortisol (*right*) response to a standardized psychosocial stress test (Trier Social Stress Test, or TSST) was attenuated after 9 days of treatment with 100 mg/d NBI-34041 (*blue lines*) compared with placebo (*black lines*), while the ACTH and cortisol response to exogenous CRH administered two days after the TSST was unchanged, suggesting a central effect of the CRHR1 antagonist (Ising et al. 2007b).

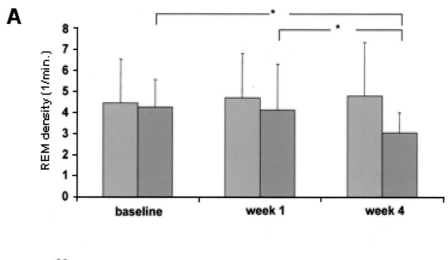

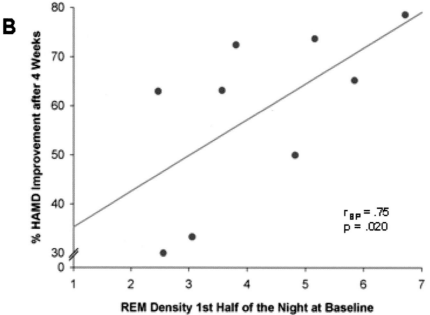

Figure 10

Elevated rapid-eye-movement (REM) density during early night sleep at baseline predicts depression improvement after four weeks of treatment with the corticotrophin-releasing hormone receptor 1 (CRHR1) antagonist NBI-30775/R121919. Four weeks of treatment with high doses (up to 160 mg/d) of the CRHR1 antagonist NBI-30775/R121919 improves REM density during sleep (*A, blue bars*), while this is not the case in patients treated with a low dose (5 to 40 mg/d) of the CRHR1 antagonist (*A, red bars*). In addition, elevated REM density during the first half of the baseline night predicts improvement of depressive symptoms after four weeks of treatment (*B*) (from Held et al. 2004). These findings further support that altered REM density could be a surrogate marker for elevated central CRH characterizing patients who will particularly benefit from CRHR1 antagonistic treatment.

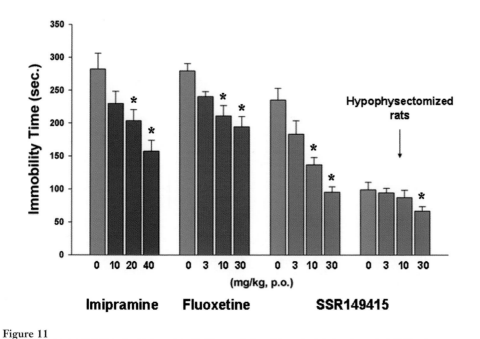

Figure 11

The V1B receptor antagonist SSR149415 shows antidepressant-like effects in the forced swim test in rats. I.p. administration of the V1B receptor antagonist SSR149415 in rats reduced the immobility time in the forced swim test in a dose-dependent manner, comparable with the effects of two reference antidepressants, imipramine and fluoxetine. This effect was also observed in hypophysectomized animals treated with the higher dose of SSR149415, confirming involvement of central V1B receptors (from Griebel et al. 2002).

model that mimics impaired GR sensitivity, which results in a dysregulation of the HPA axis and increased depression-like behavior in these animals. Compared with wild-type mice, the heterozygous GR knockout animals showed reduced hippocampal neurogenesis, which was further suppressed after stress exposure, suggesting a direct link between impaired GR signaling and reduced neurogenesis. However, a study by Surget et al. (2008) demonstrated that reduced neurogenesis is not a general requirement of stress-induced behavioral changes: Drugs acting primarily on monoaminergic pathways, however, require hippocampal neurogenesis to exert their behavioral, i.e., antidepressant-like, effects, which is in line with a previous observation demonstrating the failure of fluoxetine, a selective serotonergic reuptake inhibitor (SSRI), on behavioral effects if neurogenesis is inhibited (Santarelli et al. 2003).

Most humans who experience trauma or stressors do not develop psychopathology; only a subset of individuals who carry genetic and/or experience-related vulnerabilities develop a stress-related disorder such as depression (**Figure 3**, see color insert). Refined analysis of the physiological functions through which stress-elicited corticosteroids act in the brain converged in the hypothesis that impaired corticosteroid-receptor signaling is a key risk factor rendering an individual prone to stress-related disorders (Holsboer 2000). Neuroendocrine test results from both nonaffected individuals from families with high genetic load for depression (Holsboer et al. 1995) and from subjects having experienced early childhood trauma (Heim et al. 2008a) are in agreement with this hypothesis. Both show exaggerated stress-hormone release following dex/CRH testing, and both have an increased risk for developing depression in later life. This notion extends to morphological and neuroradiological changes as well as to observed reciprocal interactions between hippocampal corticosteroid and BDNF concentrations (Holsboer 2000).

Most studies investigating stress hormone actions in the context of adaptation and disease

have not fully taken into consideration that stress-induced cortisol hypersecretion can be protective but becomes harmful once the HPA hyperdrive is sustained. The molecular and physiological properties of MR and GR determine whether corticosteroid elevations are protective or harmful. The laboratories of Marian Joels and Ron de Kloet formulated the MR/GR balance hypothesis and showed that both receptors alone, in combination, or in tandem fulfill complementary or amplifying functions in a time-sensitive context. The MR prevents stress-elicited homeostatic disturbance opposing effects of glucocorticoid-activated GRs, which results in resilience toward stress exposure that is characterized by rapid activation and efficient termination of humoral responses (Feder et al. 2009). Imbalances between MR and GR receptor function compromise resilience toward stress exposure and increase risk for the development of a stress-related clinical condition, such as depression. Neuroendocrine tests (dex/CRH test) in genetically prone individuals, in subjects following childhood trauma, and in subjects with genetic mutations in GR and MR genes (including regulatory sequences) support this notion (DeRijk et al. 2006, van Rossum et al. 2006).

The opposing effects of MR and GR have also been studied in the context of cell survival using primary postnatal hippocampal cultures. As expected, dexamethasone, a specific GR agonist, induced apoptosis in a dose-dependent fashion, an effect that can be suppressed by an MR agonist and exacerbated with an MR antagonist (Crochemore et al. 2005). These observations further support that functional MR/GR balance is involved in hippocampal cell survival and ultimately in the regulation of stress-related psychopathology. Both receptors are downregulated following stress exposure, whereas antidepressants upregulate MR and GR in a concerted mode (Reul et al. 1993). The need for a fully functioning MR is also highlighted by a study showing that clinical efficacy of an antidepressant drug is muted if an MR antagonist is coadministered (Holsboer 1999). It is of note that MR antagonists themselves can impede neuronal cell viability, confirming the special role of central MRs that includes survival of hippocampal granule neurons but that also extends to many other characteristics (Behl et al. 1997, Joels et al. 2008, Obradovic et al. 2004, Reul et al. 2000, Yu et al. 2008) (**Figure 4**, see color insert).

Another class of steroids involved in the regulation of stress and emotion is the so-called neuroactive steroids (or neurosteroids). Neurosteroids are synthesized in the peripheral nervous system and in the brain from cholesterol or other precursors and are chemically reduced in the ring A position of the steroid molecule. They act as modulators of GABA-gated chloride channels and are able to moderate stress responses at the systemic level by enhancing ion flux into the cell in a way similar to that for benzodiazepines (Rupprecht 1997, Rupprecht & Holsboer 1999). As a consequence of this mechanism, pretreatment of rats with the neurosteroid tetrahydroprogesterone resulted in (*a*) decreased CRH response following adrenergic stimulation (Patchev et al. 1994), (*b*) attenuated endocrine response to emotional stress, and (*c*) diminished expression of MR, GR, and AVP in the brain (Patchev et al. 1996). The importance of neuroactive steroids signaling has been recently demonstrated in a study that used the drug candidate XBD173 as a tool (Rupprecht et al. 2009). This molecule is a ligand of the translocator protein enhancing neurosteroid synthesis that was demonstrated to act as an anxiolytic compound in a rodent model of panic disorder (**Figure 5**, see color insert). It was also anxiolytic in human volunteers, where anxiety was experimentally induced with cholecystokinin, an anxiogenic peptide (Rupprecht et al. 2009). This intervention produced fewer side effects than did benzodiazepines.

In recent years, our understanding of how experiences imprint on genomic regulation has profited from studies that elucidate the molecular underpinnings of epigenetic modifications in the brain. It has long been known that epigenetic mechanisms contribute to the phenotypic specification of individual cells, which all carry the same genome. More recently, however, the ways in which experiences ranging from nutritional effects to trauma can backlash upon gene regulation were studied using biochemical tools to investigate the chromatine structure of the cellular DNA. This line will ultimately lead to an understanding of how experiences can be translated into chemical reactions at the level of the genome, resulting in long-lasting changes of gene activity and subsequent physiological and behavioral consequences. It is beyond the scope of this review to go into biochemical details of epigenetic modification; the reader is referred to recent excellent reviews (e.g., Tsankova et al. 2007). What needs to be understood in this context is that many different mechanisms exist by which epigenetic marks modify genome function. The best-studied examples are histone acetylation and DNA methylation. More recently, histone methylation has been elucidated in the context of tumor development in particular. In the cell nucleus, DNA is tightly coiled around histone proteins. These proteins carry N-terminal tails to which small chemical substituents can bind in response to an incoming event that challenges cellular function (**Figure 6**, see color insert). By binding such a substituent, which in most investigated cases is an acetyl group, the chromatin (DNA-histone complex) alters its structure, allowing better access of transcription factors at the specific DNA-sequence where acetylation had occurred. Better access of transcription factors translates into changes of gene expression. The enzymes that alter chromatin structure by removing acetyl groups are histone deacetylases (HDACs), whereas acetylation is catalyzed by histone acetylases (HATs).

In contrast, at certain areas of the DNA, methyl groups can be covalently bound to a cytosine side chain at genomic regions with increased CpG (cytosin-phosphatidyl-guanosin) dinucleotide density (so-called CpG islands), which results in an even denser chromatin packaging that denies transcription factor access. Studies are now becoming feasible that decipher gene-by-environment interactions at the molecular level. Posttraumatic stress disorder (PTSD) is a clinical condition that is particularly suited to the study of these experience-related effects upon gene regulation. PTSD is characterized by unintended re-experiencing of traumatic events, avoidance of remainders of the event, and hyperarousal. The latter includes physiological signs and symptoms, such as insomnia, irritability, impaired concentration, and increased startle reactions (Yehuda 2002). A particularly interesting feature is that these patients have profound HPA axis dysregulation in terms of a blunted stress-hormone response, pointing to a hypersensitivity of the GR (de Kloet et al. 2006, Ströhle et al. 2008, Yehuda et al. 2004). A similar finding was observed in a subtype of depressed women characterized by job stress-related long-term sick leave. Unlike in major depression, these patients showed a persistent attenuation of the stress hormone response to the combined dex/CRH test (Wahlberg et al. 2009), which is also observed in PTSD patients (Ströhle et al. 2008) and in depressed patients having outlived a suicide attempt (Pfennig et al. 2005). These findings indicate that the stress-hormone regulation has undergone epigenetic modifications following chronic job stress or trauma exposure. A study of gene-activity patterns among subjects exposed to the World Trade Center attack on September 11, 2001, differentiated patients with PTSD from individuals without psychopathology (Yehuda et al. 2009). The differentially regulated genes included those involved in GR signaling, possibly explaining the neuroendocrine changes observed. This conclusion is conjectural because laboratory assessments prior to trauma were not available. The role of possibly underlying epigenetic mechanisms has nevertheless been highlighted in a study that investigated Holocaust survivors, where maternal but not paternal PTSD was associated with increased risk for PTSD in adult offspring (Yehuda et al. 2008). Studies by Weaver et al. (2004, 2005) gained further insight into the molecular mechanisms underlying stress hormone effects elicited by experience. They observed that an epigenetic modification, specifically methylation at a regulatory sequence of the GR gene, was enhanced among the offspring of mothers who provided only little maternal care, which is a risk factor for the development of PTSD-like symptoms in rodents (Siegmund et al. 2009). In agreement with these findings, evidence for childhood trauma-dependent epigenetic regulation was recently found also in human brains of suicide victims (McGowan et al. 2009). The authors reported increased methylation of the GR promoter region and decreased levels of GR transcripts in postmortem hippocampal samples of suicide victims having experienced childhood abuse as opposed to those suicide victims without such aversive experience. This can be taken as first evidence of how childhood experience imprints itself in genomic regulation of the stress hormone system. It may explain clinical findings where liability to develop depression manifests with premorbid stress hormone dysregulation, or, more specifically, why childhood trauma increases the risk for mood disorders in adulthood. Recently, the implication of such epigenetic marks has been underscored in a study where methylation patterns in 1% of the total genome across the 22 nonsex chromosomes were analyzed. It was found that these patterns were carrying more resemblance among monozygotic than among dizygotic twins, further supporting the view that molecular mechanisms, other than DNA sequence transmission, exist and facilitate the inheritance of phenotypical traits (Kaminsky et al. 2009). It was shown that variations in the FKBP5 gene involved in GR signaling interact with the severity of childhood abuse to predict adult PTSD (Binder et al. 2008). This finding further supports that the impact of environmental threads on epigenetic modifications is moderated by genetic factors. The field of epigenetics is still in its beginning, but perhaps it will become the most exciting opportunity to understand how experience-related factors are chemically imprinted. Thus, epigenetics is becoming the cornerstone of molecular psychology.

Posttraumatic stress disorder (PTSD): develops after exposure to a severe trauma and is characterized by frequent involuntary re-experiencing of the traumatic event, sleep disturbances, avoidance behavior, hyperarousal, and stress hormone variations

Epigenetics: summarizes all changes of the genome other than those resulting from an altered sequence of the nucleotides. Most result from gene-environment interactions, and some of these changes can be inherited

TRANSLATION OF CORTICOSTEROID DYSREGULATION INTO THERAPY

HPA-axis dysregulation is the most profoundly studied laboratory abnormality in stress-related disorders, and elevation of adrenocortical stress hormones has been recognized as a depression-associated feature for decades (Holsboer 2000, Sachar 1967, Vreeburg et al. 2009). A straightforward approach of blocking insidious effects of corticosteroid excess was first reported in studies where patients with Cushing's syndrome were treated with RU486 (mifepristone), a nonpeptide antagonist at progesterone receptors and at GRs (Chu et al. 2001, Nieman et al. 1985, van der Lely et al. 1991). Several reports suggested that mifepristone not only mitigates psychotic symptoms in Cushing's syndrome but also in psychotic depression (DeBattista et al. 2006). This clinical condition is almost always associated with hypercortisolism, which is suggested to account for the cognitive changes in this depressive subtype that are distinct from those in nonpsychotic major depression with absent or only moderate HPA-axis dysregulation (Belanoff et al. 2001). Mifepristone was found to counteract corticosteroid-induced cognitive impairment in rats (Oitzl et al. 1998), and short-term treatment with mifepristone was shown to reverse the aforementioned reduction of adult hippocampal neurogenesis (Mayer et al. 2006). It remains to be resolved whether mifepristone is acting as a bona fide antidepressant or whether it ameliorates psychotic features specifically. The dopamine hypothesis of psychotic depression formulated by Schatzberg et al. (1985) suggests that the psychotic subtype of depression is characterized by excessive dopaminergic neurotransmission, which is further enhanced by elevated corticosteroids (Piazza et al. 1996). More recent studies revealed that GR antagonists exert distinct effects on the HPA axis that include MR enhancement, which in light of the MR/GR-balance hypothesis (de Kloet et al. 2005) and the prominent role of both types of receptors in hippocampal neurogenesis may highlight an antidepressant mechanism different from monoamine-based drugs (Bachmann et al. 2003). In line with this view is a study by Johnson et al. (2007), who used several specific GR antagonists and found that when coadministered with a serotonergic antidepressant (SSRI) they may accelerate serotonin receptor 1A (5-HTR1A) desensitization, a pharmacological effect thought to be essential for antidepressant efficacy. Another study by the same group observed that SSRI-induced downregulation of the presynaptic serotonin-transporter is amplified by coadministration of GR antagonists (Johnson et al. 2009). Although these new applications of long-established pharmacological mechanisms will soon be further evaluated, it is obvious that they do not recuperate the pathological mechanism, which is an impaired capacity to adapt optimally to a stressor. As explained above, this condition can be inherited or acquired, and GR antagonists can help to ameliorate the adverse consequences.

Given the recent evidence about the involvement of epigenetic mechanisms that are likely imprinting impaired stress response and the subsequent risk to develop stress-related disorders, it is intriguing to interfere pharmacologically with enzymes catalyzing chemical reactions that are manipulating the epigenome. Primary candidates are HDAC inhibitors, which make modifications of the epigenome feasible (see above). Some limitations, however, exist: Currently available HDAC inhibitors lack specificity because they act across all HDAC classes, which comprise more than ten isoforms. Nevertheless, HDAC inhibitor discovery is now a top priority in the pharmaceutical industry. Such endeavors might be rewarding; for instance, a study recently showed that maternal programming of stress response by epigenetic markers is amenable to drug intervention (Weaver 2007).

CORTICOTROPHIN-RELEASING HORMONE

After Harris (1948) proposed that hypothalamic neurons produce discrete factors that regulate the release of anterior pituitary hormones, it took almost four decades until Vale and colleagues (1981) discovered and characterized corticotrophin-releasing hormone (CRH, often termed corticotrophin-releasing factor, or CRF), the principal stress hormone of the brain. It soon became clear that CRH is not only driving the HPA axis but is also coordinating many humoral and behavioral aspects of the adaptive response to stress. From a neuroanatomical perspective, this is evidenced by CRH immunoreactive fibers widely distributed throughout the brain (Swanson et al. 1983), where CRH acts as neuroregulator (Gallagher et al. 2008). CRH exerts its actions by means of two different receptor subtypes, corticotrophin-releasing hormone receptor 1 and 2 (CRHR1 and CRHR2), which present with different expression patterns in the brain. CRHR1 is expressed at different levels in neocortical areas, hippocampus, basolateral amygdala, ventral tegmental area, pontine gray, lateral dorsal tegmentum, pedunculopontine tegmental nucleus, and the anterior pituitary (Potter et al. 1994, Sanchez et al. 1999, Van Pett et al. 2000). CRHR2 is found in the lateral septum, bed nucleus of the stria terminalis, medial and cortical nuclei of the amygdala, dorsal raphe, and nucleus of the solitary tract. Both CRH receptors exist in isoforms (CRHR1α,β and CRHR2α,β,γ), several of which were shown to be nonfunctional (Dautzenberg & Hauger 2002, Grammatopoulos & Chrousos 2002). CRH is a high-affinity ligand for CRHR1; it binds with much lower affinity to CRHR2, where urocortin II (also termed stresscopin-related peptide) and urocortin III (also termed stresscopin) are preferred ligands. CRH receptors are linked to different intracellular-signaling pathways, which differ between brain regions, thus resulting in a neuroanatomically signaling specificity of CRH receptors (Arzt & Holsboer 2006). For the sake of brevity, we confine ourselves to addressing data linked to the hormonal stress response and related behavioral features including anxiety, depression, and sleep. For a more detailed description of CRHR1 and CRHR2 effects, the reader is referred to reviews by Bale & Vale (2004) and Reul & Holsboer (2002). Shortly following the discovery by Vale and colleagues (1981), who identified CRH as it occurs in ovine and rat, a Japanese group led by Numa (Takahashi et al. 1983) cloned the human CRH and found a high degree of homology.

The first clinical trials investigating the effects of CRH among psychiatric patients were able to reject the possibility that pituitary corticotrophs account for HPA hyperdrive in depression (Gold et al. 1984; Holsboer 1983; Holsboer et al. 1984, 1986). When CRH is intravenously administered to depressives in the morning, the plasma ACTH response is normal. CRH administration in the evening, however, results in blunted ACTH secretion. In contrast, among patients with Cushing's disease, where corticotrophs are excessively active, CRH induces high plasma ACTH levels. These findings, which were widely replicated, were taken as evidence that peripheral pituitary adrenocortical hyperactivity among psychiatric patients may serve as a window to the brain, revealing a central hyperactivity of CRH neurons (Holsboer 1999). Nemeroff and colleagues (1984) supported these studies: They found CRH to be elevated in the cerebrospinal fluid of depressed patients (Nemeroff et al. 1984) and identified reduced CRH binding sites in the frontal cortex of suicide victims (Nemeroff et al. 1988). The latter was taken as reflection of central CRH overabundance leading to CRH receptor desensitization, a phenomenon common to many G-protein-coupled cell membrane-located receptors. Importantly, these increased CSF CRH concentrations normalize following successful antidepressant treatment (de Bellis et al. 1993, Heuser et al. 1998). Many subsequent studies corroborated these findings, and in parallel, a host of animal experiments supported the view that increased CRH accounts not only for the endocrine stress response, but

CRHR1:
corticotrophin-releasing hormone receptor 1

also acts as a key regulator of behavioral adaptation to stress (**Figure 7**, see color insert).

Most animal studies used injections of CRH into specific brain areas, either alone or in combination with CRHR1 antagonists; other studies used antisense directed against CRH, CRHR1, and CRHR2 (for reviews, see Arborelius et al. 1999, Bale & Vale 2004, Holsboer 1999). These studies further corroborated that CRH is a mediator of anxiety-like behavior and also accounts for several features of depression-like behavior in animals and monkeys. For example, if antisense directed against CRHR1mRNA is injected into the intracerebral ventricular space of male rats, they display less anxiety-like behavior (Liebsch et al. 1999); this intervention had no effect in the Porsolt forced swim test (FST), which measures active or passive coping behavior. In contrast, antisense directed against CRHR2 had no effect on anxiety-like behavior as measured in the elevated plus-maze (see above), whereas it enhanced passive coping behavior in the FST. These behavioral analyses concluded that CRH exerts stress-like behavior via CRHR1, whereas CRHR2 activation is involved in stress coping (that is why the preferred ligand of CRHR2 was termed stresscopin by Hsu & Hsueh 2001). Given the brain-area-specific CRH/CRHR1,2-signaling capacity, those studies where CRH in transgenic mice is hypersecreted either in the whole body (Stenzel-Poore et al. 1992) or in brain areas normally not expressing CRH failed to provide entirely valid models for long-lasting CRH disinhibition (Groenink et al. 2002). A recent report by Lu et al. (2008) combined the knock-in technique of a single copy of the murine CRH cDNA into the ROSA26 locus (Zambrowicz et al. 1997) with the Cre/lox P system. By these means, the investigators were able to overexpress CRH in a spatiotemporally regulated fashion and analyzed neuroendocrine and behavioral effects of spatially confined CRH overexpression. As illustrated in **Figure 8** (see color insert), mice with CRH overexpression in the entire brain show signs of hyperarousal in a gene-dose-dependent mode, which can be blocked by a CRHR1 antagonist. This ef-

fect was absent when CRH overexpression was restricted locally to distinct brain areas. Although these data confirmed the role of stress-elicited hyperarousal, the selective deletion of CRHR1 more specifically addressed anxiety-like behavior. CRHR1-null mutants exhibited reduced anxiety-like behavior and impaired stress-hormone secretion at baseline and following stress exposure (Smith et al. 1998, Timpl et al. 1998). The confounding effect of aberrant hormone secretion—owing to the absence of pituitary CRHR1s—was avoided in a mouse where CRHR1 deletion was restricted to the forebrain. Here again it was shown that limbic CRH/CRHR1 signaling accounts for anxiety-like behavior (Müller et al. 2003). Both anxiogenic and anxiolytic-like effects after CRHR2 activation or gene deletion have been reported (Bale et al. 2000, Coste et al. 2000, Kishimoto et al. 2000). In combination with the pharmacological studies mentioned above, the overall conclusion from these and related studies is that CRHR2 facilitates recovery (coping) by curtailing initial CRHR1-mediated stress response.

CRH seems to be also involved in learning and memory. This is suggested by the presence of CRH receptors in the hippocampus, which after ligand activation convey a long-lasting enhancement of synaptic efficacy in the hippocampus (Wang et al. 1998). Intraperitoneal injection of the CRHR1 antagonist antalarmin prior to training impaired the induction of contextual fear conditioning in rats (Deak et al. 1999), and transgenic mice lacking CRHR1 showed learning deficits in a simultaneous discrimination task (Croiset et al. 2000) and in contextual fear learning (Risbrough et al. 2009). However, it is unclear to what degree these findings might be explained by a diminished arousal as a result of CRH blockade, which could have contributed to lower attention and thus worsened learning performance. It appears that optimal learning performance requires a state of balanced CRH levels in the brain, as intracerebroventricular injection of CRH to rodent brains also impairs memory performance, amplifying the negative effects of anticholinergic drugs (Steckler & Holsboer 2001).

CRH is elevated after excessive substance abuse, presumably mediating withdrawal-related negative emotional states. This was demonstrated in rat models of alcohol addiction, where elevated CRH levels were measured in the extended amygdala (Gilpin et al. 2008, Heilig & Koob 2007). In addition, CRHR1 is upregulated in the amygdala of animals showing excessive rates of alcohol self-administration, which in turn further increases the stress responsivity of the amygdala (Sandi et al. 2008). Alcohol consumption and craving behavior could be distinctly attenuated after blocking hyperactive signaling at CRH receptors (Gilpin et al. 2008, Heilig & Koob 2007). However, transgenic mice lacking CRHR1 also showed increased alcohol consumption in response to repeated stress (Sillaber et al. 2002), suggesting that a well-balanced activity of the CRH system is required to prevent stress-induced drinking.

The stress system is intimately connected with monoaminergic systems, which is not only neuroanatomically evidenced, but is also supported by functional studies (Valentino et al. 2001). Chronic elevation of CRH in the CNS causes decreased responsiveness of hippocampal serotonin to stressors (Linthorst et al. 1997). Opposite changes were observed following CRHR1 blockade by a specific antagonist (Oshima et al. 2003) or by CRHR1 gene deletion in mice (Penalva et al. 2002). In addition, noradrenergic pathways interconnect with CRH/CRHR1 signaling at a functional level. This was shown clinically by a CSF study, where a reciprocally amplifying link between a central hypernoradrenergic state and a central CRH hyperdrive had been demonstrated (Wong et al. 2000). The latter study also found hypercortisolism in parallel with CRH excess, indicating impaired negative feedback of central corticosteroid receptors upon CRH synthesis, which is in keeping with the corticosteroid receptor hypothesis of depressive states associated with hypersecretion of both cortisol and CRH (Holsboer 2000). Another example of this interaction was reported by Bissette et al. (2003), who examined the well-established stimulatory effect of CRH on the locus coeruleus (LC), the major source of norepinephrine in the brain. The authors took LC micropunches postmortem from brains of depressives and found both norepinephrine and CRH to be elevated. In agreement with this, Austin and colleagues (2003) reported evidence for specifically increased CRH levels in the LC as well as in the serotonergic raphe nuclei in brains of depressed suicide victims, further supporting the link between altered CRH and monoaminergic disturbance in depression.

THERAPEUTIC TARGETING OF CRH SIGNALING

The finding of elevated CRH in acute depression and anxiety, the anxiogenic effects of central CRH in animal models, and the fact that human CRH binds at the CRHR1 with 15-fold higher affinity over CRHR2, led to the hypothesis that selective CRHR1 antagonists are promising drug candidates for the treatment of depression, anxiety, and other stress-related disorders (Grigoriadis 2005). Initially available CRHR1 antagonists were peptides (e.g., astressin) unable to pass the blood-brain barrier; antalarmin was one of the first nonpeptide small-molecule CRHR1 antagonists exhibiting central effects in animal experiments if administered peripherally by subcutaneous or oral gavage. Intraperitoneal administration of antalarmin to mice produced anxiolytic effects in the light/dark box and in an intruder defense test (Griebel et al. 1998). Oral administration of antalarmin attenuated anxiety-related behavior in male macaques, who were exposed to a social stressor, and increased exploratory and sexual behaviors, which are generally suppressed during anxiety (Habib et al. 2000). As described in **Figure 8**, intraperitoneal injection of the CRHR1 antagonist DMP696 in central CRH-overexpressing mice reversed hyperarousal in the FST in a dose-dependent manner (Lu et al. 2008). These findings underscore the prominent role of central CRH for anxiety-related behaviors and suggest blocking of CRHR1 as a promising treatment in stress-related mental disorders.

The first clinical CRHR1 antagonist study was conducted with NBI-30775/R121919, a nonpeptide tricyclic compound initially developed by Neurocrine Biosciences in San Diego, California. This drug is well absorbed when given orally, penetrates the blood-brain barrier, and binds specifically to human CRHR1s, while binding to other receptors or transporters is absent or more than 1000-fold lower (Chen et al. 2004, Heinrichs et al. 2002, Steckler & Dautzenberg 2006). A reduction of anxiety-related behavior was observed in different animal models after oral or subcutaneous administration of NBI-30775/R121919, and the effects of exogenous CRH could be antagonized by this compound (Heinrichs et al. 2002, Keck et al. 2001). In the first clinical trial, the effects of increasing doses of NBI-30775/R121919 were evaluated in patients with major depression (Held et al. 2004, Künzel et al. 2003, Zobel et al. 2000). Patients were treated with NBI-30775/R121919 for 30 days in two dose-escalating panels, where increasing dosages from 5 to 40 mg/day or from 40 to 80 mg/day were administered. Even though the trial was designed as a safety and tolerability study, psychopathology improvement and change in sleep performance were additionally evaluated. On average, improvement in depression and anxiety scores were observed in all patients, although they were more pronounced in the group receiving higher dosages (Zobel et al. 2000). The effect size of treatment with higher dosages of NBI-30775/R121919 was well comparable with effects of the serotonergic antidepressant paroxetine demonstrated in a comparable study population treated as inpatients for severe major depression (Holsboer & Ising 2008). Similar improvement effects were observed for vegetative and cognitive aspects of depression and for suicidality, suggesting a comparable profile of action between paroxetine and the CRHR1 antagonist. Another cardinal symptom in depression is disturbed sleep, which is characterized by an imbalance between slow-wave sleep and rapid eye movement (REM) sleep (Steiger 2007b). A sleep-electroencephalogram analysis in a subgroup of

patients showed that this treatment normalized this imbalance by increasing slow-wave sleep and reducing phasic REM sleep (Held et al. 2004). An in-depth hormonal evaluation analyzing manifold endocrine systems confirmed the safety of the drug. This analysis included the pituitary-adrenocortical response to an intravenously administered test dose of exogenous CRH (CRH challenge test) and showed that plasma ACTH and cortisol responses were not affected by the drug (Zobel et al. 2000). This is of importance because it confirms that even if a dose is administered that effectively blocks central CRHR1s completely, there still remain sufficient receptors available at the anterior pituitary corticotrophs to maintain their capacity for an adequate response to exogenous stressors. Thus, the risk that patients treated with a CRHR1 antagonist might not be able to respond adequately to an acute stressor with HPA activation can be eliminated.

Another selective CRHR1 antagonist developed by Neurocrine Biosciences, NBI-34041, was tested in a human study evaluating its effects in a double-blind placebo-controlled proof-of-concept trial (Ising et al. 2007b). Participants were healthy male volunteers receiving NBI-34041 in one of three dosages (10, 50, and 100 mg/d) or placebo over a period of 14 days. Besides evaluating the safety and tolerability of the compound, the ability of NBI-34041 to improve the response to psychosocial stress after subchronic treatment was examined. This was evaluated with the Trier Social Stress Test (TSST), which is a well-standardized stress paradigm (Kirschbaum et al. 1993, Zimmermann et al. 2004). The TSST was conducted after nine days of treatment with NBI-34041. All subjects showed comparable subjectively perceived stress response in this test, whereas the hormonal response to the stressor differed between groups. The group receiving 100 mg/d NBI-34041 responded with decreased plasma ACTH and cortisol surges in the psychosocial stress test compared with the placebo group (**Figure 9**, see color insert).

The same subjects also participated in a CRH challenge test evaluating the stimulating effects of exogenous CRH on the ACTH response of the pituitary corticotrophs. This test was conducted two days after the TSST, while the subjects were maintained on NBI-34041 or placebo. As already observed for NBI-30775/R121919 (Zobel et al. 2000), NBI-34041 did not affect the pituitary response to exogenous CRH, suggesting that the hormonal effect following the psychosocial stress response in the TSST was mediated by the blockade of central CRHR1s, whereas peripheral CRHR1s at the anterior pituitary still remained fully responsive to exogenous stimulation.

Blocking central CRHR1s can be viewed as a first step in a treatment tailored to one's individual pathophysiological condition. Animal and human studies supported the view of an important contribution of CRH in mediating stress-elicited behavior including anxiety, a leading symptom of mood disorders. Nevertheless, it would be naïve to expect that interference with one single signaling pathway out of millions of molecules that exert functions within and between billions of brain cells would solve the clinical problem, and it would not come as a surprise if we would see an upsurge of clinical studies using CRHR1 antagonists in conditions where anxiety and depressive symptoms prevail, rejecting the clinical utility of this new class of drugs. A problem inherent in all clinical research of complex diseases is that diagnostic attributions, useful as they might be for creating clinical categories, tell us little about the underlying pathologies. This is particularly true for psychiatric diagnoses, which emerge from the conference room rather than the laboratory. Specifically, we have no means yet to identify patients having increased central CRH/CRHR1 signaling and who would benefit from CRHR1 antagonist treatment. The window-into-the-brain approach based on neuroendocrine assessments may be of limited help in this regard: The study administering NBI-30775/R121919 to depressed patients demonstrated only a weak predictive value on drug response after 30 days by means of a CRH-stimulation test administered after the first 10 days of treatment (Künzel et al. 2003,

Zobel et al. 2000). A recent trial by Binneman and colleagues (2008) illustrates the situation: These authors report on a comparison of 90 male patients with a DSM-IV diagnosis of recurrent major depression who were randomly assigned to CP 316.311, a selective CRHR1 antagonist, sertraline (an SSRI), or placebo. Although planned as a larger study, recruitment was stopped after an interim analysis hinted futility, leaving 54 patients equally distributed over three treatment arms for analysis, which revealed superiority of sertraline over CP 316.311 and placebo. The conclusion that CP 316.311 failed to demonstrate efficacy, however, is premature as long as the following questions remain unresolved: (a) Because CP 316.311 has an almost 10-fold-lower affinity for CRHR1s than NBI-30775/R121919, for which clinical effects were shown in a proof-of-concept study (Künzel et al. 2003, Zobel et al. 2000), it remains unclear which degree of receptor occupancy was achieved with the given dose. (b) Clinical data on a CRHR1 antagonistic treatment are of little information as long as studies remain unpublished that evaluated the compound in animal models with innate excessive CRH/CRHR1 signaling when stress exposed. (c) Because CRHR1 polymorphisms exist and are influencing antidepressant treatment response (Licinio et al. 2004), one may argue that CRHR1 polymorphisms must be shown to be equally distributed over all three treatment arms. (d) Likewise, presence of genetic variants known to be associated with faster antidepressant treatment response in general has to be reported. For example, Binder et al. (2004) have shown that a certain FKBP5 genotype is associated with hastened onset to antidepressants; and a manifold of other examples exists linking certain genotypes with clinical course (Kirchheiner et al. 2008, Kraft et al. 2007, Uhr et al. 2008). Other completed clinical trials using CRHR1 antagonists that are burdened with these and other impediments will show up and raise the possibility that they are failed rather than negative studies. What is urgently needed are reliable biomarkers that identify patients who would specifically benefit from CRHR1 antagonists. As stated above, neuroendocrine tests can give a picture of hypothalamic pituitary regulation, but contrary to initial expectations, these hormone assessments do not necessarily reflect central CRH/CRHR1-signaling activity in brain areas relevant for psychopathology. The availability of CRHR1-selective radioligands allowing one to study anatomical distribution, density, and occupancy in humans following drug administration employing positron emission tomography would be ideally suited for biomarker development. Unfortunately, such tools are yet not available.

More recent research has followed up a different approach: When rats are selectively bred for high innate anxiety, they present with a number of sleep disturbances that could be ameliorated with NBI-30775/R121919, a CRHR1 antagonist (Lancel et al. 2002). In such rodents, CRH is overexpressed (Wigger et al. 2004). In humans as well as in rats, CRH administration reduces the amount of slow wave sleep and enhances REM sleep (Ehlers et al. 1986, Holsboer et al. 1988), a pattern that is also observed in depression. Touma et al. (2008, 2009) generated a novel animal model for mood disorders by separate breeding lines selected for high, intermediate, or low HPA-activation (measured as corticosterone secretion) in response to stress. These animals were studied in a sleep-electroencephalogram laboratory for mice, where it was shown that those mice with the highest corticosterone response to stress had the highest REM sleep increase, confirming the strong link between HPA activation and REM sleep (Touma et al. 2009). More recently Kimura et al. (2009) reported that transgenic mice, where CRH overexpression is limited to the forebrain, have increased REM sleep that cannot be attributed to peripheral stress-hormone changes. In this study, the REM enhancement could be reversed by DMP696, a selective CRHR1 antagonist. In agreement with this observation, it was shown among patients with depression that increased REM density, which is an indicator of phasic REM, was suppressed after four weeks of treatment with high doses of a CRHR1 antagonist (Held et al. 2004). In a reanalysis of the data by Held et al. (2004), it could be demonstrated that REM density during the first half of the baseline night showed a strong association with improvement of depressive symptoms in response to treatment with the CRHR1 antagonist (**Figure 10**, see color insert). These results further support that altered REM density could be a surrogate marker for elevated central CRH characterizing patients who will particularly benefit from CRH antagonistic treatments.

Although we do not neglect that the balance between various sleep stages, especially REM and SWS, is regulated by many different mechanisms, work by Steiger has emphasized the important role of neuropeptides (Steiger 2007a). Longitudinal observations of patients with depression have shown both gradual normalization of HPA activity and REM sleep disturbance. Likewise, normal healthy controls from families with a high genetic load for depression also present with abnormal neuroendocrine and REM sleep findings, which led Modell et al. (2005) to submit that REM-sleep measures may serve as endophenotypes for depression. The relationship between central CRH overexpression and REM-sleep enhancement in animals and humans lends further support that REM-sleep measures may serve as surrogate markers guiding differentiated therapy.

ARGININE VASOPRESSIN

A potential role for arginine vasopressin (AVP) in the development and course of depression has been derived from clinical studies, which found elevated AVP concentrations in CSF (de Bellis et al. 1993, Heuser et al. 1998), in plasma (van Londen et al. 1997), and in PVN neurons (Purba et al. 1996). The reciprocally amplifying effects of CRH and AVP in humans were first recognized after neuroendocrine studies showed that neither CRH nor AVP when given alone can produce a plasma cortisol increase in dexamethasone-pretreated healthy male volunteers where any personal or family history of psychiatric disorder or early-life trauma had been excluded. When both neuropeptides were infused in combination (continuous infusion of AVP and a single bolus of CRH), high plasma ACTH and cortisol concentrations were observed, suggesting a synergistic action of AVP and CRH (von Bardeleben et al. 1985). This potentiating effect was predicted by basic studies (Gillies et al. 1982), and it was suggested that the phenomenon of high post-CRH levels of ACTH and cortisol in dexamethasone-pretreated depressives is reflecting elevated AVP levels originating from the PVN and resulting in AVP-driven HPA hyperactivity following emotional stressors (von Bardeleben & Holsboer 1989, de Goeij et al. 1992, Wigger et al. 2004, Wotjak et al. 1996). It had been hypothesized that the normalization of dexamethasone/CRH test results that are preceding full resolution of depressive symptoms reflects gradually improved GR and MR signaling (Holsboer 2000) that resulted in a more efficient suppression of CRH and AVP. As a consequence, AVP levels are decreased and fail to synergize with exogenously administered CRH (as part as the dexamethasone/CRH test) to overcome dexamethasone-induced ACTH suppression. Pretreatment by dexamethasone is indeed pertinent because opposite to cortisol, low dexamethasone dosages fail to cross the blood-brain barrier and result (on a functional level) in CNS hypocortisolism, which stimulates AVP (von Bardeleben & Holsboer 1989). This explanation was probed in many ways and proven valid (Hatzinger et al. 2000, Keck et al. 2002). Particularly, the antidepressant treatment effects upon HPA function in depressive patients were successfully translated in an animal model where high anxiety existed as an innate trait generated by selective breeding. These animals are characterized by an overexpression of central AVP (Landgraf 2006), and treatment with an antidepressant led to a gradual reduction of AVP hypersecretion, reflected by decreased stress-hormone response to dexamethasone/CRH-challenges (Keck et al. 2003). More recent studies are intriguing as they showed that rats with high innate anxiety carry a mutation in the AVP promoter that

denied binding of a repressor, thus explaining increased hypothalamic AVP secretion in the PVN (Murgatroyd et al. 2004). The group led by Neumann employed these rats and studied whether increased anxiety and AVP secretion affects maternal behavior, conferring behavioral traits via a higher level of maternal nursing (Bosch & Neumann 2008) and resulting in early genomic imprinting, possibly via epigenetic modifications. This finding is important because recent human genetic studies highlighted the possibility that changes in AVP/vasopressin receptor 1B (V1B) receptor signaling may contribute to the susceptibility or resilience to depression (van West et al. 2004).

THERAPEUTIC BLOCKING OF VASOPRESSIN RECEPTORS

In comparison to CRHR1 blockers, much less emphasis had been put on the discovery of centrally acting AVP receptor antagonists. In this context, two receptors, the V1A and V1B, are of interest because they are known to be involved in several stress-related behaviors (Bielsky et al. 2005). Antagonizing the V1B receptor is of particular interest, as in animal experiments chronic stress was found to increase levels of V1B receptors, and their blockade was shown to reverse stress-induced suppression of hippocampal neurogenesis (Alonso et al. 2004). The compound SSR149415 is an orally available highly selective nonpeptide V1B receptor antagonist (Serradeil-Le Gal et al. 2002) that was tested in a number of animal models of anxiety- and antidepressant-like behavior (Serradeil-Le Gal et al. 2003). In standard tests, such as the elevated plus maze (discussed above), it produced anxiolytic-like effects, which were particularly pronounced in models of traumatic stress exposure (Griebel et al. 2002). The same authors also noted antidepressant-like activity in the FST and after chronic mild stress, which was comparable to activities observed with the antidepressants fluoxetine (an SSRI) and imipramine (a pharmacologically more promiscuous tricyclic compound, blocking

V1B: vasopressin receptor 1b

reuptake of NE, 5-HT, and exerting many other effects) (**Figure 11**, see color insert). While encouraging, these reports have not used an animal model with established hyperdrive of AVP/V1b signaling but rather employed rat and mouse strains commonly used to evaluate monoamine-based drug candidates. As described for CRH/CRHR1-studies, treatment of mice centrally overexpressing CRH with CRHR1 antagonists produced results in some of these tests that were opposite of those found with the V1B antagonists. Clarification of these questions requires studies in specialized animal models and human proof-of-concept trials that include stress exposures such as those described for CRHR1 antagonists (Ising et al. 2007b).

FUTURE ROLE OF DRUGS TARGETING THE STRESS HORMONE SYSTEM

The Swiss Psychiatrist Manfred Bleuler was the first to study systematically the psychotropic effects of hormones, including those that regulate the response to stress. Since then our knowledge on molecular mechanisms by which adrenal corticosteroids and brain-derived neuropeptides exert their cellular function has multiplied, and clinical psychology has made major contributions to elaborate a clear picture of how the stress-hormone system helps to minimize adversities induced by stress exposure. In recent years, the ability to bridge the gap between cell biology and clinical psychology by means of targeted genetic engineering of mice has further advanced our understanding of the fine-tuned interplay of gene-by-environment interactions. It is also clear that attempts to sort out specific effects of individual hormones results in nontestable hypotheses because the stress-hormone system is so rich in checks and balances that any perturbation at a certain position results in adaptations at many others, obfuscating any simple conclusions. From an evolutionary standpoint, these intrinsically intertwined mechanisms seem important for adaptation to environmental challenges. Individuals with profoundly impaired stress-hormone systems have a poor likelihood of staying in good health when stressed; therefore, maintaining integrity of stress-adaptive capacity is important.

In this light, it is sobering that the vastly expanding knowledge on all levels of research has yet failed to result in successful development of drugs for stress-related disorders directly targeting stress-hormone systems. It is foreseeable that sole or adjunctive treatments with specific drugs directed toward central CRH or vasopressin signaling require a personalized approach, i.e., combinations of genotypes and biomarkers identifying those patients who potentially would benefit from interventions in stress-hormone systems (Holsboer 2008).

SUMMARY POINTS

1. Elevated corticosteroid levels exhibit detrimental effects upon cognition, especially upon the retrieval of declarative memory, and chronic exposure also exerts strong effects on mood and anxiety.

2. Early childhood trauma and genetic vulnerability factors both can result in impaired HPA axis regulation and hypercortisolemia, which in turn increases the risk to develop an affective disorder.

3. Epigenetic modifications having sustained effects on gene expression play a critical role as a molecular interface between life stress and disturbed stress-hormone regulation as well as vulnerability for depression and other stress-related disorders.

4. The balance between mineralocorticoid receptors (MRs) and glucocorticoid receptors (GRs) is a critical factor mediating the effects of hypercortisolemia. Although the endocrine stress response, cognitive impairment, and apoptosis are predominantly GR related, the effects of antidepressant treatments and hippocampal neurogenesis are related to the activity of MRs.

5. GR antagonists are assumed to normalize the disturbed MR/GR balance in stress-related disorders and are currently under investigation as potential drugs for the treatment of psychotic depression.

6. Corticotrophin-releasing hormone (CRH) and arginine vasopressin (AVP) are the major drivers of the neuroendocrine stress response in the brain. These peptides act also as neuromodulators, which are responsible for behavioral alterations, motivational deficits, cognitive impairments, and emotional responses that are typical for depression and anxiety disorders.

7. Blockade of central CRH receptor 1 and AVP receptor 1b showed antidepressant efficacy in animal models of anxiety and depression. However, clinical studies demonstrating clinical efficacy in depression and anxiety disorders are missing because biomarkers are not yet available to identify those patients who have a central overabundance of CRH and/or AVP.

DISCLOSURE STATEMENT

The authors are not aware of any biases that might be perceived as affecting the objectivity of this review.

ACKNOWLEDGMENT

We thank Isabella Wieser for excellent support in preparing figures and art work.

LITERATURE CITED

Alonso R, Griebel G, Pavone G, Stemmelin J, Le FG, Soubrie P. 2004. Blockade of CRF(1) or V(1b) receptors reverses stress-induced suppression of neurogenesis in a mouse model of depression. *Mol. Psychiatry* 9(3):278–86

Appelhof BC, Huyser J, Verweij M, Brouwer JP, van Dyck R, et al. 2006. Glucocorticoids and relapse of major depression (dexamethasone/corticotropin-releasing hormone test in relation to relapse of major depression). *Biol. Psychiatry* 59(8):696–701

Arborelius L, Owens MJ, Plotsky PM, Nemeroff CB. 1999. The role of corticotropin-releasing factor in depression and anxiety disorders. *J. Endocrinol.* 160(1):1–12

Arzt E, Holsboer F. 2006. CRF signaling: molecular specificity for drug targeting in the CNS. *Trends Pharmacol. Sci.* 27(10):531–38

Austin MC, Janosky JE, Murphy HA. 2003. Increased corticotropin-releasing hormone immunoreactivity in monoamine-containing pontine nuclei of depressed suicide men. *Mol Psychiatry* 8(3):324–32

Bachmann CG, Linthorst AC, Holsboer F, Reul JM. 2003. Effect of chronic administration of selective glucocorticoid receptor antagonists on the rat hypothalamic-pituitary-adrenocortical axis. *Neuropsychopharmacology* 28(6):1056–67

Bale TL, Contarino A, Smith GW, Chan R, Gold LH, et al. 2000. Mice deficient for corticotropin-releasing hormone receptor-2 display anxiety-like behaviour and are hypersensitive to stress. *Nat. Genet.* 24(4):410–14

Bale TL, Vale WW. 2004. CRF and CRF receptors: role in stress responsivity and other behaviors. *Annu. Rev. Pharmacol. Toxicol.* 44:525–57

Behl C, Lezoualc'h F, Trapp T, Widmann M, Skutella T, Holsboer F. 1997. Glucocorticoids enhance oxidative stress-induced cell death in hippocampal neurons in vitro. *Endocrinology* 138(1):101–6

Belanoff JK, Flores BH, Kalezhan M, Sund B, Schatzberg AF. 2001. Rapid reversal of psychotic depression using mifepristone. *J. Clin. Psychopharmacol.* 21(5):516–21

Bielsky IF, Hu SB, Ren X, Terwilliger EF, Young LJ. 2005. The V1a vasopressin receptor is necessary and sufficient for normal social recognition: a gene replacement study. *Neuron* 47(4):503–13

Binder EB, Bradley RG, Liu W, Epstein MP, Deveau TC, et al. 2008. Association of FKBP5 polymorphisms and childhood abuse with risk of posttraumatic stress disorder symptoms in adults. *JAMA* 299(11):1291–305

Binder EB, Künzel HE, Nickel T, Kern N, Pfennig A, et al. 2009. HPA-axis regulation at in-patient admission is associated with antidepressant therapy outcome in male but not in female depressed patients. *Psychoneuroendocrinology* 34(1):99–109

Binder EB, Salyakina D, Lichtner P, Wochnik GM, Ising M, et al. 2004. Polymorphisms in FKBP5 are associated with increased recurrence of depressive episodes and rapid response to antidepressant treatment. *Nat. Genet.* 36(12):1319–25

Binneman B, Feltner D, Kolluri S, Shi Y, Qiu R, Stiger T. 2008. A 6-week randomized, placebo-controlled trial of CP-316311 (a selective CRH1 antagonist) in the treatment of major depression. *Am. J. Psychiatry* 165(5):617–20

Bissette G, Klimek V, Pan J, Stockmeier C, Ordway G. 2003. Elevated concentrations of CRF in the locus coeruleus of depressed subjects. *Neuropsychopharmacology* 28(7):1328–35

Bosch OJ, Neumann ID. 2008. Brain vasopressin is an important regulator of maternal behavior independent of dams' trait anxiety. *Proc. Natl. Acad. Sci. USA* 105(44):17139–44

Brunner R, Schaefer D, Hess K, Parzer P, Resch F, Schwab S. 2005. Effect of corticosteroids on short-term and long-term memory. *Neurology* 64(2):335–37

Buchanan TW, Lovallo WR. 2001. Enhanced memory for emotional material following stress-level cortisol treatment in humans. *Psychoneuroendocrinology* 26(3):307–17

Buchanan TW, Tranel D, Adolphs R. 2006. Impaired memory retrieval correlates with individual differences in cortisol response but not autonomic response. *Learn. Mem.* 13(3):382–87

Campbell S, MacQueen G. 2004. The role of the hippocampus in the pathophysiology of major depression. *J. Psychiatr. Neurosci.* 29(6):417–26

Campolongo P, Roozendaal B, Trezza V, Hauer D, Schelling G, et al. 2009. Endocannabinoids in the rat basolateral amygdala enhance memory consolidation and enable glucocorticoid modulation of memory. *Proc. Natl. Acad. Sci. USA* 106(12):4888–93

Chen C, Wilcoxen KM, Huang CQ, Xie YF, McCarthy JR, et al. 2004. Design of 2,5-dimethyl-3-(6-dimethyl-4-methylpyridin-3-yl)-7-dipropylaminopyrazolo[1,5-a]pyrimidine (NBI 30775/R121919) and structure-activity relationships of a series of potent and orally active corticotropin-releasing factor receptor antagonists. *J. Med. Chem.* 47(19):4787–98

Chu JW, Matthias DF, Belanoff J, Schatzberg A, Hoffman AR, Feldman D. 2001. Successful long-term treatment of refractory Cushing's disease with high-dose mifepristone (RU 486). *J. Clin. Endocrinol. Metab.* 86(8):3568–73

Coluccia D, Wolf OT, Kollias S, Roozendaal B, Forster A, de Quervain DJ. 2008. Glucocorticoid therapy-induced memory deficits: acute versus chronic effects. *J. Neurosci.* 28(13):3474–78

Coplan JD, Andrews MW, Rosenblum LA, Owens MJ, Friedman S, et al. 1996. Persistent elevations of cerebrospinal fluid concentrations of corticotropin-releasing factor in adult nonhuman primates exposed to early-life stressors: implications for the pathophysiology of mood and anxiety disorders. *Proc. Natl. Acad. Sci. USA* 93(4):1619–23

Coste SC, Kesterson RA, Heldwein KA, Stevens SL, Heard AD, et al. 2000. Abnormal adaptations to stress and impaired cardiovascular function in mice lacking corticotropin-releasing hormone receptor-2. *Nat. Genet.* 24(4):403–9

Crochemore C, Lu J, Wu Y, Liposits Z, Sousa N, et al. 2005. Direct targeting of hippocampal neurons for apoptosis by glucocorticoids is reversible by mineralocorticoid receptor activation. *Mol. Psychiatry* 10(8):790–98

Croiset G, Nijsen MJ, Kamphuis PJ. 2000. Role of corticotropin-releasing factor, vasopressin and the autonomic nervous system in learning and memory. *Eur. J. Pharmacol.* 405(1–3):225–34

Datson NA, Morsink MC, Meijer OC, de Kloet ER. 2008. Central corticosteroid actions: search for gene targets. *Eur. J. Pharmacol.* 583(2–3):272–89

Dautzenberg FM, Hauger RL. 2002. The CRF peptide family and their receptors: yet more partners discovered. *Trends Pharmacol. Sci.* 23(2):71–77

de Bellis MD, Gold PW, Geracioti TD Jr, Listwak SJ, Kling MA. 1993. Association of fluoxetine treatment with reductions in CSF concentrations of corticotropin-releasing hormone and arginine vasopressin in patients with major depression. *Am. J. Psychiatry* 150(4):656–57

de Goeij DC, Dijkstra H, Tilders FJ. 1992. Chronic psychosocial stress enhances vasopressin, but not corticotropin-releasing factor, in the external zone of the median eminence of male rats: relationship to subordinate status. *Endocrinology* 131(2):847–53

de Kloet CS, Vermetten E, Geuze E, Kavelaars A, Heijnen CJ, Westenberg HG. 2006. Assessment of HPA-axis function in posttraumatic stress disorder: pharmacological and non-pharmacological challenge tests, a review. *J. Psychiatr. Res.* 40(6):550–67

de Kloet ER, Joels M, Holsboer F. 2005. Stress and the brain: from adaptation to disease. *Nat. Rev. Neurosci.* 6(6):463–75

de Quervain DJ, Roozendaal B, McGaugh JL. 1998. Stress and glucocorticoids impair retrieval of long-term spatial memory. *Nature* 394(6695):787–90

de Quervain DJ, Roozendaal B, Nitsch RM, McGaugh JL, Hock C. 2000. Acute cortisone administration impairs retrieval of long-term declarative memory in humans. *Nat. Neurosci.* 3(4):313–14

Deak T, Nguyen KT, Ehrlich AL, Watkins LR, Spencer RL, et al. 1999. The impact of the nonpeptide corticotropin-releasing hormone antagonist antalarmin on behavioral and endocrine responses to stress. *Endocrinology* 140(1):79–86

DeBattista C, Belanoff J, Glass S, Khan A, Horne RL, et al. 2006. Mifepristone versus placebo in the treatment of psychosis in patients with psychotic major depression. *Biol. Psychiatry* 60(12):1343–49

DeRijk RH, Wust S, Meijer OC, Zennaro MC, Federenko IS, et al. 2006. A common polymorphism in the mineralocorticoid receptor modulates stress responsiveness. *J. Clin. Endocrinol. Metab.* 91(12):5083–89

Ehlers CL, Reed TK, Henriksen SJ. 1986. Effects of corticotropin-releasing factor and growth hormone-releasing factor on sleep and activity in rats. *Neuroendocrinology* 42(6):467–74

Feder A, Nestler EJ, Charney DS. 2009. Psychobiology and molecular genetics of resilience. *Nat. Rev. Neurosci.* 10(6):446–57

Gallagher JP, Orozco-Cabal LF, Liu J, Shinnick-Gallagher P. 2008. Synaptic physiology of central CRH system. *Eur. J. Pharmacol.* 583(2–3):215–25

Gillies GE, Linton EA, Lowry PJ. 1982. Corticotropin releasing activity of the new CRF is potentiated several times by vasopressin. *Nature* 299(5881):355–57

Gilpin NW, Richardson HN, Koob GF. 2008. Effects of CRF1-receptor and opioid-receptor antagonists on dependence-induced increases in alcohol drinking by alcohol-preferring (P) rats. *Alcohol Clin. Exp. Res.* 32(9):1535–42

Gold PW, Chrousos G, Kellner C, Post R, Roy A, et al. 1984. Psychiatric implications of basic and clinical studies with corticotropin-releasing factor. *Am. J. Psychiatry* 141(5):619–27

Gould E, Tanapat P, McEwen BS, Flugge G, Fuchs E. 1998. Proliferation of granule cell precursors in the dentate gyrus of adult monkeys is diminished by stress. *Proc. Natl. Acad. Sci. USA* 95(6):3168–71

Grammatopoulos DK, Chrousos GP. 2002. Functional characteristics of CRH receptors and potential clinical applications of CRH-receptor antagonists. *Trends Endocrinol. Metab.* 13(10):436–44

Review article that summarizes stress effects mediated by GR and MR and describes how impaired adaptation can translate into stress disorders.

Animal study demonstrating concordant memory impairing effects of glucocorticoids and stress exposure.

Griebel G, Perrault G, Sanger DJ. 1998. Characterization of the behavioral profile of the non-peptide CRF receptor antagonist CP-154,526 in anxiety models in rodents. Comparison with diazepam and buspirone. *Psychopharmacology (Berl.)* 138(1):55–66

Griebel G, Simiand J, Serradeil-Le GC, Wagnon J, Pascal M, et al. 2002. Anxiolytic- and antidepressant-like effects of the non-peptide vasopressin V1b receptor antagonist, SSR149415, suggest an innovative approach for the treatment of stress-related disorders. *Proc. Natl. Acad. Sci. USA* 99(9):6370–75

Grigoriadis DE. 2005. The corticotropin-releasing factor receptor: a novel target for the treatment of depression and anxiety-related disorders. *Expert Opin. Ther. Targets* 9(4):651–84

Groenink L, Dirks A, Verdouw PM, Schipholt M, Veening JG, et al. 2002. HPA axis dysregulation in mice overexpressing corticotropin releasing hormone. *Biol. Psychiatry* 51(11):875–81

Habib KE, Weld KP, Rice KC, Pushkas J, Champoux M, et al. 2000. Oral administration of a corticotropin-releasing hormone receptor antagonist significantly attenuates behavioral, neuroendocrine, and autonomic responses to stress in primates. *Proc. Natl. Acad. Sci. USA* 97(11):6079–84

Hajek T, Bernier D, Slaney C, Propper L, Schmidt M, et al. 2008. A comparison of affected and unaffected relatives of patients with bipolar disorder using proton magnetic resonance spectroscopy. *J. Psychiatry Neurosci.* 33(6):531–40

Harris GW. 1948. Neural control of the pituitary gland. *Physiol. Rev.* 28(2):139–79

Hatzinger M, Hemmeter UM, Baumann K, Brand S, Holsboer-Trachsler E. 2002. The combined DEX-CRH test in treatment course and long-term outcome of major depression. *J. Psychiatr. Res.* 36(5):287–97

Hatzinger M, Wotjak CT, Naruo T, Simchen R, Keck ME, et al. 2000. Endogenous vasopressin contributes to hypothalamic-pituitary-adrenocortical alterations in aged rats. *J. Endocrinol.* 164(2):197–205

Heilig M, Koob GF. 2007. A key role for corticotropin-releasing factor in alcohol dependence. *Trends Neurosci.* 30(8):399–406

Heim C, Mletzko T, Purselle D, Musselman DL, Nemeroff CB. 2008a. The dexamethasone/corticotropin-releasing factor test in men with major depression: role of childhood trauma. *Biol. Psychiatry* 63(4):398–405

Heim C, Newport DJ, Mletzko T, Miller AH, Nemeroff CB. 2008b. The link between childhood trauma and depression: insights from HPA axis studies in humans. *Psychoneuroendocrinology* 33(6):693–710

Heinrichs SC, de Souza EB, Schulteis G, Lapsansky JL, Grigoriadis DE. 2002. Brain penetrance, receptor occupancy and antistress in vivo efficacy of a small molecule corticotropin releasing factor type I receptor selective antagonist. *Neuropsychopharmacology* 27(2):194–202

Held K, Künzel HE, Ising M, Schmid DA, Zobel A, et al. 2004. Treatment with the CRH1-receptor-antagonist R121919 improves sleep-EEG in patients with depression. *J. Psychiatr. Res.* 38(2):129–36

Hennings JM, Owashi T, Binder EB, Horstmann S, Menke A, et al. 2009. Clinical characteristics and treatment outcome in a representative sample of depressed inpatients—findings from the Munich Antidepressant Response Signature (MARS) project. *J. Psychiatr. Res.* 43(3):215–29

Heuser IJ, Bissette G, Dettling M, Schweiger U, Gotthardt U, et al. 1998. Cerebrospinal fluid concentrations of corticotropin-releasing hormone, vasopressin, and somatostatin in depressed patients and healthy controls: response to amitriptyline treatment. *Depress. Anxiety* 8(2):71–79

Heuser IJ, Yassouridis A, Holsboer F. 1994. The combined dexamethasone/CRH test: a refined laboratory test for psychiatric disorders. *J. Psychiatr. Res.* 28:341–56

Holsboer F. 1983. Prediction of clinical course by dexamethasone suppression test (DST) response in depressed patients—physiological and clinical construct validity of the DST. *Pharmacopsychiatria* 16:186–91

Holsboer F. 1999. The rationale for corticotropin-releasing hormone receptor (CRH-R) antagonists to treat depression and anxiety. *J. Psychiatry Res.* 33:181–214

Holsboer F. 2000. The corticosteroid receptor hypothesis of depression. *Neuropsychopharmacology* 23:477–501

Holsboer F. 2008. How can we realize the promise of personalized antidepressant medicines? *Nat. Rev. Neurosci.* 9(8):638–46

Holsboer F, Gerken A, von Bardeleben U, Grimm W, Beyer H, et al. 1986. Human corticotropin-releasing hormone in depression. *Biol. Psychiatry* 21(7):601–11

Holsboer F, Ising M. 2008. Central CRH system in depression and anxiety—evidence from clinical studies with CRH(1) receptor antagonists. *Eur. J. Pharmacol.* 583(2–3):350–57

Holsboer F, Lauer CJ, Schreiber W, Krieg JC. 1995. Altered hypothalamic-pituitary-adrenocortical regulation in healthy subjects at high familial risk for affective disorders. *Neuroendocrinology* 62:340–47

Holsboer F, von Bardeleben U, Gerken A, Stalla GK, Müller OA. 1984. Blunted corticotropin and normal cortisol response to human corticotropin-releasing factor in depression. *N. Engl. J. Med.* 311(17):1127

Holsboer F, von Bardeleben U, Steiger A. 1988. Effects of intravenous corticotropin-releasing hormone upon sleep-related growth hormone surge and sleep EEG in man. *Neuroendocrinology* 48(1):32–38

Holsboer-Trachsler E, Stohler R, Hatzinger M. 1991. Repeated administration of the combined dexamethasone-human corticotropin releasing hormone stimulation test during treatment of depression. *Psychiatry Res.* 38:163–71

Hsu SY, Hsueh AJ. 2001. Human stresscopin and stresscopin-related peptide are selective ligands for the type 2 corticotropin-releasing hormone receptor. *Nat. Med.* 7(5):605–11

Ising M, Horstmann S, Kloiber S, Lucae S, Binder EB, et al. 2007a. Combined dexamethasone/corticotropin releasing hormone test predicts treatment response in major depression—a potential biomarker? *Biol. Psychiatry* 62(1):47–54

Ising M, Künzel HE, Binder EB, Nickel T, Modell S, Holsboer F. 2005. The combined dexamethasone/CRH test as a potential surrogate marker in depression. *Prog. Neuropsychopharmacol. Biol. Psychiatry* 29(6):1085–93

Ising M, Zimmermann US, Künzel HE, Uhr M, Foster AC, et al. 2007b. High-affinity CRF(1) receptor antagonist NBI-34041: preclinical and clinical data suggest safety and efficacy in attenuating elevated stress response. *Neuropsychopharmacology* 32(9):1941–49

Joels M, Karst H, DeRijk R, de Kloet ER. 2008. The coming out of the brain mineralocorticoid receptor. *Trends Neurosci.* 31(1):1–7

Johnson DA, Grant EJ, Ingram CD, Gartside SE. 2007. Glucocorticoid receptor antagonists hasten and augment neurochemical responses to a selective serotonin reuptake inhibitor antidepressant. *Biol. Psychiatry* 62(11):1228–35

Johnson DA, Ingram CD, Grant EJ, Craighead M, Gartside SE. 2009. Glucocorticoid receptor antagonism augments fluoxetine-induced downregulation of the 5-HT transporter. *Neuropsychopharmacology* 34(2):399–409

Kaminsky ZA, Tang T, Wang SC, Ptak C, Oh GH, et al. 2009. DNA methylation profiles in monozygotic and dizygotic twins. *Nat. Genet.* 41(2):240–45

Karst H, Berger S, Turiault M, Tronche F, Schutz G, Joels M. 2005. Mineralocorticoid receptors are indispensable for nongenomic modulation of hippocampal glutamate transmission by corticosterone. *Proc. Natl. Acad. Sci. USA* 102(52):19204–7

Keck ME, Welt T, Müller MB, Uhr M, Ohl F, et al. 2003. Reduction of hypothalamic vasopressinergic hyperdrive contributes to clinically relevant behavioral and neuroendocrine effects of chronic paroxetine treatment in a psychopathological rat model. *Neuropsychopharmacology* 28(2):235–43

Keck ME, Welt T, Wigger A, Renner U, Engelmann M, et al. 2001. The anxiolytic effect of the CRH(1) receptor antagonist R121919 depends on innate emotionality in rats. *Eur. J. Neurosci.* 13(2):373–80

Keck ME, Wigger A, Welt T, Müller MB, Gesing A, et al. 2002. Vasopressin mediates the response of the combined dexamethasone/CRH test in hyper-anxious rats: implications for pathogenesis of affective disorders. *Neuropsychopharmacology* 26(1):94–105

Kimura M, Muller-Preuss P, Lu A, Wiesner E, Flachskamm C, et al. 2009. Conditional corticotropin-releasing hormone overexpression in the mouse forebrain enhances rapid eye movement sleep. *Mol. Psychiatry.* In press

Kirchheiner J, Lorch R, Lebedeva E, Seeringer A, Roots I, et al. 2008. Genetic variants in FKBP5 affecting response to antidepressant drug treatment. *Pharmacogenomics* 9(7):841–46

Kirschbaum C, Pirke KM, Hellhammer DH. 1993. The Trier Social Stress Test—a tool for investigating psychobiological stress responses in a laboratory setting. *Neuropsychobiology* 28(1–2):76–81

Kishimoto T, Radulovic J, Radulovic M, Lin CR, Schrick C, et al. 2000. Deletion of crhr2 reveals an anxiolytic role for corticotropin-releasing hormone receptor-2. *Nat. Genet.* 24(4):415–19

Korte SM, de Boer SF. 2003. A robust animal model of state anxiety: fear-potentiated behaviour in the elevated plus-maze. *Eur. J. Pharmacol.* 463(1–3):163–75

Kraft JB, Peters EJ, Slager SL, Jenkins GD, Reinalda MS, et al. 2007. Analysis of association between the serotonin transporter and antidepressant response in a large clinical sample. *Biol. Psychiatry* 61(6):734–42

Kronenberg G, Kirste I, Inta D, Chourbaji S, Heuser I, et al. 2009. Reduced hippocampal neurogenesis in the GR+/− genetic mouse model of depression. *Eur. Arch. Psychiatry Clin. Neurosci.* In press

Künzel HE, Zobel AW, Nickel T, Ackl N, Uhr M, et al. 2003. Treatment of depression with the CRH-1-receptor antagonist R121919: endocrine changes and side effects. *J. Psychiatr. Res.* 37(6):525–33

Lancel M, Müller-Preuss P, Wigger A, Landgraf R, Holsboer F. 2002. The CRH1 receptor antagonist R121919 attenuates stress-elicited sleep disturbances in rats, particularly in those with high innate anxiety. *J. Psychiatr. Res.* 36(4):197–208

Landgraf R. 2006. The involvement of the vasopressin system in stress-related disorders. *CNS Neurol. Disord. Drug Targets.* 5(2):167–79

Leon-Carrion J, Atutxa AM, Mangas MA, Soto-Moreno A, Pumar A, et al. 2009. A clinical profile of memory impairment in humans due to endogenous glucocorticoid excess. *Clin. Endocrinol. (Oxf.)* 70(2):192–200

Levine S. 1967. Maternal and environmental influences on the adrenocortical response to stress in weanling rats. *Science* 156(772):258–60

Levine S, Mody T. 2003. The long-term psychobiological consequences of intermittent postnatal separation in the squirrel monkey. *Neurosci. Biobehav. Rev.* 27(1–2):83–89

Licinio J, O'Kirwan F, Irizarry K, Merriman B, Thakur S, et al. 2004. Association of a corticotropin-releasing hormone receptor 1 haplotype and antidepressant treatment response in Mexican-Americans. *Mol. Psychiatry* 9(12):1075–82

Liebsch G, Landgraf R, Engelmann M, Lorscher P, Holsboer F. 1999. Differential behavioural effects of chronic infusion of CRH 1 and CRH 2 receptor antisense oligonucleotides into the rat brain. *J. Psychiatr. Res.* 33(2):153–63

Linthorst AC, Flachskamm C, Hopkins SJ, Hoadley ME, Labeur MS, et al. 1997. Long-term intracerebroventricular infusion of corticotropin-releasing hormone alters neuroendocrine, neurochemical, autonomic, behavioral, and cytokine responses to a systemic inflammatory challenge. *J. Neurosci.* 17(11):4448–60

Lu A, Steiner MA, Whittle N, Vogl AM, Walser SM, et al. 2008. Conditional CRH overexpressing mice: an animal model for stress-elicited pathologies and treatments that target the central CRH system. *Mol. Psychiatry* 13(11):1028–42

Malberg JE, Eisch AJ, Nestler EJ, Duman RS. 2000. Chronic antidepressant treatment increases neurogenesis in adult rat hippocampus. *J. Neurosci.* 20(24):9104–10

Marsicano G, Wotjak CT, Azad SC, Bisogno T, Rammes G, et al. 2002. The endogenous cannabinoid system controls extinction of aversive memories. *Nature* 418(6897):530–34

Mayer JL, Klumpers L, Maslam S, de Kloet ER, Joels M, Lucassen PJ. 2006. Brief treatment with the glucocorticoid receptor antagonist mifepristone normalises the corticosterone-induced reduction of adult hippocampal neurogenesis. *J. Neuroendocrinol.* 18(8):629–31

McClung CA, Nestler EJ. 2008. Neuroplasticity mediated by altered gene expression. *Neuropsychopharmacology* 33(1):3–17

McEwen BS. 2000. Effects of adverse experiences for brain structure and function. *Biol. Psychiatry* 48(8):721–31

McGowan PO, Sasaki A, D'Alessio AC, Dymov S, Labonte B, et al. 2009. Epigenetic regulation of the glucocorticoid receptor in human brain associates with childhood abuse. *Nat. Neurosci.* 12(3):342–48

Meijsing SH, Pufall MA, So AY, Bates DL, Chen L, Yamamoto KR. 2009. DNA binding site sequence directs glucocorticoid receptor structure and activity. *Science* 324(5925):407–10

Mitra R, Sapolsky RM. 2008. Acute corticosterone treatment is sufficient to induce anxiety and amygdaloid dendritic hypertrophy. *Proc. Natl. Acad. Sci. USA* 105(14):5573–78

Modell S, Ising M, Holsboer F, Lauer CJ. 2005. The Munich vulnerability study on affective disorders: premorbid polysomnographic profile of affected high-risk probands. *Biol. Psychiatry* 58(9):694–99

Modell S, Yassouridis A, Huber J, Holsboer F. 1997. Corticosteroid receptor function is decreased in depressed patients. *Neuroendocrinology* 65(3):216–22

Müller MB, Lucassen PJ, Yassouridis A, Hoogendijk WJ, Holsboer F, Swaab DF. 2001. Neither major depression nor glucocorticoid treatment affects the cellular integrity of the human hippocampus. *Eur. J. Neurosci.* 14(10):1603–12

CRH overexpression restricted to central neurons in mouse brains results in an anxious and hyperaroused phenotype.

Müller MB, Zimmermann S, Sillaber I, Hagemeyer TP, Deussing JM, et al. 2003. Limbic corticotropin-releasing hormone receptor 1 mediates anxiety-related behavior and hormonal adaptation to stress. *Nat. Neurosci.* 6(10):1100–7

Murgatroyd C, Wigger A, Frank E, Singewald N, Bunck M, et al. 2004. Impaired repression at a vasopressin promoter polymorphism underlies overexpression of vasopressin in a rat model of trait anxiety. *J. Neurosci.* 24(35):7762–70

Nemeroff CB, Owens MJ, Bissette G, Andorn AC, Stanley M. 1988. Reduced corticotropin releasing factor binding sites in the frontal cortex of suicide victims. *Arch. Gen. Psychiatry* 45(6):577–79

Nemeroff CB, Widerlov E, Bissette G, Walleus H, Karlsson I, et al. 1984. Elevated concentrations of CSF corticotropin-releasing factor-like immunoreactivity in depressed patients. *Science* 226(4680):1342–44

Newell-Price J, Bertagna X, Grossman AB, Nieman LK. 2006. Cushing's syndrome. *Lancet* 367(9522):1605–17

Nicolson NA. 2004. Childhood parental loss and cortisol levels in adult men. *Psychoneuroendocrinology* 29(8):1012–18

Nieman LK, Chrousos GP, Kellner C, Spitz IM, Nisula BC, et al. 1985. Successful treatment of Cushing's syndrome with the glucocorticoid antagonist RU 486. *J. Clin. Endocrinol. Metab.* 61(3):536–40

Obradovic D, Tirard M, Nemethy Z, Hirsch O, Gronemeyer H, Almeida OF. 2004. DAXX, FLASH, and FAF-1 modulate mineralocorticoid and glucocorticoid receptor-mediated transcription in hippocampal cells—toward a basis for the opposite actions elicited by two nuclear receptors? *Mol. Pharmacol.* 65(3):761–69

Oitzl MS, Fluttert M, Sutanto W, de Kloet ER. 1998. Continuous blockade of brain glucocorticoid receptors facilitates spatial learning and memory in rats. *Eur. J. Neurosci.* 10(12):3759–66

Oshima A, Flachskamm C, Reul JM, Holsboer F, Linthorst AC. 2003. Altered serotonergic neurotransmission but normal hypothalamic-pituitary-adrenocortical axis activity in mice chronically treated with the corticotropin-releasing hormone receptor type 1 antagonist NBI 30775. *Neuropsychopharmacology* 28(12):2148–59

Patchev VK, Hassan AH, Holsboer DF, Almeida OF. 1996. The neurosteroid tetrahydroprogesterone attenuates the endocrine response to stress and exerts glucocorticoid-like effects on vasopressin gene transcription in the rat hypothalamus. *Neuropsychopharmacology* 15(6):533–40

Patchev VK, Shoaib M, Holsboer F, Almeida OF. 1994. The neurosteroid tetrahydroprogesterone counteracts corticotropin-releasing hormone-induced anxiety and alters the release and gene expression of corticotropin-releasing hormone in the rat hypothalamus. *Neuroscience* 62(1):265–71

Penalva RG, Flachskamm C, Zimmermann S, Wurst W, Holsboer F, et al. 2002. Corticotropin-releasing hormone receptor type 1-deficiency enhances hippocampal serotonergic neurotransmission: an in vivo microdialysis study in mutant mice. *Neuroscience* 109(2):253–66

Pfennig A, Kunzel HE, Kern N, Ising M, Majer M, et al. 2005. Hypothalamus-pituitary-adrenal system regulation and suicidal behavior in depression. *Biol. Psychiatry* 57(4):336–42

Piazza PV, Rouge-Pont F, Deroche V, Maccari S, Simon H, Le MM. 1996. Glucocorticoids have state-dependent stimulant effects on the mesencephalic dopaminergic transmission. *Proc. Natl. Acad. Sci. USA* 93(16):8716–20

Potter E, Sutton S, Donaldson C, Chen R, Perrin M, et al. 1994. Distribution of corticotropin-releasing factor receptor mRNA expression in the rat brain and pituitary. *Proc. Natl. Acad. Sci. USA* 91(19):8777–81

Pryce CR, Ruedi-Bettschen D, Dettling AC, Weston A, Russig H, et al. 2005. Long-term effects of early-life environmental manipulations in rodents and primates: potential animal models in depression research. *Neurosci. Biobehav. Rev.* 29(4–5):649–74

Purba JS, Hoogendijk WJ, Hofman MA, Swaab DF. 1996. Increased number of vasopressin- and oxytocin-expressing neurons in the paraventricular nucleus of the hypothalamus in depression. *Arch. Gen. Psychiatry* 53(2):137–43

Reul JM, Gesing A, Droste S, Stec IS, Weber A, et al. 2000. The brain mineralocorticoid receptor: greedy for ligand, mysterious in function. *Eur. J. Pharmacol.* 405(1–3):235–49

Reul JM, Holsboer F. 2002. Corticotropin-releasing factor receptors 1 and 2 in anxiety and depression. *Curr. Opin. Pharmacol.* 2(1):23–33

Absence of CRH1 receptors in the forebrains of mice results in reduced anxiety-like behavior.

Postmortem study with brains of suicide victims revealing reduced CRH-binding sites in the frontal cortex as result of chronic CRH overexpression.

Reul JM, Stec I, Soder M, Holsboer F. 1993. Chronic treatment of rats with the antidepressant amitriptyline attenuates the activity of the hypothalamic-pituitary-adrenocortical system. *Endocrinology* 133(1):312–20

Risbrough VB, Geyer MA, Hauger RL, Coste S, Stenzel-Poore M, et al. 2009. CRF1 and CRF2 receptors are required for potentiated startle to contextual but not discrete cues. *Neuropsychopharmacology* 34(6):1494–503

Roozendaal B. 2000. 1999 Curt P. Richter award. Glucocorticoids and the regulation of memory consolidation. *Psychoneuroendocrinology* 25(3):213–38

Roozendaal B, Okuda S, de Quervain DJ, McGaugh JL. 2006. Glucocorticoids interact with emotion-induced noradrenergic activation in influencing different memory functions. *Neuroscience* 138(3):901–10

Rubinow DR, Post RM, Savard R, Gold PW. 1984. Cortisol hypersecretion and cognitive impairment in depression. *Arch. Gen. Psychiatry* 41(3):279–83

Rupprecht R. 1997. The neuropsychopharmacological potential of neuroactive steroids. *J. Psychiatr. Res.* 31(3):297–314

Rupprecht R, Holsboer F. 1999. Neuroactive steroids: mechanisms of action and neuropsychopharmacological perspectives. *Trends Neurosci.* 22(9):410–16

Rupprecht R, Rammes G, Eser D, Baghai TC, Schule C, et al. 2009. Translocator protein (18 kD) as target for anxiolytics without benzodiazepine-like side effects. *Science* 325(5939):490–93

Sachar EJ. 1967. Corticosteroids in depressive illness. II. A longitudinal psychoendocrine study. *Arch. Gen. Psychiatry* 17(5):554–67

Sanchez MM, Young LJ, Plotsky PM, Insel TR. 1999. Autoradiographic and in situ hybridization localization of corticotropin-releasing factor 1 and 2 receptors in nonhuman primate brain. *J. Comp. Neurol.* 408(3):365–77

Sandi C, Cordero MI, Ugolini A, Varea E, Caberlotto L, Large CH. 2008. Chronic stress-induced alterations in amygdala responsiveness and behavior-modulation by trait anxiety and corticotropin-releasing factor systems. *Eur. J. Neurosci.* 28(9):1836–48

Santarelli L, Saxe M, Gross C, Surget A, Battaglia F, et al. 2003. Requirement of hippocampal neurogenesis for the behavioral effects of antidepressants. *Science* 301(5634):805–9

Sapolsky RM. 2000. Glucocorticoids and hippocampal atrophy in neuropsychiatric disorders. *Arch. Gen. Psychiatry* 57(10):925–35

Sapolsky RM. 2003. Stress and plasticity in the limbic system. *Neurochem. Res.* 28(11):1735–42

Sato H, Horikawa Y, Iizuka K, Sakurai N, Tanaka T, et al. 2008. Large-scale analysis of glucocorticoid target genes in rat hypothalamus. *J. Neurochem.* 106(2):805–14

Schaaf MJ, Hoetelmans RW, de Kloet ER, Vreugdenhil E. 1997. Corticosterone regulates expression of BDNF and trkB but not NT-3 and trkC mRNA in the rat hippocampus. *J. Neurosci. Res.* 48(4):334–41

Schatzberg AF, Rothschild AJ, Langlais PJ, Bird ED, Cole JO. 1985. A corticosteroid/dopamine hypothesis for psychotic depression and related states. *J. Psychiatr. Res.* 19(1):57–64

Schüle C, Baghai TC, Eser D, Hafner S, Born C, et al. 2009. The combined dexamethasone/CRH test (DEX/CRH test) and prediction of acute treatment response in major depression. *PLoS ONE* 4(1):e4324

Selye H. 1936. A syndrome produced by diverse nocuous agents. *Nature* 138:32

Selye H. 1973. The evolution of the stress concept. *Am. Sci.* 61(6):692–99

Serradeil-Le Gal C, Derick S, Brossard G, Manning M, Simiand J, et al. 2003. Functional and pharmacological characterization of the first specific agonist and antagonist for the V1b receptor in mammals. *Stress* 6(3):199–206

Serradeil-Le Gal C, Wagnon J, Simiand J, Griebel G, Lacour C, et al. 2002. Characterization of (2S,4R)-1-[5-chloro-1-[(2,4-dimethoxyphenyl)sulfonyl]-3-(2-methoxy-phenyl)-2-oxo- 2,3-dihydro-1H-indol-3-yl]-4-hydroxy-N,N-dimethyl-2-pyrrolidine carboxamide (SSR149415), a selective and orally active vasopressin V1b receptor antagonist. *J. Pharmacol. Exp. Ther.* 300(3):1122–30

Siegmund A, Dahlhoff M, Habersetzer U, Mederer A, Wolf E, et al. 2009. Maternal inexperience as a risk factor of innate fear and PTSD-like symptoms in mice. *J. Psychiatr. Res.* In press

Sillaber I, Rammes G, Zimmermann S, Mahal B, Zieglgansberger W, et al. 2002. Enhanced and delayed stress-induced alcohol drinking in mice lacking functional CRH1 receptors. *Science* 296(5569):931–33

Smith GW, Aubry JM, Dellu F, Contarino A, Bilezikjian LM, et al. 1998. Corticotropin releasing factor receptor 1-deficient mice display decreased anxiety, impaired stress response, and aberrant neuroendocrine development. *Neuron* 20(6):1093–102

Soravia LM, Heinrichs M, Aerni A, Maroni C, Schelling G, et al. 2006. Glucocorticoids reduce phobic fear in humans. *Proc. Natl. Acad. Sci. USA* 103(14):5585–90

Steckler T, Dautzenberg FM. 2006. Corticotropin-releasing factor receptor antagonists in affective disorders and drug dependence—an update. *CNS Neurol. Disord. Drug Targets* 5(2):147–65

Steckler T, Holsboer F. 2001. Interaction between the cholinergic system and CRH in the modulation of spatial discrimination learning in mice. *Brain Res.* 906(1–2):46–59

Steiger A. 2007a. Neurochemical regulation of sleep. *J. Psychiatr. Res.* 41(7):537–52

Steiger A. 2007b. Neuroendocrinology of sleep. In *Handbook of Neurochemistry and Molecular Neurobiology—Behavioral Neurochemistry, Neuroendocrinology and Molecular Neurobiology*, ed. A Lajtha, J Blaustein, pp. 897–932. Berlin/Heidelberg: Springer

Stenzel-Poore MP, Cameron VA, Vaughan J, Sawchenko PE, Vale W. 1992. Development of Cushing's syndrome in corticotropin-releasing factor transgenic mice. *Endocrinology* 130(6):3378–86

Ströhle A, Scheel M, Modell S, Holsboer F. 2008. Blunted ACTH response to dexamethasone suppression-CRH stimulation in posttraumatic stress disorder. *J. Psychiatr. Res.* 42(14):1185–88

Surget A, Saxe M, Leman S, Ibarguen-Vargas Y, Chalon S, et al. 2008. Drug-dependent requirement of hippocampal neurogenesis in a model of depression and of antidepressant reversal. *Biol. Psychiatry* 64(4):293–301

Swanson LW, Sawchenko PE, Rivier J, Vale WW. 1983. Organization of ovine corticotropin-releasing factor immunoreactive cells and fibers in the rat brain: an immunohistochemical study. *Neuroendocrinology* 36(3):165–86

Takahashi H, Hakamata Y, Watanabe Y, Kikuno R, Miyata T, Numa S. 1983. Complete nucleotide sequence of the human corticotropin-beta-lipotropin precursor gene. *Nucleic Acids Res.* 11(19):6847–58

Timpl P, Spanagel R, Sillaber I, Kresse A, Reul JM, et al. 1998. Impaired stress response and reduced anxiety in mice lacking a functional corticotropin-releasing hormone receptor 1. *Nat. Genet.* 19(2):162–66

Touma C, Bunck M, Glasl L, Nussbaumer M, Palme R, et al. 2008. Mice selected for high versus low stress reactivity: a new animal model for affective disorders. *Psychoneuroendocrinology* 33(6):839–62

Touma C, Fenzl T, Ruschel J, Palme R, Holsboer F, et al. 2009. Rhythmicity in mice selected for extremes in stress reactivity: behavioural, endocrine and sleep changes resembling endophenotypes of major depression. *PLoS ONE* 4(1):e4325

Trapp T, Holsboer F. 1996. Heterodimerization between mineralocorticoid and glucocorticoid receptors increases the functional diversity of corticosteroid action. *Trends Pharmacol. Sci.* 17(4):145–49

Trapp T, Rupprecht R, Castren M, Reul JM, Holsboer F. 1994. Heterodimerization between mineralocorticoid and glucocorticoid receptor: a new principle of glucocorticoid action in the CNS. *Neuron* 13(6):1457–62

Tsankova N, Renthal W, Kumar A, Nestler EJ. 2007. Epigenetic regulation in psychiatric disorders. *Nat. Rev. Neurosci.* 8(5):355–67

Tyrka AR, Wier L, Price LH, Ross N, Anderson GM, et al. 2008. Childhood parental loss and adult hypothalamic-pituitary-adrenal function. *Biol. Psychiatry* 63(12):1147–54

Uhr M, Tontsch A, Namendorf C, Ripke S, Lucae S, et al. 2008. Polymorphisms in the drug transporter gene ABCB1 predict antidepressant treatment response in depression. *Neuron* 57(2):203–9

Vale WW, Spiess J, Rivier C, Rivier J. 1981. Characterization of a 41-residue ovine hypothalamic peptide that stimulates secretion of corticotropin and beta-endorphin. *Science* 213(4514):1394–97

Valentino RJ, Liouterman L, van Bockstaele EJ. 2001. Evidence for regional heterogeneity in corticotropin-releasing factor interactions in the dorsal raphe nucleus. *J. Comp. Neurol.* 435(4):450–63

Van Der Lely AJ, Foeken K, Van Der Mast RC, Lamberts SW. 1991. Rapid reversal of acute psychosis in the Cushing syndrome with the cortisol-receptor antagonist mifepristone (RU 486). *Ann. Intern. Med.* 114(2):143–44

Review about the role of epigenetic mechanisms in gene regulation and their implications for depression, drug addiction, and schizophrenia.

van Londen L, Goekoop JG, van Kempen GM, Frankhuijzen-Sierevogel AC, Wiegant VM, et al. 1997. Plasma levels of arginine vasopressin elevated in patients with major depression. *Neuropsychopharmacology* 17(4):284–92

Van Pett K, Viau V, Bittencourt JC, Chan RK, Li HY, et al. 2000. Distribution of mRNAs encoding CRF receptors in brain and pituitary of rat and mouse. *J. Comp. Neurol.* 428(2):191–212

van Rossum EF, Binder EB, Majer M, Koper JW, Ising M, et al. 2006. Polymorphisms of the glucocorticoid receptor gene and major depression. *Biol. Psychiatry* 59(8):681–88

van West D, del Favero J, Aulchenko Y, Oswald P, Souery D, et al. 2004. A major SNP haplotype of the arginine vasopressin 1B receptor protects against recurrent major depression. *Mol. Psychiatry* 9(3):287–92

von Bardeleben U, Holsboer F. 1989. Cortisol response to a combined dexamethasone-human corticotrophin-releasing hormone challenge in patients with depression. *J. Neuroendocrinol.* 1(6):485–88

von Bardeleben U, Holsboer F, Stalla GK, Müller OA. 1985. Combined administration of human corticotropin-releasing factor and lysine vasopressin induces cortisol escape from dexamethasone suppression in healthy subjects. *Life Sci.* 37(17):1613–18

Vreeburg SA, Hoogendijk WJ, van PJ, DeRijk RH, Verhagen JC, et al. 2009. Major depressive disorder and hypothalamic-pituitary-adrenal axis activity: results from a large cohort study. *Arch. Gen. Psychiatry* 66(6):617–26

Wahlberg K, Ghatan PH, Modell S, Nygren A, Ingvar M, et al. 2009. Suppressed neuroendocrine stress response in depressed women on job-stress-related long-term sick leave: a stable marker potentially suggestive of preexisting vulnerability. *Biol. Psychiatry* 65(9):742–47

Wang HL, Wayner MJ, Chai CY, Lee EH. 1998. Corticotrophin-releasing factor produces a long-lasting enhancement of synaptic efficacy in the hippocampus. *Eur. J. Neurosci.* 10(11):3428–37

Weaver IC. 2007. Epigenetic programming by maternal behavior and pharmacological intervention. Nature versus nurture: Let's call the whole thing off. *Epigenetics* 2(1):22–28

Weaver IC, Cervoni N, Champagne FA, D'Alessio AC, Sharma S, et al. 2004. Epigenetic programming by maternal behavior. *Nat. Neurosci.* 7(8):847–54

Weaver IC, Champagne FA, Brown SE, Dymov S, Sharma S, et al. 2005. Reversal of maternal programming of stress responses in adult offspring through methyl supplementation: altering epigenetic marking later in life. *J. Neurosci.* 25(47):11045–54

Wigger A, Sanchez MM, Mathys KC, Ebner K, Frank E, et al. 2004. Alterations in central neuropeptide expression, release, and receptor binding in rats bred for high anxiety: critical role of vasopressin. *Neuropsychopharmacology* 29(1):1–14

Wong ML, Kling MA, Munson PJ, Listwak S, Licinio J, et al. 2000. Pronounced and sustained central hypernoradrenergic function in major depression with melancholic features: relation to hypercortisolism and corticotropin-releasing hormone. *Proc. Natl. Acad. Sci. USA* 97(1):325–30

Wotjak CT, Kubota M, Liebsch G, Montkowski A, Holsboer F, et al. 1996. Release of vasopressin within the rat paraventricular nucleus in response to emotional stress: a novel mechanism of regulating adrenocorticotropic hormone secretion? *J. Neurosci.* 16(23):7725–32

Yehuda R. 2002. Post-traumatic stress disorder. *N. Engl. J. Med.* 346(2):108–14

Yehuda R, Bell A, Bierer LM, Schmeidler J. 2008. Maternal, not paternal, PTSD is related to increased risk for PTSD in offspring of Holocaust survivors. *J. Psychiatr. Res.* 42(13):1104–11

Yehuda R, Cai G, Golier JA, Sarapas C, Galea S, et al. 2009. Gene expression patterns associated with posttraumatic stress disorder following exposure to the World Trade Center attacks. *Biol. Psychiatry* 66(7):708–11

Yehuda R, Halligan SL, Golier JA, Grossman R, Bierer LM. 2004. Effects of trauma exposure on the cortisol response to dexamethasone administration in PTSD and major depressive disorder. *Psychoneuroendocrinology* 29(3):389–404

Yu S, Holsboer F, Almeida OF. 2008. Neuronal actions of glucocorticoids: focus on depression. *J. Steroid Biochem. Mol. Biol.* 108(3–5):300–9

Zambrowicz BP, Imamoto A, Fiering S, Herzenberg LA, Kerr WG, Soriano P. 1997. Disruption of overlapping transcripts in the ROSA beta geo 26 gene trap strain leads to widespread expression of beta-galactosidase in mouse embryos and hematopoietic cells. *Proc. Natl. Acad. Sci. USA* 94(8):3789–94

The intensity of maternal care of rat mothers influences hippocampal GR activity in the offspring by epigenetic mechanisms.

Micro-array study in PTSD demonstrating altered activity of genes involved in HPA axis regulation.

Zimmermann U, Spring K, Kunz-Ebrecht SR, Uhr M, Wittchen HU, Holsboer F. 2004. Effect of ethanol on hypothalamic-pituitary-adrenal system response to psychosocial stress in sons of alcohol-dependent fathers. *Neuropsychopharmacology* 29(6):1156–65

Zobel AW, Nickel T, Künzel HE, Ackl N, Sonntag A, et al. 2000. Effects of the high-affinity corticotropin-releasing hormone receptor 1 antagonist R121919 in major depression: the first 20 patients treated. *J. Psychiatr. Res.* 34(3):171–81

Zobel AW, Yassouridis A, Frieboes RM, Holsboer F. 1999. Prediction of medium-term outcome by cortisol response to the combined dexamethasone-CRH test in patients with remitted depression. *Am. J. Psychiatry* 156:949–51

First clinical trial showing antidepressant efficacy of a CRHR1 antagonist in major depression.

Structural Plasticity and Hippocampal Function

Benedetta Leuner and Elizabeth Gould

Department of Psychology, Neuroscience Institute, Princeton University, Princeton, New Jersey 08544; email: goulde@princeton.edu

Annu. Rev. Psychol. 2010. 61:111–40

The *Annual Review of Psychology* is online at psych.annualreviews.org

This article's doi: 10.1146/annurev.psych.093008.100359

Key Words

adult neurogenesis, anxiety, learning, memory, synapse

Abstract

The hippocampus is a region of the mammalian brain that shows an impressive capacity for structural reorganization. Preexisting neural circuits undergo modifications in dendritic complexity and synapse number, and entirely novel neural connections are formed through the process of neurogenesis. These types of structural change were once thought to be restricted to development. However, it is now generally accepted that the hippocampus remains structurally plastic throughout life. This article reviews structural plasticity in the hippocampus over the lifespan, including how it is investigated experimentally. The modulation of structural plasticity by various experiential factors as well as the possible role it may have in hippocampal functions such as learning and memory, anxiety, and stress regulation are also considered. Although significant progress has been made in many of these areas, we highlight some of the outstanding issues that remain.

Contents

INTRODUCTION

Throughout most of the twentieth century, the neuroscience community assumed that the central nervous system of mammals became structurally stable soon after birth. The complex architecture and functions of the mammalian brain argued against the possibility of structural remodeling of neural circuits during adulthood. This assumption was coupled with a lack of compelling evidence in favor of structural plasticity throughout life. Technical advances over the past several decades, however, have forced a dramatic revision of this view. It is now clear that rather than being fixed and immutable, the brain displays persistent plasticity across the lifespan.

The initial discovery of adult neurogenesis in the 1960s was largely ignored, and two decades later, groundbreaking work documenting evidence of neurogenesis in the adult bird brain was viewed as irrelevant to the mammalian brain. Since that time, however, evidence has been mounting in support of adult neurogenesis in many mammalian species. Consequently, there is now almost universal acceptance that some neurons are continually generated in adulthood and added to established neural circuits (Shors 2008). There remains controversy about the regional extent of adult neurogenesis (reviewed in Gould 2007), but the hippocampus is one brain region where consensus has been reached that the production of new granule neurons is ongoing throughout life (**Figure 1**, see color insert). Since the creation of entirely new granule neurons is accompanied by the growth of their axons, dendrites, and synapses, adult neurogenesis increases the plasticity of the hippocampus through multiple processes. In addition, preexisting granule neurons of the dentate gyrus and pyramidal neurons in areas CA3 and CA1 (**Figure 1**) undergo dynamic modifications in the form of dendritic extension and retraction, as well as synapse formation and elimination. All of these types of structural plasticity are subject to modification by a variety of factors and conditions, suggesting that they may be substrates for experience-dependent change.

In this review, we discuss the variety of traditional and emerging methodologies that have facilitated the study of structural plasticity in the adult hippocampus. We also describe evidence for lifelong structural plasticity and summarize how these processes are modulated by environmental experience, including learning and stress. Finally, the possibility that structural plasticity participates in hippocampal functions such as learning and memory, anxiety, and stress regulation will be considered. Even though much of what is known about structural plasticity, its experiential modulation, and its functional relevance comes from work done in rodents, there is evidence for adult neurogenesis and dendritic remodeling in the hippocampus of primates, including humans. Thus, information gathered from animal studies is likely to be applicable to humans and may shed light on the clinical importance of structural plasticity in the adult brain.

STRUCTURAL PLASTICITY ACROSS THE LIFESPAN

The hippocampus consists of a heterogeneous population of neurons distinguished by their age, morphological characteristics, and connectivity (**Figure 1**). The synapses and dendrites of mature neurons undergo continuous rearrangement, and entirely new neurons are formed throughout life. These various forms of structural change, which are typically associated with development, continue to occur during the postnatal period and beyond, persisting into young adulthood and throughout middle age and senescence. Despite the fact that cellular events traditionally associated with development take place in adulthood, each life stage is characterized by varying degrees of plasticity and different endpoints for structural change.

Early Postnatal Life

Although pyramidal neurons of the CA3 and CA1 regions are generated exclusively during embryonic development, the granule cell population of the dentate gyrus is produced during an extended period that begins during gestation and continues postnatally (reviewed in Seress 2007). In rodents, the granule cell layer (GCL) forms along four general gradients—caudal to rostral, suprapyramidal to infrapyramidal, tip to crest, and superficial to deep (**Figure 2**, see color insert). Thus, superficially located granule cells in the caudal tip of the suprapyramidal blade are the oldest, produced exclusively

during the embryonic period. At the time of birth, the gross structure of the GCL is mostly formed except for the rostral infrapyramidal blade, which is virtually nonexistent. During the first postnatal week, granule cell genesis is maximal, and the result is that the remainder of the GCL coalesces (Schlessinger et al. 1975). Also, a considerable amount of cell death occurs among the newly generated granule cell population at this time. The day of maximal granule cell genesis is the same day as maximal granule cell death (Gould et al. 1991a). The massive neurogenesis and concomitant cell death that occur during the early postnatal period complete the process of laying down the foundation of the GCL. New granule cells are then inserted into this foundation throughout the ensuing stages of life.

Granule cell dendrites begin to develop shortly after the production of each new cell—at first dendrites are rudimentary and bare, but in the weeks that follow, they develop numerous branches and become covered with dendritic spines (reviewed in Rahimi & Claiborne 2007). Although the exact events leading to spine formation remain to be fully determined, filopodia have been implicated in synaptogenesis and early spine development (Fiala et al. 1998). Regressive events also sculpt hippocampal circuitry during development—pruning of dendritic branches occurs on the granule cells during this time (Rahimi & Claiborne 2007). Similar events occur throughout the hippocampus—postnatal development of dendritic arbors and the formation of dendritic spines followed by dendritic pruning and synapse elimination are also features of the pyramidal neuron population (Liu et al. 2005).

Juvenile Period and Adolescence

Following the early postnatal period, continued differentiation of neuronal structure occurs in all hippocampal regions. Although levels of neurogenesis are highest perinatally, neurogenesis remains robust during the juvenile period and adolescence (He & Crews 2007,

GCL: granule cell layer

Dendritic spines: protrusions covering the surface of dendrites that are major sites of excitatory synaptic input

Filopodia: long, thin, dynamic protrusions that are the precursors of dendritic spines

Neural stem cells:
cells that self-renew
and are multipotent,
giving rise to neurons
and glia

SGZ: subgranular
zone

Progenitor cells:
proliferative progeny
of stem cells that
generate differentiated
cells but that have a
limited capacity for
self-renewal

**Immediate early
genes (IEGs):** genes
that are rapidly and
transiently expressed
in response to various
cellular stimuli that are
often used as indirect
markers for neuronal
activity

**Gamma-
aminobutyric acid
(GABA):** major
inhibitory
neurotransmitter in
the adult brain that is
excitatory to immature
neurons during
development and to
neural progenitor cells
during adult
neurogenesis

Hodes et al. 2009). In addition, spine densities increase during this time and, on pyramidal neurons, do not reach adult levels until the time of sexual maturity in both rats and monkeys (~45 days in rats and 4 years in rhesus monkeys) (Pokorný & Yamamoto 1981, Seress & Ribak 1995). In the dentate gyrus, granule cells also undergo dendritic pruning during adolescence. This dendritic regression appears to be restricted to the infrapyramidal blade during this life stage (Zehr et al. 2008), perhaps because this part of the GCL is less mature than the suprapyramidal blade.

Young Adulthood

Altman and colleagues were the first to demonstrate that neurogenesis in the dentate gyrus persists into adulthood (Altman 1962, Altman & Das 1965). Although neurogenesis is not limited to the postnatal and juvenile periods, the level of new neuron production undergoes a progressive decline during the transition into adulthood (He & Crews 2007, Hodes et al. 2009). Except for a few species of bats (Amrein et al. 2007), adult neurogenesis in the hippocampus appears to be a common characteristic of all species from rodents to primates, including humans (Cameron et al. 1993, Eriksson et al. 1998, Gould et al. 1999a, Manganas et al. 2007).

Neurogenesis in the adult brain is a complex process characterized by distinct milestones (reviewed in Kempermann et al. 2004). In adulthood, new neurons are generated from a resident population of mitotic cells that are believed to be neural stem cells, although some debate remains as to whether they should be classified as such (Bull & Bartlett 2005, Jessberger et al. 2008a, Walker et al. 2008). These putative neural stem cells have some characteristics of astroglia (Garcia et al. 2004, Seri et al. 2001) and are localized to the subgranular zone (SGZ), where they divide asymmetrically to either self-renew or give rise to progenitor cells (**Figure 2**). The progenitor cells, while committed to a neuronal phenotype, act as transit-amplifying cells, dividing again to produce additional committed daughter cells that mature and become postmitotic. As the postmitotic progeny differentiate, they migrate a short distance into the GCL, where maturation continues. Over time, newly born cells express proteins that are characteristic of granule neurons (reviewed in Christie & Cameron 2006; **Figure 3**, see color insert), elaborate dendritic projections with dendritic spines (reviewed in Ribak & Shapiro 2007; see also Toni et al. 2007, van Praag et al. 2002, Zhao et al. 2006), receive synaptic inputs (Kaplan & Hinds 1977, Markakis & Gage 1999), extend axons into the appropriate targets (Hastings & Gould 1999, Markakis & Gage 1999, Toni et al. 2008), and release glutamate as their main neurotransmitter (Toni et al. 2008). Eventually, adult-generated neurons produce action potentials (Laplagne et al. 2006, van Praag et al. 2002) and show other signs of activation, i.e., they express immediate early genes (IEGs) in response to a variety of stimuli (Kee et al. 2007; Ramirez-Amaya et al. 2006; Snyder et al. 2009a,b; Tashiro et al. 2007), thereby indicating that they become integrated into the existing hippocampal circuitry.

Numerous lines of evidence suggest that the maturational processes of adult-generated neurons follow stages characteristic of development even though they are maturing in the context of an adult hippocampus (Espósito et al. 2005; reviewed in Overstreet-Wadiche & Westbrook 2006, Ribak & Shapiro 2007). For example, like the developing brain, the inhibitory neurotransmitter gamma-aminobutyric acid (GABA) initially elicits excitatory responses in newborn cells of the adult brain (Ge et al. 2006, Karten et al. 2006). Once mature, adult-generated granule cells become indistinguishable in many ways from granule cells born during embryonic development (Ge et al. 2007, Laplagne et al. 2006). An exception to this seems to be with the axonal projection patterns of some early generated neurons—these appear to be more widely divergent than those of adult-generated granule cells (Hastings et al. 2002). This widespread divergence of axonal projections most likely occurs when embryonically generated granule cells extend axon collaterals to an immature CA3 region that subsequently grows and tows the collaterals farther apart. Late-generated granule cells do not display this feature, presumably because they are forming connections with a target area that is no longer undergoing major changes in size.

It is important to note that not all neurons produced in adulthood mature and persist. Indeed, a large proportion of newly generated neurons die within a few weeks after mitosis (Dayer et al. 2003; Gould et al. 1999b, 2001). The survival of adult-generated cells is highly sensitive to experience, suggesting that the overproduction of granule cells prepares the dentate gyrus for environmental conditions that might benefit from the incorporation of more new neurons. In the absence of these conditions, such as in laboratory control settings, these neurons are not needed and instead degenerate. The extent to which such a phenomenon reflects naturally occurring plasticity that enables a response to variable environmental demands versus an artifact of living in an abnormal laboratory setting remains unknown.

During adulthood, the morphology of mature hippocampal neurons also displays plasticity under normal conditions. For example, new spines and spine synapses form and regress on CA1 pyramidal neurons across the estrous cycle of the female rat (Woolley et al. 1990a). Similar to early postnatal spinogenesis, the mechanism by which spines are formed in the adult hippocampus likely involves the formation of filopodia and the eventual transition to a mature spine shape. Besides the production of new dendritic spines on hippocampal neurons, existing dendritic spines are also known to be quite motile and exhibit rapid changes in size and shape in adulthood (reviewed in Bonhoeffer & Yuste 2002).

Middle Age to Senescence

The hippocampus maintains the ability to undergo structural reorganization even later in life. In aged rodents and monkeys, the hippocampus produces new neurons, albeit at a much reduced level compared to young adulthood (Cameron & McKay 1999, Kuhn et al. 1996, Leuner et al. 2007a; **Figure 2**). The decline in new neuron production begins during middle-age, well before the onset of senescence, as a result of a reduction in the rate of proliferation, a loss in the number of progenitors, and a decrease in the proportion of progenitor cells that adopt a neuronal phenotype (Kuhn et al. 1996, Olariu et al. 2007, van Praag et al. 2005). These changes in turn may be a consequence of age-associated changes in extrinsic trophic signals and a reduction in the responsiveness of progenitor cells to these signals (reviewed in Klempin & Kempermann 2007). Although aging substantially reduces proliferation of neural progenitor cells and the differentiation of their progeny, dendritic morphology, including dendritic length, branching, and spine density, of new neurons is similar to those produced in the young brain (Morgenstern et al. 2008, van Praag et al. 2005). Thus, new neurons generated in the aged hippocampus maintain the capacity to achieve a level of complexity that is comparable to that of other dentate granule cells.

In contrast to the substantial reduction in the rate of neurogenesis, aging has subtler and regionally specific effects on dendritic and synaptic structure of mature hippocampal neurons (reviewed in Burke & Barnes 2006). Although the density of synaptic contacts formed onto dentate gyrus granule cells is reduced by aging (Geinisman et al. 1992), dendritic complexity and/or spine density of granule cells, as well as of pyramidal neurons of CA3 and CA1, are unaltered. Similar effects have been observed in aged humans, when patients with dementia are excluded (reviewed in Flood 1993).

METHODOLOGIES USED TO STUDY STRUCTURAL PLASTICITY IN THE ADULT BRAIN

The now widespread acceptance of structural plasticity in the intact adult brain represents a major milestone in the neuroscience community. This change in thinking has been

BrdU:
bromodeoxyuridine

fueled, at least in part, by methodological advances. The application of new techniques to the question of structural plasticity has produced a rapidly expanding literature. Findings in this subfield of neuroscience, however, have often been discrepant, raising issues about the need for a standardization of techniques and the importance of a critical evaluation of the strengths and weaknesses of the available methods.

Detection of Adult Neurogenesis

Tritiated thymidine. The earliest reports of adult neurogenesis in the mammalian brain used ^{3}H-thymidine labeling (Altman 1962, Altman & Das 1965). This method involves injecting animals with radiolabeled thymidine, which is incorporated into DNA of dividing cells. By varying the survival time after labeling, ^{3}H-thymidine can be a marker of proliferating cells (at short survival times) or their progeny (longer survival times). ^{3}H-thymidine-labeled cells are identified using autoradiographic techniques (Altman 1962). Although ^{3}H-thymidine autoradiography can be combined with immunocytochemistry for verifying neuronal phenotype (Cameron et al. 1993), colabeling is difficult to establish with certainty. Because conventional light microscopy only allows for visualizing tissue in two dimensions, it's possible that a putative ^{3}H-thymidine-labeled neuron is actually a ^{3}H-thymidine-labeled nonneuronal cell lying directly on top of a mature neuron. Another problem with this technique is that it underestimates the numbers of labeled cells because ^{3}H only exposes photographic emulsion if it is located in the upper few microns of a tissue section. With the emergence of various new techniques, this method to label newly generated cells is utilized relatively infrequently.

Bromodeoxyuridine. Currently, administration of the thymidine analog bromodeoxyuridine (BrdU) is the most widely used method to study adult neurogenesis. BrdU, like thymidine,

is injected into animals, becomes incorporated into the DNA of cells during the synthesis stage (i.e., S-phase) of the cell cycle, and depending on the survival time employed, is a marker of proliferating cells and their progeny. The use of BrdU as a marker of dividing cells has a number of advantages over ^{3}H-thymidine. First, BrdU labeling is a nonisotopic method that can be easily combined with immunohistochemistry, and unlike autoradiography, takes only a few days for incubation and staining (Wojtowicz & Kee 2006). Second, antibodies to BrdU can identify labeled nuclei throughout the thickness of the section, and labeling can be quantitatively assessed with stereological counting techniques. Third, BrdU allows for the use of fluorescent immunohistochemical methods to label newly generated cells that can be combined with multiple markers to identify phenotypes of new cells (**Figure 3**) as well as to assess the expression of neurotransmitter and growth factor receptors and IEGs. The colocalization of BrdU with these markers can then be confirmed using three-dimensional reconstruction with confocal microscopy.

BrdU labeling is relatively straightforward. However, its extensive use in studies of adult neurogenesis has raised several questions about important variables that alter experimental outcomes. Two issues appear to be critical in designing and interpreting studies involving BrdU labeling. One issue involves differences in the dose, timing, and treatment regimen of BrdU, all of which can affect the number of labeled cells. For instance, Cameron & McKay (2001) have shown that low doses of BrdU (50 mg/kg) underestimate the number of newly born cells. A single 200–300 mg/kg BrdU injection appears to label the maximal number of cells in S-phase. The other issue that can greatly influence the detection of BrdU-labeled cells involves differences in immunohistochemical methods. Antibody selection is an important consideration given that some commonly used BrdU antibodies label substantially fewer cells than others (Leuner et al. 2009; **Figure 4**). Additional variability in BrdU labeling occurs with different DNA denaturation techniques. DNA

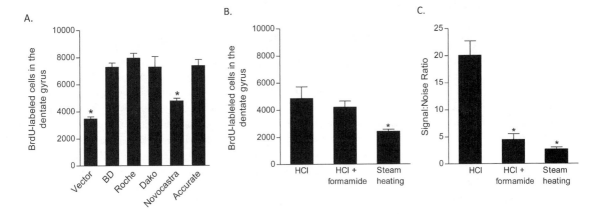

Figure 4

Methods for studies of adult neurogenesis are not equally sensitive. (*A*) BrdU antibodies do not label the same number of newborn cells in the dentate gyrus. Vector and Novocastra antibodies stain fewer BrdU-labeled cells as compared to BD, Roche, Dako, and Accurate antibodies (two-hour post-BrdU survival time). (*B*) Additional variability in BrdU labeling occurs with different DNA denaturation pretreatment methods. HCl alone and HCl + formamide pretreatments stain more newborn cells in the dentate gyrus than does steam heating. (*C*) Pretreatments also differentially affect immunoflurorescent staining for the mature neuronal marker, NeuN; greater staining is observed with HCl-alone pretreatment. $*p < 0.05$. Adapted from Leuner et al. (2009).

denaturation is required because BrdU antibodies recognize the antigen only in single-stranded DNA. Denaturation can be achieved by high or low pH, high temperature, or treatment with solvents such as formamide. These techniques alter the number of detectable BrdU-labeled cells and the intensity of staining for NeuN, a standard marker of neuronal phenotype (Leuner et al. 2009; **Figure 4**).

The two points raised above appear to be much more problematic for studies using the BrdU method than are other commonly mentioned potential pitfalls of this method. For example, numerous papers have raised the possibility that BrdU produces false positive results because it labels cells undergoing DNA repair or in the process of dying. This concern appears to be unimportant, since BrdU incorporation is specific to dividing cells even when the level of DNA repair is experimentally increased in adults (Bauer & Patterson 2005). Furthermore, no available evidence suggests that BrdU labels dying cells in the adult brain, unless they are cells that incorporated BrdU during mitosis and ultimately degenerated. Other issues raised in criticism of BrdU labeling are that it is toxic to cells and that it stimulates cell proliferation. Neither of these possibilities appears to be the

case for the adult brain. Even at high doses, BrdU does not have cytotoxic effects and does not alter cell proliferation rates (Cameron & McKay 2001, Hancock et al. 2009, Kee et al. 2002). Finally, there is no evidence that BrdU incorporation alters neuronal differentiation—the percentage of new cells that express neuronal markers and the age of those cells at which such expression can be detected is the same as with ³H-thymidine labeling.

Other nucleotide analogs. In addition to BrdU, recent reports have used iododeoxyuridine (IdU) and chlorodeoxyuridine (CldU), thymidine analogs with a structure similar to BrdU, to label newly generated cells in the adult brain (Bauer & Patterson 2005, Burns & Kuan 2005, Dupret et al. 2007, Thomas et al. 2007, Vega & Peterson 2005). These analogs can be detected individually by different antibodies that have been reported to recognize IdU or CldU exclusively. Thus, IdU and CldU have an advantage over BrdU labeling alone; both can be injected into the same animal so cells produced at different time points can be simultaneously assessed. For this technique to produce interpretable results, antibodies for one analog must not crossreact with the other.

NeuN: neuronal nuclei

GFP: green
fluorescent protein

Previous work identified antibodies that recognize IdU or CldU exclusively (Burns & Kuan 2005, Vega & Peterson 2005), although these studies did not use IdU and CldU at molarities comparable to the dose of BrdU that labels the maximal number of cells (i.e., 200–300 mg/kg; Cameron & McKay 2001). Even at higher molarities, IdU and CldU do not label as many cells as BrdU, and furthermore, antibody selectivity is lost (Leuner et al. 2009). As a result, these analogs may not provide an accurate estimate of the number of newly born cells.

Most recently, a new thymidine analog, ethynyldeoxyuridine (EdU), has been developed that reportedly has a number of benefits over the other thymidine analogs currently in use. As mentioned above, BrdU, IdU, and CldU require DNA denaturation procedures so that antigen/antibody binding can occur. This typically involves harsh pretreatments, such as the application of strong acids and/or high heat (Wojtowicz & Kee 2006), that affect histological quality as well as the detection of newborn cells (Leuner et al. 2009). In contrast, EdU does not require denaturation but instead can be detected by a fluorescent azide through a reaction known as "click chemistry" (Salic & Mitchinson 2008). This reaction is quick—it can be done in minutes as compared to hours or days—and compatible with multiple probes for fluorescent immunochemistry (Chehrehasa et al. 2009). Like BrdU, IdU, and CldU, EdU can be administered peripherally and shows strong labeling of proliferating cells that is localized within nuclei. But because this is a new technique, additional quantitative studies are needed before definitive conclusions can be made about its usefulness for studies of adult neurogenesis.

Endogenous markers. Another strategy for identifying dividing cells in the adult brain involves the detection of endogenous proteins that are only expressed in mitotically active cells (reviewed in Eisch & Mandyam 2007). Although endogenous markers, such as Ki-67, are limited in that they can only be used to examine cell proliferation, they are useful when it is not feasible to deliver thymidine analogs, such as in the study of natural populations of animals (Amrein et al. 2004, Epp et al. 2009) or postmortem human tissue (Boldrini et al. 2009, Jin et al. 2006, Reif et al. 2006). Also, endogenous markers can be used to confirm findings obtained with thymidine analogs, especially when experimental conditions may alter the availability or uptake of exogenous nucleotides. Indeed, the expression of endogenous markers mimics that of BrdU labeling, though typically more cells are stained with endogenous markers since BrdU labels only those cells that are in S-phase for at most two hours after the BrdU injection (Cameron & McKay 2001, Kee et al. 2002).

Viral vectors. An increasing number of studies use retroviral vectors that drive the expression of fluorescent proteins, most often green fluorescent protein (GFP), to label dividing cells and their progeny. Unlike the thymidine analog methods that show label dilution with cell division, viral-mediated labeling is permanent because the retroviruses incorporate into dividing cells by integrating into the genome. This technique is advantageous because it can be used to identify adult-generated neurons in living-slice preparations and characterize their electrophysiological properties (Ge et al. 2007, Laplagne et al. 2006, van Praag et al. 2002). Since the fluorescent protein is distributed throughout the entire infected neuron, retroviral-mediated labeling also enables the morphological development of newborn neurons to be examined (Espósito et al. 2005; Toni et al. 2007, 2008; Zhao et al. 2006). In addition, the regulation of adult neurogenesis by specific genes can be studied by engineering viral vectors to induce specific types of genetic manipulations (Ge et al. 2006, Jessberger et al. 2008b, Tashiro et al. 2006). However, as with the other techniques used to study adult neurogenesis, there are limitations to the application of virus-mediated cell labeling. Most notably, the retroviral method is inefficient and variable across animals, making it unsuitable for quantitative analyses. Even with improved retroviruses, the numbers of labeled cells are lower and the

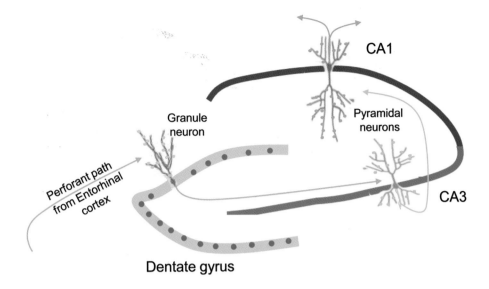

Figure 1

Schematic diagram of the hippocampus showing a mature granule neuron of the dentate gyrus and mature pyramidal neurons of areas CA3 and CA1 as well as their main axonal connections. For each of these cell types, the size and complexity of the dendritic trees as well as the size, shape, and number of dendritic spines can change. In the dentate gyrus, substantial numbers of new neurons (*red*) are also produced in adulthood.

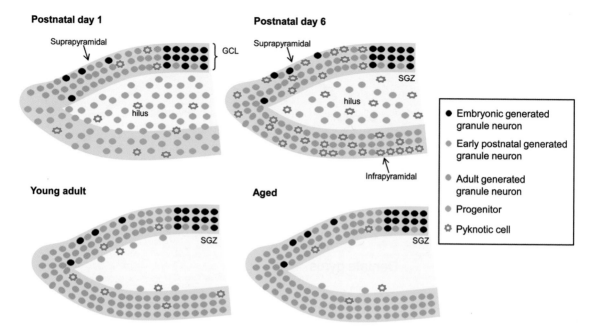

Figure 2

Cell birth and cell death in the dentate gyrus across the lifespan. On postnatal day 1, granule neurons that were generated embryonically have begun to form the tip of the suprapyramidal blade of the granule cell layer (GCL). During the first postnatal week, the GCL continues to be formed from progenitor cells located within the hilus along four general gradients—caudal to rostral, suprapyramidal to infrapyramidal, suprapyramidal tip through crest to infrapyramidal tip, and superficial to deep. Thereafter, the production of new granule neurons tapers off but remains substantial in adulthood until animals reach middle age and become aged. Alongside neurogenesis, there is substantial death of granule neurons. Cell death peaks at the end of the first postnatal week as indicated by the presence of pyknotic (i.e., dying) cells. In adulthood, substantial cell death continues, especially of newborn neurons located primarily within the subgranular zone (SGZ) or deep within the GCL.

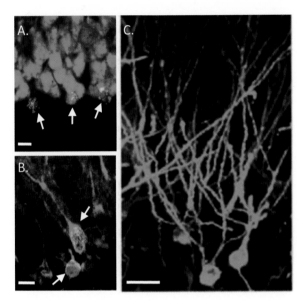

Figure 3

(*A, B*) Photomicrographs of newly born neurons (*arrows*) in the dentate gyrus of an adult rat labeled with BrdU (*red*) coexpressing (*A*) NeuN (*green*), a marker of mature neurons or (*B*) TuJ1 (*green*), a marker of immature and mature neurons. Scale bars, 10 μm. Eventually, adult-generated neurons become morphologically indistinguishable from granule neurons generated during development, like those shown in (*C*) which were labeled with the lipophilic tracer DiI. Scale bar, 25 μm. Parts of this panel have been previously published (Leuner et al. 2004, Stranahan et al. 2007).

proportion of cells expressing neuronal markers is decreased compared to BrdU incorporation (van Praag et al. 2002, Zhao et al. 2006). Another concern is that stereotaxic surgery is necessary to deliver the retrovirus to the region of interest. This delivery method is not only more labor intensive but also is potentially problematic because damage is inevitable, and injury-induced neurogenesis has been reported (Gould & Tanapat 1997). Also, the immune-mediated side effects resulting from the virus and/or surgery may cause the proliferation of microglia that incorporate the retrovirus to subsequently fuse with existing postmitotic neurons, thereby creating a false demonstration of neurogenesis, although this has only been reported for the neocortex (Ackman et al. 2006). In addition to retroviral vectors, lentiviral vectors have been employed in studies of adult neurogenesis. However, these are not specific for newborn cells and label a broader range of cell types (van Hooijdonk et al. 2009).

Reporter Mice. Transgenic mouse lines expressing genetically encoded fluorescent reporters such as GFP have become an important tool for studying adult neurogenesis (Overstreet et al. 2004, Yamaguchi et al. 2000). These lines allow for selective identification of cells at discrete developmental stages including neural stem cells, progenitor cells, and postmitotic, immature neurons (Couillard-Despres et al. 2006, Encinas et al. 2006, Overstreet et al. 2004, Yamaguchi et al. 2000). Like retroviral labeling, the full morphology of labeled cells can be visualized and electrophysiological analysis performed. Transgenic reporter lines in which the fluorescent protein is directed to the nucleus have the added benefit of quantitative analysis (Encinas et al. 2006). Moreover, the effect of specific genes or mutations on adult neurogenesis can be examined by crossing reporter mice with other genetically modified mice. Although transgenic labeling is noninvasive and thus not confounded by issues related to inflammation or injury, expression of the reporter in these mice is often transient, making it impossible to follow the same population of cells across

maturation (Overstreet et al. 2004, Yamaguchi et al. 2000). In order to overcome this issue, inducible transgenic mouse lines have been developed that permit labeling and tracking of progenitor cells and their progeny in the dentate gyrus (Imayoshi et al. 2008, Lagace et al. 2008). The inducible transgenic systems have also been useful for gene deletion and progenitor ablation studies that investigate adult neurogenesis from a mechanistic and functional perspective.

Imaging. Currently, all methods to directly study adult neurogenesis involve assessment of postmortem tissue. Investigating this process in vivo has been delayed because of a lack of non-invasive methods to detect new neurons over time. However, efforts are underway to address this gap (reviewed in Schroeder 2008). One approach has relied on the relationship between neurogenesis and angiogenesis. Since angiogenesis has been coupled to cerebral blood volume, which can be measured with magnetic resonance imaging, this method has been suggested to provide an in vivo correlate of neurogenesis (Pereira et al. 2007). Although this approach does not specifically measure neurogenesis, other work has reported the discovery of a biomarker for neural progenitor cells in humans that is detectable using magnetic resonance spectroscopy (Manganas et al. 2007). However, questions about the validity of the detection techniques and data analysis methods of this latter approach have been raised. Even so, the ability to monitor neural stem/progenitor cells in the hippocampus of live animals and humans represents a major technological breakthrough, one that would have important implications for understanding the functional consequences of adult neurogenesis as well as its role in psychiatric and neurological disorders.

Analysis of Dendritic Structure and Dendritic Spines

Golgi technique. The vast majority of studies until recently have used light microscopic analysis of brain sections stained with Golgi

Angiogenesis: the growth of new blood vessels

techniques to examine dendritic structure and dendritic spines. Several versions of this technique are currently in use, but all are based on the same principles of metallic impregnation first developed and used more than 100 years ago by Golgi and Ramon y Cajal. The Golgi technique is useful because it randomly labels a small number of cells in their entirety so that detailed information regarding dendritic branching, length, and spine density can be measured. Since more than 90% of excitatory synapses are formed on dendritic spines (reviewed in Nimchinsky et al. 2002), dendritic spine numbers obtained from Golgi-stained tissue provide an indirect measure of excitatory synaptic inputs. However, quantification of the actual number of synapses can only be done using electron microscopic procedures. Also, due to limits in resolution with light microscopy, Golgi staining doesn't reveal subtler changes in spine morphology and other aspects of spine ultrastructure.

Fluorescent labeling. More recent work has employed fluorescent labeling of neurons followed by confocal microscopy to assess dendritic and synaptic structure (Dailey et al. 1999, Kozorovitskiy et al. 2005). In this regard, intracellular microinjection of fluorescent dyes such as Lucifer yellow has been used in hippocampal slices. Cell filling has also been achieved with lipophilic fluorescent dyes such as DiI, which diffuse readily across neuronal membranes of fixed tissue (O'Brien & Lummis 2006). Crystals of the dye can be applied directly to slices, delivered ballistically with a gene gun, or inserted into small tissue blocks where it serves as a retrograde label. Not only do these approaches produce spine images of a higher resolution when viewed with a confocal microscope, allowing for the assessment of spine morphology, but when used in slices, synaptic activity can be manipulated and its effects on dendritic morphology determined.

Imaging. Two-photon laser-scanning microscopy in combination with fluorescent molecular tools has allowed for high-resolution, time-lapse imaging of spines in living slices (reviewed in Nimchinsky et al. 2002). It is now even possible to study dendritic spines in vivo using transgenic mouse lines that sparsely express genetically encoded fluorescent proteins in specific neuronal types. A "window" is created in the skulls of these mice, and when secured under a two-photon laser-scanning microscope, the same dendritic segments can be imaged over extended periods of time as well as before and after exposure to stimuli. This form of imaging has been primarily used to visualize neurons in the most superficial layers of the cortex, although preparations for in vivo imaging of hippocampal dendrites and spines have been reported (Mizrahi et al. 2004). Dynamic changes in the individual shapes of spines can be detected with this technique, but resolution is not sufficient to count numbers or identify exactly where synapses occur. There are also data to suggest that the cranial window itself can cause substantial glial activation and influence spine dynamics (Xu et al. 2007). An alternative approach involves viewing neurons through a thinned skull preparation. Results from this method have shown naturally occurring changes in dendritic spine number and shape but of a less extensive nature than that observed with a cranial window. However, examining deep structures such as the hippocampus with this method is difficult. Another limitation of current imaging techniques is that because anesthesia is required, examination of structural plasticity in an animal as it actively engages in specific behaviors cannot yet be done. With the development of miniaturized fiber optic microscopy (Flusberg et al. 2008), cellular-level imaging of the hippocampus may soon be possible in behaving animals.

EXPERIENCE MODULATES STRUCTURAL PLASTICITY

Structural plasticity in the hippocampus is sensitive to a wide range of experiences, many of which appear to have substantial effects throughout the lifespan of the animal. Within the context of adult neurogenesis, the discrete stages that characterize the progression from progenitor cell to mature granule neuron are each subject to experiential modification. In addition, hippocampal neurons produced during development are responsive to many of the same experiential factors and exhibit alterations in dendritic architecture and dendritic spines. This prolonged sensitivity of the hippocampus to experience may have positive and negative consequences. On the one hand, the extended restructuring of the hippocampus according to experiential cues may confer important adaptive plasticity. On the other hand, the perpetual capacity for structural change might render the hippocampus particularly sensitive to environmental perturbations that may have adverse consequences on hippocampal function.

Negative Versus Positive Stress

Stressors are typically defined in terms of their ability to activate the hypothalamic-pituitary-adrenal (HPA) axis and ultimately increase glucocorticoid levels (reviewed in Ulrich-Lai & Herman 2009). Most experiences known to cause HPA axis activation are aversive. Exposure to aversive stressors adversely influences numerous aspects of hippocampal structure.

With few exceptions (Bain et al. 2004, Snyder et al. 2009a, Thomas et al. 2007), new cell production in the dentate gyrus is inhibited by a variety of acute and chronic aversive experiences, including both physical and psychosocial stressors (reviewed in Mirescu & Gould 2006). Stress-induced suppression of cell proliferation has been demonstrated in various species (mouse, rat, tree shrew, monkey) and occurs throughout life, with similar results reported for the early postnatal period, young adulthood, and aging (Coe et al. 2003; Gould et al. 1997, 1998; Simon et al. 2005; Tanapat et al. 1998, 2001; Veenema et al. 2007). When stressor exposure occurs during development, the effects are enduring and can persist into adulthood (Lemaire et al. 2000, Lucassen et al. 2009, Mirescu et al. 2004). However, it is unclear whether stress experienced

in adulthood has a long-lasting influence on hippocampal neurogenesis. Prolonged effects of stress on new neuron production (Heine et al. 2004, Malberg & Duman 2003, Pham et al. 2003) and survival (Koo & Duman 2008, Thomas et al. 2007, Westenbroek et al. 2004) have been observed. Yet, others have shown that the influence of stress on adult neurogenesis is temporary, decreasing cell proliferation and immature neuron production without altering the number of new neurons that survive to maturity (Mirescu et al. 2004, Snyder et al. 2009a, Tanapat et al. 2001). The reason for these discrepancies is unknown but may be related to the duration or intensity of the stressor or timing of BrdU labeling or sacrifice relative to the stressful experience.

In addition to suppressing neurogenesis, aversive stressful experiences alter dendritic architecture in the hippocampus. For example, repeated stress in adulthood induces retraction of CA3 pyramidal neuron dendrites as well as a loss of synapses in adult male rats and tree shrews (Magariños et al. 1996, McKittrick et al. 2000, Stewart et al. 2005). Within hours of stressor onset, dendritic spine density in the CA3 region is also reduced (Chen et al. 2008). The effects of stress on dendritic architecture in other hippocampal regions have been less well-studied. Chronic stress causes dendritic regression and spine synapse loss in the dentate gyrus and CA1 (Hajszan et al. 2009, Sousa et al. 2000). Acute stress also alters dendritic spine density on CA1 pyramidal cells of adult rats, but the direction of the effect is dependent on the sex of the animal, increasing the number of dendritic spines in males but decreasing the number of dendritic spines in females (Shors et al. 2001a).

Some evidence demonstrates that glucocorticoids regulate structural plasticity in the hippocampus and are the primary mediator underlying the detrimental effects of aversive stress on hippocampal structure. First, an inhibition of neurogenesis occurs in response to natural changes in glucocorticoids across the lifespan. Neurogenesis in the dentate gyrus is maximal during the early postnatal period, when levels

HPA: hypothalamic-pituitary-adrenal

Glucocorticoid: steroid hormone released by the adrenal cortex in response to stress

of circulating glucocorticoids are low (Gould et al. 1991b) but diminished during life stages when glucocorticoids are elevated, including aging and the postpartum period (Cameron & McKay 1999; Kuhn et al. 1996; Leuner et al. 2007a,b). Second, glucocorticoid administration during the early postnatal period and in adulthood suppresses neurogenesis (Cameron & Gould 1994, Gould et al. 1991b). Conversely, removal of circulating glucocorticoids by bilateral adrenalectomy increases neurogenesis in adult and aged rats (Cameron & Gould 1994, Cameron & McKay 1999) and prevents the stress-induced reduction in neurogenesis (Mirescu et al. 2004, Tanapat et al. 2001). Third, blocking glucocorticoid receptors can reverse the reduction in neurogenesis after glucocorticoid treatment (Mayer et al. 2006) or stressor exposure (Oomen et al. 2007). Like neurogenesis, the stress-induced atrophy of CA3 pyramidal neurons is prevented by pharmacological blockade of the glucocorticoid stress response and can be mimicked by exogenous glucocorticoid administration (Magariños & McEwen 1995, Woolley et al. 1990b).

It is becoming increasingly clear, however, that glucocorticoids are not the sole factor mediating the suppressive action of stress on hippocampal structure (Gould et al. 1997, Koo & Duman 2008, Van der Borght et al. 2005a) and that the effects of glucocorticoids on structural plasticity are complex. Notably, conditions associated with elevated glucocorticoids do not necessarily have detrimental effects on structural plasticity and in some cases, those conditions can be beneficial. Physical activity is an example of this paradox—despite substantial elevations in circulating glucocorticoids, running enhances adult neurogenesis (Stranahan et al. 2006, van Praag et al. 1999, Zhao et al. 2006) and dendritic architecture (Eadie et al. 2005, Stranahan et al. 2007) in the hippocampus. Although a variety of factors are likely to contribute to stress outcomes, including stressor controllability (Shors et al. 2007), social context (Stranahan et al. 2006), and coping strategy (Veenema et al. 2007), emotional valence of the stressor seems to be a critical variable.

Since the systematic descriptions of stress by Selye (1976), a distinction has been made between negative and positive stress. Although both types of experience activate stress hormone systems and are generally arousing, positive stress is, by definition, rewarding. For example, rodents will develop a conditioned place preference to contexts in which they previously had access to a running wheel and will show signs of distress if they are denied access after chronic exposure (reviewed in Brené et al. 2007). The beneficial effects of running suggest that a rewarding stress can exert the opposite action on hippocampal structure as an aversive stress. However, since running is naturally rewarding to rodents, the possibility that these findings may not apply to other animals without a strong motivation to run must be considered. Nonetheless, the ability of this stimulus to override the negative actions of glucocorticoids is interesting and raises questions about the underlying mechanisms that enable running-induced neurogenesis despite activation of the HPA axis.

Environmental Enrichment

The first evidence that environmental complexity influences hippocampal neurogenesis was provided by Barnea & Nottebohm (1994), who showed that compared to black-capped chickadees living in captivity, those living in the wild maintained a higher number of new neurons. Similar findings have been reported in rodents using "environmental enrichment" protocols—housing conditions that enhance opportunities for social, cognitive, sensory, and motor stimulation. Compared to animals living in standard laboratory cages, hippocampal neurogenesis is enhanced in juvenile, adult, and aged rodents living in enriched environments (Kempermann et al. 1997, 1998). In adulthood, environmental enrichment is able to influence new neurons during a narrow temporal window shortly after they are produced, suggesting that there is a sensitive period during which newborn neurons are susceptible to experiential modulation (Tashiro et al. 2007).

Enriched environments have long been known to have a beneficial effect on other aspects of brain structure (reviewed in van Praag et al. 2000). Rosenzweig and colleagues (Globus et al. 1973) were the first to demonstrate that exposure to enriched settings either during development or in adulthood enhance multiple measures of neuronal structure. Rodents and monkeys living in an enriched environment have more dendritic spines and synapses as well as increased dendritic branching in the hippocampus compared to laboratory controls (Kozorovitskiy et al. 2005, Moser et al. 1994).

There is currently no consensus on the specific environmental feature that contributes to the beneficial consequences of enrichment on hippocampal structure (van Praag et al. 2000). Since environmental enrichment protocols typically include access to a running wheel, some have suggested physical activity may play an important role. For instance, exercise and living in enriched environments similarly enhance dendritic spine density and neurogenesis in the hippocampus (Eadie et al. 2005, Stranahan et al. 2007). Environmental complexity also provides a larger number of learning opportunities than are in standard housing conditions, which, as discussed below, can have a beneficial effect on neurogenesis and dendritic architecture. Regardless of the specific environmental feature that may be responsible for these effects, it is important to keep in mind that standard laboratory housing conditions are impoverished and that under these conditions, hippocampal structure may atrophy from disuse. Thus, experimental enrichment may be a reversal of the impoverishment generally found in the laboratory setting rather than enrichment over a natural setting. Indeed, like birds, some species of wild-living rodents have a greater amount of adult neurogenesis compared to those living in the laboratory (Amrein et al. 2004, Epp et al. 2009).

Learning

A variety of learning tasks that depend on the hippocampus have been shown to alter the number of new neurons in the dentate gyrus of adult rats. For example, the number of newborn cells is increased following the associative learning task of trace eyeblink conditioning (Gould et al. 1999b). This effect persists until the new neurons are at least two months old (Leuner et al. 2004). Other hippocampus-dependent tasks, such as long-delay eyeblink conditioning, as well as spatial learning in the Morris water maze and conditioned food preference, also increase the number of newborn cells (Ambrogini et al. 2000, Döbrössy et al. 2003, Dupret et al. 2007, Gould et al. 1999b, Hairston et al. 2005, Lemaire et al. 2000, Leuner et al. 2006a, Olariu et al. 2005). In contrast, learning tasks that do not require the hippocampus (i.e., short-delay eyeblink conditioning, cued water-maze training, active shock avoidance) do not change the number of newborn neurons (Gould et al. 1999b, Van der Borght et al. 2005a). However, classifying a task as hippocampal dependent or independent cannot completely account for the effects of learning on adult neurogenesis (reviewed in Shors 2008). Rather, more recent data suggest that for learning to have a stimulatory effect on neurogenesis, the task must be sufficiently difficult (Leuner et al. 2006a, Waddell & Shors 2008) and it must be learned well (Dalla et al. 2007, 2009; Leuner et al. 2004). Even so, there are several reported contradictions. Notably, spatial learning in the water-maze task has been linked to no effect or to a decrease in the number of newborn neurons in the dentate gyrus (Ambrogini et al. 2004, Döbrössy et al. 2003, Dupret et al. 2007, Ehninger & Kempermann 2006, Epp et al. 2007, Mohapel et al. 2006, Van der Borght et al. 2005b). In addition to differences in BrdU injection protocols and training paradigms employed, the maturity of the labeled adult-born cells at the time of learning may determine whether and how learning alters them. Both spatial learning and trace eyeblink conditioning encourage the survival of new cells born about one week prior to training, when these cells are immature but already differentiated into neurons (Ambrogini et al. 2000, Dupret et al. 2007, Epp et al. 2007, Gould et al. 1999b, Hairston et al. 2005). In contrast, some studies suggest that spatial learning induces the death of cells that are less mature (i.e., ≤4 days of age; Dupret et al. 2007, Mohapel et al. 2006), whereas others show that the death of older and perhaps more mature cells occurs (i.e., ≥10 days of age; Ambrogini et al. 2004). Therefore, learning may have a differential capacity to influence neurogenesis depending on the age of the cell. This is consistent with observations showing that experience-induced modulation of adult neurogenesis occurs at a critical period during an immature stage (Tashiro et al. 2007).

Further adding to the complex effects of learning on adult neurogenesis are studies showing that besides affecting cell survival and cell death, learning also influences cell proliferation, depending on the specific phase of the learning process assessed (Döbrössy et al. 2003, Dupret et al. 2007). That learning can affect cell proliferation, cell survival, and cell death has been proposed to reflect an activity-dependent selective stabilization process analogous to what occurs during development (Dupret et al. 2007). Accordingly, neurogenesis may be promoted by synaptic plasticity during learning, an idea that is consistent with electrophysiological data showing that enhanced synaptic activity associated with long-term potentiation (LTP) increases cell proliferation and cell survival (Bruel-Jungerman et al. 2006).

The purpose of a learning-induced enhancement of neurogenesis remains to be fully determined. One possibility is that these newborn neurons can contribute to learning and memory by creating a neural representation of previous experience (Aimone et al. 2009). Work showing that neurons made to survive by exposure to an enriched environment are preferentially activated at a later time to the same, but not a different, experience lends some support to the possibility that such a process takes place (Tashiro et al. 2007).

Learning has also been reported to induce dendritic spine alterations of mature hippocampal neurons. The effects of learning include changes in spine number and morphology (Knafo et al. 2004; Leuner et al. 2003; Moser et al. 1994; O'Malley et al. 1998, 2000) and changes in the number and distribution of synapses along dendrites (Andersen & Soleng 1998, Eyre et al. 2003, Geinisman et al. 2001, Miranda et al. 2006, Rusakov et al. 1997). Although a variety of learning tasks (i.e., trace eyeblink conditioning, water-maze training, olfactory discrimination, avoidance conditioning) have been associated with these alterations, there are some differences in the magnitude, time course, and location of the effects across studies. Similar to the effects of learning on adult neurogenesis, it appears that changes in spine formation are activity driven. Indeed, studies using live imaging with two-photon microscopy have shown that LTP is associated with the growth of new spines and synapses as well as changes in spine morphology (reviewed in De Roo et al. 2008, Lamprecht & LeDoux 2004).

STRUCTURAL PLASTICITY AND HIPPOCAMPAL FUNCTION

Although it is generally assumed that dendritic and synaptic rearrangement of mature neurons underlie at least some aspects of hippocampal function, the significance of adult neurogenesis remains elusive. One possibility is that new neurons are continuously added to the existing hippocampal circuitry to replace older cells that die. Because a substantial amount of cell death occurring in this region involves the adult-generated populations, adult neurogenesis as a replacement mechanism seems unlikely (Dayer et al. 2003). Instead, neurogenesis may be required for the modulation and refinement of existing neuronal circuits in the dentate gyrus (Imayoshi et al. 2008) and may serve one or several aspects of hippocampal function that cannot be accomplished exclusively by existing mature neurons. Even though the level of neurogenesis in the adult hippocampus is substantial, with an estimated 9000 new neurons produced daily in the young adult rat, this still represents only a relatively small proportion (∼0.5%) of the total population of mature granule neurons (Cameron & McKay

2001). How can so few neurons have functional significance? The answer to this question may be related to the unique properties of adult-generated neurons. One distinct feature of newborn neurons in the adult hippocampus is that they are structurally plastic during their immature stages (Hastings & Gould 1999, Toni et al. 2007, Zhao et al. 2006). Adult-generated neurons also possess, at least transiently, several electrophysiological characteristics that differ from those of mature neurons. For example, immature neurons exhibit depolarization by GABA, enhanced excitability, low LTP-induction threshold, and more robust LTP that unlike mature granule cells is insensitive to GABA inhibition (Ge et al. 2006, 2007; Karten et al. 2006; Schmidt-Hieber et al. 2004; Snyder et al. 2001; Wang et al. 2000). Collectively, these findings support the view that a somewhat small population of immature neurons might exert a substantial influence on hippocampal function.

Experimental Approaches to Study the Role of Structural Plasticity in Hippocampal Function

Several strategies have been used to link structural change to hippocampal function. One is correlative and involves evaluating whether there is a positive relationship between structural plasticity and hippocampal function. Another is more direct and involves blocking structural changes and examining whether hippocampal functions are altered. With respect to adult neurogenesis, the depletion of newborn cells has been achieved pharmacologically by systemic administration of the antimitotic agent methylazoxymethanol (MAM; Bruel-Jungerman et al. 2005, Shors et al. 2001b) or the DNA-alkylating agent temozolomide (TMZ; Garthe et al. 2009) as well as by central infusion of the mitotic blocker cytosine arabinoside (AraC; Mak et al. 2007). However, none of these agents diminish the number of newborn neurons exclusively within the dentate gyrus. Irradiation is another approach to block hippocampal neurogenesis and when applied focally, spares neurogenesis in the rest of the brain (Clelland et al. 2009, Santarelli et al. 2003, Saxe et al. 2006, Winocur et al. 2006). One downside common to all of these methods is their nonspecific side effects that may complicate the interpretation of results (Dupret et al. 2005, Monje et al. 2003). Genetic ablation of dividing progenitors may be less susceptible to this criticism, but again assessing behavioral consequences is difficult because inhibition of the dividing precursors is not restricted to the dentate gyrus (Garcia et al. 2004, Saxe et al. 2006). For this reason, virus-based strategies have been developed to prevent neurogenesis exclusively in the dentate gyrus at a specific time in adulthood (Clelland et al. 2009, Jessberger et al. 2009). However, the possibility that postmitotic neurons are affected by the virus and may contribute to behavioral alterations cannot be ruled out. Most recently, inducible genetic approaches to ablate specific populations of adult-generated neurons in a temporally and spatially precise manner have been used (Imayoshi et al. 2008, Revest et al. 2009, Zhang et al. 2008), although these too are not without practical drawbacks.

Immunohistochemical procedures to quantify whether newly born cells labeled with BrdU express IEGs is a complementary noninvasive way in which the role of adult-generated neurons in hippocampal functions has been examined and allows for a comparison of mature versus new populations of neurons (Kee et al. 2007, Ramirez-Amaya et al. 2006, Snyder et al. 2009b, Tashiro et al. 2007). Although examining the expression of IEGs in adult-generated neurons provides an indication of whether recently born neurons participate in functionally relevant hippocampal networks, it does not reveal whether new neurons are necessary for those functions. An additional downside to this approach seems to be the very small number of new neurons that stain for IEGs, even under conditions of environmental stimulation. Because of the shortcomings inherent to each strategy, it is critical that multiple, independent methods be used when examining the role of adult neurogenesis in a specific behavior.

A Possible Role in Learning and Memory

The role of the hippocampus in learning and memory has long been recognized. However, the hippocampus has been associated with a range of learning tasks (e.g., trace conditioning, contextual fear conditioning, social transmission of food preference, spatial navigation, and object recognition, to name a few) that do not readily fall into a single category, making a unifying theory of hippocampal function difficult to pin down. One reason for this may be related to findings from recent studies incorporating a subregional analysis of the hippocampus that suggests a heterogeneous distribution of function within its different subfields (reviewed in Rolls & Kesner 2006) as well as along the septotemporal axis (reviewed in Bannerman et al. 2004, Moser & Moser 1998). Despite this complexity, it has been proposed that learning and memory might require structural changes in the hippocampus (reviewed in Lamprecht & LeDoux 2004, Nottebohm 2002). In support of this, numerous positive correlations between learning and structural plasticity have been demonstrated.

In rodents, a variety of conditions that decrease adult neurogenesis in the dentate gyrus are associated with learning impairments. These include stress, increased levels of circulating glucocorticoids, and aging (Drapeau et al. 2003, Montaron et al. 2006). Similarly, adverse prenatal or early-life experiences produce persistent reductions in neurogenesis and reduced learning abilities in adulthood (Lemaire et al. 2000). Conversely, conditions that increase neurogenesis, such as environmental enrichment and physical exercise, also tend to enhance performance on hippocampal-dependent learning tasks (Kempermann et al. 1997; van Praag et al. 1999, 2005). There are also a number of studies that have found no correlation or even a negative correlation between neurogenesis and learning (reviewed in Leuner et al. 2006b). However, it is important to keep in mind that a positive correlation between the number of new neurons and learning performance implies a relationship between neurogenesis and learning, although not necessarily a causal one. Another issue to consider is that the time course for alterations in cell production may not correspond to changes in learning abilities. For example, it seems unlikely that the production of new cells would have an immediate effect on processes involved in learning because the cells probably require a certain level of differentiation to have an impact on behavior. Perhaps an even more important consideration, and one that is impossible to discount, is the fact that many of the factors known to affect neurogenesis alter other aspects of brain structure, such as dendritic architecture and synapse number. Since these types of changes are also likely to be involved in hippocampal-dependent learning, it is difficult to interpret correlations between new neurons and learning.

Because of the caveats associated with correlative studies, other work has attempted to demonstrate a casual relationship between learning and neurogenesis, but these too have yielded mixed findings (Leuner et al. 2006b). Reducing or blocking hippocampal neurogenesis disrupts various hippocampal-dependent forms of learning and memory (Clelland et al. 2009; Dupret et al. 2008; Garthe et al. 2009; Hernandez-Rabaza et al. 2009; Jessberger et al. 2009; Imayoshi et al. 2008; Madsen et al. 2003; Raber et al. 2004; Rola et al. 2004; Saxe et al. 2006; Shors et al. 2001b, 2002; Snyder et al. 2005; Winocur et al. 2006; Zhang et al. 2008). Recent findings further suggest that the correct differentiation and integration of new neurons may be necessary for acquisition of new information and the recall of memories consolidated in tasks previously performed (Farioli-Vecchioli et al. 2008). However, a large number of studies have failed to demonstrate an involvement of newly generated cells in hippocampal-dependent learning (Hernandez-Rabaza et al. 2009, Jessberger et al. 2009, Shors et al. 2002, Snyder et al. 2005, Zhang et al. 2008), and there is at least one demonstration of enhanced learning following the suppression of neurogenesis (Saxe et al. 2007). These discrepancies can be attributed to numerous factors, including the animal species and strain tested and the method of ablation, as well as the specifics of the design, analysis, and interpretation of the learning paradigm employed (Garthe et al. 2009). Another possibility is that the age of the newborn neurons may be critical in determining their specific involvement in cognitive function. On the one hand, new immature neurons (because of their unique electrophysiological properties) may participate in learning for only a discrete period after their production, thus requiring a specific timing and length of neuron depletion in order to detect a learning deficit. A depletion paradigm that is insufficient in length, uses an inappropriate interval between depletion and training, or is too long, allowing compensatory mechanisms to come into play, could lead to contradictory results. On the other hand, new neurons may be critical for learning only when they are mature and integrated into similar neural networks as preexisting neurons. There is some disagreement regarding the exact age at which this occurs as well as whether the distinct functional properties of adult-born neurons continue to exist upon maturation. Some studies suggest that young mature neurons do not retain their unique electrophysiological properties, eventually becoming part of the same functional population as old mature neurons (Ge et al. 2007, Laplagne et al. 2006). In contrast, results from other work indicate that mature newborn cells show enhanced plasticity—adult-born neurons are more likely to be activated than are older cells during spatial exploration and hippocampal-dependent spatial learning (Ramirez-Amaya et al. 2006, Snyder et al. 2009b) and are also preferentially reactivated during recall of the spatial memory (Kee et al. 2007). A third possibility, and most probable, is that neurons of different ages—young adult, mature adult, and preexisting—may be optimally suited for different functions (Aimone et al. 2009). Indeed, it has been proposed that neurogenesis serves to complement the synaptic plasticity and memory function of older neurons. In this context, new neurons would provide more synapses for learning and added processing abilities (Schinder & Gage 2004).

Numerous other theories about the functions of newborn cells in the hippocampus have been proposed, including the possibility that a rapidly changing population of adult-generated neurons may provide a temporary substrate for memory storage (Gould et al. 1999b). Accordingly, one might predict that the longevity of a new neuron would correspond to the duration of the memory that it supports. However, this is not necessarily the case since learning increases the survival of new neurons in the hippocampus where they remain for at least two months after training (Leuner et al. 2004), well beyond the time when the hippocampus is required for the retention of those memories. These findings do not exclude the possibility that new neurons participate transiently in memory storage or encoding. In fact, computational (Aimone et al. 2009) and experimental (Clelland et al. 2009) work suggests that immature neurons may be critical for creating associations between memories learned close in time (Aimone et al. 2009) and may aid in distinguishing memories closely related in space (Clelland et al. 2009). How these memories are then transferred to the prefrontal cortex, the site of long-term storage and retrieval of memories (reviewed in Frankland & Bontempi 2005), is an open question that highlights the need to investigate the consequences of structural changes in the hippocampus on related brain regions. One possibility is that the learning-induced enhancement of neurogenesis, as well as dendritic spines, alters the excitability or activity of the circuitry between the hippocampus and prefrontal cortex, which in turn alters the structure of the prefrontal cortex in a way that supports memory storage. Regardless, even if new neurons are somehow involved in a time-limited way in memory storage, they must eventually outlive their usefulness, perhaps becoming important for some other, still unknown, function.

A Possible Role in Anxiety and Depression

The involvement of the hippocampus in mood disorders is suggested by magnetic resonance imaging studies demonstrating a small reduction in hippocampal volume in depressed patients (reviewed in Campbell & MacQueen 2004). It has been proposed that reduced neurogenesis contributes to these volumetric changes, as well as the symptoms associated with depression and anxiety, and that the efficacy of antidepressant treatments may depend on their ability to restore neurogenesis to normal levels. These ideas, collectively referred to as the neurogenic hypothesis of depression, have been fueled by the observation in rodents and monkeys that stress, which predisposes some individuals to develop anxiety and depression, inhibits hippocampal neurogenesis (see discussion above), and that antidepressants, which are effective in alleviating behavioral symptoms of these disorders, stimulate neurogenesis, at least in adults (Encinas et al. 2006, Hodes et al. 2009, Malberg et al. 2000, Perera et al. 2007). Additional support for a link between adult neurogenesis and affective disorders comes from work examining the effects of focal irradiation on the behavioral effects of antidepressants. Prevention of the antidepressant-induced increase in neurogenesis blocks the ability of these treatments to reduce the behavioral signs of anxiety (Santarelli et al. 2003) or depression (Airan et al. 2007). However, the potential role for adult hippocampal neurogenesis as a mechanism underlying the etiology and treatment of mood disorders remains a matter of intense discussion and investigation (reviewed in Sahay & Hen 2007, Sapolsky 2004). This is in part because some studies have failed to demonstrate that neurogenesis is required for the behavioral effects of antidepressants (Holick et al. 2008, Surget et al. 2008), but also because stressful procedures that reduce neurogenesis do not necessarily cause a depressive phentotype in animals models (Vollmayr et al. 2003). Furthermore, it has not been shown that a disruption of hippocampal neurogenesis, either by using irradiation or antimitotic drugs, enhances susceptibility to stress (Surget et al. 2008) or induces depression-like or anxiety-related behaviors (Airan et al. 2007, Santarelli et al. 2003, Saxe et al. 2006, Shors et al. 2002).

One exception to this is a recent study showing that arresting neurogenesis leads to increased anxiety (Revest et al. 2009). Because specific depletion of newborn neurons was accomplished with an inducible transgenic strategy, it is possible that the less-specific ablation methods used in earlier work may have produced confounding behavioral perturbations. Nevertheless, the "neurogenic hypothesis of depression" continues to be controversial. Currently, there is no evidence for differences in the number of proliferating cells in the hippocampus of individuals with depression (Boldrini et al. 2009, Reif et al. 2006), although the possibility remains that other stages of neurogenesis such as survival, differentiation, or integration of new neurons into the existing hippocampal circuitry are affected. Moreover, only one study has demonstrated increased progenitor cell proliferation in depressed patients after antidepressant treatment (Boldrini et al. 2009). Further studies are necessary to determine whether this effect is associated with an improvement of depressive symptoms, a critical issue as most of the patients in this study died from suicide.

Like the role of adult neurogenesis in learning and memory, the specific involvement new neurons might have in the pathogenesis of and recovery from depression is not yet clear. However, given the complexity of mood disorders, it is important to consider that multiple mechanisms are likely to be involved (reviewed in Sahay & Hen 2007). That the anxiolytic effects of some manipulations, such as drugs that directly target the HPA axis, can be achieved even after suppression of hippocampal neurogenesis is at least one indication that neurogenesis-independent mechanisms exist (Surget et al. 2008). These may include other types of structural change (reviewed in McEwen 2005), a possibility that is supported by the demonstration that hippocampal spine synapse loss occurs in animal models of depression (Hajszan et al. 2009). Analogous effects have been observed in the hippocampus of depressed patients (Law et al. 2004).

One additional point worth mentioning is that although the hippocampus has been linked to anxiety-related behavior, lesions of the hippocampus lead to decreased, not increased, levels of anxiety (Bannerman et al. 2004). Thus, under normal conditions, the hippocampus is anxiogenic. How the addition of new neurons that are known to be excitatory to an anxiogenic brain region would lead to less anxiety is a paradox that is not addressed by the neurogenic hypothesis of depression.

A Possible Role in Stress Regulation

A less well known function of the hippocampus is its role as a negative feedback regulator of the HPA axis. The high concentration of adrenal steroid receptors in the hippocampus (reviewed in de Kloet et al. 1998) and the hippocampal projections to the hypothalamus (reviewed in Ulrich-Lai & Herman 2009) provide an indirect link between the hippocampus and regulation of the stress response. Direct evidence comes from numerous studies showing that destruction of the hippocampus prevents the efficient shut-off of the HPA axis and the return of glucocorticoid levels to their basal state after stressor exposure, whereas stimulation of the hippocampus inhibits stress-induced HPA activation (reviewed in Jacobson & Sapolsky 1991, Ulrich-Lai & Herman 2009).

Adult-generated neurons may play a role in regulating the HPA axis as suggested by work examining the effects of adverse early-life experiences on the development of the HPA axis and adult neurogenesis. In both rodents and monkeys, exposure to prenatal stress results in a persistent dampening in the production of new neurons in adulthood (Coe et al. 2003, Lemaire et al. 2000). Likewise, adult rats subjected to maternal separation in early life exhibit reduced neurogenesis (Mirescu et al. 2004). Prenatal and early postnatal stressors have additionally been associated with impaired negative feedback of the HPA axis response to stressful situations during adulthood. Taken together, these studies raise the possibility that adult-generated neurons are involved in hippocampal neuroendocrine function. This idea has been recently tested using transgenic mice in which adult

neurogenesis was conditionally suppressed. Compared to wild-type controls, mice lacking adult neurogenesis exhibited greater stress-induced activation of the HPA axis (Schloesser et al. 2009), indicating that newly born neurons may in fact contribute to the ability of the hippocampus to mediate proper inhibitory control over the HPA axis. Again, adult neurogenesis is likely not the sole mechanism involved in HPA axis regulation. Alterations in CA3 dendritic complexity caused by chronic stress have been proposed to make the hippocampus less effective in regulating the HPA axis, which in turn leads to hypersecretion of glucocorticoids, but currently there is only correlative evidence to support this view (reviewed in Conrad 2006).

Other Possible Roles

In addition to the functions already discussed, accumulating evidence suggests that hippocampal neurogenesis may be linked to social behaviors, a function first suggested by work in birds (reviewed in Gheusi et al. 2009; see also Kozorovitskiy & Gould 2004, Mak et al. 2007). Structural plasticity in the hippocampus has been proposed to play a role in a number of neuropsychiatric and neurological disorders. Although a discussion of these is beyond the scope of this review, adult neurogenesis and other forms of structural plasticity have been implicated in addiction, schizophrenia, Alzheimer's, and epilepsy (reviewed in Burke & Barnes 2006, Eisch et al. 2008, Manji et al. 2001, Russo et al. 2009, Swann et al. 2000).

OVERALL CONCLUSIONS AND DIRECTIONS

A number of outstanding issues remain before definitive conclusions about the role of structural plasticity in hippocampal function can be reached. First and foremost, given the various types of structural change that occur within the hippocampus, it is currently impossible to attribute functional alterations to one specific type. Thus, a critical direction for future research will be the development of new techniques or approaches that selectively alter one form of plasticity while sparing the others. If different forms of structural plasticity are linked mechanistically, this might be difficult to achieve. Advances in imaging technologies allowing for the observation of structural changes in behaving animals combined with molecular approaches enabling the manipulation of structural plasticity in vivo will be critical to this endeavor and will help to elucidate the role of specific types of structural change in functions mediated by the hippocampus.

Within the context of adult neurogenesis, most studies to date have focused on quantitative changes. However, it is possible that the qualitative properties of new neurons could be altered instead of, or in addition to, absolute numbers. By analyzing the response properties of young cells to different experiences and by comparing these to mature cells, information can be obtained regarding the contribution of these different populations of neurons to hippocampal functions. Along similar lines, although much has been elucidated about the maturation of young cells, it will be critical to examine whether different aspects of their development are subject to experiential modification. For example, antidepressants have been shown to not only increase neurogenesis but also to impact the maturation and synaptic plasticity of adult-born hippocampal granule cells (Wang et al. 2008). Extending this type of analysis to other factors and experiences that modulate neurogenesis will undoubtedly provide novel insights into how adult-generated cells contribute to hippocampal functions.

It is also becoming increasingly appreciated that the hippocampus is not a homogenous structure and that it exhibits differences in connectivity and function, as well as gene expression, along the longitudinal or septotemporal axis (Bannerman et al. 2004, Leonardo et al. 2006). Whereas the dorsal hippocampus participates in working and spatial memory, the ventral hippocampus is primarily involved in emotional memory and anxiety, and unlike the dorsal region, has connections to amygdala, hypothalamus, and prefrontal cortex structures associated with the HPA axis and emotion (Moser & Moser 1998, Swanson & Cowan 1977). Thus, additional consideration of the distinctions between the dorsal and ventral hippocampus is necessary and may be key to understanding the specific contributions that structural change makes to learning and memory, anxiety, and stress regulation. For instance, some newer work suggests that spatial and associative learning may have a more pronounced effect on the survival and subsequent activation of new cells in the ventral hippocampus (Dalla et al. 2009, Snyder et al. 2009b).

Finally, various forms of structural plasticity have been tied to numerous psychiatric and neurological conditions. Although no definitive link has been established because of obstacles in studying structural plasticity in the human brain, technological advances are on the horizon and should be valuable in this regard. Given that there is now widespread acceptance that the adult brain is capable of undergoing dramatic structural reorganization, it is likely only a matter of time before definitive conclusions are obtained about the precise role of structural plasticity in hippocampal functions under normal and pathological conditions.

DISCLOSURE STATEMENT

The authors are not aware of any biases that might be perceived as affecting the objectivity of this review.

ACKNOWLEDGMENTS

The work was supported by a Young Investigator Award from the National Alliance for Research on Schizophrenia and Depression to B.L. and grants from the National Institute of Mental Health to B.L. (K99MH084148) and E.G. (MH54970).

LITERATURE CITED

Ackman JB, Siddiqi F, Walikonis RS, LoTurco JJ. 2006. Fusion of microglia with pyramidal neurons after retroviral infection. *J. Neurosci.* 26:11413–22

Aimone JB, Wiles J, Gage FH. 2009. Computational influence of adult neurogenesis on memory encoding. *Neuron* 61:187–202

Airan RD, Meltzer LA, Roy M, Gong Y, Chen H, Deisseroth K. 2007. High-speed imaging reveals neuro-physiological links to behavior in an animal model of depression. *Science* 317:819–23

Altman J. 1962. Are new neurons formed in the brains of adult mammals? *Science* 135:1127–28

Altman J, Das GD. 1965. Autoradiographic and histological evidence of postnatal hippocampal neurogenesis in rats. *J. Comp. Neurol.* 124:319–35

Ambrogini P, Cuppini R, Cuppini C, Ciaroni S, Cecchini T, et al. 2000. Spatial learning affects immature granule cell survival in the adult dentate gyrus. *Neurosci. Lett.* 286:21–24

Ambrogini P, Orsini L, Mancini C, Ferri P, Ciaroni S, Cuppini R. 2004. Learning may reduce neurogenesis in the adult rat dentate gyrus. *Neurosci. Lett.* 359:13–16

Amrein I, Dechmann DK, Winter Y, Lipp HP. 2007. Absent or low rate of adult neurogenesis in the hippocampus of bats (Chiroptera). *PLoS One* 2:e455

Amrein I, Slomianka L, Lipp HP. 2004. Granule cell number, cell death and cell proliferation in the dentate gyrus of wild-living rodents. *Eur. J. Neurosci.* 20:3342–50

Andersen P, Soleng AF. 1998. Long-term potentiation and spatial training are both associated with the generation of new excitatory synapses. *Brain Res. Brain Res. Rev.* 26:353–59

Bain MJ, Dwyer SM, Rusak B. 2004. Restraint stress affects hippocampal cell proliferation differently in rat and mice. *Neurosci. Lett.* 368:7–10

Bannerman DM, Rawlins JN, McHugh SB, Deacon RM, Yee BK, et al. 2004. Regional dissociations within the hippocampus—memory and anxiety. *Neurosci. Biobehav. Rev.* 28:273–83

Barnea A, Nottebohm F. 1994. Seasonal recruitment of hippocampal neurons in adult free-ranging black-capped chickadees. *Proc. Natl. Acad. Sci. USA* 91:11217–21

Bauer S, Patterson PH. 2005. The cell cycle-apoptosis connection revisited in the adult brain. *J. Cell Biol.* 171:641–50

Boldrini M, Underwood MD, Hen R, Rosoklija GB, Dwork AJ, et al. 2009. Antidepressants increase neural progenitor cells in the human hippocampus. *Neuropsychopharmacology* 34:2376–89

Bonhoeffer T, Yuste R. 2002. Spine motility. Phenomenology, mechanisms, and function. *Neuron* 35:1019–27

Brené S, Bjørnebekk A, Aberg E, Mathé AA, Olson L, Werme M. 2007. Running is rewarding and antidepressive. *Physiol. Behav.* 92:136–40

Bruel-Jungerman E, Davis S, Rampon C, Laroche S. 2006. Long-term potentiation enhances neurogenesis in the adult dentate gyrus. *J. Neurosci.* 26:5888–93

Bruel-Jungerman E, Laroche S, Rampon C. 2005. New neurons in the dentate gyrus are involved in the expression of enhanced long-term memory following environmental enrichment. *Eur. J. Neurosci.* 21:513–21

Bull ND, Bartlett PF. 2005. The adult mouse hippocampal progenitor is neurogenic but not a stem cell. *J. Neurosci.* 25:10815–21

Burke SN, Barnes CA. 2006. Neural plasticity in the ageing brain. *Nat. Rev. Neurosci.* 7:30–40

Burns KA, Kuan CY. 2005. Low doses of bromo- and iododeoxyuridine produce near-saturation labeling of adult proliferative populations in the dentate gyrus. *Eur. J. Neurosci.* 21:803–7

Cameron HA, Gould E. 1994. Adult neurogenesis is regulated by adrenal steroids in the dentate gyrus. *Neuroscience* 61:203–9

Cameron HA, McKay RD. 1999. Restoring production of hippocampal neurons in old age. *Nat. Neurosci.* 2:894–97

Cameron HA, McKay RD. 2001. Adult neurogenesis produces a large pool of new granule cells in the dentate gyrus. *J. Comp. Neurol.* 435:406–17

Cameron HA, Woolley CS, McEwen BS, Gould E. 1993. Differentiation of newly born neurons and glia in the dentate gyrus of the adult rat. *Neuroscience* 56:337–44

Provides evidence that substantial numbers of new neurons are produced in the adult hippocampus daily.

Campbell S, MacQueen G. 2004. The role of the hippocampus in the pathophysiology of major depression. *J. Psychiatry Neurosci.* 29:417–26

Chehrehasa F, Meedeniya ACB, Dwyer P, Abrahamsen G, Mackay-Sim A. 2009. EdU, a new thymidine analogue for labeling proliferating cells in the nervous system. *J. Neurosci. Methods* 177:122–30

Chen Y, Dubé CM, Rice CJ, Baram TZ. 2008. Rapid loss of dendritic spines after stress involves derangement of spine dynamics by corticotropin-releasing hormone. *J. Neurosci.* 28:2903–11

Christie BR, Cameron HA. 2006. Neurogenesis in the adult hippocampus. *Hippocampus* 16:199–207

Clelland CD, Choi M, Romberg C, Clemenson GD Jr, Fragniere A, et al. 2009. A functional role for adult hippocampal neurogenesis in spatial pattern separation. *Science* 325:210–13

Coe CL, Kramer M, Czéh B, Gould E, Reeves AJ, et al. 2003. Prenatal stress diminishes neurogenesis in the dentate gyrus of juvenile rhesus monkeys. *Biol. Psychiatry* 54:1025–34

Conrad CD. 2006. What is the functional significance of chronic stress-induced CA3 dendritic retraction within the hippocampus? *Behav. Cogn. Neurosci. Rev.* 5:41–60

Couillard-Despres S, Winner B, Karl C, Lindemann G, Schmid P, et al. 2006. Targeted transgene expression in neuronal precursors: watching young neurons in the old brain. *Eur. J. Neurosci.* 24:1535–45

Dailey M, Marrs G, Satz J, Waite M. 1999. Concepts in imaging and microscopy. Exploring biological structure and function with confocal microscopy. *Biol. Bull.* 197:115–22

Dalla C, Bangasser DA, Edgecomb C, Shors TJ. 2007. Neurogenesis and learning: acquisition and asymptotic performance predict how many new cells survive in the hippocampus. *Neurobiol. Learn. Mem.* 88:143–48

Dalla C, Papachristos EB, Whetstone AS, Shors TJ. 2009. Female rats learn trace memories better than male rats and consequently retain a greater proportion of new neurons in their hippocampi. *Proc. Natl. Acad. Sci. USA* 106:2927–32

Dayer AG, Ford AA, Cleaver KM, Yassaee M, Cameron HA. 2003. Short-term and long-term survival of new neurons in the rat dentate gyrus. *J. Comp. Neurol.* 460:563–72

de Kloet ER, Vreugdenhil E, Oitzl MS, Joëls M. 1998. Brain corticosteroid receptor balance in health and disease. *Endocr. Rev.* 19:269–301

De Roo M, Klauser P, Garcia PM, Poglia L, Muller D. 2008. Spine dynamics and synapse remodeling during LTP and memory processes. *Prog. Brain Res.* 169:199–207

Döbrössy MD, Drapeau E, Aurousseau C, Le Moal M, Piazza PV, Abrous DN. 2003. Differential effects of learning on neurogenesis: learning increases or decreases the number of newly born cells depending on their birth date. *Mol. Psychiatry* 8:974–82

Drapeau E, Mayo W, Aurousseau C, Le Moal M, Piazza PV, Abrous DN. 2003. Spatial memory performances of aged rats in the water maze predict levels of hippocampal neurogenesis. *Proc. Natl. Acad. Sci. USA* 100:14385–90

Dupret D, Fabre A, Döbrössy MD, Panatier A, Rodríguez JJ, et al. 2007. Spatial learning depends on both the addition and removal of new hippocampal neurons. *PLoS Biol.* 5:e214

Dupret D, Montaron MF, Drapeau E, Aurousseau C, Le Moal M, et al. 2005. Methylazoxymethanol acetate does not fully block cell genesis in the young and aged dentate gyrus. *Eur. J. Neurosci.* 22:778–83

Dupret D, Revest JM, Koehl M, Ichas F, De Giorgi F, et al. 2008. Spatial relational memory requires hippocampal adult neurogenesis. *PLoS ONE* 3:e1959

Eadie BD, Redila VA, Christie BR. 2005. Voluntary exercise alters the cytoarchitecture of the adult dentate gyrus by increasing cellular proliferation, dendritic complexity, and spine density. *J. Comp. Neurol.* 486:39–47

Ehninger D, Kempermann G. 2006. Paradoxical effects of learning the Morris water maze on adult hippocampal neurogenesis in mice may be explained by a combination of stress and physical activity. *Genes Brain Behav.* 5:29–39

Eisch AJ, Cameron HA, Encinas JM, Meltzer L, Ming GL, Overstreet-Wadiche LS. 2008. Adult neurogenesis, mental health, and mental illness: hope or hype? *J. Neurosci.* 28:11785–91

Eisch AJ, Mandyam CD. 2007. Adult neurogenesis: Can analysis of cell cycle proteins move us "Beyond BrdU"? *Curr. Pharm. Biotechnol.* 8:147–65

Encinas JM, Vaahtokari A, Enikolopov G. 2006. Fluoxetine targets early progenitor cells in the adult brain. *Proc. Natl. Acad. Sci. USA* 103:8233–38

Presents a novel hypothesis about the way that new neurons support learning and memory.

Epp JR, Barker JM, Galea LA. 2009. Running wild: neurogenesis in the hippocampus across the lifespan in wild and laboratory-bred Norway rats. *Hippocampus* In press

Epp JR, Spritzer MD, Galea LA. 2007. Hippocampus-dependent learning promotes survival of new neurons in the dentate gyrus at a specific time during cell maturation. *Neuroscience* 149:273–85

Eriksson PS, Perfilieva E, Björk-Eriksson T, Alborn AM, Nordborg C, et al. 1998. Neurogenesis in the adult human hippocampus. *Nat. Med.* 4:1313–17

Espósito MS, Piatti VC, Laplagne DA, Morgenstern NA, Ferrari CC, et al. 2005. Neuronal differentiation in the adult hippocampus recapitulates embryonic development. *J. Neurosci.* 25:10074–86

Eyre MD, Richter-Levin G, Avital A, Stewart MG. 2003. Morphological changes in hippocampal dentate gyrus synapses following spatial learning in rats are transient. *Eur. J. Neurosci.* 17:1973–80

Farioli-Vecchioli S, Saraulli D, Costanzi M, Pacioni S, Cinà I, et al. 2008. The timing of differentiation of adult hippocampal neurons is crucial for spatial memory. *PLoS Biol.* 6:e246

Fiala JC, Feinberg M, Popov V, Harris KM. 1998. Synaptogenesis via dendritic filopodia in developing hippocampal area CA1. *J. Neurosci.* 18:8900–11

Flood DG. 1993. Critical issues in the analysis of dendritic extent in aging humans, primates, and rodents. *Neurobiol. Aging* 14:649–54

Flusberg BA, Nimmerjahn A, Cocker ED, Mukamel EA, Barretto RP. 2008. High-speed, miniaturized fluorescence microscopy in freely moving mice. *Nat. Methods* 5:935–38

Frankland PW, Bontempi B. 2005. The organization of recent and remote memories. *Nat. Rev. Neurosci.* 6:119–30

Garcia AD, Doan NB, Imura T, Bush TG, Sofroniew MV. 2004. GFAP-expressing progenitors are the principal source of constitutive neurogenesis in adult mouse forebrain. *Nat. Neurosci.* 7:1233–41

Garthe A, Behr J, Kempermann G. 2009. Adult-generated hippocampal neurons allow the flexible use of spatially precise learning strategies. *PLoS One* 5:e5464

Ge S, Goh EL, Sailor KA, Kitabatake Y, Ming GL, Song H. 2006. GABA regulates synaptic integration of newly generated neurons in the adult brain. *Nature* 439:589–93

Ge S, Yang CH, Hsu KS, Ming GL, Song H. 2007. A critical period for enhanced synaptic plasticity in newly generated neurons of the adult brain. *Neuron* 54:559–66

Geinisman Y, Berry RW, Disterhoft JF, Power JM, Van Der Zee EA. 2001. Associative learning elicits the formation of multiple-synapse boutons. *J. Neurosci.* 21:5568–73

Geinisman Y, deToledo-Morrell L, Morrell F, Persina IS, Rossi M. 1992. Age-related loss of axospinous synapses formed by two afferent systems in the rat dentate gyrus as revealed by the unbiased stereological dissector technique. *Hippocampus* 2:437–44

Gheusi G, Ortega-Perez I, Murray K, Lledo PM. 2009. A niche for adult neurogenesis in social behavior. *Behav. Brain Res.* 200:315–22

Globus A, Rosenzweig MR, Bennett EL, Diamond MC. 1973. Effects of differential experience on dendritic spine counts in rat cerebral cortex. *J. Comp. Physiol. Psychol.* 82:175–81

Gould E. 2007. How widespread is adult neurogenesis in mammals? *Nat. Rev. Neurosci.* 8:481–88

Gould E, Beylin A, Tanapat P, Reeves AJ, Shors TJ. 1999b. Learning enhances adult neurogenesis in the hippocampal formation. *Nat. Neurosci.* 2:260–65

Gould E, McEwen BS, Tanapat P, Galea LA, Fuchs E. 1997. Neurogenesis in the dentate gyrus of the adult tree shrew is regulated by psychosocial stress and NMDA receptor activation. *J. Neurosci.* 17:2492–98

Gould E, Reeves AJ, Fallah M, Tanapat P, Gross CG, Fuchs E. 1999a. Hippocampal neurogenesis in adult Old World primates. *Proc. Natl. Acad. Sci. USA* 96:5263–67

Gould E, Tanapat P. 1997. Lesion-induced proliferation of neuronal progenitors in the dentate gyrus of the adult rat. *Neuroscience* 80:427–36

Gould E, Tanapat P, McEwen BS, Flügge G, Fuchs E. 1998. Proliferation of granule cell precursors in the dentate gyrus of adult monkeys is diminished by stress. *Proc. Natl. Acad. Sci. USA* 95:3168–71

Gould E, Vail N, Wagers M, Gross CG. 2001. Adult-generated hippocampal and neocortical neurons in macaques have a transient existence. *Proc. Natl. Acad. Sci. USA* 98:10910–17

Gould E, Woolley CS, Cameron HA, Daniels DC, McEwen BS. 1991b. Adrenal steroids regulate postnatal development of the rat dentate gyrus: II. Effects of glucocorticoids and mineralocorticoids on cell birth. *J. Comp. Neurol.* 313:486–93

The first evidence that adult neurogenesis occurs in the human hippocampus.

The first study to achieve cellular level imaging in freely moving mice.

Gould E, Woolley CS, McEwen BS. 1991a. Naturally occurring cell death in the developing dentate gyrus of the rat. *J. Comp. Neurol.* 304:408–18

Hairston IS, Little MT, Scanlon MD, Barakat MT, Palmer TD, et al. 2005. Sleep restriction suppresses neurogenesis induced by hippocampus-dependent learning. *J. Neurophysiol.* 94:4224–33

Hajszan T, Dow A, Warner-Schmidt JL, Szigeti-Buck K, Sallam NL, et al. 2009. Remodeling of hippocampal spine synapses in the rat learned helplessness model of depression. *Biol. Psychiatry* 65:392–400

Hancock A, Priester C, Kidder E, Keith JR. 2009. Does 5-bromo-2'-deoxyuridine (BrdU) disrupt cell proliferation and neuronal maturation in the adult rat hippocampus in vivo? *Behav. Brain Res.* 199:218–21

Hastings N, Gould E. 1999. Rapid extension of axons into the CA3 region by adult-generated granule cells. *J. Comp. Neurol.* 413:146–54

Hastings NB, Seth MI, Tanapat P, Rydel TA, Gould E. 2002. Granule neurons generated during development extend divergent axon collaterals to hippocampal area CA3. *J. Comp. Neurol.* 452:324–33

He J, Crews FT. 2007. Neurogenesis decreases during brain maturation from adolescence to adulthood. *Pharmacol. Biochem. Behav.* 86:327–33

Heine V, Maslam S, Zareno J, Joëls M, Lucassen PJ. 2004. Suppressed proliferation and apoptotic changes in the rat dentate gyrus after acute and chronic stress are reversible. *Eur. J. Neurosci.* 19:131–44

Hernández-Rabaza V, Llorens-Martín M, Velázquez-Sánchez C, Ferragud A, Arcusa A, et al. 2009. Inhibition of adult hippocampal neurogenesis disrupts contextual learning but spares spatial working memory, long-term conditional rule retention and spatial reversal. *Neuroscience* 159:59–68

Hodes GE, Yang L, VanKooy J, Santollo J, Shors TJ. 2009. Prozac during puberty: distinctive effects on neurogenesis as a function of age and sex. *Neuroscience* 163:609–17

Holick KA, Lee DC, Hen R, Dulawa SC. 2008. Behavioral effects of chronic fluoxetine in BALB/cJ mice do not require adult hippocampal neurogenesis or the serotonin 1A receptor. *Neuropsychopharmacology* 33:406–17

Imayoshi I, Sakamoto M, Ohtsuka T, Takao K, Miyakawa T, et al. 2008. Roles of continuous neurogenesis in the structural and functional integrity of the adult forebrain. *Nat. Neurosci.* 11:1153–61

Jacobson L, Sapolsky R. 1991. The role of the hippocampus in feedback regulation of the hypothalamic-pituitary-adrenocortical axis. *Endocr. Rev.* 12:118–34

Jessberger S, Aigner S, Clemenson GD Jr, Toni N, Lie DC, et al. 2008b. Cdk5 regulates accurate maturation of newborn granule cells in the adult hippocampus. *PLoS Biol.* 6:e272

Jessberger S, Clark RE, Broadbent NJ, Clemson GD Jr, Consiglio A, et al. 2009. Dentate gyrus-specific knockdown of adult neurogenesis impairs spatial and object recognition memory in adult rats. *Learn. Mem.* 16:147–54

Jessberger S, Toni N, Clemenson GD Jr, Ray J, Gage FH. 2008a. Directed differentiation of hippocampal stem/progenitor cells in the adult brain. *Nat. Neurosci.* 11:888–93

Jin K, Wang X, Xie L, Mao XO, Zhu W, et al. 2006. Evidence for stroke-induced neurogenesis in the human brain. *Proc. Natl. Acad. Sci. USA* 103:13198–202

Kaplan MS, Hinds JW. 1977. Neurogenesis in the adult rat: electron microscopic analysis of light radioautographs. *Science* 197:1092–94

Karten YJ, Jones MA, Jeurling SI, Cameron HA. 2006. GABAergic signaling in young granule cells in the adult rat and mouse dentate gyrus. *Hippocampus* 16:312–20

Kee N, Sivalingam S, Boonstra R, Wojtowicz JM. 2002. The utility of Ki-67 and BrdU as proliferative markers of adult neurogenesis. *J. Neurosci. Methods* 115:97–105

Kee N, Teixeira CM, Wang AH, Frankland PW. 2007. Preferential incorporation of adult-generated granule cells into spatial memory networks in the dentate gyrus. *Nat. Neurosci.* 10:355–62

Kempermann G, Jessberger S, Steiner B, Kronenberg G. 2004. Milestones of neuronal development in the adult hippocampus. *Trends Neuroci.* 27:447–52

Kempermann G, Kuhn HG, Gage FH. 1997. More hippocampal neurons in adult mice living in an enriched environment. *Nature* 386:493–95

Kempermann G, Kuhn HG, Gage FH. 1998. Experience-induced neurogenesis in the senescent dentate gyrus. *J. Neurosci.* 18:3206–12

Klempin F, Kempermann G. 2007. Adult hippocampal neurogenesis and aging. *Eur. Arch. Psychiatry Clin. Neurosci.* 257:271–80

Knafo S, Ariav G, Barkai E, Libersat F. 2004. Olfactory learning-induced increase in spine density along the apical dendrites of CA1 hippocampal neurons. *Hippocampus* 14:819–25

Koo JW, Duman RS. 2008. IL-1beta is an essential mediator of the antineurogenic and anhedonic effects of stress. *Proc. Natl. Acad. Sci. USA* 105:751–56

Kozorovitskiy Y, Gould E. 2004. Dominance hierarchy influences adult neurogenesis in the dentate gyrus. *J. Neurosci.* 24:6755–59

Kozorovitskiy Y, Gross CG, Kopil C, Battaglia L, McBreen M, et al. 2005. Experience induces structural and biochemical changes in the adult primate brain. *Proc. Natl. Acad. Sci. USA* 102:17478–82

Kuhn HG, Dickinson-Anson H, Gage FH. 1996. Neurogenesis in the dentate gyrus of the adult rat: age-related decrease of neuronal progenitor proliferation. *J. Neurosci.* 16:2027–33

Lagace DC, Benavides DR, Kansy JW, Mapelli M, Greengard P, et al. 2008. Cdk5 is essential for adult hippocampal neurogenesis. *Proc. Natl. Acad. Sci. USA* 105:18567–71

Lamprecht R, LeDoux J. 2004. Structural plasticity and memory. *Nat. Rev. Neurosci.* 5:45–54

Laplagne DA, Espósito MS, Piatti VC, Morgenstern NA, Zhao C, et al. 2006. Functional convergence of neurons generated in the developing and adult hippocampus. *PLoS Biol.* 4:e409

Law AJ, Weickert CS, Hyde TM, Kleinman JE, Harrison PJ. 2004. Reduced spinophilin but not microtubule-associated protein 2 expression in the hippocampal formation in schizophrenia and mood disorders: molecular evidence for a pathology of dendritic spines. *Am. J. Psychiatry* 161:1848–55

Lemaire V, Koehl M, LeMoal M, Abrous DN. 2000. Prenatal stress produces learning deficits associated with an inhibition of neurogenesis in the hippocampus. *Proc. Natl. Acad. Sci. USA* 97:11032–37

Leonardo ED, Richardson-Jones JW, Sibille E, Kottman A, Hen R. 2006. Molecular heterogeneity along the dorsal-ventral axis of the murine hippocampal CA1 field: a microarray analysis of gene expression. *Neuroscience* 137:177–86

Leuner B, Falduto J, Shors TJ. 2003. Associative memory formation increases the observation of dendritic spines in the hippocampus. *J. Neurosci.* 23:659–65

Leuner B, Glasper ER, Gould E. 2009. Thymidine analog methods for studies of adult neurogenesis are not equally sensitive. *J. Comp. Neurol.* 517:123–33

Leuner B, Gould E, Shors TJ. 2006b. Is there a link between adult neurogenesis and learning? *Hippocampus* 16:216–24

Leuner B, Kozorovitskiy Y, Gross CG, Gould E. 2007a. Diminished adult neurogenesis in the marmoset brain precedes old age. *Proc. Natl. Acad. Sci. USA* 104:17169–73

Leuner B, Mendolia-Loffredo S, Kozorovitskiy Y, Samburg D, Gould E, Shors TJ. 2004. Learning enhances the survival of new neurons beyond the time when the hippocampus is required for memory. *J. Neurosci.* 24:7477–81

Leuner B, Mirescu C, Noiman L, Gould E. 2007b. Maternal experience inhibits the production of immature neurons in the hippocampus during the postpartum period through elevations in adrenal steroids. *Hippocampus* 17:434–42

Leuner B, Waddell J, Gould E, Shors TJ. 2006a. Temporal discontiguity is neither necessary nor sufficient for learning-induced effects on adult neurogenesis. *J. Neurosci.* 26:13437–42

Liu XB, Low LK, Jones EG, Cheng HJ. 2005. Stereotyped axon pruning via plexin signaling is associated with synaptic complex elimination in the hippocampus. *J. Neurosci.* 25:9124–34

Lucassen PJ, Bosch OJ, Jousma E, Krömer SA, Andrew R, et al. 2009. Prenatal stress reduces postnatal neurogenesis in rats selectively bred for high, but not low, anxiety: possible key role of placental 11beta-hydroxysteroid dehydrogenase type 2. *Eur. J. Neurosci.* 29:97–103

Madsen TM, Kristjansen PEG, Bolwig TG, Wortwein G. 2003. Arrested neuronal proliferation and impaired hippocampal function following fractionated brain irradiation in the adult rat. *Neuroscience* 119:635–42

Magariños AM, McEwen BS. 1995. Stress-induced atrophy of apical dendrites of hippocampal CA3c neurons: involvement of glucocorticoid secretion and excitatory amino acid receptors. *Neuroscience* 69:89–98

Magariños AM, McEwen BS, Flügge G, Fuchs E. 1996. Chronic psychosocial stress causes apical dendritic atrophy of hippocampal CA3 pyramidal neurons in subordinate tree shrews. *J. Neurosci.* 16:3534–40

Mak G, Enwere EK, Gregg C, Pakarainen T, Poutanen M, et al. 2007. Male-pheromone-stimulated neurogenesis in the adult female brain: possible role in mating behavior. *Nat. Neurosci.* 10:1003–11

Malberg JE, Duman RS. 2003. Cell proliferation in adult hippocampus is decreased by inescapable stress: reversal by fluoxetine treatment. *Neuropsychopharmacology* 28:1562–71

Malberg JE, Eisch AJ, Nestler EJ, Duman RS. 2000. Chronic antidepressant treatment increases neurogenesis in adult rat hippocampus. *J. Neurosci.* 20:9104–10

Manganas LN, Zhang X, Li Y, Hazel RD, Smith SD, et al. 2007. Magnetic resonance spectroscopy identifies neural progenitor cells in the live human brain. *Science* 318:980–85

Manji HK, Drevets WC, Charney DS. 2001. The cellular neurobiology of depression. *Nat. Med.* 7:541–47

Markakis E, Gage F. 1999. Adult-generated neurons in the dentate gyrus send axonal projections to field CA3 and are surrounded by synaptic vesicles. *J. Comp. Neurol.* 406:449–60

Mayer JL, Klumpers L, Maslam S, de Kloet ER, Joëls M, Lucassen PJ. 2006. Brief treatment with the glucocorticoid receptor antagonist mifepristone normalises the corticosterone-induced reduction of adult hippocampal neurogenesis. *J. Neuroendocrinol.* 18:629–31

McEwen BS. 2005. Glucocorticoids, depression, and mood disorders: structural remodeling in the brain. *Metabolism* 54:20–23

McKittrick CR, Magariños AM, Blanchard DC, Blanchard RJ, McEwen BS, Sakai RR. 2000. Chronic social stress reduces dendritic arbors in CA3 of hippocampus and decreases binding to serotonin transporter sites. *Synapse* 36:85–94

Miranda R, Blanco E, Begega A, Santín LJ, Arias JL. 2006. Reversible changes in hippocampal CA1 synapses associated with water maze training in rats. *Synapse* 59:177–81

Mirescu C, Gould E. 2006. Stress and adult neurogenesis. *Hippocampus* 16:233–38

Mirescu C, Peters JD, Gould E. 2004. Early life experience alters response of adult neurogenesis to stress. *Nat. Neurosci.* 7:841–46

Mizrahi A, Crowley JC, Shtoyerman E, Katz LC. 2004. High-resolution in vivo imaging of hippocampal dendrites and spines. *J. Neurosci.* 24:3147–51

Mohapel P, Mundt-Petersen K, Brundin P, Frielingsdorf H. 2006. Working memory training decreases hippocampal neurogenesis. *Neuroscience* 142:609–13

Monje ML, Toda H, Palmer TD. 2003. Inflammatory blockade restores adult hippocampal neurogenesis. *Science* 302:1760–65

Montaron MF, Drapeau E, Dupret D, Kitchener P, Aurousseau C, et al. 2006. Lifelong corticosterone level determines age-related decline in neurogenesis and memory. *Neurobiol. Aging* 27:645–54

Morgenstern NA, Lombardi G, Schinder AF. 2008. Newborn granule cells in the ageing dentate gyrus. *J. Physiol.* 586:3751–57

Moser MB, Moser EI. 1998. Functional differentiation in the hippocampus. *Hippocampus* 6:608–19

Moser MB, Trommald M, Andersen P. 1994. An increase in dendritic spine density on hippocampal CA1 pyramidal cells following spatial learning in adult rats suggests the formation of new synapses. *Proc. Natl. Acad. Sci. USA* 91:12673–75

Nimchinsky EA, Sabatini BL, Svoboda K. 2002. Structure and function of dendritic spines. *Annu. Rev. Physiol.* 64:313–53

Nottebohm F. 2002. Why are some neurons replaced in adult brain? *J. Neurosci.* 22:624–28

O'Brien JA, Lummis SC. 2006. Diolistic labeling of neuronal cultures and intact tissue using a hand-held gene gun. *Nat. Protoc.* 1:1517–21

Olariu A, Cleaver KM, Cameron HA. 2007. Decreased neurogenesis in aged rats results from loss of granule cell precursors without lengthening of the cell cycle. *J. Comp. Neurol.* 501:659–67

Olariu A, Cleaver KM, Shore LE, Brewer MD, Cameron HA. 2005. A natural form of learning can increase and decrease the survival of new neurons in the dentate gyrus. *Hippocampus* 15:750–62

O'Malley A, O'Connell C, Murphy KJ, Regan CM. 2000. Transient spine density increases in the mid-molecular layer of hippocampal dentate gyrus accompany consolidation of a spatial learning task in the rodent. *Neuroscience* 99:229–32

O'Malley A, O'Connell C, Regan CM. 1998. Ultrastructural analysis reveals avoidance conditioning to induce a transient increase in hippocampal dentate spine density in the 6 hour post-training period of consolidation. *Neuroscience* 87:607–13

Oomen CA, Mayer JL, de Kloet ER, Joëls M, Lucassen PJ. 2007. Brief treatment with the glucocorticoid receptor antagonist mifepristone normalizes the reduction in neurogenesis after chronic stress. *Eur. J. Neurosci.* 2612:3395–401

Overstreet LS, Hentges ST, Bumaschny VF, de Souza FS, Smart JL, et al. 2004. A transgenic marker for newly born granule cells in dentate gyrus. *J. Neurosci.* 24:3251–59

Overstreet-Wadiche LS, Westbrook GL. 2006. Functional maturation of adult-generated granule cells. *Hippocampus* 16:208–15

Pereira AC, Huddleston DE, Brickman AM, Sosunov AA, Hen R, et al. 2007. An in vivo correlate of exercise-induced neurogenesis in the adult dentate gyrus. *Proc. Natl. Acad. Sci. USA* 104:5638–43

Perera TD, Coplan JD, Lisanby SH, Lipira CM, Arif M, et al. 2007. Antidepressant-induced neurogenesis in the hippocampus of adult nonhuman primates. *J. Neurosci.* 27:4894–901

Pham K, Nacher J, Hof PR, McEwen BS. 2003. Repeated restraint stress suppresses neurogenesis and induces biphasic PSA-NCAM expression in the adult rat dentate gyrus. *Eur. J. Neurosci.* 7:879–86

Pokorný J, Yamamoto. 1981. Postnatal ontogenesis of hippocampal CA1 area in rats. II. Development of ultrastructure in stratum lacunosum and moleculare. *Brain Res. Bull.* 7:121–30

Raber J, Rola R, LeFevour A, Morhardt D, Curley J, et al. 2004. Radiation induced cognitive impairments are associated with changes in indicators of hippocampal neurogenesis. *Radiat. Res.* 162:39–47

Rahimi O, Claiborne BJ. 2007. Morphological development and maturation of granule neuron dendrites in the rat dentate gyrus. *Prog. Brain Res.* 163:167–81

Ramirez-Amaya V, Marrone DF, Gage FH, Worley PF, Barnes CA. 2006. Integration of new neurons into functional neural networks. *J. Neurosci.* 26:12237–41

Reif A, Fritzen S, Finger M, Strobel A, Lauer M, et al. 2006. Neural stem cell proliferation is decreased in schizophrenia, but not in depression. *Mol. Psychiatry* 11:514–22

Revest JM, Dupret D, Koehl M, Funk-Reiter C, Grosjean N, et al. 2009. Adult hippocampal neurogenesis is involved in anxiety-related behaviors. *Mol. Psychiatry.* In press

Ribak CE, Shapiro LA. 2007. Dendritic development of newly generated neurons in the adult brain. *Brain. Res Rev.* 55:390–94

Rola R, Raber J, Rizk A, Otsuka S, VandenBerg SR, et al. 2004. Radiation-induced impairment of hippocampal neurogenesis is associated with cognitive deficits in young mice. *Exp. Neurol.* 188:316–30

Rolls ET, Kesner RP. 2006. A computational theory of hippocampal function, and empirical tests of the theory. *Prog. Neurobiol.* 79:1–48

Rusakov DA, Davies HA, Harrison E, Diana G, Richter-Levin G, et al. 1997. Ultrastructural synaptic correlates of spatial learning in rat hippocampus. *Neuroscience* 80:69–77

Russo SJ, Mazei-Robison MS, Ables JL, Nestler EJ. 2009. Neurotrophic factors and structural plasticity in addiction. *Neuropharmacology* 56:73–82

Sahay A, Hen R. 2007. Adult hippocampal neurogenesis in depression. *Nat. Neurosci.* 10:1110–15

Salic A, Mitchinson TJ. 2008. A chemical method for fast and sensitive detection of DNA synthesis in vivo. *Proc. Natl. Acad. Sci. USA* 105:2415–20

Santarelli L, Saxe M, Gross C, Surget A, Battaglia F, et al. 2003. Requirement of hippocampal neurogenesis for the behavioral effects of antidepressants. *Science* 301:805–9

Sapolsky RM. 2004. Is impaired neurogenesis relevant to the affective symptoms of depression? *Biol. Psychiatry* 56:137–39

Saxe MD, Battaglia F, Wang JW, Malleret G, David DJ, et al. 2006. Ablation of hippocampal neurogenesis impairs contextual fear conditioning and synaptic plasticity in the dentate gyrus. *Proc. Natl. Acad. Sci. USA* 103:17501–6

Saxe MD, Malleret G, Vronskaya S, Mendez I, Garcia AD, et al. 2007. Paradoxical influence of hippocampal neurogenesis on working memory. *Proc. Natl. Acad. Sci. USA* 104:4642–46

Schinder AF, Gage FH. 2004. A hypothesis about the role of adult neurogenesis in hippocampal function. *Physiology (Bethesda)* 19:253–61

Schlessinger AR, Cowan WM, Gottlieb DI. 1975. An autoradiographic study of the time of origin and the pattern of granule cell migration in the dentate gyrus of the rat. *J. Comp. Neurol.* 159:149–75

Schloesser RJ, Manji HK, Martinowich K. 2009. Suppression of adult neurogenesis leads to increased hypothalamo-pituitary-adrenal axis response. *Neuroreport* 20:553–57

Provides the first direct evidence that newly born neurons contribute to the hippocampus's ability to mediate proper inhibitory regulation over the HPA axis.

Schmidt-Hieber C, Jonas P, Bischofberger J. 2004. Enhanced synaptic plasticity in newly generated granule cells of the adult hippocampus. *Nature* 429:184–87

Schroeder T. 2008. Imaging stem-cell-driven regeneration in mammals. *Nature* 453:345–51

Seress L. 2007. Comparative anatomy of the hippocampal dentate gyrus in adult and developing rodents, nonhuman primates and humans. *Prog. Brain Res.* 163:23–41

Seress L, Ribak CE. 1995. Postnatal development of CA3 pyramidal neurons and their afferents in the Ammon's horn of rhesus monkeys. *Hippocampus* 5:217–31

Seri B, García-Verdugo JM, McEwen BS, Alvarez-Buylla A. 2001. Astrocytes give rise to new neurons in the adult mammalian hippocampus. *J. Neurosci.* 21:7153–60

Selye H. 1976. *The Stress of Life*. New York: McGraw-Hill

Shors TJ. 2008. From stem cells to grandmother cells: how neurogenesis relates to learning and memory. *Cell Stem Cell* 3:253–58

Shors TJ, Chua C, Falduto J. 2001a. Sex differences and opposite effects of stress on dendritic spine density in the male versus female hippocampus. *J. Neurosci.* 21:6292–97

Shors TJ, Mathew J, Sisti HM, Edgecomb C, Beckoff S, Dalla C. 2007. Neurogenesis and helplessness are mediated by controllability in males but not in females. *Biol. Psychiatry* 62:487–95

Shors TJ, Miesagaes G, Beylin A, Zhao M, Rydel T, Gould E. 2001b. Neurogenesis in the adult rat is involved in the formation of trace memories. *Nature* 410:372–76

Shors TJ, Townsend DA, Zhao M, Kozorovitskiy Y, Gould E. 2002. Neurogenesis may relate to some but not all types of hippocampal-dependent learning. *Hippocampus* 12:578–84

Simon M, Czéh B, Fuchs E. 2005. Age-dependent susceptibility of adult hippocampal cell proliferation to chronic psychosocial stress. *Brain Res.* 1049:244–48

Snyder JS, Kee N, Wojtowicz JM. 2001. Effects of adult neurogenesis on synaptic plasticity in the rat dentate gyrus. *J. Neurophysiol.* 85:2423–31

Snyder JS, Glover LR, Sanzone KM, Kamhi JF, Cameron HA. 2009a. The effects of exercise and stress on the survival and maturation of adult-generated granule cells. *Hippocampus* In press

Snyder JS, Hong NS, McDonald RJ, Wojtowicz JM. 2005. A role for adult neurogenesis in spatial long-term memory. *Neuroscience* 130:843–52

Snyder JS, Radik R, Wojtowicz JM, Cameron HA. 2009b. Anatomical gradients of adult neurogenesis and activity: Young neurons in the ventral dentate gyrus are activated by water maze training. *Hippocampus* 19:360–70

Sousa N, Lukoyanov NV, Madeira MD, Almeida OF, Paula-Barbosa MM. 2000. Reorganization of the morphology of hippocampal neurites and synapses after stress-induced damage correlates with behavioral improvement. *Neuroscience* 97:253–66

Stewart MG, Davies HA, Sandi C, Kraev IV, Rogachevsky VV, et al. 2005. Stress suppresses and learning induces plasticity in CA3 of rat hippocampus: a three-dimensional ultrastructural study of thorny excrescences and their postsynaptic densities. *Neuroscience* 131:43–54

Stranahan A, Kahlil D, Gould E. 2006. Social isolation delays the positive effects of running on adult neurogenesis. *Nat. Neurosci.* 9:526–33

Stranahan A, Kahlil D, Gould E. 2007. Running induces widespread structural alterations in the hippocampus and entorhinal cortex. *Hippocampus* 17:1017–22

Surget A, Saxe M, Leman S, Ibarguen-Vargas Y, Chalon S, et al. 2008. Drug-dependent requirement of hippocampal neurogenesis in a model of depression and of antidepressant reversal. *Biol. Psychiatry* 64:293–301

Swann JW, Al-Noori S, Jiang M, Lee CL. 2000. Spine loss and other dendritic abnormalities in epilepsy. *Hippocampus* 10:617–25

Swanson LW, Cowan WM. 1977. An autoradiographic study of the organization of the efferent connections of the hippocampal formation in the rat. *J. Comp. Neurol.* 172:49–84

Tanapat P, Galea LA, Gould L. 1998. Stress inhibits the proliferation of granule cell precursors in the developing dentate gyrus. *Int. J. Dev. Neurosci.* 16:235–39

Tanapat P, Hastings NB, Rydel TA, Galea LA, Gould E. 2001. Exposure to fox odor inhibits cell proliferation in the hippocampus of adult rats via an adrenal hormone-dependent mechanism. *J. Comp. Neurol.* 437:496–504

Shows that adult-born neurons possess unique electrophysiological properties as compared to mature granule neurons in the dentate gyrus.

Tashiro A, Makino H, Gage FH. 2007. Experience-specific functional modification of the dentate gyrus through adult neurogenesis: a critical period during an immature stage. *J. Neurosci.* 27:3252–59

Tashiro A, Zhao C, Gage FH. 2006. Retrovirus-mediated single-cell gene knockout technique in adult newborn neurons in vivo. *Nat. Protoc.* 1:3049–55

Thomas RM, Hotsenpiller G, Peterson DA. 2007. Acute psychosocial stress reduces cell survival in adult hippocampal neurogenesis without altering proliferation. *J. Neurosci.* 27:2734–43

Toni N, Laplagne DA, Zhao C, Lombardi G, Ribak CE, et al. 2008. Neurons born in the adult dentate gyrus form functional synapses with target cells. *Nat. Neurosci.* 11:901–7

Toni N, Teng EM, Bushong EA, Aimone JB, Zhao C, et al. 2007. Synapse formation on neurons born in the adult hippocampus. *Nat. Neurosci.* 10:727–34

Ulrich-Lai YM, Herman JP. 2009. Neural regulation of endocrine and autonomic stress responses. *Nat. Rev. Neurosci.* 10:397–409

Van Der Borght K, Meerlo P, Luiten PG, Eggen BJ, Van Der Zee EA. 2005a. Effects of active shock avoidance learning on hippocampal neurogenesis and plasma levels of corticosterone. *Behav. Brain Res.* 157:23–30

Van Der Borght K, Wallinga AE, Luiten PG, Eggen BJ, Van Der Zee EA. 2005b. Morris water maze learning in two rat strains increases the expression of the polysialylated form of the neural cell adhesion molecule in the dentate gyrus but has no effect on hippocampal neurogenesis. *Behav. Neurosci.* 119:926–32

van Hooijdonk LW, Ichwan M, Dijkmans TF, Schouten TG, de Backer MW, et al. 2009. Lentivirus-mediated transgene delivery to the hippocampus reveals subfield specific differences in expression. *BMC Neurosci.* 10:2

van Praag H, Kempermann G, Gage FH. 1999. Running increases cell proliferation and neurogenesis in the adult mouse dentate gyrus. *Nat. Neurosci.* 2:266–70

van Praag H, Kempermann G, Gage FH. 2000. Neural consequences of environmental enrichment. *Nat. Rev. Neurosci.* 1:191–98

van Praag H, Schinder AF, Christie BR, Toni N, Palmer TD, Gage FH. 2002. Functional neurogenesis in the adult hippocampus. *Nature* 415:1030–34

van Praag H, Shubert T, Zhao C, Gage FH. 2005. Exercise enhances learning and hippocampal neurogenesis in aged mice. *J. Neurosci.* 25:8680–85

Veenema AH, de Kloet ER, de Wilde MC, Roelofs AJ, Kawata M, et al. 2007. Differential effects of stress on adult hippocampal cell proliferation in low and high aggressive mice. *J. Neuroendocrinol.* 19:489–98

Vega CJ, Peterson DA. 2005. Stem cell proliferative history in tissue revealed by temporal halogenated thymidine analog discrimination. *Nat. Methods* 2:167–69

Vollmayr B, Simonis C, Weber S, Gass P, Henn F. 2003. Reduced cell proliferation in the dentate gyrus is not correlated with the development of learned helplessness. *Biol. Psychiatry* 54:1035–40

Waddell J, Shors TJ. 2008. Neurogenesis, learning and associative strength. *Eur. J. Neurosci.* 27:3020–28

Walker TL, White A, Black DM, Wallace RH, Sah P, Bartlett PF. 2008. Latent stem and progenitor cells in the hippocampus are activated by neural excitation. *J. Neurosci.* 28:5240–47

Wang JW, David DJ, Monckton JE, Battaglia F, Hen R. 2008. Chronic fluoxetine stimulates maturation and synaptic plasticity of adult-born hippocampal granule cells. *J. Neurosci.* 28:1374–84

Wang S, Scott BW, Wojtowicz JM. 2000. Heterogeneous properties of dentate granule neurons in the adult rat. *J. Neurobiol.* 42:248–57

Westenbroek C, Den Boer JA, Veenhuis M, Ter Horst GJ. 2004. Chronic stress and social housing differentially affect neurogenesis in male and female rats. *Brain Res. Bull.* 64:303–8

Winocur G, Wojtowicz JM, Sekeres M, Snyder JS, Wang S. 2006. Inhibition of neurogenesis interferes with hippocampus-dependent memory function. *Hippocampus* 16:296–304

Wojtowicz JM, Kee N. 2006. BrdU assay for neurogenesis in rodents. *Nat. Protoc.* 1:1399–405

Woolley CS, Gould E, Frankfurt M, McEwen BS. 1990a. Naturally occurring fluctuation in dendritic spine density on adult hippocampal pyramidal neurons. *J. Neurosci.* 10:4035–39

Woolley CS, Gould E, McEwen BS. 1990b. Exposure to excess glucocorticoids alters dendritic morphology of adult hippocampal pyramidal neurons. *Brain Res.* 531:225–31

Xu HT, Pan F, Yang G, Gan WB. 2007. Choice of cranial window type for in vivo imaging affects dendritic spine turnover in the cortex. *Nat. Neurosci.* 10:549–51

The first study showing that adult-generated neurons in the mammalian brain generate action potentials and thereby become functionally integrated into the hippocampal circuitry.

Yamaguchi M, Saito H, Suzuki M, Mori K. 2000. Visualization of neurogenesis in the central nervous system using nestin promoter-GFP transgenic mice. *Neuroreport* 11:1991–96

Zehr JL, Nichols LR, Schulz KM, Sisk CL. 2008. Adolescent development of neuron structure in dentate gyrus granule cells of male Syrian hamsters. *Dev. Neurobiol.* 68:1517–26

Zhang CL, Zou Y, He W, Gage FH, Evans RM. 2008. A role for adult TLX-positive neural stem cells in learning and behavior. *Nature* 451:1004–7

Zhao C, Teng EM, Summers RG Jr, Ming GL, Gage FH. 2006. Distinct morphological stages of dentate granule neuron maturation in the adult mouse hippocampus. *J. Neurosci.* 26:3–11

RELATED RESOURCES

Andersen P, Morris R, Amaral D, Bliss T, O'Keefe J, eds. 2007. *The Hippocampus Book*. New York: Oxford Univ. Press

A Bridge Over Troubled Water: Reconsolidation as a Link Between Cognitive and Neuroscientific Memory Research Traditions

Oliver Hardt,[1] Einar Örn Einarsson,[1] and Karim Nader

Department of Psychology, McGill University, Montreal, Quebec, H3A 1B1 Canada; email: oliver.hardt@mac.com; einar.einarsson@mcgill.ca; karim.nader@mcgill.ca

Annu. Rev. Psychol. 2010. 61:141–67

First published online as a Review in Advance on October 19, 2009

The *Annual Review of Psychology* is online at psych.annualreviews.org

This article's doi:
10.1146/annurev.psych.093008.100455

0066-4308/10/0110-0141$20.00

[1]These authors contributed equally to this work and share first authorship. Correspondence may be addressed to either author

Key Words

consolidation, reconsolidation, memory updating, memory distortions

Abstract

There are two research traditions on dynamic memory processes. In cognitive psychology, the malleable nature of long-term memory has been extensively documented. Distortions, such as the misinformation effect or hindsight bias, illustrate that memories can be easily changed, often without their owner taking notice. On the other hand, effects like hypermnesia demonstrate that memory might be more reliable than these distortions suggest. In the neuroscience field, similar observations were obtained mostly from animal studies. Research on memory consolidation suggested that memories become progressively resistant to amnesic treatments over time, but the reconsolidation phenomenon showed that this stability can be transiently lifted when these memories are reactivated, i.e., retrieved. Surprisingly, both research traditions have not taken much notice of each others' advances in understanding memory dynamics. We apply concepts developed in neuroscience to phenomena revealed in cognitive psychology to illustrate how these twins separated at birth may be reunited again.

Contents

INTRODUCTION

One of the most prominent research traditions in the neurosciences of memory began more than 100 years ago with observations noting that memory is most vulnerable shortly after it has been acquired. Theodule-Armand Ribot (1881) reported in his now famous monograph, "Diseases of Memory," that amnesic patients seemed to have lost memories predominantly of their recent past, whereas more remote events could still be remembered. Ribot concluded that a biological process unfolds over time that progressively renders memories stronger, such that trauma tends to cause amnesia selectively for events newly committed to memory. Some years later, Müller & Pilzecker (1900) provided a cognitive explanation for the same phenomenon. Their studies on learning and memory moved them to propose that shortly after acquisition, a phase of reactivations of the learned material takes place that stabilizes the new memory contents. Disruptions of this assumed perseveratory activity compromise memory consolidation, leading to impaired memory.

These fundamental notions inspired two of the most successful research programs probing the biological basis of memory, mostly with animals and human patient populations. Two memory models emerged out of the broad empirical fundament laid down by these efforts—cellular and systems consolidation. The former, mostly animal-research-derived model, closely relates to the initial consolidation ideas formulated at the beginning of the past century, as it describes molecular mechanisms unfolding after learning that change synaptic efficacy and thus implement memory on the neuronal level. Like the perseveration-consolidation model, cellular consolidation posits that the extent of memory impairment following disruption of these processes will be strongest the less advanced they are. Consequently, no memory impairments are expected for amnesic treatments applied after consolidation is completed.

System consolidation, on the other hand, is a hypothesis that refers more to a memory transfer or reorganization process than a memory stabilization process, describing a time-dependent shift in brain systems that support performance. Research that gave rise to this model began with Scoville & Milner's (1957) case study of the late Henry Gustav Molaison, better known as patient H.M., who lost most of his medial temporal lobe in a surgery to relieve him from intractable epilepsy. The operation left him with a profound impairment in forming new episodic memories (anterograde amnesia) and an extensive loss of such memories, extending back years into the past (retrograde amnesia). His and similar cases, as well as animal models, suggested that such memories initially depend on the hippocampus, but come to rely on extrahippocampal, cortical areas over time.

Similar to the cellular consolidation model, systems consolidation expects a temporally graded sensitivity of memory to amnesic treatments: The less complete systems consolidation is, the more memory will be impaired following hippocampal damage.

Both cellular and systems consolidation models thus promote the idea that stability characterizes fully consolidated, i.e., long-term, memory. In cognitive psychology, however, a rich research tradition documents just the opposite, namely malleability of long-term, i.e., consolidated, memory. Bartlett's (1932) reports that over time episodic memories get systematically distorted or Loftus's (1975) demonstrations that eyewitness testimony can be quickly modified, even without the owners of these memories taking notice, seem rather opposite to the cellular and systems consolidation account.

How can these fields of memory research be reconciled? We develop the argument that memory retrieval forms the missing link between these phenomena of stability of consolidated memory on the one hand and their lability on the other. First, we describe the reconsolidation phenomenon, illustrating that reactivation, counter to the assumptions of cellular and systems consolidation, can transfer long-term memories again into a labile state, from which they, just like new memories, need to be restabilized in order to be preserved. Thus, memory transformation processes as described by cellular and systems consolidation seem to be invoked each time long-term memory is recalled and undergoes reconsolidation. We show that prominent memory malleability phenomena documented in cognitive psychology, such as the misinformation effect, hindsight bias, flashbulb memory, hypermnesia, reminiscence, and interference, all invoke memory retrieval as a central component. Departing from this observation, we suggest how consolidation and reconsolidation could explain these memory effects, and how the two concepts may help constrain theory formation both in neuroscience and in cognitive psychology.

SYNAPTIC CONSOLIDATION AND RECONSOLIDATION

Müller & Pilzecker (1900) observed in their classic studies on retroactive interference that the participants reiterated syllables they learned recently. Memory was impaired when reiteration was disrupted by, for example, presenting additional lists of syllables to learn or by any other "mental activity." In their attempts to explain the phenomenon, they suggested that "the tendency to perseverate [...] might serve to consolidate the associations among [the syllables]" (p. 68). Hebb's (1949; see also Gerard 1949) dual-trace memory theory was the first to provide a physiological explanation for Müller and Pilzecker's perseveration-consolidation concept and thus for time-dependent memory vulnerability. He proposed that new memories are stabilized by recurrent neural activity of the network (cell assembly) representing the new experience. This activity was thought to correspond to short-term memory. If left undisturbed, it leads to morphological alterations of the network's synapses, rendering the connections among the participating neurons permanent and thus allowing for regenerating the pattern of activity at a later point. This structural modification was proposed to correspond to long-term memory.

A large body of empirical evidence has been accumulated over the years since then, demonstrating that for some period after learning, termed the "consolidation interval," memories are labile and vulnerable to alteration. First, amnesia can be induced if treatments such as electroconvulsive shock (Duncan 1949) or protein synthesis inhibitors (Flexner et al. 1965) are given shortly after learning. Second, performance can be impaired if new competing learning occurs in short temporal proximity to the initial learning (Gordon & Spear 1973). Third, retention can be enhanced by administration of various compounds, such as strychnine (McGaugh & Krivanek 1970). Critically, all three manipulations are effective only when given shortly after new learning, not when given after a delay.

These and similar data form the empirical basis of the synaptic consolidation hypothesis, which states that memories are captured in the brain through changes in synaptic efficacy, and that these changes depend upon complex cellular and molecular mechanisms that lead to structural alterations underpinning potentiated synaptic function (Glickman 1961, Hebb 1949, McGaugh 1966). These changes can take several hours, during which memory becomes consolidated and enters a state referred to as long-term memory, in which memory is thought to be fixed and no longer susceptible to previously effective amnesic or enhancing treatments (McGaugh 1966). Around the 1970s, however, some anomalous effects emerged that could not be readily explained by the then dominant synaptic consolidation doctrine. On the one hand, there were studies showing recovery from amnesia (e.g., Quartermain et al. 1970, Serota 1971), and the debate arose whether the inability to remember after amnesic treatments indeed represents disrupted consolidation, i.e., actual memory loss, or rather a transient or permanent inability to retrieve memory that still is available (Lewis 1979, Miller & Springer 1974, Spear 1973). If long-term memory requires synaptic consolidation, then no recovery should be seen if the process terminated prematurely. This issue has never been resolved, as both the retrieval- and the storage-impairment positions can explain any result from studies showing memory recovery or lack thereof after amnesia, and thus the debate arrived at a stalemate (Nader & Wang 2006; but see Hardt et al. 2009b for a possible resolution).

The other challenge to the idea of memory consolidation was a small set of studies (e.g., Misanin et al. 1968, Robbins & Meyer 1970, Schneider & Sherman 1968) showing that even consolidated memories could again return to a state of vulnerability. Similar to demonstrations of a consolidation period, these studies provided evidence that memory reactivation could return consolidated memories to a transient labile state during which they were sensitive to amnesic treatments, suggesting that reactivated memory restabilizes, or reconsolidates, as

this process was to be called later. A number of those researchers who were already unconvinced by the consolidation idea argued in light of these findings instead that memories were always open to alteration and/or disruption, so long as they were in an active state, which was the state of newly formed memories or retrieved long-term memories (cf. Lewis 1979, Mactutus et al. 1979, Miller & Springer 1973, Spear & Mueller 1984). The potential of inactive memories to transfer to an active state was considered to be a basic property of memories, regardless of previous activations or the age of the memory. Contrary to this model, the synaptic consolidation idea characterizes the stabilization process as unidirectional—memories progress gradually from unstable to stable and thus become progressively resistant to disruptions.

As in the case of consolidation, three lines of evidence support the existence of a postreactivation restabilization, or reconsolidation, period. First, performance can be impaired if amnesic treatments such as electroconvulsive shock are given shortly after reactivation (Misanin et al. 1968, Schneider & Sherman 1968). Second, performance can be impaired if new competing learning occurs in short temporal proximity to the reactivation (Gordon 1977a). Third, retention can be enhanced by administration of various compounds, such as strychnine, after reactivation (Gordon 1977b). Critically, these manipulations are effective only when given shortly after reactivation but not when given after a delay.

Although the reconsolidation phenomenon runs counter to the central assumptions of the cellular consolidation hypothesis, neither the phenomenon itself nor the active/inactive memory model, which was able to explain both consolidation and reconsolidation findings, received broad attention in the following decades. For reasons that remain unclear, only a small group of researchers continued to study the new effect (a detailed review of this literature is provided by Sara 2000).

Research on memory reconsolidation was revitalized by its demonstration in auditory fear conditioning in the rat (Nader et al. 2000).

Targeting directly the brain circuitry critically mediating the behavior and its consolidation (basolateral nucleus of the amygdala), and using a drug with well-documented amnesic effects on memory consolidation (inhibition of protein synthesis with the antibiotic anisomycin), this study demonstrated that reminders could bring well-consolidated fear memories back into an unstable state, in which they could be disrupted. Memory impairments were not observed in the absence of reactivation. The conclusion, as in the original studies from the 1970s, was that reactivated consolidated memories return to an unstable state from which they must restabilize in order to persist.

Since this study, reconsolidation became an intensive area of investigation in the neurosciences, and it has been demonstrated in a range of species (including humans), in many different tasks and brain regions, and with various amnesic and enhancing agents. The fact that retrieval can return consolidated memory to an unstable state from which it must restabilize over time has been established as a fundamental memory process (for a review of the literature, see Nader & Hardt 2009).

Nevertheless, not all memories have been found to undergo reconsolidation. This property of reconsolidation was noted early on. It was thought that the induction of lability critically depended on specific parameters (Lewis 1979, Miller & Springer 1973, Spear 1973). Several boundary conditions on reconsolidation, i.e., situations in which memory that would reconsolidate no longer does, have been proposed, such as the consolidation of extinction (e.g., Eisenberg et al. 2003), memory age (e.g., Milekic & Alberini 2002), predictability of the reactivation stimulus (e.g., Lee 2009, Morris et al. 2006, Pedreira et al. 2004), training intensity (Suzuki et al. 2004, Wang et al. 2009), and mode of reactivation, i.e., whether a memory is directly or indirectly reactivated (Debiec et al. 2006).

Progress in understanding the conditions under which lability of consolidated memory will and will not be observed may provide critical insight into how certain memory

malleability effects, such as misinformation effects or hindsight bias, can be prevented. As we discuss below, these memory distortions may be mediated by retrieval-induced memory malleability, and thus a better understanding of boundary conditions on reconsolidation may directly impact our understanding of these phenomena as well.

SYSTEMS CONSOLIDATION

Retrograde Amnesia in Humans

The report describing HM's memory impairments marked the beginning of a research program aimed at identifying the brain systems and mechanisms underpinning memory. Memory impairments similar to those of HM have since been found in a number of patients with medial-temporal lobe (MTL) damage. The extent of the temporal gradient of retrograde amnesia, however, has been found to vary substantially between patients, from several months to decades (e.g., Reed & Squire 1998), and in some patients, a flat gradient, i.e., comparable amnesia for both recent and remote memories, has been documented (Kopelman & Kapur 2001). These discrepancies may be due to the size and location of the MTL lesion. Patients with damage limited to the hippocampus have shorter gradients, typically covering a decade, whereas individuals with more extensive MTL damage show even more far-reaching retrograde memory loss (Bayley et al. 2005, Reed & Squire 1998).

Furthermore, it has been suggested that the length of the gradient might differ with the type of memory tested, that is, different gradients have been observed for semantic memory (memories of facts and general knowledge), episodic memory (memories of discrete events or autobiographical episodes), and allocentric spatial memory (memories of spatial relationships between objects within an environment independent of one's viewpoint) (Nadel & Moscovitch 1997). Specifically, if damage is limited to the hippocampus, patients can present either with a lack of a retrograde gradient for semantic memories or semantic memory loss that extends back no more than about 10 years (Kapur & Brooks 1999, Manns et al. 2003, Rempel-Clower et al. 1996); gradients spanning two or three decades have been found if damage to the MTL is more extensive (Bayley et al. 2006, Bright et al. 2006). Similarly, for episodic memories, temporal retrograde gradients of a few years' length were detected if damage was limited to the hippocampus (Bayley et al. 2003). When damage extended to adjacent MTL regions, a few studies either did not find a gradient or have reported retrograde amnesia extending back for decades (Cipolotti et al. 2001, Hirano et al. 2002), whereas others have not (Bayley et al. 2003, 2005).

Although the hippocampus has been implicated in the acquisition of allocentric memories (Maguire et al. 1996), patients with large hippocampus lesions can retain spatial memories for highly familiar environments (Maguire et al. 2006, Rosenbaum et al. 2005, Teng & Squire 1999). The relatively few studies that have investigated remote spatial memory following hippocampal damage suggest that spatial memory acquired throughout childhood can remain intact (Teng & Squire 1999), whereas spatial memories acquired later in adulthood may lose some of their detail and are not as flexible for generating new routes (Maguire et al. 2006, Rosenbaum et al. 2005). These later findings suggest qualitative differences between remote hippocampus-dependent and hippocampus-independent spatial memories.

Neuroimaging Studies in Humans

Neuroimaging studies in healthy individuals have examined the role of the MTL and hippocampus in recent and remote memory. Although few studies have shown that the hippocampus is more active during the retrieval of recent than remote episodic memories (Piefke et al. 2003, Takashima et al. 2006), most findings suggest that the structure is similarly highly active for both recent and remote memories (Addis et al. 2004, Gilboa et al. 2004, Maguire 2001, Ryan et al. 2001, Steinvorth et al. 2006),

although one study found more hippocampal activity following the retrieval of remote memories than recent ones (Rekkas & Constable 2005). These differences may be due to the amount of details recalled at recent and remote time points.[1] Some studies suggest that the hippocampus is more engaged in the retrieval of detailed episodic memories (Trinkler et al. 2009), and recent memories appear more detailed than remote ones (Piefke et al. 2003), leading to stronger hippocampal activity for recent than remote memories (Addis et al. 2004). When level of detail (or emotionality) of memories was controlled, the hippocampus was activated to the same level when retrieving recent or remote memories. Further evidence supporting the idea that the hippocampus plays a specific role in supporting rich, detailed episodic memories comes from studies showing that hippocampal activation declines when over time, detailed memory recollection fades away (Eldridge et al. 2000, Viskontas et al. 2009, Yonelinas et al. 2005).

A number of neuroimaging studies on semantic memory have found equal hippocampal activation for recent and remote memories (Bernard et al. 2004, Kapur et al. 1995, Maguire 2001), whereas others have found retrograde temporal gradients for activation in the right parahippocampal cortex (Douville et al. 2005) and right entorhinal cortex (Haist et al. 2001). A recent study by Smith & Squire (2009) found reduced activity following the retrieval of more remote semantic memories than recent ones in the medial temporal lobe (including the hippocampus), and increased activity in the frontal lobe, temporal lobe, and parietal lobe.

---

[1]Two additional problems in interpreting neuroimaging studies of remote memory pertain to the incidental encoding of being tested in a scanner and the selection of baseline conditions, both factors that might mask any difference between recent and remote memories. These issues lie beyond the scope of this review, and we refer the interested reader to Squire LR, Bayley PJ. 2007. The neuroscience of remote memory. *Curr. Opin. Neurobiol.* 17:185–96; and Moscovitch M, Nadel L, Winocur G, Gilboa A, Rosenbaum RS. 2006. The cognitive neuroscience of remote episodic, semantic and spatial memory. *Curr. Opin. Neurobiol.* 16:179–90.

Animal Models of Systems Consolidation

Studying systems consolidation in animal models has two major advantages: First, memories of different ages can be studied prospectively by performing experimental manipulations at specific time points after memory acquisition. Second, animal models allow targeting of specific areas and/or specific molecular processes.

The first two studies to model retrograde amnesia used two very different paradigms, the socially transmitted food preference task (Winocur 1990) and contextual fear conditioning (Kim & Fanselow 1992). In both studies, electrolytic lesions of the dorsal hippocampus of rats were made at different time points after training. Memory of socially transmitted food preference was impaired if lesions were made 1–2 days after training, but not when applied after five days (Winocur 1990). Contextual fear memory, however, was severely impaired if lesions were made 1–14 days after training, but was intact when applied 28 days after training (Kim & Fanselow 1992). Since then, temporally graded retrograde amnesia has also been found in studies using rabbits, rats, mice, and monkeys, as well as in a number of different paradigms, following both partial and extensive lesions of the hippocampus, using various different lesioning methods (Frankland & Bontempi 2005). One important difference between gradients in human amnesic patients and those found in animal models is the timescale of the temporal gradient, which is vastly shorter in animal models, ranging from weeks to months in contrast to years and decades in humans.

In contrast to the systems consolidation hypothesis, a number of studies have found flat gradients, such that the amnesic manipulations were similarly effective at recent and remote time-points (Burwell et al. 2004, Gaffan 1993, Sutherland et al. 2001, Winocur et al. 2005). However, given the extensive hippocampal lesions in these studies, it remains possible that cortical structures involved in the expression of remote memories were affected as well. Nevertheless, in other studies even partial hippocampal lesions have consistently been found to impair memory at all time points. These studies used the Morris water maze, a spatial task that appears to always require the hippocampus (Clark et al. 2005, Martin et al. 2005, Moscovitch et al. 2006).

Indirect evidence for a special role for the hippocampus in mediating detailed aspects of spatial/contextual tasks comes from studies showing that by about four weeks after contextual fear conditioning, at a time when such memories can be expressed without a hippocampus (Kim & Fanselow 1992), animals will show generalized fear responses to novel contexts not expressed at more recent time points (Wiltgen & Silva 2007, Winocur et al. 2007). Taken together, these findings suggest that reduced hippocampus involvement correlates with more schematic, less detailed, memory.

Further corroborating evidence comes from a study in which rats were reared in a complex environment (the "village") for three months (Winocur et al. 2005). They were then trained in a specific spatial task in the village, after which they received hippocampal lesions. Interestingly, lesioned rats performed the task just as well as control animals. However, although the lesioned animals were able to perform when distal cues were substituted, they were severely impaired when spatial relations among the cues or the spatial context itself were changed (village rotated relative to distal cues; village put in a new room). These findings suggest that the rats' spared memory was less detailed than that of control animals.

Thus, similar to neuroimaging studies in humans, evidence from lesion studies in animals indicates that the hippocampus is strongly involved in mediating contextually rich, detailed memories at remote and recent time points.

Reengagement of the Hippocampus: Systems Reconsolidation

Although animal models of retrograde amnesia have provided compelling evidence for the transient role of the hippocampus in retrieving certain kinds of memories, they do not necessarily rule out the participation of the hippocampus in remote memory in intact animals. A few studies have suggested that although the hippocampus becomes dispensable for retrieving remote contextual fear memory, the structure still plays an important role in processing the memory once it has been retrieved (Debiec et al. 2002, Frankland et al. 2006, Land et al. 2000). In a study by Debiec et al. (2002), hippocampal lesions were ineffective when performed 45 days after training, indicating that at that time point, systems consolidation was complete. However, if the remote memory was reactivated immediately before applying the lesion, the animals were amnesic when tested later. Lesions of the hippocampus were only effective if performed up to two days after reactivation. Thus, an apparent hippocampus-independent memory became again transiently hippocampus-dependent, suggesting the existence of a systems reconsolidation process. Furthermore, local infusion of the protein-synthesis inhibitor anisomycin into the hippocampus at either recent or remote time points after training also resulted in memory impairment on a later test. Similar to the lesioning effect, impairment following anisomycin infusions was contingent on prior memory reactivation. Indirect evidence for the reengagement of the hippocampus and its role in mediating detailed memory comes from a study measuring the specificity of contextual fear memories in mice over time (Wiltgen & Silva 2007). After establishing that contextual fear memory becomes more generalized over a time course that corresponds to systems consolidation (~35 days), it was found that the reactivation of the memory on day 35 restored context discrimination when tested a day later as the animals now did not generalize their fear to a novel context.

Together, these findings suggest that systems consolidation, like cellular consolidation, may not be a unidirectional process of memory fixation. Rather, reactivation of a remote memory can re-engage the hippocampus and possibly restore a generalized memory back to a more detailed form.

Memory Schemas and Systems Consolidation

Interestingly, a recent study has suggested that systems consolidation can occur as quickly as within one day of learning new information, if the animal had previously acquired a "schema" allowing for incorporation of new information (Tse et al. 2007). In this study, paired-associate learning was used, and rats were trained to use different flavors of food as cues to retrieve an associative spatial memory. After weeks of training several paired-associates with different spatial properties, new associates could be learned in a single trial. Furthermore, although the memory was sensitive to lesions of the hippocampus three hours after training of such new associates, lesions two days after training had no effect on later memory expression. This suggests that the memory remains hippocampus-dependent only within these two days after training, a steeper temporal gradient of systems consolidation than has been found before in other tasks. The authors suggest that extended training on this task allowed the creation of a neocortical "schema," into which new memories could be rapidly integrated, thereby becoming quickly independent of the hippocampus. However, alternatively, this schema may also be stored in the hippocampus or the hippocampus-cortical network. Either way, these findings suggest that in order to add new learning onto an existing schema, the hippocampus only has to be involved for a short period of time to allow storage of new knowledge in cortical areas, such that it is no longer necessary for expressing the memory afterward. Interestingly, the two-day sensitivity of the new knowledge being added to the existing cortical schema is a time course similar to the one found for systems reconsolidation of contextual fear memories (Debiec et al. 2002). Systems reconsolidation of the cortically based schema memory might have been induced during the final training day. The new information could then have been incorporated into the cortical schema as it quickly underwent systems reconsolidation.

As we discuss below, memory-updating processes in humans occur very rapidly, on the order of minutes and hours (cf. the sections on misinformation effect and hindsight bias). Unlike animals, the material used in human studies usually is meaningful, such as words, pictures, and stories, and represents instances of semantic knowledge (and schemas; Bartlett 1932). Thus, in humans, the reconsolidation-induced memory modification may occur almost immediately (see also Fagen & Rovee-Collier 1983).

THEORIES OF SYSTEMS CONSOLIDATION

McClelland and associates (1995) proposed a connectionist model, building on ideas initially formulated by Marr (1971). They assume that the hippocampal system rapidly stores new episodes and "replays" them to the slower-learning neocortical system, interleaving the new episodes with previous knowledge, thus allowing for generalization as cortical memories form. This type of hippocampus-driven memory reinstatement, which in turn reinstates the neocortical memory system, can take place either in task-relevant situations or off-line, i.e., through rehearsal or reactivation during sleep. The model further proposes that reinstatement of a pattern in the hippocampal system can strengthen the hippocampal representation itself, as well as the representation in the neocortex. Thus, reactivation can reinstate memories in both hippocampal and cortical memory systems, i.e., according to the reconsolidation hypothesis, memory reactivation can induce lability in both systems. Such self-reinforcement could impede the decay of the hippocampal trace, thus delaying its systems consolidation. However, the authors note that this would possibly not happen during off-line reinstatement, i.e., during some stages of sleep when hippocampal synaptic plasticity has been found to be suppressed (Leonard et al. 1987). The connectionist model assumes that all hippocampus-dependent memories undergo a similar time-dependent consolidation process and thus does not make any distinction between more detailed

memories and more schematic ones. Therefore, findings from neuroimaging studies showing that retrieval of even very old, detailed episodic and spatial memories engages the hippocampus are not consistent with the model. The model can accommodate memory reconsolidation, as it assumes that memory reactivation can reinstate both hippocampal and cortical representations, thus making them again transiently labile. However, accounting for hippocampal reconsolidation of a memory following systems consolidation, which rendered memory expression hippocampus-independent, is more difficult.

The standard consolidation theory posits that the hippocampus plays a time-limited role in memory for all declarative memory (semantic, episodic, and spatial) (Squire & Alvarez 1995, Squire et al. 1984). The theory assumes that memory is stored in the same neocortical areas specialized in processing the relevant information and that the hippocampus is initially required for memory acquisition and later retrieval. The role of the hippocampus is to provide "indices" that link neocortical representations, which are too dispersed and weakly linked to support memory retrieval on their own. Through a gradual process of reorganization, connections between cortical regions are progressively strengthened until they become strong enough to support the memory independently of the hippocampus, such that it is no longer required or involved in later recall. Similar to the connectionist model, the standard consolidation theory is ill equipped to account for recent neuroimaging findings of hippocampal engagement in retrieval of remote, detailed, contextually rich episodic and spatial memories, and animal studies showing that the hippocampus is critical for expressing context-dependent and detailed spatial memories. Furthermore, the theory is fundamentally challenged by findings of reconsolidation as it assumes that systems consolidation is a unidirectional process.

Although partly based on the standard consolidation model, the multiple trace theory was developed as a response to some of the main tenets of that theory (Moscovitch & Nadel 1998, Nadel & Moscovitch 1997). Similar to the standard consolidation model, multiple trace theory posits that information is sparsely encoded in a hippocampal-neocortical memory trace. The hippocampus contains representations that bind together memory content in neocortical areas. In addition, the most recent version of this account puts more emphasis on the idea that the re-encoding of hippocampal memories allows the extraction of semantic memories, which are then stored independently of episodic memory and the hippocampus (Nadel et al. 2007b). This process of building up extrahippocampal semantic memory is similar to systems consolidation. The model makes the same distinctions for spatial memory, assuming that coarse topographical representations can exist independently of the hippocampus, but rich, detailed spatial memories will always require this brain structure (Rosenbaum et al. 2001). Findings from human neuroimaging studies and animal models showing the continuing involvement of the hippocampus in expressing old detailed memories (detailed, contextually rich episodic and spatial memories in humans and context-dependent memories in animals) fit well with the multiple trace model's position that the hippocampus always mediates rich episodic and spatial memories, whereas neocortical structures can support more coarse or schematic representations independently of the hippocampus. Reconsolidation has also found a place in more recent versions of multiple trace theory, as it is now assumed that reactivation of episodic memories can lead to their reinstatement in the hippocampus (Nadel et al. 2007b). However, similar to the connectionist model, it is unclear whether the model allows for reconsolidation of more schematic memories that are not mediated by the hippocampus.

None of the theories mentioned above can readily account for recent findings of rapid system consolidation after animals have acquired an associative framework or schema. All three models assume that systems consolidation of memory is a strictly time-dependent process and do not directly propose mechanisms that could hasten that process.

MEMORY MALLEABILITY EFFECTS AND RECONSOLIDATION

Many experimental demonstrations of the reconsolidation phenomenon imply that retrieval is far more than a passive read-out of memory: Retrieval transfers memory into a state of transient plasticity. In this state, memory can be modified in various ways; it can be impaired (Amorapanth et al. 2000), enhanced (Lee 2008), or distorted (Hupbach et al. 2007, Walker et al. 2003). These findings suggest a minimum of two possible functional roles for postretrieval plasticity. First, memory reactivation allows for modulation of memory strength. Second, it permits memory updating. In this sense, reconsolidation ultimately serves an adaptive purpose, as it allows existing memory to be quickly recalibrated by adding of new knowledge and weakening and strengthening of certain memory contents (for similar positions on retrieval, see, e.g., Bjork 1975, Boller & Rovee-Collier 1994, Lee 2009, McDaniel & Masson 1985, Sara 2000).

The reconsolidation phenomenon therefore directly relates to a rich tradition of research in cognitive psychology demonstrating the malleability of human memory. Under this umbrella term, we here subsume phenomena showing that memory can change with use, either in strength or in contents. Both types, we try to argue, can be explained within a unifying framework that is based on the neurobiologically sound concept of postretrieval plasticity and reconsolidation, the subsequent stabilization process.

In our overview of the literature on cognitive malleability, we first turn to changes in memory contents, phenomena that are most convincingly demonstrated by distortions of memory, such as the misinformation effect, hindsight bias, and memory interference. Psychological research on this common observation owes much to the pioneering work of Bartlett (1932). His basic method was to submit his participants to repeated free reproductions of the studied material (the most famous being an American folk talk about "The War of the Ghosts"), with recall intervals ranging from immediately to several years. Bartlett found that what participants remembered of this unusual story revealed several forms of systematic mnemonic effects that can affect memory accuracy. Bartlett's influential contribution to cognitive concepts of memory was the basic insight that memory in essence is a schema-mediated reconstruction: What can be recalled will therefore systematically deviate from the original in accordance to the schemata recruited during encoding and reconstruction. Although there was some dissent regarding whether Bartlett's findings replicate, recent studies that attentively reproduced his original method were able to find the original effects (e.g., Ahlberg & Sharps 2002, Wheeler & Roediger 1992).

An alternative explanation for schematization can be derived from a study originally designed to examine the effects of verbal labels given at encoding on later recognition. Daniel (1972) presented participants with a series of images that showed systematic variations of a base image (e.g., duck, camel). These studied instances all deviated to the same degree from their respective base object, and all were presented with the word correctly identifying it. The recognition test followed immediately, or up to two days later. In this test, the studied instance and other nonstudied instances that deviated more or less than the studied item from the base object were presented in a randomized order. Participants had better recognition memory for the studied instance shortly after the test than after a delay. Importantly, the longer the retention interval, the more often participants incorrectly identified as the studied item nonstudied instances that deviated less from the base form. Although these results may be taken as suggesting that over time memory gets restructured toward a semantic category, or schema, an equally valid alternative explanation may be that over time the perceptual component of the original memory fades away and simply is forgotten while the conceptual component, in this case, the verbal label, remains. As a consequence, recognition of forms that closely resemble the studied concept (e.g., the "typical" duck) will be more and more likely falsely recognized as the studied instance.

This memory "distortion" represents a memory transformation that, by virtue of decay of perceptual details (i.e., forgetting), reveals the embedded conceptual core. Unlike current models of memory organization reviewed in the previous section (e.g., MTT), which understand such transformations rather as the active extraction of knowledge (e.g., semanticization) than forgetting, Daniel's (1972) findings suggest that semanticization may result from a decay of perceptual (i.e., visual, olfactory, tactile, spatial, etc.) detail, thereby revealing the semantic contents underlying the memory of an experience. During later recall, then, this conceptual skeleton is used to rebuild a detailed event memory, using factual knowledge to fill in the gaps and generate vividness, which is thus largely imagined rather than experienced (cf. Schacter & Addis 2007). Such a process may explain why flashbulb memories, as we show below, are highly detailed but overall mostly inaccurate.

In a similar way, Bartlett's research suggests that encoding and retrieval processes cannot be categorically separated. In fact, encoding almost inevitably causes retrieval of related knowledge and experiences, just as retrieval may lead to the incorporation of new elements into existing memories (see also Bjork 1975). In this sense, retrieval has the potential to change what is being retrieved. That both memory processes are related was an idea expressed at the beginning of the twentieth century by Richard Semon (1904, 1909). He suggested that the engram is the result of both encoding (engraphy) and retrieval (ecphory) processes. As a consequence, the engram does not correspond only to the actual experience, but also to related engrams already present in the brain (see Schacter 2001 for a detailed discussion of Semon's work).

Hence, failures of memory, as Ribot (1881) remarked in his monograph, provide us with opportunities to discover fundamental mechanisms underpinning normal memory. However, with the notable exception of research on interference, memory distortions were rarely studied in the years that followed these early demonstrations and conceptualizations, and were regarded more as an obstacle in understanding the laws governing learning and retention. When the cognitive revolution took up speed, marked by Neisser's (1967) book establishing the field, interest in these "sins" of memory revitalized (Schacter 1999). Like Bartlett before him, Neisser argued that memories of past events are essentially complex reconstructions that regenerate an experience by piecing together whatever fragments remain from the original experience, drawing from semantic knowledge and other related episodic fragments and memories to fill in missing elements. The very act of reconstruction gives room for distortions of many kinds.

In the following section we discuss some of these distortions, which illustrate the malleability of memory, and which could potentially be explained within a framework built on the observation that memory reactivation induces plasticity and memory reconsolidation. So far, explanations of these malleability phenomena have not considered explicitly reactivation as a critical precondition for memory change to occur. A second look at the paradigms used to study the effects, however, reveals that some form of reactivation is always part of the procedure: For example, flashbulb memories are studied in repeated memory tests spaced out over weeks and months, and the consistency of these memories declines with repeated retrieval; in the misinformation paradigm, the misleading questions necessarily have to explicitly refer to the previously witnessed event; in hindsight bias studies, an explicit reference to the initial study session is made, and, in some paradigms, the original material is repeated; memory interference has been traditionally studied in a paired-associates paradigm, in which interference effects are obtained by repairing parts of the original stimulus with new items, thereby reactivating the original memory; and reminiscence, hypermnesia, and

flashbulb memories illustrate the effects of repeated retrieval on retention.

From this list of memory malleability phenomena we excluded research on false memories (Deese 1959, Roediger & McDermott 1995, Underwood 1965), as these appear related more to effects that occur during encoding, i.e., initial memory acquisition. As several authors have suggested, false memories may be the result of relatedness effects, in that associated existing knowledge and memories become automatically associated with the items to be studied (Roediger & McDermott 2000). As a consequence, during later memory recall, these unstudied but related items will also be recalled. Consider, for example, Deese's (1959) demonstration that participants who studied words that were semantically strongly associated to a word that itself was not on the list (e.g., bed, rest, awake) were likely to falsely produce the nonstudied word (e.g., sleep) when asked to free recall the studied items. Underwood (1965) reported a similar effect and suggested that implicit associated responses caused false recognition of unstudied but related words. These accounts imply at the very least that studying the stimulus material reactivated existing memories; whether or not this reactivation constitutes retrieval can be debated. However, since these effects occur during encoding, the distortion observed during later recall appears to be mediated by memory consolidation during initial encoding rather than by reconsolidation during retrieval.

Flashbulb Memories

Brown & Kulik (1977) introduced the term flashbulb memory to describe exceptionally accurate memories for public events of high salience (e.g., the Kennedy assassination, Challenger explosion, death of Michael Jackson). They believed that these memories are encoded by a unique memory process (the "now print" mechanism) that, like a camera, quickly stores a large quantity of information that, unlike a camera, not only comprises the critical event but also antecedent and subsequent events and brain states, such as knowledge about where the event was experienced, who was present, with whom the event was discussed subsequently, and how the weather was. Flashbulb memories thus appear different from other event-related memories in that they exhibit higher richness in detail and higher levels of accuracy and consistency over longer retention intervals. Since such memories also have a higher likelihood of being retold numerous times, they may pose a problem for our suggestion that retrieval induces states of plasticity that allow for memory distortions.

The vividness of recalled flashbulb memories appears to be more a function of accompanying affective states (cf. Schooler et al. 1997), which may reflect memory for the emotions experienced during witnessing the event, or which may result as a response during recall of the experience. Evidence for the claim that flashbulb memories are of higher accuracy than normal memories has been mixed and the associated debate controversial (e.g., Bohannon 1988, Conway et al. 1994, McCloskey et al. 1988, Neisser & Harsh 1992, Pillemer 1984). Recent research, however, demonstrated that flashbulb memories are no more accurate than ordinary memories, exhibiting forgetting over time and schema-mediated distortions. For example, Neisser & Harsh (1992) report that memory for the explosion of the Space Shuttle Challenger systematically declined in terms of accuracy, despite being rich in detail and accompanied by high subjective confidence in the accuracy of the recalled events. However, a study by Conway et al. (1994), comparing the memories that U.S. and U.K. citizens retained of the resignation of British Prime Minister Margaret Thatcher in November 1990 showed markedly higher recall rates for the U.K. citizens at a remote memory test (11 months after the event), as well as a much greater consistency between the remote and initial test, which was administered two weeks after the event. Two factors mediating the consistency and thus fixedness of flashbulb memories have been isolated. First, Conway et al.'s (1994) findings indicate that arousal may play a significant role

in whether flashbulb memories remain stable or are subject to alteration and forgetting. Correlations between self-reported emotional response elicited by witnessing the event and recall consistency over repeated tests suggest that higher arousal is associated with reduced malleability of flashbulb memories (e.g., Bohannon 1988). The second factor that can influence accuracy appears to be how close in time the first memory test occurs to witnessing the critical event. Because memories of events of high salience have a higher tendency to be told and retold, especially shortly after they are experienced, memory distortions may be incorporated early after the event. Thus, if the first memory test, against which consistency of later tests will be compared, is administered immediately after the event, consistency will be lower than when administering the initial assessment after a longer delay (e.g., Christianson & Engelberg 1999, Winningham et al. 2000). Given the evidence, it appears that flashbulb memories are not different from memories for ordinary events, in that they are prone to decay and distortions (e.g., McCloskey 1992, Rubin & Kozin 1984) and that their stability depends on the strength of encoding. Therefore, our conceptual suggestions regarding the genesis of long-lasting memory and memory distortions also apply to flashbulb memories.

Misleading Postevent Information

In what is probably the most widely known study of misleading questions on event memory, Loftus et al. (1978) showed participants slides of an accident involving a red Datsun. Immediately, as well as one day, two days, or one week afterward, participants were asked to answer questions about the depicted events. One was the critical misleading question, asking whether there was a "stop" sign at the in intersection where the Datsun made the fatal turn that led to the accident, while in fact there was a "yield" sign. Twenty minutes after these questions, a two-alternative forced-choice recognition test was administered, in which participants had to decide which of two slides they had originally seen. False recognition rates were highest when the misleading question was presented two weeks after witnessing the event. In an attempt to address whether motivational factors rather than distortions of memory account for the false recognition rates, in another experiment participants were debriefed right after the recognition test and then had the opportunity to state what sign they actually had seen and what sign had been mentioned in the leading question. This manipulation did not recover the original memory. Loftus and colleagues interpreted this finding as supporting their claim that misleading questions can lead to permanent memory distortions (for an alternative account based on biased guessing instead on biased memory, see McCloskey & Zaragoza 1985). Further studies have shown that neither monetary incentives for correct recognitions nor suggestions that correct recalls are associated with higher intelligence were effective in reducing the memory distortions induced by misleading postevent information (Loftus 1979b). However, Loftus (1979b) reported that "blatantly" wrong postevent information will not lead to false recognition. As we discuss below, this is another similarity between misinformation effect and hindsight bias.

Explanations of the distortion ranged from the "update and erase" model (Loftus & Loftus 1980), in which it is assumed that the original knowledge is irrecoverably replaced by the misleading information, to the idea that original and new knowledge are fused into "representational blends" (e.g., Schooler & Tanaka 1991; see also Metcalfe & Bjork 1991), to the suggestions that old and new knowledge coexist (e.g., Loftus & Loftus 1980). Recent neuroimaging work suggests that instead of retrieval, the effect depends on events during encoding (Okado & Stark 2005). However, it has not yet been determined how to best account for the phenomenon, although some explanations seem more likely than others. Recent neuroimaging work suggests the reconsolidation phenomenon could be of potential use to shed light on the memory processes involved, although the question of whether reactivation

is a necessary condition for the effect to occur might be impossible to answer because the misinformation is introduced by explicit reference to the original event. One could therefore argue that the experimental design invoked to demonstrate the misinformation effect essentially is an instance of a reconsolidation protocol. The fact that repeating the misinformation (Zaragoza & Mitchell 1996) or repeated retrieval of the misinformation (e.g., Roediger et al. 1996) enhances the misinformation effect provides support for our suggestion that at the root of this phenomenon lie retrieval-induced plasticity processes and reconsolidation. In terms of the reconsolidation notion, this memory distortion could be explained as a process that allows new information to be included in the existing memory representation, as it became plastic after reactivation (cf. Hupbach et al. 2007). Progress in research on the boundary conditions and parameters of the reconsolidation process might be of potential practical use here, as this might allow questioning eyewitnesses in a way that will not lead to memory distortion (by, for example, changing the context of the first questioning; cf. Hupbach et al. 2008). One could imagine that either the old memory is prevented from undergoing reconsolidation or that initiated reconsolidation processes following reactivation are blocked from completion such that no long-term memory distortions will be caused.

Hindsight Bias

Hindsight bias has been demonstrated for a variety of materials and experimental conditions, such as short stories, medical diagnoses, political prognoses, and knowledge questions (for reviews, see Christensen-Szalanski & Willham 1991, Hawkins & Hastie 1990). Although first studied using stories and episodes (e.g., Fischhoff 1975, 1977; Wood 1978), almanac-like questions are often used because of a nearly three-times larger effect size (Christensen-Szalanski & Wilham 1991). A typical experiment using this material consists of three phases. First, participants are asked to respond to difficult questions to which they usually do not know the answer and have to use their existing knowledge on the subject matter to provide an estimate (e.g., "How high is the Eiffel tower?"). Second, some time afterward, they are provided with additional information pertaining to the previously answered questions (e.g., they are given the actual solutions, the estimates of others, or random numbers). Finally, they are asked to recall their original answer to the question. Typically, the remembered answer is biased, such that in hindsight, it is closer to the additional information presented in the second phase than it initially had been.

It appears that the "better" the original memory (in terms of strength, precision, and detail), the smaller the probability of hindsight bias. Like the misinformation effect, hindsight bias thus dwells on the fuzziness of the knowledge that is assessed. If participants are likely to know the correct solutions to the questions presented, the obtained bias can be expected to be small (Christensen-Szalanski & Wilham 1991). Hindsight bias positively correlates with depth of anchor encoding (Wood 1978) and negatively correlates with depth of estimate encoding (e.g., Hell et al. 1988). Hindsight bias is larger the shorter the interval between anchor presentation and recollection (e.g., Erdfelder & Buchner 1998, Hell et al. 1988) and larger the longer the interval between estimation and anchor presentation (Fischhoff & Beyth 1975). Similarly, the longer the time between estimation and anchor presentation, the lower the probability to correctly recall the original answer (e.g., Fischhoff 1975, Hell et al. 1988, Pennington 1981). These time-dependent effects can be understood as a function of forgetting of the estimate over time, which decreases its probability of being retrieved (Hell et al. 1988).

It has been frequently demonstrated that participants will consider even blatantly arbitrary values: Hindsight bias was not smaller when the supplemental information was determined by a coin toss (Connolly & Bukzar 1990). Hindsight bias also cannot be reduced by informing participants about the nature of the bias (e.g., Fischhoff 1977, Pohl & Hell 1996), instructing them to "work hard" (e.g., Fischhoff 1975), or offering (financial) incentives to not be biased (e.g., Hell et al. 1988, Wood 1978). However, elimination of hindsight bias can be achieved when the supplemental information was subsequently discredited as being wrong (Hasher et al. 1981) and when participants were asked to generate alternatives or think about the opposite outcome (cf. Davies 1992, Slovic & Fischhoff 1977). Hardt & Pohl (2003) showed that the less plausible the anchor, the smaller the bias it caused, and that the plausibility ascribed to an anchor was directly correlated to the extent the anchor deviated from the individual's knowledge.

Fischhoff (1975) introduced the concept of creeping determinism to account for hindsight bias. According to this notion, the presented outcome information becomes immediately assimilated into the participant's domain knowledge, which thereby gets restructured in light of the new information in order to resolve ambiguities by "strengthening associative links with reasons supporting the answer" (Fischhoff 1977, p. 356). He suggested that this process was automatically initiated, and its impact on the knowledge representations was therefore unavoidable. A recent model of hindsight bias incorporates and extends these ideas. The selective activation, reconstruction, and anchoring (SARA) model (Pohl et al. 2003), which borrows some concepts from the search-of-associative-memory framework (Shiffrin & Raaijmakers 1992), assumes that long-term memory representations are associated with each other with links of varying strength that indicate their mutual retrieval probabilities. The closer certain memories are related, the greater the strength of their association and the higher the probability that activation of one will lead to an activation of the other. In SARA, it is assumed that presentation of supplemental information automatically initiates an encoding process that transfers this information to long-term memory, during which related memories are also retrieved. As a consequence of retrieval, the associations of the related memories are increased in strength, such that they are more likely to be recalled later. Subsequent information retrieval hence is biased toward the supplemental information and similar, related memories. These ideas are thus similar to suggestions that learning will always induce retrieval of related knowledge that has already been committed to memory (Bartlett 1932; Semon 1904, 1909) and that retrieval will lead to changes in existing memory (e.g., Bjork 1975).

The basic idea of SARA, that retrieval changes the strength of associations in long-term memory, corresponds directly to the reconsolidation hypothesis, in that reactivating long-term memory induces states of plasticity, which allow memory to be strengthened, weakened, and which permit new information to be integrated into existing memories. These memory-modification processes ultimately make memory distortions possible, although for the most part, they allow memory to be adaptive, as they permit updating existing knowledge in light of new information. Thus, SARA and the creeping determinism notion invoke concepts that are highly similar to the schema-driven quick systems consolidation found in animals (discussed in the previous section; Tse et al. 2007).

Forgetting, Interference, Reminiscence, and Hypermnesia

After more than a century of research, little agreement exists about the mechanism of forgetting, and two central controversies remain unresolved to this day. First, the lack of performance after successful training could reflect storage (i.e., consolidation) impairments, such that memory is unavailable and can therefore not be expressed, or it could be due to retrieval failure, as available memory permanently or transiently cannot be accessed (Nader & Wang 2006). The second controversy concerns the possible reasons for actual loss of memory, thus taking the position that failures to express memory reflect its unavailability rather than inaccessibility. Here two positions are debated, one that ascribes forgetting to the decay of memory traces, the other arguing that interference, not decay, causes memory decline.

The decay hypothesis was entertained for some time at the end of the nineteenth century and the beginning of the twentieth. Jost's law of forgetting represents an early formulation of the idea that the main factor determining forgetting rate is the passage of time and not the strength of a memory. Specifically, his law states that given two associations of equal strength but different age, the older will decay slower than the younger one as time progresses (Jost 1897). Thorndike's (1914) laws of use and disuse (subsumed under his "Law of Exercise") extend the idea by suggesting that trace decay over time can be prevented if memory is used or attended, which leads to a strengthening of memory. Indeed, repeated retrieval can improve memory retention, and Ballard (1913) was the first to study these effects systematically. He coined the term "reminiscence," referring to a peculiar beneficial effect repeated testing, i.e., memory retrieval, exerted on memory performance. Asking school children to memorize poems, and then subsequently testing them several times, he observed that lines of the studied poems that were not recalled on earlier tests could be recalled on later tests despite the absence of interpolated learning; in some cases, the total gain compensated forgetting, resulting in overall improved memory performance. Although reminiscence has been observed in most studies of repeated free recall tests, the effect rarely leads to the overall performance increase originally reported by Ballard (e.g., Tulving 1967). A related phenomenon of retrieval on memory performance is hypermnesia. Introduced by Erdelyi & Becker (1974), it refers to an overall increase in the number of remembered items as a function of repeated memory tests, which thus differs from reminiscence, the recall of items on later tests that were not recalled on earlier ones. Both effects can be reliably obtained in repeated-testing paradigms (Wheeler & Roediger 1992). These findings thus support, albeit indirectly, the idea that one possible reason for forgetting is memory decay.

Jost's law thus hints at the idea of memory consolidation, proposed by Müller & Pilzecker (1900) shortly thereafter, suggesting that, if not disrupted, a perseveration-consolidation process stabilizes memory over time—hence younger memories should be less stable than older memories and thus more susceptible to forgetting than older ones. It is important to note that Müller and Pilzecker considered mental processes that are unrelated to the memory being consolidated, as well as interfering intrusions of similar material as possible forces disturbing ongoing consolidation processes, but did not base their theory on a trace decay notion.

One of the earliest empirical tests of the consolidation account was Jenkins & Dallenbach's (1924) now classical study, which employed sleep as a factor in the experimental design and can therefore be considered a precursor to a research paradigm that in recent years produced important findings on memory organization (e.g., Rasch et al. 2007; Wagner et al. 2003, 2004). Jenkins & Dallenbach (1924) asked two subjects to study a list of nonsense syllables, with the difference that one subject learned the list prior to retiring for the night, while the other subject studied the syllables in the morning after waking up. The number of correctly recalled syllables was higher when recalled after sleep than wakefulness. Jenkins & Dallenbach (1924) concluded from their results that forgetting is due to "interference, inhibition, or obliteration of the old by the new" (p. 612), and not to decay, thereby supporting the notion that disrupting consolidation processes after learning will also disrupt memory. Although their results do not rule out that once consolidation is complete, passive trace decay may be a cause of forgetting, the interference account became the defacto explanation of forgetting in the decades that followed, and McGeoch's (1932) critique on passage-of-time-based decay notions as well as his outspoken support for interference processes as causal agents for forgetting contributed to this shift in focus.

A substantial body of data on memory interference phenomena has been produced using the well-known paired-associates technique. Typically, participants first study a list of word pairs (A-B), and later are presented with another list, in which words from the first list are paired with new ones (A-C). Finally, they are provided with A as a cue to retrieve C. Interference manifests as a performance impairment relative to a control group that did not study A-B initially. Some have argued that this paradigm models most everyday forgetting (Underwood 1957), but observations such as those provided by Jenkins & Dallenbach (1924) cast doubt on this claim, and later studies led ultimately to a rejection of this account (cf. Underwood & Ekstrand 1966). Alternatives have recently been suggested that attribute loss of memory more to interfering basic mental activity, which reduces available resources of brain areas involved in consolidation of new memories, such as the hippocampus (Wixted 2004). It appears that the field now approaches again notions articulated by Müller and Pilzecker at the beginning of the past century, which have been put onto a sound neurobiological basis in the past decades.

In the same spirit, we propose that memory reconsolidation processes following retrieval mediate some of these forgetting effects. The beneficial effects of repeated testing could be a function of reconsolidation processes strengthening reactivated memory (e.g., Gordon 1981). Interference effects, on the other hand, could be a function of memory modifications initiated by retrieval of existing memory in the presence of new information. The fact that interference effects are small when memory for A-B is tested shortly after learning of the A-C list, but larger when tested at time points more remote, directly supports the suggestion that reconsolidation processes underpin these distortions [for a similar account of interference in rats, see Gordon (1977a)]—a defining characteristic of memory reconsolidation is intact postreactivation of short-term memory, but impaired postreactivation of long-term memory (Nader & Hardt 2009). This pattern has also been observed in a set of recent studies on reconsolidation of human episodic memory

(Hupbach et al. 2007, 2008). Using a memory-interference paradigm, these authors showed that intrusions into memory for a list of objects were observed when participants were tested two days after learning a second list, but not when tested immediately after learning.

TOWARD A UNIFYING FRAMEWORK

Our short review of the literature on memory distortions and forgetting documents a rich tradition of research and theory formation about how memory might be organized. For the most part of its history, this research tradition took little notice of the developments in neuroscience that addressed, largely in the animal model, the same basic question, namely how brains create and maintain memories (cf. Wixted 2004). On the other hand, neuroscience research programs have often failed to recognize that their concepts born out of animal models need also account for the dynamic nature of consolidated memories. Although recent advances in cognitive neuroscience try to overcome the divide of these fields, they do so mostly by applying neuroscientific methods on human populations (e.g., Schacter et al. 1998). Approaches to unite the fields by applying theoretical concepts developed in one to study a phenomenon in the other so far have been rare [for a review of reactivation-based memory studies in human infants, see Rovee-Collier (1997)], but have become more prevalent in recent years (e.g., Easton et al. 2009, Hardt et al. 2009a, Hupbach et al. 2008, Kesner et al. 2008, Sauvage et al. 2008, Tse et al. 2007, Winocur et al. 2007).

We mentioned above two possible functions for postreactivation memory plasticity and reconsolidation. First, reconsolidation might lead to a change in the strength of the reactivated memory: Similar to consolidation processes that unfold after learning and transform a transient memory trace into a long-lasting one, reconsolidation processes following retrieval of long-term memory allow reactivated memory to be strengthened or weakened. Second,

reconsolidation may allow for modifying the contents of reactivated long-term memory by allowing new stimuli that are present at the time of retrieval to be associated with the transiently malleable memory. We assume that there may be cases when consolidation mechanisms update memory (Tronel et al. 2005) and others when reconsolidation processes are employed. For example, reconsolidation induced by exposure to the original learning environment is both necessary and sufficient to induce intrusions into memory for lists of objects without simultaneously reducing the number of correctly recalled items (Hupbach et al. 2008). It is thus an empirical question under which conditions consolidation or reconsolidation mechanisms contribute to these "sins" of memory.

A closer look at the memory malleability effects we discuss here reveals two principal types of phenomena: those characterized by retrieval-induced distortions, elicited by providing external retrieval cues, and those involving retrieval-induced memory strengthening in the absence of external cues. First, misinformation effect, hindsight bias, and interference all involve an explicit partial representation of previously learned stimuli: In the misinformation effect, participants are presented with a question that refers to an aspect of the original experience and simultaneously introduces novel information. In hindsight bias studies, participants are reminded of a previous experience and then are explicitly provided with some important information pertaining to it. In the basic interference paradigm, participants first study a list of word pairs, and later this memory is reactivated by reexposing the participants to one of the words now paired with a new one. What characterizes the results obtained from these experimental protocols is that the original memory gets distorted; alternatively, one could also interpret the distortion as the effects of a memory-updating process that, under normal conditions, produces adaptive behavior. As has been speculated for the possible functional reasons for hindsight bias: Why should participants not modify their knowledge when they are presented with information that they believe to be the solution to a question of which they did not know the exact answer? A memory system that can change quickly when relevant information becomes available will serve its owner well. Since in all reviewed cases, memory reactivation was part of the procedure to induce the observed memory change, we suggest that these experimental paradigms are methodologically equivalent to animal and human studies on memory reconsolidation.

The second type of retrieval-induced memory phenomena is illustrated by effects such as hypermnesia and reminiscence, beneficial results of repeated memory testing (and thus retrieval), leading in both cases to memory improvement. These effects are obtained in free-recall situations, in which external cues aiding retrieval are not provided, which might be a reason why reminiscence and hypermnesia effects typically co-occur. Again, we propose that retrieval induces reconsolidation of the reactivated memory. Since no new information is provided in these experimental procedures, memory updating will not be observed. Rather, the reactivated components will be strengthened. There is good reason to assume that reactivation of one element of a more complex memory leads to reactivation of the associated components (Nyberg et al. 2000; cf. spreading activation concept, Collins & Loftus 1975). Indeed, reactivation has been shown to enhance retention of a consolidated memory (Gordon & Mowrer 1980), and a recent study demonstrated that repeated retrieval of episodic memories led to an increase in the number of details recalled (Nadel et al. 2007a). Additionally, owing to forgetting and different initial strengths, not all components of a complex memory have equal recall probabilities. Therefore, retrieval-induced memory strengthening might affect subsequent recall probability differentially, leading to hypermnesia for some elements and reminiscence for others, and a similar process might be responsible for the good retention but poor accuracy of flashbulb memories, i.e., memories for highly salient events (such as the fall of the Berlin Wall) that are typically retold many times, especially shortly after they were experienced. As discussed above, repeated retrieval in the form of retelling the event has been isolated as one of the factors that contributes to the persistence of flashbulb memories. Thus, flashbulb memories appear similar to hypermnesia and reminiscence, as all these phenomena seem to be associated with repeated retrieval attempts, which, we propose, trigger memory reconsolidation processes that strengthen and stabilize the reactivated memory.

One may ask what benefits arise for cognitive psychology from our analysis suggesting that a neuroscientifically documented memory reconsolidation process lies at the root of several (cognitive) memory malleability phenomena. First, grounding a set of cognitive phenomena in biologically plausible memory processes limits the space of probable theoretical explanations for the effects and may thus reduce the number of proposed theoretical models. The same holds for the neuroscientific theories promoted to explain these phenomena: Their usefulness is also determined by how well they fare when applied to basic phenomena studied in cognitive psychology. Second, it may stimulate the development of animal models to study these phenomena in more rigorous ways, allowing interventions that directly affect the proposed mechanisms and that reveal, on a systems level, the critical brain areas mediating the memory effect. Some of these interventions may then find their way into clinical research (e.g., Brunet et al. 2008). Third, boundary conditions that have been documented for reconsolidation may explain why under certain conditions some memory distortions are not observed. For example, in rats, some strong memories do not undergo reconsolidation (e.g., Wang et al. 2009), as do certain memory types [e.g., memory for the spatial context in which something happened (Biedenkapp & Rudy 2004)]. Similarly, in humans, stronger memories are less susceptible to some memory distortions (e.g., hindsight bias is reduced for "better" memories"; repeated exposure to misleading information leads to stronger misinformation effects than do single exposures).

These boundary conditions may not only help in better understanding memory distortions, they may also be useful when the goal is to prevent rather than to demonstrate them.

What our basic framework lacks so far is an explanation for the type of memory transformations studied by Bartlett (1932), in which repeated retrieval reveals schema-consistent memory distortions as well as forgetting. Wheeler & Roediger (1992) pointed out that two of the main traditions of retrieval-induced memory alterations produce results that are hard to reconcile. Although Ballard (1913) and the research tradition that followed his footsteps demonstrated that repeated retrieval in form of free recall can lead to memory improvement (e.g., reminiscence and hypermnesia), Bartlett (1932) and the line of research he inspired consistently demonstrated that repeated retrieval in form of free recall reveals a transformation of the original memory in direction of a schema at the expense of detail and accuracy. Wheeler & Roediger (1992) isolate a factor mediating which memory effect will be observed given repeated testing. They conclude that hypermnesia and reminiscence will be observed in repeated testing when the time between the tests is brief, whereas forgetting effects as described by Bartlett will be revealed when longer times between the recurrent recalls are used.

Implied by our basic suggestion that postretrieval memory reconsolidation processes can strengthen memory is the assumption that forgetting exists as a basic memory process. As discussed in our brief review on memory interference phenomena, the nature of forgetting processes has not yet been determined, but the two main candidate mechanisms are decay of the biological substrate of memory and interference by other mental activity (cf. Wixted 2004). A possible reconsolidation-based explanation of schematization on the one hand and hypermnesia and reminiscence on the other assumes that forgetting, in one form or another, occurs after memory acquisition. Not all aspects of an experience will be encoded at the same strength, and this can depend on numerous factors, such as level-of-processing (Craik & Lockhart 1972), salience and relative distinctiveness (cf. von Restorff 1933), the amount of attention paid to a stimulus [e.g., weapon focus phenomenon (see Loftus 1979a)], or the expectations at encoding regarding how memory will be assessed later (Frost 1972). We assume that forgetting will be more pronounced for the weaker components of a complex memory than for the stronger ones. If retrieval occurs shortly after acquisition, forgetting has not led to a pronounced loss of memory, such that even weaker components of the memory will still be available and benefit from reconsolidation-mediated strengthening induced by reactivation. In these cases, hypermnesia and reminiscence will be observed. If, however, retrieval occurs later after initial learning, some of the weaker components may have faded away and only the remaining, stronger, aspects will benefit from reactivation. As Bartlett demonstrated, elements of an event that are unusual and alien, such as certain concepts in the famous "War of the Ghost" story, cannot be easily encoded, and might even during encoding suffer from a distortion by subsuming the unknown under a best-fitting existing semantic category (cf. Daniel 1972) or will not be encoded deeply, as proposed in the levels-of-processing framework. These weaker aspects of the memory for the story will thus be more quickly forgotten. If retrieval then occurs at intervals that are more widely spaced, only the still remaining components will be strengthened, which are most likely those that were consistent with existing knowledge from the beginning or were distorted such that they became consistent during encoding. This way, wider-spaced successive retrieval will reveal what is known as schematization, while shorter retrieval intervals will reveal hypermnesia and reminiscence.

The basic memory processes outlined here are part of most, if not all, networks in the brain. The system-level theories of memory organization reviewed above, such as the connectionist model, the standard model of consolidation, and the multiple trace theory do not yet capture the transformative nature of memory retrieval and need to incorporate cellular and systems reconsolidation processes into their frameworks. In a similar vein, neuroscience has largely ignored the influence of previous knowledge on new learning, which necessarily involves retrieval of relevant information during learning. Furthermore, these models have so far been silent on how to explain schematization of memory in humans and how to account for the sins of memory illustrated by the memory malleability phenomena we reviewed, and for which we tried to suggest a possible consolidation-reconsolidation, and thus neurobiologically based, conceptual foundation. The rapid progress we witnessed in recent years in the neuroscience and the cognitive neuroscience of memory holds great promise that such advances lie ahead. Ultimately, answers about the nature of memory must aim at integrating the two great research traditions, cognitive psychology and neuroscience.

DISCLOSURE STATEMENT

The authors are not aware of any biases that might be perceived as affecting the objectivity of this review.

LITERATURE CITED

Addis DR, Moscovitch M, Crawley AP, McAndrews MP. 2004. Recollective qualities modulate hippocampal activation during autobiographical memory retrieval. *Hippocampus* 14:752–62

Ahlberg SW, Sharps MJ. 2002. Bartlett revisited: reconfiguration of long-term memory in young and older adults. *J. Genet. Psychol.* 163:211–18

Amorapanth P, LeDoux JE, Nader K. 2000. Different lateral amygdala outputs mediate reactions and actions elicited by a fear-arousing stimulus. *Nat. Neurosci.* 3:74–79

Ballard PB. 1913. Obliviescence and reminiscence. *Br. J. Psychol. Monogr. Suppl.* 1:1–82

Bartlett FC. 1932. *Remembering: A Study in Experimental and Social Psychology*. Cambridge, U.K.: Cambridge Univ. Press

Bayley PJ, Gold JJ, Hopkins RO, Squire LR. 2005. The neuroanatomy of remote memory. *Neuron* 46:799–810

Bayley PJ, Hopkins RO, Squire LR. 2003. Successful recollection of remote autobiographical memories by amnesic patients with medial temporal lobe lesions. *Neuron* 38:135–44

Bayley PJ, Hopkins RO, Squire LR. 2006. The fate of old memories after medial temporal lobe damage. *J. Neurosci.* 26:13311–17

Bernard FA, Bullmore ET, Graham KS, Thompson SA, Hodges JR, Fletcher PC. 2004. The hippocampal region is involved in successful recognition of both remote and recent famous faces. *Neuroimage* 22:1704–14

Biedenkapp JC, Rudy JW. 2004. Context memories and reactivation: constraints on the reconsolidation hypothesis. *Behav. Neurosci.* 118:956–64

Bjork RA. 1975. Retrieval as a memory modifier: an interpretation of negative recency and related phenomena. In *Information Processing and Cognition*, ed. RL Solso, pp. 123–44. New York: Wiley

Bohannon NJ. 1988. Flashbulb memories for the space shuttle disaster: a tale of two theories. *Cognition* 29:179–96

Boller K, Rovee-Collier C. 1994. Contextual updating of infants' reactivated memories. *Dev. Psychobiol.* 27:241–56

Bright P, Buckman J, Fradera A, Yoshimasu H, Colchester AC, Kopelman MD. 2006. Retrograde amnesia in patients with hippocampal, medial temporal, temporal lobe, or frontal pathology. *Learn. Mem.* 13:545–57

Brown R, Kulik J. 1977. Flashbulb memories. *Cognition* 5:73–99

Brunet A, Orr SP, Tremblay J, Robertson K, Nader K, Pitman RK. 2008. Effect of postretrieval propranolol on psychophysiologic responding during subsequent script-driven traumatic imagery in post-traumatic stress disorder. *J. Psychiatr. Res.* 42:503–6

Burwell RD, Bucci DJ, Sanborn MR, Jutras MJ. 2004. Perirhinal and postrhinal contributions to remote memory for context. *J. Neurosci.* 24:11023–28

Christensen-Szalanski JJJ, Wilham CF. 1991. The hindsight bias: an individual difference analysis. *J. Personal.* 51:606–20

Christensen-Szalanski JJJ, Willham CF. 1991. The hindsight bias: a meta-analysis. *Organ. Behav. Hum. Decis. Process.* 48:147–68

Christianson S-Å, Engelberg E. 1999. Memory and emotional consistency: the MS Estonia ferry disaster. *Memory* 7:471–82

Cipolotti L, Shallice T, Chan D, Fox N, Scahill R, et al. 2001. Long-term retrograde amnesia… the crucial role of the hippocampus. *Neuropsychologia* 39:151–72

Clark RE, Broadbent NJ, Squire LR. 2005. Impaired remote spatial memory after hippocampal lesions despite extensive training beginning early in life. *Hippocampus* 15:340–46

Collins AM, Loftus EF. 1975. A spreading-activation theory of semantic processing. *Psychol. Rev.* 82:407–29

Connolly T, Bukzar EW. 1990. Hindsight bias: self-flattery or cognitive error? *J. Behav. Decis. Making* 3:205–11

Conway M, Anderson S, Larsen S, Steen F, Donnelly C, et al. 1994. The formation of flashbulb memories. *Mem. Cogn.* 22:326–43

Craik FIM, Lockhart RS. 1972. Levels of processing: a framework for memory research. *J. Verbal Learn. Verbal Behav.* 11:671–84

Daniel TC. 1972. Nature of the effect of verbal labels on recognition memory for form. *J. Exp. Psychol.* 96:152–57

Davies MF. 1992. Field dependence and hindsight bias: cognitive restructuring and the generation of reasons. *J. Res. Personal.* 26:58–74

Debiec J, Doyere V, Nader K, LeDoux JE. 2006. Directly reactivated, but not indirectly reactivated, memories undergo reconsolidation in the amygdala. *Proc. Natl. Acad. Sci. USA* 103:3428–33

Debiec J, LeDoux JE, Nader K. 2002. Cellular and systems reconsolidation in the hippocampus. *Neuron* 36:527–38

Deese J. 1959. On the prediction of occurrence of particular verbal intrusions in immediate recall. *J. Exp. Psychol.* 58:17–22

Douville K, Woodard JL, Seidenberg M, Miller SK, Leveroni CL, et al. 2005. Medial temporal lobe activity for recognition of recent and remote famous names: an event-related fMRI study. *Neuropsychologia* 43:693–703

Duncan CP. 1949. The retroactive effect of electroconvulsive shock. *J. Comp. Physiol. Psychol.* 42:32–44

Easton A, Zinkivskay A, Eacott MJ. 2009. Recollection is impaired, but familiarity remains intact in rats with lesions of the fornix. *Hippocampus.* Epub ahead of print

Eisenberg M, Kobilo T, Berman DE, Dudai Y. 2003. Stability of retrieved memory: inverse correlation with trace dominance. *Science* 301:1102–4

Erdelyi MH, Becker J. 1974. Hypermnesia for pictures: Incremental memory for pictures but not for words in multiple recall trials. *Cogn. Psychol.* 6:159–71

Erdfelder E, Buchner A. 1998. Decomposing the hindsight bias: an integrative multinomial processing tree model. *J. Exp. Psychol.: Learn. Mem. Cogn.* 24:387–414

Eldridge LL, Knowlton BJ, Furmanski CS, Bookheimer SY, Engel SA. 2000. Remembering episodes: a selective role for the hippocampus during retrieval. *Nat. Neurosci.* 3:1149–52

Fagen JW, Rovee-Collier C. 1983. Memory retrieval: a time-locked process in infancy. *Science* 222:1349–51

Fischhoff B. 1975. Hindsight is not equal to foresight: the effect of outcome knowledge on judgement under uncertainty. *J. Exp. Psychol.: Hum. Percept. Perform.* 1:288–99

Fischhoff B. 1977. Perceived informativeness of facts. *J. Exp. Psychol.: Hum. Percept. Perform.* 3:349–58

Fischhoff B, Beyth R. 1975. "I knew it would happen": remembered probabilities of once-future things. *Organ. Behav. Hum. Decis. Process.* 13:1–16

Flexner LB, Flexner JB, Stellar E. 1965. Memory and cerebral protein synthesis in mice as affected by graded amounts of puromycin. *Exp. Neurol.* 13:264–72

Frankland PW, Bontempi B. 2005. The organization of recent and remote memories. *Nat. Rev. Neurosci.* 6:119–30

Frankland PW, Ding HK, Takahashi E, Suzuki A, Kida S, Silva AJ. 2006. Stability of recent and remote contextual fear memory. *Learn Mem.* 13:451–57

Frost N. 1972. Encoding and retrieval in visual memory tasks. *J. Exp. Psychol.* 95:317–26

Gaffan D. 1993. Additive effects of forgetting and fornix transfection in the temporal gradient of retrograde amnesia. *Neuropsychologia* 31:1055–66

Gerard RW. 1949. Physiology and psychiatry. *Am. J. Psychiatry* 106:161–73

Gilboa A, Winocur G, Grady CL, Hevenor SJ, Moscovitch M. 2004. Remembering our past: functional neuroanatomy of recollection of recent and very remote personal events. *Cereb. Cortex* 14:1214–25

Glickman S. 1961. Perseverative neural processes and consolidation of the memory trace. *Psychol. Bull.* 58:218–33

Gordon WC. 1977a. Similarities of recently acquired and reactivated memories in interference. *Am. J. Psychol.* 90:231–42

Gordon WC. 1977b. Susceptibility of a reactivated memory to the effects of strychnine: a time-dependent phenomenon. *Physiol. Behav.* 18:95–99

Gordon WC. 1981. Mechanisms of cue-induced retention enhancements. In *Information Processing in Animals: Memory Mechanisms*, ed. NE Spear, JA Kleim, pp. 319–39. Hillsdale, NJ: Erlbaum

Gordon WC, Mowrer RR. 1980. An extinction trial as a reminder treatment following electroconvulsive shock. *Anim. Learn. Behav.* 8:363–67

Gordon WC, Spear NE. 1973. Effect of reactivation of a previously acquired memory on the interaction between memories in the rat. *J. Exp. Psychol.* 99:349–55

Haist F, Bowden Gore J, Mao H. 2001. Consolidation of human memory over decades revealed by functional magnetic resonance imaging. *Nat. Neurosci.* 4:1139–45

Hardt O, Hupbach A, Nadel L. 2009a. Factors moderating blocking in human place learning: the role of task instructions. *Learn Behav.* 37:42–59

Hardt O, Pohl RF. 2003. Hindsight bias as a function of anchor distance and anchor plausibility. *Memory* 11:379–94

Hardt O, Wang SH, Nader K. 2009b. Storage or retrieval deficit: the yin and yang of amnesia. *Learn. Mem.* 16:224–30

Hasher L, Attig MS, Alba JW. 1981. I knew it all along: or, did I? *J. Verbal Learn. Verbal Behav.* 20:89–96

Hawkins SA, Hastie R. 1990. Hindsight: biased judgments of past events after the outcomes are known. *Psychol. Bull.* 107:311–27

Hebb DO. 1949. *The Organization of Behavior*. New York: Wiley

Hell W, Gigerenzer G, Gauggel S, Mall M, Müller M. 1988. Hindsight bias: an interaction of automatic and motivational factors? *Cognition* 16:533–38

Hirano M, Noguchi K, Hosokawa T, Takayama T. 2002. I cannot remember, but I know my past events: remembering and knowing in a patient with amnesic syndrome. *J. Clin. Exp. Neuropsychol.* 24:548–55

Hupbach A, Gomez R, Hardt O, Nadel L. 2007. Reconsolidation of episodic memories: a subtle reminder triggers integration of new information. *Learn. Mem.* 14:47–53

Hupbach A, Hardt O, Gomez R, Nadel L. 2008. The dynamics of memory: context-dependent updating. *Learn. Mem.* 15:574–79

Jenkins JG, Dallenbach KM. 1924. Obliviscence during sleep and waking. *Am. J. Psychol.* 35:605–12

Jost A. 1897. Die Assoziationsfestigkeit in ihrer Abhängigkeit von der Verteilung der Wiederholungen. *Zeitschrift für Psychologie und Physiologie der Sinnesorgane* 14:436–72

Kapur N, Brooks DJ. 1999. Temporally-specific retrograde amnesia in two cases of discrete bilateral hippocampal pathology. *Hippocampus* 9:247–54

Kapur N, Friston KJ, Young A, Frith CD, Frackowiak RS. 1995. Activation of human hippocampal formation during memory for faces: a PET study. *Cortex* 31:99–108

Kesner RP, Hunsaker MR, Warthen MW. 2008. The CA3 subregion of the hippocampus is critical for episodic memory processing by means of relational encoding in rats. *Behav. Neurosci.* 122:1217–25

Kim JJ, Fanselow MS. 1992. Modality-specific retrograde amnesia of fear. *Science* 256:675–77

Kopelman MD, Kapur N. 2001. The loss of episodic memories in retrograde amnesia: single-case and group studies. *Philos. Trans. R. Soc. Lond. B Biol. Sci.* 356:1409–21

Land C, Bunsey M, Riccio DC. 2000. Anomalous properties of hippocampal lesion-induced retrograde amnesia. *Psychobiology* 28:476–85

Lee JL. 2008. Memory reconsolidation mediates the strengthening of memories by additional learning. *Nat. Neurosci.* 11:1264–66

Lee JL. 2009. Reconsolidation: maintaining memory relevance. *Trends Neurosci.* 32:413–20

Leonard BJ, McNaughton BL, Barnes CA. 1987. Suppression of hippocampal synaptic plasticity during slow-wave sleep. *Brain Res.* 425:174–77

Lewis DJ. 1979. Psychobiology of active and inactive memory. *Psychol. Bull.* 86:1054–83

Loftus EF. 1975. Leading questions and the eyewitness report. *Cogn. Psychol.* 7:560–72

Loftus EF. 1979a. *Eyewitness Testimony.* Cambridge, MA: Harvard Univ. Press

Loftus EF. 1979b. Reactions to blatantly contradictory information. *Mem. Cogn.* 7:368–74

Loftus EF, Loftus GR. 1980. On the permanence of stored information in the human brain. *Am. Psychol.* 35:409–20

Loftus EF, Miller DG, Burns HJ. 1978. Semantic integration of verbal information into a visual memory. *J. Exp. Psychol.: Hum. Learn. Mem.* 4:19–31

Mactutus CF, Riccio DC, Ferek JM. 1979. Retrograde amnesia for old (reactivated) memory: some anomalous characteristics. *Science* 204:1319–20

Maguire EA. 2001. Neuroimaging studies of autobiographical event memory. *Philos. Trans. R. Soc. Lond. B Biol. Sci.* 356:1441–51

Maguire EA, Frackowiak RS, Frith CD. 1996. Learning to find your way: a role for the human hippocampal formation. *Proc. Biol. Sci.* 263:1745–50

Maguire EA, Nannery R, Spiers HJ. 2006. Navigation around London by a taxi driver with bilateral hippocampal lesions. *Brain* 129:2894–907

Manns JR, Hopkins RO, Squire LR. 2003. Semantic memory and the human hippocampus. *Neuron* 38:127–33

Marr D. 1971. Simple memory: a theory for archicortex. *Philos. Trans. R. Soc. Lond. B Biol. Sci.* 262:23–81

Martin SJ, de Hoz L, Morris RGM. 2005. Retrograde amnesia: neither partial nor complete hippocampal lesions in rats result in preferential sparing of remote spatial memory, even after reminding. *Neuropsychologia* 43:609–24

McClelland JL, McNaughton BL, O'Reilly RC. 1995. Why there are complementary learning systems in the hippocampus and neocortex: insights from the successes and failures of connectionist models of learning and memory. *Psychol. Rev.* 102:419–57

McCloskey M. 1992. Special versus ordinary memory mechanisms in the genesis of flashbulb memories. In *Affect and Accuracy in Recall: The Problem of "Flashbulb" Memories*, ed. E Winograd, U Neisser, pp. 227–35. Cambridge, UK: Cambridge Univ. Press

McCloskey M, Wible CG, Cohen NJ. 1988. Is there a special flashbulb-memory mechanism? *J. Exp. Psychol.: Gen.* 117:171–81

McCloskey M, Zaragoza M. 1985. Misleading postevent information and memory for events: arguments and evidence against memory impairment hypotheses. *J. Exp. Psychol.: Gen.* 144:1–16

McDaniel MA, Masson MEJ. 1985. Altering memory representations through retrieval. *J. Exp. Psychol.: Learn. Mem. Cogn.* 11:371–85

McGaugh JL. 1966. Time-dependent processes in memory storage. *Science* 153:1351–58

McGaugh JL, Krivanek JA. 1970. Strychnine effects on discrimination learning in mice: effects of dose and time of administration. *Physiol. Behav.* 5:1437–42

McGeoch JA. 1932. Forgetting and the law of disuse. *Psychol. Rev.* 39:352–70

Metcalfe J, Bjork RA. 1991. Composite models never (well, hardly ever) compromise: reply to Schooler and Tanaka (1991). *J. Exp. Psychol.: Gen.* 120:203–10

Milekic MH, Alberini CM. 2002. Temporally graded requirement for protein synthesis following memory reactivation. *Neuron* 36:340–43

Miller RR, Springer AD. 1973. Amnesia, consolidation, and retrieval. *Psychol. Rev.* 80:69–79

Miller RR, Springer AD. 1974. Implications of recovery from experimental amnesia. *Psychol. Rev.* 81:470–73

Misanin JR, Miller RR, Lewis DJ. 1968. Retrograde amnesia produced by electroconvulsive shock after reactivation of a consolidated memory trace. *Science* 160:203–4

Morris RG, Inglis J, Ainge JA, Olverman HJ, Tulloch J, et al. 2006. Memory reconsolidation: sensitivity of spatial memory to inhibition of protein synthesis in dorsal hippocampus during encoding and retrieval. *Neuron* 50:479–89

Moscovitch M, Nadel L. 1998. Consolidation and the hippocampal complex revisited: in defense of the multiple-trace model. *Curr. Opin. Neurobiol.* 8:297–300

Moscovitch M, Nadel L, Winocur G, Gilboa A, Rosenbaum RS. 2006. The cognitive neuroscience of remote episodic, semantic and spatial memory. *Curr. Opin. Neurobiol.* 16:179–90

Müller GE, Pilzecker A. 1900. Experimentelle Beiträge zur Lehre vom Gedächtnis. *Z. Psychol. Ergänzungsband* (Suppl. No. 1):1–300

Nadel L, Campbell J, Ryan L. 2007a. Autobiographical memory retrieval and hippocampal activation as a function of repetition and the passage of time. *Neural Plast.* 2007:90472

Nadel L, Moscovitch M. 1997. Memory consolidation, retrograde amnesia and the hippocampal complex. *Curr. Opin. Neurobiol.* 7:217–27

Nadel L, Winocur G, Ryan L, Moscovitch M. 2007b. Systems consolidation and hippocampus: two views. *Debates Neurosci.* 1:55–66

Nader K, Hardt O. 2009. A single standard for memory: the case for reconsolidation. *Nat. Rev. Neurosci.* 10:224–34

Nader K, Schafe GE, LeDoux JE. 2000. Fear memories require protein synthesis in the amygdala for reconsolidation after retrieval. *Nature* 406:722–26

Nader K, Wang SH. 2006. Fading in. *Learn. Mem.* 13:530–35

Neisser U. 1967. *Cognitive Psychology.* New York: Appleton-Century-Crofts

Neisser U, Harsh N. 1992. Phantom flashbulbs: false recollections of hearing the news about Challenger. In *Affect and Accuracy in Recall: Studies of "Flashbulb" Memories*, ed. E Winograd, U Neisser, pp. 9–13. Cambridge, UK: Cambridge Univ. Press

Nyberg L, Habib R, McIntosh AR, Tulving E. 2000. Reactivation of encoding-related brain activity during memory retrieval. *Proc. Natl. Acad. Sci. USA* 97:11120–24

Okado Y, Stark CE. 2005. Neural activity during encoding predicts false memories created by misinformation. *Learn. Mem.* 2005:3–12

Pedreira ME, Perez-Cuesta LM, Maldonado H. 2004. Mismatch between what is expected and what actually occurs triggers memory reconsolidation or extinction. *Learn. Mem.* 11:579–85

Pennington DC. 1981. Being wise after the event: an investigation of hindsight bias. *Curr. Psychol. Res.* 1:271–82

Piefke M, Weiss PH, Zilles K, Markowitsch HJ, Fink GR. 2003. Differential remoteness and emotional tone modulate the neural correlates of autobiographical memory. *Brain* 126:650–68

Pillemer DB. 1984. Flashbulb memories of the assassination attempt on President Reagan. *Cognition* 16:63–80

Pohl RF, Eisenhauer M, Hardt O. 2003. SARA: a cognitive process model to simulate the anchoring effect and hindsight bias. *Memory* 11:337–56

Pohl RF, Hell W. 1996. No reduction of hindsight bias with complete information and repeated testing. *Organ. Behav. Hum. Decis. Process.* 67:49–58

Quartermain D, McEwen BS, Azmitia EC Jr. 1970. Amnesia produced by electroconvulsive shock or cycloheximide: conditions for recovery. *Science* 169:683–86

Rasch B, Buchel C, Gais S, Born J. 2007. Odor cues during slow-wave sleep prompt declarative memory consolidation. *Science* 315:1426–29

Reed JM, Squire LR. 1998. Retrograde amnesia for facts and events: findings from four new cases. *J. Neurosci.* 18:3943–54

Rekkas PV, Constable RT. 2005. Evidence that autobiographic memory retrieval does not become independent of the hippocampus: an fMRI study contrasting very recent with remote events. *J. Cogn. Neurosci.* 17:1950–61

Rempel-Clower NL, Zola SM, Squire LR, Amaral DG. 1996. Three cases of enduring memory impairment after bilateral damage limited to the hippocampal formation. *J. Neurosci.* 16:5233–55

Ribot T. 1881. *Les Maladies de la Memoire.* New York: Appleton-Century-Crofts

Robbins MJ, Meyer DR. 1970. Motivational control of retrograde amnesia. *J. Exp. Psychol.* 84:220–25

Roediger HL III, Jacoby D, McDermott KB. 1996. Misinformation effects in recall: creating false memories through repeated retrieval. *J. Mem. Lang.* 35:300–18

Roediger HL III, McDermott KB. 1995. Creating false memories: remembering words not presented in lists. *J. Exp. Psychol.: Learn. Mem. Cogn.* 21:803–14

Roediger HL III, McDermott KB. 2000. Tricks of memory. *Curr. Dir. Psychol.* 9:123–27

Rosenbaum RS, Gao F, Richards B, Black SE, Moscovitch M. 2005. "Where to?" Remote memory for spatial relations and landmark identity in former taxi drivers with Alzheimer's disease and encephalitis. *J. Cogn. Neurosci.* 17:446–62

Rosenbaum RS, Winocur G, Moscovitch M. 2001. New views on old memories: re-evaluating the role of the hippocampal complex. *Behav. Brain Res.* 127:183–97

Rovee-Collier C. 1997. Dissociations in infant memory: rethinking the development of implicit and explicit memory. *Psychol. Rev.* 104:467–98

Rubin DC, Kozin M. 1984. Vivid memories. *Cognition* 16:81–95

Ryan L, Nadel L, Keil K, Putnam K, Schnyer D, et al. 2001. Hippocampal complex and retrieval of recent and very remote autobiographical memories: evidence from functional magnetic resonance imaging in neurologically intact people. *Hippocampus* 11:707–14

Sara SJ. 2000. Retrieval and reconsolidation: toward a neurobiology of remembering. *Learn. Mem.* 7:73–84

Sauvage MM, Fortin NJ, Owens CB, Yonelinas AP, Eichenbaum H. 2008. Recognition memory: opposite effects of hippocampal damage on recollection and familiarity. *Nat. Neurosci.* 11:16–18

Schacter DL. 1999. The seven sins of memory: how the mind forgets and remembers. *Am. Psychol.* 54:182–203

Schacter DL. 2001. *Forgotten Ideas, Neglected Pioneers: Richard Semon and the Story of Memory*. Philadelphia, PA: Psychol. Press

Schacter DL, Addis DR. 2007. The cognitive neuroscience of constructive memory: remembering the past and imagining the future. *Philos. Trans. R. Soc. Lond. B Biol. Sci.* 362:773–86

Schacter DL, Norman KA, Koutstaal W. 1998. The cognitive neuroscience of constructive memory. *Annu. Rev. Psychol.* 49:289–318

Schneider AM, Sherman W. 1968. Amnesia: a function of the temporal relation of footshock to electroconvulsive shock. *Science* 159:219–21

Schooler JW, Bendiksen M, Ambadar Z. 1997. Taking the middle line: Can we accommodate both fabricated and recovered memories of sexual abuse? In *Recovered Memories and False Memories*, ed. MA Conway, pp. 251–92. Oxford, UK: Oxford Univ. Press

Schooler JW, Tanaka JW. 1991. Composites, compromises, and CHARM: What is the evidence for blend memory representations? *J. Exp. Psychol.: Gen.* 120:96–100; discussion 101–5

Scoville WB, Milner B. 1957. Loss of recent memory after bilateral hippocampal lesions. *J. Neurol. Psychiatry* 20:11–21

Semon R. 1904. *The Mneme*. London: George Allen & Unwin

Semon R. 1909. *Mnemic Psychology*. London: George Allen & Unwin

Serota RG. 1971. Acetoxycycloheximide and transient amnesia in the rat. *Proc. Natl. Acad. Sci. USA* 68:1249–50

Shiffrin RM, Raaijmakers JGW. 1992. The SAM retrieval model: a retrospective and a prospective. *From Learning Processes to Cognitive Processes: Essays in Honor of William K. Estes*, ed. AF Healy, SM Kosslyn, RM Shiffrin, pp. 69–86. Hillsdale, NJ: Erlbaum

Slovic P, Fischhoff B. 1977. On the psychology of experimental surprises. *J. Exp. Psychol.: Hum. Percept. Perform.* 3:544–51

Smith CN, Squire LR. 2009. Medial temporal lobe activity during retrieval of semantic memory is related to the age of the memory. *J. Neurosci.* 29:930–38

Spear N. 1973. Retrieval of memory in animals. *Psychol. Rev.* 80:163–94

Spear NE, Mueller CW. 1984. Consolidation as a function of retrieval. In *Memory Consolidation: Psychobiology of Cognition*, ed. H Weingartner, ES Parker, pp. 111–47. Hillsdale, NJ: Erlbaum

Squire LR, Alvarez P. 1995. Retrograde amnesia and memory consolidation: a neurobiological perspective. *Curr. Opin. Neurobiol.* 5:169–77

Squire LR, Bayley PJ. 2007. The neuroscience of remote memory. *Curr. Opin. Neurobiol.* 17:185–96

Squire LR, Cohen NJ, Nadel L. 1984. The medial temporal region and memory consolidation: a new hypothesis. In *Memory Consolidation: Psychobiology of Cognition*, ed. H Weingartner, ES Parker, pp. 185–210. Hillsdale, NJ: Erlbaum

Steinvorth S, Corkin S, Halgren E. 2006. Ecphory of autobiographical memories: an fMRI study of recent and remote memory retrieval. *Neuroimage* 30:285–98

Sutherland RJ, Weisend MP, Mumby D, Astur RS, Hanlon FM, et al. 2001. Retrograde amnesia after hippocampal damage: recent vs remote memories in two tasks. *Hippocampus* 11:27–42

Suzuki A, Josselyn SA, Frankland PW, Masushige S, Silva AJ, Kida S. 2004. Memory reconsolidation and extinction have distinct temporal and biochemical signatures. *J. Neurosci.* 24:4787–95

Takashima A, Petersson KM, Rutters F, Tendolkar I, Jensen O, et al. 2006. Declarative memory consolidation in humans: a prospective functional magnetic resonance imaging study. *Proc. Natl. Acad. Sci. USA* 103:756–61

Teng E, Squire LR. 1999. Memory for places learned long ago is intact after hippocampal damage. *Nature* 400:675–77

Thorndike EL. 1914. *Educational Psychology*. New York: Teachers College, Columbia Univ.

Trinkler I, King JA, Doeller CF, Rugg MD, Burgess N. 2009. Neural bases of autobiographical support for episodic recollection of faces. *Hippocampus* 19:718–30

Tronel S, Milekic MH, Alberini CM. 2005. Linking new information to a reactivated memory requires consolidation and not reconsolidation mechanisms. *PLoS Biol.* 3:e293

Tse D, Langston RF, Kakeyama M, Bethus I, Spooner PA, et al. 2007. Schemas and memory consolidation. *Science* 316:76–82

Tulving E. 1967. The effects of presentation and recall in free recall learning. *J. Verbal Learn. Verbal Behav.* 6:175–84

Underwood BJ. 1957. Interference and forgetting. *Psychol. Rev.* 64:49–60

Underwood BJ. 1965. False recognition produced by implicit verbal responses. *J. Exp. Psychol.* 70:122–29

Underwood BJ, Ekstrand BR. 1966. An analysis of some shortcomings in the interference theory of forgetting. *Psychol. Rev.* 73:540–49

Viskontas IV, Carr VA, Engel SA, Knowlton BJ. 2009. The neural correlates of recollection: hippocampal activation declines as episodic memory fades. *Hippocampus* 19:265–72

von Restorff H. 1933. Analyze von Vorgängen im Spurenfeld I: Über die Wirkung von Bereichsbildung im Spurenfeld. *Psychol. Forsch.* 18:299–342

Wagner U, Gais S, Haider H, Verleger R, Born J. 2004. Sleep inspires insight. *Nature* 427:352–55

Walker MP, Brakefield T, Hobson JA, Stickgold R. 2003. Dissociable stages of human memory consolidation and reconsolidation. *Nature* 425:616–20

Wang SH, de Oliveira Alvares L, Nader K. 2009. Cellular and systems mechanisms of memory strength as a constraint on auditory fear reconsolidation. *Nat. Neurosci.* 12:905–12

Wheeler MA, Roediger HL III. 1992. Disparate effects of repeated testing: reconciling Ballard's (1913) and Bartlett's (1932) results. *Psychol. Sci.* 3:240–45

Wiltgen BJ, Silva AJ. 2007. Memory for context becomes less specific with time. *Learn. Mem.* 14:313–17

Winningham RG, Hyman IE, Dinnel DL. 2000. Flashbulb memories? The effects of when the initial memory report was obtained. *Memory* 8:209–16

Winocur G. 1990. Anterograde and retrograde amnesia in rats with dorsal hippocampal or dorsomedial thalamic lesions. *Behav. Brain Res.* 38:145–54

Winocur G, Moscovitch M, Fogel S, Rosenbaum RS, Sekeres M. 2005. Preserved spatial memory after hippocampal lesions: effects of extensive experience in a complex environment. *Nat. Neurosci.* 8:273–75

Winocur G, Moscovitch M, Sekeres M. 2007. Memory consolidation or transformation: context manipulation and hippocampal representations of memory. *Nat. Neurosci.* 10:555–57

Wixted JT. 2004. The psychology and neuroscience of forgetting. *Annu. Rev. Psychol.* 55:235–69

Wood G. 1978. The "knew-it-all-along" effect. *J. Exp. Psychol.: Hum. Percept. Perform.* 4:345–53

Yonelinas AP, Otten LJ, Shaw KN, Rugg MD. 2005. Separating the brain regions involved in recollection and familiarity in recognition memory. *J. Neurosci.* 25:3002–8

Zaragoza MS, Mitchell KJ. 1996. Repeated exposure to suggestion and the creation of false memories. *Psychol. Sci.* 7:294–300

Cognitive Neural Prosthetics

Richard A. Andersen,[1] Eun Jung Hwang,[1]
and Grant H. Mulliken[2]

[1]Division of Biology, California Institute of Technology, Pasadena, California 91125;
email: andersen@vis.caltech.edu, eunjung@vis.caltech.edu

[2]McGovern Institute for Brain Research, Massachusetts Institute of Technology,
Cambridge, Massachusetts 02139; email: grantm@mit.edu

Annu. Rev. Psychol. 2010. 61:169–90

First published online as a Review in Advance on
September 28, 2009

The *Annual Review of Psychology* is online at
psych.annualreviews.org

This article's doi:
10.1146/annurev.psych.093008.100503

Key Words

decision making, planning, intention, posterior parietal cortex,
brain-machine interface, efference copy, learning, sensorimotor
transformation

Abstract

The cognitive neural prosthetic (CNP) is a very versatile method for
assisting paralyzed patients and patients with amputations. The CNP
records the cognitive state of the subject, rather than signals strictly related to motor execution or sensation. We review a number of high-level
cortical signals and their application for CNPs, including intention, motor imagery, decision making, forward estimation, executive function,
attention, learning, and multi-effector movement planning. CNPs are
defined by the cognitive function they extract, not the cortical region
from which the signals are recorded. However, some cortical areas may
be better than others for particular applications. Signals can also be extracted in parallel from multiple cortical areas using multiple implants,
which in many circumstances can increase the range of applications of
CNPs. The CNP approach relies on scientific understanding of the
neural processes involved in cognition, and many of the decoding algorithms it uses also have parallels to underlying neural circuit functions.

Contents

WHAT IS A COGNITIVE NEURAL PROSTHETIC?

Cognitive neural prosthetics (CNPs): instruments that consist of an array of electrodes, a decoding algorithm, and an external device controlled by the processed cognitive signal

Decoding algorithms: computer algorithms that interpret neural signals for the purposes of understanding their function or for providing control signals to machines

The number of patients suffering from some form of paralysis in the United States alone has been estimated to be from 1.7 million (U.S. Dept. Health Human Serv. 1995) to 5.6 million (Christopher & Dana Reeve Found. 2009). Paralysis can result from spinal cord lesion and other traumatic accidents, peripheral neuropathies, amyotrophic lateral sclerosis, multiple sclerosis, and stroke. Another 1.4 million patients have motor disabilities due to limb amputation (U.S. Dept. Health Human Serv. 1995). A majority of these patients still have sufficiently intact cortex to plan movements, but they are unable to execute them. Thus they are candidates for assistance using cortical neural prosthetics.

Figure 1 (see color insert) shows the concept of cortical neural prosthetics generally, and cognitive neural prosthetics (CNPs) more specifically. In this particular case, the patient is shown to have a spinal cord lesion, but a similar logic applies to other forms of paralysis or to amputation. The patient can still plan movements but cannot execute them. Recordings can be made from microelectrode arrays in cortex. The implants not only record the activity of populations of nerve cells but also transmit these signals wirelessly to external assistive devices. Implants can be placed in a variety of areas, and they record the intent or other cognitive variables of the subject. Decoding algorithms interpret the meaning of the recorded signals. These algorithms can be incorporated into hardware in the implant or in the external devices. The decoded neural signals are further transformed to provide control signals to operate assistive devices. In the example in **Figure 1**, these devices can include robotic limbs, functional electrical stimulation of otherwise paralyzed limbs for reanimation, wheelchair navigation, Internet access, email, telephone and other forms of computer-assisted communication, and the control of the patient's environment including television, temperature control, and calls for assistance. Elements of a cortical neural prosthetic, including the electrodes, decoding algorithms, and associated electronics, are often referred to collectively as a brain-machine interface (BMI).

In research applications, healthy monkeys are used to test cortical prosthetics. Typically, the animals have a permanently implanted array of electrodes, similar to the case for human patients. The animals control an output device with their thoughts and can do this without eliciting movements. This process is often referred to as a brain-control task. It is also called a closed-loop task since the animals receive feedback about their performance, for instance, the movement of a cursor on a computer screen controlled by their neural activity.

Many studies have involved extracting motor execution signals from motor cortex (Carmena et al. 2003, Fetz 1969, Serruya et al.

2002, Taylor et al. 2002). It was often observed that the monkeys did not need to actually move the limb to bring a cursor under brain control. In terms of the current topic, this would constitute cognitive control, in which brain signals not directly related to executing a movement can nonetheless be harnessed for the task. This control can be derived from motor imagery, planning, attention, decision making, or executive control, to name just a few of the cognitive signals that are potentially useful for neuroprosthetics. The distinction is not the brain location of the recording but rather the type of signal that is being extracted (Andersen et al. 2004a). This being said, some brain areas will no doubt be better sources of signals for particular neuroprosthetic applications. The specialization of different cortical areas is an advantage for CNPs. For example, for mute patients speech can potentially be decoded directly from speech areas rather than using a letter board and controlling a cursor from motor cortex. CNPs can also take advantage of parallel decoding, in which implants are placed in multiple cortical areas and different signals are decoded simultaneously. A prime example of this parallel decoding is the application of CNPs to complex, multi-effector movements, discussed below.

Science as a Guide for Cognitive Neural Prosthetics

One central element of neuroprosthetics is engineering. Advanced statistical and signal-processing techniques are commonly used to optimize decoding algorithms as well as develop algorithms that are adaptive. Such approaches are essential to CNPs. However, CNPs also benefit from the additional component of a scientific understanding of the brain processes being performed by the region(s) of recording. This understanding extends to functional neuroanatomy and network/circuit properties that can guide the selection of recording sites and the design and implementation of decoding algorithms. The following sections highlight examples that match cortical function, and in some cases decoding algorithms, to particular cognitive neuroprosthetic applications.

INTENDED GOALS

Neural prosthetic applications have often used trajectory signals to bring a cursor or a robotic hand to a goal (Carmena et al. 2003, Serruya et al. 2002, Taylor et al. 2002). This approach, especially for cursor control, is similar to using a mouse to drag a cursor to a location on a computer screen. However, many applications would benefit from being able to rapidly indicate a series of goals. One example would be the rapid indication of letters on a letter board for communication. Another would be to provide a sequence of movements for a robotic limb to ensure a more fluid programming of a string of movements.

The primary motor cortex (M1) contains some goal information, but goal information is strongly represented in the premotor and posterior parietal cortex (Hatsopoulos et al. 2004, Snyder et al. 1997) (**Figure 2**, see color insert). This goal information reflects the intent of the animal to make a movement to the goal.

Gnadt & Andersen (1988) first demonstrated intended eye movement signals in the lateral intraparietal area (LIP) of the posterior parietal cortex (PPC). Subsequent studies showed that neurons in the parietal reach region (PRR) of PPC encode the intent to make reach movements (Snyder et al. 1997). A variety of experiments have demonstrated intention-related activity that is not spatial attention (Cui & Andersen 2007, Gail & Andersen 2006, Quiroga et al. 2006, Scherberger & Andersen 2007, Scherberger et al. 2005, Snyder et al. 1998). These movement plans can be formed but then cancelled without executing a movement; therefore, they do not reflect motor execution but rather the higher-level plan to move (Andersen & Buneo 2002, Bracewell et al. 1996, Snyder et al. 1998). The more high-level, abstract nature of the intention signals is also evident from the finding that the intended reach activity in PRR is coded in visual rather than limb coordinates (Batista et al. 1999).

Brain-machine interface (BMI): a device that records neural activity, decodes these signals, and uses the decoded signals for operating machines

Brain-control task: a task in which the subject uses only neural signals to control an external device

Cognitive signals: neural activities related to high-level cognitive function (e.g., intention, planning, decision making, executive function, thoughts, concepts, and speech)

M1: primary motor cortex

LIP: lateral intraparietal area

PPC: posterior parietal cortex

PRR: parietal reach region

PMd: dorsal
premotor cortex

Putative human homologues of LIP and PRR have been identified in humans using functional magnetic resonance imaging (fMRI) experiments (Astafiev et al. 2003, Connolly et al. 2003, Filimon et al. 2009). Interestingly, electrical stimulation of the posterior parietal cortex in human patients invoked the conscious intention to move various body parts even though no movements resulted from the stimulation (Desmurget et al. 2009). Whereas it was possible to demonstrate intention-related activity in monkey PPC neurons, this study shows that the conscious awareness of intention also arises with increased PPC activity.

Musallam et al. (2004) demonstrated decoding of four or eight goal locations from array recordings from the PRR of PPC and the dorsal premotor cortex (PMd) in frontal cortex (**Figure 3A**, see color insert). To emphasize the cognitive nature of the signal, they decoded the persistent activity that results when monkeys plan a movement to a briefly cued location in space but while withholding the execution of the movement. This goal signal is decoded in the dark, with no stimulus present and no movement being executed; it is endogenously generated and represents the movement thought or intent of the animal. This intent can be decoded very rapidly. If a 100 ms time segment was used for decoding, it was nearly as accurate as using a 900 ms time segment. Subsequent studies in PMd showed that three goals could be decoded in rapid succession (Santhanam et al. 2006).

Many natural movements are highly coordinated concatenations of movement sequences rather than single reaches as discussed above. Frontal areas encode the parts of sequences including the directions and order of movements (Averbeck et al. 2006, Fujii & Graybiel 2003, Histed & Miller 2006, Lu & Ashe 2005, Mushiake et al. 2006, Ninokura et al. 2003, Ohbayashi et al. 2003, Tanji & Shima 1994). An early study of PRR found that only the next movement of a sequence is encoded, but the task was complex and involved the canceling of old plans and formation of new ones (Batista & Andersen 2001). In a more direct test of sequential planning in PRR, it was found that the area represents simultaneously and in parallel the first and second goals in a sequence of two movements (Baldauf et al. 2008). This dual representation was present regardless of whether the two movements were made rapidly or slowly. A nearest-neighbor decoding algorithm applied to the data revealed that the sequence of planned movements could be decoded. This decoding was done during a delay period in which there was no stimulus or movement, again emphasizing the cognitive nature of the signals encoding the sequence. Thus PRR activity encodes simultaneously and in parallel a sequence of movements, and this feature could be utilized to provide for a more fluid operation of output devices for prosthetic applications.

MOTOR IMAGERY

A basis of neural prosthetic control may be motor imagery. The fact that primary motor cortex cells can be trained to respond without evoking a movement suggests that movements can be imagined even from an area very close to the final motor output (Fetz 2007, Hochberg et al. 2006). Noninvasive studies using fMRI have provided a picture of the circuits involved in imagined movement. Motor imagery activates a subset of the areas that are also active during real movements, particularly premotor areas in the frontal lobe and areas in the posterior parietal cortex (Decety 1996, Gerardin et al. 2000, Stephan et al. 1995) (Glidden et al. 2005), and this activation can be as large as that seen for real movements [with the exception of motor cortex, which shows much less activation for imagined compared to real movements (Glidden et al. 2005)].

Another potential source of motor imagery for prosthetic control is the mirror neuron. Mirror neurons respond when a monkey makes a movement and also when the monkey observes the experimenter making the same movement (di Pellegrino et al. 1992, Fogassi et al. 2005, Gallese et al. 1996, Tkach et al. 2007). It has been proposed that mirror neurons form the basis of action understanding (Fogassi et al. 2005). It is possible that mirror neurons may also be activated during internally generated, imagined movements. If this is the case, and these cells also exist in human cortex, they may provide a source of control of complex and meaningful movements for prosthetics applications.

DECISION MAKING

Many of the cortical areas that can produce control signals are also involved in action selection. These areas represent the expected value or utility of an action. Decision making is based on choosing the alternative with the highest value. In monkey experiments, the value is generally appetitive and includes the type, amount, and probability of reward. Many areas in the parietal and frontal cortex which represent movement plans also represent the expected value of the planned action (Barraclough et al. 2004, Campos et al. 2005, Hikosaka & Watanabe 2000, Kobayashi et al. 2002, Leon & Shadlen 1999, Matsumoto et al. 2003, Platt & Glimcher 1999, Schultz 2000, Shidara & Richmond 2002, Sugrue et al. 2004, Tremblay & Schultz 2000).

Expected value can be decoded from PRR recordings in both delayed reach and brain-control tasks (Musallam et al. 2004). In the latter, the monkey plans a movement but does not execute it and instead uses the planning activity to move a cursor to a goal on a computer screen. During a session, one reward variable (type, size, or probability) changed from trial to trial. The cue size indicated on each trial whether the animal would receive the preferred or less-preferred reward for successful completion of the trial. The cue size was varied across sessions so that a large cue represented a more desirable or less desirable reward on different days. In general, the anticipation of a preferred reward led to a larger response and improved spatial tuning. The increase in activity was unlikely to be due to increased attention given that no increase in activity was seen when the non-preferred reward was aversive (saline solution). Overall, the cells carried more information for preferred reward expectation. Parallel decoding showed that expected reward and spatial loca-

tion could be decoded simultaneously. Moreover, since the cells carried more information about spatial location when higher reward was expected, the decoding performance for target location was better in high-reward trials.

A practical advantage of the reward expectation decoding results is that they provide insight into the preferences and potentially the mood of the patient. The first thing a doctor asks a patient is, "How are you feeling?" On a more general level, this study was the first to show that a very high level cognitive signal, expected value, could be decoded in brain-control trials. These results open the door to decoding many complex cognitive signals including speech, attention, executive control, and emotion for prosthetics applications.

FORWARD MODELS

Numerous studies support the idea that the brain constructs internal forward and inverse models to control movement (Atkeson 1989, Jordan & Rumelhart 1992, Kawato et al. 1987, Wolpert et al. 1995). The forward model predicts the sensory consequences of a movement by incorporating recent motor commands into a model of the movement dynamics, thereby predicting the upcoming state of the effector (e.g., the limb). The inverse model produces the motor commands necessary to achieve the desired movement.

Efference copy, and by extension a forward model, can be used to cancel the sensory effects of one's own movements (Andersen et al. 1987, Bradley et al. 1996, Claxton 1975, Crowell et al. 1998, Diedrichsen et al. 2005, Duhamel et al. 1992, Haarmeier et al. 2001, Roy & Cullen 2004, Royden et al. 1992, Shadmehr & Krakauer 2008, Weiskran et al. 1971). Another important feature of forward models is that they remove the delays that are present between movements and the resulting sensory feedback. When sensory feedback alone is used to correct movements online, these delays would normally lead to overcompensation and instability. For example, the execution of a goal-directed arm movement will result in visual signals that will take approximately 90 ms (Raiguel et al.

Forward model: a prediction of the consequences of a movement by processing the efference copy signal of motor commands

1999) and somatosensory signals that will take 20 to 40 ms (Allison et al. 1991) to reach sensorimotor cortex. Subsequent processing delays for sensorimotor integration, motor command generation, and execution result in delays of more than 100 ms for somatosensory control (Flanders & Cordo 1989) and over 200 ms for visualmotor control (Georgopoulos et al. 1981, Miall et al. 1993). However, by monitoring the movement commands through an efference copy of the command, the current state of the arm can be estimated internally well in advance of the late-arriving sensory information.

Kalman Filter

The forward model can also be incorporated into an observer framework (Goodwin & Sin 1984, Miall & Wolpert 1996) (see **Figure 4**).

The forward model derives an estimate of the upcoming or current state of the limb. Sensory events arriving later are integrated with the forward model to update and refine the estimate. This combination of the forward model and sensory feedback is called the "observer," and for linear systems with additive and Gaussian noise, the optimal observer is known as a Kalman filter (Kalman 1960).

Studies in humans have suggested that the observer may, at least in part, be located in the PPC. Lesions of the PPC produce optic ataxia in which patients have difficulty in locating and reaching to targets (Balint 1909, Perenin & Vighetto 1998, Rondot et al. 1977), in making corrective movements (Grea et al. 2002, Pisella et al. 2000), and in maintaining an estimate of the internal state of the arm (Wolpert et al. 1998). Transcranial magnetic stimulation

Sensorimotor: cortical processing and cortical areas that are involved in transforming sensory inputs to motor outputs for sensory-guided movements

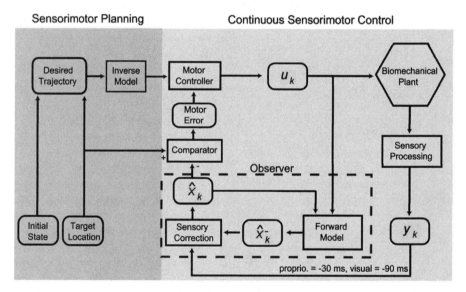

Figure 4

Sensorimotor integration for reach planning and online control. Rounded boxes denote pertinent sensorimotor variables, and computational processes are contained in the rectangular boxes. Prior to a reach, an intended trajectory is formulated as a function of both the initial state of the arm and the desired endpoint. An inverse model is used to determine a set of motor plans that will result in the desired trajectory. Motor commands, u_k, are then issued (e.g., by primary motor cortex) and subsequently executed by muscle activations (*biomechanical plant hexagon*). Following the movement onset, the state of the arm is continuously monitored and corrected if necessary. Rapid online correction is made possible by the forward model, which generates an anticipatory estimate of the next state of the arm, $\hat{x}_k^-$, as a function of the previous state and efference copy. Sensory feedback refines the a priori estimate of the forward dynamics model (observer). This a posteriori, current-state estimate, $\hat{x}_k$, can then be evaluated to make corrections for subsequent motor commands (after Desmurget & Grafton 2000).

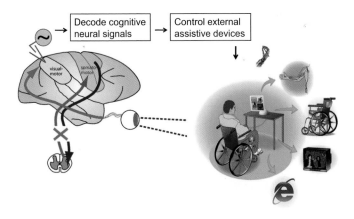

Figure 1

Schematic representation of a cognitive neural prosthetic. In this example, the patient has a lesion of the spinal cord, represented by the red X on the brain drawing on the left. The patient can still see the goal of a movement and can plan the movement, but cannot execute it. The electrodes are positioned in sensori-motor cortex in the parietal reach region, which is involved in reach planning. The recordings are decoded to obtain the meaning of the cognitive signal and then transformed into processed control signals to operate an external device. The schematic on the right indicates that this signal can be used, among other things, for controlling a robot limb, stimulating the muscles to animate the paralyzed limb, navigating a wheelchair, controlling a television, and using the Internet and email. (Modified from **www. cyberkinetics.com.**)

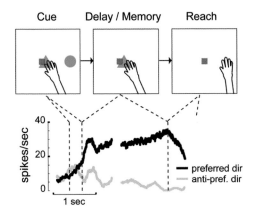

Figure 2

The representation of intended goals in the parietal reach region (PRR). The top plot shows the delayed goal-directed reach task. After the brief presentation of a cue stimulus (*green circle*), the monkey plans a reach to the cued location but delays the execution until the GO signal (extinction of the *green triangle*). The monkey's gaze is fixed on the red rectangle. The bottom plot shows the response of a typical PRR neuron during this task. Notice the sustained, elevated activity during the delay period when the monkey plans a reach to the target in the preferred direction.

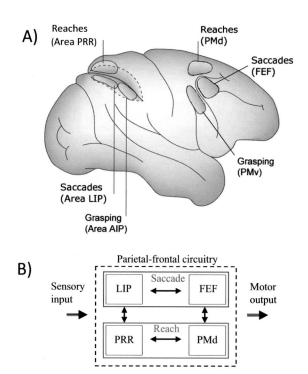

Figure 3

(*A*) Schematic of areas in the cortex where cognitive signals can be recorded for neural prosthetic applications. For reaches, these areas include the parietal reach region (PRR) and dorsal premotor cortex (PMd); for saccades, lateral intraparietal (LIP) and frontal eye field (FEF); and for grasp, anterior intraparietal area (AIP) and ventral premotor cortex (PMv). (*B*) Diagram of connections between effector-specific regions. LIP has strong corticocortical connections with FEF and PRR with PMd. There are also strong cortico-cortical connections between LIP and PRR in the parietal lobe and FEF and PMd in the frontal lobe. These additional connections could provide an avenue for integration of complex movements including hand-eye coordination. (Modified from Cohen & Andersen 2002.)

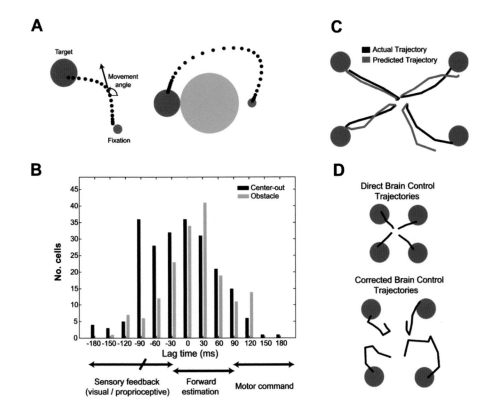

Figure 5

(*A*) Example trajectories made for direct and obstacle versions of the joystick task. (*B*) Distribution of optimal lag times (OLTs) for posterior parietal cortex (PPC) population tuned to the dynamic movement angle. Many neurons' OLTs were consistent with a forward estimate of the state of the movement angle, which did not directly reflect delayed sensory feedback to PPC, nor were they compatible with outgoing motor commands from PPC. (*C*) Example trajectory reconstructions predicted using goal-based Kalman filter decoding algorithm. (*D*) Successful trajectories made by the monkey during online brain-control trials for which the monkey moved the cursor directly to the target or needed to correct the path of the cursor. **Figures 5*A*** and **5*B*** are from Mulliken et al. (2008a) and **Figures 5*C*** and ***D*** are from Mulliken et al. (2008b).

(TMS) over the PPC interferes with the correction of trajectories or adaptation to novel force-fields (Della-Maggiore et al. 2004, Desmurget et al. 1999). PPC lesions disrupt the mental simulation of movement (Sirigu et al. 1996), and a disruption is not seen with lesions of M1 (Sirigu et al. 1995), cerebellum (Kagerer et al. 1998), or basal ganglia (Dominey et al. 1995). The movement durations are generally underestimated during simulation by these patients, suggesting a disruption of the forward model.

Neurophysiological recording experiments also suggest that a forward model may include PPC. This part of cortex receives massive feedback projections from motor structures and input from visual and somatosensory cortex and thus is ideally situated for integrating efference copy and sensory signals (Andersen et al. 1985a, 1990; Goldman-Rakic 1998; Johnson et al. 1996; Jones & Powell 1970). In an experiment designed to investigate forward models in PPC, monkeys were trained in a joystick task to move a cursor to targets either directly or around obstacles (Mulliken et al. 2008b). The obstacles afforded a more curved trajectory (**Figure 5A**, see color insert). Neurons in the PPC not only encoded the static goal of the movement endpoint, but also the dynamic heading angle of the moving cursor. The timing of the dynamic component was centered on zero lag (**Figure 5B**). Thus it was too late to represent the motor command and too early to be derived from sensory input. Rather, it appears to represent the current direction of cursor movement consistent with a forward estimate. This direction was approximately linear in space-time, indicating that it encodes a mostly linear instantaneous trajectory. Similar dynamics have recently been observed between hand kinematics and neural activity in area 5 (Archambault et al. 2009).

A subsequent experiment showed that this forward estimate could be harnessed for neuroprosthetic applications (Mulliken et al. 2008a). The trajectories of a cursor could be decoded in joystick and brain-control tasks (**Figure 5C** and **5D**). In the latter, the neural activity moved the cursor on the computer screen in real time.

A goal-based Kalman filter was also applied for decoding, which used both the forward estimate and the goal component of neural activity. This decoding method was superior to other methods that did not use a combination of the goal and trajectory information.

EFFECTOR SPECIFICITY AND COORDINATED MOVEMENTS

So far, neural prosthetics applications have focused on single effector movements, for instance a robotic limb or a cursor. However, natural movements often involve several body parts, especially for bimanual operations, hand-eye coordination, and reach-to-grasp.

Cells in parietal and premotor areas show response specificity for effectors (**Figure 3B**). For instance, in the PPC there are cells specific for reaching, eye movements, and grasp (Andersen et al. 1985a, 1990; Andersen & Buneo 2002; Sakata et al. 1997; Snyder et al. 1997). These cells tend to be clustered into cortical areas—saccade selectivity in lateral intraparietal (LIP) area, reach in PRR, and grasp in the anterior intraparietal (AIP) area. A similar clustering of specificity has been shown in the frontal lobe, with saccades for the frontal eye fields (FEFs) (Bizzi 1967, Bruce & Goldberg 1985, Bruce et al. 1985), reach for PMd (Wise 1985), and grasp for the ventral premotor cortex (PMv) (Rizzollatti et al. 1994). To date, closed-loop brain control for reach has been shown in PRR and PMd (Carmena et al. 2003, Mulliken et al. 2008a, Musallam et al. 2004, Santhanam et al. 2006) and online decoding for grasp in AIP and PMv (Townsend et al. 2007), but not for eye movements from FEF or LIP.

Reach-to-Grasp

A most natural extension of brain-control reach is reach-to-grasp. One method of approaching this problem would be to record from the limb area and hand area of M1 (Velliste et al. 2008). However, an alternative would be to record from reach (PRR/PMd) and grasp

AIP: anterior intraparietal area

FEFs: frontal eye fields

PMv: ventral premotor cortex

areas (AIP/PMv) in parietal and premotor cortex, where the movements are more abstractly represented (Baumann et al. 2009). For instance, cells in AIP and PMv represent the shapes of objects and the hand shape needed to grasp them (Baumann et al. 2009, Rizzollatti et al. 1994, Sakata et al. 1997). Thus, single cells can indicate the configuration of the hand and would not require a large number of cells for the different digits (as would perhaps be the case for M1 recordings).

Bimanual Movements

There are very few investigations of the neural mechanisms for bimanual movement. Most early studies considered M1 to be involved only in the control of the contralateral limb. However, experiments in which monkeys made bimanual movements showed that a significant number of M1 cells responded to ipsilateral movements, although less than the contralateral limb (Donchin et al. 1998). When comparing bimanual movements to single-limb movements, most M1 cells showed significant differences in activity, indicating that bimanual interactions are extremely common. These effects could not be accounted for by postural differences between the single- and two-limb tasks. The interactions were often quite complex and included facilitation, suppression, and even changes in preferred direction tuning (Donchin et al. 1998, Rokni et al. 2003). The supplementary motor area (SMA) contains a large number of bimanual-responding neurons and bimanual interactions (Donchin et al. 1998). In PRR, a recent study found a continuum of representations of the limb from pure contralateral representation to bimanual representation (Chang et al. 2008). These studies indicate a high degree of coordination between the limbs in parietal-frontal circuits and open the possibility of being able to control two limbs effectively in bimanual operations.

Hand-Eye Coordination

Recordings from eye movement areas may be used for improving the decoding of reaches.

This combination of recording from eye and reach areas utilizes the fact that eye and hand movements are coordinated and we look to where we reach. Using eye position information recorded from an external eye tracker or estimated from neural activity, the success for decoding reach targets can be improved (Batista et al. 2008). Similarly, activity in parietal and frontal areas indicates the focus of attention. Attention is automatically attracted to the target of a reach (Baldauf et al. 2006, Deubel et al. 1998) and could also be used to facilitate decoding.

Common Coordinate Frames

Cells in LIP and PRR encode visual targets mostly in eye coordinates (Andersen et al. 1985b, Batista et al. 1999). That is, they signal the location of a target with respect to the eyes, and if the gaze direction changes, the location in space for which the cells are sensitive shifts with the gaze. The spatial locations of sounds are initially extracted with respect to the head. However, when auditory stimuli are the targets of saccades or reaches, the encoding of the saccade targets in LIP and reach targets in PRR are often represented in eye coordinates (Cohen & Andersen 2000, 2002; Stricanne et al. 1996). Common coordinate frames between these areas may facilitate decoding during hand-eye coordination.

Brain-control trials from PRR have been performed with the eyes fixating straight ahead to compensate for the eye-centered encoding of stimuli. However, when the eyes are free to move, the efficiency of spatial decoding is about the same as with eyes fixed (Musallam et al. 2004). This curious observation raises several possibilities. It may be that compensations are made through updating or gain fields (Andersen et al. 1985b, Duhamel et al. 1992, Gnadt & Andersen 1988), the decoding algorithms may extract the regularities of hand-eye coordination, or PRR may change coordinate frames depending on the constraints of the task.

Relative Coordinate Frames

PMd uses a different coordinate frame for encoding reach targets from PRR. Whereas PRR uses predominantly an eye-centered coordinate frame (Batista et al. 1999, Cisek & Kalaska 2002, Pesaran et al. 2006b), PMd encodes simultaneously the target with respect to the eye (eye-centered), the target with respect to the hand (hand-centered), and the hand with respect to the eye (hand-in-eye) (Pesaran et al. 2006b). Rather than encoding the three variables in absolute spatial coordinates, it represents all three with respect to one another. This relative coding may be tailored to coordinating different body parts invariant of particular locations in the workspace. Area 5 may use a similar relative coordinate frame since it encodes reach targets with respect to the hand and the eye (Buneo et al. 2002), although the hand-in-eye coding has yet to be tested.

This relative coordinate frame encoding has potential advantages for neuroprosthetic applications. It defines a "work space," as mentioned above, which can be used for multi-effector movement tasks. Since the three relative frames are in extrinsic coordinates, it also allows inversions/transformations between coordinate frames (Pesaran et al. 2006b). Relative codes can reduce the accumulation of errors that may result from maintaining absolute encodings of spatial location (Csorba & Durrant-Whyte 1997, Dissanayake et al. 2001, Newman 1999, Olfati & Murray 2002).

EXECUTIVE FUNCTION: SENSORIMOTOR CONTEXT

Sensorimotor context determines movement goals. For instance, one may wish to reach to the location of a cookie, but reach away from the location of a bee. Most neural prosthetics research has used straightforward goal-directed movements toward a stimulus.

One method for studying context is the antimovement task (**Figure 6A**). The animal is cued to either move toward or away from a target (Boussaoud et al. 1993, Crammond &

Kalaska 1994, di Pellegrino and Wise 1993, Everling et al. 1999, Gail & Andersen 2006, Georgopoulos et al. 1989, Gottlieb & Goldberg 1999, Kalaska 1996, Schlag-Rey et al. 1997, Zhang & Barash 2000). This task has typically been used for saccades and reaches to dissociate sensory signals from movement signals. For antimovement trials, if a neuron only codes the stimulus location, it is considered sensory; if it only encodes the movement direction, it is considered movement-related; and if it codes both, it is considered sensorimotor.

The pro-/antimovement task can be structured as a sensorimotor transformation with two opposing stimulus-response mappings. The executive function for applying the abstract rule for transformation may reside in the prefrontal cortex, premotor cortex, and basal ganglia (Boettiger & D'Esposito 2005, Nixon et al. 2004, Pasupathy & Miller 2005, Petrides 1982, Toni & Passingham 1999, Wallis et al. 2001, White & Wise 1999), although rule-based activity has also been reported in the PPC (Grol et al. 2006, Stoet & Snyder 2004). This rule can then act on the sensorimotor transformation process in PPC, premotor, and motor areas. We present here a recent example from PRR, since in this case neural decoding techniques were used as part of the analysis and shed light on how a CNP could determine the abstract rule and the appropriate stimulus-response mapping (Gail & Andersen 2006).

A pro-/antireach task was used for recordings from PRR (**Figure 6A**) that had three advantages: (*a*) Four different directions for pro and anti movements were used so the spatial tuning of the cells for both rules could be determined; (*b*) briefly flashed targets were used, and delays were interposed before the "go" signal to highlight cognitive-related activity; and (*c*) the task rule to be applied was provided each time at the beginning of the trial prior to the presentation of the target cue. This last feature of the task is important for examining whether the rule can be decoded, since often the features of the target dictate the rule and lead to a confounding in time of rule-based activity with other variables such as a sensory response

Executive function: a cognitive system that manages other brain processes

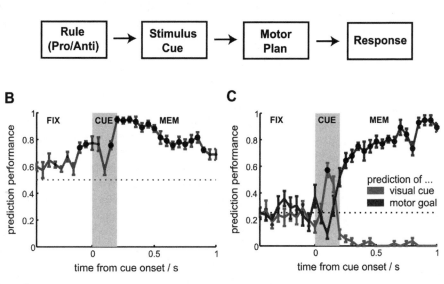

Figure 6

(*A*) Flow diagram of rule-based pro-/antimovement task. (*B*) Decoding of the task rule in PRR. The prediction of the task rule (pro/anti) was significantly above chance (50%) prior to the start of the cue period, indicating explicit task rule representations in PRR. (*C*) Dynamics of sensory versus motor decoding of direction in anti-reach trials (four-way classification of direction; 25% chance level). The performance value denotes the probability that the predicted direction coincides with the cue or motor goal position, respectively. This decode revealed a moderate transient representation of the cue position during part of the cue period (*light curve*). However, this sensory representation is quickly replaced by a strong motor goal representation in the population of PRR neurons (*dark curve*). **Figures 6B** and **6C** are from Gail & Andersen (2006).

to the target and the possible cancelling of an automatic plan toward the target in the anti-movement trials. Using this paradigm, it was found that the number of cells tuned only to the target was statistically insignificant, the number tuned only to the movement direction predominated (45%), and a small number were sensorimotor (7%). The sensorimotor cells were initially tuned to the stimulus location and then, during the delay period, were tuned to the direction of the planned movement. The fact that most cells were only tuned for movement direction rules out spatial attention as a contributing factor for those neurons.

Decode performance for task rule and direction (2 × 4, 12.5% chance) rose steeply after the brief (200 ms) presentation of the target cue, reaching 90% peak in 150 ms, and remained high during the variable delay

(1–1.5 s) before the "go" signal. A transconditional decode revealed that the cue location was only weakly coded during the brief cue presentation, through the sensorimotor cells. PRR represented the movement plan from the end of the cue throughout the delay period (**Figure 6C**). These dynamics indicate that PRR immediately transforms the sensory representation into a movement representation without any residual memory of the location of the sensory signal. Interestingly, the rule could already be predicted above chance a short time before the presentation of the target, indicating that the rule was already explicitly represented in PRR before the appearance of the target cue (**Figure 6B**). In a separate neural network modeling study based on the above experiment, it was found that the context-based information could be integrated with the sensory target location through a classic gain field mechanism (Brozovic et al. 2007). It was suggested that this context modulation may result from top-down information originating from the frontal or parietal lobe.

Recent experiments show that rule-based sensorimotor transformations can also be extended to brain-control experiments (E.J. Hwang and R.A. Andersen, personal observation). The monkeys were able to move the cursor on a computer screen in the opposite direction to a cue using cell recordings from PRR and without any overt reaches. In a second experiment, the monkeys were trained to associate an arrow presented at the straight-ahead position on a computer screen with brain-control cursor movements in the direction the arrow was pointing (Hwang & Andersen 2008).

In the above reach tasks and brain-control tasks, the rules are applied to sensorimotor transformations. However, the fact that rules and their effect on neural transformations can both be decoded from the same population of cells in PPC suggests that other types of executive functions can be decoded in other brain areas. Executive rules that lie outside sensorimotor transformation include categorization, direction of spatial attention, and the formation of abstract concepts and thoughts.

CHOOSING SIGNALS

Typically, neural prosthetic applications have relied on spiking activity of neurons as a signal source. Information from spikes is very precise and represents fundamental building blocks of the brain. Another signal that is interesting, particularly from the viewpoint of CNPs, is the local field potential (LFP) (Andersen et al. 2004b, Pesaran et al. 2006a). The LFP is determined by a number of factors, including the geometry and alignment of the sources, and thus can vary from region to region due to changes in local architecture. Also, the LFP is derived from multiple sources including synaptic potentials and action potentials and is summed over a volume of tissue that contains hundreds or thousands of cells. Still there are features of the LFPs that make them generally useful for prosthetic applications. They are often tuned, for instance, to the direction of planned reaches (Scherberger et al. 2005). Thus they can provide additional information to improve decoding when used in combination with spikes. They have a larger "listening sphere" than that of single cells. Electrode array implants generally have fixed geometries. The sampling of cells is hit or miss, and many electrodes will not be near neurons and will not yield recordings. Typically, to increase yield, lower impedance electrodes are used. This approach increases the listening sphere but also lowers the signal-to-noise ratio and makes single-cell isolation difficult. LFPs, on the other hand, sample from a large listening sphere and so the yield is much higher. Over time, the reliability of recording spikes often goes down, although the LFP signal remains largely unaffected. The basis of this decrease in performance is not completely clear, but it may include long-term encapsulation of the electrodes by glial scarring, which would be expected to have a larger effect on the more local signals of spikes compared to LFPs.

From the viewpoint of CNPs, LFPs have two primary contributions. The first is that it is actually easier to decode cognitive state from LFPs than from spikes. Recordings made from single electrodes in LIP during a memory saccade task showed that, on a single-trial basis, the direction of a planned saccade could be equally well decoded from single-cell spike activity and the LFP (Pesaran et al. 2002). On the other hand, the time of transition from planning to executing a saccade could be decoded from the LFP but not the spike recording. Interestingly, the decoding of direction was obtained from the higher-frequency (30–100 Hz) LFP spectrum and the cognitive state transition from the lower (0–20 Hz) spectrum. A similar result was found in PRR decoding from a population of PRR recording sites obtained on different days of recording (Scherberger et al. 2005). In this particular task, the monkeys made saccades or reaches on different trials so there were

Local field potential (LFP): the recorded sum of electrical activity from hundreds to thousands of neurons around the tip of a microelectrode

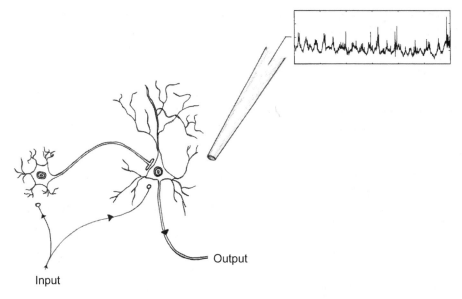

Figure 7

Example of recording sources of spikes and local field potentials. Large pyramidal neurons project out of cortex and represent the predominant source of recorded spikes due to their larger size and number. The local field potentials reflect to a large degree the synaptic potentials and thus the inputs to cortex and local processing. The stellate cell drawn on the left represents an interneuron that contributes to the local processing. The recording is a few hundred milliseconds of actual data from LIP showing both the spikes and the oscillations of the local field potential. Drawn by Christin Montz.

a variety of cognitive states that included baseline (fixating only), reach planning, saccade planning, reaching, and saccading. Whereas state could be decoded from LFPs and spikes, it took many more recording sites using spikes compared to LFPs to reach a similar performance. On the other hand, although direction could be decoded from both spikes and LFPs, the spike decodes were slightly better.

The second contribution of LFPs to CNPs is that they may provide complementary information due to some differences in source and as a result allow a broader view of overall network activity. In cortex, the largest class of neurons is the pyramidal (output) cell. Also, single-cell recording is biased toward larger cells, again the pyramidal neurons. Thus, spiking activity tends to represent the output of a cortical region (**Figure 7**). The LFP is not simply a sum of averaged spike activity but rather reflects, to a considerable degree, the mean synaptic activity that derives from inputs and intracortical pro-

cessing (Buzsaki & Draguhn 2004, Logothetis et al. 2001). Thus, a component of LFP activity in the PPC may derive from inputs into the area (**Figure 7**). An efference copy from motor areas to PPC may explain why the LFP in PPC is so sensitive to the transition from planning to executing, since the PPC output is not thought to contribute to the execution of movements (Andersen & Buneo 2002). Recently, monkeys have been trained to generate a self-paced "go" LFP signal in PPC for brain-control experiments (Hwang & Andersen 2007). The animals were trained to generate the signature LFP signal associated with the state change from planning to executing actual reaches, an increase in lower frequencies and decrease in higher frequencies, without making any movements. The feasibility of a hybrid BMI system was also demonstrated in brain-control experiments in which the direction was decoded from the PRR spike activity while the state was decoded from the LFP recorded at the same site (Hwang

& Andersen 2007). As mentioned above, the direction can be decoded from both spikes and LFPs in PRR. Additional brain-control experiments showed that using spikes and LFPs together increased decode performance compared to using either alone, demonstrating that combining information from the two sources can lead to better decodes (Hwang & Andersen 2009).

LEARNING

Most applications using brain-control tasks have shown a high degree of learning. This learning can be very rapid, over a few minutes to hours of training (Fetz 1969, Jarosiewicz et al. 2008, Moritz et al. 2008), over a period of days (Mulliken et al. 2008a), or even over a period of weeks (Carmena et al. 2003, Musallam et al. 2004, Taylor et al. 2002). This learning extends to LFPs (Hwang & Andersen 2007). Learning effects have been seen in many brain areas including the motor cortex, premotor cortex, and parietal cortex. To our knowledge, it is currently not understood which areas may show more plasticity or be better for learning particular categories of tasks.

WHAT MIGHT DECODING ALGORITHMS SAY ABOUT BRAIN PROCESSING?

A number of classes of decoding algorithms have been applied in brain-control experiments. Interestingly, many of these algorithms have parallels with brain function and may be successful, in part, because of these similarities. Bayesian decoding, which calculates maximum likelihood of an intended movement (Bokil et al. 2006, Gao et al. 2002, Scherberger et al. 2005, Shenoy et al. 2003), is one example. Recent modeling studies have suggested that cortical areas represent probability distributions and may use Bayesian inference for decision making (Beck et al. 2008). Population vector decoding has also been used in brain-control experiments (Taylor et al. 2002, Velliste et al. 2008). This algorithm was originally developed to explain how the direction of reaches is represented by populations of neurons in motor cortex (Georgopoulos et al. 1986). As mentioned above, Kalman filter decoding works well in PPC, and this cortical region has properties of state estimation that can be modeled effectively with Kalman filters (Mulliken et al. 2008a, Wu et al. 2004). Transitions between cognitive states show changes in brain activity, particularly reflected in the spectrum of LFPs but also in spike firing rates. State-space models such as finite state machines and Markov models have been successful in decoding state changes and may reflect the states and transitions between states in brain activity (Shenoy et al. 2003). Decoding has been improved by taking into account correlations between spike trains (Abbott & Dayan 1999, Averbeck et al. 2006, Brown et al. 2004, Nirenberg & Latham 2003) and the temporal regularities in responses (Musallam et al. 2004). These decoding methods that take into account correlations and dynamics may be exploiting underlying temporal coding strategies used by the brain.

CONCLUSION

The applications of CNPs are very wide ranging and rely on the decoding of signals that are neither motor execution nor sensory signals but rather rely on internal cognitive states. Although several specific examples are given in this review, in principle all cognitive states likely can be decoded with the appropriate recording technologies, placement of electrodes, and decoding algorithms. Spike activity is a major source of signal, but LFPs are also particularly useful for determining cognitive state. Extensions of signal analysis may include the measure of spike-field coherence between cortical areas, which may provide additional insights into the processing of cognitive functions, and their decoding, across cortical circuits (see Future Issues, below). CNPs may also be extended to patients' volitional control of brain stimulation, which can be applied to movement disorders, depression, epilepsy, and other brain diseases that may benefit from neural stimulation. Clearly, the future is bright for CNPs and their future application to assisting patients with brain disorders. An added benefit is that research in CNPs will continue to uncover the neural basis of cognitive functions through the basic research that forms the foundations of CNPs as well as the insights that are afforded by the operation and performance of CNPs.

SUMMARY POINTS

1. Cognitive neural prosthetics tap into brain signals that are neither motor execution commands nor sensory signals, but rather represent higher brain functions such as intention, multi-effector and sequential movement planning, attention, decision making, executive control, emotions, learning, and speech. Scientific understanding of the functional organization of cortex helps to guide the placement of electrodes and the choices of decoding algorithms.

2. Memory-guided movements are often used in examining cognitive processes that might be applicable to cognitive neural prosthetic applications. These tasks have delay components in which there is no sensory stimulus or movement, and persistent neural activity during this period represents the cognitive process under study.

3. Single goals and even sequences of intended goals can be decoded from prefrontal and parietal regions. Advantages of this approach over conventional trajectory decoding are speed (typically it takes a second or more to arrive at a goal, whereas goal endpoint decoding can be achieved in one-tenth the time) and the ability to plan ahead. Such goal decoding is ideally suited for rapid applications such as "typing" using letter boards.

4. Cognitive neural prosthetics can make use of motor imagery that appears in motor cortex and generates even greater activity, judged from fMRI experiments, in other frontal and parietal areas related to movement planning.

5. Decision variables related to reward expectation, including the amount, type, and probability of reward, can be decoded from parietal cortex. These signals may be useful for cognitive neural prosthetic applications by registering the preferences and mood of the patients.

6. Forward models, used to predict the current state of a movement and derived from efference copy signals, can be harnessed for producing trajectories for CNPs. Interestingly, these signals can be internally generated without any movement actually occurring.

7. The representation of different effectors in different cortical areas allows for the decoding of complex movements such as reach-to-grasp and bimanual movements. Common coordinate frames in some of these cortical areas, and the use of relative coordinate frames, can facilitate the use of multi-effector operations using CNPs.

8. CNPs can be used to decode executive functions. This application has been demonstrated for determining rules for sensorimotor tasks but in principle can also be applied to executive functions of categorization, directing spatial attention, and the formation of abstract concepts and thoughts.

9. Local field potentials (LFPs) can be used in addition to spike activity to enhance CNP applications. They are superior to spikes for decoding cognitive state in parietal cortex. Also, spikes and LFPs reflect to a certain degree different sources, with spikes more

indicative of cortical outputs and LFPs indicative of inputs and intracortical processing. Thus, combined use of these signals provides a larger functional view of the network in which a cortical area is embedded.

10. Certain decoding algorithms may model underlying brain processes and thus be particularly useful for CNP applications.

FUTURE ISSUES

1. A future challenge is to extend CNPs to multiple cortical areas. Recording from multiple cortical areas allows measures of LFP-LFP and spike-LFP coherences between them (Pesaran et al. 2008). These measures, particularly the spike-LFP measures, may indicate changes in communication between areas and may provide additional insights into cognitive functions and refinement of cognitive decoding algorithms.

2. Another advance would be to bring therapies using brain stimulation under volitional control of the patient. For instance, deep-brain stimulation for movement disorders such as Parkinson's disease can be controlled manually by patients, although this can be a bit cumbersome. A more direct approach would be to bring the stimulation under cognitive control, in which a patient's decoded intentions could be used to control stimulation. Such an approach could be extended to other future uses of brain stimulation, such as the control of severe depression and obsessive-compulsive disorders.

DISCLOSURE STATEMENT

The authors are not aware of any biases that might be perceived as affecting the objectivity of this review.

ACKNOWLEDGMENTS

We thank the National Institutes of Health, the Defense Advanced Research Projects Agency, the Boswell Foundation, and the McKnight Foundation for supporting this research. We also thank Drs. Eb Fetz and Michael Campos for discussions during the preparation of this review. We thank Dr. Viktor Shcherbatyuk, Tessa Yao, Kelsíe Pejsa, and Nicole Sammons for technical and editorial assistance.

LITERATURE CITED

Abbott LF, Dayan P. 1999. The effect of correlated variability on the accuracy of a population code. *Neural Comput.* 11:91–101

Allison T, McCarthy G, Wood CC, Jones SJ. 1991. Potentials evoked in human and monkey cerebral cortex by stimulation of the median nerve. *Brain* 114:2465–503

Andersen RA, Asanuma C, Cowan WM. 1985a. Callosal and prefrontal associational projecting cell populations in area 7A of the macaque monkey: a study using retrogradely transported fluorescent dyes. *J. Comp. Neurol.* 232:443–55

Andersen RA, Asanuma C, Essick C, Siegel RM. 1990. Corticocortical connection of anatomically and physiologically defined subdivisions within the inferior parietal lobe. *J. Comp. Neurol.* 296:65–113

Andersen RA, Budrick JW, Musallam S, Pesaran B, Cham JG. 2004a. Cognitive neural prosthetics. *Trends Cogn. Sci.* 8:486–93

Andersen RA, Buneo CA. 2002. Intentional maps in posterior parietal cortex. *Annu. Rev. Neurosci.* 25:189–220

Andersen RA, Essick GK, Siegel RM. 1985b. The encoding of spatial location by posterior parietal neurons. *Science* 230:456–58

Andersen RA, Essick GK, Siegel RM. 1987. Neurons of area 7 activated by both visual stimuli and oculomotor behavior. *Exp. Brain Res.* 67:316–22

Andersen RA, Musallam S, Pesaran B. 2004b. Selecting the signals for a brain-machine interface. *Curr. Opin. Neurobiol.* 14:1–7

Archambalut PS, Caminiti R, Battaglia-Mayer A. 2009. Cortical mechanisms for online control of hand movement trajectory: the role of the posterior parietal cortex. *Cereb. Cortex* doi:10.1093/cercor/bhp058

Astafiev SV, Shulman GL, Stanley CM, Snyder AZ, Van Essen DC, Corbetta M. 2003. Functional organization of human intraparietal and frontal cortex for attending, looking, and pointing. *J. Neurosci.* 23:4689–99

Atkeson CG. 1989. Learning arm kinematics and dynamics. *Annu. Rev. Neurosci.* 12:157–83

Averbeck BB, Latham PE, Pouget A. 2006. Neural correlations, population coding and computation. *Nat. Rev. Neurosci.* 7:358–66

Baldauf D, Cui H, Andersen RA. 2008. The posterior parietal cortex encodes in parallel both goals for double-reach sequences. *J. Neurosci.* 28:10081–99

Baldauf D, Wolf M, Deubel H. 2006. Deployment of visual attention before sequences of goal-directed hand movements. *Vision Res.* 46:4355–74

Balint R. 1909. Seelenlähmung des "Schauens," optische Ataxie, raumliche Storung der Aufmerksamkeit. *Monatsschr. Psychiatr. Neurol.* 25:51–81

Barraclough DJ, Conroy ML, Lee D. 2004. Prefrontal cortex and decision making in a mixed-strategy game. *Nat. Neurosci.* 7:404–10

Batista AP, Andersen RA. 2001. The parietal reach region codes the next planned movement in a sequential reach task. *J. Neurophysiol.* 85:539–44

Batista AP, Buneo CA, Snyder LH, Andersen RA. 1999. Reach plans in eye-centered coordinates. *Science* 285:257–60

Batista AP, Yu BM, Santhanam G, Ryu SI, Afshar A, Shenoy KV. 2008. Cortical neural prosthesis performance improves when eye position is monitored. *IEEE Trans. Neural. Syst. Rehabil. Eng.* 16:24–31

Baumann MA, Fluet MC, Scherberger H. 2009. Context-specific grasp movement representation in the macaque anterior intraparietal area. *J. Neurosci.* 29:6436–48

Beck JM, Ma WJ, Kiani R, Hanks T, Churchland AK, et al. 2008. Probabilistic population codes for Bayesian decision making. *Neuron* 60:1142–52

Bizzi E. 1967. Discharge of frontal eye field neurons during eye movements in unanesthetized monkeys. *Science* 157:1588–90

Boettiger CA, D'Esposito M. 2005. Frontal networks for learning and executing arbitrary stimulus-response associations. *J. Neurosci.* 25:2723–32

Bokil H, Pesaran B, Andersen RA, Mitra PP. 2006. A framework for detection and classification of events in neural activity. *IEEE Trans. Biomed. Eng.* 53:1678–87

Boussaoud D, Barth TM, Wise SP. 1993. Effects of gaze on apparent visual responses of frontal cortex neurons. *Exp. Brain Res.* 93:423–34

Bracewell RM, Mazzoni P, Barash S, Andersen RA. 1996. Motor intention activity in the macaque's lateral intraparietal area. II. Changes of motor plan. *J. Neurophysiol.* 76:1457–64

Bradley DC, Maxwell M, Andersen RA, Banks MS, Shenoy KV. 1996. Mechanisms of heading perception in primate visual cortex. *Science* 273:1544–47

Brown E, Kass RE, Mitra PP. 2004. Multiple neural spike train data analysis: state-of-the-art and future challenges. *Nat. Neurosci.* 7:456–61

Brozovic M, Gail A, Andersen RA. 2007. Gain mechanisms for contextually guided visuomotor transformations. *J. Neurosci.* 27:10588–96

Bruce CJ, Goldberg ME. 1985. Primate frontal eye fields: I. Single neurons discharging before saccades. *J. Neurophysiol.* 53:603–35

Bruce CJ, Goldberg ME, Bushnell MC, Stanton GB. 1985. Primate frontal eye fields. II. Physiological and anatomical correlates of electrically evoked eye movements. *J. Neurophysiol.* 54:714–34

Buneo CA, Jarvis MR, Batista AP, Andersen RA. 2002. Direct visuomotor transformations for reaching. *Nature* 416:632–36

Buzsaki G, Draguhn A. 2004. Neuronal oscillations in cortical networks. *Science* 304:1926–29

Campos M, Breznen B, Bernheim K, Andersen RA. 2005. The supplementary motor area encodes reward expectancy in eye movement tasks. *J. Neurophysiol.* 94:1325–35

Carmena JM, Lebedev MA, Crist RE, O'Doherty JE, Santucci DM, et al. 2003. Learning to control a brain–machine interface for reaching and grasping by primates. *PLoS* 1(2):e42

Chang SWC, Dickinson AR, Snyder LH. 2008. Limb-specific representation for reaching in the posterior parietal cortex. *J. Neurosci.* 28:6128–40

Christopher & Dana Reeve Found. 2009. *One Degree of Separation. Paralysis and Spinal Cord Injury in the United States.* Short Hills, NJ: Christopher & Dana Reeve Found.

Cisek P, Kalaska JF. 2002. Modest gaze-related discharge modulation in monkey dorsal premotor cortex during a reaching task performed with free fixation. *J. Neurophysiol.* 88:1064–72

Claxton G. 1975. Why can't we tickle ourselves? *Percept. Mot. Skills* 41:335–38

Cohen YE, Andersen RA. 2000. Eye position modulates reach activity to sounds. *Neuron* 27:647–52

Cohen YE, Andersen RA. 2002. A common reference frame for movement plans in the posterior parietal cortex. *Nat. Rev. Neurosci.* 3:553–62

Connolly JD, Andersen RA, Goodale MA. 2003. fMRI evidence for a "parietal reach region" in the human brain. *Exp. Brain Res.* 153:140–45

Crammond DJ, Kalaska JF. 1994. Modulation of preparatory neuronal-activity in dorsal premotor cortex due to stimulus-response compatibility. *J. Neurophysiol.* 71:1281–84

Crowell JA, Banks MS, Shenoy KV, Andersen RA. 1998. Visual self-motion perception during head turns. *Nat. Neurosci.* 1:732–37

Csorba M, Durrant-Whyte HF. 1997. *A new approach to map building using relative position estimates.* Presented at Soc. Photo-Optical Instrumentation Engineers Conf., Orlando, FL

Cui H, Andersen RA. 2007. Posterior parietal cortex encodes autonomously selected motor plans. *Neuron* 56:552–59

Decety J. 1996. Do imagined and executed actions share the same neural substrate? *Brain Res. Cogn. Brain Res.* 3:87–93

Della-Maggiore V, Malfait N, Ostry DJ, Paus T. 2004. Stimulation of the posterior parietal cortex interferes with arm trajectory adjustments during the learning of new dynamics. *J. Neurosci.* 24:9971–76

Desmurget M, Epstein CM, Turner RS, Prablanc C, Alexander GE, Grafton ST. 1999. Role of the posterior parietal cortex in updating reaching movements to a visual target. *Nat. Neurosci.* 2:563–67

Desmurget M, Grafton S. 2000. Forward modeling allows feedback control for fast reaching movements. *Trends Cogn. Sci.* 4:423–31

Desmurget M, Reilly KT, Richard N, Szathmari A, Mottolese C, Sirigu A. 2009. Movement intention after parietal cortex stimulation in humans. *Science* 324:811–13

Deubel H, Schneider WX, Paprotta I. 1998. Selective dorsal and ventral processing: evidence for a common attentional mechanism in reaching and perception. *Visual Cogn.* 5:81–107

Diedrichsen J, Hashambhoy Y, Rane T, Shadmehr R. 2005. Neural correlates of reach errors. *J. Neurosci.* 25:9919–31

di Pellegrino G, Fadiga L, Fogassi L, Gallese V, Rizzolatti G. 1992. Understanding motor events: a neurophysiological study. *Exp. Brain Res.* 91:176–80

di Pellegrino G, Wise SP. 1993. Visuospatial versus visuomotor activity in the premotor and prefrontal cortex of a primate. *J. Neurosci.* 13:1227–43

Dissanayake MWMG, Newman P, Clark S, Durrant-Whyte HF, Csorba M. 2001. A solution to the simultaneous localization and map building (SLAM) problem. *IEEE Trans. Rob. Autom.* 17:229–41

Dominey P, Decety J, Broussolle E, Chazot G, Jeannerod M. 1995. Motor imagery of a lateralized sequential task is asymmetrically slowed in hemi-Parkinson's patients. *Neuropsychologia* 33:727–41

Donchin O, Gribova A, Steinberg O, Berman H, Vaadia E. 1998. Primary motor cortex is involved in bimanual coordination. *Nature* 395:274–78

Duhamel JR, Colby CL, Goldberg ME. 1992. The updating of the representation of visual space in parietal cortex by intended eye movements. *Science* 255:90–92

Everling S, Dorris MC, Klein RM, Munoz DP. 1999. Role of primate superior colliculus in preparation and execution of anti-saccades and prosaccades. *J. Neurosci.* 19:2740–54

Fetz EE. 1969. Operant conditioning of cortical unit activity. *Science* 163:955–58

Fetz EE. 2007. Volitional control of neural activity: implications for brain-computer interfaces. *J. Physiol.* 579:571–79

Filimon F, Nelson JD, Huang RS, Sereno MI. 2009. Multiple parietal reach regions in humans: cortical representations for visual and proprioceptive feedback during on-line reaching. *J. Neurosci.* 29:2961–71

Flanders M, Cordo PJ. 1989. Kinesthetic and visual control of a bimanual task: specification of direction and amplitude. *J. Neurosci.* 9:447–53

Fogassi L, Ferrari PF, Gesierich B, Rozzi S, Chersi F, Rizzolatti G. 2005. Parietal lobe: from action organization to intention understanding. *Science* 308:662–67

Fujii N, Graybiel AM. 2003. Representation of action sequence boundaries by macaque prefrontal cortical neurons. *Science* 301:1246–49

Gail A, Andersen RA. 2006. Neural dynamics in monkey parietal reach region reflect context-specific sensorimotor transformations. *J. Neurosci.* 26:9376–84

Gallese V, Fadiga L, Fogassi L, Rizzolatti G. 1996. Action recognition in the premotor cortex. *Brain* 119:593–609

Gao Y, Black MJ, Bienenstock E, Shoham S, Donoghue JP. 2002. Probabilistic inference of hand motion from neural activity in motor cortex. In *Advances in Neural Information Processing Systems*, ed. TG Dietterich, S Becker, Z Ghahramani, 14:213–20. Cambridge, MA: MIT Press

Georgopoulos AP, Kalaska JF, Massey JT. 1981. Spatial trajectories and reaction-times of aimed movements: effects of practice, uncertainty, and change in target location. *J. Neurophysiol.* 46:725–43

Georgopoulos AP, Lurito JT, Petrides M, Schwartz AB, Massey JT. 1989. Mental rotation of the neuronal population vector. *Science* 143:234–36

Georgopoulos AP, Schwartz A, Kettner RE. 1986. Neuronal population coding of movement direction. *Science* 233:1416–19

Gerardin E, Sirigu A, Lehericy S, Poline JB, Gaymard B, et al. 2000. Partially overlapping neural networks for real and imagined hand movements. *Cereb. Cortex* 10:1093–104

Glidden HK, Rizzuto DS, Andersen RA. 2005. Localizing neuroprosthetic implant targets with fMRI: premotor, supplementary motor, and parietal regions. *Presented at Ann. Meet. Soc. Neurosci., Washington, DC*

Gnadt JW, Andersen RA. 1988. Memory-related motor planning activity in posterior parietal cortex of macaque. *Exp. Brain Res.* 70:216–20

Goldman-Rakic PS. 1998. Topography of cognition-parallel distributed networks in primate association cortex. *Annu. Rev. Neurosci.* 11:137–56

Goodwin GC, Sin KS. 1984. *Adaptive Filtering Prediction and Control.* Englewood Cliffs, NJ: Prentice-Hall

Gottlieb J, Goldberg ME. 1999. Activity of neurons in the lateral intraparietal area of the monkey during an antisaccade task. *Nat. Neurosci.* 2:906–12

Grea H, Pisella L, Rosetti Y, Desmurget M, Tilikete C, Grafton S. 2002. A lesion of the posterior parietal cortex disrupts on-line adjustments during aiming movements. *Neuropsychologia* 40:2471–80

Grol MJ, de Lange FP, Verstraten FAJ, Passingham RE, Toni I. 2006. Cerebral changes during performance of overlearned arbitrary visuomotor associations. *J. Neurosci.* 26:117–25

Haarmeier T, Bunjes F, Lindner A, Berret E, Thier P. 2001. Optimizing visual motion perception during eye movements. *Neuron* 32:527–35

Hatsopoulos N, Joshi J, O'Leary JG. 2004. Decoding continuous and discrete motor behaviors using motor and premotor cortical ensembles. *J. Neurophysiol.* 92:1165–74

Hikosaka K, Watanabe M. 2000. Delay activity of orbital and lateral prefrontal neurons of the monkey varying with different rewards. *Cereb. Cortex* 10:263–71

Histed MH, Miller EK. 2006. Microstimulation of frontal cortex can reorder a remembered spatial sequence. *PLoS Biol.* 4:e134

Hochberg LR, Serruya MD, Friehs GM, Mukand JA, Saleh M, et al. 2006. Neuronal ensemble control of prosthetic devices by a human with tetraplegia. *Nature* 442:164–71

Hwang EJ, Andersen RA. 2007. Decoding a "go" signal using the local field potential in the parietal reach region. *Presented at Annu. Meet. BMES, Los Angeles, CA*

Hwang EJ, Andersen RA. 2008. The parietal reach region represents the spatial goal in symbolically instructed reaches. *Presented at Annu. Meet. Soc. Neurosci. Washington, DC*

Hwang EJ, Andersen RA. 2009. Complementary multi-site LFPs and spikes for reach target location decoding in parietal region. *Presented at Ann. Meet. Soc. Neurosci., Chicago, IL*

Jarosiewicz B, Chase SM, Fraser GW, Velliste M, Kass RE, Schwartz AB. 2008. Functional network reorganization during learning in a brain-computer interface paradigm. *Proc. Natl. Acad. Sci. USA* 105:19486–91

Johnson PB, Ferraina S, Bianchi L, Caminiti R. 1996. Cortical networks for visual reaching: physiological and anatomical organization of frontal and parietal lobe arm regions. *Cereb. Cortex* 6:102–19

Jones EG, Powell TP. 1970. An anatomical study of converging sensory pathways within the cerebral cortex of the monkey. *Brain* 93:793–820

Jordan MI, Rumelhart DE. 1992. Forward models: supervised learning with a distal teacher. *Cogn. Sci.* 16:307–54

Kagerer F, Bracha V, Wunderlich DA, Stelmach GE, Bloedel JR. 1998. Ataxia reflected in the simulated movements of patients with cerebellar lesions. *Exp. Brain Res.* 121:125–34

Kalaska JF. 1996. Parietal cortex area 5 and visuomotor behavior. *Can. J. Physiol. Pharmacol.* 74:483–98

Kalman RE. 1960. A new approach to linear filtering and prediction problems. *J. Basic Engin.* March:35–46

Kawato M, Furukawa K, Suzuki R. 1987. A hierarchical neural-network model for control and learning of voluntary movement. *Biol. Cybern.* 57:169–85

Kobayashi S, Lauwereyns J, Koizumi M, Sakagami M, Hikosaka O. 2002. Influence of reward expectation on visuospatial processing in macaque lateral prefrontal cortex. *J. Neurophysiol.* 87:1488–98

Leon MI, Shadlen MN. 1999. Effect of expected reward magnitude on the response of neurons in the dorsolateral prefrontal cortex of the macaque. *Neuron* 24:415–25

Logothetis NK, Pauls J, Augath M, Trinath T, Oeltermann A. 2001. Neurophysiological investigation of the basis of the fMRI signal. *Nature* 412:150–57

Lu X, Ashe J. 2005. Anticipatory activity in primary motor cortex codes memorized movement sequences. *Neuron* 45:967–73

Matsumoto K, Suzuki W, Tanaka K. 2003. Neuronal correlates of goal-based motor selection in the prefrontal cortex. *Science* 301:229–32

Miall RC, Weir DJ, Wolpert DM, Stein JF. 1993. Is the cerebellum a Smith predictor? *J. Motor Behav.* 25:203–16

Miall RC, Wolpert DM. 1996. Forward models for physiological motor control. *Neural Netw.* 9:1265–79

Moritz CT, Perlmutter SI, Fetz EE. 2008. Direct control of paralysed muscles by cortical neurons. *Nature* 456:639–42

Mulliken GH, Musallam S, Andersen RA. 2008a. Decoding trajectories from posterior parietal cortex ensembles. *J. Neurosci.* 28:12913–26

Mulliken GH, Musallam S, Andersen RA. 2008b. Forward estimation of movement state in posterior parietal cortex. *Proc. Natl. Acad. Sci. USA* 105:8170–77

Musallam S, Corneil BD, Greger B, Scherberger H, Andersen RA. 2004. Cognitive control signals for neural prosthetics. *Science* 305:258–62

Mushiake H, Saito N, Sakamoto K, Itoyama Y, Tanji J. 2006. Activity in the lateral prefrontal cortex reflects multiple steps of future events in action plans. *Neuron* 50:631–41

Newman PM. 1999. *On the Solution to the Simultaneous Localization and Map Building Problem.* Sydney, Austral.: Univ. Sydney

Ninokura Y, Mushiake H, Tanji J. 2003. Representation of the temporal order of objects in the primate lateral prefrontal cortex. *J. Neurophysiol.* 89:2869–73

Nirenberg S, Latham PE. 2003. Decoding neuronal spike trains: How important are correlations? *Proc. Natl. Acad. Sci. USA* 100:7348–53

Nixon PD, McDonald KR, Gough PM, Alexander IH, Passingham RE. 2004. Cortico-basal ganglia pathways are essential for the recall of well-established visuomotor associations. *Eur. J. Neurosci.* 20:3165–78

Ohbayashi M, Ohki K, Miyashita Y. 2003. Conversion of working memory to motor sequence in the monkey premotor cortex. *Science* 301:233–36

Olfati R, Murray RM. 2002. Distributed cooperative control of multiple vehicle formations using structural potential functions. *Proc. 15th IFAC World Congress, Barcelona, Spain*

Pasupathy A, Miller EK. 2005. Different time courses for learning-related activity in the prefrontal cortex and striatum. *Nature* 433:873–76

Perenin MT, Vighetto A. 1998. Optic ataxia: a specific disruption in visuomotor mechanisms: 1. Different aspects of the deficit in reaching for objects. *Brain* 111:643–74

Pesaran B, Musallam S, Andersen RA. 2006a. Cognitive neural prosthetics. *Curr. Biol.* 16:77–80

Pesaran B, Nelson MJ, Andersen RA. 2006b. Dorsal premotor neurons encode the relative position of the hand, eye and goal during reach planning. *Neuron* 51:125–34

Pesaran B, Nelson MJ, Andersen RA. 2008. Free choice activates a decision circuit between frontal and parietal cortex. *Nature* 453:406–9

Pesaran B, Pezaris J, Sahani M, Mitra PM, Andersen RA. 2002. Temporal structure in neuronal activity during working memory in macaque parietal cortex. *Nat. Neurosci.* 5:805–11

Petrides M. 1982. Motor conditional associative-learning after selective prefrontal lesions in the monkey. *Behav. Brain Res.* 5:407–13

Pisella L, Grea H, Tilikete C, Vighetto A, Desmurget M. 2000. An "automatic pilot" for the hand in human posterior parietal cortex: toward reinterpreting optic ataxia. *Nat. Neurosci.* 3:729–36

Platt ML, Glimcher PW. 1999. Neural correlates of decision variables in parietal cortex. *Nature* 400:233–38

Quian Quiroga R, Snyder LH, Batista AP, Cui H, Andersen RA. 2006. Movement intention is better predicted than attention in the posterior parietal cortex. *J. Neurosci.* 26:3615–20

Raiguel SE, Xiao DK, Marcar VL, Orban GA. 1999. Response latency of macaque area MT/V5 neurons and its relationship to stimulus parameters. *J. Neurophysiol.* 82:1944–56

Rizzollatti G, Riggio L, Sheliga B. 1994. Space and selective attention. In *Attention and Performance*, ed. C Umilta, M Moscovitch, pp. 231–65. Cambridge, MA: MIT Press

Rokni U, Steinberg O, Vaadia E, Sompolinsky H. 2003. Cortical representation of bimanual movements. *J. Neurosci.* 23:11577–86

Rondot P, Recondo JD, Ribadeaudumas JL. 1977. Visuomotor ataxia. *Brain* 100:355–76

Roy JE, Cullen KE. 2004. Dissociating self-generated from passively applied head motion: neural mechanisms in the vestibular nuclei. *J. Neurosci.* 27:2102–11

Royden CS, Banks MS, Crowell JA. 1992. The perception of heading during eye movements. *Nature* 360:583–85

Sakata H, Taira M, Kusunoki M, Murata A, Tanaka Y. 1997. The TINS Lecture. The parietal association cortex in depth perception and visual control of hand action. *Trends Neurosci.* 20:350–57

Santhanam G, Ryu SI, Yu BM, Afshar A, Shenoy KV. 2006. A high-performance brain-computer interface. *Nature* 442:195–98

Scherberger H, Andersen RA. 2007. Target selection signals for arm reaching in the posterior parietal cortex. *J. Neurosci.* 27:2001–12

Scherberger H, Jarvis MR, Andersen RA. 2005. Cortical local field potential encodes movement intentions in the posterior parietal cortex. *Neuron* 46:347–54

Schlag-Rey M, Amador N, Sanchez H, Schlag J. 1997. Antisaccade performance predicted by neuronal activity in the supplementary eye field. *Nature* 390:398–401

Schultz W. 2000. Multiple reward signals in the brain. *Nat. Rev. Neurosci.* 1:199–207

Serruya MD, Hatsopoulos NG, Paninski L, Fellows MR, Donoghue JP. 2002. Instant neural control of a movement signal. *Nature* 416:141–42

Shadmehr R, Krakauer JW. 2008. A computational neuroanatomy for motor control. *Exp. Brain Res.* 185:359–81

Shenoy KV, Meeker D, Cao SY, Kureshi SA, Pesaran B, et al. 2003. Neural prosthetic control signals from plan activity. *Neuroreport* 14:591–96

Shidara M, Richmond BJ. 2002. Anterior cingulate: single neuronal signals related to degree of reward expectancy. *Science* 296:1709–11

Sirigu A, Cohen L, Duhamel JR, Pillon B, Dubois B, Agid Y. 1995. Congruent unilateral impairments for real and imagined hand movements. *Neuroreport* 6:997–1001

Sirigu A, Duhamel JR, Cohen L, Pillon B, Dubois B, Agid Y. 1996. The mental representation of hand movements after parietal cortex damage. *Science* 273:1564–68

Snyder LH, Batista AP, Andersen RA. 1997. Coding of intention in the posterior parietal cortex. *Nature* 386:167–70

Snyder LH, Batista AP, Andersen RA. 1998. Change in motor plan, without a change in the spatial locus of attention, modulates activity in posterior parietal cortex. *J. Neurophysiol.* 79:2814–19

Stephan KM, Fink GR, Passingham RE, Silbersweig D, Ceballosbaumann AO, et al. 1995. Functional anatomy of the mental representation of upper extremity movements in healthy subjects. *J. Neurophysiol.* 73:373–86

Stoet G, Snyder LH. 2004. Single neurons in posterior parietal cortex of monkeys encode cognitive set. *Neuron* 42:1003–12

Stricanne B, Andersen RA, Mazzoni P. 1996. Eye-centered, head-centered, and intermediate coding of remembered sound locations in area LIP. *J. Neurophysiol.* 76:2071–76

Sugrue LP, Corrado GS, Newsome WT. 2004. Matching behavior and the representation of value in the parietal cortex. *Science* 304:1782–87

Tanji J, Shima K. 1994. Role for supplementary motor area cells in planning several movements ahead. *Nature* 371:413–16

Taylor DM, Tillery SIH, Schwartz AB. 2002. Direct cortical control of 3D neuroprosthetic devices. *Science* 296:1829–32

Tkach D, Reimer J, Hatsopoulos NG. 2007. Congruent activity during action and action observation in motor cortex. *J. Neurosci.* 27:13241–50

Toni I, Passingham RE. 1999. Prefrontal-basal ganglia pathways are involved in the learning of arbitrary visuomotor associations: a PET study. *Exp. Brain Res.* 127:19–32

Townsend BR, Lehmann SJ, Subasi E, Scherberger H. 2007. Decoding hand grasping from primate premotor and parietal cortex. *Presented at Ann. Meet. Soc. Neurosci., San Diego, CA*

Tremblay L, Schultz W. 2000. Reward-related neuronal activity during go-nogo task performance in primate orbitofrontal cortex. *J. Neurophysiol.* 83:1864–76

U.S. Dept. Health Human Serv. 1995. Current estimates from the National Health Interview Survey, 1994. *Vital Health Stat.* 193(Pt. 1):1–260

Velliste M, Perel S, Spalding MC, Whitford AS, Schwartz AB. 2008. Cortical control of a prosthetic arm for self-feeding. *Nature* 453 1098–101

Wallis JD, Anderson KC, Miller EK. 2001. Single neurons in prefrontal cortex encode abstract rules. *Nature* 411:953–56

Weiskran L, Elliott J, Darlingt C. 1971. Preliminary observations on tickling oneself. *Nature* 230:598

White IM, Wise SP. 1999. Rule-dependent neuronal activity in the prefrontal cortex. *Exp. Brain Res.* 126:315–35

Wise SP. 1985. The primate premotor cortex: past, present, and preparatory. *Annu. Rev. Neurosci.* 8:1–19

Wolpert DM, Ghahramani Z, Jordan MI. 1995. Are arm trajectories planned in kinematic or dynamic coordinates? An adaptation study. *Exp. Brain Res.* 103:460–70

Wolpert DM, Goodbody SJ, Husain M. 1998. Maintaining internal representations: the role of the human superior parietal lobe. *Nat. Neurosci.* 1:529–33

Wu W, Black MJ, Mumford D, Gao Y, Bienenstock E, Donoghue JP. 2004. Modeling and decoding motor cortical activity using a switching Kalman filter. *IEEE Trans. Biomed. Eng.* 51:933–42

Zhang M, Barash S. 2000. Neuronal switching of sensorimotor transformations for antisaccades. *Nature* 408:971–75

RELATED RESOURCES

Berger TW, Ahuja A, Courellis SH, Deadwyler SA, Erinjippurath G, et al. 2005. Restoring lost cognitive function. *IEEE Eng. Med. Biol. Mag.* 24(5):30–44

Donoghue JP. 2008. Bridging the brain to the world: a perspective on neural interface systems. *Neuron* 60(3):511–21

Fagg AH, Hatsopoulos NG, de Lafuente V, Moxon KA, Nemati S, et al. 2007. Biomimetic brain machine interfaces for the control of movement. *J. Neurosci.* 27(44):11842–46

Fetz EE. 2007. Volitional control of neural activity: implications for brain-computer interfaces. *J. Physiol.* 579(3):571–79

Kennedy PR, Bakay RAE, Moore MM, Adams K, Goldwaithe J. 2000. Direct control of a computer from the human central nervous system. *IEEE Trans. Rehabil. Eng.* 8(2):198–202

Lebedev MA, Nicolelis MAL. 2006. Brain-machine interfaces: past, present and future. *Trends Neurosci.* 29(9):536–46

Schwartz AB, Cui XT, Weber DJ, Moran DW. 2006. Brain-controlled interfaces: movement restoration with neural prosthetics. *Neuron* 52(1):205–20

Speech Perception and Language Acquisition in the First Year of Life

Judit Gervain[1] and Jacques Mehler[2]

[1] Department of Psychology, University of British Columbia, Vancouver British Columbia, V6T 1Z4, Canada

[2] Neuroscience Sector, Scuola Internazionale Superiore di Studi Avanzati, Trieste 31014, Italy; email: mehler@sissa.it

Annu. Rev. Psychol. 2010. 61:191–218

First published online as a Review in Advance on September 28, 2009

The *Annual Review of Psychology* is online at psych.annualreviews.org

This article's doi: 10.1146/annurev.psych.093008.100408

Key Words

infancy, learning mechanisms, phonological bootstrapping, evolution of language

Abstract

During the first year of life, infants pass important milestones in language development. We review some of the experimental evidence concerning these milestones in the domains of speech perception, phonological development, word learning, morphosyntactic acquisition, and bilingualism, emphasizing their interactions. We discuss them in the context of their biological underpinnings, introducing the most recent advances not only in language development, but also in neighboring areas such as genetics and the comparative research on animal communication systems. We argue for a theory of language acquisition that integrates behavioral, cognitive, neural, and evolutionary considerations and proposes to unify previously opposing theoretical stances, such as statistical learning, rule-based nativist accounts, and perceptual learning theories.

Contents

INTRODUCTION

The emergence of language has intrigued scientists and the general public alike, but it was only in the second half of the twentieth century that a systematic empirical investigation of language acquisition began. This work was greatly inspired by the suggestion that the environment is mainly a trigger rather than a tutor for language acquisition, at least during the first years of life (Chomsky 1959). Consequently, to explain the uniquely human capacity of language, scholars proposed innate acquisition mechanisms, specific to language (Chomsky 1959). A few years later, research into the biological foundations of language was expanded, giving a better grasp of the innate dispositions

for language acquisition (Lenneberg 1967). By contrast, other researchers suggested that classical learning mechanisms, ones that humans share with other animals, may be sufficient to acquire language (Elman 1996, Tomasello 2000). Under this view, the human specificity of language arises from quantitative rather than qualitative differences between the species.

Some of these theoretical questions may be resolved by studying preverbal infants, in particular newborns, as this allows us to determine how much of our language acquisition abilities are due to dispositions detectable much before the surroundings have shaped our cognitive apparatus. Therefore, our review mostly focuses on the development of language and its underlying mechanisms during the first year of life. This choice is also justified by the growing body of research and recent advances in understanding how different mechanisms, such as statistical and distributional learning, rule extraction, as well as perceptual and memory constraints, work together during language development.

Our review discusses landmarks in language acquisition as well as their biological underpinnings. We focus on studies that connect brain, mind, and behavior. We believe that building bridges between these different levels is the way of the future and that the next decades will see the success of such integrative methodology and theory building.

In the review, we first describe the different theoretical approaches to language acquisition. We then review the increasingly important and fast-growing body of literature on the biological foundations of human language, focusing mostly on genetic and evolutionary aspects. Then we review the empirical evidence that has accumulated over the past decades in support of the theories and approaches introduced. We discuss the findings following the levels of organization in language from phonology through word segmentation and lexical acquisition to grammar. Finally, we consider some of the novel empirical findings that relate to the neural basis of language acquisition and processing in newborns and young infants. Building on these empirical findings, we argue for an integrative theory of language acquisition, proposing that rule learning, perceptual bootstrapping, and statistical learning all contribute to different levels of language acquisition, and that the most interesting objective is to understand their interactions and the division of labor among them.

THEORETICAL APPROACHES

Language acquisition came to the forefront of cognitive and developmental research when Noam Chomsky (1957, 1959) pointed out that acquiring language poses a serious learning problem. Infants never receive explicit information about the structure of the grammar that generated the utterances they are exposed to. In the absence of structural information, the finite data set that infants receive as input is compatible with an infinite number of underlying rules or grammars—a challenge to learning known in philosophy and mathematics as the induction problem.

The most important theoretical approaches to language acquisition in the past 50 years have investigated this logical problem, proposing solutions to it or denying its existence.

Nativist Approaches to Language Acquisition

Language cannot be learned exclusively from the input, yet young infants seem to acquire it with remarkable ease. Therefore, Chomsky (1959) argued that the acquisition process has to be guided by innate knowledge. This logical argument gave rise to a nativist theoretical approach to language acquisition as well as a large body of related empirical research (for a representative summary, see Guasti 2002). This view capitalizes on the observation that although they are superficially different from one another, languages of the world share a large number of structural characteristics; for example, they all use lexical categories like functors (small grammatical words, such as *he, it, on, of, this*) and content words (e.g., nouns and verbs that carry lexical meaning, such as *flower, table, run, sing*). Under the nativist view, the universal features of language design are part of our species' biological endowment and are encoded in the language faculty as innate principles. By contrast, aspects of language structure that vary (e.g., the relative order of verbs and objects or whether a language allows pronominal subjects to be dropped) are assumed to be encoded by parameters, i.e., mental switches that implement all the universal options [e.g., a verb-object (VO) order and an OV order; licensing pronoun-drop or not].

This account assumed that infants are able to detect and extract abstract regularities from the input. Indeed, Marcus et al. (1999) showed that 7-month-old infants are able to learn abstract, algebraic generalizations. In their study, infants were familiarized with an artificial grammar encoding an identity-based regularity (e.g., ABB: *wo fe fe*). In the test phase, babies showed longer looking times for items that were inconsistent with the grammar of familiarization (e.g., ABA) than for items that were consistent with it, indicating that they extracted the underlying regularity.

Under the principles and parameters view, language acquisition is mediated by setting the parameters to the values that characterize the native language. For instance, an English-learning infant will have to set the word-order parameter to VO, e.g., *eat an apple*, and the pro-drop parameter to negative, e.g., *It is raining*, but not **Is raining*, while a Japanese infant will set both parameters to the opposite value, e.g., *ringo-wo taberu* 'apple.accusative eat' "eat an apple" and *futte iru* 'raining is' "(it) is raining." However, parameters are defined over abstract linguistic entities such as verbs, nouns, and pronouns, so the infant still faces the problem of linking these abstract mental representations to actual physical entities in the speech signal (Pinker 1984).

One solution proposed to the linking problem is the use of bootstrapping mechanisms. These are heuristic learning mechanisms that exploit the universal correlations that exist between perceptually available, surface characteristics of a language and its abstract morphosyntactic properties. Three types of surface cues have been proposed to act as triggers for bootstrapping.

One approach (e.g., Pinker 1984) suggests that the relevant cue is of semantic/conceptual nature. By understanding the general meaning of some simple sentences and by knowing the meaning of some words, typically nouns, the infant can construct syntactic trees, given configurational universals, such as the phrase structure suggested by generative grammar or other linguistic theories, which are believed to be part of the innate language faculty. From these trees, the child can derive the syntactic rules of her mother tongue, which in turn

help her parse and understand more complex sentences.

A second approach (e.g., Gleitman & Landau 1994) claims that the already acquired pieces of syntactic knowledge help bootstrap the rest of syntax. The initial (productive) lexicon of the child contains a large number of nouns. This allows the infant to track the position of nouns within sentences. With this information, infants can learn the type and argument structure of verbs. In English, for instance, intransitive verbs have one noun (phrase) (NP) preceding them, transitive action verbs have one NP preceding and one following them, mental verbs have one NP preceding them and a clause following them, and so forth. Thus, upon encountering a sentence containing an initial NP and a final NP with a verb between them, the verb can be categorized as transitive.

It is important to note that these two approaches build on already acquired linguistic knowledge. But how are these initial pieces acquired? A third approach, the one we are exploring here, suggests that morphosyntactic properties are signaled by their acoustic/phonological correlates (Mehler et al. 2004; Morgan & Demuth 1996; Nespor et al. 1996, 2008). As Morgan & Demuth (1996, p. 2) put it: "[T]hese accounts propose that information available in speech may contain clues to certain fundamental syntactic distinctions [...]." This approach, unlike the other two, assumes no prior linguistic knowledge on the part of the learner and thus may explain the earliest acquisitions. Nouns and verbs, for instance, are abstract lexical categories. However, in English, nouns often bear stress on the first syllable (record N: /**'rekɔ:(r)d**/) and verbs on the last (record V: /rɪ**'kɔ:(r)d**/) (Cutler & Carter 1987, Davis & Kelly 1997). The stress pattern, then, can act as a cue to the two categories. Although this is specific to English, there seem to be phonological and prosodic cues that might signal syntactic properties universally (Mehler et al. 2004; Morgan & Demuth 1996; Nespor et al. 1996, 2008). An important focus of our review, therefore, is not only to characterize how infants perceive and learn about the acoustic, phonetic, and phonological aspects of language, but also to explore how these might bootstrap the beginnings of morphosyntax during the first year of life.

Perceptual Primitives in Language Acquisition

How the acoustic and phonological aspects of speech are related to underlying structure has received increasing attention recently. According to a recent proposal by Endress et al. (2009), language might recruit previously existing perceptual mechanisms or "primitives" and use their outputs to feed abstract linguistic computations. In the perception and memory literature, for instance, it has long been known that sequence edges are particularly salient positions, facilitating perception, learning, and recall of elements in those positions (see Endress et al. 2009 for a summary). This, the authors argue, might be related to why languages show a universal preference for word-initial and word-final morphosyntactic processes as opposed to word-internal ones; e.g., prefixing and suffixing are common among languages, whereas infixing is very rare. Indeed, Endress et al. (2005) have recently demonstrated that adult learners perform well in an artificial grammar learning task if the regularity that they need to learn (identical adjacent repetition of syllables) is at the edge of a syllable sequence, but they fail if the same regularity appears sequence internally.

Similarly, as Endress et al. (2007) have demonstrated, identical repetitions are perceived automatically as salient Gestalts by adult learners in artificial grammar paradigms. When participants' task was to learn a sequence of three tones where the second and third tones were identical, they succeeded. But they failed when the tone sequences implemented an ordinal regularity, for example, a high tone followed by a low tone followed by a middle tone. Repetitions or identity appears to be a special input configuration that is more readily perceived than are other relations of the same mathematical complexity, for example, ordinal relations.

In the following sections, we review how some perceptual primitives, for example, the detection of repetitions (Endress et al. 2005, 2007; Gervain et al. 2008a), edge salience (Endress et al. 2005, 2007), or prosodic grouping principles (Nespor et al. 2008), might help bootstrap the acquisition of morphosyntactic structure.

Statistical Approaches to Language Acquisition

Although the above described nativist position has been very influential in the past 50 years, the long tradition of empiricist approaches to language acquisition has re-emerged in the past two decades. These empiricist positions take different forms, from statistical learning approaches to connectionism (Elman et al. 1996); what they share, though, is a belief that no innate language-specific knowledge is required to explain language acquisition. Rather, language development is a piecemeal learning process that relies on general-purpose mechanisms, typically statistical in nature, shared by most perceptual and cognitive domains. No innate mental contents specific to language such as lexical categories, principles, or parameters are assumed.

These statistical learning approaches gained new momentum in the language-acquisition literature when Saffran et al. (1996) demonstrated that very young infants are able to use statistical information contained in speech and to then use such information to segment continuous speech into its constituent words. These initial results have given rise to a large body of research, partly reviewed in The Word Segmentation Problem section below, investigating the role, scope, and limitations of statistical learning in language acquisition.

These statistical accounts have also been combined with social learning theory. In Tomasello's (2000) account, infants begin by learning frequently occurring sequences in the input (e.g., *Where is the toy? Where is the cup? This is a ball. This is a dog.*). As a second step, infants discover similarities among these memorized sequences and extract semiabstract constructions or templates with a memorized component and one variable element (*Where is the _? This is a _.*). In these templates, the variable elements are not variables in a mathematical sense, as their scope might be limited to an arbitrary set of elements, for example, the members of the family, animals, or cars. Abstract, adult-like linguistic knowledge is believed to emerge only later, as young children generalize further, using the semiabstract templates. In Tomasello's (2000) view, infants and young children are aided by their social learning abilities during the stepwise abstraction process. They understand and construct the meaning of utterances not solely on the basis of the semantics of the linguistic constituents in the utterances addressed to them, but also by inferring the possible meaning from the speaker's intention, which even very young infants have been shown to have access to (Csibra & Gergely 2009, Gergely & Csibra 2003, Onishi & Baillargeon 2005).

Our review takes an integrative stance, emphasizing that innate language-specific, perceptual, and statistical mechanisms are all necessary for language acquisition. What needs to be explored is their respective roles and the interactions between them.

EVOLUTIONARY ORIGINS AND BIOLOGICAL FOUNDATIONS: APES, BIRDS, AND HUMANS

The nativist position on language acquisition grounded language in human biology. The initial investigations focused on the neurobiology of language, citing critical period effects, language acquisition in congenitally blind and deaf children, neurally based language pathologies, etc. (see Lenneberg 1967 for a classical formulation). More recently, in an attempt to investigate the most fundamental questions about language, numerous papers have explored its evolution. In parallel, studies of nonhuman animals are proceeding in the hope of determining whether human abilities have arisen in the human mind as a patchwork of different precursor systems that were present in ancestral species.

This line of research is of particular relevance for language acquisition because it raises convergent theoretical questions about innate, genetically endowed language abilities. If a predisposition for language is innate in humans, it became part of our genetic heritage during evolution. Therefore, research into nonhuman species' cognitive and communicative abilities complements studies of early infancy. Such comparative research also sheds light on the issue of language specificity. If humans and nonhuman animals share cognitive and/or learning abilities, these cannot be language specific since only our species has language. However, they may have been precursors bringing humans closer to language.

Research comparing human (infant) language acquisition and nonhuman cognitive, perceptual, and learning abilities usually takes one of two routes. Traditionally, humans' capabilities were compared to those of their closest evolutionary relatives, primates. Indeed, comparative studies between infants and primates have shown that the latter are also capable of statistical learning (Newport et al. 2004), language discrimination on the basis of rhythm (Ramus et al. 2000), and categorical phoneme perception (Morse et al. 1987), among other abilities. More recently, birdsong has been explored as a possible analogy for human language. This may, at first, appear surprising, since songbirds are not closely related to humans. However, vocal communication, like human language, plays an important role in songbirds' cognitive as well as social development, which is not the case for nonhuman primates. Songbirds' sophisticated vocalization system thus allows us to investigate not only learning and cognitive abilities underlying language as an abstract system, but also the mechanisms involved in vocalization, i.e., the relationship between perception and production. In addition, birdsong is highly complex, which allows a better comparison with human language than structurally simpler primate calls do. To quote Prather et al. (2009), "all songbirds studied to date [...] learn their song notes by imitation, a feature of human speech that is otherwise rare among animals [...]. Swamp sparrows' songs comprise repeated groups of 2–5 'notes', which are composed of short pure-tonal frequency sweeps, with note categories differing primarily in duration, bandwidth and rate of change in frequency."

Below we show the relevance of birdsong as a comparative model of speech, if not necessarily of language. Investigating birdsong from this perspective gives us the opportunity to dissociate evolutionary ancestry from adaptive pressures. Phylogenetically different vocal communication systems might have developed similar mechanisms not because of common ancestry, but as a response to similar environmental and adaptive pressures. Comparing human language to birdsong makes it possible to explore the components of human language that are the result of selection and those that arose through hereditary endowment.

Genetic Studies of Speech Production and Language

Mutations in FOXP2 cause speech, morphological, and in all likelihood, other language disorders (Gopnik & Crago 1991, Haesler et al. 2007, Marler & Peters 1981). Haesler et al. (2007) began to study whether birds also possess behaviors and neural structures related to FOXP2 mutations after patients suffering from speech dyspraxia were found to have functional abnormalities related to high levels of FOXP2 in the striatum and basal ganglia. They reasoned that if birds also had problems related to elevated levels of FOXP2, then it would be possible to use birds as a model to understand whether the genetic underpinnings of speech were similar to those of birdsongs. The authors used zebra finches because they learn their songs by "imitating" adult tutors and because they change songs seasonally. Haesler et al. (2007) noticed that the expression of FOXP2 tends to increase in Area X when zebra finches learn to sing. The levels of FOXP2 decrease before the birds begin to learn their songs. The authors experimentally lowered the level of FOXP2 in Area X during song learning and found that the experimental birds with decreased levels of FOXP2 sing in atypical ways as compared with controls. This study suggests that songbirds have mechanisms for learning their songs that are reminiscent of humans learning to speak and are susceptible to mutations in FOXP2. Since these findings, several other experiments have enriched our understanding of the expression of the genetic endowment and learning abilities (e.g., Miller et al. 2008).

Similarities Between Birdsong and Human Speech

The similarities of some mechanisms observed in songbirds and humans are indeed quite striking. Birdsong and human speech might use similar brain mechanisms: Auditory brain areas responsible for perception and motor areas responsible for production might be closely linked in both systems with single neurons responding to both perceived and produced vocalizations. For humans, the motor theory of speech, linking perception and production, was proposed decades ago (Liberman et al. 1967). More recently, Prather et al. (2008) identified similar mechanisms in swamp sparrows. The brain area HVC (high vocal center) of male swamp sparrows is engaged during song production, song perception, and learning of songs from tutors. Prather et al. (2008) investigated whether HVC neurons display both types of activity by recording from this area in freely behaving male swamp sparrows during presentation as well as production of songs. The authors found that some HVC neurons were active during singing *and* listening, which, as the authors demonstrated, was due to a motor estimation of auditory feedback. To confirm that this activity is indeed motor in nature and not simply due to auditory feedback as the bird perceives its own song, the authors played different distracting songs to birds while they were singing, so auditory feedback was disrupted. Increased neural activity was observed despite this manipulation. This, as the authors suggest, bears resemblance to the motor theory of speech perception (Liberman et al. 1967) as well as to the mirror neuron system in the frontal cortex of monkeys (Gallese et al. 1996, Rizzolatti et al. 2001).

Birdsong has been suggested as a potential analog for speech and/or language due to its complex structure. In birdsong, just like in human language, the origin of this structural complexity, whether it is genetically determined or learned, is an exciting question. Feher et al. (2009) have asked whether species-typical songs can be created de novo in zebra finches, much like language can emerge in groups of linguistic isolates in the span of a few generations (Senghas et al. 2004). Feher et al. (2009) studied juvenile birds, raised in isolation. Songs that are usually observed in isolated (ISO) birds are less structured, noisier, and contain high-pitch upsweeps, making it possible to quantify the differences observed between the wild-type (WT) and ISO type of songs. Each juvenile bird was trained by a particular ISO tutor in a soundproof cage. A number of isolated birds served as individual tutors to teach juveniles who had been deprived of prior exposure. Pupils of the first generation become tutors for other juvenile isolates, an operation that went on until the fourth generation was reached. Changes were observed in each successive training stage from the first to the fourth generation. The data show that the WT and ISO songs differ in their spectral features and duration of the acoustic state of songs, but across generations there is a progression from the ISO toward the WT song properties. The authors claim that "song culture is the result of an extended developmental process, a 'multigenerational' phenotype partly genetically encoded in a founding population and partly in environmental variables, but taking multiple generations to emerge." These findings bear strong resemblance to language emergence de novo in that more structured and more species-typical song and language emerge as a result of the acquisition/learning process, suggesting that impoverished input is sufficient to trigger the genetically encoded mechanisms responsible for song/speech.

The above reviewed evidence indicates that similarities between birdsong and speech exist at the level of neural mechanisms as well as in terms of the underlying genetic bases. But is birdsong a good model for the core property of human language, namely its structural complexity? Gardner et al. (2005) looked at canaries (*Serinus canaria*), which produce hierarchically organized songs. Songs consist of "syllables," which, when repeated, form a "phrase." Such phrases appear in young canaries after 60 days when they are raised typically, that is, in a population of singing adults. It is known that deafened juveniles produce the species-specific hierarchical organization, although syllables and phrases are impoverished. Gardner et al. (2005) exposed isolated juveniles to synthesized songs that were "ungrammatical" because they implemented a "random walk" through the syllable space. Initially, the production of the isolates seemed congruent with the random walk exposure. Upon transition to adulthood, however, normal syllables became recognizable and primitive phrasing started to emerge. At the end of the learning process, juveniles produced standard syllables, and species-typical phrasing was clearly noticeable. The authors concluded that "imitation and innate song constraints are separate processes that can be segregated in time: freedom in youth, rules in adulthood."

Gentner et al. (2000) and Prather et al. (2009) further examined song organization and perception in birds, focusing on categorical perception (for a discussion of categorical perception in humans, see The Early Sensitivity to Speech and Subsequent Phonological Development section). In the latter study, the authors systematically manipulated note duration, a learned aspect of swan sparrow song, and found that sensorimotor neurons showed a categorical response to gradually varying note duration. This neural response coincided with category boundaries observed behaviorally in the animals. Furthermore, sparrows coming from song dialects exhibiting different categorical boundaries responded according to the boundaries of their own species, indicating that boundaries were indeed learned.

In sum, it appears that birdsong and human speech are comparable in terms of their underlying neural mechanisms, the presence of innate guiding principles as well as some of their organizational properties. This, of course, does not imply that birdsong is equivalent to human language in terms of its productivity and structural complexity. Nor does it mean that songbirds' cognitive abilities are more similar to those of humans than are the cognitive abilities of primate species. Comparisons with birdsong provide us with an optimal testing ground to explore the genetic ancestry as well as the adaptive pressures that have shaped human language during the evolution of our species.

These similarities notwithstanding, human language appears to have a unique productivity and computational power not paralleled in any other species. Where do these features originate? After reviewing the abilities and mechanisms shared by humans and other animals, we turn to those that might be unique to our species.

Does a New Computational Component Cause the Emergence of Language in the Human Brain?

In an influential paper, Hauser et al. (2002) proposed that enquiries into language evolution should be incorporated into theories of language. They suggested that it may be convenient to distinguish between two aspects of the human language faculty: the language faculty in the broad sense (FLB) and the language faculty in the narrow sense (FLN). Their proposal is that the FLB is composed of various elements such as sensory motor systems, memory systems, social abilities, and so forth, whereas the FLN comprises a very limited number of computational components or a single computational component, which the authors view as quite likely to have been sufficient for the emergence of language. A similar conclusion has been drawn by other researchers with respect to mathematical abilities. "The human species is unique in its capacity to create revolutionary cultural inventions such as writing and mathematics, which dramatically enhance its native competence. From a neurobiological standpoint, such inventions are too recent for natural selection to have dedicated specific brain mechanisms to them. It has therefore been suggested that they co-opt or 'recycle' evolutionarily older circuits with a related function [...], thus enriching (without necessarily replacing) their domain of use" (Knops et al. 2009, p. 1538).

This way of presenting the theoretical framework proposes that many components (use of the vocal tract, categorical perception, etc.) are present in other animals. For a detailed discussion of which phonological abilities might be found in nonhuman species, see Yip (2006). The computational abilities required to acquire the syntax of the native language, by contrast, are unique to humans. Hauser et al. (2002) framed their paper as "a quest for the crucial evolutionary step that allowed our species to acquire the complex syntax of human languages."

In a follow-up experimental paper, Fitch & Hauser (2004) and Saffran et al. (2008) proposed that recursion, responsible for discrete infinity, might be the one and unique component of FLN. This proposal generated a great number of experiments and theoretical debates seeking to support or infirm the conjecture (Bahlman et al. 2006, Fitch et al. 2005, Friederici et al. 2006, Hauser et al. 2002, Hochmann et al. 2008, Pinker & Jackendoff 2005). Fitch & Hauser (2004) based their studies on the complexity of grammars that Chomsky (1957 and subsequent work) proposed. Chomsky made the claim that human languages are best characterized as context-free or phrase-structure grammars (PSG), not as computationally more limited finite-state grammars (FSG). Fitch & Hauser (2004) report an experiment investigating whether humans and monkeys are similar in their abilities to learn a FSG and a PSG from the simple presentation of items derived from the grammars. The authors used two artificial grammars. The FSG had items conforming to structure $(AB)^n$ with $n \leq 3$, the PSG to structure $A^n B^n$

with n ≤ 3. The authors habituated humans and cotton-top tamarin monkeys to either of these items. As and Bs were consonant-vowel syllables, with a female voice pronouncing the A syllables and a male the B syllables. In the test phase, humans had to rate new items as congruent or incongruent with the grammar they had learned, whereas monkeys were tested with a head-turn procedure to estimate whether the underlying grammar had been extracted. Humans behaved as if they had learned both grammars and monkeys as if they had the capacity to extract only the FSG grammar.

Later, Gentner et al. (2006) studied European starlings and challenged the notion that only humans can learn PSG. They used the same kinds of grammars as had Fitch & Hauser (2004), except that As and Bs corresponded to two specific categories of sounds these birds use. Before being tested, birds were trained with a protracted operant-conditioning schedule, a procedure that Fitch & Hauser (2004) did not use with the cotton-top tamarins. After this extended training phase, starlings learned the PSG.

Perruchet & Rey (2005) criticized Fitch & Hauser (2004) on different grounds, arguing that in Fitch & Hauser's (2004) study, humans did not actually need to establish nonadjacent dependencies to succeed and cannot therefore be assumed to have extracted the underlying structure of the $A^n B^n$ items. Indeed, the distributional properties and/or the rhythmic properties of Fitch & Hauser's (2004) material offer a better explanation of how humans processed the $A^n B^n$ items. Indeed, Hochmann et al. (2008) showed that human participants in the test did not dismiss $A^2 B^3$ or $A^3 B^2$ as incongruent with the grammar $A^n B^n$. Moreover, when interrogated at the end of the experiment, those few participants who did dismiss such items reported that they explicitly counted the number of As and Bs and only accepted sequences with equal numbers. Despite these empirical issues, the theoretical proposal made by Hauser et al. (2002) remains highly interesting and invites further research.

We follow this brief review of the evolutionary aspects of human language and animals' abilities with a detailed discussion of young infants' speech and language-processing capacities to provide an empirical basis for the evaluation of the theoretical and evolutionary claims introduced so far.

THE EARLY SENSITIVITY TO SPEECH AND SUBSEQUENT PHONOLOGICAL DEVELOPMENT

Newborn infants show surprising speech-processing abilities from birth. They prefer forward-going speech and primate vocalizations over acoustically matched nonspeech sounds or backward speech (Dehaene-Lambertz et al. 2002; Pena et al. 2003; Vouloumanos & Werker 2004, 2007), their mother's voice over other female voices (Mehler et al. 1978), and their native language over unfamiliar languages (Mehler et al. 1988, Moon et al. 1993). These early language discrimination abilities might represent some form of imprinting to the properties of the native language upon the first encounter immediately after birth, or alternatively the result of exposure to the maternal language in utero. Newborns can make most of the phonemic distinctions attested in the world's languages (Dehaene-Lambertz & Dehaene 1994, Eimas et al. 1971, Werker & Tees 1984b), and they are able to distinguish languages they have never heard before on the basis of their rhythmical characteristics (Mehler et al. 1988; Nazzi et al. 1998; Ramus et al. 1999, 2000). Newborns are also able to detect the acoustic cues that signal word boundaries (Christophe et al. 1994), discriminate words with different patterns of lexical stress (Sansavini et al. 1997), and distinguish function words (e.g., *it, this, in, of, these, some*) from content words (e.g., *baby, table, eat, slowly, happy*) on the basis of their different acoustic characteristics (Shi et al. 1999). These early, innate abilities lay the foundations for later language learning.

Acquisition of the Native Phonology

One of the most fundamental and at the same time most surprising perceptual abilities of newborns is that they are able to discriminate most sound contrasts used in the world's languages. In other words, they are born as "citizens of the world," ready to learn any natural language. Just like adults, newborns perceive these sounds categorically (Eimas et al. 1971, Liberman et al. 1957), perceiving acoustic variation from within a phoneme boundary as the same sound and the same acoustic variation spanning adult phoneme boundaries as being different sounds.

During the first year of life, as a result of exposure to the native language, this initial universal discrimination narrows down to the phonemes, that is, minimal meaningful differences (e.g., *pin* versus *bin*), of the native language (Werker & Tees 1984a). Discrimination of most nonnative contrasts is lost (Werker & Tees 1984a), whereas it is maintained or even enhanced for native contrasts (Kuhl et al. 2006). English, for instance, only has a dental /d/ sound, whereas Hindi discriminates between a retroflex /D/ and a dental /d/. Newborns and young infants born into English-speaking environments readily discriminate the Hindi sounds. But after eight months of exposure to English, where the two categories are not distinguished, English-learning infants start losing the discrimination (Werker & Tees 1984a). Indeed, English-speaking adults find it very hard to discriminate this contrast. Hindi infants and adults, as a result of exposure to Hindi, maintain it.

What learning mechanism might account for this learning-by-forgetting (Mehler 1974, Mehler & Dupoux 1994) or perceptual attunement (Scott et al. 2007) process? It has been suggested that native phonological categories might be established through a distributional learning mechanism (Maye et al. 2002). In a language like English, where there is only one /d/ sound, most actual realizations that infants encounter will cluster around a prototypical /d/ pronunciation, so the distribution of English /d/ sounds will have a mode around the most typical acoustic parameters for /d/. On the other hand, in Hindi, where there are two /d/ sounds, the same acoustic space will show a bimodal distribution, as there will be many instances around the typical /D/ sound as well as around the typical /d/ sound. As a result, in English, infants will be exposed to a unimodal distribution, and in Hindi, a bimodal one. It has been shown that infants are sensitive to this statistical distribution, and they create a single phoneme category when exposed to a unimodal distribution, whereas they establish two categories if the distribution in the input is bimodal (Maye et al. 2002). In their study, Maye and colleagues (2002) used the /da/-/ta/ continuum, where the two syllables are distinguished by the onset of voicing (voice onset time, or VOT). Since /d/ is a voiced consonant, in /da/, voicing starts at 0 msec, that is, immediately at the onset of the syllable, whereas in /ta/, the consonant is voiceless; thus, voicing starts only at the onset of the vowel. By delaying VOT incrementally, a continuum was created from /da/ with VOT at 0 msec through six syllables with VOT at 20 msec, 40 msec, etc., to /ta/ with VOT at 140 msec. One group of 6- to 8-month-old infants, the unimodal group, was exposed to a frequency distribution along this continuum where syllables in the middle (instances 4 and 5 with VOT 60 msec and 80 msec, respectively) had the highest frequency of occurrence. A second group, the bimodal group, was exposed to a distribution where tokens closer to the end points (with VOT 20 msec and 120 msec) were the most frequent ones. When tested on the discrimination of the end points of the continuum, /da/ and /ta/, the bimodal group showed better discrimination than the unimodal group (Maye et al. 2002).

These results suggest that infants have the ability to track the frequency of sound tokens in the input and might use this information to tune into native phonemic categories (Best & McRoberts 2003, Kuhl 2004, Maye et al. 2002).

The Early Sensitivity to Rhythm and Its Potential Bootstrapping Role

The previous sections have illustrated the challenge of acquiring one's native language. However, some infants successfully acquire not only one, but two or more languages at the same time. How do these infants discriminate between their languages?

Linguists have long recognized that languages differ perceptibly in their sound patterns and, in particular, in their rhythm (Abercrombie 1967, James 1940, Ladefoged 1993, Pike 1945). Initially, these differences were described as categorical and were derived from the isochrony principle, that is, as a function of the linguistic unit that has a constant duration in a given language. According to this view, languages fall into one of three rhythmic classes. In stress-timed languages such as English, Dutch, or Polish, the isochronous unit is the time between two subsequent stressed syllables. For example, in the sentence *Pronunciation is important in English*, the duration of time between the stressed syllables (in bold) is roughly the same. In syllable-timed languages, such as Spanish or Italian, the unit of isochrony is the syllable, that is, syllables are roughly of equal duration. For instance, in *tavolo* 'table' (Italian), no vowel is reduced, so all syllables are of the same length. In mora-timed languages, such as Japanese or Tamil, the isochronous unit is the mora. The mora is the measure of syllable weight [light/short syllables such as *a* (the indefinite article) consist of one mora; heavy/long syllables such as *see* consist of two morae].

These differences in rhythm are intuitive and easy to perceive for adults. If infants have the same sensitivity to linguistic rhythm, it might help them discriminate their languages, at least when those are from different rhythmical classes. Such an early sensitivity was indeed observed by Mehler et al. (1988), who showed that newborns were able to discriminate their future native language from a rhythmically different language, even if both were low-pass filtered, suppressing phoneme identity. This initial finding, suggesting that language

discrimination relies upon suprasegmental, rhythmical cues, was extended by Nazzi et al. (1998), showing that rhythmical differences were sufficient for discrimination; familiarity with the languages was not necessary. These authors found that French newborns readily discriminated between low-pass filtered utterances in English and Japanese, two languages they had never heard before.

These results established that rhythm might serve as an initial cue to language discrimination. However, the exact acoustic features corresponding to the subjective percept of rhythm were still unknown. The isochrony principle proved incorrect, as empirical investigations obtained no isochrony for the relevant units (Dauer 1983), and several languages were found that showed characteristics of both stress-timed and syllable-timed rhythm (Nespor 1990). Rhythmicity thus appeared to be a gradient rather than a categorical property (Nespor 1990). Building on these observations, Ramus et al. (1999) proposed an operational definition for rhythm and rhythmical classification as a function of three acoustic parameters: (*a*) %V, the proportion of vowels/vocalic space relative to the total length of an utterance, (*b*) ΔV, the variability in the length of vocalic spaces, and (*c*) ΔC, the variability in the length of consonant clusters. The authors measured these parameters in naturalistic recordings of speech in eight languages (e.g., English, Dutch, French, Italian, Japanese) and found that languages clustered into groups similar to the traditional rhythmical classes when plotted in two-dimensional spaces defined by any two of the three acoustic parameters. This definition recreated the traditional classification and accounted for languages previously found to be ambiguous (Nespor 1990) with respect to classification or currently undergoing change, because continuous rather than categorical measures were used. It is important to note that work by Grabe & Low (2002), also using a computational definition of rhythm, failed to recreate the traditional rhythmic classes. However, as subsequent work by Ramus (2002) suggests, there were important methodological differences between Ramus et al.'s (1999) and Grabe & Low's (2002) studies, which might account for the different findings. Grabe & Low (2002) analyzed speech from one speaker per language, whereas Ramus et al. (1999) recorded four speakers for each language, thus obtaining a measure that matched the general pattern of languages more closely than did the idiosyncrasies of individual speakers.

The classification in terms of %V, ΔV, and ΔC suggested that it wasn't specific segmental identity that defined rhythm, but rather the relative length and variability of vocalic and consonantal spaces. Ramus & Mehler (1999) and Ramus et al. (1999) tested this prediction in a series of experiments in which they replaced individual vowels by /a/ and individual consonants by /s/. Utterances resynthesized this way suppressed phonemic and consequently lexical identity, but preserved the proportion of vowels and consonants in the signal. Adults as well as newborns were able to discriminate utterances from two rhythmically different languages when this resynthesis was applied. However, they failed when both vowels and consonants were transformed into /a/, suppressing the difference between them. These results clearly established that the three parameters relating to the ratio of vowels and consonants in the speech signal were necessary and sufficient acoustic cues for rhythm-based language discrimination at birth. The discrimination of rhythmically similar languages emerges at around age 4 months; it has been hypothesized to rely on more subtle cues, such as phoneme identity or phonotactics (Bosch & Sebastián-Gallés 2001, Ramon-Casas et al. 2009).

In addition to language discrimination, linguistic rhythm might also serve as a bootstrapping cue for morphosyntax. Languages belonging to different rhythmic classes also show different morphosyntactic properties. For instance, mora-timed languages, that is, languages with a high value for %V, such as Japanese, tend to have simple syllabic structure, agglutinating morphology, and object-verb (OV) word order, whereas languages with lower %V values, such as English or Polish, typically have complex syllable structure, inflecting morphology, and VO word order (Fenk-Oczlon & Fenk 2005). Given these correlations, Mehler et al. (2004) have proposed that rhythm might act as a bootstrap for general morphosyntactic type. The proposal hasn't been tested empirically, but it is of potential importance because it links a robust acoustic cue, detected even by neonates, to the most general and most abstract morphosyntactic properties.

THE WORD SEGMENTATION PROBLEM: LEARNING MECHANISMS AND PERCEPTUAL PRIMITIVES

Parallel to the task of breaking the syntactic code of their native language, infants also need to start building a lexicon. According to an increasingly widespread view (see Swingley 2009 for a review), lexical acquisition starts as early as the second half of the first year of life, when infants begin to segment potential word forms out of the continuous speech stream they hear. These forms are believed not yet to be reliably associated with meaning; nevertheless, they play a significant role not only in building the lexicon, but also in morphosyntactic acquisition. In other words, lexical acquisition starts much before infants utter their first words.

Learning word forms is a challenging task since speech is continuous: Most word boundaries are not marked by pauses, and words typically do not occur in isolation. Yet the sensitivity to potential word forms appears as early as birth. Newborns are able to discriminate identical phoneme sequences that only differ in that some span a word boundary, whereas others don't (e.g., *panorama typique* versus *mathématicien*, respectively; Christophe et al. 1994). This result provides a good example of infants' early sensitivity to perceptual Gestalts like edges and to prosodic structure in general. In addition, newborns are also able to discriminate word forms with different patterns of lexical stress (Sansavini et al. 1997).

These early sensitivities notwithstanding, extracting and storing a relatively large number of word forms from speech starts only at about age 6 to 8 months. Several mechanisms have been proposed to account for this feat. Statistical learning has been proposed as a general-purpose, potentially universal mechanism, which might be operational early on, whereas language-specific mechanisms, which require some familiarity with the native language, such as tracking allophonic variation, phonotactics, or stress patterns, are suggested to emerge somewhat later (Swingley 2005).

Statistically Based Word Segmentation

Proponents of structural linguistics (Harris 1955) and information theory (Shannon 1948) have long recognized that the statistical information encoded in language provides cues to its constituent units (e.g., morphemes and words) and structural patterns. Some words are much more frequent, that is, more probable, than others in absolute terms (e.g., *this*, *it*, *in*, *are*, *dog*, *time*) or in a given context (e.g., *chips* after *fish and*. . .; *do* or *is* at the beginning of a sentence).

Building on these observations, Hayes & Clark (1970) tested whether adult participants can use statistical information to extract words from a continuous stream of sine-wave speech analogs and found successful segmentation. Later, Saffran et al. (1996) showed that 8-month-old infants could use statistical information, more specifically transition probabilities (TPs; i.e., the probability with which one syllable predicts the next or the previous one), to segment a continuous stream of syllables, where syllables within a word predicted one another with a probability of 1.00, while syllables spanning word boundaries had TPs of 0.33. Infants could use dips in TPs to identify word boundaries.

Statistical learning has been shown to be a robust, domain-general, age-independent, and not specifically human ability. It operates over speech sounds as well as tones (Kudo et al. 2006) and visual stimuli (Fiser & Aslin 2002a,b). It is performed by newborns (Teinonen et al. 2009), infants at 8 and 13 months (Saffran et al. 1996), and adults (Pena et al. 2002). Moreover, nonhuman species, such as tamarin monkeys (Hauser et al. 2001) and rats (Toro & Trobalon 2005), are also able to learn statistical information.

Perceptual and Linguistic Constraints on Statistical Learning

Saffran et al.'s (1996) results shed new light on the well-known fact that humans are powerful statistical learners. But how is statistical learning used in language acquisition? A recent set of studies suggests that statistics are not used across the board for learning language. Rather, they are recruited for specific learning tasks—in particular, word segmentation and lexical acquisition—triggered by cues in the speech signal, and their application is limited by linguistic constraints.

Inspired by the fact that both morphology and syntax make use of constructions with distant dependencies, Pena et al. (2002), Newport & Aslin (2004), and Newport et al. (2004) asked the question whether transition probabilities between nonadjacent items can be learned. Pena et al. (2002) found that adults readily segmented out trisyllabic words from an artificial language when they were defined by high TPs between the first and the last syllables (A X C). However, subjects failed to generalize the pattern to novel X items unless (subliminal) segmentation cues were inserted into the stream to facilitate the original segmentation task, allowing participants to better process the regularity (Pena et al. 2002). These results suggest that cues in the signal, for example, pauses, act as triggers for different processing mechanisms, for example, statistics versus rule generalization.

A second and related issue that arises is the nature of the units or representations to which statistical computations apply. Bonatti et al. (2005) observed that adults readily segment over nonadjacent consonants, but not over nonadjacent vowels. This finding was further confirmed by Toro et al. (2008), who devised a series of artificial grammar experiments to show that consonants and vowels serve as preferential input to different kinds of learning mechanisms. They found that participants performed well when their task was to do statistical computations over consonants or rule-learning over vowels (the rule to be learned was a repetition-based generalization). But their performance dropped to chance in the opposite case, i.e., statistical computations over vowels and rule-learning over consonants. Taken together, these studies indicate that not all linguistic representations are equally suitable for statistical learning. Consonants seem to be the primary target, while vowels are preferentially recruited for rule learning.[1] These findings converge with certain observations in linguistics (Nespor et al. 2003) suggesting that consonants and vowels have different linguistic functions. Consonants are believed to be responsible for encoding the lexicon; e.g., consonantal stems carry the semantic contents of lexical items in Semitic languages. By contrast, vowels are claimed to signal morphological form and syntactic function, e.g., Ablaut phenomena in Germanic languages, *sing, sang, sung*. These studies provide further evidence that statistical computations are selectively triggered and constrained by cues in the input, and their primary function is lexical segmentation.

However, the use of statistics for segmentation and word-form learning might not be universal. In some languages, such as Chinese or infant-directed English, most words are monosyllabic, rendering statistical computations vacuous (Yang 2004, Yang & Gambell 2004). Morphologically complex languages, such as Hungarian (*ház-a-i-nk-ból*

'house.possessive.plural.1stpl.from' "from our houses") and Turkish, might pose the opposite problem, as it is not clear what unit would be segmented out: complex word forms or individual stems and suffixes.

Taken together, these studies indicate that statistical segmentation alone is not sufficient to solve the task of extracting word forms from continuous speech. Other cues, taking into account the morphophonological properties of individual languages, are needed to complement statistical computations.

Language-Specific Cues to Segmentation

Although words are not separated by clear pauses in continuous speech, there are some acoustic and phonological features that correlate reliably enough with word boundaries to allow successful segmentation in most cases. At least three such cues have been identified in the literature, mostly on the basis of English: word-level stress patterns, phonotactic regularities, and allophonic variation.

Many languages assign word-level stress to a specific position within words; for example, Hungarian, has strictly word-initial stress. But even in languages where stress is not fixed but is lexically determined for each word, there are predominant patterns that can serve as heuristic cues. In English, word-level stress is lexically determined, but most bisyllabic nouns follow a strong-weak, that is, trochaic pattern (e.g., *doctor, infant*) Thus, segmenting speech at strong syllables is a potentially useful heuristic known as the metrical segmentation strategy (Cutler 1994, Cutler & Carter 1987). Indeed, Jusczyk et al. (1999) found that 7.5-month-old English-exposed infants show a trochaic bias, treating heavy syllables as word-initial (**doctor, can**dle). Importantly, the bias required words to be multisyllabic. Heavy monosyllables (*dock, can*) were not recognized (Jusczyk et al. 1999), but trisyllabic words with initial stress (strong-weak-weak) were treated as familiar, whereas weak-strong-weak and weak-weak-strong patterns were not (Curtin et al.

---

[1] It needs to be noted that Newport & Aslin (2004) found successful statistical segmentation for vowels as well as consonants. However, they used an artificial speech stream that allowed immediate repetitions of the same word frame, making the statistical patterns highly salient, whereas Bonatti et al.'s (2005) and Toro et al.'s (2008) stream had no immediate repetitions. It seems, then, that vowels might also be used for statistical computations under special conditions, such as the informationally highly redundant stream used by Newport & Aslin (2004).

2001). Importantly, the metrical segmentation strategy is a heuristic tool, since some English bisyllables are not trochaic, but iambic (e.g., *gui'tar*). In these cases, the strategy predicts initial missegmentation. This was confirmed empirically: 7.5-month-olds who readily recognize trochaic words in continuous passages failed to show similar recognition for iambs (Jusczyk et al. 1999).

Legal and illegal phoneme distributions, that is, phonotactics, also provide information about word boundaries. In English, the sequence /br/ is frequent word initially, but it is rare word internally. Therefore, it is a good candidate for a potential word onset. Conversely, words frequently end in /nt/, which is therefore a possible cue to the end of words. In a task where infants were exposed to CVCCVC (C, consonant; V, vowel) sequences with word-internally frequent or infrequent CC clusters, they segmented the sequences into two words in the latter case, but not in the former case (Mattys et al. 1999; Mattys & Jusczyk 2001a,b).

Variation in the realization of phonemes, known as allophony, can also indicate word boundaries. In English, for instance, aspirated stop consonants appear at the onsets of stressed syllables, whereas their unaspirated allophones appear elsewhere (Church 1987). At 9 months of age, infants are able to posit word boundaries based on allophonic (e.g., night rates versus nitrates) and distributional cues, and at 10.5 months, allophonic cues alone are sufficient for successful segmentation (Jusczyk et al. 1999).

The Interaction of Statistical and Language-Specific Cues

The above cues are mostly heuristic in nature and might lead to missegmentation in less frequent or atypical cases. Such missegmentations can be induced in experimental conditions (Jusczyk et al. 1999) and can also be observed in young children's spontaneous production (Slobin 1997). However, infants acquire the majority of the word forms they know without error. This implies that they are using more than just one cue at a time, since converging cues yield more accurate segmentation.

Several studies have shown that young infants are indeed capable of using different cues simultaneously. When stress and phonotactic cues provide conflicting information about word boundaries, 9-month-old infants prefer to rely on stress cues (Mattys et al. 1999; Mattys & Jusczyk 2001a,b). When stress and statistical information are contrasted, 6-month-olds follow the statistical information (Saffran & Thiessen 2003), whereas 8-month-olds use stress cues (Johnson & Jusczyk 2001). This shift indicates a move from universal to more language-specific strategies as infants gain increasing familiarity with their native language.

Artificial grammar learning work with adults also indicates that statistical information and prosody are both computed in segmentation tasks, and prosody is typically used to constrain statistics in linguistically meaningful ways, as discussed above. If, for instance, the continuous speech stream is not monotonous as used in Saffran et al.'s (1996) original work, but has utterance-like intonational contours overlaid on it, then participants readily segment statistically coherent words inside prosodic contours, but not spanning two contours (Shukla et al. 2007). Similarly, while participants erroneously recognize "phantom words" in artificial speech streams, that is, words that never occurred in the stream, but their pair-wise syllable transitions have high probabilities (e.g., *fekula* was never heard, but *fe-ku* and *ku-la* appeared in the stream with high TPs), this false recognition can be suppressed if the stream contains prosodic cues to word boundaries, such as pauses or word-final lengthening (Endress & Mehler 2009).

Early Form-Meaning Associations

As suggested above, infants start learning words as early as age 6 to 8 months by extracting potential word forms from the input using statistical as well as phonological cues (see Swingley 2009 for a review). In order to develop a lexicon, they also need to start matching these word forms with possible meanings. Learning the full meaning of words, especially abstract words or grammatical functors, requires advanced abilities, such as categorization, understanding referentiality, and solving the induction problem for meaning (Nazzi & Bertoncini 2003, Quine 1960, Waxman & Gelman 2009). We do not discuss these complex and advanced forms of word learning here. We only review the earliest stages of lexical acquisition, when a linguistic label gets associated with a perceptually available, concrete object.

These early associations were investigated by Stager & Werker (1997), who showed that infants use their phonological knowledge and representations differently at different stages of the word-learning process. At 8 months, before word learning en masse begins, infants readily discriminate a minimal pair of word forms, *bih* and *dih*, and they are also able to associate them with two different objects. At 14 months, which is the beginning of the word-learning stage, infants succeed in the simple phonetic discrimination task, but fail to distinguish the two words when they are used in a labeling context, that is, associated with two distinct objects. They succeed, however, even in this context if the words are very distinct, for example, *lif* and *neem*. At 17 months, when word learning is in full swing, infants succeed again in both tasks. The authors accounted for these results by arguing that phonological knowledge is recruited for word learning in different ways at different developmental stages. When starting to associate word forms with meanings, infants need to pay attention to the details of both and establish an association between them. At this early stage, infants might not attribute more importance to the minimal phonemic difference between two words than to other properties of the words, such as the speaker's gender. Given the high cognitive demands of the association task, a minimal phonemic difference might go unnoticed. At later stages, when infants become experienced word learners, label-object associations become less taxing for the cognitive systems; thus, even minor differences can be more readily utilized.

Confirmation for the cognitive load hypothesis comes from recent studies that found successful associations in 14-month-olds with minimally different labels when the cognitive load of the task was reduced, e.g., by using words known to the infants (Fennell & Werker 2003), by prefamiliarizing them with the objects (Fennell & Werker 2004), by giving them a visual choice between two objects in a test (Yoshida et al. 2009), or by making the acoustic difference between words more salient (Curtin et al. 2009) or more relevant for the task (Thiessen 2007).

BROAD LEXICAL CATEGORIES: FUNCTORS AND CONTENT WORDS

Words in the lexicon are organized into hierarchical categories. The most general and cross-linguistically universal divide is the one between closed-class functors (free or bound), such as articles, pronouns, and pre- or postpositions, and open-class content words, such as nouns, verbs, and adjectives. The most important difference between these two broad categories is functional: Functors signal morphosyntactic structure (e.g., plurality, tense, and argument structure), whereas content words carry lexical meaning. In addition, there are a number of statistical and acoustic/phonological differences between them. Functors have very high token frequencies. In corpora, they often account for 30% to 50% of the whole input (Gervain et al. 2008b, Kučera & Francis 1967). Content words typically have much lower token frequencies. By contrast, they are acoustically more salient, as they carry stress, consist of multiple syllables, and have at least one nonreduced vowel (Morgan et al. 1996).

It is well known that young children often omit functors in their early productions (Guasti 2002), which raised the question of whether they are able to perceive and represent functors at all. An early study (Shipley et al. 1969) showed that children whose linguistic production was at the telegraphic phase (i.e., contained no function words) nevertheless understood instructions better if the instructions themselves were not telegraphic, but contained function words as well. Later, Gerken et al. (1990) established that the omission of functors in early production stems from a limitation on production and not on perception or encoding. In a series of imitation experiments with 2- to 3-year-old children, they found that children tend to omit weak, unstressed monosyllabic morphemes, typically functors, but not strong, stressed ones, typically content words, even if both are nonsense non-English words. Also, they imitate nonexisting content words with greater ease if they appear in the environment of real English function words as opposed to environments of nonsense function words. Moreover, children make a distinction between those nonsense functors that follow the usual consonant patterns of English functors and those that do not. Taken together, these results indicate that even though young children produce few functors, they build fairly detailed representations of them, which they can use in segmenting and labeling the incoming speech stream. In a later experiment, Gerken & McIntosh (1993) obtained similar results for sentence comprehension.

The above experiments were carried out with children who already have substantial knowledge of the grammar of their native language. But segmentation and labeling cues are most relevant at the beginning of acquisition to break up the input. Indeed, Shi et al. (1999) asked whether newborns are able to distinguish functors and content words on the basis of the phonological differences between them. Their findings indicate that newborn infants of both English-speaking and non-English-speaking mothers are able to categorically discriminate between English function and content words presented in isolation. By 6 months of age, infants start to show a preference for content words (Shi & Werker 2001), and by 11 months, they are also able to represent frequent functors in some phonological detail (Shi et al. 2006). They are also able to use functors, frequent and infrequent ones alike, to segment out a following content word (Shi et al. 2006).

Höhle & Weissenborn (2003) obtained similar results, showing functor versus content word discrimination in 7- to 9-month-old German infants exposed to continuous speech.

On the basis of the findings described above, it is not unreasonable to assume that the function word versus content word distinction is available to infants very early on, and although functors might not frequently appear in infants' earliest productions, they might be among their earliest word form representations, serving to bootstrap the early content words categories, e.g., nouns and verbs. Borrowed from the structuralist-generativist linguistic tradition, the idea that functors are fundamental for the categorization of content words has recently gained empirical support from corpus studies (Mintz 2002, Redington et al. 1998).

WORD ORDER AND OTHER TYPOLOGICAL DIFFERENCES

The acquisition and production of the first words at around the age of one year mark an important milestone in young infants' language development. Multiword utterances appear much later, after the second birthday. However, the acquisition of the most basic syntactic properties of the native language, such as word order, might actually start much earlier, during the first year of life, in parallel with and possibly in relation to early speech perception and word-learning abilities. Indeed, Brown (1973) has shown that infants get basic word order right from their first productions, which suggests that word order is a property that they have acquired prior to the production of multiword utterances.

How do infants acquire word order so early? According to the lexicalist position (Tomasello 2000), infants and young children initially do not represent word order in an abstract form. Rather, they learn relatively fixed constructions, often specific to individual lexical items, usually individual verbs (for example, *eat* is preceded by a noun phrase, the *eater*, and is followed by a noun phrase, the *eatee*). The generativist account, by contrast, assumes that even young learners have general and abstract word-order representations encoding the relative order of the phrasal head and its complements and specifiers. For example, in a language with a head-complement, these technical terms are always spelled with capital initials; in linguistics, it would be better to follow this conventional order: objects follow verbs, nouns follow prepositions, etc. (e.g., *eat an apple*; *on the table*). One way to differentiate between these two accounts is to show that infants have some rudimentary representation of word order prior to the acquisition of a sizeable lexicon.

Recent results suggest that such a prelexical word-order representation might be created early on using frequency as a bootstrapping cue (Gervain et al. 2008b). As discussed above, functors are more frequent than content words. In addition, their position relative to utterance boundaries correlates with the general word order of languages (Gervain et al. 2008b, Morgan et al. 1996). In Italian, for instance, the general word order is VO; therefore, functors that head a phrase appear phrase initially (for example, prepositions: *sul tavolo* on-the table 'on the table'). By contrast, in Japanese, functors heading phrases are final (for example, postpositions: *Tokyo ni* Tokyo to 'to Tokyo'). In infant-directed speech corpora in these two languages, the distribution of frequent words, that is, functors, was exactly the opposite. In Italian, most two-word phrases at utterance boundaries started with a frequent word, that is, functor, whereas in Japanese, most of these phrases ended in a frequent word. Importantly, 8-month-old infants appear to be sensitive to these distributional differences. When exposed to a structurally ambiguous artificial speech stream in which frequent and infrequent nonwords alternated and the beginning and the end of the stream was ramped in amplitude to mask phase information, Japanese infants preferred to parse the stream into frequent-final units, whereas Italian infants showed longer looking times for frequent-initial test items (Gervain et al. 2008b). This suggests that prelexical infants show a rudimentary initial representation of word order, at least in terms of the relative

positions of frequent and infrequent words, that is, typically functors and content words. This finding has been confirmed by recent results (J. Hochmann, A. Endress, and J. Mehler, manuscript under review) suggesting that infants do indeed treat frequent words as functors and infrequent ones as content words. When infants were given the choice to pair either the frequent words or the infrequent words with objects, they chose the infrequent ones as possible labels for naming objects (J. Hochmann, A. Endress, and J. Mehler, manuscript under review).

However, unlike Italian and Japanese, some languages do not show a consistent word-order pattern. German, for example, uses both OV and VO orders within the verb phrase, depending on the syntactic context. Also, some infants grow up with an OV and a VO language simultaneously (for example, Japanese and English). In these cases, frequency alone does not provide enough information about word order, since both frequent-initial and frequent-final phrases occur in the input. This implies that further cues are necessary to bootstrap word order. One cue that has been suggested in the literature is prosody. Nespor et al. (2008) found that the location and the acoustic realization of prosodic prominence correlate with word order both across and within languages. Thus, in OV languages such as Turkish and in phrases with OV order within mixed languages such as German, prominence within prosodic phrases is initial, and it is implemented as a pitch contrast (high-low), whereas in VO languages such as Italian or French as well as in the VO phrases of mixed languages, a durational contrast is utilized, and prominence is final (short-long). If infants can use this prosodic cue in conjunction with frequency, then a more precise and fine-grained representation of word order can be acquired, even in cases where the two word orders, OV and VO, occur within a single language.

It has been argued that this grouping, that is, prominence-initial for pitch or intensity contrasts and prominence-final for durational contrasts, is an auditory bias that applies to speech and nonspeech stimuli alike (the iambic-trochaic law; Hayes 1995). More recently, some data have been reported suggesting that the grouping principle might emerge as a result of language experience (Iversen et al. 2008; K.A. Yoshida, J.R. Iversen, A.D. Patel, R. Mazuka, H. Nito, J. Gervain, and F. Werker, manuscript under revision). However, these results are not conclusive, as other studies have found no language-related differences (R. Bion, S. Benavides, and M. Nespor, manuscript under review; Hay & Diehl 2007). Irrespective of whether this bias is independent of language experience or a result of it, infants might use it as a cue to word order at a very early age.

The hypothesis that even prelexical infants might possess some simple word order representations, possibly bootstrapped by frequency and prosody, received independent confirmation from studies using naturalistic stimuli in German. Weissenborn et al. (1996) found that German infants were sensitive to word order violations in German subordinate clauses.

THE NEURAL CORRELATES OF LANGUAGE IN YOUNG INFANTS

With the advancement of brain imaging techniques, it has become increasingly possible to pursue the original agenda of the research on the biological foundations of language with infant populations. Researchers have started charting the brain areas and circuits dedicated to language and speech perception in newborns and young infants.

One of the most important findings of this increasing body of research is that the newborn and infant brain shows a functional organization for language processing that is similar to that of the adult brain (Dehaene-Lambertz et al. 2002, 2008; Gervain et al. 2008a; Pena et al. 2003; Taga & Asakawa 2007). This organization appears to be at least partly under genetic control and develops even without experience with language (e.g., in congenitally deaf individuals; Dehaene-Lambertz et al. 2008).

More specifically, it has been observed that 3-month-old infants as well as newborns show a left-hemisphere advantage when listening to speech as compared with reversed speech and silence (Bortfeld et al. 2009, Dehaene-Lambertz et al. 2002, Pena et al. 2003). This early left lateralization has been confirmed using diffusion tensor imaging, a technique that is able to track white matter fascicles and myelination. The left hemisphere showed advanced development in 2-month-old infants (Dubois et al. 2008). Interestingly, those aspects of language processing that are usually right lateralized in adults, e.g., the processing of prosody, also appear to be right lateralized in infants (Homae et al. 2006, 2007).

In addition to this general lateralization pattern, recent results have allowed identification of the areas involved in language processing at a more fine-grained level. Gervain et al. (2008a), using near-infrared spectroscopy, have found that the newborn brain is able to extract identical, adjacent repetitions of syllables from speech stimuli. The repetitions were detected as some kind of perceptual Gestalt or primitive by the left (and to a lesser extent by the right) temporal areas immediately upon exposure. Over the course of the study, the repeated exposure to dozens of different stimuli, all instantiating the same underlying regularity (AAB: "mubaba," "penana," etc.), also gave rise to an increased response in the left frontal areas, suggesting the general pattern has been learned or extracted from the stimuli. This connection between the temporal areas, responsible for auditory processing, and the frontal areas, involved in higher-level learning and memory, has also been documented in a series of studies by Dehaene-Lambertz and her collaborators (Dehaene-Lambertz & Baillet 1998; Dehaene-Lambertz & Gliga 2004; Dehaene-Lambertz et al. 2006, 2008). These authors used activation speed to identify a circuit of areas, from the primary auditory cortex through the superior temporal gyrus to the inferior frontal area, which respond to speech in a hierarchical, cascading fashion, possibly integrating over increasingly large and/or abstract linguistic units.

These results indicate that brain organization shows structural and functional specialization for language from the start. This is not to say, though, that language experience has no role to play. We demonstrated above how language experience shapes phonological and morphosyntactic development during the first year of life when measured behaviorally. In the past decade, numerous studies emerged documenting the underlying neural changes (for a recent review, see Kuhl & Rivera-Gaxiola 2008). For instance, Kuhl et al. (2008) found that at 7.5 months, better discrimination abilities for native phonemes, measured using electrophysiological techniques, correlate with the rate of later language development. This finding suggests that behavioral attunement to the native language is mediated by brain structures that become specifically responsive to frequently encountered, i.e., native, linguistic contrasts, which in turn promotes further learning of linguistic distinctions relevant for the native language and suppresses sensitivity to nonnative contrasts. Word learning also shows electrophysiological signatures at an early age. Familiar words evoke responses that are different in amplitude as well as in scalp distribution measurements from responses to unfamiliar words from about 9 months of age (Molfese 1990, Vihman et al. 2007).

Most of these studies were carried out with infants exposed to just one language. In many linguistic communities, though, exposure to multiple languages is the norm. An increasing body of research is now attempting to understand how such an environment affects phonological discrimination and categorization (Bosch & Sebastián-Gallés 1997, Conboy & Mills 2006, Mehler et al. 2004, Weikum et al. 2007, Werker & Byers-Heinlein 2008).

Interestingly, exposure to two languages from birth seems to affect development in other cognitive domains as well. In a series of experiments, Kovács & Mehler (2009a,b) have explored why bilingually raised children, having to learn twice as much about language as their monolingual peers, display a speed of acquisition comparable to that of monolingual infants. In the first study, Kovács & Mehler (2009a) compared 7-month-old monolingual and bilingual groups in an eye-tracker task, where they had to learn to anticipate where a puppet would appear on the screen immediately after a trisyllabic word was heard. Both groups performed equally well in this task. During the second phase of the experiment, immediately after the first phase, both groups had to learn that the puppet appeared on the opposite side of the screen. Bilinguals learned this second task as fast as the first one, whereas monolinguals' performance was at chance. The authors concluded that continuous exposure to two languages during early infancy enhances the executive functions, attesting that the plasticity of certain brain regions prevents infants from potential confusion. In a second experiment with 12-month-olds, the same authors showed that when two structures, namely AAB and ABA, were used to cue infants to look to one side of the screen upon exposure to AAB and to the other side when ABA was heard (the presentation was interleaved), monolinguals learned to respond to the simpler structure AAB and were at chance for the other structure, whereas bilinguals learned both structures. The authors concluded, "The advantage of bilinguals may be related to the precocious development of control and selection abilities... This in turn may help them to learn more efficiently each of their languages. Such powerful learning abilities allow bilinguals to pass the linguistic milestones at the same rate as monolinguals" (Kovács & Mehler 2009b).

CONCLUSION

In this review, we presented theoretical approaches and underlying mechanisms proposed to explain infants' first steps into language. We have reviewed evidence suggesting that nativist and empiricist proposals are incomplete if they fail to include innate dispositions and learning in a broader, integrative, biologically anchored language acquisition theory. In addition, we have shown that a third type of mechanism, perceptual and memory constraints, needs to be evoked to provide a full account of early acquisition.

This integrative stance proposes that the three mechanisms are triggered by different properties of the input. For instance, statistical computations are evoked when the learner encounters an unsegmented speech stream. These computations selectively target some linguistic units, e.g., consonants, but not others, e.g., vowels. However, if the speech stream is already segmented, rule extraction and generalization mechanisms are used. In sum, the three processing and learning mechanisms complement as well as constrain each other.

Such an interaction of complementary mechanisms is not surprising from a biological point of view. Indeed, from an evolutionary perspective, the recruitment of a mechanism for a novel function is frequently observed (Jacob 1977). Therefore, it is plausible to assume that several of the mechanisms underlying our linguistic abilities are shared with other species. However, it remains true that only humans have language. Therefore, the quest is still on to identify the specific set of abilities that has emerged during our unique evolutionary history.

We have attempted to illustrate above how research into cognitive abilities and brain organization in young infants, in conjunction with information about the precursors that we share with other organisms, may shed light on the specifically human abilities that make us a language-learning animal.

DISCLOSURE STATEMENT

The authors are not aware of any biases that might be perceived as affecting the objectivity of this review.

LITERATURE CITED

Abercrombie D. 1967. *Elements of General Phonetics*. Edinburgh: Edinburgh Univ. Press

Abramson AS, Lisker L. 1970. Discriminability along the voicing continuum: cross-language tests. In *Proceedings of the Sixth International Congress of Phonetic Sciences*. Prague: Academia

Bahlmann J, Gunter TC, Friederici AD. 2006. Hierarchical and linear sequence processing: an electrophysiological exploration of two different grammar types. *J. Cogn. Neurosci.* 18(11):1829–42

Best CT, McRoberts GW. 2003. Infant perception of non-native consonant contrasts that adults assimilate in different ways. *Lang. Speech* 46(2):183–216

Bonatti LL, Pena M, Nespor M, Mehler J. 2005. Linguistic constraints on statistical computations: the role of consonants and vowels in continuous speech processing. *Psychol. Sci.* 16(6):451–59

Bortfeld H, Fava E, Boas DA. 2009. Identifying cortical lateralization of speech processing in infants using near-infrared spectroscopy. *Dev. Neuropsychol.* 34(1):52–65

Bosch L, Sebastián-Gallés N. 1997. Native-language recognition abilities in 4-month-old infants from monolingual and bilingual environments. *Cognition* 65(1):33–69

Bosch L, Sebastián-Gallés N. 2001. Early language differentiation in bilingual infants. In *Trends in Bilingual Acquisition*, ed. J Cenoz, F Genesee, pp. 71–93. Amsterdam: Benjamins

Brown RW. 1973. *A First Language: The Early Stages*. Cambridge, MA: Harvard Univ. Press

Chomsky N. 1957. *Syntactic Structures*. The Hague: Mouton

Chomsky N. 1959. A review of B.F. Skinner's verbal behavior. *Language* 35(1):26–58

Christophe A, Dupoux E, Bertoncini J, Mehler J. 1994. Do infants perceive word boundaries? An empirical study of the bootstrapping of lexical acquisition. *J. Acoust. Soc. Am.* 95(3):1570–80

Church KW. 1987. Phonological parsing and lexical retrieval. *Cognition* 25:53–69

Conboy BT, Mills DL. 2006. Two languages, one developing brain: event-related potentials to words in bilingual toddlers. *Dev. Sci.* 9(1):F1–12

Csibra G, Gergely G. 2009. Natural pedagogy. *Trends Cogn. Sci.* 13(4):148–53

Curtin S, Fennell CT, Escudero P. 2009. Weighting of acoustic cues explains patterns of word-object associative learning. *Dev. Sci.* 12(5):725–31

Curtin S, Mintz TH, Byrd D. 2001. Coarticulatory cues enhance infants' recognition of syllable sequences in speech. *Proc. 25th Annu. Boston Univ. Conf. Lang. Dev.*, pp. 190–201. Somerville, MA: Cascadilla Press

Cutler A. 1994. Segmentation problems, rhythmic solutions. *Lingua* 92:81–104

Cutler A, Carter DM. 1987. The predominance of strong initial syllables in the English vocabulary. *Comput. Speech Lang.* 2:133–42

Dauer RM. 1983. Stress-timing and syllable-timing reanalyzed. *J. Phonetics* 11:51–62

Davis SM, Kelly MH. 1997. Knowledge of the English noun-verb stress difference by native and nonnative speakers. *J. Mem. Lang.* 36(3):445–60

Dehaene-Lambertz G, Baillet S. 1998. A phonological representation in the infant brain. *Neuroreport* 9(8):1885–88

Dehaene-Lambertz G, Dehaene S. 1994. Speed and cerebral correlates of syllable discrimination in infants. *Nature* 370(6487):292–95

Dehaene-Lambertz G, Dehaene S, Hertz-Pannier L. 2002. Functional neuroimaging of speech perception in infants. *Science* 298(5600):2013–15

Dehaene-Lambertz G, Gliga T. 2004. Common neural basis for phoneme processing in infants and adults. *J. Cogn. Neurosci.* 16:1375–87

Dehaene-Lambertz G, Hertz-Pannier L, Dubois J, Dehaene S. 2008. How does early brain organization promote language acquisition in humans? *Eur. Rev.* 16(4):399–411

Dehaene-Lambertz G, Hertz-Pannier L, Dubois J, Meriaux S, Roche A, et al. 2006. Functional organization of perisylvian activation during presentation of sentences in preverbal infants. *Proc. Natl. Acad. Sci. USA* 103(38):14240–45

Dubois J, Hertz-Pannier L, Cachia A, Mangin J, Le Bihan D, Dehaene-Lambertz G. 2008. Structural asymmetries in the infant language and sensori-motor networks. *Cereb. Cortex* 19:414–23

Eimas PD, Siqueland ER, Jusczyk PW, Vigorito J. 1971. Speech perception in infants. *Science* 171(968):303–6

Elman JL, Bates EA, Johnson MH, Karmiloff-Smith A, Parisi D, Plunkett K. 1996. *Rethinking Innateness: A Connectionist Perspective on Development*. Cambridge, MA: MIT Press

Endress AD, Dehaene-Lambertz G, Mehler J. 2007. Perceptual constraints and the learnability of simple grammars. *Cognition* 105(3):577–614

Endress AD, Mehler J. 2009. The surprising power of statistical learning: when fragment knowledge leads to false memories of unheard words. *J. Mem. Lang.* 60(3):351–67

Endress AD, Nespor M, Mehler J. 2009. Perceptual and memory constraints on language acquisition. *Trends Cogn. Sci.* In press

Endress AD, Scholl BJ, Mehler J. 2005. The role of salience in the extraction of algebraic rules. *J. Exp. Psychol.: Gen.* 134(3):406–19

Feher O, et al. 2009. De novo establishment of wild-type song culture in the zebra finch. *Nature* 459(28):564–68

Fenk-Oczlon G, Fenk A. 2005. Crosslinguistic correlations between size of syllables, number of cases, and adposition order. In *Sprache und Natürlichkeit, Gedenkband für Willi Mazerthaler*, ed. G Fenk-Oczlon, C Winkler, pp. 350–57. Tübingen: Narr

Fennell CT, Werker JF. 2003. Early word learners' ability to access phonetic detail in well-known words. *Lang. Speech* 46(2):245–64

Fennell CT, Werker JF. 2004. Infant attention to phonetic detail: knowledge and familiarity effects. *Proc. 28th Annu. Boston Univ. Conf. Lang. Dev.*, pp. 165–76. Boston, MA

Fiser J, Aslin RN. 2002a. Statistical learning of higher-order temporal structure from visual shape sequences. *J. Exp. Psychol.: Learn. Mem. Cogn.* 28(3):458–67

Fiser J, Aslin RN. 2002b. Statistical learning of new visual feature combinations by infants. *Proc. Natl. Acad. Sci. USA* 99(24):15822–26

Fitch WT, Hauser MD. 2004. Computational constraints on syntactic processing in a nonhuman primate. *Science* 303(5656):377–80

Fitch WT, Hauser MD, Chomsky N. 2005. The evolution of the language faculty: clarifications and implications. *Cognition* 97(2):179–210; discussion 211–25

Friederici AD, Bahlmann J, Heim S, Schubotz RI, Anwander A. 2006. The brain differentiates human and non-human grammars: functional localization and structural connectivity. *Proc. Natl. Acad. Sci. USA* 103(7):2458–63

Gallese V, Fadiga L, Fogassi L, Rizzolatti G. 1996. Action recognition in the premotor cortex. *Brain* 119:593–609

Gardner TJ, Naef F, Nottebohm F. 2005. Freedom and rules: the acquisition and reprogramming of a bird's learned song. *Science* 308(5724):1046–49

Gentner TQ, Hulse SH, Bentley GE, Ball GF. 2000. Individual vocal recognition and the effect of partial lesions to HVc on discrimination, learning, and categorization of conspecific song in adult songbirds. *J. Neurobiol.* 42(1):117–33

Gentner TQ, Fenn KM, Margoliash D, Nusbaum HC. 2006. Recursive syntactic pattern learning by songbirds. *Nature* 440(7088):1204–7

Gergely G, Csibra G. 2003. Teleological reasoning in infancy: the naive theory of rational action. *Trends Cogn. Sci.* 7(7):287–92

Gerken L, Landau B, Remez R. 1990. Function morphemes in young children's speech perception and production. *Dev. Psychol.* 26:204–16

Gerken L, McIntosh B. 1993. Interplay of function morphemes and prosody in early language. *Dev. Psychol.* 29(3):448–57

Gervain J, Macagno F, Cogoi S, Pena M, Mehler J. 2008a. The neonate brain detects speech structure. *Proc. Natl. Acad. Sci. USA* 105(37):14222–27

Gervain J, Nespor M, Mazuka R, Horie R, Mehler J. 2008b. Bootstrapping word order in prelexical infants: a Japanese-Italian cross-linguistic study. *Cogn. Psychol.* 57:56–74

Gleitman LR, Landau B. 1994. *The Acquisition of the Lexicon*. Cambridge, MA: MIT Press

Gopnik M, Crago MB. 1991. Familial aggregation of a developmental language disorder. *Cognition* 39:1–50

Grabe E, Low EL. 2002. Durational variability in speech and the rhythm class hypothesis. In *Papers in Laboratory Phonology*, ed. C Gussenhoven, N Warner, pp. 515–46. Berlin: Mouton de Gruyter

Guasti MT. 2002. *Language Acquisition: The Growth of Grammar*. Cambridge, MA: MIT Press

Haesler S, Rochefort C, Georgi B, Licznerski P, Osten P, Scharff C. 2007. Incomplete and inaccurate vocal imitation after knockdown of FoxP2 in songbird basal ganglia nucleus area X. *PLoS Biol.* 5(12):2885–97

Harris Z. 1955. From phoneme to morpheme. *Language* 31:190–222

Hauser MD, Chomsky NA, Fitch WT. 2002. The faculty of language: What is it, who has it, and how did it evolve? *Science* 298(5598):1569–79

Hauser MD, Newport EL, Aslin RN. 2001. Segmentation of the speech stream in a non-human primate: statistical learning in cotton-top tamarins. *Cognition* 78(3):B53–64

Hay JS, Diehl RL. 2007. Perception of rhythmic grouping: testing the iambic/trochaic law. *Percept. Psychophys.* 69(1):113–22

Hayes B. 1995. *Metrical Stress Theory: Principles and Case Studies*. Chicago: Univ. Chicago Press

Hayes JR, Clark HH. 1970. Experiments in the segmentation of an artificial speech analogue. In *Cognition and the Development of Language*, ed. JR Hayes, pp. 221–34. New York: Wiley

Hochmann J-R, Azadpour M, Mehler. 2008. Do humans really learn AnBn artificial grammars from exemplars? *Cogn. Sci.* 32:1021–36

Höhle B, Weissenborn J. 2003. German-learning infants' ability to detect unstressed closed-class elements in continuous speech. *Dev. Sci.* 6(2):122–27

Homae F, Watanabe H, Nakano T, Asakawa K, Taga G. 2006. The right hemisphere of sleeping infant perceives sentential prosody. *Neurosci. Res.* 54(4):276–80

Homae F, Watanabe H, Nakano T, Taga G. 2007. Prosodic processing in the developing brain. *Neurosci. Res.* 59(1):29–39

Iversen JR, Patel AD, Ohgushi K. 2008. Perception of rhythmic grouping depends on auditory experience. *J. Acoust. Soc. Am.* 124(4):2263–71

Jacob F. 1977. Evolution and tinkering. *Science* 196(4295):1161–66

James AL. 1940. *Speech Signals in Telephony*. London: Sir Isaac Pitman & Sons

Johnson EK, Jusczyk PW. 2001. Word segmentation by 8-month-olds: when speech cues count more than statistics. *J. Mem. Lang.* 44(4):548–67

Jusczyk PW, Hohne EA, Bauman A. 1999. Infants' sensitivity to allophonic cues to word segmentation. *Percept. Psychophys.* 61:1465–76

Jusczyk PW, Houston DM, Newsome MR. 1999. The beginnings of word segmentation in English-learning infants. *Cogn. Psychol.* 39(3):159–207

Knops A, Thirion B, Hubbard EM, Michel V, Dehaene S. 2009. Recruitment of an area involved in eye movements during mental arithmetic. *Science* 324(5934):1583–85

Kovács AM, Mehler J. 2009a. Cognitive gains in 7-month-old bilingual infants. *Proc. Natl. Acad. Sci. USA* 106(16):6556–60

Kovács AM, Mehler J. 2009b. Flexible learning of multiple speech structures in bilingual infants. *Science*. In press

Kučera H, Francis WN. 1967. *Computational Analysis of Present-Day American English*. Providence, RI: Brown Univ. Press

Kudo N, Nonaka Y, Mizuno K, Okanoya K. 2006. *Statistical learning and word segmentation in neonates: an ERP evidence*. Presented at Annu. Meet. XVth Bienn. Int. Conf. Infant Studies, Kyoto, Japan

Kuhl PK. 2004. Early language acquisition: cracking the speech code. *Nat. Rev. Neurosci.* 5(11):831–43

Kuhl PK, Conboy BT, Coffey-Corina S, Padden D, Rivera-Gaxiola M, Nelson T. 2008. Phonetic learning as a pathway to language: new data and native language magnet theory expanded (NLM-e). *Philos. Trans. R. Soc. Lond. B Biol. Sci.* 363(1493):979–1000

Kuhl PK, Rivera-Gaxiola M. 2008. Neural substrates of language acquisition. *Annu. Rev. Neurosci.* 31:511–34

Kuhl PK, Stevens E, Hayashi A, Deguchi T, Kiritani S, Iverson P. 2006. Infants show a facilitation effect for native language phonetic perception between 6 and 12 months. *Dev. Sci.* 9(2):F13–21

Ladefoged P. 1993. *A Course in Phonetics*. New York: Harcourt Brace Jovanovich

Lenneberg EH. 1967. *The Biological Foundations of Language*. New York: Wiley

Liberman AM, Cooper FS, Shankweiler DP, Studdert-Kennedy M. 1967. Perception of the speech code. *Psychol. Rev.* 74(6):431–61

Liberman AM, Harris KS, Hoffman HS, Griffith BC. 1957. The discrimination of speech sounds within and across phoneme boundaries. *J. Exp. Psychol.* 54:358–68

Marcus GF, Vijayan S, Rao SB, Vishton PM. 1999. Rule learning by seven-month-old infants. *Science* 283(5398):77–80

Marler P, Peters S. 1981. Sparrows learn adult song and more from memory. *Science* 213:780–82

Mattys SL, Jusczyk PW. 2001a. Do infants segment words or recurring contiguous patterns? *J. Exp. Psychol.: Hum. Percept. Perform.* 27(3):644–55

Mattys SL, Jusczyk PW. 2001b. Phonotactic cues for segmentation of fluent speech by infants. *Cognition* 78(2):91–121

Mattys SL, Jusczyk PW, Luce PA, Morgan JL. 1999. Phonotactic and prosodic effects on word segmentation in infants. *Cogn. Psychol.* 38(4):465–94

Maye J, Werker JF, Gerken L. 2002. Infant sensitivity to distributional information can affect phonetic discrimination. *Cognition* 82(3):B101–111

Mehler J. 1974. Apprendre par désapprendre. In *L'Unité de l'homme: essais et discussions*, ed. E Morin, M Piatelli-Palmarini, pp. 187–319. Paris: Éditions du Seuil

Mehler J, Bertoncini J, Barriere M, Gerschenfeld DJ. 1978. Infant recognition of mother's voice. *Perception* 7:491–97

Mehler J, Dupoux E. 1994. *What Infants Know: The New Cognitive Science of Early Development*. Cambridge, MA: Blackwell

Mehler J, Jusczyk PW, Lambertz G, Halsted N, Bertoncini J, Amiel-Tison C. 1988. A precursor of language acquisition in young infants. *Cognition* 29:143–78

Mehler J, Sebástian-Gallés N, Nespor M. 2004. Biological foundations of language: language acquisition, cues for parameter setting and the bilingual infant. In *The New Cognitive Neuroscience*, ed. M Gazzaniga, pp. 825–36. Cambridge, MA: MIT Press. 3rd ed.

Miller JE, et al. 2008. Birdsong decreases protein levels of FoxP2, a molecule required for human speech. *J. Neurophysiol.* 100(4):2015–25

Mintz TH. 2002. Category induction from distributional cues in an artificial language. *Mem. Cogn.* 30(5):678–86

Molfese DL. 1990. Auditory evoked responses recorded from 16-month-old human infants to words they did and did not know. *Brain Lang.* 38(3):345–63

Moon C, Cooper RP, Fifer WP. 1993. Two-day-olds prefer their native language. *Infant Behav. Dev.* 16(4):495–500

Morgan JL, Demuth K. 1996. *Signal to Syntax: Bootstrapping from Speech to Grammar in Early Acquisition.* Hillsdale, NJ: Erlbaum

Morgan JL, Shi R, Allopenna P. 1996. Perceptual bases of rudimentary grammatical categories: toward a broader conceptualization of bootstrapping. In *Signal to Syntax*, ed. JL Morgan, K Demuth, pp. 263–83. Hillsdale, NJ: Erlbaum

Morse PA, Molfese D, Laughlin NK, Linnville S, Wetzel F. 1987. Categorical perception for voicing contrasts in normal and lead-treated rhesus monkeys: electrophysiological indices. *Brain Lang.* 30(1):63–80

Nazzi T, Bertoncini J. 2003. Before and after the vocabulary spurt: two modes of word acquisition? *Dev. Sci.* 6(2):136–42

Nazzi T, Bertoncini J, Mehler J. 1998. Language discrimination by newborns: toward an understanding of the role of rhythm. *J. Exp. Psychol.: Hum. Percept. Perform.* 24(3):756–66

Nespor M. 1990. On the rhythm parameter in phonology. In *Logical Issues in Language Acquisition*, ed. I Roca, pp. 157–75. Dordrecht: Foris

Nespor M, Guasti MT, Christophe A. 1996. Selecting word order: the rhythmic activation principle. In *Interfaces in Phonology*, ed. U Kleinhenz, pp. 1–26. Berlin: Akademie Verlag

Nespor M, Pena M, Mehler J. 2003. On the different roles of vowels and consonants in speech processing and language acquisition. *Lingue e Linguaggio* 2:203–31

Nespor M, Shukla M, van de Vijver R, Avesani C, Schraudolf H, Donati C. 2008. Different phrasal prominence realization in VO and OV languages. *Lingue e Linguaggio* 7(2):1–28

Newport EL, Aslin RN. 2004. Learning at a distance I. Statistical learning of non-adjacent dependencies. *Cogn. Psychol.* 48(2):127–62

Newport EL, Hauser MD, Spaepen G, Aslin RN. 2004. Learning at a distance II. Statistical learning of non-adjacent dependencies in a non-human primate. *Cogn. Psychol.* 49(2):85–117

Onishi KH, Baillargeon R. 2005. Do 15-month-old infants understand false beliefs? *Science* 308(5719):255–58

Pena M, Bonatti LL, Nespor M, Mehler J. 2002. Signal-driven computations in speech processing. *Science* 298(5593):604–7

Pena M, Maki A, Kovacic D, Dehaene-Lambertz G, Koizumi H, et al. 2003. Sounds and silence: an optical topography study of language recognition at birth. *Proc. Natl. Acad. Sci. USA* 100(20):11702–5

Perruchet P, Rey A. 2005. Does the mastery of center-embedded linguistic structures distinguish humans from nonhuman primates? *Psychon. Bull. Rev.* 12(2):30713

Pike KL. 1945. *The Intonation of American English.* Ann Arbor: Univ. Mich. Press

Pinker S. 1984. *Language Learnability and Language Development.* Cambridge, MA: Harvard Univ. Press

Pinker S, Jackendoff R. 2005. The faculty of language: What's special about it? *Cognition* 95(2):201–36

Prather JF, Nowicki S, Anderson RC, Peters S, Mooney R. 2009. Neural correlates of categorical perception in learned vocal communication. *Nat. Neurosci.* 12(2):221–28

Prather JF, Peters S, Nowicki S, Mooney R. 2008. Precise auditory-vocal mirroring in neurons for learned vocal communication. *Nature* 451:305–10

Quine WV. 1960. *Word and Object.* Cambridge, MA: MIT Press

Ramon-Casas M, Swingley D, Sebástian-Gallés N, Bosch L. 2009. Vowel categorization during word recognition in bilingual toddlers. *Cogn. Psychol.* 59(1):96–121

Ramus F. 2002. Acoustic correlates of linguistic rhythm: perspectives. In *Proceedings of Speech Prosody 2002*, ed. B Bel, I Marlien, pp. 115–20. Aix-en-Provence, France

Ramus F, Hauser MD, Miller C, Morris D, Mehler J. 2000. Language discrimination by human newborns and by cotton-top tamarin monkeys. *Science* 288(5464):349–51

Ramus F, Mehler J. 1999. Language identification with suprasegmental cues: study based on speech resynthesis. *J. Acoust. Soc. Am.* 105(1):512–21

Ramus F, Nespor M, Mehler J. 1999. Correlates of linguistic rhythm in the speech signal. *Cognition* 73(3):265–92

Redington M, Chater N, Finch S. 1998. Distributional information: a powerful cue for acquiring syntactic categories. *Cogn. Sci.* 22(4):425–69

Rizzolatti G, Fogassi L, Gallese V. 2001. Neurophysiological mechanisms underlying the understanding and imitation of action. *Nat. Rev. Neurosci.* 2(9):661–70

Saffran JR, Aslin RN, Newport EL. 1996. Statistical learning by 8-month-old infants. *Science* 274(5294):1926–28

Saffran JR, Hauser M, Seibel R, Kapfhamer J, Tsao F, Cushman F. 2008. Grammatical pattern learning by human infants and cotton-top tamarin monkeys. *Cognition* 107(2):479–500

Saffran JR, Thiessen ED. 2003. Pattern induction by infant language learners. *Dev. Psychol.* 39(3):484–94

Sansavini A, Bertoncini J, Giovanelli G. 1997. Newborns discriminate the rhythm of multisyllabic stressed words. *Dev. Psychol.* 33(1):3–11

Scott LS, Pascalis O, Nelson CA. 2007. A domain-general theory of the development of perceptual discrimination. *Curr. Dir. Psychol. Sci.* 16(4):197–201

Senghas A, Kita S, Özyürek A. 2004. Children creating core properties of language: evidence from an emerging sign language in Nicaragua. *Science* 305(5691):1779–82

Shannon CE. 1948. A mathematical theory of communication. *Bell Syst. Tech. J.* 27:379–423, 623–56

Shi R, Cutler A, Werker J, Cruickshank M. 2006. Frequency and form as determinants of functor sensitivity in English-acquiring infants. *J. Acoust. Soc. Am.* 119(6):EL61–67

Shi R, Werker JF. 2001. Six-month-old infants' preference for lexical words. *Psychol. Sci.* 12(1):71–76

Shi R, Werker JF, Morgan JL. 1999. Newborn infants' sensitivity to perceptual cues to lexical and grammatical words. *Cognition* 72(2):B11–21

Shipley EF, Smith CS, Gleitman LR. 1969. A study in the acquisition of language: free responses to commands. *Language* 45:322–42

Shukla M, Nespor M, Mehler J. 2007. An interaction between prosody and statistics in the segmentation of fluent speech. *Cogn. Psychol.* 54(1):1–32

Slobin DI. 1997. *The Crosslinguistic Study of Language Acquisition.* Hillsdale, NJ: Erlbaum

Stager CL, Werker JF. 1997. Infants listen for more phonetic detail in speech perception than in word-learning tasks. *Nature* 388(6640):381–82

Swingley D. 2005. Statistical clustering and the contents of the infant vocabulary. *Cogn. Psychol.* 50(1):86–132

Swingley D. 2009. Contributions of infant word learning to language development. *Philos. Trans. Royal Soc. B.* In press

Taga G, Asakawa K. 2007. Selectivity and localization of cortical response to auditory and visual stimulation in awake infants aged 2 to 4 months. *NeuroImage* 36(4):1246–52

Teinonen T, Fellman V, Naatanen R, Alku P, Huotilainen M. 2009. Statistical language learning in neonates revealed by event-related brain potentials. *BMC Neurosci.* 10:21

Thiessen ED. 2007. The effect of distributional information on children's use of phonemic contrasts. *J. Mem. Lang.* 56(1):16–34

Tomasello M. 2000. Do young children have adult syntactic competence? *Cognition* 74(3):209–53

Toro JM, Nespor M, Mehler J, Bonatti LL. 2008. Finding words and rules in a speech stream: functional differences between vowels and consonants. *Psychol. Sci* 19(2):137–44

Toro JM, Trobalon JB. 2005. Statistical computations over a speech stream in a rodent. *Percept. Psychophys.* 67(5):867–75

Vihman MM, Thierry G, Lum J, Keren-Portnoy T, Martin P. 2007. Onset of word form recognition in English, Welsh, and English-Welsh bilingual infants. *Appl. Psycholinguistics* 28(3):475–93

Vouloumanos A, Werker JF. 2004. Tuned to the signal: the privileged status of speech for young infants. *Dev. Sci.* 7(3):270

Vouloumanos A, Werker JF. 2007. Listening to language at birth: evidence for a bias for speech in neonates. *Dev. Sci.* 10(2):159–64

Waxman SR, Gelman SA. 2009. Early word-learning entails reference, not merely associations. *Trends Cogn. Sci.* 13(6):258–63

Weikum WM, Vouloumanos A, Navarra J, Soto-Faraco S, Sebastián-Gallés N, Werker JF. 2007. Visual language discrimination in infancy. *Science* 316(5828):1159

Weissenborn J, Höhle B, Kiefer D, Cavar D. 1996. Children's sensitivity to word-order violations in german: evidence for very early parameter-setting. *Proc. 22nd Annu. Boston Univ. Conf. Lang. Dev*, pp. 756–77. Boston, MA

Werker JF, Byers-Heinlein K. 2008. Bilingualism in infancy: first steps in perception and comprehension. *Trends Cogn. Sci.* 12(4):144–51

Werker JF, Tees RC. 1984a. Cross-language speech perception: evidence for perceptual reorganization during the first year of life. *Infant Behav. Dev.* 7(1):49–63

Werker JF, Tees RC. 1984b. Phonemic and phonetic factors in adult cross-language speech perception. *J. Acoust. Soc. Am.* 75(6):1866–78

Yang CD. 2004. Universal grammar, statistics or both? *Trends Cogn. Sci.* 8(10):451–56

Yang C, Gambell T. 2004. Statistics learning and universal grammar: modeling word segmentation. In *COLING 2004: Psycho-Computational Models of Human Language Acquisition*, pp. 51–54. Geneva, Switzerland

Yip MJ. 2006. The search for phonology in other species. *Trends Cogn. Sci.* 10(10):442–46

Yoshida KA, Fennell CT, Swingley D, Werker JF. 2009. Fourteen-month-old infants learn similar sounding words. *Dev. Sci.* 12(3):412–18

Yoshida KA, Iversen JR, Patel AD, Mazuka R, Nito H, et al. 2009. The development of perceptual grouping biases in infancy. *Cognition*. Manuscript under revision

An Odor is Not Worth a Thousand Words: From Multidimensional Odors to Unidimensional Odor Objects

Yaara Yeshurun and Noam Sobel

Department of Neurobiology, The Weizmann Institute of Science, Rehovot, 76100, Israel;
email: yaara.yeshurun@weizmann.ac.il; noam.sobel@weizmann.ac.il

Annu. Rev. Psychol. 2010. 61:219–41

First published online as a Review in Advance on
October 19, 2009

The *Annual Review of Psychology* is online at
psych.annualreviews.org

This article's doi:
10.1146/annurev.psych.60.110707.163639

0066-4308/10/0110-0219$20.00

Key Words

olfaction, coding, pleasantness, verbal, perception

Abstract

Olfaction is often referred to as a multidimensional sense. It is multidimensional in that ~1000 different receptor types, each tuned to particular odor aspects, together contribute to the olfactory percept. In humans, however, this percept is nearly unidimensional. Humans can detect and discriminate countless odorants, but can identify few by name. The one thing humans can and do invariably say about an odor is whether it is pleasant or not. We argue that this hedonic determination is the key function of olfaction. Thus, the boundaries of an odor object are determined by its pleasantness, which—unlike something material and more like an emotion—remains poorly delineated with words.

Contents

THE MECHANISMS OF SMELL

In this article, we first briefly review the mechanisms and neural substrates that together underlie the perception of smell. Because we make a claim on the human psychology of smell, we detail evidence obtained from humans rather than from other animals wherever possible. We review several lines of evidence that together bring us to suggest a novel definition for odor objects. We propose that odor objects, unlike visual objects, reflect a combination of molecules in the external world combined with an internal state of emotion and homeostasis that together generate a given pleasantness that is itself the odor object.

OLFACTION STARTS WITH A SNIFF

Sniffs are not inconsequential to the eventual olfactory percept (Kepecs et al. 2006, Mainland & Sobel 2006, Schoenfeld & Cleland 2006) that they influence in at least two ways. First, sniffs influence the quantity and quality of the molecules perceived. How sniffs influence odor quantity is plainly evident: The more vigorous the sniff, the more odor molecules are delivered to the olfactory system. Consistent with this, and similar to other senses subserved by a sensory-motor apparatus, an olfactomotor system can modify sniffs within ~160 ms of odorant onset (Johnson et al. 2003) in order to optimize detection threshold (Sobel et al. 2000) and maintain olfactory constancy (Teghtsoonian & Teghtsoonian 1984). In turn, the way in which sniffs influence odor quality is more complicated: Odorant molecules can differ in their sorption, namely their tendency to cross the olfactory mucosa (Mozell & Jagodowicz 1973). Furthermore, sorption interacts with sniff airflow rate to produce varying patterns of activity across the olfactory mucosa (Kent et al. 1996). In simple terms, this is because higher rates of airflow will favor high sorption, and lower airflow will favor low sorption (Mozell et al. 1991). Thus, a given sniff airflow rate will optimize perception for particular odorants as a reflection of their sorption. Furthermore, because mammals have a different rate of airflow in each nostril during a given sniff (Gilbert & Rosenwasser 1987, Principato & Ozenberger 1970), each nostril is therefore optimized for slightly different odorants. In other words, a typical mammalian sniff provides the brain with two simultaneous slightly offset images of the olfactory world (Sobel et al. 1999).

In addition to influencing the quantity and quality of the molecules perceived, the second influence of sniffs on olfaction is through driving neural activity patterns throughout the olfactory system. This is evident in clean-air sniff-induced activity at the olfactory epithelium (Grosmaitre et al. 2007), bulb (Adrian 1942), and cortex (Sobel et al. 1998, Zelano et al. 2005). The exact manner by which sniff-induced neural activity influences the eventual olfactory percept remains unclear. Finally, considering the importance of sniffing, it is noteworthy that much of our notion on function within the olfactory system was obtained through experiments in anesthetized rodents that were not sniffing. In our view, this may have significantly affected our notion of processing in this system.

Once an odor is sniffed, it is processed within an olfactory neuroanatomy that has been remarkably conserved in mammals (Ache & Young 2005) and consists of three primary processing stages: epithelium, bulb, and cortex.

OLFACTORY EPITHELIUM

Transduction of an odorant molecule starts with its transport to the olfactory epithelium by sniffing. In humans, the epithelia are located bilaterally ~7 cm up the nasal passage, lining the cribriform plate and extending to the nasal turbinates (Clerico et al. 2003). Here the odorant molecules cross a mucous membrane through a process that combines passive diffusion and possibly active transport (Pelosi 2001, Pevsner et al. 1985) in order to then bind with transmembrane G-protein-coupled olfactory receptors at the ciliated end of olfactory receptor neurons (Nakamura & Gold 1987, Pace et al. 1985). The mammalian olfactory receptor repertoire contains ~1000 different receptor types (Buck & Axel 1991). Each olfactory receptor neuron expresses only one (Chess et al. 1994, Nef et al. 1992, Ressler et al. 1993, Strotmann et al. 1992, Vassar et al. 1993) or two (Goldman et al. 2005) of these receptor types, and the ~1000 types are distributed at unknown proportions across millions of olfactory receptor neurons. Genetic analysis has suggested that humans functionally express ~350 of these receptor types (Glusman et al. 2001), within ~12 million olfactory receptor neurons (Moran et al. 1982). It is currently held that each receptor type can bind with a number of different odorants, and each odorant can bind with a number of different receptor types, thus generating a potentially massive combinatorial space for coding smell (Breer 2003, Firestein 2001). The bipolar sensory neurons, which continuously regenerate throughout the life span (Graziadei et al. 1979, Graziadei & Monti Graziadei 1983), can be considered "transition neurons" between the peripheral nervous system and central nervous system (Doucette 1991). They send one dendrite-like process to the olfactory epithelium, and the other axon-like process joins the olfactory nerve bundle (cranial nerve I) to cross through the cribriform plate and synapse at specialized neuropoil termed "glomeruli" on the surface of the ipsilateral olfactory bulb (**Figure 1**; see color insert). The epithelium is obviously a key structure in olfaction, and damage to the human epithelium can lead to anosmia (a complete loss of smell) (Dalton 2004, Doty & Mishra 2001).

OLFACTORY BULB

The path from epithelium to bulb entails a striking case of neural convergence whereby all neurons expressing the same type of receptor converge to one of two mirror-glomeruli in the olfactory bulb (Mombaerts et al. 1996, Ressler et al. 1994, Tsuboi et al. 1999, Vassar et al. 1994). The result of this connectivity, whereby each glomerulus now "represents" one receptor type, is a stereotyped map where odor identity can be represented in the spatiotemporal patterns of glomerular activation (Cleland et al. 2007, Leon & Johnson 2003). Within the glomeruli, the receptor axons contact dendrites of either mitral or tufted output neurons and periglomerular interneurons. The mitral and tufted cell axons join to form the lateral olfactory tract that is the output from the bulb to the ipsilateral primary olfactory cortex in the ventral portions of the temporal lobe (**Figure 1**). Consistent with its key role in formation of the olfactory percept, the olfactory bulb receives more afferents from cortex than efferents to cortex (Kay & Freeman 1998). This suggests the olfactory bulb as a candidate site for much of the extensive contextual influences on olfactory perception (Kay & Freeman 1998), a major topic that is discussed later in this review. Finally, considering the prominent position of the olfactory bulb in the stream of olfactory processing, a series of studies that found only minimal olfactory impairments following extensive olfactory-bulb lesions remains puzzling (Slotnick & Bisulco 2003).

Epithelium-to-bulb connectivity was uncovered mostly in rodents. Considering this rule of convergence, whereby all receptor neurons expressing a particular receptor type converge on the same glomerulus, combined with the expectation of ~350 functional olfactory receptor types expressed in humans (Glusman et al. 2001), one might predict that the human olfactory bulb would have about 700 glomeruli. However, the few studies that addressed this in human tissue identified nearly eightfold the number of expected glomeruli (Maresh et al. 2008). Thus, the rules underlying the organization of the human olfactory bulb and its relation to the epithelium may be slightly different than are the rules in rodents.

Nevertheless, the human olfactory bulb plays a key role in odor processing. Undeveloped olfactory bulbs are associated with anosmia (MacColl et al. 2002), and reduced bulb volume is associated with poor olfactory detection and discrimination (Buschhuter et al. 2008).

OLFACTORY CORTEX

By current definition, primary olfactory cortex consists of all brain regions that receive direct input from the mitral and tufted cell axons of the olfactory bulb (Allison 1954; Carmichael et al. 1994; de Olmos et al. 1978; Haberly 2001; Price 1973, 1987, 1990; Shipley 1995). These comprise most of the paleocortex, including (by order along the olfactory tract) the anterior olfactory cortex (also referred to as the anterior olfactory nucleus) (Brunjes et al. 2005), the ventral tenia tecta, anterior hippocampal continuation and indiusium griseum, the olfactory tubercle, piriform cortex, the anterior cortical nucleus of the amygdala, the periamygdaloid cortex, and the rostral entorhinal cortex (Carmichael et al. 1994). This definition of primary olfactory cortex as "all regions that receive direct input from the olfactory bulb" has recently been reevaluated, primarily because the definition is unhelpful when considering function (Cleland & Linster 2003, Haberly 2001, Sobel et al. 2003). One cannot assign *a function* to primary olfactory cortex when primary olfactory cortex is a label legitimately applied to a large proportion of the mammalian brain. With this in mind, there has been a growing tendency to use the term "primary olfactory cortex" for piriform cortex alone. Piriform cortex, the largest component of primary olfactory cortex in mammals, lies along the olfactory tract at the junction of temporal and frontal lobes and continues onto the dorsomedial aspect of the temporal lobe. Beyond these primary regions, olfactory information is projected throughout the brain, most prominently to orbitofrontal gyri and the insular cortex (Small & Prescott 2005).

The specific functional roles of human primary olfactory cortex remain poorly understood. Lesion studies have implicated primary olfactory cortex in odor discrimination (Zatorre & Jones-Gotman 1991), odor memory (Rausch et al. 1977), odor identification (Jones-Gotman & Zatorre 1988), and olfactory learning (Dade et al. 2002). The interesting aspect of this list is the faculty not listed, namely, we know of no reports on complete anosmia following focal cortical lesions in humans. In other words, we know of no olfactory equivalent to cortical blindness.

Imaging studies have implicated primary cortex in various olfactory tasks: Odor intensity coding, where, as a rule, increased intensity was associated with increased activation (Anderson et al. 2003; Rolls et al. 2003, 2008;

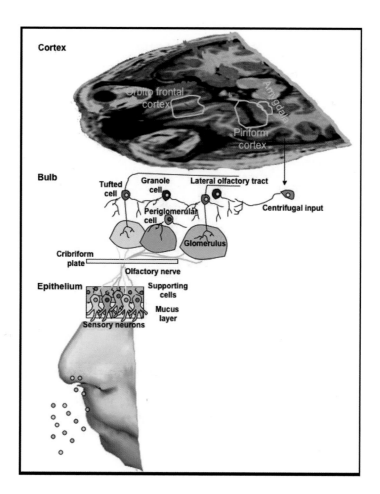

Figure 1

The olfactory neuroanatomy. Odor molecules are transported, by sniffing, to the olfactory epithelium, where they cross a mucus membrane to then bind with olfactory receptors. A neural signal is then transmitted through the olfactory nerve to the olfactory bulb. Following extensive bulbar processing resulting from interbulb, intrabulb, and cortex-to-bulb projections, the resultant signal is then projected via the lateral olfactory tract to primary olfactory cortex (piriform and amygdala are highlighted in the figure) and from there to secondary olfactory cortex (medial orbitofrontal cortex is highlighted in the figure).

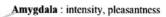

Medial orbito frontal cortex: pleasant odorants, sniffing, odor memory

Lateral Orbito frontal Cortex: unpleasant odorants, odor memory

Piriform cortex: intensity, sniffing, odor anticipation, pleasantness, odor memory

Cerebellum: sniffing, intensity

Amygdala : intensity, pleasantness

Entorhinal cortex: intensity

Parahippocampus: familiarity

Primary Visual areas: pleasantness, edibility

Not in this MRI slice:

Anterior Cingulate: pleasantness, intensity of trigeminal odorants

Broka: remembering odor intensity, familiarity

Insula cortex: pleasantness, discrimination

Olfactory tubercle: irritation

Inferior frontal gyrus: intensity, intensity memory, familiarity

Parietal cortex: memory, attention, familiarity, discrimination

Precuneus: familiarity, odor recognition, odor naming

Figure 2

One magnetic resonance imaging slice captures most cortical regions implicated in olfaction. In other words, olfaction can be thought of as a ventral brain network. That said, several nonventral cortical areas have also been implicated in several olfactory tasks.

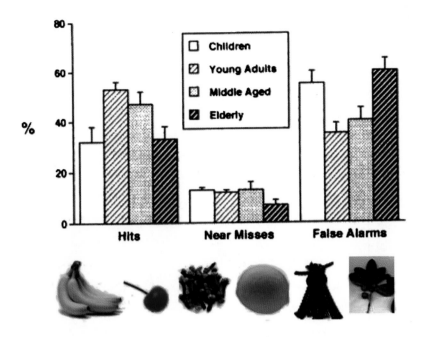

Figure 4

Poor human odor identification and naming. Percent correct (hits), near-miss, and far-miss (false alarms) identification (±SEM) for children, young adults, middle-aged, and elderly persons (from de Wijk & Cain 1994a). Images represent the odor sources used in this experiment: banana, cherry, cloves, lemon, licorice, and wintergreen.

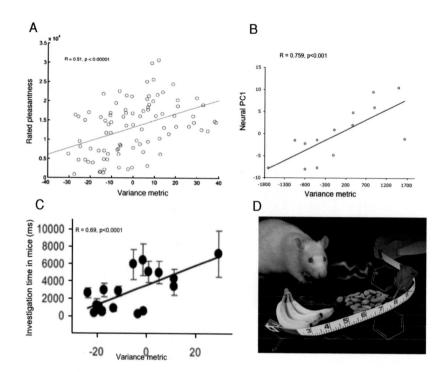

Figure 5

Pleasantness as the principal dimension of smell. (*A*) Khan et al. (2007) found that the first principal component of molecular structure (PC1), referred to as the variance metric, predicted the pleasantness of 90 different odorants as assessed by 20 subjects (adapted from Haddad et al 2008b). (*B*) The PC1 (variance metric) predicted the difference in neural activity at mouse olfactory receptor neurons (mouse data from Sato et al. 1994; correlation explained in Haddad et al. 2008a). (*C*) The PC1 (variance metric) predicted behavioral preferences in mice (adapted from Mandairon et al. 2009). (*D*) A graphic illustration of the notion of an olfactory metric that we argue reflects the axis of maximal variance in odor structure and the axis of pleasantness in perception (from Haddad et al. 2008b).

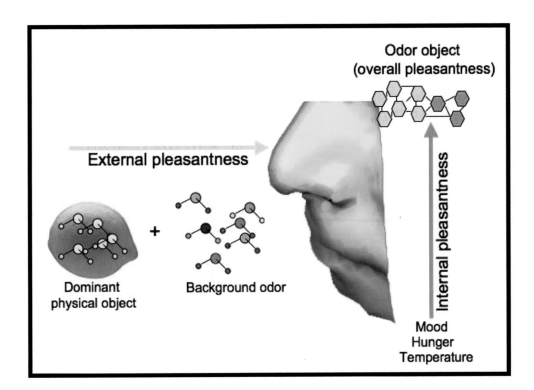

Figure 6

Definition of odor objects. We suggest that an odor object is the integration of the external odor pleasantness with the internal pleasantness. The external pleasantness is the combined pleasantness of the odor emanated from the dominant source of odor (physical object) together with the background odor (*blue hexagons*). The internal pleasantness is the subjective state at the moment of coding: mood, hunger, fear, temperature, etc. (*purple hexagons*). Brain odor-object representation is the overall pleasantness (*blue* and *purple hexagons* combined). Thus, we argue that given an external stimulus similar to the blue hexagons alone, the brain may try to complete the pattern by generating the appropriate purple hexagons, namely an emotion or homeostatic state.

Royet et al. 2001; Winston et al. 2005); pleasantness coding, where, as a rule, reduced pleasantness was associated with increased activation (Anderson et al. 2003, Gottfried et al. 2002, Grabenhorst et al. 2007, Rolls et al. 2003, Royet et al. 2000, Zald & Pardo 1997); familiarity coding, where, as a rule, increased familiarity was associated with increased activation regardless of task (Qureshy et al. 2000, Royet et al. 1999, Savic & Berglund 2004); olfactory attention, whereby a gating function has been ascribed to piriform cortex (Rolls et al. 2008, Zelano et al. 2005); and olfactory memory, whereby piriform cortex functioned as an olfactory analogue of the visuospatial sketchpad where odors were reflected in ongoing activity during active maintenance (Dade et al. 1998, 2001; Savic et al. 2000; Zelano et al. 2009) (**Figure 2**; see color insert).

One study directly explored the role of primary olfactory cortex in odor identity coding. In order to determine whether the piriform cortex encodes information about perceptual or structural determinants of odor, lemon-like and vegetable-like odorants that contained alcohol or aldehyde functional groups were presented in a functional magnetic resonance imaging (fMRI) cross-adaptation paradigm. A double dissociation in odor coding was revealed. Posterior piriform coded odor quality, and anterior piriform coded odor structure, in this case, functional group (Gottfried et al. 2006).

Two overriding aspects to the anatomy of olfaction have been highlighted as unique among the distal senses. The first is that olfaction is the only sense in which information does not propagate from periphery to cortex through the thalamus. As noted, olfactory information goes from epithelium to bulb to cortex, without a thalamic relay. Piriform cortex then projects to orbitofrontal cortex both directly and, through a thalamic path, indirectly. The functional significance of this thalamic path remains unclear, although it may play a role in olfactory attention (Plailly et al. 2008).

The second unique aspect of olfactory neuroanatomy is its ipsilateral unilateral connectivity. Most anatomical evidence suggests that each epithelium projects to its ipsilateral bulb that in turn projects to its ipsilateral primary cortex (Powell et al. 1965). That said, recent functional evidence in both rodents (Cross et al. 2006, McBride & Slotnick 1997, Wilson 1997) and humans (Porter et al. 2005, Savic & Gulyas 2000) suggests apparently equal levels of ipsilateral and contralateral functional connectivity from nostril to cortex, thus rendering the question of laterality less clear.

The above neuroanatomy is the substrate of human olfaction. Using this substrate, humans can perform tasks that are on one hand astonishingly keen, yet on the other hand astonishingly dull. Here we detail both ends of performance.

HUMANS ARE ASTONISHINGLY GOOD AT ODOR DETECTION AND DISCRIMINATION

Humans possess an extraordinary, if underappreciated, sense of smell (Shepherd 2004, Zelano & Sobel 2005). Nowhere is this more evident than in odor detection (**Figure 3A**). The odorant ethyl mercaptan, which is often added to propane as a warning agent, can be detected at concentrations below 1 part per billion (ppb) and perhaps as low as 0.2 ppb (Whisman et al. 1978). This is equivalent to approximately three drops of odorant within an Olympic-size swimming pool—given two pools, a human could detect by smell which pool contained the three drops of odorant. Extremely low detection thresholds have been reported for the odorants d-limonene and ozone as well (Cain et al. 2007). Finally, a report by the Japan Sanitation Center (Nagata & Takeuchi 1990) suggested humans can detect isoamyl mercaptan at 0.77 parts per trillion! This, to our knowledge, is the lowest reported human detection threshold.

Feats of detection are not limited to the olfaction lab. For example, consumers detected an off-odor in mineral water bottles that was undetected by the modern analytical in-line detection devices that were supposed to reject contaminated bottles (Widen et al. 2005). Humans not only are inherently good at odor detection, but they also can

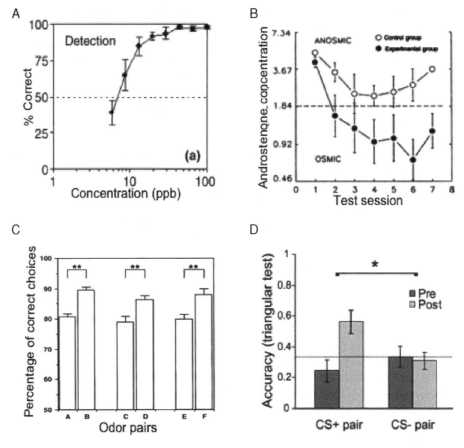

Figure 3

Keen human odor detection and discrimination. (*A*) Correct detection of ozone corrected for guessing (averages ± SEM). The is significantly beyond the 50% chance level by ∼10 parts per billion (ppb) (adapted from Cain et al. 2007). (*B*) Androstenone detection thresholds declined in an exposed group, but not in an unexposed group. The dashed line represents the functional definition of androstenone anosmia (adapted from Wysocki et al. 1989). (*C*) Discrimination between similar odorants: *column A*, odor pairs that involved two hexenols; *column B*, odor pairs that involved a hexanol and a hexenol; *column C*, odor pairs that involved two *cis*-hexenols; *column D*, odor pairs that involved two trans-hexenols; *column E*, odor pairs that involved hexenols sharing the same geometry but differing in the position of the double bond by only one carbon atom; and *column F*, odor pairs that involved hexenols sharing the same geometry but differing in the position of the double bond by two carbon atoms (adapted from Laska 2005). (*D*) Odor discrimination accuracy was at chance (dashed line) for CS+ and CS− pairs before conditioning, but selectively improved for the CS+ pair after conditioning. Error bars, ±SEM (adapted from Li et al. 2008).

improve with practice. Repeated exposure to an odorant leads to enhanced olfactory sensitivity and decreased detection thresholds for a number of different odorants (Cain & Gent 1991, Dalton et al. 2002, Engen & Bosack 1969) (**Figure 3B**). Furthermore, humans who were completely unable to detect the odor of androstenone developed the ability to detect it

after repeated exposure (Wysocki et al. 1989). There is an ongoing debate as to the point of plasticity underlying these improvements in olfaction with exposure or practice. A study with androstenone-anosmic mice (mice unable to detect androstenone despite otherwise intact olfaction) found evidence in favor of epithelial rather than cortical plasticity. Exposure of a surgically disconnected androstenone-anosmic mouse epithelium to androstenone enabled later androstenone-detection once the epithelium-to-bulb projection regenerated in those mice (Yee & Wysocki 2001). In other words, events at the isolated epithelium gave rise to behavioral plasticity. An additional study measured electrical evoked responses (EOGs) stemming from the human olfactory epithelium concurrent with an androstenone exposure paradigm and found changes in the EOG pattern with lowered detection thresholds, leading the authors to conclude that an epithelial modification occurred over time (Wang et al. 2004). In contrast, in favor of cortical plasticity, systematically exposing only one nostril of human androstenone anosmics to androstenone led to improved detection in both the exposed and the unexposed nostril (Mainland et al. 2002). This suggests that plasticity occurred at a substrate common to both nostrils, namely cortex. A conclusion consistent with all the data is that exposure may induce changes at both the peripheral and central levels. Repeated exposure may indeed lead to increased expression of receptors at the epithelial level (Yee & Wysocki 2001) and to an increased ability of the brain to make sense of what was a previously senseless message (Mainland et al. 2002). The recent identification of the specific human olfactory receptor that is primarily responsible for the detection of androstenone (Keller et al. 2007) may now enable a more direct investigation of this question.

Humans are not only good at detecting odorants, they are also good at discriminating one odorant from another, either in terms of concentration or molecular identity. Humans can discriminate between two odorants that differ in concentration by as little as 7% (the olfactory "just noticeable difference") (Cain 1977), and even smaller changes in the relative proportion of a component in a mixture can change the perception of the mixture (Le Berre et al. 2008). Humans can also discriminate the smallest alterations in molecular structure, such as between odorants equal in number of carbons but differing in functional group (Laska et al.

2000) or equal in functional group but differing in chain length by one carbon only (Laska & Freyer 1997) (**Figure 3C**). Moreover, humans are able to discriminate between various pairs of enantiomers (mirror-image molecules) such as (+) and (−) carvone. Still, discrimination is not always easy. Humans fail to discriminate some enantiomer pairs (Laska & Teubner 1999), unfamiliar odors are harder to discriminate than familiar odors (Mingo & Stevenson 2007), and the ability to discriminate the number of odorants in a mixture is limited to four (Laing & Glemarec 1992), even when the odors are "poor blending" odors (Livermore & Laing 1998).

In turn, like odor detection, odor discrimination can improve with learning and practice (Rabin 1988). Increased familiarization was associated with a decrease in discrimination errors of initially unfamiliar odors (Jehl et al. 1995). Odor enantiomers that were initially indiscriminable became discriminable after one of the enantiomers was associated with an electric shock (Li et al. 2008) (**Figure 3D**). Subjects working in perfume retail outlets were significantly better at odor discrimination compared with subjects not working in such odorous environments (Hummel et al. 2004), and wine tasters were superior to naive controls at odor discrimination (Bende & Nordin 1997).

Whereas discrimination between common molecules in the laboratory is outstanding, it may be even better between molecules that are ecologically meaningful. For example, human participants could use smell to discriminate their own T-shirt from 100 identical T-shirts worn by others for 24 hours (Lord & Kasprzak 1989). If the latter sounds more like an olfactory feat of a dog, a separate amusing study found that humans can in fact discriminate their pet dog from other dogs using smell alone (i.e., the humans smelled the dogs. . .) (Wells & Hepper 2000). More ecologically relevant, however, is that human mothers could discriminate between the smell of their baby and other babies (Porter et al. 1983), five- to eight-year-old children could discriminate between the smell of their three- to four-year-old siblings and other children (Porter & Moore 1981), and nine-year-old children could discriminate between the smells of their close friends (Mallet & Schaal 1998). Many of these discriminations are achieved despite low confidence or awareness (Lundstrom et al. 2008). Furthermore, these discriminatory powers may be innate: Babies can discriminate the smell of their breast-feeding mothers from other mothers by six days after birth (Macfarelane 1975, Schaal et al. 1980), and newborn babies cry less when exposed to the odor of amniotic fluid (which was present in the intrauterine environment) than to the odor of their mother's breasts (Varendi et al. 1998). Breast-feeding infants, at approximately two weeks of age, discriminated between their mother's axillary odor and odors produced by either nonparturient or unfamiliar lactating women (Cernoch & Porter 1985).

HUMANS ARE ASTONISHINGLY BAD AT ODOR IDENTIFICATION AND NAMING

Whereas humans underestimate their detection and discrimination abilities, they overestimate their ability to identify and name odors (Cain et al. 1998, Jonsson et al. 2005, Jonsson & Olsson 2003, Lawless & Engen 1977) (**Figure 4**; see color insert). This inability is subjectively striking when revealed to those who don't study olfactory psychophysics and hence appreciate it as fact. For example, in an effort to describe the eventual point of this review to a family member, author NS asked this family member to close her eyes, and then held in front of her nose a jar of peanut butter, which he asked her to name. This adult "subject," who despite eating peanut butter every day is otherwise neurologically intact, could not identify or name the odor. When she opened her eyes, she was astonished at her inability to name this odor that was otherwise so familiar. Because this inability is key to the main suggestion later made in this review, we invite the reader to conduct a similar "experiment" on him/herself, or friends and family, using the refrigerator as a

relatively safe source for odorants. The outcome is always striking. Indeed, humans are unable to name by smell at least 50% of the odorous household items they use daily (Cain 1979, de Wijk et al. 1995, Lawless & Engen 1977). The dissociation between knowledge about an odor concurrent with inability to name it is evident already at childhood. When smelling dangerous household products, children correctly named 15% of the odors, but correctly rated edibility of 79% of the same odors (De Wijk & Cain 1994a). Finally, the poor odor-name bond is symmetrical—matching a name to an odor was as difficult as matching an odor to a name (Olsson & Jonsson 2008).

Like detection and discrimination, naming ability improves when odor familiarity increases (Homewood & Stevenson 2001) and further improves with explicit practice. Five practice sessions of naming 80 odorants resulted in a shift from 36 to 61 correctly named (Cain 1979). The ability to name odors increases significantly when rather than free recall, subjects can choose between alternative labels. Even for common odors such as banana, licorice, and clove, performance in cued identification far exceeded that in free identification (de Wijk & Cain 1994b). Because of this, the benchmark test used for scoring olfactory identification is not a free recall test, but rather a four-alternative forced-choice test. The University of Pennsylvania Smell Identification Test (Doty et al. 1984a,b) consists of 40 microencapsulated odorants that subjects have to scratch and sniff. For each odorant, the task is to choose from four alternative labels the one that best describes each odor. This test is one of the only "norms" in olfaction research and has been used to characterize an olfactory impairment in numerous diseases (Doty 2005).

To conclude, humans are bad at naming an odor, especially if they don't have labels to choose from. This difficulty may reflect a form of competition between language and olfaction over common neural substrates (Lorig 1999), or it may reflect a fundamental aspect of odor objects that renders them particularly difficult to name. This possibility is considered later.

VERBAL AND VISUAL INFLUENCE ON ODOR PERCEPTION

Humans are very good at detecting an odorant but are poor at naming it. The poor ability to name odors using olfactory information alone renders the process of odor naming and identification highly susceptible to interference from other modalities. For example, in one study, odorants were presented with an explicitly described source as either synthetic ("this is a synthetic rotten egg") or natural ("this is natural rose"). When pleasant odors were labeled "natural," they were rated as more familiar than when labeled "synthetic" (Herz 2003). Similarly, when an isovaleric and butyric acid mixture was labeled "parmesan cheese," it was rated as more familiar than when labeled "vomit" (Herz & von Clef 2001). In another experiment, each odor was presented three times under different names that referred to either a pleasant, unpleasant, or neutral odor source. For example, the odorant pyridine was presented with the label "sea weed," "rotten fish" or "fifty-three." Odorants were rated as more intense when presented with unpleasant names than with neutral or pleasant names (Djordjevic et al. 2008).

Visual information, particularly color, also affects odor characteristics. When a white wine was artificially colored red with an odorless dye, a panel of 54 expert tasters shifted to using olfactory characteristics of red wine in order to describe the concoction (Morrot et al. 2001). Odor solutions were also rated as smelling more intense when colored than when colorless (Zellner & Kautz 1990). Furthermore, a cherry-flavored drink colored orange was perceived as smelling orange flavored (Dubose et al. 1980), and when it was colored red, subjects performed better at identifying the solution by smell than when they performed the task blindfolded or when a lemon-flavored drink was colored red (Zellner et al. 1991). Additionally, olfactory detection was faster and more accurate when odors appeared in the context of visual cues that were semantically congruent (vanillin odor—picture of ice cream) as compared with incongruent (vanillin odor—picture of bread) (Gottfried & Dolan 2003).

This susceptibility in odor perception extends to ecological odors as well. For example, when a label "participant's baby's name" or "someone else's baby" was added correctly to a diaper, mothers rated their own baby's diaper as less displeasing. However, when the diapers were mislabeled, no difference in pleasantness was rated (Case et al. 2006). Thus, verbal labels inverted the percept of an odor. This inversion was evident not only in perception, but also in brain activity. In an fMRI experiment, subjects smelled an odor mixture that was composed of isovaleric acid and cheddar cheese flavor. The mixture was labeled on different trials as "cheddar cheese" or "body odor," and as a control, delivery of clean air was paired with the same labels. Brain regions involved in pleasantness representation were significantly more activated by odor and by clean air when labeled "cheddar cheese" than when labeled "body odor" (de Araujo et al. 2005). The influence of nonolfactory and especially verbal information on olfactory identification can be seen as facilitating a process of olfactory pattern completion or constancy (Stevenson & Boakes 2003); this is discussed in more detail below.

PLEASANTNESS AS THE PRIMARY AXIS OF OLFACTORY PERCEPTION

The studies cited above demonstrate that humans are good at detecting and discriminating smells but are poor at naming them, and humans readily change the name or label they apply to an odor as a reflection of interference from language or vision. However, humans consistently and rapidly apply to an odor verbal labels identifying its pleasantness.

Odorant pleasantness was the primary aspect of odor spontaneously used by subjects in olfactory discrimination tasks (Schiffman 1974), and odorant pleasantness was the primary criterion spontaneously used by subjects to combine odorants into groups (Berglund et al. 1973, Schiffman et al. 1977). When using large numbers of verbal descriptors to describe odorants, pleasantness repeatedly emerged as the primary dimension in multidimensional analyses of the resultant descriptor space (Khan et al. 2007, Moskowitz & Barbe 1977, Zarzo 2008). Studies with newborns suggested that at least some aspects of olfactory pleasantness may be innate (Soussignan et al. 1997, Steiner 1979). For example, neonates' behavioral markers of disgust (wrinkling nose, raising upper lip) discriminated between vanillin judged as being pleasant and butyric acid judged as being unpleasant by adult raters (Soussignan et al. 1997). Moreover, there is agreement in the assessments of pleasantness by adults and children for various pure odorants (Schmidt & Beauchamp 1988) and personal odors (Mallet & Schaal 1998). Interestingly, fathers and daughters, and brothers and sisters, rated each other's odor as unpleasant, a phenomenon that has been considered in the context of a mechanism for incest avoidance (Weisfeld et al. 2003). The primacy of pleasantness is further borne out in the physiological responses to odors. Pleasant and unpleasant odorants were evaluated at different speeds (Bensafi et al. 2002a) and generated different autonomic responses (Bensafi et al. 2002b). Furthermore, pleasant and unpleasant odorants are appraised by dissociable neural substrates, as evidenced in both electrophysiological recordings (Alaoui-Ismaili et al. 1997, Kobal et al. 1992, Masago et al. 2001, Pause & Krauel 2000) and functional neuroimaging studies (Anderson et al. 2003, Gottfried et al. 2002, Grabenhorst et al. 2007, Rolls et al. 2003, Royet et al. 2000, Zald & Pardo 1997). The task most frequently used to test brain representation of odor pleasantness was to present subjects with a set of pleasant and unpleasant odorants and ask them to rate odor pleasantness. These tasks consistently revealed orbitofrontal cortex involvement in representing odor pleasantness (Anderson et al. 2003, Rolls et al. 2003, Royet et al. 2001). More specifically, pleasant odors increased activation in posterior medial orbitofrontal cortex, and unpleasant odors increased activation in the lateral orbitofrontal cortex (Gottfried et al. 2002, Grabenhorst et al. 2007, Rolls et al. 2003). In addition, there was evidence for the separate and simultaneous representation of positive (in medial orbitofrontal cortex) and negative (in dorsal anterior cingulate and mid-orbitofrontal cortex) hedonic value of a mixture that was composed of one pleasant and one unpleasant odorant (Grabenhorst et al. 2007). Odor pleasantness was also reflected in piriform cortex (Zelano et al. 2007). Additional regions that have been implicated in odor pleasantness processing are anterior cingulate, ventral insula, superior frontal gyrus, and motor area BA 8 (Fulbright et al. 1998; Gottfried et al. 2002; Rolls et al. 2003, 2008; Royet et al. 2000, 2003; Winston et al. 2005; Zelano et al. 2007). Increased activity for odor hedonic judgments was also evident in primary visual areas (Royet et al. 2001), suggesting that rating odor pleasantness may involve visual imagery of the odor source.

The role of the amygdala in odor pleasantness processing is controversial. Whereas some studies reported increased amygdala activation for unpleasant versus pleasant odors (Gottfried et al. 2002, Royet et al. 2003, Zald & Pardo 1997), another study suggested that amygdala activation may preferentially reflect the intensity rather than the valence of odors (Anderson et al. 2003). An alternative consistent with all the data is that the amygdala does not preferentially respond to intensity or valence per se, but rather to a combination of the two (Winston et al. 2005). When valence was held constant, the amygdala responded robustly to odor intensity for pleasant and unpleasant smells but did not similarly respond for neutral smells. In turn, when intensity was held constant (at high concentrations), the amygdala was preferentially activated by positive and negative valence but not by neutral valence.

Finally, odor pleasantness is paramount not only when considering odor perception or odorant-induced brain activation, but also emerges when considering odor molecules alone. Khan et al. (2007) applied principal components analysis to more than 1600 molecular features of more than 1500 odorants to identify the principal physicochemical axis of odor space. They found that the resultant axis, the first principal component of molecular structure, i.e., the axis that best explains the variance in odor structure, was significantly correlated to the perception of odorant pleasantness. This implies that pleasantness is indeed "written into" the molecular structure of odors. Uncovering this relationship allowed Khan et al. (2007) to predict the pleasantness of novel molecules based on their structure alone (**Figure 5A**; see color insert). Furthermore, Haddad et al. (2008a) later demonstrated that this axis can be used as an odorant metric that explains a large portion of the variance in neural activity across a wide range of species (**Figure 5B**) (Haddad et al. 2008b). Critically, this same metric later predicted behavioral preferences not only in humans but in mice as well (**Figure 5C**) (Mandairon et al. 2009). Taken together, these lines of evidence combine to highlight pleasantness as the principal perceptual axis of smell (**Figure 5D**).

All that said, pleasantness does not explain all the variance in olfactory perception, nor does physicochemical structure explain all the variance in pleasantness. For example, odor pleasantness is dependent on odor intensity (Doty 1975, Henion 1971, Moskowitz et al. 1976) and familiarity (Delplanque et al. 2008, Distel et al. 1999, Distel & Hudson 2001, Jellinek & Koster 1983), and it varies across individuals and cultures (Ayabe-Kanamura et al. 1998, Moncrieff 1966, Pangborn 1975, Wysocki et al. 1991) as well as within individuals over time (Cain & Johnson 1978, Hudson 1999). Finally, despite its perceptual primacy, the perception of odorant pleasantness, like other odor aspects, can also be significantly influenced by visual and verbal information. Thus, in the previously described studies where a verbal or visual label altered odor intensity, familiarity, identity, and brain activity, the visual and verbal labels similarly influenced pleasantness (Case et al. 2006, de Araujo et al. 2005, Herz 2003, Herz & von Clef 2001).

Taken together, findings indicate that humans are good at detecting and discriminating odorants but bad at naming odorants, and the one label they readily apply to an odor is its pleasantness. This label is reflected in human behavior and neurophysiology, and, critically, it reflects the axis that best explains the variance within the structure of molecules that have a smell. If an odor primarily denotes pleasantness, than what is an odor object? For example, what is the odor object "banana"? Or in fact, is there an odor object "banana"?

DEFINING ODOR OBJECTS

It seemed that this poor ignorant Monarch—
as he called himself—was persuaded that the
Straight Line which he called his Kingdom,
and in which he passed his existence, consti-
tuted the whole of the world, and indeed the
whole of Space.

FlatLand, A Romance of Many Dimensions
Edwin A. Abbott, 1884

The *Merriam-Webster* definition for object is:

a: something material that may be perceived by the senses; *b*: something that when viewed stirs a particular emotion.

Most previous considerations of olfactory objects used the above definition *a* of an object. Akin to the visual object "banana," the olfactory object "banana" was considered as an amalgamation of molecules that can be separated from the background molecules to stand out as an object reflecting something material—a banana.

In contrast, we propose that the above definition *b* is the more appropriate framework for defining odor objects. We suggest that an odor object is the integration of the odor's inherent pleasantness (Khan et al. 2007) with the subjective state at the moment of coding: mood, hunger, fear, etc. Therefore, an odor object is not the odor of the banana but rather an integration of the pleasantness of the banana odor with the subjective state at which it was encountered. Thus, whereas by our definition banana odor when you are hungry is a different object from banana odor when you are satiated, according to definition *a*, these are the same object—banana.

Similarly, according to our definition, milk odor and sour-milk odor are completely different olfactory objects because they differ in their perceived pleasantness, whereas according to definition *a*, these are the same object—milk. On the other hand, by our definition, if grapes and melon have exactly the same pleasantness for a specific person, then olfactory-wise, grapes and melon are the same object for that person. Below, we consider this point of view within four arguments.

ARGUMENT 1: AN ODOR OBJECT IS A GIVEN PLEASANTNESS

The primary function of olfaction can be viewed as to signal approach or withdrawal. This signal is best represented by pleasantness. Approach is the proper response to an edible food, a safe environment, or a fertile mate, and they all indeed generally smell pleasant. Withdrawal is the proper response to a poison or a predator, and they indeed generally smell unpleasant. In other words, because approach and withdrawal is the realm of olfaction, the language of olfaction is pleasantness, and an olfactory object is a given pleasantness.

If olfaction can tell us only about an odor's given pleasantness, then how can we know, for example, that a given odor is "strawberry"? The immediate answer to this is that usually we cannot know. As reviewed above, presented with an odor alone, humans usually fail to spontaneously provide the odor with a label. They do, however, provide a label under two conditions: What we here call the "olfactory laymen condition"—when offered alternative names (either verbally or visually), or more rarely under what we here call the "olfactory expert condition"—when an odor name is spontaneously generated. Our explanation for the laymen solution is that even through limited experience and learning, we have learned to link the given pleasantness of strawberry to a particular visual image, a particular context, and a particular name. Thus, once our nose puts us "in the ballpark" in terms of the exact

pleasantness, we can complete the task by linking this pleasantness to one of a few optional solutions when offered, as long as one option will be significantly closer than the others in terms of pleasantness. In turn, the olfactory expert solution is to become so incredibly refined through experience and learning that the resolution on the pleasantness scale is fine enough to determine a strawberry by the molecular input alone. In other words, we claim that there is a pleasantness score nearly unique to strawberry, shared by only very few, if any, olfactory objects in the world, that will then smell exactly like strawberry. A simplistic analogy can be made using color. Imagine you perceived only color when visually inspecting a strawberry. Asked to identify what the "red" was, you would probably fail. Yet if you were asked whether the "red" was a strawberry, banana, or lemon, you would choose strawberry based on your previous experience. Humans can discriminate millions of colors. Now imagine that you spend your life picking strawberries, and you have learned the very unique shade of red that is shared by strawberries and only very few, if any, additional objects. If presented with this unique color, you may indeed spontaneously identify it as strawberry, not raspberry or Ferrari. In other words, even with a unidimensional scale, you could become very refined at identifying discrete objects, especially if this unidimensional scale were made of the relative inputs of 1000 (olfaction) rather than 3 (vision) different types of receptors. An ultimate unidimensional representation can explain the high level of olfactory performance retained following lesions to the olfactory bulb (Slotnick & Bisulco 2003). If the end representation of olfactory objects were multidimensional, then losing parts of the olfactory bulb would entail losing dimensions of the object, resulting in a different object. In contrast, if the representation is unidimensional, losing parts of the olfactory bulb will merely generate an impoverished object but not a different one.

Our notion of an odor object that does not correspond to a visual object contrasts with ideas developed by Richardson & Zucco (1989) and Stevenson & Wilson (2007), who likened olfactory objects to visual objects. Stevenson & Wilson (2007) proposed that an odor object differs from a visual object in that the former reflects synthetic processing. Yet they further detailed that olfactory objects are the result of a pattern-matching system that recognizes discrete sets of spatial and temporal olfactory features and that the object is dissociated from its background by rapid central adaptation (Stevenson & Wilson 2007). They wrote, "Most odours are composed of 10s or 100s of volatile components, yet they are perceived as unitary perceptual events against a continually shifting olfactory background." We agree that a pattern-matching system that recognizes discrete sets of spatial and temporal olfactory features indeed exists; however, the pattern matching is not for the odor of the physical object but rather is for the overall pleasantness. We suggest that the odor of the physical object, and the background odor, are perceived as a unitary perceptual event, and their separation is dependent on additional nonolfactory sensory information and context.

Because our hypothesis and the current prevalent hypotheses on odor objects and their separation from background are clearly opposed, we propose a simple experiment that juxtaposes these two approaches. Blindfolded subjects could be presented with two olfactory objects, one edible and one inedible, placed simultaneously side-by-side in front of their nose (for example, a bar of chocolate and a used diaper). Subjects would be informed that there are two objects in front of them, and they would be asked to determine their edibility. According to the notion of objects akin to visual objects that can be separated from the odor background (Stevenson & Wilson 2007), subjects should say, "one item is edible and the other is not." In contrast, according to our theory, whereby the entire landscape would form one odor object, subjects would give only one answer: either both objects are edible, or both are inedible (we presume that subjects will refer to two objects rather

than only one because they were explicitly informed of their presence; otherwise, we expect blindfolded subjects to perceive only one object spontaneously).

ARGUMENT 2: A GIVEN PLEASANTNESS IS THE COMBINATION OF EXTERNAL AND INTERNAL FACTORS

This argument is of course not novel on its own, yet it forms a critical component of our novel definition of olfactory objects (**Figure 6**; see color insert). Cabanac (1971) proposed the word "alliesthesia" to describe a condition where a given external stimulus can be perceived as either pleasant or unpleasant depending upon signals coming from inside the body. Both hunger and ambient temperature have been studied as contexts for olfactory alliesthesia.

Fasting subjects initially rated the smell of orange syrup as pleasant but shifted its rating to unpleasant following glucose ingestion (Cabanac et al. 1973). Similarly, hunger or satiety modulated the hedonic facial responses to milk in three-day-old neonates (Soussignan et al. 1999).

The immediate effects of changes in environmental temperature on odor pleasantness ratings were studied to examine the influence of temperature on metabolic reserves (Russek et al. 1979). As expected, at 40°C hungry subjects rated alimentary odors as less pleasant than at 20°C. However, temperature had no influence on the perceived pleasantness of nonalimentary odors.

In an fMRI study aimed at revealing the brain mechanisms underlying olfactory alliesthesia, subjects were scanned with two food odors and then scanned again after eating one of the odor-corresponding foods to satiety (O'Doherty et al. 2000). The representation of the satiated food changed in the orbitofrontal region, namely secondary olfactory cortex. In other words, an internal state (in this case, satiety) influenced the olfactory representation in the brain.

ARGUMENT 3: THE INTERNAL SIGNALS ARE ANALOGOUS TO THE DIFFERENT VIEW ANGLES IN VISION

Humans are able to view an object from different angles yet still know that it is the same object. This phenomenon of visual invariance, which is demonstrated by mental rotation (Shepard & Metzler 1971), is based on multiple representations of the image viewed from various points (Edelman 1999). We propose that the different internal states that modulate overall pleasantness in olfaction are analogous to the different viewing angles in vision, and the ability to perceive an olfactory object as constant despite changing internal states reflects a form of olfactory mental rotation. Furthermore, we predict that if an internal state shifts beyond a certain threshold, the object will no longer be perceived as the same. There are many examples of shifts in olfactory perception as a function of shifts in internal state, such as shifts in olfaction across the menstrual cycle (Navarrete-Palacios et al. 2003) and in pregnancy (Nordin et al. 2004), shifts in olfaction associated with depression (Pollatos et al. 2007), and shifts in olfaction associated with hunger (Cabanac et al. 1973). This prediction could be tested in an experiment that would introduce two groups of subjects, one hungry and one satiated, to a novel food with a novel odor (for example, a carambola, also called starfruit). In this model, the two groups would learn two different odors: "hungry carambola" and "satiated carambola." Subjects would then later be tested at various levels of hunger/satiety for identification of the smell of carambola in a four-alternative forced-choice paradigm, and their reaction time would be measured. We predict that reaction time would correlate with hunger/satiety and, critically, that the direction of this correlation for subjects who learned the odor "hungry carambola" would be opposite that of those who learned the odor "satiated carambola." Of course, modality controls, such as a picture of the fruit, would need to be used in order to address the possibility of state-dependent learning, regardless of our theory (Tulving 1983).

ARGUMENT 4: ODOR IS A "SENSORY EMOTION"

We define an odor object as the combination of its external molecular components and internal state components. In agreement with most models of odor perception, given an olfactory stimulus, we expect the olfactory system to generate a form of pattern completion. Thus, given the external component of the stimulus, the system may attempt to complete the pattern by generating the internal component. Hence, the well-known tendency of odors to elicit emotions (Chu & Downes 2002, Epple & Herz 1999, Herz et al. 2004, Herz 2004, Herz & Cupchik 1995, Herz & Schooler 2002, Kirk-Smith et al. 1983) may merely be a form of olfactory object constancy and pattern completion. The ability of food odors to generate hunger or nausea may similarly be olfactory object constancy and pattern completion. For example, under our definition of olfactory object, the smell of steak when you are satiated is a different object from the smell of steak when you are hungry. The molecules of steak alone are a partial stimulus. Thus, the system will try to complete the object by generating the appropriate accompanying internal state. Thus, if you are slightly hungry, the better fit and more appropriate pattern completion will be for the odor object "hungry steak," and the smell will indeed generate hunger. In turn, if you are slightly satiated, then the better fit and the more appropriate pattern completion will be for the odor object "satiated steak," and the smell will generate nausea.

Indeed, odors not only elicit mood and emotion (Chu & Downes 2002, Diego et al. 1998, Epple & Herz 1999, Herz et al. 2004, Herz 2004, Herz & Cupchik 1995, Herz & Schooler 2002, Kirk-Smith et al. 1983, Knasko 1995, Lehrner et al. 2005, Weber & Heuberger 2008), but odor perception also shares many common characteristics with mood and emotion.

First, they share a common neural substrate, namely the limbic system, which is the neural substrate of emotion (LeDoux 2007) and largely corresponds to primary and secondary olfactory cortex, most notably amygdala and orbitofrontal cortex, respectively (Price 1987, 1990; Rolls 2004).

Second, pleasantness is the principal dimension of perception in both emotion (Fontaine et al. 2007) and olfaction (Khan et al. 2007).

Third, the combination of superior detection and discrimination concurrent with inferior verbalization is common to emotion and olfaction. For olfaction, this has been extensively detailed above; for emotion, a trivial example is that of love: We can all detect it and discriminate it from other emotions yet mostly fail to describe it in words (Levine 2005).

Fourth, odors and emotions share a similar status in memory in that both are not subject to recall, given that both are not subject to imagery. Olfactory imagery has been a topic of debate (Stevenson & Case 2005). In our view, what is mentally recreated during efforts of olfactory imagery is a given pleasantness. This is consistent with olfactory imagery-related activation of the olfactomotor system (Bensafi et al. 2003) and olfactory imagery-related activation of the brain (Bensafi et al. 2007). Thus, when trying to imagine the odor of strawberry, one can mentally recreate a low-acuity version of the pleasantness of strawberry. However, several objects may share the low-acuity pleasantness of strawberry, and hence this remains an impoverished form of imagery.

CONCLUSION

In this review, we have seen that the functional neuroanatomy of olfaction is highly conserved across mammals. Humans are poor at odor naming but, similar to other mammals, are keen at odor detection and discrimination. With poor access to language, the principal axis of human odor perception remains odor pleasantness.

Furthermore, we propose that poor odor naming reflects the unique nature of odor objects which, unlike visual objects, consist of an external component made of molecules and an internal component of emotional and homeostatic state that together generate a given pleasantness. This given pleasantness is the object. In summary, and echoing the quotation at the beginning of this section, we view olfaction as FlatLand (Abbott 1884), a realm in which unidimensional representations provide a wealth of information that—when augmented with multisensory and contextual information, both external and internal—generates the richness of smell. We highlight several lines of evidence that support this hypothesis, and propose novel experiments wherever the current literature did not provide data that either support or negate our ideas. We submit that our definition of odor objects, although far removed from current notions, is in fact consistent with much of the physiological and psychological data, that it explains several previously unexplained phenomena in olfaction, and most critically, that it is testable.

DISCLOSURE STATEMENT

The authors are not aware of any biases that might be perceived as affecting the objectivity of this review.

LITERATURE CITED

Abbott EA. 1884. *FlatLand: A Romance of Many Dimensions.* London: Seely

Ache BW, Young JM. 2005. Olfaction: diverse species, conserved principles. *Neuron* 48:417–30

Adrian ED. 1942. Olfactory reactions in the brain of the hedgehog. *J. Physiol.* 100:459–73

Alaoui-Ismaili O, Robin O, Rada H, Dittmar A, Vernet-Maury E. 1997. Basic emotions evoked by odorants: comparison between autonomic responses and self-evaluation. *Physiol. Behav.* 62:713–20

Allison A. 1954. The secondary olfactory areas in the human brain. *J. Anat.* 88:481–88

Anderson AK, Christoff K, Stappen I, Panitz D, Ghahremani DG, et al. 2003. Dissociated neural representations of intensity and valence in human olfaction. *Nat. Neurosci.* 6:196–202

Ayabe-Kanamura S, Schicker I, Laska M, Hudson R, Distel H, et al. 1998. Differences in perception of everyday odors: a Japanese-German cross-cultural study. *Chem. Senses* 23:31–38

Bende M, Nordin S. 1997. Perceptual learning in olfaction: professional wine tasters versus controls. *Physiol. Behav.* 62:1065–70

Bensafi M, Pierson A, Rouby C, Farget V, Bertrand B, et al. 2002a. Modulation of visual event-related potentials by emotional olfactory stimuli. *Neurophysiol. Clin.* 32:335–42

Bensafi M, Porter J, Pouliot S, Mainland J, Johnson B, et al. 2003. Olfactomotor activity during imagery mimics that during perception. *Nat. Neurosci.* 6:1142–44

Bensafi M, Rouby C, Farget V, Bertrand B, Vigouroux M, Holley A. 2002b. Autonomic nervous system responses to odours: the role of pleasantness and arousal. *Chem. Senses* 27:703–9

Bensafi M, Sobel N, Khan RM. 2007. Hedonic-specific activity in piriform cortex during odor imagery mimics that during odor perception. *J. Neurophysiol.* 98:3254–62

Berglund B, Berglund U, Engen T, Ekman G. 1973. Multidimensional analysis of 21 odors. *Scand. J. Psychol.* 14:131–37

Breer H. 2003. Olfactory receptors: molecular basis for recognition and discrimination of odors. *Anal. Bioanalytical Chem.* 377:427–33

Brunjes PC, Illig KR, Meyer EA. 2005. A field guide to the anterior olfactory nucleus (cortex). *Brain Res.* 50:305–35

Buck L, Axel R. 1991. A novel multigene family may encode odorant receptors: a molecular basis for odor recognition. *Cell* 65:175–87

Buschhuter D, Smitka M, Puschmann S, Gerber JC, Witt M, et al. 2008. Correlation between olfactory bulb volume and olfactory function. *Neuroimage* 42:498–502

Cabanac M. 1971. Physiological role of pleasure. *Science* 173:1103–7

Cabanac M, Pruvost M, Fantino M. 1973. Negative alliesthesia for sweet stimuli after varying ingestions of glucose (author's transl. from French). *Physiol. Behav.* 11:345–48

Cain WS. 1977. Differential sensitivity for smell: "noise" at the nose. *Science* 195:796–98

Cain WS. 1979. To know with the nose: keys to odor identification. *Science* 203:467–70

Cain WS, de Wijk R, Lulejian C, Schiet F, See LC. 1998. Odor identification: perceptual and semantic dimensions. *Chem. Senses* 23:309–26

Cain WS, Gent JF. 1991. Olfactory sensitivity: reliability, generality, and association with aging. *J. Exp. Psychol.: Hum. Percept. Perform.* 17:382–91

Cain WS, Johnson F Jr. 1978. Lability of odor pleasantness: influence of mere exposure. *Perception* 7:459–65

Cain WS, Schmidt R, Wolkoff P. 2007. Olfactory detection of ozone and D-limonene: reactants in indoor spaces. *Indoor Air* 17:337–47

Carmichael ST, Clugnet MC, Price JL. 1994. Central olfactory connections in the macaque monkey. *J. Comp. Neurol.* 346:403–34

Case TI, Repacholi BM, Stevenson RJ. 2006. My baby doesn't smell as bad as yours—the plasticity of disgust. *Evol. Hum. Behav.* 27:357–65

Cernoch JM, Porter RH. 1985. Recognition of maternal axillary odors by infants. *Child Dev.* 56:1593–98

Chess A, Simon I, Cedar H, Axel R. 1994. Allelic inactivation regulates olfactory receptor gene-expression. *Cell* 78:823–34

Chu S, Downes JJ. 2002. Proust nose best: Odors are better cues of autobiographical memory. *Mem. Cogn.* 30:511–18

Cleland TA, Johnson BA, Leon M, Linster C. 2007. Relational representation in the olfactory system. *Proc. Natl. Acad. Sci. USA* 104:1953–58

Cleland TA, Linster C. 2003. Central olfactory structures. See Doty 2003, pp. 165–80

Clerico DM, To WC, Lanza DC. 2003. Anatomy of the human nasal passages. See Doty 2003, pp. 1–16

Cross DJ, Flexman JA, Anzai Y, Morrow TJ, Maravilla KR, Minoshima S. 2006. In vivo imaging of functional disruption, recovery and alteration in rat olfactory circuitry after lesion. *Neuroimage* 32:1265–72

Dade LA, Jones-Gotman M, Zatorre RJ, Evans AC. 1998. Human brain function during odor encoding and recognition. A PET activation study. *Ann. N. Y. Acad. Sci.* 855:572–74

Dade LA, Zatorre RJ, Evans AC, Jones-Gotman M. 2001. Working memory in another dimension: functional imaging of human olfactory working memory. *Neuroimage* 14:650–60

Dade LA, Zatorre RJ, Jones-Gotman M. 2002. Olfactory learning: convergent findings from lesion and brain imaging studies in humans. *Brain* 125:86–101

Dalton P. 2004. Olfaction and anosmia in rhinosinusitis. *Curr. Allergy Asthma Rep.* 4:230–36

Dalton P, Doolittle N, Breslin PA. 2002. Gender-specific induction of enhanced sensitivity to odors. *Nat. Neurosci.* 5:199–200

de Araujo IE, Rolls ET, Velazco MI, Margot C, Cayeux I. 2005. Cognitive modulation of olfactory processing. *Neuron* 46:671–79

de Olmos J, Hardy H, Heimer L. 1978. The afferent connections of the main and the accessory olfactory bulb formations in the rat: an experimental HRP-study. *J. Comp. Neurol.* 15:213–44

de Wijk RA, Cain WS. 1994a. Odor identification by name and by edibility: life-span development and safety. *Hum. Factors* 36:182–87

de Wijk RA, Cain WS. 1994b. Odor quality: discrimination versus free and cued identification. *Percept. Psychophys.* 56:12–18

de Wijk RA, Schab FR, Cain WS. 1995. Odor identification. In *Memory for Odors*, ed. FR Schab, pp. 21–37. Mahwah, NJ: Erlbaum

Delplanque S, Grandjean D, Chrea C, Aymard L, Cayeux I, et al. 2008. Emotional processing of odors: evidence for a nonlinear relation between pleasantness and familiarity evaluations. *Chem. Senses* 33:469–79

Diego MA, Jones NA, Field T, Hernandez-Reif M, Schanberg S, et al. 1998. Aromatherapy positively affects mood, EEG patterns of alertness and math computations. *Int. J. Neurosci.* 96:217–24

Distel H, Ayabe-Kanamura S, Martinez-Gomez M, Schicker I, Kobayakawa T, et al. 1999. Perception of everyday odors—correlation between intensity, familiarity and strength of hedonic judgement. *Chem. Senses* 24:191–99

Distel H, Hudson R. 2001. Judgement of odor intensity is influenced by subjects' knowledge of the odor source. *Chem. Senses* 26:247–51

Djordjevic J, Lundstrom JN, Clement F, Boyle JA, Pouliot S, Jones-Gotman M. 2008. A rose by any other name: Would it smell as sweet? *J. Neurophysiol.* 99:386–93

Doty RL. 1975. Examination of relationships between pleasantness, intensity, and concentration of 10 odorous stimuli. *Percept. Psychophys.* 17:492–96

Doty RL. 2003. *Handbook of Olfaction and Gustation*. New York: Marcel Dekker

Doty RL. 2005. Clinical studies of olfaction. *Chem. Senses* 30(Suppl. 1):i207–9

Doty RL, Mishra A. 2001. Olfaction and its alteration by nasal obstruction, rhinitis, and rhinosinusitis. *Laryngoscope* 111:409–23

Doty RL, Shaman P, Dann M. 1984a. Development of the University of Pennsylvania Smell Identification Test: a standardized microencapsulated test of olfactory function. *Physiol. Behav.* 32:489–502

Doty RL, Shaman P, Kimmelman CP, Dann MS. 1984b. University of Pennsylvania Smell Identification Test: a rapid quantitative olfactory function test for the clinic. *Laryngoscope* 94:176–78

Doucette R. 1991. PNS-CNS transitional zone of the first cranial nerve. *J. Comp. Neurol.* 312:451–66

Dubose CN, Cardello AV, Maller O. 1980. Effects of colorants and flavorants on identification, perceived flavor intensity, and hedonic quality of fruit-flavored beverages and cake. *J. Food Sci.* 45:1393–99

Edelman S. 1999. *Representation and Recognition in Vision*. London: Bradford Books

Engen T, Bosack TN. 1969. Facilitation in olfactory detection. *J. Comp. Physiol. Psychol.* 68:320–26

Epple G, Herz RS. 1999. Ambient odors associated to failure influence cognitive performance in children. *Dev. Psychobiol.* 35:103–7

Firestein S. 2001. How the olfactory system makes sense of scents. *Nature* 413:211–18

Fontaine JR, Scherer KR, Roesch EB, Ellsworth PC. 2007. The world of emotions is not two-dimensional. *Psychol. Sci.* 18:1050–57

Fulbright RK, Skudlarski P, Lacadie CM, Warrenburg S, Bowers AA, et al. 1998. Functional MR imaging of regional brain responses to pleasant and unpleasant odors. *AJNR Am. J. Neuroradiol.* 19:1721–26

Gilbert AN, Rosenwasser AM. 1987. Biological rhythmicity of nasal airway patency: a re-examination of the "nasal cycle." *Acta Otolaryngol.* 104:180–86

Glusman G, Yanai I, Rubin I, Lancet D. 2001. The complete human olfactory subgenome. *Genome Res.* 11:685–702

Goldman AL, Van Der Goes van Naters W, Lessing D, Warr CG, Carlson JR. 2005. Coexpression of two functional odor receptors in one neuron. *Neuron* 45:661–66

Gottfried JA, Deichmann R, Winston JS, Dolan RJ. 2002. Functional heterogeneity in human olfactory cortex: an event-related functional magnetic resonance imaging study. *J. Neurosci.* 22:10819–28

Gottfried JA, Dolan RJ. 2003. The nose smells what the eye sees: crossmodal visual facilitation of human olfactory perception. *Neuron* 39:375–86

Gottfried JA, Winston JS, Dolan RJ. 2006. Dissociable codes of odor quality and odorant structure in human piriform cortex. *Neuron* 49:467–79

Grabenhorst F, Rolls ET, Margot C, da Silva MA, Velazco MI. 2007. How pleasant and unpleasant stimuli combine in different brain regions: odor mixtures. *J. Neurosci.* 27:13532–40

Graziadei PP, Levine RR, Monti Graziadei GA. 1979. Plasticity of connections of the olfactory sensory neuron: regeneration into the forebrain following bulbectomy in the neonatal mouse. *Neuroscience* 4:713–27

Graziadei PP, Monti Graziadei AG. 1983. Regeneration in the olfactory system of vertebrates. *Am. J. Otolaryngol.* 4:228–33

Grosmaitre X, Santarelli LC, Tan J, Luo M, Ma M. 2007. Dual functions of mammalian olfactory sensory neurons as odor detectors and mechanical sensors. *Nat. Neurosci.* 10:348–54

Haberly LB. 2001. Parallel-distributed processing in olfactory cortex: new insights from morphological and physiological analysis of neuronal circuitry. *Chem. Senses* 26:551–76

Haddad R, Khan R, Takahashi YK, Mori K, Harel D, Sobel N. 2008a. A metric for odorant comparison. *Nat. Methods* 5:425–29

Haddad R, Lapid H, Harel D, Sobel N. 2008b. Measuring smells. *Curr. Opin. Neurobiol.* 18:438–44

Henion KE. 1971. Odor pleasantness and intensity: a single dimension? *J. Exp. Psychol.* 90:275–79

Herz R, Schankler C, Beland S. 2004. Olfaction, emotion and associative learning: effects on motivated behavior. *Motiv. Emot.* 28:363–83

Herz RS. 2003. The effect of verbal context on olfactory perception. *J. Exp. Psychol.: Gen.* 132:595–606

Herz RS. 2004. A naturalistic analysis of autobiographical memories triggered by olfactory visual and auditory stimuli. *Chem. Senses* 29:217–24

Herz RS, Cupchik GC. 1995. The emotional distinctiveness of odor-evoked memories. *Chem. Senses* 20:517–28

Herz RS, Schooler JW. 2002. A naturalistic study of autobiographical memories evoked by olfactory and visual cues: testing the Proustian hypothesis. *Am. J. Psychol.* 115:21–32

Herz RS, von Clef J. 2001. The influence of verbal labeling on the perception of odors: evidence for olfactory illusions? *Perception* 30:381–91

Homewood J, Stevenson RJ. 2001. Differences in naming accuracy of odors presented to the left and right nostrils. *Biol. Psychol.* 58:65–73

Hudson R. 1999. From molecule to mind: the role of experience in shaping olfactory function. *J. Comp. Physiol. A* 185:297–304

Hummel T, Guel H, Delank W. 2004. Olfactory sensitivity of subjects working in odorous environments. *Chem. Senses* 29:533–36

Jehl C, Royet JP, Holley A. 1995. Odor discrimination and recognition memory as a function of familiarization. *Percept. Psychophys.* 57:1002–11

Jellinek JS, Koster EP. 1983. Perceived fragrance complexity and its relationship to familiarity and pleasantness 0.2. *J. Soc. Cosmet. Chem.* 34:83–97

Johnson BN, Mainland JD, Sobel N. 2003. Rapid olfactory processing implicates subcortical control of an olfactomotor system. *J. Neurophysiol.* 90:1084–94

Jones-Gotman M, Zatorre RJ. 1988. Olfactory identification deficits in patients with focal cerebral excision. *Neuropsychologia* 26:387–400

Jonsson FU, Olsson H, Olsson MJ. 2005. Odor emotionality affects the confidence in odor naming. *Chem. Senses* 30:29–35

Jonsson FU, Olsson MJ. 2003. Olfactory metacognition. *Chem. Senses* 28:651–58

Kay LM, Freeman WJ. 1998. Bidirectional processing in the olfactory-limbic axis during olfactory behavior. *Behav. Neurosci.* 112:541–53

Keller A, Zhuang H, Chi Q, Vosshall LB, Matsunami H. 2007. Genetic variation in a human odorant receptor alters odour perception. *Nature* 449:468–72

Kent PF, Mozell MM, Murphy SJ, Hornung DE. 1996. The interaction of imposed and inherent olfactory mucosal activity patterns and their composite representation in a mammalian species using voltage-sensitive dyes. *J. Neurosci.* 16:345–53

Kepecs A, Uchida N, Mainen ZF. 2006. The sniff as a unit of olfactory processing. *Chem. Senses* 31:167–79

Khan R, Luk C, Flinker A, Aggarwal A, Lapid H, et al. 2007. Predicting odor pleasantness from odorant structure: pleasantness as a reflection of the physical world. *J. Neurosci.* 27:10015–23

Kirk-Smith MD, Van Toller C, Dodd GH. 1983. Unconscious odour conditioning in human subjects. *Biol. Psychol.* 17:221–31

Knasko SC. 1995. Pleasant odors and congruency: effects on approach behavior. *Chem. Senses* 20:479–87

Kobal G, Hummel T, Vantoller S. 1992. Differences in human chemosensory evoked-potentials to olfactory and somatosensory chemical stimuli presented to left and right nostrils. *Chem. Senses* 17:233–44

Laing DG, Glemarec A. 1992. Selective attention and the perceptual analysis of odor mixtures. *Physiol. Behav.* 52:1047–53

Laska M. 2005. Olfactory discrimination ability for aliphatic c6 alcohols as a function of presence, position, and configuration of a double bond. *Chem. Senses* 30:755–60

Laska M, Ayabe-Kanamura S, Hubener F, Saito S. 2000. Olfactory discrimination ability for aliphatic odorants as a function of oxygen moiety. *Chem. Senses* 25:189–97

Laska M, Freyer D. 1997. Olfactory discrimination ability for aliphatic esters in squirrel monkeys and humans. *Chem. Senses* 22:457–65

Laska M, Teubner P. 1999. Olfactory discrimination ability of human subjects for ten pairs of enantiomers. *Chem. Senses* 24:161–70

Lawless H, Engen T. 1977. Associations to odors: interference, mnemonics, and verbal labeling. *J. Exp. Psychol. Hum. Learn. Mem.* 3:52–59

Le Berre E, Beno N, Ishii A, Chabanet C, Etievant P, Thomas-Danguin T. 2008. Just noticeable differences in component concentrations modify the odor quality of a blending mixture. *Chem. Senses* 33:389–95

LeDoux J. 2007. The amygdala. *Curr. Biol.* 17:R868–74

Lehrner J, Marwinski G, Lehr S, Johren P, Deecke L. 2005. Ambient odors of orange and lavender reduce anxiety and improve mood in a dental office. *Physiol. Behav.* 86:92–95

Leon M, Johnson BA. 2003. Olfactory coding in the mammalian olfactory bulb. *Brain Res. Brain Res. Rev.* 42:23–32

Levine SB. 2005. What is love anyway? *J. Sex Marital Ther.* 31:143–51

Li W, Howard JD, Parrish TB, Gottfried JA. 2008. Aversive learning enhances perceptual and cortical discrimination of indiscriminable odor cues. *Science* 319:1842–45

Livermore A, Laing DG. 1998. The influence of odor type on the discrimination and identification of odorants in multicomponent odor mixtures. *Physiol. Behav.* 65:311–20

Lord T, Kasprzak M. 1989. Identification of self through olfaction. *Percept. Mot. Skills* 69:219–24

Lorig TS. 1999. On the similarity of odor and language perception. *Neurosci. Biobehav. Rev.* 23:391–98

Lundstrom JN, Boyle JA, Zatorre RJ, Jones-Gotman M. 2008. The neuronal substrates of human olfactory based kin recognition. *Hum. Brain Mapp.* 30:2571–80

MacColl G, Bouloux P, Quinton R. 2002. Kallmann syndrome: adhesion, afferents, and anosmia. *Neuron* 34:675–78

Macfarelane A. 1975. Olfaction in the development of social preferences in the human neonate. *Ciba Found. Symp.* 33:103–17

Mainland JD, Bremner EA, Young N, Johnson BN, Khan RM, et al. 2002. Olfactory plasticity: One nostril knows what the other learns. *Nature* 419:802

Mainland JD, Sobel N. 2006. The sniff is part of the olfactory percept. *Chem. Senses* 31:181–96

Mallet P, Schaal B. 1998. Rating and recognition of peers' personal odors by 9-year-old children: an exploratory study. *J. Gen. Psychol.* 125:47–64

Mandairon N, Poncelet J, Bensafi M, Didier A. 2009. Humans and mice express similar olfactory preferences. *PLoS ONE* 4:e4209

Maresh A, Rodriguez Gil D, Whitman MC, Greer CA. 2008. Principles of glomerular organization in the human olfactory bulb—implications for odor processing. *PLoS ONE* 3:e2640

Masago R, Shimomura Y, Iwanaga K, Katsuura T. 2001. The effects of hedonic properties of odors and attentional modulation on the olfactory event-related potentials. *J. Physiol. Anthropol. Appl. Hum. Sci.* 20:7–13

McBride SA, Slotnick B. 1997. The olfactory thalamocortical system and odor reversal learning examined using an asymmetrical lesion paradigm in rats. *Behav. Neurosci.* 111:1273–84

Mingo SA, Stevenson RJ. 2007. Phenomenological differences between familiar and unfamiliar odours. *Perception* 36:931–47

Mombaerts P, Wang F, Dulac C, Chao SK, Nemes A, et al. 1996. Visualizing an olfactory sensory map. *Cell* 87:675–86

Moncrieff RW. 1966. *Odour Preferences*. London: Leonard Hill

Moran DT, Rowley JC, Jafek BW, Lovell MA. 1982. The fine structure of the olfactory mucosa in man. *J. Neurocytol.* 11:721–46

Morrot G, Brochet F, Dubourdieu D. 2001. The color of odors. *Brain Lang.* 79:309–20

Moskowitz HR, Barbe CD. 1977. Profiling of odor components and their mixtures. *Sens. Processes* 1:212–26

Moskowitz HR, Dravnieks A, Klarman LA. 1976. Odor intensity and pleasantness for a diverse set of odorants. *Percept. Psychophys.* 19:122–28

Mozell MM, Jagodowicz M. 1973. Chromatographic separation of odorants by the nose: retention times measured across in vivo olfactory mucosa. *Science* 181:1247–49

Mozell MM, Kent P, Murphy S. 1991. The effect of flow rate upon the magnitude of the olfactory response differs for different odorants. *Chem. Senses* 16:631–49

Nagata Y, Takeuchi N. 1990. Measurement of odor threshold by triangle odor bag method. *Bull. Jpn. Environ. Sanit. Cent.* 17:77–89

Nakamura T, Gold GH. 1987. A cyclic nucleotide-gated conductance in olfactory receptor cilia. *Nature* 325:442–44

Navarrete-Palacios E, Hudson R, Reyes-Guerrero G, Guevara-Guzman R. 2003. Lower olfactory threshold during the ovulatory phase of the menstrual cycle. *Biol. Psychol.* 63:269–79

Nef P, Hermansborgmeyer I, Artierespin H, Beasley L, Dionne VE, Heinemann SF. 1992. Spatial pattern of receptor expression in the olfactory epithelium. *Proc. Natl. Acad. Sci. USA* 89:8948–52

Nordin S, Broman DA, Olofsson JK, Wulff M. 2004. A longitudinal descriptive study of self-reported abnormal smell and taste perception in pregnant women. *Chem. Senses* 29:391–402

O'Doherty J, Rolls ET, Francis S, Bowtell R, McGlone F, et al. 2000. Sensory-specific satiety-related olfactory activation of the human orbitofrontal cortex. *Neuroreport* 11:893–97

Olsson MJ, Jonsson FU. 2008. Is it easier to match a name to an odor than vice versa? *Chemosensory Percept.* 1:184–89

Pace U, Hanski E, Salomon Y, Lancet D. 1985. Odorant-sensitive adenylate cyclase may mediate olfactory reception. *Nature* 316:255–58

Pangborn RM. 1975. Cross-cultural aspects of flavour preference. *Food Technol.* 29:34–36

Pause BM, Krauel K. 2000. Chemosensory event-related potentials (CSERP) as a key to the psychology of odors. *Int. J. Psychophysiol.* 36:105–22

Pelosi P. 2001. The role of perireceptor events in vertebrate olfaction. *Cell. Mol. Life Sci.* 58:503–9

Pevsner J, Trifiletti RR, Strittmatter SM, Snyder SH. 1985. Isolation and characterization of an olfactory receptor protein for odorant pyrazines. *Proc. Natl. Acad. Sci. USA* 82(9):3050–54

Plailly J, Howard JD, Gitelman DR, Gottfried JA. 2008. Attention to odor modulates thalamocortical connectivity in the human brain. *J. Neurosci.* 28:5257–67

Pollatos O, Kopietz R, Linn J, Albrecht J, Sakar V, et al. 2007. Emotional stimulation alters olfactory sensitivity and odor judgment. *Chem. Senses* 32:583–89

Porter J, Anand T, Johnson B, Khan RM, Sobel N. 2005. Brain mechanisms for extracting spatial information from smell. *Neuron* 47:581–92

Porter RH, Cernoch JM, McLaughlin FJ. 1983. Maternal recognition of neonates through olfactory cues. *Physiol. Behav.* 30:151–54

Porter RH, Moore JD. 1981. Human kin recognition by olfactory cues. *Physiol. Behav.* 27:493–95

Powell TP, Cowan WM, Raisman G. 1965. The central olfactory connexions. *J. Anat.* 99:791–813

Price JL. 1973. An autoradiographic study of complementary laminar patterns of termination of afferent fibers to the olfactory cortex. *J. Comp. Neurol.* 150:87–108

Price JL. 1987. The central olfactory and accessory olfactory systems. In *Neurobiology of Taste and Smell*, ed. TE Finger, WL Silver, pp. 179–203. New York: Wiley Intersci.

Price JL. 1990. Olfactory system. In *The Human Nervous System*, ed. G Paxinos, pp. 979–1001. San Diego, CA: Academic

Principato JJ, Ozenberger JM. 1970. Cyclical changes in nasal resistance. *Arch. Otolaryngol.* 91:71–77

Qureshy A, Kawashima R, Imran MB, Sugiura M, Goto R, et al. 2000. Functional mapping of human brain in olfactory processing: a PET study. *J. Neurophysiol.* 84:1656–66

Rabin MD. 1988. Experience facilitates olfactory quality discrimination. *Percept. Psychophys.* 44:532–40

Rausch R, Serafetinides EA, Crandall PH. 1977. Olfactory memory in patients with anterior temporal lobectomy. *Cortex* 13:445–52

Ressler KJ, Sullivan SL, Buck LB. 1993. A zonal organization of odorant receptor gene-expression in the olfactory epithelium. *Cell* 73:597–609

Ressler KJ, Sullivan SL, Buck LB. 1994. Information coding in the olfactory system: evidence for a stereotyped and highly organized epitope map in the olfactory bulb. *Cell* 79:1245–55

Richardson JT, Zucco GM. 1989. Cognition and olfaction: a review. *Psychol. Bull.* 105:352–60

Rolls ET. 2004. Convergence of sensory systems in the orbitofrontal cortex in primates and brain design for emotion. *Anat. Rec. A Discov. Mol. Cell Evol. Biol.* 281:1212–25

Rolls ET, Grabenhorst F, Margot C, da Silva MA, Velazco MI. 2008. Selective attention to affective value alters how the brain processes olfactory stimuli. *J. Cogn. Neurosci.* 20:1815–26

Rolls ET, Kringelbach ML, de Araujo IE. 2003. Different representations of pleasant and unpleasant odours in the human brain. *Eur. J. Neurosci.* 18:695–703

Royet JP, Hudry J, Zald DH, Godinot D, Gregoire MC, et al. 2001. Functional neuroanatomy of different olfactory judgments. *Neuroimage* 13:506–19

Royet JP, Koenig O, Gregoire MC, Cinotti L, Lavenne F, et al. 1999. Functional anatomy of perceptual and semantic processing for odors. *J. Cogn. Neurosci.* 11:94–109

Royet JP, Plailly J, Delon-Martin C, Kareken DA, Segebarth C. 2003. fMRI of emotional responses to odors: influence of hedonic valence and judgment, handedness, and gender. *Neuroimage* 20:713–28

Royet JP, Zald D, Versace R, Costes N, Lavenne F, et al. 2000. Emotional responses to pleasant and unpleasant olfactory, visual, and auditory stimuli: a positron emission tomography study. *J. Neurosci.* 20:7752–59

Russek M, Fantino M, Cabanac M. 1979. Effect of environmental temperature on pleasure ratings of odors and tastes. *Physiol. Behav.* 22:251–56

Sato T, Hirono J, Tonoike M, Takebayashi M. 1994. Tuning specificities to aliphatic odorants in mouse olfactory receptor neurons and their local distribution. *J. Neurophysiol.* 72:2980–89

Savic I, Berglund H. 2004. Passive perception of odors and semantic circuits. *Hum. Brain Mapp.* 21:271–78

Savic I, Gulyas B. 2000. PET shows that odors are processed both ipsilaterally and contralaterally to the stimulated nostril. *Neuroreport* 11:2861–66

Savic I, Gulyas B, Larsson M, Roland P. 2000. Olfactory functions are mediated by parallel and hierarchical processing. *Neuron* 26:735–45

Schaal B, Montagner H, Hertling E, Bolzoni D, Moyse A, Quichon R. 1980. Olfactory stimulations in mother-child relations. *Reprod. Nutr. Dev.* 20:843–58

Schiffman S, Robinson DE, Erickson RP. 1977. Multidimensional-scaling of odorants—examination of psychological and physiochemical dimensions. *Chem. Senses Flavor* 2:375–90

Schiffman SS. 1974. Physicochemical correlates of olfactory quality. *Science* 185:112–17

Schmidt HJ, Beauchamp GK. 1988. Adult-like odor preferences and aversions in three-year-old children. *Child Dev.* 59:1136–43

Schoenfeld TA, Cleland TA. 2006. Anatomical contributions to odorant sampling and representation in rodents: zoning in on sniffing behavior. *Chem. Senses* 31:131–44

Shepard RN, Metzler J. 1971. Mental rotation of three-dimensional objects. *Science* 171:701–3

Shepherd GM. 2004. The human sense of smell: Are we better than we think? *PLoS Biol.* 2:E146

Shipley MT. 1995. Olfactory system. In *The Rat Nervous System*, ed. G Paxinos, pp. 899–928. San Diego, CA: Academic

Slotnick B, Bisulco S. 2003. Detection and discrimination of carvone enantiomers in rats with olfactory bulb lesions. *Neuroscience* 121:451–57

Small DM, Prescott J. 2005. Odor/taste integration and the perception of flavor. *Exp. Brain Research.* 166:345–57

Sobel N, Johnson BN, Mainland J, Yousem DM. 2003. Functional neuroimaging of human olfaction. See Doty 2003, pp. 251–73

Sobel N, Khan RM, Hartley CA, Sullivan EV, Gabrieli JD. 2000. Sniffing longer rather than stronger to maintain olfactory detection threshold. *Chem. Senses* 25:1–8

Sobel N, Khan RM, Saltman A, Sullivan EV, Gabrieli JD. 1999. The world smells different to each nostril. *Nature* 402:35

Sobel N, Prabhakaran V, Desmond JE, Glover GH, Goode RL, et al. 1998. Sniffing and smelling: separate subsystems in the human olfactory cortex. *Nature* 392:282–86

Soussignan R, Schaal B, Marlier L. 1999. Olfactory alliesthesia in human neonates: Prandial state and stimulus familiarity modulate facial and autonomic responses to milk odors. *Dev. Psychobiol.* 35:3–14

Soussignan R, Schaal B, Marlier L, Jiang T. 1997. Facial and autonomic responses to biological and artificial olfactory stimuli in human neonates: re-examining early hedonic discrimination of odors. *Physiol. Behav.* 62:745–58

Steiner JE. 1979. Human facial expressions in response to taste and smell stimulation. *Adv. Child Dev. Behav.* 13:257–95

Stevenson RJ, Boakes RA. 2003. A mnemonic theory of odor perception. *Psychol. Rev.* 110:340–64

Stevenson RJ, Case TI. 2005. Olfactory imagery: a review. *Psychon. Bull. Rev.* 12:244–64

Stevenson RJ, Wilson DA. 2007. Odour perception: an object-recognition approach. *Perception* 36:1821–33

Strotmann J, Wanner I, Krieger J, Raming K, Breer H. 1992. Expression of odorant receptors in spatially restricted subsets of chemosensory neurons. *Neuroreport* 3:1053–56

Teghtsoonian R, Teghtsoonian M. 1984. Testing a perceptual constancy model for odor strength: the effects of sniff pressure and resistance to sniffing. *Perception* 13:743–52

Tsuboi A, Yoshihara S, Yamazaki N, Kasai H, Asai-Tsuboi H, et al. 1999. Olfactory neurons expressing closely linked and homologous odorant receptor genes tend to project their axons to neighboring glomeruli on the olfactory bulb. *J. Neurosci.* 19:8409–18

Tulving E. 1983. *Elements of Episodic Memory.* New York: Oxford Univ. Press

Varendi H, Christensson K, Porter RH, Winberg J. 1998. Soothing effect of amniotic fluid smell in newborn infants. *Early Hum. Dev.* 51:47–55

Vassar R, Chao SK, Sitcheran R, Nunez JM, Vosshall LB, Axel R. 1994. Topographic organization of sensory projections to the olfactory-bulb. *Cell* 79:981–91

Vassar R, Ngai J, Axel R. 1993. Spatial segregation of odorant receptor expression in the mammalian olfactory epithelium. *Cell* 74:309–18

Wang L, Chen L, Jacob T. 2004. Evidence for peripheral plasticity in human odour response. *J. Physiol.* 554:236–44

Weber ST, Heuberger E. 2008. The impact of natural odors on affective states in humans. *Chem. Senses* 33:441–47

Weisfeld GE, Czilli T, Phillips KA, Gall JA, Lichtman CM. 2003. Possible olfaction-based mechanisms in human kin recognition and inbreeding avoidance. *J. Exp. Child Psychol.* 85:279–95

Wells DL, Hepper PG. 2000. The discrimination of dog odours by humans. *Perception* 29:111–15

Whisman M, Goetzinger J, Cotton F, Brinkman D. 1978. Odorant evaluation: a study of ethanethiol and tetrahydrothiophene as warning agents in propane. *Environ. Sci. Technol.* 12:1285–88

Widen H, Leufven A, Nielsen T. 2005. Identification of chemicals, possibly originating from misuse of refillable PET bottles, responsible for consumer complaints about off-odours in water and soft drinks. *Food Additives Contam.* 22:681–92

Wilson DA. 1997. Binaral interactions in the rat piriform cortex. *J. Neurophysiol.* 78:160–69

Wilson DA, Stevenson RJ. 2003. The fundamental role of memory in olfactory perception. *Trends Neurosci.* 26:243–47

Winston JS, Gottfried JA, Kilner JM, Dolan RJ. 2005. Integrated neural representations of odor intensity and affective valence in human amygdala. *J. Neurosci.* 25:8903–7

Wysocki CJ, Dorries KM, Beauchamp GK. 1989. Ability to perceive androstenone can be acquired by ostensibly anosmic people. *Proc. Natl. Acad. Sci. USA* 86:7976–78

Wysocki CJ, Pierce JD, Gilbert AN. 1991. Geographic, cross-cultural, and individual variation in human olfaction. In *Smell and Taste in Health and Disease*, ed. TV Getchell, pp. 287–314. New York: Raven

Yee KK, Wysocki CJ. 2001. Odorant exposure increases olfactory sensitivity: olfactory epithelium is implicated. *Physiol. Behav.* 72:705–11

Zald DH, Pardo JV. 1997. Emotion, olfaction, and the human amygdala: amygdala activation during aversive olfactory stimulation. *Proc. Natl. Acad. Sci. USA* 94:4119–24

Zarzo M. 2008. Psychologic dimensions in the perception of everyday odors: pleasantness and edibility. *J. Sensory Stud.* 23:354–76

Zatorre RJ, Jones-Gotman M. 1991. Human olfactory discrimination after unilateral frontal or temporal lobectomy. *Brain* 114(Pt. 1A):71–84

Zelano C, Bensafi M, Porter J, Mainland J, Johnson B, et al. 2005. Attentional modulation in human primary olfactory cortex. *Nat. Neurosci.* 8:114–20

Zelano C, Montag J, Johnson B, Khan R, Sobel N. 2007. Dissociated representations of irritation and valence in human primary olfactory cortex. *J. Neurophysiol.* 97:1969–76

Zelano C, Montag J, Khan R, Sobel N. 2009. A specialized odor memory buffer in primary olfactory cortex. *PLoS One* 4:e4965

Zelano C, Sobel N. 2005. Humans as an animal model for systems-level organization of olfaction. *Neuron* 48:431–54

Zellner DA, Bartoli AM, Eckard R. 1991. Influence of color on odor identification and liking ratings. *Am. J. Psychol.* 104:547–61

Zellner DA, Kautz MA. 1990. Color affects perceived odor intensity. *J. Exp. Psychol.: Hum. Percept. Perform.* 16:391–97

Somesthetic Senses

Mark Hollins

Department of Psychology, University of North Carolina at Chapel Hill, Chapel Hill, North Carolina 27599; email: mhollins@email.unc.edu

Annu. Rev. Psychol. 2010. 61:243–71

First published online as a Review in Advance on October 19, 2009

The *Annual Review of Psychology* is online at psych.annualreviews.org

This article's doi: 10.1146/annurev.psych.093008.100419

Key Words

attention, emotion, pain, pain modulation, texture perception, thermoreception, touch

Abstract

This is a review of recent advances in our understanding of the sensory modalities of touch, temperature sensitivity, and pain. Most of the research described is psychophysical or perceptual in nature, but physiological and imaging studies are included when they sharpen issues or reveal underlying mechanisms. Coverage of touch research comprises the subjects of acuity, vibrotaction and texture perception, perception of location and movement, tactile attention, and cross-modal phenomena. For pain, the covered topics are central sensitization, pain-touch and pain-pain interactions, placebo effects, the role of attention and emotion in pain, and the genetics of pain. For touch, the topics are arranged roughly in order of increasing cognitive involvement, but such an ordering is not feasible for pain, where attitudes and expectations can substantially affect even the most "sensory" of judgments.

Contents

Somesthetic senses: sensory systems that respond to stimulation of the skin and deeper tissues of the body

Thermoreception: the detection and perception (typically as coolness, coldness, warmth, or heat) of stimulation that changes the temperature of the skin

Tactile acuity: the ability to resolve spatial aspects of tactile stimulation, such as the orientation of a grating pressed against the skin

INTRODUCTION

In many ways, somesthesis (touch and other forms of bodily sensibility) is unique among sensory systems. It is the most diverse, comprising a family of submodalities that respond in a variety of ways to mechanical, thermal, and chemical energy; it has the largest sensory surface, even if we ignore internal structures and consider only the skin; it reflects the most balanced emphasis on spatial information (in which vision is pre-eminent) and temporal information (the specialty of the auditory system); it is the one most closely interwoven with affect, both positive and negative; and of the senses, it is the most essential to life.

The sense of touch, broadly defined, has also played a crucial role in sensory science, yielding paradigm-shifting discoveries on topics ranging from sensory discrimination and the specificity of sensory nerve endings to (more recently)

the brain's capacity for plasticity. Current work offers many new insights, as described in this review. Some newly discovered principles underline the distinctive role and nature of somesthesis; others—especially at the cognitive level—emphasize similarities and interactions across modalities.

This review covers research on the somesthetic senses of touch, thermoreception, and pain, during the period 1998–2008. The last such review in these pages was by Craig & Rollman (1999), and an attempt has been made to provide continuity with their survey while minimizing overlap.

In surveying this broad subject within the space available, it has been necessary to be selective in the choice of citations. For example, when a series of articles report closely related experiments, only key references are given; and studies prior to the reviewed period are generally omitted, even if they helped lay the groundwork for research that is discussed. The citations given are sufficient, however, to give readers access to the extended literature. Finally, it has only been possible to give incidental coverage to some topics, most notably haptics, the study of active exploration (especially) by the hand; Jones & Lederman (2006) provide an authoritative review of this expanding field. Research on the sense of touch in persons who are visually impaired is also omitted; work in this area has recently been brought together by Heller & Ballesteros (2006).

Psychophysical research is emphasized throughout, with physiological and neuroimaging work cited only sparingly. For erudite coverage of the anatomy and physiology of the hand, see Mountcastle's 2005 monograph.

We begin with touch; later sections are devoted to thermal sensation and to pain.

TOUCH

Tactile Acuity

Classically, the premier measure of tactile acuity was the two-point threshold. In this paradigm, two points are simultaneously touched to the skin, and the subject reports whether one or two were felt; the smallest separation that supports a "two" report is the threshold. Although many discoveries (most notably the systematic variations in acuity across the body surface) were made with this method, it gradually became clear that experimental subjects could base their responses on a variety of criteria. In recent years a consensus has emerged (Craig & Johnson 2000) that more precise and analytical measures should generally be used in place of the two-point threshold.

The fact that subjects can use different criteria is interesting, however, for it suggests that tactile acuity is a complex phenomenon, to which multiple processes contribute. To dissect these, Craig (1999) asked subjects to discriminate among three distinct stimuli, pressed against the index fingerpad. One was a tactile grating, with ridges parallel to the long axis of the finger; a second was an identical grating but oriented at 90° to the first; the third stimulus was a smooth surface. Craig found that subjects were better at identifying the smooth surface than they were at distinguishing the two orientations of grating from one another.

Gibson & Craig (2002) proposed that the relatively easy smooth-grooved discrimination is largely mediated by intensity cues, with ridge edges contributing to overall stimulus effectiveness, whereas the grating orientation task is accomplished by the use of spatial information. In support of this view, they demonstrated that orientation task performance varies substantially with the locus of stimulation, as does receptor spacing, whereas performance on the smooth-grooved task does not. Recent work has shown, however, that the distinction between types of information used in the two tasks is more nuanced than was originally thought: In the smooth-grooved task, subjects detect the grating's inhomogeneities although they do not perceive their spatial layout (Craig et al. 2008).

A shortcoming of the grating orientation task is that it is difficult to use except on the hand and face: Acuity elsewhere is so poor as to require a grating too large to be practicable.

A gap-detection task, however, addresses this concern: It can be used on the arm as well as the hand, and performance varies steeply with innervation density, implying spatial processing (Gibson & Craig 2005).

The physiological basis of spatial processing has been explored by Bensmaïa et al. (2006b), building on earlier work by Johnson and colleagues (for an overview, see Johnson 2002). Bensmaïa et al. (2006b) recorded from mechanoreceptive afferents serving the fingerpad of the macaque monkey, while tactile gratings were pressed against it. Activity of a neuron was modulated as the grating was stepped across its receptive field. The depth of this modulation increased with groove and ridge width (these were always equal to each other), no doubt accounting for the fact that coarse gratings are easier to resolve. These physiological results demonstrate that responses from a population of afferents with offset receptive fields are capable of providing the spatial information on which grating orientation judgments depend.

As expected, Bensmaïa and colleagues (2006b) found that modulation was greater in slowly adapting type 1 (SA1) afferents than in rapidly adapting (RA) afferents; this result is consistent with the widely accepted view that SA1 afferents (which terminate as Merkel disks in the skin) are the premier conveyors of spatial information. Interestingly, vibrating the gratings (e.g., at 80 Hz) while they were being held against the skin had virtually no influence on the amount of spatial information carried by the afferents, but reduced the grating-orientation acuity of human observers presented with the same stimuli (Bensmaïa et al. 2006a). Since this interference does not occur in the afferents, it must reflect events in the central nervous system. Bensmaïa and colleagues hypothesized that relatively blurred signals from RAs, which are vibration-sensitive, might be combining with and thus degrading the precise spatial signals carried by SA1s. They confirmed this idea by showing that adapting out the RA channel with strong vibration improved subjects' performance on the spatial task.

Slowly adapting type 1 (SA1) channel: a semi-independent anatomical and functional system consisting of Merkel disks (pressure-sensitive cutaneous mechanoreceptors) and their neural connections

RA: rapidly adapting mechanoreceptor

Vibrotaction

Understanding of the way in which the somatosensory system responds to dynamic stimulation has also advanced in the past decade, with some earlier ideas supported by new evidence, while others have been overturned.

Continuing to refine the multichannel model of vibrotaction that has gradually evolved from the pioneering work of Verrillo (1962), Gescheider et al. (2001) used an adapting-effectiveness measure to define the tuning curves of the RA, Pacinian (PC), and slowly adapting type 2 (SA2) channels. The results are consistent with tuning curves obtained earlier using masking procedures (Bolanowski et al. 1988) but extend them over a wider frequency range. An elegant synthesis of work on the multichannel model has recently appeared (Gescheider et al. 2009).

Vibrotactile stimuli are perceived as having both intensity and pitch, and these subjective properties vary as a complex function of stimulus amplitude and frequency (Hollins & Roy 1996, Roy & Hollins 1998). To explore intensity coding, Muniak et al. (2007) compared magnitude estimates from human participants with physiological responses recorded from primary afferents in anesthetized monkeys. They used a mathematical model to demonstrate that subjective intensity can be accounted for by an additive combination of signals from the SA1, RA, and PC channels. (The SA2 channel is not present in monkeys, and even in humans it appears to play little role in vibrotaction.)

With regard to vibrotactile frequency judgments, the view that they are based on temporal coding (Mountcastle et al. 1969) has been widely accepted. However, it has since been found that trial-to-trial changes in the accuracy of monkey frequency discrimination closely reflect concurrent variations in the rate of firing of its S1 neurons (Salinas et al. 2000). The implication is that a neural rate code may contribute to vibratory pitch. The frequencies employed by Salinas et al. were in the range to which the RA system is primarily responsive; when a wider range of frequencies is involved, pitch coding may include a comparison of activity levels in different mechanoreceptive channels (Roy & Hollins 1998).

Texture Perception

Texture, in a broad sense, means any mechanical properties that influence the feel of a surface. A multidimensional scaling (MDS) study in which subjects were asked to rate the differentness of everyday surfaces from one another showed that roughness and hardness are the two main dimensions of texture space, with a slipperiness/stickiness dimension playing a secondary role for some individuals (Hollins et al. 2000a). Additional dimensions may come into play when specialized sets of surfaces are used.

Research during the past decade has demonstrated that at least two sensory coding mechanisms contribute to the roughness/smoothness of a surface. It had previously been shown, in a series of studies summarized by Johnson (2002), that the roughness of a surface could be predicted on the basis of spatial variations in activity within the population of SA1 afferents in the stimulated skin. They found the roughest surfaces to be those with texture elements that activated some of these afferents while being far enough apart (about 3 mm on the fingerpad) to leave a roughly equal number of intervening SA1s unstimulated; the relationship between roughness and element spacing is, however, modulated by a variety of other geometrical parameters (Meftah et al. 2000). Johnson's work has provided physiological confirmation of a spatial code for roughness, psychophysically demonstrated much earlier by Lederman (1974).

A number of subsequent findings showed, however, that a spatial code cannot account for the roughness/smoothness of very fine surfaces (those with spatial periods below about 200 μm). For example, coarse surfaces are equally discriminable whether they move across the fingerpad or remain stationary, a result consistent with a spatial code; fine textures, on the other hand, become indiscriminable when they are held motionless against the skin (Hollins &

Risner 2000). The authors proposed that lateral stimulus movement creates vibrations that are detected by mechanoreceptors and form the basis for the perceived roughness of fine surfaces. Hollins et al. (2000b) demonstrated that vibrotactile signals can manifest themselves perceptually as roughness. They found that surreptitiously vibrating a surface as the finger moved across it made it feel rougher, even for subjects who later reported no awareness of the vibration.

To determine whether vibration per se, rather than some other concomitant of stimulus movement, is essential for fine-texture perception, Hollins et al. (2001) measured the discriminability of surfaces before and after they desensitized vibrotactile channels with strong 100-Hz vibration. This adaptation did not affect the discriminability of the coarse surfaces, but it virtually abolished discriminability for the fine surfaces. In a second experiment using selective adaptation with low- and high-frequency vibrations, Hollins et al. (2001) showed that activity in the Pacinian channel was necessary for perception of the fine textures.

Taken together, these studies provide considerable support for the duplex theory of roughness, i.e., the view that roughness is mediated by two neural codes—a spatial code for coarse textures and a vibrotactile code for fine textures. A substantive understanding of the vibrotactile code required, however, that cutaneous vibrations be recorded and analyzed. Bensmaïa & Hollins (2003, 2005) made such recordings by tracking the movements of a small magnet riding on the skin as a variety of fine surfaces were drawn across the fingerpad. Fourier analysis revealed that when periodic surfaces (etched arrays of microscopic truncated pyramids) were used, the fundamental frequency of the recorded vibrations corresponded to the frequency at which texture elements swept across a given location on the skin; this confirmed the validity of the method. A rich assortment of higher frequencies (including harmonics) was also present, so that each surface, including papers, cloths, and other everyday surfaces, had a distinctive

vibratory signature that could conceivably mediate its distinctive "feel," given the independently demonstrated ability of subjects to discriminate complex vibrations based on their harmonic structure (Bensmaïa et al. 2005). Roughness, however, was found to be a fairly straightforward function of the calculated overall effectiveness of vibration in activating Pacinian corpuscles (Bensmaïa and Hollins 2003). Research with surfaces moving across an artificial fingertip (Scheibert et al. 2009) has shown that fingerprint ridges promote this stimulation of Pacinians by amplifying vibration frequencies to which they are sensitive.

Some surfaces have a microtexture superimposed on a macrotexture, like corduroy. Gescheider et al. (2005) have shown that judgments of the roughness of texturally complex surfaces are normally based primarily on macrotexture. However, when subjects are asked to rate the roughness of individual texture elements, they give responses that can be reduced by 250-Hz adaptation and are thus mediated by vibrotaction. The subjects were also able to combine both types of signals into estimates of "overall" roughness, a result that strongly supports the duplex theory.

Despite this degree of synthesis, roughness perception remains an active, and sometimes controversial, research area. Among the views for which evidence has been put forward are that a spatial code can account for roughness of fine as well as coarse textures (Yoshioka et al. 2001) and that texture element height (Miyaoka et al. 1999), tangential force variations (Smith et al. 2002), and temporal coding (Cascio & Sathian 2001) contribute to perceived roughness.

All of the studies described in this section were concerned with direct touch; it is also possible to perceive textures (real or virtual) through a probe, such as a stylus. This indirect touch differs in instructive ways from direct touch. For example, roughness is determined not by the properties of the texture alone, but also by the relative dimensions of probe and surface features; this indicates that the interaction

Pacinian channel: a semi-independent anatomical and functional system consisting of Pacinian corpuscles (large, vibration-sensitive mechanoreceptors) and their neural connections; also called the PC channel

between probe and surface is determinative (Klatzky & Lederman 1999, Klatzky et al. 2003) and implies that the same is true (although the interactions are more subtle) in direct touch. Some differences between direct and indirect touch, such as the partial blurring of perceptual dimensions in the latter (Hollins et al. 2004, 2005), presumably reflect the fact that indirect touch is relatively impoverished with respect to spatial information. Other comparisons of direct and indirect touch have been made by Hollins et al. (2006), LaMotte (2000), and Yoshioka et al. (2007).

Perception of Location and Movement

One of the most important components of the sense of touch is the ability to localize a cutaneous stimulus. Measured with isolated taps, localization is quite accurate; vibratory stimuli, however, appear to be less precisely localized, perhaps because they produce traveling waves and (at high frequencies) vigorously stimulate Pacinian corpuscles, which have large, diffuse receptive fields. Cholewiak & Collins (2003) measured localization on the forearm, using an array of vibrators extending nearly from the elbow to the wrist. Randomly selected vibrators were individually activated, and the participant was asked to identify them. Performance was good when tactors near the elbow or wrist were activated, but surprisingly poor when vibration was delivered to positions near the middle of the forearm: Apparently there is something perceptually distinctive about stimulation at a joint. The results were only partly accounted for by the fact that the elbow and wrist stimuli formed the ends of an array. Analogous findings were obtained with a belt of tactors worn around the waist (Cholewiak et al. 2004), where the navel and spine apparently serve as landmarks. van Erp (2008) found, using a triangulation method, that such stimuli are mislocalized primarily in terms of their distance along radii from the center of the torso, perhaps reflecting the fact that our girth changes frequently! Work on this topic is motivated partly by a desire to facilitate the development of cutaneous devices that can convey spatial information not visually available.

Localization becomes more problematic when two or more stimuli, at neighboring positions, are presented in close temporal proximity (interstimulus interval <0.3 s). A variety of experimental paradigms have been used to study the resulting interactions, but it may be that a common set of mechanisms accounts for all of them. The basic finding is that the distance between two stimuli is increasingly underestimated as the interstimulus interval between them grows shorter.

Cholewiak (1999) explored the limits of this spatiotemporal interaction by presenting pairs of taps under a variety of conditions and asking subjects to give magnitude estimates of the overall spatial extent of the resulting sensory experience. The same basic pattern of results was obtained on thigh, palm, and fingertip. At small separations (less than the traditional two-point threshold for that body site), perceived extent depended on temporal separation only, suggesting that the local sign associated with a spot on the skin meanders somewhat; above the two-point threshold, perceived extent was a positive function of both spatial and temporal stimulus separation; finally, at very large separations (e.g., 30 cm on the thigh), time ceased to influence perceived distance.

Despite their similarities, the different examples of spatiotemporal interaction have some distinctive features. Consider, for example, cutaneous saltation (Geldard 1982), a phenomenon usually demonstrated with three taps, the first two (T1 and T2) at one location, and the third (T3) at a different location. In this situation, stimulation appears to "hop" from the initially stimulated locus to an intermediate spot and then to the location of the final tap; the attraction of the second tap toward the third one is a manifestation of spatiotemporal interaction. Saltation is so compelling that subjects cannot distinguish between it and a control condition in which T2 is actually delivered to the intermediate locus (Eimer et al. 2005). A unique feature of saltation is that taps cannot be induced to cross the midline; however,

Eimer et al. (2005) showed (by delivering taps to juxtaposed forearms) that the perceptual attraction responsible for it does cross the midline. With T1 and T2 delivered to one arm and T3 to the other, T2 hopped along the first arm in the direction (in external coordinates) of T3, but not between arms.

Few recent studies have examined the perception of continuous movement, but a set of experiments by Pei et al. (2008), using a dense array of independently controllable probes to present tangible patterns to the index fingerpad, sheds light on this issue. They used several paradigms that are familiar from research on the visual perception of movement, including the field-of-bars paradigm in which a two-dimensional array (i.e., rows and columns) of short, vertical bars drifts past a stationary circular aperture. The bars actually move along a diagonal, but the perception is that they move in a more nearly horizontal direction, and the illusion grows stronger as trial duration is shortened to 200 ms. Pei et al. (2008) propose that, as in vision, a developing percept is initially dominated by local cues (in this case movement of the mostly vertical edges of the bars perpendicular to their orientation), but that these elements are gradually combined into a more realistic overall impression.

The existence of a tactile movement aftereffect (MAE) offers another parallel with visual movement perception. In the visual MAE, adaptation to a moving pattern, such as a grating, causes a subsequently viewed test stimulus to appear to drift in the opposite direction; the effect is believed to result from desensitization of direction-specific motion detectors. Hollins & Favorov (1994) reported such an effect for touch following vigorous stimulation of the hand with moving bars; during the test phase, the subject's hand rested on stationary bars. In a larger study, however, Lerner & Craig (2002) found that only a minority of subjects reported a unidirectional MAE under these conditions. Watanabe et al. (2007) have now shown that more reliable MAEs can be obtained when care is taken to activate the RA channel during both adaptation and test: Their motion

stimulus was a set of three pins, vibrating at 30 Hz, that were activated sequentially.

Affective Touch

Research described in the preceding sections supports the view that precise, discriminative judgments about tactile stimuli depend on signals in myelinated mechanoreceptive afferents. However, we also have a system of unmyelinated mechanoreceptors, the C-tactile (CT) afferents, which respond to sustained gentle pressure and slow movement (Vallbo et al. 1999). In neurological patients who lack myelinated mechanoreceptors, and whose ability to detect light touch therefore presumably depends on the CT system, Olausson et al. (2002, 2008) found that tactile stimuli elicit only vague, pleasant sensations that are difficult to localize. They proposed that these afferents, stimulation of which activates limbic structures rather than somatosensory cortex, may contribute to emotional responses to caress-like interpersonal touch (the "affective touch hypothesis"). Consistent with this idea, McGlone et al. (2007) found that a soft brush sweeping along the skin feels most pleasant at those velocities (1–3 cm/s) that are most effective in activating CT afferents. More research is needed to definitively evaluate this intriguing hypothesis.

Tactile Attention

We can attend to a tactile stimulus as well as we can to a visual or auditory one, and there is now a considerable literature on the nature of this process—or rather, family of processes. The present review covers only psychophysical work, but rapid progress is also being made in understanding the physiology of tactile attention: Key papers by Chapman & Meftah (2005) and Roy et al. (2007) provide access to the literature on this topic.

The rules of attention for touch are quite similar to those for other modalities. For example, tactile attention can be drawn to a particular location by a sudden stimulus, as demonstrated by Spence & McGlone (2001). Subjects

Cross-modal:

involving an interaction between sensory modalities, as when an auditory stimulus modifies tactile perception

in their study held a sponge cube in each hand, using thumb and forefinger. Two small vibrators were embedded in each cube, and the subject's task was to indicate, by operating foot pedals, whether the target vibrator activated on a trial was an upper or a lower one. A fraction of a second before the target, both vibrators on one side were briefly activated. The subject knew that this cue was nonpredictive in that it was delivered to the same hand as the target only half the time. Nevertheless, performance was faster and more accurate on these ipsilateral trials, showing that attention was exogenously (i.e., reflexively) drawn to the cued hand. The effect of cuing was most marked when the target followed the cue at a stimulus-onset asynchrony (SOA) of 300 ms.

Tactile attention, having been exogenously attracted to a given location, is at longer SOAs withdrawn from it, so that detection of a target there is slower than under baseline conditions (Spence et al. 2000). This phenomenon, called inhibition of return, has been extensively investigated in other modalities; it is believed to make scanning of a receptor surface more efficient by preventing attention from lingering in any one place. In touch it can last for several seconds (Cohen et al. 2005).

Another constraint on target processing, familiar to vision researchers, is the attentional blink. In this paradigm, a rapid stream of perhaps two dozen stimuli, such as alphanumeric characters, is presented. A few of the stimuli are distinctive (say, numbers among letters) and serve as targets; the subject's task is to identify them. When two such target characters are presented in close temporal proximity, subjects are often unable to identify the second one correctly, suggesting that attention, after being focused on the first target, is passing through a brief refractory state. Hillstrom et al. (2002) have now shown, in a series of experiments using vibrations differing in frequency and other properties as both targets and distractors, that the processing of tactile information is also subject to this transient impairment. The generality of the attentional blink is consistent with the view (Luck & Vecera 2002) that it reflects the limited capacity of a cognitive process—working memory.

The nature of the spatial framework within which attention is deployed has been studied by Lakatos & Shepard (1997). They instructed subjects to voluntarily shift attention from one body site to another and to indicate as quickly as possible whether a tactile stimulus (a jet of air) was being directed at the second location. Assuming that this judgment could only be made once attention reached the target location, the authors used response time as a measure of the time needed for attention to shift. This RT was an increasing function of the distance between the two sites. Importantly, it was the straightline Euclidean distance between the two sites, not the path length along the body surface, that gave the best prediction of RT. Results obtained when the arms or legs were moved to alter Euclidean, but not cutaneous, distance confirmed this interpretation. Other data supporting the conclusion that attention operates within a representation of external space have been reported by Kennett et al. (2002) and Soto-Faraco et al. (2004).

Attention space appears to be multimodal because decisions about a tactile stimulus, such as whether it is pulsed or steady, are speeded when a visual or auditory cue has drawn attention to the target site (Spence et al. 1998). Yet when stimuli in different modalities are simultaneously presented in different locations, it is possible, within limits (Martino & Marks 2000), to attend to one modality while ignoring the other. When this occurs, the attended stimulus may seem to occur slightly before the neglected one, a perceptual phenomenon called prior entry. Spence et al. (2001) have documented prior entry (pairing a visual stimulus with a tactile one) in the absence of response bias, a possible confound in some early studies.

Finally, attentional mechanisms may also be at work in a cross-modal version of prepulse inhibition, a well-studied auditory phenomenon in which a soft warning sound reduces the startle response to a loud sound presented a fraction of a second later. In the intermodal paradigm, the startle stimulus is still a sound, but the warning stimulus is a vibratory burst delivered to the ball of the thumb 120 ms earlier (Hill & Blumenthal 2005). Interestingly, prepulse inhibition occurs only if the vibration is high enough in frequency to activate the Pacinian channel.

Cross-Modal Effects

Considered as specific illusions or phenomena, cross-modal effects are extremely diverse. Some, like those considered above, are attentional in nature. Others serve to make our perceptual experience as coherent and unitary as possible. For example, when inputs from different modalities are fully compatible, as when we view an object while touching it, these inputs will combine into a unified, multimodal perceptual experience; on the other hand, when the inputs are totally incompatible, one of them is likely to be perceptually suppressed or neglected.

The most interesting situations, however, are those in which the signals from two modalities are only moderately incompatible, such as the sight and feel (simultaneously and in spatial register) of two textured surfaces, one of which is coarser than the other. Here, both sensory inputs may influence the subject's responses, even when he/she is instructed to rely exclusively on one modality. For example, Guest & Spence (2003) found that speeded sorting of visually presented textile samples was rendered less accurate by the simultaneous tactile presentation of other samples of a different roughness. However, when subjects were instead asked to judge only the touched samples, simultaneously presented visual textures did not intrude. Touch was the more difficult sense to ignore, even for pairs of surfaces that were more visually than tactually discriminable.

This example of intermodal interference may reflect distraction or alternation rather than genuine perceptual modification, but other studies offer clear evidence of perceptual effects. For example, Jousmäki & Hari (1998) presented to subjects, through headphones, the sound they were currently making by rubbing their hands together. By amplifying or otherwise modifying the sound, the experimenters were able to systematically influence subjects' perception of the texture of their own skin, reported on a rating scale. Guest et al. (2002) extended this work, showing that increasing the sound level made the skin feel both rougher and drier.

Yau et al. (2009b) elucidated the sensory processing underlying this type of interaction using simpler stimuli. They found that vibrotactile frequency discrimination was impaired by the presentation of an auditory tone (or noise band) simultaneously with one of the vibrations in a trial, but only if the auditory and tactile stimuli were similar in frequency content. Furthermore, the perceived "pitch" of the vibration appeared to be altered—pulled toward the frequency of the accompanying sound. The results suggest the presence of temporal frequency channels to which both tactile and auditory signals have access. When we move a finger across a surface, both sounds and cutaneous vibrations are usually produced; by combining inputs from these two modalities, the brain may be creating a supramodal representation of texture that makes efficient use of all available information (Yau et al. 2009a).

A similar approach has been used by Bensmaïa et al. (2006c) to document effects of visual movement on the perception of tactile movement. Subjects indicated on each trial which of two tactile gratings, one of which was accompanied by a drifting visual grating, was moving faster. When the visual and tactile stimuli moved in the same direction, the former (if its temporal frequency was high enough) increased the apparent speed of the latter; opposing movement had more complex effects. Disrupting the synchrony of visual and tactile stimuli eliminated the effect, suggesting that it depends on the perceptual system attributing them both to a single event.

Even closer cooperation between visual and tactile signals has been reported in recent work on apparent movement. When a flash from a light-emitting diode attached to one index finger is followed a fraction of a second later by a tap on the other index finger, subjects may experience movement from one finger to the other (Harrar et al. 2008); however, the effect is not as compelling as when both stimuli are in the same modality, and it does not show the same relationship (Korte's third law) between SOA and spatial separation. These two studies of perceived movement document robust, but not always smooth, interaction of visual and tactile signals.

Sometimes the exact nature of the perceptual blend or compromise that occurs depends on task demands. Heller et al. (1999) asked subjects to touch an object while viewing it through a reducing lens and then to indicate the object's size using either a visual or haptic matching array. Regardless of the modality used for matching, subjects reported the object to be of intermediate size. When pressed for more precise judgments, however, subjects tended to rely more on a single modality—the one in which matches were being made.

In conflicts dealing with whether or where stimulation occurred, however, vision generally dominates. For example, seeing a laser beam shined onto a rubber hand can make subjects feel that their own hand is being stimulated (Durgin et al. 2007). And "mirror therapy," in which a normal, moving limb is seen by reflection to occupy the place of a diseased or missing one, appears to reduce clinical pain in some cases (Ramachandran & Rogers-Ramachandran 1996), although much of the evidence for its effectiveness is anecdotal, as noted by Moseley et al. (2008). It is sometimes suggested that interactions between cortical areas (perhaps combined with cortical reorganization in clinical cases) contribute to such phenomena.

Another sort of interaction between the senses is one in which information obtained through one modality is compared with information acquired later through another modality. For example, Norman et al. (2004) asked subjects to examine two objects (plastic replicas of bell peppers) sequentially and to say whether they were same or different. Performance was not significantly worse in cross-modal conditions than when both stimuli were presented

haptically and was only moderately worse than when both were presented visually. The data suggest a close relationship between haptic and visual representations of shape. A similar pattern of results was obtained by Pensky et al. (2008), who studied memory for common objects using an old/new paradigm; the new objects presented at test were same-name foils for studied objects, ensuring that perceptual, rather than verbal, memory was being measured.

Also consistent with the existence of a representation shared by the visual and somatosensory systems is the fact that presentation of an object primes the subsequent naming of the same object, whether in the same or the other modality (Reales & Ballesteros 1999). Priming was equally strong whether subjects were instructed, in the study phase, to encode the objects physically (by rating their volume) or semantically. The authors conclude that the stored representations are probably presemantic, structural, and amodal.

However, representations of an object created when it is examined visually or haptically are unlikely to be identical, as shown by Newell et al. (2001). They measured the ability of subjects to recognize, in one modality, objects (nonsense shapes made with LEGO® blocks) that had previously been presented either to the same or to the other modality. The novel feature of this experiment is that objects were sometimes turned front-to-back between study and test. This maneuver interfered with the recognition of objects presented twice in the same modality, but it enhanced cross-modal recognition—presumably because grasping an object yields considerable information about its "back."

An important feature of the visual system is that shape information is processed somewhat separately from information about the location of an object. Recent research indicates that this distinction between a ventral "what" stream and a dorsal "where" stream applies to the somatosensory system as well (Reed et al. 2005). The question of how much functional integration across modalities there is within each stream was examined by Chan & Newell (2008).

They asked subjects to compare two stimuli and say whether they were the same or different either in shape or in the location of a small component. Between presentation of the two stimuli, a second task was administered. This interfering task produced more disruption of the primary task when the two were of the same kind (i.e., what or where) than when they were not. This difference was robust when both tasks were within the same modality, but was still present to some degree when one task was visual and the other tactile.

THERMORECEPTION

One of the classic discoveries in somesthesis was that warmth and cold are separate submodalities, activated by stimulation of different spots on the skin. Recent research has shown that these two systems differ in a number of ways. Detection thresholds (expressed as change from baseline temperature) for both vary widely, and generally in parallel, over the body surface (Essick et al. 2004, Stevens & Choo 1998), but warm threshold is consistently larger than cold threshold.

In fact, Green & Cruz (1998) have provided evidence that there are regions of skin several square cm in area that are completely devoid of warm spots; here, temperature increases are detected only at the threshold of nociception. Equivalent cold-insensitive regions have not been found.

Other differences were found by Greenspan et al. (2003), who had subjects immerse a hand or foot in water of various temperatures and rate the thermal intensity, affect, and pain (if any) that was experienced. It was found that if two temperatures, one warm and one cold, produced equally intense thermal ratings, the cold stimulus consistently evoked a more negative affect than the warm one—even at temperatures so mild that both stimuli were judged pleasant.

As stimulus temperatures increasingly deviate from resting skin temperature, they gradually become unpleasant, then are tinged with a stinging or burning quality, and eventually produce frank pain. It has traditionally been assumed that this subjective continuum reflects a gradual transition from stimulation of warm and cold fibers to stimulation of nociceptors, but it has recently been discovered (Green & Pope 2003) that sensations of stinging and burning can be evoked even by very mild cooling (e.g., to 27°C), probably because some nociceptors are sensitive to this slight drop in temperature. Green et al. (2008) suggest that some nociceptors may express more than one temperature-sensitive receptor protein (see section on Genetics of Pain), so that they respond both to mild and to extreme temperatures.

This "innocuous-cold nociception" is rarely noted because it is normally blocked by the tactile signals evoked when a cool object comes into contact with the skin; by resting a thermode on the skin before lowering its temperature, Green & Pope (2003) were able to minimize tactile stimulation and thereby release the pain signals from inhibition. Even nociceptive spots can be found with a variant of this approach (Green et al. 2008).

An enduring challenge for researchers is the thermal grill illusion, in which an array of interspersed warm and cool bars causes a strong sensation of heat, sometimes described as burning pain. A widely accepted explanation for the illusion is that activity in warm fibers interferes centrally with the ability of cold fibers to suppress signals from cold-sensitive nociceptors (Craig & Bushnell 1994). This "unmasking" mechanism accounts well for the frank pain experienced when stimulation by the cool bars is intense enough to activate polymodal nociceptors. With milder temperatures, however, the dominant algorithm appears to be addition of warm and cold signals to produce synthetic heat (Bouhassira et al. 2005, Green 2002), an idea first proposed more than a century ago.

In summary, recent research indicates that the "temperature sense" is more complicated than it was thought to be just a few years ago, given new evidence of the sensitivity of some nociceptors to mild temperatures and of previously unrecognized submodality interactions.

Nociception: the detection and perception (typically as pain) of stimulation that is damaging or potentially damaging

PAIN

In previous sections of this review, we discussed components of somesthesis that allow us to learn about objects and events in the world around us. The information we receive in this way is often accompanied by affect, which may be either positive (the pleasure of a kiss) or negative (the discomfort of feeling sweaty on a hot day). The affect often has both sensory and cognitive aspects, as in these examples. The contribution that activity in CT afferents may make to positive affect has already been described.

The remainder of this review focuses on the pain system, a component of the somatosensory system that is intrinsically associated with negative affect and that is dedicated to detecting injury or potential injury. Acute pain, as from a sprained ankle, plays a useful role by warning of harm and by enforcing inactivity, but chronic pain is largely negative in its impact. The suffering and disability that it causes, with resulting costs associated with treatment and lost productivity, make it a major public health problem. In many cases, persistent pain cannot be adequately controlled by analgesic drugs.

A remarkable characteristic of pain is its susceptibility to modulation. Intense pain signals modify the pathways over which they travel, making them more supportive of later pain. At the same time, dedicated systems counteract these changes and dramatically reduce pain under some conditions. The first three sections deal with sensory processes that modulate pain; the fourth discusses the converse phenomenon in which pain triggers an impairment of light touch; and the next three sections concern mutual influences between pain and cognitive processes. The review concludes with a discussion of the role of genetics in pain. The primary emphasis throughout is on behavioral research; for coverage of the underlying physiology, see reviews by Mannion & Woolf (2000) on plasticity and by Apkarian et al. (2005) on brain mechanisms. Work on specific chronic pain conditions is described only when this helps to make a general point about pain processing.

Hyperalgesia: a sensory disturbance in which noxious stimulation causes abnormally intense pain; often occurs in conjunction with allodynia

Allodynia: a sensory disturbance in which normally innocuous stimulation causes pain

Review of the extensive literature on the topic of sex differences in pain is beyond the scope of the present article; an edited volume by Fillingim (2000) provides an accessible introduction to many avenues of research in this expanding field. In some but not all situations, females have higher pain sensitivity and responsiveness than do males, and physiological mechanisms and sociocultural factors both contribute to these differences (Berkley 1997). Greenspan et al. (2007) provide a consensus report on optimal research strategies and promising directions for future work in the area.

Central Sensitization

Sensitization is a long-lasting increase in pain sensitivity that occurs following an intense noxious event. Shutting a file drawer on a finger, for example, produces not only ongoing pain, but also an extreme sensitivity to further stimulation. This sensitivity includes both hyperalgesia (increased responsiveness to noxious stimulation) and allodynia (pain in response to normally innocuous stimulation). It is now appreciated that both peripheral and central changes can contribute to sensitization. For example, an injection of capsaicin (the molecule that makes chili peppers "hot") into the skin produces a small region of increased heat sensitivity that is due mainly to sensitization of nociceptors (primary hyperalgesia), as well as a much larger region of enhanced mechanical sensitivity (secondary hyperalgesia and allodynia) reflecting an increased ability of signals from myelinated tactile afferents to stimulate central neurons (Torebjörk et al. 1992). Here, even gentle touch is painful.

Experimental studies of hyperalgesia and allodynia most often involve stimulation of the skin, but sensitization can be demonstrated in deeper tissues as well. For example, allodynia localized to a muscle occurs when it is subjected to prolonged eccentric exercise, i.e., gradual relaxation under tension, as when a weight is lowered. This mild, diffuse injury to the muscle produces a tenderness to palpation called delayed-onset muscle soreness (DOMS).

Barlas et al. (2000) showed that pressure-pain threshold on the biceps was abnormally low two days after exercise, but that this allodynia was abolished if afferent signals from A (that is, myelinated) fibers were blocked by a tourniquet around the upper arm. The implication is that DOMS, like allodynia in skin, involves a distortion by the central nervous system of signals carried by non-nociceptors (in this case probably stretch receptors). That DOMS produces a qualitative change in the sensory effects of large-fiber activity was confirmed by Weerakkody et al. (2003), who applied steady, painful pressure to a muscle and then superimposed vibration, which is an effective stimulus for large afferents. In muscles without DOMS, the vibration reduced the ongoing pressure-pain (an example of mechanoreceptor-induced analgesia, discussed below), but in muscles with DOMS, vibration increased the pain.

An important pathophysiological aspect of allodynia is that, in addition to being painful in itself, it can promote further pain. For example, Kim et al. (2007) showed that secondary hyperalgesia, induced in the rat paw by capsaicin injection, could be maintained for weeks by gentle vibratory stimulation, confined to a 30-minute daily period, of the affected region. The implication is that once allodynia is established, the mechanoreceptive afferents that trigger it also acquire the ability to maintain and enhance the sensitized state, a role normally reserved for signals in C fibers.

These examples of prolonged central sensitization can be distinguished from a more transient phenomenon called temporal summation, in which a brief, noxious stimulus, such as a pulse of heat repeatedly applied to the same spot or adjacent spots on normal skin, becomes increasingly painful. The increase in responsiveness happens in the spinal cord, through an augmentation process called "windup" (Mendell & Wall 1965); it occurs only for signals reaching the dorsal horn in unmyelinated (C) nociceptors, not the small myelinated (Aδ) ones.

Given that both temporal summation and central sensitization involve central changes, is the former simply a mild, transient engagement of the same mechanisms that cause the latter? To address this question, Magerl et al. (1998) injected capsaicin into the skin of the forearm, producing a region of secondary hyperalgesia. Temporal summation was then assessed here and in a faraway control site. Testing was more painful in the hyperalgesic zone, but temporal summation was no more pronounced, suggesting that the two processes are independent. Electrophysiological work in the rat, however, indicates that they have some features in common (Li et al. 1999).

Some persistent pain conditions, such as temporomandibular disorder (TMD; Maixner et al. 1998) and fibromyalgia (Price et al. 2002), involve abnormal temporal summation as well as central sensitization. For example, windup, once established, can be maintained in a healthy subject only if noxious pulses continue at short intervals; but in someone with fibromyalgia, the intervals can be as long as 12 s (Staud et al. 2004). Moreover, some pain patients show a gradual buildup of allodynia, which can be viewed as a slow form of temporal summation (Fillingim et al. 1998). For an extended discussion of temporal summation's relevance to pathological pain, see Price (1999).

In most of these studies, and in others described in the following sections, subjects were asked to indicate the intensity of their pain either by responding verbally with a number on a predefined scale or by adjusting or marking on a visual analog scale (VAS). Both types of scales are typically bounded at both ends, extending, for example, from 0 (no pain) to 100 (most intense pain imaginable), and may have some internal structure as well. The two methods have complementary advantages: Numerical scales are well suited to situations in which a series of discrete responses are needed in rapid succession, whereas visual analog scales with electronic readout allow continuous records of pain intensity to be obtained (Maixner et al. 1998). A detailed comparison of the two types of scales has been made by Price et al. (1994).

TMD: temporomandibular disorder

VAS: visual analog scale

Mechanoreceptor-Induced Analgesia

The fact that pain can be reduced by light mechanical stimulation, as when we gently rub a bruise, was first documented experimentally by Wall & Cronly-Dillon (1960). This phenomenon and its apparent physiological basis (indirect inhibition, by low-threshold mechanoreceptors, of secondary neurons in the dorsal horn) played an important role in the development of the Gate Control Theory of Pain (Melzack & Wall 1965). Yet the effect is a modest one when vibratory stimulation is localized or of only moderate intensity. Watanabe et al. (1999) in fact found that pain from electric shocks was not at all ameliorated by 120 Hz vibration at 40–50 dB above threshold, applied either locally or to a remote region of the body. Roy et al. (2003) reported that although vibration significantly reduced spontaneous pain in a clinical (TMD) population, some subjects experienced an increase in pain, apparently a mild version of the allodynia described by Fillingim et al. (1998).

A definitive account of vibratory analgesia is made difficult by the inherent subjectivity of pain report and by the possibility that distraction contributes to the effect. To address these issues, Hollins et al. (2003) made use of a forced-choice procedure to measure (healthy) subjects' ability to detect the "pinprick" of faint laser stimulation of the forearm. Detectability declined gradually as the amplitude of a nearby vibration increased, and the range of effective vibration frequencies indicated that at least two mechanoreceptor populations contributed to the effect.

Some research on mechanoreceptor-induced analgesia has used transcutaneous electrical nerve stimulation (TENS) rather than vibration to activate large afferents. TENS is typically administered with devices that allow the intensity of stimulation to be adjusted over a considerable range: At low current the device produces a tingling sensation that presumably reflects the activation primarily of low-threshold mechanoreceptors, while higher current recruits nociceptive afferents as

well. Using low intensities, Chesterton et al. (2002) found that the pressure-pain threshold on the hand was raised by TENS applied to the forearm but not to the shin. This squares with the prediction that mechanoreceptor-induced analgesia should be segmental or, at most, confined to neighboring dermatomes (see Yarnitsky et al. 1997) because of the local interactions in the dorsal horn that it is thought to reflect.

Chesterton et al. (2002) used a sham-control and a double-blind design to minimize placebo effects, but not all studies have been so rigorous. A review of the literature by Sluka & Walsh (2003) indicates that procedures and stimulus parameters are so variable in TENS research as to leave the question of its clinical utility in need of further evaluation.

Diffuse Noxious Inhibitory Controls

In contrast to the generally modest decrease in pain that can be produced by vibration, a stronger analgesia often occurs when the suppressing stimulus is itself painful. Moreover, the effectiveness of this noxious "conditioning" stimulus is typically independent of its distance on the body from the test stimulus. An early study by LeBars et al. (1979) showed, in lightly anesthetized rats, that responses of cells in the dorsal horn to noxious stimulation of a test site (the hindpaw) were reduced by a second noxious stimulus delivered to any of a variety of other locations, such as the tail or muzzle. The effect did not occur in rats whose spinal cord had been severed from the brainstem, proving the involvement of supraspinal structures, now known to include the periaqueductal gray (PAG) and the rostral ventral medulla. LeBars et al. called the phenomenon "diffuse noxious inhibitory controls" (DNIC), a term which is now rather widely applied to reduction of one pain by another in a different location.

Price & McHaffie (1988) demonstrated a psychophysical correlate of the LeBars et al. physiological effect and discovered that second pain (i.e., dull pain mediated by C fibers) is more affected than first pain (sharp pain mediated by

Aδ fibers). This difference has since been confirmed physiologically by McMullan & Lumb (2006).

A direct comparison of the analgesic effects of vibratory and noxious stimuli is provided by the Watanabe et al. (1999) study described above. They used a painful intramuscular injection of hypertonic saline as a noxious conditioning stimulus; when delivered to a remote site, this was quite effective in reducing the painfulness of the electrical test stimulus, demonstrating the occurrence of DNIC. Analgesia did not occur when the injection was delivered within the same dermatome as the test stimulus, perhaps indicating a spread of pain between these two forearm sites. In any case, the results contrast with the ineffectiveness of vibration at either conditioning site.

An analogous comparison can be made between the effects of low- and high-intensity TENS in the Chesterton et al. (2002) study: Low-intensity TENS was effective in raising pressure-pain threshold, but only during stimulation and only when applied locally; high-intensity TENS was effective only when presented to the remote site, but this effect outlasted stimulation by at least a half-hour. Despite the many differences between the studies, they both support the widespread view that DNIC is more robust than mechanoreceptor-induced analgesia and that it follows different rules.

A focus of much current research on DNIC is the fact that it appears to differ considerably in magnitude from one individual to another. For example, its strength has been reported to vary as a function of gender (Granot et al. 2008, Staud et al. 2003) and ethnicity (Campbell et al. 2008, Mechlin et al. 2005). In addition, it is weak in people with some chronic pain conditions (Lautenbacher & Rollman 1997, Pielsticker et al. 2005), and there is a negative statistical association between DNIC and the presence of pain that affects everyday functioning (Edwards et al. 2003b); remarkably, a lack of DNIC during presurgical testing predicts the development of chronic postsurgical pain (Yarnitsky et al. 2008). A consistent finding in these studies is that the relationship between DNIC and clinical pain is a negative one, suggesting that robust DNIC may help to prevent or reduce the chronification of pain.

Some individuals appear not just to lack DNIC but to show the opposite effect. For example, in a study of the way in which temporal summation of heat pulses was affected by a contralateral conditioning stimulus, college-age subjects showed clear DNIC, but an older group (mean age = 63) showed instead an enhancement of temporal summation (Edwards et al. 2003a). This and other findings (Ren & Dubner 2002) suggest that descending pain modulation is complex, with both excitatory and inhibitory components. Even innocuous events, such as gum chewing (Mohri et al. 2005), may trigger descending DNIC-like signals.

Touch Gating

For decades, there have been scattered reports in the clinical literature that chronic pain conditions are sometimes accompanied by impairments of light touch. Recent research supports these case reports, as illustrated by several studies comparing individuals with chronic facial pain (TMD) and healthy controls. When vibratory test stimuli were applied to the face in or near the painful region, detection threshold was slightly elevated in those with TMD (Hollins et al. 1996), and frequency discrimination threshold dramatically so, whereas amplitude discrimination was virtually unaffected (Hollins & Sigurdsson 1998). These results suggest that cortical processing of somesthetic information, shown in earlier research to be essential for frequency discrimination (LaMotte & Mountcastle 1979), is disturbed in this chronic pain population. Consistent with this view is the fact that a more integrative perceptual ability, discerning the objective orientation of a tangible contour despite changes in the orientation of the hand, also tends to be reduced in people with TMD (Higashiyama et al. 2006).

These and other clinical studies (Geber et al. 2008) demonstrate that chronic pain is often accompanied by disturbances of somesthesis, but they cannot establish a cause-and-effect relationship. Apkarian et al. (1994) showed, however, that touch is also impaired by experimental (contact heat) pain, a phenomenon they called touch gating. Vibrotactile detection threshold was higher, and perceived magnitude of suprathreshold vibrations lower, when the contactor and its surround were painfully hot than when they were at an innocuous temperature. Later work showed that the effect declines with increasing distance between the test site and the locus of pain; that cold pain also closes the touch gate (Bolanowski et al. 2000); and that vibrotactile amplitude discrimination is not affected (Bolanowski et al. 2001), a finding that parallels the TMD results of Hollins & Sigurdsson (1998). Touch gating has also been obtained when the experimental pain is caused by electric shock, by intradermal capsaicin injection (Geber et al. 2008), or by injection of hypertonic saline into a muscle (Stohler et al. 2001).

Although mechanoreceptor-induced analgesia and touch gating may psychophysically appear to be opposite but otherwise equivalent processes, the anatomy of the nervous system dictates that these two "gates" be in very different locations. Mechanoreceptor-induced pain gating is largely a segmental process, albeit one influenced by descending signals. Touch gating, however, cannot be effected in the spinal cord because tactile primary afferents ascend all the way to the brainstem; interactions within the cortex (Apkarian 1995, Tommerdahl et al. 1996) or other parts of the brain provide a more likely explanation.

Since intense pain activates a widespread network of cortical areas, some of which adjoin or overlap (and therefore potentially interact with) regions that are involved in cognition and emotion, it is perhaps not surprising that pain has been reported to affect, and to be affected by, these higher-level processes as well. The following sections briefly examine pain's interactions with psychological processes beyond perception.

Placebo Effects

An example of the influence of higher-level factors on pain is the effect of a placebo, that is, a treatment that has no intrinsic physiological (in the case of a drug, pharmacological) ability to reduce pain, but that may be expected by the subject to do so. Recent studies have shown that the placebo effect is not simply a reduction in anxiety or a generalized feeling of well-being, but rather is a specific, often localized, reduction in pain. Expectation on the part of the subject is key, as shown by Price et al. (1999). These authors applied painful heat to three locations on the forearm after "treating" two of the sites with inert skin cream described as two different analgesic creams. Different temperatures were then applied to the sites, creating the impression that one cream was more effective than the other. After this learning phase, a final set of trials was carried out with the creams in place and the same temperature applied to all three sites. A graded placebo effect occurred, with subjects' pain assessments conforming to their expectations, measured between the two sets of trials. Benedetti et al. (1999) showed that such expectation-based placebo effects are mediated by endogenous opioids, even when they are localized.

Placebo effects may sometimes result from classical conditioning, brought about by earlier positive experiences with doctors and medicines. Does such conditioning work simply because it sets up expectations of benefit? The data of Price et al. (1999) are consistent with this interpretation, but work by Amanzio & Benedetti (1999) suggests that the effects of expectation and conditioning are at least partially separate. In their study, tolerance for ischemic pain was measured under a variety of conditions extending over several days. For two days, subjects received (i.e., were conditioned with) either morphine or a nonopioid analgesic; on the following day, placebo effects were measured, with instructions varied to either encourage or discourage expectations of analgesia. The authors found that the opioid antagonist naloxone consistently reversed expectancy effects but blocked only those conditioning effects that were created by opioid administration.

The placebo response, like DNIC, appears to depend on descending modulation of pain signals. In an fMRI study, Bingel et al. (2006) recorded both psychophysical and brain responses to painful laser pulses delivered to the back of the hand; a placebo response was produced by telling subjects that skin cream applied to a hand was a powerful analgesic. The rostral anterior cingulate cortex (rACC) was more activated when a placebo response occurred than when it did not; at those times, the PAG also gave an increased BOLD response. The authors interpret their findings to mean that the rACC plays a key role in initiating the placebo response, activating the PAG and other structures that produce descending signals.

Pain and Attention

Pain has been shown to compromise performance on a variety of cognitive tasks, and distraction appears to contribute importantly to these effects (see review by Eccleston & Crombez 1999). That is, pain is such a salient event that it captures attention, appropriating processing resources that would otherwise contribute to performance on competing tasks.

Effects of pain on memory may serve as an example. Kuhajda et al. (1998) asked subjects to read a list of words, classifying each one as affectively positive or negative. Later, subjects were presented with the same ("old") words, interspersed with new ones, and were asked to say whether each word was old or new. Different groups of subjects were subjected to pain during either the study (initial presentation) phase, the test phase, or both, by immersion of a hand in cold water. Recognition memory was impaired by pain at either study or test. A follow-up study (Kuhajda et al. 2002) used clinical (headache) rather than experimental pain. Study and test sessions were on different days; subjects notified the experimenters when they were in the appropriate pain/no pain state (based on random assignment) so that a session could be promptly

arranged. Only headache at test significantly affected performance in this experiment, perhaps because subjects with headaches took longer at the initial task, compensating for their distracted state.

Is attention really the key mediator of pain's effect on memory? To address this question, Grisart & Van Der Linden (2001) used a procedure introduced by Jacoby et al. (1993) to disentangle the contributions of controlled (i.e., conscious and therefore by definition attention-using) processing and automatic processing to memory performance. Chronic pain patients and healthy controls studied a list of words and then were tested by being asked to complete word stems either with words from the initial list or (in separate blocks) with words not on the original list. Comparison of scores on these two tests enabled the authors to conclude that controlled memory processes were disrupted in the patients while automatic processes were not. This result supports the view that pain affects memory by monopolizing attentional resources.

Some research has addressed the converse question of whether pain can be influenced, i.e., reduced, by distracting subjects from it. A review of early literature by McCaul & Malott (1984) concluded that the answer is yes, within limits. Complex, attention-demanding tasks are moderately effective in distracting subjects from mild pain but are not helpful against strong pain. In agreement with earlier findings, Tracey et al. (2002) found that asking subjects to distract themselves from a painful stimulus by thinking of something else produced lower retrospective pain ratings; it also led to increased activity in the PAG, a brainstem structure involved in descending pain modulation. This result suggests that distraction causes pain to be actively suppressed.

If distraction from pain reduces its intensity, a state of heightened attentiveness to noxious stimuli should increase their perceived intensity. Some individuals, including a large proportion of those with chronic pain conditions such as fibromyalgia, appear to be especially alert for sensations that are aversive or threatening, an attentional habit called hypervigilance (Chapman 1978). Does hypervigilance contribute to the enhanced pain sensitivity of fibromyalgia patients? That it may do so is suggested by findings of McDermid et al. (1996), who capitalized on the fact that hypervigilance generalizes beyond somesthesis, at least to the auditory modality. They showed that the amplitude at which auditory stimuli become intolerably loud is reduced in hypervigilant patients, an increase in sensitivity that is presumably attentional in origin. In further support of a role for attentional factors, Hollins et al. (2009) showed by direct scaling that even gentle pressure, too weak to be judged unpleasant, is perceptually amplified in hypervigilant pain patients. The authors interpreted this result to mean that the clinical history of these individuals has produced a heightened attentional focus on all pressure stimuli, regardless of intensity. Rollman (2009) provides a thoughtful perspective on still-unresolved issues in hypervigilance research.

Pain and Emotion

Attention and emotion both influence pain, but Villemure et al. (2003) showed that they do so in somewhat different ways. Subjects were presented simultaneously with noxious heat stimuli on the forearm and with odorants. Two stimuli of each type were successively presented within a trial, and the subject's task was to say whether the second stimulus of a particular type was stronger than or equal to the first. In some blocks of trials, the subject made judgments about the noxious stimuli, and in other blocks, about the odorants; in this way attention was manipulated. Pain intensity, reported afterward, was lower when subjects attended to the odorant than when they attended to the painful heat. Ratings of pain unpleasantness, however, showed a different pattern: They were less affected by attention than by whether the odorant was pleasant or unpleasant. Bad smells made pain more unpleasant, regardless of which modality was attended. The results suggest that distraction is of limited value when clinical

pain is strong enough to provoke an emotional reaction.

The distinction between pain intensity and unpleasantness has become one of the central themes of pain research in recent years, and neuroimaging has revealed that to some degree, different brain regions mediate these dimensions, the anterior cingulate cortex (ACC) being one of the areas consistently implicated in pain affect. Rainville et al. (1999), for example, experimentally dissociated pain unpleasantness and intensity by telling hypnotized subjects that a noxious stimulus was either very unpleasant or only mildly so; the ACC was more strongly activated in the former subjects than in the latter. Some limbic areas are also activated by emotional distress not arising from nociception (e.g., social exclusion: Eisenberger et al. 2003; empathy for another person's pain: Singer et al. 2004), an overlap that probably accounts for the metaphorical description of these states as painful and for the mutual interaction between pain and negative emotional states.

An example of this interaction was provided by Rainville et al. (2005), who instructed hypnotized subjects to immerse a hand in hot water and to experience either negative (e.g., anger) or positive (anticipation of relief) feelings about the pain. Ratings of both pain intensity and unpleasantness were increased by the negative emotions and reduced by the positive ones. Negative emotions do not always increase pain, however. Rhudy & Meagher (2003) found that VAS ratings of the pain caused by radiant heat to a finger were reduced by the threat of sudden, painful electric shocks to the same or a different finger. This fear-induced hypoalgesia is consistent with animal research, but it contrasts with the usual effect (i.e., hyperalgesia) of negative emotions in humans. The authors suggest that the high level of arousal accompanying their subjects' fear may have tipped the balance in favor of hypoalgesic processes.

Emotions do not have to be explicitly about pain in order for them to influence pain. For example, subjects experience noxious heat stimuli as more painful after they have been induced (by a sad story) into feeling empathy for another person (Loggia et al. 2008). In a similar vein, Meagher et al. (2001) used slide shows to induce either negative (e.g., attack scenes) or positive (couples in erotic poses) emotional states just before subjects immersed a hand in painfully cold water. Compared to a neutral condition, pain threshold (defined as the time at which ratings rose above zero) was generally lower when subjects were experiencing negative emotions and higher during positive ones. Rhudy et al. (2005) used comparable slides to induce emotions, but more briefly. Positive, negative, and neutral slides, presented for 6 s each, were interspersed in an extended series, during which electric shocks to the ankle were delivered at unpredictable intervals. VAS ratings of pain intensity were lower for shocks delivered during the viewing of positive as opposed to negative scenes, supporting the findings of Meagher et al. (2001). Moreover, the withdrawal reflex triggered by the shock was more vigorous during negative than positive slides. Emotions thus can activate descending pathways that influence even spinal processing of nociceptive information.

The studies described show that emotions (or more precisely, neural responses to emotion-inducing stimuli) cause changes in experimental pain. With persistent pain, unfortunately, causal relationships are much less clear. Emotional states are often statistically associated with persistent pain conditions, but how the linkage develops in a given individual is not known. However, some insight into the mechanism has been provided regarding the positive association that has been reported between anger scores and the severity of some types of chronic pain (Bruehl et al. 2002, Materazzo et al. 2000). Experiments with naloxone have revealed an impairment of endogenous opioid systems in some individuals, which appears to partially mediate the relationship between level of anger-out (the tendency to express anger) and pain intensity (Bruehl et al. 2003). A review by Bruehl et al. (2006) puts this and related findings into a theoretical context.

Emotions trigger autonomic activity that is the cause of many physiological changes, which may in turn influence pain. For example, anxiety can raise blood pressure, and there is substantial evidence for a negative relationship between blood pressure and pain sensitivity (e.g., Campbell et al. 2004, Dworkin et al. 1994). Conversely, painful stimulation can cause autonomic reactions that influence emotional state. This is a large field of research that is beyond the scope of the present review.

Emotion and cognition (including attention) have so far been described as distinct, but in everyday life they often blend together: Our attention is drawn to emotional stimuli; emotional events are retained in memory; and judgment sometimes involves weighing emotional consequences. Chronic pain is often found in association with subtle behavioral "styles" that have both cognitive and emotional aspects. For example, Apkarian et al. (2004) found that chronic pain patients are impaired on a gambling task that involves a mixture of emotional and cognitive processes. Participants were asked to choose repeatedly from several piles of cards that specified financial gains and losses. Some piles specified small gains and losses, while others specified larger contingencies and a less-favorable net outcome. After sampling all the piles, control participants settled for the small-stakes piles, while patients tended to gravitate to the riskier, less favorable ones. The authors believe (based on comparison with other tasks) that chronic pain selectively disrupts the ability to use emotional information in a measured way in decision-making.

One of the most studied psychological aspects of persistent pain is catastrophizing, a tendency in some individuals to regard their pain as something they are unable to cope with. Catastrophizing has both emotional aspects (feeling overwhelmed) and cognitive aspects (judging that certain activities are impossible). Indeed, catastrophizing can be seen as a coping mechanism the patient uses to elicit social support (Sullivan et al. 2001), albeit a counterproductive one that increases distress and fosters disability. Some interventions aim to reduce catastrophizing and other negative thoughts as a way to ameliorate the patient's overall situation

(Gil et al. 1996, Thorn et al. 2007). Catastrophizing is just one psychological aspect of persistent pain; Keefe et al. (2004) provide a review of research in this area.

Genetics of Pain

There is currently an exponential growth of research on the genetics of pain, with a wide range of approaches being employed. Only a few examples are given here.

The most closely interrelated series of discoveries concerns a family of membrane proteins that, by admitting calcium to neurons when appropriately stimulated, produce transient receptor potentials. It has long been appreciated that these "TRP" proteins play a role in transduction in several modalities, but their involvement in pain was only recently discovered, by Caterina et al. (1997, 2000). They showed that one member of this family, TRPV1, is responsive both to noxious heating and to capsaicin. Presumably capsaicin is adaptive because of its ability to produce painful sensations of heat and thus to discourage foraging mammals. Knockout mice lacking the gene that codes for TRPV1 have a reduced sensitivity to heat and do not develop heat hyperalgesia. Other members of the TRP family respond to different temperatures and to a variety of chemicals that provoke thermally tinged sensations, such as camphor and menthol. An introduction to this topic and a comprehensive review of existing research are provided by Story & Cruz-Orengo (2007) and Dhaka et al. (2006), respectively.

An intriguing study by Mogil et al. (2003) illustrates the complexity of pain genetics. The melanocortin-1 receptor gene, which controls the metabolic pathway by which melanin is synthesized, also influences pain sensitivity, but only in females. The authors found that in men, ratings of thermal and ischemic pain were reduced by pentazocine, an opioid, whether or not they had an active form of the gene; but in females, pentazocine was effective only in individuals lacking the gene (most of whom had red hair). In females, the gene apparently compromises the NMDA-dependent mechanism by which pentazocine has its effect.

Diatchenko and colleagues (2005) reported that another gene, which codes for the enzyme catecholamine-O-methyltransferase (COMT), is responsible for substantial and clinically significant variations in pain sensitivity within the general population. Three common haplotypes (variants) of this gene were found to be associated with scores reflecting the overall sensitivity of human research participants to experimental pain. The more active the COMT produced by a given haplotype, the lower (on average) was the individual's pain sensitivity. Zubieta et al. (2003) found that even a single-nucleotide polymorphism causing the substitution of one amino acid for another at a specific site in the COMT molecule can produce changes in pain processing that are observable not only psychophysically, but also by means of neuroimaging (positron emission tomography). COMT is widely distributed in the nervous system and is involved in the regulation of catecholamine and enkephalin levels, so there may be several routes by which it modulates pain processing; Nackley et al. (2007) showed, in rats, that inhibiting COMT causes hyperalgesia by allowing β_2- and β_3-adrenergic receptors to become overly active. It should be noted, however, that COMT genotype is not always found to be an important predictor of pain sensitivity (Kim et al. 2004), and the topic remains controversial (Diatchenko et al. 2007, Kim & Dionne 2007).

Despite these solid advances, or perhaps because of them, it is worth emphasizing that pain experiences are always the result of a complex interplay of genetic and experiential factors. A twin study, recently conducted in Norway, showed that both types of factors make substantial contributions to variations in pain sensitivity across individuals (Nielsen et al. 2008). Moreover, the factors responsible for sensitivity to heat pain overlapped only moderately with those responsible for sensitivity to cold-pressor pain.

CONCLUDING REMARKS

The conceptual and methodological diversity of the work reviewed here is a striking manifestation of the continuing expansion of the field of somatosensory research. This growth reflects both psychophysical discoveries (the main focus of this review) and advances made using other methods, notably electrophysiology and neuroimaging.

Part of this growth involves the continuing development of broad themes or principles that apply throughout somesthesis (and, indeed, in other sensory systems). One of these is the body's use of multiple mechanisms to achieve a certain result, as in the use of two codes for tactile roughness and two broad classes of nociceptors. Another broad theme is the ubiquitous occurrence of interactions between signals of different types, which can reinforce but more often interfere with one another. Examples are the compromising of tactile acuity by signals from RA afferents and the (more beneficial) reduction in pain resulting from stimulation of mechanoreceptors. A third theme is the important role that cognition (especially attention) plays in somesthesis. This has been examined with remarkable precision in the past decade, as refined methods of cognitive psychology have increasingly been brought to bear on touch and pain.

In addition to this increased knowledge of principles of operation that apply broadly, the research has given us a more nuanced understanding of the relationships among somesthetic submodalities. Revisions are occurring in the traditional associations between receptor classes and sensory qualities: For example, the fact that nociceptive sensations can sometimes be evoked (in normal skin) by mild cooling complicates the distinction between thermoreception and nociception.

Despite this blurring of some submodality borders, however, there has been an increased appreciation of differences between touch and pain, particularly regarding their susceptibility to modulation. Tactile percepts can be modified by contextual or cognitive factors, but these changes are modest compared to pathophysiological alterations that occur in pain, such as the allodynia that renders the stroke of a cotton wisp excruciating. The susceptibility of pain to modulation over a range of time scales is now recognized as one of its hallmarks and is one of the central organizing themes of current pain research.

Finally, it is worth noting that research on touch and research on pain, like touch and pain themselves, differ in some ways. Both fields are progressing rapidly, but in touch, the increase in knowledge is roughly linear, whereas pain research continues along an exponential trajectory that began several decades ago. Another difference between the fields, at least as regards psychophysical work, is that pain research relies primarily on subjective scaling, whereas touch researchers are able, in addition, to use criterion-free forced-choice methods to measure threshold. This precision in measurement, combined with a growing emphasis on computational modeling, is giving the field of touch substantial predictive power in certain areas. Pain research, with its robust phenomena and elegant experimental designs, will benefit from continued refinement of its methods of psychophysical measurement.

DISCLOSURE STATEMENT

The author is not aware of any biases that might be perceived as affecting the objectivity of this review.

ACKNOWLEDGMENTS

I am indebted to Sliman Bensmaïa and Daniel Harper for their helpful comments on an earlier version of the manuscript. Preparation of this review was supported by NIH grants NS045685 and NR009993.

LITERATURE CITED

Amanzio M, Benedetti F. 1999. Neuropharmacological dissection of placebo analgesia: expectation-activated opioid systems versus conditioning-activated specific subsystems. *J. Neurosci.* 19:484–94

Apkarian AV. 1995. Functional imaging of pain: new insights regarding the role of the cerebral cortex in human pain perception. *Semin. Neurosci.* 7:279–93

Apkarian AV, Bushnell MC, Treede R-D, Zubieta J-K. 2005. Human brain mechanisms of pain perception and regulation in health and disease. *Eur. J. Pain* 9:463–84

Apkarian AV, Sosa Y, Krauss BR, Thomas PS, Fredrickson BE, et al. 2004. Chronic pain patients are impaired on an emotional decision-making task. *Pain* 108:129–36

Apkarian AV, Stea RA, Bolanowski SJ. 1994. Heat-induced pain diminishes vibrotactile perception: a touch gate. *Somatosens. Mot. Res.* 11:259–67

Barlas P, Walsh DM, Baxter GD, Allen JM. 2000. Delayed onset muscle soreness: effect of an ischaemic block upon mechanical allodynia in humans. *Pain* 87:221–25

Benedetti F, Arduino C, Amanzio M. 1999. Somatotopic activation of opioid systems by target-directed expectations of analgesia. *J. Neurosci.* 19:3639–48

Bensmaïa S, Hollins M. 2005. Pacinian representations of fine surface texture. *Percept. Psychophys.* 67:842–54

Bensmaïa S, Hollins M, Yau J. 2005. Vibrotactile intensity and frequency information in the Pacinian system: a psychophysical model. *Percept. Psychophys.* 67:828–41

Bensmaïa SJ, Craig JC, Johnson KO. 2006a. Temporal factors in tactile spatial acuity: evidence for RA interference in fine spatial processing. *J. Neurophysiol.* 95:1783–91

Bensmaïa SJ, Craig JC, Yoshioka T, Johnson KO. 2006b. SA1 and RA afferent responses to static and vibrating gratings. *J. Neurophysiol.* 95:1771–82

Bensmaïa SJ, Hollins M. 2003. The vibrations of texture. *Somatosens. Mot. Res.* 20:33–43

Bensmaïa SJ, Killebrew JH, Craig JC. 2006c. Influence of visual motion on tactile motion perception. *J. Neurophysiol.* 96:1625–37

Berkley KJ. 1997. Sex differences in pain. *Behav. Brain Sci.* 20:371–80

Bingel U, Lorenz J, Schoell E, Weiller C, Büchel C. 2006. Mechanisms of placebo analgesia: rACC recruitment of a subcortical antinociceptive network. *Pain* 120:8–15

Bolanowski SJ, Gescheider GA, Fontana AM, Niemiec JL, Tromblay JL. 2001. The effects of heat-induced pain on the detectability, discriminability, and sensation magnitude of vibrotactile stimuli. *Somatosens. Mot. Res.* 18:5–9

Bolanowski SJ Jr, Gescheider GA, Verrillo RT, Checkosky CM. 1988. Four channels mediate the mechanical aspects of touch. *J. Acoust. Soc. Am.* 84:1680–94

Bolanowski SJ, Maxfield LM, Gescheider GA, Apkarian AV. 2000. The effects of stimulus location on the gating of touch by heat- and cold-induced pain. *Somatosens. Mot. Res.* 17:195–204

Bouhassira D, Kern D, Rouaud J, Pelle-Lancien E, Morain F. 2005. Investigation of the paradoxical painful sensation ("illusion of pain") produced by a thermal grill. *Pain* 114:160–67

Bruehl S, Burns JW, Chung OY, Ward P, Johnson B. 2002. Anger and pain sensitivity in chronic low back pain patients and pain-free controls: the role of endogenous opioids. *Pain* 99:223–33

Bruehl S, Chung OY, Burns JW. 2006. Anger expression and pain: an overview of findings and possible mechanisms. *J. Behav. Med.* 29:593–606

Bruehl S, Chung OY, Burns JW, Biridepalli S. 2003. The association between anger expression and chronic pain intensity: evidence for partial mediation by endogenous opioid dysfunction. *Pain* 106:317–24

Campbell CM, France CR, Robinson ME, Logan HL, Geffken GR, Fillingim RB. 2008. Ethnic differences in diffuse noxious inhibitory controls. *J. Pain* 9:759–66

Campbell TS, Hughes JW, Girdler SS, Maixner W, Sherwood A. 2004. Relationships of ethnicity, gender, and ambulatory blood pressure to pain sensitivity: effects of individualized pain rating scales. *J. Pain* 5:183–91

Cascio CJ, Sathian K. 2001. Temporal cues contribute to tactile perception of roughness. *J. Neurosci.* 21:5289–96

Caterina MJ, Leffler A, Malmberg AB, Martin WJ, Trafton J, et al. 2000. Impaired nociception and pain sensation in mice lacking the capsaicin receptor. *Science* 288:306–13

Activity in one mechanoreceptive channel can interfere with acuity judgments that depend on signals in another channel.

Caterina MJ, Schumacher MA, Tominaga M, Rosen TA, Levine JD, Julius D. 1997. The capsaicin receptor: a heat-activated ion channel in the pain pathway. *Nature* 389:816–24

Chan JS, Newell FN. 2008. Behavioral evidence for task-dependent "what" versus "where" processing within and across modalities. *Percept. Psychophys.* 70:36–49

Chapman CE, Meftah E-M. 2005. Independent controls of attentional influences in primary and secondary somatosensory cortex. *J. Neurophysiol.* 94:4094–107

Chapman CR. 1978. Pain: the perception of noxious events. In *The Psychology of Pain*, ed. RA Sternbach, pp. 169–202. New York: Raven

Chesterton L, Barlas P, Foster NE, Lundeberg T, Wright CC, Baxter GD. 2002. Sensory stimulation (TENS): effects of parameter manipulation on mechanical pain thresholds in healthy human subjects. *Pain* 99:253–62

Cholewiak RW. 1999. The perception of tactile distance: influences of body site, space, and time. *Perception* 28:851–75

Cholewiak RW, Brill JC, Schwab A. 2004. Vibrotactile localization on the abdomen: effects of place and space. *Percept. Psychophys.* 66:970–87

Cholewiak RW, Collins AA. 2003. Vibrotactile localization on the arm: effects of place, space, and age. *Percept. Psychophys.* 65:1058–77

Cohen JC, Bolanowski SJ, Verrillo RT. 2005. A direct comparison of exogenous and endogenous inhibition of return and selective attention mechanisms in the somatosensory system. *Somatosens. Mot. Res.* 22:269–79

Craig AD, Bushnell MC. 1994. The thermal grill illusion: unmasking the burn of cold pain. *Science* 265:252–55

Craig JC. 1999. Grating orientation as a measure of tactile spatial acuity. *Somatosens. Mot. Res.* 16:197–206

Craig JC, Johnson KO. 2000. The two-point threshold: not a measure of tactile spatial resolution. *Curr. Dir. Psychol. Sci.* 9:29–32

Craig JC, Rhodes RP, Gibson GO, Bensmaïa SJ. 2008. Discriminating smooth from grooved surfaces: effects of random variations in skin penetration. *Exp. Brain Res.* 188:331–40

Craig JC, Rollman GB. 1999. Somesthesis. *Annu. Rev. Psychol.* 50:305–31

Dhaka A, Viswanath V, Patapoutian A. 2006. TRP ion channels and temperature sensation. *Annu. Rev. Neurosci.* 29:135–61

Diatchenko L, Nackley AG, Slade GD, Belfer I, Max MB, et al. 2007. Responses to Drs. Kim and Dionne regarding comments on Diatchenko et al. Catechol-*O*-methyltransferase gene polymorphisms are associated with multiple pain-evoking stimuli. *Pain* 2006;125:216–24. *Pain* 129:366–70

Diatchenko L, Slade GD, Nackley AG, Bhalang K, Sigurdsson A, et al. 2005. Genetic basis for individual variations in pain perception and the development of a chronic pain condition. *Hum. Mol. Genet.* 14:135–43

Durgin FH, Evans L, Dunphy N, Klostermann S, Simmons K. 2007. Rubber hands feel the touch of light. *Psychol. Sci.* 18:152–57

Dworkin BR, Elbert T, Rau H, Birbaumer N, Pauli P, et al. 1994. Central effects of baroreceptor activation in humans: attenuation of skeletal reflexes and pain perception. *Proc. Nat. Acad Sci. USA* 91:6329–33

Eccleston C, Crombez G. 1999. Pain demands attention: a cognitive-affective model of the interruptive function of pain. *Psychol. Bull.* 125:356–66

Edwards RR, Fillingim RB, Ness TJ. 2003a. Age-related differences in endogenous pain modulation: a comparison of diffuse noxious inhibitory controls in healthy older and younger adults. *Pain* 101:155–65

Edwards RR, Ness TJ, Weigent DA, Fillingim RB. 2003b. Individual differences in diffuse noxious inhibitory controls (DNIC): association with clinical variables. *Pain* 106:427–37

Eimer M, Forster B, Vibell J. 2005. Cutaneous saltation within and across arms: a new measure of the saltation illusion in somatosensation. *Percept. Psychophys.* 67:458–68

Eisenberger NI, Lieberman MD, Williams KD. 2003. Does rejection hurt? An fMRI study of social exclusion. *Science* 302:290–92

Essick G, Guest S, Martinez E, Chen C, McGlone F. 2004. Site-dependent and subject-related variations in perioral thermal sensitivity. *Somatos. Mot. Res.* 21:159–75

Fillingim RB, Fillingim LA, Hollins M, Sigurdsson A, Maixner W. 1998. Generalized vibrotactile allodynia in a patient with temporomandibular disorder. *Pain* 78:75–78

Demonstrates that pain can be reduced in two ways by electrical stimulation: mechanoreceptor-induced analgesia and diffuse noxious inhibitory controls.

Fillingim RBE. 2000. *Sex, Gender, and Pain: Progress in Pain Research and Management, Vol. 17.* Seattle: Intl. Assoc. Study Pain Press

Geber C, Magerl W, Fondel R, Fechir M, Rolke R, et al. 2008. Numbness in clinical and experimental pain—a cross-sectional study exploring the mechanisms of reduced tactile function. *Pain* 139:73–81

Geldard FA. 1982. Saltation in somesthesis. *Psychol. Bull.* 92:136–75

Gescheider GA, Bolanowski SJ, Greenfield TC, Brunette K. 2005. Perception of the tactile texture of raised dot patterns: a multidimensional analysis. *Somatosens. Mot. Res.* 22:127–140

Gescheider GA, Bolanowski SJ, Hardick KR. 2001. The frequency selectivity of information-processing channels in the tactile sensory system. *Somatosens. Mot. Res.* 18:191–201

Gescheider GA, Wright JH, Verrillo RT. 2009. *Information-Processing Channels in the Tactile Sensory System.* Scientific Psychology Series, ed. SW Link, JT Townsend. New York: Psychol. Press

Gibson GO, Craig JC. 2002. Relative roles of spatial and intensive cues in the discrimination of spatial tactile stimuli. *Percept. Psychophys.* 64:1095–107

Gibson GO, Craig JC. 2005. Tactile spatial sensitivity and anisotropy. *Percept. Psychophys.* 67:1061–79

Gil KM, Wilson JJ, Edens JL, Webster DA, Abrams MA, et al. 1996. Effects of cognitive coping skills training on coping strategies and experimental pain sensitivity in African American adults with sickle cell disease. *Health Psychol.* 15:3–10

Granot M, Weissman-Fogel I, Crispel Y, Pud D, Granovsky Y, et al. 2008. Determinants of endogenous analgesia magnitude in a diffuse noxious inhibitory control (DNIC) paradigm: Do conditioning stimulus painfulness, gender and personality variables matter? *Pain* 136:142–49

Green BG. 2002. Synthetic heat at mild temperatures. *Somatosens. Mot. Res.* 19:130–38

Green BG, Cruz A. 1998. "Warmth-insensitive fields": evidence of sparse and irregular innervation of human skin by the warmth sense. *Somatosens. Mot. Res.* 15:269–75

Green BG, Pope JV. 2003. Innocuous cooling can produce nociceptive sensations that are inhibited during dynamic mechanical contact. *Exp. Brain Res.* 148:290–99

Green BG, Roman C, Schoen K, Collins H. 2008. Nociceptive sensations evoked from "spots" in the skin by mild cooling and heating. *Pain* 135:196–208

Greenspan JD, Craft RM, LeResche L, Arendt-Nielsen L, Berkley KJ, et al. 2007. Studying sex and gender differences in pain and analgesia: a consensus report. *Pain* 132:S26–45

Greenspan JD, Roy EA, Caldwell PA, Farooq NS. 2003. Thermosensory intensity and affect throughout the perceptible range. *Somatosens. Mot. Res.* 20:19–26

Grisart JM, Van Der Linden M. 2001. Conscious and automatic uses of memory in chronic pain patients. *Pain* 94:305–13

Guest S, Catmur C, Lloyd D, Spence C. 2002. Audiotactile interactions in roughness perception. *Exp. Brain Res.* 146:161–71

Guest S, Spence C. 2003. Tactile dominance in speeded discrimination of textures. *Exp. Brain Res.* 150:201–7

Harrar V, Winter R, Harris LR. 2008. Visuotactile apparent motion. *Percept. Psychophys.* 70:807–17

Heller MA, Ballesteros SE. 2006. *Touch and Blindness: Psychology and Neuroscience.* Mahwah, NJ: Erlbaum

Heller MA, Calcaterra JA, Green SL, Brown L. 1999. Intersensory conflict between vision and touch: the response modality dominates when precise, attention-riveting judgments are required. *Percept. Psychophys.* 61:1384–98

Higashiyama A, Hollins M, Maixner W. 2006. Tactile orientation constancy: Do proprioception and attention affect the tactile vertical? *Jpn. Psychol. Res.* 48:255–69

Hill BD, Blumenthal TD. 2005. Inhibition of acoustic startle using different mechanoreceptive channels. *Percept. Psychophys.* 67:741–47

Hillstrom AP, Shapiro KL, Spence C. 2002. Attentional limitations in processing sequentially presented vibrotactile targets. *Percept. Psychophys.* 64:1068–82

Hollins M, Bensmaïa SJ, Karlof K, Young F. 2000a. Individual differences in perceptual space for tactile textures: evidence from multidimensional scaling. *Percept. Psychophys.* 62:1534–44

Hollins M, Bensmaïa SJ, Washburn S. 2001. Vibrotactile adaptation impairs discrimination of fine, but not coarse, textures. *Somatosens. Mot. Res.* 18:253–62

Hollins M, Favorov O. 1994. The tactile movement aftereffect. *Somatosens. Mot. Res.* 11:153–62

When examining a surface that has both macrotexture and microtexture, subjects can attend separately to these differently-processed components.

Under some conditions, mild cooling can evoke sensations of stinging or burning, a result that complicates the distinction between thermoreception and nociception.

Hollins M, Fox A, Bishop C. 2000b. Imposed vibration influences perceived tactile smoothness. *Perception* 29:1455–65

Hollins M, Harper D, Gallagher S, Owings EW, Lim PF, et al. 2009. Perceived intensity and unpleasantness of cutaneous and auditory stimuli: an evaluation of the generalized hypervigilance hypothesis. *Pain* 141:215–21

Hollins M, Lorenz F, Harper D. 2006. Somatosensory coding of roughness: the effect of texture adaptation in direct and indirect touch. *J. Neurosci.* 26:5582–88

Hollins M, Lorenz F, Seeger A, Taylor R. 2005. Factors contributing to the integration of textural qualities: evidence from virtual surfaces. *Somatosens. Mot. Res.* 22:193–206

Hollins M, Risner SR. 2000. Evidence for the duplex theory of tactile texture perception. *Percept. Psychophys.* 62:695–705

Hollins M, Roy EA. 1996. Perceived intensity of vibrotactile stimuli: the role of mechanoreceptive channels. *Somatosens. Mot. Res.* 13:273–86

Hollins M, Roy EA, Crane SA. 2003. Vibratory antinociception: effects of vibration amplitude and frequency. *J. Pain* 4:381–91

Hollins M, Seeger A, Pelli G, Taylor R. 2004. Haptic perception of virtual surfaces: scaling subjective qualities and interstimulus differences. *Perception* 33:1001–19

Hollins M, Sigurdsson A. 1998. Vibrotactile amplitude and frequency discrimination in temporomandibular disorders. *Pain* 75:59–67

Hollins M, Sigurdsson A, Fillingim L, Goble A. 1996. Vibrotactile threshold is elevated in temporomandibular disorders. *Pain* 67:89–96

Jacoby LL, Toth JP, Yonelinas AP. 1993. Separating conscious and unconscious influences of memory: measuring recollection. *J. Exp. Psychol.: Gen.* 122:139–54

Johnson K. 2002. Neural basis of haptic perception. In *Stevens' Handbook of Experimental Psychology*, ed. H Pashler, S Yantis, Vol. 1, pp. 537–83. New York: Wiley. 3rd ed.

Jones LA, Lederman SJ. 2006. *Human Hand Function*. New York: Oxford Univ. Press

Jousmäki V, Hari R. 1998. Parchment-skin illusion: sound-biased touch. *Curr. Biol.* 8:R190

Keefe FJ, Rumble ME, Scipio CD, Giordano LA, Perri LM. 2004. Psychological aspects of persistent pain: current state of the science. *J. Pain* 5:195–211

Kennett S, Spence C, Driver J. 2002. Visuo-tactile links in covert exogenous spatial attention remap across changes in unseen hand posture. *Percept. Psychophys.* 64:1083–94

Kim H, Dionne RA. 2007. Comment on Diatchenko et al. Catechol-*O*-methyltransferase gene polymorphisms are associated with multiple pain-evoking stimuli. *Pain* 2006; 125:216–24. *Pain* 129:365–66

Kim H, Neubert JK, San Miguel A, Xu K, Krishnaraju RK, et al. 2004. Genetic influence on variability in human acute experimental pain sensitivity associated with gender, ethnicity and psychological temperament. *Pain* 109:488–96

Kim HK, Schattschneider J, Lee I, Chung K, Baron R, Chung JM. 2007. Prolonged maintenance of capsaicin-induced hyperalgesia by brief daily vibration stimuli. *Pain* 129:93–101

Klatzky RL, Lederman SJ. 1999. Tactile roughness perception with a rigid link interposed between skin and surface. *Percept. Psychophys.* 61:591–607

Klatzky RL, Lederman SJ, Hamilton C, Grindley M, Swendsen RH. 2003. Feeling textures through a probe: effects of probe and surface geometry and exploratory factors. *Percept. Psychophys.* 65:613–31

Kuhajda MC, Thorn BE, Klinger MR. 1998. The effect of pain on memory for affective words. *Ann. Behav. Med.* 20:31–35

Kuhajda MC, Thorn BE, Klinger MR, Rubin NJ. 2002. The effect of headache pain on attention (encoding) and memory (recognition). *Pain* 97:213–21

Lakatos S, Shepard RN. 1997. Constraints common to apparent motion in visual, tactile, and auditory space. *J. Exp. Psychol.: Hum. Percept. Perform.* 23:1050–60

LaMotte RH. 2000. Softness discrimination with a tool. *J. Neurophysiol.* 83:1777–86

LaMotte RH, Mountcastle VB. 1979. Disorders in somesthesis following lesions of parietal lobe. *J. Neurophysiol.* 42:400–19

Lautenbacher S, Rollman GB. 1997. Possible deficiencies of pain modulation in fibromyalgia. *Clin. J. Pain* 13:189–96

Le Bars D, Dickenson AH, Besson J-M. 1979. Diffuse noxious inhibitory controls (DNIC). I. Effects on dorsal horn convergent neurones in the rat. *Pain* 6:283–304

Lederman SJ. 1974. Tactile roughness of grooved surfaces: the touching process and the effects of macro- and microsurface structure. *Percept. Psychophys.* 16:385–95

Lerner EA, Craig JC. 2002. The prevalence of tactile motion aftereffects. *Somatosens. Mot. Res.* 19:24–29

Li J, Simone DA, Larson AA. 1999. Windup leads to characteristics of central sensitization. *Pain* 79:75–82

Loggia ML, Mogil JS, Bushnell MC. 2008. Empathy hurts: compassion for another increases both sensory and affective components of pain perception. *Pain* 136:168–76

Luck SJ, Vecera SP. 2002. Attention. In *Stevens' Handbook of Experimental Psychology*, ed. H Pashler, S Yantis, Vol. 1, pp. 235–86. New York: Wiley. 3rd ed.

Magerl W, Wilk SH, Treede R-D. 1998. Secondary hyperalgesia and perceptual wind-up following intradermal injection of capsaicin in humans. *Pain* 74:257–68

Maixner W, Fillingim R, Sigurdsson A, Kincaid S, Silva S. 1998. Sensitivity of patients with painful temporo-mandibular disorders to experimentally evoked pain: evidence for altered temporal summation of pain. *Pain* 76:71–81

Mannion RJ, Woolf CJ. 2000. Pain mechanisms and management: a central perspective. *Clin. J. Pain* 16:S144–56

Martino G, Marks LE. 2000. Cross-modal interaction between vision and touch: the role of synesthetic correspondence. *Perception* 29:745–54

Materazzo F, Cathcart S, Pritchard D. 2000. Anger, depression, and coping interactions in headache activity and adjustment: a controlled study. *J. Psychosom. Res.* 49:69–75

McCaul KD, Malott JM. 1984. Distraction and coping with pain. *Psychol. Bull.* 95:516–33

Provides support for the hypothesis that hypervigilance can generalize beyond pain to other sensory modalities.

McDermid AJ, Rollman GB, McCain GA. 1996. Generalized hypervigilance in fibromyalgia: evidence of perceptual amplification. *Pain* 66:133–44

McGlone F, Vallbo AB, Olausson H, Loken L, Wessberg J. 2007. Discriminative touch and emotional touch. *Can. J. Exp. Psychol.* 61:173–83

McMullan S, Lumb BM. 2006. Midbrain control of spinal nociception discriminates between responses evoked by myelinated and unmyelinated heat nociceptors in the rat. *Pain* 124:59–68

Meagher MW, Arnau RC, Rhudy JL. 2001. Pain and emotion: effects of affective picture modulation. *Psychosom. Med.* 63:79–90

Mechlin MB, Maixner W, Light KC, Fisher JM, Girdler SS. 2005. African Americans show alterations in endogenous pain regulatory mechanisms and reduced pain tolerance to experimental pain procedures. *Psychosom. Med.* 67:948–56

Meftah EM, Belingard L, Chapman CE. 2000. Relative effects of the spatial and temporal characteristics of scanned surfaces on human perception of tactile roughness using passive touch. *Exp. Brain Res.* 132:351–61

Melzack R, Wall PD. 1965. Pain mechanisms: a new theory. *Science* 150:971–79

Mendell LM, Wall PD. 1965. Responses of single dorsal cord cells to peripheral cutaneous unmyelinated fibers. *Nature* 206:97–99

Miyaoka T, Mano T, Ohka M. 1999. Mechanisms of fine-surface-texture discrimination in human tactile sensation. *J. Acoust. Soc. Am.* 105:2485–92

Mogil JS, Wilson SG, Chesler EJ, Rankin AL, Nemmani KVS, et al. 2003. The melanocortin-1 receptor gene mediates female-specific mechanisms of analgesia in mice and humans. *Proc. Natl. Acad. Sci. USA* 100:4867–72

Mohri Y, Fumoto M, Sato-Suzuki I, Umino M, Arita H. 2005. Prolonged rhythmic gum chewing suppresses nociceptive response via serotonergic descending inhibitory pathways in humans. *Pain* 118:35–42

Moseley GL, Gallace A, Spence C. 2008. Is mirror therapy all it is cracked up to be? Current evidence and future directions. *Pain* 138:7–10

Mountcastle VB. 2005. *The Sensory Hand. Neural Mechanisms of Somatic Sensation.* Cambridge, MA: Harvard Univ. Press

Mountcastle VB, Talbot WH, Sakata H, Hyvarinen J. 1969. Cortical neuronal mechanisms in flutter-vibration studied in unanesthetized monkeys. Neuronal periodicity and frequency discrimination. *J. Neurophysiol.* 32:452–84

Muniak MA, Ray S, Hsiao SS, Dammann JF, Bensmaia SJ. 2007. The neural coding of stimulus intensity: linking the population response of mechanoreceptive afferents with psychophysical behavior. *J. Neurosci.* 27:11687–99

Nackley AG, Tan KS, Fecho K, Flood P, Diatchenko L, Maixner W. 2007. Catechol-*O*-methyltransferase inhibition increases pain sensitivity through activation of both b2- and b3-adrenergic receptors. *Pain* 128:199–208

Newell FN, Ernst MO, Tjan BS, Bülthoff HH. 2001. Viewpoint dependence in visual and haptic object recognition. *Psychol. Sci.* 12:37–42

Nielsen CS, Stubhaug A, Price DD, Vassend O, Czajkowski N, Harris JR. 2008. Individual differences in pain sensitivity: genetic and environmental contributions. *Pain* 136:21–29

Norman JF, Norman HF, Clayton AM, Lianekhammy J, Zielke G. 2004. The visual and haptic perception of natural object shape. *Percept. Psychophys.* 66:342–51

Olausson H, Cole J, Rylander K, McGlone F, Lamarre Y, et al. 2008. Functional role of unmyelinated tactile afferents in human hairy skin: sympathetic response and perceptual localization. *Exp. Brain Res.* 184:135–40

Olausson H, Lamarre Y, Backlund H, Morin C, Wallin BG, et al. 2002. Unmyelinated tactile afferents signal touch and project to insular cortex. *Nat. Neurosci.* 5:900–4

Pei YC, Hsiao SS, Bensmaia SJ. 2008. The tactile integration of local motion cues is analogous to its visual counterpart. *Proc. Natl. Acad. Sci. USA* 105:8130–35

Pensky AEC, Johnson KA, Haag S, Homa D. 2008. Delayed memory for visual-haptic exploration of familiar objects. *Psychon. Bull. Rev.* 15:574–80

Pielsticker A, Haag G, Zaudig M, Lautenbacher S. 2005. Impairment of pain inhibition in chronic tension-type headache. *Pain* 118:215–23

Price DD. 1999. *Psychological Mechanisms of Pain and Analgesia: Progress in Pain Research and Management. Vol. 15.* Seattle: Intl. Assoc. Study Pain Press

Price DD, Bush FM, Long S, Harkins SW. 1994. A comparison of pain measurement characteristics of mechanical visual analogue and simple numerical rating scales. *Pain* 56:217–26

Price DD, McHaffie JG. 1988. Effects of heterotopic conditioning stimuli on first and second pain: a psychophysical evaluation in humans. *Pain* 34:245–52

Price DD, Milling LS, Kirsch I, Duff A, Montgomery GH, Nicholls SS. 1999. An analysis of factors that contribute to the magnitude of placebo analgesia in an experimental paradigm. *Pain* 83:147–56

Price DD, Staud R, Robinson ME, Mauderli AP, Cannon R, Vierck CJ. 2002. Enhanced temporal summation of second pain and its central modulation in fibromyalgia patients. *Pain* 99:49–59

Rainville P, Bau QVH, Chrétien P. 2005. Pain-related emotions modulate experimental pain perception and autonomic responses. *Pain* 118:306–18

Rainville P, Carrier B, Hofbauer RK, Bushnell MC, Duncan GH. 1999. Dissociation of sensory and affective dimensions of pain using hypnotic modulation. *Pain* 82:159–71

Ramachandran VS, Rogers-Ramachandran D. 1996. Synaesthesia in phantom limbs induced with mirrors. *Proc. Roy. Soc. B* 263:377–86

Reales JM, Ballesteros S. 1999. Implicit and explicit memory for visual and haptic objects: cross-modal priming depends on structural descriptions. *J. Exp. Psychol.: Learn. Mem. Cogn.* 25:644–63

Reed CL, Klatzky RL, Halgren E. 2005. What vs. where in touch: an fMRI study. *NeuroImage* 25:718–26

Ren K, Dubner R. 2002. Descending modulation in persistent pain: an update. *Pain* 100:1–6

Rhudy JL, Meagher MW. 2003. Negative affect: effects on an evaluative measure of human pain. *Pain* 104:617–26

Rhudy JL, Williams AE, McCabe KM, Nguyen MATV, Rambo P. 2005. Affective modulation of nociception at spinal and supraspinal levels. *Psychophysiology* 42:579–87

Rollman GB. 2009. Perspectives on hypervigilance. *Pain* 141:183–84

Roy A, Steinmetz PN, Hsiao SS, Johnson KO, Niebur E. 2007. Synchrony: a neural correlate of somatosensory attention. *J. Neurophysiol.* 98:1645–61

Roy EA, Hollins M. 1998. A ratio code for vibrotactile pitch. *Somatosens. Mot. Res.* 15:134–45

Roy EA, Hollins M, Maixner W. 2003. Reduction of TMD pain by high-frequency vibration: a spatial and temporal analysis. *Pain* 101:267–74

Neuroimaging and psychophysical data support the idea that unmyelinated mechanoreceptive afferents help trigger the emotional response to interpersonal touch.

Demonstrates that a placebo can cause analgesia that is restricted to a specific skin region, if that is what the subject expects.

Since emotional state affects the strength of a spinal nociceptive reflex, emotional processing must influence descending modulatory systems.

Salinas E, Hernández A, Zainos A, Romo R. 2000. Periodicity and firing rate as candidate neural codes for the frequency of vibrotactile stimuli. *J. Neurosci.* 20:5503–15

Scheibert J, Leurent S, Prevost A, Debrégeas G. 2009. The role of fingerprints in the coding of tactile information probed with a biomimetic sensor. *Science* 323:1503–6

Singer T, Seymour B, O'Doherty J, Kaube H, Dolan RJ, Frith CD. 2004. Empathy for pain involves the affective but not sensory components of pain. *Science* 303:1157–62

Sluka KA, Walsh D. 2003. Transcutaneous electrical nerve stimulation: basic science mechanisms and clinical effectiveness. *J. Pain* 4:109–21

Smith AM, Chapman CE, Deslandes M, Langlais J-S, Thibodeau M-P. 2002. Role of friction and tangential force variation in the subjective scaling of tactile roughness. *Exp. Brain Res.* 144:211–23

Soto-Faraco S, Ronald A, Spence C. 2004. Tactile selective attention and body posture: assessing the multisensory contributions of vision and proprioception. *Percept. Psychophys.* 66:1077–94

Spence C, Lloyd D, McGlone F, Nicholls MER, Driver J. 2000. Inhibition of return is supramodal: a demonstration between all possible pairings of vision, touch, and audition. *Exp. Brain Res.* 134:42–48

Spence C, McGlone FP. 2001. Reflexive spatial orienting of tactile attention. *Exp. Brain Res.* 141:324–30

Spence C, Nicholls MER, Gillespie N, Driver J. 1998. Cross-modal links in exogenous covert spatial orienting between touch, audition, and vision. *Percept. Psychophys.* 60:544–57

Spence C, Shore DI, Klein RM. 2001. Multisensory prior entry. *J. Exp. Psychol.: Gen.* 130:799–832

Staud R, Price DD, Robinson ME, Mauderli AP, Vierck CJ. 2004. Maintenance of windup of second pain requires less frequent stimulation in fibromyalgia patients compared to normal controls. *Pain* 110:689–96

Staud R, Robinson ME, Vierck CJ Jr, Price DD. 2003. Diffuse noxious inhibitory controls (DNIC) attenuate temporal summation of second pain in normal males but not in normal females or fibromyalgia patients. *Pain* 101:167–74

Stevens JC, Choo KK. 1998. Temperature sensitivity of the body surface over the life span. *Somatosens. Mot. Res.* 15:13–28

Stohler CS, Kowalski CJ, Lund JP. 2001. Muscle pain inhibits cutaneous touch perception. *Pain* 92:327–33

Story GM, Cruz-Orengo L. 2007. Feel the burn. *Am. Sci.* 95:326–33

Sullivan MJL, Thorn B, Haythornthwaite JA, Keefe F, Martin M, et al. 2001. Theoretical perspectives on the relation between catastrophizing and pain. *Clin. J. Pain* 17:52–64

Thorn BE, Pence LB, Ward LC, Kilgo G, Clements KL, et al. 2007. A randomized clinical trial of targeted cognitive behavioral treatment to reduce catastrophizing in chronic headache sufferers. *J. Pain* 8:938–49

Tommerdahl M, Delemos KA, Vierck CJ Jr, Favorov OV, Whitsel BL. 1996. Anterior parietal cortical response to tactile and skin-heating stimuli applied to the same skin site. *J. Neurophysiol.* 75:2662–70

Torebjörk HE, Lundberg LER, LaMotte RH. 1992. Central changes in processing of mechanoreceptive input in capsaicin-induced secondary hyperalgesia in humans. *J. Physiol.* 448:765–80

Tracey I, Ploghaus A, Gati JS, Clare S, Smith S, et al. 2002. Imaging attentional modulation of pain in the periaqueductal gray in humans. *J. Neurosci.* 22:2748–52

Vallbo ÅB, Olausson H, Wessberg J. 1999. Unmyelinated afferents constitute a second system coding tactile stimuli of the human hairy skin. *J. Neurophysiol.* 81:2753–63

van Erp JBF. 2008. Absolute localization of vibrotactile stimuli on the torso. *Percept. Psychophys.* 70:1016–23

Verrillo RT. 1962. Investigation of some parameters of the cutaneous threshold for vibration. *J. Acoust. Soc. Am.* 34:1768–73

Villemure C, Slotnick BM, Bushnell MC. 2003. Effects of odors on pain perception: deciphering the roles of emotion and attention. *Pain* 106:101–8

Wall PD, Cronly-Dillon JR. 1960. Pain, itch, and vibration. *Arch. Neurol.* 2:365–75

Watanabe I, Svensson P, Arendt-Nielsen L. 1999. Influence of segmental and extrasegmental conditioning stimuli on cortical potentials evoked by painful electrical stimulation. *Somatosens. Mot. Res.* 16:243–50

Watanabe J, Hayashi S, Kajimoto H, Tachi S, Nishida S. 2007. Tactile motion aftereffects produced by appropriate presentation for mechanoreceptors. *Exp. Brain Res.* 180:577–82

Weerakkody NS, Percival P, Hickey MW, Morgan DL, Gregory JE, et al. 2003. Effects of local pressure and vibration on muscle pain from eccentric exercise and hypertonic saline. *Pain* 105:425–35

Yarnitsky D, Crispel Y, Eisenberg E, Granovsky Y, Ben-Nun A, et al. 2008. Prediction of chronic postoperative pain: pre-operative DNIC testing identifies patients at risk. *Pain* 138:22–28

Measurements with an artificial fingertip show that fingerprints amplify vibrations that play a key role in the perception of fine textures.

This elegantly designed experimental study shows that attention and emotion can modulate pain in different ways.

Yarnitsky D, Kunin M, Brik R, Sprecher E. 1997. Vibration reduces thermal pain in adjacent dermatomes. *Pain* 69:75–77

Yau JM, Hollins M, Bensmaia SJ. 2009a. Textural timbre: the perception of surface microtexture depends in part on multimodal spectral cues. *Commun. Integr. Biol.* 2:1–3

Yau JM, Olenczak JB, Dammann JF, Bensmaia SJ. 2009b. Temporal frequency channels are linked across audition and touch. *Curr. Biol.* 19:561–66

Yoshioka T, Bensmaia SJ, Craig JC, Hsiao SS. 2007. Texture perception through direct and indirect touch: an analysis of perceptual space for tactile textures in two modes of exploration. *Somatosens. Mot. Res.* 24:53–70

Yoshioka T, Gibb B, Dorsch AK, Hsiao SS, Johnson KO. 2001. Neural coding mechanisms underlying perceived roughness of finely textured surfaces. *J. Neurosci.* 21:6905–16

Zubieta J-K, Heitzeg MM, Smith YR, Bueller JA, Xu K, et al. 2003. COMT val[158]met genotype affects μ-opioid neurotransmitter responses to a pain stressor. *Science* 299:1240–43

Learning: From Association to Cognition

David R. Shanks

Division of Psychology and Language Sciences, University College London,
London WC1H 0AP United Kingdom; email: d.shanks@ucl.ac.uk

Annu. Rev. Psychol. 2010. 61:273–301

First published online as a Review in Advance on
September 15, 2009

The *Annual Review of Psychology* is online at
psych.annualreviews.org

This article's doi:
10.1146/annurev.psych.093008.100519

0066-4308/10/0110-0273$20.00

Key Words

association, awareness, blocking, cognition, conditioning, inference,
reasoning

Abstract

Since the very earliest experimental investigations of learning, tension
has existed between association-based and cognitive theories. Associationism accounts for the phenomena of both conditioning and "higher"
forms of learning via concepts such as excitation, inhibition, and reinforcement, whereas cognitive theories assume that learning depends
on hypothesis testing, cognitive models, and propositional reasoning.
Cognitive theories have received considerable impetus in regard to both
human and animal learning from recent research suggesting that the key
illustration of cue selection in learning, blocking, often arises from inferential reasoning. At the same time, a dichotomous view that separates
noncognitive, unconscious (implicit) learning from cognitive, conscious
(explicit) learning has gained favor. This review selectively describes key
findings from this research, evaluates evidence for and against associative and cognitive explanatory constructs, and critically examines both
the dichotomous view of learning as well as the claim that learning can
occur unconsciously.

Contents

INTRODUCTION

It seems unlikely that any investigator would carry out an Instructed Conditioning study with a motor response since, in plain English, this would consist of telling S to move his finger. However, common sense is not a good guide when predicting the behavior of investigators operating in an S-R framework. Experiment 6 in Hunter (1938) consists of producing finger withdrawal conditioning by saying, "Lift your finger," or "Don't lift your finger." If Ss didn't make a finger withdrawal response to "Lift your finger," they were shocked. To insure objectivity the commands were presented by telephone. The Ss conditioned. (Brewer 1974, p. 14)

Brewer's lampooning of studies conducted within the framework of stimulus-response (S-R) behaviorism, on the grounds that they ignored the ubiquitous involvement of conscious thinking in learning and memory, will doubtless make many modern researchers reflect with amusement and relief on how far experimental psychology has come since those

S-R: stimulus-response

Associationism: the assumption that learning can be understood in terms of the formation and expression of excitatory or inhibitory associations, formed via reinforcement

Implicit learning: synonymous with unconscious learning. Also termed "procedural" in contrast to "declarative" (conscious) learning

dark days. The present review takes Brewer's seminal re-evaluation of the relationship between learning and cognition as its starting point. One conclusion of Brewer's assault was the notion that processes of association formation and reinforcement are largely irrelevant for the understanding of human learning. Another conclusion was that learning invariably arises from the operation of conscious cognitive processes. This review reassesses these fundamental hypotheses about learning in the light of contemporary research.

Associationism has dominated the history of learning theory. This prominence originates from the work in the early part of the past century by Edward Thorndike, for whom an understanding of the reinforcement processes that cause strengthening of S-R connections (e.g., the Laws of Effect and Exercise) was a central concern. Related to his associationist philosophy, Thorndike also believed that learning could occur unconsciously or implicitly: he was the pioneer of what we now know as the field of implicit learning (Thorndike 1931). Because he viewed reinforcing events as being effects that automatically stamped in S-R bonds, rather than as providing information, Thorndike was eager to show that rewards and punishments can affect learning even when the individual is unaware that such learning is taking place, and he conducted numerous studies (reviewed by Postman 1962) attempting to establish this. Thus Thorndike combined two positions, assigning a key role to reinforcement processes in learning together with the claim that these learning processes can proceed independently of awareness.

A very different view of learning can be traced back to the Gestaltists (especially Köhler and Koffka) and field theorists (particularly Tolman) who took an opposing position on the effect versus information issue. For them, events did not provide the opportunity for gradual trial-and-error learning, but rather set the context for the development of insight and problem solving. Tolman in particular argued that reinforcement is not a necessary condition for learning; instead, cognitive relationships (hypotheses or cognitive maps) are formed between stimuli or events as a result of contiguity and organizational principles (see the review of learning by Melton 1950, in the very first *Annual Review of Psychology*). Debate between S-R and field theories, and the importance of phenomena such as latent learning, dominated much of experimental psychology up until the cognitive revolution (see Holland 2008).

By the time Brewer (1974) came to review the literature, it was abundantly plain that the traditional S-R theory of conditioning, including core notions such as the automatic and unconscious stamping in (i.e., reinforcement) of associative links, was not appropriate for either classical or operant (instrumental) conditioning, nor did it provide an adequate framework for such important applied problems as understanding the development of phobias (Rachman 1977). Evidence that conditioning of autonomic, motor, as well as more complex responses only occurs in parallel with expectancies and awareness convinced Brewer that all conditioning is the result of cognitive processing, in particular of the formation and testing of conscious hypotheses. Although tension has existed between associative and cognitive views of learning for a century, the topic has received renewed attention in the past few years. The considerable evidence that awareness necessarily accompanies learning has been challenged recently as the study of implicit learning has gained momentum. The present article reviews some of the current evidence from this area and asks whether Brewer's position remains the most viable interpretation: Is learning intrinsically a conscious process? On the other hand, much recent research has retained the strongly antiassociationist perspective, which Brewer championed, regarding concepts like reinforcement as superfluous. Recent evidence bearing on this issue is also reviewed.

In exploring the relationship between associative and cognitive processing, this article examines a fundamental theme that has remained unresolved since the early days of experimental psychology. Recent research is reviewed, mostly published since 2000, covering contributions from the areas of associative and contingency learning, and implicit learning and memory. A guiding question is whether our explanatory scope for explaining the richness of learning would be seriously curtailed if concepts such as excitation and reinforcement were abandoned. Plainly, it is not sufficient to reject traditional S-R theory. Instead, cognitive theories that dispense with associative constructs must be contrasted with those modern theories that incorporate cognitive constructs such as attention and awareness while also assigning a fundamental role to association formation. Extraordinarily rich explanations of learning phenomena have been achieved by models built out of automatic link machinery (i.e., connectionist, neural network, or parallel distributed processing accounts) in which representations are coded subsymbolically (McClelland & Rumelhart 1986, Rumelhart & McClelland 1986, Thomas & McClelland 2008). Such models demonstrate massive "emergentism," in that processes that seem cognitive and high level emerge from the operations and interactions of very elementary processing units. These processes yield knowledge structures and states of activation which, when sufficiently strong and stable, constitute the contents of consciousness (see Maia & Cleeremans 2005). It is against this contemporary associationist framework that the present review compares the alternative propositional-cognitive theory.

ROLE OF COGNITION IN LEARNING

Should we think of learning as the automatic formation of a mental link or bond between a cue (or CS) and an outcome (or US), or instead as the acquisition of a propositional belief representing the relationship between them? One counterintuitive but well-documented empirical observation forcefully captures the paradox of learning and cognition. This is the finding that verbal instructions seem to be largely interchangeable with experienced events. The mere instruction that a tone will be followed by shock is sufficient to cause an

Conditioning: in classical or Pavlovian conditioning, a conditioned stimulus (CS; e.g., a tone) predicts an unconditioned stimulus (US; e.g., food or shock). As a result of learning, the response normally evoked by the US (e.g., salivation or freezing) or a similar response comes to be evoked by the CS

CS: conditioned stimulus

US: unconditioned stimulus

increase in skin conductance that is indistinguishable from that obtained when the tone is actually paired with shock (e.g., Cook & Harris 1937, McNally 1981). In more recent research, Lovibond (2003) has shown that this interchangeability extends to more subtle designs including blocking (described below). The paradox is that if true conditioning, with events that are actually experienced, engages (Brewer notwithstanding) an automatic and unconscious learning mechanism, then how can verbal, cognitive, conscious instructions make contact with that mechanism? Contrary to commonly held belief, we seem to be faced with the conclusion that conditioning in fact gives rise to conscious, cognitive, propositional representations rather than to automatic, unconscious ones. This is precisely the position adopted by many contemporary researchers (De Houwer 2009, Mitchell et al. 2009), in which associative processes are jettisoned.

In the past few years, the cognitive approach (now commonly referred to as propositional or inferential) has kindled renewed attention and emphasis. To what extent, then, do cognitive processes penetrate learning? Should constructs such as reinforcement and excitation play any role in our explanatory frameworks?

Blocking: Associative Accounts

The signature phenomenon of blocking (Kamin 1969) has played a key role in the history of learning theory and has been central in the debate between proponents of associative and cognitive theories. Blocking is the fundamental demonstration that learning about the relationship between two events depends on not just their frequency of pairing, but also on the extent to which one provides information about the other. Consider the pairing of a cue and an outcome, or of a conditioned stimulus (CS) with an unconditioned stimulus (US). When cues A and B are paired together and predict an outcome, the extent to which learning accrues to A is diminished if B has previously, in the absence of A, been paired with the outcome (see **Table 1**). Thus blocking refers to a two-stage design in which B is established as a reliable predictor of the outcome in stage 1 (denoted B+), with A and B occurring together and jointly predicting the outcome in stage 2 (denoted AB+). As a concrete example, laboratory studies with human participants might describe a hypothetical individual suffering from allergic reactions to some foods but not others. On day 1 the individual eats tomatoes and suffers an allergic reaction, and on day 2 she eats tomatoes together with pasta and again suffers a reaction. The participant's task is to judge the extent to which pasta is associated with the reaction, and blocking refers to the fact that the initial tomatoes-allergy pairing will weaken the perceived pasta-allergy connection.

Standard associationist accounts of blocking rely on concepts such as excitation,

> **Blocking:** the fundamental demonstration of cue selection in learning. When a pair of cues A and B predicts an outcome, the degree of learning about the A-outcome relationship is reduced (blocked) if B has previously on its own predicted that outcome

Table 1 Experimental designs relating to blocking

Condition	Pretraining	Stage 1	Stage 2	Test	Comment
Blocking		B+	AB+	A	B+ trials reduce responding to A at test
Blocking control			AB+	A	Responding to A at test is strong
Backward blocking		AB+	B+	A	B+ trials reduce responding to A at test
Subadditivity	C+/D+/CD+	B+	AB+	A	Pretraining reduces blocking (i.e., enhances responding to A)
Additivity	C+/D+/CD++	B+	AB+	A	Pretraining enhances blocking (i.e., reduces responding to A)
Maximality	+	B+	AB+	A	Pretraining reduces blocking (i.e., enhances responding to A)
Submaximality	++	B+	AB+	A	Pretraining enhances blocking (i.e., reduces responding to A)

Note: A–D: cues or conditioned stimuli. + indicates occurrence of the outcome or unconditioned stimulus. ++ indicates an outcome of larger magnitude.

reinforcement, associability, and surprise (Dickinson 1980, Mackintosh 1983, Rescorla & Wagner 1972). In the classic Rescorla-Wagner theory, for instance, an excitatory association is assumed to form in stage 1 between B and the outcome, with the latter playing the role of reinforcer. In stage 2, the reinforcing power of the outcome is diminished because its occurrence is no longer surprising—it is predicted by the presence of cue B. Thus the outcome does not serve as a reinforcer of the A-outcome association, and little learning accumulates to A. This theory, whose history and influence is reviewed by Miller et al. (1995), has played such a central role in recent learning theory that it has in effect acted as the departure point for almost all subsequent theories. Its influence arose in considerable part from its ability to explain the blocking effect Kamin discovered.

Although subject to numerous theoretical subtleties (Mackintosh 1975, Pearce & Hall 1980), this explanatory framework is supported by a wealth of evidence (Mackintosh 1983), including such diverse findings as that learning is retarded for a blocked cue that is subsequently paired with an entirely new outcome (Le Pelley et al. 2007), that blocking occurs in organisms not generally assumed to be endowed with cognitive capacities (including the marine mollusc *Hermissenda*; Rogers & Matzel 1996), and that the dopamine system in the brain appears to provide a reinforcing mechanism with just the required formal properties (Fletcher et al. 2001, Waelti et al. 2001). Although the modern associationist perspective differs in numerous ways from the classic S-R theories of Tolman, Guthrie, Hull, and others, in its fundamental form it incorporates many of the concepts Brewer was so determined to reject (for a review of the intellectual transition from early to contemporary learning theories, see Mowrer & Klein 2001).

It is also important to note that associative models of learning have often inaccurately been described as assuming automatic transfer of activation from the CS representation to the US representation. In reality, modern asso-

ciative theories have placed great emphasis on attentional, controlled processing and related concepts such as limited-capacity working memory (Mackintosh 1975, Pearce & Hall 1980, Wagner 1981), and the role of attention in human as well as animal conditioning has been recognized for many years (Dawson & Schell 1982). The important question, of course, is whether cognitive concepts such as these, and the evidence for their role, ultimately require abandoning the associationist perspective.

Blocking: Cognitive Accounts

Waldmann & Holyoak (1990, 1992) were the instigators of the cognitive challenge to the associationist account of blocking. Their key observation was that associations have no semantic properties, whereas human learning seems to be highly sensitive to such properties. For instance, on the associationist theory, it should not matter whether cues and outcomes are described as causes and effects, respectively, or as effects and causes. Imagine an experimental task in which the participant is shown information about substances in the blood of a hypothetical patient together with information about whether the patient is suffering from a target disease. From an associative perspective, the task involves learning connections between the substance (cue or CS) and the disease (outcome or US). However, the substance could be described as a cause of or as an effect of the disease, and Waldmann & Holyoak (1990, 1992) showed that from a rational perspective these interpretations can have radically different implications. Indeed, they argued that blocking would only be expected in a cause-effect scenario and not in an effect-cause scenario, and they presented experimental evidence consistent with this prediction.

Later research has confirmed that the interpretation of events, over and above their simple pairing, can substantially modulate blocking, but this research has also shown that learning is sometimes quite immune to the way events are described (e.g., Cobos et al. 2002, López et al. 2005, Waldmann 2000). For example,

López et al. (2005) presented participants with a simulated device in which switches and lights on one side of a box were connected to lights on the other side of the box. Participants either saw trials in which the cue played the role of a cause and the outcome the role of an effect, or vice versa. The main finding was that this causal interpretation had no effect except in conditions where López et al. (2005) went to extreme lengths to emphasize the causal nature of the task to participants. Thus there do seem to be conditions in which the associationist theory provides an appropriate account of participants' behavior, although we are some way from a full understanding of the boundary conditions for such an account.

In related work, Matute and her colleagues (Matute et al. 2002, Vadillo et al. 2005) have extensively studied aspects of the precise format of questions probing associative knowledge. Suppose participants observe trials in which various medicines are related to allergic reactions. Probe questions might ask to what extent a medicine *causes* the allergic reaction, the extent to which it predicts or indicates the reaction, or the extent to which medicine and allergy co-occur. Contrary to the simple idea that a single associative connection underlies all such judgments, these studies reveal qualitative differences between different judgment questions. For example, Vadillo et al. (2005) found that causal and prediction judgments could be dissociated. Yet as Vadillo et al. themselves noted, a slightly more subtle associative account would have no difficulty accounting for this finding. Such an account would assume that causal judgments are assessed by simply probing the associative strength of the target cue on its own, while prediction judgments are based on the combined associative strength of the target cue plus the context.

Recall that the essence of associative approaches is that they assume that presentation of a cue calls to mind (given sufficient attentional resources and so on) the outcome with which it was associated. Now consider a situation in which a cue competition effect such as blocking occurs (B+ in stage 1 followed by

AB+ in stage 2). It has been known for many years (Dickinson et al. 1984) that associative or causal judgments for A will be low in comparison to a control condition in which the initial B+ trials are omitted (see **Table 1**). But studies have also shown that judgments of the probability of the outcome given cue A will manifest a blocking-like effect (De Houwer et al. 2007, Lagnado & Shanks 2002, López et al. 1998, Price & Yates 1993). This is a striking result because the probability of the outcome given cue A, $P(O/A)$, is unaffected by whether or not B+ trials are presented in stage 1. Associative theories explain this effect by proposing that A's associative weight, which is reduced in the blocking condition, is part of the evidence used to make a probability judgment. Even though the probabilities are objectively the same in the two conditions, the cue much more strongly makes us think of the outcome in the control than in the blocking condition, and this mental activation unavoidably biases our probability judgment. Explaining the bias in terms of inferential processes appears difficult. Similar effects emerge in terms of memory for the relationship between a blocked cue and its associated outcome (discussed below).

De Houwer et al. (2002) took a different approach to explore cognitive influences in blocking. They proposed that blocking arises from a chain of reasoning from the premise "the outcome is as probable and intense after B as after AB" to the conclusion "therefore A is not a cause of the outcome." They also noted, however, that such an inference is valid only if the effect is not occurring at its maximal possible level. The inference only follows if there is room for the outcome to occur with greater probability or intensity. To test this analysis, they described the outcome in a blocking design as occurring with an intensity of 10 on a scale from 0–10 (maximal condition). De Houwer et al. (2002) speculated that if blocking arises as a result of reasoning, rather than from associative processes, then their participants should be unsure about the status of the blocked cue A under these conditions. In stage 1 they learned that cue B predicted the outcome, and then in stage 2 they observed A and B occurring together with the same outcome. Such information is insufficient to distinguish between A having no relationship with the outcome versus it having a strong relationship that is masked by a ceiling effect. If B is already causing the outcome with maximal intensity, then A cannot increase or alter that outcome, even if it does have a causal relationship with the outcome. De Houwer et al. (2002) contrasted the maximal condition with a submaximal one in which the same events were presented, but the outcome was always described as occurring with intensity 10/20. Hence, in this case the failure of A to change the magnitude of the outcome in stage 2 is significant, as it could have done so: The outcome still has room to increase in magnitude, but did not do so. Consistent with this analysis, De Houwer et al. (2002) observed much stronger blocking in the submaximal condition and argued that this finding is fundamentally inconsistent with associative theories of blocking.

In a related modification to the standard blocking design (see **Table 1**), a number of authors (Beckers et al. 2005, Lovibond et al. 2003, Mitchell & Lovibond 2002) have given their participants pre-exposure designed to confirm or contradict the idea that cues have additive causal value. If participants believe cues are additive, then the failure of cue B to cause an increase in the outcome's magnitude indicates that it is ineffective, and blocking should be substantial. However, if they believe that cues are subadditive (i.e., that two cues, each of which causes an outcome with magnitude M, do not produce an outcome of magnitude 2M when paired together), then the failure of B to increase the outcome's magnitude is not evidence that B lacks any causal power. In that event, blocking should be much weaker in the subadditive condition, and this is the pattern commonly observed (Beckers et al. 2005, Lovibond et al. 2003, Mitchell & Lovibond 2002).

These maximality and additivity effects have been the subject of extensive further research since their original discovery. For instance, Beckers et al. (2006) have reported additivity

effects in conventional conditioning procedures with rats and concluded that similar inferential reasoning processes and "remarkable cognitive abilities" (p. 100) are employed. In their studies, both subadditivity (C+, D+, CD+) and additivity (C+, D+, CD++, where ++ denotes a US with higher magnitude) pretraining influenced blocking, the former reducing it and the latter enhancing it. Moreover, maximality pretraining also had an influence: specifically, a pretreatment in which the animals received unsignaled large magnitude (++) as well as smaller (+) shocks led to an enhancement of blocking, consistent with the inference that the blocked cue could have, but did not, increase the magnitude of the US and therefore must have been an ineffective cue.

Are these findings inconsistent with associationist accounts, as has often been claimed? Perhaps the presence of the effects in laboratory rats should lead us to look particularly carefully for simpler explanations. And indeed there is a strong counterargument that additivity effects might have a rather different basis, at least in some circumstances. Wheeler et al. (2008) reported an additivity pretraining effect, namely that subadditivity pretraining attenuated blocking. Specifically, they presented rats in a fear-conditioning preparation with trials in which C, D, and the compound CD all signaled the US (C+, D+, CD+), thus providing information that the causal consequences of combining cues were not additive. Then in the main training stage the rats received B+ followed by AB+ trials in a typical blocking arrangement prior to an assessment of conditioned responding to the target CS A. Wheeler et al. (2008) found that the subadditivity pretreatment substantially weakened the blocking effect—that is, enhanced learning about A—consistent with the inferential theory. The subadditive trials indicate that the outcome of the combination of two reliable cues is not additive, and hence in the main stage of the experiment the animals might have reasoned that A was a perfectly valid predictor of the US, despite not increasing the US's magnitude. Yet Wheeler et al. (2008) went on to show that their subadditivity pretreatment

Maximality: information (e.g., 20/20) implying that an outcome is occurring at its ceiling level. Contrast with submaximality (e.g., 10/20)

Additivity: trials (e.g., C+, D+, CD++, where ++ denotes a high-magnitude outcome) that imply that the predictive value of cues adds when they are combined. Contrast with subadditivity (e.g., C+, D+, CD+)

Inferential theory: assumes that cue selection effects are the result of inferences from beliefs. In blocking, for example, little weight is assigned to the blocked cue because participants assume cue additivity and reason that the cue does not increase the magnitude of the outcome

was sensitive to a number of manipulations typically found to impair generalization. For example, a change of context from the pretreatment to the blocking phase reduced the impact of the subadditivity trials. This suggests the possibility that the effect emerges not because of controlled inference, but rather because the pretreatment allows the formation of some associative structures that generalize (or fail to generalize under a context switch) to the blocking phase.

The nature of this putative generalization mechanism has been explored by Haselgrove (2009). One common way of building generalization into associative theories is to assume that stimuli are composed of multiple elements and that some of these elements may be shared between nominally distinct stimuli. Consider the additivity design employed by Beckers et al. (2006) and Wheeler et al. (2008) in which blocking of A after B+ and AB+ trials is attenuated if subadditivity is demonstrated in a previous learning phase with C+, D+, and CD+ trials. Haselgrove (2009) noted that most of the stimuli used in these experiments came from the same modality (auditory) and suggested that this might enhance generalization between them. To model this, Haselgrove conducted a simple simulation of this experimental design using the Rescorla-Wagner theory, but assuming that one additional element or cue was present on every trial. Surprisingly, this simple model reproduced the key finding that the pretreatment stage reduced blocking, and the reason for this was that the common element accrued asymptotic associative strength in the pretreatment stage, such that when A was presented in the blocking test (with the common element assumed also to be present), a high level of responding was predicted. Haselgrove (2009) also showed that the model predicted the contrasting effect of an enhancement of blocking after additivity pretraining (i.e., C+, D+, CD++), as observed by Beckers et al. (2006), as well as after submaximality pretraining, and concluded that the inferential basis for the additivity effect, at least in rats, is far from proven.

Schmajuk & Larrauri (2008) also tested a connectionist model with the events of a typical additivity design. In their model, associative connections are updated by a reinforcement process, and the connections have no symbolic reference. Although different from Haselgrove's (2009) model in some important respects, it also reproduced the additivity effect. Schmajuk & Larrauri (2008) conclude that it is not necessary to interpret additivity effects in terms of propositional reasoning.

Another line of research has considered the possibility that maximality and additivity effects have their influence not via changing hypotheses and reasoning about cue combinations but rather by inducing shifts between elemental and configural processing. There is now a considerable body of evidence suggesting that organisms (both human and nonhuman) can represent stimuli in rather flexible ways (Melchers et al. 2008). In particular, the same nominal stimulus can be coded either as an irreducible configuration or as the sum of a set of elements. For instance, in a human Pavlovian conditioning study by Melchers et al. (2004a), participants initially saw either a feature-neutral discrimination or a matched control discrimination. The control discrimination (A+, AB+, C−, CB−) afforded an elemental solution: Correct responses are made on all trials if the participant learns a strong positive association between cue A and the US, with all other cues having associative weights of zero, and assuming additivity of cue weights. Despite being almost identical, the feature-neutral discrimination (A−, AB+, C+, CB−) cannot be solved this way; there is no set of weights for the individual elements that yield correct responses across all trial types. Hence this problem requires a more complex solution, such as the formation of configural representations in which AB and CD are represented as distinct from the sum of their constituent parts.

To test the hypothesis that participants indeed solved these discriminations in qualitatively different ways, Melchers et al. (2004a) next gave both groups a new discrimination (EX+, FX−, followed by test trials with E and F) and found very different behavior as a function of the initial problem. Specifically, greater responding to E than to F was evident in the group pretrained on the control discrimination but not in the one pretrained on the feature-neutral one. Such a pattern is consistent with the hypothesis that the group trained on the control discrimination transferred an elemental strategy to the new problem, broke the EX and FX compounds into elements, and assigned a positive weight to E and weights of zero to F and X, whereas the group trained on the feature-neutral discrimination transferred a configural strategy in which compounds and elements are treated as independent.

Building on this idea, Livesey & Boakes (2004; see also Williams et al. 1994) reported that a range of manipulations thought to enhance elemental processing increased blocking (in much the same way as additivity instructions), whereas manipulations assumed to enhance configural processing decreased blocking (as with subadditivity instructions). Strikingly, by presenting the cues in a configural manner, Livesey & Boakes (2004) were able to eliminate blocking even when an additivity pretreatment stage was provided. Such a result raises the strong possibility that maximality and additivity effects have some of their influence via shifting the balance between elemental and configural processing. However, whether this account can explain all of the relevant results is unclear. Beckers et al. (2005) found, for example, that additivity information affected blocking even when it was presented after the target trials, an outcome difficult to reconcile with the idea that the locus of additivity effects resides solely in their influence on the way the blocking stimuli are coded. Lastly, a subtractivity pretreatment employed by Mitchell et al. (2005b) affected blocking in the way predicted by a reasoning account.

Retrospective Revaluation

Cognitive interpretations have also been offered for the phenomenon of backward blocking (Dickinson & Burke 1996, Shanks 1985, Van Hamme & Wasserman 1994) and other examples of retrospective revaluation. In a backward blocking design (**Table 1**), trials in which A and B are paired with the outcome precede B-outcome trials. According to traditional theories (Rescorla & Wagner 1972), blocking (reduced judgments of the relationship between A and the outcome) should not occur under such circumstances; yet numerous studies have confirmed that it does. The inferential explanation is that individuals reason just as they do in forward blocking. B and AB predict the same outcome, thus they conclude that A is not an independent cause.

But once again the main findings are not incompatible with associationism. In an elegant analysis, for instance, Ghirlanda (2005) showed that a range of retrospective effects including backward blocking are in fact entirely compatible with the Rescorla-Wagner theory, provided a suitable scheme for stimulus representation is employed. Traditional applications of the theory simply assume that each stimulus is represented by a single unit or node in a network. Under such circumstances, it is true that backward blocking cannot be predicted. However, Ghirlanda (2005) showed that this conclusion does not hold when each cue is instead represented via a pattern of activity distributed over a large number of units. Ghirlanda (2005) reported simulations in which arrays of 50 units coded each elemental stimulus, yielding backward blocking (reduction of judgments for A after AB+, B+ training) as well as its converse, unovershadowing (increase in judgments for A after AB+, B− training) and backward conditioned inhibition (negative judgments for A after AB−, B+ training). A key element of distributed coding schemes is that they allow distinct cues to activate overlapping sets of elements, thus capturing the fundamental principle of stimulus generalization. Kruschke (2008) has reported similar theoretical developments for dealing with retrospective revaluation, but in the context of models driven by Bayesian considerations. Kruschke assumes that knowledge is not captured by a single strength of association, but instead by a distribution of degrees of belief over a range of

Retrospective revaluation: indirect change in a cue's associative strength resulting from later information. An example is backward blocking (when B+ trials follow AB+ ones, they cause a reduction in responding to A)

hypotheses, with these beliefs being optimally adjusted in response to learning feedback.

Another prominent development is Dickinson & Burke's (1996) proposal that the formation of a within-compound association between cues A and B in a backward blocking design plays a key role in the retrospection effect. In the first stage, these cues are combined and jointly predict the outcome (AB+). It is assumed that participants not only learn associations between each of the cues and the outcome, but also between the cues themselves. In the second stage, B is presented in isolation and predicts the outcome (B+). Dickinson & Burke's (1996) revised associative theory proposes that B activates the representation of A in the second stage via the within-compound association formed in the first stage. While the physically presented cue, B, undergoes a normal increment in associative strength when the outcome is presented, the associatively activated representation of A undergoes a change of the opposite polarity. Hence the B+ trials lead to a reduction in A's associative strength. Learning is governed by associative processes and by reinforcement as conceptualized in the traditional theory.

Melchers et al. (2004b) proposed an alternative account based more on memory retrieval processes than on associative activation. On this account, participants access trial types from memory and replay them mentally [a similar notion is central to McClelland et al.'s (1995) connectionist theory of the relationship between the hippocampal and neocortical memory systems]. Hence AB+ trials are recalled and rehearsed during stage two when B+ trials are observed. If such replayed trials function much like experienced trials, then backward blocking would emerge as a simple result of the ongoing adjustment of associative strengths and would not be the product of true reasoning. The concepts of within-compound associations (Dickinson & Burke 1996) and memory-based rehearsal (Melchers et al. 2004b) are obviously closely related.

These associative accounts are supported by a range of evidence. Aitken et al. (2001)

reported that retrospective changes are related to the strength of the critical within-compound association. In another set of tests, Melchers et al. (2004b, 2006; see also Vandorpe et al. 2007) found that the magnitude of the retrospective change was related to participants' memory for the trial pairings and proposed that it is only if the AB pairing can be recalled that downward adjustments in A's strength can be induced. Importantly, Melchers et al. (2004b, 2006) and Vandorpe et al. (2007) also found that there was no corresponding correlation between forward blocking and participants' memory for the compound trials. This is as expected by standard associative theories, because forward blocking (B+ followed by AB+) is driven simply by competition between A and B on the AB trials. Any association between A and B is irrelevant for such competition.

As noted by Mitchell et al. (2005a) and Vandorpe et al. (2007), however, these retrospective revaluation effects are also consistent with cognitive accounts. Having observed AB+ trials, participants can infer that A has some predictive value, but when they subsequently observe B+ trials, they should now alter that conclusion because they have information indicating that A adds nothing beyond what B signals. Such a chain of inference assigns an important role to memory in that the adjustment of belief about A requires recollection of the AB pairing. On the other hand, forward blocking is not expected to be similarly dependent on memory. In this case (B+ followed by AB+), individuals can infer during the AB trials that A is nonpredictive so long as they remember the B+ trials, and there is no necessity for memory of the conjunction of A and B. Hence the asymmetry observed by Melchers et al. (2004b, 2006) and Vandorpe et al. (2007), where backward but not forward blocking correlates with memory for the cue compound, is compatible with a cognitive account.

Indeed, Mitchell et al. (2005a) and Vandorpe et al. (2007) have argued that the patterns of behavior in the retrospective case are better explained by inference than by associative mechanisms. In an ingenious experiment, Mitchell et al. (2005a) succeeded in reversing the normal backward blocking effect such that B+ trials presented subsequent to AB+ ones actually caused an increase rather than a decrease in ratings for cue A. They achieved this result by employing a method akin to the additivity manipulation described previously, in which they pretrained participants to believe that compounds predictive of the outcome must be composed of elements with equivalent predictive values. Mitchell et al. (2005a) thus concluded that their participants solved the task via deliberate inference, akin to that observed in other rule-learning designs (Shanks & Darby 1998). Associative approaches might seek to explain this result in terms of a shift between elemental and configural processing. The reversal of blocking observed by Mitchell et al. (2005a) is consistent with configural-based associative theory, assuming there was some generalization between the A and B cues.

An even more striking empirical example of backward blocking is the second-order effect reported by De Houwer & Beckers (2002a,b; Melchers et al. 2004b). In their three-stage procedure, participants first saw cues AB paired with the outcome (AB+) and then were shown trials in which cues AC were paired with the outcome (AC+). Finally, trials were presented in which B occurred either with or without the outcome (B+ or B−). To give a concrete illustration, imagine that the foods avocado and banana cause an allergic reaction and that, subsequently, avocado and cheese also cause the allergy. Finally, banana in isolation either causes or does not cause the allergy. Consider a participant for whom B was paired with the outcome in the final stage. On a cognitive reasoning account, such a participant might be expected to infer that since B is a good predictor, then A must be a poor predictor: This is a standard backward blocking effect. However, the participant might go on to infer that if A is a poor predictor, then C is a good one. Thus, even though B is never paired with C, the final stage trials (B+ or B−) might alter the attribution of predictive significance to C, and this is exactly the result observed by De Houwer

& Beckers (2002a,b). The occurrence of the allergy in the presence of banana (B+) led to a concomitant increase in the judged relationship between cheese (C) and the allergy, while conversely its nonoccurrence led to a decrease. Although it is true that such a result might signal the importance of reasoning in blocking-like designs, Melchers et al. (2004b) found that the magnitude of the retrospective change in second-order blocking was again related to participants' memory for the trial pairings and argued that the data were therefore compatible with an alternative account based on associative reinforcement combined with rehearsal of previous trial types.

Blocking: Memory for the Blocked Cue

The role of memory in cue learning has been central to the evaluation of another prediction that distinguishes associative and cognitive models. As noted above, the classic associative analysis of blocking (B+ trials followed by AB+ trials) proposes that the accumulation of associative strength by B in the first stage endows it with the capacity to compete more effectively with cue A in the compound stage. This competition can arise because the outcome, being unsurprising, is not processed (Rescorla & Wagner 1972) or because cue A is only weakly attended to and hence not processed (Mackintosh 1975, Pearce & Hall 1980). Either way, the consequence of these processing failures is that only a very weak association (if any) is formed between cue A and the outcome, resulting in low judgments of the A-outcome association. A clear prediction from such an analysis is that there should be a further manifestation of blocking, namely poor memory for the outcome paired with A. Thus not only should participants judge the association to be weak, but they also should find it hard to recall that the outcome co-occurred with A because that cue will fail to activate the outcome representation associatively. The opposite prediction, however, follows from inferential accounts. Indeed, these must assume that the

A-outcome relationship is strongly recalled. Participants are assumed to reason roughly as follows: "If A predicts the outcome, then the effect of AB would have been greater than that of B alone. B and AB predicted the same outcome, thus A is not predictive." Intrinsic to this chain of inference is that participants must remember that AB predicted the outcome, which is to say they must code the fact that A (in conjunction with B) was paired with the outcome.

This hypothesis has been tested in recent experiments. Mitchell et al. (2006) devised a blocking task with many different foods as the cues and with allergies as the outcomes, such that recall could be tested. In addition to revealing blocking on judgments, the results were clear in showing that recall of the outcome associated with cue A was poor in comparison with appropriate control cues. This pattern is exactly as predicted by the associative account. A further important aspect of Mitchell et al.'s (2006) experiments was that these results were obtained in a task in which subadditivity pretraining was employed. Recall that such pretraining ought to eliminate or at least reduce blocking. In providing evidence that the outcome is no larger following a compound of predictive cues than with the cues in isolation, subadditivity pretraining leaves the predictive status of B ambiguous. The fact that forward blocking (on both predictive judgments and recall measures) was observed thus seems to offer strong support for the associative analysis and is difficult to reconcile with inferential accounts, although other data involving more complex designs have favored the latter (Mitchell et al. 2005c, 2007).

Scully & Mitchell (2008) conducted a simpler test of cue memory in the context of extinction rather than blocking. After pairing a cue with an outcome (A+), the cue was then extinguished (A−). In a subsequent test, ratings of the A-outcome relationship were reduced as a result of the extinction phase. More importantly, cued recall of the outcome paired with A in the first stage was significantly impaired in comparison to a nonextinguished control cue. Such a result is again problematic for inferential

accounts. The basic extinction result (on contingency judgments) can be explained very easily by assuming that participants compute some measure of the statistical contingency between the cue and the outcome. For example, an inferential account might incorporate rules based on the metric ΔP [defined as the difference between the probability of the outcome given the cue, $P(O/C)$, and the probability of the outcome in the absence of the cue, $P(O/\sim C)$], which would yield a lower measure for an extinguished cue compared to a control cue because the extinction (A−) trials reduce $P(O/C)$. (For discussion of the possible psychological reality of these and similar rules, see Cheng 1997; Cheng & Holyoak 1995; Perales & Shanks 2007, 2008). However, such an account provides no reason to anticipate poor memory for the initial A+ pairings. Indeed, to the extent that the calculation of $P(O/C)$ requires a record of the history of trial outcomes, good recollection of the pairings would seem to be necessary. Of course, inferential accounts could be supplemented with additional processes to accommodate memory failure, but these processes would have to include precisely the sorts of interference mechanisms that associative theory has devoted much effort to developing (Bouton 1993).

Whereas the Mitchell et al. (2006) study described above assessed memory for the extent to which a blocked cue can prompt recall of its associated outcome, other research has asked the related question of whether a weakened memory representation is formed for the blocked cue itself. It was noted above that some (but not all) associative analyses assume that blocking arises from a failure adequately to process the blocked cue (Mackintosh 1975, Pearce & Hall 1980). Griffiths & Mitchell (2008) devised an ingenious modification of a blocking task again using foods as the cues and allergies as the outcome, but added the feature that categories of foods (e.g., fruits) played the role of cues A and B in a blocking design. These categories were composed of instances (e.g., apples, bananas) such that each actual instance only appeared once in the training stage. At test, new and old instances from the critical categories were presented, and participants rated the likelihood of each instance causing the food allergy, as well as making a conventional old/new recognition memory judgment. Blocking of predictive ratings was, as usual, observed. Griffiths & Mitchell's (2008) most striking finding, however, was that recognition of the instances of the blocked category was significantly poorer than that of appropriate control cues, consistent with associative theories that attribute blocking to a reduction in attention to and processing of the blocked cue. In sum, then, these studies examining memory in the context of blocking designs provide quite strong support for the involvement of associative processes. As Griffiths & Mitchell (2008) also note, their procedure provides a novel bridge between studies of associative learning and research on recognition and other forms of memory, and hence opens up several promising avenues for further work.

This draws to a close the review of recent studies guided by cognitive or inferential views of learning. There is no doubt that this research has considerably enriched our understanding of basic learning processes in both humans and animals. An extensive body of evidence can be marshaled in support of the radical claim that associative processes play no role in learning. However, although manipulations designed to alter individuals' beliefs have certainly been shown to influence behavior, it remains possible that the locus of some or all such manipulations is in their effects on associative rather than inferential processes. Associative theory has, over the decades, often succeeded in explaining phenomena initially thought to be beyond its bounds, and there are solid reasons to believe that the same may apply to some of the findings described here (e.g., additivity effects). Results such as the effects of cue competition on memory and judgment for a blocked cue seem, in contrast, to provide positive evidence for basic associative processes, and it remains a challenge, therefore, to inferential accounts to explain such findings. A view of learning in which knowledge is formed out of associative connections between distributed representations of events remains viable, perhaps offering a middle way between the extreme cognitivism of inferential accounts and the equally extreme reductionism of S-R theory.

AWARENESS AND LEARNING

Brewer's (1974) view of conditioning was that in humans it is invariably accompanied by contingency awareness. There has been a wealth of research on this topic since the 1970s, so it is natural to ask whether a contemporary perspective would lead us to revise this conclusion. The outcome of one recent review (Lovibond & Shanks 2002) tended to confirm Brewer's position. After analyzing experimental results on Pavlovian autonomic conditioning, conditioning with subliminal stimuli, eyeblink conditioning, conditioning in amnesia, evaluative conditioning, and conditioning under anesthesia, Lovibond & Shanks (2002) concluded that there were no strong grounds for revising the view that awareness is a necessary condition for learning in these preparations. In the present section, some recent studies of eyeblink, fear, and evaluative conditioning are described prior to a selective review of implicit learning studies using other experimental procedures, such as motor sequence learning.

Eyeblink Conditioning

The voluminous literature on human skeletal conditioning has been supplemented by a small number of studies published since the review period covered by Lovibond & Shanks (2002). An important distinction in such studies is between trace conditioning procedures, in which there is a temporal gap between the termination of the CS and the onset of the US, and delay conditioning, in which the onset of the US occurs before the termination of the CS. It is generally agreed that awareness, typically measured by a postconditioning assessment of contingency knowledge, is necessary for the acquisition of responding in typical laboratory trace eyeblink conditioning preparations (Clark & Squire 1998, Lovibond & Shanks 2002). However, the possibility of delay conditioning in the absence of awareness is much more controversial.

Two recent studies (Bellebaum & Daum 2004, Knuttinen et al. 2001) failed to obtain evidence of conditioning in the absence of contingency awareness. A study by Smith et al. (2005), however, did obtain such evidence. Specifically, participants were presented with two auditory stimuli (a tone and white noise), one of which predicted an airpuff to the eye. Smith et al. (2005) observed reliable delay conditioning in participants classified subsequently as being unaware of the correct CS-US relationship. The status of this work is difficult to gauge, however, because a subsequent attempt to replicate the key findings yielded no evidence whatsoever of unaware conditioning. Lovibond and colleagues (P.F. Lovibond, J.J.C. Loo, G. Weidemann, and C.J. Mitchell, manuscript submitted) reported two experiments that used the same methods and procedure and in addition introduced some further variables (e.g., contrasting short versus long awareness questionnaires). Even for participants treated identically to those of Smith et al. (2005), awareness was a necessary condition for the observation of differential conditioning. Plainly, whatever the basis of these discrepant findings, it would be premature to abandon the conclusion from earlier studies that awareness and conditioning tend to be associated rather than dissociated.

Fear Conditioning

In studies of fear conditioning, the US is typically a shock or loud noise, and the CR is a change in skin conductance. The literature on awareness and fear conditioning has been supplemented by a handful of recent studies. Knight et al. (2003) devised a novel delay conditioning procedure for studying unconscious fear conditioning. One tone CS (CS+) predicted the US (loud noise), whereas another tone (CS−) did not, but during acquisition the intensity of the CSs was varied to render some of them imperceptible. Participants indicated whenever they heard a tone and also

continuously registered their expectancy of the US on a rating scale. Knight et al. (2003) reported that unperceived CSs evoked differential CRs but not differential US expectancy ratings. That is to say, when the tone CS+ could not be detected, it failed to evoke a conscious report of expectancy of the loud noise but did evoke a conditioned change in skin conductance.

This impressive demonstration of unaware learning was subsequently replicated in two further studies by Knight et al. (2006, 2009). Knight et al. (2006) reported at the same time that the effect was not observed in trace conditioning, where differential conditioned responding only occurred to perceived CSs. In the delay condition that replicated the earlier Knight et al. (2003) study, statistical analysis found that differential CRs to unperceived CSs yielded a t value of 1.86, significant at 0.05 (one-tailed, $df = 12$). A comparable analysis found that differential expectancy ratings yielded a t value of 1.68 which is nonsignificant at 0.05. In a neuroimaging study employing the same procedure, Knight et al. (2009) obtained similar results, with CR differentiation yielding a reliable t value of 2.46 compared to expectancy ratings reported to be nonsignificant at $t = 2.05$ ($df = 14$ in both cases, though this latter effect is significant one-tailed). Hence, the conclusion of unaware conditioning in these two replications rests on one effect falling on just one side of the critical t value and the other effect falling on just the other side. Firmer replication evidence is needed to allow the Knight et al. (2003) result to be properly evaluated.

Moreover, in a careful study employing signal detection methods, unperceived CSs in fear conditioning did not elicit differential skin conductance responses (Cornwell et al. 2007), and other research has found that fear conditioning in delay as well as trace procedures is dependent on awareness. For instance, Weike et al. (2007) used a conventional procedure in which faces served as CS+ and CS− and shock as the US in trace and delay conditioning preparations. Differential skin conductance conditioned responses only occurred in participants classified by a postconditioning test as contingency aware. As Weike et al. (2007, p. 178) noted, "electrodermal conditioning seems to primarily index cognitive learning of the rules or circumstances in which a specific stimulus is signaling an aversive event, which is a declarative and explicit memory." Weike et al. (2007) did report that a different measure of fear, potentiated startle responses, developed in participants unaware of the CS-US contingency in delay conditioning, but this result is hard to interpret as it occurred only on trials administered prior to the awareness questionnaire and not on ones presented after it. Dawson et al. (2007), in contrast, found a good association between startle modulation and awareness.

Evaluative Conditioning

Evaluative conditioning refers to the transfer of affect or liking from one stimulus to another as a result of the pairing of those stimuli. This may be an important mechanism involved in the development of people's likes and dislikes for such everyday things as faces, consumer goods, and music. In a typical experiment, pictures judged pre-experimentally as being affectively neutral are paired with ones rated as highly liked or disliked. The neutral pictures therefore serve as CSs and the affectively valenced ones as USs. The common finding is that affective reactions to the CS pictures are pulled in the direction of the US pictures with which they are associated, such that a neutral picture paired with a highly liked picture itself comes to be liked; the converse is true for a neutral picture paired with a disliked picture. The important question is whether participants have to be aware of the nature of the stimulus pairings in order to show these learning effects. Is it necessary to be aware that a certain CS picture was paired with a liked or disliked US picture in order for its valence to change? Lovibond & Shanks (2002) (see also Field & Davey 1999, Shanks & Dickinson 1990) highlighted a number of methodological concerns in some of the studies included in their review but concluded that the more careful ones demonstrated (with the possible exception of evaluative conditioning of tastes—see below) that contingency awareness is indeed necessary.

More recent studies serve to confirm this conclusion. For example, Pleyers et al. (2007) and Stahl et al. (2009) paired images (e.g., consumer products; the CSs) with positively or negatively valenced US pictures. Evaluative conditioning only occurred for those CSs for which participants were contingency aware. Dawson et al. (2007) used faces as their CSs and USs and embedded CS-US pairings in a short-term visual memory test. Instead of measuring evaluative conditioning via explicit ratings, they measured skin conductance. Again, evaluative conditioning only occurred when participants were aware of the CS-US pairings.

A study by Walther & Nagengast (2006) again showed evaluative conditioning accompanied by above-chance awareness—as measured by a recognition test—at the group level. These authors claimed, however, that the conditioning effect they observed was significant only in participants classified as performing at or below chance in the recognition test and not in those performing above chance. Apart from the fact that the interaction between awareness group and conditioning was not in fact statistically significant in their data, the method of examining learning effects post hoc in a subgroup of participants classified as unaware can lead to highly questionable conclusions. This widely used technique is almost guaranteed to generate apparent but potentially misleading evidence of unaware learning.

To illustrate this point, consider the following extremely simple simulation. Suppose data for a number of hypothetical participants are generated, each producing a conditioning score. Assume also that this score is based on a normally distributed variable x with a mean of 30 and standard deviation of 20. Hence x represents the knowledge underlying the participant's conditioned responding. The mean conditioning score for the group is of course about 30, but a proportion of participants will score at or below zero, taken here to reflect chance performance. Next, assume that the awareness score is also based on x, but with added noise. Specifically, the awareness score is derived for each value of x by simply adding a uniformly distributed random number, for example between -40 and 40. The critical point is that the conditioning and awareness scores are both based on the same underlying knowledge, x. The only difference is that noise is added to generate the awareness score. If one now selects all the participants who score at or below zero on the awareness measure, what is their average conditioning score? The answer is that it is about 10 (SD $\approx$ 15), reliably greater than zero. This in statistical terms is just a regression-to-the-mean effect (the expected value of a normal variable x conditional upon $x + e < 0$, where e is a random variable with mean 0, is not constrained to be less than or equal to zero), but it illustrates that the practice of looking at conditioning (or any other measure) in a sample of participants selected post hoc as scoring at or below chance on an awareness measure is a very dangerous practice. Above-chance conditioning may be evident in such a subsample even though conditioning and awareness derive solely (except for random noise) from the same underlying source.

As mentioned above, there were a small number of studies (e.g., Baeyens et al. 1990) on evaluative conditioning with tastes that Lovibond & Shanks (2002) highlighted as providing tantalizing evidence of unaware learning and thus meriting further research. Two studies have indeed followed up this earlier work. Dickinson & Brown (2007) replicated the Baeyens et al. (1990) procedure, which involves presenting participants with compound drinks that are both flavored (e.g., vanilla) and colored (e.g., blue) as well as being pleasant or unpleasant. Pleasant tastes were created by adding sugar; unpleasant ones had the bitter substance polysorbate 20 added to them. From a conditioning perspective, pleasantness can be considered the US and the flavors and colors as CSs, and evidence of evaluative conditioning would comprise pairing-dependent changes in likability ratings for the flavors or colors when presented in isolation. Thus a participant might come to increase her liking of vanilla as a result of blue-vanilla-sugar pairings, or decrease

her liking ratings for red drinks as a result of red-banana-polysorbate pairings. At the end of the experiment, awareness for the various CS-US contingencies can be assessed by presenting colorless flavors or flavorless colors without any US. Although Dickinson & Brown (2007) introduced a number of procedural improvements on the original Baeyens et al. (1990) procedure, they nonetheless replicated the key observation, namely evidence of flavor evaluative conditioning in the absence of awareness. More specifically, liking ratings of the flavors changed as a consequence of their pairings with sugar/polysorbate. Strikingly, participants were able to recall the color-US pairings but not the flavor-US ones. Thus participants did show some degree of contingency awareness, but it was not related to evaluative conditioning: They knew the color contingencies and not the flavor ones, but showed conditioning of flavors.

Wardle et al. (2007) introduced some further procedural improvements such as counterbalancing the order of presentation of the evaluative conditioning and contingency awareness tests and using a better format for the awareness questions. Whereas Dickinson & Brown (2007) asked participants to identify which flavor went with a particular US, in Wardle et al.'s procedure they tasted a flavor and rated their confidence that it went with sugar or polysorbate. Under such circumstances, Wardle et al. (2007) found high levels of flavor-US and color-US awareness, as well as evaluative conditioning of the flavors (but not of the colors). Thus the key evidence of unaware conditioning was no longer observed. When Wardle et al. (2007) broke down their data according to contingency awareness, they found that flavor evaluative conditioning was confined to those participants who demonstrated awareness. Notwithstanding the earlier cautions expressed about such analyses, the results revealed no evidence of evaluative conditioning in unaware participants. Moreover, when Wardle et al. (2007) reanalyzed Dickinson & Brown's (2007) data by separating aware from unaware participants, they obtained the same pattern. Thus, whatever the final picture to emerge from this intriguing line of research, it seems safe to conclude that it has not as yet yielded strong evidence of unconscious learning.

The Perruchet Effect

In the Lovibond & Shanks (2002) review, one other empirical result was highlighted as providing potentially convincing evidence of unaware learning. This is the Perruchet effect, which arises in conditions of partial reinforcement. Perruchet (1985) used an eyeblink conditioning preparation in which the CS was reinforced on 50% of trials. In the trial sequence, runs of CS-alone or CS-US trials occurred. When a run comprised CS-alone trials, Perruchet found that the likelihood of the conditioned response declined across trials. For example, if there happened to be a sequence of four CS-alone trials, the likelihood of a CR would tend to decline across these four trials. Conversely, in a run of CS-US trials, the likelihood of the CR would tend to increase across trials. Such changes are consistent with the increments and decrements in associative strength that would be predicted by any reinforcement-based learning theory. Perruchet (1985) reported, however, that participants' expectation of the US showed exactly the opposite pattern. In a run of CS-alone trials, expectation of the US increased the longer the run, consistent with the well-known gambler's fallacy. In a run of CS-US trials, expectation of the US decreased the longer the run. Thus, the Perruchet effect comprises a striking dissociation between conditioned responding and awareness, and hence evidence for unaware learning. Participants seem to have thought that the next trial must contain an outcome different from the preceding ones in order to maintain the 50% reinforcement probability. Perruchet et al. (2006) obtained a similar pattern in a reaction time (RT) experiment. Here, the CS was a warning tone and the US an imperative stimulus to which participants had to respond with a rapid button-press. While expectancy ratings showed the gambler's fallacy pattern, RTs became slower with runs of CS-alone trials and faster with runs of CS-US ones.

Recent follow-up studies on this intriguing phenomenon have raised as many questions as they have answered, however. Both the gambler's fallacy aspect of the results (the changes in conscious expectancy with run length) and the behavioral part of the results are matters of dispute. The circumstances for assessing expectancy are hardly ideal. In Perruchet et al.'s (2006) studies, participants moved a pointer on a dial to indicate their moment-by-moment expectancy that the target would occur on the next trial. These expectancies, measured at a point just before presentation of the target, were the primary data. But suppose the participant only changed his/her expectancy rating every few seconds. With a very short cue (<1 sec) and a stimulus-onset asynchrony of only 500 msec, the participant has virtually no time to register any CS-dependent change in expectancy. Suppose that, for whatever reason, expectancy of the target is not the same in the intertrial interval as it is when the CS is actually present. The method would provide almost no chance of detecting such changes. Perruchet et al. (2006) acknowledged this issue and took some steps to ameliorate it, but without a much longer stimulus-onset asynchrony it is hard to be confident in their results. In short, although the gambler's fallacy is unquestionably observed in many situations, it is difficult to accept uncritically the claim that it occurs here and that expectancy ratings are largest after runs of cue-alone trials.

Turning to the other part of the dissociation, recall that CRs and speeded button-presses show a pattern whereby responses are less likely or rapid after a run of CS-alone trials than a run of CS-US trials. A key question is whether these changes in responding are genuinely associative in nature. If they are not, then the result may have less to do with learning and more to do with performance aspects of the task, such as US-recency effects. To investigate whether the effect is truly associative, Mitchell

Perruchet effect: while CRs increase across a run of CS-US trials, US expectancy ratings decrease, and vice versa for a series of CS-alone trials

RT: reaction time

et al. repeated the Perruchet et al. (2006) RT study but arranged backward pairings or random occurrences of the warning stimulus (CS) and imperative stimulus (US). Under such circumstances, participants have no opportunity to use the warning stimulus to prepare for the US. Despite this, Mitchell et al. (2009) saw the same behavioral effect as in the standard forward-pairing condition. They also observed the typical pattern when the CSs were omitted entirely. The obvious conclusion is that changes in RT to the imperative stimulus have nothing to do with learning predictive relationships, but rather are a consequence of runs of motor responses. When there is a run of CS-US trials, for example, then the frequency of the US (and hence of responses to the imperative stimulus) is high, whereas when there is a run of CS-alone trials, the frequency of the US declines. It seems that in the RT experiment it is variation in the frequency of responses that determines reaction times, unconnected to learning anything about the relationship between the CS and US.

Weidemann et al. (2009) reported a similar analysis in the context of eyeblink conditioning rather than speeded button pressing. In this case, the associative basis of the effect seems more secure. They found that the behavioral effect (fewer CRs after a run of CS-alone trials than a run of CS-US trials) was not the consequence of US (airpuff) recency. Thus, there is some reason to believe that the Perruchet effect in eyeblink conditioning represents genuine evidence of unaware learning, in that conditioned eyeblink responses follow a pattern that is completely opposite to the pattern displayed in expectancy ratings. However, the effect in other behavioral preparations such as speeded button pressing seems much less secure. Plainly this is an area where more research is needed and where firm conclusions must await the outcome of that research.

What of other experimental procedures within the broad domain of implicit learning? Numerous tasks have been developed and explored over the past few years, such as artificial grammar learning, the learning of sequential dependencies in speeded RT settings, and the learning of contextual cues in visual search. We now turn to a brief review of some of this evidence.

Sequence Learning

Nissen & Bullemer (1987) devised a simple procedure in which a visual target appeared on each trial at one of four locations in a display, and the participant's task was to press the appropriate key for that location as fast as possible. Targets moved from location to location according to a fixed, but nonsalient, sequence (later studies have employed noisy or probabilistic sequences). Although participants were not instructed about the presence of the sequence, they nonetheless showed evidence of sequence learning in that their RTs were faster than in a control condition with random target locations, an effect that has been replicated in numerous subsequent studies. This task, with its heavy emphasis on perceptual-motor speed, provides an ideal method for studying implicit learning: If participants readily learn the target sequence as evidenced by speeded RTs, are they also aware of the sequence? Or can procedural learning occur even in the absence of sequence awareness?

To avoid the likelihood that verbal responses to postexperimental questions underestimate awareness, researchers have developed alternative tests to assess awareness. In one such test, participants are asked to report their conscious sequence knowledge by reproducing or generating the training sequence or parts of it. In another test, they observe sequence chunks and signal whether they are old (that is, from the learned sequence) or new. With such tests, Gaillard et al. (2009), Jiménez et al. (2006), Norman et al. (2006, 2007), Perruchet & Amorim (1992), Perruchet et al. (1997), Shanks & Johnstone (1999), Shanks et al. (2003, 2005, 2006), Stefaniak et al. (2008), and Wilkinson & Shanks (2004) have all reported clear associations between learning and awareness, and indeed Perruchet et al. (1997) and Shanks & Johnstone (1999) have shown that above-chance performance on a test of awareness can precede any reliable degree of chronometrically measured sequence learning. Bremner et al. (2007) discovered, remarkably, that 2-year-olds were able to report their sequence knowledge in a generation test.

Some studies have reported sequence learning in the absence of awareness as measured by generation or recognition tests (e.g., Dennis et al. 2006; Fu et al. 2009, Vandenberghe et al. 2006), but these results are hard to interpret. For example, Dennis et al. (2006) reported that sequence learning in young participants was accompanied by awareness, but not in older participants. Yet, in one experiment, the older group did show awareness. Fu et al. (2008) reported that after short amounts of sequence training, participants lacked awareness in that they generated the learned sequence even when instructed to avoid doing so. Taking control as an index of awareness (Jacoby 1991), Fu et al. (2008) concluded that under these circumstances, sequence knowledge was not consciously accessible. However, in a subsequent report, Fu et al. (2009) failed to observe this effect when they used a slightly different generation test for assessing awareness, although they did obtain other apparent evidence of implicit learning.

Vandenberghe et al. (2006) trained both amnesic and control participants with a deterministic sequence comprising a fixed 12-location sequence or with a probabilistic sequence in which the majority of targets appeared at preordained locations while the minority appeared at unexpected locations. Vandenberghe et al. (2006) concluded that although control participants were able to learn both types of sequences, amnesics could learn only the deterministic ones (although learning of probabilistic sequences in amnesia is possible: see Shanks et al. 2006). On subsequent tests (generation and recognition) of sequence awareness, there was evidence that participants in the control group trained on a deterministic sequence were conscious of that sequence (replicating the findings of Wilkinson & Shanks 2004), whereas controls trained on a probabilistic sequence and

amnesics trained with a deterministic sequence were not. Vandenberghe et al. (2006) therefore concluded that in the latter cases, learning was implicit. However, they did not report statistical tests to confirm the reliability of deterministic sequence learning in the amnesic group, and with only six participants in this group, it is by no means clear that learning occurred. The results for the controls trained on probabilistic sequences must also be treated with caution. Participants in comparable conditions of experiments by Shanks et al. (2003, 2005) and Fu et al. (2008) showed substantial levels of sequence awareness, despite being trained for only about half as many trials. Until more is known about the basis of these discrepant results, null results such as those of Vandenberghe et al. (2006) should be treated with caution.

Also relevant are data from brain imaging studies of implicit and explicit learning. Plainly, data showing that different neural networks are activated under implicit and explicit learning conditions would provide powerful support for the idea that learning can be dissociated from awareness. In fact, this does not seem to be the case. In a careful functional magnetic resonance neuroimaging study, Willingham et al. (2002) defined an implicit condition as one in which recognition was at chance and an explicit condition as one above chance in recognition. These investigators found that the same neural systems (e.g., left prefrontal cortex, left inferior parietal cortex, and right putamen) were activated in both conditions but that additional regions were activated in the explicit condition (e.g., premotor cortex). This seems to challenge the idea of distinct implicit and explicit learning processes. Even under implicit conditions, Willingham et al. (2002) did find a difference (albeit nonsignificant) between recognition ratings for old and new test sequences of a comparable magnitude to those typically found. Thus, it seems reasonable to conjecture that Willingham et al.'s implicit and explicit groups merely represented participants with weaker and stronger sequence knowledge.

Visual Search and Contextual Cuing

Another task that has gained some popularity for the study of implicit learning involves the contextual cuing of target locations in a visual search setting. Suppose that a target such as a horizontal letter T appears among a set of horizontal L distracters, and the participant's task is to indicate the orientation of the T. Suppose also that on some trials the configuration of distracters is repeated from earlier trials, and that in these repeated displays the location of the target is constant. If the participant is able to learn about the repeated displays, and that the location of the target is reliably cued by a familiar distracter context, then faster localization responses might be made to repeated compared to unique displays. Chun & Jiang (1998), who devised this task, showed that participants could indeed learn about repeated configurations and make especially fast responses to them while apparently being unaware of the repetition of displays (see also Chun & Jiang 2003).

Later studies have replicated these results but have also suggested that participants are generally aware of the display repetitions, provided that their awareness is assessed appropriately. Smyth & Shanks (2008) measured awareness with two methods. In one, participants were shown repeated displays, but with the T replaced by another distracter L, and were asked to indicate where they thought the missing T would be located. When this test incorporated only 12 trials, no evidence of awareness was obtained (that is, performance was at chance despite the fact that in the preceding target-search part of the experiment, RTs were faster to repeated displays). However, when the number of trials was increased to 48, thus increasing the reliability and power of the test, above-chance performance was observed. For instance, reliability increased from $r = 0.09$ to $r = 0.46$. Thus, evidence that learning in the contextual cuing task is unconscious comes from studies in which the assessment of awareness is unreliable. Smyth & Shanks (2008) also evaluated awareness in a test in which participants were simply shown repeated and unique displays and asked to report which ones they had seen previously. This test once again revealed above-chance levels of awareness. Such above-chance recognition was also observed by Preston & Gabrieli (2008) and Vaidya et al. (2007, Exp. 2). In the influential study by Chun & Phelps (1999), contextual cuing was observed in control but not amnesic individuals. The authors argued that the task assesses implicit learning because recognition was statistically at chance. Yet, the mean recognition hit and false-alarm rates (0.37 versus 0.32 for the controls, 0.64 versus 0.42 for the amnesics) for old and new displays suggest the alternative possibility that a real awareness effect was masked by unreliability in their measure and low statistical power.

Nevertheless, a common finding in this research is that awareness (as measured by recognition, for example) and implicit performance tend to be uncorrelated. For instance, in the Preston & Gabrieli (2008) and Smyth & Shanks (2008) studies, the correlations were close to zero, and implicit performance was no greater for recognized than for unrecognized configurations. In the Smyth & Shanks (2008) study, it was also the case that analyses of contextual cuing in "unaware" participants showed reliable learning effects (see also Howard et al. 2004). But for the reason described above, these findings still do not constitute clear evidence of implicit learning. In addition to the possibility that the awareness test was unreliable (Howard et al. 2004 tested awareness with only 12 test displays), such dissociations are predicted by single-system models that do not incorporate the implicit–explicit distinction (Shanks & Perruchet 2002, Shanks et al. 2003) when items or participants are selected post hoc. Suppose that there is a single knowledge base that controls performance both in an implicit test, such as contextual cuing, and in an explicit test, such as recognition. Suppose also, however, that independent sources of noise or error contribute to each performance measure. As noted above, under such circumstances, it will inevitably be the case that simulated participants selected after the fact as scoring at or below chance on the explicit measure will score above chance on the implicit one, and likewise for configurations selected post hoc on the same basis. Indeed, these models can even predict correlations of zero between implicit and explicit measures, despite them arising from the same underlying representation (Berry et al. 2006, Kinder & Shanks 2003).

Thus the evidence is rather compelling that awareness is a necessary condition for learning across a wide range of experimental preparations. On this substantial issue, Brewer (1974) seems to have been correct in his conclusion.

CONCLUSIONS AND FUTURE DIRECTIONS

This review of recent research on the roles of associative and cognitive processes in human learning points to two main conclusions: first, that learning across a range of preparations and conditions is almost invariably accompanied by awareness of the experimental contingency; and second, that although manipulations of individuals' beliefs can profoundly affect the way they acquire information, associationist concepts continue to play a key role in explaining learning.

These conclusions run counter to the current zeitgeist in the psychology of learning. The study of implicit (i.e., unconscious) learning has become a very substantial and distinct research topic, influencing other areas such as developmental psychology and cognitive neuroscience, and perpetuating a belief going back at least as far as Thorndike (1931) that learning can proceed independently of awareness. The present review suggests that the core concept at the heart of this research area commands remarkably little empirical support. The present review also suggests that the current fashion for viewing learning as an entirely cognitive, inferential process faces a number of challenges. Certainly, cognitive processes penetrate very deeply into many of the subprocesses that contribute to learning, yet associationist concepts such as reinforcement and activation are

nevertheless implied by some of the key findings considered here.

An important question is the extent to which so-called dual-process theories have utility in helping us to understand learning. These theories (Broadbent et al. 1986, Evans 2008, Kahneman 2003, Sloman 1996) propose that the mind is composed of two systems, one automatic, implicit, nonrational, and unconscious and the other slow, effortful, rational, explicit, and conscious. Thus the first system is consistent with unconscious learning and the second with inferential reasoning. The present review should make it clear that the need for two systems has yet to be established, at least in relation to learning. It is quite debatable whether any significant forms of learning can proceed automatically or unconsciously, nor is it the case that apparently rational forms of learning can be explained only by reasoning-like processes: We have seen several examples of phenomena, such as retrospective revaluation, that can be explained associatively as well as they can inferentially.

Of course, advocates of dual-process theories draw support from a range of domains in addition to learning, including decision-making, reasoning, and many aspects of social cognition. There are numerous examples of what appear to be powerful unconscious influences on behavior (Nisbett & Wilson 1977, Wilson 2002). Yet it is equally important to note that sophisticated theoretical and methodological analysis of consciousness has been applied to few domains more thoroughly than it has to the field of learning. When examples of apparent unconscious influences in other domains have been subjected to the same level of scrutiny, it has not been uncommon to find that the evidence for such influences is considerably weakened; good illustrations are Maia & McClelland's (2004) demonstration of the role of awareness in the Iowa Gambling Task, and the extensive evidence that attitudes measured implicitly (e.g., by the Implicit Association Test) are often not truly unconscious (Gawronski et al. 2006). It is plain that future research with more demanding tests of awareness will allow much firmer conclusions to be drawn about the limits of unconscious processing.

The phenomenon of blocking has been central to the research reviewed here. It is of course possible that what appear to be instances of the same phenomenon in fact arise for different reasons. For instance, blocking might be a single name for a set of related outcomes that arise from overlapping or even independent processes. It was mentioned above that blocking can be observed in marine molluscs as well as in humans and numerous species in between; plainly that does not imply that it occurs for the same reason. Perhaps associative principles are more important in some species or circumstances, and cognitive ones in others. Although such a possibility must be borne in mind, it must also be recognized that the similarities between blocking in different species run very deep. In both humans and rats, for example, blocking is sensitive to manipulations of additivity information. Indeed, it has proven quite difficult to find any associative learning phenomena that appear to be qualitatively different across species or across contexts within a species (such as across implicit and explicit learning conditions in humans). Thus, supporters of dual-process theories face the important challenge in future work of demonstrating such qualitative differences more convincingly than has been achieved so far.

It is also entirely reasonable to take the view that whereas unconscious learning has proven hard to demonstrate in the sorts of preparations reviewed here (e.g., eyeblink conditioning), it does nonetheless occur in other circumstances. Typical experimental procedures for studying implicit learning tend to employ single laboratory sessions with meaningless stimuli (tones and lights), so perhaps forms of more gradual learning with meaningful stimuli are being ignored. It is undoubtedly important that future work attempts to extend beyond simple laboratory tasks. Yet a good deal of research has been undertaken in which learning is studied over quite prolonged periods during which expertise is established (e.g., 10,000 repetitions in table tennis: Koedijker et al. 2008) and with

meaningful (e.g., linguistic: Leow & Bowles 2005) materials and numerous perceptual and motor as well as cognitive tasks, without yielding stronger evidence.

The major alternative to the inferential and dual-process perspectives derives both from traditional associative learning theory but also from the success of the connectionist project in human cognition (McClelland & Rumelhart 1986, Rumelhart & McClelland 1986, Thomas & McClelland 2008). It is not possible to review this project in detail here, but its essential components are the critical role played by associative processes together with the appreciation that when such processes operate across distributed representations, high-level reasoning-like behavior may emerge. The simulation by Ghirlanda (2005) described above is a striking illustration of this, in that it showed how retrospective revaluation (the apparently inferential readjustment of the weight assigned to a cue) may result from activation and incremental learning within a simple network of neuron-like processing units. Although connectionist models are in principle consistent with unconscious learning, it is often assumed that stable states of activation within the brain, subject to selective attention, are precisely those states of which we are conscious (Maia & Cleeremans 2005).

Although the present review has focused on studies explicitly designed to test and compare associative and inferential accounts, other findings not reviewed here continue to defy explanation in anything other than associative terms. Principle among these is the nonrational aspect of many conditioned behaviors, a point made forcefully by Dickinson (1980, 2009; see also Shanks 1990). In a procedure such as fear conditioning, for example, presentation of a CS that predicts an aversive US such as shock evokes a range of responses including sweating and elevated heart rate, yet there is no rational basis for these responses. Or consider the even more striking example of pigeon autoshaping, a major source of evidence in the study of conditioned behavior. If a keylight signals the presentation of food, the pigeon will approach and peck it. Although the approach behavior might be the product of rational inference—if the pigeon "believes" that approach will cause food to be obtained—it is hard to see any chain of inferences that would cause the pigeon to peck the keylight. Such pecking does not affect the delivery of food, and indeed pigeons will continue to peck even when pecking causes omission of the food. The form of the response (the pigeon appears to try to eat a keylight that predicts food and drink one that predicts water) strongly suggests Pavlov's original mechanism of stimulus substitution, whereby the CS becomes associated with and takes the place of the US. It is very hard to see any involvement of cognitive or inferential operations in this type of learning and behavior.

Many gaps remain in our knowledge of the contributions of cognitive and associative processes to learning. Perhaps the most important item for the research agenda is to gain a fuller understanding of the limits of associative principles in explaining additivity and related effects on blocking. As described in this review, it has been clearly demonstrated that the outcome of a blocking experiment, in both humans and animals, can be radically altered by pretreatments designed to demonstrate the additivity or nonadditivity of cues. Yet the precise locus of these effects is still unknown. It is possible that they operate by altering the beliefs that form the basis for inferences about predictive value, but it is also possible that configural processing or generalization are the key mechanisms that are affected by such manipulations. These and related questions will surely feature prominently in future research seeking to understand the inferential and associative aspects of learning.

SUMMARY POINTS

1. A review of the literature illustrates that although they are based on radically different principles, cognitive and associative accounts of learning can both encompass a broad range of empirical phenomena. Decisive tests are difficult to devise.

2. Forty years after its discovery, the phenomenon of blocking continues to lie at the heart of theoretical debate. Explanations in terms of the automatic formation of associations are certainly inadequate.

3. Learning is strongly influenced by pretreatments that provide information about the additivity or nonadditivity of cue weights and by other manipulations of beliefs relevant to inferential reasoning.

4. There is a substantial body of results, including the effects of cue competition on memory and judgment, that provides evidence for associative processes such as activation and reinforcement.

5. Robust and replicable instances of unconscious learning have failed to emerge in the experimental literature, consistent with the view that awareness is a necessary condition for all forms of learning, including conditioning.

6. Although its basis is not yet fully understood, the Perruchet effect represents perhaps the most clear-cut current evidence for independent implicit and explicit learning systems.

DISCLOSURE STATEMENT

The author is not aware of any biases that might be perceived as affecting the objectivity of this review.

LITERATURE CITED

Aitken MRF, Larkin MJW, Dickinson A. 2001. Re-examination of the role of within-compound associations in the retrospective revaluation of causal judgements. *Q. J. Exp. Psychol.* 54B:27–51

Baeyens F, Eelen P, Van den Bergh O, Crombez G. 1990. Flavor-flavor and color-flavor conditioning in humans. *Learn. Motiv.* 21:434–55

Beckers T, De Houwer J, Pineño O, Miller RR. 2005. Outcome additivity and outcome maximality influence cue competition in human causal learning. *J. Exp. Psychol.: Learn. Mem. Cogn.* 31:238–49

Argues that inferential causal reasoning underlies blocking in animal conditioning.

Beckers T, Miller RR, De Houwer J, Urushihara K. 2006. Reasoning rats: forward blocking in Pavlovian animal conditioning is sensitive to constraints of causal inference. *J. Exp. Psychol.: Gen.* 135:92–102

Bellebaum C, Daum I. 2004. Effects of age and awareness on eyeblink conditional discrimination learning. *Behav. Neurosci.* 118:1157–65

Berry CJ, Henson RNA, Shanks DR. 2006. On the relationship between repetition priming and recognition memory: insights from a computational model. *J. Mem. Lang.* 55:515–33

Bouton ME. 1993. Context, time, and memory retrieval in the interference paradigms of Pavlovian learning. *Psychol. Bull.* 114:80–99

Bremner AJ, Mareschal D, Destrebecqz A, Cleeremans A. 2007. Cognitive control of sequential knowledge in 2-year-olds: evidence from an incidental sequence-learning and-generation task. *Psychol. Sci.* 18:261–66

Brewer WF. 1974. There is no convincing evidence for operant or classical conditioning in adult humans. In *Cognition and the Symbolic Processes*, ed. WB Weimer, DS Palermo, pp. 1–42. Hillsdale, NJ: Erlbaum

Broadbent DE, Fitzgerald P, Broadbent MHP. 1986. Implicit and explicit knowledge in the control of complex systems. *Br. J. Psychol.* 77:33–50

Cheng PW. 1997. From covariation to causation: a causal power theory. *Psychol. Rev.* 104:367–405

Cheng PW, Holyoak KJ. 1995. Complex adaptive systems as intuitive statisticians: causality, contingency, and prediction. In *Comparative Approaches to Cognitive Science*, ed. HL Roitblat, J-A Meyer, pp. 271–302. Cambridge, MA: MIT Press

Chun MM, Jiang Y. 1998. Contextual cueing: implicit learning and memory of visual context guides spatial attention. *Cogn. Psychol.* 36:28–71

Chun MM, Jiang Y. 2003. Implicit, long-term spatial contextual memory. *J. Exp. Psychol.: Learn. Mem. Cogn.* 29:224–34

Chun MM, Phelps EA. 1999. Memory deficits for implicit contextual information in amnesic subjects with hippocampal damage. *Nat. Neurosci.* 2:844–47

Clark RE, Squire LR. 1998. Classical conditioning and brain systems: the role of awareness. *Science* 280:77–81

Cobos PL, López FJ, Caño A, Almaraz J, Shanks DR. 2002. Mechanisms of predictive and diagnostic causal induction. *J. Exp. Psychol.: Anim. Behav. Process.* 28:331–46

Cook SW, Harris RE. 1937. The verbal conditioning of the galvanic skin reflex. *J. Exp. Psychol.* 21:202–10

Cornwell BR, Echiverri AM, Grillon C. 2007. Sensitivity to masked conditioned stimuli predicts conditioned response magnitude under masked conditions. *Psychophysiology* 44:403–6

Dawson ME, Rissling AJ, Schell AM, Wilcox R. 2007. Under what conditions can human affective conditioning occur without contingency awareness? Test of the evaluative conditioning paradigm. *Emotion* 7:755–66

Dawson ME, Schell AM. 1982. Electrodermal responses to attended and nonattended significant stimuli during dichotic listening. *J. Exp. Psychol.: Hum. Percept. Perform.* 8:315–24

The first report of higher-order retrospective revaluation.

De Houwer J. 2009. The propositional approach to associative learning as an alternative for association formation models. *Learn. Behav.* 37:1–20

De Houwer J, Beckers T. 2002a. Higher-order retrospective revaluation in human causal learning. *Q. J. Exp. Psychol.* 55B:137–51

De Houwer J, Beckers T. 2002b. Second-order backward blocking and unovershadowing in human causal learning. *Exp. Psychol.* 49:27–33

Demonstrates effects on blocking of maximality/ submaximality information.

De Houwer J, Beckers T, Glautier S. 2002. Outcome and cue properties modulate blocking. *Q. J. Exp. Psychol.* 55A:965–85

De Houwer J, Vandorpe S, Beckers T. 2007. Statistical contingency has a different impact on preparation judgements than on causal judgements. *Q. J. Exp. Psychol.* 60:418–32

Dennis NA, Howard JH, Howard DV. 2006. Implicit sequence learning without motor sequencing in young and old adults. *Exp. Brain Res.* 175:153–64

Dickinson A. 1980. *Contemporary Animal Learning Theory.* London: Cambridge Univ. Press

Dickinson A. 2009. What are association formation models? *Learn. Behav.* 37:21–24

Dickinson A, Brown KJ. 2007. Flavor-evaluative conditioning is unaffected by contingency knowledge during training with color-flavor compounds. *Learn. Behav.* 35:36–42

Dickinson A, Burke J. 1996. Within-compound associations mediate the retrospective revaluation of causality judgements. *Q. J. Exp. Psychol.* 49B:60–80

Dickinson A, Shanks DR, Evenden JL. 1984. Judgement of act-outcome contingency: the role of selective attribution. *Q. J. Exp. Psychol.* 36A:29–50

Evans JSBT. 2008. Dual-processing accounts of reasoning, judgment, and social cognition. *Annu. Rev. Psychol.* 59:255–78

Field AP, Davey GCL. 1999. Reevaluating evaluative conditioning: a nonassociative explanation of conditioning effects in the visual evaluative conditioning paradigm. *J. Exp. Psychol. Anim. Behav. Process.* 25:211–24

Fletcher PC, Anderson JM, Shanks DR, Honey R, Carpenter TA, et al. 2001. Responses of human frontal cortex to surprising events are predicted by formal associative learning theory. *Nat. Neurosci.* 4:1043–48

Fu QF, Dienes Z, Fu XL. 2009. Can unconscious knowledge allow control in sequence learning? *Conscious. Cogn.* In press

Fu QF, Fu XL, Dienes Z. 2008. Implicit sequence learning and conscious awareness. *Conscious. Cogn.* 17:185–202

Gaillard V, Destrebecqz A, Michiels S, Cleeremans A. 2009. Effects of age and practice in sequence learning: a graded account of ageing, learning and control. *Eur. J. Cogn. Psychol.* 21:255–82

Gawronski B, Hofmann W, Wilbur CJ. 2006. Are "implicit" attitudes unconscious? *Conscious. Cogn.* 15:485–99

Ghirlanda S. 2005. Retrospective revaluation as simple associative learning. *J. Exp. Psychol.: Anim. Behav. Process.* 31:107–11

Griffiths O, Mitchell CJ. 2008. Selective attention in human associative learning and recognition memory. *J. Exp. Psychol.: Gen.* 137:626–48

Haselgrove M. 2009. Reasoning rats or associative animals? A common-element analysis of the effects of additive and subadditive pretraining on blocking. *J. Exp. Psychol.: Anim. Behav. Process.* In press

Holland PC. 2008. Cognitive versus stimulus-response theories of learning. *Learn. Behav.* 36:227–41

Howard JH, Howard DV, Dennis NA, Yankovich H, Vaidya CJ. 2004. Implicit spatial contextual learning in healthy aging. *Neuropsychology* 18:124–34

Jacoby LL. 1991. A process dissociation framework: separating automatic from intentional uses of memory. *J. Mem. Lang.* 30:513–41

Jiménez L, Vaquero JMM, Lupiáñez J. 2006. Qualitative differences between implicit and explicit sequence learning. *J. Exp. Psychol.: Learn. Mem. Cogn.* 32:475–90

Kahneman D. 2003. A perspective on judgment and choice: mapping bounded rationality. *Am. Psychol.* 58:697–720

Kamin LJ. 1969. Selective association and conditioning. In *Fundamental Issues in Associative Learning*, ed. NJ Mackintosh, WK Honig, pp. 42–64. Halifax: Dalhousie Univ. Press

Kinder A, Shanks DR. 2003. Neuropsychological dissociations between priming and recognition: a single-system connectionist account. *Psychol. Rev.* 110:728–44

Knight DC, Nguyen HT, Bandettini PA. 2003. Expression of conditional fear with and without awareness. *Proc. Natl. Acad. Sci.* 100:15280–83

Knight DC, Nguyen HT, Bandettini PA. 2006. The role of awareness in delay and trace fear conditioning in humans. *Cogn. Affect. Behav. Neurosci.* 6:157–62

Knight DC, Waters NS, Bandettini PA. 2009. Neural substrates of explicit and implicit fear memory. *NeuroImage* 45:208–14

Knuttinen M-G, Power JM, Preston AR, Disterhoft JF. 2001. Awareness in classical differential eyeblink conditioning in young and aging humans. *Behav. Neurosci.* 115:747–57

Koedijker JM, Oudejans RRD, Beek PJ. 2008. Table tennis performance following explicit and analogy learning over 10,000 repetitions. *Int. J. Sport Psychol.* 39:237–56

Illustrates the role of within-compound associations in retrospective revaluation.

Demonstrates that retrospective revaluation effects can be simulated by a simple associative network, with a suitable stimulus coding scheme.

Kruschke JK. 2008. Bayesian approaches to associative learning: from passive to active learning. *Learn. Behav.* 36:210–26

Lagnado DA, Shanks DR. 2002. Probability judgment in hierarchical learning: a conflict between predictiveness and coherence. *Cognition* 83:81–112

Le Pelley ME, Beesley T, Suret MB. 2007. Blocking of human causal learning involves learned changes in stimulus processing. *Q. J. Exp. Psychol.* 60:1468–76

Leow RP, Bowles MA. 2005. Attention and awareness in SLA. In *External and Internal Factors in Adult SLA*, ed. C Sanz, pp. 179–203. Washington, DC: Georgetown Univ. Press

Livesey EJ, Boakes RA. 2004. Outcome additivity, elemental processing and blocking in human causality judgements. *Q. J. Exp. Psychol.* 57B:361–79

López FJ, Cobos PL, Caño A. 2005. Associative and causal reasoning accounts of causal induction: symmetries and asymmetries in predictive and diagnostic inferences. *Mem. Cogn.* 33:1388–98

López FJ, Cobos PL, Caño A, Shanks DR. 1998. The rational analysis of human causal and probability judgment. In *Rational Models of Cognition*, ed. M Oaksford, N Chater, pp. 314–52. London: Oxford Univ. Press

Lovibond PF. 2003. Causal beliefs and conditioned responses: retrospective revaluation induced by experience and by instruction. *J. Exp. Psychol.: Learn. Mem. Cogn.* 29:97–106

Lovibond PF, Been S-L, Mitchell CJ, Bouton ME, Frohardt R. 2003. Forward and backward blocking of causal judgment is enhanced by additivity of effect magnitude. *Mem. Cogn.* 31:133–42

Lovibond PF, Shanks DR. 2002. The role of awareness in Pavlovian conditioning: empirical evidence and theoretical implications. *J. Exp. Psychol.: Anim. Behav. Process.* 28:3–26

Mackintosh NJ. 1975. A theory of attention: variations in the associability of stimuli with reinforcement. *Psychol. Rev.* 82:276–98

Mackintosh NJ. 1983. *Conditioning and Associative Learning.* Oxford, UK: Clarendon

Maia TV, Cleeremans A. 2005. Consciousness: converging insights from connectionist modeling and neuroscience. *Trends Cogn. Sci.* 9:397–404

Maia TV, McClelland JL. 2004. A reexamination of the evidence for the somatic marker hypothesis: what participants really know in the Iowa gambling task. *Proc. Natl. Acad. Sci. USA* 102:16075–80

Matute H, Vegas S, De Marez PJ. 2002. Flexible use of recent information in causal and predictive judgments. *J. Exp. Psychol.: Learn. Mem. Cogn.* 28:714–25

McClelland JL, McNaughton BL, O'Reilly RC. 1995. Why there are complementary learning systems in the hippocampus and neocortex: Insights from the successes and failures of connectionist models of learning and memory. *Psychol. Rev.* 102:419–57

McClelland JL, Rumelhart DE. 1986. *Parallel Distributed Processing: Explorations in the Microstructure of Cognition. Vol. 2: Psychological and Biological Models.* Cambridge, MA: MIT Press

McNally RJ. 1981. Phobias and preparedness: instructional reversal of electrodermal conditioning to fear-relevant stimuli. *Psychol. Rep.* 48:175–80

Melchers KG, Lachnit H, Shanks DR. 2004a. Past experience influences the processing of stimulus compounds in human Pavlovian conditioning. *Learn. Motiv.* 35:167–88

Melchers KG, Lachnit H, Shanks DR. 2004b. Within-compound associations in retrospective revaluation and in direct learning: a challenge for comparator theory. *Q. J. Exp. Psychol.* 57B:25–53

Melchers KG, Lachnit H, Shanks DR. 2006. The comparator theory fails to account for the selective role of within-compound associations in cue selection effects. *Exp. Psychol.* 53:316–20

Melchers KG, Shanks DR, Lachnit H. 2008. Stimulus coding in human associative learning: flexible representations of parts and wholes. *Behav. Process.* 77:413–27

Melton AW. 1950. Learning. *Annu. Rev. Psychol.* 1:9–30

Miller RR, Barnet RC, Grahame NJ. 1995. Assessment of the Rescorla-Wagner model. *Psychol. Bull.* 117:363–86

Mitchell CJ, De Houwer J, Lovibond PF. 2009. The propositional nature of human associative learning. *Behav. Brain Sci.* 32:183–246

Mitchell CJ, Killedar A, Lovibond PF. 2005a. Inference-based retrospective revaluation in human causal judgments requires knowledge of within-compound relationships. *J. Exp. Psychol.: Anim. Behav. Process.* 31:418–24

Mitchell CJ, Livesey E, Lovibond PF. 2007. A dissociation between causal judgement and the ease with which a cause is categorized with its effect. *Q. J. Exp. Psychol.* 60:400–17

Mitchell CJ, Lovibond PF. 2002. Backward and forward blocking in human electrodermal conditioning: blocking requires an assumption of outcome additivity. *Q. J. Exp. Psychol.* 55B:311–29

Mitchell CJ, Lovibond PF, Condoleon M. 2005b. Evidence for deductive reasoning in blocking of causal judgments. *Learn. Motiv.* 36:77–87

Mitchell CJ, Lovibond PF, Gan CY. 2005c. A dissociation between causal judgment and outcome recall. *Psychon. Bull. Rev.* 12:950–54

Mitchell CJ, Lovibond PF, Minard E, Lavis Y. 2006. Forward blocking in human learning sometimes reflects the failure to encode a cue-outcome relationship. *Q. J. Exp. Psychol.* 59:830–44

Mitchell CJ, Wardle SG, Lovibond PF, Weidemann G, Chang BPI. 2009. Is Perruchet's dissociation between cued reaction time and outcome expectancy evidence for two separate associative learning processes? *J. Exp. Psychol.: Learn. Mem. Cogn.* In press

Mowrer RR, Klein SB. 2001. The transitive nature of contemporary learning theory. In *Handbook of Contemporary Learning Theories*, ed. RR Mowrer, SB Klein, pp. 1–21. Mahwah, NJ: Erlbaum

Nisbett RE, Wilson TD. 1977. Telling more than we can know: verbal reports on mental processes. *Psychol. Rev.* 84:231–59

Nissen MJ, Bullemer P. 1987. Attentional requirements of learning: evidence from performance measures. *Cogn. Psychol.* 19:1–32

Norman E, Price MC, Duff SC. 2006. Fringe consciousness in sequence learning: the influence of individual differences. *Conscious. Cogn.* 15:723–60

Norman E, Price MC, Duff SC, Mentzoni RA. 2007. Gradations of awareness in a modified sequence learning task. *Conscious. Cogn.* 16:809–37

Pearce JM, Hall G. 1980. A model for Pavlovian learning: variations in the effectiveness of conditioned but not of unconditioned stimuli. *Psychol. Rev.* 87:532–52

Perales JC, Shanks DR. 2007. Models of covariation-based causal judgment: a review and synthesis. *Psychon. Bull. Rev.* 14:577–96

Perales JC, Shanks DR. 2008. Driven by power? Probe question and presentation format effects on causal judgment. *J. Exp. Psychol.: Learn. Mem. Cogn.* 34:1482–94

Perruchet P. 1985. A pitfall for the expectancy theory of human eyelid conditioning. *Pavlov. J. Biol. Sci.* 20:163–70

Perruchet P, Amorim M-A. 1992. Conscious knowledge and changes in performance in sequence learning: evidence against dissociation. *J. Exp. Psychol.: Learn. Mem. Cogn.* 18:785–800

Perruchet P, Bigand E, Benoit-Gonin F. 1997. The emergence of explicit knowledge during the early phase of learning in sequential reaction time tasks. *Psychol. Res.* 60:4–13

Perruchet P, Cleeremans A, Destrebecqz A. 2006. Dissociating the effects of automatic activation and explicit expectancy on reaction times in a simple associative learning task. *J. Exp. Psychol.: Learn. Mem. Cogn.* 32:955–65

Pleyers G, Corneille O, Luminet O, Yzerbyt V. 2007. Aware and (dis)liking: Item-based analyses reveal that valence acquisition via evaluative conditioning emerges only when there is contingency awareness. *J. Exp. Psychol.: Learn. Mem. Cogn.* 33:130–44

Postman L. 1962. Rewards and punishments in human learning. In *Psychology in the Making: Histories of Selected Research Problems*, ed. L Postman, pp. 331–401. New York: Knopf

Preston AR, Gabrieli JDE. 2008. Dissociation between explicit memory and configural memory in the human medial temporal lobe. *Cereb. Cortex* 18:2192–207

Price PC, Yates JF. 1993. Judgmental overshadowing: further evidence of cue interaction in contingency judgment. *Mem. Cogn.* 21:561–72

Rachman S. 1977. The conditioning theory of fear-acquisition: a critical examination. *Behav. Res. Ther.* 15:375–87

Rescorla RA, Wagner AR. 1972. A theory of Pavlovian conditioning: variations in the effectiveness of reinforcement and nonreinforcement. In *Classical Conditioning II: Current Theory and Research*, ed. AH Black, WF Prokasy, pp. 64–99. New York: Appleton-Century-Crofts

Early demonstration of additivity effects in human blocking.

Demonstration of the Perruchet effect in a human reaction time task.

Rogers RF, Matzel LD. 1996. Higher-order associative processing in *Hermissenda* suggests multiple sites of neuronal modulation. *Learn. Mem.* 2:279–98

Rumelhart DE, McClelland JL. 1986. *Parallel Distributed Processing: Explorations in the Microstructure of Cognition. Vol. 1: Foundations.* Cambridge, MA: MIT Press

Schmajuk N, Larrauri J. 2008. Associative models can describe both causal learning and conditioning. *Behav. Process.* 77:443–45

Scully AL, Mitchell CJ. 2008. Extinction in human learning and memory. *Q. J. Exp. Psychol.* 61:1472–78

Shanks DR. 1985. Forward and backward blocking in human contingency judgement. *Q. J. Exp. Psychol.* 37B:1–21

Shanks DR. 1990. On the cognitive theory of conditioning. *Biol. Psychol.* 30:171–79

Shanks DR, Channon S, Wilkinson L, Curran HV. 2006. Disruption of sequential priming in organic and pharmacological amnesia: a role for the medial temporal lobes in implicit contextual learning. *Neuropsychopharmacology* 31:1768–76

Shanks DR, Darby RJ. 1998. Feature- and rule-based generalization in human associative learning. *J. Exp. Psychol.: Anim. Behav. Process.* 24:405–15

Shanks DR, Dickinson A. 1990. Contingency awareness in evaluative conditioning: a comment on Baeyens, Eelen, and Van den Bergh. *Cogn. Emot.* 4:19–30

Shanks DR, Johnstone T. 1999. Evaluating the relationship between explicit and implicit knowledge in a sequential reaction time task. *J. Exp. Psychol.: Learn. Mem. Cogn.* 25:1435–51

Shanks DR, Perruchet P. 2002. Dissociation between priming and recognition in the expression of sequential knowledge. *Psychon. Bull. Rev.* 9:362–67

Shanks DR, Rowland LA, Ranger MS. 2005. Attentional load and implicit sequence learning. *Psychol. Res.* 69:369–82

Shanks DR, Wilkinson L, Channon S. 2003. Relationship between priming and recognition in deterministic and probabilistic sequence learning. *J. Exp. Psychol.: Learn. Mem. Cogn.* 29:248–61

Sloman SA. 1996. The empirical case for two systems of reasoning. *Psychol. Bull.* 119:3–22

Smith CN, Clark RE, Manns JR, Squire LR. 2005. Acquisition of differential delay eyeblink classical conditioning is independent of awareness. *Behav. Neurosci.* 119:78–86

Smyth AC, Shanks DR. 2008. Awareness in contextual cuing with extended and concurrent tests. *Mem. Cogn.* 36:403–15

Stahl C, Unkelbach C, Corneille O. 2009. On the respective contributions of awareness of unconditioned stimulus valence and unconditioned stimulus identity in attitude formation through evaluative conditioning. *J. Personal. Soc. Psychol.* 97:404–20

Stefaniak N, Willems S, Adam S, Meulemans T. 2008. What is the impact of the explicit knowledge of sequence regularities on both deterministic and probabilistic serial reaction time task performance? *Mem. Cogn.* 36:1283–98

Thomas MSC, McClelland JL. 2008. Connectionist models of cognition. In *The Cambridge Handbook of Computational Psychology*, ed. R Sun, pp. 23–58. London: Cambridge Univ. Press

Thorndike EL. 1931. *Human Learning.* New York: Century

Vadillo MA, Miller RR, Matute H. 2005. Causal and predictive-value judgments, but not predictions, are based on cue-outcome contingency. *Learn. Behav.* 33:172–83

Vaidya CJ, Huger M, Howard DV, Howard JH. 2007. Developmental differences in implicit learning of spatial context. *Neuropsychology* 21:497–506

Van Hamme LJ, Wasserman EA. 1994. Cue competition in causality judgments: the role of nonpresentation of compound stimulus elements. *Learn. Motiv.* 25:127–51

Vandenberghe M, Schmidt N, Fery P, Cleeremans A. 2006. Can amnesic patients learn without awareness? New evidence comparing deterministic and probabilistic sequence learning. *Neuropsychologia* 44:1629–41

Vandorpe S, de Houwer J, Beckers T. 2007. The role of memory for compounds in cue competition. *Learn. Motiv.* 38:195–207

Waelti P, Dickinson A, Schultz W. 2001. Dopamine responses comply with basic assumptions of formal learning theory. *Nature* 412:43–48

Wagner AR. 1981. SOP: a model of automatic memory processing in animal behavior. In *Information Processing in Animals: Memory Mechanisms*, ed. NE Spear, RR Miller, pp. 5–47. Hillsdale, NJ: Erlbaum

Waldmann MR. 2000. Competition among causes but not effects in predictive and diagnostic learning. *J. Exp. Psychol.: Learn. Mem. Cogn.* 26:53–76

Waldmann MR, Holyoak KJ. 1990. Can causal induction be reduced to associative learning? *Proceedings 12th Ann. Conf. Cogn. Sci. Soc.*, pp. 190–97. Hillsdale, NJ: Erlbaum

Waldmann MR, Holyoak KJ. 1992. Predictive and diagnostic learning within causal models: asymmetries in cue competition. *J. Exp. Psychol.: Gen.* 121:222–36

Walther E, Nagengast B. 2006. Evaluative conditioning and the awareness issue: assessing contingency awareness with the four-picture recognition test. *J. Exp. Psychol.: Anim. Behav. Process.* 32:454–59

Wardle SG, Mitchell CJ, Lovibond PF. 2007. Flavor evaluative conditioning and contingency awareness. *Learn. Behav.* 35:233–41

Weidemann G, Tangen JM, Lovibond PF, Mitchell CJ. 2009. Is Perruchet's dissociation between eyeblink conditioned responding and outcome expectancy evidence for two learning systems? *J. Exp. Psychol.: Anim. Behav. Process.* 35:169–76

Weike AI, Schupp HT, Hamm AO. 2007. Fear acquisition requires awareness in trace but not delay conditioning. *Psychophysiology* 44:170–80

Wheeler DS, Beckers T, Miller RR. 2008. The effect of subadditive pretraining on blocking: limits on generalization. *Learn. Behav.* 36:341–51

Wilkinson L, Shanks DR. 2004. Intentional control and implicit sequence learning. *J. Exp. Psychol.: Learn. Mem. Cogn.* 30:354–69

Williams DA, Sagness KE, McPhee JE. 1994. Configural and elemental strategies in predictive learning. *J. Exp. Psychol.: Learn. Mem. Cogn.* 20:694–709

Willingham DB, Salidis J, Gabrieli JDE. 2002. Direct comparison of neural systems mediating conscious and unconscious skill learning. *J. Neurophysiol.* 88:1451–60

Wilson TD. 2002. *Strangers to Ourselves: Discovering the Adaptive Unconscious.* Cambridge, MA: Belknap

Contrasts learning about cause-effect (predictive) and effect-cause (diagnostic) relationships.

Evolving the Capacity to Understand Actions, Intentions, and Goals

Marc Hauser[1],* and Justin Wood[2]

[1] Departments of Psychology and Human Evolutionary Biology, Harvard University, Cambridge, Massachusetts 02138; email: mdh102559@gmail.com

[2] Department of Psychology, University of Southern California, Los Angeles, California 90089

Annu. Rev. Psychol. 2010. 61:303–24

First published online as a Review in Advance on August 19, 2009

The *Annual Review of Psychology* is online at psych.annualreviews.org

This article's doi: 10.1146/annurev.psych.093008.100434

0066-4308/10/0110-0303$20.00

*Both authors contributed equally to this manuscript.

Key Words

motor representations, mirror neurons, mental states, evolution, morality

Abstract

We synthesize the contrasting predictions of motor simulation and teleological theories of action comprehension and present evidence from a series of studies showing that monkeys and apes—like humans—extract the meaning of an event by (*a*) going beyond the surface appearance of actions, attributing goals and intentions to the agent; (*b*) using details about the environment to infer when an action is rational or irrational; (*c*) making predictions about an agent's goal and the most probable action to obtain the goal, within the constraints of the situation; (*d*) predicting the most probable outcome of actions even when they are physiologically incapable of producing the actions; and (*e*) combining information about means and outcomes to make decisions about social interactions, some with moral relevance. These studies reveal the limitations of motor simulation theories, especially those that rely on the notion of direct matching and mirror neuron activation. They provide support, however, for a teleological theory, rooted in an inferential process that extracts information about action means, potential goals, and the environmental constraints that limit rational action.

Contents

INTRODUCTION

To understand another's action, it is necessary to go beyond the movement of limbs in space. One must infer that each action is directed toward proximate and ultimate goals, linked to the individual agent. Making this inference enables us to comprehend novel actions, predict future actions, and learn from the prior successes and failures of earlier actions. Further, by probing beneath the surface appearance of actions, we are able to distinguish between intentionally and accidentally caused harms; this capacity is a critical stepping-stone for building a moral agent, an individual who can evaluate both the means and the consequences of actions and then decide what the moral high ground should look like.

Although interest in action comprehension has a long, interdisciplinary history (Davidson 2001, Hart & Honore 1985, Kirsh 1991, Michotte 1962), recent work in the neurosciences and developmental psychology has reinvigorated research, raising new problems, especially in terms of the coordination of action production and perception. For example, although we appear to simulate our own motor production routines when observing the actions of others, damage to motor systems need not diminish perceptual and conceptual comprehension. Further, infants generate rich representations of others' goals and intentions without being able to produce anything comparable (Gallese et al. 2004; Gergely & Csibra 2003; Mahon & Caramazza 2008, 2009).

Recent work on nonhuman animals, especially the monkeys and apes, has entered these debates, allowing further elaboration of at least three different questions that we address here. First, to what extent are the mechanisms subserving action comprehension, especially the capacity to infer goals and intentions, shared across species and implemented in a variety of contexts? Second, to what extent does an animal's motor capacity contribute to action comprehension, and how has the evolution of particular motor capacities in our own species contributed to action comprehension? Third, to what extent do the domain-general mechanisms that support action comprehension (e.g., general processes of visual perception, categorization, and memory) interface with other systems (e.g., folk intuitions about goals and intentions) to support more socially complex interactions that arise in morally relevant situations? In a nutshell, do nonhuman animals have what we might properly consider the precursors or foundations to human morality?

We begin our discussion by providing a succinct review of the dominant theories in the field, starting with simulation/embodiment and ending with the teleological stance. We then turn to recent behavioral experiments on primates that help adjudicate between these different perspectives and open the door to new predictions and experiments.

Mental Simulation and Embodiment

Since Rizzolatti and colleagues (di Pellegrino et al. 1992; Gallese et al. 1996; Rizzolatti et al. 1996, 1999) made their discovery of mirror neurons in the macaque premotor cortex, the cognitive neurosciences have witnessed an explosion of new studies looking at the relationship between action production and perception systems. Two dominant theories—simulation (Gallese & Goldman 1998) and embodied cognition (Lakoff & Johnson 1999)—suggest that action comprehension relies critically on the capacity to produce the same action. Thus, I understand hair cutting because I can replay the act of holding and cutting hair with scissors, or because my concept of "scissor" entails not only information about the object but also information about what to do with the object (Barsalou et al. 2003, Pulvermuller 2005). However, the observation of motor system activation does not license the conclusion that motor information is necessary or causally involved in action understanding (Mahon & Caramazza 2008). It is equally plausible that action understanding involves purely perceptual, nonmotor processes, and that once an action is understood, it interfaces with the motor system that provides instructions for how to use an object. Thus, we have a concept of "scissor" that includes abstract details of the object (shape, size, material) together with instructions for how to use it. On this view, understanding the meaning of an object or action involves, but does not require, a motor representation. At present, none of the existing data provide definitive evidence in support of one side or the other. Thus, although verbs of action, together with the perception of action, trigger corresponding motor areas (Pulvermuller 2005), these studies can't distinguish between concepts that entail motor information and concepts that do not but that

interface to the motor systems with instructions. Similarly, although apraxic patients can't produce motor-appropriate actions with objects that they semantically comprehend, this doesn't mean that action comprehension is entirely divorced from action production. Specifically, these patients incurred damage in adulthood, after the relevant ontological competence had already been acquired.

The Teleological Stance

Though neither simulation theory nor embodied cognition can provide a complete account of action comprehension, both point to the significant interfaces between action production and perception systems. The teleological stance is one theoretical approach that can account for action comprehension in cases where the observer lacks a motor routine of the observed action (Gergely & Csibra 2003). On this view, interpreting another's actions relies on an inferential process that considers the target goal and the environmental constraints that limit or facilitate goal achievement. Thus, if we witness an agent illuminating a light switch with his knee, while both hands are free, this strikes us as irrational. If this same knee-switch action arises while the agent holds books in his hands, we conclude that the agent is acting in a goal-directed, rational fashion, given constraints on using his hands. Importantly, this theory has been used to argue that infants show great sensitivity to the environmental contexts in which agents act in and on the world, using this information to infer goals (Csibra et al. 1999, 2003; Csibra & Gergely 1998; Gergely et al. 1995, 2002; Gergely & Csibra 2003). Furthermore, a wide variety of animal studies (reviewed below) provide parallel support (Buttlemann et al. 2007, Range et al. 2007, Rochat et al. 2008, Wood et al. 2007b). Finally, when such events are presented to human subjects in a scanner (Brass et al. 2007), the blood-oxygen-level-dependent (BOLD) response reveals selective activation in the superior-temporal sulcus (STS) as opposed to in the mirror neuron system (e.g., inferior frontal gyrus, premotor cortex); this suggests that the STS is critically involved in the processing of intentionally mediated actions and in the absence of motor input.

Integrating insights from both motor-rich (simulation, embodiment) and motor-poor (teleological) theories of action comprehension is attractive as they provide different angles on the same problem, set up different predictions about the psychological components of action comprehension, and enable a broad comparative approach to understanding how organisms interpret and predict the actions of others.

Action Comprehension in a Comparative Context

We suggest that behavioral studies of nonhuman primates can enrich the study of action comprehension in unique ways (Wood & Hauser 2008). First, such studies shed light on its evolutionary origins by revealing whether nonhuman primates and human infants and adults recruit similar mechanisms during action comprehension. Many of the studies reviewed here, for example, suggest that some components of action comprehension are shared with species across the animal kingdom; we discuss this topic in more detail below.

Second, much of the evidence in favor of motor simulation comes from physiological studies with macaque monkeys. In a series of now classic experiments, Rizzolatti and colleagues discovered that some neurons in area F5 of the macaque premotor cortex activate both when an individual observes an experimenter act on an object and when the individual acts in the same way (Rizzolatti et al. 1996, 1999, 2001b). Given the parallel pattern of activation for the production of an action and the perception of the same action, these cells have been named mirror neurons. These neurons are highly sensitive to the details of an event, especially the motor patterns underlying reaching and grasping an object considered as a goal. For example, whereas some neurons fire both during the observation and execution of a hand grasping an object with pincer grip (the thumb and index finger), the same neurons do not fire when a set of pliers grasps the same object (Rizzolatti et al. 1996, 2001b). Despite the wealth of neurophysiological data, however, there is little research connecting the physiological activity of these neurons to behavior, especially social behavior. Filling in this gap is particularly important given that the mirror neuron system in humans has been argued to support imitation, mental state attribution, empathy, and language (see below), processes for which there is either no evidence or very thin evidence in primates. The majority of evidence linking these capacities to the mirror neuron system is correlational (i.e., mirror neurons activate both during action observation and production), making it virtually impossible to determine whether and in what ways the mirror neuron system supports these capacities. With regard to action comprehension, for example, the mirror neuron system might reflect processes that are either necessary or sufficient for computing the intentional state of an actor (Rizzolatti et al. 2001b), or they might reflect processes that are not directly related to action comprehension (Csibra 2007), such as preparation for imitation. Studies of action comprehension in free-ranging animals can provide a unique perspective on this issue by examining whether their spontaneous behavior accords more closely with the predictions of motor simulation, the teleological stance, or some combination of the two. Further, and as discussed in detail below, studies of nonhuman animals can provide causal evidence regarding whether motor capacities are necessary for action comprehension (Wood et al. 2007a).

Third, studies of nonhuman animals allow more control over an individual's experiences, critical for testing the necessary and sufficient processes for action comprehension and enactment. We can teach animals how to perform new actions, use species with restricted motor capacities (e.g., animals vary considerably in their dexterity), and modify an individual's visual experiences (e.g., by restricting their experience of seeing others perform actions). This type of experimental control turns out to be crucial for distinguishing between motor simulation and the teleological stance with regard to action comprehension because individuals that develop in a normal environment will both have motor experience of their own actions as well as visual experience of seeing others act in motorically familiar ways. Thus, in these animals, it is impossible to distinguish the respective roles of motor and visual experiences in action comprehension. However, when these experiences can be controlled, it becomes possible to isolate their respective roles for action comprehension.

Action Comprehension in Nonhuman Primates

There is a rich comparative literature focusing on how animals respond to different behaviors, including their social interactions and communicative signals. Here we focus on recent behavioral work with macaques (*Macaca*), given that this genus was targeted for the original physiological studies (species *nemestrina* in the case of cellular recordings, *mulatta* in the case of behavior) and that the experiments were explicitly designed to test different aspects of the simulation and teleological hypotheses (Hauser et al. 2007; Wood et al. 2007a,b, 2008).

In a series of studies designed to map out how rhesus monkeys respond to different aspects of an action in the service of drawing inferences about the agent's goals and intentions (Wood et al. 2007b, 2008), an experimenter presented two potential food sources (overturned coconut shells) to a subject, acted on one, and then walked away, allowing the subject to selectively approach. Although coconuts are native to the island on which these animals live, rhesus cannot open the hard outer shells themselves and, therefore, only obtain the desired inner fruit when the coconuts have been opened and discarded by a human. Thus, it logically follows that if rhesus monkeys comprehend the experimenter's action as goal directed, then they should selectively approach the coconut contacted as this maximizes the odds of obtaining food.

Results showed that rhesus selectively approached the targeted container when the experimenter grasped the coconut with his hand, foot, or with a precision grip involving the pointer finger and thumb (**Figure 1**, see color insert). Control conditions ruled out the possibility that rhesus approached the contacted coconut shell because they preferred to inspect objects handled by a human experimenter without making the inference that the experimenter was acting on a coconut containing hidden food (Wood et al. 2008). These results support the hypothesis that, in the absence of training, rhesus monkeys spontaneously infer the goals and intentions underlying a human experimenter's actions.

Further experiments examined the limits of this ability by testing whether rhesus comprehend the meaning of actions that fall outside of their species-typical motor repertoire. Rhesus do not spontaneously use tools in the wild (although they can be trained to do so in laboratory settings). Thus, for this population of individuals, actions involving tools are not part of the species-specific motor repertoire. Accordingly, Wood et al. (2008) examined whether rhesus comprehend tool-related actions as goal directed in this two-option social foraging context. In striking contrast to their behavior when observing actions that are part of the motor repertoire, rhesus failed to use the tool-related actions as cues to infer the location of hidden food. When the experimenter touched one of the coconuts with a pole or a machete, or grasped the coconut with a pair of pliers—all familiar objects used by personnel on the island— rhesus approached the two coconuts at chance levels (see **Figure 1**). Their failure to perceive the machete action as goal-directed toward hidden food is particularly surprising because coconuts are regularly opened on the island by humans using machetes, often in full view of the monkeys. Nevertheless, rhesus failed to perceive this action as goal directed. However, this same population of monkeys can make other types of inferences about tools, including the importance of their design features in causing particular transformations or achieving particular outcomes (Hauser & Spaulding 2006, Santos et al. 2003). Thus, the monkeys' failure to perceive tool-related actions as goal directed is not the result of a general inability to reason about actions involving tools; rather, it appears to reflect domain-specific limits on action perception.

How do rhesus monkeys distinguish between intentional and accidental actions? Do they simply differentiate between actions that do, and do not, involve tools, perceiving only the former as goal directed? Or, like human infants and adults, can they make more fine-grained distinctions, such as that between intentional and accidental hand actions? To test this, Wood et al. (2007b, 2008) examined how rhesus monkeys reason about an accidental hand-flop gesture in which the experimenter flopped the back of his hand onto the coconut in a manner that does not appear, from a human perspective, as goal directed (Woodward 1999). In accord with our own comprehension of this action, rhesus also failed to perceive the hand-flop action as goal directed, approaching the two coconuts at chance levels (see **Figure 1**).

Together, these studies show that when assessing the meaning of actions, rhesus are highly sensitive to the action means used to achieve a goal. For example, they perceived a hand-grasp action as goal directed but a hand-flop action as accidental, despite the fact that in both conditions, the experimenter's body and eye gaze were directed toward the targeted coconut shell.

Building Bridges Between Natural Foraging Behavior and Patterns of Neural Activation

Neurophysiological studies show that the mirror neuron system activates both when individuals perform an action and when they observe another individual perform a similar action (e.g., Rizzolatti et al. 2001b). Similarly, the experiments reviewed above suggest that rhesus monkeys perceive actions as goal directed toward hidden food only when the observed actions are part of their species-specific motor repertoire. This raises the possibility that the mirror neuron system is, in some way, connected with rhesus monkeys' behavior in this natural foraging context. If so, then the natural foraging behavior of rhesus should also accord with other signatures of mirror neuron activation. Wood et al. (2008) tested this hypothesis, generating three significant results. First, physiological studies show that mirror neurons activate both when subjects observe a complete action as well as when some of the elements that comprise the action are absent (Umilta et al. 2001). Similarly, rhesus were able to comprehend the meaning of an action both from a full visual description of an action as well as from an incomplete description that arises under occlusion (see **Figure 1**).

Second, mirror neurons activate only when the subject observes object-directed actions; that is, these neurons do not activate when the monkey observes an object alone, an individual mimicking an action, or an individual making intransitive gestures (Rizzolatti et al. 1996, 2001b). Similarly, rhesus did not perceive an action as goal directed toward an object when the experimenter performed an intransitive gesture (i.e., reaching directly next to an object; see **Figure 1**).

Third, mirror neurons in the inferior parietal lobe show different activation patterns to the same act (e.g., grasping) when this act is part of a different event (e.g., eating versus placing the same object; Fogassi 2005). Similarly, when presented with the same act (grasping the coconut) embedded within different contexts ("grasping to obtain food" versus "grasping the coconut for balance while standing"), rhesus evaluated the action by attending to the broader context, perceiving only the former action as goal directed toward food.

These results are exciting because they provide evidence for common signature limits between neurophysiological studies using cellular recordings with restrained animals and behavioral studies of animals in natural, ecologically relevant contexts. In the same way that neurophysiologists have described a set of properties that characterize the activation of mirror neurons during the perception of goal-directed actions, so too have ethologists described a parallel set of properties that trigger understanding of others' goals. This suggests that mirror neurons are in some way connected with rhesus monkeys' capacity to comprehend the meaning of actions and that they evolved to solve ecologically relevant problems. What is not clear from these results, however, is whether the mirror neuron system plays a functional role in the comprehension of actions, or whether mirror neuron activation, as well as rhesus monkeys' social foraging behavior, depends on an additional teleological mechanism that computes the meaning of an action. That is, the parallel between mirror neuron activation and monkeys' social foraging behavior is correlational.

To explore the role of teleological mechanisms in action comprehension, we tested the limits of the rhesus monkeys' capacity to comprehend actions across three contexts in which the theories of motor simulation and teleological inference make contrasting predictions. First, we examined whether an individual needs an exact motor representation of an action in order to comprehend its meaning. Second, we examined whether motor representations of actions are sufficient for action comprehension. Third, we examined whether event comprehension can occur in the absence of action observation.

ARE EXACT MOTOR REPRESENTATIONS NECESSARY FOR ACTION COMPREHENSION?

Motor simulation and the teleological stance make contrasting predictions regarding the range of actions that can be successfully interpreted by an observer. Under the motor simulation account, the visual properties of an observed action are mapped onto the observer's premotor system. This causes the motor system to "resonate," thereby allowing the observer to understand the goal of the observed action as if she were performing the action

herself (see Rizzolatti et al. 2001b). The resonance of the motor system is, therefore, proposed to be causally involved in and, critically, necessary for the comprehension of an action. Thus, if an observer lacks a motor representation that is similar to the one being observed,[1] then she should be unable to comprehend the action. In contrast, the teleological stance proposes that action comprehension is based on a reasoning process that operates over the visual properties of a context, such as the action means, the apparent target goal, and the environmental constraints that limit or facilitate goal achievement. This process does not depend directly on the motor system (see Brass et al. 2007): Although the output of this process may activate motor regions of the brain, action comprehension, including the agent's goal, is computed by nonmotor processes.

On the direct matching hypothesis, action comprehension should fail in situations where the motor action observed is outside the range of physically producible actions. To test this possibility, Wood and colleagues (2007a) explored the capacity of rhesus monkeys to understand the functional consequences of throwing. Humans, but no other animals, have evolved the capacity for accurate, high-momentum throwing, a morphological specialization with significant adaptive consequences in fighting and prey capture. The fact that only humans have the capacity (and underlying motor representations) to perform accurate, high-momentum throwing raises the question of whether they are also the only species with the capacity to comprehend the meaning of throwing actions, a prediction that follows from the motor simulation theory in which comprehension of observed actions occurs through the activation of the observer's own motor representations.

---

[1] It is not entirely clear what the architects of the direct matching hypothesis have in mind when they say that action comprehension relies on motor routines that are in the repertoire. This could either mean actions that the organism typically produces or ones that it can physically produce even if it never does so. Obviously, actions that are in the repertoire can be produced, but those that can be produced need not be.

The rhesus monkeys living on the island of Cayo Santiago provided a unique opportunity to test whether exact motor representations of observed actions are necessary for action comprehension because many of these individuals have observed humans throw objects,[2] but like other monkeys, they don't throw (i.e., throwing is outside of the species-typical repertoire), and due to the lack of relevant musculature, are incapable of throwing (i.e., throwing is outside of the physically possible range of motor actions). Nonetheless, we can ask whether they might comprehend the meaning of throwing by presenting them with a human experimenter performing a throwing action and observing their patterns of response.

The method worked as follows: An experimenter approached a lone monkey and revealed a rock in one hand. He then performed an overhand throw toward the subject but without releasing the rock. The dependent measure was whether the subject moved from its current location, an adaptive response and measure of avoidance in the face of a potential threat.

When rhesus observed the experimenter perform an overhand throw in their direction, 85% of the subjects moved away. This shows that these individuals are able to predict the outcome of a throwing action and interpret it as a potential threat, despite lacking exact motor representations of throwing actions. However, this result can be explained through two very different types of mechanisms. One possibility is that the behavior was based on a general associative learning mechanism, forging an association between some aspect of the throwing motion (e.g., the overhand motion, the rock, or the thrower's eye gaze) and a negative consequence (i.e., a looming object). Alternatively, rhesus might have recruited a more specialized teleological mechanism that evaluates various characteristics of an event, such as the path of

motion, the object involved in the throw, the thrower's attention, and the various environmental constraints that arise when an individual attempts to strike a target goal by throwing. Unlike a general associative mechanism, this interpretive system should demonstrate flexibility in its capacity to generalize knowledge of one kind of action—such as the familiar overhand throw—to related but novel actions.

To distinguish between these competing mechanisms, Wood et al. (2007a) explored how rhesus respond to throwing actions with which they have little to no experience observing (see **Figure 2** for a visual description of the throws and the corresponding results). The associative learning mechanism predicts that rhesus should show an avoidance response whenever the throwing action contains a property, or a collection of properties, associated with the negative outcome—for example, the overhand pattern of movement and/or the presence of the rock. In contrast, the teleological mechanism predicts that rhesus should show the avoidance response only when all of the properties of the observed throw are sufficient to make it a viable threat. Furthermore, this mechanism should be able to generalize knowledge of an overhand throw to novel actions that the subject has little to no experience observing.

When the experimenter performed a novel underhand throwing motion that rhesus had little to no experience observing, they nevertheless showed identical levels of avoidance (85% avoidance response) compared to the overhand throw. In contrast, rhesus showed less avoidance when the experimenter performed throwing actions that lacked all of the kinematic components of an overhand throw (i.e., moving arm backward: 30% avoidance response; rotating shoulder forward: 45% avoidance response; extending forearm forward: 35% avoidance response). Similarly, rhesus showed less avoidance when the throw was performed with an empty hand (15% avoidance response) or with a soft food object rather than a rock (5% avoidance response), at a slower speed (i.e., overhand throw was performed at one-third of normal speed: 35% avoidance response), toward a

---

[2]Because some rhesus monkeys sometimes aggressively approach human experimenters on the island, it is sometimes necessary for the experimenters to pick up rocks and simulate throwing; here, as in the experiments, individuals are never contacted with the rocks, but merely witness the act of throwing, with rocks released away from the animal, if at all.

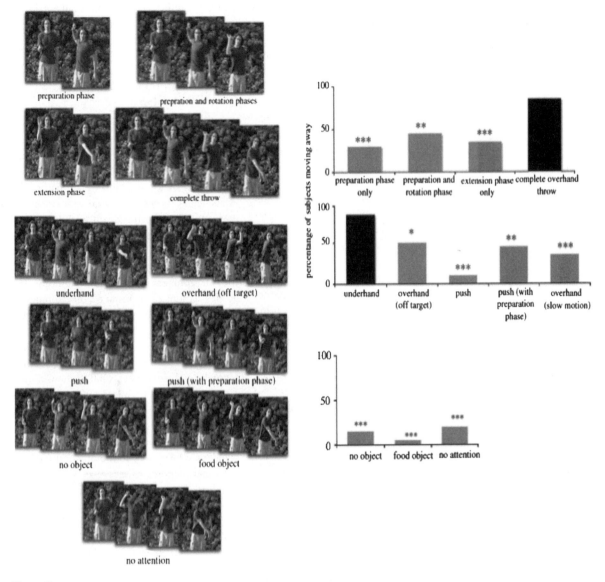

Figure 2

(*left*) Illustration of the key frames of the throwing actions presented to rhesus monkeys. (*right*) Results illustrating the percentage of subjects moving from their current location after observing the throws. Gray bars signify statistically significant differences compared with the complete overhand throw with a rock (chi-square, two-tailed predictions); ***$p < 0.001$, **$p < 0.01$, *$p < 0.05$. Data reported in Wood et al. (2007a).

different direction from the subject (i.e., experimenter looked at, but performed the overhand throw 90° away from, the subject: 50% avoidance response), or with a trajectory that could not produce sufficient torque to serve as a threat (i.e., experimenter moved arm straight toward the subject: 10% avoidance response). Rhesus also showed less avoidance when the experimenters performed the overhand throw but directed their eye gaze 90° in a different direction (20% avoidance rate), indicating that the underlying action-comprehension mechanism performs an analysis of the kinematics of the motion pattern and combines this with information about the actor's eye gaze.

An associative learning mechanism cannot readily explain this pattern of behavior. Rhesus showed low levels of avoidance in response to the overhand throwing motion when it was performed with an empty hand or a soft food object, or when the action was performed with a rock but the experimenter looked away from the subject. The pattern of motion was identical in all of these cases, and yet rhesus only perceived the throw as a threat when all of the relevant properties were sufficient for the throw to constitute a threat. Similarly, rhesus showed identical levels of avoidance to the overhand and underhand throwing motions, despite their lack of experience with an underhand throw. These results are highly consistent with the hypothesis that individuals reason about actions using a teleological mechanism that evaluates various visual characteristics of an event. This mechanism operates over at least four kinds of information: (a) the kinematics of the motor action, (b) the object involved in the action, (c) the actor's direction of eye gaze, and (d) the position of the subject.

These results suggest that exact motor representations of observed actions are unnecessary for comprehension of those actions. This presents a strong challenge to the motor simulation theory of action comprehension and specifically the direct-matching hypothesis. On this view, the visual properties of observed actions (which are initially devoid of meaning; Rizzolatti et al. 2001) acquire their meaning once they have been mapped to the observer's premotor system. Because the input to motor simulation is limited to the visual properties of the action, all actions with identical visual properties should be interpreted in the same way by a direct-matching mechanism. This prediction was not supported by the data. Many of the throwing actions had identical visual properties and yet were interpreted in very different ways. Other characteristics of the event, such as the kind of object involved in the throw and the observer's head and body orientation, had a significant influence on rhesus monkeys' interpretation of throwing events.[3]

ARE MOTOR REPRESENTATIONS SUFFICIENT FOR ACTION COMPREHENSION?

Another approach to distinguishing between motor simulation and the teleological stance is to examine the type of information evaluated within a given context. The teleological stance assigns a goal to an action by evaluating the efficiency of the agent's action with respect to environmental constraints on goal attainment (see Gergely & Csibra 2003). Thus, comprehension of an action involves information about potential goals, the action means, and the environmental constraints limiting the agent's actions. For instance, developmental studies of human infants indicate that individuals read beneath the surface appearance of behavior by referencing each action against a backdrop of environmental constraints. Gergely and colleagues (2002) showed that when 14-month-old infants watched an experimenter use her head to illuminate a box, infants imitated this precise action only if the experimenter's hands were free to move and could have been used to illuminate the box; if the experimenter's hands were occupied, and could not be used, then the infants used their hands. Infants most likely inferred that since the experimenter could have used her hands, but used her head instead, the head must confer some advantage for illuminating the box. This finding converges with others showing that young infants make inferences about actions, goals, and environmental constraints when watching the motions of simple geometric figures (see Gergely & Csibra 2003). For example, 12-month-old infants were habituated to a

---

[3] Studies of mirror neurons in the macaque premotor cortex also show that activation of these neurons depends on contextual properties of an event. Although these results have traditionally been interpreted as consistent with a direct-matching mechanism, they are, in fact, more consistent with a teleological mechanism (see Csibra 2007).

computer-animated event in which a circle approached and contacted another circle by jumping over a barrier that separated them (Gergely et al. 1995). During the test phase, the experimenters changed the constraints of the situation by removing the barrier. Infants then observed the same jumping motion pattern as in the habituation trials or a perceptually novel straight-line approach. Infants looked longer at the jumping pattern, but failed to dishabituate to the perceptually novel straight-line approach. These results suggest that human infants assess whether an agent's actions are rational by evaluating how the intervening environmental circumstances constrain the achievement of a target goal; as such, they infer properties of mental life that are not transparent from the surface appearance of behavior. Is this capacity the product of specifically human evolution or do nonhuman animals also evaluate others' behavior using this same kind of interpretative system?

To investigate this question, Wood and colleagues (2007b) used the two-option social foraging method described above. As noted, rhesus perceive a hand-grasp action as goal directed but perceive a hand-flop action as accidental. What kind of psychological mechanism generated this distinction? One possibility is that rhesus analyzed the actions using their own motor system. Thus, the hand-grasp action was perceived as intentional because this action is part of the rhesus motor repertoire, whereas the hand-flop action was perceived as accidental because rhesus do not produce this action in goal-directed contexts (even though they of course can, motorically speaking, produce the action). An alternative account is that rhesus interpreted these actions in relation to the broader environment in which they occurred. Thus, subjects may have judged the hand flop as accidental because, in this particular situation, the experimenter could have used the more rational grasping action in order to contact the coconut shell.

Do rhesus assess the meaning of actions by evaluating whether an action is rational given the constraints of the situation? Using the two-option approach measure, subjects observed an experimenter perform the same elbow touch action under two contrasting environmental circumstances: in one condition, the experimenter's acting hand was occupied by holding an object, and in the second condition, the experimenter's acting hand was free. If rhesus evaluate actions through direct-matching motor simulation, then they should show the same pattern of searching in both the hand-occupied and hand-empty conditions because the surface properties of the actions—and thus, what will be mapped onto the motor system—are nearly identical. However, if rhesus take into account the environmental constraints facing the experimenter, then only the hand-occupied condition should be perceived as a rational, goal-directed action. Given that the experimenter's acting hand was occupied at the moment of gesturing, his elbow provides an alternative means to contact the target goal. Accordingly, the hand-empty condition would not be perceived as a rational, goal-directed action because at the time, the experimenter could have used his unoccupied acting hand to grasp and indicate the target container, leaving the subject uncertain as to the target goal. Therefore, subjects should not infer that the experimenter's goal was to contact the box with the potentially concealed food.

Results showed that rhesus used the elbow touch as a cue to find the hidden food when the experimenter's acting hand was occupied but not when it was free. A similar pattern of results was found with cotton-top tamarins and chimpanzees (Wood et al. 2007b). Furthermore, other laboratories testing macaques, chimpanzees, and domestic dogs have obtained convergent evidence using a variety of methods, ranging from violation of expectancy looking-time measures (Rochat et al. 2008) to selective imitation (Buttelmann et al. 2007, Range et al. 2007). Buttelmann and colleagues (2007), for example, examined whether chimpanzees evaluate the environmental constraints that limit rational action when imitating others' movements. Chimpanzees observed a human experimenter use an unusual body part to operate an apparatus (i.e., she pressed it with her forehead). In one condition, the action was performed while the experimenter's hands were occupied, whereas in a second condition, the action was performed while the experimenter's hands were free. If chimpanzees evaluate environmental constraints when imitating others' actions, then they should be more likely to use the unusual body part when the experimenter performed the action while her hands were free and unoccupied. Results support this prediction. Like human infants (Gergely et al. 2002), chimpanzees imitated the unusual action more often when the experimenter performed the action with unoccupied hands (Buttelmann et al. 2007).

Is this capacity unique to nonhuman primates, or do other species also imitate others' actions by evaluating the constraints that limit goal-directed behavior? Remarkably, Range and colleagues (2007) showed that domestic dogs also selectively imitate others' actions. An observer dog watched a demonstrator dog pull a rod using either its paw or its mouth. In one condition, the demonstrator dog performed the action while concurrently carrying a ball in its mouth, whereas in a second condition, the action was performed while the dog's mouth was empty. Thus, in the first condition, the presence of the ball in the demonstrator dog's mouth justified the use of the less preferred paw action because in this particular context, she could not use her mouth to perform the action. In the first trial after observing this action, the observer dogs selectively imitated the less preferred paw action only when the demonstrator dog modeled the action with a ball in its mouth. Thus, dogs, like children and chimpanzees, evaluate the environmental constraints that limit rational goal-directed action when imitating others' movements.

Together, these studies show that nonhuman animals infer the meaning of an action by evaluating action means in relation to the environmental constraints imposed on the agent in relation to a potential goal state. Action comprehension cannot, therefore, depend on a direct-matching motor simulation

mechanism that solely evaluates the properties of the observed action (Rizzolatti et al. 2001b).

Intriguingly, these behavioral studies with nonhuman animals converge with recent functional magnetic resonance imaging data obtained with human adults (Brass et al. 2007). Subjects were presented with actions similar to those presented to human infants (Gergely et al. 2002) and nonhuman animals (Buttelmann et al. 2007, Range et al. 2007, Wood et al. 2007b) while in a scanner. For example, subjects observed an actor operate an apparatus using an unfamiliar body part while her hands were either empty or occupied. The BOLD response revealed that the STS activated differently to the hands-empty and hands-occupied actions, suggesting that this region of the brain supports action-comprehension tasks that require integrating information about environmental constraints with observed movements in order to infer the actor's intention. In contrast, the mirror neuron system activated equally to the hands-empty and hands-occupied actions, suggesting that mirror neurons do not evaluate information about the constraints that limit rational action. Thus, although mirror neurons may activate when observing others' actions, they do not process information that is critical for determining an agent's underlying intention.

Convergent evidence for this conclusion comes from a study showing that the mirror neuron system does not distinguish between animate agents and inanimate objects (Wheatley et al. 2007). Subjects were presented with an identically moving shape that was perceived as either an animate agent (e.g., an ice skater) or an inanimate object (e.g., a spinning top) based on the background scene alone. The BOLD response revealed equal activation in the mirror neuron system regardless of whether the shape was perceived as an agent or an inanimate object. This suggests that although the mirror neuron system may play a role in elucidating the actions of all objects, it does not play a specialized role in evaluating the underlying intentions that motivate the actions of animate agents. In contrast, the STS system was modulated by the perceived animacy of the shape.

ACTION PREDICTION IN THE ABSENCE OF ACTION OBSERVATION

The studies discussed above show that animals use environmental constraints to interpret the actions of others. What happens, however, when there are no actions at all, and subjects must predict an agent's goals based on other features of the environment? Motor simulation predicts that action comprehension occurs when an organism observes an action and then simulates that action within its motor system. It thus logically follows that in a context where an organism does not observe an action at all, then its motor system will not resonate. If event comprehension depends on motor resonance, then monkeys will fail to comprehend an event in the absence of observing an action.

Studies of chimpanzees provide one test of these ideas even though they were not designed for this purpose. In particular, Hare et al. (2000) carried out experiments in which a subordinate and dominant chimpanzee were placed in a competitive situation, sitting in opposite rooms, with a center room containing two bananas. In one test condition, the subordinate could see a banana behind an occluder, but the dominant could not; both subordinate and dominant could, however, see a second banana located in the open. When the door to the subordinate's room was opened first, the subordinate dashed out and grabbed the occluded banana. The subordinate's behavior was thus based on an inference about what the dominant could see, and thus, what the dominant would most likely do. Said differently, subordinate chimpanzees generated an appropriate prediction about the dominant's most likely behavior in the absence of any action at all.

These results are consistent with a teleological mechanism that provides meaning to an event by analyzing the action means, potential goals, and the environmental constraints. As Gergely & Csibra (2003) have shown in their elegant studies of human infants, if individuals are provided with information about two of these three kinds of information, then they can infer the third component. Similarly, when chimpanzees are provided with information about two components of an event, such as potential goals (the food) and environmental constraints (the barrier), they can predict which action the other chimpanzee is most likely to perform and react accordingly.

To conclude this section, evidence from three different contexts reveals that nonhuman primates' capacity for action comprehension accords strongly with predictions of the teleological stance but not with predictions of a motor simulation mechanism.

A SHARED SYSTEM OF ACTION COMPREHENSION: EVOLUTIONARY ROOTS AND ONTOGENETIC BEGINNINGS

A number of developmental studies show that within the first year of life, human infants begin to predict the goals of others' actions. For example, in a now classic study, Woodward (1998) habituated preverbal infants to a human agent who reached for one of two objects that were placed side-by-side on a stage. Following habituation, the experimenter concealed the stage from the infant's view, switched the location of the objects, and then, in view of the subject, reached for either the same object as in the habituation period (goal-consistent trials) or for the other object (goal-inconsistent trials). Infants looked longer during the goal-inconsistent trials, suggesting that they are able to encode the actions of others as goal directed. However, infants failed to show this pattern of looking when an inanimate object touched the target objects or the human agent flopped the back of his hand on the target object in a manner that appeared accidental (Woodward 1999). Recall that rhesus monkeys show a parallel pattern of action understanding, perceiving hand-reaching actions as goal directed, but actions involving inanimate objects and a hand flop as accidental (Wood et al. 2007b, 2008).

Follow-up studies examined the extent to which infants' capacity for action comprehension depends on their own ability to produce those actions. For example, when tested with the method described above, five-month-old infants, but not three-month-old infants, looked longer during the test trials when the hand reached for the new object in the old location compared to when the hand reached for the old object in the new location. This suggests that at five months of age, infants can infer that agents will perform future actions toward the same object. However, when three-month-old infants were provided with sticky mittens before the experiment—which allowed them to grasp and manipulate objects despite underdeveloped motor dexterity—these infants were able to encode an experimenter's hand-grasp actions as goal directed (Sommerville & Woodward 2005, Sommerville et al. 2005). Similarly, older infants were able to encode means-end actions as goal directed when they were taught how to produce these actions (Sommerville & Woodward 2005).

Human infants acquire the capacity to discriminate intentional from accidental actions during the first year of development (e.g., Gergely & Csibra 2003, Woodward 1999); similarly, adult rhesus monkeys and chimpanzees can make the same kinds of inferences about others' actions (e.g., Buttelmann et al. 2007; Call et al. 2004; Hauser et al. 2007; Wood et al. 2007a,b, 2008). This suggests that human and nonhuman primates share a common system of action comprehension.

ACTION COMPREHENSION AND THE BUILDING BLOCKS OF MORALITY

For socially living species, such as the primates, action comprehension often arises in a social context, including threats from a dominant, requests for coalitionary support, grooming, mating, and the exchange of resources. For observers of these interactions or those directly involved, it is important to assess not only the actual or expected outcomes, but also the means by which they are achieved. Thus, although an individual may obtain food by theft, as a result of another's offering, or by tolerated taking, each

of these modes of attainment, matched for outcome (i.e., food obtained), differs in terms of its social relevance. Theft violates an animal's sense of property or ownership; food offers represent cases of altruism or cooperation; and tolerated taking is either altruistic or possibly accidental depending upon the possessor's attentional state (e.g., if looking away, toleration turns into theft under inattention). In the case of human primates, these events represent morally relevant actions with consequences for the welfare of other group members. For nonhuman primates, they represent the building blocks upon which our own moral sense evolved. Here we explore these foundations further.

Call and colleagues (2004) developed a task for chimpanzees in which a human experimenter presented subjects with an opportunity to reach for and obtain food. Across conditions, the outcome was held constant (the chimpanzees never obtained the food), but the manner of food presentation was manipulated. For example, in the "clumsy" condition, the experimenter repeatedly tried to give food to the chimpanzee through the target hole, but failed, dropping it out of reach. In the "unable" condition, the experimenter tried to give food to the chimpanzee, but the hole was blocked. In the "unwilling" condition, the experimenter placed the food in view, stared at the chimpanzee, but refused to place it in the hole. Finally, in the "tease" condition, the experimenter brought the food toward the opening and as soon as the chimpanzee reached for it, the experimenter pulled it away. Results showed clear patterns of response, suggesting sensitivity to the means underlying the experimenter's actions as opposed to the outcomes. That is, chimpanzees were more likely to leave the test area early and/or bang on the apparatus in the unwilling and tease conditions compared with the clumsy and unable conditions.

Several recent studies have explored the role that inequities play in economic decision making, as such outcomes play a critical role in social interactions. The key issue in this work is whether animals are sensitive to the distribution of rewards and, in particular, the social consequences of equal as opposed to unequal distributions. In many studies of justice, perceptions of fairness are essential (Hauser 2006, Rawls 1971). As such, studies of how animals compute and act upon fairness serve as an important foundation for thinking about the evolution of human morality and the legal systems that often emerge from it. One of the earliest treatments of this problem was Brosnan & de Waal's (2003) study of brown capuchin monkeys. After subjects were trained to trade tokens for food rewards, they watched a conspecific acquire and eat a high-value food item, and then they were given the opportunity to acquire and eat a lower-value food item. Subjects consistently refused to trade the token for the lower-value food. Brosnan & de Waal (2003) interpreted this result as evidence for inequity aversion and a sense of fairness.

Although the capuchins' response to food distribution suggests that they are sensitive to more than the mere outcome of a transaction, the results are at odds with those obtained in studies of humans, and several important criticisms of this work emerged soon after. In particular, when humans confront inequities, rejections occur only insofar as their actions negatively affect their social partner. In the Brosnan & de Waal (2003) experiments, however, when an individual rejects the lower-quality food, the only cost is to self: that is, rejecting the low-quality food does not affect the paired individual for the trial because this individual maintains access to the high-quality food traded. Several conceptual and experimental follow-ups also pointed to the fact that because rejection rates were comparable in the social and nonsocial condition, it was not possible to rule out the effect of frustration as the driving force behind rejections (Dubreuil et al. 2006; Roma et al. 2006a,b; Wynne 2004). That is, subjects may have rejected unfair offers not because the other individual was getting a better offer but rather because they were frustrated at not being able to obtain the higher-value food item. Though subsequent experiments confirmed the validity of these critiques (Dubreuil et al. 2006, Roma et al. 2006a), Brosnan, de

Waal, and their colleagues have since replicated the original findings with relevant controls and found that their results cannot be explained by frustration (van Wolkenten et al. 2007). Further, there are now parallel findings with chimpanzees (Brosnan et al. 2005) and dogs (Range et al. 2009), though even in these cases the story is not entirely clear (Brauer et al. 2006).

In summary, although there is still much controversy surrounding the results on inequity aversion in animals, it appears that animals are sensitive to the distribution of rewards, in both social and nonsocial contexts, responding negatively when an outcome appears unfair.

A final approach concerns an exploration of the foundations of the Golden Rule, and specifically, the possibility that animals engage in reciprocal altruism. Beginning with the theoretical clarifications by Trivers (1971) concerning the evolution of reciprocity, several studies soon appeared, claiming to find evidence of reciprocal altruism. These studies have failed to replicate, can be interpreted in terms other than reciprocity, or provide only weak support because the requisite conditions are highly artificial and the patterns of exchanges are infrequent and thus relatively insignificant in evolutionary terms. Here, however, we discuss one example because it explicitly explored the relative contribution of outcomes as opposed to means in deciding whether to cooperate.

Hauser and colleagues (2003) ran experiments on cotton-top tamarin monkeys designed to test three properties of a reciprocal relationship: altruistic contingency, reputation tracking, and distinguishing intentional from accidental outcomes. Genetically unrelated tamarins played in four different games, each requiring an actor to decide whether to pull a tool that would deliver food to self, a partner, or both (**Figure 3**). In game 1, individual subjects played against one of two trained confederates, one "nice" cooperative tamarin trained to pull the tool 100% of the time and one "mean" uncooperative tamarin trained to never pull the tool. In this game, pulling the tool resulted in one piece of food for the recipient and no food for the actor, thus, it was considered an

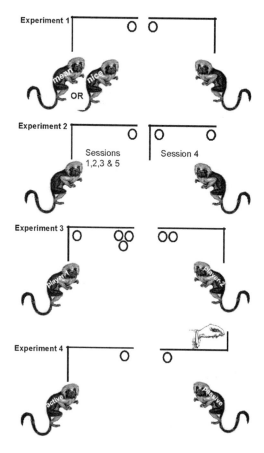

Figure 3

Four different games played by genetically unrelated cotton-top tamarins (Hauser et al. 2003). In Experiment 1, each subject played alternating sessions (24 trials; 12 trials each) with either a nice stooge (trained to pull the tool 100% of the time) or a mean stooge (trained to pull the tool 0% of the time). In Experiment 2, subjects played a reciprocating altruism game (i.e., no food for actor but one piece for recipient) for the first three sessions; in the fourth session a byproduct mutualism game was played (i.e., a piece of food for the actor and recipient); and in the final session, a reciprocating altruism game was played. In Experiment 3, one subject was assigned to the player-1 position (pulling provided one piece to the actor and three pieces to the recipient) and one subject was assigned to the player-2 position (pulling provided no food for the actor and two pieces to the recipient). In Experiment 4, the active tamarin could pull as an altruistic act (no food for self, one for the recipient), while the passive tamarin had no opportunity to pull; instead, when the tool switched to the passive tamarin's side, the experimenter pushed the tool on 100% of the trials, thus mimicking the payoff structure for the nice stooge in Experiment 1.

criticisms immediately arise. First, identifying cooperators requires an ability to recognize the partner's motivations—do they incur a cost in order to cooperate (altruism) or do they only cooperate when they also benefit (mutualism)? Experiments 2 and 3 explored this possibility. Second, subjects may pull more when they themselves receive food, and this situation arises most when playing against the nice confederate who always delivers food. In other words, the higher rates of pulling when paired with the nice confederate might be simply a reflection of the higher rates of reinforcement, a situation that could just as easily be achieved by a machine delivering food. Experiment 4 attempted to test this alternative account.

Summarizing across all three experiments, results show that tamarins are sensitive to the means by which food is delivered, cooperating more with those individuals who altruistically give food than those who deliver food as an accidental byproduct of an otherwise selfish behavior. Further, if a human delivers food on behalf of a tamarin, this payoff has no impact on the cooperative instincts of a partnered tamarin. These studies show that cooperation in tamarins depends on more than the patterns of reinforcement. A tamarin has to deliver the payoffs and has to do so on the basis of genuinely altruistic behavior.

Together, these studies suggest that tamarins are sensitive to some of the important proximal ingredients that enter into reciprocity, including altruistic contingency, reputation tracking, and distinguishing the means by which outcomes are obtained. That said, when one explores the longer-term pattern of cooperation observed in these experiments together with studies of a wide variety of other species, it is clear that tamarins are incapable of sustaining reciprocity because even a rather brief period of defection causes the cooperative relationship to unravel. In particular, based on a game theoretic analysis of the tamarin results from the nonstooge games, it is clear that after two consecutive rounds of defection, tamarins stop pulling in the altruistic condition and never recover the reciprocally cooperative relationship

altruistic act. Here, subjects pulled significantly more often when paired with the nice stooge than with the mean stooge. This suggests that tamarins can distinguish recipients based on their cooperative tendencies and that they respond contingently. However, two

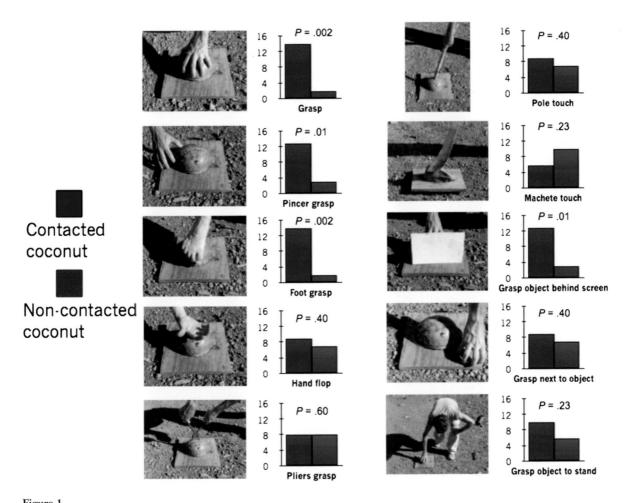

Figure 1

Illustration of the final frame of the actions presented to rhesus monkeys in the two-option forced-choice social foraging method, along with the corresponding results showing the number of subjects that selectively inspected the coconut shell that the experimenter acted toward versus the coconut shell that the experimenter did not act toward. Data reported in Wood et al. (2008).

(Chen & Hauser 2005). Thus, although tamarins may have some of the cognitive prerequisites for reciprocity, these capacities appear insufficient to sustain reciprocity. Moreover, the reciprocity observed among tamarins only emerges under fairly artificial conditions, including the presentation of discrete packages of food, highly predictable periods of interaction, and with individuals trained to be pure cooperators or defectors.

The most recent entry into the literature on reciprocity in animals comes from an elegant study of chimpanzees by Melis et al. (2008). One reason for its elegance comes from the fact that the design was based on an extensive set of prior and highly relevant experimental findings. Owing to both their natural tendencies to cooperate under a variety of circumstances and their demonstrated skills in captivity, chimpanzees have all of the apparent prerequisites to support reciprocal relationships. Specifically, chimpanzees engage in coalitionary attacks on neighboring communities when there is a significant imbalance of power, usually in the ratio of three to one, use within-community coalitions of two to three individuals (kin and nonkin; Langergraber et al. 2007) to overtake a single dominant, and coordinate individual movement and positioning while hunting for prey and sharing food (Gilby 2006, Muller & Mitani 2005). Chimpanzees show clear evidence of individual recognition (Parr 2003), live in relatively stable communities that enable opportunities for repeated social interactions, have the capacity for numerical quantification (Beran et al. 2008, Boysen et al. 1996, Kawai & Matsuzawa 2000) and the ability to delay gratification beyond that of most other animals and in some cases, even humans (Evans & Beran 2007, Rosati et al. 2007), are sensitive to equitable distributions of resources (Brosnan et al. 2005, 2008), engage in prosocial tendencies in nonfood contexts (Warneken et al. 2007, Warneken & Tomasello 2006), discriminate intentional from accidental outcomes (Call et al. 2004), and use prior reputation to enlist the most likely collaborators in a task requiring joint action (Melis et al. 2006). Together, these capacities provide the essential ingredients to initiate and sustain reciprocity.

In their experiment, Melis and colleagues (2008) asked whether chimpanzees would preferentially choose to reciprocate an altruistic action toward a previously nice and cooperative stooge over a previously mean and uncooperative stooge. As mentioned above, previous work had already demonstrated that chimpanzees recruit collaborators in a joint action task (i.e., two subjects must work together to obtain a reward; defection by one eliminates the opportunity for either to obtain food) and preferentially select the most collaborative collaborator (Melis et al. 2006). In Experiment 1, subjects first learned that the nice stooge always provided them with access to a rope that, when jointly pulled, provided access to food, whereas the mean stooge never provided access. Once they learned these action contingencies, subjects were then given an opportunity to allow either the nice or mean stooge to join them at the pulling tray. In the first block of trials, 12.5% picked the nice stooge, 62.5% picked the mean stooge, and 25% were indifferent. In the second block of trials, 37.5% picked the nice stooge (only one subject with a strong preference), 37.5% picked the mean stooge, and 25% were indifferent. Although there was a slight increase in the preference for the nice stooge over the baseline period, this effect was only just significant at the $p < 0.05$ level and with a 1-tailed test. Thus, based on analyses of individual preferences, there was, at best, only weak evidence of reciprocity.

In Experiment 2, the nice stooge altruistically opened the door for the subject to get food, whereas the mean stooge opened the door to selfishly get food for himself. Would the chimpanzees assess their partner's prior reputation and use this information to give the nice stooge more frequent access to the pulling tray when compared to the mean stooge? Pooling across individuals, there was no evidence that subjects opened the door more often for the nice than the mean stooge. On an individual level, only 12.5% showed a significant difference between stooges in the predicted direction, opening the door on every trial for the nice stooge and never for the mean stooge. In summary, and as the authors note, this study provides only weak evidence of reciprocity in chimpanzees.

Although chimpanzees appear to have the cognitive prerequisites to support reciprocal altruism, ultimately, their ability to engage in reciprocity appears to be no better than that of the many other animals that have been tested in either natural conditions or captivity (Hammerstein 2003, Stevens & Hauser 2004). Our suggestion is that although chimpanzees have the capacity to delay gratification, quantify potential payoffs, detect inequities, and punish individuals for norm violations, these ingredients do not combine to create a system for reciprocity. In contrast, from a very young age, human children endowed with similar capacities are able to integrate these into one system that ultimately enables them to develop and sustain reciprocal relationships (Fehr & Fischbacher 2005, Tomasello et al. 2005, Trivers 1971). This integration of different systems is, we believe, one of the distinguishing features of human cognition (see below; Hauser 2009, Rozin 2000).

CONCLUSIONS

The primary goal of this review is to place the study of action comprehension into a broad comparative context and, specifically, to frame the problem in terms of two competing hypotheses that attempt to explain how we and other organisms come to understand the meaning of actions. On the simulation hypothesis, including its neurophysiologically instantiated sister, the direct-matching hypothesis, action comprehension operates by means of personal simulation, with an explicit and necessary recruitment of motor representations. On the alternative, teleological hypothesis, action comprehension operates by drawing inferences from goals, action means, and the environmental constraints that limit rational action. Although the teleological stance doesn't rule out the possibility that motor systems are involved in action comprehension, they are not necessary.

Our contribution to this work, reviewed here, has been to situate previously published and ongoing studies of nonhuman animal behavior within this rich psychological, neurobiological, and philosophical framework. In particular, we showed that in several studies of nonhuman primates, including studies of macaques (the genus targeted for the original mirror neuron studies), individuals were sensitive to the details of an action vis-à-vis a target goal, both when that goal was explicitly presented (e.g., showing a piece of food disappear into a box) and implicitly inferred (e.g., following a communicative gesture to a box). Many of these behavioral studies show sensitivities that parallel the activation patterns of mirror neurons, which have been characterized in studies carried out by Rizzolatti and his colleagues over the past decade. For example, whereas mirror neurons activate to a pincer grip targeting a piece of food, the same neurons fail to respond when a hand grasps a pair of pliers and uses the pliers—in a pincer grip form—to target a piece of food. Similarly, whereas free-ranging rhesus monkeys selectively approach a coconut shell that is grasped with a pincer grip, they approach the two coconut shells at chance levels when one shell is grasped with a pair of pliers.

Several studies of primate behavior are, however, inconsistent with the simulation theory and more directly consistent with the teleological stance. Thus, studies of apes, monkeys, and dogs indicate that individuals draw inferences about goals based on environmental constraints that dictate considerations of rational as opposed to irrational behavior. Thus, although pointing with an elbow is not within the repertoire of any nonhuman primate, if a human elbow contacts a target box while the actor concurrently holds a board with the acting hand, then this gesture is perceived as a communicative action with a particular goal; the same elbow point is not so perceived when the acting hand is free and, presumably, could be used to point or grasp the target box. Thus, the same action is interpreted differently depending on context. Stronger evidence against the simulation account comes from the study of throwing. Although rhesus monkeys don't throw and lack the musculature to throw, they analyze in great detail the kinematics of human throwing, showing sensitivity to the position of the arm at the starting point, its trajectory to a termination point, the position of the head and eyes, and the item thrown. With this information, they are able to predict the most probable outcome of a throwing gesture, deciding when to flee versus when to approach. The simulation account, or the direct-matching hypothesis more specifically, cannot explain this finding. These data are, however, highly consistent with the teleological account of action comprehension.

In the final set of studies that we reviewed, we attempted to link the broad topic of action comprehension to the more narrow topic of socially relevant actions and, in particular, actions that may form the substrate for our evolved moral sense. In particular, we argued that in order for a moral system to get off the ground, it must minimally distinguish between means and outcomes, such as the distinction between intended and accidental outcomes (e.g., punching someone has significant moral consequences, whereas accidentally tripping someone does not). In several studies of monkeys and apes, there is evidence that individuals use aspects of an agent's intentions and goals to evaluate the nature of the outcome. Thus, even though chimpanzees may never obtain food from an experimenter holding the food, they show greater signs of frustration when the experimenter teases the individual than when the experimenter is clumsy or unable to provide food. Further, tamarins are more likely to reciprocate with individuals who altruistically provide food than with individuals who deliver food as a byproduct of otherwise selfish behavior.

Much of this work is in its infancy. What we find exciting is that for the first time, studies of action comprehension entail all four of what Tinbergen (1963) described as the essential causal questions to account for a behavior. That is, we are beginning to understand how action comprehension evolved (issues of phylogeny), its adaptive significance (how it contributes to survival and reproductive success), how it develops within individuals, and its underlying neural mechanisms in both humans and nonhuman animals. Many questions remain. For example, although phylogenetic considerations make it clear that humans must have a mirroring system given the neurophysiological data from macaques, the imaging work makes it difficult to establish given the spatial resolution of this technique. For example, although several studies show that areas activated for the perception of action are also activated for the production of the same action (Rizzolatti et al. 2001a), it is possible that these areas consist of discrete populations, some proportion of cells firing in response to perception and a different proportion firing to production. On a functional level, problems also arise. Thus, even if the computational function of mirror neurons in macaques and humans is the same, their role in cognition is clearly different. Thus, the human mirror neuron system appears to play some role in imitation and in the comprehension of disgust. But monkeys don't imitate and do not show a facial expression analogous to disgust. Furthermore, some have argued that mirror neurons play a role in language (Rizzolatti & Arbib 1998), and yet, monkeys clearly don't have language. Thus, we are faced with a situation where mirror neurons may have evolved for some function, and then over evolutionary time and with neural reorganization, may have been co-opted in human brains for a variety of novel cognitive functions. This possibility seems to be generally true of the human brain, with its massive capacity to link cognitive representations across domains and recruit a number of domain-general generative mechanisms to support a finite but highly variable range of potential representations (Hauser 2009).

DISCLOSURE STATEMENT

The authors are not aware of any biases that might be perceived as affecting the objectivity of this review.

LITERATURE CITED

Barsalou LW, Simmons WK, Barbey AK, Wilson CD. 2003. Grounding conceptual knowledge in modality-specific systems. *Trends Cogn. Sci.* 7:84–92

Beran M, Evans T, Harris E. 2008. When in doubt, chimpanzees rely on estimates of past reward amounts. *Proc. R. Soc. London B: Biol. Sci.* 276:309–14

Boysen ST, Berntson GG, Hannan MB, Cacioppo JT. 1996. Quantity-based inference and symbolic representations in chimpanzees (*Pan troglodytes*). *J. Exp. Psychol.: Anim. Behav. Process.* 22:76–86

Brass M, Schmitt RM, Spengler S, Gergeley G. 2007. Investigating action understanding: inferential processes versus action simulation. *Curr. Biol.* 17:2117–21

Brauer J, Call J, Tomasello M. 2006. Are apes really inequity averse? *Proc. R. Soc. London B: Biol. Sci.* 273:3123–28

Brosnan SF, de Waal FBM. 2003. Monkeys reject unequal pay. *Nature* 425:297–99

Brosnan SF, Grady M, Lambeth S, Schapiro S, Beran M, Zak P. 2008. Chimpanzee Autarky. *PLoS ONE* 3:e1518

Brosnan SF, Schiff HC, de Waal FBM. 2005. Tolerance for inequity may increase with social closeness in chimpanzees. *Proc. R. Soc. London B: Biol. Sci.* 272:253–58

Buttelmann D, Carpenter M, Call J, Tomasello M. 2007. Enculturated chimpanzees imitate rationally. *Dev. Sci.* 10:F31–38

Call J, Hare B, Carpenter M, Tomasello M. 2004. "Unwilling" versus "unable": chimpanzees' understanding of human intentional action. *Dev. Sci.* 7:488–98

Chen MK, Hauser M. 2005. Modeling reciprocation and cooperation in primates: evidence for a punishing strategy. *J. Theor. Biol.* 235:5–12

Csibra G. 2007. Action mirroring and action interpretation: an alternative account. In *Sensorimotor Foundations of Higher Cognition. Attention and Performance XXII*, ed. P Haggard, pp. 435–59. Oxford, UK: Oxford Univ. Press

Csibra G, Biro S, Koos O, Gergely G. 2003. One-year-old infants use teleological representations of actions productively. *Cogn. Sci.* 27:111–33

Csibra G, Gergely G. 1998. The teleological origins of mentalistic action explanation: a developmental hypothesis. *Dev. Sci.* 1:255–59

Csibra G, Gergely G, Biro S, Koos D, Brockbank M. 1999. Goal attribution without agency cues: the perception of "pure reason" in infancy. *Cognition* 72:237–67

Davidson D. 2001. *Essays on Actions and Events.* Oxford, UK: Oxford Univ. Press

di Pellegrino G, Fadiga L, Fogassi L, Gallese V, Rizzolatti G. 1992. Understanding motor events: a neurophysiological study. *Exp. Brain Res.* 91:176–80

Dubreuil D, Gentile MS, Visalberghi E. 2006. Are capuchin monkeys (*Cebus apella*) inequity averse? *Proc. R. Soc. London B: Biol. Sci.* 273:1223–28

Evans T, Beran M. 2007. Chimpanzees use self-distraction to cope with impulsivity. *Biol. Lett.* 3:599–602

Fehr E, Fischbacher U. 2005. The economics of strong reciprocity. In *Moral Sentiments and Material Interests*, ed. H Gintis, S Bowles, RT Boyd, E Fehr, pp. 151–92. Cambridge, MA: MIT Press

Fogassi L. 2005. Parietal lobe: from action organization to intention understanding. *Science* 308:662–67

Gallese V, Fadiga L, Fogassi L, Rizzolatti G. 1996. Action recognition in the premotor cortex. *Brain* 119:593–609

Gallese V, Goldman A. 1998. Mirror neurons and the simulation theory of mind-reading. *Trends Cogn. Sci.* 2:493–501

Gallese V, Keysers C, Rizzolatti G. 2004. A unifying view of the basis of social cognition. *Trends Cogn. Sci.* 8:398–403

Gergely G, Bekkering H, Kiraly I. 2002. Rational imitation in preverbal infants. *Nature* 415:755

Gergely G, Csibra G. 2003. Teleological reasoning in infancy: the naive theory of rational action. *Trends Cogn. Sci.* 7:287–92

Gergely G, Nadasdy Z, Csibra G, Biro S. 1995. Taking the intentional stance at 12 months of age. *Cognition* 56:165–93

Gilby IC. 2006. Meat sharing among the Gombe chimpanzees: harassment and reciprocal exchange. *Anim. Behav.* 71:953–63

Hammerstein P. 2003. Why is reciprocity so rare in social animals? A protestant appeal. In *Genetic and Cultural Evolution of Cooperation*, ed. P Hammerstein, pp. 83–94. Cambridge, MA: MIT Press

Hare B, Call J, Agnetta B, Tomasello M. 2000. Chimpanzees know what conspecifics do and do not see. *Anim. Behav.* 59:771–85

Hart HLA, Honore T. 1985. *Causation in the Law*. Oxford, UK: Oxford Univ. Press

Hauser M. 2006. *Moral Minds*. New York: Ecco/Harper Collins

Hauser M, Spaulding B. 2006. Wild rhesus monkeys generate causal inferences about possible and impossible physical transformations in the absence of experience. *Proc. Natl. Acad. Sci. USA* 103:7181–85

Hauser M, Spelke ES. 2004. Evolutionary and developmental foundations of human knowledge: a case study of mathematics. In *The Cognitive Neurosciences, Vol. 3*, ed. M Gazzaniga, pp. 325–41. Cambridge, MA: MIT Press

Hauser M, Wood JN, Glynn DD. 2007. Wild, untrained and nonenculturated rhesus monkeys correctly read the goal-relevant gestures of a human agent. *Proc. R. Soc. London B: Biol. Sci.* 274:1913–18

Hauser MD. 2009. The possibility of impossible cultures. *Nature* 460:190–96

Hauser MD, Chen MK, Chen F, Chuang E. 2003. Give unto others: genetically unrelated cotton-top tamarin monkeys preferentially give food to those who altruistically give food back. *Proc. R. Soc. London B: Biol. Sci.* 270:2363–70

Kawai N, Matsuzawa T. 2000. Numerical memory span in a chimpanzee. *Nature* 403:39–40

Kirsh D. 1991. *Foundations of Artificial Intelligence*. Cambridge, MA: MIT Press

Lakoff G, Johnson M. 1999. *Philosophy in the Flesh: The Embodied Mind and Its Challenge to Western Thought*. New York: Basic Books

Langergraber KE, Mitani JC, Vigilant L. 2007. The limited impact of kinship on cooperation in wild chimpanzees. *Proc. Natl. Acad. Sci. USA* 104:7786–90

Mahon BZ, Caramazza A. 2008. A critical look at the embodied cognition hypothesis and a new proposal for grounding conceptual content. *J. Physiol.* 102:59–70

Melis AP, Hare B, Tomasello M. 2006. Chimpanzees recruit the best collaborators. *Science* 311:1297–300

Melis AP, Hare B, Tomasello M. 2008. Do chimpanzees reciprocate received favours? *Anim. Behav.* 76:951–62

Michotte A. 1962. *The Perception of Causality*. London: Methuen

Muller MN, Mitani JC. 2005. Conflict and cooperation in wild chimpanzees. *Adv. Stud. Behav.* 35:275–331

Parr LA. 2003. The discrimination of faces and their emotional content by chimpanzees (*Pan troglodytes*). *Ann. N. Y. Acad. Sci.* 1000:56–78

Pulvermuller F. 2005. Brain mechanisms linking language and action. *Nat. Rev. Neurosci.* 6:576–82

Range F, Horn LVZ, Huber L. 2009. Absence of reward induced aversion to inequity in dogs. *Proc. Natl. Acad. Sci. USA* 106:340–45

Range F, Viranyi Z, Huber L. 2007. Selective imitation in domestic dogs. *Curr. Biol.* 17:1–5

Rawls J. 1971. *A Theory of Justice*. Cambridge, MA: Harvard Univ. Press

Rizzolatti G, Arbib MA. 1998. Language within our grasp. *Trends Neurosci.* 21:188–94

Rizzolatti G, Fadiga L, Fogassi L, Gallese V. 1999. Resonance behaviors and mirror neurons. *Arch. Ital. Biol.* 137

Rizzolatti G, Fadiga L, Gallese V, Fogassi L. 1996. Premotor cortex and the recognition of motor actions. *Cogn. Brain Res.* 3:131–41

Rizzolatti G, Fogassi L, Gallese V. 2001. Neurophysiological mechanisms underlying the understanding and imitation of action. *Nat. Rev. Neurosci.* 2:661–70

Rochat M, Serra E, Fadiga L, Gallese V. 2008. The evolution of social cognition: goal familiarity shapes monkeys' action understanding. *Curr. Biol.* 18:227–32

Roma PG, Silberberg A, Ruggiero AM, Suomi SJ. 2006a. Capuchin monkeys, inequity aversion, and the frustration effect. *J. Comp. Psychol.* 120:67–73

Roma PG, Silberberg A, Ruggiero AM, Suomi SJ. 2006b. On inequity aversion in nonhuman primates. *J. Comp. Psychol.* 120:76

Rosati A, Stevens J, Hare B, Hauser M. 2007. The evolutionary origins of human patience: temporal preferences in chimpanzees, bonobos, and human adults. *Curr. Biol.* 17:1663–68

Rozin P. 2000. Evolution and adaptation in the understanding of behavior, culture, and mind. *Am. Behav. Sci.* 43(6):970–86

Santos LR, Miller CT, Hauser M. 2003. Representing tools: how two nonhuman primate species distinguish between the functionally relevant and irrelevant features of tools. *Anim. Cogn.* 6:269–81

Sommerville JA, Woodward AL. 2005. Pulling out the intentional structure of human action: the relation between action production and processing in infancy. *Cognition* 95:1–30

Sommerville JA, Woodward AL, Needham A. 2005. Action experience alters 3-month-old infants' perception of others' actions. *Cognition* 96:B1–11

Stevens JR, Hauser MD. 2004. Why be nice? Psychological constraints on the evolution of cooperation. *Trends Cogn. Sci.* 8:60–65

Tinbergen N. 1963. On aims and methods in ethology. *Zeitschrift fur Tierpsychologie* 20:410–33

Tomasello M, Carpenter M, Call J, Behne T, Moll H. 2005. Understanding and sharing intentions: the origins of cultural cognition. *Behav. Brain Sci.* 28:1–17

Trivers RL. 1971. The evolution of reciprocal altruism. *Q. Rev. Biol.* 46:35–57

Umilta MA, Kohler E, Gallese V, Fogassi L, Fadiga L, et al. 2001. I know what you are doing: a neurophysiological study. *Neuron* 31:155–65

van Wolkenten M, Brosnan SF, de Waal FBM. 2007. Inequity responses of monkeys modified by effort. *Proc. Natl. Acad. Sci. USA* 47:18854–59

Warneken F, Hare B, Melis A, Hanus D, Tomasello M. 2007. Spontaneous altruism by chimpanzees and young children. *PLoS Biol.* 5:5–10

Warneken F, Tomasello M. 2006. Altruistic helping in human infants and young chimpanzees. *Science* 311:1301–3

Wheatley T, Milleville SC, Martin A. 2007. Understanding animate agents: distinct roles for the social network and mirror system. *Psychol. Sci.* 18:469–74

Wood JN, Hauser MD. 2008. Action comprehension in nonhuman primates: motor simulation or inferential reasoning? *Trends Cogn. Sci.* 12:461–65

Wood JN, Glynn DD, Hauser MD. 2007a. The uniquely human capacity to throw evolved from a nonthrowing primate: an evolutionary dissociation between action and perception. *Biol. Lett.* 3:360–64

Wood JN, Glynn DD, Phillips BC, Hauser MD. 2007b. The perception of rational, goal-directed action in nonhuman primates. *Science* 317:1402–5

Wood JN, Hauser M, Glynn DD. 2008. Rhesus monkeys' understanding of actions and goals. *Soc. Neurosci.* 3:60–68

Woodward AL. 1998. Infants selectively encode the goal object of an actor's reach. *Cognition* 69:1–34

Woodward AL. 1999. Infants' ability to distinguish between purposeful and nonpurposeful behaviors. *Infant Behav. Dev.* 17:515–21

Wynne CDL. 2004. Fair refusal by capuchin monkeys. *Nature* 428:140

Child Maltreatment and Memory

Gail S. Goodman,[1] Jodi A. Quas,[2]
and Christin M. Ogle[1]

[1]Department of Psychology, University of California, Davis, California 95616;
email: ggoodman@ucdavis.edu, cmogle@ucdavis.edu

[2]Department of Psychology and Social Behavior, University of California, Irvine,
California 92697; email: jquas@uci.edu

Annu. Rev. Psychol. 2009. 61:325–51

First published online as a Review in Advance on
September 30, 2009

The *Annual Review of Psychology* is online at
psych.annualreviews.org

This article's doi:
10.1146/annurev.psych.093008.100403

0066-4308/09/0110-0325$20.00

Key Words

memory development, emotion regulation, trauma, autobiographical
memory, eyewitness memory, child sexual abuse

Abstract

Exposure to childhood trauma, especially child maltreatment, has important implications for memory of emotionally distressing experiences. These implications stem from cognitive, socio-emotional, mental health, and neurobiological consequences of maltreatment and can be at least partially explained by current theories concerning the effects of childhood trauma. In this review, two main hypotheses are advanced: (*a*) Maltreatment in childhood is associated with especially robust memory for emotionally distressing material in many individuals, but (*b*) maltreatment can impair memory for such material in individuals who defensively avoid it. Support for these hypotheses comes from research on child abuse victims' memory and suggestibility regarding distressing but nonabusive events, memory for child abuse itself, and autobiographical memory. However, more direct investigations are needed to test precisely when and how childhood trauma affects memory for emotionally significant, distressing experiences. Legal implications and future directions are discussed.

Contents

CHILD MALTREATMENT AND MEMORY

Scientific studies of memory development have flourished in recent decades, resulting in important insights. Noteworthy examples include advances in the understanding of early explicit memory processes (Bauer 2004), the role of the sense of self and social reconstruction in early event memory formation (Howe & Courage 1997, Nelson & Fivush 2004), long-term memory for childhood experiences (Bauer 2006), children's eyewitness capabilities (Eisen et al. 2002), effects of emotion on children's memory (Howe et al. 2008, Quas & Fivush 2009), and neural mechanisms that underlie the development of various mnemonic processes (Paz-Alonso et al. 2008). Only recently, however, have these insights extended into the specific area of child maltreatment and memory. Given the important theoretical and practical implications of understanding how individuals exposed to child maltreatment remember and recount

Child maltreatment: Acts of commission or omission by a caregiver that result in physical, sexual, or psychological abuse, or neglect of a child. Such acts can result in alterations to normative development

DRM task: Deese-Roediger-McDermott task

prior experiences, particularly stressful ones, it seems prudent, in a single article, to review this emerging body of research.

Scientific research on maltreatment and event memory is still in its infancy, and conclusions are therefore tentative. Nevertheless, important trends are emerging. For example, short of abuse or neglect so severe as to result in brain insult or injury (including as a result of prenatal exposure to drugs; e.g., Streissguth 2007), there is so far little reason to believe that maltreatment per se is associated with deviations in basic memory processes (Beers & De Bellis 2002, Howe et al. 2006, Porter et al. 2005). Evidence for this tentative conclusion comes from Howe et al. (2004, 2009), who studied performance on Deese-Roediger-McDermott (DRM) false memory tasks (i.e., tasks in which semantically related words are presented, with one highly related item—the critical lure—omitted; memory for the words is later tested, and of particular interest are recall and recognition errors in which the never-presented critical lure is falsely remembered; Deese 1959, Roediger & McDermott 1995). Performance on the DRM false memory tasks of children with maltreatment histories did not differ from that of nonmaltreated controls. Porter et al. (2005) also reported no significant difference between child sexual abuse victims and a comparison group in memory performance on the Test of Memory and Learning (Reynolds & Bigler 1996), which includes subtests measuring verbal memory and delayed recall, although significant differences in performance on tasks related to attention and concentration were revealed.

Despite these indications that there are no general memory differences between maltreated and nonmaltreated children, the focus of the present review is on why maltreatment and associated traumatization may have important implications for memory, especially memory for traumatic or negative experiences, and on empirical findings concerning event memory in children and adults who suffered maltreatment in childhood. This review also touches on theoretical issues, methodological challenges, empirical findings, legal implications, and next steps in this line of inquiry.

CONCEPTUAL FRAMEWORK

One framework for thinking about maltreatment and memory, although merely heuristic, that may help to organize and interpret the relevant literature includes two dimensions along which studies can vary. The first dimension concerns the type of stimulus or to-be-remembered information, and the other concerns the life experiences and background of the participant in question. For simplicity, these dimensions can be represented by a 2 (type of stimulus) X 2 (childhood background) factorial classification scheme.

Considering first the type-of-stimulus dimension, in many studies, the stimulus is fairly neutral or even mildly positive (e.g., stories, brief interactions with an adult; Carter et al. 1996). But in other studies, the to-be-remembered information is distressing or trauma-related (e.g., stressful medical procedures, anogenital examinations; Merritt et al. 1994, Saywitz et al. 1991). This difference in stimulus type can have a profound effect on memory (Christianson 1992), regardless of the childhood history of the person under study.

The second dimension concerns study participants' backgrounds, that is, whether or not they experienced childhood trauma or have a history of maltreatment. In most memory studies, the participants do not have known histories of trauma or maltreatment. Yet, as reviewed here, traumatized individuals—for present purposes, those who have been exposed to child maltreatment—may remember at least some kinds of information with greater clarity than do untraumatized or nonmaltreated individuals.

This framework helps to eliminate confusion that can arise between, for example, the traumatic nature of the stimulus and the traumatic background of the participants. In some studies, the to-be-remembered information is so stressful that it can be described as "traumatic," but the participants may have no known maltreatment history (e.g., Goodman et al.

1997, Merritt et al. 1994). In other studies, the memories under examination may be for neutral or mildly positive information (e.g., interactions with adults), but the participants may have been maltreated during childhood (Goodman et al. 2001). With these two dimensions in mind, this review focuses mainly on the cell of the classification scheme in which the stimuli are stressful or trauma-related and the participants have been maltreated during childhood, although findings from studies falling in the other classification cells are mentioned when relevant.

MALTREATMENT: DEFINITIONS AND CONSEQUENCES

Before turning to theory and research on maltreatment and memory, it is useful to consider the acts that define child maltreatment and the consequences of such acts. This brief review lays the foundation for the argument that the experience of maltreatment can affect individuals' memory—or at least recounting—of stressful experiences.

Defining Maltreatment

Acts of physical abuse, sexual abuse, neglect, and/or psychological abuse, all of which are considered forms of maltreatment, constitute profound failures of caregivers to foster normal child development. Legally, definitions of maltreatment vary somewhat across states, with some jurisdictions considering exposure to domestic violence to be an additional form of child abuse. Victims of maltreatment are often deprived of experiences that are necessary for healthy adaptation according to theories of normal development (Cicchetti & Toth 2006). Fortunately, resilience and protective factors may buffer against the adverse effects (Masten et al. 2008). Still, children who have suffered maltreatment are at risk for problems across several domains of functioning, not only in childhood, but throughout life.

The prevalence of the different forms of maltreatment varies depending on how each is

Trauma: psychological injury resulting from an extraordinary stressful or life-threatening situation, accompanied by feelings of extreme helplessness and fear

defined and measured. Child neglect is generally considered to be the most frequent form of maltreatment to which children are exposed (Children's Bureau 2009), although many children experience more than one form (Rossman & Rosenberg 1998). The different forms may well have different implications for memory, a possibility not always examined directly by researchers. Instead, in some studies, researchers have collapsed the various forms of maltreatment into a single "maltreated" category. In other studies, researchers have focused exclusively on a single category, most often child sexual abuse.

The intense focus on child sexual abuse stems, in part, from legal applications of the research findings. Memory in child sexual abuse victims has been the topic of great controversy, in part because of the clinical construct of "repressed memory" and in part because of the many allegations of sexual abuse in daycare settings. Findings from studies of child abuse victims can have a major impact on legal cases, forensic interview practices, and social policy decisions, and this use of psychological research has further fueled the controversy. Often absent from discussions of these matters, however, is a scientific understanding of memory for distressing events in victims of childhood trauma. It is possible that child maltreatment and its emotional sequelae do not affect memory. Alternatively, maltreatment may have either beneficial or deleterious effects, or both, on remembering.

Consequences of Maltreatment

There is an impressive body of research concerning the potential effects of maltreatment on a wide range of cognitive, socio-emotional, and neuropsychological outcomes. It is not feasible to review this entire body of work here (see Cicchetti & Toth 2005, Myers et al. 2001), but several outcomes have important implications for memory and are especially worthy of consideration.

Regarding cognitive effects of maltreatment, some studies indicate developmental delays in maltreated children, especially those who have suffered physical abuse or neglect (see Veltman & Browne 2001 for review). Delays are at times evident across a range of cognitive processes, including intelligence, short-term memory, language, and executive function (Carrick et al. 2009, Cicchetti et al. 2003). In general, maltreated children perform at a level one to two years behind age-matched and demographically matched peers. However, delays in cognitive development and performance are not always found (e.g., Alessandri 1991, Trickett & McBride-Chang 1995), and the issue is still under debate (Ayoub et al. 2006).

To the extent that delays do exist, one straightforward implication is that maltreated children's performance on cognitive tasks, including memory measures, should be similar to the performance of younger nonmaltreated children rather than the performance of same-age nonmaltreated peers. Given the strong associations between children's age, on the one hand, and improved memory and reduced suggestibility (see Eisen et al. 2002 for review), on the other hand, relative deficits in the performance of maltreated children might be expected. As will be seen, however, the expectation is not always confirmed.

A second issue relevant to maltreated children is how well they understand and can adequately answer questions in a memory interview, given studies indicating language delays, on average, in maltreated children (e.g., Culp et al. 1991, Eigsti & Cicchetti 2004). More limited language abilities, in the areas of both production and comprehension, may reduce the coherence or amount of detail in children's descriptions of past events. Limited language abilities may also reduce children's ability to answer suggestive or potentially confusing legal questions (Saywitz et al. 1991, Zajac & Hayne 2003), a possibility confirmed in some (e.g., Carter et al. 1996) but not all of the relevant empirical studies of typically developing children. Negative associations between language skills and response accuracy may be more robust when there is greater variability in language ability, as is likely the case among maltreated children.

Cognitive delays could potentially affect maltreated children's memory performance regardless of the content of the to-be-remembered information. However, content does matter. If wide-ranging cognitive measures predicted memory function, maltreated children, with their generally more limited cognitive and linguistic abilities, should perform less well than nonmaltreated children on a variety of memory-related tasks, including those assessing autobiographical memory, event memory, and short-term working memory. However, as mentioned above and as discussed below, deficits in memory performance are not always found in maltreated samples. In fact, they sometimes exhibit memory advantages.

Maltreatment is more consistently associated with a host of socio-emotional consequences. For present purposes, one important socio-emotional outcome is the ability to regulate emotion, which includes the "extrinsic and intrinsic processes responsible for monitoring, evaluating, and modifying emotional reactions, especially their intensive and temporal features, to accomplish one's goals" (Thompson 1994, pp. 27–28). This can involve, for example, neurophysiological responses, attentional processes, interpretations, attributions, and coping behaviors. Compared to nonmaltreated children, maltreated youth are more affectively labile and negative in their reactions (suggesting poor emotion regulation), and they are less likely to engage in positive or appropriate emotion-regulation strategies (Shields & Cicchetti 1998). Both physically and sexually abused children, as well as neglected children, have difficulties in regulating emotions (e.g., Shipman & Zeman 2001, Toth et al. 2000).

Maltreatment is also associated with increased attentiveness to certain kinds of emotional information. For instance, on average, maltreated children recognize negative emotions (e.g., anger) and can label negative emotional expressions quickly (e.g., Camras et al. 1983, Masten et al. 2008, Pollak & Sinha 2002). At the same time, however, maltreated children have more difficulty disengaging from negative stimuli, regulating their responses,

and responding appropriately (Maughan & Cicchetti 2002). Maltreated children also tend to interpret ambiguous behavior as hostile (Dodge et al. 1995). All of these factors may lead to quick but prolonged stress responses and difficulty reducing arousal (Pollak et al. 1998). A similar type of vigilance is evident in traumatized adults who have a history of victimization, especially if they have symptoms of post-traumatic stress disorder (PTSD). These adults exhibit greater attention to and often better memory for trauma-related information—for example, on emotional Stroop and directed-forgetting tasks (McNally et al. 2000, Vrana et al. 1995). The implications of this vigilance are straightforward: Compared to children and adults who have not been exposed to maltreatment, children and adults formerly exposed to maltreatment should attend to negative emotional information more quickly and for longer durations, hence leading to better encoding and subsequently better memory for that information.

Nevertheless, there are likely to be individual differences in maltreated children's attentiveness to distressing information based on the emotion-regulation strategies they use to process upsetting (or potentially upsetting) experiences. Both coping research and attachment research have found that avoidant coping strategies are employed in a subset of individuals to limit the processing of distressing information (Lazarus & Folkman 1984, Mikulincer & Shaver 2008). Such limits on processing are likely to affect memory (Fraley et al. 2000) and thus may lead certain individuals to exhibit poorer memory for emotional information, at least in part as a result of more limited encoding.

Another socio-emotional consequence of maltreatment is maltreated individuals' perceptions of social relationships and their relative lack of trust in other people. In childhood, maltreated individuals hold more negative beliefs about others' (e.g., caregivers') responsiveness following an emotion-eliciting event, and they often believe that other people will be unsupportive or coercive (Macfie et al. 1999, Shipman & Zeman 2001). Such beliefs are perhaps not

Emotion regulation: the processes of monitoring, evaluating, and modifying emotional reactions to accomplish one's goals

Post-traumatic stress disorder (PTSD): a psychological condition that may develop following a life-threatening experience; symptoms include re-experiencing, hyperarousal, and avoidance of trauma cues

Attachment: mental representations developed in infancy of the caretaker-child relationship that guide emotion regulation and interpretation of others' behaviors and intentions

surprising given that maltreated children are more likely to have insecure attachments to caregivers (Crittenden 1988, Egeland & Sroufe 1981). Moreover, their attachment representations are often sustained over time: Relationship difficulties are evident in adolescents and adults with a childhood history of exposure to violence and maltreatment (e.g., Feerick et al. 2002, Scott et al. 2003).

One interesting implication of maltreated individuals' tendency to be insecurely attached and their often-biased beliefs about others concerns their reactions to stressful interview procedures, as sometimes used in forensic contexts. For instance, maltreated children's expectations that others will react unsupportively may reduce their willingness to disclose information in an interview, especially information that is troubling (Lyon et al. 2009). They may therefore need special reassurances and encouragement, as provided by a supportive, trained forensic interviewer. But the nature of this support and reassurance is important—for example, whether it indicates overall interviewer warmth (e.g., Carter et al. 1996, Quas & Lench 2007) or involves reassuring children about specific alleged event details, the latter of which may, at least in some children, increase inaccuracies (see Lyon et al. 2008).

Mental health problems and symptoms, especially trauma-related PTSD symptoms and dissociative states, are related to child maltreatment and may also affect memory. PTSD is one of the most common diagnoses assigned to traumatized children (Browne & Finkelhor 1986). Despite some disagreement about the extent and nature of experiences that cause PTSD (see McNally 2003), its symptomology includes re-experiencing traumas and emotional numbing, as well as more discrete symptoms (e.g., sleep disturbances, difficulty concentrating, exaggerated startle responses). Some of the symptoms (e.g., intrusive memories or flashbacks) may be characteristic of memory for traumatic events generally, aside from psychopathology (Rubin et al. 2008). Of interest is the degree to which already existing PTSD symptoms affect memory for new emotion-provoking stimuli, a topic

that has received considerable attention in the adult PTSD literature (McNally 2003). It has not been addressed as much in the developmental literature (but see Moradi et al. 2000), as discussed below in this review.

Regarding dissociation, the clinical understanding of this condition has been the subject of recent debates (Giesbrecht et al. 2008). Theoretically, a child engages in dissociation as a defense against painful experiences—that is, as a psychological method of removing oneself from a traumatic situation (Janet 1889). This kind of cognitive avoidance or emotion regulation is thought to protect the child from overwhelming stress (Carlson et al. 1997), which may be caused by maltreatment. And, by avoiding attending to an ongoing stressor, the child's encoding of and later memory for that event should be reduced. The "zoning out" response then may become an enduring coping strategy when faced with subsequent stressors (Koopman et al. 1994, Lynn & Rhue 1994) and, as a result, may reduce memory for other kinds of negative events but simultaneously may not have an effect on memory for neutral information or unemotional experiences. This possibility has not been adequately explored in samples of maltreated children, who should, in theory, have higher rates of dissociation than nonmaltreated children. But one should note an alternative perspective as well: It has recently been proposed that dissociation itself is largely an effect of suggestibility, fantasy proneness, and cognitive failures, possibly genetically based, which means that individuals who score high on measures of dissociation may falsely report trauma histories (Giesbrecht et al. 2008).

Finally, it is important to consider the emerging body of research on the effects of chronic stress on neuropsychological development, including regulation of the hypothalamic-pituitary-adrenal (HPA) axis. According to the glucocorticoid toxicity hypothesis, prolonged elevation of glucocorticoids, such as cortisol, following chronic stress (such as that involving exposure to maltreatment) leads to dysregulation of the HPA axis and eventually damages cortisone-receptor rich areas of the hippocampus (Sapolsky 1996). There is evidence linking the hippocampus to declarative memory, including declarative memory for emotional information, and evidence linking HPA axis activation to declarative memory for emotional information (McGaugh 2004). Although research often fails to directly examine whether HPA axis dysregulation affects memory for emotional information, adverse effects on neural structures implicated in encoding and consolidation of emotional information that result from HPA axis dysregulation certainly could manifest themselves in later differences in memory of that information (e.g., Carrion et al. 2007, Wiik & Gunnar 2009).

More generally, however, research on adult victims of maltreatment, often those diagnosed as having PTSD, supports the glucocorticoid toxicity hypothesis (e.g., Bremner & Narayan 1998, Stein et al. 1997). Bremner & Narayan (1998) for example, reported that women diagnosed with PTSD and having a childhood history of maltreatment had significantly smaller left-side hippocampal volumes. Similar findings were reported by Vythilingam et al. (2002), who found reduced hippocampal volume in depressed women with a history of childhood abuse. Related studies of children are more equivocal, however. Although one study found a significant association between PTSD symptoms and reduced hippocampal volume in children (Carrion et al. 2007), most studies have failed to find such associations in children with abuse histories (De Bellis et al. 2002, Woon & Hedges 2008). Although preliminary, some studies suggest that the effects of previous child abuse on brain structure in adulthood may vary depending on whether the child abuse occurred during times of rapid neural development or especially high plasticity (Andersen et al. 2008). Finally, it is possible that the effects of maltreatment on hippocampal volume and functioning vary not only depending on age of exposure, but also on the stage of adulthood in which the effects are measured, because the long-term effects of childhood abuse may intensify with age (Golier et al. 2002).

In addition to studies specifically investigating links between HPA axis regulation and neural functioning following maltreatment, other studies have examined links between trauma exposure in children and perturbations in other cortical regions (e.g., the prefrontal cortex) and subcortical structures (e.g., De Bellis et al. 2002) that affect cognitive functioning across numerous domains (e.g., executive control, working memory, attention, emotion regulation). These studies suggest that the links between maltreatment and neural structures depend on the presence of psychopathology and, again, the age of the individuals being studied (De Bellis et al. 2002, Richert et al. 2006; but see Gilbertson et al. 2002).In general, then, cortisol studies and neuroscience evidence suggest adverse effects of traumatization following child maltreatment on HPA axis regulation and also possibly on neural regions heavily implicated in cognitive and mnemonic processes. Moreover, there are hints that these effects vary with age and may actually be stronger in adulthood than in childhood among individuals with a history of maltreatment. Finally, evidence from adults indicates that effects must be considered in conjunction with psychopathology, specifically PTSD. Continued research, including longitudinal studies, is clearly needed to directly relate biological measures to emotional memory in maltreated individuals.

Summary

Maltreatment places individuals at risk for a variety of adverse outcomes, many of which have implications for children's and adults' memories. Although one class of potential consequences of maltreatment, cognitive delays, could produce general deficits in maltreated children's mnemonic capabilities, or at least their reporting of events, regardless of the type of memory task involved, the findings to date have provided little support for this possibility. Socio-emotional and mental health consequences of maltreatment may affect attentional focus and the emotion-regulation strategies employed to cope with stressors, sometimes enhancing memory and sometimes interfering with it. Certain mental health problems (e.g., PTSD), which in conjunction with maltreatment appear to be linked to changes in neural structures (e.g., frontal lobe integrity, hippocampal volume), may be involved in attention, encoding, and consolidation of memory. At present, research linking maltreatment, psychopathology, and neuropsychological functioning is still in its infancy, and much remains to be known about how development, severity of maltreatment, and a host of other factors, operating directly and in conjunction with psychopathology, affect brain functioning over time, and how all of these factors relate to memory.

THEORETICAL ISSUES

Numerous theoretical issues arise when one studies child maltreatment and memory. The current focus is on theoretical ideas concerning (*a*) child maltreatment victims' possible overfocus on trauma cues, which can enhance memory, and (*b*) repression or other defensive emotion-regulation processes aimed at suppressing or avoiding disturbing memories. Theoretical issues related to memory monitoring and memory error are also considered.

Much of the theory brought to bear on the domain of trauma and memory is geared to memory in nonabused adults who encounter traumatic stimuli or events. Although debate continues, Christianson (1992) proposed that during traumatic events, attention becomes focused on the main stressor, which is then remembered particularly well. This appears now to be an empirically supported rule, at least in general: The more traumatic the event, the better its core features are remembered. Neuroscience research confirms that amygdala activation in emotional situations predicts heightened memory for negative information and events (McGaugh 2004, Phelps 2006).

However, studies leading to this conclusion have generally involved one-time laboratory exposure to distressing stimuli, such as a photograph of a disfigured face, viewed by college students (e.g., Christianson & Nilsson 1984). What if a person is chronically confronted with traumatic stimuli and events? And what if such exposure begins in childhood? Studies of normal college students are not likely to answer these questions definitively.

One possible result of chronic exposure to stressful events, perhaps especially when such exposure occurs in childhood, is that a person will come to focus on stressors and on cues associated with them (i.e., threat or trauma cues). This will then become a general personality trait or processing strategy. In the context of maltreatment, the process identified by Christianson (1992) may become habitual, especially when a person believes he or she is encountering trauma-related information. In this case, the individual may be hypervigilant to negative information, perhaps as part of a self-protective mechanism. Such a person is, in effect, in a chronic fear state, or at least can be more easily thrust into a state of fear than can a nontraumatized person.

This fear state may produce what Foa and her colleagues call "fear networks" (Foa et al. 1991, Foa & Rothbaum 1992). According to Foa, traumatized individuals (e.g., those with PTSD) develop fear networks, which are semantic/episodic mental structures that store trauma-related information. These structures guide both attention and memory. If a person has PTSD, these fear structures may be readily activated, resulting in intrusive memories, such as flashbacks. Consistent with the idea of fear networks, research indicates that traumatized adults overfocus on trauma cues and have difficulty ignoring trauma-related stimuli (e.g., McNally et al. 1998).

A person's knowledge base concerning trauma-related information likely expands as a result of traumatic experiences, and this knowledge could then lead to better memory for trauma-related information. However, in comparing people who have experienced the same kinds of traumatic events, only the more traumatized ones overfocus on trauma. Moreover, following successful therapy, the overfocusing disappears (e.g., McNally et al. 1990).

Thus, normal memory mechanisms associated with knowledge do not seem to account for certain individuals' trauma-related overfocus tendencies.

Instead, research suggests that more-traumatized individuals are most likely to remember their abuse experiences and remember them particularly well relative to less-traumatized individuals (Alexander et al. 2005). They should be least likely to forget the abuse and therefore unlikely to exhibit "repressed memory" or "lost and then recovered memory" of traumatic experiences such as child sexual abuse. There is still a possibility, however, that such individuals will overinterpret other events as being trauma-related or have memory-monitoring problems, which might result in memory errors (Bremner et al. 2000, Windmann & Krüger 1998).

Alternatively, it has been proposed by some researchers (e.g., Terr 1990, van der Kolk 1997) that "special memory mechanisms" such as repression and dissociation come into play, at least for a subset of individuals. These mechanisms are believed to result in lost memory of traumatic experiences, especially when the experiences are associated with self-blame, helplessness, or repeated trauma. Child sexual abuse is often characterized by feelings of self-blame and helplessness, and sexual abuse is often continued over time. Thus, repression or dissociation might be likely in cases of repeated child sexual abuse.

Repression is very difficult to prove, however, and dissociation during a traumatic event is difficult to study. As a result, many researchers and clinicians have challenged these notions. A better construct might be emotion regulation (Compas 1998, Lazarus & Folkman 1984, Thompson 1994), because measurable differences in emotion regulation may be associated with differences in memory (Richards & Gross 2006). There appears to be a subgroup of individuals who are motivated not to think about negative experiences and to employ defensive processes that dampen or inhibit trauma memories, which include trying not to think about the trauma, not talking about it with other

people, and not rehearsing the information. It is not clear whether such avoidant strategies result in "lost" memory, but it is likely that they can weaken memories of traumatic events, and perhaps this amounts to lost memory in some cases.

Emotion-regulation strategies play a key role in theories about overgeneral memory (Williams & Broadbent 1986). Adolescents and adults who have overly general memories recount their memories in broad, general terms without reference to time and place (e.g., "I used to go to my friend's house" as opposed to "I remember that one Friday after school, I went to my friend's house to do homework together. We ended up playing music instead."). Williams (1996) proposed that individuals who suffer repeated childhood traumas have difficulty advancing beyond the level of general memory retrieval that is characteristic of young children (Nelson & Fivush 2004). The motivation for developing overly general memories, according to Williams & Broadbent (1986) and Williams and colleagues (2007), is that children who have suffered negative childhood events retrieve information in generic form as a means of controlling negative affect. That is, traumatized children are hypothesized to learn a defensive style (functional avoidance) for coping with negative memories. When memories of traumatic events are triggered, often automatically, they may be accompanied by strong negative affect, which activates executive control processes to truncate retrieval and thus dampen recall of specific, episodic memory (Dalgleish et al. 2007, Williams et al. 2007).

Although in the short term, functional avoidance may be adaptive, in the long run it is associated with maladjustment (e.g., depression). Williams (1996) also hypothesized that over time, functional avoidance affects what is encoded; new events are encoded in a more-schematic or less-detailed form. Although one difficulty with Williams's model is distinguishing among several possible explanations for overly general memory, such as automatic avoidance or unwillingness to discuss painful experiences, the model has generated

Overgeneral memory: tendency to recall events in broad, general terms without reference to time and place when asked to provide specific incidents

Functional avoidance: a defensive coping strategy whereby memory retrieval is truncated at a generic level to avoid negative affect associated with memories

useful research and discussion (e.g., Brewin 2007). Avoidance is likely to be an important emotion-regulation strategy with implications for memory (Dalgleish et al. 2008).

Windmann & Krüger (1998) proposed a different theory, one that focuses on commission errors on memory tasks. These authors proposed, first, that humans are generally predisposed to overattend to traumatic material because the amygdala is adapted to respond to such information for the sake of survival; but, second, that traumatized individuals overinterpret neutral stimuli as trauma related, resulting in commission errors. Consistent with this proposal, Pollak et al. (2000) found that child physical-abuse victims exhibited a liberal response bias when perceiving facial expressions of possible anger (but see Pollak & Sinha 2002). For adults with self-reported maltreatment histories, more commission errors are found on DRM false memory tasks, indicating less-rigorous memory monitoring (Bremner et al. 2000, Zoellner et al. 2000). From the perspective of attachment theory (Bowlby 1980), insecure attachment, which is common in maltreated samples of children and adults, may lead to greater suggestibility and compliance (Chae et al. 2009).

In general, there are probably situations in which child maltreatment or traumatization increases the likelihood of misinterpretations and memory errors. However, it seems, based on empirical findings (e.g., Alexander et al. 2005), that trauma victims often remember trauma-related material particularly well, without an increased rate of commission errors. The differences in outcome—bias or accuracy—are probably related to emotion-regulation strategies.

In the developmental literature, there has been relatively little theorizing about maltreated children's memory. Common theoretical questions about nonmaltreated children's memory—for example, what are the effects of stress on children's memory and suggestibility; do children have greater source- or memory-monitoring problems than adults; are children's memory reports more easily influenced by social factors?—have rarely been discussed in relation to maltreated children. Developmental theories regarding source monitoring, gist versus verbatim processing, trace disintegration, and theory of mind have been infrequently used to explain the effects of maltreatment (e.g., see Courage & Cowan 2008 for review). Moreover, theories concerning PTSD and repression have centered mainly on adults who, at least eventually, remember childhood victimization.

One theoretical account that provides an overarching framework for considering maltreatment and memory development was recently proposed by Ayoub et al. (2006). Based on Fischer's (1980) dynamic skill theory, a general theory of cognitive development, Ayoub et al. (2006) proposed that maltreated children may have deficits in some cognitive domains but also possess complex special skills related to their experiences, even when psychopathology is present. Such children are hypothesized to have more advanced skills than nonmaltreated children for dealing with negative information and negative contexts. This bias emerges around 4 years of age, possibly as a result of increases in general cognitive capabilities. If child abuse occurs before that age, a more generalized fear response is hypothesized to develop, causing information broadly to be viewed as possibly threatening. However, especially if maltreatment recurs, as it often does, traumatogenic responses, such as fragmentation of thoughts and feelings (an emotion-regulation strategy for controlling anxieties and fears), can become habitual, resulting in greater dissociation and less integration and coordination of memories (Ayoub et al. 2006).

This theory has the advantage of explaining unevenness in the cognitive development of maltreated children (e.g., sometimes evincing deficits, sometimes not; Carrick et al. 2009) and the interplay of emotion regulation and memory performance, all within a general developmental framework. The theory is consistent with the prediction that maltreated children will show a bias in memory for negative information depending on emotion-regulation strategies. However, given the idea that traumatogenic responses become more habitual with repeated experience, it is also possible to predict, based on the theory, that the effects of maltreatment on memory will emerge with greater clarity with age, including into adulthood, a derivation from the theory supported to some extent by the evidence reviewed above.

METHODOLOGICAL CONCERNS

In testing theoretical ideas about maltreatment and memory, one faces a number of methodological challenges. The extent to which studies have addressed these challenges affects not only the interpretation of results, but also the generalizability of findings. Here, several such challenges are described as examples of the complexities associated with conducting research on maltreatment and memory. The empirical studies discussed below should be considered in light of the methodological issues raised here.

First, it is important to distinguish between a history of maltreatment and past or current psychopathology. That is, one can have a history of childhood maltreatment but not have past or current disorders (e.g., PTSD) or symptoms. Indeed, some research designs include three groups: child sexual abuse victims with PTSD, child sexual abuse victims without PTSD, and nonabused controls with no PTSD. If the first group suffers in performance relative to the latter two, this would be attributed to the PTSD, not sexual abuse per se. Yet when these findings are reviewed, it is sometimes claimed that abuse was associated with the deficits. The problem is exacerbated in the case of studies in which one cannot readily distinguish maltreatment history from other forms of traumatization or psychopathology. In the studies discussed in this review, there is sometimes no way to differentiate between effects of child maltreatment and effects of psychopathology or traumatization.

Second, when a sample of people is labeled as maltreated, one must keep in mind that maltreatment experiences vary widely and may co-occur with other life stressors that affect memory (e.g., Johnson et al. 2005). For example, children enduring a single occurrence of sexual abuse (e.g., fondling) by a stranger but otherwise living in stable supportive families may react quite differently to their experiences than children who are under chronic stress and the threat of repeated assault (e.g., prolonged incest or repeated physical abuse) and are living in highly dysfunctional families in dangerous, crime-ridden neighborhoods. Also, children who suffer neglect (acts of omission rather than commission) may have different kinds of experiences than those who are actively abused, which then differentially affect cognitive and psychosocial functioning (Fries et al. 2008, Gunnar et al. 2001). Moreover, many children suffer from multiple forms of maltreatment (e.g., neglect and abuse). Operationalizing "child maltreatment" is not a straightforward matter, given the range of abuse experiences; the prevalence of multiple forms of maltreatment; and the effects of multiple stressors such as poverty, domestic violence, depression, residing in high-crime neighborhoods, and being exposed to substance use and abuse (Toth et al. 2009).

Third, because much of the research on maltreatment and memory, including the memories of adults who were victimized as children, has focused on the experience of sexual abuse, it is important to understand the difficulties that arise when operationalizing child sexual abuse. Unlike other forms of abuse, for which there is often hard evidence (e.g., bruises on the child), physical evidence is relatively rare in child sexual abuse cases (Adams et al. 1994, Heger et al. 2002), and allegations often rely on victims' reports, which may be contradicted by those of the accused party. Although many researchers believe that most reports of child sexual abuse are likely to be true (e.g., Lindsay & Read 1995), those researchers who study child sexual abuse and memory are justifiably concerned about the possibility of false reports. Despite these challenges, researchers often have to rely on alleged victims' retrospective reports if they wish to classify research participants as sexually abused or not. To the extent that misclassification occurs, overly conservative tests of hypotheses or distortion of findings may result.

Fourth, the age of first maltreatment and the chronicity of maltreatment may independently and jointly affect the level of traumatization and possibly the memories of maltreated individuals. For example, models of development and risk (e.g., Keiley et al. 2001) posit that traumas occurring earlier rather than later in childhood have particularly deleterious effects on psychological functioning. Also, as mentioned above, recurrent maltreatment may produce fundamental changes in the brain, particularly in regions involved in stress regulation. Chronic stress during periods of rapid neural growth, which are common in infancy and early childhood, may have different effects than similar stressful experiences in developmental periods not characterized by such growth. Whether and how these effects influence memory is not yet clear, but studies that fail to consider age, specifically age of abuse onset, may fail to detect important group differences.

Finally, when conducting research on child maltreatment, researchers obviously cannot randomly assign children to groups (e.g., abused versus nonabused). Consequently, considerable caution is needed when attempting to make causal inferences about the effects of child maltreatment on memory: There are many co-occurring and confounded variables to disentangle. Nevertheless, carefully designed studies have provided important insights into the possible effects of child maltreatment on children's memory development, and converging evidence allows several tentative conclusions to be drawn.

MALTREATMENT AND MEMORY: EMPIRICAL EVIDENCE

Given the potential adverse consequences of maltreatment on children's development, and the implications of these consequences for memory, it is not surprising that researchers have begun to examine mnemonic processes in individuals exposed to child maltreatment, even with the inevitable methodological challenges inherent in this kind of research. One line of inquiry has relied on the traditional eyewitness model to examine the accuracy of maltreated children's memory for documented prior experiences. In this model, children are exposed to an event and their memory and suggestibility are then tested as an analogue to children experiencing a crime and subsequently providing eyewitness testimony. A related but separate set of studies has investigated long-term memory in adults for documented child abuse, usually sexual abuse. A third set of studies has examined autobiographical memory in individuals exposed to maltreatment. In these latter studies, accuracy is of less concern than the extent, type, and detail of memories from childhood. These three areas of research are reviewed in the following sections.

Maltreatment, Memory, and Suggestibility in Children

Research on maltreated children's memory and suggestibility emerged as a natural extension of investigations of children's eyewitness capabilities. Given that results of studies of nonabused children's eyewitness memory were being applied to children involved in legal cases, it was important to investigate whether such findings really generalize to children who frequently come into contact with the legal system—in particular to victims of child maltreatment. It was especially important to determine how well maltreated children can remember emotionally distressing experiences and how well they can resist misleading suggestions. Fortunately, researchers have begun to address these issues.

In several studies, the accuracy of maltreated children's memory for a variety of events, including stressful ones, has been examined (e.g., Chae et al. 2006, Eisen et al. 2002, Goodman et al. 2001). To preview the results, which are described in detail below, maltreated children can remember prior experiences quite well, even those that were potentially stressful, although some of the common consequences of maltreatment do in fact differentially relate to these children's memory and suggestibility. Moreover, several predictors of memory accuracy in nonmaltreated children (e.g., age) operate similarly in maltreated children. Finally, children with maltreatment histories seem to remember trauma-related information particularly well, although those with stronger dissociative tendencies and more severe trauma symptoms, who often have more intense physiological reactions during stressful events (probably reflecting inadequate emotion-regulation strategies), make more memory errors than do other maltreated children.

For example, in an initial study that emerged from Eisen et al.'s (2002) program of research concerning maltreated children's memory, 3- to 16-year-olds were interviewed about details of an anogenital examination they had received a few days previously as part of a five-day inpatient abuse-assessment program. Their alleged maltreatment experiences varied widely and included physical and/or sexual abuse as well as neglect. Moreover, some children with no prior maltreatment histories were in the program due to suspicions of abuse or neglect that were then not substantiated, providing a nonabused control group. Because the anogenital examination was standardized and well documented, the accuracy of children's memory could be verified. Among the findings was, first, that typical age-patterns emerged: Older children provided more details and answered more specific questions accurately compared to younger children. Second, children rarely erred when asked abuse-related misleading questions (e.g., whether the doctor had undressed the child when in fact the doctor had not), as is often observed when nonmaltreated children are asked one-time abuse-related misleading questions (e.g., Rudy & Goodman 1991). Still, the younger maltreated children (e.g., 3-year-olds) were more susceptible to such errors. The relatively low error rates may reflect children's relatively greater resistance to suggestions involving unpleasant (e.g., embarrassing, taboo) rather than neutral or positive acts, a finding often observed in eyewitness studies with nonmaltreated children as well (Bruck & Ceci 1999, Saywitz et al. 1991, Schaaf et al. 2008; but see Otgaar et al. 2008).

Eisen and colleagues' study design enabled them to examine relations between children's memory and intellectual and mental health problems, which may have arisen following exposure to maltreatment. First, when age was statistically controlled, higher intelligence predicted better memory. Second, general psychopathology, as assessed with a measure of global functioning (higher scores reveal more problems), was positively associated with errors to misleading questions about the anogenital examination. Thus, poor adjustment was linked to suggestibility. However, few abuse-related differences in memory were found: In most respects, children with different forms of substantiated abuse performed comparably (e.g., sexual abuse victims compared with physical abuse victims) to the control children, who had no known history of child maltreatment.

Of special importance, in a second more refined but similar study of maltreated children undergoing forensic evaluations because of alleged abuse, Eisen and colleagues (2007) reported that children with sexual abuse histories were particularly accurate in answering questions about the anogenital examination. This finding may reflect a heightened focus on trauma-related information by children exposed to this form of maltreatment. Katz et al. (1995) had previously reported that children with substantiated child sexual abuse remembered an anogenital examination better than children whose claims of abuse were unsubstantiated. Thus, the basic findings have been confirmed in two independent studies.

Eisen and colleagues (2007) also found that greater dissociative tendencies and higher cortisol levels in children with more trauma symptoms were associated with increased memory error for an anogenital examination and a venipuncture, whereas cortisol level and trauma symptoms were not associated with increased error for children who reported fewer dissociative tendencies. In other words, dissociation predicted increased errors when it was coupled with other trauma symptoms and a large physiological response to the stressor. This may indicate greater memory error in traumatized children who are confronted with a highly stressful event and who use dissociation as an emotion-regulation strategy. Thus, when highly dissociative children with other trauma symptoms become distressed, their memory for stressful events may be impaired, supporting theoretical ideas about emotion regulation and memory (but see Howe et al. 2006).

It is also important to consider that some of the memory errors committed by maltreated children may be attributable to their reactions to interview contexts rather than to memory difficulties per se. As mentioned, maltreated children are at risk for socio-emotional problems. Such problems may influence the children's ability to answer questions in interviews, regardless of how well they actually remember a prior event. Maltreated children, for example, are often more likely than nonmaltreated children to be classified as having insecure attachment representations, and tend to have lower levels of trust in others (Crittenden 1988, Egeland & Sroufe 1981). Although associations between attachment and memory in maltreated children have not been directly examined, insecure attachment has been linked to greater stress responses during negative events (Edelstein et al. 2005, Goodman et al. 1997) and to poorer memory and increased suggestibility (Goodman et al. 1997; see also Alexander et al. 2002). The latter pattern has been observed most consistently when children are questioned about prior negative experiences, perhaps because discussing those experiences activates internal working models and attachment-related emotion-regulation strategies. Because maltreated children are at risk for insecure attachment representations and socio-emotional dysfunction, they may be especially sensitive to an interviewer's demeanor. Nonmaltreated children are often more accurate when questioned by a supportive rather than an emotionally neutral or distant interviewer (Carter et al. 1996, Quas & Lench, 2007), particularly when they are asked to recount a stressful event (Kellstrand et al. 2009). Accordingly, emotion regulation during a forensic interview may be especially important for maltreated children: Those who are nervous during interviews may benefit from supportive interviewers who in effect help the

children regulate their anxieties, insecurities, and emotions.

Adults' and Adolescents' Memory for Child Maltreatment

A controversial topic has been adults' memory for childhood abuse, particularly sexual abuse. Three issues have received considerable attention in research on eyewitness memory accuracy among adults who as children were maltreated. One issue is the degree to which adults can completely forget childhood traumas, such as child sexual abuse, by using a repressive coping strategy. A second issue concerns the accuracy of memory on the part of individuals who in fact remember their former abuse. A third issue is suggestibility and false reports about childhood maltreatment.

One problem with most studies relevant to these issues is that reports of child sexual abuse are retrospective. Thus, one has to rely on a person's memory to determine whether the abuse occurred and also to gauge the extent of the abuse. Because memory (or lack thereof) is the core issue under study, it is problematic to rely on self-reports of child sexual abuse as an independent variable. Instead, it is essential to conduct prospective research in which documented cases of child sexual abuse are followed up later.

Several influential prospective studies have examined whether adults remember documented sexual abuse from childhood (Goodman et al. 2003, Widom & Morris 1997, Williams 1994). Williams (1994), for instance, recontacted young women who, as children, had visited an emergency clinic because of alleged sexual abuse. When recontacted, these young adult women were interviewed about a variety of positive and negative events, including unwanted sexual contact in childhood. More than one-third of the women failed to disclose the documented sexual abuse from childhood, although many reported other sexual assault experiences. Williams thus concluded that a sizeable minority of women can completely forget child sexual abuse. Goodman et al. (2003) conducted a similarly designed study in which 174 young adults and older adolescents who had been involved as children in criminal cases because of sexual abuse were questioned about childhood victimization and legal experiences. Goodman et al. found a nondisclosure rate of approximately 16%. Individuals who were younger, lacked maternal support following discovery of the abuse, and had experienced less-severe abuse were less likely to disclose. Also, higher scores on a measure of current dissociative tendencies were associated with failure to disclose the abuse or with having forgotten it. To the extent that dissociation may indicate an avoidant coping strategy, this finding points again to emotion-regulation strategies affecting memory for distressing information. Together, the results of these studies suggest that, although most individuals can recall child sexual abuse, a small percentage cannot (although it is impossible to fully differentiate lack of willingness to disclose from actual forgetting).

Other studies have focused not on the question of whether individuals remember documented child sexual abuse but instead on the accuracy of memory among individuals who in fact remember abuse. Overall, memories of child maltreatment appear to be retained quite well over time, similar to findings suggesting that emotional events in general are retained much better over time than are mundane or nonemotional events (Alexander et al. 2005). Moreover, several possible consequences of abuse have been linked to later memory accuracy. Greenhoot and coworkers (2005) reported that adolescents who as children had the most negative attitudes toward their abuser (e.g., blamed him the most) provided the most accurate memory reports. Alexander and colleagues (2005) found robust memory for documented child sexual abuse in young adults, especially when those adults also reported high levels of PTSD symptoms.

To summarize the results of the different studies thus far; first, most adults can remember child maltreatment, including sexual abuse, but a few seem to completely forget. Second, being older when the abuse began, enduring more se-

vere abuse, and being less prone to dissociation help to guard against complete loss of memory (Goodman et al. 2003). And third, memories of prior maltreatment can be retained quite well over temporal spans ranging into adulthood, and certain more traumatic responses (e.g., PTSD) may later actually be associated with enhanced memory for maltreatment.

Nevertheless, there may still be a subgroup who either forget the abuse or do not remember it well. As mentioned, dissociation predicted "lost memory" in the Goodman et al. (2003) study. Emotion-regulation strategies, such as "defensive exclusion" (a term used in attachment theory that is similar to "functional avoidance" and "distancing coping" as defined below) may explain these memory problems better than "repression" in the Freudian sense. Because of the importance of this issue to the present review, a study by Edelstein et al. (2005), which examined the relation between adult attachment and long-term memory for child sexual abuse, is described in some detail. According to previous research, although distress or negative emotion generally enhances memory, individuals with avoidant attachment styles have memory deficits for highly negative, emotional information (Fraley et al. 2000). Thus, Edelstein et al. (2005) hypothesized an interaction between abuse severity and avoidant attachment: Individuals low on avoidant attachment (which can be viewed as a type of emotion-regulation strategy; Mikulincer & Shaver 2008) were expected to demonstrate the most accurate memory for severe abuse, whereas individuals high on avoidance were expected to show worse memory for more severe abuse. The nature of the victims' abuse experiences varied widely (e.g., from fondling over one's clothes to being kidnapped and raped at gunpoint), which permitted a test of this hypothesis.

Adults with documented histories of child sexual abuse were interviewed 12 to 21 years after the alleged abuse ended. Detailed information (derived from prosecutors' files, police reports, etc.) regarding participants' prior abuse experiences was examined to assess memory accuracy for abuse. That is, memory accuracy was evaluated based on discrepancies between current memory reports and original documentation of abuse collected during the victims' childhoods. The degree to which participants discussed their abuse experiences with friends and family members was also assessed. Adult attachment was measured using the Relationship Questionnaire (Bartholomew & Horowitz 1991).

The expected interaction between abuse severity and avoidant attachment was apparent. Child sexual abuse victims with low scores on avoidant attachment showed greater memory accuracy for cases of severe abuse, whereas victims scoring high on avoidant attachment demonstrated poorer memory for severe abuse. Furthermore, avoidant individuals were less likely to have discussed the abuse with others. Frequency of discussion was inversely related to memory accuracy for the abuse, such that the less one talked about the abuse, the less accurate was the memory of the abuse. Attachment anxiety was unrelated to memory accuracy, irrespective of abuse severity. These findings reveal the importance of understanding the influence of emotion regulation, in this case as reflected in avoidant attachment, in investigations of maltreatment victims' memory for emotional real-life events (Chae et al. 2009).

It is also possible that some abuse victims show deficits in source monitoring and therefore are more prone to false memory. Recently, Clancy, McNally, and colleagues (2000) and Geraerts and colleagues (2005, 2009) compared memory in women who reported recovered memories of childhood sexual abuse to that of women with continuous memories of childhood sexual abuse. These studies indicate that individuals reporting recovered memories of child sexual abuse are more likely than nonabused controls to create false memories in the laboratory (Clancy et al. 2000; Geraerts et al. 2005, 2009). In one such study, Geraerts et al. (2009) compared rates of DRM false memory in four groups: individuals who indicated that they had previously recovered memories of childhood sexual abuse through suggestive therapy, individuals who indicated that they had previously

recovered memories of childhood sexual abuse spontaneously, individuals who indicated they had continuous memory of childhood sexual abuse, and control individuals who indicated no sexual abuse in childhood or adulthood. Those who reported recovered memory in suggestive therapy exhibited heightened DRM false memory compared to those reporting spontaneously recovered memories, individuals reporting continuous memories of abuse, and controls. Geraerts et al. (2009) concluded that "To the extent that this pattern on the DRM task is indicative of a broader deficit in monitoring the source of one's memories, this finding suggests that such reports of recovered memories should be viewed with a cautious eye, as they may reflect the unwitting interaction of suggestive therapy with preexisting deficits in source memory" (p. 96).

Of interest, individuals who had spontaneously recovered child sexual abuse memories exhibited increased proneness to forget prior incidents of remembering. Geraerts et al. (2009) speculate that this group may show an enhanced ability to suppress unwanted thoughts, especially if those thoughts concern negative experiences. They write, "Memory for prior thoughts concerning the target child sexual abuse event might have been more effectively suppressed by members of this group, relative to other subjects, because those thoughts were unpleasant, and such suppression would have impaired the long-term accessibility of those memories" (p. 97). They recommend inclusion of personality tests in future research. Rather than personality per se, these findings again raise the issue of emotion-regulation strategies affecting memory of abuse.

Overall, McNally & Geraerts (2009) propose that a subset of people who report lost memory of child sexual abuse did not experience the abuse as traumatic. Although they may have thought of it at the time as confusing, disgusting, or scary, they may not have realized that it was sexual or abusive. As a result, they failed to think about the abuse for many years or forgot previous recollections. When they do remember, perhaps because of reminders, they may be shocked to realize that they indeed suffered child sexual abuse. This explanation does not require the special memory mechanism of repression.

The findings suggest that victims generally remember childhood abuse all too well, but a subset may temporarily or perhaps even permanently forget it. Lack of willingness to disclose cannot be completely ruled out, however. Emotion-regulation strategies may play an important role in determining who does and who does not fail to remember documented child abuse.

Autobiographical Memory

Scientific investigations of autobiographical memory in child victims of abuse are surprisingly few in number, although a larger body of research has examined autobiographical memory in adults with histories of maltreatment. Here the study of autobiographical memory (memory for one's life course, especially important life events) is referenced in terms of research in which documentation of the events is typically absent (although there are a few exceptions).

A small number of studies has examined deficits, or at least self-report of deficits, in childhood memories in victimized adults. Edwards et al. (2001) uncovered deficits in episodic memory for childhood experiences in adults with histories of child abuse. Sexually abused and physically abused participants were twice as likely to self-report gaps in their autobiographical memory compared to nonabused participants. Experiencing repeated abuse, abuse by a relative, and more severe abuse were especially powerful predictors of self-reported memory loss. However, in other studies, individuals who suffered more severe child sexual abuse reported having experienced more forgetting despite actually remembering the abuse better (Ghetti et al. 2006). Thus, self-reports of forgetting may not predict memory accuracy for traumatic events. As stated above, prospective memory studies suggest that child abuse victims can have quite accurate and detailed

memory for specific documented events related to their traumas (Alexander et al. 2005).

Studies of "overgeneral" memory, mentioned earlier, provide important insights into the effects of child maltreatment and trauma on autobiographical memory. A great deal of research on overgeneral memory has involved assessments of how trauma history in combination with PTSD relates to the specificity of individuals' memory reports. The themes in this area of research are similar to those in the study of lost memory of child sexual abuse. Accordingly, Williams (1996) proposed that individuals who have suffered maltreatment may be motivated to block conscious access to autobiographical memories (e.g., of abuse incidents or of childhood experiences in general) or at least to avoid public discussion of them because of the negative affect aroused by the memories (functional avoidance). Such avoidance is believed to contribute to overgeneral memory as opposed to memory specificity. However, some have questioned the robustness of the phenomenon given that most memories recalled by trauma victims and others are at the specific rather than the general level (Howe et al. 2006).

Nonetheless, in support of Williams's theory, Kuyken & Brewin (1995) found that adults with histories of child maltreatment who also reported PTSD symptoms produced overgeneral memories at particularly high rates (but see Kuyken et al. 2006, Moore & Zoellner 2007). Of interest, for an overly general autobiographical memory style to emerge, it appears that the adverse events must occur in childhood (e.g., see Stokes et al. 2004): Traumatic events in adulthood alone do not lead to overgeneral autobiographical memory (e.g., Kangas et al. 2005).

However, other research on the specificity of autobiographical memory suggests that childhood trauma alone does not produce autobiographical memory disruptions. No relations were found between child maltreatment and the specificity of autobiographical memory retrieval in (a) adolescents with histories of physical abuse, assessed during memory interviews about family conflict (Orbach et al. 2001); (*b*) adolescents with child sexual abuse histories in response to affective cue words (Johnson et al. 2005); (*c*) adults with child sexual abuse histories (Hunter & Andrews 2002, Stokes et al. 2008); and (*d*) adults with histories of childhood maltreatment (i.e., emotional abuse, sexual abuse, physical abuse, physical neglect, or emotional neglect) in response to affective cue words (Wessel et al. 2001).

Consistent with our point of view, results implicate emotion-regulation mechanisms as influences on the quality of autobiographical recollections and suggest that the influence of these mechanisms is related to post-traumatic reactions. Harris et al. (2009) examined the relation between coping and autobiographical memory specificity in adolescents and adults with child sexual abuse histories and found that reduced autobiographical memory specificity was related to the tendency to use avoidant forms of coping (e.g., distancing coping). In a similar study, Ogle et al. (2009) examined the specificity of autobiographical recall about childhood incidents in relation to symptoms of post-traumatic stress in adolescents (14- to 17-year-olds) and adults (18- to 37-year-olds) with and without documented child sexual abuse histories. For the participants with abuse histories, PTSD symptoms predicted heightened specificity (see also Kuyken et al. 2006).

Several variations in the experimental methodology and in the clinical diagnostic characteristics of the samples in these studies may help to explain discrepancies in the research findings. These variations include reliance on retrospective self-reports of childhood maltreatment versus documented cases of maltreatment, the inclusion of samples with broadly defined childhood maltreatment groups versus samples with child sexual abuse histories only, memory specificity coded from general memory interviews versus reports elicited by affective cue words, and timed versus untimed retrieval tasks. Furthermore, differences in the qualitative nature of abuse experiences (e.g., age of abuse onset, abuse duration, abuse severity, and subsequent trauma-related sequelae) may also have affected the extent to which relations between child maltreatment and autographical memory emerged. Overall, it appears that maltreatment per se is related over time to more specific autobiographical memories in many victims, but to fewer memories of specific former experiences in the subset of victims who use a more avoidant coping strategy—that is, who engage in avoidant emotion-regulation strategies.

APPLIED ISSUES

The vast majority of research on such topics as memory development, distress and memory, and children's eyewitness memory has not examined memory processes in precisely the children who are likely to end up in legal cases, namely those exposed to maltreatment. When children who have suffered abuse become involved in a legal case, the accuracy of their reports can be critical. Given that children are often questioned about alleged maltreatment (e.g., sexual abuse, witnessing domestic violence, physical abuse; Goodman et al. 1999), it is critical to understand how well these children in particular can remember such experiences and answer forensically relevant questions. Adults who were victims of child maltreatment are also at times called upon to provide information to authorities or testify in court, where the accuracy of their long-term memory for traumas experienced in childhood is likely to be called into question. A full understanding of maltreatment and memory must include the strengths and weaknesses of the memories of maltreated, possibly traumatized, children and adults. Finally, maltreatment victims may react differently than nonvictims to forensic interviews, further highlighting the importance not only of evaluating this group's memory abilities but also of identifying methods of considering their particular needs in forensic interviews.

CONCLUSIONS AND FUTURE DIRECTIONS

The topic of this review—how maltreatment affects memory for negative emotional experiences—is ripe for further systematic investigation. Although several theories and many studies provide a basis for predictions concerning how maltreatment may affect memory processes, the field is still relatively new. This review, therefore, has had to be less of a straightforward summary of a well-established literature and more of an attempt to integrate theories and findings from several lines of research (e.g., on cognitive processes, socioemotional consequences of maltreatment, and autobiographical memory in traumatized individuals; theories about distress and memory and about attention and adaptation following traumatic experiences). Predictions based on this integrative review include (*a*) that maltreatment should lead to enhanced memory for negative emotionally laden or stressful information in most individuals, but also (*b*) that certain subsets of maltreated individuals may have memory deficits for negative or traumatic experiences. Maltreated individuals' heightened attention to and vigilance regarding negative emotional information (Maughan & Cicchetti 2002, Pollak et al. 1998) may encourage extended processing of and recurrent thoughts about negative information. However, because some individuals—those who rely on avoidant coping strategies—try to suppress, inhibit, or ignore potentially traumatic memories, they may actually weaken or even eliminate these memories over time. These predictions are based on converging evidence from several research domains. What is needed at this point are more direct tests of these predictions that will identify the mechanisms responsible for the effects of maltreatment on emotional memory and elucidate their development, which seems likely to be affected by rapid neural development in certain age periods.

One especially important line of research would probe how predictors of memory in traumatized adults relate to maltreated children's memory. Although a few studies have examined memory accuracy for stressful events among maltreated children, this research has largely failed to reveal—or has left unstudied—whether the same predictors of memory performance are found in traumatized children and adults. For instance, among adults with trauma histories, those with higher levels of traumatization often pay greater attention to and more accurately remember trauma-related information (Alexander et al. 2005, Vrana et al. 1995), with traumatization operationalized in terms of abuse severity or PTSD (see Bremner et al. 2000, Goodman et al. 2003). A few researchers have begun to examine the role that these factors play in children's memory (e.g., Eisen et al. 2007), although additional research is needed to identify the extent to which the traumatization contributes to enhanced memory and the extent to which such enhancement emerges in childhood, a time of considerably fewer available coping resources.

A second important need is for more direct tests of emotion-regulation strategies and attention patterns in both maltreated individuals and nonmaltreated ones. Much research has already been conducted on conscious and unconscious methods of regulating emotions (Gross 2006). Some of this work has a strong developmental perspective and has revealed, for example, age-related changes in the strategies children employ when faced with negative, stressful, or challenging stimuli and environments. Research on children's coping skills has also been conducted with vulnerable children, such as those with asthma or leukemia (Chen et al. 2000, Fivush & Sales 2006), so it may be possible to identify common strategies used by children of different ages when faced with different kinds of stressors. Although it seems likely that emotion regulation is a major mediator of the relation between maltreatment and memory, little research has been devoted to understanding coping strategies used by maltreated individuals or the role these strategies play in affecting memory. Nor has sufficient research examined coping strategies in adults who were maltreated as children.

A third topic for further research would be early autobiographical memory in young maltreated children. As noted earlier, studies of the autobiographical memories of adults who were maltreated as children indicate that they often have overly general early autobiographical memories. Although a great deal of research has been carried out on early autobiographical memory in young children, virtually none of it has included maltreated children. Nevertheless, several of the theories proposed to explain autobiographical memory development in normal samples may apply to maltreated children. For instance, according to Howe & Courage (1997), the emergence of the cognitive self, which occurs between approximately 18 and 24 months, marks the onset of autobiographical memory and concurrently the end of infantile amnesia. At that age, children develop an internal representation of the self that enables them to organize personally experienced events around a personal theme, leading to the formation of autobiographical memories. Nelson and colleagues' social interactionist model (e.g., Nelson & Fivush 2004) posits that, through complex social interactions with familiar adults, children gradually learn what information about prior experiences is worth discussing and rehearsing and hence what should be stored in an autobiographical memory system.

Maltreated children, however, often have a fractionated sense of self that includes feelings of being unworthy and unloved, and of shame (Feiring 2005). Maltreated children often suffer from language delays, possibly because they have fewer rich interactions with caregivers, especially positive ones. Finally, maltreated children are at risk for insecure attachment relationships (Cicchetti & Toth 2006). Whether and how these different early self-perceptions, language and communication problems, and troubled early family relationships affect children's emerging autobiographical memory needs to be examined. The knowledge gleaned by studying maltreated children's early autobiographical memories could shed light on the developmental time course of overgeneralization of autobiographical memories. Such studies may also help identify certain children at risk for defensive emotion-regulation processes.

These suggestions for future research are not the only ones that might advance the study of maltreatment and memory. But these kinds of research will provide a better understanding of the processes involved in enhanced memory for negative emotional events among many individuals exposed to child maltreatment, while at the same time clarifying the use of defensive-avoidance by some formerly maltreated individuals. As empirical results accumulate, not only will the theoretical understanding of maltreatment and memory advance, but so will the ability to provide clear, concrete, and practical recommendations to legal, clinical, and policy professionals about memory for distressing events among individuals exposed to child maltreatment.

FUTURE ISSUES

1. Future research should examine the extent to which predictors of memory performance in adults maltreated as children also predict memory performance in maltreated children themselves. Although several predictors of memory have been identified for adults who had been maltreated in childhood, relatively few of these have been studied developmentally in maltreated children.

2. According to the current review, it is theoretically possible that trauma-related psychopathology in children and/or adults with child maltreatment histories may contribute to particularly robust memory, especially for trauma-related information. However, the precise nature of this effect, including its developmental time course, has not yet been sufficiently examined in relation to eyewitness and autobiographical memory, and as such is an important next step in this line of research.

3. Few extant studies have investigated memory accuracy for stressful events among maltreated children. Additional research is needed to advance a scientific understanding of the accuracy of maltreated children's memories of stressful events as well as of their propensity to be misled when recounting such events.

4. Future research should examine coping strategies and memory in individuals with maltreatment histories. One set of studies should identify coping strategies commonly employed by maltreated children when faced with stressors and how such strategies influence memory. This research would contribute significantly to the study of emotion regulation in maltreated populations. Another set of studies should examine coping strategies in adults who were maltreated as children and identify associations between the use of these strategies and memory processes.

5. Investigations of early autobiographical memory in maltreated children are needed. Results will provide insight into a number of important theoretical issues, including the developmental time course of overgeneralization of autobiographical memories as observed in adolescents and adults.

6. According to the current review, compared to nonmaltreated individuals, maltreated children and adults may exhibit certain memory advantages, as opposed simply to greater memory error, especially for trauma-related information. However, research aimed at further exploring the possibility of increased memory error in maltreated children and adults is needed to advance a comprehensive understanding of the influence of maltreatment on memory development.

DISCLOSURE STATEMENT

The authors are not aware of any biases that might be perceived as affecting the objectivity of this review.

ACKNOWLEDGMENT

Writing of this article was supported in part by a grant from the National Science Foundation (Grant 0545413). Any opinions, findings, conclusions, or recommendations expressed in this article are those of the authors and do not necessarily reflect the views of the National Science Foundation.

LITERATURE CITED

Adams JA, Harper K, Knudson S, Revilla J. 1994. Examination findings in legally confirmed child sexual abuse: It's normal to be normal. *Pediatrics* 94:310–17

Alessandri SM. 1991. Play and social behavior in maltreated preschoolers. *Dev. Psychopathol.* 3:191–205

Alexander KW, Quas JA, Goodman GS. 2002. Theoretical advances in understanding children's memory for distressing events: the role of attachment. *Dev. Rev.* 22:490–519

Alexander KW, Quas JA, Goodman GS, Ghetti S, Edelstein RS, et al. 2005. Traumatic impact predicts long-term memory for documented child sexual abuse. *Psychol. Sci.* 16:33–40

Andersen SL, Tomada A, Vincow ES, Valente E, Polcari A, Teicher MH. 2008. Preliminary evidence for the sensitive periods in the effect of childhood sexual abuse on regional brain development. *J. Neuropsychiatry Clin. Neurosci.* 20:292–301

This article is important in describing possible effects of attachment on encoding, storage, and retrieval of information in children's memory.

Presents an overarching theoretical framework for considering maltreatment and development.	Ayoub CC, O'Conner E, Rappolt-Schlichtmann G, Fischer KW, Rogosch FA. 2006. Cognitive and emotional differences in young maltreated children: a translational application of dynamic skill theory. *Dev. Psychopathol.* 18:679–706

Bartholomew K, Horowitz LM. 1991. Attachment styles among young adults: a test of a four-category model. *J. Personal. Soc. Psychol.* 61:226–44

Bauer PJ. 2004. Getting explicit memory off the ground: steps toward construction of a neuro-developmental account of changes in the first two years of life. *Dev. Rev.* 24:347–73

Bauer PJ. 2006. Event memory. In *Handbook of Child Psychology. Vol. 2: Cognition, Perception, and Language*, ed. D Kuhn, RS Siegler, W Damon, RM Lerner, pp. 373–425. Hoboken, NJ: Wiley. 6th ed.

Beers SR, De Bellis MD. 2002. Neuropsychological function in children with maltreatment-related posttraumatic stress disorder. *Am. J. Psychiatry* 159:483–86

Bowlby J. 1980. *Attachment and Loss.* New York: Basic Books

Bremner JD, Narayan M. 1998. The effects of stress on memory and the hippocampus throughout the life cycle: implications for childhood development and aging. *Dev. Psychopathol.* 10:871–85

Bremner JD, Shobe KK, Kihlstrom JF. 2000. False memories in women with self-reported childhood sexual abuse: an empirical study. *Psychol. Sci.* 11:333–37

Brewin CR. 2007. Autobiographical memory for trauma: update on four controversies. *Memory* 15:227–48

Browne A, Finkelhor D. 1986. Impact of child sexual abuse: a review of the research. *Psychol. Bull.* 99:66–77

Bruck M, Ceci SJ. 1999. The suggestibility of children's memory. *Annu. Rev. Psychol.* 50:419–39

Camras LA, Grow JG, Ribordy SC. 1983. Recognition of emotional expression by abused children. *J. Clin. Child Psychol.* 12:325–28

Carlson EB, Armstrong J, Loewenstein R. 1997. Reported amnesia for childhood abuse and other traumatic events in psychiatric inpatients. In *Recollections of Trauma: Scientific Evidence and Clinical Practice. NATO ASI Series. Series A: Life Sciences*, ed. JD Read, SD Lindsay, 291:395–401. New York: Plenum

Carrick NC, Quas JA, Lyon TD. 2009. Maltreated and nonmaltreated children's evaluations of emotional fantasy. *Child Abuse Negl.* In press

Carrion VG, Weems CF, Reiss AL. 2007. Stress predicts brain changes in children: a pilot longitudinal study on youth stress, posttraumatic stress disorder, and the hippocampus. *Pediatrics* 119:509–16

Carter CA, Bottoms BL, Levine M. 1996. Linguistic and socioemotional influences on the accuracy of children's reports. *Law Hum. Behav.* 20:335–58

Chae Y, Eisen M, Goodman GS, Qin J. 2006. *Maltreated Children's Memory: Accuracy, Suggestibility, and Psychopathology*. Presented at Annu. Meet. Assoc. Psychol. Sci., 18th, New York

Chae Y, Ogle CM, Goodman GS. 2009. Remembering negative childhood experiences: an attachment theory perspective. In *Emotion and Memory in Development: Biological, Cognitive, and Social Considerations*, ed. JA Quas, R Fivush, pp. 3–27. New York: Oxford Univ. Press

Chen E, Zeltzer LK, Craske MG, Katz ER. 2000. Children's memories for painful cancer treatment procedures: implications for distress. *Child Dev.* 71:933–47

Christianson SA. 1992. Emotional stress and eyewitness memory: a critical review. *Psychol. Bull.* 112:284–309

Christianson SA, Nilsson LG. 1984. Functional amnesia as induced by a psychological trauma. *Mem. Cogn.* 12:142–55

Cicchetti D, Rogosch FA, Maughan A, Toth SL, Bruce J. 2003. False belief understanding in maltreated children. *Dev. Psychopathol.* 15:1067–91

Cicchetti D, Toth SL. 2005. Child maltreatment. *Annu. Rev. Clin. Psychol.* 1:409–38

Cicchetti D, Toth SL. 2006. Building bridges and crossing them: translational research in developmental psychopathology. *Dev. Psychopathol.* 18:619–22

Clancy SA, Schacter DL, McNally RJ, Pitman RK. 2000. False recognition in women reporting recovered memories of sexual abuse. *Psychol. Sci.* 11:26–31

Compas BE. 1998. An agenda for coping research and theory: basic and applied developmental issues. *Int. J. Behav. Dev.* 22:231–37

Courage M, Cowan N. 2008. *The Development of Memory in Infancy and Childhood.* New York: Psychol. Press

Crittenden PK. 1988. Dangerous behavior and dangerous contexts: a 35-year perspective on research on the developmental effects of child physical abuse. In *Violence Against Children in the Family and the Community*, ed. PK Trickett, CJ Schellenbach, pp. 11–38. Washington, DC: Am. Psychol. Assoc.

Culp A, Watkins RV, Lawrence H, Letts D, Kelly D, Rice M. 1991. Maltreated children's language and speech development. *First Lang.* 11:377–89

Dalgleish T, Golden AJ, Barrett LF, Au Yeung C, Murphy V, et al. 2007. Reduced specificity of autobiographical memory and depression: the role of executive control. *J. Exp. Psychol.* 136:23–42

Dalgleish T, Rolfe J, Golden AM, Dunn BD, Barnard PJ. 2008. Reduced autobiographical memory specificity and posttraumatic stress: exploring the contributions of impaired executive control and affect regulation. *J. Abnorm. Psychol.* 117:236–41

De Bellis MD, Keshavan MS, Shifflett H, Iyengar S, Beers SR, et al. 2002. Brain structures in pediatric maltreatment-related posttraumatic stress disorder: a sociodemographically matched study. *Biol. Psychiatry* 52:1066–78

Deese J. 1959. On the prediction of occurrence of certain verbal intrusions in free recall. *J. Exp. Psychol.* 58:17–22

Dodge KA, Pettit GS, Bates JE, Valente E. 1995. Social information-processing patterns partially mediate the effect of early physical abuse on later conduct problems. *J. Abnorm. Psychol.* 104:632–43

Edwards VJ, Fivush R, Anda RF, Felitti VJ, Nordenberg DF. 2001. Autobiographical memory disturbances in childhood abuse survivors. *J. Aggress. Maltreat. Trauma* 4:247–63

Edelstein RS, Ghetti S, Quas JA, Goodman GS, Alexander KW, et al. 2005. Individual differences in emotional memory: adult attachment and long-term memory for child sexual abuse. *Personal. Soc. Psychol. Bull.* 31:1537–48

Egeland B, Sroufe LA. 1981. Attachment and early maltreatment. *Child Dev.* 52:44–52

Eigsti IM, Cicchetti D. 2004. The impact of child maltreatment on expressive syntax at 60 months. *Dev. Sci.* 7:88–102

Eisen ML, Goodman GS, Qin J, Davis S, Crayton J. 2007. Maltreated children's memory: accuracy, suggestibility, and psychopathology. *Dev. Psychol.* 43:1275–94

Eisen ML, Quas JA, Goodman GS, eds. 2002. *Memory and Suggestibility in the Forensic Interview*. Mahwah, NJ: Erlbaum Provides comprehensive reviews of children's and adults' eyewitness memory and suggestibility research.

Feerick MM, Haugaard JJ, Hien DA. 2002. Child maltreatment and adulthood violence: the contribution of attachment and drug abuse. *Child Maltreat.* 7:226–40

Feiring C. 2005. Emotional development, shame, and adaptation to child maltreatment. *Child Maltreat.* 10:307–10

Fischer KW. 1980. A theory of cognitive development: the control and construction of hierarchies of skills. *Psychol. Rev.* 87:477–531

Fivush R, Sales JM. 2006. Coping, attachment, and mother-child narratives of stressful events. *Merrill-Palmer Q.* 52:125–50

Foa EB, Feske U, Murdock TB, Kozak MJ, McCarthy PR. 1991. Processing of threat-related information in rape victims. *J. Abnorm. Psychol.* 100:156–62

Foa EB, Rothbaum BO. 1992. Post-traumatic stress disorder: clinical features and treatment. In *Aggression and Violence Throughout the Life Span*, ed. RD Peters, RJ McMahon, VL Quinsey, pp. 155–70. Thousand Oaks, CA: Sage

Fraley RC, Garner JP, Shaver PR. 2000. Adult attachment and the defensive regulation of attention and memory: examining the role of preemptive and postemptive defensive processes. *J. Personal. Soc. Psychol.* 79:816–26

Fries ABW, Shirtcliff EA, Pollak SD. 2008. Neuroendocrine dysregulation following early social deprivation in children. *Dev. Psychobiol.* 50:588–99

Geraerts E, Lindsay DS, Merckelbach H, Jelicic M, Raymaekers L, et al. 2009. Cognitive mechanisms underlying recovered-memory experiences of childhood sexual abuse. *Psychol. Sci.* 20:92–98

Geraerts E, Smeets E, Jelicic M, van Heerden J, Merckelbach H. 2005. Fantasy proneness, but not self-reported trauma, is related to DRM performance of women reporting recovered memories of childhood sexual abuse. *Conscious. Cogn.* 14:602–12

Ghetti S, Edelstein RS, Goodman GS, Cordòn IM, Quas JA, et al. 2006. What can subjective forgetting tell us about memory for childhood trauma? *Mem. Cogn.* 34:1011–25

Giesbrecht T, Lynn SJ, Lilienfeld S, Merckelbach H. 2008. Cognitive processes in dissociation: an analysis of core theoretical assumptions. *Psychol. Bull.* 134:617–47

Gilbertson MW, Shenton ME, Ciszewski A, Kasai K, Lasko NB. 2002. Smaller hippocampal volume predicts pathologic vulnerability to psychological trauma. *Nat. Neurosci.* 5:1242–47

Golier JA, Yehuda R, Lupien SJ, Harvey PD, Grossman R, Elkin A. 2002. Memory performance in Holocaust survivors with posttraumatic stress disorder. *Am. J. Psychiatry* 159:1682–88

Goodman GS, Bottoms BL, Rudy L, Davis SL, Schwartz-Kenney BM. 2001. Effects of past abuse experiences on children's eyewitness memory. *Law Hum. Behav.* 25:269–98

Goodman GS, Ghetti S, Quas JA, Edelstein RS, Alexander KW, et al. 2003. A prospective study of memory for child sexual abuse: new findings relevant to the repressed-memory controversy. *Psychol. Sci.* 14:113–18

Goodman GS, Quas JA, Batterman-Faunce JM, Riddlesberger MM, Kuhn J. 1997. Children's reactions to and memory for a stressful event: influences of age, anatomical dolls, knowledge, and parental attachment. *Appl. Dev. Sci.* 1:54–75

Goodman GS, Quas JA, Bulkley J, Shapiro C. 1999. Innovations for child witnesses: a national survey. *Psychol. Public Policy Law* 5:255–81

Greenhoot AF, McCloskey L, Glisky E. 2005. A longitudinal study of adolescents' recollections of family violence. *Appl. Cogn. Psychol.* 19:719–43

Gross JJ, ed. 2006. *Handbook of Emotion Regulation*. Thousand Oaks, CA: Sage

Gunnar MR, Morison SJ, Chisholm K, Schuder M. 2001. Salivary cortisol levels in children adopted from Romanian orphanages. *Dev. Psychopathol.* 13:611–28

Harris L, Block SD, Ogle CM, Urquiza AJ, Timmer SG, et al. 2009. *The relation between coping style and autobiographical memory specificity in maltreated and nonmaltreated adolescents and young adults*. Presented at Annu. Meet. Assoc. Psychol. Sci., 21st, San Francisco, CA

Heger A, Ticson L, Velasquez O, Bernier R. 2002. Children referred for possible sexual abuse: medical findings in 2384 children. *Child Abuse Negl.* 26:645–59

Howe ML, Cicchetti D, Toth SL. 2006. Children's basic memory processes, stress, and maltreatment. *Dev. Psychopathol.* 18:759–69

Howe ML, Cicchetti D, Toth SL, Cerrito BM. 2004. True and false memories in maltreated children. *Child Dev.* 75:1402–17

Howe ML, Courage ML. 1997. The emergence and early development of autobiographical memory. *Psychol. Rev.* 104:499–523

Howe ML, Goodman GS, Cicchetti D, eds. 2008. *Stress, Trauma and Children's Memory Development: Neurobiological, Cognitive, Clinical, and Legal Perspectives*. New York: Cambridge Univ. Press

Howe ML, Toth SL, Cicchetti D. 2009. *Can maltreated children suppress true and false memories for emotional information?* Presented at Biennial Meet. Soc. Res. Child. Dev., Denver, CO

Hunter ECM, Andrews B. 2002. Memory for autobiographical facts and events: a comparison of women reporting childhood sexual abuse and non-abused controls. *Appl. Cogn. Psychol.* 16:575–88

Janet P. 1973/1889. *L'automatisme Psychologigue*. Paris: Société Pierre Janet

Johnson RJ, Greenhoot AF, Glisky E, McCloskey LA. 2005. The relations among abuse, depression, and adolescents' autobiographical memory. *J. Clin. Child Adolesc. Psychol.* 34:235–47

Kangas M, Henry JL, Bryant RA. 2005. A prospective study of autobiographical memory and posttraumatic stress disorder following cancer. *J. Consult. Clin. Psychol.* 73:293–99

Katz SM, Schonfeld DJ, Carter AS, Leventhal JM, Cicchetti D. 1995. The accuracy of children's reports with anatomically correct dolls. *J. Dev. Behav. Pediatr.* 16:71–76

Keiley MK, Howe TR, Dodge KA, Bates JE, Petit GS. 2001. The timing of child physical maltreatment: a cross-domain growth analysis of impact on adolescent externalizing and internalizing problems. *Dev. Psychopathol.* 13:891–912

Kellstrand E, Quas JA, Larson RP, Clark S, Sumaroka M. 2009. *Eyewitness identification abilities in children and adolescents: influence of stress and interview context*. Presented at Bienn. Meet. Society Res. Child Dev., Denver, CO

Koopman C, Classen C, Spiegel DA. 1994. Predictors of posttraumatic stress symptoms among survivors of the Oakland/Berkeley, Calif., firestorm. *Am. J. Psychiatry* 151:888–94

Kuyken W, Brewin CR. 1995. Autobiographical memory functioning in depression and reports of early abuse. *J. Abnorm. Psychol.* 104:585–91

Offers the most thorough and integrative review to date of emotion regulation research and theory.

Reviews research on trauma and children's memory; several of the findings lay scientific groundwork for the present article.

Kuyken W, Howell R, Dalgleish T. 2006. Overgeneral autobiographical memory in depressed adolescents with, versus without, a reported history of trauma. *J. Abnorm. Psychol.* 115:387–96

Lazarus RS, Folkman S. 1984. *Stress, Appraisal and Coping.* New York: Springer

Lindsay DS, Read JD. 1995. "Memory work" and recovered memories of childhood sexual abuse: scientific evidence and public, professional, and personal issues. *Psychol. Public Policy Law* 1:846–908

Lynn SJ, Rhue JW, eds. 1994. *Dissociation: Clinical and Theoretical Perspectives.* New York: Guilford

Lyon TD, Malloy LC, Ahern E, Quas JA. 2009. Children's reasoning about disclosing adult transgressions: effects of maltreatment, child age, and adult identity. *Child Dev.* In press

Lyon TD, Malloy LC, Quas JA, Talwar VA. 2008. Coaching, truth induction, and young maltreated children's false allegations and false denials. *Child Dev.* 79:914–29

Macfie J, Toth SL, Rogosch FA, Robinson J, Emde RN, Cicchetti D. 1999. Effect of maltreatment on preschoolers' narrative representations of responses to relieve distress and of role reversal. *Dev. Psychol.* 35:460–65

Masten CL, Guyer AE, Hodgdon H, McClure EB, Charney DS, et al. 2008. Recognition of facial emotions among maltreated children with high rates of post-traumatic stress disorder. *Child Abuse Negl.* 32:139–53

Maughan A, Cicchetti D. 2002. Impact of child maltreatment and interadult violence on children's emotion regulation abilities and socioemotional adjustment. *Child Dev.* 73:1525–42

McGaugh JL. 2004. The amygdala modulates the consolidation of memories of emotionally arousing experiences. *Annu. Rev. Neurosci.* 27:1–28

McNally RJ. 2003. *Remembering Trauma*. Cambridge, MA: Belknap/Harvard Univ. Press

McNally RJ, Clancy SA, Schacter DL, Pitman RK. 2000. Cognitive processing of trauma cues in adults reporting repressed, recovered, or continuous memories of childhood sexual abuse. *J. Abnorm. Psychol.* 109:355–59

McNally RJ, Geraerts E. 2009. A new solution to the recovered memory debate. *Perspect. Psychol. Sci.* 4:126–34

McNally RJ, Metzger LJ, Lasko NB, Clancy SA, Pitman RK. 1998. Directed forgetting of trauma cues in adult survivors of childhood sexual abuse with and without posttraumatic stress disorder. *J. Abnorm. Psychol.* 107:596–601

McNally RJ, Riemann BC, Kim E. 1990. Selective processing of threat cues in panic disorder. *Behav. Res. Ther.* 28:407–12

Merritt KA, Ornstein PA, Spicker B. 1994. Children's memory for a salient medical procedure: implications for testimony. *Pediatrics* 94:17–23

Mikulincer M, Shaver PR. 2008. Adult attachment and affect regulation. In *Handbook of Attachment*, ed. J Cassidy, PR Shaver, pp. 503–31. New York: Guilford

Moore SA, Zoellner LA. 2007. Overgeneral autobiographical memory and traumatic events: an evaluative review. *Psychol. Bull.* 133:419–37

Moradi AR, Taghavi R, Neshat-Doost HT, Yule W, Dalgleish T. 2000. Memory bias for emotional information in children and adolescents with posttraumatic stress disorder: a preliminary study. *J. Anxiety Dis.* 14:521–34

Myers JEB, Berliner L, Briere J, Hendrix CT, Jenny C, Reid TA, eds. 2001. *APSAC Handbook on Child Maltreatment.* Thousand Oaks, CA: Sage. 2nd ed.

Nelson K, Fivush R. 2004. The emergence of autobiographical memory: a social cultural developmental theory. *Psychol. Rev.* 111:486–511

Ogle CM, Harris L, Block SD, Larsen RP, Pineda R, et al. 2009. *Autobiographical memory specificity, abuse severity, and trauma-related psychopathology in adolescents and young adults.* Presented at Annu. Meet. Assoc. Psychol. Sci., 21st, San Francisco, CA

Orbach Y, Lamb ME, Sternberg KJ, Williams JMG, Dawud-Noursi S. 2001. The effect of being a victim or witness of family violence on the retrieval of autobiographical memories. *Child Abuse Negl.* 25:1427–37

Otgaar H, Candel I, Merckelbach H. 2008. Children's false memories: easier to elicit for a negative than for a neutral event. *Acta Psychol.* 128:350–54

Paz-Alonso PM, Ghetti S, Donohue SE, Goodman GS, Bunge SA. 2008. Neurodevelopmental correlates of true and false recognition. *Cerebral Cortex* 18:2208–16

Phelps EA. 2006. Emotion and cognition: insights from studies of the human amygdala. *Annu. Rev. Psychol.* 57:27–53

Offers a clinical and scientific analysis of individuals', primarily adults', memories of trauma.

Comprehensive and integrative review of research on overgeneral autobiographical memory in individuals exposed to trauma.

Pollak SD, Cicchetti D, Hornung K, Reed A. 2000. Recognizing emotion in faces: developmental effects of child abuse and neglect. *Dev. Psychol.* 36:679–88

Pollak SD, Cicchetti D, Klorman R. 1998. Stress, memory, and emotion: developmental considerations from the study of child maltreatment. *Dev. Psychopathol.* 10:811–28

Pollak SD, Sinha P. 2002. Effects of early experience on children's recognition of facial displays of emotion. *Dev. Psychol.* 38:784–91

Porter C, Lawson JS, Bigler ED. 2005. Neurobehavioral sequelae of child sexual abuse. *Child Neuropsychol.* 11:203–20

Quas JA, Fivush R, eds. 2009. *Emotion and Memory in Development: Biological, Cognitive, and Social Considerations.* New York: Oxford Univ. Press

Quas JA, Lench HC. 2007. Arousal at encoding, arousal at retrieval, interviewer support, and children's memory for a mild stressor. *Appl. Cogn. Psychol.* 21:289–305

Reynolds CR, Bigler ED. 1996. Factor structure, factor indexes, and other useful statistics for interpretation of the Test of Memory and Learning (TOMAL). *Arch. Clin. Neuropsychol.* 11:29–43

Richards JM, Gross JM. 2006. Personality and emotional memory: how regulating emotion impairs memory for emotional events. *J. Res. Personal.* 40:631–51

Richert KA, Carrion VG, Karchemskiy A, Reiss AL. 2006. Regional differences of the prefrontal cortex in pediatric PTSD: an MRI study. *Depress. Anxiety* 23:17–25

Roediger HL III, McDermott KB. 1995. Creating false memories: remembering words not presented on lists. *J. Exp. Psychol.: Learn. Mem. Cogn.* 21:803–14

Rossman R, Rosenberg M, eds. 1998. *Multiple Victimization of Children: Conceptual, Developmental, Research, and Treatment Issues.* Binghamton, NY: Haworth

Rubin DC, Berntsen D, Bohni MK. 2008. A memory-based model of posttraumatic stress disorder: evaluating basic assumptions underlying the PTSD diagnosis. *Psychol. Rev.* 115:985–1011

Rudy L, Goodman GS. 1991. Effects of participation on children's reports: implications for children's testimony. *Dev. Psychol.* 27:527–38

Sapolsky RM. 1996. Why stress is bad for your brain. *Science* 273:749–50

Saywitz KJ, Goodman GS, Nicholas E, Moan SF. 1991. Children's memories of a physical examination involving genital touch: implications for reports of child sexual abuse. *J. Consult. Clin. Psychol.* 59:682–91

Schaaf JM, Alexander KW, Goodman GS. 2008. Children's false memory and true disclosure in the face of repeated questions. *J. Exp. Child Psychol.* 100:157–85

Scott KL, Wolfe DA, Wekerle C. 2003. Maltreatment and trauma: tracking the connections in adolescence. *Child Adolesc. Psychiatr. Clin. N. Am.* 12:211–30

Shields A, Cicchetti D. 1998. Reactive aggression among maltreated children: the contributions of attention and emotion dysregulation. *J. Clin. Child Psychol.* 27:381–95

Shipman KL, Zeman J. 2001. Socialization of children's emotion regulation in mother-child dyads: a developmental psychopathology perspective. *Dev. Psychopathol.* 13:317–36

Stein MB, Koverola C, Hanna C, Torchia MG. 1997. Hippocampal volume in women victimized by childhood sexual abuse. *Psychol. Med.* 27:951–59

Stokes DJ, Dritschel BH, Bekerian DA. 2004. The effect of burn injury on adolescent autobiographical memory. *Behav. Res. Ther.* 42:1357–65

Stokes DJ, Dritschel BH, Bekerian DA. 2008. Semantic and episodic autobiographical memory recall for memories not directly associated with childhood sexual abuse. *J. Fam. Violence* 23:429–35

Streissguth A. 2007. Offspring effects of prenatal alcohol exposure from birth to 25 years: the Seattle Prospective Longitudinal Study. *J. Clin. Psychol. Med. Settings* 14:81–101

Terr L. 1990. *Too Scared to Cry: Psychic Trauma in Childhood.* New York: Harper & Row

Thompson RA. 1994. Emotion regulation: a theme in search of definition. *Monogr. Soc. Res. Child Dev.* 59:25–52

Toth SL, Cicchetti D, Macfie J, Maughan A, Vanmeenen K. 2000. Narrative representations of caregivers and self in maltreated pre-schoolers. *Attachment Hum. Dev.* 2:271–305

Toth SL, Harris LS, Goodman GS, Cicchetti D. 2009. Influence of violence and aggression on children's psychological development: trauma, attachment, and memory. In *Aggression and Violence*, ed. M Mikulincer, PR Shaver. Washington, DC: Am. Psychol. Assoc. Books. In press

Presents state-of-the-art reviews of emotion and memory development research, including emotion regulation and coping.

Trickett PK, McBride-Chang C. 1995. The developmental impact of different forms of child abuse and neglect. *Dev. Rev.* 15:311–37

U.S. Dept. Health Human Serv., Admin. Child. Youth Families. 2009. *Child Maltreatment 2007*. Washington, DC: U.S. Gov. Print. Office

Van Der Kolk BA. 1997. Traumatic memories. In *Trauma and Memory: Clinical and Legal Controversies*, ed. PS Appelbaum, LA Uyehara, MR Elin, pp. 243–60. New York: Oxford Univ. Press

Veltman MWM, Browne KD. 2001. Three decades of child maltreatment research: implications for the school years. *Trauma Violence Abuse* 2:215–39

Vrana SR, Roodman A, Beckham JC. 1995. Selective processing of trauma-relevant words in posttraumatic stress disorder. *J. Anxiety Dis.* 9:515–30

Vythilingam M, Heim C, Newport J, Miller AH, Anderson E, et al. 2002. Childhood trauma associated with smaller hippocampal volume in women with major depression. *Am. J. Psychiatry* 159:2072–80

Wessel I, Meeren M, Peeters F, Arntz A, Merckelbach H. 2001. Correlates of autobiographical memory specificity: the role of depression, anxiety, and childhood trauma. *Behav. Res. Ther.* 39:409–21

Widom CS, Morris S. 1997. Accuracy of adult recollections of childhood victimization, Part 2: childhood sexual abuse. *Psychol. Assess.* 9:34–46

Wiik KL, Gunnar MR. 2009. Development and social regulation of stress neurobiology in human development: implications for the study of traumatic memories. In *Emotion and Memory in Development: Biological, Cognitive, and Social Considerations*, ed. JA Quas, R Fivush, pp. 256–77. New York: Oxford Univ. Press

Williams LM. 1994. Recall of childhood trauma: a prospective study of women's memories of child sexual abuse. *J. Consult. Clin. Psychol.* 62:1167–76

Williams JMG. 1996. Depression and the specificity of autobiographical memory. In *Remembering Our Past: Studies in Autobiographical Memory*, ed. DC Rubin, pp. 244–67. New York: Cambridge Univ. Press

Williams JMG, Barnhofer T, Crane C, Hermans D, Raes F, et al. 2007. Autobiographical memory specificity and emotional disorder. *Psychol. Bull.* 133:122–48

Williams JMG, Broadbent K. 1986. Autobiographical memory in suicide attempters. *J. Abnorm. Psychol.* 95:144–49

Windmann S, Krüger T. 1998. Subconscious detection of threat as reflected by an enhanced response bias. *Conscious. Cogn.* 7:603–33

Woon FL, Hedges DW. 2008. Hippocampal and amygdala volumes in children and adults with childhood maltreatment-related posttraumatic stress disorder: a meta-analysis. *Hippocampus* 18:729–36

Zajac R, Hayne H. 2003. I don't think that's what really happened: the effect of cross-examination on the accuracy of children's reports. *J. Exp. Psychol.* 9:187–95

Zoellner LA, Foa EB, Brigidi BD, Przeworski A. 2000. Are trauma victims susceptible to "false memories?" *J. Abnorm. Psychol.* 109:517–24

Proposes a new theoretical framework for understanding the mechanisms underlying overgeneral autobiographical memory, and reviews related research.

RELATED RESOURCES LISTS/LINKS

Bottoms BL, Najdowski C, Goodman GS, eds. 2009. *Children as Victims, Witnesses, and Offenders: Psychological Science and the Law*. New York: Guilford. 412 pp.

Child Welfare Information Gateway. **http://www.childwelfare.gov/**

Children's Bureau. **http://www.acf.hhs.gov/programs/cb/**

McNally RJ. 2003. Progress and controversy in the study of posttraumatic stress disorder. *Annu. Rev. Psychol.* 54:229–52

National Center on Posttraumatic Stress Disorder. **http://www.ncptsd.va.gov/ncmain/index.jsp**

Pipe ME, Lamb ME, Orbach Y, Cederborg AC, eds. 2007. *Child Sexual Abuse: Disclosure, Delay, and Denial*. Mahwah, NJ: Erlbaum. 318 pp.

Patterns of Gender Development

Carol Lynn Martin[1] and Diane N. Ruble[2]

[1]Arizona State University, School of Social and Family Dynamics, Program in Family and Human Development, Tempe, Arizona 85287-3701; email: cmartin@asu.edu

[2]Department of Psychology, New York University, New York, New York 10003; email: diane.ruble@nyu.edu

Annu. Rev. Psychol. 2009. 61:353–81

The *Annual Review of Psychology* is online at psych.annualreviews.org

This article's doi:
10.1146/annurev.psych.093008.100511

Key Words

gender typing, stereotypes, dynamic systems, sex segregation, timescales

Abstract

A comprehensive theory of gender development must describe and explain long-term developmental patterning and changes and how gender is experienced in the short term. This review considers multiple views on gender patterning, illustrated with contemporary research. First, because developmental research involves understanding normative patterns of change with age, several theoretically important topics illustrate gender development: how children come to recognize gender distinctions and understand stereotypes, and the emergence of prejudice and sexism. Second, developmental researchers study the stability of individual differences over time, which elucidates developmental processes. We review stability in two domains—sex segregation and activities/interests. Finally, a new approach advances understanding of developmental patterns, based on dynamic systems theory. Dynamic systems theory is a metatheoretical framework for studying stability and change, which developed from the study of complex and nonlinear systems in physics and mathematics. Some major features and examples show how dynamic approaches have been and could be applied in studying gender development.

Contents

INTRODUCTION

Understanding the changes that correspond with the passage of time is a hallmark of developmental studies, including the study of gender development. Gender developmental scientists are concerned with age-related changes in gender typing, and more broadly, with many issues about the emergence and patterning of gendered behaviors and thinking. Description of these changes is vitally important as it informs theoretical approaches to gender development. Using a broad lens on age-related changes provides important information describing how development occurs, but shorter time frames are also useful for identifying processes that may underlie developmental patterns. Gender developmental scientists are beginning to conceptualize temporal change and measurement of relevant variables over time in more nuanced ways and with new methods and analytic strategies.

Our goal in this article is not to provide an extensive review of changes in gender over childhood, but instead to focus on the perspective of developmental patterning. In selecting issues to review, we attempted to find a set of issues that would provide insights into processes underlying gender development while also being representative of contemporary issues and future directions in the field. First, to highlight developmentalists' interest in average or normative changes across age, we review the timeline of gender development for the emergence of gender understanding and stereotyping and how discrimination and prejudice develop in childhood. Second, we examine continuities within individuals over time as an important theoretical complement to the first focus on mean-level, normative patterns over time. Longitudinal studies are reviewed to examine whether individual differences are stable over time in two areas of gender typing: sex segregation and activities and interests. Finally, we discuss how dynamic systems theory may be applied in gender development and describe its potential for understanding patterns over different time frames.

HOW EARLY DO CHILDREN ACQUIRE GENDER CONCEPTS AND EXHIBIT PREJUDICE AND DISCRIMINATION?

The first few years of life and into adolescence have been the focus of much theorizing and empirical research on gender development. Major questions have arisen about the timeline of gender development, and resolving these issues is central to understanding processes underlying gender development. In this section, we discuss two key aspects of gender development. First, the earliest emergence of gender understanding and behaviors provides insights about the origins of sex differences and the prominence of gender as a social category, and so it is not surprising that these topics have been highlighted in contemporary research on gender development. Second, because of the far-ranging implications for human social interactions, we review research evidence concerning the emergence of gender prejudice and discrimination.

Do Infants Understand and Use Gender?

A major issue that has driven research is whether children's basic understanding of gender identity motivates and organizes the development of gender-typed behaviors, an idea proposed by "self-socialization" theories of gender development. Self-socialization perspectives posit that children actively seek information about what gender means and how it applies to them and that an understanding of gender categories motivates behavior such that, in essence, they socialize themselves (see Martin et al. 2002). In contrast, others (Bussey & Bandura 1999, Campbell et al. 2002) have argued that gender understanding must not play an important role in the emergence of gendered behaviors because some gender-typed behaviors emerge prior to age two, presumably earlier than children's understanding or identification

with gender. The evidence needed to resolve this controversy concerns whether behavior becomes increasingly gender typed with the onset of basic gender understanding, and recent findings have extended our knowledge of these fundamental issues. Much has been written about these topics and about the surrounding controversies (Bandura & Bussey 2004; Martin et al. 2002, 2004); here, we provide an overview and update of the evidence.

When do children begin to recognize that there are two types of people—males and females—and when are they able to link this information to other qualities to form basic stereotypes? A related question is, when do children recognize their own sex? Infants as young as three to four months of age distinguish between categories of female and male faces, as demonstrated in habituation and preferential looking paradigms (Quinn et al. 2002). By about six months, infants can discriminate faces and voices by sex, habituate to faces of both sexes, and make intermodal associations between faces and voices (e.g., Fagan & Singer 1979, Miller 1983, Younger & Fearing 1999). By 10 months, infants are able to form stereotypic associations between faces of women and men and gender-typed objects (e.g., a scarf, a hammer), suggesting that they have the capacity to form primitive stereotypes (Levy & Haaf 1994). Infants' early associative networks about the sexes may not carry the same conceptual or affective associations that characterize those of older children or adults, although the nature of these associations has yet to be examined in any depth (see Martin et al. 2002).

Because of the difficulties associated with testing infants, it has been challenging to determine when children first recognize their own or others' sex. Early studies suggested that labeling and understanding of gender may not emerge until about 30 months of age, but more recent studies have moved the age of understanding gender identity and labeling downward. In a study using a preferential looking paradigm, about 50% of 18-month-old girls showed knowledge of gender labels ("lady," "man"), but boys did not, and 50% of

18- and 24-month-old boys and girls showed above-chance understanding of the label "boy" (Poulin-Dubois et al. 1998). In another non-verbal testing situation, 24- and 30-month old children knew the gender groups to which they and others belonged (Stennes et al. 2005). Similarly, most 24- and 28-month-old children select the correct picture in response to gender labels provided by an experimenter (Campbell et al. 2002, Levy 1999).

A recent study examined the naturally occurring instances of gender labels (e.g., girl, boy, woman, man, lady, guy) as indicators of knowledge of gender categories and assessed whether the onset of use of these terms related to children's observed free play with toys (Zosuls et al. 2009). Information about gender labels was obtained from examining bi-weekly parent diaries of children's speech from 10 months of age onward. Zosuls and colleagues (2009) also analyzed videotapes of the children at 17 months and 21 months playing with a set of toys varying from high to neutral in gender typing. The results showed that 25% of children used gender labels by 17 months and 68% by 21 months. On average, girls produced labels at 18 months, one month earlier than did boys. These labeling results were used to predict changes in gender-typed behavior with the two most strongly gender-typed toys (trucks and dolls). Children who knew and used gender labels were more likely than other children to show increases in gender-typed play with toys.

Taken together, these studies suggest that most children develop the ability to label gender groups and to use gender labels in their speech between 18 and 24 months. As proposed by self-socialization theorists, the results from the Zosuls et al. study (2009) suggest that developing this ability has consequences: Knowing basic gender information was related to increased play with strongly stereotyped toys. These findings are consistent with research suggesting that children develop awareness of their own "self" at roughly 18 months and then begin to actively engage in information seeking about what things mean and how they should behave (Baldwin & Moses 1996).

When Do Children Develop Stereotypes?

Developmental researchers have identified that rudimentary stereotypes develop by about two years of age (Kuhn et al. 1978), and many children develop basic stereotypes by age three (Signorella et al. 1993). Children first show an understanding of sex differences associated with adult possessions (e.g., shirt and tie), physical appearance, roles, toys, and activities, and recognize some abstract associations with gender (e.g., hardness as male; softness as female) (Leinbach et al. 1997, Weinraub et al. 1984). Children develop stereotypes about physical aggression at an early age, and by age 4½, children believe that girls show more relational aggression than boys (Giles & Heyman 2005). Interestingly, even when researchers examine children's spontaneous associations about boys and girls, a consistent pattern is found from preschool through fourth/fifth grade: girls are seen as nice, wearing dresses, and liking dolls, and boys are seen as having short hair, playing active games, and being rough (Miller et al. 2009).

As children grow older, the range of stereotypes about sports, occupations, school tasks, and adult roles expands, and the nature of the associations becomes more sophisticated (e.g., Sinno & Killen 2009). Specifically, early in childhood, children make vertical associations between the category label ("girls," "boys") and qualities (e.g., "boys like trucks"). They appear slower to make horizontal inferences (e.g., recognizing that trucks and airplanes are associated with being "masculine"), which tend to appear around age eight. For instance, when told about an unfamiliar sex-unspecified child who likes trucks, older children but not younger ones predict that the child also likes playing with airplanes (Martin et al. 1990). Concreteness of gendered items influences the ability of younger children to make these property-to-property inferences (Bauer et al. 1998). In contrast, adults often rely on individuating information rather than the person's sex to make similar types of judgments (Deaux & Lewis 1984). The difficulty that children have with these judgments suggests that they may not understand within-sex individual differences.

Meta-analytic studies find that stereotypes become more flexible with age (Signorella et al. 1993). A longitudinal study of children from 5 to 10 years of age showed a peak in the rigidity of stereotypes at either 5 or 6 years of age and then an increase in flexibility two years later. Neither the timing nor the level of peak rigidity affected the developmental trajectory, suggesting that children generally follow the same normative path across development despite variations in when rigidity starts and how extreme it becomes (Trautner et al. 2005).

Many questions remain to be answered about the developmental progression in learning the content of stereotypes and in exploring individual differences in patterns of development. For instance, when do children first begin to assume that there are similarities within one sex and dissimilarities between the sexes? Theorists are interested in examining the roles that personal interests and idiosyncratic knowledge play in the development or hindrance in stereotype formation (Liben & Bigler 2002, Martin & Ruble 2004). Furthermore, how children apply stereotypes once they have learned them is an issue of continuing interest in the field.

When Do Children Exhibit Prejudice and Discrimination?

Recent conceptual analyses suggest a range of factors that likely contribute to the development of stereotypes and prejudice, such as highly salient categorizing dimensions (e.g., sex) (Martin & Ruble 2004) and labeling of these dimensions by others (Bigler et al. 1997). Because recent reviews of Developmental Intergroup Theory have covered the influence of these factors and discussed studies of children's responses to novel stereotyping situations (Arthur et al. 2008, Bigler & Liben 2007), the focus here is on the age-related changes in cognitive and behavioral expressions of gender prejudice and discrimination, not with their origins.

Attitudes about the two sexes. How do children's evaluations of the two sexes change with age? This question involves a number of different kinds of attitudes and beliefs; we focus on two: (*a*) ingroup/outgroup biases, and (*b*) perceptions of status differences and discrimination. There has been relatively little research on these topics, but interest has increased recently.

Ingroup/outgroup biases. Children's growing awareness of membership in a social group (i.e., male or female) becomes an evaluative process through self-identification and thus affects how positively children regard the ingroup relative to the outgroup (Ruble et al. 2004). Some research suggests that as early as preschool, children report feeling more positively about their own sex (Yee & Brown 1994), and differential liking is also seen among older children (e.g., Heyman 2001, Verkuyten & Thijs 2001). Studies are mixed regarding age trends, depending on the measure. Those examining negative versus positive trait ratings suggest that intergroup biases decline in elementary school (e.g., Egan & Perry 2001, Powlishta et al. 1994), consistent with increasing stereotype flexibility described above; but studies tapping more affective reactions (e.g., liking the ingroup better) do not show this decline (e.g., Yee & Brown 1994), at least not until early adolescence (Verkuyten & Thijs 2001).

We do not yet know whether and when ingroup favoritism is associated with outgroup derogation. That is, do children actually dislike or have hostile attitudes toward the other sex, or is it simply that children like their own sex better? Because many studies use difference scores, ingroup positivity and outgroup negativity are often confounded (Brewer 2001, Cameron et al. 2001). Moreover, Kowalski (2007) reports that studies of young children's interactions do involve evaluative comments between boys and girls but rarely involve animosity, suggesting that some researchers may have misinterpreted children's positive ingroup feelings in structured interviews as overt rejection of the other group. Recent research suggests that when they are decoupled, ingroup positivity effects are stronger than outgroup negativity among elementary school children (Susskind & Hodges 2007). It is also not clear whether young girls' willingness to judge boys as "bad," for example, indicates outright hostility (Rudman & Glick 2008) or if, instead, such judgments reflect stereotypes about boys getting into trouble (e.g., Heyman 2001). On the other hand, studies showing that the other sex is disliked (e.g., Yee & Brown 1994) are consistent with a conclusion of negative outgroup evaluation. An important issue for future research concerns this distinction between cognitive and affective aspects of intergroup bias and its connection to the development of gender prejudice (Halim & Ruble 2009).

A distinction in the adult literature between hostile and benevolent sexism (Glick & Fiske 2001) represents a potentially very useful conceptualization for future developmental research. The idea is that, unlike most forms of prejudice toward outgroups, negative intergroup attitudes between males and females are likely to be complicated by intimate interdependence and thus are likely to be ambivalent, involving benevolent as well as hostile aspects. For example, women may be viewed as competitors seeking to gain power over men, but they may also be viewed as angelic (put on a pedestal) and vulnerable, in need of protection. Men may be resented for their dominance over women but also admired as providers and heroes. Applying this distinction to the developmental course of intergroup attitudes, Rudman & Glick (2008) argued that ambivalence does not characterize gender prejudice in young children, but rather that it moves from a simple form of childhood hostility toward competing groups to ambivalent sexism.

This is an interesting proposal with important implications, but questions remain. First, outgroup negativity in young children can be interpreted differently, as suggested above; their perceptions may be simple and competitive, but not extreme enough to be characterized as hostile. Perhaps, instead, children's need to master important categorical distinctions coupled with relatively limited cognitive skills make it threatening when peers cross gender boundaries (Kowalski 2007). Second, young children's attitudes may involve some complexity and ambivalence, but of a different sort than for adults. For example, young children may dislike members of the other sex because they are boring (about girls) or rough (about boys) while still holding positive views about other characteristics of other-sex peers, such as girls are nice and boys play exciting games. Moreover, children begin to anticipate adult roles at an early age, and benevolent feelings could arise from a "princess" anticipating her "prince" or the expectation by two young opposite-sex friends that they will one day be husband and wife. Further examination of different interpretations of preschoolers' ingroup bias is important because knowing what it represents is critical to knowing when to intervene to minimize sexism.

Awareness of status differences and discrimination.

When do children become aware of the status difference applied to males and masculine activities relative to females and feminine activities in most cultures? Although studies of gender stereotypes in young children show that they attribute greater power to males and helplessness to females (Ruble et al. 2006), only a few studies have examined perceptions of inequality directly. First, research has found awareness of status differences in occupations typically held by men and women (Liben et al. 2001, Teig & Susskind 2008). Children as young as 6 years understood that jobs more likely to be held by men (e.g., business executive) are higher in status than female-typical jobs, but only older children (11-year-olds) associated fictitious "male" jobs as being higher in status (Liben et al. 2001). A study of perceptions of a high-status job—the U.S. presidency—found that 87% of children aged 5–10 years knew that only men had been presidents, though knowledge increased significantly with age (Bigler et al. 2008).

Second, research has examined the development of children's general perceptions of gender inequalities (Neff et al. 2007). The findings showed a notable increase between 7 and 15 years of age in beliefs that males are granted more power and respect than females.

Finally, a few recent studies examined children's perceptions of gender discrimination. First, in the study of the presidency, only approximately 30% of the 5- to 10-year-old children attributed the lack of women presidents to discrimination, although this percentage increased with age. Instead, the most frequent explanation was ingroup bias: that men would not vote for women. These findings suggest that even young children are aware of how ingroup biases shape behavior and that they perceive such reasons as more important than institutional discrimination in determining the selection of the president (Bigler et al. 2008). In a second study, children in two age groups (5–7 and 8–10 years) responded to a set of hypothetical stories about teachers deciding whether a boy or a girl did better on an activity (Brown & Bigler 2005). The findings showed that the younger children were somewhat aware of gender discrimination, but such perceptions were higher in the older group. Children perceived discrimination, however, only when explicitly told that the teacher may be biased, not when the context was ambiguous.

Taken together, these studies suggest that children's awareness of the differential status of the sexes and gender discrimination are relatively late-developing phenomena. Young children show limited awareness, but only when contextual cues (e.g., explicit mention of biases) or social experiences (knowledge of status of real occupations) make inequities obvious. More subtle awareness of inequities may not emerge until later in elementary school. The slow development of this more "public" evaluation, such as recognizing status and power differences and institutional discrimination, is in stark contrast to the early developing "personal" regard shown by ingroup biases, suggesting different developmental underpinnings of the two types.

Gender prejudice and discrimination. In what ways might developmental changes in stereotypic beliefs and intergroup attitudes play out in actual choices and behavior? What little research there is on gender prejudice development has primarily focused on two types: (*a*) negative reactions to peers' violations of gender norms and (*b*) preferential treatment.

Reactions to gender norm violations. Because preschoolers have strong beliefs that boys and girls do different things, they would be expected to respond negatively to gender norm violations. Several early studies found support for this prediction (Huston 1983). For example, when 3- to 5-year-olds were videotaped while playing with either a male- or female-typed toy (e.g., soldiers; dollhouse) in the presence of a same-sex peer, children were punished (e.g., ridiculed) by the peer when playing with cross-sex toys (Langlois & Downs 1980).

Recent research has supported and expanded these findings. For example, teachers report that kindergarten children tend to respond in one of three ways to gender norm violations: correction ("give that girl puppet to a girl"), ridicule, and "identity negation" (e.g., "Jeff is a girl") (Kowalski 2007). Interestingly, one recent study found that preschool children are able to identify children who are more likely to enforce the gender rules and gender-segregated boundaries (McGuire et al. 2007). Preschoolers were asked, "Who in your classroom says you shouldn't play because you are a boy/girl?" The findings showed that children who had greater exposure to "gender enforcer" peers were more likely to limit their play to same-sex peers. These findings suggest that there may be individual differences in overt "sexist" behavior as early as preschool, and that the actions of these gender "police" contribute more broadly to the maintenance of gender distinctions in the classroom.

Because children show age-related increases in the flexibility of stereotypes and other aspects of gender category knowledge, such as gender constancy and the ability to make multiple classifications, their negative reactions to gender norm violations should decline after preschool. Unfortunately, age trends in older children have received little attention, though examples of such behavior abound. Based on extensive qualitative ethnographic observations in middle-elementary school, Thorne (1993) found that boys who violated norms for masculinity were teased, shunned, or referred to as "girls." For example, one girl excluded a boy from jump rope because "...you don't know how to do it, to swing it. You gotta be a girl" (p. 45). Other research documented the various "rules" that children have about maintaining gender boundaries and found that children who maintain boundaries are more popular with peers (Sroufe et al. 1993). Finally, research with children exhibiting extreme gender-nonnormative behaviors suggests that girls and especially boys are teased and rejected by peers (Zucker & Bradley 1995).

Studies using hypothetical stories also indicate that children make negative judgments of, and consider unpopular, peers who engage in gender-atypical behavior, especially boys. In contrast to the implications from the more behavioral studies described above, however, many of these studies fail to find negative evaluations of gender-atypical behaviors before middle-elementary school (e.g., Berndt & Heller 1986), and children often show increased negativity with age, although findings are mixed (Ruble et al. 2006). The findings in the judgment studies may be influenced by the qualities and salience of the stimuli as well as by children's cognitive abilities and gender knowledge (Arthur et al. 2008, Lutz & Ruble 1995). For example, one recent study showed a dramatic decrease in negative judgments between 5 and 7 years of age, which was mediated by increasing gender knowledge—specifically, gender constancy (Ruble et al. 2007b).

Thus, conclusions about evidence of sexism in young children drawn from judgment studies can be different from conclusions drawn from studies of actual behaviors. This observation raises interesting questions for future research about what exactly children are reacting to when they demonstrate seemingly sexist behaviors or attitudes toward peers engaging in atypical behavior. First, children's liking or popularity judgments in hypothetical situations may reflect egocentric considerations, such as preferring targets engaged in activities typical of their own sex (e.g., girls preferring male targets with feminine interests) (Alexander & Hines 1994, Zucker et al. 1995). Thus, young children's liking for gender nonconforming targets may not reflect their tolerance for gender nonconformity but instead their personal interest in masculine or feminine activities.

Second, it is not clear if the sexist behaviors found in preschool children (e.g., hitting a boy who wears fingernail polish) are based on global negative evaluations of such children as being gender atypical or if they reflect a more limited evaluation of a specific instance of a child breaking a rule (such as stealing cookies). Children's judgments of gender atypicality are likely influenced by additional factors such as their perceptions of the targets' dissimilarity to same-sex others (e.g., Egan & Perry 2001) and/or awareness of within-sex variability. Moreover, it may be only when children begin to recognize and understand the stability of behavior that individual atypical behaviors coalesce into a broader and more negative view of the person as being deviant (Ruble & Dweck 1995). Unfortunately, developmental changes in children's perceptions of others' gender typicality have received little attention. This is surprising because perceptions of gender typicality are key to understanding reactions to gender norm violations and what they mean. Whether preschoolers' negative judgments and reactions reflect sexism and, if so, what form of sexism are interesting questions for future research.

Preferential treatment. Given that the ingroup liking bias occurs at a young age, one might expect that children would show favoritism toward their own sex. When affiliative behavior is measured, children begin to show preferential selection of same-sex peers starting at age 3 (La Freniere et al. 1984). Children also preferentially allocate resources to their own-sex group, beginning in preschool (Yee & Brown 1994).

Other research has examined ingroup favoritism in terms of children's responses to hypothetical stories about excluding peers from gender stereotypic activities, such as a ballet or baseball "club" (Killen et al. 2008). In these studies, there has been little evidence that children were more likely to choose same-sex members. Instead, children's exclusion and inclusion decisions were found to vary across age depending on exactly what they were told about the situation. When children were asked about a single child who wanted to join the club, most children responded that exclusion was wrong (e.g., to exclude a boy from a ballet club), even though they knew the stereotypes. Consistent with findings of increasing flexibility of stereotypes with age, however, this was true for only about 60% of preschoolers (Theimer et al. 2001) versus 90% of older children (Killen & Stangor 2001). When children were asked to select between a boy and a girl of equal competence, age differences in the influence of gender stereotypes on inclusion decisions appeared to be even stronger. Children in the study of preschoolers selected the stereotyped choice (e.g., the girl for the ballet class) (Theimer et al. 2001). Older children, however, preferred the counterstereotypic choice (Killen & Stangor, 2001) and offered justifications based on equal access (e.g., boys don't get a chance to take ballet). Such "fairness" considerations in inclusion decisions coupled with relatively low levels of exclusion are surprising in that they seem inconsistent with the observations of behavioral exclusion described above. Perhaps only a few children engage in exclusion (e.g., the "gender police"), or hypothetical situations might allow children to think instead of answering impulsively and thus may not invoke ingroup favoritism as much as more personal, immediate situations might.

In short, it appears that gender prejudice and discrimination begin as early as preschool; this finding is particularly evident in research examining actual behavior, whether naturalistic or experimental. That is, preschoolers respond negatively to violations of gender norms and favor ingroup members in actual choices of play partners (sex segregation) and allocation of resources. Findings of studies examining responses in hypothetical situations appear to be more mixed, however. From these studies, it appears that the form and bases of gender prejudice and discrimination vary across age and context. For example, in young children, prejudice may reflect simple same-sex liking biases or relatively straightforward applications of gender norms, whereas at older ages, prejudice may involve differential evaluation of capabilities and past history and thus be more closely linked to knowledge of status differences and discrimination. The few studies examining these issues have involved very different paradigms. Thus, findings that apparently conflict across studies cannot be evaluated without future research.

HOW STABLE ARE INDIVIDUAL DIFFERENCES IN GENDER TYPING?

It seems intuitively obvious that individuals vary greatly in how gender typed they are. Some girls are extremely "girly" and refuse to go anywhere without wearing a dress, often pink and frilly, whereas other girls have no such interest and instead prefer playing ball with the boys. Some men can handle any kind of tool (except kitchen tools!), whereas others lack such mechanical facility. It is commonly assumed that attributes associated with being a typical male or female are seen early on, show at least some continuity across time, and influence personal preferences and behaviors throughout life.

How much empirical support is there for these assumptions? Maccoby (2002) has argued that there is not much. According to her analysis, this is because different manifestations of gender typing in childhood do not cohere and because there is considerable situational variation in how gender typed a given child seems. Instead, she suggests that gender typing at this age may be more of a group phenomenon rather than something that reflects the dispositions of relatively more or less gender-typed children. Thus, she advocates a shift in research focus away from individual differences in gender-related outcomes and toward the study of how gender is manifested in groups of males and females.

Although we agree wholeheartedly about the importance of studying group-based elements of gender, we suggest that it may be premature to dismiss the importance of examining gender typing as an individual difference variable. Variation across contexts and domains of gender typing does not preclude the possibility that some aspects show stability across time within individuals. For example, some boys may show an interest in moving parts or vehicles that persists in different forms into adulthood, even if that interest shows no connection to rough-and-tumble play or to other male-typical interests and behaviors. Surprisingly, researchers have rarely directly examined the stability of gender-typed interests and behaviors, and the existing database is piecemeal and sketchy (Huston 1983, Powlishta et al. 1993). This is unfortunate, because knowing more about which aspects of gender typing are stable is critical to a full understanding of the nature and processes involved in gender development.

In the sections below, we provide a detailed analysis of longitudinal studies of gender typing in children and what the studies show about stability. We then reevaluate the evidence that led to Maccoby's (2002) conclusions that examining individual differences in gender typing is not productive.

Evidence of the Stability of Gender Typing from Longitudinal Studies

What do longitudinal studies of gender development tell us about stability? Although gender typing can involve a number of different features, we limit the present review to behavioral-type variables (e.g., play with same-sex peers; interests and activities) rather than cognitive-type variables such as stereotyping or gender identity. We do this because much research on gender typing has concerned young children's peer and activity preferences. It is also partly

because cognitive variables show considerable variation during childhood (Ruble et al. 2006) and may not be conducive to demonstrating stability, at least in young children.

Surprisingly, the few longitudinal studies of gender typing that exist have paid relatively little attention to this issue of stability. This may be partly because it has not been a primary component of major theories of gender development. Because most theories emphasize the factors that lead to gender typing, longitudinal studies have often focused on such issues as how contextual, socialization, or social-cognitive factors at one point in time affect gender-typing at a later point in time (e.g., McHale et al. 2004) rather than on the stability of gender typing across time. Other longitudinal studies have focused on normative changes in gender-typed behaviors or cognitions, such as attitudes or stereotyping (e.g., Bartini 2006).

In interpreting the theoretical significance of such studies, however, it is essential to determine whether gender typing represents some continuing characteristic of individuals that influences future beliefs and behaviors or whether it is better viewed as linked to a particular developmental time point or context, with little future implications (Serbin et al. 1993). Moreover, identifying the factors that lead children to be more or less gender typed should help distinguish among alternative theories of gender typing (Powlishta et al. 1993). Thus, information about which elements of gender typing are stable, over what period of time, and during which developmental periods seems essential to the study of gender development.

Longitudinal studies examining the stability of sex segregation. Some studies have used observational methods to examine the stability of preferences for spending time with same-sex versus other-sex others. Different types of assessments have been used: (*a*) split-half correlations (e.g., across odd versus even weeks), (*b*) cross-situational stability (e.g., across indoor and outdoor play); and (*c*) test-retest (temporal) stability (whether sex segregation scores are correlated over some period of time).

The findings have been mixed, both across studies and across measures, and most studies have involved small samples and relatively short time periods (six months or less). To illustrate, Maccoby & Jacklin (1987) reported nonsignificant test-retest reliability over a one-week period among $4\frac{1}{2}$-year-olds (0.39) and among $6\frac{1}{2}$-year-olds (0.17). They did find cross-situational (indoor-outdoor) stability in preschoolers, but for girls only (0.44). Powlishta et al. (1993) used a split-half reliability procedure across odd and even days over a four- to six-month period and found that sex segregation showed significant stability for preschool boys (0.73) but not for girls (0.20). Lloyd & Duveen (1992) found significant temporal stability (0.40) in children ranging in age from about 4 to 7 years when they correlated the proportion of same-sex play from one term to the next. Turner et al. (1993) also examined temporal stability in a large sample (n = 161) of 4- to $4\frac{1}{2}$-year-old children from two countries across eight sessions. Sex segregation scores in sessions one to four were correlated with sessions five to eight at significant or marginal levels (0.3 to 0.7).

As a final example of studies examining relatively short-term stability, Martin & Fabes (2001) assessed sex segregation over two consecutive academic terms for preschool and kindergarten children. Observations took place inside and outside every weekday for six months. This study is unusual because of the large number of observations (about 300 per child) and because of the use of multiple forms of stability assessment. First, split-half procedures (odd and even weeks) showed high and significant correlations for both sexes and for younger and older children (0.69–0.84). Second, as suggested by Epstein (1980), they calculated stability coefficients with data aggregated over differing lengths of time, a procedure that reduces error of measurement. The one-week coefficients were low (below 0.3), but as the number of weeks of aggregated data increased, the stability coefficients showed large increases, such that when data were aggregated over eight-week periods, stability coefficients

rose to the 0.5 to 0.6 range and continued to rise across larger units of time. Finally, they found considerable temporal stability (>0.7) across the two academic terms. These findings suggest that a relatively large number of observations, spread over time, may be needed to observe stability in sex segregation. Thus, prior conclusions about a lack of individual stability in same-sex peer preferences may be misleading.

In short, some longitudinal studies show reasonably impressive stability of individual differences in sex segregation. One problem with these studies, however, is that stability is examined within a group context that does not change. That is, stability may be found not because of individual differences in same-sex preferences, but rather because groups are formed early in the class year, and these structures are maintained (Maccoby & Jacklin 1987). Thus, the results of longitudinal studies involving longer periods of time are of considerable interest.

Unfortunately, few studies have examined temporal stability for longer than six months, and, as with short-duration research, the findings are mixed. For example, Maccoby & Jacklin (1987) examined stability in sex segregation in children across a two-year period ($4\frac{1}{2}$ to $6\frac{1}{2}$ years). Given the low level of short-term stability found in this study, as described above, the authors did not expect to find, and did not find, much evidence of temporal stability, except for a significant correlation (0.31) over time for boys, but only for outdoor play. In contrast, Serbin et al. (1993) did find long-term temporal stability from one year to the next using a peer-nomination procedure (e.g., participants selecting photos of the children with whom they most like to play) in 5- to 12-year-olds. It is not clear exactly why this paper-and-pencil measure might yield more stable estimates, but it may be that the situational variation in observations was eliminated and that only the strongest relationships were assessed this way. Regardless, it is impressive that temporal stability was found across a time period when classrooms had changed.

Taken together, despite some nonsignificant findings, it seems fair to conclude that individual differences in sex segregation do show both internal consistency (split-half reliability) and temporal stability, given sufficient power and numbers of observations. Although observational data suggest that a child may vary in same-sex play from week to week, when observations are aggregated across multiple weeks, stability is seen. It would be helpful in future research to use data-aggregation procedures to see how many weeks of observations are needed to show temporal stability across one year or more. It would also be worthwhile to examine how long individual differences in segregation are maintained. For example, do preschool preferences predict preferences in middle-elementary school?

Longitudinal studies of the stability of interests and activity preferences. Studies of other indices of gender typing have been somewhat more consistent in finding temporal stability. Some observational studies of preschoolers and/or kindergartners have shown short-term, test-retest temporal stability in stereotyped toy and activity choices during free play (e.g., Maccoby & Jacklin, 1987, Martin & Fabes 2001). Other observational studies have shown significant stability in terms of split-half consistency (e.g., Connor & Serbin 1977, Powlishta et al. 1993). In addition, gender-stereotyped activity preferences have shown moderate to high stability over varying periods of time, as assessed with test-retest reliability involving pencil-and-paper measures completed either by the children themselves (e.g., Edelbrock & Sugawara 1978, Golombok & Rust 1993) or by parents about their children (e.g., Golombok & Rust 1993).

One recent, impressive study examined the stability of gender typing using pencil-and-paper measures (Golombok et al. 2008). This study warrants a more detailed look because it involved a much longer time period (from age $2\frac{1}{2}$ to 8 years) and a much larger sample (more than 2700 girls and 2700 boys) than has been typical. When the children were ages $2\frac{1}{2}$, $3\frac{1}{2}$,

and 5 years old, parents completed a toy and activity questionnaire (Pre-School Activities Inventory, or PSAI; Golombok & Rust 1993) about their child's preferences; at age 8, the children completed an age-appropriate modified version, the Children's Activities Inventory (CAI). To examine temporal stability during the preschool years (test-retest reliability), intercorrelations in PSAI scores were examined among all three time points (ages $2\frac{1}{2}$, $3\frac{1}{2}$, and 5 years). Stability coefficients for the PSAI were high: 0.6–0.7 for adjacent time points and 0.5 from $2\frac{1}{2}$ to 5 years. These levels are comparable to or even higher than those reported in earlier studies and thus demonstrate moderate to high stability in gender-typed interests and activities over time periods ranging from 1 to $2\frac{1}{2}$ years.

Golombok et al. (2008) also examined stability between the preschool years and age 8, though not with test-retest correlations. Instead, at age $3\frac{1}{2}$, boys and girls separately were divided into nine categories of gender typing based on PSAI scores; children who varied in their categories were compared on CAI scores. For both sexes, the children who were most gender typed at age $3\frac{1}{2}$ continued to be so at age 8. A similar analysis compared CAI scores at age 8 with scores indicating the trajectory (acceleration in gender-typed interests) from ages $2\frac{1}{2}$ to 5 years. As predicted, children showing the greatest increase in gender typing at a young age were those with higher levels of gender-typical behavior at age 8.

These findings are interesting in part because the trends run counter to what would be expected from regression to the mean, in that the children who were most gender typed to start with became relatively more so over time. Moreover, the findings suggested the possibility that individual differences in gender typing may be more stable in children who are relatively high or low in gender typing when young, a pattern that was particularly marked for the least gender-typed girls. It would be of great interest in future research to examine the stability and trajectory of gender typing among children at the extremes, such as tomboys or girly girls.

Taken together, longitudinal studies of gender-typed interests and activities show fairly compelling evidence of stability of individual differences. Future research needs to examine stability across one year or more using observations rather than paper-and-pencil measures to be certain that the apparent stability of gender typing reflects actual behaviors rather than stability in self- or parent perceptions.

Interpretations and Conclusions About the Evidence from Longitudinal Studies

As we discussed in the introduction to this section, Maccoby (2002) suggested that the study of individual differences in gender typing was no longer productive on the basis of various types of evidence, most notably: (*a*) the idea that sex typing is multidimensional and lacks coherence, and (*b*) the situational variability of gender typing. In our review of the longitudinal data, we identified some reasons why prior findings might have led to Maccoby's conclusions. Most importantly, the longitudinal studies suggest that a lack of power and insufficient reliability may have made it difficult to observe temporal stability within domains or coherence across domains. The case is particularly clear for studies of sex segregation. The studies of very short-term stability suggest that children do vary from day-to-day and week-to-week in the proportion of time spent with same- versus other-sex peers. Over greater numbers of data points and amounts of time, however, relative consistency of individual children can be seen (e.g., Martin & Fabes 2001). This observation also speaks to the apparent lack of coherence seen across different indices of gender typing. Indeed, when stable, reliable measures are used, coherence across indices is often observed (e.g., Martin & Fabes 2001, Serbin et al. 1993). In short, based on the findings reviewed, we conclude that the study of individual differences in gender typing may be more productive than has recently been thought. Nevertheless, we also urge caution: It would be unreasonable to conclude that gender typing is strong and stable throughout life, because the database is limited in a number of ways.

First, it is not clear how long such differences remain stable. For example, gender-typed behavior is perhaps most visible in young children, when rigid distinctions appear in children's appearance and play. Many if not most preschool girls show some manifestation of extreme "girliness," refusing to wear anything but a dress, often pink and frilly, whereas boys are draped with superman capes or are holding swords and acting as superheroes (Dunn & Hughes 2001, Halim et al. 2009, Maccoby 1998, Ruble et al. 2007a). We know almost nothing about the stability of such behaviors after preschool, however. It may be necessary to examine how one kind of gender typing at one age relates to a different kind at a later age (McHale et al. 2004). Does a lack of interest in dresses predict later interest in sports or playing with boys? Future research using both longitudinal and retrospective methods may provide answers to such questions.

Second, it is not clear which forms of gender typing may be most stable and best characterize the essence of individual differences. The review of longitudinal studies focused on two frequently examined elements of gender typing (sex segregation and interests/activity preferences). Other aspects of gender development may turn out to be more fundamental, however, at least at some ages. One such candidate is a sense of oneself in relation to males and females. How important or central is gender to self-concept? How typical does one feel as a male or female? Multi-dimensional theories of social identity demonstrate the significance of such distinctions after the early elementary school years (Ashmore et al. 2004, Egan & Perry 2001). Moreover, perhaps stable individual differences are characterized not only by general feelings of typicality and centrality but also by the specific nature of one's fit with gender (Tobin et al. 2009). For example, one preadolescent girl may recognize that she is not a typical female in the sense of having more interest than other females have in sports and less interest in room decoration or make-up, but she may feel part of girls as a group and want to look and act feminine in manner. Other children's sense of gender may emphasize avoiding gender-typical characteristics that they dislike: a girl may eschew the giggly, girly stuff; a boy may try to distance himself from macho elements of maleness.

Finally, future research might examine whether stable individual differences in certain gender-related cognitions emerge after preschool. Most children pass through a phase of believing that it is morally wrong for a boy to wear nail polish or for a girl to play football, but this typically ends by early elementary school (Ruble et al. 2006). Thus, individual differences in tolerance of gender-atypical behaviors may be found later. Indeed, recent research has shown quite high levels of stability (0.5–0.6) in gender role attitudes over a two-year period in 10- to 12-year-olds (McHale et al. 2004). Also, a recent study provided direct support for the idea that once the period of rigidity has passed, individual differences may emerge. Stable individual differences in reactions to gender role violations were found across two time points and related to self-esteem only for children 5 years or older, past peak rigidity (Lurye et al. 2008).

In short, our analysis of longitudinal research suggests that conclusions about the lack of evidence for stable individual differences in gender typing may have been limited by looking too hard and with too few data points for some unified construct. Although gender typing is clearly multi-dimensional, there may be stable elements in some components (e.g., behavior/interests) but not in others (e.g., attitudes/stereotypes), at least at particular ages. Perhaps, then, it would be productive to examine individual differences in gender typing as a developmentally malleable construct. Developmental factors may limit the extent to which biological predispositions can be expressed, change the way children are cognitively capable of thinking about gender, and expose them to varying social influences. Thus, the form of gender typing that is paramount may vary at different phases of life, and different combinations of biological, cognitive, and socialization processes could contribute to individual differences in gender typing at different times.

HOW DOES THE STUDY OF GENDER DEVELOPMENT BENEFIT FROM DYNAMIC ANALYSES?

Gender development research has been guided by theories that offer differing explanations about the origins of gender typing and sex differences. These theories emphasize a variety of different processes, including cognitive developmental changes (e.g., Bigler & Liben 2007, Kohlberg 1966, Martin & Halverson 1981), socialization (Bussey & Bandura 1999, Mischel 1966), and proximal (McCarthy & Arnold 2008) and distal biological influences (e.g., evolutionary pressures) (see Ruble et al. 2006 for a review of these theories as well as the multiple distinctions currently being made for each type of process). Despite differences, a common element among these theories is reliance on data collected at one or few time points, and in rare cases, multiple assessments are made over time and then are aggregated. Aggregation and limited assessment methods provide information about concurrent relations and long-term patterns; however, these methods sacrifice important information about variability over time, and are not focused on assessing short-term, moment-to-moment changes.

By applying methods and concepts used in the physical and biological sciences, the variation that most psychologists have considered error or background noise may be found to contain "the dynamic signature of purposive behavior" (Van Orden et al. 2003, p. 331). Dynamic studies of this background noise in behavior are beginning to reveal new and potentially important insights about a range of psychological and social processes, including motor development (e.g., Adolph et al. 2003, Kelso 1995), emotional development (Lewis & Granic 2000), dyadic play (Steenbeek & van Geert 2008), structure of the self (Nowak et al. 2000), cognitive development (van Geert 2003), and stereotyping (e.g.,

Correll 2008). This revolutionary approach to describing and understanding patterns, based on complexity theory (Waldrop 1992) or commonly labeled "dynamic systems approach" or "dynamic systems theory" (Thelen & Smith 1998), has been gaining ground across fields.

Dynamic systems (DS) approaches have potential for illuminating processes involved in gender development by providing both conceptual and methodological advances that enable researchers to assess fine-grained as well as larger-grained developmental temporal variations (Lichtwarck-Aschoff et al. 2008) and, especially important for developmental research, to delineate relationships between different timescales (e.g., Lewis 2002). A comprehensive theory of gender development needs to describe and explain long-term developmental changes but must also describe how gender is experienced and plays out in short-term interactions with objects and people. DS approaches provide conceptual underpinnings and methods for identifying patterns of behavior change over time, and in some cases, how these patterns may relate to one another.

The DS approach is appealing for a number of other reasons. Gender-related topics (e.g., work and family issues) have taken center stage in heated discussions about the roles of nature versus nurture, mainly concerning the origins and nature of sex differences. Because the DS approach advocates no distinctions between the sources of influence on a system (Oyama 2000), it offers a rapprochement for debates about nature versus nurture. Furthermore, the DS approach has potential to provide a theoretical umbrella that would incorporate aspects of many gender development theories. Specifically, adopting a DS approach suggests new ways to collect, analyze, and describe data but provides limited guidance on which parameters to study; existing theories help to fill that gap.

Thus far, DS analysis of gender development has been limited to a few topics: sexual orientation (e.g., Diamond 2007), children's sex segregation (Martin 2008, Martin et al. 2005), and mother-infant interactions (Fausto-Sterling et al. 2008). Below, we provide a description of basic concepts of DS approaches and then employ topics in gender development and review empirical studies to illustrate some of the major features of dynamic approaches (see Thelen & Smith 1994, 1998, 2006).

Dynamics and Complex Systems: Basic Concepts

Dynamic analyses are applied to complex systems, which are systems characterized by simple, interrelated interacting elements, where the interactions of these elements give rise to higher-order global patterns (e.g., Waldrop 1992). This process, called self-organization, does not require a higher-order agent and is not preprogrammed. Structures arise as the elements spontaneously organize and reorganize into emergent systems that are larger and more complex (e.g., Williams 1997). Examples of complex systems abound: heart-rate variability, army ant swarms, termite nest building, and the formation of hurricanes.

Scientists interested in applying dynamic systems must first identify and define the variable that represents the system of interest, called the collective variable (Thelen & Smith 2006). The collective variable should be clearly defined and observable, and understanding how it behaves over different conditions is important. In developmental psychology, some classic examples of collective variables that have been studied include walking, reaching, and word learning.

Dynamic systems are marked by fluctuations from factors internal and external to the system, and this inherent activity provides potential for changes to occur in the system. In some cases, the system dampens down the fluctuations, allowing stability; in other cases, the system is "perturbed," that is, it loses coherence, exhibits high degrees of variability, and may experience a qualitative change (i.e., phase shift) to a new coordinated state. As dynamic systems experience fluctuations, they have certain preferred states that occur with a high probability under certain conditions (called attractors). When displaced from these preferred states, the system tends to return there (Thelen & Smith 2006). Some of these attractors are strong; others are weaker and have less "pull" on behavior. Other states act as repellors because behavior never or seldom settles there.

A goal for researchers is to understand and map both the immediate and longer-term stability/variability of complex systems. Researchers strive to identify the shifts among states because this is when the agents of change are most easily identified. These change agents (called control parameters) may be obvious (e.g., practice facilitating learning), but they also may appear incidental or minor (Thelen & Smith 2006). For instance, in a classic study, King & West (1988) found that male cowbird song development was influenced by a seemingly unimportant factor—the patterning of brief wing flickering in female cowbirds. In developmental research, an aspect of language development that may appear unrelated to another domain of language development has been identified as an agent of change: Children who show a fast rate of word learning are limited in their ability to access well-known words (Gershkoff-Stowe & Smith 1997). Regardless of their salience, such agents of change are more easily identified at transition points because they vary with changes in the collective variable.

Children's Play Choices: Sex Segregation as a Dynamic System

Children's tendency to assort by sex is an example of a complex system. Sex segregation is a pervasive, early-developing pattern that increases over childhood until interactions are so segregated that boys and girls have been described as growing up in separate cultures (Maccoby & Jacklin 1987). A DS analysis of sex segregation may focus on the patterns that emerge over time in a child's choice of play partners and examine how these choices vary over the school year. Important variables to examine when children first begin congregating with peers (e.g., in a new class) might include

social factors (e.g., each child's prior experiences with peers) as well as biological factors (e.g., hormone levels) or biosocial influences, such as the child's temperament (e.g., being inhibited). Children's choices are interdependent with others in the class: Choices are constrained by who is available to play on a given day, at a given time, and depend upon the choices made by others in the class immediately before the child decides to find a partner. Degrees of freedom for choosing a partner are lost the more other children have already claimed a partner.

Through repeated interactions and reshuffling, patterns of play may change as interactions become increasingly governed by children's experiences with classmates; their responsiveness to bids, play styles, and shared interests. Individual children may settle into particular patterns of play with particular partners. For instance, from individual children's experiences, more and longer-playing same-sex dyads may emerge in the system. As these processes play out over longer time intervals, a child's dyadic play may grow into larger groups of same-sex children, and these groupings may be formed and maintained depending upon the interests of children or the desires or openness of the initial dyad to including other children. Interestingly, simulations have demonstrated that even when individuals show only very slight preferences for similar others, segregation emerges (Schelling 1971, Wilensky 1997).

Play patterns can also be viewed from the perspective of the entire class. A series of bird's-eye snapshots of a playground would show that the number of children in class who are involved in sex-segregated play varies as pairings and groupings of children form and break up, with groupings shifting over time. With more children involved in same-sex groupings, these groups may have enhanced appeal, and so other children will be drawn into the groups, thus illustrating how the higher-order structure of same-sex groups may also influence patterning of interactions. Sex segregation as an emergent structure of the system may become increasingly evident at both the individual-child and classroom levels. Although no one person directed the class or an individual child to choose same-sex partners for play, sex segregation can emerge, suggesting a self-organizing system.

Variability in Systems: Gender-Typed Activities, Sex Segregation, and Gender Identity

Dynamic systems analyses involve studying temporal patterning—how a system transforms from one state to another over time. Scientists studying a system need to understand the short- and long-term stability and change in the system so the regular variability is distinguishable from extreme variability. Extreme variability holds particular fascination as it may signal a shift of a system from one kind of attractor to a new kind of attractor, or to a more highly organized state. For this reason, scientists using dynamic analyses may use cross-sectional data to narrow their focus to the time frames of most interest and then collect intensive data about variations in the primary variables of interest as well as about potential agents of change.

A gender application to illustrate this point would be the theoretically important issue of how gender-typed toy choices emerge. Since cross-sectional research suggests that boys begin to show gender-typed toy choices (e.g., playing with trucks) around the age of two (Berenbaum et al. 2008, Ruble et al. 2006), bracketing this time with intensive data collection about toy choices would be particularly interesting. Also, to better understand factors influencing such choices, other information about the play situation (e.g., other available toys, presence of peers), parents (e.g., stereotypic beliefs), and children (e.g., gender knowledge, activity level) should be collected. Developmental changes in any of these may influence boys' sense of control or feelings of pressure concerning toy selection. Studies of fine-grained changes from day-to-day or moment-to-moment gain import, and multiple data points are needed to detect these patterns.

When children enter preschool, qualitative changes may occur in their toy and activity choices. Preschool is a dramatically different setting from that at home; more peers of both sexes are available as play partners, and adult supervision may be low. Dynamic analyses involving longitudinal data about toy choices at home and school would shed light on this transition. Analysis of the activities children engage in at home versus at preschool, and the presence and reactions of peers, would provide insights into whether children's preferences change dynamically in preschool, where many toys are available, peers may tease them for "gender-inappropriate" play, and adults may react differently than their parents.

Fine-grained data have been collected on young children's peer choices, making this topic suitable for illustrating both stability and variability in dynamic systems. Controversy has arisen about the stability of sex segregation (see How Stable Are Individual Differences in Gender Typing section, above), but it appears that as more snapshots of behavior are aggregated, sex segregation becomes more stable until it reaches a moderately high level (Martin & Fabes 2001). The stability of sex segregation may be questioned in part because of the variability in this behavior from day-to-day. To illustrate this more clearly, notice the day-to-day variation in children's play partners, based on observations conducted during the fall term for four children depicted in **Figure 1**. Variability is apparent, although two children also show strong same-sex preferences day-to-day, but the other two children do not. There also is stability over time; children's patterns remain similar into the spring term of data collection. Extending this type of analysis to explore when and how variations occur would be fascinating.

Another approach for applying dynamic analysis is to focus on the potential instability of constructs believed to be stable. Walking is a stable feature of most humans' behavior, but the exact form of walking at any given time depends on many different factors, including the type of surface being walked upon (e.g., thick

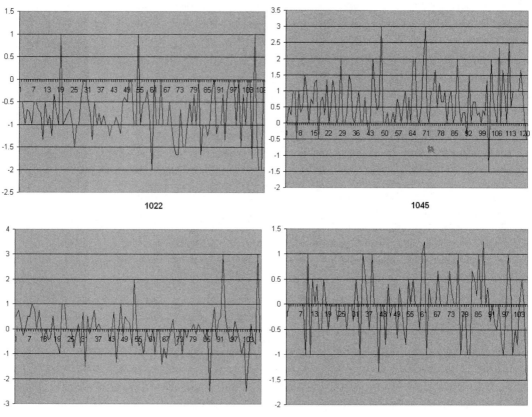

Figure 1

Day-to-day variations in children's play partner choices as a function of sex of child and long-term patterning. Observed play partner choices were summed and averaged per day of observation using the following: Each boy play partner was given a +1; each girl was given a −1. Children with ID numbers 1032 and 1022 were girls; children with ID numbers 1041 and 1045 were boys. For girls, data below the 0 point represent same-sex peer play; for boys, data above the 0 point represent same-sex play. The graphs at the top (1032 and 1041) represent patterns of children who tend to show long-term preferences for same-sex play; the graphs at the bottom represent patterns of children who tend to show long-term preferences for playing with both sexes. Variability is apparent in all the graphs (DiDonato & Martin 2009).

rug versus tiled floor, slope of surface). Most researchers think of gender identity as being a stable feature, but if we consider when variations in gender identity might occur, it broadens the perspective on gender identity. An interesting analysis would be to explore variations in feelings (e.g., gender typicality, comfort) and displays of gender identity (e.g., style of dressing, voice, gestures) over different types of social "surfaces" (e.g., being in a sports bar, holding a baby) (Martin 2000). Analysis of moment-to-moment changes in the patterning

of gender identity may reveal surprising insights about gender development (a similar point is made about identity formation in Lichtwarck-Aschoff et al. 2008). For instance, collecting intensive time-series data about feelings of gender typicality (e.g., "How similar do you feel to your own sex right now?") over a range of situations may illustrate that feelings of gender typicality are strong and show little variability in situations where one is a minority member, but that gender typicality is low but more variable when one is in a same-sex situation.

Dynamic Contexts: Gender Cognitions and Socialization

An important feature of dynamic analysis is how "context" is viewed. Although context is considered important in gender theories, it is often conceptualized as being distal (i.e., cultural contexts). In contrast, DS theorists view context as a dynamic characteristic of interactions, one that is temporally and spatially close and is an aspect of the interaction process itself (Steenbeek & van Geert 2008). Even influences typically considered distal, stable, or abstract are represented and carried forward in time by their embodiment within everyday interactions. For instance, gender stereotypes and gender identity become embodied as children dynamically engage in "gendering"—remembering gender and acting on gender—incorporating the immediate contextual factors, and this being carried forward to the next moment of knowing and acting on gender.

Developmental processes that occur in real time then carry over and become consolidated and generalized across different contexts (Fischer & Bidell 1998), and these then influence and constrain behavior (e.g., Lewis 2000) (although there is controversy about the extent to which this happens) (for review of the issue, see Witherington 2007). For instance, as toddlers come to understand their sex, become motivated by same-sex expectations, and begin to develop stereotypes, these features can be carried into interactions with others. The patterning and display of the gendered self may evolve into new forms (e.g., styles of dress, play partners, activities), which vary from moment-to-moment and over longer time periods. Thinking of gender as being enacted in each interaction is similar to proposals from sociological research traditions focusing on the social construction of gender (West & Zimmerman 1991).

Gender socialization provides a good example of how both the child's and parents' cognitions are enacted in moment-to-moment interactions through the dynamic embodiment of gender. Parental expectations about what it means to have a child who is either a boy or girl (expectations colored by cultural values, etc.) become displayed as actions with the child (e.g., glances, touching, toy offering), and these embodied expectations interact with the child's phenotypic and early behavioral features. Thus, gender socialization involves parents and siblings, peers, other socialization agents, and the individual child, who all act and interact in varied contexts.

Methods and Analyses of Dynamic Systems

Studying complex systems involves identifying the collective variables that capture the behavior of interest and then collecting a long time series of data to watch the emergence of behaviors. Social scientists may avoid dynamic analyses because they expect that they will have to collect thousands of observations to identify complex patterns of behavior. However, even shorter time frames and smaller sets of time-series data may reveal important features that traditional methods may not disclose (Williams 1997), especially when investigators use some of the newly proposed analytic techniques (e.g., Finan et al. 2008).

The recognition and study of complex systems have promoted development of an array of techniques designed to understand these systems, including techniques for nonlinear dynamics, time-series analyses, data visualization (e.g., Lamey et al. 2004), and computer simulations to model the behavior of systems (e.g., Griffin et al. 2004, Schafer et al. 2009). This new and expanded toolbox provides better ways of describing, analyzing, and interpreting temporal data of all types (Ward 2002). The mathematics involved in describing systems can be complex and unfamiliar to psychologists (e.g., May 1976); thus, DS ideas often are applied heuristically for thinking about patterns and for directing the kinds of data that are obtained rather than using the toolkit of analyses that describe obtained time-series data. However, psychologists have become increasingly interested in developing and applying these analytic tools (see Boker & Wenger 2007, van Geert 2003).

For instance, Thelen and colleagues (2001) conducted rigorous modeling of a developmental phenomenon involving touching patterns of infants (the A-not-B effect), which was originally identified by Piaget. Others are refining and expanding upon DS approaches to better integrate these ideas with connectionist models (e.g., Spencer & Schoner 2003) and neurobiology (Lewis 2005). Regardless of how it is employed, DS perspectives hold promise for revealing patterns of gender development previously unrecognized.

Dynamic Analyses of Gendered Play Partners and Activities

Not all the applications of DS to gender development are as abstract as we have presented above. In this section, we outline specific examples of studies that have been conducted to apply a dynamic systems approach to gender development.

Data visualization, attractors, and repellors in children's sex segregation. In a dynamic view of sex segregation, children are seen to settle into certain behavioral patterns. This illustrates a characteristic of a dynamic system: Despite a large number of possible patterns among system elements, only a few ever stabilize. Dynamic analyses have been used to study the patterns of children's play partners in preschool classes and the role of gender in these interactions. Martin and colleagues (2005) used a new data-visualization tool, called state space grids (SSGs), to explore the extent to which preschool children showed attraction for same-sex and behaviorally similar children. Developmental scientists interested in applying DS methods (e.g., Granic & Lamey 2002, Hollenstein et al. 2004) recognized the need for a methodology to visualize system dynamics; thus, they developed the SSG technique (e.g., Lewis et al. 1999).

SSGs involve mapping of dimensions onto a state space to determine the regularity or stability of the patterns (for a description of how to use GridWare, see Hollenstein 2007).

In Martin et al. (2005), SSGs were constructed based on children's choices of play partners derived from scan observations of three classes of preschool children over several months in order to examine whether sex of peers and behavioral tendencies act as attractors. Children were divided into types using cluster analysis: externalizing, internalizing, and socially competent children; play patterns of target children with types of peers (rather than one other child) were analyzed using SSGs. If children's play partner choices related strongly to behavioral similarity, then competent children should choose other competent children regardless of sex; if their selections relate to sex, then children should choose on the basis of similar sex regardless of behavior.

Attractors were characterized in three ways. First, a high number of individual interactions in the state space regions representing play with same-sex peers or particular peer qualities (e.g., externalizing) would indicate that those spaces are attractors. If same-sex peers act as attractors, then we would expect, for instance, that girls would have more interactions in the "girl peer" region than in the "boy peer" region. Second, when a region is an attractor, children should enter it quickly; for instance, early in the time series, girls would be expected to play with girls and would have few (or no) interactions with boys before they move into the "girl peer" region. Third, if a region is an attractor, children should return to the region quickly. Whenever girls leave the "girl peer" region, they would be expected to have relatively few interactions with boys before moving back to playing with girls.

The results supported these ideas. Same-sex peers were strong attractors for children: Both sexes had more than twice as many interactions with same-sex than with other-sex peers, were faster to return to same-sex peers, and started playing with them more quickly. Interestingly, these patterns were apparent even in the first 20 observations obtained on children after only several weeks of preschool. **Figure 2** illustrates a typical pattern for a girl's first 20 interactions. The SSG shows data from a competent girl, whose first coded play bout is with a girl (open circle), and the pattern shows that she plays with girls more than with boys. Externalizing and social competence also contributed to behavioral states, but patterns varied by sex of child and peer (e.g., boys were more attracted to externalizing boys than to externalizing girls). As **Figure 2** illustrates, the competent girl played much more with competent girls than with other girls, but she did not play with competent boys at all. Overall, the findings suggest that both the sex of peers and their behavioral qualities help fashion the social organization in the classroom.

In a similar study, Martin (2008) compared patterns of children who were highly gender typed in play to those with less gender-typed play patterns in order to examine whether children who differed in their overall patterns showed differences early in the time series of observations. Interestingly, within the first 20 observed interactions, highly gender-typed children experienced more positive emotions with same-sex than with other-sex peers; less gender-typed children showed no difference. These findings suggest that children who have early positive emotional experiences with same-sex peers but not with other-sex peers incorporate these experiences into their play, such that same-sex peers have increasing appeal, whereas other-sex peers lose their appeal. In this way, emotional experiences with peers appear to contribute to the overall patterning of children's play and to sex segregation in the class.

These studies use data-visualization techniques to illustrate a new approach to examining peer interaction patterns and suggest that both the sex of peers and peers' behavior act as attractors. Additional research involving moment-to-moment coding of behavior and new techniques for analyzing group patterns will allow for even more detailed dynamic analyses of children's behavior with peers.

Self-organized criticality in the temporal patterning of children's gendered behavior. Many complex systems show a particularly intriguing pattern of organization, called

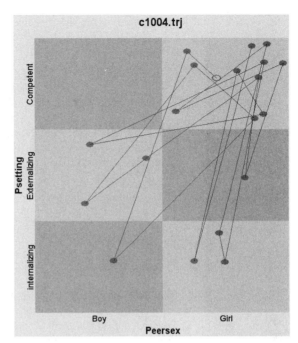

Figure 2

A socially competent girl's state space grid, illustrating her patterns of play with peers of different sexes and different behavioral qualities over the first 20 observed interactions. The x-axis represents the sex of the peer with whom the target girl interacts; the y-axis represents the behavioral quality of the peers as determined by clustering teacher ratings of children's behavior. Each solid circle represents a single observed interaction, and the open circle represents the first observed interaction (with a socially competent girl). Lines between circles represent the ordering of observations. This girl showed strong sex selection: 16 of her first 20 interactions were with girls. She also showed a preference for interacting with socially competent girls but not boys (Martin 2008).

self-organization near a critical state. These systems are balanced between enough stability to maintain order and enough instability or variation to be adaptive to change (Bak et al. 1989). Adaptability is enhanced because new alternatives can be generated as needed in response to varying circumstances (e.g., Van Orden et al. 2003). In physiological systems, self-organized criticality is associated with well-being and health, and its loss or deterioration is related to disease, depression, and aging (Goldberger 1996, Linkenkaer-Hansen et al. 2005, Sosnoff & Newell 2008).

Self-organization near a critical state involves "self-similarity" across time-scales; in other words, if one small portion of the time series is magnified, its appearance is similar to the larger time series in which it is embedded. That is, small-scale patterns reflect the patterns that would be expected at larger scales, such that identifying a regularity in a 2-minute window of time may share similarity to a pattern found in a 16-minute window, and both may share similarity to a pattern found on a much longer timescale (e.g., developmental changes that occur from early to later childhood). This self-organization near a critical state is represented by the presence of long-term, positively correlated variability in a time series (Treffner & Kelso 1999, Van Orden et al. 2003). Time series with completely independent data do not exhibit self-similarity. Given the implications for understanding different timescales and how they relate to one another, the implications of finding self-similarity in systems are far-ranging, especially for developmental scientists.

DiDonato (2008) applied both dynamic and traditional analyses to explore whether children's gendered behavior shows self-organized criticality and whether temporal patterns relate to children's adjustment. Brief observations of preschool children's activities and play partners were conducted daily over several months. By combining gender typing of activities and play partners across observations each day, DiDonato derived a single indicator of gendered behavior. Each child's time series was plotted and analyzed for self-organized criticality (e.g., Hurst 1951), and the results indicated this pattern, suggesting that children exhibited flexibility in their gendered behavior. For example, the implication of the findings is that a girl who normally plays with girls may adapt her behavior by playing with a boy if he is playing with her favorite toy. Furthermore, flexibility in gendered behavior was positively related to adjustment in girls but not in boys. Boys' restricted gender roles may constrain the relation between flexible behavior and adjustment.

These findings have implications for debates about how gender roles relate to adjustment and provide a compelling example of how both traditional and dynamic approaches can be combined to yield more information than would either approach alone. In this case, the short-term

patterning of activities and partners related to adjustment, and it suggests that further explorations of changes in children's gendered behavior at different timescales are warranted.

In sum, DS approaches have potential for providing a new lens for viewing gender development. DS approaches adopt unique views of context, focus on describing variability, provide information about patterning of behavior over both short and longer developmental time frames, and suggest new techniques and different methods of data analyses and collection. Adopting a DS approach also has the potential to provide an all-encompassing theoretical umbrella and deflates controversy surrounding the roles of nature and nurture in gender development. At a broader level, DS approaches cross-cut disciplinary boundaries, bridging methods and concepts across disciplines. Highlights of the appeal of exploring DS approaches include discovering new answers to old problems, recognizing new types of questions, and ultimately advancing alternative accounts of gender development.

CONCLUSIONS

Children's gender development unfolds over long time frames of average or normative change, over shorter time frames such as the emergence of relatively stable individual preferences in with whom or with what to play during the early school years, and over much shorter time frames—micro timescales—such as when an individual child selects an outfit to wear or carries on an interaction with a peer over a toy. In the present review, we illustrated each of these time frames in terms of a few specific current, and sometimes controversial, topics in the field of gender development.

First, we took the long view, examining normative changes from infancy through middle adolescence in key aspects of children's beliefs and behaviors regarding gender distinctions. In this way, we were able to speak to the question of temporal ordering of different elements of gender development and, thereby, analyze certain controversies within the field about how early children understand gender distinctions and how that understanding relates to behavior. Moreover, the analysis of temporal ordering helps generate hypotheses for future research about what indications of gender prejudice, such as ingroup favoritism, might represent for young children who can understand gender stereotypes but not necessarily status inequities between the sexes.

Normative trends involve only averages across individuals; they do not, however, inform us about whether there are stable individual differences in expressions of gender typing. Whether there are continuities in individual gender typing over time has been another important but controversial topic in gender development. For instance, identifying stability in sex segregation would suggest that individual children vary in their preferences and that sex segregation is not simply due to situational variability or normative constraints as had previously been assumed. Thus, in the second section, we reviewed studies of longitudinal change within individuals over shorter periods of time. We discovered that there is more stability in sex segregation and gender-typed activities and preferences than previously thought. However, future research must determine how long stability exists and over which periods of development.

Another advantage of normative trends is that they indicate at what points developmentally it would be useful to search for stable individual differences, such as after periods of rapid change, as when children first enter preschool. In the third section, we described a new tool for taking advantage of such opportunities. Dynamic systems theory provides a coherent set of principles and methods for examining change over differing time frames. Socialization, cognitive, and biological processes can be explored over multiple time frames using techniques that focus on temporal patterning of behavior. Dynamic systems theory complements existing theories by providing more nuanced views of gender at different timescales. For instance, sex segregation exhibits both variability and stability from a dynamic perspective. Particularly intriguing is the potential for small-scale patterns to provide insights into large-scale patterns. For systems that exhibit self-similarity, a pattern that appears at a microlevel time frame mimics the pattern found at a more macrolevel time frame. Considering similarity across timescales is an idea that, in our view, has no counterpart in developmental research or theorizing.

Developmental research on gender has primarily focused attention on the longer timescales to assess normative developmental patterning. Less attention has been focused on shorter timescales to explore individual patterns and stability of behavior, and very little has been done to explore gender development in terms of micro timescales. We hope our review has made it clear that comprehensive explanations of gender need to consider each of these timescale perspectives.

DISCLOSURE STATEMENT

The authors are not aware of any biases that might be perceived as affecting the objectivity of this review.

ACKNOWLEDGMENTS

This review was supported by a grant from the National Institute of Child Health and Human Development (1 R01 HD45816) and a grant from the T. Denny Sanford Foundation awarded to Carol Lynn Martin; a National Institute of Child Health and Human Development Research Grant (1 R01 HD04994) to Diane N. Ruble; and a National Science Foundation IRADS grant (0721383). We are very grateful to Faith Greulich for assistance in preparing the manuscript and to Nia Amazeen, Matt DiDonato, May Ling Halim, Tom Hollenstein, and Kristina Zosuls for comments on an earlier draft.

LITERATURE CITED

Adolph KE, Vereijken B, Shrout PE. 2003. What changes in infant walking and why. *Child Dev.* 74:475–97

Alexander GM, Hines M. 1994. Gender labels and play styles: their relative contribution to children's selection of playmates. *Child Dev.* 65:869–79

Arthur AE, Bigler RS, Liben LS, Gelman SA, Ruble DN. 2008. Gender stereotyping and prejudice: a developmental intergroup perspective. In *Intergroup Attitudes and Relations in Childhood Through Adulthood*, ed. S Levy, M Killen, pp. 66–85. New York: Oxford Univ. Press

Ashmore RD, Deaux K, McLaughlin-Volpe T. 2004. An organizing framework for collective identity: articulation and significance of multidimensionality. *Psychol. Bull.* 130:80–114

Bak P, Chen K, Creutz M. 1989. Self-organized criticality in the "Game of Life." *Nature* 342:780–81

Baldwin DA, Moses LK. 1996. The ontogeny of social information gathering. *Child Dev.* 67:1915–39

Bandura A, Bussey K. 2004. On broadening the cognitive, motivational, and sociocultural scope of theorizing about gender development and functioning: comment on Martin, Ruble, and Szkrybalo (2002). *Psychol. Bull.* 130:691–701

Bartini M. 2006. Gender role flexibility in early adolescence: developmental change in attitudes, self-perceptions, and behaviors. *Sex Roles* 55:233–45

Bauer PJ, Liebl M, Stennes L. 1998. Pretty is to dress as brave is to suitcoat: gender-based property-to-property inferences by 4-1/2-year-old children. *Merrill-Palmer Q.* 44:355–77

Berenbaum SA, Martin CL, Hanish LD, Briggs PT, Fabes RA. 2008. Sex differences in children's play. In *Sex Differences in the Brain: From Genes to Behavior*, ed. JB Becker, KJ Berkley, N Geary, E Hampson, JP Herman, EA Young, pp. 275–90. Oxford, UK: Oxford Univ. Press

Berndt TJ, Heller KA. 1986. Gender stereotypes and social inferences: a developmental study. *J. Personal. Soc. Psychol.* 50:889–98

Bigler RS, Arthur AE, Hughes JM. 2008. The politics of race and gender: children's perceptions of discrimination and the U.S. presidency. *Anal. Soc. Issues Public Policy* 8:1–30

Bigler RS, Jones LC, Lobliner DB. 1997. Social categorization and the formation of intergroup attitudes in children. *Child Dev.* 68:530–43

Bigler RS, Liben LS. 2007. Developmental intergroup theory: explaining and reducing children's social stereotyping and prejudice. *Curr. Dir. Psychol. Sci.* 16:162–66

Boker SM, Wenger MJ. 2007. *Data Analytic Techniques for Dynamical Systems*. Mahwah, NJ: Erlbaum

Brewer MB. 2001. Ingroup identification and intergroup conflict: When does ingroup love become outgroup hate? In *Social Identity, Intergroup Conflict, and Conflict Reduction*, ed. RD Ashmore, L Jussim, D Wilder, pp. 17–41. New York: Oxford Univ. Press

Brown CS, Bigler RS. 2005. Children's perceptions of discrimination: a developmental model. *Child Dev.* 76:533–53

Bussey K, Bandura A. 1999. Social cognitive theory of gender development and differentiation. *Psychol. Rev.* 106:676–713

Cameron JA, Alvarez JM, Ruble DN, Fuligni AJ. 2001. Children's lay theories about ingroups and outgroups: reconceptualizing research on "prejudice." *Personal. Soc. Psychol. Rev.* 5:118–28

Campbell A, Shirley L, Caygill L. 2002. Sex-typed preferences in three domains: Do two-year-olds need cognitive variables? *Br. J. Psychol.* 93:203–17

Connor JM, Serbin LA. 1977. Behaviorally-based masculine and feminine activity preference scales for preschoolers: correlates with other classroom behaviors and cognitive tests. *Child Dev.* 48:1411–16

Correll J. 2008. $1/f$ noise and effort on implicit measures of bias. *J. Personal. Soc. Psychol.* 94:48–59

Deaux K, Lewis LL. 1984. Structure of gender stereotypes: inter-relationships among components and gender label. *J. Personal. Soc. Psychol.* 46:991–1004

Diamond L. 2007. A dynamic systems approach to the development and expression of female same-sex sexuality. *Perspect. Psychol. Sci.* 2:142–61

DiDonato MD. 2008. *Children's gendered behavior and psychological adjustment: longitudinal and dynamic relations.* Thesis, Arizona State Univ., Tempe

DiDonato MD, Martin CL. 2009. Variations in children's play patterns day to day. Tempe, AZ. Manuscript in preparation.

Dunn J, Hughes C. 2001. "I got some swords and you're dead!": violent fantasy, antisocial behavior, friendship, and moral sensibility in young children. *Child Dev.* 72:491–505

Edelbrock C, Sugawara AI. 1978. Acquisition of sex-typed preferences in preschool children. *Dev. Psychol.* 14:614–23

Egan SK, Perry DG. 2001. Gender identity: a multidimensional analysis with implications for psychosocial adjustment. *Dev. Psychol.* 37:451–63

Epstein S. 1980. The stability of behavior: II. Implications for psychological research. *Am. Psychol.* 35:790–806

Fagan JF, Singer LT. 1979. The role of simple feature differences in infants' recognition of faces. *Infant Behav. Dev.* 2:39–45

Fausto-Sterling A, Coll CG, Schooler D. 2008. *Towards a dynamic study of gender in infant development.* Presented at Gender Dev. Conf., San Francisco

Finan PH, Hessler EE, Amazeen PG, Butner J, Zautra AJ, Tennen H. 2009. Nonlinear oscillations in pain prediction accuracy. *Nonlinear Dynamics Psychol. Life Sci.* In press

Fischer KW, Bidell TR. 1998. Dynamic development of psychological structures in action and thought. In *Handbook of Child Psychology: Vol. 1. Theoretical Models of Human Development*, ed. RM Lerner, pp. 313–99. New York: Wiley

Gershkoff-Stowe L, Smith LB. 1997. A curvilinear trend in naming errors as a function of early vocabulary growth. *Cogn. Psychol.* 34:37–71

Giles JW, Heyman GD. 2005. Young children's beliefs about the relationship between gender and aggressive behavior. *Child Dev.* 76:107–21

Glick P, Fiske ST. 2001. Ambivalent sexism. In *Advances in Experimental Social Psychology*, ed. MP Zanna, pp. 115–88. Thousand Oaks, CA: Academic

Goldberger AL. 1996. Non-linear dynamics for clinicians: chaos theory, fractals, and complexity at the bedside. *Lancet* 347:1312–14

Golombok S, Rust J. 1993. The Pre-school Activities Inventory: a standardized assessment of gender role in children. *Psychol. Assess.* 5:131–36

Golombok S, Rust J, Zervoulis K, Croudace T, Golding J, Hines M. 2008. Developmental trajectories of sex-typed behavior in boys and girls: a longitudinal general population study of children aged 2.5–8 years. *Child Dev.* 79:1583–93

Granic I, Lamey AV. 2002. Combining dynamic-systems and multivariate analyses to compare the mother-child interactions of externalizing subtypes. *J. Abnorm. Child Psychol.* 30:265–83

Griffin WA, Hanish LD, Martin CL, Fabes RA, Barcelo H, Greenwood P. 2004. PlayMate: new data, new rules, and model validity. In *Agent 2004: Social Dynamics: Interaction, Reflexivity and Emergence*, ed. DL Sallach, CM Macal, MJ North, pp. 339–51. Univ. Chicago & Argonne Natl. Lab.

Halim ML, Ruble DN. 2009. Gender identity and stereotyping in early and middle childhood. In *Handbook of Gender Research in Psychology*, ed. JC Chrisler, DR McCreary. New York: Springer-Verlag. In press

Halim ML, Ruble DN, Greulich F, Lurye LE, Zosuls KM. 2009. Pink frilly dresses: early obsessions and social identity. Manuscript submitted

Heyman GD. 2001. Children's interpretation of ambiguous behavior: evidence for a "boys are bad" bias. *Soc. Dev.* 10:230–47

Hollenstein T. 2007. State space grids: analyzing dynamics across development. *Int. J. Behav. Dev.* 31:384–96

Hollenstein T, Granic I, Stoolmiller M, Snyder J. 2004. Rigidity in parent-child interactions and the development of externalizing and internalizing behavior in early childhood. *J. Abnorm. Child Psychol.* 32:598–602

Hurst HE. 1951. Long term storage capacity of reservoirs. *Trans. Am. Soc. Civil Eng.* 116:770–99

Huston AC. 1983. Sex typing. In *Handbook of Child Psychology: Socialization, Personality, and Social Development*, ed. EM Hetherington, pp. 387–467. New York: Wiley

Kelso JAS. 1995. *Dynamic Patterns: The Self Organization of Brain and Behavior.* Cambridge, MA: MIT Press

Killen M, McGlothlin H, Henning A. 2008. Implicit biases and explicit judgments: a developmental perspective. In *Intergroup Attitudes and Relations in Childhood Through Adulthood*, ed. SR Levy, M Killen, pp. 126–45. Oxford, UK: Oxford Univ. Press

Killen M, Stangor C. 2001. Children's social reasoning about inclusion and exclusion in gender and race peer group contexts. *Child Dev.* 72:174–86

King A, West M. 1988. Searching for the functional origins of cowbird song in eastern brown-headed cowbirds (*Molothrus ate rater*). *Anim. Behav.* 36:1575–88

Kohlberg LA. 1966. A cognitive-developmental analysis of children's sex role concepts and attitudes. In *The Development of Sex Differences*, ed. EE Maccoby, pp. 82–173. Stanford, CA: Stanford Univ. Press

Kowalski K. 2007. The development of social identity and intergroup attitudes in young children. In *Contemporary Perspectives on Social Learning in Early Childhood Education*, ed. ON Saracho, B Spodek, pp. 51–84. Charlotte, NC: Inform. Age Publ.

Kuhn D, Nash SC, Brucken L. 1978. Sex role concepts of two- and three-year-olds. *Child Dev.* 49:445–51

La Freniere P, Strayer FF, Gauthier R. 1984. The emergence of same-sex affiliative preferences among preschool peers: a developmental/ethological perspective. *Child Dev.* 55:1958–65

GridWare (Version 1.1). Freeware available at http://www.oise.utoronto.ca/ssg/gridware.php

Lamey AV, Hollenstein T, Lewis MD, Granic I. 2004. GridWare (version 1.1B). http://statespacegrids.org

Langlois JH, Downs AC. 1980. Mothers, fathers, and peers as socialization agents of sex-typed play behaviors in young children. *Child Dev.* 51:1237–47

Leinbach MD, Hort BE, Fagot BI. 1997. Bears are for boys: metaphorical associations in young children's gender stereotypes. *Cogn. Dev.* 12:107–30

Levy GD. 1999. Gender-typed and non-gender-typed category awareness in toddlers. *Sex Roles* 41:851–73

Levy GD, Haaf RA. 1994. Detection of gender-related categories by 10-month-old infants. *Infant Behav. Dev.* 17:457–59

Lewis MD. 2000. The promise of dynamic systems approaches for an integrated account of human development. *Child Dev.* 71:36–43

Lewis MD. 2002. Interacting time scales in personality (and cognitive) development: intentions, emotions, and emergent forms. In *Microdevelopment: Transition Processes in Development and Learning*, ed. N Granott, J Parziale, pp. 183–212. New York: Cambridge Univ. Press

Lewis MD. 2005. Bridging emotion theory and neurobiology through dynamic systems modeling. *Behav. Brain Sci.* 28:105–30

Lewis MD, Granic I. 2000. *Emotion, Development, and Self-Organization: Dynamic Systems Approaches to Emotional Development*. Cambridge, UK: Cambridge Univ. Press

Lewis MD, Lamey AV, Douglas L. 1999. A new dynamic systems method for the analysis of early socioemotional development. *Dev. Sci.* 2:457–75

Liben LS, Bigler RS. 2002. The developmental course of gender differentiation. In *Monographs of the Society for Research in Child Development*, ed. W Overton, pp. vii–147. Cambridge, MA: Blackwell Sci.

Liben LS, Bigler RS, Krogh HR. 2001. Pink and blue collar jobs: children's judgments of job status and job aspirations in relation to sex of worker. *J. Exp. Child Psychol.* 79:346–63

Lichtwarck-Aschoff A, van Geert P, Bosma H, Kunnen S. 2008. Time and identity: a framework for research and identity formation. *Dev. Rev.* 28:370–400

Linkenkaer-Hansen K, Monto S, Rytsala H, Suominen K, Isometsa E, Kahkonen S. 2005. Breakdown of long-range temporal correlations in theta oscillations in patients with major depressive disorder. *J. Neurosci.* 25:10131–37

Lloyd B, Duveen G. 1992. *Gender Identities and Education: The Impact of Starting School*. New York: St. Martin's Press

Lurye LE, Zosuls KM, Ruble DN. 2008. Gender identity and adjustment: understanding the impact of individual and normative differences in sex typing. *New Dir. Child Adolesc. Dev.* 120:31–46

Lutz SE, Ruble DN. 1995. Children and gender prejudice: context, motivation, and the development of gender conceptions. In *Annals of Child Development*, ed. R Vasta, pp. 131–66. London: Jessica Kingsley Publ.

Maccoby EE. 1998. *The Two Sexes: Growing Up Apart, Coming Together*. Cambridge, MA: Belknap

Maccoby EE. 2002. Gender and group process: a developmental perspective. *Curr. Dir. Psychol. Sci.* 11:54–58

Maccoby EE, Jacklin CN. 1987. Gender segregation in childhood. In *Advances in Child Development and Behavior, Vol. 20*, ed. WR Hayne, pp. 239–87. Orlando, FL: Academic

Martin CL. 2000. Cognitive theories of gender development. In *The Developmental Social Psychology of Gender*, ed. T Eckes, HM Trautner, pp. 91–121. Mahwah, NJ: Erlbaum

Martin CL. 2008. *Moving beyond the dyad: dynamic systems, gender, and social relationships in young children*. Presented at Gender Dev. Conf., San Francisco, CA

Martin CL, Fabes RA. 2001. The stability and consequences of young children's same-sex peer interactions. *Dev. Psychol.* 37:431–46

Martin CL, Fabes RA, Hanish LD, Hollenstein T. 2005. Social dynamics in the preschool. *Dev. Rev.* 25:299–327

Martin CL, Halverson C. 1981. A schematic processing model of sex typing and stereotyping in children. *Child Dev.* 52:1119–34

Martin CL, Ruble DN. 2004. Children's search for gender cues: cognitive perspectives on gender development. *Curr. Dir. Psychol. Sci.* 13:67–70

Martin CL, Ruble DN, Szkrybalo J. 2002. Cognitive theories of early gender development. *Psychol. Bull.* 128:903–33

Martin CL, Ruble DN, Szkrybalo J. 2004. Recognizing the centrality of gender identity and stereotype knowledge in gender development and moving toward theoretical integration: reply to Bandura and Bussey (2004). *Psychol. Bull.* 130:702–10

Martin CL, Wood CH, Little JK. 1990. The development of gender stereotype components. *Child Dev.* 61:1891–904

May RM. 1976. Simple mathematical models with very complicated dynamics. *Nature* 261:64–72

McCarthy MM, Arnold AP. 2008. Sex differences in the brain: What's old and what's new? In *Sex Differences in the Brain: From Genes to Behavior*, ed. JB Becker, KJ Berkley, N Geary, E Hampson, JP Herman, EA Young, pp. 15–33. Oxford, UK: Oxford Univ. Press

McGuire J, Martin CL, Fabes RA, Hanish LD. 2007. *The role of "gender enforcers" in young children's peer interactions.* Poster presented at Biennial Mtg. Soc. Res. Child Dev., Boston, MA

McHale SM, Kim J, Whiteman S, Crouter AC. 2004. Links between sex-typed time use in middle-childhood and gender development in early adolescence. *Dev. Psychol.* 40:868–81

Miller C, Lurye LE, Zosuls KM, Ruble DN. 2009. Accessibility of gender stereotype domains: developmental and gender differences in children. *Sex Roles* 60: 870–81

Miller CL. 1983. Developmental changes in male/female voice classification by infants. *Infant Behav. Dev.* 6:313–30

Mischel W. 1966. A social learning view of sex differences in behavior. In *The Development of Sex Differences*, ed. E Maccoby, pp. 57–81. Stanford, CA: Stanford Univ. Press

Neff KD, Cooper CE, Woodruff AL. 2007. Children's and adolescents' developing perceptions of gender inequality. *Soc. Dev.* 16:682–99

Nowak A, Vallacher RR, Tesser A, Borkowski W. 2000. Society of the self: the emergence of collective properties in self-structure. *Psychol. Rev.* 107:39–61

Oyama S. 2000. *Evolution's Eye: A Systems View of the Biology-Culture Divide*. Durham, NC: Duke Univ. Press

Poulin-Dubois D, Serbin LA, Derbyshire A. 1998. Toddlers' intermodal and verbal knowledge about gender. *Merrill-Palmer Q.* 44:338–54

Powlishta KK, Serbin LA, Doyle A, White DR. 1994. Gender, ethnic, and body type biases: the generality of prejudice in childhood. *Dev. Psychol.* 30:526–36

Powlishta KK, Serbin LA, Moller LC. 1993. The stability of individual differences in gender typing: implications for understanding gender segregation. *Sex Roles* 29:723–37

Quinn PC, Yahr J, Kuhn A, Slater AM, Pascalis O. 2002. Representation of the gender of human faces by infants: a preference for female. *Perception* 31:1109–21

Ruble DN, Alvarez J, Bachman M, Cameron J, Fuligni A, et al. 2004. The development of a sense of self: the development and implications of children's collective identity. In *The Development of the Social Self*, ed. M Bennett, F Sani, pp. 29–76. East Sussex, UK: Psychol. Press

Ruble DN, Dweck CS. 1995. Self-perceptions, person conceptions, and their development. In *Social Development. Review of Personality and Social Psychology*, ed. N Eisenberg, Ch. 15, pp. 109–39. Thousand Oaks, CA: Sage

Ruble DN, Lurye LE, Zosuls KM. 2007a. Pink frilly dresses (PFD) and early gender identity. *Princeton Report Knowledge (P-ROK)* 2:2

Ruble DN, Martin CL, Berenbaum SA. 2006. Gender development. In *Handbook of Child Development*, ed. N Eisenberg, pp. 858–932. New York: Wiley

Ruble DN, Taylor LJ, Cyphers L, Greulich FK, Lurye LE, Shrout PE. 2007b. The role of gender constancy in early gender development. *Child Dev.* 78:1121–36

Rudman LA, Glick P. 2008. *The Social Psychology of Gender: How Power and Intimacy Shape Gender Relations.* New York: Guilford. 386 pp.

Schafer DR, Light JM, Fabes RA, Hanish LD, Martin CL. 2009. Fundamental principles of network formation among preschool children. *Soc. Networks.* In press

Schelling TC. 1971. Dynamic models of segregation. *J. Math. Sociol.* 1:143–86

Serbin LS, Powlishta KK, Gulko J. 1993. The development of sex typing in middle childhood. In *Monographs of the Society for Research in Child Development*, ed. WC Bronson, pp. v–74. Chicago, IL: Univ. Chicago Press

Signorella ML, Bigler RS, Liben LS. 1993. Developmental differences in children's gender schemata about others: a meta-analytic review. *Dev. Rev.* 13:147–83

Sinno SM, Killen M. 2009. Moms at work and dads at home: children's evaluations of parental roles. *Appl. Dev. Sci.* 13:16–29

Sosnoff JJ, Newell KM. 2008. Age-related loss of adaptability to fast time scales in motor variability. *J. Gerontol. Ser. B: Psychol. Sci. Soc. Sci.* 63:344–52

Spencer JP, Schoner G. 2003. Bridging the representational gap in the dynamic systems approach to development. *Dev. Sci.* 6:392–412

Sroufe LA, Bennett C, Englund M, Urban J, Shulman S. 1993. The significance of gender boundaries in preadolescence: contemporary correlates and antecedents of boundary violation and maintenance. *Child Dev.* 64:455–66

Steenbeek H, van Geert P. 2008. An empirical validation of a dynamic systems model of interaction: Do children of different sociometric statuses differ in their dyadic play? *Dev. Sci.* 11:253–81

Stennes LM, Burch MM, Sen MG, Bauer PJ. 2005. A longitudinal study of gendered vocabulary and communicative action in young children. *Dev. Psychol.* 41:75–88

Susskind JE, Hodges C. 2007. Decoupling children's gender-based in-group positivity from out-group negativity. *Sex Roles* 56:707–16

Teig S, Susskind JE. 2008. Truck driver or nurse? The impact of gender roles and occupational status on children's occupational preferences. *Sex Roles* 58:848–63

Theimer CE, Killen M, Stangor C. 2001. Young children's evaluations of exclusion in gender-stereotypic peer contexts. *Dev. Psychol.* 37:18–27

Thelen E, Schoner G, Scheier C, Smith LB. 2001. The dynamics of embodiment: a field theory of infant perseverative reaching. *Behav. Brain Sci.* 24:1–34

Thelen E, Smith LA. 1994. *A Dynamic Systems Approach to the Development of Cognition and Action.* Cambridge, MA: Bradford/MIT Press

Thelen E, Smith LB. 1998. Dynamic systems theories. In *Handbook of Child Psychology*, ed. W Damon, pp. 563–634. New York: Wiley

Thelen E, Smith LB. 2006. Dynamic systems theories. In *Handbook of Child Psychology: Theoretical Models of Human Development*, ed. RM Lerner, pp. 258–312. New York: Wiley

Thorne B. 1993. *Gender Play: Girls and Boys in School.* New Brunswick, NJ: Rutgers Univ. Press

Tobin DD, Menon M, Menon M, Spatta BC, Hodges EVE, Perry DG. 2009. The intrapsychics of gender: a model of self-socialization. *Psychol. Rev.* Manuscript under review

Trautner HM, Ruble DN, Cyphers L, Kirsten B, Behrendt R, Hartman P. 2005. Rigidity and flexibility of gender stereotypes in children: developmental or differential? *Infant Child Dev.* 14:365–80

Treffner PJ, Kelso JAS. 1999. Dynamic encounters: long memory during functional stabilization. *Ecol. Psychol.* 11:103–37

Turner P, Gervai J, Hinde RA. 1993. Gender-typing in young children: preferences, behaviour, and cultural differences. *Br. J. Dev. Psychol.* 11:323–42

van Geert P. 2003. Dynamic systems approaches and modeling of developmental processes. In *Handbook of Developmental Psychology*, ed. J Valsiner, KJ Connolly, pp. 640–72. London: Sage

Van Orden GC, Holden JG, Turvey MT. 2003. Self-organization of cognitive performance. *J. Exp. Psychol.: Gen.* 132:331–50

Verkuyten M, Thijs J. 2001. Ethnic and gender bias among Dutch and Turkish children in late childhood: the role of social context. *Infant Child Dev.* 10:203–17

Waldrop MM. 1992. *Complexity: The Emerging Science at the Edge of Order and Chaos.* New York: Simon & Schuster

Ward LM. 2002. *Dynamic Cognitive Science.* Cambridge, MA: Bradford

Weinraub M, Clemens LP, Sockloff A, Etheridge R, Gracely E, Myers B. 1984. The development of sex role stereotypes in the third year: relationships to gender labeling, gender identity, sex-typed toy preferences, and family characteristics. *Child Dev.* 55:1493–503

West C, Zimmerman DH. 1991. Doing gender. In *The Social Construction of Gender,* ed. J Lorber, SA Farrell, pp. 13–37. Thousand Oaks, CA: Sage

Wilensky U. 1997. NetLogo segregation model. In *Learning and Computer-Based Modeling.* Evanston, IL: Northwestern Univ. http://ccl.northwestern.edu/netlogo/models/Segregation. Center for Connected Learning and Computer-Based Modeling, Northwestern Univ., Evanston, IL

Williams GP. 1997. *Chaos Theory Tamed.* Washington, DC: Joseph Henry Press

Witherington DC. 2007. The dynamic systems approach as a metatheory for development psychology. *Hum. Dev.* 50:127–53

Yee M, Brown R. 1994. The development of gender differentiation in young children. *Br. J. Soc. Psychol.* 33:183–96

Younger BA, Fearing DD. 1999. Parsing items into separate categories: developmental change in infant categorization. *Child Dev.* 70:291–303

Zosuls KM, Ruble DN, Tamis-LeMonda CS, Shrout PE, Bornstein MH, Greulich FK. 2009. The acquisition of gender labels in infancy: implications for sex-typed play. *Dev. Psychol.* 45:688–701

Zucker KJ, Bradley SJ. 1995. *Gender Identity Disorder and Psychosexual Problems in Children and Adolescents.* New York: Guilford

Zucker KJ, Wilson-Smith DN, Kurita JA, Stern A. 1995. Children's appraisals of sex-typed behavior in their peers. *Sex Roles* 33:703–25

A NetLogo model that can be run with varying parameters; illustrates the emergence of segregation in a system.

Social and Emotional Aging

Susan T. Charles[1] and Laura L. Carstensen[2]

[1]Department of Psychology and Social Behavior, University of California, Irvine, California 96297; email: scharles@uci.edu

[2]Department of Psychology, Stanford University, Stanford, California 94305; email: laura.carstensen@stanford.edu

Annu. Rev. Psychol. 2009. 61:383–409

The *Annual Review of Psychology* is online at psych.annualreviews.org

This article's doi: 10.1146/annurev.psych.093008.100448

Key Words

emotion regulation, aging, well-being, affective well-being

Abstract

The past several decades have witnessed unidimensional decline models of aging give way to life-span developmental models that consider how specific processes and strategies facilitate adaptive aging. In part, this shift was provoked by the stark contrast between findings that clearly demonstrate decreased biological, physiological, and cognitive capacity and those suggesting that people are generally satisfied in old age and experience relatively high levels of emotional well-being. In recent years, this supposed "paradox" of aging has been reconciled through careful theoretical analysis and empirical investigation. Viewing aging as adaptation sheds light on resilience, well-being, and emotional distress across adulthood.

Contents

INTRODUCTION

In the most fundamental ways, social and emotional functioning changes little with age. At no point in life does the need to feel embedded in a larger social group lessen (Baumeister & Leary 1995, Charles & Mavandadi 2003, Maslow 1943, Snowden 2001), nor do the devastating consequences of isolation diminish (Berkman et al. 2000, Mellor et al. 2008). Intense, strong emotions remain, and the integrity of the constellation of physiological, facial, and subjective feelings associated with specific emotions is in old age what it was in youth (Levenson et al. 1991, Tsai et al. 2000). Though modest changes have been documented, personality traits also remain largely stable into old age. And in late life, as at earlier times, the experience of negative emotions affects physiological functioning and ultimately physical health.

Yet social and emotional life does change with age. Social networks narrow. Experienced emotions are more predictable and less labile. Negative emotions become more infrequent (until very old age) and social roles change quantitatively and qualitatively. Investments in meaningful relationships increase. Compromised physical functioning renders effortful some social activities that once were completed with ease. Sensory losses strain conversations. And physiological functioning is regulated less efficiently. Understanding stability and change with age demands consideration of interactions between improved self-regulation on the one hand and decreased physical reserves on the other. The current review examines social and emotional aspects of aging—presenting what we have learned and pointing to areas that demand additional investigation.

Below we first discuss the importance of social and emotional processes for physical and cognitive well-being across the adult life span. We then present theories describing mechanisms responsible for these changes and discuss how such mechanisms may have far-reaching influences on social functioning and cognitive processing. Rather than a paradox—namely, the stark contrast between physical declines and psychological improvements—a coherent picture of aging is emerging. Improved self-regulation and changes in priorities that favor meaningful activities result in distinctly positive developmental shifts. When life is controllable and social supports are strong, older people fare better than their younger counterparts. However, when stressors are unavoidable and exposure is prolonged, physiological regulation suffers. We follow with an overview of age-related changes in neurological and physiological processes and the ways in which they correspond to changes in cognition and behavior. We suggest that by integrating information about age-related changes, we can predict the circumstances necessary for continued reports of strong social network ties and high levels of emotional and physical well-being, as well as circumstances that may lead to significant distress in old age.

SOCIAL AND EMOTIONAL PROCESSES AND WELL-BEING ACROSS THE ADULT LIFE SPAN

People who perceive their friends and family members as supportive during times of need have a stronger sense of meaning in their lives; that is, they live their lives with a broader purpose, adhering to a value system that fits within the larger social world (Krause 2007). In addition, people with strong social networks report greater emotional well-being in day-to-day life as well as when they experience stressful life events (see classic review by Cohen & Wills 1985). Both structural—i.e., the number and type of social partners in a given network—and functional—i.e., the perceived or actual receipt of support—aspects of social networks

contribute to emotional well-being (Cohen & Wills 1985).

In old age, social spheres also influence cognitive functioning. A growing number of studies have found that older adults embedded in strong social networks and high levels of social activity are less likely than their more socially disengaged peers to experience declines in cognitive functioning (e.g., Barnes et al. 2004, Zunzunegui 2003, Wilson et al. 2007). Epidemiologist Laura Fratiglioni and colleagues of the Kungsholmen Project found that positive social networks may even be protective against cognitive decline (Fratiglioni et al. 2000). In a prospective study that followed more than 1200 older adults who were tested over a three-year period, they observed that those with strong and positive social networks were 60 percent less likely to show signs of dementia three years later. Older people who engage in volunteer activities that are either socially or mentally demanding also perform better on cognitive tasks than do older adults engaged in solitary activities with low cognitive demands (Singh-Manoux et al. 2003). Social support is related not only to staving off decline, but also to regaining functioning; stronger social networks and emotional support assessed soon after a stroke are associated with greater improvements in cognitive functioning six months later even after controlling for age and education (Glymour et al. 2008). The authors of the work above note that future studies need to rule out the possibility that prodromal symptoms of cognitive decline undetected by clinical interviews may be causing social withdrawal, yet they are encouraged by the strength of their findings that social interactions may play a causal role in staving off cognitive decline or aiding in recovery after serious illness.

Structural aspects of social networks are also related to higher levels of cognitive functioning. Older men who live alone at any point during a five-year period, for example, are twice as likely to experience cognitive declines as those who live with others (van Gelder et al. 2006). The benefits of structural aspects of social networks on cognitive functioning among older adults pertain to the larger social context as well, as measured by characteristics of the neighborhood or the overall lifestyle of the individual (see review by Barnes et al. 2008). For example, the socioeconomic status of British urban neighborhoods significantly predicts the cognitive status of older adults residing in them independent of individual socioeconomic status and controlling for health, depression, and other potential confounding factors (Lang et al. 2008).

Positive emotions experienced during social interactions are considered a central reason why social interactions may benefit cognitive functioning (Blanchard-Fields et al. 2008). People who report less satisfaction with their networks show greater declines in cognitive functioning over time (Hughes et al. 2008). Similarly, in one study, better emotional support was prospectively linked to better cognitive performance eight years later (Seeman et al. 2001). As stated above, causal directions are difficult to discern and need to be further studied (see review by Barnes et al. 2008). However, clinical studies that randomly assign participants to social or nonsocial interventions show similar advantages of socially engaging activity on cognitive performance (Stine-Morrow et al. 2008).

Social Processes and Physical Health Outcomes

In addition to better cognitive functioning, people who report stronger social networks are at lower risk for morbidity and mortality (see review by Berkman et al. 2000, House et al. 1988, Ryff & Singer 2001). The effects described in this literature are large. The effect size of strong social networks is comparable to traditional medical indicators such as high cholesterol and smoking. Pressman & Cohen (2007) found that authors who heavily referenced social roles in their life stories lived five years longer, on average, than those who did not. Using an innovative and indirect approach, they counted the number of relational words that psychologists and fiction writers had used in their

autobiographies, words such as "father," "brother," or "sister," as well as inclusive pronouns such as "we," compared to individual pronouns such as "I." They found a strong relationship between the use of relationship words and length of life.

It is becoming increasingly clear that relationships need to be emotionally meaningful and positive. Researchers have found, for example, that positive affect in early adulthood predicts mortality at older ages (Danner et al. 2001). In another study, positive affect (defined by having a positive attitude and deriving happiness in everyday activities) predicted survival ten years later among octogenarians (Lyyra et al. 2006). Emotional experience has been tied to physical indicators related to health status, such as blood pressure (Ong & Allaire 2005) and immune response (Graham et al. 2006), and is related to both physical morbidity and mortality (see review by Ryff & Singer 2001). In contrast, negative social exchanges are related to poorer health and more frequent endorsements of depressive symptoms (Newsom et al. 2008, Rook 1984). In addition, women who report low levels of emotional support (unrelated to access to instrumental assistance) are twice as likely to die as older women with high levels of emotional support (Lyyra & Heikkinen, 2006).[1] In a psychosocial intervention with patients who had coronary heart disease, Burg et al. (2005) observed that participants who had a partner and perceived higher levels of social support at baseline were less likely to die than those who had no partner and perceived lower levels of social support. Importantly, this effect remained after controlling for type of treatment and other potential confounds such as age and health-related indicators. In yet another study, older adults who reported being useful to their friends and family had lower rates of disability and mortality after a seven-year period compared to

---

[1]In the Hyyra & Heikkinen (2006) study, significant effects were not observed in men; however, other studies have found the effects of positive social experiences and decreased mortality for both genders (see review by Pressman & Cohen 2005).

older adults who rated themselves lower on perceived usefulness (Gruenewald, Karlamangla, Greendale, Singer, & Seeman, 2007). In the study of elderly Swedes described above, Fratigiolini et al. (2000) found similar effects for the relationship between cognition and social support. In that study, only people who reported positive social relations benefitted from the contact.

Early Origins of Healthy Relationships

To understand the full influence of social relationships on mental, physical, and cognitive health in adulthood, assessing the current circumstances of older adults is insufficient. Early childhood environments are critical for shaping emotional development (e.g., Ainsworth & Wittig 1969, Bowlby 1969). Attachment styles that young adults recall having with their parents in childhood are similar to the ones they report having with their current romantic partners (Shaver et al. 2000). Recent studies show that early relationships have effects on social, emotional, and physical functioning that extend into adulthood (e.g., Antonucci et al. 2004, Morris et al. 2007, Shaver et al. 2000). Older adults who reported that they had secure attachments with their parents in childhood endorse higher levels of positive emotions and lower levels of negative emotions when characterizing their daily emotional experiences in comparison with those who report less secure attachments to early caregivers (Consedine & Magai 2003). Perhaps the most obvious reason for the continued influence of these early relationships into adulthood is that they last: Some of the most important social relationships are highly stable throughout life. One study, for example, found that mothers continue to serve as important attachment figures for younger and middle-aged adults, second only to romantic partners in their ability to fulfill attachment needs (Doherty & Feeney 2004). Within the broader social network, other family members and friends form a constellation of social partners that provide relational stability across adulthood (Antonucci 1994, Magai 2001). However, it appears that the story is even more complicated. Repetti et al. (2002) argue convincingly that among children who are genetically vulnerable, the experience of cold and neglectful families in childhood alters functioning of brain systems (e.g., the hypothalamic-pituitary-adrenal axis) that regulate stress in enduring ways that can lead to chronic disease and early death.

Indeed, early experiences predict physical and mental health outcomes later in life. People who had childhoods marked by emotional neglect or adversity are more likely to report smaller social networks and emotional isolation in old age (Wilson et al. 2006). Among older adults, a history of childhood physical or sexual abuse is related to poorer physical and mental health (Draper et al. 2008) as well as poorer cognitive functioning (Luecken 2006). Stressful childhood experiences are also related to cardiovascular disease (Batten et al. 2004) and greater reactivity of the immune system among women (Lemieux et al. 2008).

Even less severe experiences, such as insecure attachments with caregivers or a stressful childhood marked by frequent moves, also relate to health outcomes in adulthood (Consedine & Magai 2003, Luecken 2006). For instance, younger, middle-aged, and older adults who report low levels of parental support in childhood have higher levels of depressive symptoms and a greater number of chronic health conditions than do same-aged peers who report higher levels of parental support (Shaw et al. 2004).

SOCIAL PATTERNS ACROSS ADULTHOOD

Older adults identify fewer social partners in their networks than do younger adults, a pattern observed in diverse groups including European Americans, African Americans, Germans, and Hong Kong Chinese (Fung et al. 2001, 2008). Researchers originally attributed age-related decreases in social network size to losses that are associated with aging: decreases in social roles, deaths of friends and family members, and increased functional limitations that reduce social involvement (see review by Carstensen & Charles 1998). However, an apparent pruning process appears to begin in peoples' thirties and forties, long before the age-related losses begin (Carstensen 1992). Research suggests that aging people play active roles in reducing social networks into smaller, more intimate forms across adulthood (Carstensen, 1993, 2006; Carstensen et al. 1999). Importantly, smaller networks that have high concentrations of emotionally close partners appear to benefit mental health (Lang & Carstensen 1994). Age-related decreases are driven primarily by excluding less meaningful, casual acquaintances (Fung et al. 2001, Yeung et al. 2008). Notably, the number of emotionally close social partners remains highly stable (Fung et al. 2001, Lang & Carstensen 1994) or slightly increases with age (Yeung et al. 2008).

Experimental studies suggest that changes in network composition are voluntary. When asked about their desire to interact with potential social partners, older adults most often express preferences for familiar and emotionally close social partners, whereas younger adults are as likely to choose novel social partners (Fredrickson & Carstensen 1990, Fung et al. 1999). Older adults report the highest level of positive emotional experiences when interacting with family members, higher than the level reported by younger adults (Charles & Piazza 2007), whereas younger adults report higher levels of positive affect when interacting with new friends than do older adults. And whereas younger adults with relatively few peripheral partners in their networks report lower levels of happiness, this is not so for older adults (Lang & Carstensen 2002). Time use also distinguishes older and younger adults. Older people appear to carefully select activities that are personally and emotionally meaningful (Hendricks & Cutler 2004). Importantly, selective investments appear to hold benefits. Older adults who provide social support to others report higher levels of positive emotions, lower levels of negative emotions, greater purpose in life, and even reduced mortality (Greenfield & Marks 2004, Krause 2006). Thus, although social networks are smaller in old age, reduced size of networks appears to benefit satisfaction. Of course, network size can become too small, such that people are at risk for isolation. But generally speaking, the closeness and importance of relationships is more important than network size in old age.

EMOTIONAL WELL-BEING

Emotional well-being and distress depend centrally on social relationships. The most commonly reported daily stressors are interpersonal tensions (Almeida 2005), and interpersonal stressors can lead to high levels of emotional distress (Almeida & Kessler 1998, Rook 1984). With age, older adults are more satisfied with their social networks (Carstensen 1992). They report having experienced higher levels of positive emotions with members of their family members than do younger adults (Charles & Piazza 2007) and more positive than negative exchanges (Newsom et al. 2005). Older adults also report fewer negative interactions with members of their social networks than do younger adults (Birditt & Fingerman 2003) and smaller increases in distress when they encounter interpersonal tensions (Birditt et al. 2005). The emotional experiences of older adults may reflect these social experiences. Older adults report high levels of emotional well-being, often even higher than those reported by younger adults.

Emotional well-being refers to the subjective experience of positive and negative emotions. This construct is defined in terms of happiness, life satisfaction, or the balance between positive and negative affect. In all studies using these definitions, increases in emotional well-being are consistently observed across people in their thirties, forties, fifties, and into their sixties. In cross-sectional studies, for example, older age is related to lower levels of negative affect (Carstensen et al. 2000, Diener & Suh 1997, Mroczek & Kolarz 1998) and lower rates of anxiety and major depressive disorder (see reviews by Blazer 2003, Piazza & Charles 2006). Reports of anger also decrease for successively older adults (Phillips et al. 2006; see review by Magai 2001). In longitudinal studies examining this same age range, older age is related to lower levels of negative affect (Charles et al. 2001), increases in life satisfaction (Mroczek & Spiro 2005), and stable levels of positive affect (Charles et al. 2001).

Findings about age differences in emotional well-being in people 60 years and older are less consistent. One cross-sectional study found upturns in negative affect (Diener & Suh 1997) after age 65, although another study found continued decreases once the investigators controlled for the number of chronic health problems and level of functional limitation (Kunzman et al. 2000). When asked about depressive symptoms, participants in their sixties and seventies reported upturns in depressive symptoms associated with age in cross-sectional (Diener & Suh 1997, Haynie et al. 2001) and longitudinal studies (Davey et al. 2004). To place in perspective the extent of these upturns observed in the mid sixties, however, the negative affect reported by the oldest old in these studies fails to reach levels reported by young adults (e.g., Diener & Suh 1997). Moreover, another study showed that reports of depressive symptoms, including feeling sad, blue, or depressed, decreases linearly with age among people ranging from 60 to 84 years old (Kobau et al. 2004), and still another study found a very slight decrease in negative affect over a 23-year period among people who entered the study when they were aged 65 or older (Charles et al. 2001).

Researchers find slight decreases (Diener & Suh 1997) or plateaus (Carstensen et al. 2000) in positive affect among successively older age groups. In longitudinal analyses, positive affect decreases slightly (Charles et al. 2001), as does life satisfaction (Mroczek & Spiro 2005). These decreases are very slight, however, such that the life satisfaction reported at age 80 is similar to the levels reported by people in their forties (Mroczek & Spiro 2005). In another study, the decrease in positive affect among the older adults equaled about a 12% decrease on the scale across more than 20 years (Charles

et al. 2001). Considering findings from studies of positive and negative emotional experience together, older adults are reporting relatively high levels of well-being, and they consistently report higher levels of positive affect than negative affect (e.g., Charles et al. 2001, Diener & Suh 1997). When decreases in well-being are observed, they generally occur after age 60 and are small in magnitude. Even centenarians report overall high levels of emotional well-being (Jopp & Rott 2006).

Some researchers posit that high-intensity emotions, such as exhilaration and enthusiasm, are more likely to decrease with age than are low-arousal emotions, such as contentment or feeling at peace (Diener et al. 1985, Lawton et al. 1992). In support of the hypothesis that age differences in emotion depend on the physiological arousal they evoke, a meta-analysis including more than 100 studies that examined age differences in emotional experience reveals that age-related declines are driven predominantly by high-arousal negative and positive emotions; low-arousal positive emotions, for example, do not show a significant decrease in this meta-analysis (Pinquart 2001).

UNDERSTANDING SOCIAL AND EMOTIONAL TRAJECTORIES ACROSS ADULTHOOD

The earliest theories of social aging posited that profound qualitative changes occur in psychological functioning in later life. Disengagement theory, which dominated the study of social aging for decades, maintained that as people reach old age, they become emotionally distanced and detached from loved ones in symbolic preparation for death (Cumming & Henry 1961). As empirical investigation grew, however, observed patterns did not support key postulates of disengagement theory. Social networks do indeed decrease in size, yet the typical psychological profile of aging is generally positive and socially engaged (see review by Charles & Carstensen 2007). More recent models reconcile social and emotional trajectories.

Selective Optimization with Compensation

Selective Optimization with Compensation, developed by Baltes & Baltes (1990), offers a meta-model or heuristic to account for interactions between persons and situations within a life-span perspective (see also Marsiske et al. 1995). According to this model, across adulthood, people become increasingly aware of age-related gains and losses. Because social, cognitive, and functional reserves are often diminished with age, resources are carefully allocated. As a result, people select goals that (*a*) are important and (*b*) can be realistically obtained in later life. These goals are often selected at the cost of other, less important priorities that are eventually discarded. As goals are prioritized, people engage in behaviors that optimize their abilities to achieve these goals. If their goals cannot be met using their usual strategies, people may engage in compensatory activities, such as enlisting the help of others. Applying this model to social relationships, the maintenance of emotionally close relationships, sometimes accompanied by even higher levels of well-being, reflects selection and optimization. The discarding of peripheral relationships creates more time and energy for these important relationships.

Socioemotional Selectivity Theory

Socioemotional selectivity theory (SST) maintains that motivation changes as people age and time horizons shrink (Carstensen 1993, 2006; Carstensen et al. 1999). According to SST, awareness of the temporal horizons influences goals. Whether conscious or subconscious, awareness of constraints on time activates changes in goal hierarchies. People who are young and healthy typically view the future as expansive. When people perceive a seemingly endless temporal horizon, they prioritize goals that prepare them for a long and nebulous future. Goals focused on gaining knowledge and information for their future possibilities are prioritized over other goals. However, as people age and time horizons are constrained, goals increasingly emphasize emotion and meaning.

Life Experience

Experience also changes the ways that people approach social situations (Blanchard-Fields 2007; Hess & Auman 2001; Hess et al. 1999, 2005; Leclerc & Hess 2007). In particular, life experiences affect how people process and respond to emotional information (e.g., Blanchard-Fields 2007, Charles & Piazza 2009, Magai et al. 2006). It appears that older adults, in comparison with younger adults, are more sensitive to emotional cues when making social inferences (see review by Hess 2005). Hess and colleagues have conceptualized social expertise as the extent to which people make social judgments consistent with the values of society (Hess & Auman 2001, Hess et al. 2005; see review by Hess 2005). Hess builds on work suggesting that in the United States, cultural norms about judgments of social behavior guide people to weigh negative information about a person's moral character, such as the extent to which a person is honest or wicked, more heavily than information about a person's abilities, such as his or her athletic or intellectual prowess. The reverse is true about positive information. In several studies, Hess and his colleagues have shown that older adults in comparison with younger adults weigh negative information about moral character more heavily than information about abilities when judging strangers and rating their likability (Hess et al. 2005, Leclerc & Hess 2007).

Strength and Vulnerability Integration

According to the Strength and Vulnerability Integration theory (Charles & Piazza 2009), people change their perspective as a result of time left to live (as posited by socioemotional selectivity theory) and increase their knowledge about how to regulate their emotions and their social lives from experience garnered from time lived. These changes in perspective and knowledge enable older people to navigate their environments so that they successfully avoid negative experiences. Importantly, the Strength and Vulnerability Integration theory also maintains that biological systems become less flexible with age. Physiological and subjective processes do not have a perfect correspondence, yet they inform one another, particularly when people experience high levels of physiological arousal. Consequently, whereas older people regulate low levels of negative distress quite well, they have greater difficulty when they experience distress for relatively long periods of time. When older people employ strategies that allow them to avoid negative emotional experiences, they experience higher levels of well-being than do younger adults. When situations creating high levels of distress are unavoidable, age-related advantages in well-being disappear and may even reverse in direction (Charles & Piazza 2009). Unfortunately, unavoidable negative situations often increase with age, such as experiencing the loss of people who provide life with meaning, experiencing functional limitations that cause pain and daily hassles, and meeting the demands of caregiving.

AGE DIFFERENCES IN PROCESSING, REMEMBERING, AND ACTING ON EMOTIONS

Social and emotional experiences change with age. Social partners that are meaningful and important are preserved, more peripheral social ties are discarded, and anger and distress are experienced less frequently. Positive affect remains highly stable, only decreasing in some studies among the oldest old. Researchers have identified reasons why these changes occur, with models and theories agreeing that perspective changes with age. This perspective increases the importance of emotionally meaningful experiences and the desire to maintain high levels of well-being. These goals, in turn, influence thoughts and behaviors related to social and emotional experiences.

Appraisals

Emotion theorists have long emphasized the importance of cognitive appraisal in determining emotional experience and well-being. Specific thoughts are related to specific emotions: For example, hopelessness, helplessness, and irrevocable loss are associated with sadness; perceptions that someone or something is standing in the way of a goal are associated with anger; appraisals of threats are related to anxiety (Levine et al. 2006). Whether a person perceives a situation as a challenge or a threat predicts associated emotional distress (Lazarus 1991). Research examining appraisals in response to laboratory stimuli or autobiographical events have found that older adults appraise and remember events less negatively and more positively with age.

Age differences in how people perceive and appraise emotional material have been widely documented. Even very early in processing, before explicit appraisals can occur, older age is associated with selective attention toward positive stimuli and away from negative stimuli (Isaacowitz et al. 2006, Mather & Carstensen 2003). Yet once people appraise information, findings suggest that younger adults are more likely to dwell on this negative information than are older adults (Charles & Carstensen 2008). In a study where younger and older adults listened to negative comments directed toward them and were asked to voice aloud their responses to these comments, younger adults were more likely to react to these negative comments by making disparaging remarks toward the people speaking and reflecting on what they had just heard. Older adults, in contrast, made few comments about what they had heard and instead made comments that were less negative and focused less on the criticisms. Older adults also made fewer requests for more information about the motives of the people speaking; that is, they appeared less engaged in the conflict (Charles & Carstensen 2008).

Older adults also describe negative situations in their own lives less negatively. When evaluating relatively minor but negative daily stressors they had experienced across the week, older age was related to lower levels of perceived severity (Charles & Almeida 2007). Even controlling for types of situations, older adults have more positive appraisals of social situations than do younger and middle-aged adults (Lefkowitz & Fingerman 2003, Story et al. 2007). In a laboratory study, adult daughters and their mothers engaged in a problem-solving task (Lefkowitz & Fingerman 2003). Afterward, they were asked about the emotions they experienced during this interaction. Mothers reported greater frequencies of positive affect and less negative affect than did adult daughters. Another study compared interactions among older married spouses to those of younger married spouses (Story et al. 2007). Each couple was videotaped as they discussed an area of conflict between the two of them. When asked about the behavior of their spouses, older adults rated their spouse's actions more positively than did objective raters who coded these interactions. Younger couples made no such positively biased appraisals.

More positive appraisals are consistent with the writings of older adults. In one study, people ranging in age from the late teens to mid-eighties were asked to imagine themselves in different social interactions and then to describe how they and their social partner would feel (Löckenhoff et al. 2008). An example of such a scenario is one where a person who is usually quite critical pays you a compliment. Older adults reported that they would feel less anger and anxiety than did younger adults. They also reported that their social partner would feel less sadness than did the younger adults. Overall, findings pointed to age-related increases in inferences of positive emotions and age-related decreases for negative emotions. In another study where people were asked to write about past life events, older age was related to greater use of positive words and fewer negative words in a large sample including more than 3000 people ranging from age 8 to 85 (Pennebaker & Stone 2003). The age-related increase in positive content was most pronounced when comparing across people who were aged 50 and older. The same pattern was observed when researchers examined the positive and negative content of published writings (including plays, books, and poetry) of ten long-lived famous

authors (Pennebaker & Stone 2003). More positive appraisals with age extend to more general perceptions as well. For example, benevolent beliefs about the world—including beliefs about the world in general and beliefs about the goodness of people—were highest among older adults relative to younger adults (Poulin & Cohen Silver 2008).

More positive appraisals may explain why older adults report fewer regrets in life, defined by such statements beginning with "I should have done," than do younger adults (Riediger & Freund 2008). Age-related differences in regret are consistent across both minor and major decisions and life experiences. For example, in laboratory studies where people are asked to evaluate options and then make a choice between several different products, older adults list more positive attributes to their chosen products and are more satisfied with their choices (Kim et al. 2008).

Another study also produced findings suggesting that older adults may experience less "buyer's remorse" than do younger adults; after choosing between two items described by an equal number of positive and negative attributes, younger and older adults were later asked to remember those attributes (Mather et al. 2005). Older adults were more accurate at later recognizing the positive features than negative features of their chosen options than were younger adults, who recognized the positive and negative features equally well. Even in situations as extreme as unresolved issues pertaining to the death of a loved one, older adults report lower levels of regret across the two years of bereavement compared with younger adults (Torges et al. 2008).

As noted above, research suggests that personality traits are quite stable across adulthood (see review by McCrae et al. 2000). Nonetheless, the few changes that do emerge suggest age-related reductions in negative thoughts. Researchers examined the trajectory of neuroticism across 12 years among men aged 40 and older (Mroczek & Spiro 2003). They found that neuroticism decreased with age until around age 80. After age 80, neuroticism showed slight increases, such that the level of neuroticism projected at age 100 for the sample was the same level as that reported when people were in their seventies. Levels of extraversion—the personality trait related to more positive appraisals, sociability, and positive emotions—remained stable over time. The tendency to ruminate about negative events, another fairly stable trait characterized in one study by recurring and unintentional thoughts about anger-provoking situations, was also lower among older adults compared with their younger counterparts (McConatha & Huba 1999).

Memory

Studies of appraisals often require people to evaluate recent events. For example, commonly used questionnaires query people about emotions experienced across the prior few weeks (Affect Balance Scale: Bradburn 1969; Center for Epidemiological Studies-Depression: Radloff 1977) or the previous month (psychological distress: Kessler et al. 2002). Whether appraising their quality of daily life, overall life satisfaction, or the perceived emotional support received from friends and family, people often reflect over their current status, and researchers have examined these more general responses more often than a person's current emotional experience. As a result, these reports rely strongly on memory. Memories of past events factor strongly into how people appraise their lives and evaluate their affective well-being. In studies examining memory for positive, neutral, and negative stimuli, findings often suggest that the memory of older adults is less negative, and sometimes even more positive, than that of younger adults.

Researchers have found that younger adults have a negative bias when processing emotional stimuli (Rozin & Royzman 2001). They have pondered why the "bad is stronger than good" (Baumeister & Leary 1995). A growing number of studies, however, suggest that older adults do not share this bias toward negative information. Instead, older adults compared with younger adults remember both positive and negative information to equal degrees (Kensinger et al.

2007) and sometimes remember more positive than negative information (Charles et al. 2003). The age-related shift in the ratio of positive to negative material processed in memory and attention is termed the "positivity effect" (Mather & Carstensen 2005).

Within the theoretical context of SST, the positivity effect reflects adaptations to different parts of the life course. Early in life, there is demand to maximally absorb information; negative stimuli generally hold more information than positive stimuli. With experience and age, however, many of life's negative lessons have been learned. Furthermore, as time horizons grow shorter, people are in some sense relieved of the burden of preparing for the future. Motivation to preserve emotional balance shifts attention to positive aspects of life.

In studies of autobiographical memory, older adults are biased storytellers, recalling their past more positively than they reported at the time (Kennedy et al. 2004, Ready et al. 2007). Even negative memories are recalled more positively among older than younger adults (Comblain et al. 2005). These findings are consistent with those from laboratory studies (Grady et al. 2007, Kensinger 2008, Leigland et al. 2004, Mather & Knight 2005; see review by Carstensen et al. 2006). For example, in one study, older adults viewed positive, negative, and neutral images and were later asked to recall what they had seen and then to distinguish these images from newly presented items (Charles et al. 2003). Results showed that younger adults recognized and recalled a greater proportion of negative images than positive or neutral ones. Compared with younger adults, older adults remembered a greater proportion of positive images relative to neutral and negative ones. Other studies confirm the relatively more positive memories—either through remembering a greater amount of positive material or a smaller amount of negative material—among older adults than younger adults. For example, another study found that older adults' memory for negative pictures was worse relative to their memory for positive or neutral pictures as compared with younger adults (Grühn et al. 2007). Even studies that find no age-related bias in overall memory performance see evidence of a positivity bias when examining the types of appraisals and errors that people make when recalling information. For example, older adults report a greater familiarity for positive words than for negative words (Spaniol et al. 2008) and a greater age-related tendency to make false memory errors for positive stimuli than negative stimuli (Fernandes et al. 2008).

Behavioral Responses

Thoughts—either current appraisals or memories for prior events—guide behavior. The above research indicates that older adults prioritize emotional material, such that they appraise situations less negatively and their memories are generally less negative and more positive. Their actions are consistent with decreases in negative, and increases in positive, experiences. They report more satisfaction when interacting with family members than do younger adults (Carstensen 1992, Charles & Piazza 2007) and acknowledge fewer daily stressors in their lives (Almeida 2005).

Even among people with strong social networks, however, interpersonal tensions are unavoidable. They are also the most frequently reported stressors for adults regardless of age (Almeida 2005) and create the highest levels of stress across all types of stressors reported during the course of a week (Almeida & Kessler 1998). Although positive interpersonal exchanges are related to higher levels of well-being, their effects are far weaker than those of negative experiences. The effects of positive social exchanges are limited to positive emotional experiences (Newsom et al. 2008; see review by Rook 1998). In contrast, reports of negative exchanges are linked to higher levels of depression, lower positive emotional well-being, and worse self-reported health (Newsom et al. 2008; see review by Rook 1998). The avoidance of negative exchanges, then, holds both emotional and health-related benefits. Older adults navigate their environments such that negative

experiences occur less frequently compared with the reports of younger adults (see review by Charles & Carstensen 2007). Older age is related to a decreased report of interpersonal tensions and to attenuated affective responses when conflicts occur (Birditt et al. 2005).

One of the reasons why older adults report less distress in response to a negative interpersonal exchange appears to be that they engage in behaviors that prevent escalation of tense situations more often than do younger adults. For example, when asked how they would respond to emotionally complex interpersonal tensions, older age is related to endorsements of more passive actions such as doing nothing or letting the situation pass (see review by Blanchard-Fields 2007). Older adults also recommend these more passive strategies to others who are faced with negative interpersonal situations (Charles et al. 2001). These behaviors are in line with the goals of older adults when faced with an interpersonal conflict: Older adults often report goals such as preserving goodwill (Coats & Blanchard-Fields 2008, Sorkin & Rook 2006). When ages are compared, older adults report goals of social harmony more so than do younger adults, who are more likely to report goals of problem-solving and resolution of the conflict (Birditt & Fingerman 2003). Older adults also engage in strategies that reduce the negativity of conflictual situations, such as infusing negative comments with positive ones when discussing a conflict with their spouse (Levenson et al. 1994).

Studies further indicate that age-related decreases in affective distress in response to interpersonal problems may be the result of these disengagement strategies. Older age is related to less affective reactivity when people report that they found themselves in a tense social situation but chose not to engage in the argument; when people report having the argument, younger, middle-aged, and older adults all show similar rises in affective distress (Charles et al. 2009). In addition, older adults who identify the preservation of goodwill as their goal during a negative interaction report the greatest success in achieving this goal, whereas older adults who have a goal of getting someone to change report higher levels of distress and the lowest success rate of achieving this goal when recounting the altercation (Sorkin & Rook 2006). Moreover, experts' ratings are consistent with the endorsements of older adults, as they also deem more passive responses as the best strategies when faced with tense interpersonal exchanges (Blanchard-Fields et al. 2007).

In summary, with age, people come to negotiate their environments such that they experience stressors less often, particularly social stressors. Older people appraise their worlds as more benign and appear to defuse tense situations more effectively. On reports of overall affective well-being, people who are 60 and 70 years old report lower levels of negative affect and higher levels of satisfaction than do people in their twenties and thirties (Charles et al. 2001). Thus, the cognitive, emotional, and social patterns that characterize older adults are quite positive. Yet these stable and sometimes improved patterns occur within an aging biological system—one that is characterized predominantly by decline. Below we turn to the biological systems that underlie aging.

AGE, BIOLOGY, AND SOCIOEMOTIONAL PROCESSES

Almost every physiological and biological process studied across the adult life span shows evidence of age-related decline. The brain decreases in size, with cross-sectional studies indicating small age-related declines when comparing people in their mid-twenties to those around age 50, at which time the rate of neuronal loss and decrease in overall brain volume accelerates (DeCarli et al. 2005; see review by Raz & Rodrigue 2006). The difference in brain volume is indicated by larger sulci and enlarged ventricles correlating with older age. Neurons reduce in size and density, and damage to the mitochondria and loss of myelinated fibers are more prevalent with age when comparing the brains of consecutively older adults who are age 60 and older (see review by Raz 2005; Raz et al. 2005). Neurons are also less

efficient; for example, they are less effective at inhibiting the activity of surrounding neurons. Decreases are pervasive, but the rate of decline varies across different loci. For example, the amygdala, a more primitive region of the brain critical for detecting emotional stimuli, shows less pronounced age differences relative to other areas of the brain (Grieve et al. 2005, Mu et al. 1999). In contrast, the prefrontal cortex shows the most dramatic age differences, characterized by age-related increases until the mid-twenties, a plateau with very small rates of decline until the mid-fifties, and then an accelerated decline in later life (Raz & Rodrigue 2006).

The prefrontal cortex is critically involved in tasks requiring rapid learning and quick judgments. This region of the brain has been thought to play important roles in social behavior and in processing emotion-related thoughts, behaviors, and goals (see review by Davidson et al. 2007). Studies often reveal age-related differences in performances that parallel the age-related declines in brain structure. For example, in one study, researchers gave mazes and maps to people ranging from age 18 to 93 and told them to select the quickest and most efficient routes (Salthouse & Siedlecki 2007). Results indicate an age-related decrease in performance with age, with an acceleration of these age-related declines starting in the early sixties. Similarly, the ability to remember both the information and its source (e.g., did the participant hear the information or read it?) shows small declines from ages 20 to 50, but more rapid age-related declines after age 50 (Siedlecki et al. 2005). Thus, age differences in tasks requiring fluid intelligence—the ability to learn quickly, respond rapidly to often-changing situations, and flexibly weigh disparate information—decrease with age.

Finding Benefits in Decline

Given the declines observed for many cognitive tasks, early emotion theorists assumed the trajectory of emotional experience would parallel these physiological declines (Banham 1951).

Findings provide a more complex picture of how people process emotional information. Some age-related declines may paradoxically aid older adults in their increased focus on emotion-related information. For example, researchers have discussed the age-related decrease in the ability to inhibit irrelevant information—the result of a decline in the ability of neurons to suppress the activity of surrounding neurons (e.g., Darowski et al. 2008). Emotional aspects of information are often deemed irrelevant, so failure to inhibit this information may increase its salience to older adults. Research supports this contention. For example, in an incidental-memory study, adults ranging from age 20 to 83 were asked to read a passage from a story and then, about 15 minutes later, they were asked to recount all that they could remember. With each successively older age group, people recalled a greater proportion of emotional information than nonemotional information (Carstensen & Turk-Charles 1994). When recalling information about a laboratory task, the performance of older adults is marked by a greater focus on emotional rather than on perceptual details (Johnson et al. 1996, Mather et al. 1999). Older adults in comparison with younger adults also weigh emotional information more heavily than nonemotional information when making confidence ratings for their memory performance (Hashtroudi et al. 1990).

Age-related increases in the salience of emotional material also explain discrepant age differences in working memory. A vast number of studies show reliable age-related declines in working memory and inhibitory processing; these changes correlate with decreases in white-matter integrity in the anterior area of the brain (Kennedy & Raz 2009). When researchers use emotional stimuli, however, age differences do not follow the seemingly predictable pattern of decline (Mikels et al. 2005). In this study, older and younger adults viewed a positive, a negative, and a neutral image followed by a screen with a three-second interval. At the interval, they were shown a second image and asked to compare this new image to the previously viewed one,

based on either its brightness or the emotional intensity that it evoked. When comparing pictures on brightness, younger adults once again outperformed older adults. When comparing emotional intensity, however, older adults were similar to younger adults in their performance for negative images and actually outperformed younger adults when rating the intensity of positive stimuli (Mikels et al. 2005). Working memory is dependent not only on biological factors influencing white matter integrity, but also on motivational influences. The age difference in task performance suggests a greater motivation and focus on positive stimuli.

In addition, slower processing speed may provide seemingly paradoxical benefits. The function of emotions is often placed in evolutionary terms, which stress rapid responses where "fight or flight" patterns determine survival. In the modern social world, rapid responses may not be the best response. Snapping at someone with a fast retort may not be as wise as pausing before responding to an interpersonal slight. When responding to negative interpersonal conflicts, faster responses may not translate to an adaptive response. Further research is needed to test this premise.

The Downside of Biological Changes

The effects of poorer inhibitory functioning and decreased speed point to serendipitous benefits from brain-related declines for emotional well-being. This deduction, however, would be premature to apply to all aspects of emotional functioning. Although poorer physiological inhibitory control may make emotions more salient, as research has suggested (e.g., see review by Zacks & Hasher 1997), poorer executive functioning is not related to increased focus on positive over negative emotional stimuli. Mather and her colleagues have found that cognitive control is fundamental to emotion-regulation success among older adults (Kryla-Lighthall & Mather 2009, Mather & Knight 2005; see review by Mather 2006). For example, older adults who were allowed to attend to positive, negative, and neutral images remembered more positive than negative images (Mather & Knight 2005). Older adults who were distracted by a divided-attention task, however, failed to show the positivity bias and instead displayed a negativity bias similar to their younger counterparts. Importantly, the positivity effect is not observed for all studies examining age differences in memories or attention for emotional material, a discontinuity that underscores the dependency of the positivity effect on motivational efforts and cognitive-control abilities (see review by Mather & Carstensen 2005). Indeed, the positivity effect is most pronounced among older adults who have the cognitive capacity necessary and the unrestricted freedom to focus on the information they prioritize, as opposed to other information such as facts, over emotional content (Kryla-Lighthall & Mather 2009).

Poorer inhibitory control may also pose problems when individuals are recovering from high levels of activation. When people perceive high levels of threat, their body mobilizes for action. As part of this process, the hypothalamus delivers corticotropin-releasing hormone, which begins a cascade of reactions that end in the release of cortisol into the bloodstream. Cortisol passes through the blood-brain barrier, and its presence signals the hypothalamus to decrease further release of corticotropin-releasing hormone. The glucocorticoid cascade hypothesis describes how age is related to a decreased ability to down-regulate the further activation of this stress cycle (Sapolsky et al. 1986; Wilkinson 1997, 2001; but see Kudielka et al. 2004). According to this hypothesis, older age is related to a reduced ability of neurons in the hypothalamus to inhibit this activity, consistent with findings showing that high-affinity receptors responsible for feedback inhibition in the hypothalamus decrease with age (Dodt et al. 1994; see review by Ferrari et al. 2003). Furthermore, dysregulation of high-affinity receptors and an imbalance between high- and low-affinity glucocorticoid receptors are more common with age (Dodt et al. 1994, Giordano et al. 2005). The glucocorticoid cascade hypothesis originated from animal studies but has

expanded to encompass human aging as well (Bakke et al. 2004; see reviews by Bjorntorp 2002, Otte et al. 2005).

The cardiovascular system is also less flexible. For example, the vasculature, including veins, arteries, and aortic-pulmonary valves, thickens and become more rigid with age. This reduced flexibility renders the heart less able to respond quickly, as evidenced by a smaller elevation in heart rate in response to both emotional and nonemotional stressors (Deschenes et al. 2006; see review by Levenson 2000). As a result, older adults may be less likely to respond physiologically to brief, relatively minor events. For situations that elicit sustained, high levels of arousal, however, these age-related changes in cardiovascular activity may lead to prolonged activation. Reductions in heart-rate variability (see review by De Meersman & Stein 2006) and inflexibility of the vasculature may contribute to poorer regulation of the system once activated. Consistent with this premise, Uchino and his colleagues have found that older age is related to greater increases in blood pressure in response to stressors both in cross-sectional (Uchino et al. 1999) and longitudinal studies (Uchino et al. 2005).

Predicting Patterns of Age Differences in Emotional Well-Being

Older age is related to increases in the ability to regulate emotions. The relative importance of emotion-related goals increases with age (Carstensen 2006) such that people engage in thoughts and actions that decrease exposure to negative situations and sometimes increase their exposure to positive events. Many of these strengths lie in social processes whereby older adults navigate their social worlds such that they report fewer social conflicts (Birditt & Fingerman 2003) and solve interpersonal problems, often more effectively than do younger adults (Blanchard-Fields et al. 2007). These strengths may even be enhanced by some age-related changes in physiological functioning. Decreases in inhibitory processes may have the consequence of paradoxically improving the ability of emotion-related aspects of stimuli relative to nonemotional features (see review by Isaacowitz et al. 2000).

When faced with high levels of sustained arousal, however, decreased flexibility may prolong the emotional experience for older adults and leave them more vulnerable to emotional distress. Taking these findings together, we predict that older adults will experience high levels of distress and no age-related advantages when they are either unable to employ, or are ineffective in their ability to avoid, high levels of emotional arousal. When older adults are unable to prioritize emotional goals, benefit from prior experience, or engage in thoughts and behaviors that allow them to avoid experiencing high, sustained levels of emotional arousal, age will no longer confer benefits to well-being.

When Older Adults Do Not Prioritize Emotional Goals

When asked to remember a sequence of events, people often focus on factual, nonemotional information. Cognitive psychologists long considered emotional aspects of information to be the nuisance variable, irrelevant information that leaked into memories only as a result of inhibitory failures (see review by Isaacowitz et al. 2000). When emotions are instead valued and emotional information measured, older adults often excel in these cognitive tasks more than do younger adults (see review by Carstensen et al. 2006, Carstensen & Mikels 2005, Mather & Carstensen 2005).

By manipulating the importance of emotional goals, researchers have illustrated situations where age-related increases in memory for emotion-related stimuli are found; there are situations where these age differences in memory performance disappear completely (see review by Carstensen et al. 2006). For example, age-related increases in positivity of past memories disappear if people are asked to recall their past as accurately as they can as opposed to thinking about how they were feeling at the time of the events (Kennedy et al. 2004). When asked to evaluate the positive and negative attributes

of a given product they chose from a set of options, older adults recalled their chosen product more positively than when they were not told to engage in such evaluations (Thomas & Hasher 2006). When evaluating different health insurance options, older adults attended to and recalled more positive than negative aspects of the different options when they evaluated their options after they were instructed to think about how they were feeling while engaged in the task (Löckenhoff & Carstensen 2007). When they were told instead to focus on the facts of each plan, the age-related bias for positive information disappeared. Studies that ask people to attend to all information, as opposed to those giving people the option of viewing a subset of the stimuli, often do not show the positivity effect (see review by Peters et al. 2007).

Similarly, older adults are just as attentive to threatening stimuli as are younger adults (Mather & Knight 2006). In daily life, then, we speculate that older adults do not direct their attention away from negative information and toward positive information in situations when they are threatened or when they do not have the time or ability to act consistently with their motivational goals. For example, a grandmother raising a grandchild must attend to potential problems and challenges that accompany raising a child. This motivation to attend to negative experiences may explain why older adults who are raising children are twice as likely as noncustodial grandparents to report high levels of depressive symptoms (Minkler et al. 1997, 2000). Indeed, the ease with which the positivity effect is eliminated suggests that it may represent chronically activated "default" motivation, but when conditions demand attention to the negative, older people can and do activate other goals.

Exceptions That Make the Rule

Researchers speculate that older adults regulate their emotions more effectively, in part, because accrued life experiences lead to expertise in social and emotional regulation (e.g., Blanchard-Fields 2007, Magai 2001). This expertise is gathered throughout life by managing daily social interactions and resolving negative stressors. Of course, exposure does not insure greater expertise. A subset of people appears to benefit little from experience.

Neuroticism is a personality trait defined as emotional instability, where higher levels of neuroticism are associated with chronic emotional activation and reactivity (Eysenck 1967). People scoring high on neuroticism, or emotional instability, report greater numbers of interpersonal stressors in their daily lives, more negative appraisals of these stressors, and greater negative reactivity in response (Gunthert et al. 1999, Suls & Martin 2005). Neuroticism is strongly associated with negative affect (Charles & Almeida 2006). People high in neuroticism often dwell on past events and have more negative reactions to recurring problems in a pattern known as the "neurotic cascade" (Suls & Martin 2005). High levels of neuroticism increase the risk for divorce, lower occupational status (Roberts et al. 2007), worse physical health (Charles et al. 2008), and a greater number of negative life events (e.g., Farmer et al. 2002). Thus, higher levels of neuroticism are related to poorer interpersonal relationships and less successful problem resolution.

A growing number of studies suggest that people who score high on neuroticism do not experience age-related benefits in emotional functioning. People who score high in neuroticism report relatively stable levels of negative affect with age, in contrast to reductions in negative affect reported by their same-aged peers (Charles et al. 2001). Similarly, people high in neuroticism reported stable levels of life-satisfaction, not the increases in life-satisfaction that are observed among people low in neuroticism (Mroczek & Spiro 2005). In addition, older age is generally related to either similar or lower levels of affective reactivity to daily stressors (Birditt et al. 2005, Neupert et al. 2007). Among people who score high on levels of neuroticism, however, older age is related to greater affective reactivity (Mroczek & Almeida 2004).

Researchers speculate that after years of encountering negative stressors, people high in neuroticism become more sensitive and reactive to them, a phenomenon they term the "kindling effect" (Mroczek & Almeida 2004, Mroczek et al. 2006). The kindling effect is similar to the neurotic cascade in that people high in neuroticism grow more sensitive and reactive to negative experiences over time. Instead of learning from experience and becoming better at maintaining well-being, people high in neuroticism experience high levels of negative affect and are at increased risk for depression (e.g., Kendler et al. 2006). One interpretation of these findings is that people scoring high in neuroticism do not learn from their experiences and modify their emotion-regulation strategies to decrease their exposure and reactivity to negative experiences, particularly negative life experiences.

Failure to Use Cognitive and Behavior Emotion-Regulation Strategies

Older adults are motivated to maintain their affective well-being, and they engage in emotion-regulation strategies that allow them to do so. We predict at least three circumstances in which older adults are unable to employ these strategies effectively and that often increase in prevalence with age. First, older adults must have the cognitive capacity necessary to engage in emotion-regulation strategies. Mather and her colleagues posit that the positivity bias observed among older adults is dependent on cognitive-control strategies (see review by Kryla-Lighthall & Mather 2009). Older adults who perform best on demanding working-memory tasks requiring cognitive control show the greatest bias toward positive information and away from negative information (Mather & Knight 2005). In tasks with low cognitive demand, older adults displayed the positivity bias on tasks of attention and memory (Knight et al. 2007, Mather & Knight 2005). When engaged in divided-attention tasks, however, older adults display no positivity bias. This position is consistent with studies that have found strong associations between poorer cognitive functioning and greater depressive symptomatology (Wilson et al. 2004, Yaffe et al. 1999).

Situations in which emotion-regulation strategies favored by older adults—e.g., avoidance or distraction—are ineffective or impossible to employ present a second circumstance where older adults may not have advantages in emotion regulation compared with younger adults. For example, having a chronic illness is related to higher rates of negative affect (Charles & Almeida 2006). Given the higher prevalence rates of chronic illnesses with age (Rook et al. 2007), a logical conclusion would be that older adults report higher levels of negative affect than do younger adults. Yet older adults continue to report higher levels of positive affect and lower levels of negative affect than do younger adults in comparisons of groups of people with different numbers of reported health conditions (Piazza et al. 2007). An older adult with two levels of chronic illnesses, for example, reports the same level of negative affect as does a younger adult with no chronic health conditions. This age-related advantage in negative affect is no longer present, however, when people experience a stressful event (Piazza et al. 2007). When placed in a situation where they report an event sufficient to elicit high levels of stress, age was not related to affective reactivity.

A third circumstance where older adults may not continue to show strong age-related increases in well-being over time is when they experience losses to their social network. A loss in social belonging, such as that commonly caused by bereavement, is related to increases in negative distress for people of all ages (e.g., Turvey et al. 1999). Unfortunately, the likelihood of bereavement, from loss of family or friends, increases with age. Moreover, loneliness is strongly related to depression among older adults even after controlling for marital status (Barg et al. 2006, Cacioppo et al. 2006), and researchers suggest that the effects of loneliness on physiological functioning may even be stronger among older adults than younger adults (Hawkley & Cacioppo 2007). Further research will need to explore this possibility.

CONCLUSION

There have been notable strides in understanding social and emotional aspects of aging over the past two decades. Social relationships and emotional well-being benefit from experience and time perspective. Experience confers improved regulatory skills; shorter time perspectives lead older people to place greater priority on meaningful aspects of life. Older adults appear to navigate social environments well and use social regulation, particularly social selection, to maintain relatively high levels of well-being. Cognitive resources are also deployed selectively: Attention and memory increasingly favor positive material as people grow older. A growing number of studies have acknowledged biological changes involved in aging and begun to examine how these processes influence, and are influenced by, social and emotional aspects of aging. Namely, when faced with unavoidable or inescapable negative events, older adults experience relatively high levels of physiological distress that can be highly disruptive to physical and mental health. Under such circumstances, social isolation greatly exacerbates the disruption. In summary, in everyday life older adults show social and emotional functioning that is equal to or superior to that of younger adults. When faced with prolonged and unavoidable stress, however, age-related advantages appear to be compromised.

DISCLOSURE STATEMENT

The authors are not aware of any biases that might be perceived as affecting the objectivity of this review.

ACKNOWLEDGMENTS

This work was supported by NIA Grant RO1-8816 awarded to Laura L. Carstensen and NIA Grant R01-AG023845 awarded to Susan Charles.

LITERATURE CITED

Ainsworth MDS, Wittig BA. 1969. Attachment and exploratory behavior of one-year-olds in a strange situation. In *Determinants of Infant Behavior*, ed. BM Foss, Vol. 4, pp. 111–36. London: Methuen

Almeida DM. 2005. Resilience and vulnerability to daily stressors assessed via diary methods. *Curr. Dir. Psychol. Sci.* 14(2):64–68

Almeida DM, Kessler RC. 1998. Everyday stressors and gender differences in daily distress. *J. Personal. Soc. Psychol.* 75(3):670–80

Antonucci TC. 1994. A life-span view of women's social relations. In *Women Growing Older*, ed. BF Turner, LE Troll, pp. 239–69. Thousand Oaks, CA: Sage

Antonucci TC, Akiyama H, Takahashi K. 2004. Attachment and close relationships across the life span. *Attach. Hum. Dev.* 6(4):353–70

Bakke M, Tuxen A, Thomsen CE, Bardow A, Alkjaer T, Jensen BR. 2004. Salivary cortisol level, salivary flow rate, and masticatory muscle activity in response to acute mental stress: a comparison between aged and young women. *Gerontology* 50(6):383–92

Baltes PB, Baltes MM. 1990. Selective optimization with compensation. In *Successful Aging: Perspectives from the Behavioral Sciences*, ed. PB Baltes, MM Baltes, pp. 1–34. New York: Cambridge Univ. Press

Banham KM. 1951. Senescence and the emotions: a genetic theory. *J. Genet. Psychol.* 78(2):175–83

Barg FK, Huss-Ashmore R, Wittink MN, Murray GF, Bogner HR, Gallo JJ. 2006. A mixed-methods approach to understanding loneliness and depression in older adults. *J. Gerontol. Ser. B: Psychol. Sci. Soc. Sci.* 61(6):S329–39

Barnes LL, Cagney KA, Mendes de Leon CF. 2008. Social resources and cognitive function in older persons. In *Handbook of Cognitive Aging*, ed. SM Hofer, DF Alwin, pp. 603–10. Thousand Oaks, CA: Sage

Barnes LL, Mendes de Leon CF, Wilson RS, Bienias JL, Evans DA. 2004. Social resources and cognitive decline in a population of older African Americans and whites. *Neurology* 63(12):2322–26

Batten SV, Aslan M, Maciejewski PK, Mazure CM. 2004. Childhood maltreatment as a risk factor for adult cardiovascular disease and depression. *J. Clin. Psychiatry* 65(2):249–54

Baumeister R, Leary MR. 1995. The need to belong: desire for interpersonal attachments as a fundamental human motivation. *Psychol. Bull.* 117(3):497–529

Berkman LF, Glass T, Brissette I, Seeman TE. 2000. From social integration to health: Durkheim in the new millennium. *Soc. Sci. Med.* 51(6):843–57

Birditt KS, Fingerman KL. 2003. Age and gender differences in adults' descriptions of emotional reactions to interpersonal problems. *J. Gerontol. Ser. B: Psychol. Sci. Soc. Sci.* 58(4):P237–45

Birditt KS, Fingerman KL, Almeida DM. 2005. Age differences in exposure and reactions to interpersonal tensions: a daily diary study. *Psychol. Aging* 20(2):330–40

Bjorntorp P. 2002. Alterations in the ageing corticotropic stress-response axis. *Novartis Found. Symp.* 242:46–58; discussion 58–65

Blanchard-Fields F. 2007. Everyday problem solving and emotion: an adult developmental perspective. *Curr. Dir. Psychol. Sci.* 16(1):26–31

Blanchard-Fields F, Horhota M, Mienaltowski A. 2008. Social context and cognition. In *Handbook of Cognitive Aging: Interdisciplinary Perspectives*, ed. SM Hofer, DF Alwin, pp. 614–28. Los Angeles, CA: Sage

Blanchard-Fields F, Mienaltowski A, Seay RB. 2007. Age differences in everyday problem-solving effectiveness: older adults select more effective strategies for interpersonal problems. *J. Gerontol. Ser. B: Psychol. Sci. Soc. Sci.* 62(1):P61–64

Blazer DG. 2003. Depression in late life: review and commentary. *J. Gerontol. Ser. A: Biol. Sci. Med. Sci.* 58(3):M249–65

Bradburn NM. 1969. *The Structure of Psychological Well-Being*. Chicago: Aldine

Bowlby J. 1969. *Attachment and Loss. Volume 1: Attachment.* New York: Basic Books

Burg MM, Barefoot J, Berkman L, Catellier DJ, Czajkowski S, et al. 2005. Low perceived social support and post-myocardial infarction prognosis in the enhancing recovery in coronary heart disease clinical trial: the effects of treatment. *Psychosom. Med.* 67(6):879–88

Cacioppo JT, Hughes ME, Waite LJ, Hawkley LC, Thisted RA. 2006. Loneliness as a specific risk factor for depressive symptoms: cross-sectional and longitudinal analyses. *Psychol. Aging* 21(1):140–51

Carstensen LL. 1992. Social and emotional patterns in adulthood: support for socioemotional selectivity theory. *Psychol. Aging* 7(3):331–38

Carstensen LL. 1993. Motivation for social contact across the life span: a theory of socioemotional selectivity. In *Nebraska Symposium on Motivation*, ed. JE Jacobs, pp. 209–54. Lincoln: Univ. Nebraska Press

Carstensen LL. 2006. The influence of a sense of time on human development. *Science* 312(5782):1913–15

Carstensen LL, Charles ST. 1998. Emotion in the second half of life. *Curr. Dir. Psychol. Sci.* 7(5):144–49

Carstensen LL, Isaacowitz D, Charles ST. 1999. Taking time seriously: a theory of socioemotional selectivity. *Am. Psychol.* 54(3):165–81

Carstensen LL, Mikels JA. 2005. At the intersection of emotion and cognition: aging and the positivity effect. *Curr. Dir. Psychol. Sci.* 14(3):117–21

Carstensen LL, Mikels JA, Mather M. 2006. Aging and the intersection of cognition, motivation and emotion. In *Handbook of the Psychology of Aging*, ed. JE Birren, KW Schaie, pp. 343–62. San Diego, CA: Academic. 6th ed.

Carstensen LL, Pasupathi M, Mayr U, Nesselroade JR. 2000. Emotional experience in everyday life across the adult life span. *J. Personal. Soc. Psychol.* 79(4):644–55

Carstensen LL, Turk-Charles S. 1994. The salience of emotion across the adult life span. *Psychol. Aging* 9(2):259–64

Charles ST, Almeida DM. 2006. Daily reports of symptoms and negative affect: Not all symptoms are the same. *Psychol. Health* 21(1):1–17

Charles ST, Almeida DM. 2007. Genetic and environmental effects on daily life stressors: more evidence for greater variation in later life. *Psychol. Aging* 22(2):331–40

Charles ST, Carstensen LL. 2007. Emotion regulation and aging. In *Handbook of Emotion Regulation*, ed. JJ Gross, pp. 307–20. New York: Guilford

Charles ST, Carstensen LL. 2008. Unpleasant situations elicit different emotional responses in younger and older adults. *Psychol. Aging* 23(3):495–504

Charles ST, Carstensen LL, McFall RM. 2001. Problem-solving in the nursing home environment: age and experience differences in emotional reactions and responses. *J. Clin. Geropsychol.* 7(4):319–30

Charles ST, Gatz M, Kato K, Pedersen NL. 2008. Physical health 25 years later: the predictive ability of neuroticism. *Health Psychol.* 27(3):369–78

Charles ST, Mather M, Carstensen LL. 2003. Aging and emotional memory: the forgettable nature of negative images for older adults. *J. Exp. Psychol: Gen.* 132(2):310–24

Charles ST, Mavandadi S. 2003. Relationships and health across the life span. In *Growing Together: Personal Relationships Across the Life Span*, ed. F Lang, K Fingerman, pp. 240–67. New York: Cambridge Univ. Press

Charles ST, Piazza JR. 2007. Memories of social interactions: age differences in emotional intensity. *Psychol. Aging* 22(2):300–9

Charles ST, Piazza JR. 2009. Strength and vulnerability across the lifespan: an integration of literature on aging, emotional well-being and emotion regulation. *Soc. Pers. Psychol. Compass.* In press

Charles ST, Piazza JR, Luong G, Almeida DM. 2009. Now you see it, now you don't: age differences in affective reactivity to social tensions. *Psychol. Aging* In press

Charles ST, Reynolds CA, Gatz M. 2001. Age-related differences and change in positive and negative affect over 23 years. *J. Personal. Soc. Psychol.* 80(1):136–51

Coats AH, Blanchard-Fields F. 2008. Emotion regulation in interpersonal problems: the role of cognitive-emotional complexity, emotion regulation goals, and expressivity. *Psychol. Aging* 23(1):39–51

Cohen S, Wills TA. 1985. Stress, social support, and the buffering hypothesis. *Psychol. Bull.* 98(2):310–57

Comblain C, D'Argembeau A, Van Der Linden M. 2005. Phenomenal characteristics of autobiographical memories for emotional and neutral events in older and younger adults. *Exp. Aging Res.* 31(2):173–89

Consedine NS, Magai C. 2003. Attachment and emotion experience in later life: the view from emotions theory. *Attach. Hum. Dev.* 5(2):165–87

Cumming E, Henry WE. 1961. *Growing Older: The Process of Disengagement.* New York: Basic Books

Danner DD, Snowdon DA, Friesen WV. 2001. Positive emotions in early life and longevity: findings from the nun study. *J. Personal. Soc. Psychol.* 80(5):804–13

Darowski ES, Helder E, Zacks RT, Hasher L, Hambrick DZ. 2008. Age-related differences in cognition: the role of distraction control. *Neuropsychology* 22(5):638–44

Davey A, Halverson CFJ, Zonderman AB, Costa PTJ. 2004. Change in depressive symptoms in the Baltimore Longitudinal Study of Aging. *J. Gerontol. Ser. B: Psychol. Sci. Soc. Sci.* 59(6):P270–77

Davidson RJ, Fox A, Kalin NH. 2007. Neural bases of emotion regulation in nonhuman primates and humans. In *Handbook of Emotion Regulation*, ed. JJ Gross, pp. 47–68. New York: Guilford

DeCarli C, Massaro J, Harvey D, Hald J, Tullberg M, et al. 2005. Measures of brain morphology and infarction in the Framingham Heart Study: establishing what is normal. *Neurobiol. Aging* 26(4):491–510

De Meersman RE, Stein PK. 2006. Vagal modulation and aging. *Biol. Psychol.* 74(2):165–73

Deschenes MR, Carter JA, Matney EN, Potter MB, Wilson MH. 2006. Aged men experience disturbances in recovery following submaximal exercise. *J. Gerontol. Ser. A: Biol. Sci. Med. Sci.* 61A(1):63–71

Diener E, Sandvik E, Larsen RJ. 1985. Age and sex effects for emotional intensity. *Dev. Psychol.* 21(3):542–46

Diener E, Suh ME. 1997. Subjective well-being and age: an international analysis. In *Annual Review of Gerontology and Geriatrics*, ed. KW Schaie, MP Lawton, Vol. 17, pp. 304–24. New York: Springer

Dodt C, Theine KJ, Uthgenannt D, Born J, Fehm HL. 1994. Basal secretory activity of the hypothalamo-pituitary-adrenocortical axis is enhanced in healthy elderly. An assessment during undisturbed night-time sleep. *Eur. J. Endocrinol.* 131(5):443–50

Doherty NA, Feeney JA. 2004. The composition of attachment networks throughout the adult years. *Pers. Relat.* 11(4):469–88

Draper B, Pfaff JJ, Pirkis J, Snowdon J, Lautenschlager NT, et al. 2008. Long-term effects of childhood abuse on the quality of life and health of older people: results from the depression and early prevention of suicide in general practice project. *J. Am. Geriatr. Soc.* 56(2):262–71

Eysenck HJ. 1967. *The Biological Basis of Personality.* Springfield, IL: Thomas

Farmer A, Redman K, Harris T, Mahmood A, Sadler S, Pickering A, et al. 2002. Neuroticism, extraversion, life events and depression: The Cardiff Depression Study. *Br. J. Psychiatry* 181(2):118–22

Fernandes M, Ross M, Wiegand M, Schryer E. 2008. Are the memories of older adults positively biased? *Psychol. Aging* 23(2):297–306

Ferrari AU, Radaelli A, Centola M. 2003. Invited review: aging and the cardiovascular system. *J. Appl. Physiol.* 95(6):2591–97

Fratiglioni L, Wang HX, Ericsson K, Maytan M, Winblad B. 2000. Influence of social network on occurrence of dementia: a community-based longitudinal study. *Lancet* 355(9212):1315–19

Fredrickson BL, Carstensen LL. 1990. Choosing social partners: how old age and anticipated endings make people more selective. *Psychol. Aging* 5(3):335–47

Fung HH, Carstensen LL, Lang FR. 2001. Age-related patterns in social networks among European Americans and African Americans: implications for socioemotional selectivity across the life span. *Int. J. Aging Hum. Dev.* 52(3):185–206

Fung HH, Carstensen LL, Lutz AM. 1999. Influence of time on social preferences: implications for life-span development. *Psychol. Aging* 14(4):595–604

Fung HH, Stoeber FS, Yeung DY, Lang FR. 2008. Cultural specificity of socioemotional selectivity: age differences in social network composition among Germans and Hong Kong Chinese. *J. Gerontol. Ser. B: Psychol. Sci. Soc. Sci.* 63B(3):P156–64

Giordano R, Bo M, Pellegino M, Vezzari M, Baldi M, et al. 2005. Hypothalamus-pituitary-adrenal hyperactivity in human aging is partially refractory to stimulation by mineralocorticoid receptor blockade. *J. Clin. Endocrinol. Metab.* 90(10):5656–62

Glymour MM, Weuve J, Fay ME, Glass T, Berkman LF. 2008. Social ties and cognitive recovery after stroke: Does social integration promote cognitive resilience? *Neuroepidemiology* 31(1):10–20

Grady CL, Hongwanishkul D, Keightley M, Lee W, Hasher L. 2007. The effect of age on memory for emotional faces. *Neuropsychology* 21(3):371–80

Graham JE, Christian LM, Kiecolt-Glaser JK. 2006. Stress, age, and immune function: toward a lifespan approach. *J. Behav. Med.* 29(4):389–400

Greenfield EA, Marks NF. 2004. Formal volunteering as a protective factor for older adults' psychological well-being. *J. Gerontol. Ser. B: Psychol. Sci. Soc. Sci.* 59(5):S258–64

Grieve SM, Clark CR, Williams LM, Peduto AJ, Gordon E. 2005. Preservation of limbic and paralimbic structures in aging. *Hum. Brain Mapp.* 25(4):391–401

Gruenewald TL, Karlamangla AS, Greendale GA, Singer BH, Seeman TE. 2007. Feelings of usefulness to others, disability, and mortality in older adults: the MacArthur study of successful aging. *J. Gerontol. Ser. B: Psychol. Sci. Soc. Sci.* 62(1):P28–37

Grühn D, Scheibe S, Baltes PB. 2007. Reduced negativity effect in older adults' memory for emotional pictures: the heterogeneity-homogeneity list paradigm. *Psychol. Aging* 22(3):644–49

Gunthert KC, Cohen LH, Armeli S. 1999. The role of neuroticism in daily stress and coping. *J. Personal. Soc. Psychol.* 77(5):1087–100

Hashtroudi S, Johnson MK, Chrosniak LD. 1990. Aging and qualitative characteristics of memories for perceived and imagined complex events. *Psychol. Aging* 5(1):119–26

Hawkley LC, Cacioppo JT. 2007. Aging and loneliness: downhill quickly? *Curr. Dir. Psychol. Sci.* 16(4):187–91

Haynie DA, Berg S, Johansson B, Gatz M, Zarit SH. 2001. Symptoms of depression in the oldest old: a longitudinal study. *J. Gerontol. Ser. B: Psychol. Sci. Soc. Sci.* 56(2):P111–18

Hendricks J, Cutler SJ. 2004. Volunteerism and socioemotional selectivity in later life. *J. Gerontol. Ser. B: Psychol. Sci. Soc. Sci.* 59(5):S251–57

Hess TM. 2005. Memory and aging in context. *Psychol. Bull.* 131(3):383–406

Hess TM, Auman C. 2001. Aging and social expertise: the impact of trait-diagnostic information on impressions of others. *Psychol. Aging* 16(3):497–510

Hess TM, Bolstad CA, Woodburn SM, Auman C. 1999. Trait diagnosticity versus behavioral consistency as determinants of impression change in adulthood. *Psychol. Aging* 14(1):77–89

Hess TM, Osowski NL, Leclerc CM. 2005. Age differences in sensitivity to diagnostic cues and the flexibility of social judgments. *Psychol. Aging* 20(3):447–59

House JS, Landis KR, Umberson D. 1988. Social relationships and health. *Science* 241(4865):540–45

Hughes TF, Andel R, Small BJ, Borenstein AR, Mortimer JA. 2008. The association between social resources and cognitive change in older adults: evidence from the Charlotte County Healthy Aging Study. *J. Gerontol. Ser. B: Psychol. Sci. Soc. Sci.* 63(4):P241–44

Isaacowitz DM, Carstensen LL, Charles ST. 2000. Emotion and cognition. In *The Handbook of Aging and Cognition*, ed. FIM Craik, TA Salthouse, pp. 593–631. Mahwah, NJ: Erlbaum. 2nd ed.

Isaacowitz DM, Wadlinger HA, Goren D, Wilson HR. 2006. Is there an age-related positivity effect in visual attention? A comparison of two methodologies. *Emotion* 6(3):511–16

Johnson MK, Nolde SF, De Leonardis DM. 1996. Emotional focus and source monitoring. *J. Mem. Lang.* 35(2):135–56

Jopp D, Rott C. 2006. Adaptation in very old age: exploring the role of resources, beliefs, and attitudes for centenarians' happiness. *Psychol. Aging* 21(2):266–80

Kendler KS, Gatz M, Gardner CO, Pederson G. 2006. A Swedish National Twin Study of lifetime major depression. *Am. J. Psychiatry* 163(1):109–14

Kennedy KM, Raz N. 2009. Aging white matter and cognition: differential effects of regional variations in diffusion properties on memory, executive functions, and speed. *Neuropsychologia* 47(3):916–27

Kennedy Q, Mather M, Carstensen LL. 2004. The role of motivation in the age-related positivity effect in autobiographical memory. *Psychol. Sci.* 15(3):208–14

Kensinger EA. 2008. Age differences in memory for arousing and nonarousing emotional words. *J. Gerontol. Ser. B: Psychol. Sci. Soc. Sci.* 63(1):P13–18

Kensinger EA, Garoff-Eaton RJ, Schacter DL. 2007. Effects of emotion on memory specificity in young and older adults. *J. Gerontol. Ser. B: Psychol. Sci. Soc. Sci.* 62(4):P208–15

Kessler RC, Andrews G, Colpe LJ, Hiripi E, Mroczek DK, et al. 2002. Short screening scales to monitor population prevalences and trends in nonspecific psychological distress. *Psychol. Med.* 32(6):959–76

Kim S, Healey MK, Goldstein D, Hasher L, Wiprzycka UJ. 2008. Age differences in choice satisfaction: a positivity effect in decision making. *Psychol. Aging* 23(1):33–38

Knight M, Seymour TL, Gaunt JT, Baker C, Nesmith K, Mather M. 2007. Aging and goal-directed emotional attention: distraction reverses emotional biases. *Emotion* 7(4):705–14

Kobau R, Safran MA, Zack MM, Moriarty DG, Chapman D. 2004. Sad, blue, or depressed days, health behaviors and health-related quality of life, Behavioral Risk Factor Surveillance System, 1995–2000. *Health Qual. Life Outcomes* 2:40

Krause N. 2006. Neighborhood deterioration, social skills, and social relationships in late life. *Int. J. Aging Hum. Dev.* 62(3):185–207

Krause N. 2007. Longitudinal study of social support and meaning in life. *Psychol. Aging* 22(3):456–69

Kryla-Lighthall N, Mather M. 2009. The role of cognitive control in older adults' emotional well-being. In *Handbook of Theories of Aging*, ed. V Berngtson, D Gans, N Putney, M Silverstein, pp. 323–44. New York: Springer. 2nd ed.

Kudielka BM, Buske-Kirschbaum A, Hellhammer DW, Kirschbaum C. 2004. HPA axis responses to laboratory psychosocial stress in healthy elderly adults, younger adults, and children: impact of age and gender. *Psychoneuroendocrinology*, 29(1):83–98

Kunzman U, Little TD, Smith J. 2000. Is age-related stability of subjective well-being a paradox? Cross-sectional and longitudinal evidence from the Berlin Aging Study. *Psychol. Aging* 15(3):511–26

Lang FR, Carstensen LL. 1994. Close emotional relationships in late life: further support for proactive aging in the social domain. *Psychol. Aging* 9(2):315–24

Lang FR, Carstensen LL. 2002. Time counts: future time perspective, goals and social relationships. *Psychol. Aging* 17(1):125–39

Lang IA, Llewellyn DJ, Langa KM, Wallace RB, Huppert FA, Melzer D. 2008. Neighborhood deprivation, individual socioeconomic status, and cognitive function in older people: analyses from the English Longitudinal Study of Ageing. *J. Am. Geriatr. Soc.* 56(2):191–98

Lawton MP, Kleban MH, Rajagopal D, Dean J. 1992. Dimensions of affective experience in three age groups. *Psychol. Aging* 7(2):171–84

Lazarus RS. 1991. *Emotion and Adaptation*. London: Oxford Univ. Press

Leclerc CM, Hess TM. 2007. Age differences in the bases for social judgments: tests of a social expertise perspective. *Aging Res.* 33(1):95–120

Lefkowitz ES, Fingerman KL. 2003. Positive and negative emotional feelings and behaviors in mother-daughter ties in late life. *J. Fam. Psychol.* 17(4):607–17

Leigland LA, Schulz LE, Janowsky JS. 2004. Age-related changes in emotional memory. *Neurobiol. Aging* 25(8):1117–24

Lemieux A, Coe CL, Carnes M. 2008. Symptom severity predicts degree of T cell activation in adult women following childhood maltreatment. *Brain Behav. Immun.* 22(6):994–1003

Levenson RW. 2000. Expressive, physiological, and subjective changes in emotion across adulthood. In *Psychology and the Aging Revolution: How We Adapt to Longer Life*, ed. SH Qualls, N Abeles, pp. 123–40. Washington, DC: Am. Psychol. Assoc.

Levenson RW, Carstensen LL, Friesen WV, Ekman P. 1991. Emotion, physiology, and expression in old age. *Psychol. Aging* 6(1):28–35

Levenson RW, Carstensen LL, Gottman JM. 1994. Influence of age and gender on affect, physiology, and their interrelations: a study of long-term marriages. *J. Personal. Soc. Psychol.* 67(1):56–68

Levine LJ, Safer MA, Lench HC. 2006. Remembering and misremembering emotions. In *Judgments Over Time: The Interplay of Thoughts, Feelings, and Behaviors*, ed. LJ Sanna, E Chin-Ho Chang, pp. 271–92. Oxford, UK: Oxford Univ. Press

Löckenhoff CE, Carstensen L. 2007. Aging, emotion, and health-related decision strategies: motivational manipulation can reduce age differences. *Psychol. Aging* 22(1):134–46

Löckenhoff CE, Costa PT, Lane RD. 2008. Age differences in descriptions of emotional experience in oneself and others. *J. Gerontol. Ser. B: Psychol. Sci. Soc. Sci.* 63(2):P92–99

Luecken LJ. 2006. Early family adversity and cognitive performance in aging: a lifespan developmental model. *J. Soc. Clin. Psychol.* 25(1):33–52

Lyyra T, Heikkinen R. 2006. Perceived social support and mortality in older people. *J. Gerontol. Ser. B: Psychol. Sci. Soc. Sci.* 61(3):S147–52

Lyyra T, Törmäkangas TM, Read S, Rantanen T, Berg S. 2006. Satisfaction with present life predicts survival in octogenarians. *J. Gerontol. Ser. B: Psychol. Soc. Sci.* 61(6):P319–26

Magai C. 2001. Emotions over the lifespan. In *Handbook of the Psychology of Aging*, ed. JE Birren, KW Schaie, pp. 399–426. San Diego, CA: Academic. 5th ed.

Magai C, Consedine N, Krivoshekova YS, Kudadjie-Gyamfi E, McPherson R. 2006. Emotion experience and expression across the adult life span: insights from a multimodal assessment study. *Psychol. Aging* 21(2):303–17

Marsiske M, Lang FR, Baltes PB, Baltes MM. 1995. Selective optimization with compensation: life-span perspectives on successful human development. In *Compensation for Psychological Deficits and Declines: Managing Losses and Promoting Gains*, ed. RA Dixon, L Backman, pp. 35–79. Hillsdale, NJ: Erlbaum

Maslow AH. 1943. A theory of human motivation. *Psychol. Rev.* 50(4):370–96

Mather M. 2006. A review of decision making processes: weighing the risks and benefits of aging. In *When I'm 64: Committee on Aging Frontiers in Social Psychology, Personality, and Adult Developmental Psychology*, ed. LL Carstensen, CR Hartel, pp. 145–73. Washington, DC: Natl. Acad. Press

Mather M, Carstensen LL. 2003. Aging and attentional biases for emotional faces. *Psychol. Sci.* 14(5):409–15

Mather M, Carstensen LL. 2005. Aging and motivated cognition: the positivity effect in attention and memory. *Trends Cogn. Sci.* 9(10):496–502

Mather M, Johnson MK, De Leonardis DM. 1999. Stereotype reliance in source monitoring: age differences and neuropsychological test correlates. *Cogn. Neuropsychol.* 16(3–5):437–58

Mather M, Knight MR. 2005. Goal-directed memory: the role of cognitive control in older adults' emotional memory. *Psychol. Aging* 20(4):544–70

Mather M, Knight MR. 2006. Angry faces get noticed quickly: threat detection is not impaired among older adults. *J. Gerontol. Ser. B: Psychol. Sci. Soc. Sci.* 61(1):P54–57

Mather M, Knight MR, McCaffrey M. 2005. The allure of the alignable: younger and older adults' false memories of choice features. *J. Exp. Psychol.: Gen.* 134(1):38–51

McConatha JT, Huba HM. 1999. Primary, secondary, and emotional control across adulthood. *Curr. Psychol.* 18(2):164–70

McCrae RR, Costa PT Jr, Ostendorf F, Angleitner A, Hrebrikova M, et al. 2000. Nature over nurture: temperament, personality, and lifespan development. *J. Personal. Soc. Psychol.* 78(1):173–86

Mellor D, Stokes M, Firth L, Hayashi Y, Cummins R. 2008. Need for belonging, relationship satisfaction, loneliness, and life satisfaction. *Personal. Individ. Differ.* 45(3):213–18

Morris AS, Silk JS, Steinberg L, Myers SS, Robinson LR. 2007. The role of the family context in the development of children's emotion regulation. *Soc. Dev.* 16(2):361–88

Mikels JA, Larkin GR, Reuter-Lorenz PA, Carstensen LL. 2005. Divergent trajectories in the aging mind: changes in working memory for affective versus visual information with age. *Psychol. Aging* 20(4):542–53

Minkler M, Fuller-Thomson E, Miller D, Driver D. 1997. Depression in grandparents raising grandchildren: results of a national longitudinal study. *Arch. Fam. Med.* 6(5):445–52

Minkler M, Fuller-Thomson E, Miller D, Driver D. 2000. Grandparent caregiving and depression. In *Grandparents Raising Grandchildren: Theoretical, Empirical, and Clinical Perspectives*, ed. B Hayslip Jr, R Goldberg-Glen, pp. 207–19. New York: Springer

Mroczek DK, Almeida DM. 2004. The effect of daily stress, personality, and age on daily negative affect. *J. Personal.* 72(2):355–78

Mroczek DK, Kolarz CM. 1998. The effect of age on positive and negative affect: a developmental perspective on happiness. *J. Personal. Soc. Psychol.* 75(5):1333–49

Mroczek DK, Spiro A. 2003. Modeling intraindividual change in personality traits: findings from the Normative Aging Study. *J. Gerontol. Ser. B: Psychol. Sci. Soc. Sci.* 58(3):P153–65

Mroczek DK, Spiro A. 2005. Change in life satisfaction over 20 years during adulthood: findings from the VA Normative Aging Study. *J. Personal. Soc. Psychol.* 88(1):189–202

Mroczek DK, Spiro A, Griffin PW, Neupert S. 2006. Social influences on adult personality, self-regulation and health. In *Social Structures, Aging and Self-Regulation*, ed. KW Schaie, L Carstensen, pp. 69–84. New York: Springer

Mu Q, Xie J, Wen Z, Weng Y, Shuyun Z. 1999. A quantitative MRI study of the hippocampal formation, the amygdala, and the temporal horn of the lateral ventricle in healthy subjects 40 to 90 years of age. *Am. J. Neuroradiol.* 20(2):207–11

Neupert S, Almeida DM, Charles ST. 2007. Age differences in reactivity to daily stressors: the role of personal control. *J. Gerontol. Ser. B: Psychol. Sci. Soc. Sci.* 62(4):P216–25

Newsom JT, Mahan TL, Rook KS, Krause N. 2008. Stable negative social exchanges and health. *Health Psychol.* 27(3):78–86

Newsom JT, Rook KS, Nishishiba M, Sorkin DH, Mahan TL. 2005. Understanding the relative importance of positive and negative social exchanges: examining specific domains and appraisals. *J. Personal. Soc. Psychol.* 60(6):304–12

Ong AD, Allaire JC. 2005. Cardiovascular intraindividual variability in later life: the influence of social connectedness and positive emotions. *Psychol. Aging* 20(3):476–85

Otte C, Hart S, Neylan TC, Marmar CR, Yaffe K, Mohr DC. 2005. A meta-analysis of cortisol response to challenge in human aging: importance of gender. *Psychoneuroendocrinology* 30(1):80–91

Pennebaker J, Stone LD. 2003. Words of wisdom: language use over the lifespan. *J. Personal. Soc. Psychol.* 85(2):291–301

Peters E, Hess TM, Västfjäll D, Auman C. 2007. Adult age differences in dual information processes: implications for the role of affective and deliberative processes in older adults' decision making. *Perspect. Psychol. Sci.* 2(1):1–23

Phillips LH, Henry JD, Hosie JA, Milne AB. 2006. Age, anger regulation and well being. *Aging Ment. Health* 10(3):250–56

Piazza JR, Charles ST. 2006. Mental health and the baby boomers. In *The Baby Boomers at Midlife: Contemporary Perspectives on Middle Age*, ed. SK Whitbourne, SL Willis, pp. 111–46. Hillsdale, NJ: Erlbaum

Piazza JR, Charles ST, Almeida DM. 2007. Living with chronic health conditions: age differences in affective well-being. *J. Gerontol. Ser. B: Psychol. Sci. Soc. Sci.* 62(6):P313–21

Pinquart M. 2001. Correlates of subjective health in older adults: a meta-analysis. *Psychol. Aging* 16(3):414–26

Poulin M, Cohen Silver R. 2008. World benevolence beliefs and well-being across the life span. *Psychol. Aging* 23(1):13–23

Pressman SD, Cohen S. 2005. Does positive affect influence health? *Psychol. Bull.* 131(6):925–71

Pressman SD, Cohen S. 2007. Use of social words in autobiographies and longevity. *Psychosom. Med.* 69(3):262–69

Radloff LS. 1977. The CES-D scale. *Appl. Psychol. Meas.* 1(3):385–401

Raz N. 2005. The aging brain observed in vivo. In *Cognitive Neuroscience of Aging*, ed. R Cabeza, L Nyberg, DC Park, pp. 19–57. New York: Oxford Univ. Press

Raz N, Lindenberger U, Rodrigue KM, Kennedy KM, Head D, et al. 2005. Regional brain changes in aging healthy adults: general trends, individual differences and modifiers. *Cereb. Cortex* 15(11):1676–89

Raz N, Rodrigue KM. 2006. Differential aging of the brain: patterns, cognitive correlates and modifiers. *Neurosci. Biobehav. Rev.* 30(6):730–48

Ready RE, Weinberger MI, Jones KM. 2007. How happy have you felt lately? Two diary studies of emotion recall in older and younger adults. *Cogn. Emot.* 21(4):728–57

Repetti RL, Taylor SE, Seeman TE. 2002. Risky families: family social environments and the mental and physical health of offspring. *Psychol. Bull.* 128(2):330–66

Riediger M, Freund A. 2008. Me against myself: motivational conflicts and emotional development in adulthood. *Psychol. Aging* 23(2):126–40

Roberts BW, Kuncel N, Shiner R, Caspi A, Goldberg LR. 2007. The power of personality: the comparative analysis of the predictive validity of personality traits, SES, and IQ. *Perspect. Psychol. Sci.* 2(4):313–45

Rook KS. 1984. The negative side of social interaction: impact on psychological well-being. *J. Personal. Soc. Psychol.* 46(5):1097–108

Rook KS. 1998. Investigating the positive and negative sides of personal relationships: through a glass darkly? In *The Dark Side of Close Relationships*, ed. BH Spitzberg, WR Cupach, pp. 369–93. Mahwah, NJ: Erlbaum

Rook KS, Charles ST, Heckhausen J. 2007. Aging and health. In *Handbook of Health Psychology*, ed. HS Friedman, RC Silver, pp. 234–62. New York: Oxford Univ. Press

Rozin P, Royzman EB. 2001. Negativity bias, negativity dominance, and contagion. *Personal. Soc. Psychol. Rev.* 5(4):296–320

Ryff CD, Singer BH. 2001. Integrating emotions into the study of social relationships and health. In *Emotion, Social Relationships, and Health*, ed. CD Ryff, BH Singer, pp. 3–22. Oxford, UK: Oxford Univ. Press

Salthouse TA, Siedlecki KL. 2007. An individual difference analysis of false recognition. *Am. J. Psychol.* 120(3):429–58

Sapolsky RM, Krey LC, McEwen BS. 1986. The neuroendocrinology of stress and aging: the glucocorticoid cascade hypothesis. *Endocrinol. Rev.* 7(3):284–301

Seeman TE, Lusignolo TM, Albert M, Berkman L. 2001. Social relationships, social support, and patterns of cognitive aging in healthy, high-functioning older adults: MacArthur Studies of Successful Aging. *Health Psychol.* 20(4):243–55

Shaver PR, Belsky J, Brennan KA. 2000. The adult attachment interview and self-reports of romantic attachment: associations across domains and methods. *Pers. Relat.* 7(1):25–43

Shaw BA, Krause N, Chatters LM, Connell CM, Ingersoll-Dayton B. 2004. Emotional support from parents early in life, aging, and health. *Psychol. Aging* 19(1):4–12

Siedlecki KL, Salthouse TA, Berish DE. 2005. Is there anything special about the aging of source memory? *Psychol. Aging* 20(1):19–32

Singh-Manoux A, Richards M, Marmot M. 2003. Leisure activities and cognitive function in middle age: evidence from the Whitehall II study. *J. Epidemiol. Community Health* 57(11):907–13

Snowden LR. 2001. Social embeddedness and psychological well-being among African Americans and Whites. *Am. J. Community Psychol.* 29(4):519–36

Sorkin D, Rook KS. 2006. Dealing with negative social exchanges in later life: coping responses, goals, and effectiveness. *Psychol. Aging* 21(4):715–25

Spaniol J, Voss A, Grady CL. 2008. Aging and emotional memory: cognitive mechanisms underlying the positivity effect. *Psychol. Aging* 23(4):859–72

Stine-Morrow EAL, Parisi JM, Morrow DG, Park DC. 2008. The effects of an engaged lifestyle on cognitive vitality: a field experiment. *Psychol. Aging* 23(4):778–86

Story TN, Berg CA, Smith TW, Beveridge R, Henry NJM, Pearce G. 2007. Age, marital satisfaction, and optimism as predictors of positive sentiment override in middle aged and older married couples. *Psychol. Aging* 24(4):719–27

Suls J, Martin R. 2005. The daily life of the garden-variety neurotic: reactivity, stressor exposure, mood spillover, and maladaptive coping. *J. Personal.* 73(6):1485–510

Thomas RC, Hasher L. 2006. The influence of emotional valence on age differences in early processing and memory. *Psychol. Aging* 21(4):821–25

Torges CM, Stewart AJ, Nolen-Hoeksema S. 2008. Regret resolution, aging, and adapting to loss. *Psychol. Aging* 23(1):169–80

Tsai JL, Levenson RW, Carstensen LL. 2000. Autonomic, subjective, and expressive responses to emotional films in older and younger Chinese Americans and European Americans. *Psychol. Aging* 15(4):684–93

Turvey CL, Carney C, Arndt S, Wallace RB, Herzog R. 1999. Conjugal loss and syndromal depression in a sample of elders aged 70 years or older. *Am. J. Psychiatry* 156(10):1596–601

Uchino BN, Holt-Lunstad J, Bloor LE, Campo RA. 2005. Aging and cardiovascular reactivity to stress: longitudinal evidence for changes in stress reactivity. *Psychol. Aging* 20(1):134–43

Uchino BN, Uno D, Holt-Lunstad J, Flinders JB. 1999. Age-related differences in cardiovascular reactivity during acute psychological stress in men and women. *J. Gerontol. Ser. B: Psychol. Sci. Soc. Sci.* 54(6):339–46

van Gelder BM, Tijhuis M, Kalmijn S, Giampaoli S, Nissinen A, Kromhout D. 2006. Marital status and living situation during a 5-year period are associated with a subsequent 10-year cognitive decline in older men: the FINE Study. *J. Gerontol. Ser. B: Psychol. Sci. Soc. Sci.* 61(4):213–19

Wilkinson CW, Peskind ER, Raskind MA. 1997. Decreased hypothalamic-pituitary adrenal axis sensitivity to cortisol feedback inhibition in human aging. *Neuroendocrinology* 65(1):79–90

Wilkinson CW, Petrie EC, Murray SR, Colasurdo EA, Raskind MA, Peskind ER. 2001. Human glucocorticoid feedback inhibition is reduced in older individuals: Evening Study. *J. Clin. Endocrinol. Metab.* 86(2):545–50

Wilson RS, Krueger KR, Arnold SE, Schneider JA, Kelly JF, et al. 2007. Loneliness and risk of Alzheimer disease. *Arch. Gen. Psychiatry* 64(2):234–40

Wilson RS, Krueger KR, Arnold SE, Barnes LL, Mendes de Leon CF, et al. 2006. Childhood adversity and psychosocial adjustment in old age. *Am. J. Geriatr. Psychiatry* 14(4):307–15

Wilson RS, Mendes de Leon CF, Bennett DA, Bienias JL, Evans DA. 2004. Depressive symptoms and cognitive decline in a community population of older persons. *J. Neurol. Neurosurg. Psychiatry* 75(1):126–29

Yaffe K, Blackwell T, Gore R, Sands L, Reus V, Browner WS. 1999. Depressive symptoms and cognitive decline in nondemented elderly women: a prospective study. *Arch. Gen. Psychiatry* 56(5):425–30

Yeung DY, Fung HH, Lang FR. 2008. Self-construal moderates age differences in social network characteristics. *Psychol. Aging* 23(1):222–26

Zacks R, Hasher L. 1997. Cognitive gerontology and attentional inhibition: a reply to Burke and McDowd. *J. Gerontol. Ser. B: Psychol. Sci. Soc. Sci.* 52(6):P274–83

Zunzunegui MV, Alvarado BE, Del Ser T, Otero A. 2003. Social networks, social integration, and social engagement determine cognitive decline in community-dwelling Spanish older adults. *J. Gerontol. B: Psychol. Sci. Soc. Sci.* 58B(2):S93–100

Human Development in Societal Context

Aletha C. Huston and Alison C. Bentley

Department of Human Ecology, University of Texas at Austin, Austin, Texas 78712;
email: achuston@mail.utexas.edu, alison.bentley@mail.utexas.edu

Annu. Rev. Psychol. 2010. 61:411–37

First published online as a Review in Advance on
July 2, 2009

The *Annual Review of Psychology* is online at
psych.annualreviews.org

This article's doi:
10.1146/annurev.psych.093008.100442

0066-4308/10/0110-0411$20.00

Key Words

poverty, ecological theory, children, policy, social inequality

Abstract

Low family socioeconomic position is a net of related conditions—
low income, material deprivation, single-parent family structure, low
educational level, minority ethnic group membership, and immigrant
status. According to ecological theory, proximal contexts experienced
by children, including family, material resources, out-of-school experiences, schools, neighborhoods, and peers, are mediators of poverty
effects. Developmental timing of exposure to poverty conditions and
the processes by which effects occur differ for cognitive and social domains of development. Understanding how contexts combine and interact is as important as understanding their independent influences.
Effects may be cumulative, but advantages in one context can also ameliorate disadvantages in others. Although research is typically based on
unidirectional causal models, the relations between the developing child
and the contexts he or she experiences are reciprocal and transactional.
Finally, although income inequality has increased greatly, little is known
about the influences of relative poverty and social inequality on human
development.

Contents

Social inequality:
inequality in a variety of domains including economics, family life, education, neighborhoods, and housing

Human development: change in behavior or perception resulting from the interplay of the person's biological characteristics and the environment

INTRODUCTION

Our national ideology portrays the United States as a land of opportunity where anyone can achieve success, wealth, and power regardless of family heritage or early circumstances. We deny strong influences of social context and structure, touting instead personal qualities as the major determinants of success or failure. These views are reflected in our economic and social policies, which rest on the assumption that individuals bear the primary responsibility for their own poverty or wealth and their own success or failure. Of course, this national myth has never been entirely correct. Family education, position, wealth, and having white Anglo-Saxon ancestry have always conferred advantages, but their importance has become more salient over the past generation or two in part because social inequality based on income, ethnic group, and education has increased in the United States and to a lesser extent in other western democracies since the 1970s (Neckerman 2004).

In this review, we take family socioeconomic position as a point of departure to understand how some societal contexts set the conditions for children's development. Poverty and social disadvantage are not literally contexts, but are "social addresses" (Bronfenbrenner 1989) that signal or summarize a set of correlated contexts and experiences. Poverty is not simply low income or absence of material goods; it is part of an interrelated net of circumstances that can include single-parent families, low levels of education, and belonging to a minority or immigrant group.

We begin with a conceptual framework based on an ecological theory of human development, then proceed to three major sections of the review examining (*a*) the societal contexts associated with poverty for children in the twenty-first century; (*b*) the relations of these contexts to children's development, using both naturalistic research and studies of public policies; and (*c*) the proximal processes that mediate the relations of these contexts to development. Most of the research discussed is based on United States populations, but some international comparisons are included.

DEFINITIONS AND CONCEPTUAL FRAMEWORKS

An ecological model incorporating the relations among personal characteristics, proximal processes, context, and time is used to frame our understanding of the relations of poverty to children's development. Human development is defined as "change during the life course in enduring patterns of behavior or perception resulting from the interplay of biological characteristics of the person and the environment" (Bronfenbrenner & Crouter 1983, p. 359). The child is embedded in an expanding set of contexts as illustrated in **Figure 1** (see color insert). An environmental context is "any event or condition outside the organism that affects or is affected by a person's development" (Bronfenbrenner & Crouter 1983, p. 359). The model is dynamic, including contexts with which children have direct contact (microsystems) and those that affect development indirectly (exosystems and macrosystems) (Bronfenbrenner & Morris 1998, 2006). Using this ecological perspective, we make context the anchor point of our analysis, organizing the discussion around person variables, processes, and time as they relate to the contexts of interest (see Eamon 2001a for similar analysis).

As noted above, poverty is often part of a net of correlated social address characteristics, including single-mother family structure, low parent education, minority ethnic group membership, and immigrant status. These in turn affect the contexts surrounding the child within and outside the home. A large literature showing that family environment and parenting mediate some of the effects of socioeconomic status (SES) on children has been well reviewed in this publication (Bradley & Corwyn 2002, Conger & Donnellan 2007). As Eamon (2001a) pointed out, "Theories of the effects of poverty on proximal processes in the microsystem of the family have the most research support, but processes in other microsystems such as the peer group and school and in other levels of the ecological environment may also explain the relation between economic deprivation and children's socioemotional functioning" (p. 256). Following this suggestion, we give particular attention to proximal contexts beyond parenting, including material hardship, child care, schooling, neighborhoods, and peer groups.

Lack of space precludes extensive review of person-by-context interactions, but we do examine age differences and the developmental timing of exposure to contexts of poverty. We acknowledge that biological and genetic characteristics of individuals may contribute to the variations in development associated with the social addresses we are studying, but a thorough consideration of these topics is beyond the scope of this review (see Lerner 2003 for discussion of these issues).

Some researchers have tried to parse the conditions correlated with poverty in order to identify the effects of one component (e.g., income or family structure) independently of the others. We argue here that understanding how contexts combine and interact is equally important. Two hypotheses describe how the effects of contexts may combine. One approach is akin to cumulative disadvantage theories (e.g., Sameroff & Seifer 1995), considering the combined effects of contexts as greater than the sum of their individual components. According to this hypothesis, the advantages or disadvantages conferred by the multiple settings and contexts of poverty are cumulative and often multiplicative, leading to larger effects than would be predicted from a simple additive model. Alternatively, their relations may be compensatory or interactive. Advantages in one context may compensate for disadvantages in another, or combinations of components may lead to different contextual environments for children. For example, poverty in immigrant families may co-occur with different family processes and have different effects on children than poverty in native-born families partly because such families have different types of social capital (Fuligni & Yoshikawa 2003). Moreover, immigrants differ considerably in patterns of achievement and assimilation into their adopted countries, suggesting the importance of a range of cultural values, social supports, and prior experiences.

Much of the research on poverty and SES is based on unidirectional causal models, in part because their goal is to identify contexts that can be changed through intervention, but models incorporating reciprocal interaction of persons and environments are more consistent with ecological theory. "Development takes place through increasingly complex processes in which an active organism interacts with persons, objects, and symbols in its immediate

Environmental context: any external event or condition that affects or is affected by a person's development

SES: socioeconomic status

Social capital: results from children's interactions and relationships with parents and other people

environment" (Bronfenbrenner & Morris 1998, p. 797). That is, the relations of individuals to contexts are transactional. Patterns of children's behavior that result from the contexts of poverty may in turn affect those contexts through eliciting responses from others; for example, a small advantage in language development may lead adults to verbalize to the child, further expanding the child's language repertoire. As children get older, they actively select environments (e.g., play activities, peers) that in turn cultivate particular patterns of skills and behavior (Scarr & McCartney 1983). Almost all of the literature investigating poverty effects is based on a unidirectional model, but we note transactional processes where possible.

Poverty is typically defined by absolute levels of resources, but individuals may also be affected by relative poverty—that is, by how their circumstances compare to others around them. For example, absolute levels of material deprivation in many developing countries are vastly worse than those in economically developed countries, but relative poverty in any country matters because individuals compare themselves to the expectations in their own society. Relative poverty may have more influence in the United States than in European countries because there are fewer cash supports and social services to reduce inequality of resources between rich and poor. Although psychological theories of relative deprivation have been in existence for many years, little or no research on poverty has used them as a framework. There has been considerable attention, however, to economic inequality, largely because it gives rise to social inequality in many domains including family life, education, neighborhoods, and housing (Neckerman 2004). Social exclusion, a related concept used widely in European policy discussions, includes inequalities in basic living, family economic participation, housing, health, education, public space, and social participation, as well as the subjective experience of social exclusion (Kahn & Kamerman 2002).

In summary, several themes guide our analysis: (*a*) poverty is defined by an interrelated set of characteristics beyond low income and lack of material goods; (*b*) developmental change and developmental timing of exposure to contexts are of particular importance; (*c*) the effects of social address characteristics are mediated by proximal contexts and processes; (*d*) understanding how contexts combine is as important as understanding their individual effects; (*e*) the relations between the developing child and the contexts he or she experiences are reciprocal and transactional; and (*f*) relative as well as absolute levels of resources may define important features of poverty.

SOCIAL ADDRESS VARIATIONS IN THE UNITED STATES

Family economic status, family structure, parents' educational levels, and ethnic group are not only correlated in the population; they are also causally interrelated in the sense that they affect one another. For example, low education limits earning potential; single-mother family structure limits family income; discrimination limits economic opportunities for minority ethnic groups; poverty limits educational opportunity. The broad concept of socioeconomic status reflects the interrelations of education and income, but minority ethnic group status and single-mother family structure are now well established as important correlates for understanding SES influences on children.

Income and Wealth

Poverty. The U.S. government publishes poverty thresholds, adjusted for family size and for annual changes in the Consumer Price Index, that are intended to define the minimum income necessary for basic essentials. Because this index has been widely criticized, several alternatives have been proposed. The Baseline Basic Budget poverty definition (Hernandez et al. 2008) was created using recommendations from a National Research Council review of the poverty threshold (Citro & Michael 1995). Another index used for most international comparisons sets poverty at 50% of the national median income. A number of scholars use 200%

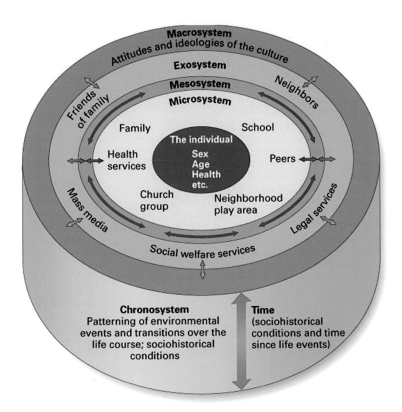

Figure 1

Bronfenbrenner's ecological model. Published with permission of McGraw-Hill Companies.

of the poverty threshold, describing families between 100% and 200% of the threshold as low-income (e.g., Sawhill 2003). In 2008, the poverty threshold was $21,834 for a family of four; twice that level would be $43,668.

Although poverty rates vary annually, they have remained stubbornly high in the United States. The official poverty rate for children has fluctuated since the early 1980s; it reached a high of 22% in 1993 and decreased to 16% in 2000. In 2007, 18% of children in the United States lived in families with incomes below the poverty threshold, but rates were higher for children under age 6 (20%). Similarly, the percentage of children living below 200% of poverty has remained relatively steady, ranging from 38% to 42% (National Center for Children in Poverty 2009). Although one might expect the percentages to increase with economic downturns, there is not a one-to-one correspondence because wages and employment at the bottom of the income scale do not always follow improvements in the economy overall.

Income inequality. Increasing income inequality—the gap between the highest and lowest incomes within a society—may be as important as absolute levels of income or poverty (Blank et al. 2006). Income inequality has been increasing worldwide, but the discrepancy between rich and poor is greater in the United States than in most other countries (Rainwater & Smeeding 2003). From 1980 through 2005, the number of U.S. children living in middle-income (200%–399% of poverty threshold) families declined from 41% to 32%. At the same time, the percentage of children living in families with high income (more than 400% of poverty) was higher in 2005, at 30%, than in 1980, at 17%, and the percentage in very-high-income (600%+) families went from 4% to 14% (Federal Interagency Forum on Child and Family Statistics 2008). Inequality in wealth is greater than that in income. As of the early 2000s, the top 10% of the income distribution had 68% of the wealth, and the top 1% had 34% of the wealth (Scholtz & Levine 2004).

Conditions Correlated with Poverty

Single-mother families, people with low education, members of certain minority ethnic groups (e.g., African Americans, Latinos, and American Indians), and immigrants are more likely to be poor than their counterparts, and all of these statuses are correlated with one another, though not perfectly.

Family structure. About 38% of U.S. children are born to unmarried mothers; the rate for African Americans is 60%. Single-mother families are much more likely to be poor than two-parent married families. In 2006, children living in families headed by a female with no husband present experienced a poverty rate of 42% compared to 8% for children living in married-couple families. About half of the children in African American and Hispanic single-mother families lived in poverty (Federal Interagency on Child and Family Statistics 2008).

Low levels of education and educational inequality. Education has become increasingly important for earnings, with wages stagnating or dropping at the low-skill end of the continuum. From 1979 to 2004, real wages and employment rates of men with less than a high school education declined; wages remained steady for high school graduates, and they increased for those with more than a high school education. Wage declines were especially severe for African American men. Although employment rates for women increased among all educational groups, wages dropped slightly for high school drop-outs; wages for women with higher education increased more than for those with lower levels of education (Blank et al. 2006). All of these trends have magnified the advantages of higher education and the disadvantage associated with low education.

Given this context, inequality of educational opportunity is especially disturbing. From the earliest years through higher education, children from low-income families have less access to high-quality educational experiences than do

Financial capital:
material and economic
resources

those from high-income families. Inequality is greatest at the beginning and end of the typical educational career—in preschool and post high school, when private means are especially important (Kane 2004). For example, the wealthiest 20% of American families spend almost five times as much for preschool as the poorest 20%, and wealthy families are more likely to use regulated child care (Meyers et al. 2004). On the other hand, inequality in public expenditures on K–12 schooling has declined, largely because of court cases requiring states to distribute funds equitably across geographic areas. Nevertheless, public expenditures in the richest 5% of schools are still double those in the poorest 5% (Neckerman 2004).

African American and Hispanic children. Over one-third of U.S. children are African American (15%) or Hispanic (21%). Despite some increases in opportunity for underrepresented minorities, the rates of poverty among families of African American and Hispanic children are much higher than those for non-Hispanic White children. In 2006, 10% of White, non-Hispanic children lived in poverty, compared with 33% of Black children and 27% of Hispanic children (Federal Interagency Forum on Child and Family Statistics 2008). African American children are especially likely to live in chronic rather than transitory poverty because their families have fewer resources on which to fall back in difficult times (McLoyd 1998). The rates of poverty vary for different Latino groups partly because of variations in educational attainment, language fluency, and cultural background. People from Mexico are more likely to be poor than those from Guatemala and El Salvador; people from South America have relatively low poverty rates, probably because of better parent education. Poverty is high among Puerto Ricans despite the fact that they are U.S. citizens (Sullivan et al. 2008).

Immigrant children. Almost one-fourth of U.S. children live in an immigrant family, broadly defined as a family with at least one parent who was not born in the United States (Hernandez et al. 2008). Immigrant children are somewhat more likely to live in low-income, two-parent homes than are children born to natives. In 2007, 21% of children in immigrant families lived below the poverty threshold compared to 17% of native-born children, and 49% lived in low-income families compared to 36% of native-born children (Annie E. Casey Foundation 2009). Immigrant children are more likely than native-born children to live with two parents (84% versus 76%) (Hernandez et al. 2008), but are also more likely to face barriers resulting from parents' linguistic isolation and low levels of education. In 2007, 26% of their parents did not have a high school education, and 27% lived in households experiencing high linguistic isolation, which is one form of social exclusion (Annie E. Casey Foundation 2009). Twenty percent of school-age children spoke a language other than English at home, and five percent had difficulty speaking English (Federal Interagency on Child and Family Statistics 2008).

Some socioeconomic indicators of poverty may operate differently for immigrant families than for native-born families. For instance, immigrants with low education levels may have high levels compared to the average person in their country of origin, and high levels of education in their native countries may not qualify them for equivalent income or social status in the United States. Immigrant parents' income may not be a good indicator of family resources because household income is generated by other family members, including children and grandparents, and because many families send substantial amounts of money back to their home countries. Although immigrant families may have lower levels of human and financial capital than do native-born families, the greater prevalence of two-parent families and supportive communities may offer social capital that ameliorates the effects of poverty on children's skills and trajectories (Fuligni & Yoshikawa 2003).

Contexts of Poverty

In summary, child poverty in the United States often, but not always, occurs in families with single mothers, among parents with low levels of education, in families of color, and among some immigrant groups. Across many groups, poverty and low educational attainment appear to be integrally associated (Blank et al. 2006). For example, increased poverty rates in immigrant families from 1970 to the late 1990s occurred disproportionately among children of parents with lower levels of education, but were not greater among racial/ethnic minorities (Van Hook et al. 2004). On the other hand, language barriers are more common among Hispanic and immigrant families than among other poor families. Single-mother family structures are especially prevalent for African American, and to a lesser extent, for Hispanic poor families, but are relatively infrequent among immigrant families.

In a recent review of family structure and income inequality, McLanahan & Percheski (2008) argue for a complex interaction such that "increases in income inequality may lead to increases in single motherhood, particularly among less educated women. Single motherhood in turn decreases intergenerational economic mobility by affecting children's material resources and the parenting they experience. Because of the unequal distribution of family structure by race and the negative effects of single motherhood, family structure changes exacerbate racial inequalities" (p. 257). This view implies that the net of correlates surrounding poverty may become tighter over time, especially as the inequalities associated with education become more pronounced.

INCOME/POVERTY AND CHILDREN'S DEVELOPMENT

Children growing up in poverty are at a disadvantage in almost every domain of development; the disadvantage is more severe for children living in chronic poverty than for those whose family poverty is transitory (Duncan & Brooks-Gunn 2000). Because so many characteristics are associated with poverty, much of the research in the past several years has been devoted to disaggregating the effects of different components of poverty. Specifically, investigators have asked: Are the effects of poverty due to income per se, or are they primarily a result of the correlated conditions involved in low SES—single-parent family structure, low parent education, or ethnic minority status? Family structure and income have received the most attention, probably because they can be modified by policy more readily than education or ethnic group. It is possible, and even likely, however, that the contributions of these correlated conditions cannot be completely disaggregated because their effects are cumulative or interactive. For example, the effects of low income among African Americans may be exacerbated by societal discrimination, isolation in high-poverty neighborhoods, and high rates of single-mother families.

A related set of issues revolves around social causation versus social selection. According to social causation theories, social and structural conditions cause poverty and its sequellae, including children's physical, intellectual, and social development. Social selection theorists propose that individual characteristics based in genetics, personality, motivation, or other unknown factors select people into poverty and also affect their children's development. Conger & Donnellan (2007) recently argued for an interactionist perspective incorporating both social causation and social selection—a point of view akin to a transactional model—but most empirical research has been designed to test a unidirectional social causation model, using a range of methods to identify the causal effects of poverty net of selection bias. This research, described in the following section, provides modest support for a causal effect of poverty on children's development. Obviously, these data do not exclude the possibility that selection also occurs.

Income Effects

Economists have been especially interested in determining the causal effects of income that are independent of correlated social conditions as well any individual personality characteristics, abilities, and motivations that may select people into poverty or low SES. Using a range of methods to control for selection effects and omitted variables bias, Mayer (1997) and Blau (1999) both concluded that income had a small effect on a range of outcomes for children. Because almost all investigations agree that income has greater effects at the lower ranges, linear models may underestimate its effects. For example, in analyses of a large longitudinal dataset using sibling comparisons to control for family characteristics, the effects of income variation on educational attainment were much greater at the lower end of the income distribution than at other points on the distribution (Duncan et al. 1998). The association of income with psychological adjustment may be curvilinear, with children in the middle faring best. One investigator has found some evidence that children living in very-high-income families have more problems of psychological adjustment than do those in middle-income families (Luthar 2003).

Most of the research by economists and sociologists investigates such distal adolescent events as educational attainment, early pregnancy, and dropping out of school. In two analyses of young children's development over the first six years of life, income changes within families predicted concurrent changes in children's cognitive performance and social behavior, primarily for families living in or near poverty (Dearing et al. 2001, 2006). Within-family changes are less subject to selection bias than between-family comparisons, though it is still possible that unobserved characteristics of parents affect both income changes and children's behavior.

Experiments are usually considered the best method for establishing causal relations. In the late 1960s and early 1970s, four "income maintenance" experiments were designed to test the effects of a guaranteed minimum income offered through a "negative income tax" that provided refunds to poor families. Thousands of adults with children in several parts of the country were randomly assigned to receive refunds or to a control group (Rossi & Lyall 1978). Unfortunately, minimal information was collected about children in the participating families because the major purpose was to learn whether adults would reduce their work effort. There were, however, some positive effects on school attendance and achievement for elementary-school-age children as well as scattered effects on nutrition and the percent of children born with low birth weight (Salkind & Haskins 1982).

A second wave of policy experiments tested variations in welfare policy designed to move low-income single mothers into employment. Some policies offered earnings supplements that raised total income for employed participants. In the absence of earnings supplements, income did not increase when people moved from receiving welfare to earning a paycheck. Young children's school achievement improved when their families participated in policies offering earnings supplements (i.e., when family income increased), but did not improve when no earnings supplements were provided (i.e., when family income remained unchanged). Because each policy had multiple components, a two-stage regression technique was used to isolate the effects of income from other policy features; income accounted for a significant portion of the improvement in children's achievement (Morris et al. 2009). Nonexperimental longitudinal studies of transitions from welfare to work are consistent with these findings, showing little effect on children or on income (Chase-Lansdale et al. 2003, Kalil & Dunifon 2007). In sum, when single mothers move from welfare to work, their children benefit only if income increases along with employment.

The effects of income changes that did not result from parent employment were evaluated in a natural experiment in a rural community when a casino opened on an Indian reservation, providing every American Indian with an income supplement that increased annually. Indian children whose families were lifted out of poverty after the casino opened showed reductions in conduct and oppositional defiant disorders, but there were no effects on anxiety and depression. Similar decreases in symptoms occurred for non-Indian children whose families moved out of poverty, suggesting that income changes resulting from factors other than the casino could account for the results (Costello et al. 2003).

In sum, both naturalistic and experimental research supports the hypothesis that family income positively influences children's school achievement and social emotional development, at least at the lower ranges of income. Small increments that move families out of poverty produce modest improvements for children.

Developmental Timing and Developmental Domain

Poverty during early and middle childhood appears to have greater effects on achievement and educational trajectories than does poverty in adolescence. In analyses of two nationally representative longitudinal studies, family income during the period from birth through age five predicted educational attainment and achievement better than income after age five (Duncan et al. 1998, Votruba-Drzal 2006). Similarly, in the welfare policy experiments, positive effects on children's achievement were greatest for those who were three to five years old when their parents entered the program; in fact, there were some negative effects for those in early adolescence (ages 11–13) when their parents entered the programs (Morris et al. 2005). Similarly, the positive effects on school performance in the income maintenance experiments occurred for elementary-age children but not for adolescents (Salkind & Haskins 1982).

For social and deviant behavior, however, the developmental timing of poverty appears to be less important. Poverty in both early

and middle childhood predicted children's behavior problems in a longitudinal analysis of a nationally representative sample (Votruba-Drzal 2006). In another comparison of children experiencing poverty from birth to age three with those whose families were poor from ages four to nine, behavior problems were slightly more common among those in the later poverty group; children in poverty in both age periods had higher rates of problems still (NICHD Early Child Care Research Network 2005). Similarly, examining poverty across the elementary years, Ackerman et al. (2004) found a slight tendency for more recent poverty to predict behavior problems in fifth grade. Concurrent income during adolescence was related to nonmarital childbearing, even with controls for income in earlier time periods (Duncan et al. 1998).

In short, early poverty appears to be especially damaging to children's achievement trajectories and school careers, but both early and later poverty appear to affect such behaviors as externalizing problems and nonmarital child bearing. These developmental patterns suggest that different pathways may link family income to different developmental domains. There is some preliminary evidence, for example, that the conditions of poverty affect neuropsychological processes involved in self-regulation that may be especially vulnerable in the early years (Noble et al. 2007). We consider the proximal mediators of these differences by developmental level and developmental domain in a later section.

Disaggregating Income from Other Aspects of Poverty

Family structure and stability. Efforts to disaggregate the effects of income from those of family structure indicate that each is important, but that income may be somewhat more important for educational attainment, and family structure may have more influence on behavior problems. One review of several early studies suggests that about half of the income gap in school completion between children with

Human capital:
persons' skills and abilities. Typically defined as parents' educational level as well as the time parents spend with children

single and married parents can be attributed to income, but that family structure accounts for more of the variation in adolescent pregnancy (McLanahan 1997), a conclusion that is supported by the finding that "father absence" puts girls at special risk for early pregnancy and sexual behavior (Ellis et al. 2003). In another analysis, children's educational attainment was higher when they lived in the same nuclear family from birth to 18 than in single-mother or blended families; the difference was largely accounted for by differences in income (Ginther & Pollack 2004).

Family structure is confounded with family instability. Single-mother families are more likely than married couples to have unstable family structures as a result of changes in resident and marital partners. Changes in family structure during the preschool years predicted children's behavior problems at both first and fifth grades, even with controls for income and family structure at birth in one longitudinal study (Cavanagh & Huston 2008). In another analysis, increases in income during the period from age two through first grade predicted reduced behavior problems, but only at times when mothers lived with a partner. When mothers were single, changes in income had no relation to children's behavior problems (Dearing et al. 2006). Temporal changes and instability in family processes partly accounted for the effects of income on cognitive-linguistic development and fully accounted for income effects on social behavior (Mistry et al. 2004). Finally, the rates of educational and social problems for children in stepfamilies are similar to those for children in single-mother families, even though the stepfamilies have considerably higher incomes (Ginther & Pollack 2004, McLanahan 1997). In short, there is evidence that not only family structure but also family stability is important for children's cognitive development and especially for their social development. One implication of this pattern is that a stable single-mother family may support development better than one in which partners come and go.

Parent educational attainment. Parents' low levels of educational attainment are another strand in the web of poverty. Although parent education is one of the best predictors of children's intellectual functioning, it is hopelessly confounded with other parent and child characteristics and with other features of poverty. Nevertheless, a few recent studies provide evidence that increases in education, at least for mothers with low initial educational attainment, may lead to slight improvements in children's intellectual performance. In one policy experiment, the National Evaluation of Welfare to Work Study, single mothers were assigned to a Human Capital condition offering opportunities for limited amounts of education or to a Labor Force Attachment condition requiring participants to search for work immediately. The control group remained eligible for cash welfare. Using a two-stage regression procedure, the investigators demonstrated a modest effect of parents' educational gains on children's performance on achievement tests (Gennetian et al. 2008). Similarly, in a longitudinal study of young children, increases in maternal education between the time children were two and three years old predicted improvements in children's language performance at age three, but only for mothers with no initial post–high school training (Magnuson et al. 2009).

Variations by race/ethnic group. By the time children enter school, African American and Hispanic children receive lower average scores on measures of cognitive development, school readiness, and achievement than do non-Hispanic White children. In a recent review of approaches to closing these racial and ethnic gaps, the editors concluded that increasing income and parental education would have only modest effects; direct intervention in the form of early childhood education appears to be a more promising approach (Rouse et al. 2005). There is some evidence that chronic poverty has more negative effects on behavior and emotional problems of White children than of African American children, partly because there is a strong association among Whites between poverty and mother's prior history of delinquency and current marital status. For Hispanic children, mothers' psychological resources were the strongest mediator between persistent poverty and child problems (McLeod & Nonnemaker 2000).

Immigrant children. Despite the fact that recent immigrants have relatively high rates of poverty, first generation children—children born in the United States whose parents immigrated into the country—have better educational performance and attainment than do children from later generations—a phenomenon described as the "immigrant paradox." Selection and acculturation may partially account for this anomaly as mothers of first-generation children have higher levels of education than do mothers of the later-generation children. Longer exposure to experiences of discrimination, poor-quality schools, few educational and employment opportunities, as well as changes in beliefs, attitudes, and behaviors may also be reasons for the paradox (Palacios et al. 2008).

Cumulative Effects of Poverty Components

Theories of cumulative advantage or disadvantage are based on the assumption that the influences of various components of poverty depend more on the number of sources of disadvantage than on any one factor (Sameroff & Seifer 1995). Sources may be additive, but most of these theories consider them multiplicative, such that combinations of factors have greater effects than the sum of their components. Cumulative theories are based on the assumption that combinations of income, family structure, parent education, and ethnic minority status, for example, have greater impact than the sum of their individual contributions, and that the number of disadvantages is more important than the particular type of disadvantage.

This approach is implicit in an analysis attempting to explain racial and ethnic gaps in achievement. In a nationally representative study of school-age children, an SES index combining income, single-family structure, parent education, and a number of contextual and personal characteristics accounted for about half a standard deviation of the gap in the reading and math scores of African American and Hispanic children compared to non-Hispanic White children (Duncan & Magnuson 2005). In another analysis of very young children (ages two to three), an SES index composed of maternal education, income, and welfare receipt predicted cognitive performance and children's behavior problems; maternal education was the strongest component of SES (Mistry et al. 2008a).

Two studies tested the hypothesis that the positive effects of two social policy experiments offering earnings supplements to low-income parents who were employed—the Minnesota Family Investment Program (MFIP) and New Hope—were mediated by changes in cumulative risk or advantage conferred by the policies tested. In one study comparing the two social policy experiments, the cumulative poverty-related risk index had nine components: income poverty, material deprivation, unemployment, welfare receipt, food insufficiency, parental depression, parenting stress, and parental warmth. Both policy approaches reduced cumulative poverty-related risk, and there were significant linear relations of cumulative poverty-related risk to parent-reported child behavior problems and school achievement. Evidence for mediation was less strong, however. Cumulative poverty-related risk partially mediated the impacts of MFIP on children's behavior problems and of New Hope on school achievement, but in the latter case, only among children of long-term welfare recipients (Gassman-Pines & Yoshikawa 2006).

Walker (2008) created an index of cumulative advantage conferred by the New Hope program that included nonparental care (center-based child care, out-of-school structured activities), home quality (physical conditions of home, family stability, parenting

MFIP: Minnesota Family Investment Program

quality, parent psychological well-being), parental employment (hours, amount, quality), and family earnings (parent earnings). The cumulative environmental advantage produced by the New Hope program partially accounted for improvements in children's academic achievement, but did not account for the program impacts on children's academically relevant noncognitive skills (e.g., expectancies of success and classroom study skills).

Relative Versus Absolute Poverty

Virtually all of the available research examining relations of poverty to children's development uses indicators of absolute levels of poverty. With increasing attention to income inequality and social exclusion, it is disappointing to find almost no attempts to examine inequality or relative poverty as predictors of children's development. Psychological theories of relative deprivation would lead to the hypothesis that relative poverty would affect developmental trajectories, but the literature testing such ideas is scant. Few investigations include measures of children's perceptions of their family's social and economic status, but ethnographic research offers numerous examples of children and adults feeling shame or embarrassment about their housing, clothes, or other conspicuous signs of poverty (Weisner et al. 2006). In the New Hope experiment, a test of a poverty-reduction intervention, parents talked about using additional funds not only to meet material needs (e.g., utility bills, food, and rent), but also for less tangible but important needs (e.g., birthday and Christmas presents for their children or an occasional family meal at a fast-food restaurant). Meeting the less tangible needs was a more important predictor of children's lowered behavior problems than was the ability to meet material needs (Mistry et al. 2008b).

PROXIMAL CONTEXTS THAT MEDIATE EFFECTS OF POVERTY

Thus far, we have discussed the relations of poverty and its associated social address

characteristics to children's development. We turn now to proximal contexts that mediate the relations of poverty and SES to development, following the hints in the literature that the processes may differ for cognitive and socioemotional development, for children of different ages, and for children in different cultural groups. We group proximal contexts into (a) parents and family, (b) physical conditions (e.g., food, shelter, pollutants), (c) out-of-home settings (e.g., preschool), (d) schools, and (e) neighborhoods and peers. Because all of these contexts differ as a function of poverty and SES, we are particularly interested in understanding their combined and interactive effects.

Although contexts are often conceptualized as separate entities, we take seriously the basic transactional premise of ecological theory that contexts and individuals not only interact but also influence one another. Families are affected not only by schools and neighborhoods, but parents and children also influence the environments in which children live. Many scholars treat this transactional process as a source of selection bias that clouds the ability to detect the causal effects of child care or neighborhoods, for example, on families and on children's development. Much of the research on family process, for example, is explicitly or implicitly based on a unidirectional causal model in which poverty affects some aspects of parenting, which in turn mediate effects on children. But parents are actors as well as recipients of social influences, making decisions about residence, jobs, schooling, and care settings for their children. These instrumental activities are sometimes described as family management. Parents living in poverty may have fewer options than other parents do, but they make choices among those options, often giving priority to the needs of their children (e.g., Scott et al. 2002). Children's capabilities and behavior affect parents' patterns of interaction with them as well as parents' decisions about such environments as child care and school. Transactional models are more difficult to test empirically than unidirectional models, but they are also probably more accurate.

Family Processes

Family processes and parenting are the primary foci of much of the theory and research investigating how the conditions of poverty are transmitted to children. Two major theories guide this research. In economic or family investment theory, resources available to children are classified as financial, human, and social capital. Financial capital comprises material and economic resources; human capital consists of skills and abilities and is typically defined as parents' educational level as well as the time parents spend with children; social capital results from children's interactions and relationships with parents and other people (Foster 2002a). Family stress theories posit economic stress as an influence on parents' psychological stress, resulting in lowered warmth and increased harshness with children, which in turn leads to poor child adjustment (e.g., McLoyd 1998). An elaboration on the family stress hypothesis incorporating reciprocal relations of family processes and SES appears in Conger and Donnellan (2007).

Both family investment and family stress theories have extensive empirical support that is not reviewed here because of space constraints (for reviews, see Bornstein & Bradley 2003, Bradley & Corwyn 2002, Conger & Donnellan 2007, McLoyd et al. 2006). We limit our discussion to two points. First, different processes appear to be important for different developmental domains. Second, although some processes appear to operate similarly across racial and ethnic groups, there are a few important differences as well.

Cognitive and social development. Based on family investment theory, both human and social capital in the home have been investigated as mediators of material poverty effects on children's development. In most investigations, these constructs are operationalized as cognitive stimulation, including such activities as reading and educational toys, visits to places in the community, and language interactions with the child. Family stress models by contrast emphasize parental warmth and harsh punishment as likely mediators. Although cognitive stimulation and positive parenting practices tend to co-occur, there is some evidence that cognitive stimulation in the home mediates the effects of family income on children's intellectual development more strongly and consistently than do parental warmth and punishment. The latter typically mediate poverty effects on behavior problems and psychological adjustment better than do indicators of human and social capital.

Using a nationally representative sample of children ages three to five, Yeung et al. (2002) demonstrated that much of the association between income and children's reading and math scores was mediated by a stimulating family learning environment. In contrast, family income was associated with children's behavior problem scores primarily through maternal emotional distress and parenting practices. In another longitudinal study, the relation between modest improvements in maternal education and children's language development from ages two to three years was partially mediated by improvements in cognitive stimulation in the home (Magnuson et al. 2009). In tests of a large number of potential mediators of poverty effects on children's reading and math scores in another nationally representative longitudinal study, cognitive stimulation in the home was the strongest mediator of poverty effects; parenting style (warmth) was weaker (Guo & Harris 2000). The effects of neighborhood SES were mediated by the family literacy environment, consistent parenting, and punitive parenting in an analysis of a Canadian longitudinal study. The literacy environment and consistent parenting were the pathways to children's verbal ability; punitive parenting predicted behavior problems and, more weakly, verbal ability (Kohen et al. 2008).

Racial and ethnic variations. For the most part, similar patterns apply across different racial and ethnic groups as well as for immigrant children. In an analysis of two- and three-year-old children's development, there was greater similarity than difference in the processes by which SES was related to immigrant and native children's preschool outcomes. Both language/literacy stimulation and maternal supportiveness mediated the relations of SES to children's cognitive performance; parenting stress mediated the effects of SES on children's aggressive behavior for native-born, but not immigrant, households (Mistry et al. 2008a). Among older children, learning stimulation predicted vocabulary, reading, math, and behavior problems similarly for White, African American, and Hispanic samples, but learning stimulation was less strong as a predictor for behavior problems than for cognitive development (Bradley et al. 2003).

In two analyses of a nationally representative sample of children from kindergarten through fifth grade, poverty and family investment were measured more completely than in earlier studies. Income and material hardship were evaluated separately as indexes of poverty, and the family investment measure included participation in out-of-school structured activities and other activities outside the home as well as cognitive stimulation within the home. Both material hardship and low income predicted lowered family investment and parenting stress. In the overall models, family investment was the major path to children's cognitive development; family stress and lack of positive parenting formed the major path to behavior problems. The models for White, African American, and Hispanic families followed similar patterns, but varied in the strength of the associations among constructs (Gershoff et al. 2007, Raver et al. 2007).

Income change and parenting. Although longitudinal studies support the hypothesis that family processes mediate the effects of poverty, there is mixed evidence about whether improvements in income and material well-being translate into changes in parenting practices. In a large sample of single mothers receiving welfare, those who moved into employment, particularly stable employment, had substantial increases in income and psychological well-being, but there were few changes in the quality of parenting or children's home environments over an 18-month period (Coley et al. 2007). Income increases over a four-year period did, however, predict improved cognitive stimulation in children's home environments in another investigation, particularly for low-income households (Votruba-Drzal 2003). In a Michigan sample, mothers who moved from welfare to combining welfare and work decreased in harsh parenting and increased in positive parenting. Although there were concomitant decreases in children's problem behaviors, they were not mediated by parenting (Dunifon et al. 2003).

In experiments testing policies designed to move single mothers into employment, there were mixed effects on mothers' psychological well-being and parenting practices. Even when income and resources increased, participation in the experimental policies increased depressive symptoms for mothers of preschool children. There were no significant effects on parenting and children's behavior. For mothers whose children were school-age, by contrast, programs reduced depressive symptoms, increased parental warmth and cognitive stimulation, and reduced behavior problems (Morris et al. 2009, Walker et al. 2008).

Both the family investment and family stress models posit the direction of influence from parent to child, but there is some evidence for transactional processes. Over the first three years of life, parenting quality mediated the effects of family resources on children's cognitive development, but children's early cognitive performance also contributed to higher parenting quality (Lugo-Gil & Tamis-LeMonda 2008). It appears that children created their parenting environment as well as being influenced by it. This model has implications for early intervention and for the possible mechanisms by which contexts may have cumulative effects. In one analysis, the investigators demonstrated that infants from low-income families who received intensive high-quality child care demonstrated improved language development, which carried over to the home where babies elicited language interactions from adults (Burchinal et al. 1997).

Among preschool and older children, the New Hope policy experiment led to reduced behavior problems, which in turn led to improved parenting control three years later (Epps & Huston 2007).

Material Deprivation

Poverty implies material deprivation—food insecurity, unsafe and inadequate housing (or, at the extreme, eviction and homelessness), inability to pay rent and utility bills, and doing without needed health care, all of which have direct impacts on health, cognitive, and social development. Many poor children experience food insecurity in the form of reduced food choices, but a relatively small number (0.6% of the population) have spells of serious food insecurity in which they are hungry and skip meals altogether. Housing problems are frequent among the poor as they often live in physically inadequate and crowded spaces, and high costs lead to frequent moves that can result in changes of neighborhood and schools for children as well as in homelessness (Federal Interagency on Child and Family Statistics 2008).

Indices of material deprivation are correlated with income poverty, particularly near the low end of the income distribution, but the two are not identical (Mayer 1997). Among a sample of low-income single mothers studied over six years, hardships decreased monotonically across quintiles of income, but mothers' mental health was also related to perceived hardship independently of income (Sullivan et al. 2008). In another sample of single mothers, a shift from welfare to stable employment led to better income as well as to reduced financial strain and food insecurity (Coley et al. 2007). Few investigations of poverty effects on children include indicators of material deprivation separately from family income. One exception is a path analysis showing that both income and material deprivation contributed independently to predicting parents' investments and positive parenting, which in turn predicted children's cognitive and social-emotional competence (Gershoff et al. 2007).

The physical environments experienced by children living in poverty pose relatively high risks of air, water, and noise pollution, which can in turn affect children's health as well as cognitive and social development (Evans 2006, Federal Interagency on Child and Family Statistics 2008). For example, children living in poverty are more likely than nonpoor children to have elevated blood lead levels, particularly if they are African American, and poor children in rural areas have higher exposure to pesticides than do more affluent children. One set of authors estimates that elevated exposure to lead and other pollutants could account for up to one-fourth of a standard deviation in achievement test scores (Dilworth-Bart & Moore 2006).

Finally, the physical and social environments of poverty can produce high levels of stress that require children to expend both cognitive and emotional resources in vigilance and self-protection. The large literatures on cumulative effects of the physical and social environments of poverty and on the relations of physical environmental variables to development are well reviewed by Evans (2006).

Out-of-Home Settings

Although families are generally acknowledged to be the most important single contextual influence on children, most children spend time in child care and early education settings during the preschool years and in schools and other out-of-school settings throughout childhood and adolescence. The institutions and social systems surrounding a family can have both direct and indirect effects on children as well as on parents.

Preschool and child care. The majority of preschool-aged children spend time in child care and early education settings outside their homes, being cared for by people other than their parents. Intervention programs such as Head Start and high-quality preschools contribute to children's academic skills and, in some cases, to competent social behavior (Karoly et al. 2005). It is especially noteworthy, therefore, that children in poor families are likely to receive lower-quality child care than those in more affluent families do and that even programs specifically designed to promote learning for socially disadvantaged children vary in quality by family income.

On average, the child care received by children from low-income families is of lower quality than that received by those from higher-income families (Huston 2004). The one exception is that, in some instances, children in very poor families receive higher-quality care than those in near-poor families, probably because the very poor have access to child care subsidies. In analyses of quality when children were ages two, three, and four-and-a-half in the NICHD Study of Early Child Care, there were U-shaped relations of family income to teacher education and training, but on observational measures of the quality of cognitive and social interactions, quality was lowest for poor children and highest for the affluent (Dowsett et al. 2008). Similar patterns were found in an earlier study of child care centers in several states (Phillips et al. 1994). The U-shaped relation probably also applies at the college level, with youth from very poor families being eligible for more types of financial aid than are those from families that have modest incomes.

Child care centers attended by preschool children offer more opportunities for cognitive stimulation and other aspects of quality than do the unregulated home settings used by low-income families, but the variability within each type of care is quite large (Li Grining & Coley 2006). Nevertheless, three- and four-year-olds from low-income families are less likely than children from higher-income families to be enrolled in organized preschool programs. The disparity is reduced at age five, when many children attend publicly supported kindergartens (Bainbridge et al. 2005). Even among children who are eligible for Head Start, all of whom are economically disadvantaged, those who enroll are somewhat less disadvantaged than those who do not enroll (Foster 2002b).

Pre-kindergarten programs designed to prepare children for school entry are now widespread, and there is good evidence that they contribute to entry-level academic skills (Gormley & Gayer 2005). Observations of 692 classrooms were used to detect patterns of varying emotional and instructional support along with varying teacher characteristics. The poorest-quality profile was associated with classroom poverty level, suggesting that the children who need the highest-quality educational experiences are least likely to receive it (LoCasale-Crouch et al. 2007). Children who did receive sensitive and stimulating interactions with the teacher and high instructional quality performed better on language, preacademic, and social skills at the end of the kindergarten year (Burchinal et al. 2008).

In short, the most disadvantaged children are least likely to attend center-based child care or organized preschools early in their lives, and the programs they do attend are likely to be of lower quality than the programs used by higher-income families. This inequality of exposure to high-quality early education and child care can be juxtaposed against a large body of evidence showing that children from disadvantaged backgrounds can profit from such programs (e.g., Karoly et al. 2005, McLoyd et al. 2006). In one analysis, the authors estimate that an intensive early education program could raise achievement by as much as 0.5 standard deviations (Duncan et al. 2007). Even "ordinary" center-based child care appears to provide a small advantage in cognitive functioning and achievement in comparison to typical home-based child care (NICHD Early Child Care Research Network & Duncan 2003).

Although high-quality programs contribute to intellectual development for children from low-income families, they also promote cognitive development for children from more affluent families. In an analysis of three studies of child care quality, Burchinal et al. (2000) concluded that there was no evidence that quality had larger effects for poor than for non-poor children, although there was some evidence for greater effects on non-White than on White children. By contrast, children from low-income families benefited from an academically oriented prekindergarten program more than did those from higher-income families (Gormley & Gayer 2005). Some have argued that high-quality early education programs may increase rather than decrease inequality in achievement because more disadvantaged children are less likely to participate. These discussions point out a conundrum in social goals—reducing an income gap may conflict with the goal of helping all children to develop optimally.

Schools. Children from low-income families attend schools of lower quality, on average, than do more affluent children. Although reduced, funding disparities continue despite legal requirements for equitable distribution of public support (Books 2004, Neckerman 2004). Overall, children from low-income families attend schools with less-qualified teachers than do more affluent children (Lankford et al. 2002). At a more proximal level, processes within the classroom and the school differ by income. In one longitudinal study, over 1600 first- and third-grade classrooms from diverse regions in the United States were observed. In classrooms attended by children from low-income families, as compared with those attended by children from more affluent families, classroom climate was less positive and supportive, teachers engaged in less high-quality instruction, and teachers spent more time disciplining children. Children in classrooms with a positive climate were more involved in classroom activities and were less disruptive; hence such classrooms offered better learning environments (NICHD Early Child Care Research Network 2006). In a sample of rural African American students, those in classrooms with high levels of organization, rule clarity, and student involvement had relatively low levels of both externalizing and internalizing behavior problems (Brody et al. 2002).

School quality is determined not only by the practices and policies of the adults running the school, but also by the population of students attending it. The overall social class composition of a school predicts the performance and behavior of its students; moreover, school characteristics can to some degree compensate for family SES differences. Two analyses show that family characteristics predict children's entering skills in reading, but that the percent of low-income children in the school predicts the rate with which reading skills grow over the elementary school years (Aikens & Barbarin 2008, Hauser-Cram et al. 2006). Individual growth in reading was also lower in schools with high numbers of children with reading deficits (Aikens & Barbarin 2008). Among Latino adolescents, attending schools with relatively high average SES was associated with better performance on English vocabulary, but predicted grade point average only for first-generation students (Ryabov & Van Hook 2007). In another adolescent sample, schools with higher average SES levels had more positive social climates, which in turn mediated the positive relations of school SES to self-reported school engagement. These patterns were consistent across different racial and ethnic groups (Benner et al. 2008).

School quality may also be an important factor in the persistence or fade-out of benefits that children receive from Head Start and other early intervention programs, but the data are slim and inconsistent. In one nationally representative sample, the benefits of center-based preschools on children's achievement lasted into first grade only in large classrooms with relatively low quality of reading instruction, suggesting that high quality in either preschool or school might compensate for lower quality in the other context (Magnuson et al. 2007). Using a longer time perspective, however, Currie & Thomas (2000) demonstrated that the benefits of Head Start for African American children lasted when children had high-quality instruction, but not when they attended lower-quality schools, suggesting a cumulative effect of preschool and school experiences.

Neighborhood. Although some children attend schools outside their neighborhood, schools and neighborhoods are partially overlapping contexts for many children. People with low incomes tend to live in neighborhoods with others who are poor, and neighborhood disadvantage is typically indexed by poverty rates as well as by rates of crime and violence. Separating the effects of individual characteristics from those of the neighborhoods in which they live poses methodological challenges, but the evidence supports the conclusion that neighborhood characteristics contribute modestly to children's development independently of families. In their extensive review of the literature, Leventhal & Brooks-Gunn (2000) conclude that high neighborhood SES contributes to school achievement and educational attainment, and that low neighborhood SES increases the likelihood of deviant and problem behavior. One large-scale investigation indicates, however, that the association of neighborhood SES with achievement test scores and behavior problems holds true only for White children and for African American children who live in predominantly Black neighborhoods (Turley 2003).

Conceptual frameworks explaining the effects of neighborhood disadvantage on children's development include several potential pathways. Institutional resources vary. For example, poor neighborhoods differ from affluent neighborhoods in opportunities for recreation, grocery stores with healthy food, public services, quality child care and schools, out-of-school programs, jobs for adults, and transportation. A second pathway is shared values and norms along with community enforcement of those norms or collective efficacy. Sampson (2006) has demonstrated that neighborhoods with high levels of collective efficacy have lower crime rates than others that are equally poor but have low efficacy. Because peer values and behavior contribute to individual children's developmental pathways, the presence of deviant peers in the neighborhood is an important mechanism for neighborhood effects. One group of investigators argues that the high percentage of children relative to adults (i.e., child saturation), which

characterizes low-income neighborhoods, increases the influence of peers (Hart et al. 2008). Finally, the stresses of living in a low-income neighborhood can affect parenting warmth and discipline (e.g., Pinderhughes et al. 2001). Although one might expect that neighborhood qualities would become increasingly important with age as children become less dependent on parents, the research is fairly consistent in showing effects of neighborhood poverty on intellectual skills (O'Brien Caughy & O'Campo 2006) and behavior problems (Hart et al. 2008) from preschool-age through adolescence.

For our purposes, the important question is whether neighborhood characteristics mediate the effects of family poverty. That is, are some of the correlates of poverty due to the neighborhoods in which poor people live? There is some evidence that parenting practices mediate the effects of neighborhood disadvantage on children's achievement (Eamon 2005) and behavior (Kohen et al. 2008), though not all studies agree (Caughy et al. 2008). Both social norms and social cohesion of relationships also mediate the effects of neighborhood poverty on young children's verbal skills and behavior problems (Caughy et al. 2008, Eamon 2005, Kohen et al. 2008).

Disadvantaged neighborhoods magnify individual family poverty effects in part by increasing the likelihood of associating with deviant peers, which in turn increases the likelihood of aggression and antisocial behavior. Parents who are nurturant and involved, along with community resources, can counteract deviant peer pressure (Brody et al. 2001, Eamon 2001b). As children reach the later elementary grades and early adolescence, opportunities for supervised activities in the community may be protective (Mahoney et al. 2005). In one investigation, aggressive children who lived in unsafe neighborhoods were especially likely to show increases in externalizing behavior problems in seventh grade if they spent unsupervised time with peers (Pettit et al. 1999).

Experiments investigating the effects of changing neighborhoods constitute another approach to identifying the causal role of neighborhoods in transmitting the effects of family poverty. In the 1970s, a lawsuit against the Chicago Housing Authority led to the Gautreaux program, in which public housing residents were offered an opportunity to move. Some moved to White suburbs, and others moved within Chicago to largely Black neighborhoods, creating a pseudoexperiment. Follow-ups indicated that youth in the White suburbs did significantly better than those who moved within the city on educational attainment, employment, and wages (Kaufman & Rosenbaum 1992).

These encouraging findings led to the Moving to Opportunity experiment, a large-scale investigation in which public housing residents in five cities were randomly assigned to one of three conditions: (a) vouchers to move to private housing in a low-poverty neighborhood, (b) vouchers for private housing in any neighborhood of their choice, or (c) a control group that was not offered vouchers for private housing. About half of the families in the treatment groups actually moved; the other half stayed in public housing. Both quantitative and qualitative assessments of the children and adolescents in the affected families show no effects of treatments on school achievement and educational attainment, possibly because the schools attended by the children changed less than the neighborhoods did (Sanbonmatsu et al. 2006). The effects on deviant behavior varied. Females whose families had the opportunity to move to low-poverty areas had lower frequencies of arrests for violent and property crimes, relative to the control group. Males also had reduced arrests for violent crime, but had increased problem behaviors and arrests for property crime (Kling et al. 2005). One reason may have been that the males tended to associate with the most deviant peers in their new neighborhoods or to return to their old neighborhoods.

Summary. The effects of poverty on children's cognitive and social development are mediated through family processes, but also through material deprivation as well as the accumulation of experiences in child care, in school, with peers, and in neighborhoods and communities. Much of the literature is designed to identify the separate contributions of these contexts, but they probably interact in a dynamic fashion rather than being additive. Although family processes are more important than any single context outside the home, families do not operate in a vacuum. Parents are affected by the schools and neighborhoods that surround them, and parents also select and affect the institutional contexts experienced by their children.

CONCLUSIONS AND IMPLICATIONS FOR FUTURE RESEARCH

We began with the theme that children's experiences of poverty often occur as part of a correlated web of social conditions, including single-parent family structure, low parent education, minority ethnic group membership, and immigrant status. These conditions, alone or in combination, contribute to patterns of developmental change. As ecological theory would predict, developmental timing of contextual experiences matters, and the relations of context to development vary for different developmental domains. Specifically, early childhood appears to be a period of particular vulnerability to the effects of poverty, family structure, and related experiences on children's cognitive and academic development. The processes identified by family investment theory—including material resources and cognitive stimulation in the home, child care, early education, and neighborhood settings—appear to be important mediators of socioeconomic differences in academic achievement and ultimate educational attainment.

Social behavior and emotional development appear to be subject to the influences of poverty experienced throughout childhood and adolescence. The processes described in family stress theory—parental stress, positive parenting practices, and absence of harsh punishment—appear to be particularly important mediators of socioeconomic conditions for children's psychological well-being and behavior problems. Single-parent family structure, instability of family composition, and low neighborhood SES are also important aspects of poverty influencing behavior problems and deviant social behavior. One caveat is that information about negative and dysfunctional behavior is much more extensive than evidence about positive social behavior and psychological well-being, reflecting what appears to be a disproportionate concentration on social problems to the exclusion of positive aspects of development in much of the extant research. Positive and problem behaviors are not the opposite ends of a continuum. In the New Hope experiment, which increased a range of resources for children and families, there were long-lasting effects on an index of positive behavior that measured social competence, autonomy, and compliance with adult rules, but not on behavior problems (Huston et al. 2008).

Contexts combine and interact at the level of social address variables and at the level of proximal experiences. One cannot completely disentangle the social address variables, and a strictly additive model probably is not correct. Instead, social address variables probably are cumulative and multiplicative, at least for poor, single-mother, poorly educated, and minority families. Income alone accounts for significant but relatively small amounts of variation in development; adding material deprivation improves predictive accuracy to some extent. There is support for a cumulative model in studies showing that the number of advantages or disadvantages rather than any one contextual change mediates the effects of improved earnings (Gassman-Pines & Yoshikawa 2006, Walker 2008), and advantages conferred in preschool continue when children subsequently experience high-quality schools (Currie & Thomas 2000).

Poverty effects also vary by ethnic group and sometimes by family structure in ways that suggest compensatory effects. For example, the universal prekindergarten program evaluated in Oklahoma had stronger effects on children from low-income families than on those from more affluent families, and impacts were

greatest for Hispanic children with less effect on White non-Hispanic children (Gormley & Gayer 2005). Evidence that preschool programs partially close the achievement gap between White non-Hispanic and both African American and Hispanic children indirectly supports a compensatory model (Magnuson & Waldfogel 2005).

A relatively recent body of research on immigrant populations has begun to elucidate the variations in how poverty and social disadvantage affect development, with particular emphasis on social capital. Children of recent immigrants achieve well and have relatively few behavior problems despite the fact that their families often have low incomes and limited levels of education. Most theorists emphasize the social capital and values characterizing their families and communities as factors that counteract the effects of poverty. Immigration and migration are increasing throughout the world, and the United States is becoming increasingly multiethnic. We are now beginning to see a body of research examining contextual influences and processes across ethnic and cultural groups that allows better understanding of the similarities and differences in the processes influencing development. Future research could provide more nuanced and theoretically informed understanding of both social address issues and the operation of proximal processes in mediating and moderating the effects of family income and family poverty on children's development.

Reciprocal or transactional causal models have considerable intellectual appeal and have been used extensively in developmental research, yet most empirical research on poverty and its related contexts is based on unidirectional models in which poverty and other social address variables affect family or other contexts, which in turn influence child development. Poverty and its correlates are in varying degrees exogenous in the sense that they are unlikely to be affected directly by children, but most of them can be affected by parents' characteristics and behavior. The fact that parents' skills, personalities, and motivations influence family income, family structure, and educational level is often treated as a methodological problem of selection bias, but it can also be built into more sophisticated models that incorporate interactions of persons with situations. At the level of proximal contexts, the case for reciprocal influences is even stronger because both children and parents can affect family environments, schools, and neighborhoods as well as responding to them. A small body of evidence supports models in which contexts affect children who in turn affect the same or a different context. Moreover, some of the important features of schools and neighborhoods are the characteristics of the other people who inhabit them (e.g., the percent living in poverty); each individual contributes in some sense to these group and community settings.

The concentration on unidirectional models is based partly in the difficulty of demonstrating reciprocal processes empirically, but it also results from the policy goals inherent in much of the research on socioeconomic contexts. Policy research is oriented to actions that can ameliorate social problems, and policy can affect income, material well-being, and some of the other correlates of poverty more easily than it can change individuals. We would argue that transactional models do not imply that the processes involved cannot be altered by intervention. Suppose, for example, that exposure to child care providers who provide a rich language environment improves a child's language development, which in turn leads the child to interact with providers in ways that elicit even richer language interactions, and so on. Intervention at any point in that process could alter the entire sequence just as altering one part of a dynamic system creates changes in the rest of the system. We believe that the field is ready for more research that takes transactional models seriously, and that such models will not only generate better scientific understanding of development, but also will produce more nuanced understanding of policy-relevant processes.

Although income inequality, social inequality, and relative poverty are widely discussed, there is almost no quantitative empirical research designed to identify the effects of relative economic position independently of absolute poverty level. Such research could lead to considering individuals' perceptions rather than actual material resources. Social comparison theories appear well suited to understand the effects of relative poverty but are not often used explicitly for this purpose. The closest body of literature is the investigation of income loss, showing that large losses in income produce strains in families that can translate into psychological distress and other problems for children and youth (Conger & Donnellan 2007, McLoyd 1998). Income loss may have effects on both parents and children not only through material deprivation, but also through negative social comparison.

This review has been restricted largely to poverty in the United States with occasional inclusion of other developed countries, but other parts of the world, particularly sub-Saharan Africa and south Asia, have levels of poverty that are orders of magnitude worse than those in developed countries. For example, the rates of neonatal death in southern and central Africa and south Asia range from 36 to 45 per 1000 births, compared to 3 for developed countries (United Nations Children's Fund 2008). Although ecological theory might be useful in conceptualizing the research for these populations, the questions and issues are quite different, focusing on survival, basic education, preventive health measures, and economic opportunity, among others. Research on social programs in developing countries offers one pathway for additional understanding of how social ecologies affect child development (for example, see Lomel'i 2008).

These conclusions point to a number of fruitful directions for future research, including explicit examination of developmental change (as opposed to developmental differences among groups); more careful delineation of the processes affecting cognitive and social development; further investigation of developmental timing of poverty; more theoretically guided treatments of the interplay among contexts; methodologically sound tests of transactional models; investigation of relative as well as absolute poverty; and integration of policy research in the United States with that in other countries.

SUMMARY POINTS

1. Poverty is part of an interrelated web of correlated conditions—low income, material deprivation, single-parent family structure, low educational level, minority ethnic group, and immigrant status.

2. Developmental change and developmental timing of exposure to poverty contexts are of particular importance.

3. The effects of poverty and its associated characteristics are likely to be mediated by proximal contexts and processes with which the child has direct interaction.

4. Understanding how contexts combine and interact is as important as understanding their individual effects.

5. The relations between the developing child and the contexts he or she experiences are reciprocal and transactional.

6. Relative as well as absolute levels of resources may define important features of poverty.

FUTURE ISSUES

1. As the United States becomes increasingly multiethnic, it will be more important to understand ethnic and cultural variations in how the societal contexts associated with poverty influence children's development.

2. Empirical tests of transactional models are possible, given the availability of large nationally representative datasets and increasingly powerful statistical tools.

3. Research on contexts outside the family has begun to appear, but more investigation of school and neighborhood settings as contexts could contribute useful information to the field.

4. Economic, anthropological, and human developmental perspectives joined in interdisciplinary approaches have produced some valuable advances in the field and will continue to be productive avenues, particularly for understanding the interplay between structural conditions and individual processes.

5. Current policy research is concerned almost entirely with United States conditions and policies. A broader range of knowledge would be generated by integration of approaches across nations with different levels of affluence and different policy environments.

DISCLOSURE STATEMENT

The authors are not aware of any biases that might be perceived as affecting the objectivity of this review.

LITERATURE CITED

Ackerman BP, Brown EP, Izard CE. 2004. The relations between persistent poverty and contextual risk and children's behavior in elementary school. *Dev. Psychol.* 40:367–77

Aikens NL, Barbarin O. 2008. Socioeconomic differences in reading trajectories: the contribution of family, neighborhood, and school contexts. *J. Educ. Psychol.* 100:235–51

Annie E Casey Foundation. 2009. Kids Count Data Center. **http://www.kidscount.org/datacenter/profile_results.jsp?r=1&d=1&c=12&x=136&y=12**

Bainbridge J, Meyers MK, Tanaka S, Waldfogel J. 2005. Who gets an early education? Family income and the enrollment of three- to five-year-olds from 1968 to 2000. *Soc. Sci. Q.* 86:725–45

Benner AD, Graham S, Mistry RS. 2008. Discerning direct and mediated effects of ecological structures and processes on adolescents' educational outcomes. *Dev. Psychol.* 44:840–54

Blank RM, Danziger SH, Schoeni RF. 2006. Work and poverty during the past quarter-century. In *Working and Poor: How Economic and Policy Changes are Affecting Low-Wage Workers*, ed. RM Blank, SH Danziger, RF Schoeni, pp. 1–20. New York: Sage

Blau DM. 1999. The effect of income on child development. *Rev. Econ. Stat.* 81:261–76

Books S. 2004. *Poverty and Schooling in the U.S.: Contexts and Consequences*. Mahwah, NJ: Erlbaum

Bornstein MH, Bradley RH, eds. 2003. *Socioeconomic Status, Parenting, and Child Development*. Mahwah, NJ: Erlbaum

Bradley RH, Corwyn RF. 2002. Socioeconomic status and child development. *Annu. Rev. Psychol.* 53:371–99

Bradley RH, Corwyn RF, Bornstein MH. 2003. Age and ethnic variations in family process mediators of SES. See Bornstein & Bradley 2003, pp. 161–88

Brody GH, Dorsey S, Forehand R, Armistead L. 2002. Unique and protective contributions of parenting and classroom processes to the adjustment of African American children living in single-parent families. *Child Dev.* 73:274–86

Brody GH, Ge X, Conger RD, Gibbons FX, Murry VM, et al. 2001. The influence of neighborhood disadvantage, collective socialization, and parenting on African American children's affiliation with deviant peers. *Child Dev.* 72:1231–46

Bronfenbrenner U. 1989. Ecological systems theory. In *Annals of Child Development: Six Theories of Child Development-Revised Formulations and Current Issues*, ed. R Vasta, 6:187–249. Boston: JAI

Bronfenbrenner U, Crouter A. 1983. The evolution of environmental models in developmental research. In *Handbook of Child Psychology. Vol. 1. History, Theory, and Methods*, ed. W Kessen, PH Mussen, pp. 357–414. New York: Wiley

Bronfenbrenner U, Morris PA. 1998. The ecology of developmental processes. In *Handbook of Child Psychology. Vol. 1: Theoretical Models of Human Development*, ed. W Damon, RM Lerner, pp. 993–1028. New York: Wiley. 5th ed.

Bronfenbrenner U, Morris PA. 2006. The bioecological model of human development. In *Handbook of Child Psychology. Vol. 1: Theoretical Models of Human Development*, ed. W Damon, RM Lerner, pp. 793–828. New York: Wiley. 6th ed.

Burchinal MR, Campbell FA, Bryant DM, Wasik BH, Ramey CT. 1997. Early intervention and mediating processes in cognitive performance of children in low-income African American families. *Child Dev.* 68:935–54

Burchinal MR, Howes C, Pianta R, Bryant D, Early D, et al. 2008. Predicting child outcomes at the end of kindergarten from the quality of prekindergarten teacher-child interactions and instruction. *Appl. Dev. Sci.* 12:140–53

Burchinal MR, Peisner-Feinberg ES, Bryant DM, Clifford RM. 2000. Children's social and cognitive development and child-care quality: testing for differential associations related to poverty, gender, or ethnicity. *Appl. Dev. Sci.* 4:149–65

Caughy MOB, Nettles SM, O'Campo PJ. 2008. The effect of residential neighborhood on child behavior problems in first grade. *Am. J. Community Psychol.* 42:39–50

Cavanagh SE, Huston AC. 2008. The timing of family instability and children's social development. *J. Marriage Fam.* 70:1258–69

Chase-Lansdale PL, Moffit RA, Lohman BJ, Cherlin AJ, Coley RL, et al. 2003. Mothers' transitions from welfare to work and the well-being of preschoolers and adolescents. *Science* 299:1548–52

Citro CF, Michael RT. 1995. *Measuring Poverty: A New Approach*. Washington, DC: Natl. Acad. Press

Coley RL, Lohman BJ, Votruba-Drzal E, Pittman LD, Chase-Lansdale PL. 2007. Maternal functioning, time, and money: the world of work and welfare. *Child. Youth Serv. Rev.* 29:721–41

Conger RD, Donnellan MB. 2007. An interactionist perspective on the socioeconomic context of human development. *Annu. Rev. Psychol.* 58:175–99

Costello EJ, Compton SN, Keller G, Angold A. 2003. Relations between poverty and psychopathology. *J. Am. Med. Assoc.* 290:2023–29

Currie J, Thomas D. 2000. School quality and the longer-term effects of Head Start. *J. Hum. Resour.* 35:755–74

Dearing E, McCartney K, Taylor BA. 2001. Change in family income-to-needs matter more for children with less. *Child Dev.* 72:1779–93

Dearing E, McCartney K, Taylor BA. 2006. Within-child associations between family income and externalizing and internalizing problems. *Dev. Psychol.* 42:237–52

Dilworth-Bart JE, Moore CF. 2006. Mercy mercy me: social injustice and the prevention of environmental pollutant exposures among ethnic minority and poor children. *Child Dev.* 77:247–65

Dowsett CJ, Huston AC, Imes AE, Gennetian L. 2008. Structural and process features in three types of child care for children from high and low income families. *Early Child. Res. Q.* 23:69–93

Duncan GJ, Brooks-Gunn J. 2000. Family poverty, welfare reform, and child development. *Child Dev.* 71:188–96

Duncan GJ, Ludwig J, Magnuson KA. 2007. Reducing poverty through preschool interventions. *Future Child.* 17:143–60

Duncan GJ, Magnuson KA. 2005. Can family socioeconomic resources account for racial and ethnic test score gaps? *Future Child.* 15:35–54

Duncan GJ, Yeung WJ, Brooks-Gunn J, Smith JR. 1998. How much does childhood poverty affect the life chances of children? *Am. Sociol. Rev.* 63:406–23

Dunifon R, Kalil A, Danziger SH. 2003. Maternal work behavior under welfare reform: How does the transition from welfare to work affect child development? *Child Youth Serv. Rev.* 25:55–82

Eamon MK. 2001a. The effects of poverty on children's socioemotional development: an ecological systems analysis. *Soc. Work* 46:256–67

Eamon MK. 2001b. Poverty, parenting, peer and neighborhood influences on young adolescent antisocial behavior. *J. Soc. Serv. Res.* 28:1–23

Eamon MK. 2005. Social-demographic, school, neighborhood, and parenting influences on the academic achievement of Latino young adolescents. *J. Youth Adolesc.* 34:163–74

Ellis BJ, Bates JE, Dodge KA, Fergusson DM, Horwood LJ, et al. 2003. Does father absence place daughters at special risk for early sexual activity and teenage pregnancy? *Child Dev.* 75:801–21

Epps SR, Huston AC. 2007. Effects of a poverty intervention policy demonstration on parenting and child behavior: a test of the direction of effects. *Soc. Sci. Q.* 88:344–65

Evans GW. 2006. Child development and the physical environment. *Annu. Rev. Psychol.* 57:423–51

Federal Interagency Forum on Child and Family Statistics. 2008. *America's Children in Brief: Key National Indicators of Well-Being, 2008.* Fed. Interagency Forum Child Fam. Stat., Washington, DC: U.S. Gov. Print. Off. **http://www.childstats.gov/pdf/ac2008/ac_08.pdf**

Foster EM. 2002a. How economists think about family resources and child development. *Child Dev.* 73:1904–14

Foster EM. 2002b. Trends in multiple and overlapping disadvantages among Head Start enrollees. *Child. Youth Serv. Rev.* 24:933–54

Fuligni AJ, Yoshikawa H. 2003. Socioeconomic resources, parenting, and child development among immigrant families. See Bornstein & Bradley 2003, pp. 107–24

Gassman-Pines A, Yoshikawa H. 2006. The effects of antipoverty programs on children's cumulative level of poverty-related risk. *Dev. Psychol.* 42:981–99

Gennetian LA, Magnuson K, Morris PA. 2008. From statistical associations to causation: what developmentalists can learn from instrumental variables techniques coupled with experimental data. *Dev. Psychol.* 44:381–94

Gershoff ET, Aber JL, Raver CC, Lennon MC. 2007. Income is not enough: incorporating material hardship into models of income associations with parenting and child development. *Child Dev.* 78:70–95

Ginther DK, Pollack RA. 2004. Family structure and children's educational outcomes: blended families, stylized facts and descriptive regressions. *Demography* 41:671–96

Gormley WT, Gayer T. 2005. Promoting school readiness in Oklahoma. *J. Hum. Resour.* 40:533–58

Guo G, Harris KM. 2000. The mechanisms mediating the effects of poverty on children's intellectual development. *Demography* 37:431–47

Hart D, Atkins R, Matsuba MK. 2008. The association of neighborhood poverty with personality change in childhood. *J. Personal. Soc. Psychol.* 94:1048–61

Hauser-Cram P, Warfield ME, Stadler J, Sirin SR. 2006. School environments and the diverging pathways of students living in poverty. In *Middle Childhood: Contexts of Development*, ed. AC Huston, M Ripke, pp. 198–217. New York: Cambridge Univ. Press

Hernandez DF, Denton NA, Macarney SE. 2008. Children in immigrant families: looking to America's future. *Soc. Policy Rep.* 22:1–23

Huston AC. 2004. Child care for low-income families: problems and promises. In *Work-Family Challenges for Low-Income Parents and Their Children*, ed. AC Crouter, A Booth, pp. 139–64. New York: Erlbaum

Huston AC, Gupta AE, Bentley AC, Dowsett C, Ware A, Epps SR. 2008. *New Hope's Effect on Social Behavior, Parenting, and Activities at Eight Years.* New York: MDRC

Kane TJ. 2004. College-going and inequality. See Neckerman 2004, pp. 319–53

Kahn AJ, Kamerman SB. 2002. Social exclusion: a better way to think about childhood deprivation? In *Beyond Child Poverty: The Social Exclusion of Children*, pp. 11–36. New York: Inst. Child Fam. Policy Columbia Univ.

Kalil A, Dunifon R. 2007. Maternal work and welfare use and child well-being: evidence from six years of data from the Women's Employment Study. *Child. Youth Serv. Rev.* 29:742–61

Karoly LA, Kilburn MR, Cannon JS. 2005. *Early Childhood Interventions: Proven Results, Future Promise.* Santa Monica, CA: Rand

Kaufman JE, Rosenbaum JE. 1992. The education and employment of low-income Black youth in White suburbs. *Educ. Eval. Policy Anal.* 14:229–40

Kling JR, Ludwig J, Katz LF. 2005. Neighborhood effects on crime for male and female youth: evidence from a randomized housing voucher experiment. *Q. J. Econ.* 120:87–130

Kohen DE, Leventhal T, Dahinten VS, McIntosh CN. 2008. Neighborhood disadvantage: pathways of effects for young children. *Child Dev.* 79:156–69

Lankford H, Loeb S, Wyckoff J. 2002. Teacher sorting and the plight of urban schools: a descriptive analysis. *Educ. Eval. Policy Anal.* 24:37–62

Lerner RM. 2003. What are SES effects effects of? A developmental systems perspective. See Bornstein & Bradley 2003, pp. 231–55

Leventhal T, Brooks-Gunn J. 2000. The neighborhoods they live in: the effects of neighborhood residence on child and adolescent outcomes. *Psychol. Bull.* 126:309–37

Li Grining CP, Coley RL. 2006. Child care experiences in low-income communities: developmental quality and maternal views. *Early Child. Res. Q.* 21:125–41

LoCasale-Crouch J, Konold T, Pianta RC, Howes C, Burchinal M, et al. 2007. Observed classroom quality profiles in state-funded prekindergarten programs and associations with teacher, program, and classroom characteristics. *Early Child. Res. Q.* 22:3–17

Lomel'i EV. 2008. Conditional cash transfers as social policy in Latin America: an assessment of their contributions and limitations. *Annu. Rev. Sociol.* 34:475–99

Lugo-Gil J, Tamis-LeMonda CS. 2008. Family resources and parenting quality: links to children's cognitive development across the first three years. *Child Dev.* 79:1065–85

Luthar SS. 2003. The culture of affluence: psychological costs of material wealth. *Child Dev.* 74:1581–93

Magnuson KA, Waldfogel J. 2005. Early childhood care and education: effects on ethnic and racial gaps in school readiness. *Future Child.* 15:169–96

Magnuson KA, Ruhm CJ, Waldfogel J. 2007. The persistence of preschool effects: Do subsequent classroom experiences matter? *Early Child. Res. Q.* 22:18–38

Magnuson KA, Sexton H, Davis-Kean PE, Huston AC. 2009. Increases in maternal education and children's language skills at age 3: evidence from the NICHD Study. *Merrill Palmer Q.* 55:319–50

Mahoney JL, Larson RW, Eccles JS. 2005. *Organized Activities as Contexts of Development: Extracurricular Activities, After-School and Community Programs.* Mahwah, NJ: Erlbaum

Mayer SE. 1997. *What Money Can't Buy: Family Income and Children's Life Chances*. Cambridge, MA: Harvard Univ. Press

McLanahan S. 1997. Parent absence or poverty: Which matters more? In *Consequences of Growing Up Poor*, ed. GJ Duncan, JB Gunn, pp. 35–48. New York: Sage

McLanahan S, Percheski C. 2008. Family structure and the reproduction of inequalities. *Annu. Rev. Sociol.* 34:257–76

McLeod JD, Nonnemaker JM. 2000. Poverty and child emotional and behavioral problems: racial/ethnic differences in processes and effects. *J. Health Soc. Behav.* 41:137–61

McLoyd VC. 1998. Socioeconomic disadvantage and child development. *Am. Psychol.* 53:185–204

McLoyd VC, Aikens NL, Burton LM. 2006. Childhood poverty, policy, and practice. In *Child Psychology in Practice*, ed. KA Renninger, I Sigel, pp. 700–75. New York: Wiley

Meyers MK, Rosenbaum DT, Ruhm C, Waldfogel J. 2004. Inequality in early childhood education and care: What do we know? See Neckerman 2004, pp. 223–70

Mistry RS, Biesanz JC, Chien N, Howes C, Benner AD. 2008a. Socioeconomic status, parental investments, and the cognitive and behavioral outcomes of low-income children from immigrant and native households. *Early Child. Res. Q.* 23:193–212

Mistry RS, Biesanz JC, Taylor LC, Burchinal MR, Cox MJ. 2004. Family income and its relation to preschool children's adjustment for families in the NICHD Study of Early Child Care. *Dev. Psychol.* 40:727–45

Mistry RS, Lowe ED, Benner AD, Chien N. 2008b. Expanding the family economic stress model: insights from a mixed-methods approach. *J. Marriage Fam.* 70:196–209

Morris PA, Duncan GJ, Clark-Kauffman E. 2005. Child well-being in an era of welfare reform: the sensitivity of transition in development to policy change. *Dev. Psychol.* 41:919–32

Morris PA, Gennetian LA, Duncan GJ, Huston AC. 2009. How welfare policies affect child and adolescent school performance: investigating pathways of influence with experimental data. In *Welfare Reform and Its Long-Term Consequences for America's Poor*, ed. J Ziliak. New York: Cambridge Univ. Press

National Center for Children in Poverty. 2009. *Demographics of Poor Children*. **http://www.nccp.org/profiles/US_profile_7.html**

Neckerman KM, ed. 2004. *Social Inequality*. New York: Sage

NICHD Early Child Care Research Network. 2005. Duration and developmental timing of poverty and children's cognitive and social development from birth through third grade. *Child Dev.* 76:795–810

NICHD Early Child Care Research Network. 2006. The relations of classroom contexts in the early elementary years to children's classroom and social behavior. In *Developmental Contexts in Middle Childhood: Bridges to Adolescence and Adulthood*, ed. AC Huston, M Ripke, pp. 217–36. New York: Cambridge Univ. Press

NICHD Early Child Care Research Network, Duncan GJ. 2003. Modeling the impacts of child care quality on children's preschool cognitive development. *Child Dev.* 74:1454–75

Noble KG, McCandliss BD, Farah MJ. 2007. Socioeconomic gradients predict individual differences in neurocognitive abilities. *Dev. Sci.* 10:464–80

O'Brien Caughy M, O'Campo PJ. 2006. Neighborhood poverty, social capital, and the cognitive development of African American preschoolers. *Am. J. Community Psychol.* 37:141–54

Palacios N, Guttmannova K, Chase-Lansdale PL. 2008. Early reading achievement of children in immigrant families: Is there an immigrant paradox? *Dev. Psychol.* 44:1381–95

Pettit GS, Bates JE, Dodge KA, Meece DW. 1999. The impact of after-school peer contact on early adolescent externalizing problems is moderated by parental monitoring, perceived neighborhood safety, and prior adjustment. *Child Dev.* 70:768–78

Phillips DA, Voran M, Kisker E, Howes C, Whitebook M. 1994. Child care for children in poverty: opportunity or inequity? *Child Dev.* 65:472–92

Pinderhughes EE, Nix R, Foster EM, Jones D. 2001. Parenting in context: impact of neighborhood poverty, residential stability, public services, social networks, and danger on parental behaviors. *J. Marriage Fam.* 63:941–53

Rainwater L, Smeeding TM. 2003. *Poor Kids in a Rich Country: America's Children in Comparative Perspective*. New York: Sage

Raver CC, Gershoff ET, Aber JL. 2007. Testing equivalence of mediating models of income, parenting, and school readiness for White, Black, and Hispanic children in a national sample. *Child Dev.* 78:96–115

Rossi PH, Lyall KC. 1978. An overview evaluation of the NIT experiment. In *Evaluation Studies Review Annual*, ed. TD Cook, ML Del Rosario, KM Hennigan, MM Mark, WMK Trochim, pp. 412–27. Beverly Hills, CA: Sage

Rouse C, Brooks-Gunn J, McLanahan S. 2005. Introducing the issue. School readiness: closing racial and ethnic gaps. *Future Child.* 15:5–14

Ryabov I, Van Hook J. 2007. School segregation and academic achievement among Hispanic children. *Soc. Sci. Res.* 36:767–88

Salkind NJ, Haskins R. 1982. Negative income tax: the impact on children from low-income families. *J. Fam. Issues* 3:165–80

Sameroff AJ, Seifer R. 1995. Accumulation of environmental risk and child mental health. In *Children of Poverty: Research, Health, and Policy Issues*, ed. HE Fitzgerald, BM Lester, BS Zuckerman, pp. 233–58. New York: Garland

Sampson RJ. 2006. Collective efficacy theory: lessons learned and directions for future inquiry. In *Taking Stock*, ed. RJ Sampson, pp. 149–67. New Brunswick, NJ: Transaction

Sanbonmatsu L, Kling JR, Duncan GJ, Brooks-Gunn J. 2006. Neighborhoods and academic achievement: results from the MTO Experiment. *J. Hum. Resour.* 41:649–91

Sawhill I. 2003. *One Percent for the Kids: New Policies, Brighter Futures for America's Children*. Washington, DC: Brookings Inst.

Scarr S, McCartney K. 1983. How people make their own environments: a theory of genotype–environment effects. *Child Dev.* 54:424–35

Scholtz JK, Levine K. 2004. U.S. Black-White wealth inequality. See Neckerman 2004, pp. 895–930

Scott EK, Edin K, London AS, Mazelis JM, Duncan GJ, Chase Lansdale PL. 2002. My children come first: welfare-reliant women's post-TANF views of work-family trade-offs and marriage. In *For Better or for Worse: Welfare Reform and the Well-Being of Children and Families*, ed. GJ Duncan, PL Chase Lansdale, pp. 132–53. New York: Sage

Sullivan JX, Turner L, Danziger S. 2008. The relationship between income and material hardship. *J. Policy Anal. Manag.* 27:63–81

Turley Lopez RN. 2003. When do neighborhoods matter? The role of race and neighborhood peers. *Soc. Sci. Res.* 32:61–79

United Nations Children's Fund (UNICEF). 2008. *The State of the World's Children 2009: Maternal and Newborn Health*. http://www.unicef.org/sowc09/

Van Hook J, Brown SL, Kwenda MN. 2004. A decomposition of trends in poverty among children of immigrants. *Demography* 41:649–70

Votruba-Drzal E. 2003. Income changes and cognitive stimulation in young children's home learning environments. *J. Marriage Fam.* 65:341–55

Votruba-Drzal E. 2006. Economic disparities in middle childhood development: Does income matter? *Dev. Psychol.* 42:1154–67

Walker JT. 2008. *Cumulative environmental advantage and children's achievement: a mediation analysis of the effects of an employment support and antipoverty program*. Master's thesis, Univ. Texas, Austin

Walker JT, Imes AE, Huston AC. 2008. Effects of welfare and employment policies on children's social behavior: Is family stress a pathway? Paper presented at Meet. Assoc. Public Policy Manag., Los Angeles.

Weisner TS, Yoshikawa H, Lowe ED, ed. 2006. *Making It Work: Low-Wage Employment, Family Life, and Child Development*. New York: Russell Sage Found.

Yeung WJ, Linver MR, Brooks-Gunn J. 2002. How money matters for young children's development: parental investment and family processes. *Child Dev.* 73:1861–79

Epigenetics and the Environmental Regulation of the Genome and Its Function

Tie-Yuan Zhang and Michael J. Meaney

Sackler Program for Epigenetics and Psychobiology of McGill University, Douglas Mental Health University Institute and the Singapore Institute for Clinical Sciences, Montreal, Quebec, H4H 1R3 Canada; email: michael.meaney@mcgill.ca

Annu. Rev. Psychol. 2010. 61:439–66

The *Annual Review of Psychology* is online at psych.annualreviews.org

This article's doi:
10.1146/annurev.psych.60.110707.163625

Key Words

maternal care, stress responses, DNA methylation, gene x environment interactions, glucocorticoid receptor

Abstract

There are numerous examples in psychology and other disciplines of the enduring effects of early experience on neural function. In this article, we review the emerging evidence for epigenetics as a candidate mechanism for these effects. Epigenetics refers to functionally relevant modifications to the genome that do not involve a change in nucleotide sequence. Such modifications include chemical marks that regulate the transcription of the genome. There is now evidence that environmental events can directly modify the epigenetic state of the genome. Thus studies with rodent models suggest that during both early development and in adult life, environmental signals can activate intracellular pathways that directly remodel the "epigenome," leading to changes in gene expression and neural function. These studies define a biological basis for the interplay between environmental signals and the genome in the regulation of individual differences in behavior, cognition, and physiology.

Contents

INTRODUCTION

Psychology has seen a major transition in personality theory. Personality traits were once thought to emerge under the dominion of influences associated with "nurture." The postnatal family environment was considered as the primary candidate force in the development of individual differences in personality. This perspective changed dramatically in response to integration of the biological sciences into personality psychology. First, evolutionary approaches established the idea that the brain and its development, like any other organ, are subject to evolutionary forces. Second, behavioral genetics (Ebstein 2006, Kendler 2001, Plomin & Rutter 1998) provided evidence for a relation between variation at the level of the genome and that in personality and mental health. Although efforts to quantify the independent contribution of genetic and environmental

influences are fraught with complications (e.g., gene–environment interactions, nongenomic mechanisms of inheritance), measures of concordance in specific traits between monozygotic and dizygotic twins, among other approaches, suggest a pervasive influence of genetic variation. Indeed, it is impossible to imagine that the function of brain cells could occur independent of variations in the genes that encode for proteins that regulate neuronal functions.

Genomic variation at the level of nucleotide sequence is associated with individual differences in personality and thus with vulnerability and resistance to a wide range of chronic illness (Ebstein 2006, Meyer-Lindenberg & Weinberger 2006, Rutter 2007). Such variations can take multiple forms, including variation at the level of (*a*) a single nucleotide (i.e., single-nucleotide polymorphisms or SNPs), (*b*) variation in the number of nucleotide repeats (i.e., variable number of tandem repeats or VNTRs), or (*c*) chromosomal reorganization. Each form of variation can potentially alter genomic function and thus phenotype. The challenge for psychology is that of conceptually integrating findings from genetics into the study of personality and our understanding of the pathophysiology of mental illness. How and under what conditions does genomic variation influence brain development and function? How might relevant findings from the field of genetics influence the design of public policy and therapies in psychology?

It is important to note the simple fact that genes encode for protein, not function. Thus, as described below, the effects of genetic variation are contextually determined and best considered as probabilistic. Cellular function can only be understood in terms of the constant dialogue that occurs between the genome and its environment. The environment regulates the cellular signals that control the operation of the genome. The objective of this review is to describe recent advances in molecular biology, notably in the field of epigenetics, and to suggest that epigenetic mechanisms are an ideal candidate mechanism for the effects of environmental signals, including events such

Phenotype: any observable characteristic or trait of an organism, such as its morphology, development, biochemical or physiological properties, or behavior as social interactions, on the structure and function of the genome (Harper 2005). The intent is to first consider the processes by which cellular signals, referred to as transcription factors, regulate the activity (or expression) of a gene. The biological primacy of gene–environment interactions is apparent from the simple realization that the levels and the activity of these transcription factors is controlled by environmental signals. Thus the operation of the genome is dependent upon context. The question concerns the mechanisms responsible for such contextual influences. We suggest that epigenetics is one such process and can account, in part, for instances in which environmental events occurring at any time over the lifespan exert a sustained effect on genomic function and phenotype.

Epigenetics signals refer to a series of chemical modifications to the DNA or to regions surrounding the DNA. The transcriptional activity of the genome is regulated by signals, transcription factors, that physically bind to specific DNA sites. The importance of epigenetics mechanisms lies in the ability to regulate the ease with which transcription factors can access the DNA. Epigenetic signals can thus determine the capacity for environmental regulation of the genome. There is emerging evidence for the idea that epigenetic marks are directly altered in early life by environmental events and thus influence the development of individual differences in specific neural functions that underlie cognition and emotion. More recent studies suggest that dynamic alterations in these same epigenetic signals are crucial for the synaptic remodeling that mediates learning and memory. Thus, epigenetics provides a remarkable insight into the biology that governs the function of the genome in response to environmental signals.

GENE TRANSCRIPTION

The most compelling evidence for the predominance of gene–environment interactions in cellular function emerges from the study of gene transcription [Gilbert (2006) provides a very clear and well-illustrated description]. The transcription of the genome is a highly regulated event. At the heart of this process lies a class of proteins referred to as transcription factors. As the name implies, these proteins have the ability to bind to regulatory elements of the gene and to activate or repress gene transcription. Importantly, the expression and activation of the transcription factors themselves are dynamically regulated by environmental signals. Many of the earliest cellular responses to environmental stimuli involve either the activation of pre-existing transcriptional signals through chemical modifications such as phosphorylation (i.e., the addition of a phosphate) of specific amino acids of the protein, or an increase in gene expression that results in the rapid synthesis of proteins (e.g., immediate early gene products) that then serve to regulate the activity of other genes. This includes genes that are involved in synaptic plasticity. The binding of transcription factors to DNA sites is the biological machinery for the dynamic gene–environment interactions that result in altered rates of gene transcription.

Figure 1 portrays the organization of the glucocorticoid receptor gene as an example of genomic organization and a target for discussion below. The schema is actually somewhat misleading. For reasons of graphic simplicity, we often describe the organization of a gene or the interactions between transcription factors and DNA as if the DNA were a linear molecule to which transcription factors gain unimpeded access. The reality of protein–DNA interactions is very different. **Figure 2** (see color insert) presents the classic crystallographic analysis of the organization of DNA (Luger et al. 1997). DNA is organized into units referred to as nucleosomes, each of which contains about 145–150 base pairs wrapped around a core region of histone proteins (Turner 2001). The histones and DNA together are referred to as chromatin; the nucleosome is the organization of chromatin. Under normal conditions there is a tight physical relation between the histone proteins and its accompanying DNA, resulting in a rather closed nucleosome

Gene transcription: the synthesis of RNA under the direction of DNA. RNA synthesis is the process of transcribing DNA nucleotide sequence information into RNA sequence information

Receptor: a protein embedded in either the plasma membrane or cytoplasm of a cell to which a mobile signaling molecule (ligand) may bind. The signaling molecule can be a peptide, a hormone, a pharmaceutical drug, or a toxin, and when such binding occurs, the receptor goes into a conformational change that ordinarily initiates a cellular response

Chromatin: the combination of DNA, RNA, and protein that makes up chromosomes. The major components of chromatin are DNA and histone proteins

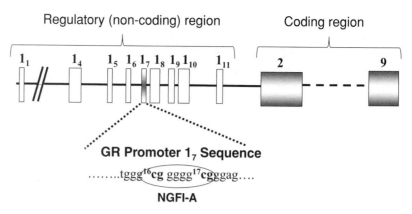

Figure 1

A schema describing the organization of the rat glucocorticoid receptor gene including 9 exon regions. Exons 2–9 participate in the coding for the glucocorticoid receptor protein. Exon 1 is composed of multiple regulatory regions, each of which is capable of activating gene transcription (i.e., promoter sequences). The activity of the various exon 1 promoters is tissue-specific, with evidence suggesting that certain promoters are more active in areas such as liver or thymus, and others are more active in brain (e.g., exon 1_7; based on McCormick et al. 2000; see Turner & Muller 2005 for comparable data in humans). The use of multiple promoters permits regulation in one tissue independently from other regions (i.e., increased glucocorticoid receptor in pulmonary tissues prior to birth that is necessary for respiratory competency at parturition, while maintaining reduced glucocorticoid receptor levels in brain, where glucocorticoid effects might inhibit neurogenesis). The consensus binding site for nerve growth factor–inducible factor A (NGFI-A) lying within the exon 1_7 promoter is highlighted. The reader should note that this organization is not necessarily typical. Regulatory elements (promoters or enhancers) can exist between exons (i.e., within introns) or at sites that are either 5′ or 3′ to the coding region, sometimes at considerable distances.

configuration. This restrictive configuration is maintained, in part, by electrostatic bonds between the positively charged histones and the negatively charged DNA. The closed configuration impedes transcription factor binding and is associated with a reduced level of gene expression. An increase in transcription factor binding to DNA and the subsequent activation of gene expression commonly requires chemical modification of the chromatin that occurs on the histone proteins. The primary targets for such events are the amino acids that form the histone tails extending from the nucleosome (**Figure 2**). These modifications alter chromatin in a manner that either increases or decreases the ability of transcription factors to access regulatory sites on the DNA that control gene transcription.

Chromatin Modifications

The dynamic alteration of chromatin structure is achieved through modifications to the histone proteins at the amino acids that form the histone protein tails that extend out from the nucleosome (**Figure 2**). These modifications are achieved through a series of enzymes that bind to the histone tails and modify the local chemical properties of specific amino acids (Grunstein 1997, Hake & Allis 2006, Jenuwein & Allis 2001). For example, the enzyme histone acetyltransferase transfers an acetyl group onto specific lysines on the histone tails. The addition of the acetyl group diminishes the positive charge, loosening the relation between the histones and DNA, opening the chromatin and improving the ability of transcription factors to access DNA sites. Thus, histone acetylation at specific lysine sites is commonly associated with active gene transcription.

The functional antagonists of the histone acetyltransferases are a class of enzymes known as histone deacetylases (HDACs). These enzymes remove acetyl groups and prevent further acetylation, thus maintaining a closed chromatin structure, decreasing transcription factor and gene expression. Both the acetylation and deacetylation of histones are dynamic processes that are regulated by environmental signals. Indeed, a number of proteins that were known to be associated with transcriptional activation (e.g., transcriptional cofactors) have been identified as histone acetyltransferases. These factors enhance the efficacy of transcription factors by opening chromatin and thus increasing the binding of the factor to the regulatory regions of the gene.

The reader should note that there are actually multiple modifications to histone tails, including methylation (in this case on the histones), phosphorylation, and ubiquitination. For the sake of simplicity, the discussion is limited to histone acetylation/deacetylation.

Regulation of Glucocorticoid Receptor Expression

The neurotransmitter serotonin (5-hydroxytryptamine; 5-HT) regulates glucocorticoid receptor gene transcription in hippocampal neurons (**Figure 3**, see color insert; Mitchell et al. 1990, 1992; Weaver et al. 2007). This effect is dependent upon the binding of the transcription factor nerve growth factor–inducible factor A (NGFI-A) to a specific binding site on the exon 1_7 glucocorticoid (GR) promoter (**Figure 1**). The importance of this interaction can be precisely defined. For example, mutating a single nucleotide, in this case simply exchanging a cytosine for an adenine, in the region of the promoter that normally binds NGFI-A abolishes the ability of NGFI-A to associate with the exon 1_7 promoter and eliminates the effect of NGFI-A on gene transcription (Weaver et al. 2007). However, the ability of NGFI-A to bind to the exon 1_7 promoter is regulated by another protein, a transcriptional cofactor, the CREB-binding protein, that is activated by the same 5-HT-cyclic adenosine monophosphate (cAMP)/cyclic nucleotide–dependent kinases (PKA)-signaling cascade that results in the increased levels of NGFI-A (**Figure 3**). The

CREB-binding protein is a histone acetyltransferase. The association of the CREB-binding protein with the exon 1_7 promoter is accompanied by an increase in the acetylation of a specific lysine on the tail of histone 3 of the exon 1_7 promoter (Weaver et al. 2004, 2007). Thus, 5-HT activates both NGFI-A and the CREB-binding protein. Interestingly, NGFI-A and the CREB–binding protein physically associate with one another prior to DNA binding. The CREB–binding protein acetylates histones associated with the exon 1_7 promoter, enhancing the ability of NGFI-A to bind and activate gene transcription.

Environmental signals alter 5-HT activity. Indeed, the effect of 5-HT on glucocorticoid receptor expression reflects the dependency of gene transcription on signals that derive from environmental events (note that the relevant environmental event may be internal or external to the organism; e.g., a change in the availability of glucose, an electrical impulse, or a social interaction). Such effects underlie the dynamic interdependence of gene and environment. However, psychologists, and in particular developmental psychologists, are familiar with more enduring environmental influences; instances where experience in early life has shaped neural development and function in a manner that is sustained into adulthood. Such effects are considered as the basis for environmental influences over the development of individual differences. In certain cases, the sustained effects of early experience have been associated with structural alterations in neural circuits that mediate specific functions. The process of sexual differentiation among vertebrates provides excellent examples where environmental signals lead to differences in morphology and thus to gender. However, more recent studies suggest another form of environmentally regulated plasticity that exists at the level of genome itself. Such effects appear to involve the modification of epigenetic marks on the DNA. These studies suggest that environmental events alter the activity of specific intracellular signals that modify the nature of the epigenetic marks at specific sites

Histone acetyltransferases: enzymes that acetylate lysine amino acids on histone proteins by transferring an acetyl group from acetyl CoA to form ε-N-acetyl lysine. Histone acetylation is associated with the activation of gene transcription

Promoter: a region of DNA that facilitates the transcription of a particular gene. Promoters are typically located near the genes they regulate, on the same strand and upstream from the coding region in the genome, leading to sustained effects on gene expression and thus neural function.

ENVIRONMENTAL PROGRAMMING OF GENE EXPRESSION

Studies in developmental psychobiology and physiology are replete with examples of the environmental programming of gene expression. Such studies commonly report that a variation in the early environment associates with changes in gene expression and biological function that persists into adulthood and thus well beyond the duration of the relevant environmental event. In the rat, for example, prenatal nutrient deprivation or enhanced exposure to hormonal signals associated with stress stably alter, or program, the activity of genes in the liver and other sites that are associated with glucose and fat metabolism, including the gene for the glucocorticoid receptor (Bateson et al. 2004; Gluckman & Hanson 2004, 2007; Jirtle & Skinner 2007; Meaney et al. 2007; Seckl & Holmes 2007). These findings are assumed to represent instances in which the operation of a genomic region in adulthood varies as a function of early environmental influences. The results of recent studies suggest that such "programming" effects can derive from gene–environment interactions in early life that lead to a structural alteration of the DNA, which in turn mediates the effects on gene expression as well as more complex levels of phenotype (Jirtle & Skinner 2007, Meaney 2007, Meaney & Szyf 2005). These studies were performed in rodents but were inspired by the vast literature reporting the pervasive effects of family environment on health outcomes in humans (Repetti et al. 2002). No less compelling are the results of studies on "maternal effects" in plants, insects, reptiles, and birds showing that variations in nongenomic signals of maternal origin associate with sustained effects on the phenotype of the offspring (Cameron et al. 2005, Mousseau & Fox 1998, Rossiter 1998).

The objective of these studies is to examine the biological mechanisms whereby variations in mother–infant interactions might directly influence gene expression and behavior (Meaney 2001). Such studies focus on variations in maternal behavior that lie within the normal range for the species, in this case the Norway rat, and that occur in the absence of any experimental manipulations (i.e., naturally occurring variations in mother–pup interactions). Variations on maternal care in the rat are studied with simple, albeit very time-consuming, observations on animals in their home cages (Champagne 2008, Champagne et al. 2003). One behavior, pup licking/grooming (LG), emerges as highly variable across mothers. Pup LG is a major source of tactile stimulation for the neonatal rat that regulates endocrine and cardiovascular function in the pup (Hofer 2005, Levine 1994, Schanberg et al. 1984). The question then was whether such variations in pup LG might directly alter the development of individual differences in behavior and physiology. For the studies reviewed here, the focus is on the development of individual differences in defensive responses.

Subsequent findings revealed considerable evidence for the effect of maternal care on the behavioral and endocrine responses to stress in the offspring. The male or female adult offspring of mothers that naturally exhibit increased levels of pup LG (i.e., the offspring of high-LG mothers) show more modest behavioral and endocrine responses to stress compared to animals reared by low-LG mothers (Caldji et al. 1998, Francis et al. 1999, Liu et al. 1997, Menard et al. 2004, Toki et al. 2007, Weaver et al. 2004). Specifically, the offspring of high-LG mothers show reduced fearfulness and more modest hypothalamic-pituitary-adrenal (HPA) responses to stress. Cross-fostering studies, where pups born to high-LG mothers are fostered at birth to low-LG mothers (and vice versa), reveal a direct relationship between maternal care and the postnatal development of individual differences in behavioral and HPA responses to stress (Caldji et al. 2000, 2003; Francis et al. 1999; Weaver et al. 2004). In these studies, the rearing mother determined the phenotype of

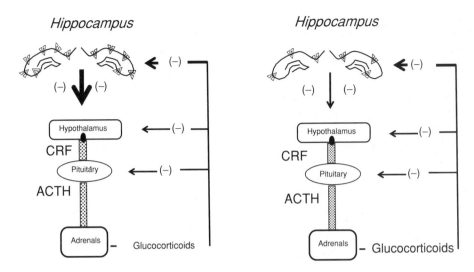

Hippocampus

Hippocampus

Figure 4

A schema outlining the function of the hypothalamic-pituitary-adrenal axis, the nexus of which are the corticotropin-releasing factor (CRF) neurons of the paraventricular nucleus of the hypothalamus. CRF is released into the portal system of the anterior pituitary, stimulating the synthesis and release of adrenocorticotropin (ACTH), which then stimulates adrenal glucocorticoid release. Glucocorticoids act on glucocorticoid receptors in multiple brain regions, including the hippocampus, to inhibit the synthesis and release of CRF (i.e., glucocorticoid negative feedback). The adult offspring of high-LG mothers, by comparison to those of low-LG dams, show (*a*) increased glucocorticoid receptor expression, (*b*) enhanced negative-feedback sensitivity to glucocorticoids, (*c*) reduced CRF expression in the hypothalamus, and (*d*) more modest pituitary-adrenal responses to stress.

the offspring. Thus variations within a normal range of parental care can dramatically alter phenotypic development in the rat.

The effects of maternal care on the development of defensive responses to stress in the rat involve alterations in the function of the corticotrophin-releasing factor (CRF) systems in selected brain regions (**Figure 4**). The CRF system furnishes the critical signal for the activation of behavioral, emotional, autonomic, and endocrine responses to stressors (Bale & Vale 2004, Koob et al. 1994, Plotsky et al. 1989). As adults, the offspring of high-LG mothers show decreased CRF expression in the hypothalamus as well as reduced plasma ACTH and glucocorticoid responses to acute stress by comparison to the adult offspring of low-LG mothers (Francis et al. 1999; Liu et al. 1997; Weaver et al. 2004, 2005). Circulating glucocorticoids act at glucocorticoid receptor sites in corticolimbic structures, such as the hippocampus, to regulate HPA activity (**Figure 4**). Such feedback effects

commonly inhibit hypothalamic CRF expression. The high-LG offspring showed significantly increased hippocampal glucocorticoid receptor expression, enhanced glucocorticoid negative feedback sensitivity, and decreased hypothalamic CRF levels. Indeed, the magnitude of the glucocorticoid response to acute stress is significantly correlated with the frequency of pup LG during the first week of life, as is the level of both hippocampal glucocorticoid receptor and hypothalamic CRF expression (all r's >0.70; Liu et al. 1997). Importantly, pharmacological manipulations that block the effect of the glucocorticoid receptor eliminate the maternal effect on the HPA response to stress, suggesting that the differences in hippocampal glucocorticoid receptor expression are directly related to those at the level of HPA function.

Pup LG is a major source of tactile stimulation for the neonate. Experimental models that directly apply tactile stimulation, through the stroking of the pup with a brush, provide direct evidence for the importance of tactile stimulation derived from pup LG. Thus, stroking pups over the first week of life increases hippocampal glucocorticoid receptor expression (Jutapakdeegul et al. 2003) and dampens behavioral and HPA responses to stress (Burton et al. 2007, Gonzalez et al. 2001). Likewise, manipulations of lactating mothers that directly increase the frequency of pup LG also increase hippocampal glucocorticoid receptor expression and decrease HPA responses to stress (Francis et al. 1999, Toki et al. 2007). Manipulations, notably stressors imposed on the mother, that decrease pup LG are associated with increased behavioral and HPA responses to stress and are associated with decreased hippocampal glucocorticoid receptor expression and increased hypothalamic expression of CRF (Champagne & Meaney 2006, Fenoglio et al. 2005).

The offspring of the high-LG and low-LG mothers also differ in behavioral responses to novelty (Caldji et al. 1998, Francis et al. 1999, Zhang et al. 2004). As adults, the offspring of the high-LG mothers show decreased startle responses, increased open-field exploration, and shorter latencies to eat food provided in a novel environment. There are also behavioral differences in response to more precise forms of threat. Thus, the offspring of low-LG mothers show greater burying of an electrified probe in the defensive burying paradigm (Menard et al. 2004), which involves an active response to a threat. These differences in behavioral responses to stress are associated with altered activity in the CRF system that links the amygdala (and bed nucleus of the stria terminalis) to the noradrenergic cells of the locus coeruleus (Caldji et al. 1998, Zhang et al. 2004).

The results of these studies suggest that the behavior of the mother toward her offspring can "program" stable changes in gene expression that then serve as the basis for individual differences in behavioral and neuroendocrine responses to stress in adulthood. The maternal effects on phenotype are associated with sustained changes in the expression of genes in brain regions that mediate responses to stress

and form the basis for stable individual differences in stress reactivity. These findings provide a potential mechanism for the influence of parental care on vulnerability/resistance to stress-induced illness over the lifespan. But the critical issue is simply that of how maternal care might stably affect gene expression. How are variations in the social interactions between the mother and her offspring biologically embedded so as to stably alter the activity of specific regions of the genome? The answers to these questions appear to involve the ability of social interactions in early development to structurally modify relevant genomic regions. For the sake of this review, we focus on the maternal effect on the regulation of hippocampal glucocorticoid receptor expression.

EPIGENETIC REGULATION OF THE GENOME

The molecular processes that lead to the initiation of gene transcription involve modifications to the histone proteins that form the core of the nucleosome (**Figure 2**). Such modifications open chromatin, permitting transcription factor binding and the activation of gene transcription. A second level of regulation occurs not on the histone proteins, but rather directly on the DNA. Indeed, the classic epigenetic alteration is that of DNA methylation, which involves the addition of a methyl group (CH_3) onto cytosines in the DNA (Bird 1986, Holliday 1989, Razin & Riggs 1980). DNA methylation is associated with the silencing of gene transcription. This effect appears to be mediated in one of two ways (Bird 2002). First, wide swaths of densely methylated DNA preclude transcription factor binding to DNA sites, thus silencing gene expression. The second manner is subtler and probably far more prevalent in regions with more dynamic variations in gene transcription, such as the brain. In this case, selected cytosines are methylated, and the presence of the methyl group attracts a class of proteins know as methylated-DNA binding proteins (Klose & Bird 2007). These proteins, in turn, attract an entire cluster of

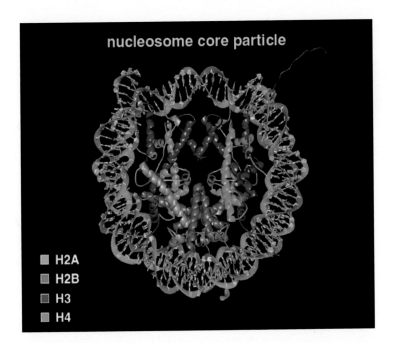

Figure 2

Crystallographic image of the nucleosome showing 145–150 base pairs wrapped around a histone complex that is composed of histone 2A, 2B, 3, and 4 proteins. The tight configuration is maintained, in part, by electrostatic bonds. Modifications, such as acetylation, to the histone regulate transcription factor binding and occur primarily at the histone tails protruding out of the nucleosome (pictured is the blue tail of histone 3).

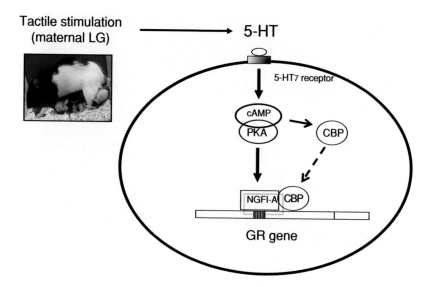

Figure 3

A summary of in vivo studies with hippocampal tissue samples from neonates and in vitro studies using primary hippocampal cell cultures. In vivo, an increased frequency of pup licking/grooming (LG) from the mother associates with hippocampal 5-hydroxytryptamine (5-HT) turnover, activation of a 5-HT7 receptor positively coupled to cyclic adenosine monophosphate (cAMP) and cyclic nucleotide dependent kinases (PKA) and the induction of nerve growth factor–inducible factor A (NGFI-A) expression. In vivo, increased pup LG or artificial tactile stimulation induces NGFI-A expression as well as that of the cAMP-response element-binding protein (CREB)-binding protein, both of which show greater binding to the exon 1_7 promoter in the neonatal offspring high-LG compared with low-LG mothers. Results of in vitro studies show that blockade of cAMP, PKA, or NGFI-A abolish the effect of 5-HT of glucocorticoid receptor expression. GR, glucocorticoid.

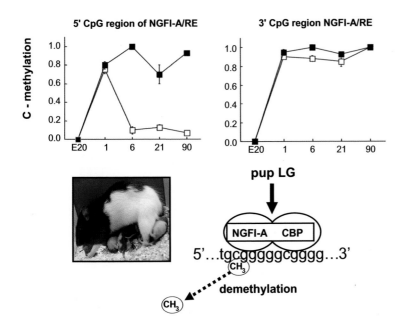

Figure 5

(*Top panels*) A summary of the developmental changes in the methylation status of the 5′ and 3′ CpG (see **Figure 1**) of the nerve growth factor–inducible factor A (NGFI-A) consensus sequence lying within the exon 1_7 glucocorticoid receptor promoter. Note that neither CpG site is methylated in late fetal life, followed by a period of de novo methylation following birth. The critical alteration at the 5′ CpG site involves an apparent demethylation of the site. (*Bottom panels*) A working hypothesis for the experience (maternal care)-driven remodeling of the epigenetic state of the NGFI-A consensus-binding sequence over the first week of postnatal life in the offspring of high-LG mothers. The binding of a NGFI-A/CREB-binding protein (CBP) complex actively targets the as yet unidentified demethylase process resulting in the removal of the methyl group from the 5′ CpG site of the NGFI-A-binding site (Meaney & Szyf 2005). (Top panel adapted from Weaver et al. 2004.)

proteins that form a repressor complex, which includes active mediators of gene silencing. The HDACs are a critical component of the repressor complex. HDACs prevent histone acetylation and favor a closed chromatin state that constrains transcription factor binding and gene expression (**Figure 2** and see above). Compounds that inhibit HDACs can thus increase transcription from methylated DNA.

When we think of genomic influences, we most commonly imagine effects associated with variation in nucleotide sequence. Yet this is only one form of information contained within the genome. Despite the reverence afforded DNA, a gene is basically like any other molecule in the cell; it is subject to physical modifications. As described above, these modifications alter the structure and chemical properties of the DNA and thus gene expression. Collectively, the modifications to the DNA and its chromatin environment can be considered as an additional layer of information that is contained within the genome. This information is thus epigenetic in nature (the name derives from the Greek *epi* meaning "upon" and *genetics*). The acetylation of histone proteins or the methylation of DNA are examples of epigenetic modifications. Epigenetic modifications do not alter the sequence composition of the genome. Instead, these epigenetic marks on the DNA and the histone proteins of the chromatin regulate the operation of the genome. Thus, "epigenetics" has been defined as a functional modification to the DNA that does not involve an alteration of sequence (Waddington 1957). Although this definition has been subjected to revision (Bird 2007, Hake & Allis 2006), the essential features of epigenetic mechanisms are (*a*) structural modifications to chromatin either at the level of the histone proteins (**Figure 2**) or the DNA, (*b*) the associated regulation of the structure and function of chromatin, (*c*) the downstream effects on gene expression, and (*d*) the fact that these effects occur in the absence of any change in nucleotide sequence.

The methylation of DNA in mammals is an active biochemical modification that selectively targets cytosines and is achieved through the actions of enzymes, DNA methyltransferases, that transfer the methyl groups from methyl donors. There are two critical features to DNA methylation: First, it is a stable chemical modification, and second, it is associated with the silencing of gene transcription (Bestor 1998, Bird 2002, Bird & Wolffe 1999, Razin 1998).

Until very recently, it was thought that DNA methylation patterns on the genome were overlaid upon the genome only during early periods in embryonic development. Indeed, DNA methylation is considered as a fundamental feature of cell differentiation. It is important to consider a simple feature of cell biology: All cells in the body generally share the same DNA. Thus, the processes of cell specialization, whereby liver cells specialize in functions related to energy metabolism and brain cells establish the capacity for learning and memory, involve silencing certain regions of the genome in a manner that is specific for each cell type. Genes associated with gluconeogenesis are silenced in brain cells but remain active in liver cells. Such processes define the function of the cell type (e.g., Fan et al. 2005). DNA methylation is considered as a mechanism for the genomic silencing that underlies cell specialization. Such events occur early in development and are considered to be highly stable, such that dedifferentiation (whereby a cell loses its specialization) is rare and often is associated with organ dysfunction.

Thus DNA methylation was considered both unique to early periods in development and irreversible. Experimental models commonly used to study DNA methylation further reinforced this view. DNA methylation-induced gene silencing mediates two of the most commonly studied examples of the epigenetic silencing of genes, namely X-chromosome inactivation and gene imprinting. Mammalian females bear two copies of the X-chromosome. The inactivation of one copy of the X-chromosome occurs in all mammalian females and is essential for normal function (i.e., maintaining a constant gene dosage in males and females). The silencing of the X-chromosome is associated with DNA methylation (Mohandas et al. 1981, Riggs & Pfieffer 1992; but also see Hellman & Chess 2007 for a more current update). The second example of epigenetic-mediated gene silencing is that of gene imprinting (da Rocha & Ferguson-Smith 2004, Reik 2001), a remarkable subject in its own right and one with considerable implications for growth and development (Charalambous et al. 2007). For humans and other mammals, the expression of specific genes is determined by the parent of origin. For certain genes, the copy derived from the mother is active while that emanating from the father is silenced—a maternally imprinted gene. In other cases, it is the reverse: The copy of the gene inherited from the father is active while that from the mother is silenced—a paternally imprinted gene. The silent copy is methylated in DNA regions that regulate gene expression and thus is inactive. Again, the epigenetic marks associated with gene imprinting are established very early in life. These marks, as well as those associated with X-chromosome inactivation, are largely stable.

Collectively, these models have left biologists with the impression that under normal conditions, DNA methylation occurs early in embryonic life and is irreversible. DNA methylation was considered to be an actively dynamic process only during periods of cell division and differentiation (see above) such that in mature postmitotic cells, further alteration of methylation patterns was improbable. Moreover, the extensive loss of cytosine methylation in the models described above is associated with pathology. This perspective was further reinforced by findings showing that an alteration of DNA methylation at critical genomic targets (i.e., tumor suppressors) is associated with cancer (Eden et al. 2003, Feinberg 2007, Laird 2005).

At this point, dynamic changes in DNA methylation were of considerable interest for developmental biologists but somewhat less so for psychologists, who study the aftermath of more subtle variations in neuronal differentiation that occur in later periods of development or even in the fully mature brain. The issue for developmental psychologists concerns less the process by which cells specialize as neurons and more the issues related to why neurons in one individual function differently from those of another, or how neurons might dynamically later alter functional properties in relation to experience (i.e., activity-dependent neuronal plasticity). The studies reviewed below provide an important revision to this perspective. There is now considerable evidence in neuroscience and other fields, including immunology and endocrinology/metabolism, that the state of DNA methylation at specific genomic sites is indeed dynamic even in adult animals (Bird 2007, Jirtle & Skinner 2007, Meaney & Szyf 2005). Moreover, alterations in DNA methylation are emerging as a candidate mechanism for the effects of early experience in individual differences in neural function as well as in learning and memory. Thus, although the assumptions concerning DNA methylation appear valid for the examples cited above, recent studies reveal that DNA methylation patterns are actively modified in mature (i.e., fully differentiated) cells including, and perhaps especially, neurons, and that such modifications can occur in animals in response to cellular signals driven by environmental events (Jirtle & Skinner 2007, Meaney & Szyf 2005, Sweatt 2009). For example, variations in the diet of mice during gestation or later in development, such as the early postweaning period, can stably alter the methylation status of the DNA (Cooney et al. 2002, Waterland & Jirtle 2003, Waterland et al. 2006, Whitelaw & Whitelaw 2006). Likewise, both mature lymphocytes (Bruniquel & Schwartz 2003, Murayama et al. 2006) and neurons (e.g., Champagne 2008, Champagne et al. 2006, Lubin et al. 2008, Martinowich et al. 2003, Sweatt 2009) show changes in the DNA methylation patterns at critical genomic regions in response to environmental stimuli that stably alter cellular function. The ability of environmental signals to actively remodel epigenetic marks that regulate gene expression is a rather radical change in our understanding of the environmental regulation of gene expression. Such epigenetic modifications are thus a candidate mechanism for the environmental programming of gene expression.

Epigenetics and the Social Environment

The section below describes studies of the molecular basis for the effects of maternal care on the development of individual differences in gene expression and stress responses. The mechanism for this interaction is epigenetic, involving alterations in DNA methylation at specific sites in the genome. In summary, variations in mother–infant interactions in the rat alter the extra- and intracellular environment of neurons in selected brain regions. Such alterations directly modify the epigenetic marks on regions of the DNA that regulate the transcription of the glucocorticoid receptor, which in turn regulates the HPA response to stress. These epigenetic marks are stable, enduring well beyond the period of maternal care, and provide a molecular basis for a stable maternal effect on the phenotype of the offspring. Thus, the behavior of the mother directly alters cellular signals that then actively sculpt the epigenetic landscape of the offspring, influencing the activity of specific regions of the genome and the phenotype of the offspring.

The critical feature of the maternal effects described above is that of persistence. The differences in the frequency of pup LG between high- and low-LG mothers are limited to the first week of postnatal life. And yet the differences in gene expression and neural function are apparent well into adulthood. How might the effects of an essentially social interaction stably alter the expression of the genes that regulate the activity of neural systems that mediate endocrine and behavioral responses to stress? To address this question, we focused on the sustained effect of maternal care on glucocorticoid receptor gene transcription in the hippocampus as a model system for the environmental programming of gene expression.

The focus of the epigenetic studies is the NGFI-A consensus sequence in the exon 1₇ promoter (**Figure 1**) that activates glucocorticoid receptor expression in hippocampal neurons. The tactile stimulation associated with pup LG increases 5-HT activity in the hippocampus. In vitro studies with cultured hippocampal neurons show that 5-HT acts on 5-HT$_7$ receptors to initiate a series of intracellular signals that culminate with an increase in the expression of NGFI-A as well as in the CREB-binding protein (**Figure 3**). Comparable effects occur in vivo. Manipulations that increase pup LG by lactating rats result in an increased level of cAMP as well as NGFI-A (Meaney et al. 2000). Pups reared by high-LG mothers show increased NGFI-A expression in hippocampal neurons as well as an increased binding of NGFI-A to the exon 1₇ promoter sequence (Weaver et al. 2007, Zhang et al. 2009). Moreover, the binding of NGFI-A to the exon 1₇ promoter sequence is actively regulated by mother–pup interactions, such that there is increased NGFI-A bound to the exon 1₇ promoter immediately following a nursing bout, but not at a period that follows 25 minutes without mother–pup contact (Zhang et al. 2009).

NGFI-A and the CREB-binding protein form a complex that binds directly to the exon 1₇ promoter sequence and actively redesigns the methylation pattern at this region of the genome (Weaver et al. 2004, 2007). Thus, as adults, the offspring reared by high-LG mothers show very modest levels of methylation at the 5′ CpG of the NGFI-A consensus sequence (**Figure 5**, see color insert). This effect on methylation is very precise. Located only a few nucleotides removed from this site is the 3′ CpG site (**Figures 1** and **5**), the methylation status of which is unaffected by maternal care.

A rather novel aspect of the effect of maternal care on DNA methylation was apparent in the results of a simple developmental study examining the methylation status of the 5′ and 3′ CpG sites from late in fetal life to adulthood (Weaver et al. 2004). Neither the 5′ nor the 3′ CpG sites within the NGFI-A binding region is methylated in hippocampal neurons from fetal rats, whereas both sites are heavily methylated on the day following birth, with no difference as a function of maternal care.

These findings reflect what is referred to as de novo methylation, whereby a methyl group is applied to previously unmethylated sites. However, between the day following birth and the end of the first week of life, the 5' CpG is demethylated in pups reared by high-LG, but not low-LG, mothers. This difference then persists into adulthood. Importantly, the period over which the demethylation occurs falls precisely within that time when high- and low-LG mothers differ in the frequency of pup LG; the difference in pup LG between high- and low-LG mothers is not apparent in the second week of postnatal life (Caldji et al. 1998, Champagne 2008, Champagne et al. 2003).

The demethylation of the 5' CpG site occurs as a function of the same 5-HT-activated signals that regulate glucocorticoid receptor gene expression in cultured hippocampal neurons (Weaver et al. 2007). Thus, when hippocampal neurons of embryonic origin are placed in culture and treated with 5-HT, which mimics the extracellular signal associated with maternal LG, the 5' CpG site is demethylated; there is no effect at the 3' CpG site. The binding of NGFI-A to the exon 1_7 site is critical. Hippocampal neurons that are rendered incapable of increasing NGFI-A expression through antisense or siRNA treatment show neither the demethylation of the 5' CpG site nor the increase in glucocorticoid receptor expression (Weaver et al. 2007). Likewise, a mutation of the NGFI-A site (exchanging a C for an A at the 3' CpG site) that completely abolishes the binding of NGFI-A to the exon 1_7 promoter also prevents the demethylation of the 5' CpG. Finally, the infection of hippocampal neurons with a virus containing a nucleotide construct engineered to express high levels of NGFI-A produces demethylation of the 5' CpG of the exon 1_7 promoter sequence and increases glucocorticoid receptor expression.

These findings suggest that maternal licking of pups increases NGFI-A levels in the hippocampal neurons of the offspring, thus altering DNA methylation. But there is a complication. If DNA methylation blocks transcription factor binding and the 5' CpG site of the exon 1_7 promoter is heavily methylated in neonates, then how might maternally activated NGFI-A bind to and remodel the exon 1_7 region? And why is the effect apparent at the 5' but not the 3' CpG? The answer to these questions appears to involve other transcriptional signals that are affected by maternal care. Levels of the transcription factor–specific protein-1 (SP-1) and the CREB-binding protein are also increased in the hippocampus of pups reared by high-LG mothers (Weaver et al. 2007, Zhang et al. 2009). The exon 1_7 promoter contains a DNA sequence that binds SP-1, and this region overlaps with that for NGFI-A. SP-1 can actively target both methylation and demethylation of CpG sites (Brandeis et al. 1994). The 5'CpG site is the region of overlap in the binding sites. The CREB-binding protein, on the other hand, acts as a histone acetyltransferase, an enzyme capable of acetylating histone tails, including the exon 1_7 region, opening chromatin and permitting the binding of transcription factors such as NGFI-A and SP-1. Increasing histone acetylation can lead to transcription factor binding at previously methylated sites and the subsequent demethylation of these regions (Fan et al. 2005, Szyf et al. 2005). Thus, we suggest that the binding of this complex of proteins, NGFI-A, the CREB-binding protein, and SP-1 is critical in activating the process of demethylation. The results to date are certainly consistent with this model, but we should note that we have yet to firmly establish the identity of the enzyme that is responsible for the demethylation of the 5' CpG site.

These findings suggest that maternally induced increases in hippocampal NGFI-A levels can initiate the remodeling of DNA methylation at the regions of the DNA that regulate glucocorticoid receptor expression. The NGFI-A transcription factor binds to multiple sites across the genome. If NGFI-A-related complexes target demethylation, then one might assume that other NGFI-A-sensitive regions should show a maternal effect on DNA methylation and gene expression comparable to that observed with the glucocorticoid receptor. Zhang and colleagues (2009) showed that the hippocampal expression of the *GAD1* gene that encodes for glutamic acid decarboxylase, an enzyme in the production of the neurotransmitter GABA, is increased in the adult offspring of high-LG mothers. This effect is associated with altered DNA methylation of an NGFI-A response element in a manner comparable to that for the glucocorticoid receptor gene. Moreover, as with the effect on the glucocorticoid receptor, an in vitro increase in NGFI-A expression mimics the effects of increased pup LG. The function of GABAergic neurons in the limbic system is also regulated by maternal care (Caldji et al. 1998, 2000, 2003) and is a major target for anxiolytic agents. These findings are therefore likely relevant for the decreased fearfulness observed in the adult offspring of high-LG mothers.

In summary, the maternally induced changes in specific intracellular signals in hippocampal neurons can physically remodel the genome. The increased binding of NGFI-A that derives from pup LG appears critical for the demethylation of the exon 1_7 promoter. We suggest that this process involves accompanying increases in SP-1 and the CREB-binding protein, and that the combination of these factors results in the active demethylation of the exon 1_7 promoter. It should be noted that there are important features of this model that remain to be clearly defined, including the identification of the enzyme that is directly responsible for the demethylation. Nevertheless, the events described to date represent a model by which the biological pathways activated by a social event may become imprinted onto the genome. This imprint is then physically apparent in the adult genome, resulting in stable alterations (or programming) of gene expression.

THE FUNCTIONAL IMPORTANCE OF THE SOCIAL IMPRINT

A critical issue is that of relating the epigenetic modifications at specific DNA regions to function. The presence of a methyl group on the 5' CpG of the NGFI-A binding site is functionally related to glucocorticoid receptor gene expression in adult animals. In vitro studies reveal that the methylation of the 5'CpG site reduces the ability of NGFI-A to bind to the exon 1_7 promoter and activate glucocorticoid receptor transcription (Weaver et al. 2007). These findings are consistent with the model described above, whereby DNA methylation impedes transcription factor binding and thus the activation of gene expression. The next question concerns the in vivo situation and function at a level beyond that of gene expression.

In contrast to the situation with neonates, there is no difference in NGFI-A expression as a function of maternal care among adult animals: Hippocampal levels of NGFI-A are comparable in the adult offspring of high- and low-LG mothers. However, the altered methylation of the exon 1_7 promoter would suggest differences in the ability of NGFI-A to access its binding site on the exon 1_7 promoter. Chromatin-immunoprecipitation assays, which permit measurement of the interaction between a specific protein and a defined region of the DNA, reveal increased NGFI-A association with the exon 1_7 promoter in hippocampi from adult offspring of high- compared to low-LG mothers (Weaver et al. 2004, 2005). This difference occurs despite the comparable levels of NGFI-A. These findings show that in the living animal, under normal conditions, there is more NGFI-A associated with the exon 1_7 promoter in hippocampal neurons of adult animals reared by high- compared with low-LG mothers.

There is also evidence that directly links the maternal effect on the epigenetic state of the exon 1_7 promoter to the changes in glucocorticoid receptor expression and HPA responses to stress. Recall that the methylation of specific CpG sites can diminish transcription factor binding through the recruitment of repressor complexes that include HDACs. The HDACs deacetylate histone tails, thus favoring a closed chromatin configuration. Indeed, the exon 1_7 promoter is more prominently acetylated in hippocampi from adult offspring of high- compared with low-LG mothers

(Weaver et al. 2004, 2005). This finding is consistent with the increased transcription of the glucocorticoid receptor gene in animals reared by high- versus low-LG mothers. A subsequent study (Weaver et al. 2004) examined the effects of directly blocking the actions of the HDACs in the adult offspring of high- and low-LG mothers by directly infusing an HDAC inhibitor into the hippocampus daily for four consecutive days. The treatment with the HDAC inhibitor produces a series of predictable results that reflect a cause-effect relation between DNA methylation and gene expression. First, as expected, HDAC blockade eliminates the differences in the acetylation of the histone tails (open chromatin) of the exon 1_7 promoter in hippocampal samples from high- and low-LG mothers. Second, the increased histone acetylation of the exon 1_7 promoter in the offspring of low-LG mothers is associated with an increase in the binding of NGFI- A to the exon 1_7 promoter in the offspring of low-LG mothers, eliminating the maternal effect on NGFI-A binding to the exon 1_7 promoter. Comparable levels of NGFI-A binding to the exon 1_7 promoter then eliminate the maternal effect on hippocampal glucocorticoid receptor expression, such that glucocorticoid receptor levels in the adult offspring of low-LG mothers treated with the HDAC inhibitor are comparable to those in animals reared by high-LG mothers. And most importantly, the infusion of the HDAC inhibitor reversed the differences in the HPA response to stress.

HDAC inhibition increases NGFI-A binding to the exon 1_7 promoter in the offspring of low-LG mothers. The studies with neonates reveal that increased NGFI-A binding results in the demethylation of the 5′ CpG. In vitro, the introduction of a viral tool that leads to the increased expression of NGFI-A is sufficient to demethylate the exon 1_7 promoter. Weaver et al. (2007) argue that the binding of NGFI-A is critical for the demethylation of the 5′CpG site. The same effect is apparent in vivo and even with the adult animals used in the studies described above. HDAC infusion into the hippocampus increases NGFI-A binding to the exon 1_7 promoter in the adult offspring of low-LG mothers and decreases the level of methylation of the 5′CpG site on the exon 1_7 promoter. Another study (Weaver et al. 2005) showed that the reverse pattern of results could be obtained in response to the infusion of methionine into the hippocampus. The methionine infusion produced greater methylation of the 5′CpG in the offspring of high-LG mothers, decreased NGFI-A binding and GR expression, and increased HPA responses to stress (Weaver et al. 2005).

Although these studies employ rather crude pharmacological manipulations, the results are critical as they suggest that fully mature neurons in an adult animal express the necessary enzymatic machinery to demethylate or remethylate DNA. The importance of this plasticity at the level of DNA methylation is revealed in subsequent studies of cognition (see below), which suggest that dynamic modification of DNA methylation in critical neuronal populations in adult animals is involved in specific forms of learning and memory.

ACTIVITY-DEPENDENT REGULATION OF THE EPIGENOME

The maternal effect on the epigenetic state of the glucocorticoid receptor exon 1_7 promoter and glucocorticoid receptor gene expression is apparent over the first week of life and occurs in response to an increased NGFI-A signal in hippocampal neurons. The increased expression of NGFI-A and its binding to the exon 1_7 GR promoter over the first week of life are activated by maternal behavior (Weaver et al. 2007, Zhang et al. 2009). An increase in the expression of NGFI-A is associated with synaptic plasticity and with learning and memory (Dragunow 1996, Jones et al. 2001, Knapska & Kaczmarek 2004, Li et al. 2005, O'Donovan et al. 1999). Thus it is not surprising that the offspring of high-LG mothers show increased synaptic density both in early life (Liu et al. 2000) and in adulthood (Bagot et al. 2009, Bredy et al. 2003, Champagne et al. 2008, Liu et al. 2000).

Such events occur as a function of a series of activity-dependent changes in neuronal activity triggered by the action of glutamate at the NMDA receptor site (Ali & Salter 2001, Bear & Malenka 1994, Malenka & Nicoll 1993, Morris & Frey 1997). Thus, it is possible that environmentally driven changes in neuronal transcriptional signals could potentially remodel the methylation state of specific regions of the DNA (Meaney & Szyf 2005, Sng & Meaney 2009). These effects could, in turn, prove essential for sustained alterations in synaptic function.

Learning and long-term memory commonly require changes in gene expression and protein synthesis (Alberini et al. 1995, Kandel 2001, Lynch 2004). As described above, gene transcription is associated with chromatin remodeling engineered by enzymes that modify the histone proteins within chromatin complexes. A number of the intracellular signals that are crucial for learning and memory are in fact enzymes that modify histone proteins. One example is that of the CREB-binding protein, which functions as a histone acetyltransferase and is strongly implicated in cognitive function (e.g., Alarcon et al. 2004). Thus, contextual fear conditioning, which is a hippocampus-dependent learning paradigm whereby an animal associates a novel context with an aversive stimulus, is accompanied by increased acetylation of histone H3 (Levenson et al. 2004). Likewise, there is evidence for the importance of epigenetic modifications of histones in the amygdala during fear conditioning (Yeh et al. 2004). Interestingly, extinction of the conditioned fear response is associated with increased histone acetylation in the prefrontal cortex, which mediates the inhibition of conditioned fear responses (Bredy et al. 2007). The CREB-binding protein is probably involved in the relevant histone modifications. Mice that are heterozygous for a dysfunction form of the CREB-binding protein show significant impairments in multiple forms of hippocampal-dependent, long-term memory (Bourtchouladze et al. 2003, Korzus et al. 2004, Wood et al. 2006; also see Guan et al. 2002,

Vecsey et al. 2007). Importantly, the cognitive impairments are reversed with HDAC administration, suggesting that CREB-binding protein-induced histone acetylation mediates effects on learning and memory.

There is also evidence for the importance of dynamic changes in DNA methylation at specific sites during learning and memory. Fear conditioning results in the rapid methylation and transcriptional silencing of the gene for protein phosphatase 1 (PP1), which suppresses learning. The same training results in the demethylation and transcriptional activation of the synaptic plasticity gene reelin. These findings imply that both DNA methylation and demethylation might be involved in long-term memory consolidation.

BDNF has been implicated in adult neural plasticity, including learning and memory (West 2001). The genomic structure of the *Bdnf* gene contains multiple promoters that generate mRNAs containing different noncoding exons spliced upstream of a common coding exon (Timmusk et al. 1993). This organization is somewhat like that described above for the glucocorticoid receptor (**Figure 1**). In the case of BDNF, the exon IV promoter in rat is activated upon membrane depolarization in cultured cortical and hippocampal neurons by means of KCl, which leads to calcium influx, activating signaling cascades and inducing the expression of an array of genes that are involved in neural plasticity (West 2001).

Importantly, the activity-dependent *Bdnf* gene is also regulated through epigenetic modifications that involve dynamic changes in DNA methylation and the association of methylated-DNA binding proteins to the relevant sites on the *bdnf* promoter. Thus, increased DNA methylation of the exon IV promoter at sites that bind to transcriptional activators is associated with the presence of the methylated-DNA-binding protein, MeCP2, and a decreased level of *bdnf* expression. This transcriptionally quiescent state prior to depolarization is also associated with the presence of histone deacetylases (i.e., HDAC1) and mSIN3A, which form a common repressor complex. Membrane depolarization of the neuron leads to a decrease in CpG methylation and a dissociation of MeCP2-related repressor complex from the exon IV promoter. As described above for the glucocorticoid receptor, the decrease in CpG methylation is then associated with an increase in histone acetylation and the binding of the transcription factor, CREB. CREB is known to activate *bdnf* expression. These data suggest that DNA methylation at a particular site can suppress activity-dependent transcription of *Bdnf*. These findings also indicate that DNA methylation patterns in postmitotic neurons can undergo dynamic changes in response to neuronal activation, and a lower level of DNA methylation correlates with a higher level of *Bdnf* gene transcription in neurons.

Interestingly, MeCP2 levels increase as neurons mature (Zoghbi 2003). The high level of MeCP2 protein in mature neurons is consistent with a possible role for MeCP2 in synaptic remodeling associated with learning and memory (Zhou et al. 2006). Further supporting a role for MeCP2 in mature synaptic function and plasticity, Mecp2-null mice exhibit abnormalities in dendritic arborization (Chen et al. 2003, Kishi & Macklis 2004), basal synaptic transmission (Moretti et al. 2006), presynaptic function (Asaka et al. 2006, Moretti et al. 2006, Nelson et al. 2006), excitatory synaptic plasticity (Asaka et al. 2006, Moretti et al. 2006), and hippocampal and amygdalar learning (Moretti et al. 2006, Pelka et al. 2006). Zhou et al. (2006) found that neuronal activity (membrane depolarization) is associated with a phosphorylation of MeCP2 at Serine421 that led to its dissociation from the *bdnf* exon IV promoter and an increase in *bdnf* expression (also see Chen et al. 2003). Importantly, activity-dependent increases in BDNF levels are blocked in cells bearing a mutant version of MeCP2 that is unable to undergo phosphorylation. Glutamate is a primary neural signal for synaptic plasticity, and both glutamate as well as the direct activation of its NMDA receptor produced MeCP2 phosphorylation in neurons. Glutamate activates NMDA receptors, resulting in a neuronal calcium influx and the activation of calcium-modulated kinase II

(CaMKII), which regulates synaptic plasticity (Lisman et al. 2002). Zhou et al. (2006) found that CaMKII actively phosphorylates MeCP2.

The protein phosphorylation occurring at MeCP2 in response to neuronal activation is a transient event. The results described above (Martinowich et al. 2003) suggest that neuronal activation can lead to changes in DNA methylation, which is a potentially more stable, epigenetic alteration that could conceivably result in a long-term change in *bdnf* expression. Thus far, this review has considered the relation between DNA methylation, histone acetylation/deacetylation, transcription factor binding, and gene expression. However, there is evidence that the chromatin alterations can alter DNA methylation. Thus, HDAC inhibitors result in an increase in histone acetylation, enhanced transcription factor binding, and decreased DNA methylation. Such effects were described above in relation to DNA methylation and glucocorticoid receptor expression (Weaver et al. 2004, 2005). Thus, it is possible that (*a*) neuronal activation leads to the transient phosphorylation of MeCP2 and its dissociation from the exon IV *bdnf* promoter and (*b*) an increase in histone acetylation and CREB binding, producing increased *bdnf* expression; and that (*c*) the histone acetylation and CREB binding are also associated with DNA demethylation, as described above in the case of the glucocorticoid receptor for histone acetylation and NGFI-A binding. Such events could underlie a common process of activity-dependent modification of DNA methylation (Meaney & Szyf 2005).

Studies by Sweatt and colleagues suggest that the changes in DNA methylation at the exon IV *bdnf* promoter are involved in specific forms of learning and memory (Sweatt 2009). *Bdnf* gene expression increases in the hippocampus with contextual and spatial learning and appears essential for the synaptic remodeling that accompanies such forms of learning and memory (Hall et al. 2000, Linnarsson et al. 1997). NMDA receptor activation is critical for both contextual (Maren & Quirk 2000) and spatial (Morris et al. 2003) learning as well as for the increase in *bdnf expression* that accompanies such events. Lubin et al. (2008) found that contextual fear conditioning was associated with a demethylation of the exon IV *bdnf* promoter and an increase in *bdnf* expression: Both effects were blocked with a glutamate receptor antagonist. Taken together, these findings suggest that the activity-dependent changes in neuronal activity that associate with learning and memory induce a dynamic alteration in DNA methylation that, in turn, subserves the sustained changes in gene expression critical for long-term memory. Although this remains a working hypothesis, the findings discussed above further emphasize the degree to which neuronal activation can structurally remodel the genome and alters its operation.

Interestingly, there is also evidence that environmental influences prevailing during early development may determine the capacity for such activity-driven, epigenetic modifications. Disruptions to mother–infant interactions during early development are associated with alterations in hippocampal *bdnf* expression (Branchi et al. 2006; Lippman et al. 2007; Roceri et al. 2002, 2004; but also see Griesen et al. 2005) and increased DNA methylation at the exon IV *bdnf* promoter (Roth et al. 2009). Rearing mice in a communal nest, with three mothers and their litters, increases maternal care toward the offspring, which in turn is associated with increased BDNF expression (Branchi et al. 2006). And in the rat, the offspring of high-LG mothers show decreased MeCP2 association with the exon IV *bdnf* promoter (Weaver et al. 2007) and increased *bdnf* expression (Liu et al. 2000). Such maternal effects might bias in favor of reduced capacity for epigenetic remodeling at this critical site and restrain synaptic plasticity associated with learning and memory.

Summary (and Perhaps Some Constraints)

Studies over the past five years have created considerable enthusiasm for epigenetic models of the effects of early experience, synaptic plasticity, and neural function. The hypothesis underlying this approach considers epigenetic effects on gene expression as a candidate mechanism for the effects of environmental signals on the future behavior of the organism. This hypothesis is particularly attractive for those examining the sustained effects of early experience or of chronic, biologically relevant events in adulthood (e.g., environmental enrichment, chronic stress) on gene expression and neural function. Mature neurons undergo considerable changes in phenotype and are therefore an ideal cell population for epigenetic regulation. Nevertheless, there are constraints on the influence of epigenetic marks. For example, the effects of DNA methylation on gene expression are influenced by the organization of the relevant genomic region. DNA methylation appears to have a reduced effect on gene expression in regions that have a very high density of cytosine-guanine paired sites (Weber et al. 2007). Moreover, much of the DNA within a cell is packed tightly in heterochromatin (Fraser & Bickmore 2007) and is probably inaccessible to environmentally induced chromatin remodeling signals. Thus, the infusion of an HDAC inhibitor directly into the adult hippocampus alters the expression of only about 2% of all the genes normally expressed in the rat hippocampus (Weaver et al. 2006). Were the entire genome subject to dynamic epigenetic regulation such as described above for the *bdnf* gene, then we could expect this percentage to be substantially higher. It is likely that there is a pool of genes that retains the capacity for dynamic environmental regulation through epigenetic mechanisms. Of course this begs questions concerning the factors that determine the nature and contents of such pools. These considerations notwithstanding, it appears that with neurons, a number of genes are closely related to synaptic plasticity and neural function and are subject to dynamic regulation through epigenetic mechanisms, including DNA methylation.

Epigenetics refers to a collection of chemical modifications that occur to histones or directly on the DNA. These modifications, in turn, alter gene transcription. One might argue that in defining such mechanisms we have, in effect, simply better defined the processes that regulate gene transcription. Although the value of such findings is obvious for molecular biology, how might such processes revise our thinking at the level of the systems sciences? We suggest that these findings provide researchers with a renewed appreciation of the environmental regulation of cellular activity. We now understand the physical basis for the Hebbian synapse (Hebb 1958), whereby environmental signals activate intracellular pathways that result in the remodeling of synaptic connections in a manner that influences subsequent activity at relevant sites. There is a physical reference for the process of neuroplasticity. Epigenetic modifications provide the mechanism for a comparable level of plasticity at the level of the genome. We once thought of synaptic connections as being fixed, immutable to further changes beyond some critical period in development. Studies of synaptic plasticity revised our appreciation of the brain, revealing instead a dynamic tissue, subject to constant remodeling through the environmental activation of activity-dependent synaptic plasticity. The study of epigenetics suggests a comparable process at the level of the genome, also once considered a constant, static source of influence. Indeed, we must emphasize that epigenetic modifications do not alter DNA sequence. The product of the glucocorticoid receptor gene is unaffected by epigenetic marks. However, it appears that the operation of the genome is indeed subject to environmental regulation in a manner that may be no less dynamic than that of synaptic connections.

Recent studies from Nestler and colleagues reveal considerable epigenetic modification at specific genomic sites associated with chronic stress or repeated exposure to psychostimulant drugs, both of which produce sustained influences on behavior (Nestler 2009, Renthal et al. 2009). Although such effects have yet to be reported for DNA methylation, modifications of histone proteins are associated with exposure to drugs of abuse and stressors in rodent models (Renthal et al. 2009, Renthal & Nestler

2008). These findings suggest that epigenetic states, including DNA methylation, are altered by a wide range of biologically relevant events (Meaney & Szyf 2005, Renthal & Nestler 2008, Szyf et al. 2005). Such epigenetic modifications might therefore underlie a wide range of stable changes in neural function following exposure to highly salient events (e.g., chronic stress, drugs of abuse, reproductive phases such as parenting) and are thus logical mechanisms for environmentally induced alterations in mental health (Akbarian & Huang 2009, Jiang et al. 2008, Tsankova et al. 2007).

EPIGENETICS AND MENTAL HEALTH

Emerging evidence links the alterations in gene expression associated with DNA methylation to psychiatric illness. Cortical dysfunction in schizophrenia is associated with changes in GABAergic circuitry (Benes & Berretta 2001). This effect is associated with a decrease in the expression of the $GAD1$ gene that encodes for a specific form of glutamic acid decarboxylase (GAD_{67}), one to two key enzymes for GABA synthesis in cortical interneurons. There is compelling evidence for the decreased expression of GAD_{67} in cortical tissues from schizophrenic patients (Akbarian & Huang 2006, Costa et al. 2004). The dysregulated GAD_{67} expression in the chandelier GABA neurons is thought to result in disruption of synchronized cortical activity and impairment of executive functions in schizophrenia subjects (Lewis et al. 2005). Likewise, allelic variation in $GAD1$ is associated with schizophrenia (Straub et al. 2007).

In addition to GAD_{67}, there is also a decrease in cortical expression of reelin in schizophrenic brains (Eastwood & Harrison 2003); reelin is closely associated with synaptic plasticity. The same GABAergic neurons in the schizophrenic brain that express reelin and GAD_{67} exhibit an increase in DNA methyltransferases 1 (DNMT1; Veldic et al. 2004). DNMT1 is a member of a family of enzymes that transfers a methyl group from the methyl donor *S*-adenosyl-methionine (SAM) onto cytosines, thus producing DNA methylation. The promoter for the *reelin* gene shows increased methylation in the brains of patients with schizophrenia compared with control subjects (Abdolmaleky et al. 2005, Grayson et al. 2005). Kundakovic et al. (2007) showed that the inhibition of DNMT1 in neuronal cell lines resulted in the increased expression of both reelin and GAD_{67}. The increase in gene expression was associated with a decreased association of MeCP2, further suggesting that these differences are associated with alteration in DNA methylation. Recall that maternal care directly alters DNA methylation of the GAD_{67} promoter in the rat (Zhang et al. 2009). This effect is associated with a decrease in DNMT1 expression and reduced MeCP2 association with the *GAD1* promoter.

An important question is that of the developmental origins of such differences in DNA methylation. A set of recent studies (McGowan et al. 2009) suggests that epigenetic modifications might occur in humans in response to variations in parent–offspring interactions. DNA was extracted from hippocampal samples obtained from victims of suicide or from individuals who had died suddenly from other causes (auto accidents, heart attacks, etc.). The samples were obtained from the Québec Suicide Brain Bank, which conducts forensic phenotyping that includes a validated assessment of psychiatric status and developmental history (e.g., McGirr et al. 2008). The studies examined the methylation status of the exon 1_F promoter of the glucocorticoid receptor, which corresponds to the exon 1_7 promoter in the rat (Turner & Muller 2005). The results showed increased DNA methylation of the exon 1_F promoter in hippocampal samples from suicide victims compared with controls, but only if suicide was accompanied with a developmental history of child maltreatment. Child maltreatment, independent of psychiatric state, predicted the DNA methylation status of the exon 1_F promoter. As in the previous rodent studies, the methylation state of the exon 1_F promoter also determined the ability of NGFI-A to bind to the promoter and activate gene transcription. Although such studies are obviously correlational and limited by postmortem approaches, the results are nevertheless consistent with the hypothesis that variations in parental care can modify the epigenetic state of selected sites of the human genome. Moreover, the findings are also consistent with studies that link childhood abuse to individual differences in stress responses (Heim et al. 2000). Childhood abuse is associated with an increase in pituitary ACTH responses to stress among individuals with or without concurrent major depression. These findings are particularly relevant, since pituitary ACTH directly reflects central activation of the HPA stress response, and hippocampal glucocorticoid receptor activation dampens HPA activity. The findings in humans are consistent with the rodent studies cited above investigating epigenetic regulation of the glucocorticoid receptor gene and with the hypothesis that early life events can alter the epigenetic state of relevant genomic regions, the expression of which may contribute to individual differences in the risk for psychopathology (Holsboer 2000, Neigh & Nemeroff 2006, Schatzberg et al. 1985).

Certain limitations need to be considered as we integrate epigenetics into the study of psychopathology. The study of epigenetic mechanisms in humans is complicated by the fact that epigenetic marks are often tissue-specific. For example, the brain contains some neurons that synthesize and release dopamine as a neurotransmitter and others that rely on acetylcholine. We might assume that among dopaminergic neurons, the genes associated with the capacity for acetylcholine production are silenced, likely through some level of epigenetic regulation. Such processes are inherent in the specialization of brain cells, as with all other differentiated cells in the body. This process of specialization involves epigenetic regulation and implies that the epigenetic marks vary from cell type to cell type. Indeed, there is considerable variation in epigenetic marks from one brain region to another, perhaps even more so than variation within the same brain region across individuals (Ladd-Acosta et al. 2007). Brain samples are for the most part beyond direct examination in the living individual at the level of molecular analysis. This often leaves us with measures of DNA extracted from blood or saliva and with the question of whether the epigenetic marks within such samples actually reflect those within the relevant neuronal population. Thus, for the time being advances in the study of "neuroepigenetics" will rely heavily on relevant models with nonhuman species as well as complementary studies of samples from postmortem human brains.

CONCLUSIONS

It is now evident that genomic variation at the level of nucleotide sequence is associated with individual differences in personality and thus with vulnerability and resistance to a wide range of chronic illness (Ebstein 2006, Meyer-Lindenberg & Weinberger 2006, Rutter 2007). The challenge is how to conceptually integrate the findings from genetics into psychology. The operation of the genome is regulated by cellular signals that are responsive to environmental conditions. Thus, the effects of genetic variation are contextually determined and therefore best considered as probabilistic. Genetic variations influence cellular activity and, depending upon current and past environmental conditions, will bias toward particular functional outcomes. The molecular events that mediate gene transcription reveal the interdependence of gene and environment (Sokolowski 2001, Sokolowski & Wahlsten 2001). Oddly, what is perhaps the most profound comment on this issue dates back several years. In response to a question from a journalist considering the relative importance of nature versus nurture in defining individual differences in personality, Hebb responded that such comparisons are akin to asking what contributes more to the area of rectangle, the length or the width? The recent flush of studies examining gene x environment effects on personality and vulnerability/resistance to mental illness (Caspi et al. 2003, Meaney 2009, Rutter 2007, Suomi 2006)

reflects the interdependence of genetic and environmental influences, such that the effects at one level can only be understood within the context of the other. Indeed, developmental processes are best considered as the outcome of a constant dialog between the genome and its environment (Bateson 1994; Gottelieb 1997, 1998; Lewontin 1974).

The gene x environment perspective is critical in the establishment of an understanding of the development of individual differences in neural function and personality. Until recently, most experimental approaches were limited to identifying factors that could influence neural development. Our own studies of maternal care in the rat are a case in point. This research examines the effects of variation in maternal care in animals that are housed from weaning onward under identical conditions. We systematically minimize variation from weaning onward. This approach permits conclusions as to the potential effects of variations in maternal care but cannot estimate the importance of such effects for individual differences in adult function under natural conditions. Indeed, environmental enrichment in the postweaning period can reverse effects associated with the variations in maternal care (Bredy et al. 2004, Champagne & Meaney 2006, Zhang et al. 2006). Likewise, studies of monozygotic-dizygotic twins examine what are, in effect, differences in parental gene dosage while minimizing variation in the early environment. Such approaches have provided convincing evidence that genetic factors can influence the development of individual differences, but do not identify how. Indeed, the challenge is to define how, when, and under which conditions specific genetic or environment factors operate to regulate development. Herein lies the enormous contribution of the gene x environment perspective, particularly when integrated into longitudinal studies of development.

The excitement concerning the findings in the area of epigenetics derives from the realization that such mechanisms could form the biological basis for the interplay between environmental signals and the genome. The studies reviewed here suggest that (*a*) epigenetic remodeling occurs in response to the environmental activation of the classic "activity-dependent" cellular signaling pathways that are associated with synaptic plasticity, (*b*) epigenetic marks, particularly DNA methylation, are actively remodeled over early development in response to environmental events that regulate neural development and function, and (*c*) epigenetic marks at histone proteins and the DNA are subject to remodeling in response to environmental influences even at later stages in development. We have highlighted examples of environmental influences that are of obvious relevance for psychologists. However, increasing evidence from animal studies indicates that prenatal and early postnatal environmental factors, including nutritional supplements, xenobiotic chemicals, and reproductive technologies, can alter the epigenetic state of specific genomic regions (Jirtle & Skinner 2007).

These findings suggest that epigenetic remodeling might serve as an ideal mechanism for phenotypic plasticity—the process whereby the environment interacts with the genome to produce individual differences in the expression of specific traits. One could easily imagine that such processes mediate observed discordances between monozygotic twins (Petronis 2006, Weksberg et al. 2002). Thus, differences at the level of experience might lead to discordance in the nature of the epigenetic marks at specific sites in the genome, leading to differences in phenotype despite a common genotype. If this is the case, then one might expect an increasing degree of discordance in epigenetic marks over time among monozygotic twins, and there is indeed evidence for such an effect (Fraga et al. 2005). The same processes are likely to account for instances of statistical gene–environment interactions, whereby the genotype–phenotype relation is apparent in one environmental context but not in another (Sokolowski & Wahlsten 2000). In such cases, we could imagine an environmentally regulated epigenetic mark that alters the functional consequences of a genomic variation in sequence. Because the operation of the genome is determined by both sequence-based variation as well as epigenetic state, the process of environmentally regulated plasticity of the epigenome emerges as an exciting context for the integration of genetics and psychology.

DISCLOSURE STATEMENT

The authors are not aware of any biases that might be perceived as affecting the objectivity of this review.

ACKNOWLEDGMENTS

Research support for MJM is provided by the National Institutes of Health, the Canadian Institutes for Health Research, the Natural Sciences and Engineering Research Council of Canada, and the Human Frontiers Science Program. Research support for T-YZ is provided by the National Alliance for Research in Schizophrenia and Affective Disorders.

LITERATURE CITED

Abdolmaleky HM, Cheng K, Russo A, Smith CL, Faraone SV, et al. 2005. Hypermethylation of the reelin (RELN) promoter in the brain of schizophrenic patients: a preliminary report. *Am. J. Med. Genet. B Neuropsychiatr. Genet.* 134:60–66

Akbarian S, Huang HS. 2006. Molecular and cellular mechanisms of altered GAD1/GAD67 expression in schizophrenia and related disorders. *Brain Res. Brain Res. Rev.* 52:293–304

Akbarian S, Huang HS. 2009. Epigenetic regulation in human brain-focus on histone lysine methylation. *Biol. Psychiatry* 65:198–203

Alarcon JM, Malleret G, Touzani K, Vronskaya S, Ishii S, et al. 2004. Chromatin acetylation, memory, and LTP are impaired in CBP+/− mice: a model for the cognitive deficit in Rubinstein-Taybi syndrome and its amelioration. *Neuron* 42(6):947–59

Alberini CM, Ghirardi M, Huang YY, Nguyen PV, Kandel ER. 1995. A molecular switch for the consolidation of long-term memory: cAMP-inducible gene expression. *Ann. N. Y. Acad. Sci.* 758:261–86

Ali DW, Salter MW. 2001. NMDA receptor regulation by Src kinase signaling in excitatory synaptic transmission and plasticity. *Curr. Opin. Neurobiol.* 11(3):336–42

Asaka Y, Jugloff DG, Zhang L, Eubanks JH, Fitzsimonds RM. 2006. Hippocampal synaptic plasticity is impaired in the Mecp2-null mouse model of Rett syndrome. *Neurobiol. Dis.* 21:217–27

Bagot RC, van Hasselt FN, Champagne DL, Meaney MJ, Krugers HJ, Joëls M. 2009. Maternal care determines rapid effects of stress mediators on synaptic plasticity in adult rat hippocampal dentate gyrus. *Neurobiol. Learn. Mem.* In press

Bale TL, Vale WW. 2004. CRF and CRF receptors: role in stress responsivity and other behaviors. *Annu. Rev. Pharmacol. Toxicol.* 44:525–57

Bateson P. 1994. The dynamics of parent-offspring relationships in mammals. *Trends Ecol. Evol.* 9:399–403

Bateson P, Barker D, Clutton-Brock T, Deb D, D'Udine B, et al. 2004. Developmental plasticity and human health. *Nature* 430:419–21

Bear MF, Malenka RC. 1994. Synaptic plasticity: LTP and LTD. *Curr. Opin. Neurobiol.* 4(3):389–99

Benes FM, Berretta S. 2001. GABAergic interneurons: implications for understanding schizophrenia and bipolar disorder. *Neuropsychopharmacology* 25:1–27

Bestor TH. 1998. Gene silencing. Methylation meets acetylation. *Nature* 393:311–12

Bird AP. 1986. CpG-rich islands and the function of DNA methylation. *Nature* 321:209–13

Bird AP. 2002. DNA methylation patterns and epigenetic memory. *Genes Dev.* 16:6–21

Bird AP. 2007. Perceptions of epigenetics. *Nature* 447:396–98

Bird AP, Wolffe AP. 1999. Methylation-induced repression—belts, braces, and chromatin. *Cell* 99:451–54

Bourtchouladze R, Lidge R, Catapano R, Stanley J, Gossweiler S, et al. 2003. A mouse model of Rubinstein-Taybi syndrome: Defective long-term memory is ameliorated by inhibitors of phosphodiesterase 4. *Proc. Natl. Acad. Sci. USA* 100:10518–22

Branchi I, D'Andrea I, Fiore M, Di Fausto V, Aloe L, Alleva E. 2006. Early social enrichment shapes social behavior and nerve growth factor and brain-derived neurotrophic factor levels in the adult mouse brain. *Biol. Psychiatry* 60:690–96

Brandeis M, Frank D, Keshet I, Siegfried Z, Mendelsohn M, et al. 1994. Sp1 elements protect a CpG island from de novo methylation. *Nature* 371:435–38

Bredy TW, Humpartzoomian RA, Cain DP, Meaney MJ. 2003. The influence of maternal care and environmental enrichment on hippocampal development and function in the rat. *Neuroscience* 118:571–76

Bredy TW, Wu H, Crego C, Zellhoefer J, Sun YE, Barad M. 2007. Histone modifications around individual BDNF gene promoters in prefrontal cortex are associated with extinction of conditioned fear. *Learn. Mem.* 14:268–76

Bredy TW, Zhang TY, Grant RJ, Diorio J, Meaney MJ. 2004. Peripubertal environmental enrichment reverses the effects of maternal care on hippocampal development and glutamate receptor subunit expression. *Eur. J. Neurosci.* 20:1355–62

Bruniquel D, Schwartz RH. 2003. Selective, stable demethylation of the interleukin-2 gene enhances transcription by an active process. *Nat. Immunol.* 4:235–40

Burton CL, Chatterjee D, Chatterjee-Chakraborty M, Lovic V, Grella SL, et al. 2007. Prenatal restraint stress and motherless rearing disrupts expression of plasticity markers and stress-induced corticosterone release in adult female Sprague-Dawley rats. *Brain Res.* 1158:28–38

Caldji C, Diorio J, Meaney MJ. 2003. Variations in maternal care alter GABAA receptor subunit expression in brain regions associated with fear. *Neuropsychopharmacology* 28:150–59

Caldji C, Francis DD, Sharma S, Plotsky PM, Meaney MJ. 2000. The effects of early rearing environment on the development of GABAA and central benzodiazepine receptor levels and novelty-induced fearfulness in the rat. *Neuropsychopharmacology* 22:219–29

Caldji C, Tannenbaum B, Sharma S, Francis DD, Plotsky PM, Meaney MJ. 1998. Maternal care during infancy regulates the development of neural systems mediating the expression of behavioral fearfulness in adulthood in the rat. *Proc. Natl. Acad. Sci. USA* 95:5335–40

Cameron N, Parent C, Champagne FA, Fish E, Ozaki-Kuroda K, Meaney MJ. 2005. The programming of individual differences in defensive responses and reproductive strategies in the rat through variations in maternal care. *Neurosci. Biobehav. Rev.* 29:843–65

Caspi A, Sugden K, Moffitt TE, Taylor A, Craig IW, et al. 2003. Influence of life stress on depression: moderation by a polymorphism in the 5-HTT gene. *Science* 301:386–89

Champagne DL, Bagot RC, van Hasselt F, Ramakers G, Meaney MJ, et al. 2008. Maternal care alters dendritic length, spine density and synaptic potentiation in adulthood. *J. Neurosci.* 28:6037–45

Champagne FA. 2008. Epigenetic mechanisms and the transgenerational effects of maternal care. *Front. Neuroendocrinol.* 29:386–97

Champagne FA, Francis DD, Mar A, Meaney MJ. 2003. Naturally-occurring variations in maternal care in the rat as a mediating influence for the effects of environment on the development of individual differences in stress reactivity. *Physiol. Behav.* 79:359–71

Champagne FA, Meaney MJ. 2006. Stress during gestation alters postpartum maternal care and the development of the offspring in a rodent model. *Biol. Psychiatry* 59:1227–35

Champagne FA, Weaver ICG, Diorio J, Dymov S, Szyf M, Meaney MJ. 2006. Maternal care regulates methylation of the estrogen receptor alpha 1b promoter and estrogen receptor alpha expression in the medial preoptic area of female offspring. *Endocrinology* 147:2909–15

Charalambous M, da Rocha ST, Ferguson-Smith AC. 2007. Genomic imprinting, growth control and the allocation of nutritional resources: consequences for postnatal life. *Curr. Opin. Endocrinol. Diabetes Obes.* 14:3–12

Chen WG, Chang Q, Lin Y, Meissner A, West AE, et al. 2003. Derepression of BDNF transcription involves calcium-dependent phosphorylation of MeCP2. *Science* 302:793–95

Cooney CA, Dave AA, Wolff GL. 2002. Maternal methyl supplements in mice affect epigenetic variation and DNA methylation of offspring. *J. Nutr.* 132:2393–400

Costa E, Davis JM, Dong E, Grayson DR, Guidotti A, et al. 2004. A GABAergic cortical deficit dominates schizophrenia pathophysiology. *Crit. Rev. Neurobiol.* 16:1–23

da Rocha ST, Ferguson-Smith AC. 2004. Genomic imprinting. *Curr. Biol.* 14:R646–99

Dragunow M. 1996. A role for immediate-early transcription factors in learning and memory. *Behav. Genet.* 26(3):293–99

Eastwood SL, Harrison PJ. 2003. Interstitial white matter neurons express less reelin and are abnormally distributed in schizophrenia: towards an integration of molecular and morphologic aspects of the neurodevelopmental hypothesis. *Mol. Psychiatry* 769:821–31

Ebstein RP. 2003. Relation of shyness in grade school children to the genotype for the long form of the serotonin transporter promoter region polymorphism. *Am. J. Psychiatry* 160:671–76

Ebstein RP. 2006. The molecular genetic architecture of human personality: beyond self-report questionnaires. *Mol. Psychiatry* 11:427–45

Eden A, Gaudet F, Waghmare A, Jaenisch R. 2003. Chromosomal instability and tumors promoted by DNA hypomethylation. *Science* 300:455

Fan G, Martinowich K, Chin MH, He F, Fouse SD, et al. 2005. DNA methylation controls the timing of astrogliogenesis through regulation of JAK-STAT signaling. *Development* 132:3345–56

Feinberg AP. 2007. Phenotypic plasticity and the epigenetics of human disease. *Nature* 447:433–40

Fenoglio KA, Brunson KL, Avishai-Eliner S, Stone BA, Kapadia BJ, Baram TZ. 2005. Enduring, handling-evoked enhancement of hippocampal memory function and glucocorticoid receptor expression involves activation of the corticotropin-releasing factor type 1 receptor. *Endocrinology* 146:4090–96

Fraga MF, Ballestar E, Paz MF, Setien F, Ballestar ML, et al. 2005. Epigenetic differences arise during the lifetime of monozygotic twins. *Proc. Natl. Acad. Sci. USA* 102:10604–9

Francis DD, Diorio J, Liu D, Meaney MJ. 1999. Nongenomic transmission across generations in maternal behavior and stress responses in the rat. *Science* 286:1155–58

Fraser P, Bickmore W. 2007. Nuclear organization of the genome and the potential for gene regulation. *Nature* 447:413–17

Gilbert SF. 2006. *Developmental Biology*. Sunderland, MA: Sinauer

Gluckman PD, Hanson MA. 2004. Living with the past: evolution, development, and patterns of disease. *Science* 305:1733–36

Gluckman PD, Hanson MA. 2007. Developmental plasticity and human disease: research directions. *J. Intern. Med.* 261:461–71

Gonzalez A, Lovic V, Ward GR, Wainwright PE, Fleming AS. 2001. Intergenerational effects of complete maternal deprivation and replacement stimulation on maternal behavior and emotionality in female rats. *Dev. Psychobiol.* 38:11–32

Gottlieb G. 1997. *Synthesizing Nature-Nurture*. Mahwah, NJ: Erlbaum

Gottlieb G. 1998. Normally occurring environmental and behavioral influences on gene activity: from central dogma to probabilistic epigenesis. *Psychol. Rev.* 105:792–892

Grayson DR, Jia X, Chen Y, Sharma RP, Mitchell CP, et al. 2005. Reelin promoter hypermethylation in schizophrenia. *Proc. Natl. Acad. Sci. USA* 102:9341–46

Grunstein M. 1997. Histone acetylation in chromatin structure and transcription. *Nature* 389:349–52

Guan Z, Giustetto M, Lomvardas S, Kim JH, Miniaci MC, et al. 2002. Integration of long-term-memory-related synaptic plasticity involves bidirectional regulation of gene expression and chromatin structure. *Cell* 111:483–93

Hake SB, Allis CD. 2006. Histone H3 variants and their potential role in indexing mammalian genomes: the "H3 barcode hypothesis." *Proc. Natl. Acad. Sci. USA* 103:6428–35

Hall J, Thomas KL, Everitt BJ. 2000. Rapid and selective induction of BDNF expression in the hippocampus during contextual learning. *Nat. Neurosci.* 3:533–35

Harper LV. 2005. Epigenetic inheritance and the intergenerational transfer of experience. *Psychol. Bull.* 131:340–60

Hebb DO. 1958. *Textbook of Psychology*. Philadelphia, PA: Saunders

Heim C, Newport DJ, Heit S, Graham YP, Wilcox M, et al. 2000. Pituitary-adrenal and autonomic responses to stress in women after sexual and physical abuse in childhood. *J. Am. Med. Assoc.* 284:592–97

Hellman A, Chess A. 2007. Gene body-specific methylation on the active X chromosome. *Science* 315:1141–43

Hofer MA. 2005. The psychobiology of early attachment. *Clin. Neurosci. Res.* 4:291–300

Holliday R. 1989. DNA methylation and epigenetic mechanisms. *Cell Biophys.* 15:15–20

Holsboer F. 2000. The corticosteroid receptor hypothesis of depression. *Neuropsychopharmacology* 23:477–501

Jenuwein T, Allis CD. 2001. Translating the histone code. *Science* 293:1074–80

Jiang Y, Langley B, Lubin FD, Renthal W, Wood MA, et al. 2008. Epigenetics in the nervous system. *J. Neurosci.* 28:11753–59

Jirtle RL, Skinner MK. 2007. Environmental epigenomics and disease susceptibility. *Nat. Rev. Genet.* 8:253–62

Jones MW, Errington ML, French PJ, Fine A, Bliss TV, et al. 2001. A requirement for the immediate early gene Zif268 in the expression of late LTP and long-term memories. *Nat. Neurosci.* 4:289–96

Jutapakdeegul N, Casalotti SO, Govitrapong P, Kotchabhakdi N. 2003. Postnatal touch stimulation acutely alters corticosterone levels and glucocorticoid receptor gene expression in the neonatal rat. *Dev. Neurosci.* 25:26–33

Kandel ER. 2001. The molecular biology of memory storage: a dialogue between genes and synapses. *Science* 294(5544):1030–38

Kendler KS. 2001. Twin studies of psychiatric illness: an update. *Arch. Gen. Psychiatry* 58(11):1005–14

Kishi N, Macklis JD. 2004. MECP2 is progressively expressed in post-migratory neurons and is involved in neuronal maturation rather than cell fate decisions. *Mol. Cell. Neurosci.* 27:306–21

Klose RJ, Bird AP. 2007. Genomic DNA methylation: the mark and its mediators. *Trends Biochem. Sci.* 31:89–97

Knapska E, Kaczmarek L. 2004. A gene for neuronal plasticity in the mammalian brain: Zif268/Egr-1/NGFI-A/Krox-24/TIS8/ZENK? *Prog. Neurobiol.* 74(4):183–211

Koob GF, Heinrichs SC, Menzaghi F, Pich EM, Britton KT. 1994. Corticotropin-releasing factor, stress and behavior. *Semin. Neurosci.* 6:221–29

Korzus E, Rosenfeld MG, Mayford M. 2004. CBP histone acetyltransferase activity is a critical component of memory consolidation. *Neuron* 42:961–72

Kundakovic M, Chen Y, Costa E, Grayson DR. 2007. DNA methyltransferase inhibitors coordinately induce expression of the human reelin and glutamic acid decarboxylase 67 genes. *Mol. Pharmacol.* 71:644–53

Ladd-Acosta C, Pevsner J, Sabunciyan S, Yolken RH, Webster MJ, et al. 2007. DNA methylation signatures within the human brain. *Am. J. Hum. Genet.* 81:1304–15

Laird PW. 2005. Cancer epigenetics. *Hum. Mol. Genet.* 14(Spec. No. 1):R65–76

Levenson JM, O'Riordan KJ, Brown KD, Trinh MA, Molfese DL, Sweatt JD. 2004. Regulation of histone acetylation during memory formation in the hippocampus. *J. Biol. Chem.* 279:40545–59

Levine S. 1994. The ontogeny of the hypothalamic-pituitary-adrenal axis. The influence of maternal factors. *Ann. N. Y. Acad. Sci.* 746:275–88

Lewis DA, Hashimoto T, Volk DW. 2005. Cortical inhibitory neurons and schizophrenia. *Nat. Rev. Neurosci.* 6:312–24

Lewontin RC. 1974. The analysis of variance and the analysis of causes. *Am. J. Hum. Genet.* 26:400–11

Linnarsson S, Björklund A, Ernfors P. 1997. Learning deficit in BDNF mutant mice. *Eur. J. Neurosci.* 9:2581–87

Lippmann M, Bress A, Nemeroff CB, Plotsky PM, Monteggia LM. 2007. Long-term behavioural and molecular alterations associated with maternal separation in rats. *Eur. J. Neurosci.* 25:3091–98

Lisman J, Schulman H, Cline H. 2002. The molecular basis of CaMKII function in synaptic and behavioral memory. *Nat. Rev. Neurosci.* 3:175–90

Liu D, Diorio J, Day JC, Francis DD, Mar A, Meaney MJ. 2000. Maternal care, hippocampal synaptogenesis and cognitive development in the rat. *Nat. Neurosci.* 3:799–806

Liu D, Diorio J, Tannenbaum B, Caldji C, Francis DD, et al. 1997. Maternal care, hippocampal glucocorticoid receptors and HPA responses to stress. *Science* 277:1659–62

Lubin FD, Roth TL, Sweatt JD. 2008. Epigenetic regulation of *bdnf* gene transcription in the consolidation of fear memory. *J. Neurosci.* 28:10576–86

Luger K, Mader AW, Richmond RK, Sargent DF, Richmond TJ. 1997. Crystal structure of the nucleosome coreparticle at 2.8 A resolution. *Nature* 389:251–60

Lynch MA. 2004. Long-term potentiation and memory. *Physiol. Rev.* 84:87–136

Malenka RC, Nicoll RA. 1993. NMDA-receptor-dependent synaptic plasticity: multiple forms and mechanisms. *Trends Neurosci.* 16(12):521–27

Maren S, Quirk GJ. 2000. Neuronal signaling of fear memory. *Nat. Rev. Neurosci.* 5:844–52

Martinowich K, Hattori D, Wu H, Fouse S, He F, et al. 2003. DNA methylation-related chromatin remodeling in activity-dependent BDNF gene regulation. *Science* 302:890–93

McCormick JA, Lyons V, Jacobson MD, Noble J, Diorio J, et al. 2000. 5′-heterogeneity of glucocorticoid receptor messenger RNA is tissue specific: differential regulation of variant transcripts by early-life events. *Mol. Endocrinol.* 14:506–17

McGirr A, Renaud J, Seguin M, Alda M, Turecki G. 2008. Course of major depressive disorder and suicide outcome: a psychological autopsy study. *J. Clin. Psychiatry* 69:966–70

McGowan PO, Sasaki A, Dymov S, Turecki G, Szyf M, Meaney MJ. 2009. Differential methylation of a neuron-enriched glucocorticoid receptor gene promoter in human hippocampus is associated with early child trauma and adult psychopathology. *Nature Neurosci.* 12:342–48

Meaney MJ. 2001. The development of individual differences in behavioral and endocrine responses to stress. *Annu. Rev. Neurosci.* 24:1161–92

Meaney MJ. 2007. Social influences on sexual differentiation in mammals. *Adv. Genet.* 59:173–215

Meaney MJ. 2009. Epigenetics and the biological definition of gene x environment interactions. *Child Dev.* In press

Meaney MJ, Diorio J, Donaldson L, Yau J, Chapman K, Seckl JR. 2000. Handling alters the expression of messenger RNAs for AP-2, NGFI-A and NGFI-B in the hippocampus of neonatal rats. *J. Neurosci.* 20:3936–45

Meaney MJ, Szyf M. 2005. Maternal effects as a model for environmentally-dependent chromatin plasticity. *Trends Neurosci.* 28:456–63

Meaney MJ, Szyf M, Seckl JR. 2007. Epigenetic mechanisms of perinatal programming of hypothalamic-pituitary-adrenal function and health. *Trends Mol. Med.* 13:269–77

Menard J, Champagne D, Meaney MJ. 2004. Maternal care alters behavioral and neural activity patterns in the defensive burying paradigm. *Neuroscience* 129:297–308

Meyer-Lindenberg A, Weinberger DR. 2006. Intermediate phenotypes and genetic mechanisms of psychiatric disorders. *Nat. Rev. Neurosci.* 7:818–27

Mitchell JB, Rowe W, Boksa P, Meaney MJ. 1990. Serotonin regulates type II corticosteroid receptor binding in hippocampal cell cultures. *J. Neurosci.* 10:1745–52

Mitchell JB, Betito K, Rowe W, Boksa P, Meaney MJ. 1992. Serotonergic regulation of type II corticosteroid receptor binding in cultured hippocampal cells: the role of serotonin-induced increases in cAMP levels. *Neuroscience* 48:631–39

Mohandas T, Sparkes RS, Shapiro LJ. 1981. Reactivation of an inactive human X chromosome: evidence for X inactivation by DNA methylation. *Science* 211:393–96

Moretti P, Levenson JM, Battaglia F, Atkinson R, Teague R, et al. 2006. Learning and memory and synaptic plasticity are impaired in a mouse model of Rett syndrome. *J. Neurosci.* 26:319–27

Morris RGM, Frey U. 1997. Hippocampal synaptic plasticity: role in spatial learning or the automatic recording of attended experience? *Philos. Trans. R. Soc. Lond. B Biol. Sci.* 352:1489–503

Morris RGM, Moser EI, Riedel G, Martin SJ, Sandin J, et al. 2003. Elements of a neurobiological theory of the hippocampus: the role of activity-dependent synaptic plasticity in memory. *Philos. Trans. R. Soc. Lond. B Biol. Sci.* 358:773–86

Mousseau TA, Fox CW. 1998. The adaptive significance of maternal effects. *Trends Ecol. Evol.* 13:403–7

Murayama A, Sakura K, Nakama M, Yasuzawa-Tanaka K, Fujita E, et al. 2006. A specific CpG site demethylation in the human interleukin 2 gene promoter is an epigenetic memory. *EMBO J.* 25:1081–92

Neigh GN, Nemeroff CB. 2006. Reduced glucocorticoid receptors: consequence or cause of depression? *Trends Endocrinol. Metab.* 17:124–25

Nelson ED, Kavalali ET, Monteggia LM. 2006. MeCP2-dependent transcriptional repression regulates excitatory neurotransmission. *Curr. Biol.* 16:710–16

Nestler EJ. 2009. Epigenetic mechanisms in psychiatry. *Biol. Psychiatry* 65:189–90

O'Donovan KJ, Tourtellotte WG, Millbrandt J, Baraban JM. 1999. The EGR family of transcription-regulatory factors: progress at the interface of molecular and systems neuroscience. *Trends Neurosci.* 22(4):167–73

Pelka GJ, Watson CM, Radziewic T, Hayward M, Lahooti H, et al. 2006. Mecp2 deficiency is associated with learning and cognitive deficits and altered gene activity in the hippocampal region of mice. *Brain* 129:887–98

Petronis A. 2006. Epigenetics and twins: three variations on the theme. *Trends Genet.* 22(7):347–50

Plomin R, Rutter M. 1998. Child development, molecular genetics, and what to do with genes once they are found. *Child Dev.* 69:1223–42

Plotsky PM, Cunningham ET Jr, Widmaier EP. 1989. Catecholaminergic modulation of corticotropin-releasing factor and adrenocorticotropin secretion. *Endocr. Rev.* 10:437–58

Razin A. 1998. CpG methylation, chromatin structure and gene silencing—a three-way connection. *EMBO J.* 17:4905–4908

Razin A, Riggs AD. 1980. DNA methylation and gene function. *Science* 210:604–10

Reik WJ. 2001. Genomic imprinting: parental influence on the genome. *Nature* 2:21–32

Renthal W, Maze I, Krishnan V, Covington HE 3rd, Xiao G, Kumar A, et al. 2009. Histone deacetylase 5 epigenetically controls behavioral adaptations to chronic emotional stimuli. *Neuron* 56:517–29

Renthal W, Nestler EJ. 2008. Epigenetic mechanisms in drug addiction. *Trends Mol. Med.* 14:341–50

Repetti RL, Taylor SE, Seeman TE. 2002. Risky families: family social environments and the mental and physical health of offspring. *Psychol. Bull.* 128:330–66

Riggs AD, Pfeifer GP. 1992. X-chromosome inactivation and cell memory. *Trends Genet.* 8:169–74

Roceri M, Cirulli F, Pessina C, Peretto P, Racagni G, Riva MA. 2004. Postnatal repeated maternal deprivation produces age-dependent changes of brain-derived neurotrophic factor expression in selected rat brain regions. *Biol. Psychiatry* 55:708–14

Roceri M, Hendriks W, Racagni G, Ellenbroek BA, Riva MA. 2002. Early maternal deprivation reduces the expression of BDNF and NMDA receptor subunits in rat hippocampus. *Mol. Psychiatry* 7:609–16

Rossiter MC. 1998. The role of environmental variation in parental effects expression. In *Maternal Effects as Adaptations*, ed. TA Mousseau, CW Fox, pp. 112–36. London: Oxford Univ. Press

Roth TL, Lubin FD, Funk AJ, Sweatt JD. 2009. Lasting epigenetic influence of early-life adversity on the BDNF gene. *Biol. Psychiatry* 65:760–69

Rutter M. 2007. Gene-environment interdependence. *Dev. Sci.* 10:12–18

Schanberg SM, Evoniuk G, Kuhn CM. 1984. Tactile and nutritional aspects of maternal care: specific regulators of neuroendocrine function and cellular development. *Proc. Soc. Exp. Biol. Med.* 175:135–46

Schatzberg AF, Rothschild AJ, Langlais PJ, Bird ED, Cole JO. 1985. A corticosteroid/dopamine hypothesis for psychotic depression and related states. *J. Psychiatr. Res.* 19:57–64

Seckl JR, Holmes MC. 2007. Mechanisms of disease: glucocorticoids, their placental metabolism and fetal "programming" of adult pathophysiology. *Nat. Clin. Pract. Endocrinol. Metab.* 3:479–88

Sng J, Meaney MJ. 2009. Environmental regulation of the neural epigenome. *Epigenomics*. In press

Sokolowski MB. 2001. *Drosophila*: Genetics meets behavior. *Nat. Rev. Genet.* 2(11):879–90

Sokolowski MB, Wahlsten D. 2001. Gene-environment interaction and complex behavior. In *Methods in Genomic Neuroscience*, ed. SO Moldin, pp. 3–27. Boca Raton, FL: CRC Press

Straub RE, Lipska BK, Egan MF, Goldberg TE, Kleinman JE. 2007. Allelic variation in GAD1 (GAD67) is associated with schizophrenia and influences cortical function and gene expression. *Mol. Psychiatry* 12:854–69

Suomi SJ. 2006. Risk, resilience, and gene x environment interactions in rhesus monkeys. *Ann. N. Y. Acad. Sci.* 1094:83–104

Sweatt JD. 2009. Experience-dependent epigenetic modifications in the central nervous system. *Biol. Psychiatry* 65:191–97

Szyf M, Weaver IC, Champagne FA, Diorio J, Meaney MJ. 2005. Maternal programming of steroid receptor expression and phenotype through DNA methylation in the rat. *Front. Neuroendocrinol.* 26:139–62

Timmusk T, Palm K, Metsis M, Reintam T, Paalme V, et al. 1993. Multiple promoters direct tissue-specific expression of the rat BDNF gene. *Neuron* 10:475–79

Toki S, Morinobu S, Imanaka A, Yamamoto S, Yamawaki S, Honma K. 2007. Importance of early lighting conditions in maternal care by dam as well as anxiety and memory later in life of offspring. *Eur. J. Neurosci.* 25:815–29

Tsankova N, Renthal W, Kumar A, Nestler EJ. 2007. Epigenetic regulation in psychiatric disorders. *Nat. Rev. Neurosci.* 8:355–67

Turner B. 2001. *Chromatin Structure and the Regulation of Gene Expression*. Cambridge, MA: Blackwell Sci.

Turner JD, Muller CP. 2005. Structure of the glucocorticoid receptor (NR3C1) gene 5'untranslated region: identification and tissue distribution of multiple new human exon 1. *J. Mol. Endocrinol.* 35:283–92

Vecsey CG, Hawk JD, Lattal KM, Stein JM, Fabian SA, et al. 2007. Histone deacetylase inhibitors enhance memory and synaptic plasticity via CREB: CBP-dependent transcriptional activation. *J. Neurosci.* 27:6128–40

Veldic M, Caruncho HJ, Liu S, Davis J, Satta R, et al. 2004. DNA-methyltransferase 1 mRNA is selectively overexpressed in telencephalic GABAergic interneurons of schizophrenia brains. *Proc. Natl. Acad. Sci. USA* 101:348–53

Waddington CH. 1957. *The Strategy of the Genes*. New York: MacMillan

Waterland RA, Jirtle RL. 2003. Transposable elements: targets for early nutritional effects on epigenetic gene regulation. *Mol. Cell Biol.* 23:5293–300

Waterland RA, Lin JR, Smith CA, Jirtle RL. 2006. Post-weaning diet affects genomic imprinting at the insulin-like growth factor 2 (Igf2) locus. *Hum. Mol. Genet.* 15:705–16

Weaver ICG, Cervoni N, D'Alessio AC, Champagne FA, Seckl JR, et al. 2004. Epigenetic programming through maternal behavior. *Nature Neurosci.* 7:847–54

Weaver ICG, Champagne FA, Brown SE, Dymov S, Sharma S, et al. 2005. Reversal of maternal programming of stress responses in adult offspring through methyl supplementation: altering epigenetic marking later in life. *J. Neurosci.* 25:11045–54

Weaver ICG, Meaney MJ, Szyf M. 2006. Maternal care effects on the hippocampal transcriptome and anxiety-mediated behaviors in the offspring that are reversible in adulthood. *Proc. Natl. Acad. Sci. USA* 103:3480–85

Weaver ICG, DiAlessio AC, Brown SE, Hellstrom IC, Dymov S, et al. 2007. The transcription factor NGFI-A mediates epigenetic programming: altering epigenetic marking through immediate early genes. *J. Neurosci.* 27:1756–68

Weber M, Hellmann I, Stadler MB, Ramos L, Paabo S, et al. 2007. Distribution, silencing potential and evolutionary impact of promoter DNA methylation in the human genome. *Nat. Genet.* 39:457–66

Weksberg R, Shuman C, Caluseriu O, Smith AC, Fei YL, et al. 2002. Discordant KCNQ1OT1 imprinting in sets of monozygotic twins discordant for Beckwith-Wiedemann syndrome. *Hum. Mol. Genet.* 11:1317–25

West AE. 2001. Calcium regulation of neuronal gene expression. *Proc. Natl. Acad. Sci. USA* 98:11024–31

Whitelaw NC, Whitelaw E. 2006. How lifetimes shape epigenotype within and across generations. *Hum. Mol. Genet.* 15:R131–37

Wood MA, Attner MA, Oliveira AM, Brindle PK, Abel T. 2006. A transcription factor-binding domain of the coactivator CBP is essential for long-term memory and the expression of specific target genes. *Learn. Mem.* 13:609–17

Yeh SH, Lin CH, Gean PW. 2004. Acetylation of nuclear factor-κB in rat amygdala improves long-term but not short-term retention of fear memory. *Mol. Pharmacol.* 65:1286–92

Zhang T, Haws P, Wu Q. 2004. Multiple variable first exons: a mechanism for cell- and tissue-specific gene regulation. *Genome Res.* 14:79–89

Zhang TY, Bagot R, Parent C, Nesbitt C, Bredy TW, et al. 2006. Maternal programming of defensive responses through sustained effects on gene expression. *Biol. Psychiatry* 73:72–89

Zhang TY, Hellstrom I, Diorio J, Wei X-L, Meaney MJ. 2009. Maternal regulation of hippocampal GAD1 expression is associated with transcriptional regulation through promoter methylation. Manuscript submitted

Zhou Z, Hong EJ, Cohen S, Zhao WN, Ho HY, et al. 2006. Brain-specific phosphorylation of MeCP2 regulates activity-dependent Bdnf transcription, dendritic growth, and spine maturation. *Neuron* 52:255–69

Zoghbi HY. 2003. Postnatal neurodevelopmental disorders: meeting at the synapse? *Science* 302:826–30

Goals, Attention, and (Un)Consciousness

Ap Dijksterhuis[1] and Henk Aarts[2]

[1]Behavioral Science Institute, Radboud University Nijmegen, 6500 HE Nijmegen, The Netherlands; email: a.dijksterhuis@psych.ru.nl

[2]Department of Psychology, Utrecht University, 3508 TC Utrecht, The Netherlands; email: h.aarts@uu.nl

Annu. Rev. Psychol. 2010. 61:467–90

First published online as a Review in Advance on June 30, 2009

The *Annual Review of Psychology* is online at psych.annualreviews.org

This article's doi: 10.1146/annurev.psych.093008.100445

0066-4308/10/0110-0467$20.00

Key Words

volition, consciousness, unconscious

Abstract

In this article, literature from neuroscience, cognitive psychology, and social cognition is integrated to discuss the relation between goals, attention, and consciousness. Goals are the tools with which people engage in volitional behavior. Whereas goal pursuit was traditionally assumed to be strongly related to consciousness, recent research and theorizing suggest that goals guide behavior through attention, and this guidance can occur outside of a person's awareness. The crucial explanatory role of goals and attention in behavior, as well as the relative unimportance of consciousness, is examined in the context of social cognition research on goal priming. Furthermore, three research domains are discussed that are relevant for the understanding of the implementation of volitional behavior: implicit learning, evaluative conditioning, and unconscious thought. It is concluded that these processes are goal dependent and that they need attention, but that they can generally proceed without awareness. Finally, when people are consciously aware of their behavior or their goals, the effects can be beneficial as well as detrimental.

Contents

INTRODUCTION

Don't know what I want but I know how to
get it.

The Sex Pistols

The ability to engage in volitional behavior is
often considered to be a uniquely human trait.
Human behavior is motivated by, and directed
at, goals. When we set, strive for, and attain our
goals, we have a sense of agency or willfulness
in that we experience ourselves as the cause of
our own behavior as a result of decisions and
actions. Volition, then, is a fundamental feature
of the way people see and define themselves.

People have long assumed that volition and
consciousness are intimately linked. We know
what we want, and when we act on what we
want, we do so by making a conscious decision.
Moreover, when we make a conscious decision
to act—such as to buy a new pair of jeans, to
call a friend, or to order a pepperoni pizza—it
feels as if that conscious decision is the first and
foremost cause of the act that follows. Whereas
it is accepted that many mundane behaviors are
automatized in that they bypass consciousness

(Bargh & Chartrand 1999), the field of psychology has not yet fully come to grips with the role
of consciousness in behavior that is (or at least
feels as if it is) clearly volitional.

The idea that consciousness is necessary to
evoke volitional behavior was severely shaken
by a famous experiment by Libet and colleagues
(1983). They asked participants to freely choose
when to move their index fingers and measured
the movement itself, to report their conscious
decision to start the movement, and the onset
of the brains' readiness potentials preparing the
movement. As expected, the conscious decision
preceded the act itself (roughly by a quarter of
a second). However, readiness potentials could
be identified up to a full second before the actual
movement, clearly demonstrating that the brain
started to prepare the movement long before
consciousness became involved.

Libet's work was—and still is—
controversial. Arguably, the most important
problem in interpreting Libet's findings is that
one can contend that the movement still starts
with a conscious decision (van de Grind 2002).
After all, the chain of events starts with an
experimenter telling participants that they have
to move their finger and, obviously, participants
are consciously aware of this instruction. One
could conclude that participants unconsciously
decided *when* to make the actual movement,
but not *whether* to make the movement in the
first place.

Recently, Soon and colleagues (2008) extended the findings by Libet and colleagues.
They changed the paradigm in such a way that
participants not only chose when to engage in
a specific act, but also which one of two possible acts to make. They replicated Libet's work
and found readiness potentials (in the supplementary motor area, or SMA) some time before participants reported making a conscious
decision as to which act to engage in. More importantly, they found activity predictive of the
specific act in the frontal and parietal cortex up
to 10 seconds before the actual act. In other
words, we unconsciously choose which behavior to engage in long before we are consciously
aware of it.

Goals: the mental
representation of
behaviors or
behavioral outcomes
that are associated with
positive affect. They
determine our actions

Volition: also often
called the will. The
process by which we
"decide" to engage in a
particular behavior

Consciousness: the
ability to be aware of
things. Contents of
consciousness are
assumed to be available
for verbal report

The assumption that the role of consciousness in volitional behavior is much more modest than long assumed is also emphasized by recent research showing that goals and higher cognitive processes that rely on cortical brain areas can be modulated by unconscious stimuli. In a recent experiment, for instance, Lau & Passingham (2007) instructed participants to either prepare a phonological judgment or a semantic judgment on an upcoming word. In some trials, however, they were subliminally primed to do the opposite. On these trials, it was found that brain activity in areas relevant to the instructed task was reduced, whereas activity related to the primed task was enhanced. The cognitive control system, in other words, can be activated by subliminal stimuli. In addition, Pessiglione and colleagues (2007) showed that strength of motivation can be subliminally primed. Participants in their experiment did a task whereby they could win money on successive trials by squeezing a handgrip. The amount of money at stake (a pound versus a penny) was subliminally primed during each trial, and it indeed affected force of handgrip, along with skin conductance and activation in the ventral palladium, an area known to be devoted to emotional and motivational output of the limbic system. Pushing the bar even higher, Bijleveld et al. (2009) recently showed that people recruit more resources in response to high (as compared to low) subliminal reward cues, but only when the reward required considerable mental effort to obtain. This research demonstrates that people use reward information in a strategic manner to recruit resources, without this information ever reaching conscious awareness.

These findings concur with a growing body of literature from the social cognition domain showing that goals can affect higher cognitive processes and overt behavior without conscious awareness of the goal. For example, Bargh and colleagues (2001) unobtrusively exposed participants to words such as "strive" and "succeed" to prime an achievement goal and then gave them the opportunity to perform well by giving them a set of anagrams. Participants primed with an achievement goal outperformed those

who were not primed with the goal. Bargh et al. (2001) also demonstrated that such goal priming leads to qualities associated with motivational states or "goal-directedness," such as persistence and increased effort (for other such demonstrations, see, e.g., Aarts et al. 2008, Fitzsimons & Bargh 2003, Lakin & Chartrand 2003, Shah et al. 2002).

In summary, people become consciously aware of an act only after they unconsciously decide to engage in it. In addition, at least some volitional behavior does not require any conscious awareness at all: Goals and motivation can be unconsciously primed.

In the present contribution, we aim to explore how goals, attention, and consciousness are related to gain a better understanding of how people can engage in goal-directed, volitional behavior in the absence of conscious awareness. The central message and organizing theme is the following: People have long assumed that consciousness plays a leading role in guiding volitional behavior, but we contend that the lead role is actually for goals and for attention. They are the stars of the play called volitional behavior. Goals guide attention and thereby often behavior, and both goals and attention are largely independent from consciousness. To bolster this claim, literature from social psychology, cognitive psychology, and neuroscience on the relation between goals, attention, and (un)consciousness, is reviewed in this article.

In the next section, the key concepts are defined, and more importantly, recent research on their relations is discussed in the context of social cognition research on goal priming. Because goals seem to originate in the unconscious (e.g., Libet et al. 1983, Soon et al. 2008), it is essential to understand how such unconsciously evoked goals may control volitional behavior. Furthermore, if goals are capable of directing attention and behavior outside of awareness, it is possible that goals modulate bottom-up information processes relevant for the creation and implementation of volitional behavior. Accordingly, we review recent developments in three lines of research against the background

Unconscious: all the psychological processes of which we are not aware at a given moment in time

Attention: the extent to which incoming information is processed

of the proposed relationship between goals, attention, and consciousness. Specifically, implicit learning, evaluative conditioning, and unconscious thought are elaborated upon as instances of bottom-up processes that may be moderated by goals and attention in the absence of awareness. Finally, the possible role of consciousness in volitional behavior is analyzed, whereby a framework is presented about when conscious awareness is beneficial and when it is (potentially) harmful for effective goal-directed behavior.

GOALS, ATTENTION, AND CONSCIOUSNESS

Goals are conceptualized as mental representations of behaviors or behavioral outcomes that are desirable or rewarding to engage in or to attain. Most goals are linked to lower-level acts and skills and thus provide a reference point for cognition and action (Aarts & Dijksterhuis 2000, Hommel 1996, Jeannerod 1997, Vallacher & Wegner 1987). Goals are the starting point and/or reference point of almost all behavior. Furthermore, the notion that goals are rewarding to attain suggests that goals control behavior through cognitive as well as motivational processes (Bargh et al. 2009, Custers & Aarts 2005). Accordingly, any behavior or outcome that is represented in terms of a result of more concrete action can potentially operate as a goal if one is motivated or encouraged by the external environment to attain it.

An abundance of recent evidence (reviewed more fully below) demonstrates that goals can be activated unconsciously by features of the environment (Aarts & Dijksterhuis 2000, Bargh & Gollwitzer 1994, Bargh et al. 2001, Kruglanski et al. 2002). Given that people unconsciously "decide" what goals to pursue merely as a consequence of priming by the environment, goals must be mentally represented (Bargh & Gollwitzer 1994). In a recent research program, Custers & Aarts (2005) unveiled the structure of such goal representations. They selected behaviors that were pretested as neutral (doing puzzles, studying, going for a walk) and conditioned

these activities with positive, neutral, or negative words. This was done subliminally: The participants could consciously detect the valenced words but not the activities that were conditioned. The results showed that participants later wanted to engage in the positively conditioned activities but not in the other activities. In another experiment, participants were promised they could engage in the conditioned activity after doing a filler task. Participants who were promised they could do something that was positively conditioned and that they wanted to engage in completed the filler task faster than did other participants. In summary, when the representation of a behavior becomes unconsciously associated with positive affect, it becomes a goal that motivates people to maintain and achieve it.

Attention is commonly referred to as the selective processing of one aspect while ignoring other irrelevant aspects. About one million fibers leave each human eye, meaning that we have to deal with about one megabyte of raw data each second (Koch & Tsuchiya 2006). It is impossible to process all this information on higher levels. Because information-processing capacity involved in the control of higher-level cognition and behavior is limited, attention facilitates which stimuli and actions get access to these capacity-limited processes. Therefore, attention must be flexibly applied to different processes (Kahneman 1973, Moors & de Houwer 2006). As Moors & De Houwer (2006) pointed out, early stages of information processing (sensory analysis) generally require no attention, whereas later stages require an increasing amount. Given that attention is a limited resource, some of these later processing stages do indeed continue because enough attention is devoted to them, whereas other processes are "filtered out" by lack of attention.

Whether incoming information is attended to or not—that is, whether incoming information is processed on higher stages—is determined both by bottom-up and top-down processes (Corbetta & Shulman 2002, Dehaene et al. 2006, Koch & Tsuchiya 2006). Bottom-up (exogenous) attentive processes are involuntary and elicited by stimulus saliency, such as brightness or speed of movement and stimuli that are of instinctive or learned biological importance (Koch & Ullman 1985). However, most attentive processes are driven by top-down (endogenous) concerns, and this is where goals come into play. Both the amount and duration of attention devoted to incoming information is determined by active goals: Incoming information that is relevant for goal attainment is attended to much more than information that is irrelevant. If one is thirsty, drinks attract more attention than things one cannot drink (e.g., Aarts et al. 2001).

As a general rule, attention in the service of goals involves two interconnected faculties that usually act in close harmony: stability or focus (the ability to keep information active for action or further processing) and flexibility (the ability to be flexible enough to switch to, and take advantage of, contextual variations). The balance between focus and flexibility is crucial for goals to do their work effectively. Disturbance of this balance, however, leads to inferior performance (e.g., Aston-Jones & Cohen 2005). This is elaborated upon below.

Defining consciousness is a complex and thorny issue that psychologists (and philosophers) have struggled with for a long time. In this contribution, we consider conscious processes as processes that are accompanied by awareness of certain aspects of the process and/or awareness of relevant contents. In experimental research, conscious awareness of process or content can be assessed by investigating whether people are able to verbalize processes or contents. If they are, a process can be said to be conscious. Driving is conscious, as when people drive they are (at times at least) consciously aware of sitting in a car, and they are able to verbalize this. It is enough to be aware of some aspects of the process for it to qualify as a conscious process (Dijksterhuis 2009). For instance, speaking is conscious because we are aware of our speaking while we do it. However, the processes guiding the production of speech are largely unconscious, and we are not aware of the search for each word. We are never aware of all aspects of a psychological process. Each and every conscious process is accompanied by (or is a residual of) unconscious processes.

In short, goals direct attention in the service of goal pursuit, and certain aspects of the attention process may enter consciousness or not. Although goals can control behavior in the absence of conscious awareness, goals guide these behavioral effects by modulating attention processes. In the next section, we examine how goals, attention, and consciousness are related.

THE RELATION BETWEEN ATTENTION AND CONSCIOUSNESS

It is important to realize that there is no one-to-one relation between attention and consciousness. Researchers who advocate the importance of unconscious processes by demonstrating that important psychological processes do not need any conscious guidance (e.g., Bargh et al. 1996, 2001; Dijksterhuis & Nordgren 2006; Libet et al. 1983; Reber 1967) often meet with resistance because it feels as if consciousness simply must be involved in these important processes. However, attention is the guiding principle here, not conscious awareness. Part of the confusion arises because attention (especially top-down attention) and consciousness are correlated in real-life experiences. When one pays more attention to an incoming stimulus, the probability that one becomes consciously aware of it increases.

However, attention and consciousness are distinct. More and more recent research and theorizing is aimed at understanding the distinction, and there is now some agreement that psychological processes can best be understood as falling into one of the cells of a 2 × 2 taxonomy based on whether stimuli are attended to or not and whether they are reportable or not (that is, whether one is consciously aware of them or not; Baars 1997, Damasio 1999, Dehaene et al. 2006, Koch & Tsuchiya 2006, Lamme 2003, Wegner & Smart 1997). An abundance of priming research shows that stimuli that do not reach conscious awareness can still influence various psychological processes, including overt behavior (see, e.g., Dijksterhuis & Bargh 2001 for a review), but some degree of attention to these stimuli is necessary for these effects to occur. Likewise, recent research shows that people can engage in rather complicated activities in the absence of conscious awareness (Bargh et al. 2001, Dijksterhuis et al. 2006); however, these processes are goal dependent and most likely do require a certain degree of attention. Conversely, people can be (generally fleetingly) consciously aware of stimuli without paying much attention to them.

Whereas recent theorizing is mostly based on findings on visual perception, Wegner & Smart (1997) applied the 2×2 taxonomy to a broader domain. They distinguished between activation level and consciousness. Specifically, in addition to states of no activation (no attention and no consciousness) and full activation (both attention and consciousness), they also distinguished states of deep activation (stimuli that are attended to but are unconscious) and surface activation (stimuli that are not attended to but are conscious). An example of deep activation, based on Wegner's own work (e.g., Wegner 1994), is thoughts that are temporarily suppressed. Such thoughts are highly active but do not appear in consciousness, at least not as long as suppression is successful. Good examples of surface activation are the sort of fleeting thoughts we may have when we daydream or associate freely. We do not pay attention to them, but they can briefly appear in consciousness.

THE RELATION BETWEEN GOALS AND CONSCIOUSNESS

Volitional behavior was traditionally associated with consciousness, in that goal pursuit was assumed to be the consequence of a conscious intention to perform a specified behavior or to attain a goal. According to this notion, people experience themselves to be the agent of their behaviors and goal pursuits, as these experiences of self-agency are the result of consciously forming, pursuing, and attaining one's goals.

However, recent research challenges this view. There is a bulk of experimental work showing that the mere activation of a goal representation guides behavior and higher cognitive processes involved in goal-directed behavior in the absence of a person's conscious awareness. The idea that goals can direct behavior unconsciously is based on the notion that goals are part of knowledge networks that include representations of the goal itself, actions, procedures, and objects that may aid goal pursuit as well as situational or contextual features related to the goal (Aarts & Dijksterhuis 2000, 2003; Bargh & Gollwitzer 1994; Cooper & Shallice 2006; Kruglanski et al. 2002). These knowledge networks enable people to act on goals without intentional control or without explicit expectancies. Thus, goal-directed behavior can start outside of conscious awareness because goal representations can be primed by, and interact with, behavioral and contextual information.

Part of the research on unconscious goal pursuit deals with habit formation processes (Aarts & Dijksterhuis 2000, Bargh 1990, Fishbach et al. 2003, Moskowitz et al. 2004, Shah 2003). Specifically, for goal pursuit to become automatized, one needs some practice with the selection and execution of the most effective action in the goal-relevant situation. Indeed, there is evidence showing that people immediately activate the means to reach a goal upon the unconscious instigation of that goal, but only when that goal-directed behavior has been performed frequently in the past and has become a habit (Aarts & Dijksterhuis 2000, Hommel 2000, Sheeran et al. 2005).

Other studies have tested whether goal priming facilitates the utilization of skills associated with the goal even though these skills have not been previously applied to the task at hand. In a demonstration of this idea, Holland et al. (2005) examined whether the mere perception of odor is capable of directly activating goals. They exposed some participants to the scent of all-purpose cleaner without participants' conscious awareness of the presence of the scent. Because the scent of all-purpose cleaner was assumed to enhance the accessibility of the goal of cleaning, Holland et al. (2005) hypothesized that participants exposed to the scent would spontaneously start to be cleaner. Participants were requested to eat a very crumbly cookie in the lab, and indeed, participants exposed to the scent put in more effort to keep their direct environment clean and crumb-free, even though the task and situation in which they applied their skills of cleaning were novel. These results indicate that goal activation can encourage people to exploit new opportunities in novel settings without awareness of the operation of the goal.

Goals inferred from another person's actions can also be activated in a perceiver and can control subsequent behavior without conscious intent, thus leading to goal contagion (Aarts et al. 2004, Dik & Aarts 2007, Loersch et al. 2008). As Hassin et al. (2005) have demonstrated, goal inferences can occur spontaneously, without conscious intentions and awareness. Building on this knowledge, Aarts and colleagues (2004) briefly exposed participants to a short script either implying the goal of earning money or not. After reading the goal-implying scenario, participants were told that they could participate in a lottery in which they could win money, but only if there was enough time left. They were then given a computer task, and the question was whether participants would speed up their performance as a means to ensure that they could participate in the goal-relevant task. Results showed that participants who were exposed to the behavior implying the goal of earning money were indeed faster than those in the control condition. These behavioral changes occurred without conscious intent and were more pronounced when the desire to earn money was relatively strong. These findings were replicated in another experiment with heterosexual male students and the goal of seeking casual sex.

Goals may also be automatically activated by being primed with significant others. Research has shown that goals and resultant actions are activated when people are exposed to the names of friends, parents, and spouses. Fitzsimons &

Bargh (2003) showed that subliminal priming of the names of one's parents triggers the motivation to achieve and that exposure to names of good friends primes the habitual goal and resultant concrete behavior of helping (see also Shah 2003). A recent line of experimentation replicated and extended these subliminal goal-priming effects in the realm of social stereotypes (Aarts et al. 2005a, Custers et al. 2008). Specifically, it was tested and confirmed that priming members of social groups that contain the representation of a goal that is believed to be held by that group causes people to automatically pursue the goals (e.g., the goal of helping or making money that are stereotypical for nurses or stockbrokers, respectively). Finally, Fitzsimons et al. (2008) showed that goals can even be activated by the perception of objects that are associated with goals. For instance, exposing people to a Mac computer leads to the goal to be creative in comparison to exposing people to an IBM computer.

Taken together, the results of a large body of research over the past ten years indicate that goal-directed volitional behavior can be evoked outside of awareness. Specifically, goal priming causes us to initiate and exhibit lower-level acts and skills that are available in our repertoire and associated with the primed goal without conscious intent and awareness of the actual goal causing the behavior. Importantly, the observation that our goal pursuits can emerge unconsciously suggests that conscious intentions and goals are distinct concepts that can operate independently from each other, served by different processes and brain networks (Frith et al. 2000, Haynes et al. 2007, Lau et al. 2004). Whereas intentions refer to our conscious reflection or deliberation on attaining a behavioral goal, goals are representations of desired states or outcomes that guide overt behavior without conscious awareness.

The idea that our goal pursuits also materialize unconsciously may sound counterintuitive because the actions we conduct and the outcomes they produce are often accompanied with conscious experiences of self-agency. How can much of our behavior unfold outside conscious awareness if we have those pervasive agency experiences? A possible way to understand this issue is to suggest that our conscious experience of self-agency is an inference that occurs fluently and perfunctorily after action performance and is not accurate per se (Prinz 2003, Wegner 2003). This inferential character of experiences of self-agency has become apparent in a number of recent studies (Aarts et al. 2005b, 2009a,b; Dijksterhuis et al. 2008; Jones et al. 2008; Sato 2009; Sato & Yasuda 2005; Wegner & Wheatley 1999) demonstrating that these experiences are the result of a match between the outcome of an action and knowledge about the outcome that was made active just prior to its occurrence.

In one study (Aarts et al. 2005b), participants and the computer each moved a single gray square in opposite directions on a rectangular path consisting of eight white tiles. Participants' task was to press a key to stop the rapid movement of the squares. This action turned one of the eight tiles black. In reality, the computer determined which of the tiles would turn black. From a participant's perspective, though, this black tile could represent the location of either her square or the computer's square at the time she pressed the stop key. Thus, the participant or computer could have caused the square to stop on the position (outcome), rendering the exclusivity of causes of outcomes ambiguous (Wegner & Wheatley 1999). Participants either consciously set the intention to stop on a position or were subliminally primed with that position before they saw the presented stop on the corresponding location. To measure experiences of self-agency, participants rated the extent to which they felt to have caused the square to stop on the presented location. Results showed that both intention and priming lead to an increased sense of self-agency, suggesting that online self-agency experiences were primarily based on a match between preactivated and actual outcomes, irrespective of the conscious or unconscious source of this activation. These and other findings indicate that agency experiences not only arise from our conscious goals, but also

accompany the unconscious activation of goal representations, leading us to believe that the outcomes of our behaviors were consciously intended, whereas in fact they were influenced by cues in our environment outside our conscious awareness.

THE RELATION BETWEEN GOALS AND ATTENTION

Attention is a functional process that selects and biases the incoming flow of information and internal representations in the service of effective goal achievement. Thus, the content of attention represents the goals that are active at a specific moment in time. One of the most important roles for attention is to translate goals into overt behavior (Monsell & Driver 2000). If a goal can always be executed directly in the very same environment, attention would merely reflect the translation of a perceived relevant stimulus into a response in real-time. However, because goals cannot always be enacted directly in the same situation, we often have to take temporal and spatial aspects into account. Moreover, the social environment often poses conflicts on our goals such that interfering information needs to be ignored or inhibited for effective goal performance to proceed. In short, attention does not only orient and alert the person to goal-relevant information; it also plays a supervisory role in translating goals into behavior (Posner & Fan 2007).

Indeed, recent research has started to model goal-directed behavior in terms of executive control processes (Funahashi 2001, Miller & Cohen 2001, Miyake & Shah 1999). An important aim of this research is to understand how people maintain and manipulate information in the service of goal pursuit and to provide a neurocognitive account for the ability to guide attention and action in accord with goals. A common framework proposed in this research is that the prefrontal cortex (PFC), anterior cingulate cortex, and posterior parietal cortex are the main areas taking care of attentional and control processes, consistent with theories of PFC function and the involvement of these areas in the distributed working memory system. Importantly, these cortical areas are believed to be part of a network for conscious processes, and hence are implicated in volitional behavior (Baars & Franklin 2003, Baddeley 1993, Haggard 2008, Smith & Jonides 1999). Thus, the functionality and structure of executive control and working memory are examined by presenting participants explicitly with materials that they explicitly have to work on. That is, participants are explicitly instructed to actively maintain goal information over time or to ignore irrelevant information to keep focused on the goal task at hand, thereby (often unstated) assuming that these processes also occur during self-motivated performance. However, under this working assumption, it is difficult to understand how goal pursuit is supported by attention and higher cognitive processes that make use of executive control structures without the person being aware of it. That is, how can goal-directed attention to, and transformation of, relevant information occur outside of conscious awareness?

One way to approach this issue is to propose that, in principle, the operation of higher cognitive processes does not care much about the conscious state of the individual. In other words, conscious and unconscious goals partly rely on the same functional architecture of attention and information processing in which the same cognitive functions or hardware are recruited and shared to translate goals into behavior (Aarts 2007, Badgaiyan 2000, Hassin et al. 2009). Thus, goals modulate attention processes, irrespective of the conscious or unconscious source of the activation of the goal. Although this may be a controversial proposition, there is some recent evidence for it.

First, from research on working memory, we know that the activation of semantic items decays in short-term memory over very short periods of time, usually within a couple of seconds, unless some intervention or goal holds the items active (Baddeley & Logie 1999, McKone 1995). Exploiting this notion, research has demonstrated that an unconsciously activated goal can maintain relevant information active as well.

For instance, Aarts et al. (2007) examined how the mental accessibility of a desired goal after a short interval changes as a function of subliminally priming the goal. In one of their studies, participants were either primed with the goal to socialize or not, and after a delay of two minutes, the accessibility of the goal was tested in a lexical decision task by measuring the speed of recognizing words related to the goal. Results showed that the representation of the goal remained accessible when participants were primed to attain the goal, but that the sustained activation faded away quickly as soon as desire to attain that goal was gone. Similar persistent activation effects of unconsciously activated desired goal-states have been obtained in other studies (Aarts et al. 2004, Bargh et al. 2001), suggesting that some kind of focus or rehearsal process keeps goal-relevant information active unconsciously.

Furthermore, recent work has started to explore whether humans can keep their eyes on their ongoing goal pursuit in a unconscious manner when competing goals or temptations conflicts with these pursuits. For instance, if one wants to lose weight, one has to be able to resist the temptation to eat a late-night snack. People usually engage in this type of attention process when they have to deal with interference that stems from other goals or temptations that compete for attention and behavior, a process that is commonly conceived of as requiring conscious and intentional control (see, e.g., work on delay of gratification; Mischel et al. 1989). However, there are studies that tell a somewhat different story. For instance, Shah and colleagues (2002) demonstrated that when participants are unconsciously instigated to pursue a given goal (by subliminal exposure to words representing the goal, e.g., studying), they inhibited competing accessible goals (e.g., going out); moreover, this inhibition facilitated the achievement of the unconsciously activated goal. These findings provide support for the existence of an unconscious attention/inhibition mechanism that shields goals from distracting thoughts (see also Aarts et al. 2007, Fishbach et al. 2003, Papies et al. 2008).

In summary, several lines of research suggest that goals can be translated into overt behavior outside the person's awareness of the activation and operation of the goal. Furthermore, unconscious goal pursuit is supported by attention that operates on higher cognitive processes according to principles of executive control and working memory. And these processes (and the information on which they operate) seem to run below the threshold of consciousness.

In the next section, recent developments in three research areas are reviewed, with the above framework in mind. Specifically, we elaborate on implicit learning, on evaluative conditioning, and on unconscious thought, whereby we postulate that these processes are goal dependent, that they require some attention, but that they do not need conscious guidance.

IMPLICIT LEARNING

In order to stay one step ahead in the world, humans and other animals use the world's regularities in order to anticipate events. Furthermore, learning regularities that pertain to rules of predictive relations is especially important for optimal guidance of goal-directed behavior (e.g., one needs to know which action leads to the attainment of a goal). People are able to learn complex rules and relations between events that they encounter in a bottom-up fashion without being aware of them. In the seminal work by Reber (1967, 1993; for a recent review, see Frensch & Runger 2003) on implicit learning, participants were presented with sets of letter strings, such as "XXRTRXV" and "AABEBAP." These strings obey specific rules that are unbeknownst to the participants. However, after an initial learning phase during which participants are repeatedly presented with such strings, they can to some extent classify new strings as to whether they follow the learned rule or not. Interestingly, participants can do without being able to verbalize the rules, which reflects actual human speech: We follow grammatical rules, often without being able to explain these rules.

What exactly people can learn without conscious guidance is still a matter of debate, and we concede that to which implicit learning is dependent on goals and on attention still warrants further investigation. However, it is our contention that people can indeed learn complex rules and relations without being consciously aware of them (Halford et al. 2005, Lewicki et al. 1992, Nissen & Bullemer 1987), but that these learning processes are goal dependent and do require at least some attention. Jimenez & Mendez (1999), for instance, conducted various studies in which participants engaged in sequential learning under either single- or dual-task conditions. Although they found that general attentional load hardly affected learning, it also became clear that participants do need selective attention to the crucial information. In order to learn a relation between two components, participants had to be able to hold the two components in working memory simultaneously.

Recently, Eitam et al. (2008) extended this work by showing that implicit learning is influenced by goals. They primed half their participants with the goal to achieve, whereas the others were not primed. Participants then engaged in a dynamic, complex learning task, based on the research by Berry & Broadbent (1984). Their research clearly demonstrated that participants who were primed with achievement performed considerably better than control participants—that is, they implicitly learned more. However, the ability to consciously describe what they had learned was equally poor in both conditions. In other words, goals affected implicit learning without any improvement in conscious recognition of what was learned.

The principle of implicit learning has also been examined in the context of associative versus predictive relations. Whereas it is generally assumed that bidirectional structures (i.e., associations) can be learned automatically and without conscious awareness, the formation of more precise structures that capture the predictive relation between events (e.g., predictive or causal rules) are assumed to require strategic processing and conscious awareness of the events and their relation (Berry & Dienes 1993, Sloman 1996). These assumptions mainly follow from the idea that learning mechanisms that rely on bottom-up processes (e.g., Hebbian associative learning) are able to operate outside of awareness, whereas top-down processes (e.g., predictive relations or rule-based learning) are generally assumed to require conscious awareness (e.g., Hayes & Broadbent 1988, Keele et al. 2003, Lewicki et al. 1987, Reber 1989). These assumptions were explicitly tested in recent research by Alonso et al. (2006). In a learning phase, in which participants had to categorize target words (e.g., dog, chair) as members of two categories (animal, furniture), each target was preceded by one of two additional category labels (body and plant) that were to be ignored by the participant, but fully predicted the category of the target word. Alonso and colleagues reasoned that the structure of the learned relation between primes and targets could be revealed by testing this relation in the reverse direction: If the learned relation was bidirectional (association), priming the target categories of the learning phase should facilitate members of the related category that served as a prime in the learning phase. This should not, however, be the case for unidirectional structures (predictive relation).

In order to investigate the role of awareness, participants were either explicitly asked to report the relation at the end of the experiment (Study 1) or conscious awareness was actively prevented by presenting the category primes in the learning phase subliminally (Study 2). It was found that when participants were consciously aware of the predictive relations in the learning phase, no facilitation in the reversed order was observed in the test phase, whereas such facilitation was demonstrated for participants who were unaware of the relation, or for participants for whom awareness was actively prevented by presenting the primes subliminally in the learning phase. These findings suggest that bidirectional memory structures (i.e., associations) are formed without awareness, whereas awareness of the predictive relation between events leads to the formation of unidirectional structures. Hence, these findings seem to support the general belief that the formation of bidirectional associations can occur without conscious awareness of the relation, but that such awareness is needed for the formation of unidirectional structures that capture the predictive relation between events.

The finding that learning of predictive relations requires conscious awareness of the relation seems to be at odds with the literature on implicit learning. Most relevant to the current discussion, it may be the case that awareness of the relations is confounded with attention, and hence, learning of predictive relations may occur without conscious awareness when, for example, participants are primed with the goal to process predictive relations. In a recent test of this idea, Custers & Aarts (2009) employed the learning and test phase utilized by Alonso et al. (2006). However, before participants engaged in the learning phase, they performed a task that either unobtrusively primed the goal to process co-occurring stimuli in terms of predictive relations or did not. The idea here is that the implicit goal that is used in a prior task transfers to the later learning phase and determines whether primes and targets are stored in unidirectional or bidirectional memory structures, even when awareness of the relation is actively prevented by presenting the category primes subliminally in the learning phase. Indeed, the data across three experiments showed that goal priming led to unidirectional memory structures: The target words from the learning phase speeded up the recognition of the category primes in the no-goal prime condition, whereas no such facilitation in the reversed order was observed in the goal prime condition. These effects even showed up when the category primes were presented subliminally in the learning phase. These results suggest that conscious awareness is not the critical moderator that determines how predictive relations are acquired. The acquisition relies on top-down processes in which attention is directed outside of awareness by processing goals relevant for the task at hand.

EVALUATIVE CONDITIONING

When an object (the conditioned stimulus, or CS) is repeatedly paired with a familiar object that already has a positive or negative valence (the unconditioned stimulus, or US), this object takes on the valence of the object it is paired with. Evaluative conditioning is fundamental to the shaping of preferences and goals, and it has been applied in many different domains. Most initial demonstrations (e.g., Razran 1940) were done in the context of persuasion, whereby a message was paired with a positive CS. Evaluative conditioning (EC) has been applied to heighten self-esteem (e.g., Baccus et al. 2004, Dijksterhuis 2004), to increase motivation strength in goal-directed behavior (e.g., Custers & Aarts 2005, Ferguson 2007), and to understand clinical phenomena such as spider phobia (Merkelbach et al. 1993). Jones and colleagues (2004) reported an engaging demonstration of the effects of evaluative conditioning. People generally find the letters in their own name more positive than other letters. Because of this, people like objects—including other people—more when they are associated with letters in their own name. For this reason, people are disproportionately likely to marry others whose first or last names resemble their own!

Early demonstrations of the effects were open to alternative explanations such as demand effects (Razran 1940, Staats & Staats 1958), as participants were often explicitly aware of the possible relation between the CS and the US and/or of the intentions of the experimenter. However, recent demonstrations have dealt with such problems. Various researchers have shown that evaluative conditioning occurs when either the CS or the US, or even both, are presented subliminally (e.g., Custers & Aarts 2005, Dijksterhuis 2004, Krosnick et al. 1992, Murphy et al. 1995, Niedenthal 1990), rendering any alternative explanation that requires conscious awareness highly unlikely. Krosnick et al. (1992), for instance, presented their participants with nine slides of a target person engaging in routine daily activities. These slides were preceded by slides of positive or negative events (e.g., a child with a Mickey Mouse doll versus a bloody shark) presented for a mere 13 milliseconds. Later, participants were asked to evaluate the target person. A target person paired with positive stimuli was evaluated more positively in general and was rated as having a nicer personality compared to a target person paired with negative stimuli.

Despite the findings with subliminal stimuli, whether conscious awareness of the contingencies is necessary for EC effects to occur is still a matter of debate. However, Field & Moore (2005) recently obtained evidence for the central role of attention rather than consciousness. In their first experiment, some participants could process the conditioned stimuli (CSi) under normal conditions, whereas for others attention was depleted with a distractor task. Indeed, only nondistracted participants—that is, participants who could pay sufficient attention to the CSi—demonstrated EC effects, whereas distracted participants did not. Awareness of the contingency between CSi and unconditioned stimuli (USi) did not affect the results. In a second experiment, Field & Moore (2005) manipulated attention while they presented the USi subliminally and found comparable effects: Attention drove the EC effects, whereas contingency awareness played no role.

Pleyers et al. (2007) correctly reasoned that the conclusions of Field & Moore (2005) were based on findings where participants were all aware of the contingencies (i.e., attention-enhanced condition) or where no evaluative conditioning effect was found (i.e., distraction condition). Such a strategy may be suboptimal, and Pleyers and colleagues (2007) have suggested that contingency awareness should not be measured for each participant, but rather on the level on each CS-US combination for each participant. In their experiments, they showed EC effects for CS-US combinations that participants were aware of, and no EC effects for CS-US combinations that participants were not aware of. Interestingly, a close reading of their data reveals that the vast majority of their participants were aware of all CS-US pairings, whereas the remaining few were not aware of any pairings. There were no participants who were aware of roughly half the pairings and not the others. This suggests that the way in which the CS-US combinations were constructed (a picture of a consumer product together with another positive or negative feature) caused most participants to be aware of the relation, and that this awareness (including the few instances in which participants did not attend to or missed the relation) correlated with the evaluative conditioning effect. Given the results on conditioning with subliminal stimuli, it is more likely that the seeming contingency awareness is merely the consequence of some other factor that is necessary for conditioning, most likely attention. That is, it is likely that conditioning is goal dependent and that a certain degree of attention—driven by processing goals—is necessary during encoding for conditioning to be able to occur.

Later work by Corneille and colleagues (2009) supports this interpretation. If EC is dependent on attention rather than on consciousness, it should also be responsive to goals. They gave some participants CS-US pairings while instructing them to pay attention to similarities, whereas other were instructed to pay attention to differences. Indeed, they found larger EC effects among people who paid attention to the similarities, demonstrating that processing goals and thereby attention influence EC effects. Priluck & Till (2004) recently found that EC effects are stronger among highly involved people and people scoring high in need for cognition.

Given these findings, it is likely that EC effects are dependent on processing goals and on attention and that effects of contingency awareness are merely obtained because contingency awareness generally increases with more attention.

UNCONSCIOUS THOUGHT

Recently, evidence has been collected showing that an important stage of a decision process can also occur outside of conscious awareness.

When people have processed information about various choice alternatives, how do they form a preference for one of the alternatives? Traditionally, people have thought that conscious deliberation is necessary. However, it is possible that people can engage in unconscious thought and that conscious thought is not necessary to arrive at a decision. In fact, because consciousness is often poor at weighting the relative importance of attributes (Wilson et al. 1993), unconscious thought may be preferable for arriving at a preference in a complex decision situation (Dijksterhuis 2004, Dijksterhuis et al. 2006, Dijksterhuis & Nordgren 2006).

In a typical experiment on unconscious thought, participants read information pertaining to a choice problem. More specifically, they would be presented with information about four different apartments, whereby each apartment was described by 12 different aspects (Dijksterhuis 2004). One apartment had many more positive attributes (and therefore fewer negative attributes) than the others. After participants had read all the information, some were asked to choose between the apartments immediately. Others were given some time to consciously think before they chose, whereas a third group was distracted for a while and then asked to choose. Participants in this latter group were performing a very taxing working memory task, preventing conscious thought. Instead, they were hypothesized to engage in unconscious thought. What was found with this paradigm is that unconscious thinkers make better decisions than do either conscious thinkers or immediate choosers, in that they choose alternatives with more positive and fewer negative characteristics (for more details, see Dijksterhuis 2004, Dijksterhuis et al. 2006, Dijksterhuis & Nordgren 2006, Ham et al. 2009). Moreover, similar effects were obtained with participants who chose an actual object (such as a poster) rather than a hypothetical one, with quality of choice operationalized as postchoice satisfaction (Dijksterhuis et al. 2006, Dijksterhuis & van Olden 2006).

In a recent set of experiments, it was shown that unconscious thought is a goal-dependent process (Bos et al. 2008; see also Zhong et al. 2008). In the experiments, participants were again given information about a decision problem. All participants were distracted before they made a decision. However, one group was told that they would later be asked some questions about the decision problem before they were distracted (as in previous experiments). The other group was told that they were done with the decision problem and would not be asked anything about it later on. In other words, one group had the goal to further process the information, whereas the other group had no such goal. Results showed that the former group made better decisions than did the latter. Hence, unconscious thought is a goal-dependent process. Without a goal to reach a decision, unconscious thought is not elicited.

The idea that people can think unconsciously has met with considerable resistance (e.g., Payne et al. 2008, Weber & Johnston 2009). However, as our current framework suggests, the fact that we can think without consciousness does not mean it does not require attention. Indeed, the fact that unconscious thought is goal dependent but takes place without conscious guidance strongly suggests that it does require attention. Preliminary results (F. van Harreveld, A. Dijksterhuis, & M.W. Bos, manuscript in preparation) show that performance on the working memory task during unconscious thought covaries with the successfulness of unconscious thought, in that performance on the distracter task suffers from unconscious thought and vice versa. This indicates that unconscious thought uses working memory resources. This conclusion is corroborated by other recent findings showing that effects of unconscious goals on attention and behavior are impeded when people have to perform a secondary working memory task (Aarts et al. 2008, Oikawa 2004).

The conclusion of this section is that implicit learning, evaluative conditioning, and unconscious thought are almost certainly not dependent on conscious awareness. However, they are goal directed and they do require attention (Bargh et al. 2001, Bos et al. 2008, Custers & Aarts 2009, Eitam et al. 2008, Field & Moore 2005).

FOCUS, FLEXIBILITY, AND THE TWO-FACED ROLE OF CONSCIOUSNESS

Volitional behavior involves the initiation and maintenance of goal pursuit. However, in many cases this is only half the story. Once a goal has been established, people often have to compare their desired state with their actual state and react to arising discrepancies in order to maintain their goal (Powers 1973). Furthermore, new goals may enter the scene that may ask for action. Given the potential interference of distracting information on the one hand and the dynamic nature of our world on the other, people often face the challenge to remain focused to maintain and stabilize one's goals and, at the same time, to be flexible and to adjust behavior to adapt to changing circumstances. Although operating in an antagonistic way, both aspects of attention are needed for optimal goal pursuit. Adaptive volitional behavior requires a context-dependent balance between focus and flexibility.

Whereas recent research recognizes the importance of a balance between focus and flexibility for effective goal pursuit, little is known about the mechanisms involved in establishing this balance. Research with frontal-lobe patients suggests that the frontal brain areas are involved in this process. Frontal-lobe patients display rigid behaviors and less flexibility in tasks that require switching between cognitive rules (Luria 1973, Shallice 1988, Stuss & Levine 1992). Furthermore, these patients seem to be unable to suppress impulses and well-practiced habits in response to objects and tools, also known as utilization behavior (Lhermitte 1983).

The idea that frontal cortical areas are involved in the dynamic balance between focus and flexibility raises the possibility that consciousness plays a prominent role in this process. Although tempting, this suggestion is empirically questionable. For instance, studies using a set-switching task or selective visual attention task have shown that the balance between focus and flexibility is modulated by the incidental activation of positive affect or reward cues (Della Libera & Chelazzi 2006, Dreisbach & Goschke 2004, Muller et al. 2007). According to Cohen and colleagues (Aston-Jones & Cohen 2005, Cohen et al. 2004), the regulation of the balance is hard-wired in the brain. Although the neurological basis is not yet fully delineated, it appears that flexible action is driven by subcortical output that releases dopamine in the PFC. This release is elicited by rewards or other positive cues that signal the incentive value of a goal (Berridge 2007). Furthermore, enhanced focus is more likely to ensue when action is required to keep the goal active and to shield it from distraction. Such goal-related monitoring processes are supposed to be controlled by the anterior cingulate cortex, which triggers the release of norepinephrine in the locus coeruleus, thereby enhancing focused attention processes in the PFC.

Thus, the balance between focus and flexibility is driven by the rewards and requirements associated with the goals that motivate the person to achieve them. Given the finding that reward-priming effects on decision making and resource recruitment can be brought about unconsciously (e.g., Bijleveld et al. 2009, Pessiglione et al. 2007) and given the human capacity to monitor goal-directed behavior unconsciously (e.g., Custers & Aarts 2007, Fourneret & Jeannerod 1998), it appears that the dynamic balance between focus and stability can occur in the absence of conscious awareness. This line of reasoning is consistent with research in social cognition that considers the motivation and attentional operation of goals to emerge from unconscious interactions of representations of goals and positive affect that can act as an incentive or effort mobilizer (Aarts et al. 2008, Custers & Aarts 2005).

The analysis above suggests that focus and flexibility are in good balance when unconscious goals interact with the environment in a proper way. However, this should not lead to the conclusion that consciousness does not play any role at all in goal-directed volitional behavior. Sometimes, the balance between focus and flexibility is imperfect or severely disturbed and people become aware of their unconscious goals. Indeed, research shows that the probability that unconsciously activated goals reach conscious awareness increases when goal progress is obstructed (Bongers et al. 2009), and it is this episode of conscious awareness that is said to typify a shift from unconscious, automated behavior to conscious, willful behavior (e.g., James 1890, Norman & Shallice 1986). However, how this state of conscious awareness unfolds and whether it serves a causal role in guiding volitional behavior is an essential problem in its own right and remains a topic of intriguing theorizing and empirical scrutiny (Aarts et al. 2007, Blackmore 2003, Bongers & Dijksterhuis 2009). Although we cannot solve the issue here, allow us to speculate on how conscious awareness of behavior may influence the balance between focus and flexibility.

Specifically, assuming that conscious awareness of goals directs attention in a similar way to that of unconscious goals, effects on behavior may depend on whether conscious attention co-occurs with and is directed at the imperfect balance between focus and flexibility during the process of goal pursuit. When conscious attention coincides with and is directed at restoring an imperfect balance, it may improve performance and adaptive behavior. However, when conscious awareness of goals emerges while the balance between focus and flexibility operates adequately—that is, when keeping one's eye on the goal and tuning behavior to changing circumstances act in close harmony—performance may not benefit from conscious awareness. In fact, it may even be jeopardized by conscious awareness. Such impairments may arise when people are explicitly forced to focus conscious attention on their behavior, thereby disturbing rather than promoting a good balance. A few examples of both beneficial and harmful effects of conscious awareness are given below.

Beneficial effects may occur when an imperfect balance during unconscious goal pursuit is encountered that requires a mode of information processing that cannot be relied on outside of conscious awareness. Specifically, we may encounter a deadlock, such as when goal-directed behavior is obstructed in such a way that neither focus nor flexibility is adaptive to deal with the problem. Often, this implies the planning of a course of action that is totally new or that has never been executed before in the situation at hand. According to Global Workspace Theory (e.g., Baars 1997, 2002), conscious awareness then helps to mobilize and integrate brain functions that otherwise operate independently in the process of building up an action that is not available in the person's repertoire. It offers a "facility for accessing, disseminating, and exchanging information, and for exercising global coordination and control" (Baars 1997, p. 7).

In research on the cognitive underpinnings of action planning, it has been suggested that planning integrates sensori-motor information regarding one's future behavior into a novel action representation that should be capable of bridging the gap between goals and behavior (Hommel et al. 2001). Furthermore, various studies have shown that conscious planning can lead to more successful goal achievement when such plans establish links between representations of relevant actions and cues (Gollwitzer & Sheeran 2006). That is, forming implementation intentions as to when, where, and how one will act to attain one's goal helps the progress of goal pursuit. Importantly, once the plan is formed, subsequent action initiation and performance display features of automaticity, in the sense that the action can be directly triggered by and executed in the anticipated environment without much conscious intervention. Thus, it seems that the obstruction of unconscious goal pursuit can benefit from the conscious awareness it evokes by rendering plans that specify how one needs to proceed. As soon as goal pursuit is reinitiated, the imbalance between focus and flexibility is restored, and unconscious goals can continue to do their work.

Whereas conscious awareness can clearly help goal pursuit, there is also support for detrimental effects of externally forced conscious awareness on goals. We briefly discuss three examples here. The first example pertains to the attentional blink phenomenon (e.g., Chun & Potter 1995, Marois & Ivanoff 2005, Raymond et al. 1992). When participants are asked to detect two briefly presented target stimuli within a stream of distracter stimuli, they show an impaired ability to identify the second of the two targets when they are presented in close succession. Whereas this attentional blink effect is generally thought to reflect a fundamental cognitive limitation, recent research indicates that an overinvestment of conscious attention to the stream of stimuli may drive the effect (Colzato et al. 2008; Olivers & Nieuwenhuis 2005, 2006). This research has demonstrated that a reduction in conscious attention limits the number of items in the stream that are fully processed, and as a consequence, this reduces the attentional blink effect. Also, incidental activation of positive affect or higher central dopaminergic function during the task decreases the attentional blink effect, a finding that is in line with the idea that positive affect modulates the balance between rigidly focusing on a task and a more flexible mode of processing. In short, conscious attention to goals can cause people to concentrate too hard and this promotes rather than prevents the occurrence of a rigid mode of information processing as reflected in the attentional blink effect.

Another line of research that reveals the potential for impairment in performance as a result of externally cued conscious awareness comes from research on decision making. Whereas conscious thought about a decision problem is sometimes helpful to reach more rational decisions (see, e.g., Newell et al. 2007), an abundance of research shows that conscious thought can also interfere with sound decision making (Dijksterhuis & Nordgren 2006, Reyna & Brainerd 1995, Schooler et al. 1993, Wilson & Schooler 1991). Some consider these findings counterintuitive (see, e.g., Weber & Johnston 2009), and this reaction is probably evoked by the attempt of some people to maintain that consciousness plays a crucial causal role in decision making and behavior in general. However, the findings on unconscious thought are fully in line with the current theorizing. When people make goal-directed decisions they can well deal with unconsciously (that is, when there is a good balance between focus and flexibility), conscious thought–elicited normative pressure or experimental instructions (Schooler et al. 1993) can interfere with decision making. One major problem is that people can often weight the relative importance of attributes quite well unconsciously (Dijksterhuis & Nordgren 2006, Wilson & Schooler 1991) and that conscious thought leads to biases in this weighting process, for instance because conscious thought tends to lead verbalizable information to receive too much weight and nonverbalizable information to receive too little weight (Reyna & Brainerd 1995, Schooler et al. 1993, Wilson & Schooler 1991). This jeopardizes the decision process.

A third area of study concerns skills. Skillful behavior can generally ensue without conscious awareness, and skills are often stored as abstract high-level patterns that serve a goal. When thirsty, for instance, grasping a glass and bringing it to one's mouth usually serves to take a sip. When goals guide attention in good balance between focus and flexibility, the person can unconsciously execute individual action sequences that capture the essential structure of the skill (e.g., when and how much a hand should be opened to reach for the glass) and adjust to changes in circumstances (e.g., different distance to and/or weight of the glass). It has been shown that consciously focusing on the execution of specific components of a complex motor skill can impair performance (e.g., Baumeister 1984, Beilock & Carr 2001, Lewis & Linder 1997). For instance, experienced soccer players handle the ball better with their dominant foot when they are distracted from executing a skill (e.g., dribbling) than when they are asked to consciously focus on specific action components. An explanation for this choking-under-pressure effect is that the conscious attention to separate components overrules the more efficient organizational structure of the skill. In other words, it disturbs the balance

between focus and flexibility in the unconscious execution of a skill in the environment that usually is guided by the goal. This causes the building blocks of the skill to function as separate components, in a similar way as before the skill was acquired. Once the structure breaks down, each component is executed separately, which takes more time and leaves more room for error.

CONCLUSIONS

Goals are the tools with which people engage in volitional behavior. They define what we find desirable to attain and thereby what we strive for. Goals exert their effects on behavior by modulating attention. Generally, information that can serve goal attainment is attended to more than information that is irrelevant for achieving goals.

Whereas goal pursuit was traditionally assumed to be strongly related to consciousness, recent research strongly suggests this not to be the case. Indeed, goal pursuit often proceeds entirely unconsciously. The role of consciousness in domains such as implicit learning, evaluative conditioning, and unconscious thought is still debated, in that some are willing to accept the idea that such important processes can ensue without conscious guidance, whereas others are not willing to endorse the viewpoint. However, recent research from various areas strongly suggests such processes to be dependent on goals and on attention but not on conscious awareness per se.

When people try to attain goals, attention serves to maintain a balance between focus and flexibility. That is, when people engage in goal pursuit, they face the challenge to remain focused and, at the same time, to be flexible and to adjust behavior to adapt to changing circumstances. Sometimes this balance is imperfect, and when people become consciously aware of their goals or behaviors because of endogenous factors, this generally helps to restore the balance between focus and flexibility. However, when the balance is adequate but people become consciously aware of their goals or behaviors for exogenous reasons (e.g., normative pressure, experimental instructions), the balance can be disturbed, which will jeopardize goal pursuit.

SUMMARY POINTS

1. Attention is largely determined by goals.

2. Consciousness and attention may be correlated in real life (such that stimuli that are attended to are more likely to enter consciousness), but they are independent.

3. Processes that we may think we need consciousness for are usually dependent on attention and not on consciousness.

4. Goal pursuit is dependent on both focus (the ability to keep the same information active) and flexibility (the ability to respond to changing circumstances).

5. Attention is responsible for a balance between focus and flexibility.

6. Conscious intervention may help to restore the balance between focus and flexibility. However, it can also disturb an already appropriate balance.

FUTURE ISSUES

1. The distinction between consciousness and attention should be more critically examined in studies showing that information processing and performance are dependent on goals.

2. The empirical study of the causal status of our conscious experiences of wilfulness in guiding behavior is underdeveloped.

3. What are the exact mechanisms that cause nonconscious goals to enter consciousness?

4. When exactly is consciousness helping the balance between focus and flexibility, and when is it harmful?

DISCLOSURE STATEMENT

The authors are not aware of any biases that might be perceived as affecting the objectivity of this review.

ACKNOWLEDGMENTS

Work on this review was supported by two VICI-grants from NWO (453-05-004 and 453-06-002). We thank Ruud Custers, Harm Veling, and Hans Marien for their valuable input.

LITERATURE CITED

Aarts H. 2007. Unconscious authorship ascription: the effects of success and effect-specific information priming on experienced authorship. *J. Exp. Soc. Psychol.* 43:119–26

Aarts H, Chartrand TL, Custers R, Danner U, Dik G, et al. 2005a. Social stereotypes and automatic goal pursuit. *Soc. Cogn.* 23:465–90

Aarts H, Custers R, Holland RW. 2007. The nonconscious cessation of goal pursuit: when goals and negative affect are coactivated. *J. Personal. Soc. Psychol.* 92:165–78

Aarts H, Custers R, Marien H. 2008. Preparing and motivating behavior outside of awareness. *Science* 319:1639

Aarts H, Custers R, Marien H. 2009. Priming and authorship ascription: when nonconscious goals turn into conscious experiences of self-agency. *J. Personal. Soc. Psychol.* 96:967–79

Aarts H, Custers R, Veltkamp M. 2008. Goal priming and the affective-motivational route to nonconscious goal pursuit. *Soc. Cogn.* 26:497–519

Aarts H, Custers R, Wegner DM. 2005b. On the inference of personal authorship: enhancing experienced agency by priming effect information. *Conscious. Cogn.* 14:439–58

Aarts H, Dijksterhuis A. 2000. Habits as knowledge structures: automaticity in goal-directed behavior. *J. Personal. Soc. Psychol.* 78:53–63

Aarts H, Dijksterhuis A. 2003. The silence of the library: environment, situational norm, and social behavior. *J. Personal. Soc. Psychol.* 84:18–28

Aarts H, Dijksterhuis A, De Vries P. 2001. On the psychology of drinking: being thirsty and perceptually ready. *Br. J. Psychol.* 92:631–42

Aarts H, Gollwitzer PM, Hassin RR. 2004. Goal contagion: perceiving is for pursuing. *J. Personal. Soc. Psychol.* 87:23–37

Aarts H, Oikawa M, Oikawa H. 2009. Cultural and universal routes to authorship ascription: effects of outcome priming on experienced self-agency in The Netherlands and Japan. *J. Cross-Cult. Psychol.* In press

Alonso D, Fuentes LJ, Hommel B. 2006. Unconscious symmetrical inferences: a role of consciousness in event integration. *Conscious. Cogn.* 15:386–96

Aston-Jones G, Cohen JD. 2005. An integrative theory of locus coeruleus-norepinephrine function: adaptive gain and optimal performance. *Annu. Rev. Neurosci.* 28:403–50

Baars BJ. 1997. *In the Theater of Consciousness: The Workspace of the Mind*. New York: Oxford Univ. Press

Baars BJ. 2002. The conscious access hypothesis: origins and recent evidence. *Trends Cogn. Sci.* 6:47–52

Baars BJ, Franklin S. 2003. How conscious experience and working memory interact. *Trends Cogn. Sci.* 7:166–72

Baccus JR, Baldwin MW, Packer DJ. 2004. Increasing implicit self-esteem through classical conditioning. *Psychol. Sci.* 15:498–502

Baddeley AD. 1993. Working memory and conscious awareness. In *Theories of Memory*, ed. A Collins, S Gathercole, pp. 11–28. Hillsdale, NJ: Erlbaum

Baddeley AD, Logie RH. 1999. The multiple-component model. In *Models of Working Memory: Mechanisms of Active Maintenance and Executive Control*, ed. A Miyake, P Shah, pp. 28–61. Cambridge, UK: Cambridge Univ. Press

Badgaiyan RD. 2000. Executive control, willed actions, and nonconscious processing. *Hum. Brain Mapp.* 9:38–41

Bargh JA. 1990. Auto-motives: preconscious determinants of thought and behavior. In *Handbook of Motivation and Cognition*, ed. ET Higgins, RM Sorrentino, Vol. 2, pp. 93–130. New York: Guilford

Bargh JA, Chartrand TL. 1999. The unbearable automaticity of being. *Am. Psychol.* 54:462–79

Bargh JA, Chen M, Burrows L. 1996. Automaticity of social behavior: direct effects of trait construct and stereotype activation on action. *J. Personal. Soc. Psychol.* 71:230–44

Bargh JA, Gollwitzer PM. 1994. Environmental control of goal-directed action: automatic and strategic contingencies between situations and behavior. In *Integrative Views of Motivation, Cognition, and Emotion. Nebraska Symposium on Motivation*, ed. WD Spaulding, Vol. 41, pp. 71–124. Lincoln, NE: Univ. Nebraska Press

Bargh JA, Gollwitzer PM, Lee-Chai A, Barndollar K, Trotschel R. 2001. The automated will: nonconscious activation and pursuit of behavioral goals. *J. Personal. Soc. Psychol.* 81:1014–27

Bargh JA, Gollwitzer PM, Oettingen G. 2009. Motivation. In *The Handbook of Social Psychology*, ed. ST Fiske, DT Gilbert, G Lindzey. Boston, MA: McGraw-Hill. 5th ed. In press

Baumeister RF. 1984. Choking under pressure: self-consciousness and paradoxical effects on incentives on skillful performance. *J. Personal. Soc. Psychol.* 46:610–20

Beilock SL, Carr TH. 2001. On the fragility of skilled performance: What governs choking under pressure? *J. Exp. Psychol. Gen.* 130:701–25

Berridge KC. 2007. The debate over dopamine's role in reward: the case for incentive salience. *Psychopharmacology* 191:391–431

Argues and explains how conscious and unconscious goals (partly) rely on the same functional architecture of attention and information processing in which the same cognitive functions or hardware are recruited and shared to translate goals into behavior.

A highly readable, though somewhat dated, introduction to what is now a dominant view on the role of consciousness.

A very comprehensive article by the father of automaticity research in social psychology.

The most influential article on unconscious goal activation, written by the people who thought of it first.

Berry D, Dienes ZP. 1993. *Implicit Learning: Theoretical and Empirical Issues*. Hove, UK: Erlbaum

Berry DC, Broadbent DE. 1984. On the relationship between task performance and associated verbalizable knowledge. *Q. J. Exp. Psychol. A Hum. Exp. Psychol.* 36:209–31

Bijleveld E, Custers R, Aarts H. 2009. The unconscious eye opener: Pupil dilation reveals strategic recruitment of mental resources upon subliminal reward cues. *Psychol. Sci.* In press

Blackmore S. 2003. *Consciousness: An Introduction*. New York: Oxford Univ. Press

Bongers KCA, Dijksterhuis A. 2009. Goals and consciousness. In *Encyclopedia of Consciousness*, ed. W Banks. Amsterdam: Elsevier. In press

Bongers KCA, Dijksterhuis A, Spears R. 2009. Self-esteem regulation after success and failure to attain unconsciously activated goals. *J. Exp. Soc. Psychol.* 45:468–77

Bos MW, Dijksterhuis A, Baaren RB. 2008. On the goal-dependency of unconscious thought. *J. Exp. Soc. Psychol.* 44:1114–20

Chun MM, Potter MC. 1995. A two-stage model for multiple target detection in rapid serial visual presentation. *J. Exp. Psychol.* 21:109–27

Cohen JD, Aston-Jones G, Gilzenrat MS. 2004. A systems-level theory on attention and cognitive control: guided activation, adaptive gating, conflict monitoring, and exploitation versus exploration. In *Cognitive Neuroscience of Attention*, ed. M Posner, pp. 71–90. New York: Guilford

Colzato LS, Slagter HA, Spapé MMA, Hommel B. 2008. Blinks of the eye predict blinks of the mind. *Neuropsychologia* 46:3179–83

Cooper RP, Shallice T. 2006. Hierarchical schemas and goals in the control of sequential behavior. *Psychol. Rev.* 113:887–916

Corbetta M, Shulman GL. 2002. Control of goal-directed and stimulus-driven attention in the brain. *Nat. Rev. Neurosci.* 3:201–15

Corneille O, Yzerbyt VY, Pleyers G, Mussweiler T. 2009. Beyond awareness and resources: evaluative conditioning may be sensitive to processing goals. *J. Exp. Soc. Psychol.* 45:279–82

Custers R, Aarts H. 2005. Positive affect as implicit motivator: on the nonconscious operation of behavioral goals. *J. Personal. Soc. Psychol.* 89:129–42

Custers R, Aarts H. 2007. In search of the unconscious sources of goal pursuit: accessibility and positive affective valence of the goal state. *J. Exp. Soc. Psychol.* 43:312–18

Custers R, Aarts H. 2009. Learning of predictive relations between events depends on goals, not necessarily on awareness. Manuscript under review

Custers R, Maas M, Wildenbeest M, Aarts H. 2008. Nonconscious goal pursuit and the surmounting of physical and social obstacles. *Eur. J. Soc. Psychol.* 38:1013–22

Damasio AR. 1999. *The Feeling of What Happens: Body and Emotion in the Making of Consciousness*. New York: Harcourt

Dehaene S, Changeux JP, Naccache L, Sackur J, Sergent C. 2006. Conscious, preconscious, and subliminal processing: a testable taxonomy. *Trends Cogn. Sci.* 10:204–11

Della Libera C, Chelazzi L. 2006. Visual selective attention and the effects of monetary rewards. *Psychol. Sci.* 17:222–27

Dijksterhuis A. 2004. I like myself but I don't know why: enhancing implicit self-esteem by subliminal evaluative conditioning. *J. Personal. Soc. Psychol.* 86:345–55

Dijksterhuis A. 2009. Automaticity and the unconscious. In *The Handbook of Social Psychology*, ed. ST Fiske, DT Gilbert, G Lindzey. Boston, MA: McGraw-Hill. 5th ed. In press

Dijksterhuis A, Bargh JA. 2001. The perception-behavior expressway: automatic effects of social perception on social behavior. *Adv. Exp. Soc. Psychol.* 33:1–40

Dijksterhuis A, Bos MW, Nordgren LF, Van Baaren RB. 2006. On making the right choice: the deliberation-without-attention effect. *Science* 311:1005–7

Dijksterhuis A, Nordgren LF. 2006. A theory of unconscious thought. *Perspect. Psychol. Sci.* 1:95–109

Dijksterhuis A, Preston J, Wegner DM, Aarts H. 2008. Effects of subliminal priming of self and God on self-attribution of authorship for events. *J. Exp. Soc. Psychol.* 44:2–9

Dijksterhuis A, van Olden Z. 2006. On the benefits of thinking unconsciously: unconscious thought can increase postchoice satisfaction. *J. Exp. Soc. Psychol.* 42:627–31

Empirical groundwork to come to a definition of goals.

A theory that specifies how conscious and unconscious thought work and a summary of the early findings on unconscious thought and decision making.

Dik G, Aarts H. 2007. Behavioral cues to others' motivation and goal pursuits: the perception of effort facilitates goal inference and contagion. *J. Exp. Soc. Psychol.* 43:727–37

Dreisbach G, Goschke T. 2004. How positive affect modulates cognitive control: reduced perseveration at the cost of increased distractibility. *J. Exp. Psychol. Learn. Mem. Cogn.* 30:343–53

Eitam B, Hassin RR, Schul Y. 2008. Nonconscious goal pursuit in novel environments: the case of implicit learning. *Psychol. Sci.* 19:261–67

Ferguson MJ. 2007. On the automatic evaluation of end-states. *J. Personal. Soc. Psychol.* 92:596–611

Field AP, Moore AC. 2005. Dissociating the effects of attention and contingency awareness on evaluative conditioning effects in the visual paradigm. *Cogn. Emot.* 19:217–43

Fishbach A, Friedman RS, Kruglanski AW. 2003. Leading us not unto temptation: momentary allurements elicit overriding goal activation. *J. Personal. Soc. Psychol.* 84:296–309

Fitzsimons GM, Bargh JA. 2003. Thinking of you: nonconscious pursuit of interpersonal goals associated with relationship partners. *J. Personal. Soc. Psychol.* 84:148–64

Fitzsimons GM, Chartrand TL, Fitzsimons GJ. 2008. Automatic effects of brand exposure on motivated behavior: how apple makes you "think different." *J. Consum. Res.* 35:21–35

Fourneret P, Jeannerod M. 1998. Limited conscious monitoring of motor performance in normal subjects. *Neuropsychologia* 36:1133–40

Frensch PA, Runger D. 2003. Implicit learning. *Curr. Dir. Psychol. Sci.* 12:13–18

Frith CD, Blakemore S-J, Wolpert DM. 2000. Abnormalities in the awareness and control of action. *Philos. Trans. R. Soc. Lond.* 355:1771–88

Funahashi S. 2001. Neuronal mechanisms of executive control by the prefrontal cortex. *Neurosci. Res.* 39:147–65

Gollwitzer PM, Sheeran P. 2006. Implementation intentions and goal achievement: a meta-analysis of effects and processes. *Adv. Exp. Soc. Psychol.* 38:69–120

Haggard P. 2008. Human volition: towards a neuroscience of will. *Nat. Rev. Neurosci.* 9:934–46

Halford GS, Baker R, McCredden JE, Bain JD. 2005. How many variables can humans process? *Psychol. Sci.* 16:70–76

Ham J, Van Den Bos K, Van Doorn E. 2009. Lady Justice thinks unconsciously: unconscious thought can lead to more accurate justice judgments. *Soc. Cogn.* In press

Hassin RR, Aarts H, Eitam B, Custers R, Kleiman T. 2009. Nonconscious goal pursuit and the effortful control of behavior. In *Oxford Handbook of Human Action: Mechanisms of Human Action*, ed. E Morsella, JA Bargh, PM Gollwitzer, pp. 549–68. New York: Oxford Univ. Press

Hassin RR, Aarts H, Ferguson MJ. 2005. Automatic goal inferences. *J. Exp. Soc. Psychol.* 41:129–40

Hayes NA, Broadbent DE. 1988. Two modes of learning for interactive tasks. *Cognition* 28:249–76

Haynes JD, Sakai K, Rees G, Gilbert S, Frith C, Passingham RE. 2007. Reading hidden intentions in the human brain. *Curr. Biol.* 17:323–28

Holland RW, Hendriks M, Aarts H. 2005. Nonconscious effects of scent on cognition and behavior. *Psychol. Sci.* 16:689–93

Hommel B. 1996. The cognitive representation of action: automatic integration of perceived action effects. *Psychol. Res.* 59:176–86

Hommel B. 2000. The prepared reflex: automaticity and control in stimulus-response translation. See Monsell & Driver 2000, pp. 221–42

Hommel B, Müsseler J, Aschersleben G, Prinz W. 2001. The theory of event coding (TEC): a framework for perception and action planning. *Behav. Brain Sci.* 24:849–78

James W. 1890. *The Principles of Psychology*. New York: Henry Holt

Jeannerod M. 1997. *The Cognitive Neuroscience of Action*. New York: Blackwell

Jimenez L, Mendez C. 1999. Which attention is needed for implicit sequence learning? *J. Exp. Psychol. Learn. Mem. Cogn.* 25:236–59

Jones JT, Pelham BW, Carvallo M, Mirenberg MC. 2004. How do I love thee? Let me count the Js: implicit egotism and interpersonal attraction. *J. Personal. Soc. Psychol.* 87:665–83

Jones SR, de-Wit L, Fernyhough C, Meins E. 2008. A new spin on the wheel of fortune: priming of action-authorship judgements and relation to psychosis-like experiences. *Conscious. Cogn.* 17:576–86

An up-to-date assessment of what neuroscience "knows" about volition.

Kahneman D. 1973. *Attention and Effort*. Englewood Cliffs, NJ: Prentice-Hall

Keele SW, Ivry R, Mayr U, Hazeltine E, Heuer H. 2003. The cognitive and neural architecture of sequence representation. *Psychol. Rev.* 110:316–39

Eloquently discusses the independence of attention and consciousness.

Koch C, Tsuchiya N. 2006. Attention and consciousness: two distinct brain processes. *Trends Cogn. Sci.* 11:16–22

Koch C, Ullman S. 1985. Shifts in selective visual attention: towards the underlying neural circuitry. *Hum. Neurobiol.* 4:219–27

Krosnick JA, Betz AL, Jussim LJ, Lynn AR. 1992. Subliminal conditioning of attitudes. *Personal. Soc. Psychol. Bull.* 18:152–62

Kruglanski AW, Shah JY, Fishbach A, Friedman R, Chun WY, Sleeth-Keppler D. 2002. A theory of goal systems. *Adv. Exp. Soc. Psychol.* 34:311–78

Lakin JL, Chartrand TL. 2003. Using nonconscious behavioral mimicry to create affiliation and rapport. *Psychol. Sci.* 14:334–39

Lamme VAF. 2003. Why visual attention and awareness are different. *Trends Cogn. Sci.* 7:12–18

Lau HC, Passingham RE. 2007. Unconscious activation of the cognitive control system in the human prefrontal cortex. *J. Neurosci.* 27:5805–11

Lau HC, Rogers RD, Haggard P, Passingham RE. 2004. Attention to intention. *Science* 303:1208–10

Lewicki P, Czyzewska M, Hoffman H. 1987. Unconscious acquisition of complex procedural knowledge. *Learn. Mem.* 13:523–30

Lewicki P, Hill T, Czyzewska M. 1992. Nonconscious acquisition of information. *Am. Psychol.* 47:796–801

Lewis BP, Linder DE. 1997. Thinking about choking? Attentional processes and paradoxical performance. *Personal. Soc. Psychol. Bull.* 23:937–44

Lhermitte F. 1983. "Utilization behavior" and its relation to lesions of the frontal lobes. *Brain* 106:237–55

Possibly the most important psychological experiment ever.

Libet B, Gleason CA, Wright EW, Pearl DK. 1983. Time of conscious intention to act in relation to onset of cerebral activity (readiness-potential): the unconscious initiation of a freely voluntary act. *Brain* 106:623–42

Loersch C, Aarts H, Payne KB, Jefferis VE. 2008. The influence of social groups on goal contagion. *J. Exp. Soc. Psychol.* 44:1555–58

Luria AR. 1973. *The Working Brain*. New York: Basic Books

Marois R, Ivanoff J. 2005. Capacity limits of information processing in the brain. *Trends Cogn. Sci.* 9:296–305

McKone E. 1995. Short-term implicit memory for words and nonwords. *J. Exp. Psychol. Learn. Mem. Cogn.* 21:1108–26

Merkelbach H, de Jong PJ, Arntz A, Schouten E. 1993. The role of evaluative learning and disgust sensitivity in the etiology and treatment of spider phobia. *Adv. Behav. Res. Ther.* 15:243–55

Miller EK, Cohen JD. 2001. An integrative theory of prefrontal cortex function. *Annu. Rev. Neurosci.* 24:167–202

Mischel W, Shoda Y, Rodriguez MI. 1989. Delay of gratification in children. *Science* 244:933–38

Miyake A, Shah P. 1999. *Models of Working Memory: Mechanisms of Active Maintenance and Executive Control.* Cambridge, UK: Cambridge Univ. Press

Monsell S, Driver J. 2000. *Control of Cognitive Processes: Attention and Performance XVIII.* Cambridge, MA: MIT Press

Moors A, De Houwer J. 2006. Automaticity: a theoretical and conceptual analysis. *Psychol. Bull.* 132:297–326

Moskowitz GB, Li P, Kirk ER. 2004. The implicit volition model: on the preconscious regulation of temporarily adopted goals. *Adv. Exp. Soc. Psychol.* 36:317–414

Muller J, Dreisbach G, Goschke T, Hensch T, Lesch KP, Brocke B. 2007. Dopamine and cognitive control: the prospect of monetary gains influences the balance between flexibility and stability in a set-shifting paradigm. *Eur. J. Neurosci.* 26:3661–68

Murphy ST, Monahan JL, Zajonc RB. 1995. Additivity of nonconscious affect: combined effects of priming and exposure. *J. Personal. Soc. Psychol.* 69:589–602

Newell BR, Lagnado DA, Shanks DR. 2007. *Straight Choices: The Psychology of Decision Making.* New York: Routledge

Niedenthal PM. 1990. Implicit perception of affective information. *J. Exp. Soc. Psychol.* 26:505–27

Nissen MJ, Bullemer P. 1987. Attentional requirements of learning: evidence from performance measures. *Cogn. Psychol.* 19:1–32

Norman DA, Shallice T. 1986. Attention to action: willed and automatic control of behavior. In *Consciousness and Self-Regulation*, ed. GE Schwartz, D Shapiro, Vol. 4, pp. 1–18. New York: Plenum

Oikawa M. 2004. Moderation of automatic achievement goals by conscious monitoring. *Psychol. Rep.* 95:975–80

Olivers CNL, Nieuwenhuis S. 2005. The beneficial effect of concurrent task-irrelevant mental activity on temporal attention. *Psychol. Sci.* 16:265–69

Olivers CNL, Nieuwenhuis S. 2006. The beneficial effects of additional task load, positive affect, and instruction on the attentional blink. *J. Exp. Psychol. Hum. Percept. Perform.* 32:364–79

Papies EK, Stroebe W, Aarts H. 2008. The allure of forbidden food: on the role of attention in self-regulation. *J. Exp. Soc. Psychol.* 44:1283–92

Payne J, Samper A, Bettman JR, Luce MF. 2008. Boundary conditions on unconscious thought in complex decision making. *Psychol. Sci.* 19:1118–23

Pessiglione M, Schmidt L, Draganski B, Kalisch R, Lau H, et al. 2007. How the brain translates money into force: a neuroimaging study of subliminal motivation. *Science* 316:904–6

Pleyers G, Corneille O, Luminet O, Yzerbyt V. 2007. Aware and (dis)liking: Item-based analyses reveal that valence acquisition via evaluative conditioning emerges only when there is contingency awareness. *J. Exp. Psychol. Learn. Mem. Cogn.* 33:130–49

Posner MI, Fan J. 2007. Attention as an organ system. In *Neurobiology of Perception and Communication: From Synapse to Society. De Lange Conference IV*, ed. J Pomerantz. Cambridge, UK: Cambridge Univ. Press

Powers WT. 1973. *Behavior: The Control of Perception*. Chicago: Aldine

Priluck R, Till BD. 2004. The role of contingency awareness, involvement, and need for cognition in attitude formation. *J. Acad. Mark. Sci.* 32:329–44

Prinz W. 2003. How do we know about our own actions? In *Voluntary Action: Brains, Minds, and Sociality*, ed. S Maasen, W Prinz, G Roth, pp. 21–33. New York: Oxford Univ. Press

Raymond JE, Shapiro KL, Arnell KM. 1992. Temporary suppression of visual processing in an RSVP task: an attentional blink. *J. Exp. Psychol. Hum. Percept. Perform.* 18:849–60

Razran GHS. 1940. Conditioned response changes in rating and appraising sociopolitical slogans. *Psychol. Bull.* 37:481

Reber AS. 1967. Implicit learning of artificial grammars. *J. Verbal Learn. Verbal Behav.* 6:855–63

Reber AS. 1989. Implicit learning and tacit knowledge. *J. Exp. Psychol. Gen.* 118:219–35

Reber AS. 1993. *Implicit Learning and Tacit Knowledge: An Essay on the Cognitive Unconscious*. London: Oxford Univ. Press

Reyna VF, Brainerd CJ. 1995. Fuzzy-trace theory: an interim synthesis. *Learn. Individ. Differ.* 7:1–75

Sato A. 2009. Both motor prediction and conceptual congruency between preview and action-effect contribute to explicit judgment of agency. *Cognition* 110:74–83

Sato A, Yasuda A. 2005. Illusion of sense of self-agency: Discrepancy between the predicted and actual sensory consequences of actions modulates the sense of self-agency, but not the sense of self-ownership. *Cognition* 94:241–55

Schooler JW, Ohlsson S, Brooks K. 1993. Thoughts beyond words: when language overshadows insight. *J. Exp. Psychol. Gen.* 122:166–83

Shah JY. 2003. Automatic for the people: how representations of others may automatically affect goal pursuit. *J. Personal. Soc. Psychol.* 84:661–81

Shah JY, Friedman R, Kruglanski AW. 2002. Forgetting all else: on the antecedents and consequences of goal shielding. *J. Personal. Soc. Psychol.* 83:1261–80

Shallice T. 1988. *From Neuropsychology to Mental Structure*. Cambridge, UK: Cambridge Univ. Press

Sheeran P, Aarts H, Custers R, Rivis A, Webb TL, Cooke R. 2005. The goal-dependent automaticity of drinking habits. *Br. J. Soc. Psychol.* 44:47–63

Sloman SA. 1996. The empirical case for two systems of reasoning. *Psychol. Bull.* 119:3–22

Smith EE, Jonides J. 1999. Storage and executive processes in the frontal lobes. *Science* 283:1657–61

Soon CS, Brass M, Heinze HJ, Haynes JD. 2008. Unconscious determinants of free decisions in the human brain. *Nat. Neurosci.* 11:543–45

A remarkable recent experiment that can be seen as an important follow-up on the Libet work.

Staats AW, Staats CK. 1958. Attitudes established by classical conditioning. *J. Abnorm. Soc. Psychol.* 11:187–92

Stuss DT, Levine B. 1992. Adult clinical neuropsychology: lessons from studies of the frontal lobe. *Annu. Rev. Psychol.* 33:401–33

Vallacher RR, Wegner DM. 1987. What do people think they're doing? Action identification and human behavior. *Psychol. Rev.* 94:3–15

van de Grind W. 2002. Physical, neural, and mental timing. *Conscious. Cogn.* 11:241–64

Van Harreveld F, Dijksterhuis A, Bos MW. 2009. Unconscious thought and working memory. Manuscript in preparation

Weber E, Johnston E. 2009. Mindful decision making. *Annu. Rev. Psychol.* 60:53–85

Wegner DM. 1994. Ironic processes of mental control. *Psychol. Rev.* 101:34–52

Wegner DM. 2003. *The Illusion of Conscious Will*. Cambridge, MA: MIT Press

Wegner DM, Smart L. 1997. Deep cognitive activation: a new approach to the unconscious. *J. Consult. Clin. Psychol.* 65:984–95

Wegner DM, Wheatley TP. 1999. Why it feels as if we're doing things: sources of the experience of will. *Am. Psychol.* 54:480–92

Wilson TD, Lisle DJ, Schooler JW, Hodges SD, Klaaren KJ, LaFleur SJ. 1993. Introspecting about reasons can reduce postchoice satisfaction. *Personal. Soc. Psychol. Bull.* 19:331–39

Wilson TD, Schooler JW. 1991. Thinking too much: Introspection can reduce the quality of preferences and decisions. *J. Personal. Soc. Psychol.* 60:181–92

Zhong CB, Dijksterhuis A, Galinsky AD. 2008. The merits of unconscious thought in creativity. *Psychol. Sci.* 19:912–18

A beautiful book that explains how conscious experience leads to feelings of free will.

RELATED RESOURCE

Wilson TD. 2002. *Strangers to Ourselves*. Cambridge, MA: Belknap

Negotiation

Leigh L. Thompson, Jiunwen Wang,
and Brian C. Gunia

Kellogg School of Management, Northwestern University, Evanston, Illinois 60208;
email: leighthompson@kellogg.northwestern.edu

Annu. Rev. Psychol. 2010. 61:491–515

First published online as a Review in Advance on
October 7, 2009

The *Annual Review of Psychology* is online at
psych.annualreviews.org

This article's doi:
10.1146/annurev.psych.093008.100458

Key Words

mixed-motive interaction, decision making, bargaining, value
creation, value claiming

Abstract

Negotiation occurs whenever people cannot achieve their own goals
without the cooperation of others. Our review highlights recent empirical research that investigates this ubiquitous social activity. We selectively review descriptive research emerging from social psychology
and organizational behavior. This research examines negotiation behavior and outcomes at five levels of analysis: intrapersonal, interpersonal,
group, organizational, and virtual. At each level, we review research on
negotiation processes and outcomes, and we discuss the implications of
various processes and outcomes for the two functions of negotiation:
value creation (integrative negotiation) and value claiming (distributive
negotiation).

Contents

INTRODUCTION

Anytime people cannot achieve their goals without the cooperation of others, they are negotiating. By this definition, negotiation is a ubiquitous social activity. Research on negotiation has been influenced by a wide variety of fields, including mathematics, management, organizational behavior, social psychology, cognitive psychology, economics, communication studies, sociology, and political science. The products of this multidisciplinary approach have been intense theoretical development and an impressive body of empirical findings.

Negotiation research has undergone several phases, characterized by different paradigms of thought. For example, during the 1980s, negotiation research was heavily influenced by game theory and behavioral decision theory. During the 1990s, negotiation research was strongly influenced by social psychology. At the turn of the millennium, negotiation research has become decidedly cognitive in flavor. Each generation of research has provided scholars with a new vantage point from which to examine the complex dance of negotiation.

One of the most important theoretical distinctions in negotiation scholarship is the one defining normative and descriptive research (Raiffa 1982). Normative research, largely derived from game theory, economics, and mathematics, proposes optimal models of the negotiation problem and prescribes what people would do if they were wise and all-knowing (cf. Luce & Raiffa 1957, Nash 1951). In this review, we focus on descriptive research, which recognizes that negotiators do not always behave in a game-theoretic, optimal fashion. The way negotiators actually behave usually departs significantly from normative, economic models (but not necessarily from behavioral economic models; Camerer 2003). For example, whereas normative models predict that people will/should almost always defect in a prisoner's dilemma or social dilemma, actual defection rates are dramatically lower than 100% (Camerer 2003, Komorita & Parks 1995). Moreover, normative models of negotiation dictate that parties should reach Pareto-optimal settlements, defined as agreements that cannot be improved upon without hurting one or both of the parties' outcomes. However, very few negotiators reach Pareto-optimal outcomes on a regular basis (Thompson 2009, Thompson & Hastie 1990).

Our focus is limited to descriptive research influenced by social psychology and its close cousin, organizational behavior—both of which have strongly influenced negotiation research since 1980. We focus on empirical studies that examine the individual negotiator within one or more of five systems—intrapersonal, interpersonal, group, organizational, and virtual. We use these systems as a guide for organizing our review. Within each system, we focus on two overarching themes: integrative negotiation and distributive negotiation, described further below.

The Intrapersonal, Interpersonal, Group, Organizational, and Virtual Systems

We use the term "intrapersonal system" to signify the ways that negotiation behavior and outcomes depend upon the perceptions and inner experiences of the negotiator. For example, the intrapersonal system might include research on how an individual's sense of power influences his or her negotiation behavior, satisfaction, and outcomes. The interpersonal system refers to the ways that negotiators' behavior and outcomes depend upon the presence of the other party or parties—negotiations in the context of others, and the dyadic aspects of negotiation behavior. Investigations of how a negotiator's mood influences the other party's behavior and the ultimate negotiation outcome exemplify this system. The group system encompasses social dynamics that extend beyond a single dyad—for example, group identity, cultural identity, coalitions, and conformity. The organizational system represents a higher level of analysis and examines the negotiator as embedded in a larger network or marketplace. For example, some studies at this level investigate how negotiators choose optimal counterparties in a marketplace of negotiators. Finally, the virtual system focuses on how negotiators' medium of interaction—such as face-to-face, phone, or email—affects the nature and quality of negotiation processes and outcomes. Several studies have investigated whether negotiators are more likely to discover mutual value when negotiating face-to-face or via computer (cf. Morris et al. 2002, Naquin & Paulson, 2003, Purdy et al. 2000).

Integrative and Distributive Negotiation

Whereas the independent variables or causal factors underlying negotiation have been highly eclectic and strongly influenced by the contemporary theoretical milieu, the dependent variables under investigation have remained consistent across several decades. The main reason for this consistency is the influence of economics on negotiation research. Within negotiation research, the two dependent variables that appear in virtually every published study of negotiation are negotiation processes and outcomes.

Negotiation processes include negotiators' behaviors, cognitions, emotions, and motivations. For example, much social psychological research has focused on negotiator satisfaction and the perceived relationship between the parties (see Curhan et al. 2006 for a review). Negotiation outcomes include the integrative and distributive features of the agreement. By "integrative," we mean the extent to which the negotiated outcome satisfies the interests of both parties in a way that implies the outcome cannot be improved upon without hurting one or more of the parties involved (i.e., Pareto optimality) (Pareto 1935). A classic example of Pareto optimality is the story of the two sisters who quarreled bitterly over a single orange (Fisher & Ury 1981). The sisters resolved the dispute by cutting the orange in half, such that each sister received exactly 50%. Later, the sisters discovered that one only needed the juice whereas the other only needed the rind; unfortunately they had failed to realize this during the negotiation itself. Cutting the orange in half was not an integrative outcome, because another feasible solution would have simultaneously improved both sisters' outcomes—one sister could have received all of the juice and the other all of the rind. This solution would have fully maximized both parties' interests. The fact that another feasible solution would have been better for both parties suggests that the actual outcome was suboptimal or Pareto inefficient, as opposed to integrative.

Negotiation: an interpersonal decision-making process necessary whenever we cannot achieve our objectives single-handedly. Negotiations include not only the one-on-one business meetings, but also multiparty, multicompany, and multimillion-dollar deals. People negotiate in their personal lives (e.g., with their spouses, children, schoolteachers, neighbors) as well as in their business lives

Pareto-optimal: Pareto optimality, or Pareto efficiency, is an important concept in economics with broad applications in game theory, engineering, and the social sciences. The term is named after Vilfredo Pareto, an Italian economist who used the concept in his studies of economic efficiency and income distribution. Informally, Pareto-optimal situations are those in which any change to make any person better off would make someone worse off

Integrative: negotiations are integrative when all creative opportunities are leveraged and no resources are left on the table

The distributive aspect of negotiation refers to how negotiators divide or apportion scarce resources among themselves. For example, in the classic ultimatum game (Güth et al. 1982, Ochs & Roth 1989), one person ("player 1") receives a fixed amount of money (say $100) to divide with another person. Player 1 proposes a split of the $100; if player 2 agrees, the proposed split takes effect. If player 2 rejects the proposal, each party gets $0. The split that Player 1 proposes can be perceived to be fair or acceptable to player 2, leading player 2 to accept the offer. In this case, the distributive aspect of the negotiation is the proportion of the original $100 that each negotiator receives.

Recently, the initial focus on the economic outcomes of negotiation has widened to include investigations of subjective outcomes. Whereas rational behavior in negotiation is usually equated with the maximization of economic gain, joint or individual, some have argued that it is equally appropriate to consider social-psychological outcomes, such as the quality of the relationship, the degree of trust between parties, each negotiator's satisfaction, and each person's willingness to negotiate with the other in the future. In an attempt to measure subjective concerns, Curhan and his colleagues surveyed people on what they value in negotiation (Curhan et al. 2006). Four distinct considerations emerged: feelings about instrumental outcomes (i.e., how much money they made), feelings about themselves (e.g., how competent they were in the negotiation), feelings about the process (e.g., whether the conversation was constructive) and feelings about the relationship (i.e., whether the negotiation preserved or strengthened it).

INTRAPERSONAL LEVEL

Negotiation research at the intrapersonal level of analysis clearly recognizes the multiparty nature of negotiation, but it emphasizes how the inner experience of the negotiator impacts negotiation processes and outcomes, and vice-versa. We focus on three interrelated intrapersonal constructs that have received significant research attention in recent years—power, gender, and affect. Many studies of power, gender, and affect in negotiations follow from research stimulated by the work of Steele (Steele & Aronson 1995), Banaji (Blair & Banaji 1996), Greenwald (Greenwald et al. 1996), Bargh (Bargh & Pietromonaco 1982), and others on the behavioral effects of unconscious priming. This research examines how subtle, below-threshold activation of concepts influences above-threshold behaviors. In negotiations, above-threshold behaviors substantially impact negotiation processes and outcomes, which may unconsciously activate other cognitions and behaviors.

Power

Power refers to an individual's relative ability to alter other people's outcomes (Keltner et al. 2003). Several studies examine psychological power as a state, operationalized through priming, but others examine power as a trait or individual difference. Although negotiators may have several sources of structural power (French & Raven 1959), the most commonly investigated source of power is the negotiator's best alternative to a negotiated agreement (BATNA; Fisher & Ury 1981).

A negotiator's BATNA has become the primary indicator of a negotiator's relative power in negotiation. The BATNA concept was formally introduced by Fisher and Ury in 1981; however, the concept actually traces back to the social exchange theory of Thibaut & Kelley (1959). Exchange theory cites rewards (borrowed from psychology) and resources (borrowed from economics) as the foundation of interpersonal exchanges. Rewards refer to the benefits a person enjoys from participating in a relationship (Thibaut & Kelley 1959), whereas resources are any commodities, material or symbolic, that can be transmitted through interpersonal behavior (Foa & Foa 1975) and give one person the capacity to reward another (Emerson 1976). Satisfaction with an exchange relationship is derived in part from the evaluation of the outcomes available in a relationship.

Outcomes are equal to the rewards obtained from a relationship minus the costs incurred.

People in social exchanges compare the outcomes of the current exchange with the outcomes they could achieve in an alternative exchange—these alternative outcomes are operationalized as the "comparison level of alternatives," or CLalt. When the CLalt exceeds the outcomes available in a current relationship, the person is more likely to leave the relationship. The concept of CLalt is parallel to BATNA. When one's BATNA is better than an agreement one can reach with a particular negotiation counterpart, one should choose to not agree and exercise the BATNA instead.

Negotiators' BATNAs are strongly related to their reservation point (RP). RPs are the quantification of a negotiator's BATNA (Raiffa 1982). According to Raiffa (1982), a negotiator's RP is the point at which a negotiator is indifferent between reaching a deal with party A or walking away from the table and exercising his/her BATNA. For a seller, prices exceeding reservation points are acceptable; for a buyer, prices less than reservation points are acceptable. RPs are generally operationalized as the value attached to a negotiator's BATNA, plus or minus the value of any idiosyncratic preferences they attach to reaching agreement versus exercising the BATNA.

Just as BATNA traces to Thibaut & Kelley's (1959) earlier concept of CLalt, reservation price traces to Walton & McKersie's (1965) concept of resistance point, described in their book *A Behavioral Theory of Labor Relations*. Resistance point is a negotiator's subjectively determined bottom line—the point at which negotiators are indifferent between reaching agreement and walking away, in the midst of the negotiation. Walton & McKersie (1965) postulated that negotiators who had more attractive resistance points were in a more powerful position because they could simply offer the other party just enough to meet their resistance point and claim the rest (the surplus) for themselves. Although the concept of reservation price has largely displaced the concept of resistance point

in recent academic research, resistance points provided an important theoretical step toward specifying the concept of bargaining zone. Bargaining zone is basically the overlap between two negotiators' RPs—the buyer's RP minus the seller's RP. If this number is positive, a zone of possible agreement (ZOPA) is said to exist; if it is negative, no ZOPA exists.

Research studying the effects of power have documented that there is a strong, causal relationship between the attractiveness of a negotiator's BATNA and the negotiator's ability to claim resources in a given negotiation (Galinsky & Mussweiler 2001, Magee et al. 2007, Mussweiler & Strack 1999). Negotiators with attractive BATNAs are considered "powerful"; these negotiators are decidedly more assertive in negotiations. For example, powerful people move first, both by initiating negotiations and by making the first offer (Magee et al. 2007). When power is primed (by instructing people to write about a time when they felt powerful or to perform a word-completion task involving words about power), these individuals often make the first offer in negotiations. If the concept of BATNA is a measure of structural power, then chronic tendencies to dominate others in social relationships reflect personal power. Both structural and personal power can improve negotiators' outcomes by leading them to make the first offer (Galinsky & Mussweiler 2001, Magee et al. 2007, Mussweiler & Strack 1999).

Although having power may increase a negotiator's propensity to make a first offer, this may depend on the nature of the negotiation. Specifically, it is reasonable to assume that if both negotiators have attractive BATNAs, their motivation to reach mutual agreement is not as high as that of two negotiators with very poor alternatives. Thus, the effects of one's power in a negotiation may depend on the size of the bargaining zone. Given that BATNAs establish the minimum level of benefits one would receive, irrespective of what occurs in the negotiation, their influence quickly diminishes once benefits equivalent to the BATNA value have been attained.

Reservation point: determined not by what the negotiator wishes and hopes for, but rather by what her BATNA represents. A reservation point is a quantification of a negotiator's BATNA with respect to other alternatives

Bargaining zone: the range between negotiators' reservation points. Between a buyer and a seller, the bargaining zone will be between the highest price a buyer is willing to pay and the lowest price a seller is willing to sell for

In one study, strong BATNAs improved negotiators' outcomes more when the bargaining zone was small rather than large (Kim & Fragale 2005). When the bargaining zone was large, power tended to derive more from a negotiator's contribution to the negotiation. In this case, contribution refers to the benefits that a negotiator contributes beyond the value of the counterparty's BATNA. For instance, if the counterparty is selling a house and has a BATNA (e.g., another buyer offering $200K for the house) and the negotiator offers $210K for the house, the difference, or $10K, is the contribution.

Once an offer equaled the value of one's BATNA in Kim and Fragale's research, outcomes depended more on the extent to which the counterparty could contribute value beyond the BATNA. Contributions thus exerted an important influence on negotiation outcomes, especially as the potential agreement became more valuable (relative to negotiators' BATNAs).

Gender

Power is manifested and expressed by negotiators in many ways. For example, power can depend upon structural factors (e.g., BATNA) or on personal characteristics. A negotiator's structural power can change when environmental conditions change, but personal power is, for the most part, fixed. For example, a negotiator who is selling her house and has an attractive offer from a very motivated buyer has a lot of structural power; however, if the buyer suddenly withdraws the offer on the house (perhaps due to a failed home inspection), the negotiator's power plummets. Conversely, a negotiator who is a vice president of a major company and has a lot of personal charm also holds high power, which is more resilient to temporary fluctuations of the market (except in the case of losing her job!). One important source of personal power is gender.

To exert influence in a negotiation, gender must be activated or made salient (Kray & Thompson 2005). In a series of investigations

modeled after Steele & Aronson (1995), Kray et al. (2001) did just this. Specifically, they investigated whether the mere activation of gender (and its accompanying stereotypes) impacts negotiation performance. The prevailing stereotype is that women are less assertive and agentic than men. Because many people see negotiation as a situation requiring assertive and agentic behavior, stereotypically female traits may seem inconsistent with negotiation once the connection is made salient. For these reasons, the mere mention of negotiation might create an internal conflict within women: On one hand, they may believe that performing well requires them to engage in counterstereotypical behaviors. On the other hand, they may believe that others expect them to behave in an accommodating, nonassertive fashion.

Kray et al. (2001) hypothesized that the mention of gender might operate much like stereotype threat (Steele & Aronson 1995). Gender salience might thus operate like a low-power state, preventing women from acting assertively. In their study, women did, in fact, get worse outcomes than did men in mixed-gender negotiations, when an implicit gender stereotype was subtly activated. However, it was reasoned that explicit activation of the gender stereotype may allow women to counteract it. As predicted, explicitly activated gender stereotypes led to a stereotype-reactance effect, in which women actually outperformed men by claiming more resources (presumably in an attempt to defy the stereotype). Women effectively said, "Well, unassertive behavior and accommodation may be the cultural stereotype of women, but it is surely not me!"

In another series of studies, Kray and colleagues (2004) reasoned that negotiation, like other social activities, can be construed as either a masculine or feminine activity. The masculine construal of negotiation involves agency and assertiveness. It is also possible to construe successful negotiation as understanding human behavior, perceiving nonverbal cues, and building trust. Arguably, these skills are more consistent with the classic female stereotype. Indeed, women outperformed men when traditionally feminine traits were linked with negotiation success, and each gender outperformed the other when the other gender was linked with negotiation ineffectiveness (Kray et al. 2001).

The implications of stereotype activation may also depend on whether negotiators have high or low power (Kray et al. 2004). Specifically, activation of an explicit male stereotype led to negotiated outcomes that favored the high-power negotiator, whereas activation of an explicit female stereotype led to more integrative, win-win outcomes that were beneficial for both parties, much like the sisters who discovered the juice-and-rind tradeoff.

Other studies (Small et al. 2007) examine gender differences in the willingness to initiate negotiation (Babcock et al. 2006, Bowles et al. 2007; but see Gerhart & Rynes 1991), tracing these differences to power differences. Because women traditionally have less power than do men in U.S. society (Eagly & Wood 1982), they initiate negotiations less often; however, this difference is attributable to the fact that situations framed as "negotiation" conflict with politeness norms that prevail in low-power groups (Babcock et al. 2006). Consistent with this reasoning and the links between gender and power, framing negotiations as opportunities to "ask" eliminated gender differences in negotiation initiation, as did priming psychological power (Kray et al. 2001). Along similar lines, Bowles et al. (2007) traced differences in the initiation of negotiation behavior to observers' reactions. Both male and female observers penalized female job candidates for initiating negotiations. Consistent with Small et al.'s (2007) politeness argument, participants rated women who initiated negotiations as less nice and more demanding. Moreover, women were less likely than were men to initiate negotiations with a male (but not a female) evaluator.

Another stream of gender research examines what happens when women do, in fact, initiate negotiation. Although gender differences in actual negotiation behavior have received exhaustive research attention (e.g., Deal 2000, Gerhart & Rynes 1991, Major et al. 1984, Stevens et al. 1993, Watson 1994), recent meta-analyses (Stuhlmacher & Walters 1999, Walters et al. 1998) characterize such differences as modest and context dependent. According to these meta-analyses, women negotiate slightly more cooperatively than do men, but situational factors such as relative power of the negotiator, integrative potential of the task, and mode of communication often override this effect. In addition, other individual differences (i.e., social motives) explain cooperation in negotiation more readily than gender does. For example, negotiators with a prosocial motive behave more cooperatively (and achieve better outcomes) than do those with an egoistic motive (De Dreu et al. 2000). Gender differences seem to explain relatively little variance by comparison, and it is possible that the variance they do explain reflects underlying gender differences in social motives.

There are behavioral implications of gender-dependent power. For example, does maintaining steady eye contact have different power implications for male and female negotiators (Swaab & Swaab 2009)? When negotiators made eye contact (and when visual access was possible), agreement quality was maximized for women but minimized for men (Swaab & Swaab 2009). Apparently, women and men had different affective experiences during negotiation. When men made eye contact, perceived power differences were exacerbated, creating a sense of discomfort that undermined agreement quality.

Affect

Forgas's (1995) affect infusion model considers the impact of mood on cognitive processing, identifying two overarching conditions under which mood is likely to affect information processing. The first condition is when situations require cognition about difficult, peripheral subjects; the second is when situations require judgment of obscure, atypical subjects (Forgas 1995). According to the affect infusion model, the adoption of information processing style also depends on a combination of factors such as the novelty, complexity, and salience of the task, and the personality, motivation, affective state, and cognitive capacity of the person involved in the judgment process.

The implication for negotiation processes and outcomes is that feeling good or feeling bad should have important consequences for negotiator cognition and strategies (Lanzetta 1989). In one study, positive mood generated superior individual outcomes in negotiations with integrative potential characterized by cooperative negotiation strategies (Forgas 1998). In another study, positive mood decreased evasive and equivocal communications, especially in high-conflict negotiations (Forgas & Cromer 2004).

One line of research qualifies these findings by demonstrating that the impact of affect depends on power. For example, agreement quality was better predicted by the chronic, positive affect of high-power negotiators than that of low-power negotiators (Anderson & Thompson 2004). Apparently, the more powerful negotiator's emotions were more influential than the less powerful negotiator's emotions. Furthermore, trait-positive affect, combined with high structural power (i.e., a strong BATNA), helped negotiation dyads reach more integrative agreements without harming either negotiator's individual outcomes (Anderson & Thompson 2004). Recently, investigations of negative affect such as anger expressions have also been examined (Sinaceur & Tiedens 2006). Anger expressions produced concessions from negotiators with a poor BATNA, presumably because the angry negotiator communicated "toughness." This finding contrasts somewhat with earlier investigations in which feelings of high anger and low compassion produced lower joint outcomes, but not lower individual outcomes (Allred et al. 1997). Similarly, when negotiators expressed positive affect, negative affect, or neutral affect in a take-it-or-leave-it ultimatum, positive-affect negotiators were most likely to have their ultimatum accepted. Negative-affect negotiators were the least successful (Kopelman et al. 2000).

Other research examined the relationship between economic outcomes, negotiator

behavior, and satisfaction (an affective response to negotiation). For example, a negotiator's focus on RP or aspirations influences feelings of success in a negotiation (Thompson 1995). Negotiators with low RPs felt more successful than did those with high RPs, even though their final settlements were identical. Furthermore, negotiators with low aspirations felt more successful than did negotiators with high aspirations, even though the final settlement was identical. Aspirations influenced negotiators' perceptions of success more than did RPs. In general, aspirations, relative to RPs, exerted a more powerful influence on the demands people made to others in negotiations and how successful they felt about negotiated outcomes.

Along similar lines, negotiators might feel dissatisfied when the counterparty accepts their first offer (Galinsky et al. 2002). Apparently, when the counterparty immediately accepts one's first offer, a counterfactual thought process is produced (e.g., "Oh no, I should have asked for more!"). This counterfactual thought process results in dissatisfaction, even when negotiators' outcomes were objectively superior to agreements reached later in negotiations. Thoughts about how much better they could have done overwhelmed negotiators' objective outcomes. These findings are consistent with studies demonstrating that negotiators' satisfaction depends heavily on the comparison value on which they focus attention: Negotiators who focused on their target price consistently achieved better outcomes but were less satisfied than those who focused on their BATNA (Galinsky et al. 2002). Yet, focusing on the target price during a negotiation and the BATNA after a negotiation allowed negotiators to achieve superior outcomes without the accompanying dissatisfaction.

An array of negative cognitions and emotions confront negotiators who fail to reach deals (O'Connor & Arnold 2001). For example, negotiators who failed to reach agreement (i.e., impassed) found themselves caught in a distributive spiral such that they interpreted their performance as unsuccessful, experienced negative emotions, and developed negative perceptions of their counterpart and the process. Moreover, they were less willing to work with their counterpart in the future, planned to share less information and behave less cooperatively, and lost faith in negotiation as an effective means of managing conflicts (O'Connor & Arnold 2001).

INTERPERSONAL LEVEL

Economic and Social Psychological Foundations

Traditionally, negotiation at the interpersonal level has been viewed via the lens of mixed-motive interaction. The concept of mixed-motive interaction was first introduced by economist Thomas Schelling (1960) to refer to situations where two or more parties face a conflict between two motives: cooperation (the integrative aspects of negotiation) and competition (the distributive aspects). In negotiations, individuals must cooperate to avoid impasse and reach mutual agreement, but compete to gain sufficient resources for themselves. Two-person bargaining is thus a classic example of a mixed-motive interaction. Indeed, Lax & Sebenius (1986b) emphasize that all negotiators must balance the "twin tasks" of negotiation: creating value and claiming value.

The interpersonal system in negotiation was also richly stimulated by basic research in the areas of emotional contagion, mimicry, and behavioral synchrony (Chartrand & Bargh 1999). One finding in these areas, for example, is that people tend to engage in face rubbing, foot shaking, and smiling more in the presence of someone who engages in that behavior (Chartrand & Bargh 1999). Another is that behavioral mimicry increases liking and rapport between interaction partners (Tiedens & Fragale 2003). Beyond behavioral mimicry, more complex interpersonal mimicry such as mood contagion (see Neumann & Strack 2000) and dominance complementarity (see Tiedens & Fragale 2003) have also been documented. Mood contagion effects demonstrate that people easily assume the moods of others. Dominance complementarity findings demonstrate that people respond to others' dominant behavior with a submissive stance, and vice versa. Furthermore, they demonstrate that when one party complements dominant behavior with submissive behavior, this facilitates interpersonal liking (Tiedens & Fragale 2003).

Interpersonal Effects of Emotions in Negotiation

Emotions influence negotiations at the interpersonal as well as intrapersonal level. In fact, research on emotions in negotiation bridges the intrapersonal and interpersonal level. Two specific emotions, anger and happiness, have received particular attention from negotiation researchers (Van Kleef et al. 2004a). Participants in one study received information about the emotional state (anger, happiness, or none) of their opponent (Van Kleef et al. 2004a). Consistent with the research noted above, participants conceded more to an angry opponent than to a happy one. Apparently, people used emotion information to infer the other's limit (i.e., their RP), and they adjusted their demands accordingly. However, this effect was absent when the other party made large concessions. Angry communications (unlike happy ones) induced fear and thereby mitigated the effect of the opponent's experienced emotion. Negotiators were especially influenced by their opponent's emotions when they were motivated to consider them (Van Kleef et al. 2004b).

The processes and mediators behind the interpersonal effects of emotions may be influenced by the extent to which individuals are motivated to process information systematically and deeply (De Dreu & Carnevale 2003, Van Kleef et al. 2004b). For instance, participants in one study (Van Kleef et al. 2004b) received information about the opponent's emotion (anger, happiness, or none). Those in the angry condition received a message saying "this offer makes me really angry," whereas those in the happy condition received a message saying "I am happy with this offer." As predicted, negotiators conceded more to an angry opponent than to a happy one, but only when they had low (rather than high) need for cognitive closure—a measure of their chronic motivation to process information systematically. Also, participants were only affected by the other's emotion under low rather than high time pressure, because time pressure reduced their capacity for information processing. Finally, negotiators were only influenced by their opponent's emotions when they had low (rather than high) power, presumably because high-power negotiators had less need and were less motivated to process this information. These results support the motivated information-processing model, which argues that negotiators are only affected by their opponent's emotions if they are motivated to consider them.

Interpersonal Improvisation in Negotiation

Other research has utilized a more qualitative approach to unpack interpersonal processes in negotiations. Beyond the focus on economic outcomes in negotiations, negotiators may sometimes also be focused on relationship processes and outcomes (McGinn & Keros 2002).

Specifically, McGinn & Keros (2002) highlight the improvisation and the logic of exchange in socially embedded transactions. Socially embedded transactions take into account the fact that negotiators can have deep social ties or share mutual social ties with one another. This is in contrast to the arm's length transaction between individuals, in which individuals share little familiarity or affect and no prolonged past or expected future ties (Granovetter 1973, Podolny & Baron 1997, Uzzi 1997).

By improvisation, McGinn & Keros (2002) conjecture that most people at the outset of a negotiation do not construe it as such. This is because, whereas arm's length transactions are often guided by a logic of profit maximization, embedded transactions (such as between friends) go beyond the focus on outcomes alone;

they tend to focus on rules of friendships as opposed to rules of the market.

In a qualitative fashion, McGinn & Keros (2002) used a sense-making lens to illuminate microprocesses underlying socially embedded transactions, investigating how social networks affect the logic of exchange governing the transaction. Transcript analysis of two-party negotiations revealed that most pairs of negotiators quickly coordinated a shared logic of exchange and improvised in accord with its implied rules throughout their interaction. The improvisation took the form of opening up, working together, or haggling. Negotiators used three dynamic processes—trust testing, process clarification, and emotional punctuation—when they had difficulty moving the interaction toward a coherent, mutually agreed-upon pattern. Social embeddedness, or the extent to which an individual shares other social connections with another individual (Granovetter 1973), eases coordination within negotiation (McGinn & Keros 2002).

Subjective Value in Negotiation

As noted above, negotiators have noneconomic, relational concerns as well as economic ones. Besides their concern with economic gains, negotiators are also concerned about their feelings about the self, the negotiation process, and the relationship (Curhan et al. 2006). Moreover, the "subjective value" accrued from these components of negotiation have long-lasting impact (Curhan et al. 2009). For example, the subjective value that actual managers derived from job offer negotiations predicted their subsequent job attitudes and turnover intentions better than the economic value they achieved: Subjective value measured at the outset of a negotiation predicted managers' job satisfaction and likelihood of quitting a full one year later. Curiously, negotiators' economic outcomes (i.e., their actual salaries) did not predict satisfaction or turnover. Arguably, the subjective value gained from a negotiation may have more long-lasting impact than the actual economic gains from the negotiation.

However, one potentially important consideration is whether subjective value conflicts with economic value in negotiations. To examine this, negotiators who held relational goals were compared with negotiators who held economic goals. If relational goals hinder economic gain, then it would be reasonable to expect negotiators to underperform relative to economically motivated negotiators (Curhan et al. 2008). Indeed, negotiators in egalitarian organizations reached less-efficient (i.e., worse) economic outcomes but had higher relational capital than did those who negotiated in hierarchical organizations. By directly pitting economic gain against relational considerations, this study showed how the structure of one's environment (egalitarian versus hierarchical) can influence one's own goals and therefore negotiation outcomes.

Trust and Tactics

Mutual trust is an essential ingredient in effective organizations (see Dirks & Ferrin 2001) and negotiations (Kimmel et al. 1980). Trust, defined as the intention to accept vulnerability based upon positive expectations of the counterpart's behavior and intentions (Rousseau et al. 1998), allows negotiators to exchange the information necessary for integrative agreements. Distrusting negotiators are reluctant to share information or ask questions, believing that their counterparts will take advantage of shared information and respond to their questions dishonestly. Conversely, trusting negotiators believe their counterparts will use information to identify integrative agreements. They also tend to believe information that the counterpart shares, accepting it as sincere and accurate (Parks et al. 1996). As a result, trusting negotiators exchange more information about preferences and priorities and achieve more integrative outcomes (Butler 1995, Kimmel et al. 1980, Pruitt & Kimmel 1977, Weingart et al. 1993).

Despite the importance of trust, violations of trust are common (see Elangovan & Shapiro 1998 for a review), jeopardizing the integrativeness of negotiation outcomes. Given the mixed-motive nature of negotiation, it is tempting for negotiators to use deception to maximize their personal gain. Yet, deception is likely to compromise trust. Thus, an important question is when people will lie in negotiations. People tend to lie when the lures of temptation and uncertainty align with powerless and anonymous victims (Tenbrunsel & Diekmann 2007). The more negotiators stand to gain economically, the more likely they are to lie (Bazerman et al. 1998). Moreover, the more uncertainty negotiators have about material factors, the more likely they are to lie. Of course, liars often garner a reputation as such, making it more difficult for them to win counterparts' trust in the future (Glick & Croson 2001).

Given that negotiators may sometimes resort to deceptive tactics in negotiations, another important consideration is how interpersonal trust broken by deceptive behavior can be restored. One theory holds that broken trust can never be fully restored, even if the trust breaker performs a series of consistently trustworthy actions (Schweitzer et al. 2006), such as fulfilled promises, apologies, and consistently reliable behavior. A promise to change behavior can significantly speed the trust recovery process, but prior deception harms the effectiveness of a promise in accelerating trust recovery. Another perspective holds that apologies can effectively restore trust when the trust violation concerns a matter of competence, but not when it concerns a matter of integrity (Kim et al. 2004).

In a given negotiation, tactics such as threats, bluffs, and disclaimers can affect negotiators' relationships and the grounds for their trust. For example, a buyer-seller simulation with two negotiation periods examined the behavioral and attitudinal consequences of threats, bluffs, and disclaimers (Shapiro & Bies 1994). Some negotiators received a threat stated as a disclaimer, whereas others did not. Changes in negotiators' evaluations of their partner and negotiation outcomes were examined after some were led to believe their partner had stated a false threat (a bluff). Negotiators who used threats were perceived as more powerful, but they were also perceived as less cooperative and achieved lower integrative agreements than those who did not use threats.

Relationships and Negotiations

Perhaps the most straightforward question one could investigate about the interpersonal aspects of negotiation is whether people involved in a relationship can fashion integrative agreements better than strangers can. Kelley (1982) studied how couples negotiate problems of interdependence. Yet, the first study that truly examined how people in relationships, versus strangers, negotiate was Fry et al.'s (1983) study of dating couples. Paradoxically, strangers were more likely to reach win-win (mutually beneficial agreements) than were dating couples, although the effect did not reach conventional levels of significance. The authors' reasoning was that couples (and perhaps friends) are uncomfortable asserting their own needs and therefore are more willing to settle for suboptimal agreements.

The orientation that friends bring to a negotiation seems to dictate the outcomes they achieve. Pairs of friends who are similar in communal orientation are most likely to capitalize on joint interests (Thompson & DeHarpport 1998). However, when friends are dissimilar in communal orientation, their ability to identify compatible issues declines precipitously. Friends who are high in communal orientation are more likely to allocate resources equally than are friends low in communal orientation. The existence of friendships also has significant implications for one's negotiation outcomes (Seidel et al. 2000). Seidel and colleagues analyzed more than 3000 actual salary negotiations and found that having friends in high places within the relevant organization improved salary negotiation outcomes.

Whereas the studies reviewed above tend to focus on economic outcomes, negotiations also involve symbolic resources such as identity and legitimacy. Glynn (2000) studied identity and legitimacy during a musicians' strike at the Atlanta Symphony Orchestra. Glynn analyzed the musicians and administrators as competing parties vying for the legitimacy to define the core identity of the orchestra. Embedded within the multilayered negotiation, Glynn reports, "were conflicts over status and power and, implicitly, control over the resources that would confer such status and power" (p. 291). This study illustrates that relationships not only influence negotiations, but negotiations can reconstitute and reshape relationships.

GROUP LEVEL

The group system focuses on how group dynamics influence negotiation processes and outcomes. In this section, we selectively focus on four major streams of research at the group level: social and group identity, relational and collective identity, group culture, and teams and the discontinuity effect. Some of this research uses paradigms derived from game theory (e.g., social dilemmas), but we include it in this review because it speaks directly to descriptive negotiation research.

Social and Group Identity

According to the group identity perspective, which is part of a larger social identity tradition (e.g., Tajfel et al. 1971), the stronger an individual's group identity, the less sharply he or she distinguishes between self-interest and collective interest. For negotiation, this implies that distributive (personal gains) are less focal than integrative (mutual gains) for negotiators who consider counterparts members of their group. This conjecture has been examined most directly in the social dilemma literature, which examines situations where individual and collective interest are largely opposed.

There are two perspectives concerning choice in a social dilemma situation. From a purely economic point of view, the rational choice is to defect because it yields greater outcomes. Of course, if everyone defects, then the collective welfare of the group suffers. The social psychological viewpoint is that defection is undesirable and people are best served when everyone puts self-interest aside and chooses to maximize group interests. Kramer & Brewer (1984) pioneered the study of group identity in social dilemma and negotiation research. By emphasizing the common fate among group members and the salience of a superordinate group identity, they showed that the degree of cooperation in social dilemmas increases (Brewer & Kramer 1986, Kramer & Brewer 1984). Another way of inducing group identity is to extend the length of time a person expects to be part of a group. In one study (Mannix & Loewenstein 1993), people who expected to be part of a group for a long time were more concerned with the welfare of the group than were people who anticipated a fleeting interaction. Moreover, negotiators who perceived that other group members would leave cooperated less than did those who expected the group to remain intact (Mannix & Loewenstein 1993).

These studies suggest that making group identity salient tends to activate different negotiation processes, producing different outcomes. Yet, the importance of group identity in mixed-motive interactions such as negotiation has not gone unchallenged. Kerr & Kaufman-Gilliland (1994) examined the impact of social identity on cooperation in social dilemmas. In a carefully constructed set of studies, they found strong support for the idea that it is negotiators' verbal promises that increase cooperation in social dilemmas, not simply the extent to which negotiators feel identified with their group.

Relational and Collective Identity

Recently, work on identity has moved from the extent to which individuals feel they are a part of their group to the nature of the identity. For example, Markus & Kitayama (1991) focused on whether people hold independent or interdependent identities, or self-construals. A person who holds an independent self-construal defines himself or herself in terms of the attributes, preferences, and traits that make him

or her unique and autonomous. In contrast, a person with an interdependent self-construal is more likely to define himself or herself in terms of his or her social and group relationships (Gardner et al. 1999, Markus & Kitayama 1991). In a one-on-one, dispute-negotiation context, Seeley et al. (2007) primed independent versus interdependent self-construals and found that negotiators with interdependent self-construals were more generous than were independent negotiators. However, this effect completely reversed in a team-on-team context, such that teams with independent self-construals (i.e., highly defined by their own attributes) were more generous than teams with interdependent self-construals (i.e., defined with reference to the other team). All of these effects held primarily for high-power negotiators. The implication is that interdependent self-construals seem to evoke a benevolent use of power in dyadic contexts but a more exploitative use of power in intergroup contexts.

Very little research has examined the possibility of reverse causality between negotiation and social identity—that the negotiation process itself could influence people's identity. Thompson (1993) examined how negotiation affects intergroup relations. People who negotiated with an out-group member developed more favorable evaluations of the out-group, whereas people who negotiated with an in-group member were more likely to show in-group favoritism. However, when the negotiation situation dictated that negotiators could not reach a mutually beneficial agreement, the positive effects of interpersonal negotiation disappeared. Thus, negotiation with out-group members improves intergroup relations in negotiations with integrative potential. Furthermore, outcomes are comparable regardless of the counterpart's group membership. Whereas individuals expecting to negotiate with out-group members thought they would obtain lower outcomes than those expecting to negotiate with in-group members, the value of the actual outcomes achieved did not differ.

Culture

One important aspect of group identity is culture, or the distinctive characteristics of a particular social group (Lytle et al. 1995). Culture is manifest in a group's values, beliefs, norms, and behavioral patterns. An underlying feature of Western cultures is the use of formal logic and avoidance of contradiction (Nisbett et al. 2001). In contrast, in non-Western cultures, cognition is characterized by a holistic system of thought. Individuals view themselves as embedded and interdependent with a larger social context. They also tend to focus their cognitive attention on relationships and context (Peng & Nisbett 1999).

One result of this difference in systems of thought is that negotiators from different cultures make more or less use of emotional appeals. Emotional appeals are relatively inconsistent with formal logic. Thus, negotiators from non-Western cultures tend to make more emotional appeals than do U.S. negotiators (Drake 1995). For instance, Taiwanese negotiators used more normative statements referring to social roles and relationships than did U.S. negotiators (Drake 1995). Conversely, U.S. negotiators used more statements emphasizing logic and reasoning than did Taiwanese negotiators.

Another important cultural difference between Western negotiators and non-Western negotiators is the motivation that they bring to the negotiating table. Motivation is the focused and persistent energy that drives cognition and behavior (Mook 2000). Motivation impacts how negotiators approach negotiations and evaluate outcomes. In Western cultures, negotiators tend to judge negotiation outcomes by the joint profit that accrues and the value that they themselves claim (Lax & Sebenius 1986c, Neale & Bazerman 1992). However, in non-Western cultures, negotiators may care more about relational capital—the mutual trust, knowledge, and commitment that can accrue from negotiating—more than economic outcomes (Gelfand et al. 2006).

For example, Japanese negotiators place a high value on relational capital: They prefer and even insist on negotiating with people with whom they have a relationship or social network, even if it means forgoing potential economic benefits (Graham & Sano 1989, Yamagishi & Yamagishi 1994). Indian managers, on the other hand, may assume lower relational capital in the form of mutual trust than do American managers, and negotiations may serve to reaffirm their assumptions (Gunia et al. 2009). In two studies, Indian managers' lower level of trust led to low joint gains relative to the gains of American managers.

Culture also has important effects on how individuals perceive causality. Psychological research has demonstrated that members of Western cultures tend to make the fundamental attribution error more often than do members of non-Western cultures (Nisbett et al. 2001, Peng & Nisbett 1999). That is, they underestimate the impact of situational factors and overestimate the impact of others' dispositional factors in causing events (Ross 1977). The result for negotiation is that U.S. negotiators tend to make dispositional attributions for their counterpart's behaviors and discount potential situational attributions (Morris et al. 1999). Dispositional attributions for negative behaviors lead to negative consequences in negotiations. Specifically, dispositional attributions led to competitive perceptions of the situation and counterpart, resulting in a preference for adversarial instead of collaborative procedures.

Groups and the Discontinuity Effect

A central question in group research is whether "two heads are better than one" (Insko et al. 1987, 1988, 1990; Schopler et al. 1991, 1993). This question was first addressed using a simple prisoner's dilemma game in which negotiators were offered a cooperative (trusting) choice or a defecting (self-interested, exploitive) choice. Overwhelmingly, one-on-one negotiators made more cooperative choices than did group-on-group negotiators, under identical payoffs. Insko et al. (1987) coined the term "discontinuity effect" to describe the empirical finding that one-on-one negotiation behavior cannot be simply extrapolated to group-on-group negotiation behavior. Schopler & Insko (1992) argued that the discontinuity effect was driven by group members' fear of being exploited by the out-group as well as their greed for additional payoffs.

Thompson et al. (1996) examined the discontinuity effect in a markedly different negotiation paradigm, in which parties' interests were not completely opposed and a mutually attractive, optimal outcome existed but was not apparent to negotiators. This paradigm was similar to the sisters-and-orange parable in the introduction. In terms of integrative outcomes, group-on-group configurations produced more integrative agreements than did solo-on-solo or solo-on-group. In terms of distributive outcomes, groups earned more than solos. The authors reasoned that in such a negotiation, information processing is paramount; indeed, groups asked more relevant questions, shared more information, and formed more accurate judgments than did solos (see also Peterson & Thompson 1997). The group-on-group configuration apparently allowed negotiators to seek and process more of the relevant information.

Morgan & Tindale (2002) attempted to resolve the disparate findings between Insko et al. (1987) and Thompson et al. (1996). Morgan and Tindale's insight was that the disparate-appearing findings were based upon dramatically different negotiation tasks: Insko and colleagues used a prisoner's dilemma task, whereas Thompson and colleagues used an integrative bargaining task; the tasks differ in many important ways (see Thompson 2009 for a review of the differences). In Morgan & Tindale's (2002) study, negotiators were allowed to reach an agreement on either a cooperative or competitive integrative bargaining task in one of three formats (group versus group, group versus single, or one-on-one). Next, negotiators were asked to choose between maintaining the agreed-upon settlement or defecting within a prisoner's dilemma payoff structure. Groups continued to show the discontinuity effect, such

that they opted to defect. This was true even when they had performed better than the solo negotiator with whom they had just negotiated. Groups shared motives for defection that differ depending upon the nature of the task and opponent (Morgan & Tindale 2002).

ORGANIZATIONAL LEVEL

The organizational system represents a higher level of analysis than the previous levels; it examines the negotiator as embedded in a larger network or marketplace. This level of analysis is crucial because in organizations and in markets, dyads rarely operate in isolation from their social context. Instead, each negotiator typically participates in multiple dyadic relationships, and these dyadic relationships aggregate to form a complex social structure that surrounds each dyad and influences trust, expectations, and interpersonal perceptions.

Heider (1958) documented that two people can be connected by a third party, who strengthens or disturbs the relationship among the two. Contemporary sociologists have also documented how dyadic relationships and interpersonal behavior may be influenced by the overall network structure in which the dyad is embedded (e.g., Burt & Knez 1996, Coleman 1990, Granovetter 1985). Despite these foundations, relatively little research has examined how negotiation dyads operate within their larger social context. In this section, we review three streams of negotiation research at the organizational level. The first two examine how interpersonal connections (choosing negotiation partners and reputations) influence negotiation processes. The third looks at how organizational or institutional forces impact negotiations.

Choice of Negotiation Partner

A critical issue facing employees and employers, buyers and suppliers, and joint venture partners is whom to select as a negotiation partner. The vast majority of studies in the existing negotiation literature have simply assigned negotiation partners (Tenbrunsel et al. 1999). One of the earliest studies that examined this problem of search and deliberation in partner choice was Sondak & Bazerman's (1989) study of matching in quasi-markets. In this paradigm, a large market of buyers and sellers was created and negotiators were told to partner with whomever they pleased, to make a deal. The main finding was that substantial economic suboptimality exists as the result of selection mismatches. People may choose to negotiate with their friends, even though the integrative potential of negotiating with a stranger may be higher (see also Northcraft et al. 1998). Similarly, when people had the option to choose their friend as negotiation partner in a simulated housing market, they often stopped searching and reached a deal with the friend—overlooking other, potentially fruitful negotiation relationships. Ultimately, this led to market inefficiencies (Tenbrunsel et al. 1999).

Reputation and Negotiation Through Time

One consideration that influences the integrative and distributive outcomes negotiators achieve in organizational systems is their reputation. Much sociological and macro organizational research has documented the importance of reputation in markets (e.g., Raub & Weesie 1990). In one investigation (Glick & Croson 2001), the impact of reputations among management students in a semester-long negotiation course was examined. Students rated one another on the basis of firsthand experience, from least cooperative to the most cooperative. Four reputational profiles emerged: the "liar-manipulator" (who will do anything to gain advantage), "tough-but-honest" (very tough negotiator who makes few concessions but will not lie), "nice-and-reasonable" (makes concessions), and "cream puff" (makes concessions and is conciliatory regardless of what the other does). Once reputations spread through the market, behavior changed. People acted much tougher when dealing with perceived liar-manipulators, for example. Furthermore,

people used tough or manipulative tactics in a defensive fashion with liar-manipulators and tough-but-honest negotiators, but used them in an opportunistic fashion with cream puffs (Glick & Croson 2001).

Other research examined how reputation is related to history of negotiation behavior, also in an MBA class (Anderson & Shirako 2008). The development of reputations was tracked among individuals who engaged in multiple negotiation tasks across several weeks. Reputations were only mildly related to the actual history of behavior. However, the link between reputation and behavior was much stronger for some individuals than others. The link was strongest for those who were well known and received the most social attention. In contrast, behavior had little impact on the reputations of lesser-known individuals.

Another, similar perspective suggests that dyadic negotiation is not an isolated event, but rather influences subsequent dyadic negotiations (O'Connor et al. 2005). Specifically, the quality of the deals negotiators reached at any point in time were strongly influenced by their previous bargaining experiences. Negotiators who reached an impasse in a prior negotiation were more likely either to impasse in their next negotiation or to reach deals of low joint value relative to those who had reached an initial agreement. Notably, the impact of past performance on subsequent deals was just as strong for negotiators who changed partners on the second occasion. These results highlight the role of bargaining history as a predictor of negotiation behavior. Moreover, they suggest that, at least in some cases, negotiations should be conceptualized as interrelated exchanges rather than discrete incidents.

Organizations also impact negotiations via institutional forces. One controversial perspective argues that organizations or institutions may serve as barriers to negotiations (Wade-Benzoni et al. 2002). Specifically, normative factors (obligations, operating procedures), cognitive factors (cultural values, cognitive frameworks), and regulatory factors (regulations and laws) may impede negotiations.

For example, organizations with cultures emphasizing strict adherence to procedure may discourage negotiation by explicitly prohibiting it (normative factor) or by preventing employees from even perceiving it as a viable alternative (cognitive factor). The value-laden lens that organizationally embedded actors bring may also lead to impasse or prevent people from reaching economically efficient outcomes.

VIRTUAL LEVEL

Given the ubiquity of computer-mediated communication technology in business communications, consumer transactions, and interpersonal relationships, virtual negotiation is currently a fertile ground for research (Nadler & Shestowsky 2006).

A straightforward question one might ask is whether negotiation is best conducted face-to-face or via computer-mediated communication technology. Answers to this question are surprisingly mixed (see Nadler & Shestowsky 2006 for a review). In some cases, negotiators who interact via computer-mediated technology are less likely to reach integrative outcomes than are negotiators who interact face-to-face (Arunachalam & Dilla 1995, Barefoot & Strickland 1982) or via paper and pencil (Griffith & Northcraft 1994). On the other hand, some studies report no reliable effect of communication medium (Morris et al. 2002, Naquin & Paulson 2003, Purdy et al. 2000).

With regard to confidence and satisfaction, parties who negotiate face-to-face feel more confident in their performance and satisfied with their negotiation outcome than do those who negotiate via computer (Naquin & Paulson 2003, Purdy et al. 2000, Thompson & Coovert 2003). Moreover, compared to parties who negotiate face-to-face, parties who negotiate via email desire less future interaction with their counterpart (Naquin & Paulson 2003). Despite these differences in subjective outcomes, studies that examined the emotional content of messages in email and face-to-face negotiations

found no differences between the two mediums (Morris et al. 2002).

Moderators and Mediators

Though the effects of information technology on interpersonal outcomes in negotiation may currently seem inconclusive, some studies have identified important mediators that may help to explain the effects of technology on negotiation in the future. For instance, negotiators behave more honestly when negotiating face-to-face than via writing (Valley et al. 1998). The communication medium in which bargaining takes place also affects the efficiency and distribution of outcomes (Valley et al. 1998). Face-to-face communication may facilitate more truth-telling and trust than communication via writing, thus influencing negotiation outcomes.

However, negotiators may sometimes behave less cooperatively when they have visual access to one another than when they do not (Carnevale & Isen 1986, Carnevale et al. 1981). In one investigation, researchers examined the influence of positive affect and visual access on the process and outcome of negotiation in an integrative bargaining task (Carnevale & Isen 1986). Only when negotiators were face-to-face and not in a positive affective state were there heavy use of contentious tactics, reduced tradeoffs, and few integrative solutions. In other words, when negotiators had visual access and were potentially experiencing negative affect, they were more likely to use contentious tactics.

Other research has examined contexts in which email negotiations may fail or succeed. For instance, Moore et al. (1999) proposed that there were "long" and "short" routes to success in electronically mediated negotiations. A long route to success would involve many of the aspects of deliberate cognitive processing; a short route would involve more heuristic, superficial processing of information (Fiske 1988, Sloman 2002).

To understand why email negotiations often fail, another study (Moore et al. 1999) examined two distinct elements of negotiators' relationships: shared membership in a social group and mutual self-disclosure. Some participants negotiated with a member of an out-group (a student at a competitor university), whereas others negotiated with a member of an in-group (a student at the same university). In addition, some negotiators exchanged personal information with their counterparts, such as their hometown and hobbies, whereas others did not. When neither common in-group status nor a personalized relationship existed between negotiators, email negotiations were more likely to end in impasse. These results were attributable to the positive influence of mutual self-disclosure and common group membership on negotiation processes and rapport between negotiators, especially in a relatively impersonal context like email.

CONCLUSION

Our review has focused on a subset of research findings that have strongly impacted the study and practice of negotiation. The research findings span several decades, but the investigations meaningfully build upon one another because the key criteria by which scholars evaluate the quality of negotiation has remained essentially unchanged since the dawn of negotiation research. Modern negotiation research has greatly benefitted from its economic roots, which have provided rigorous methods by which to measure the mutual value created by two or more parties, each motivated to pursue their own interests. The robust empirical fact that most negotiators fail to fully maximize their own gains (as well as mutual gains) when seated at the bargaining table has greatly fueled the fires of negotiation research.

Our focus on intrapersonal, interpersonal, group, organizational and virtual systems has allowed us to examine the wide lens through which the apparently simple task of negotiation may be meaningfully studied. The intrapersonal system provides the most close-up view of negotiation, taking us into the mind and heart of the negotiator, who is either anticipating or engaging in a negotiation. The

interpersonal system is particularly meaningful in negotiation research because the dyadic process allows us to examine the presence or absence of interpersonal phenomena such as behavioral synchrony and mutual gaze, which cannot be reduced to the intrapersonal level. The group and organizational systems have been influenced by rich social psychological, as well as sociological and organizational, traditions. Negotiation research, like the universe, appears to be expanding rather than contracting. Indeed, the virtual level has allowed globally dispersed researchers themselves to collaborate while investigating negotiation at a virtual level. Rather than reporting to a physical laboratory, today's research participants often negotiate via computer with people they will never meet.

It is curious how some research topics within the domain of social and organizational psychology sustain themselves over time, whereas others are mere flashes in the pan. Negotiation and bargaining research, by nearly any standard, has withstood the test of time. There are several reasons for its longevity. First, the multidisciplinary nature of negotiation has brought scholars together, especially from social psychology and organizational behavior and also from game theory and economics. These multidisciplinary collaborations have created a rich network of negotiation scholars that lead to shared volumes, conferences, and even jobs and research positions, thereby ensuring the longevity of the field. Nearly every business school offers a course in negotiation that many MBA students take, requiring a cadre of trained faculty members. The faculties often receive their training in PhD programs or in postdoctoral programs that focus primarily on negotiation. Graduate students are attracted to such positions and develop research ideas that are relevant to the broad array of negotiation theory.

A second factor that has contributed to the continued popularity of negotiation research is the fact that it is considered an essential business, if not a life, skill. The demand for negotiation skills spurs the development of negotiation books, courses, seminars, cases, and teaching materials that require theoretical rigor and background. The existence of a normative theory by which to evaluate the performance of negotiators provides a foundation for meaningful research and theory. The existence of descriptive theory provides meaningful insights into negotiations as they typically unfold.

If there is a downside to negotiation research it might be that negotiation has done more taking than giving, meaning that often the negotiation scholarship is essentially about social or organizational phenomena that could frankly be studied as easily in other contexts. For example, one might study behavioral synchrony or mirroring in negotiation, but it is equally plausible to study these same phenomena in other contexts, like small, collaborative teams or job interviews. Similarly, more than two decades of research have focused on extending Kahneman et al.'s (1982) research on judgment biases (e.g., framing, anchoring, overconfidence) to two-party negotiations (for a review, see Neale & Bazerman 1994). Despite this prodigious borrowing, our review suggests that negotiation research has yielded many insights of its own and is poised to yield many more in the future.

SUMMARY POINTS

1. Intrapersonal processes such as one's psychological power and mood impact negotiation processes and outcomes.

2. Interpersonal processes such as display of emotions also impact negotiation processes and outcomes.

3. When negotiation takes place not between individuals but rather between groups, group identity, culture, and structure of negotiation will affect whether groups (teams of negotiators) do better than solo negotiators.

4. The social context and network in which one is embedded also influences negotiations, through choice of negotiation partner and formation of reputation.

5. When negotiations are not face-to-face but rather are computer-mediated, many variables come into play in determining whether computer-mediated negotiations harm or facilitate negotiations.

DISCLOSURE STATEMENT

The authors are not aware of any biases that might be perceived as affecting the objectivity of this review.

LITERATURE CITED

Allred KG, Mallozzi JS, Matsui F, Raia CP. 1997. The influence of anger and compassion on negotiation performance. *Organ. Behav. Hum. Decis. Process.* 70(3):175–87

Anderson C, Shirako A. 2008. Are individuals' reputations related to their history of behavior? *J. Personal. Soc. Psychol.* 94(2):320–33

Anderson C, Thompson LL. 2004. Affect from the top down: how powerful individuals' positive affect shapes negotiations. *Organ. Behav. Hum. Decis. Process.* 95(2):125–39

Arunachalam V, Dilla WN. 1995. Judgment accuracy and outcomes in negotiation—a causal-modeling analysis of decision-aiding effects. *Organ. Behav. Hum. Decis. Process.* 61(3):289–304

Babcock L, Gelfand M, Small D, Stayhn H. 2006. Gender differences in the propensity to initiate negotiations. In *Social Psychology and Economics*, ed. D De Cremer, M Zeelenberg, JK Murnighan, pp. 239–62. Mahwah, NJ: Erlbaum

Barefoot JC, Strickland LH. 1982. Conflict and dominance in television-mediated interactions. *Hum. Relat.* 35(7):559–66

Bargh JA, Pietromonaco P. 1982. Automatic information processing and social perception: the influence of trait information presented outside of conscious awareness on impression formation. *J. Personal. Soc. Psychol.* 43(3):437–49

Bazerman MH, Tenbrunsel AE, Wade-Benzoni K. 1998. Negotiating with yourself and losing: making decisions with competing internal preferences. *Acad. Manag. Rev.* 23(2):225–41

Berderskey C, McGinn KL. 2009. Open to negotiation: phenomenological assumptions and knowledge dissemination. *Organ. Sci.* In press

Blair IV, Banaji MR. 1996. Automatic and controlled processes in stereotype priming. *J. Personal. Soc. Psychol.* 70(6):1142–63

Bowles HR, Babcock L, Lai L. 2007. Social incentives for gender differences in the propensity to initiate negotiations: Sometimes it does hurt to ask. *Organ. Behav. Hum. Decis. Process.* 103(1):84–103

Brewer MB, Kramer RM. 1986. Choice behavior in social dilemmas: effects of social identity, group size, and decision framing. *J. Personal. Soc. Psychol.* 50(3):543–49

Butler JK. 1995. Behaviors, trust, and goal achievement in a win-win negotiating role play. *Group Organ. Manag.* 20(4):486–501

Burt RS, Knez M. 1996. A further note on the network structure of trust: reply to Krackhardt. *Rationality Soc.* 8(1):117–20

Camerer C. 2003. *Behavioral Game Theory: Experiments in Strategic Interaction.* New York: Russell Sage Found./ Princeton, NJ: Princeton Univ. Press

Carnevale PJD, Isen AM. 1986. The influence of positive affect and visual access on the discovery of integrative solutions in bilateral negotiation. *Organ. Behav. Hum. Decis. Process.* 37(1):1–13

Carnevale PJD, Pruitt DG, Seilheimer SD. 1981. Looking and competing: accountability and visual access in integrative bargaining. *J. Personal. Soc. Psychol.* 40(1):111–20

Chartrand TL, Bargh JA. 1999. The Chameleon effect: the perception-behavior link and social interaction. *J. Personal. Soc. Psychol.* 76(6):893–910

Coleman JS. 1990. *Foundations of Social Theory.* Cambridge, MA: Harvard Univ. Press

Curhan JR, Elfenbein HA, Xu H. 2006. What do people value when they negotiate? Mapping the domain of subjective value in negotiation. *J. Personal. Soc. Psychol.* 91(3):493–512

Curhan JR, Neale MA, Ross L, Rosencranz-Engelmann J. 2008. Relational accommodation in negotiation: effects of egalitarianism and gender on economic efficiency and relational capital. *Organ. Behav. Hum. Decis. Process.* 107(2):192–205

Deal JJ. 2000. Gender differences in the intentional use of information in competitive negotiations. *Small Group Res.* 31(6):702–23

De Dreu CKW, Carnevale PJ. 2003. Motivational bases of information processing and strategy in conflict and negotiation. In *Advances in Experimental Social Psychology*, ed. MP Zanna, 35:235–91. New York: Academic

De Dreu CKW, Weingart LR, Kwon S. 2000. Influence of social motives on integrative negotiation: a meta-analytic review and test of two theories. *J. Personal. Soc. Psychol.* 78(5):889–905

Dirks KT, Ferrin DL. 2001. The role of trust in organizational settings. *Organ. Sci.* 12(4):450–67

Drake LE. 1995. Negotiation styles in intercultural communication. *Int. J. Confl. Manag.* 6(1):72–90

Eagly AH, Wood W. 1982. Inferred sex differences in status as a determinant of gender stereotypes about social influence. *J. Personal. Soc. Psychol.* 43(5):915–28

Elangovan AR, Shapiro DI. 1998. Betrayal of trust in organizations. *Acad. Manag. Rev.* 23(3):547–66

Emerson RM. 1972. Exchange theory: Part II. Exchange relations in networks. In *Sociological Theories in Progress*, ed. J Berger, M Zelditch, B Anderson, 2:58–87. Boston, MA: Houghton Mifflin

Fisher R, Ury W. 1981. *Getting to Yes: Negotiating Agreement Without Giving In.* Boston, MA: Houghton Mifflin

Fiske ST. 1988. Compare and contrast: Brewer's dual-process model and Fiske et al.'s continuum model. In *Advances in Social Cognition, Vol. 1: A Dual Model of Impression Formation*, ed. TK Srull, RS Wyer, pp. 65–76. Hillsdale, NJ: Erlbaum

Foa UG, Foa EB. 1975. *Resource Theory of Social Exchange.* Morristown, NJ: General Learning Press

Forgas JP. 1995. Mood and judgment: the affect infusion model (AIM). *Psychol. Bull.* 117(1):39–66

Forgas JP. 1998. On feeling good and getting your way. *J. Personal. Soc. Psychol.* 74(3):565–77

Forgas JP, Cromer M. 2004. On being sad and evasive: affective influences on verbal communication strategies in conflict situations. *J. Exp. Soc. Psychol.* 40(4):511–18

French JRP, Raven B. 1959. The bases of social power. In *Studies in Social Power*, ed. D Cartwright, pp. 150–67. Ann Arbor, MI: Inst. Soc. Res.

Fry WR, Firestone IJ, Williams DL. 1983. Negotiating process and outcome of stranger dyads and dating couples. Do lovers lose? *Basic Appl. Soc. Psychol.* 4:1–16

Galinsky AD, Mussweiler T. 2001. First offers as anchors: the role of perspective-taking and negotiator focus. *J. Personal. Soc. Psychol.* 81(4):657–69

Galinsky AD, Mussweiler T, Medvec VH. 2002. Disconnecting outcomes and evaluations: the role of negotiator focus. *J. Personal. Soc. Psychol.* 83(5):1131–40

Galinsky AD, Seiden VL, Kim PH, Medvec VH. 2002. The dissatisfaction of having your first offer accepted: the role of counterfactual thinking in negotiations. *Personal. Soc. Psychol. Bull.* 28(2):271–83

Gardner WL, Gabriel S, Lee AY. 1999. "I" value freedom, but "we" value relationships: self-construal priming mirrors cultural differences in judgment. *Psychol. Sci.* 10(4):321–26

Gelfand MJ, Major VS, Raver J, Nishii L, O'Brien KM. 2006. Negotiating relationally: the dynamics of the relational self in negotiations. *Acad. Manag. Rev.* 31(2):427–51

Gerhart B, Rynes S. 1991. Determinants and consequences of salary negotiations by male and female MBA graduates. *J. Appl. Psychol.* 76(2):256–62

Glick S, Croson R. 2001. Reputation in negotiations. In *Wharton on Making Decisions*, ed. S Hoch, H Kunreuther, pp. 177–86. New York: Wiley

Glynn MA. 2000. When cymbals become symbols: conflict over organizational identity within a symphony orchestra. *Organ. Sci.* 11(3):285–99

Graham JL, Sano Y. 1989. *Smart Bargaining*. New York: Harper Business

Granovetter M. 1973. The strength of weak ties. *Am. J. Sociol.* 78:1360–80

Granovetter M. 1985. Economic action and social structure: the problem of embeddedness. *Am. J. Sociol.* 91(3):481–510

Greenwald AG, Draine SC, Abrams RL. 1996. Three cognitive markers of unconscious semantic activation. *Science* 273(5282):1699–702

Griffith TL, Northcraft GB. 1994. Distinguishing between the forest and the trees: media, features, and methodology in electronic communication research. *Organ. Sci.* 5(2):272–85

Gunia BC, Brett JM, Kamdar D. 2009. Paying a price: the consequences of cultural assumptions about trust in negotiation. Manuscript under review

Güth W, Schmittberger R, Schwarze B. 1982. An experimental analysis of ultimatum bargaining. *J. Econ. Behav. Organ.* 3(4):367–88

Heider F. 1958. *The Psychology of Interpersonal Relations*. New York: Wiley

Insko CA, Hoyle RH, Pinkley RL, Hong GY, Slim RM, et al. 1988. Individual-group discontinuity: the role of a consensus rule. *J. Exp. Soc. Psychol.* 24(6):505–19

Insko CA, Pinkley RL, Hoyle RH, Dalton B, Hong GY, et al. 1987. Individual versus group discontinuity: the role of intergroup contact. *J. Exp. Soc. Psychol.* 23(3):250–67

Insko CA, Schopler J, Hoyle RH, Dardis GJ, Graetz KA. 1990. Individual-group discontinuity as a function of fear and greed. *J. Personal. Soc. Psychol.* 58(1):68–79

Kahneman D, Slovic P, Tversky A. 1982. *Judgment Under Uncertainty: Heuristics and Biases*. London: Cambridge Univ. Press

Kelley HH. 1982. *Personal Relationships: Their Structure and Processes*. Hillsdale, NJ: Erlbaum

Keltner D, Gruenfeld DH, Anderson C. 2003. Power, approach, and inhibition. *Psychol. Rev.* 110(2):265–84

Kerr NL, Kaufman-Gilliland CM. 1994. Communication, commitment, and cooperation in social dilemmas. *J. Personal. Soc. Psychol.* 66(3):513–29

Kim PH, Ferrin DL, Cooper CD, Dirks KT. 2004. Removing the shadow of suspicion: The effects of apology versus denial for repairing competence- versus integrity-based trust violations. *J. Appl. Psychol.* 89(1):104–18

Kim PH, Fragale AR. 2005. Choosing the path to bargaining power: an empirical comparison of BATNAs and contributions in negotiation. *J. Appl. Psychol.* 90(2):373–81

Kimmel MJ, Pruitt DG, Magenau JM, Konar-Goldband E, Carnevale PJD. 1980. Effects of trust, aspiration, and gender on negotiation tactics. *J. Personal. Soc. Psychol.* 38:9–22

Komorita SS, Parks CD. 1995. Interpersonal relations: mixed-motive interaction. *Annu. Rev. Psychol.* 46:183–207

Kopelman S, Rosette AS, Thompson LL. 2000. The three faces of Eve: strategic displays of positive, negative, and neutral emotions in negotiations. *Organ. Behav. Hum. Decis. Process.* 99:81–101

Kramer RM, Brewer MB. 1984. Effects of group identity on resource use in a simulated commons dilemma. *J. Personal. Soc. Psychol.* 46(5):1044–57

Kray LJ, Reb J, Galinsky AD, Thompson LL. 2004. Stereotype reactance at the bargaining table: the effect of stereotype activation and power on claiming and creating value. *Personal. Soc. Psychol. Bull.* 30(4):399–411

Kray LJ, Thompson LL. 2005. Gender stereotypes and negotiation performance: an examination of theory and research. *Res. Organ. Behav.* 26:103–82

Kray LJ, Thompson LL, Galinsky A. 2001. Battle of the sexes: gender stereotype confirmation and reactance in negotiations. *J. Personal. Soc. Psychol.* 80(6):942–58

Lanzetta JT. 1989. Expectations of cooperation and competition and their effects on observers' vicarious emotional responses. *J. Personal. Soc. Psychol.* 56:543–54

Lax DA, Sebenius JK. 1986a. Three ethical issues in negotiation. *Negotiation J. Process Dispute Settlement* 2(4):363–70

Lax DA, Sebenius JK. 1986b. Interests—the measure of negotiation. *Negotiation J. Process Dispute Settlement* 2(1):73–92

Lax DA, Sebenius JK. 1986c. *The Manager as Negotiator, Bargaining for Cooperative and Competitive Gain.* New York: Free Press

Luce RD, Raiffa H. 1957. *Games and Decisions: Introduction and Critical Survey.* New York: Wiley

Lytle A, Brett JM, Barsness Z, Tinsley CH, Janssens M. 1995. A paradigm for confirmatory cross-cultural research in organizational behavior. In *Research in Organizational Behavior*, ed. LL Cummings, BM Staw, 17:167–214. Greenwich, CT: JAI

Magee JC, Galinsky AD, Gruenfeld DH. 2007. Power, propensity to negotiate, and moving first in competitive interactions. *Personal. Soc. Psychol. Bull.* 33(2):200–12

Major B, Vanderslice V, Mcfarlin DB. 1984. Effects of pay expected on pay received: the confirmatory nature of initial expectations. *J. Appl. Soc. Psychol.* 14(5):399–412

Mannix EA, Loewenstein GF. 1993. Managerial time horizons and interfirm mobility: an experimental investigation. *Organ. Behav. Hum. Decis. Process.* 56(2):266–84

Markus HR, Kitayama S. 1991. Culture and the self: implications for cognition, emotion, and motivation. *Psychol. Rev.* 98(2):224–53

McGinn KL, Keros AT. 2002. Improvisation and the logic of exchange in socially embedded transactions. *Adm. Sci. Q.* 47(3):442–73

Mook J. 2000. *Motivation.* New York: Prentice Hall

Moore DA, Kurtzberg TR, Thompson LL, Morris MW. 1999. Long and short routes to success in electronically mediated negotiations: group affiliations and good vibrations. *Organ. Behav. Hum. Decis. Process.* 77(1):22–43

Morgan PM, Tindale RS. 2002. Group vs individual performance in mixed-motive situations: exploring an inconsistency. *Organ. Behav. Hum. Decis. Process.* 87(1):44–65

Morris M, Nadler J, Kurtzberg T, Thompson LL. 2002. Schmooze or lose: social friction and lubrication in e-mail negotiations. *Group Dyn. Theory Res. Pract.* 6(1):89–100

Morris MW, Larrick RP, Su SK. 1999. Misperceiving negotiation counterparts: when situationally determined bargaining behaviors are attributed to personality traits. *J. Personal. Soc. Psychol.* 77(1):52–67

Mussweiler T, Strack F. 1999. Comparing is believing: a selective accessibility model of judgmental anchoring. In *European Review of Social Psychology*, ed. W Stroebe, M Hewstone, Vol. 10, pp. 135–68. Chichester, UK: Wiley

Nadler J, Shestowsky D. 2006. Negotiation, information technology, and the problem of the faceless other. In *Negotiation Theory and Research*, ed. LL Thompson, pp. 145–72. New York: Psychol. Press

Naquin CE, Paulson GD. 2003. Online bargaining and interpersonal trust. *J. Appl. Psychol.* 88(1):113–20

Nash J. 1951. Non-cooperative games. *Ann. Math.* 54(2):286–95

Neale MA, Bazerman MH. 1992. Negotiator cognition and rationality: a behavioral decision-theory perspective. *Organ. Behav. Hum. Decis. Process.* 51(2):157–75

Neale MA, Bazerman MH. 1994. *Negotiating Rationally*. New York: Free Press

Neumann R, Strack F. 2000. "Mood contagion": the automatic transfer of mood between persons. *J. Personal. Soc. Psychol.* 79(2):211–23

Nisbett RE, Peng KP, Choi I, Norenzayan A. 2001. Culture and systems of thought: holistic versus analytic cognition. *Psychol. Rev.* 108(2):291–310

Northcraft GB, Preston JN, Neale MA, Kim P, Thomas-Hunt M. 1998. Non-linear preference functions and negotiated outcomes. *Organ. Behav. Hum. Decis. Process.* 73:54–75

Ochs J, Roth AE. 1989. An experimental study of sequential bargaining. *Am. Econ. Rev.* 79:355–84

O'Connor KM, Arnold JA. 2001. Distributive spirals: negotiation impasses and the moderating role of disputant self-efficacy. *Organ. Behav. Hum. Decis. Process.* 84(1):148–76

O'Connor KM, Arnold JA, Burris ER. 2005. Negotiators' bargaining histories and their effects on future negotiation performance. *J. Appl. Psychol.* 90(2):350–62

Pareto V. 1935. *The Mind and Society: A Treatise on General Sociology*. New York: Harcourt Brace

Parks CD, Henager RF, Scamahorn SD. 1996. Trust and messages of intent in social dilemmas. *J. Confl. Resolut.* 40:134–51

Peng KP, Nisbett RE. 1999. Culture, dialectics, and reasoning about contradiction. *Am. Psychol.* 54(9):741–54

Peterson E, Thompson LL. 1997. Negotiation teamwork: the impact of information distribution and accountability on performance depends on the relationship among team members. *Organ. Behav. Hum. Decis. Process.* 72(3):364–83

Pham MT. 2007. Emotion and rationality: a critical review and interpretation of empirical evidence. *Rev. Gen. Psychol.* 11(2):155–78

Podolny JM, Baron JN. 1997. Resources and relationships: social networks and mobility in the workplace. *Am. Sociol. Rev.* 62:673–93

Pruitt DG, Kimmel MJ. 1977. Twenty years of experimental gaming: critique, synthesis, and suggestions for the future. *Annu. Rev. Psychol.* 28:363–92

Purdy JM, Nye P, Balakrishnan PV. 2000. The impact of communication media on negotiation outcomes. *Int. J. Confl. Manag.* 11(2):162–87

Raiffa H. 1982. *The Art and Science of Negotiation*. Cambridge, MA: Harvard Univ. Press

Raub W, Weesie J. 1990. Reputation and efficiency in social interactions: an example of network effects. *Am. J. Sociol.* 96(3):626–54

Ross LD. 1977. The intuitive psychologist and his shortcomings: distortions in the attribution process. In *Advances in Experimental Social Psychology*, ed. L Berkowitz, 10:173–220. New York: Academic

Rousseau DM, Sitkin SB, Burt RS, Camerer C. 1998. Not so different after all: a cross-discipline view of trust. *Acad. Manag. Rev.* 23(3):393–404

Schelling TC. 1960. *The Strategy of Conflict*. Cambridge, MA: Harvard Univ. Press

Schopler J, Insko CA. 1992. The discontinuity effect in interpersonal and intergroup relations: generality and mediation. *Eur. Rev. Soc. Psychol.* 3:121–51

Schopler J, Insko CA, Graetz KA, Drigotas S, Smith VA, Dahl K. 1993. Individual-group discontinuity: further evidence for mediation by fear and greed. *Personal. Soc. Psychol. Bull.* 19(4):419–31

Schopler J, Insko CA, Graetz KA, Drigotas SM, Smith VA. 1991. The generality of the individual-group discontinuity dffect: variations in positivity-negativity of outcomes, players' relative power, and magnitude of outcomes. *Personal. Soc. Psychol. Bull.* 17(6):612–24

Schweitzer ME, Hershey JC, Bradlow ET. 2006. Promises and lies: restoring violated trust. *Organ. Behav. Hum. Decis. Process.* 101(1):1–19

Seeley E, Gardner W, Thompson L. 2007. The role of the self-concept and social context in determining the behavior of power-holders: self-construal in intergroup vs. dyadic dispute resolution negotiations. *J. Personal. Soc. Psychol.* 93(4):614–31

Seidel ML, Polzer JT, Stewart KJ. 2000. Having friends in high places: effects of social networks on discrimination in salary negotiations. *Adm. Sci. Q.* 45:1–24

Shapiro DL, Bies RJ. 1994. Threats, bluffs, and disclaimers in negotiations. *Organ. Behav. Hum. Decis. Process.* 60(1):14–35

Sinaceur M, Tiedens LZ. 2006. Get mad and get more than even: when and why anger expression is effective in negotiations. *J. Exp. Soc. Psychol.* 42(3):314–22

Sloman SA. 2002. Two systems of reasoning. In *Heuristics and Biases: The Psychology of Intuitive Judgment*, ed. T Gilovich, D Griffin, D Kahneman, pp. 379–96. London: Cambridge Univ. Press

Small DA, Gelfand M, Babcock L, Gettman H. 2007. Who goes to the bargaining table? The influence of gender and framing on the initiation of negotiation. *J. Personal. Soc. Psychol.* 93(4):600–13

Sondak H, Bazerman MH. 1989. Matching and negotiation processes in quasi-markets. *Organ. Behav. Hum. Decis. Process.* 44(2):261–80

Steele CM, Aronson J. 1995. Stereotype threat and the intellectual test: performance of African-Americans. *J. Personal. Soc. Psychol.* 69(5):797–811

Stevens CK, Bavetta AG, Gist ME. 1993. Gender differences in the acquisition of salary negotiation skills: the role of goals, self-efficacy, and perceived control. *J. Appl. Psychol.* 78(5):723–35

Stuhlmacher AF, Walters AE. 1999. Gender differences in negotiation outcome: a meta-analysis. *Pers. Psychol.* 52(3):653–77

Swaab RI, Swaab DF. 2009. Sex differences in the effects of visual contact and eye contact in negotiations. *J. Exp. Soc. Psychol.* 45(1):129–36

Tajfel H, Billig MG, Bundy RP, Flament C. 1971. Social categorization and intergroup behavior. *Eur. J. Soc. Psychol.* 1(2):149–77

Tenbrunsel AE, Wade-Benzoni KA, Moag J, Bazerman MH. 1999. The negotiation matching process: relationships and partner selection. *Organ. Behav. Hum. Decis. Process.* 80(3):252–83

Tenbrunsel AE, Diekmann K. 2007. When you are tempted to deceive. *Negotiation* 1:9–11

Thibaut JW, Kelley HH. 1959. *The Social Psychology of Groups*. New York: Wiley

Thompson L. 1993. The impact of negotiation on intergroup relations. *J. Exp. Soc. Psychol.* 29(4):304–25

Thompson L. 1995. The impact of minimum goals and aspirations on judgments of success in negotiations. *Group Decis. Negotiation* 4:513–24

Thompson L, Peterson E, Brodt SE. 1996. Team negotiation: an examination of integrative and distributive bargaining. *J. Personal. Soc. Psychol.* 70(1):66–78

Thompson LF, Coovert MD. 2003. Teamwork online: the effects of computer conferencing on perceived confusion, satisfaction, and postdiscussion accuracy. *Group Dyn. Theory Res. Pract.* 7(2):135–51

Thompson LL. 2009. *The Mind and Heart of the Negotiator*. Upper Saddle River, NJ: Prentice Hall. 4th ed.

Thompson LL, Hastie R. 1990. Social perception in negotiation. *Organ. Behav. Hum. Decis. Process.* 47(1):98–123

Thompson LL, DeHarpport T. 1998. Relationships, good incompatibility, and communal orientation in negotiations. *Basic Appl. Soc. Psychol.* 20(1):33–44

Tiedens LZ, Fragale AR. 2003. Power moves: complementarity in dominant and submissive nonverbal behavior. *J. Personal. Soc. Psychol.* 84(3):558–68

Uzzi B. 1997. Social structure and competition in interfirm networks: the paradox of embeddedness. *Adm. Sci. Q.* 42:35–67

Valley KL, Moag J, Bazerman MH. 1998. "A matter of trust": Effects of communication on the efficiency and distribution of outcomes. *J. Econ. Behav. Organ.* 34(2):211–38

van Kleef GA, De Dreu CKW, Manstead ASR. 2004a. The interpersonal effects of anger and happiness in negotiations. *J. Personal. Soc. Psychol.* 86(1):57–76

Van Kleef GA, De Dreu CKW, Manstead ASR. 2004b. The interpersonal effects of emotions in negotiations: a motivated information processing approach. *J. Personal. Soc. Psychol.* 87(4):510–28

Wade-Benzoni KA, Hoffman AJ, Thompson LL, Moore DA, Gillespie JJ, Bazerman MH. 2002. Barriers to resolution in ideologically based negotiations: the role of values and institutions. *Acad. Manag. Rev.* 27(1):41–57

Walters AE, Stuhlmacher AF, Meyer LL. 1998. Gender and negotiator competitiveness: a meta-analysis. *Organ. Behav. Hum. Decis. Process.* 76(1):1–29

Walton RE, McKersie RB. 1965. *A Behavioral Theory of Labor Negotiations: An Analysis of a Social Interaction System*. New York: McGraw-Hill

Watson C. 1994. Gender versus power as a predictor of negotiation behavior and outcomes. *Negotiation J.* 10(2):117–27

Weingart LR, Bennet RJ, Brett JM. 1993. The impact of consideration of issues and motivational orientation on group negotiation process and outcome. *J. Appl. Psychol.* 78:504–17

Yamagishi T, Yamagishi M. 1994. Trust and commitment in the United States and Japan. *Motiv. Emot.* 18(2):129–66

Personality Development: Continuity and Change Over the Life Course

Dan P. McAdams[1] and Bradley D. Olson[2]

[1] Department of Psychology, and School of Education and Social Policy, Northwestern University, Evanston, Illinois 60208; email: dmca@northwestern.edu

[2] School of Education and Social Policy, Northwestern University, Evanston, Illinois 60208; email: b-olson@northwestern.edu

Annu. Rev. Psychol. 2010. 61:517–42

First published online as a Review in Advance on June 17, 2009

The *Annual Review of Psychology* is online at psych.annualreviews.org

This article's doi:
10.1146/annurev.psych.093008.100507

0066-4308/10/0110-0517$20.00

Key Words

personality traits, temperament, motives and goals, narrative identity, lifespan development

Abstract

The development of personality across the human life course may be observed from three different standpoints: the person as actor (behaving), agent (striving), and author (narrating). Evident even in infancy, broad differences in social action patterns foreshadow the long-term developmental elaboration of early temperament into adult dispositional traits. Research on personal strivings and other motivational constructs provides a second perspective on personality, one that becomes psychologically salient in childhood with the consolidation of an agentic self and the articulation of more-or-less stable goals. Layered over traits and goals, internalized life stories begin to emerge in adolescence and young adulthood, as the person authors a narrative identity to make meaning out of life. The review traces the development of traits, goals, and life stories from infancy through late adulthood and ends by considering their interplay at five developmental milestones: age 2, the transition to adolescence, emerging adulthood, midlife, and old age.

Contents

Nomothetic research: the study of numerous individuals in personality psychology, with the goal of testing hypotheses and deriving laws about people in general

INTRODUCTION: PERSONALITY PSYCHOLOGY AND THE WHOLE PERSON

Ever since Allport (1937) and Murray (1938) envisioned personality psychology as the scientific study of psychological individuality, personality psychologists have focused their investigations on those most important differences in social and emotional functioning that distinguish one whole person from the next. Every human life is a variation on a general evolutionary design, developing over time and in culture (McAdams & Pals 2006). For a cognitively gifted and exquisitely social species like ours, what are those broad psychological variations on the general design that are of most consequence for adaptation to group life? And how does the scientific exploration of those most consequential individual differences help us understand the whole life of an individual person as that life develops over time? Whereas personality psychologists have historically struggled to reconcile the competing agendas of what Allport called nomothetic research and the idiographic case study, their efforts to measure and validate the most socially consequential variations in overall psychological functioning aim ultimately to provide an overall framework for understanding the individual human life. At the end of the day, personality psychology must provide a conception of the person that is full and rich enough to shed scientific light on the single case.

Over the past two decades, personality psychologists have made significant advances in identifying many of the most socially consequential features of psychological individuality. A substantial scientific literature supports the construct validity of a wide range of personality variables, from dispositional traits subsumed within the well-known Big Five taxonomy (McCrae & Costa 2008) to motives, goals, values, and the specific self-schemata featured in social-cognitive theories on personality (Mischel 2004). It is now abundantly clear that personality variables are robust predictors of behavior, especially when behavior is aggregated across different situations and over time. Moreover, personality predicts important life outcomes, such as the quality of personal relationships, adaptation to life challenges, occupational success, societal involvement, happiness, health, and mortality (Lodi-Smith & Roberts 2007, Ozer & Benet-Martinez 2006). Illustrating the power of personality, a recent review of longitudinal studies demonstrated that personality traits perform as well as measures of IQ and social class in predicting mortality, divorce, and occupational attainment (Roberts et al. 2007).

In taking a life-course developmental perspective on personality, the current review traces temporal continuity and change in a broad range of features comprising psychological individuality, from the temperament traits that arise in the first months of life to the self-narratives that adults construct to make meaning out of their lives. Building on an integrative framework that has gained considerable currency in personality psychology over the past decade (McAdams & Pals 2006, Sheldon 2004, Singer 2005), the review first organizes recent research findings in terms of three developmental layers of psychological individuality—dispositional traits (the person as actor), characteristic adaptations (the person as agent), and integrative life narratives (the person as author). Personality traits sketch a dispositional outline of psychological individuality; adaptations fill in the motivational and social-cognitive details; and life stories speak to the full meaning of the individual life. Then, the review considers what these three kinds of personality constructs—traits, adaptations, and narratives—look like in the individual life at each of five developmental milestones—around age 2, the transition to adolescence, emerging adulthood, midlife, and old age.

THE PERSON AS ACTOR: THE DISPOSITIONAL PERSPECTIVE

Dispositional traits are broad, internal, and comparative features of psychological individuality that account for consistencies in behavior, thought, and feeling across situations and over time. Typically assessed via self-report questionnaires or observer ratings, dispositional traits position an individual on a series of bipolar, linear continua that describe the most basic and general dimensions upon which persons are typically perceived to differ. Amid a number of well-validated factor-analytic approaches to sorting through the vast universe of trait concepts, the most popular trait taxonomy on the scene today is the Big Five model of personality traits (John et al. 2008a). Following the program established by McCrae & Costa (2008), the five factors have been named extraversion, neuroticism, agreeableness, conscientiousness, and openness to experience. Each of the five factors, furthermore, encompasses a range of more specific traits, or what McCrae & Costa (2008) call facets. For example, their version of extraversion includes dimensions of warmth, gregariousness, assertiveness, activity, excitement seeking, and positive emotionality. The first two factors in the five-factor scheme—extraversion and neuroticism—roughly parallel the trait factors of positive emotionality and negative emotionality respectively, as articulated in what is now often called the Big Three model (Clark & Watson 2008). The third dimension of the Big Three is a factor of constraint (versus disinhibition), or the tendency to act in an overcontrolled versus undercontrolled manner.

Whether they subscribe to some variation of the Big Five, the Big Three, or none of the above, most personality psychologists today see the personality trait as the bedrock, basic unit of psychological individuality. Dispositional traits are "basic" in at least two ways. First, traits like extraversion and agreeableness describe the most fundamental and least contingent differences between actors that are most readily detected as researchers observe different people's overt actions across situations and over time. So basic are traits in this sense that some of the same individual-difference dimensions may be consistently observed among nonhuman animals, even well beyond primates (Weinstein et al. 2008). Second, dispositional traits speak to broad differences and consistencies that appear even at the very beginning of the human life span. As soon as human beings begin to act in a social arena (e.g., the infant with a caregiver), basic differences in their performance as social actors may be observed. Some actors seem generally cheerful; others distressed. Some actors consistently approach opportunities for social rewards; others show marked inhibition.

Idiographic case study: the study of the individual case in personality psychology, with the goal of understanding a particular life in depth

Dispositional traits: broad internal dimensions of personality thought to account for general consistencies in behavior, thought, and feeling observed across situations

Big Five: five broad factors repeatedly derived from factor-analytic studies of traits: extraversion, neuroticism, openness to experience, agreeableness, and conscientiousness

Characteristic adaptations: goals, plans, projects, values, possible selves, and other contextualized features of personality capturing individual differences in motivation

Emerging adulthood: the developmental period in the life course spanning the late teens through the mid-twenties

Although it is probably not right to suggest that newborn infants possess full-fledged personality traits, the broad differences in temperament that may be observed in the early months of life signal the eventual emergence of a dispositional signature for personality.

From Temperament to Traits

Temperament is the "early-in-life framework" out of which personality traits develop (Saucier & Simonds 2006, p. 118). Tracing that development, however, is one of the great challenges facing personality science today. As a first step, an increasing number of researchers and theorists have sought to line up the most well established temperament dimensions, based largely on maternal ratings and laboratory observations, with self-report adult personality traits subsumed within the Big Five and related taxonomies (Hampson et al. 2007, Shiner 2006). In their authoritative review of the literature on child and adult personality, for example, Caspi et al. (2005) proposed that (*a*) a surgency factor in child temperament (encompassing positive affectivity and positive approach) may herald the development of adult traits traditionally subsumed within the extraversion and positive emotionality domain, (*b*) temperament dimensions of anxious/fearful distress and irritable distress (Rothbart et al. 2000) may foreshadow the development of neuroticism or negative emotionality in adulthood (with irritable distress perhaps also a precursor to low agreeableness), and (*c*) childhood capacities for focused attention and effortful control (Kochanska et al. 2000), as well as aspects of behavioral inhibition in children (Fox et al. 2005), may underlie the development of the adult traits of conscientiousness, constraint, and aspects of agreeableness.

Longitudinal data supporting clear linkages between child temperament and adult personality traits are relatively scarce to date, but some instructive findings have appeared. The landmark longitudinal study of 1000 children born in Dunedin, New Zealand documented statistically significant associations between age-3

temperaments and personality traits at age 26 (Caspi et al. 2003a). Undercontrolled 3-year-olds (impulsive, negativistic, and distractible) tended to show high levels of self-report and peer-report neuroticism and low levels of agreeableness and conscientiousness as young adults, whereas children described as especially inhibited at age 3 (socially reticent and fearful) grew up to show significantly higher levels of constraint and low levels of extraversion. In a 19-year longitudinal study, Asendorpf et al. (2008) found that boys and girls who at ages 4–6 were rated by their parents as especially inhibited were more likely in young adulthood (mid-20s) to rate themselves as highly inhibited, to show internalizing problems, and to be delayed in assuming adult roles regarding work and intimate relationships. In addition, boys rated by their parents as especially aggressive showed higher levels of young-adult delinquency.

As broad dimensions of emotional expression and behavioral style apparent at or near the beginning of the human lifespan, temperament is assumed to reflect the person's native endowment. To the extent, then, that basic temperament dimensions like positive affectivity and anxious/fearful distress resemble stripped down, less-cognitively elaborated adult traits like extraversion and neuroticism, it is tempting to assume that the former gradually morph over time into the latter via a process of genetically driven unfolding. Nonetheless, a simple story of genetic determinism does not work (Krueger & Johnson 2008, Roberts et al. 2008). Studies of identical and fraternal twins have repeatedly demonstrated that adult personality traits show substantial heritability quotients (around 50%, and sometimes higher), that shared environments like overall parenting styles and family income typically account for little of the variance observed in traits (but for a notable exception, see Borkenau et al. 2001), and that nonshared environments, therefore, appear to exert a substantial effect on the development of traits, though the precise mechanisms of that effect remain unknown. In their review of research on trait genetics, Krueger et al. (2006) conclude that the primary source for stability in temperament across time is genetics, with unique environmental influences (nonshared environments) accounting for change. Yet research on molecular genetics has found it very difficult to identify reliable associations between single candidate genes and dispositional traits (Munafo et al. 2003). It appears that any given dispositional trait is probably influenced by a multitude of genes and that genes interact with environments, at multiple levels and in complex ways, in the development of personality traits.

Phenotypic temperament differences, rooted as they are in genetic differences between people, partly drive the effects of environments themselves. The temperamentally smiley and approachable infant may tend to evoke warm and friendly responses from others, which over time become the "environments" that help to reinforce and elaborate initial temperamental tendencies, sending that smiley child, it would seem, down the road toward high extraversion (and perhaps high agreeableness) in adulthood. Genetically driven differences in behavioral style may eventually determine the kinds of environments that the individual chooses to be in. At school and in the neighborhood, little extraverts-to-be may select highly social, lively settings in which to interact, reinforcing the high-extraversion tendencies that, in a sense, were there all along. Caspi et al. (2005) and Roberts et al. (2008) list a number of mechanisms like these—tendencies to react to, interpret, select, manipulate, or reject environments in accord with one's initial temperament/trait tendencies—to suggest that genes and environments conspire, with genes taking the lead role, in the gradual elaboration of childhood temperament into dispositional traits in adulthood.

Gene-environment interactions are demonstrated when genetic differences are viewed as moderating the influence of environments on traits or when environmental differences are viewed as moderating the influence of genes on traits. For example, Caspi et al. (2003b) showed that the effects of a functional polymorphism

in the promoter region of the serotonin transporter (5-HTT) gene on depressive tendencies in young adults depend on one's history of stressful life events. Those individuals who carried at least one short allele of the 5-HTT gene (indicating a less efficient reuptake of serotonin in the synaptic cleft) and who had experienced at least four major stressful events in their lives tended to show higher levels of depression and suicidality than other young adults in the study. Employing a similar logic, Kaufman et al. (2004) found that children carrying at least one short allele of the 5-HTT gene and who had a history of parental abuse were more likely to evidence depression compared to other maltreated children, if and only if their caregivers themselves reported that they were under high stress. Haeffel et al. (2008) focused on the dopamine transporter gene. They found that male adolescents who carried a particular polymorphism in this gene were more likely to exhibit depression if and only if they also reported severe maternal rejection.

Differential Continuity of Traits

Differential continuity refers to the extent to which individual differences in a given trait hold steady over time. Do people retain their relative positions in a distribution of trait scores upon successive assessments? Over a period of days or weeks, differential continuity is essentially synonymous with the test-retest reliability of the trait measures employed (Watson 2004). Over longer periods of time, however, successive assessments of traits speak to the continuity of individual differences (temporal stability) in personality.

Differential continuity tends to increase with age. In a comprehensive meta-analysis of longitudinal studies, Roberts & DelVecchio (2000) determined that stability coefficients for dispositional traits were lowest in studies of children (averaging 0.41), rose to higher levels among young adults (around 0.55), and then reached a plateau for adults between the ages of 50 and 70 (averaging 0.70). Their overall findings held for each of the Big Five trait

Gene-environment interactions: instances wherein genetic differences may moderate the influence of environments on development of traits (or environmental differences moderate the influence of genes on traits)

Differential continuity: temporal stability of individual differences in personality construct scores

Mean-level change:
the extent to which
personality construct
scores rise or fall (on
average) over
developmental time

dimensions, for both males and females, and for different measurement methods. Terraciano et al. (2006) reviewed longitudinal data to suggest that differential continuity may plateau at an earlier age, perhaps in the 30s or 40s. Personality traits in children (often viewed as aspects of temperament) are typically assessed via parental reports or laboratory observations (Durbin et al. 2007), whereas adult traits are typically indexed by self-report. It is generally acknowledged that young children do not have the requisite self-reflective skills to rate themselves on temperament/trait dimensions. Interestingly, there is evidence to suggest that the same may hold true for some adolescents. In a large Internet sample ranging in age from 10 to 20 years, Soto et al. (2008) found that self-ratings of personality traits were more structurally inconsistent and less coherent among the younger participants. Lockenhoff et al. (2008) found that differential continuity for self-report scales was lower among African Americans, compared to whites, and among individuals with less education. They speculated that the lower temporal stability could be a function of either (a) poorer test-taking skills or less motivation among African Americans and less-educated participants (rendering their assessments less reliable) or (b) greater instability in the lives of disadvantaged groups, which itself might make for less differential continuity in traits.

How strong is the case for the temporal stability of individual differences in dispositional traits? Personality psychologists appear to differ in their answers to this question, even as they look at the same empirical findings. The high stability coefficients observed for adults have convinced some observers that individual differences in personality traits are pretty well set once people reach a certain age, say about age 40 (McCrae & Costa 2008). Adding more credence to that point of view are the findings from some studies of children's traits showing dramatically higher indices of differential continuity than those observed by Roberts & DelVecchio (2000) (e.g., De Fruyt et al. 2006). On the other side are arguments that underscore the extent

to which people may gradually shift their relative positions in trait distributions over time, especially in the first half of the life course. For example, Fraley & Roberts (2005) show that test-retest correlations tend to decay as the time intervals between assessments get longer, typically approaching an asymptote in the range of 0.20 to 0.30.

Showing just how difficult it is to document strong differential continuity over the very long haul from childhood to middle age, especially in the face of very different assessment strategies employed at different points in time, are the results from a 40-year longitudinal study assessing Big Five traits from teacher ratings in elementary school and self-reports at midlife for 799 participants (Hampson & Goldberg 2006). Although statistically significant in most cases, the correlations of temporal stability proved to be surprisingly low: 0.29 for extraversion, 0.25 for conscientiousness, 0.16 for openness to experience, 0.08 for agreeableness, and 0.00 for neuroticism. It is important to note that the relatively modest reliabilities for the elementary-school teacher ratings in this study were surely instrumental in lowering the correlations found for long-term temporal stability. Nevertheless, the vanishingly small coefficients obtained for agreeableness and neuroticism caution against blithe assumptions regarding long-term differential continuity. The developmental path from childhood dimensions to adult traits is not a straightforward and easy-to-predict thing.

Developmental Trends for Traits Across the Life Course

The extent to which persons hold their relative positions in a trait distribution over time (differential continuity) is conceptually and statistically distinct from the extent to which the average values (mean levels) of scores on any given trait within a group rise or fall over the life course. Typically referred to as mean-level change, the latter issue speaks to developmental trends in trait levels: Are 40-year-olds more conscientious on the average than

20-year-olds? Do people tend to become more neurotic as they age?

Although exceptions to the rule can be found, data from both cross-sectional and longitudinal studies of dispositional traits suggest that as people move into and through their early-to-middle-adult years, they appear to become more comfortable with themselves as adults, less inclined to moodiness and negative emotions, more responsible and caring, more focused on long-term tasks and plans, and less susceptible to extreme risk-taking and the expression of unbridled internal impulses. What Caspi et al. (2005) deem the maturity principle in personality dispositions states that people become more dominant, agreeable, conscientious, and emotionally stable over the course of adult life, or at least up through late middle age. In terms of the Big Five, mean-level scores for traits subsumed within the broad domains of conscientiousness (especially facets emphasizing industriousness and impulse control) and agreeableness appear to increase from adolescence through late midlife, and scores subsumed within neuroticism tend to decrease over that period (e.g., Donnellan & Lucas 2008, Helson & Soto 2005, Jackson et al. 2009, Lonnqvist et al. 2008, McCrae et al. 1999, Srivastava et al. 2003).

Roberts et al. (2006) conducted a meta-analysis of 92 longitudinal studies, analyzing mean scores on traits by age decades, from age 10 to age 70. Most of the studies were from North American samples of participants, with largely white and middle-class samples. Conscientiousness scores showed mainly a gradual and steady increase across the age span, but the increase in agreeableness was less smooth. Average agreeableness scores crept up slowly (and nonsignificantly) to age 50, showed a sharp increase from 50 to 60, and then leveled off again. Neuroticism decreased through age 40 and then leveled off. Extraversion showed a mixed picture. Extraversion-spectrum traits related to social dominance tended to show increases through age 30, whereas extraversion-spectrum traits related to social vitality tended to decrease after age 50. Openness to experience showed a curvilinear trend: an increase up to age 20 and then a decrease after age 50.

Roberts et al. (2006) argued that increases in conscientiousness and agreeableness and decreases in neuroticism from adolescence through midlife reflect the developing adult's increasing investment in normative social roles related to family, work, and civic involvement. By contrast, Costa & McCrae (2006) explained the same trends as a product of biological maturation, suggesting that human beings may be genetically programmed to mature in the directions shown by research on dispositional traits. In the view of Costa & McCrae (2006), increases in agreeableness and conscientiousness may be correlated with increasing investment in certain social roles, but both developmental trends—changes in traits and roles—are a function of an unfolding biological program that helps to assure that adults care for the next generation and take on the social responsibilities that group life among human beings demands.

Studies of mean-level changes in dispositional traits mask individual differences in just how much particular people change. Not all individuals follow, for example, the normative increase in conscientiousness scores with age. Some people change more than others, and some change in ways that are contrary to general population trends, a phenomenon that is sometimes referred to as interindividual differences in intraindividual change (Mroczek et al. 2006). An interesting finding in this regard appears to be a variation on the maturity principle. Those individuals who tend to change the least over time are often those who already show the dispositional signature associated with maturity—low neuroticism and high agreeableness, conscientiousness, and extraversion (Donnellan et al. 2007, Johnson et al. 2007, Lonnqvist et al. 2008). The finding suggests that people who have already attained maturity with respect to dispositional traits do not "need to" change any further, whereas those who have yet to reach maturity have a longer way to go. Differences in intraindividual change may also be a function of family and social experiences. Young adults who settle into

Maturity principle: the normative tendency for people to show increases on conscientiousness and agreeableness traits and decreases on neuroticism as they move from adolescence through late middle age

serious-partner relationships (e.g., marriage) tend to show decreases in neuroticism and increases in conscientiousness that are stronger than normative trends (Neyer & Lehnart 2007). Increases in occupational success and satisfaction may cause increases in extraversion (Scollon & Diener 2006). Certain nonnormative changes in traits can also signal trouble ahead. For instance, Mroczek & Spiro (2007) found that high levels of neuroticism and increases in neuroticism over time tended to predict higher levels of mortality for older men.

THE PERSON AS AGENT: THE MOTIVATIONAL PERSPECTIVE

Despite the fact that the dispositional trait is a bedrock concept for the study of psychological individuality, personality psychologists have never been fully satisfied with traits. Allport (1937) deemed the trait to be the central unit of analysis in personality studies, but Murray (1938) cast his lot with the rival concept of need, or motive. Many of the most prominent personality theorists of the first half of the twentieth century made but passing reference to dispositional traits. Freud, Adler, Horney, Fromm, Erikson, Rogers, Maslow, Kelly, Rotter, and Bandura all placed motivational or social-cognitive constructs at the center of their theories, emphasizing the dynamics of human behavior, social learning and cognitive schemata, strategies and coping mechanisms, developmental challenges and stages, and the ever-changing details of individual adaptation to the social world. In the 1970s, more empirically minded critics took trait theories to task for neglecting the role of environments and social-learning constructs in the prediction of behavior (Mischel 2004). Even as researchers today pile up impressive findings speaking to the differential continuity and mean-level developmental trends for dispositional traits, a wide assortment of research programs in personality psychology continue to flourish outside the trait mainstream, as if their primary allegiance were to Murray over Allport (Deci & Ryan 1991, Little 1999, Schultheiss & Pang

2007). Rather than dispositional traits, many of these alternative perspectives in personality psychology focus on what McAdams & Pals (2006) call characteristic adaptations.

More particularized and contextualized than dispositional traits, characteristic adaptations include motives, goals, plans, strivings, strategies, values, virtues, schemas, and a range of other personality constructs that speak mainly to the motivational aspects of human life. What do people want? What do they value? How do people seek out what they want and avoid what they fear? How do people develop plans, goals, and programs for their lives? How do people think about and cope with the conflicts and challenges they face? What psychological and social tasks await people at particular stages or times in their lives? Conceptions of personality that directly address questions like these tend to place human agency at the center of personality inquiry. In Mischel's (2004) language, personality is an "organized, dynamic, agentic system functioning in the social world" (p. 2). Many personality psychologists proclaim that human beings are self-determining and self-regulating agents who organize their lives around goal pursuit. Life is about choice, goals, and hope—the hope that individuals can achieve their most desired goals (Deci & Ryan 1991, Freund & Riediger 2006). As agentic, self-determining beings, people do more than merely act in more-or-less consistent ways across situations and over time. As agents, people make choices; they plan their lives; they will their very identity into being.

The Agentic Self: Intentionality and the Articulation of Goals

Whereas features of temperament may be apparent in the first few days of life, a sense of personal agency emerges gradually over the early years of personality development (Walls & Kollat 2006). It begins with a dawning appreciation of human intentionality (Tomasello 1999). By the time they reach their first birthday, infants will behave in ways to suggest that they understand what others are trying to do.

They will imitate and improvise upon intentional behaviors shown by adults at much higher rates than random behaviors. They will attend to objects and events toward which adults express interest and positive emotions, as if to suggest that they, too, may want what others want. By age four, children have consolidated a "theory of mind" (Wellman et al. 2001)—a folk-psychological understanding that says people's behavior is motivated by their desires and their beliefs. In the early school years, children begin to formulate and assess their own goal-directed efforts in specific domains of experience. They develop specific beliefs and expectancies about what kinds of desired goals they can and cannot achieve, what sorts of things they need to do to achieve certain goals, what kinds of thoughts and plans they should develop to promote goal attainment, what they should hope for, and when they should give up.

By age 7 or 8, children have readily identifiable and well-articulated goals, and they see themselves as more-or-less self-determining, goal-directed agents whose aspirations take up increasing space in consciousness and show increasing influence on daily behavior (Walls & Kollat 2006). Some of the goals developed by school-aged children may be expressions or derivatives of the three basic needs identified by McClelland (1985)—motives for achievement, power, and intimacy/affiliation (Winter et al. 1998). Goals may also flow from basic, self-determining needs for autonomy, competence, and relatedness (Sheldon et al. 2001). Others may be more idiosyncratic and reflective of family, school, neighborhood, and other social influences. Goals may relate to developing temperament dimensions in complex ways. But the goals themselves, and the social-cognitive superstructure built around them, are not the same thing as the temperament traits. By age 7 or 8, a second layer of personality has begun to form. As basic dispositions continue to shape the actor's unique emotional and behavioral style, the agentic self articulates a personalized psychology of motivation, spelling out its own intentions, plans, desires, goals, values, programs, expectancies, and goal-related strategies. Layered over the actor's developing dispositional profile, then, is a motivational agenda that will come to encompass the personality's most salient characteristic adaptations.

Roberts et al. (2004) discovered positive relations between goals and dispositional traits in a four-year longitudinal study of 298 college students. For example, the researchers found that, compared to introverts, extraverts expressed high levels of enthusiasm for a greater number and variety of personal goals. Agreeableness was positively related with social and relationship goals and negatively related to aesthetic goals. Openness was related to valuing aesthetic, social, and hedonistic goals and rating economic and religious goals as less important. Roberts et al. (2004) concluded that the correlations between certain trait dimensions and ratings of goal importance were not so high as to suggest that traits subsume goals, or vice versa. Over the four-year span, moreover, ratings on goals showed levels of differential continuity (0.56) that were comparable to those shown for traits (0.61), though (unlike traits) the mean-level values of goal ratings tended to be lower at the end of the study than they were at the beginning. The authors suggested that goals follow a different developmental sequence than traits follow. Over the course of college, the students may have winnowed down their enthusiasm for the full range of goals and by their senior years focused on those goals most consistent with their long-term aims in life.

Goals Over the Life Course

Goals may be conceived at many different levels. They may range from short-term tasks, such as getting my car fixed today or finishing this paper by the end of the month, to such lifelong aims as attaining financial security. They include approach goals such as training for a marathon and avoidance goals such as staying away from men who remind me of my first husband (Elliot et al. 2001). Goals vary with respect to level of abstraction, breadth, difficulty, realism, strength, and a range of other factors that spell out their salience and function in the social ecology of an individual life. Personality researchers tend to focus on mid-range goals with some staying power—goals that are broad enough and stable enough to organize people's future selves while still concrete and immediate enough to be reflected in current behavior. To that end, they have formulated such goal constructs as personal strivings (Emmons 1986), personal projects (Little 1999), and life longings (Scheibe et al. 2007).

Freund & Riediger (2006) describe goal constructs like these as "the building blocks of adult personality" (p. 353). Goals speak directly to how general themes in an adult's life, including dispositional traits, may be played out in particular and contextually nuanced patterns of behavior. Although goals sometimes connect thematically to traits, often they do not. People's goals may even contradict their traits. An introverted 40-something man may decide that his new, number-one goal in life is to find a mate. To launch the project, he may need to engage in many behaviors and move through many states and situations that do not seem especially "introverted." He resolves to do it. The developmental project trumps his dispositional traits. Should he achieve the goal, he may settle back into his day-to-day dispositional routine.

Developmental studies of goal constructs in personality examine changes in the content and structure of goals over time and changes in the particular ways people think about, draw upon, pursue, and relinquish goals. Research conducted in modern societies suggests that among young adults, goals related to education, intimacy, friendships, and careers are likely to be especially salient; middle-aged adults focus their goals on the future of their children, securing what they have already established, and property-related concerns; and older adults show more goals related to health, retirement, leisure, and understanding current events in the world (Freund & Riediger 2006). Goals indicative of prosocial societal engagement—generativity, civic involvement, improving one's community—become more pronounced as people move into midlife and remain relatively strong for many adults well into their retirement years (McAdams et al. 1993, Peterson & Duncan 2007). Goals in early adulthood often focus on expanding the self and gaining new information, whereas goals in later adulthood may focus more on the emotional quality of ongoing relationships (Carstensen et al. 2000).

The ways in which people manage multiple and conflicting goals may change over time. Young adults seem better able to tolerate high levels of conflict among different life goals, but midlife and older adults manage goals in ways to minimize conflict (Riediger & Freund 2008). In trying to reconcile their goals to environmental constraints, young adults are more likely to engage in what Wrosch et al. (2006) call "primary control strategies," which means that they try actively to change the environment to fit their goal pursuits. By contrast, midlife and older adults are more likely to employ secondary control strategies, which involve changing the self to adjust to limitations and constraints in the environment. With some exceptions, older adults seem to approach goals in a more realistic and prudent manner, realizing their limitations and conserving their resources to focus on those few goals in life they consider to be most important (Ogilvie et al. 2001). Compared to young adults, they are often better able to disengage from blocked goals and to rescale personal expectations in the face of lost goals. As adults move into and through their midlife years, they become more adept at selecting goals that offer the best chances for reward, optimizing their efforts to attain the best payoffs from their projects and strivings, and compensating for their own limitations and losses in goal pursuit (Baltes 1997).

THE PERSON AS AUTHOR: THE SELF-NARRATIVE PERSPECTIVE

Beginning in the 1980s, psychologists developed new theories of personality that explicitly conceived of the developing person as a storyteller who draws upon the images, plots, characters, and themes in the sociocultural world to author a life (Hermans et al. 1992, McAdams 1985, Singer & Salovey 1993, Tomkins 1987).

Layered on top of dispositional traits and characteristic adaptations is an internalized and evolving story of the self—a narrative identity—that aims to provide a person's life with some semblance of unity, purpose, and meaning (McAdams 2008, McLean et al. 2007). Narrative identity is the storied understanding that a person develops regarding how he or she came to be and where he or she is going in life. It is a narrative reconstruction of the autobiographical past and imagined rendering of the anticipated future, complete with demarcated chapters, key scenes (high points, low points, turning points), main characters, and intersecting plot lines (Conway & Pleydell-Pearce 2000, McAdams 1985). In modern societies, people begin to work on their narrative identities in late adolescence and young adulthood, when individuals are challenged to explore the many adult roles, ideologies, and occupations society offers so as to commit themselves eventually to a psychosocial niche in the adult world and a unifying configuration of the self (Erikson 1963). By the time a person reaches the 20s, therefore, his or her personality has likely expanded and deepened to encompass dispositional traits, characteristic motives and goals, and the first draft of an internalized narrative of the self.

If dispositional traits sketch an outline and characteristic adaptations fill in the details of psychological individuality, narrative identity gives individual lives their unique and culturally anchored meanings. The complex interplay between culture and psychological individuality is especially evident in narrative identity. In constructing self-narratives, people draw on the stories that they learn as active participants in culture; stories about childhood, adolescence, adulthood, and aging; stories distinguishing between what culture glorifies as good characters and vilifies as bad characters; stories dramatizing full and fragmented lives that may strike the reader/viewer as exciting, frightening, infuriating, enlightening, admirable, heroic, dignified, ignoble, disgusting, wise, foolish, or boring (Bruner 1990). Culture, therefore, provides each person with an extensive anthology of stories from which the person may draw in the authoring of narrative identity. Self-authorship involves fashioning the raw materials of a life-in-culture into a suitable narrative form. The author must creatively appropriate the resources at hand while, knowingly or not, working within the bounds set by social, political, ideological, and economic realities; by family background and educational experiences; by gender and role expectations; and by the person's own dispositional traits and characteristic adaptations.

Narrative identity: an internalized and evolving life story that a person begins to develop in late adolescence to provide life with meaning and purpose

The Developmental Emergence of Narrative Identity

Human beings begin life as social actors. By mid-childhood, they have become social agents. It is not until adolescence or young adulthood, however, that they become self-authors in society. To be sure, young children can tell stories about the self. As autobiographical memory consolidates itself in the preschool years, young children begin to share accounts of personal events with others. Parents typically encourage children to talk about their personal experiences as soon as they are verbally able to do so (Fivush & Nelson 2004). By the time they reach kindergarten, children typically know that such narrative accounts should follow a canonical story grammar, involving a character/agent who moves in a goal-directed fashion over time, typically confronting obstacles of some kind, reacting to those obstacles to push the plot forward toward a concluding resolution. Cultural factors may loom large for self-storytelling in childhood. For example, studies of conversations between mothers and their young children show that East Asian parents tend to discourage children from touting their own actions in the telling of past events while framing these narrative accounts as opportunities for teaching lessons about life (Wang 2006). By contrast, North American parents are more likely to encourage the child's exploration of thoughts and feelings and to see narrative accounts of events as opportunities for self-expression.

Self-authorship, however, requires more than merely telling stories about what happened yesterday or last year. To construct a narrative identity, the person must envision his or her entire life—the past reconstructed and the future imagined—as a story that portrays a meaningful sequence of life events to explain how the person has developed into who he or she is now and may develop into who he or she may be in the future. In an influential review, Habermas & Bluck (2000) demonstrated how some of the requisite cognitive skills for self-authorship do not typically come online until adolescence. To construct an integrative life story, the person must first know how a typical life is structured—when, for example, a person leaves home, how schooling and work are sequenced, the expected progression of marriage and family formation, what people do when they retire, when people typically die, and so on. These kinds of normative expectations, shaped as they are by both biology and culture, are what Habermas & Bluck (2000) call the "cultural concept of biography." Children begin to internalize the cultural concept of biography in elementary school, but considerable learning in this domain will also occur in adolescence.

Critical to the ability to explain the development of a person over time is what Habermas & Bluck (2000) call "causal coherence." With increasing age, adolescents are better able to provide narrative accounts that explain how one event caused, led up to, transformed, or in some way was/is meaningfully related to subsequent events in one's life. An adolescent girl may explain, for example, why she rejects her parent's liberal political values—or why she feels shy around boys, or how it came to be that her junior year in high school represented a turning point in her understanding of herself—in terms of personal experiences from the past that she has selected and reconstructed to make a coherent personal narrative. She will explain how one event led to another, which led to another, and so on. She will likely share her account with others and monitor the feedback she receives in order to determine whether her attempt at causal coherence makes sense (Thorne 2000). Furthermore, she may now identify an overarching theme, value, or principle that integrates

many different episodes in her life and conveys the gist of who she is and what her biography is all about—a cognitive operation that Habermas & Bluck (2000) call "thematic coherence." In their analyses of life narratives constructed between the ages of 8 and 20, Habermas & de Silveira (2008) show that causal and thematic coherence are relatively rare in autobiographical accounts from late childhood and early adolescence but increase substantially through the teenage years and into early adulthood.

Self-Narrative Over the Life Course

The lion's share of empirical research on self-narratives has examined (a) relations between particular themes and forms in life narratives on the one hand and other personality variables (such as traits and motives) on the other, (b) life-narrative predictors of psychological well-being and mental health, (c) variations in the ways that people make narrative sense of suffering and negative events in life, (d) the interpersonal and social functions of and effects on life storytelling, (e) uses of narrative in therapy, and (f) the cultural shaping of narrative identity (McAdams 2008). To date, there exist few longitudinal studies of life stories, and no long-term efforts, of the sort found in the trait literature, to trace continuity and change in narrative identity over decades of adult development. Nonetheless, the fact that researchers have tended to collect life-narrative data from adults of many different ages, rather than focusing on the proverbial college student, provides an opportunity to consider a few suggestive developmental trends.

Because a person's life is always a work in progress and because narrative identity, therefore, may incorporate new experiences over time, theorists have typically proposed that life stories should change markedly over time. Yet, if narrative identity is to be conceived as a layer of personality itself, then a modicum of differential continuity should be expected. But how should it be assessed? By determining the extent to which a person "tells the same story" from Time 1 to Time 2? If yes, does the "same story" mean identifying the same key events in a life? Showing the same kinds of narrative themes? Exhibiting the same sorts of causal or thematic connections? In a three-year longitudinal study that asked college students to recall and describe 10 key scenes in their life stories on three different occasions, McAdams et al. (2006) found that only 28% of the episodic memories described at Time 1 were repeated three months later (Time 2), and 22% of the original (Time 1) memories were chosen and described again three years after the original assessment (Time 3). Despite change in manifest content of stories, however, McAdams et al. (2006) also documented noteworthy longitudinal consistencies (in the correlation range of 0.35 to 0.60) in certain emotional and motivational qualities in the stories (such as positive emotional tone and strivings for power/achievement) and in the level of narrative complexity. Furthermore, over the three-year period, students' life-narrative accounts became more complex, and they incorporated a greater number of themes suggesting personal growth and integration. Other life-narrative studies have linked themes of personal growth and integration to measures of psychosocial maturity (e.g., Bauer et al. 2005, King & Hicks 2006).

Cross-sectional studies suggest that up through middle age, older adults tend to construct more complex and coherent life narratives than do younger adults and adolescents (Baddeley & Singer 2007). One process through which this developmental difference is shown is autobiographical reasoning, which is the tendency to draw summary conclusions about the self from autobiographical episodes (McLean et al. 2007). Autobiographical reasoning tends to give a life narrative greater causal and thematic coherence (Habermas & Bluck 2000). Pasupathi & Mansour (2006) found that autobiographical reasoning in narrative accounts of life turning points increases with age up to midlife. Middle-aged adults showed a more interpretive and psychologically sophisticated approach to life storytelling, compared to younger people. Bluck & Gluck (2004)

asked adolescents (age 15–20), younger adults (age 30–40), and older adults (age 60 and over) to recount personal experiences in which they demonstrated wisdom. Younger and older adults were more likely than the adolescents to narrate wisdom scenes in ways that connected the experiences to larger life themes or philosophies, yet another manifestation of autobiographical reasoning. Singer et al. (2007) found that adults over the age of 50 narrated self-defining memories that expressed a more positive narrative tone and greater integrative meaning compared to those of college students. Findings like these dovetail with Pennebaker & Stone's (2003) demonstration, based on laboratory studies of language use and analyses of published fiction, that adults use more positive and fewer negative affect words, and demonstrate greater levels of cognitive complexity, as they age. The findings are also consistent with a broader research literature in lifespan developmental psychology showing that middle-aged adults tend to express the most complex, individuated, and integrated self-conceptions (e.g., Diehl et al. 2001), and with research on autobiographical recollections showing a positivity memory bias among older adults (e.g., Kennedy et al. 2004).

PUTTING IT TOGETHER: DEVELOPMENTAL MILESTONES

The idea that the individual moves through a series of clearly demarcated stages of personality development is no longer a fashionable notion in the study of psychological individuality (see sidebar, Culture and the Three Layers of Personality). Temperament and trait models suggest a rather more continuous course of development, with few predictable epochs of transition or moments of sudden change. Life-narrative studies show that people readily think of their own lives as dividing into stages, chapters, and transitional scenes, but each person does this in a different way. Life-course perspectives in the social sciences (Levy et al. 2005) emphasize the unpredictable effects of off-time events, serendipity, and societal

Autobiographical reasoning: the tendency to draw summary (semantic) conclusions about the self from autobiographical episodes

CULTURE AND THE THREE LAYERS OF PERSONALITY

The complex relationships between culture and personality may play out somewhat differently for each of the three layers of personality described in this review (McAdams & Pals 2006). From the first perspective of the person as actor, cultures provide different display rules and norms for the expression of trait-based behavior. For example, Japanese extraverts growing up in Kyoto may express their high levels of sociability and positive affectivity in ways that differ dramatically from how their equally extraverted middle-American counterparts express the same tendencies in Columbus, Ohio. High neuroticism may translate into eating disorders and cutting behavior among upper-middle-class American teenaged girls, whereas the same levels of emotional instability may manifest itself as magical thinking and an extreme fear of enemies among teenaged girls in Ghana (Adams 2005). Whether different cultures promote the development of particular dispositional traits over others, however, is a tricky issue. Some studies report mean-level differences in trait scores across cultures (Schmitt et al. 2007), but skeptics argue that these differences are difficult to interpret because people may use local, social-comparison norms when making trait judgments about themselves and others (Heine et al. 2008). To put it simply, if Japanese participants implicitly compare themselves to other Japanese (because these are the people they know) in making trait judgments about themselves and, likewise, Canadians compare themselves to Canadians, then how might we interpret a finding suggesting that Canadians tend to score higher than Japanese on, say, the trait of agreeableness?

From the second perspective of the person as agent, cultures may show clearer influences on the content and importance of different motives and goals. For example, the well-known distinction between cultural individualism and collectivism and the corresponding emphasis upon independent and interdependent self-construals, respectively (Markus & Kitayama 1991), appears to map much more clearly onto layer-2 personality constructs—such as goals, motives, and values—than onto layer-1 traits. A large and growing body of research suggests that whereas individualist Western cultures may encourage the development of personal goals that privilege the expansion and actualization of the self, collectivist East Asian cultures may more strongly encourage the development of personal goals that aim to promote social harmony and the well-being of one's self-defining

(Continued)

change while still suggesting that development is structured by biological constraints, age-graded norms and role expectations, and by a succession of culturally informed developmental tasks. Whereas personality development may be too gradual and too culturally contingent to follow a lock-step progression of discrete stages, it does nonetheless show enough structure and direction such that developmental milestones may be identified to mark progressive change as well as continuity. A milestone is a marker along the developmental road. The placement of markers is somewhat arbitrary in personality development, but at each point marked the viewer may get an overall sense of what the whole of personality looks like and how far along it has come.

The current review conceives of dispositional traits, characteristic adaptations, and life narratives as three layers of personality, each following its own developmental course. Traits emerge first, as broad individual differences in temperament exhibited by social actors. As temperament dispositions continue to develop and consolidate in childhood, characteristic motives and goals begin to appear, revealing the person's newfound status as a striving agent. In adolescence and young adulthood, a third layer begins to emerge, even as traits and goals continue to evolve. For reasons that are cognitive, social, cultural, and existential, the person eventually becomes an author of his or her own life, constructing and living within a narrative identity that spells out who he or she was, is, and will be in time and culture. Stories are layered over goals, which are layered over traits. It is expected, nonetheless, that dispositional traits, characteristic adaptations, and narrative identity should relate to each other in complex, meaningful, and perhaps predictable ways; for after all, this is all about the development of a whole person. What traits, adaptations, and stories may look like, therefore, and how they may relate to each other may be examined at five particular developmental milestones: age 2, the transition to adolescence, emerging adulthood, midlife, and old age.

Age 2: Self and Other

The rudiments of psychological individuality appear in the first few weeks of life. Temperament differences in characteristic mood, soothability, attention, response intensity, and inhibition provide early hints of a personality yet to come. Parents react to their infant's temperament, and those responses are assumed to have some impact on the development of personality over the long haul. Genotypically driven differences interact with environments in complex ways and on multiple levels as early differences gradually elaborate into more-or-less consistent, trait-like trends in the quality of social action and emotional experience. Temperament differences likely have more immediate impacts on the development of the caregiver-infant attachment bond. Irritable babies (and their caregivers) may have an especially difficult time establishing the smooth, goal-corrected partnership that is so characteristic of securely attached infants and toddlers (Saarni 2006). Secure attachment may be easier to achieve with temperamentally easy babies.

The establishment of a secure attachment bond may be seen as the first great psychosocial goal in personality development (Mikulincer & Shaver 2007). But it is not a goal that the infant self-consciously sets out to achieve. In a general sense, social behavior is goal-directed from the beginning of life, and indeed intentional, goal-directed behavior begins to capture the infant's attention by age one (Tomasello 1999). But it is not until the second and third years of life that the hints of an agentic, goal-directed self begin to show themselves, and then only haltingly. Around 18 months of age, infants/toddlers begin to recognize themselves in mirrors and show a range of other behaviors suggesting that they now have a sense of themselves as selves. The onset of self-recognition behavior roughly coincides with the emergence of social/moral emotions such as pride, embarrassment, shame, and eventually guilt (Tangney et al. 2007). Around the time of the child's second birthday, a sense of what William James conceived as a reflexive, duplex self—an I who

groups. Some evidence also suggests that collectivist cultures may stress avoidance goals suggestive of a prevention focus in motivation, whereas more individualistic cultures may stress approach goals suggestive of a promotion focus (Elliot et al. 2001). Of course, cultural differences in goals are matters of degree rather than either/or, and not all studies find large cultural differences (Oyserman et al. 2002). Nonetheless, it would appear that culture's impact on personality may be more readily apparent with respect to goals than traits.

Finally, culture may exert its most profound influences at the level of life narratives (Hammack 2008, McAdams 2006). Stories capture and elaborate metaphors and images that are especially resonant in a given culture. Stories distinguish what culture glorifies as good characters and vilifies as bad characters, and they present the many varieties that fall between. Culture, therefore, may provide each person with a menu of stories about how to live, and each person chooses from the menu. For example, McAdams (2006) showed how highly generative American adults tend to construct their own life stories by drawing upon inspiring American narratives such as rags-to-riches stories and redemptive tales of emancipation and self-fulfillment. Identity choices are constrained and shaped by the unique circumstances of persons' social, political, and economic worlds; by their family backgrounds and educational experiences; and by their dispositional traits and characteristic motives, values, and goals. A person authors a narrative identity by selectively appropriating and personalizing the stories provided by culture.

observes the Me—is beginning to emerge. A social actor from day one, the 2-year-old is now a self-conscious social actor who keenly observes his or her own actions and those of the other actors in the social environment.

At the milestone marker of age 2, the toddler reveals broad and more-or-less consistent individual differences in temperament. The outlines of a dispositional profile can be clearly seen, even though considerable elaboration and change will surely follow (Durbin et al. 2007). Whereas the social actor is beginning to come into profile, the social agent and author are still waiting in the wings. Nonetheless, the age-2 milestone does afford a glimpse of what is to come. The emergence of an I/Me self in the second and third years of life lays the groundwork for both agency and authorship. What parents describe as "the terrible twos" refers mainly to the child's willful nature, its budding autonomy and egocentric desire to do what it wants to do, no matter what. As a willful, intentional agent, the 2-year-old pushes hard an agenda of desire. Desires make for immediate goals. In a few years, more stable goals will begin to crystallize and a clearer outline of personality's second layer will become visible. Similarly, self-recognition behaviors signal the emergence of what Howe & Courage (1997) call an "autobiographical self." The child begins to remember, own, and tell autobiographical memories around the age of 2, "my" little stories about things that happened to "me," and about things "I" intended (wanted, desired) to do. The increasingly autonomous 2-year-old self takes the first steps toward becoming a goal-directed striver and autobiographical narrator, foreshadowing the expressions of both agency and authorship in personality.

The Transition to Adolescence

Whether viewed as a period of storm and stress or an uncertain limbo sandwiched between two well-defined developmental epochs, adolescence has traditionally been conceived as a transitional phase, identified roughly as the teenaged years. Yet marking its beginning and end has become increasingly problematic. On the front edge of things, hormonal and psychological shifts heralding a transition to come seem to occur years before the advent of puberty's most obvious signs—as early as age 8 or 9. On the back end, surveys of Americans and Europeans show that an increasing number of individuals in their mid-20s still do not consider themselves adults and have not as yet assumed those roles traditionally associated with adulthood—stable jobs, marriage, parenthood (Arnett 2000). Furthermore, the psychosocial issues facing individuals in their early teens (e.g., peer pressure, delinquency) appear to be dramatically different from those facing college freshmen and sophomores (e.g., vocation, intimacy). In that it seems to begin earlier and end

later than once expected and in that its beginning looks nothing like its ending, adolescence is not what it used to be, if it ever was. In that light, it is instructive to identify two different milestones in personality development—one marking the end of childhood itself (roughly age 8–12) and another marking what Arnett (2000) describes as emerging adulthood.

The preteen period, marking the end of childhood and the beginning of adolescence, reveals a rich and newly complexified portrait of psychological individuality. Factor analytic studies of personality ratings suggest that it is around this time that a clear five-factor structure begins to appear for dispositional traits (Roberts et al. 2008). There is a sense, then, in which the structure of dispositional traits is beginning to stabilize, on the eve of adolescence. At the same time, individual differences in self-esteem have begun to emerge. According to Harter (2006), children's self-esteem scores tend to be fairly high and not especially differentiated before the age of 7 or 8. But thereafter self-esteem drops for many children and begins to show more-or-less consistent individual differences. Harter (2006) considers a wide range of explanations for these striking findings, including (a) rising expectations from parents and teachers regarding children's achievement and (b) children's newfound tendency, rooted in cognitive development, to compare themselves to one another in systematic ways. During the same developmental period, researchers typically note the first clear signs of depression (especially in girls) and increases in antisocial behavior (especially in boys). Scores on openness to experience also begin to rise in the preteen years.

By the time they are on the verge of adolescence, children have developed clear goals and motives that structure their consciousness and shape their behavior from one situation to the next and over time. They are now also able to evaluate the worth and progress of their own goal pursuits and projects as they play out across situations and over time. They begin to see what they need to do to achieve those goals on which their self-esteem depends, be they in the realm of athletics, friendship, school-work, or values. They also begin to withdraw investment in goals that seem fruitless—goals for which their own skills and traits, or environmental contingencies and affordances, may be poorly suited. At the same time, older children and young adolescents may hold grandiose fantasies about accomplishment, fame, or notoriety in the future. What Elkind (1981) described as the "personal fable" begins to emerge around this time—a fantastical first draft of narrative identity. The same cognitive skills and developments that enable preteens to evaluate themselves and their goal pursuits (positively or negatively) vis-à-vis their peers may also help launch their first full autobiographical projects, as evidenced in early adolescent diaries, fantasies, and conversations (McAdams 2008). It is during the transition to adolescence, revealed Habermas & Bluck (2000), that individuals begin to see in full what makes up an entire life, from birth through childhood, career, marriage, parenting, and so on, to death. Their first efforts at imagining their own life stories may be unrealistic, grandiose, and somewhat incoherent. But authors have to begin somewhere.

Emerging Adulthood

Arnett (2000) has argued that the period running from about age 17 up through the mid-20s constitutes an integral developmental epoch in and of itself, which he calls emerging adulthood. This demarcation makes good sense in modern postindustrial societies wherein schooling and the preparation for adult work extend well into the 20s and even beyond. The betwixt-and-between nature of what was once called adolescence appears to be extending for almost a decade beyond the teenage years for many young men and women today, who are putting off marriage and parenthood until their late 20s and 30s. The movement through this developmental period is strongly shaped by class and education. Less-educated, working-class men and women may find it especially difficult to sustain steady and gainful employment during this period. Some get married and/or

begin families anyway, but others may drift for many years without the economic security required to become a full stakeholder in society. Those more privileged men and women headed for middle-class professions may require many years of schooling and/or training and a great deal of role experimentation before they feel they are able to settle down and assume the full responsibilities of adulthood. Many social and cultural factors in modern societies have come together to make emerging adulthood the prime time in the life course for the exploration and development of what Erikson (1963) described as ego identity.

Emerging adulthood marks the beginning of a gradual upward swing for dispositional traits associated with conscientiousness and agreeableness and a decline in neuroticism. As emerging adults eventually come to take on the roles of spouse, parent, citizen, and stakeholder, their traits may shift upward in the direction of greater warmth and care for others, higher levels of social responsibility, and greater dedication to being productive, hard-working, and reliable. Even as temporal stability in individual differences increases, significant mean-level changes in personality traits are to be expected in the 20s and 30s (Roberts et al. 2008). And individual differences in traits combine with many other factors, including gender, to shape life trajectories during this time. For example, longitudinal data from the Berkeley Guidance Study showed that shy (low-extraversion) women in the middle years of the twentieth century were more likely to follow gender-conventional patterns of marriage, homemaking, and motherhood, whereas shy men were more likely to delay marriage, parenthood, and stable careers, and attained less achievement in their careers (Fox et al. 2005).

For the second and third layers of personality, emerging adulthood marks the exploration of and eventual commitment to new life goals and the articulation of a new and ideally integrative understanding of one's life story. Emerging adults begin to see life as a complex and multifaceted challenge in role performance and goal pursuit. At the same time, they seek to integrate the many different roles, goals, and selves they are managing within an organized identity pattern that provides life with some semblance of unity, purpose, and meaning. Narrative theories of identity describe this effort as a process of orchestrating different voices of the self within an ongoing narrative conversation (Hermans et al. 1992) or integrating different personifications of the self within a single self-defining life story (McAdams 1985). In any case, the main psychosocial task of emerging adulthood is to author a narrative identity. By the time young people have finally "emerged" from emerging adulthood, they have ideally articulated and internalized a more-or-less coherent story of who they were, are, and will be. The story affirms their former and ongoing explorations and their newly established commitments, and it sets them up, psychosocially speaking, for the daunting challenges of generative adulthood in the modern world.

Midlife Tipping Points

In many lives, personality development reaches something of a crescendo in middle adulthood. Against the backdrop of ever-increasing differential continuity in dispositional traits, conscientiousness and agreeableness rise to their apex and neuroticism may bottom out (Roberts et al. 2006). Generativity strivings may peak as midlife adults invest heavily in their families and communities (Peterson & Duncan 2007). Personal agency may be distributed across a broad spectrum of goals and responsibilities, as midlife adults negotiate the roles of parent, grandparent, child of aging parents, aunt and uncle, provider and breadwinner, colleague, neighbor, lifelong friend, citizen, leader, and so on. For the most active and generative adults, this is the prime of life, even as role demands and conflicting goals threaten to overwhelm them. Their life stories express the psychologically energizing themes of agency, communion, integration, and growth (Bauer et al. 2005). For many others, however, it is a time of tremendous disappointment, mounting frustration, and what Erikson (1963) described as

midlife stagnation. The long-awaited maturation expected for dispositional traits never really happens; goals are repeatedly nipped in the bud; narrative identity reveals an impoverished psychological life in which positive scenes are often contaminated by bad endings and long-term aspirations are repeatedly quashed.

Two decades of research on life stories shows that American adults in their 40s and 50s demonstrate dramatic individual differences in narrative identity (McAdams 2006). Those reporting low levels of generativity, high levels of depression, and depleted psychological resources construct life stories that fail to affirm progress and growth. Plots go round and round in vicious circles, and positive-affect scenes are often spoiled by negative outcomes. By contrast, those who score high on self-report measures of generativity and overall mental health tend to construct redemptive self-narratives wherein protagonists repeatedly overcome obstacles and transform suffering into personal enhancement and prosocial engagement. These stories often begin with the juxtaposition of emotionally positive scenes, wherein the child is made to feel blessed or special, with emotionally negative scenes, wherein he or she learns early on that other people are not so fortunate and that the world is a dangerous place. As the gifted protagonist journeys forth into an unredeemed world, he or she encounters all manner of adversity, but throughout the narrative bad things usually turn good, giving the plot a clear upward trajectory. The redemptive life stories constructed by psychologically healthy and generative American adults in their midlife years draw upon the quintessentially American discourses of atonement, emancipation, recovery, and upward social mobility (McAdams 2006). Illustrating the complex interplay of personal authorship and cultural influence, the stories reprise cultural themes—both cherished and contested—that may be traced back to such canonical American sources as the spiritual testimonials of Puritans and the autobiography of Benjamin Franklin, and forward to today's Hollywood movies, the self-help industry, and Oprah.

Nonetheless, scattered research findings on personality development across the life course show how the crescendo of midlife eventually subsides. There may be psychological tipping points in midlife when development changes direction, in a sense, or flattens out into a plateau. For example, cognitive and affective complexity appears to peak out for many people in their 50s and then declines (Diehl et al. 2001, Helson & Soto 2005). At some point, midlife adults may begin to scale back goal pursuits and focus their energies on those areas, typically family related, wherein they have made their strongest investments. As they begin to experience the physical and information-processing declines that begin even in early midlife, adults may select goals and strategies for accomplishing goals that optimize their best skills and compensate for areas of weakness (Freund & Riediger 2006). Strategies of primary control (changing the environment to fit one's needs and goals) may gradually give way to strategies of secondary control (changing the self to fit the environment) (Wrosch et al. 2006). At some point in the midlife years, adults appear to shift their perspective on life from one emphasizing expansion, activation, primary control, and information seeking to one emphasizing contraction, protection, secondary control, and the quality of emotional life. The shift is not likely to be sudden, may occur in some domains before others, and is sure to play out in different ways and according to different timetables for different people. But however and whenever it happens, the shift marks a tipping from a life narrative of ascent to one of maintenance and eventual decline.

On Endings: The Incomplete Architecture of Personality Development

In a classic paper, Baltes (1997) argued that human ontogeny manifests an "incomplete architecture" (p. 366) with increasing age. The bad news, in Baltes's view, is that evolutionary selection pressures make for decreasing genome-based plasticity and biological potential after early adulthood. The good news is that culture-based resources help to compensate and maintain a favorable gain/loss ratio for many modern adults well into middle age and the early retirement years. Eventually, however, losses outstrip gains and the structure of a life begins to unravel. At the end of the developmental course, cultural resources fail to ameliorate biological constraints. Adjustment breaks down in very old age. In sharp contrast, then, to romantic notions about an enlightened and transcendent final stage of personality development (e.g., Jung 1961), Baltes characterized the psychology of advanced aging in terms of deterioration, breakdown, and entropy.

Personality researchers have not devoted considerable resources as yet to the study of old age. Yet some findings appear to support the picture of an incomplete architecture for personality in old age. Over the age span of 74 to 103, for example, Smith & Baltes (1999) found increasingly negative affective states with age. Martin et al. (2002) observed decreasing differential continuity in traits among the very old and increasing scores on fatigue, depression, and suspiciousness. Teachman (2006) observed that the trend toward lower neuroticism with age appears to reverse itself in the mid-70s. Mroczek & Almeida (2004) observed an increase with age in the kindling effects of stress, such that small stresses seem more likely to add up to ignite debilitating negative reactions among older adults.

Continuing a trend from midlife, old age necessitates the increasing use of secondary control strategies for goals, including goal disengagement. As losses begin to overwhelm gains, older adults must conserve dwindling resources to invest in only the most essential goals. With advanced aging, goals may center largely on health concerns. With respect to narrative identity, elderly adults may draw increasingly on reminiscences as they review the life they have lived (Serrano et al. 2004). Positive memory biases among older people may give life stories a softer glow, while the tendency to recall fewer specific and more generalized memories with age may simplify life stories (Singer et al. 2007). In the wake of memory loss and increasing frailty, however, the oldest adults may no longer be psychologically involved in the construction of narrative identity. Should serious dementia follow, authorship may fade away, and so too, strong agency, as the oldest old return instead to those most basic issues of living day to day as social actors, conserving energy to focus on the moments left in life, surviving and holding on as well as possible, before death closes the door.

CONCLUSION

The development of personality across the human life course is a complex and multilayered affair. The guiding framework for this review suggests that personality develops as a dynamic constellation of dispositional traits (the person as actor), characteristic goals and motives (the person as agent), and integrative life stories (the person as author). Recent research has examined continuity and change with respect to these three layers of personality. For example, recent research on dispositional traits shows (*a*) increasing temporal stability with age and (*b*) predictable development trends in mean levels of traits over the adult lifespan, while examining the potential effects of gene-by-environment interactions, social roles and social investments, and overall maturational trends to explain patterns of continuity and change in traits. Studies focused on motivational constructs have documented changes in the content and structuring of goals across the life course and developmental trends in the way people think about, draw upon, pursue, control, cope with, and relinquish goals. For the third layer of personality, recent research demonstrates that life narratives increase in complexity and coherence up through midlife while reflecting a range of psychological content whose meanings often reflect cultural themes. Recent empirical findings and theoretical advances suggest that the future is bright for the study of personality development over the full span of life, from birth through old age. Researchers will continue to explore the biological underpinnings and social/cultural contexts of the developing whole person as he or she moves through the life course in the guises of actor, agent, and author.

SUMMARY POINTS

1. As it develops over the human life course, personality may be viewed as a constellation of dispositional traits (the person as actor), characteristic adaptations (the person as agent), and integrative life stories (the person as author) situated in time and culture.

2. Early temperament dimensions gradually develop into the dispositional traits observed in adulthood through complex, dynamic, and multileveled interactions between genes and environments over time.

3. Whereas it is difficult to show especially strong associations between personality ratings in childhood and corresponding dispositional trait scores in adulthood (though some longitudinal associations have been documented), temporal stability for individual differences in traits increases over the life course, reaching impressively high levels in the middle-adult years.

4. Cross-sectional and longitudinal studies show that mean-level scores for most traits subsumed within the broad categories of conscientiousness and agreeableness increase, and neuroticism decreases, from adolescence through late middle age.

5. Motives, goals, and related characteristic adaptations emerge as salient features of personality in middle childhood. Over the life course, the content, structure, organization, and pursuit of goals may change to reflect normative and idiosyncratic shifts in the social ecology of daily life.

6. In late adolescence and young adulthood, individuals typically begin to reconstruct the autobiographical past and imagine the future to develop an internalized life story, or narrative identity, that provides their life with a modicum of meaning and purpose. In personality development, life stories are layered over goals and motives, which are layered over dispositional traits.

7. As dispositional traits show normative trends toward greater maturity from adolescence to middle adulthood, goals and narratives show an increasing concern with commitments to family, civic involvement, and productive activities aimed at promoting the next generation. In midlife, redemptive life narratives tend to support generativity and psychosocial adaptation.

8. From late midlife through old age, personality development may reveal a plateau and eventual descent, as trait scores show some negative reversals, goals focus more on maintenance of the self and coping with loss, and life narratives express an inexorable decline in the power of self-authorship.

DISCLOSURE STATEMENT

The authors are not aware of any biases that might be perceived as affecting the objectivity of this review.

ACKNOWLEDGMENTS

This work was supported by a grant from the Foley Family Foundation to establish the Foley Center for the Study of Lives at Northwestern University. The authors thank Jonathan Adler, Emily Durbin, Tilman Habermas, Jeff McCrae, Kate McLean, Ken Sheldon, and Josh Wilt for their comments on an early draft of the manuscript.

LITERATURE CITED

Adams G. 2005. The cultural grounding of personal relationship: enemyship in North American and West African worlds. *J. Personal. Soc. Psychol.* 88:948–68

Allport GW. 1937. *Personality: A Psychological Interpretation.* New York: Holt, Rinehart & Winston

Arnett JJ. 2000. Emerging adulthood: a theory of development from the late teens through the twenties. *Am. Psychol.* 55:469–80

Asendorpf JB, Denissen JJA, van Aken MAG. 2008. Inhibited and aggressive preschool children at 23 years of age: personality and social transitions into adulthood. *Dev. Psychol.* 44:997–1011

Baddeley J, Singer JA. 2007. Charting the life story's path: narrative identity across the life span. In *Handbook of Narrative Research Methods*, ed. J Clandinin, pp. 177–202. Thousand Oaks, CA: Sage

Baltes PB. 1997. On the incomplete architecture of human ontogeny: selection, optimization, and compensation as foundation of developmental theory. *Am. Psychol.* 52:366–80

Bauer JJ, McAdams DP, Sakaeda AR. 2005. Interpreting the good life: growth memories in the lives of mature, happy people. *J. Personal. Soc. Psychol.* 88:203–17

Bluck S, Gluck J. 2004. Making things better and learning a lesson: experiencing wisdom across the lifespan. *J. Personal.* 72:543–72

Borkenau P, Riemann R, Spinath FM, Angleitner A. 2001. Genetic and environmental influences on observed personality: evidence from the German Observational Study of Adult Twins. *J. Personal. Soc. Psychol.* 80:655–68

Bruner JS. 1990. *Acts of Mind.* Cambridge, MA: Harvard Univ. Press

Carstensen LL, Pasupathi M, Mayr U, Nesselroade JR. 2000. Emotional experience in everyday life across the adult life span. *J. Personal. Soc. Psychol.* 79:644–55

Caspi A, Harrington HL, Milne B, Amell JW, Theodore RF, Moffitt TE. 2003a. Children's behavioral styles at age 3 are linked to their adult personality traits at age 26. *J. Personal.* 71:495–513

Caspi A, Roberts BW, Shiner RL. 2005. Personality development: stability and change. *Annu. Rev. Psychol.* 56:453–84

Caspi A, Sugden K, Moffitt TE, Taylor A, Craig I, et al. 2003b. Influence of life stress on depression: moderation of a polymorphism in the 5-HTT gene. *Science* 301:386–89

Clark LA, Watson D. 2008. Temperament: an organizing paradigm for trait psychology. See John et al. 2008b, pp. 265–86

Conway MA, Pleydell-Pearce CW. 2000. The construction of autobiographical memories in the self memory system. *Psychol. Rev.* 107:261–88

Costa PT, McCrae RR. 2006. Age changes in personality and their origins: comment on Roberts, Walton, and Viechtbauer (2006). *Psychol. Bull.* 132:26–28

De Fruyt F, Bartels M, Van Leeuwen KG, De Clercq B, Decuyper M, Mervielde I. 2006. Five types of personality continuity in childhood and adolescence. *J. Personal. Soc. Psychol.* 91:538–52

Deci E, Ryan RM. 1991. A motivational approach to self: integration in personality. In *Nebraska Symposium on Motivation: 1990,* ed. R Dienstbier, RM Ryan, pp. 237–88. Lincoln: Univ. Nebraska Press

Diehl M, Hastings CT, Stanton JM. 2001. Self-concept differentiation across the adult life span. *Psychol. Aging* 16:643–54

Donnellan MB, Conger RD, Burzette RG. 2007. Personality development from late adolescence to young adulthood: differential stability, normative maturity, and evidence for maturity-stability hypothesis. *J. Personal.* 75:237–63

Donnellan MB, Lucas RE. 2008. Age differences in the Big Five across the life span: evidence from two national samples. *Psychol. Aging* 23:558–66

Durbin CE, Hayden EP, Klein DN, Olino TM. 2007. Stability of laboratory-assessed temperament emotionality traits from ages 3 to 7. *Emotion* 7:388–99

Elkind D. 1981. *Children and Adolescents.* New York: Oxford Univ. Press. 3rd ed.

Elliot AJ, Chirkov VI, Kim Y, Sheldon KM. 2001. A cross-cultural analysis of avoidance (relative to approach) personal goals. *Psychol. Sci.* 12:505–10

Emmons RA. 1986. Personal strivings: an approach to personality and subjective well-being. *J. Personal. Soc. Psychol.* 51:1058–68

Erikson EH. 1963. *Childhood and Society.* New York: Norton. 2nd ed.

Fivush R, Nelson C. 2004. Culture and language in the emergence of autobiographical memory. *Psychol. Sci.* 15:573–77

Fox NA, Henderson HA, Marshall PJ, Nichols KE, Ghera MM. 2005. Behavioral inhibition: linking biology and behavior within a developmental framework. *Annu. Rev. Psychol.* 56:235–62

Fraley RC, Roberts BW. 2005. Patterns of continuity: a dynamic model for conceptualizing the stability of individual differences in psychological constructs across the life course. *Psychol. Rev.* 112:60–74

Freund AM, Riediger M. 2006. Goals as building blocks of personality and development in adulthood. See Mroczek & Little 2006, pp. 353–72

Habermas T, Bluck S. 2000. Getting a life: the emergence of the life story in adolescence. *Psychol. Bull.* 126:748–69

Habermas T, de Silveira C. 2008. The development of global coherence in life narratives across adolescence: temporal, causal, and thematic aspects. *Dev. Psychol.* 44:707–21

Haeffel GJ, Getchell M, Kiposov RA, Yrigollen CM, DeYoung CG, et al. 2008. Association between polymorphisms in the dopamine transporter gene and depression. *Psychol. Sci.* 19:62–69

Documents differential continuity from early childhood to young adulthood on traits related to impulse control.

Reviews literature to argue that cognitive skills for narrative identity develop in adolescence.

Hammack PL. 2008. Narrative and the cultural psychology of identity. *Personal. Soc. Psychol. Rev.* 12:222–47

Hampson SE, Andrews JA, Barckley M, Peterson M. 2007. Trait stability and continuity in childhood: relating sociability and hostility to the five-factor model of personality. *J. Res. Personal.* 41:507–23

Hampson SE, Goldberg LR. 2006. A first large cohort study of personality trait stability over the 40 years between elementary school and midlife. *J. Personal. Soc. Psychol.* **91:763–79**

Harter S. 2006. Developmental and individual difference perspectives on self-esteem. See Mroczek & Little 2006, pp. 311–34

Heine SJ, Buchtel EE, Norenzayan A. 2008. What do cross-national comparisons of personality traits tell us? *Psychol. Sci.* 19:309–13

Helson R, Soto CJ. 2005. Up and down in middle age: monotonic and nonmonotonic changes in roles, status, and personality. *J. Personal. Soc. Psychol.* 89:194–204

Hermans HJM, Kempen HJG, van Loon RJP. 1992. The dialogical self: beyond individualism and rationalism. *Am. Psychol.* 47:23–33

Howe ML, Courage ML. 1997. The emergence and early development of autobiographical memory. *Psychol. Rev.* 104:499–523

Jackson JJ, Bogg T, Walton KE, Wood D, Harms PD, et al. 2009. Not all conscientiousness scales change alike: a multimethod, multisample study of age differences in the facets of conscientiousness. *J. Personal. Soc. Psychol.* 96:446–59

John OP, Naumann LP, Soto CJ. 2008a. Paradigm shift to the integrative Big Five trait taxonomy: history, measurement, and conceptual issues. See John et al. 2008b, pp. 114–58

John OP, Robins RW, Pervin LA, eds. 2008b. *Handbook of Personality: Theory and Research.* New York: Guilford. 3rd ed.

Johnson W, Hicks BM, McGue M, Iacono WG. 2007. Most of the girls are alright, but some aren't: personality trajectory groups from ages 14 to 24 and some associations with outcomes. *J. Personal. Soc. Psychol.* 93:266–84

Jung CG. 1961. *Memories, Dreams, Reflections.* New York: Vintage

Kaufman J, Yang B, Douglas-Palomberi H, Houshyar S, Lipschitz D, et al. 2004. Social supports and serotonin transporter gene moderate depression in maltreated children. *Proc. Natl. Acad. Sci. USA* 101:17316–21

Kennedy Q, Mather M, Carstensen LL. 2004. The role of motivation in age-related positivity effect in autobiographical memory. *Psychol. Sci.* 15:208–14

King LA, Hicks JA. 2006. Narrating the self in the past and future: implications for maturity. *Res. Hum. Dev.* 3:121–38

Kochanska G, Murray KT, Harlan ET. 2000. Effortful control in early childhood: continuity and change, antecedents, and implications for social development. *Dev. Psychol.* 36:220–32

Krueger RF, Johnson W. 2008. Behavioral genetics and personality: a new look at the integration of nature and nurture. See John et al. 2008b, pp. 287–310

Krueger RF, Johnson W, Kling KC. 2006. Behavior genetics and personality development. See Mroczek & Little 2006, pp. 81–108

Levy R, Ghisletta P, LeGoff J-M, Spini D, Widmer E, eds. 2005. *Towards an Interdisciplinary Perspective on the Life Course.* London: Elsevier

Little BR. 1999. Personality and motivation: personal action and the conative evolution. In *Handbook of Personality: Theory and Research*, ed. LA Pervin, OP John, pp. 501–24. New York: Guilford. 2nd ed.

Lockenhoff CE, Terracciano A, Bienvenu OJ, Patriciu NS, Nestadt G, et al. 2008. Ethnicity, education, and the temporal stability of personality traits in the East Baltimore Epidemiologic Catchment Area Study. *J. Res. Personal.* 42:577–98

Lodi-Smith J, Roberts BW. 2007. Social investment and personality: a meta-analysis of the relationship of personality traits to investment in work, family, religion, and volunteerism. *Personal. Soc. Psychol. Rev.* 11:68–86

Lonnqvist JE, Markinen S, Paunonen S, Henriksson M, Verkasalo M. 2008. Psychosocial functioning in young men predicts their personality stability over 15 years. *J. Res. Personal.* 42:599–621

Markus H, Kitayama S. 1991. Culture and the self: implications for cognition, emotion, and motivation. *Psychol. Rev.* 98:224–53

Forty-year longitudinal study showing surprisingly low levels of temporal stability for some trait ratings.

Authoritative overview of the role of genes and environments in the development of dispositional traits.

Martin P, Long MV, Poon LW. 2002. Age changes and differences in personality traits and states of the old and very old. *J. Gerontol. Psychol. Sci.* 57B:144–52

McAdams DP. 1985. *Power, Intimacy, and the Life Story: Personological Inquiries into Identity.* New York: Guilford

McAdams DP. 2006. *The Redemptive Self: Stories Americans Live By.* New York: Oxford Univ. Press

McAdams DP. 2008. Personal narratives and the life story. See John et al. 2008b, pp. 241–61

McAdams DP, Bauer JJ, Sakaeda A, Anyidoho NA, Machado MA, et al. 2006. Continuity and change in the life story: a longitudinal study of autobiographical memories in emerging adulthood. *J. Personal.* 74:1371–400

McAdams DP, de St. Aubin E, Logan RL. 1993. Generativity among young, midlife, and older adults. *Psychol. Aging* 8:221–30

McAdams DP, Pals JL. 2006. A new Big Five: fundamental principles for an integrative science of personality. *Am. Psychol.* 61:204–17

McClelland DC. 1985. *Human Motivation.* Glenview, IL: Scott Foresman

McCrae RR, Costa PT. 2008. The five-factor theory of personality. See John et al. 2008b, pp. 159–81

McCrae RR, Costa PT, de Lima MP, Simoes A, Ostendorf F, Angleitner A, et al. 1999. Age differences in personality across the adult life span: parallels in five cultures. *Dev. Psychol.* 35:466–77

McLean KC, Pasupathi M, Pals JL. 2007. Selves creating stories creating selves: a process model of self-development. *Personal. Soc. Psychol. Rev.* 11:262–78

Mikulincer M, Shaver P. 2007. *Attachment in Adulthood.* New York: Guilford

Mischel W. 2004. Toward an integrative science of the person. *Annu. Rev. Psychol.* 55:1–22

Mroczek DK, Almeida DM. 2004. The effect of daily stress, personality, and age on daily negative affect. *J. Personal.* 72:355–78

Mroczek DK, Almeida DM, Spiro A, Pafford C. 2006. Modeling intraindividual stability and change in personality. See Mroczek & Little 2006, pp. 163–80

Mroczek DK, Little TD, eds. 2006. *Handbook of Personality Development.* Mahwah, NJ: Erlbaum

Mroczek DK, Spiro A. 2007. Personality change influences mortality in older men. *Psychol. Sci.* 18:371–76

Munafo MR, Clark TG, Moore LR, Payne E, Walton R, Flint J. 2003. Genetic polymorphisms and personality in healthy adults: a systematic review and meta-analysis. *Mol. Psychiatry* 8:471–84

Murray HA. 1938. *Explorations in Personality.* New York: Oxford Univ. Press

Neyer FJ, Lehnart J. 2007. Relationships matter in personality development: evidence from an 8-year longitudinal study across young adulthood. *J. Personal.* 75:535–68

Ogilvie DM, Cohen F, Solomon S. 2001. A comparison of personal project motives in three age groups. *Basic Appl. Soc. Psychol.* 23:207–15

Oyserman D, Coon HM, Kemmelmeier M. 2002. Rethinking individualism and collectivism: evaluation of theoretical assumptions and meta-analysis. *Psychol. Bull.* 128:3–72

Ozer DJ, Benet-Martinez V. 2006. Personality and the prediction of consequential outcomes. *Annu. Rev. Psychol.* 57:401–21

Pasupathi M, Mansour E. 2006. Adult age differences in autobiographical reasoning in narratives. *Dev. Psychol.* 42:798–808

Pennebaker JW, Stone LD. 2003. Words of wisdom: language use over the life span. *J. Personal. Soc. Psychol.* 85:291–301

Peterson BE, Duncan LE. 2007. Midlife women's generativity and authoritarianism: marriage, motherhood, and 10 years of aging. *Psychol. Aging* 22:411–19

Riediger M, Freund AM. 2008. Me against myself: motivational conflicts and emotional development in adulthood. *Psychol. Aging* 23:479–94

Roberts BW, DelVecchio WF. 2000. The rank-order consistency of personality traits from childhood to old age. *Psychol. Bull.* 126:3–25

Roberts BW, Kuncel NR, Shiner R, Caspi A, Goldberg LR. 2007. The power of personality: the comparative validity of personality traits, socioeconomic status, and cognitive ability for predicting important life outcomes. *Persp. Psychol. Sci.* 2:313–45

Roberts BW, O'Donnell M, Robins RW. 2004. Goal and personality trait development in emerging adulthood. *J. Personal. Soc. Psychol.* 87:541–50

Roberts BW, Walton KE, Viechtbauer W. 2006. Patterns of mean-level change in personality traits across the life course: a meta-analysis of longitudinal studies. *Psychol. Bull.* 132:1–25

Psychological and cultural/historical studies of the life stories of highly generative American adults at midlife.

Comprehensive overview of research and theory on the five-factor model of dispositional traits.

Meta-analysis of 92 longitudinal studies showing clear developmental trends for dispositional traits.

Roberts BW, Wood D, Caspi A. 2008. The development of personality traits in adulthood. See John et al. 2008b, pp. 375–98

Rothbart MK, Ahadi SA, Evans DE. 2000. Temperament and personality: origins and outcomes. *J. Personal. Soc. Psychol.* 78:122–35

Saarni C. 2006. Emotion regulation and personality development in childhood. See Mroczek & Little 2006, pp. 245–62

Saucier G, Simonds J. 2006. The structure of personality and temperament. See Mroczek & Little 2006, pp. 109–28

Scheibe S, Freund AM, Baltes PB. 2007. Toward a developmental psychology of *Sehnsucht* (life longings): the optimal (utopian) life. *Dev. Psychol.* 43:778–95

Schmitt DP, Allik J, McCrae RR, Benet-Martinez V, Alcalay L, et al. 2007. The geographic distribution of Big Five personality traits: patterns and profiles of human self-description across 56 nations. *J. Cross-Cult. Psychol.* 38:173–212

Schultheiss OC, Pang JS. 2007. Measuring implicit motives. In *Handbook of Research Methods in Personality Psychology*, ed. RW Robins, RC Fraley, RF Krueger, pp. 323–44. New York: Guilford

Scollon CN, Diener E. 2006. Love, work, and changes in extraversion and neuroticism over time. *J. Personal. Soc. Psychol.* 91:1152–65

Serrano JP, Latorre JM, Gatz M, Montanes J. 2004. Life review therapy using autobiographical retrieval practice for older adults with depressive symptomatology. *Psychol. Aging* 19:272–77

Sheldon KM. 2004. *Optimal Human Being: An Integrated Multi-Level Perspective.* Mahwah, NJ: Erlbaum

Sheldon KM, Elliot AJ, Kim Y, Kasser T. 2001. What is satisfying about satisfying events? Testing 10 candidate psychological needs. *J. Personal. Soc. Psychol.* 80:325–39

Shiner RL. 2006. Temperament and personality in childhood. See Mroczek & Little 2006, pp. 213–30

Singer JA. 2005. *Personality and Psychotherapy: Treating the Whole Person.* New York: Guilford

Singer JA, Rexhaj B, Baddeley J. 2007. Older, wider, and happier? Comparing older adults' and college students' self-defining memories. *Memory* 15:886–98

Singer JA, Salovey P. 1993. *The Remembered Self.* New York: Free Press

Smith J, Baltes PB. 1999. Trends and profiles of psychological functioning in very old age. In *The Berlin Aging Study: Aging from 70 to 100*, ed. PB Baltes, KU Mayer, pp. 197–226. Cambridge, UK: Cambridge Univ. Press

Soto CJ, John OP, Gosling SD, Potter J. 2008. The developmental psychometrics of Big Five self-reports: acquiescence, factor structure, coherence, and differentiation from ages 10 to 20. *J. Personal. Soc. Psychol.* 94:718–37

Srivastava S, John OP, Gosling SD, Potter J. 2003. Development of personality in early and middle adulthood: set like plaster or persistent change? *Dev. Psychol.* 84:1041–53

Tangney JP, Stuewig J, Mashek DJ. 2007. Moral emotions and moral behavior. *Annu. Rev. Psychol.* 58:345–72

Teachman BA. 2006. Aging and negative affect: the rise and fall and rise of anxiety and depressive symptoms. *Psychol. Aging* 21:201–7

Terraciano A, Costa PT, McCrae RR. 2006. Personality plasticity after age 30. *Personal. Soc. Psychol. Bull.* 32:1–11

Thorne A. 2000. Personal memory telling and personality development. *Personal. Soc. Psychol. Rev.* 4:45–56

Tomasello M. 1999. Having intentions, understanding intentions, and understanding communicative intentions. In *Developing Theories of Intention: Social Understanding and Self-Control*, ed. PD Zelazo, JW Astington, DR Olson, pp. 63–75. Mahwah, NJ: Erlbaum

Tomkins SS. 1987. Script theory. In *The Emergence of Personality*, ed. J Aronoff, AI Rabin, RA Zucker, pp. 147–216. New York: Springer

Walls TA, Kollat SH. 2006. Agency to agentic personalities: the early to middle childhood gap. See Mroczek & Little 2006, pp. 231–44

Wang Q. 2006. Culture and the development of self-knowledge. *Curr. Dir. Psychol. Sci.* 15:182–87

Watson D. 2004. Stability versus change, dependability versus error: issues in the assessment of personality over time. *J. Res. Personal.* 38:319–50

Links three layers of personality to clinical work with adults.

Weinstein TAR, Capitanio JP, Gosling SD. 2008. Personality in animals. See John et al. 2008b, pp. 328–48

Wellman HM, Cross D, Watson J. 2001. Meta-analysis of theory of mind development: the truth about false belief. *Child Dev.* 72:655–84

Winter DG, John OP, Stewart AJ, Klohnen EC, Duncan LE. 1998. Traits and motives: toward an integration of two traditions in personality research. *Psychol. Rev.* 105:230–50

Wrosch C, Heckhausen J, Lachman ME. 2006. Goal management across adulthood and old age: the adaptive value of primary and secondary control. See Mroczek & Little 2006, pp. 399–421

Self-Regulation at Work

Robert G. Lord, James M. Diefendorff,
Aaron M. Schmidt, and Rosalie J. Hall

Department of Psychology, University of Akron, Akron, Ohio 44325-4301;
email: rlord@uakron.edu; jdiefen@uakron.edu; aschmidt@uakron.edu; rjhall@uakron.edu

Annu. Rev. Psychol. 2010. 61:543–68

First published online as a Review in Advance on
June 17, 2009

The *Annual Review of Psychology* is online at
psych.annualreviews.org

This article's doi:
10.1146/annurev.psych.093008.100314

0066-4308/10/0110-0543$20.00

Key Words

motivation, negative feedback loops, goal-performance discrepancies,
multilevel processes

Abstract

Self-regulation at work is conceived in terms of within-person processes
that occur over time. These processes are proposed to occur within a
hierarchical framework of negative feedback systems that operate at
different levels of abstraction and with different time cycles. Negative
feedback systems respond to discrepancies in a manner that reduces
deviations from standards (i.e., goals). This is in contrast to positive
feedback systems in which discrepancies are created, which can lead to
instability. We organize our discussion around four hierarchical levels—
self, achievement task, lower-level task action, and knowledge/working
memory. We theorize that these levels are loosely connected by multiple constraints and that both automatic and more conscious processes
are essential to self-regulation. Within- and cross-level affective and
cognitive processes interact within this system to motivate goal-related
behaviors while also accessing needed knowledge and protecting current intentions from interference. Complications common in the work
setting (as well as other complex, real-life settings) such as the simultaneous pursuit of multiple goals, the importance of knowledge access
and expertise, and team and multiperson processes are also discussed.
Finally, we highlight the usefulness of newer research methodologies
and data-analytic techniques for examining such hierarchical, dynamic,
within-person processes.

Contents

INTRODUCTION

Our understanding of motivated behavior in the workplace increasingly relies on a dynamic self-regulatory framework to understand how individuals allocate volitional, cognitive, and affective resources across multiple tasks (Kanfer et al. 2008; Vancouver 2005, 2008). Work motivation has traditionally been approached from a between-person perspective that typically uses cross-sectional methods and emphasizes individual differences (Latham & Pinder 2005). In contrast, recent trends emphasize longitudinal and within-person approaches. We view this as a challenging but positive change. This emphasis has required applied researchers to (a) rethink theory, (b) adopt new methodologies and analytic techniques, (c) carefully consider how the phenomena of interest unfold over time and in the context of competing work tasks and social demands, and (d) incorporate knowledge from research on basic cognitive and affective processes, as well as advances in neuroscience that have implications for dynamic models. Ultimately, we believe a focus on understanding dynamic self-regulatory processes has the potential to address previous calls to integrate the wide variety of motivation theories (Locke & Latham 2004).

Why is this shift to more dynamic theories and models occurring? One reason is the increased recognition that although cross-sectional research contributes to our understanding of performance based on observations of stable differences between persons, many of our theories, as well as our subjective experiences, tell us that self-regulatory processes vary within individuals. Moreover, many of the practical motivational issues that managers wish to better understand are at least implicitly within-person in nature (e.g., "how do I *keep* my current employees motivated?"). Dalal & Hulin's (2008) review finds many variables traditionally studied by motivational researchers exhibit a great deal of within-person variability, e.g., 29% to 78% of variance in performance was within persons, and proximal motivational predictors such as affect (47% to 78%) and goal level (31% to 38%) also showed substantial variability. We believe a large proportion of this within-person variability reflects internal self-regulatory processes engaged to adapt to changing situational and environmental features.

Importantly, generalizing from between-person research findings to within-person motivational theories can be misleading, even when the same set of variables is considered. For example, cross-sectional, between-person research consistently shows positive associations between self-efficacy and performance (Stajkovic & Luthans 1998). Yet within-person research finds self-efficacy can be negatively associated with subsequent performance

(Vancouver et al. 2001, 2002) when high self-efficacy leads one to coast, but low self-efficacy motivates greater effort expenditure. This example serves as a general warning that cross-sectional studies may do little to inform our understanding of within-person self-regulatory processes; studies of within-person processes will require fresh expectations about critical constructs and the nature of relationships among them.

The work context has several aspects that may make it of special interest to researchers focused on self-regulation. First, because workers are expected to self-manage much of their behavior, mechanisms that allow for internalization and tying of goals to the self are especially critical. Second, work goals are often pursued under time pressures and deadlines that may modify the nature of self-regulatory processes. Third, many work situations require juggling the simultaneous pursuit of multiple goals (Schmidt & DeShon 2007). Fourth, employees often have relevant formal education, job training, and prior job experience, thus function as expert information processors. Because effective performance draws on this expertise as well as conscious processing (Newell 1990), self-regulation includes the management of knowledge access as well as the management of selective attention, emotions, and behavioral processes. Finally, success at work often requires regulation of interpersonal behaviors directed toward supervisors, coworkers, customers, etc., while simultaneously meeting task demands. Although each of these features can be present in nonwork contexts, they may be more prominent when individuals pursue goals at work.

Our review begins with a description of basic self-regulatory processes, building on research that explicitly addresses self-regulation across time. Initially, we focus on single tasks and a unitary criterion, and then extend this model to include multiple tasks and criteria. This description is informed by relevant works from cognitive, affective, personality, and social areas of psychology, which provide a foundation for understanding the nature of dynamic

self-regulatory systems and their emergence from more fundamental intrapersonal processes. By extending this model, we hope to advance research on work motivation by incorporating ideas from research on dynamic processes, affect, goal content, and multiple goals. Importantly, we argue that self-regulation at work is shaped by multiple external constraints, including social and organizational factors, in addition to those constraints originating from internal sources.

SELF-REGULATION

Self-Regulation: A General Model

Self-regulation includes "processes involved in attaining and maintaining (i.e., keeping regular) goals, where goals are internally represented (i.e., within the self) desired states" (Vancouver & Day 2005, p. 158). Thus, at the center of most theories of self-regulation are the ideas that individuals set goals, compare their progress against the goals, and make modifications to their behaviors or cognitions if there is a discrepancy between a goal and the current state (Karoly 1993). These variables and their interrelationships comprise the negative feedback loop (see **Figure 1**), which consists of an input function, a reference value, a comparator, and an output function (Carver & Scheier 1998). The input function senses how one is currently performing. The reference value is an image of a desired state such as a task goal that is actively maintained by the system. The comparator matches the input with a standard or goal to determine if there is a discrepancy between them. If a difference is detected, the output function is engaged to bring the subsequent input in line with the goal. This output may include behavioral changes aimed at increasing or decreasing effort, as well cognitive changes aimed at altering one's interpretation of the standard, input, or discrepancy. (Negative feedback loops can be contrasted with positive feedback loops, which have all of the same components but consist of individuals setting standards higher than current performance so as

Constraints: connections between units in a system that transfer activation or inhibition, helping to activate or inhibit the receiving unit

Negative feedback loops: compare sensed inputs to internal standards and respond to detected discrepancies from those standards with self-corrective actions

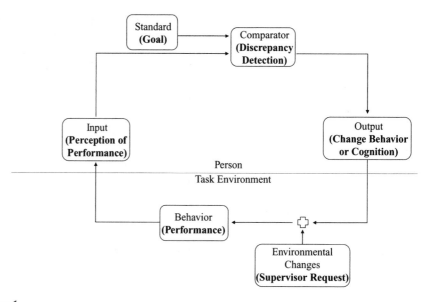

Figure 1

Negative feedback loop.

to create a discrepancy or enlarge an existing discrepancy.)

This general approach also assumes a hierarchical structure in which short-term, concrete goals are low in the hierarchy, and long-term, abstract goals are high in the hierarchy. Lower-level goals can be conceptualized as the means by which higher-level goals are attained (Lord & Levy 1994). This is considered a structural model of self-regulation, describing variables and their interrelationships but not the content or form of any particular goal or behavior (Diefendorff & Lord 2008).

Accounting for Different Levels of Consciousness and the Role of Affect

Any viable model of self-regulation at work must address two fundamental issues. First, both conscious and unconscious processes influence behavior. Although we intentionally and consciously focus on the external task environment and on task-related memories and knowledge, regulation of environmental inputs and other task-relevant information may be largely determined by more automatic processes (Johnson et al. 2006). In addition,

goals are often automatically activated by environmental primes or cues arising from social sources (e.g., significant others) or from the recognition of means (i.e., subgoals) that can be used to achieve goals (Shah & Kruglanski 2003). For example, when experimental participants were subliminally primed with father-related words (e.g., "dad"), their father's approach to working on tasks affected participants' approaches to working on an experimental task and the emotions that task feedback produced (Shah 2003, Study 3). The unconscious, automatic nature of many self-regulatory processes has been sadly underemphasized and understudied in contemporary research on work motivation (Locke & Latham 2004).

The second issue is that affective and cognitive systems must operate concurrently and with multiple points of connection to shape self-regulation. Cognition and affect are integrated at fundamental levels and influence each other over time (Allen et al. 2008, LeDoux 1995). Effective self-regulation must allow both for focused attention on current goal-related activities and for rapid reorientation toward new, important information. The affective system plays an important role in achieving this balance; it

Hierarchical structure: the embedding of more concrete, narrow feedback loops within more encompassing, abstract loops

is fast, automatic, and can interrupt and reorient conscious processing (LeDoux 1995, Simon 1967). Dopamine, an affect-related neurotransmitter, also modulates the maintenance of goals in the prefrontal cortex (and indirectly goal-related information) (Diefendorff & Lord 2008, O'Reilly et al. 1999). Thus, affect can quickly clear the conscious workspace when reorientation is required.

These gating and biasing functions of affect are important micro-level regulators of cognition and behavior. They can operate in such a manner because perceptual systems have direct routes to affective centers such as the amygdala (LeDoux 1995), which, in turn, are connected to the prefrontal cortex (Allen et al. 2008). Affect can also have other important functions such as helping to elicit appropriate coping responses, helping to manage goal conflict, or guiding current and future regulatory processes. A general model of self-regulation must account for dynamic interrelations between affect and cognition at multiple levels of consciousness.

Level of Abstraction, Cycle Time, and Self-Regulation

Level of abstraction and cycle time. Self-regulation is future-oriented and takes place within the onward flow of time. It occurs at various levels of abstraction. We discuss four broad levels of abstraction, which we term micro, low, intermediate, and high. Each level is associated with different types of self-regulatory loops—i.e., negative feedback loops that compare desired states to actual states with the objective of detecting and reducing discrepancies.

Importantly, the level of abstraction inversely relates to the cycle times of feedback loops associated with that level. Cycle time is the time required for information to cycle through the entire loop. Longer cycle times tend to be associated with higher-level, more abstract constructs (Johnson et al. 2006, Lord & Levy 1994). For example, self-regulation in terms of possible selves may have a cycle time measured in years as individuals try out and

modify various provisional selves as they adjust to new roles (Ibarra 1999). At the intermediate level of abstraction, self-regulation around achievement tasks may have a cycle time of only a few minutes, hours, or perhaps days, as a goal is attempted and feedback received. At lower levels of abstraction, specific actions such as typing a word while writing may take only a few seconds, with feedback and correction operating on a similar scale. Finally, still lower levels involving the regulation of muscle movement, knowledge access, or experienced affect may have cycle times of a fraction of a second, with part or all of the components in a self-regulatory cycle operating unconsciously. Importantly, these differing cycle times imply that the nature and content of self-regulatory processes also may differ radically at different levels, as we suggest in **Table 1**.

Cross-level linkages and emergence. Table 1 contains many terms and constructs that are not yet defined. It serves as a rough roadmap for this review as we discuss each of the four cycle levels. Some of our coverage is guided primarily by existing research on self-regulation at work, but other discussion is based on inferences from theory and research on cognition, affect, and neurocognition.

One topic implied by **Table 1**—how the various levels are linked—warrants initial discussion. A common approach to explaining links across levels is to posit a hierarchical arrangement in which higher-level processes exert supervisory control over lower-level processes. That is, in the Focus row of **Table 1**, referents to the left specify the selection of constructs to their right, e.g., possible selves influence one's choice of achievement tasks. Research on metacognitive processes and on control theory (e.g., Carver & Scheier 1998, Powers 1973) fits this hierarchical perspective. Supervisory or hierarchical control operates best when adjacent levels use similar processes (e.g., conscious deliberation) so the output of one level can feed directly into an adjacent level (e.g., intermediate-level goals access lower-level scripts). Such models imply hierarchical, top-down control of actions,

Scripts: knowledge structures containing organized sequences of actions that are needed to accomplish higher-level goals

Table 1 Aspects of self-regulatory and motivational theories by cycle level

	CYCLE LEVEL			
	High	*Intermediate*	*Low*	*Micro*
Focus	Possible selves	Achievement task	Integrated task behaviors	Behavioral components
Time	Months/years	Minutes/hours/days	Several seconds	Tens of milliseconds
	Major components of dynamic self-regulatory processes			
Referent establishment	Culture, social, value constraints	Conscious choice or automatic priming	Conscious choice, habit, unconscious goal emergence	Spreading activation from goals, working memory, and environment
Planning, goal maintenance	Provisional self is developed	Goal commitment	Goal shielding	Priming and inhibition-gated neurotransmitters
Action	Working self-concept is activated	New actions composed and executed	Driven by appropriate scripts or schemas	
Evaluation and feedback	Interpreted relevant to self	Interpreted relevant to task	Learning in neural networks updates expectancies	Neurotransmitter release and uptake

but as we illustrate, bottom-up control or sequential linkages among goals at the same level are also common.

When cycle times at two levels differ vastly, or when they emphasize very different types of processes, direct hierarchical supervision falters as a linking mechanism. For example, conscious deliberative processing operates too slowly to control switching from one behavior to another in complex scripts (e.g., well-learned dance steps) or to control the access of knowledge from working memory. Structured knowledge may create links, as when one activity automatically primes subsequent activities and when this procedure operates within knowledge structures cued by higher levels. For example, setting forks on the table may automatically prime getting napkins and may be cued by higher level goals related to getting ready for dinner. But in other circumstances, there may be no direct links between adjacent hierarchical levels. Instead, higher levels may merely create constraints on processes that run fairly autonomously at lower levels. For example, having an "effective worker" identity may not directly specify how one's job should be performed, but rather will impose more general constraints on task activities.

Constraints are connections between units in a system that transfer activation or inhibition from one unit to another, making it more or less likely that the receiving unit will become sufficiently active to affect behavior. Often, multiple constraints must operate in concert to create sufficient input to activate a lower-level process. When higher levels create constraints, lower-level processes may be guided by structures that emerge spontaneously as a result of these internal constraints combined with any relevant external constraints from task environments (Carver & Scheier 2002, Johnson et al. 2006). For example, an active collective identity may promote cooperation (i.e., an internal constraint from a higher level), but cooperative achievement task goals may emerge only when one encounters coworkers who are liked and need help (i.e., an external constraint originating in the task environment). DeShon & Gillespie (2005) successfully use the idea of cross-level constraints to articulate how particular goal orientations emerge from higher-level personality and goal structures.

Cross-level constraints can also operate in a bottom-up fashion, as when readily available means or task strategies prime higher-level goals. For example, in four experimental studies Shah & Kruglanski (2003) found that means like studying and exercising made goals related to education and fitness more accessible and also that priming means associated with a task increased persistence and performance, but priming means related to an alternative goal reduced task performance and persistence. Cross-level links can also conflict (Sherman et al. 2008), as when lower-level environmental cues prime behaviors inconsistent with higher-level goals (e.g., one eats desserts that look appealing but are inconsistent with higher-level self-relevant health goals).

Dynamics of Self-Regulation

Idealized, conscious flow, and phase models. Most dynamic models are represented by flow diagrams such as that shown in **Figure 1**, by a sequence of phases, or by a combination of these approaches. Models such as the one depicted in **Figure 1** show how simple regulation occurs based on sensed feedback, but they do not show how such systems are created in the first place. Phase theories help explain how self-regulatory systems may be created. For example, Gollwitzer (1990) identified four self-regulatory phases, which have associated mindsets. These mindsets prepare the person to act, and they appropriately tune information processing to facilitate the operations required in each phase. Typically, goals are established (deliberative mindset), planning occurs (implemental mindset), goal striving takes place (actional mindset), and goal evaluation/revision concludes this process (evaluative mindset). Often the phases are followed in this order, but individuals can also move back and forth among phases. Gollwitzer's model guided our organization of the components of dynamic processes in the bottom portion of **Table 1** (but note at the micro level it is not helpful to distinguish between planning and action phases).

Nature and control of processing and the importance of knowledge. Because most existing motivational theory applied to work situations has focused on achievement tasks, conscious processing has been emphasized. Yet many important dynamic aspects of self-regulatory processing, such as accessing relevant knowledge or learning from feedback, may operate automatically and very quickly. Knowledge management is particularly important because individuals often have considerable experience in their jobs. As experience accumulates, performance becomes increasingly determined by knowledge that is automatically accessed from long-term memory and is less dependent on attention-demanding processes that create needed knowledge on the spot (Anderson 1987, Kanfer & Ackerman 1989, Newell 1990).

Goal-relevant information has easier access to working memory than does information related to competing goals (Diefendorff et al. 1998, Johnson et al. 2006, Shah et al. 2002). How well individuals maintain goals then also influences how well they can access relevant knowledge. Interestingly, automatic management of knowledge access works better for important goals than for unimportant goals (Diefendorff et al. 1998, Shah et al. 2002). Managing working memory is also a critical aspect of effective supervisory control by a higher hierarchical level because activation of other processes spreads from constructs held in working memory in a manner that is biased by goals (Anderson 1987, Lord & Levy 1994, O'Reilly et al. 1999).

Time and deadlines. Importantly, self-regulatory processes may differ as a function of the time remaining for goal pursuit. Deadlines are often an integral aspect of goal assignments (Locke & Latham 1990). Shorter deadlines increase the difficulty of reaching a given level of performance and thus often increase motivation (Steel & König 2006). The pace of work often increases as deadlines draw tighter and time pressure mounts. However, overly imposing or impossible deadlines can result in performance decrements (Andrews & Farris 1972). Additionally, creativity may be impaired by time pressure (Amabile et al.

Knowledge management: the automatic process by which one accesses and maintains goal-relevant knowledge while it is needed for goal pursuit

2002), likely due to the narrowed attentional focus and systematic processing often invoked by anxiety. Steel & König's (2006) temporal motivation theory models the motivating power of approaching deadlines, arguing that the perceived utility of a given activity increases exponentially as the deadline nears. These and similar ideas have been applied to the pervasive phenomenon of procrastination: They imply that immediately rewarding background temptations (e.g., Internet and email) may possess greater utility than do organizationally important activities until their deadlines draw near.

Summary of the General Model of Self-Regulation

In short, self-regulatory processes are controlled and integrated not only by a conscious executive system that uses information deliberately, but also by goal structures maintained in the frontal lobes and affective systems in the midbrain that collaborate to automatically manage goal maintenance, knowledge access, and attention regulation. Active identities and affective states also exert strategic control on several aspects of information processing. Although we can analyze self-regulation in terms of separate levels, and most theories of motivation we review pertain to just one of the levels in **Table 1**, self-regulation in real-world settings requires the collaboration of multiple systems that operate on different time scales and are found in different neural locations. Furthermore, self-regulation may be indirectly or directly influenced by stable attributes of the person and situation, although additional work on these cross-level influences on goal-directed behavior is needed. With this initial understanding of the dynamic, multilevel nature of self-regulation as an underlying framework, we discuss the literature on self-regulation at work for each of the levels represented by the four columns in **Table 1**, noting that it is becoming increasingly clear that the basic processes of self-regulation operate differently at different levels of the hierarchy.

SELF-REGULATION AT ALTERNATIVE HIERARCHICAL LEVELS

High-Level Regulation of the Self

The self is a richly connected, developing knowledge structure widely viewed as important for self-regulation (Markus & Wurf 1987). Indeed, the brain appears to have a specific network of structures that supports introspection and creates autobiographical memories by integrating internal and external information (Raichle et al. 2001). (Interestingly, this network is suppressed below baseline activation when one focuses on task goals, allowing pursuit of task activities without self-relevant distractions.) Autobiographical memories allow a sense of the self to continue through time (Kihlstrom et al. 2003). One's time perspective can influence how the self is construed. Distant self-construals (e.g., "me next year") are more abstract, less complex, and more coherent than construals of the self in the near future (Wakslak et al. 2008). Distant self-construals are also less tied to context than are near selves and are thought to be more closely tied to a stable set of personality traits than are near selves.

Work settings both build on existing selves (in the form of identities) and shape new identities. For example, the sense of self as a leader may develop over a surprisingly long time (Day et al. 2009), with roots in activities going as far back as grade school (Komives et al. 2005). A leader identity in turn may influence many motivated choices and self-regulatory activities in the workplace, ranging from proactive creation of opportunities for one's own self to actions that empower others to demonstrate initiative and exhibit self-leadership.

Work settings shape identities through many mechanisms. The overarching culture and values of a work setting can create powerful sets of constraints on the self, which in turn result in a sense of the self as an organizational member with specific roles and relations to others. There are important dynamic trends within work contexts, particularly when roles change as a result of promotion, developmental assignments, restructuring, and other new demands. For example, Ibarra (1999) posits that managers develop provisional selves when trying out new roles. Provisional selves operate like the standard in any control system, but they may be quickly modified or discarded based on social feedback or fit with one's active ideal selves. Research by Lockwood & Kunda (1997) in an academic setting found that beginning and advanced students had very different reactions to other high-performing social referents. This effect may be interpreted in terms of provisional possible selves: For beginning students, the performance level of the referent was likely compared to a far self-construal, perceived as attainable, and thus motivating; for advanced students, the comparison was likely to a near self-construal, with the high-performing referent being perceived as an unattainable comparison standard.

Considerable research shows possible selves are influenced by significant others (Andersen & Chen 2002), with unique selves being developed and activated in different social relations. Organizational leaders may play a particularly important role in this process (Lord and Brown 2004, Shamir et al. 1993), and self-identities developed with one supervisor can generalize to other similar supervisors (Ritter & Lord 2007). Groups are also important in refining organizational identities (van Knippenberg et al. 2004), with social justice binding individual identities to groups and social injustice isolating individuals from groups (Lind 2001). Leary & Baumeister (2000) argued that the need to belong is so powerful and adaptive that one function of the self is to continually update where we stand in the opinions of others, and the resulting self-esteem provides an internal meter of the soundness of our interpersonal connections and likely access to socially mediated resources. In short, a variety of individual and collective social processes influence the development and maintenance of one's organizational self, and this development may occur throughout one's organizational life, although changes are most intense for newcomers and individuals who are changing organizational roles.

One's organizational self-identity also creates cognitive, motivational, and affective constraints that guide more achievement-focused activities. At any one moment, only a portion of the self is active and directing achievement-related activities. Markus & Wurf (1987) labeled this momentarily active self the working self-concept (WSC), arguing that it has a direct role in regulating behavior. Various examples can be given of the nature of these dynamics. For instance, De Cremer & van Knippenberg (2002) found that self-sacrificing supervisors elicit corresponding collective selves in subordinates, fostering cooperative work behavior. Self-benefiting supervisors activate individual-level self-identities, with resulting higher levels of subordinate competitive behaviors. In addition, the self has important associations with motivational orientations: Selves defined in terms of "ideals" elicit different regulatory orientations than selves that emphasize "oughts" (Shah & Higgins 2001). Furthermore, appraisal of an organizational event's potential to benefit or harm the self shapes affective reactions to that event. In short, the WSC is influenced by many organizational and social factors, and it has important motivational, affective, and cognitive consequences for self-regulation.

Intermediate-Level Self-Regulation

Most research on self-regulation in work settings focuses on regulation at an intermediate level around task or action goals. Regardless of whether the studies have been conducted in the field or laboratory, the goals in question have tended to be of short duration and are often achievement based. Importantly, intermediate-level self-regulation involves both controlled and automatic processes (Carver & Scheier 1998, Lord & Levy 1994, Vancouver 2005). Setting task goals is often viewed as a conscious process, but a comprehensive understanding of self-regulation in work settings must acknowledge the extent to which automatic processes play important roles in the regulation of task goals, as well as sometimes determining which goals are selected for action. For example, goal

Working self-concept (WSC): the momentarily active portion of the self-concept that regulates motivational processes

Goal shielding: the processes by which active goals and related information are protected from interference from information related to competing goals shielding, which maintains focus on task activities and prevents derailment by distracting activities (e.g., the planning- and action-phase rows in **Table 1**), is generally thought to be relatively automatic. Task progress is monitored and evaluated, with adjustment to behavior and goals occurring through both conscious and automatic processes.

Another key point is that self-regulation consumes not only regulatory resources, but also attentional resources (Schmeichel & Baumeister 2004, Schmeichel et al. 2008, Vohs et al. 2008). This is particularly true when tasks are novel (Kanfer & Ackerman 1989). In addition, outcomes of self-regulatory processes may have affective consequences that individuals attempt to manage, often without full consciousness and in manners that may detract from the total attentional resources available to devote to the task (Baumeister et al. 2007, Boekaerts & Corno 2005).

Theories of self-regulation that emphasize the functioning of feedback loops (e.g., control theory) have been criticized as being overly mechanical (Bandura & Locke 2003); however, recent findings suggest they are only one component of a more complex human system with cognitive, emotional, and physiological constraints. One challenge for applied research is to understand how these seemingly diverse elements are organized into a coherent, dynamic system. The following sections review current thinking on some of the pieces of that system, which focus on goal setting and selection, goal striving, and feedback processes.

Goal setting and goal selection. Conscious self-regulation begins when an action goal is chosen (Carver & Scheier 1998). Although goals can differ on a large number of attributes (Austin & Vancouver 1996), the dimensions most commonly discussed in organizational research are goal difficulty and specificity. A large body of goal-setting research finds that difficult, specific goals, if accepted, lead to higher performance than do easy or do-your-best goals (Locke & Latham 1990) as long as the goals are attainable and commitment to the goal is

maintained (Hollenbeck & Klein 1987). When choosing to pursue a goal (or to commit to an assigned goal), individuals mentally simulate how much effort it would take to reach each potential goal as well as what the potential outcomes of goal pursuit might be (Aspinwall & Taylor 1997). Klein et al. (2008) characterized this goal-selection process as occurring "at multiple levels within goal hierarchies, flowing from broad overarching goals to middle-level 'working goals' and down to lower-level subgoals and behavioral sequences" (p. 110).

Yet even when goals have been consciously adopted, processes that are less conscious may influence goal choice and self-regulation around those goals. For example, affect may indirectly influence goal selection (Hom & Arbuckle 1986), likely through effects on expectancy and valence judgments (Seo et al. 2004). Emerging research suggests that affect also can have direct effects on motivated behavior that do not operate through conscious processes (Bargh 1990). For instance, high activation emotions may lead individuals to exert more energy in the pursuit of desired goals and in the avoidance of undesired goals (Cacioppo et al. 1999). Other research links emotional information to physical movement, such that positive emotions are aligned with approach behaviors such as faster responses for pressing a computer key, and negative emotions are aligned with avoidance behaviors such as faster responses for moving off of a key (Seibt et al. 2008).

As mentioned, although self-regulation is generally thought to be initiated by setting conscious goals (Carver & Scheier 1998), goals in the workplace also may emerge from sets of constraints (Carver & Scheier 2002, DeShon & Gillespie 2005, Johnson et al. 2006), or they may reflect unconscious processes that seem to have effects on behavior that are similar to conscious goals (Chartrand et al. 2008). For example, in a review of 64 independent studies, Ouellette & Wood (1998) found that habit rather than conscious intention was important for frequently performed behaviors (e.g., coffee and alcohol consumption, seat belt use, class and church attendance, most types of exercise), which occur under stable enabling conditions, but conscious intentions provide a better explanation for infrequent behaviors (e.g., voting, giving blood, obtaining a flu shot), which generally occur under unstable shifting conditions that do not provide constant sets of supportive cues. Wood et al. (2002) used an experience-sampling methodology to examine behavior that reflected both rational cognitions and more intuitive, automatic cognitions. They found that habitual actions that tended to be performed daily (such as getting ready for work) were frequently produced by more intuitive, automatic processes that occurred while individuals were thinking of something else.

The potential role of unconscious processes in goal selection was further elaborated by Lord et al. (2003), who used neural network modeling to show that in stable, familiar situations, neural networks can learn to select alternatives that maximize expected utility (i.e., the product of valance, instrumentalities, and expectancies). They also showed that this automatic selection process is sensitive to shifts in constraints from higher-level goals. Such research is consistent with Vallacher & Wegner's (1985) Action Identification Theory, which maintains that as tasks become more familiar, attention shifts to higher levels in self-regulatory hierarchies, but when difficulties are encountered, attention can again be allocated to lower-level activities. Thus, attention and conscious processing may be flexibly applied to self-regulation, although only to a relatively narrow slice of goal hierarchies (Austin & Vancouver 1996, Lord & Levy 1994).

Goal selection, particularly in work situations, often reflects social processes. Other individuals can prime goals, creating "goal contagion" effects (Aarts et al. 2008, Fitzsimons & Bargh 2003). When this process is repeated, workplaces develop climates that foster particular types of goals (Dragoni 2005). Work supervisors (or other significant figures) may play a particularly important role in such processes by communicating appropriate self-regulatory standards or by activating alternative identities (Lord & Brown 2004, Shamir et al. 1993), which then constrain the goals that emerge. Supervisors can also assign goals directly to subordinates.

Goal striving. Once goals are established, they provide a standard to which feedback is continually compared as a means of regulating behavior and effort. Several factors complicate this dynamic goal-striving process. First, although effort is mobilized to address goal-performance discrepancy (GPD; typically defined as performance minus goal), the relation between GPDs and increases in effort or performance is nonlinear. Large negative GPDs can motivate large increases in performance if self-efficacy is maintained, but they can also reduce effort when they lead to discouragement and task withdrawal (Carver & Scheier 1998). When GPDs direct attention to the self rather than the task, they can also negatively influence task performance (Kluger & DeNisi 1996, Vancouver & Tischner 2004). Ironically, when GPDs are positive (performance exceeds goals) and self-efficacy is high, individuals may coast, reducing effort and performance and perhaps allocating effort to other tasks (Carver & Scheier 1998, Schmidt & DeShon 2009, Vancouver et al. 2002).

In addition to GPDs, individuals are sensitive to the velocity of discrepancy reduction; that is, the rate at which they move toward or away from desired standards (Carver & Scheier 1990, 1998). Chang et al. (2009, Study 2) manipulated velocity and found it was positively related to goal commitment, which in turn influenced task persistence. Building on the seminal theory of Carver & Scheier (1990), the strongest support has been provided for the positive effects of high velocity on the outcome of task satisfaction (Chang et al. 2009, Elicker et al. 2009, Lawrence et al. 2002). Because velocity incorporates information on the time course of performance, Johnson et al. (2006) argued that it may be particularly relevant to self-evaluation (i.e., "Am I an effective employee?"), which may explain its potential to produce strong affective reactions. As already mentioned, because individuals regulate affect

Goal-performance discrepancy (GPD): the distance from an internal standard; represented by subtracting performance from task goal levels

Velocity: the rate at which one is approaching internal standards or reducing a GPD in a given time period along with task performance (Baumeister et al. 2007), low velocity and the associated negative affect can lead to task disengagement through processes such as reduced attention or lowered goals (Elicker et al. 2009). However, sometimes disengagement may have positive health benefits associated with stress reduction and may allow faster re-engagement of more adaptive alternative goals (Wrosch et al. 2007).

Understanding successful goal striving also requires a consideration of selective attention, which serves as a mechanism linking the intermediate and the micro levels. Lord & Levy (1994) suggested a key function of self-regulation is to protect working memory and that processes of inhibiting competing schema and of activating goal-relevant information are essential to effective self-regulation and performance. Early support for this idea comes from Diefendorff et al. (1998), who found that students who were better at inhibiting distracting information in a cognitive-reaction time task were better able to achieve important life goals.

Shah et al. (2002) demonstrated that activated goals inhibit information related to competing goals and that individual differences in the strength of this inhibitory process (tenacity, in their terms) affected goal shielding. Johnson et al. (2006) provided the most systematic study of the effects of goals on attention regulation. Their meta-analysis showed instantiating goals increase accessibility of goal-relevant information relative to neutral information (based on 41 effects) and also reduce accessibility of information related to competing goals (based on 27 effects). Interestingly, when goals are completed, they are then suppressed relative to baseline conditions, and goal-relevant information becomes less accessible (based on 22 effects). Such research clearly establishes the important link between one's current motivational intentions and the knowledge that is easily available to guide task activities.

Thus, selective attention processes serve a dual function of shielding motivation and of enhancing performance by facilitating access to relevant knowledge. Performance is generally believed to rely on both motivation and ability; in this context, ability can be thought of as having access to relevant knowledge. There may be many work tasks for which knowledge differences have a greater effect on performance than do motivational differences. If some workers are experts (i.e., have extensive training and work experience), whereas others are novices, performance will primarily be a function of differences in task-specific ability (Newell 1990). An implication of this point is that attempts to increase performance by increasing goal difficulty will have limited success to the extent that performance also relies on access to knowledge that may not be readily available.

Feedback. For many tasks, individuals receive periodic external feedback (performance appraisals, informal social responses, customer reactions) that complements the self-generated feedback they create while doing tasks. External feedback often partitions activities into discrete episodes and momentarily focuses individuals on the re-evaluation of appropriateness of goals and the maintenance of task engagement. The sign and magnitude of GPDs are critical influences on subsequent actions. Many studies show downward revision of goals when large negative GPDs exist and show increases in goals when GPDs are positive (Campion & Lord 1982, Donovan & Hafsteinsson 2006, Ilies & Judge 2005, Kernan & Lord 1990). Several studies qualify the relationship of GPD to goal revision, showing it is stronger late in performance cycles and when internal attributions are made (Donovan & Williams 2003, Williams et al. 2000), or when learning or performance-avoidance goal orientations are salient (Radosevich et al. 2004). In addition, affect also appears to be an important mediator of within-person goal revision (Ilies & Judge 2005).

With a few notable exceptions, most empirical work has focused on the effects of negative GPDs. Donovan & Hafsteinsson (2006) found the effect of positive GPDs on goal levels was moderated by self-efficacy and by performance and learning goal orientations. Specifically, the GPD–goal setting relationship was stronger when self-efficacy and performance goal orientation were high and learning goal orientation was low. Tolli & Schmidt (2008) examined both positive and negative feedback (GPDs), finding performance feedback and causal attributions interactively influenced self-efficacy, which then influenced goal revision. Elicker et al. (2009) also showed velocity related positively to increases in goal levels when goals were high in importance. But with low goal importance, velocity negatively related to goal revision, perhaps reflecting a coasting response invoked when performance was perceived to be going well. Finally, in an interesting study that probed possible explanations for increasing goals above one's prior performance, Phillips et al. (1996) found that both higher-level achievement needs and one's desire to maintain high performance were associated with setting goals higher than past performance.

In contrast to the complex and often moderated effects of GPD on performance, a more straightforward relationship exists between GPDs and satisfaction. Satisfaction is greater the more performance exceeds prior goals (Elicker et al. 2009, Ilies & Judge 2005, Kernan & Lord 1991, Thomas & Mathieu 1994). These effects are stronger when internal causal attributions are made (Thomas & Mathieu 1994). High velocity also contributes to task satisfaction (Elicker et al. 2009) and job satisfaction (Chang et al. 2009) over and above the effects of discrepancies. The positive affect generated by high velocity may have indirect effects on performance if it spills over into the next self-regulatory cycle.

Summary and extensions for intermediate-level self-regulation. Intermediate levels of self-regulatory processes have received the most attention to date by organizational researchers, with emphasis on the role of goals and goal-performance discrepancies as they function within negative feedback loops. Early studies by organizational scholars who were focused on workplace applications tended to employ goals that were held in consciousness and

that often were assigned. More recent work has broadened this focus, but as discussed above, an increasing body of research indicates that substantial work activity appears to be regulated by standards other than conscious, assigned goals, including (a) goals whose selection is biased by unconscious affective influences, (b) goals emerging from sets of multiple external constraints (e.g., social factors) whose influences are largely unconscious, and (c) habit.

Although a basic mechanism associated with GPDs in feedback loops has been established, there are challenges in accurately modeling the resulting performance during goal striving. GPD effects appear to be nonlinear and asymmetric with respect to the effects of negative versus positive discrepancies. Workers are likely sensitive (perhaps even differentially sensitive) not only to the distance from a goal or standard (i.e., GPDs), but also to the rate at which that distance is changing (i.e., velocity). The importance of attentional focus and knowledge access to protecting and facilitating goal striving has recently become clear. We have less knowledge about how to actually apply this understanding to specific work situations in order to increase performance. The capacity of external feedback to influence the parsing of goal striving into episodes raises interesting questions for future applied research about the optimal timing of feedback provision. The ongoing state of the organization's feedback environment may be an important contextual factor for self-regulation around intermediate goals (Steelman et al. 2004).

Lower-Level Self-Regulation

Achievement goals often affect behavior indirectly through their activating or inhibiting effects on shorter-term self-regulatory processes with very simple objectives (e.g., reading a document). We separate this level from that associated with achievement tasks for several reasons. First, activities at this level often require less attention and are more knowledge-dependent. For example, Schank & Ableson (1977) explained that these short-term goals were often organized into knowledge structures called scripts, and Gioia & Poole (1984) discussed the relevance of scripts to organizational behavior. Scripts often specify the sequence of events needed to accomplish higher-level goals, but they can be flexibly applied in a manner that is sensitive to context. Many familiar work tasks are guided by a script structure (e.g., a staff meeting), and scripts can substitute for conscious goal selection in familiar, stable situations, a phenomenon that also can be understood in terms of habit (Ouellette & Wood 1998). Second, recent neurocognitive research also supports the distinction between these two levels. Neuroimaging studies indicate that there are different control structures in the brain for very short-term task activities compared to higher-level systems that maintain task focus for achievement tasks (Dosenbach et al. 2008).

Self-regulation at lower levels is much faster than at the two levels previously discussed. It is generally more dependent on automatically accessing appropriate behaviors based on cues from higher-level achievement goals or the situation than on conscious search or problem solving. For example, booting up one's computer requires some attention to the task environment, but retrieval of appropriate sequences from memory (e.g., mousing, entering login and password) is much faster and more efficient than is consciously thinking about needed actions. Environmental cueing of actions at this level can be facilitated by the formation of implementation intentions (Gollwitzer & Schaal 1998), which specify the conditions under which one will exert effort toward goal pursuit (Gollwitzer et al. 2008). Implementation intentions are formed by creating if-then statements that tie action to an anticipated environmental circumstance (i.e., when, where). When a cue is encountered, the goal-directed behavior is enacted (e.g., "When I go to lunch, I will drop off my report"). In other words, implementation intentions create a production system that operates automatically to elicit relevant action when the cue ("if" statement) is encountered, but this is a flexible system and the action only occurs as long as

the higher-level goal (dropping off a report) is maintained (Gollwitzer et al. 2008). Research has shown that forming implementation intentions leads to better performance (Gollwitzer & Brandstätter 1997), with these effects operating through self-regulatory processes rather than through goal-related cognitions, such as choice or efficacy beliefs (Diefendorff & Lord 2003).

Goal setting creates an implicit bias in the accessibility (O'Reilly et al. 1999) and evaluation of the favorableness (Ferguson 2008) of goal-relevant stimuli so that individuals are cognitively and affectively ready to pursue goal-related activities. However, this effect occurs only when goals are actively pursued (Ferguson 2008, Johnson et al. 2006). Thus, goal activation at an intermediate level creates cross-level effects on the activation and evaluation of actions at lower levels. Implementation intentions may also elicit such effects.

Cross-level effects associated with the nature of achievement goals may also influence regulatory processes at this lower level. For example, having a learning goal may help to focus attention on task factors, thus facilitating learning and acceptance of feedback. Having a performance goal may direct attention toward comparisons to others, making learning less likely and increasing defensiveness. Also, achievement-related anxiety can draw performance away from task activities and orient it toward the self (Vancouver & Tischner 2004), especially when self-rated anxiety is high (Simpson et al. 2001).

Cross-level influences can also operate in the other direction. As task skill develops, many work tasks can be accomplished automatically. This frees attentional resources for focusing on other factors in the work environment, thus facilitating meta-cognitive activities associated with higher levels in hierarchies (Anderson 1987). Because self-regulatory cycles are completed quickly at this lower level, the resulting self-regulatory activities are often tightly integrated with one's task environment as well as with higher-level goals—consider the act of driving a car, which requires rapid and relatively automatic behaviors to be performed, but with a consideration of driving conditions and an awareness of where one is headed.

Very Fast, Micro-Level Regulation

There is also a still faster micro level in which regulation occurs that is important to understand because it determines information access and working memory content. The content of working memory is particularly important because it determines what knowledge is accessed and maintained, allowing easy reliance on previously learned work behaviors. It is at this level that goal shielding is likely to occur. And, because activation spreads from high activation sources such as goals and working memory contents, the resulting activation of other structures is often regulated indirectly by processes such as goal shielding and working memory protection (Lord & Levy 1994). Thus, various tracks in scripts are likely automatically cued by higher-level goals and working memory contents rather than being consciously selected.

As shown in **Table 1**, activation and inhibition are key self-regulatory processes at this level. We have already discussed how these two processes contribute to the biasing effects of achievement goals, but there is also an important micro-level link between activation/inhibition and affective processes. It is widely known that the prefrontal cortex exerts brain-wide executive control through projections to many parts of the brain (Braver et al. 2002, O'Reilly et al. 1999). It does this by actively maintaining the patterns of activity represented by goals and the means to achieve them, a process mediated by the neurotransmitter dopamine. O'Reilly and colleagues (1999) argue that goals, which are maintained in the prefrontal cortex, must exhibit both a resistance to interference from new information (to maintain focus on necessary tasks until they are completed) and a receptivity to new information (in order to adapt to changing circumstances). These conflicting requirements are managed by dopamine availability in the following manner: When task success is anticipated, dopamine

levels are high, positive affect is experienced, and the biasing function of patterns or images in the prefrontal cortex is enhanced; however, when task difficulty is encountered and reward expectations decrease, dopamine levels are reduced, and the gate for new information is opened, enhancing sensitivity to a broader context and alternative goals.

Such processes are important in three respects. First, they help us understand how affect could mediate the effects of performance discrepancies on goal change as reported by Ilies & Judge (2005). An increase in dopamine is experienced as rewarding, and it also triggers approach behavior and goal maintenance. Second, these processes suggest a broad and subtle means of adjusting one's task involvement in a rather automatic fashion. When things are going well and task requirements challenge but do not exceed one's abilities, attentional focus is automatically maintained and a sense of flow and positive affect is experienced (Csikszentmihalyi 1990). Yet when doubts about potential success develop, attention disengages, allowing one to protect the self from more severe disappointment and negative feedback associated with unexpected failure. Such a mechanism may help explain why self-efficacy (Vancouver & Day 2005) or positive expectancies (Carver & Scheier 1998) are associated with task persistence and why negative feedback interpreted at the level of the self (rather than the task) is so damaging (Kluger & DeNisi 1996). Finally, because information access is very fast [Newell (1990) estimates it to occur in about 10 ms], it may be more effective to regulate information access by an emotional gating mechanism than by a relatively slow conscious process. The implications of such processes for applied motivation are discussed more fully by Diefendorff & Lord (2008).

Self-regulation and multiple cycle levels. We have stressed that self-regulation involves the joint functioning of multiple levels of abstraction, which correspond roughly to the cycle times shown in **Table 1**. Thus, one may be performing a work task that is guided by a conscious achievement goal. However, at the same time, (*a*) this occurs in the context of an active WSC, (*b*) lower-level actions may be automatically cued by scripts activated by the environment, task, and achievement goal structures, (*c*) these processes co-occur with an affective tone associated with success or failure on the achievement task and periodic assessment of goal progress, and (*d*) these factors together activate information in working memory while protecting it from interference. When self-regulation works effectively, processes at various levels and with various feedback cycles complement each other, but because of their different cycle times, are only loosely connected.

COMPLICATIONS IN THE WORKPLACE

Multiple Goals

As jobs become increasingly multifaceted, effectively dividing one's time and energy across multiple tasks has become critical for success. Unfortunately, goals sometimes conflict, with time spent on one goal coming at the expense of others (time spent on research versus time spent on teaching). A growing body of research has begun to identify factors influencing goal prioritization; GPDs appear to play a particularly important role in this process, too (Kernan & Lord 1990, Schmidt & DeShon 2007, Schmidt & Dolis 2009, Schmidt et al. 2009, Vancouver 1997). In laboratory settings where participants are presented with multiple goals, all possessing the same deadline, participants typically divide their regulatory resources by need. That is, they allocate more time toward goals that are furthest from attainment, particularly when the tasks are highly dynamic, with external factors contributing unpredictably to progress toward goal attainment.

Discrepancy-driven allocation allows attention to be flexibly reallocated to address changing circumstances, rather than rigidly maintaining current focus regardless of the situation (Carver & Scheier 1998, DeShon & Gillespie

2005, Lord & Levy 1994). This discrepancy-driven allocation strategy may be less prominent when the task environment is stable (it is clear from the outset what level of performance is necessary to achieve the task goals) and also when individuals perceive little likelihood of achieving both goals (Schmidt & Dolis 2009, Schmidt et al. 2009). Rather, under such conditions, there is a tendency to allocate more resources towards the goal closest to attainment. However, Steel & König's (2006) temporal motivation theory also suggests that differences in deadlines between multiple tasks may exert a heavy influence on goal prioritization. Goals with more immediate deadlines gain greater salience. Research is needed to integrate these varying perspectives on multiple-goal prioritization.

Goal difficulty also plays a role in resource allocation. Erez et al. (1990) found that differences in goal difficulty across two concurrent tasks (e.g., an easy goal for one task and a difficult goal for another) predicted resource allocation and performance. More resources are devoted to the more difficult goal, resulting in higher performance on that task. Yet, as difficulty increases, the resources required for attainment also increase and may eventually exceed the supply (Navon & Gopher 1979). Thus, concurrent assignment of difficult goals for multiple tasks may overburden individuals and necessitate tradeoffs, so that increased performance for one task comes at the expense of another (e.g., Schmidt & Dolis 2009). This finding serves as a caution to managers seeking to increase subordinates' performance on multiple tasks competing for limited resources.

Although it is underexplored, affect may influence multiple-goal processes. Carver & Scheier (1998) propose that positive affect can signal when a goal is well maintained and effort can be reallocated to other concerns, while negative affect can indicate a necessity for greater effort and sustained attention. Beal et al. (2005) argue that regulation of affect may draw cognitive resources from focal concerns, essentially functioning as a competing demand. However, they further argue that affective experiences can influence response tendencies, such as positive moods increasing the likelihood that prosocial goals will become active. Although empirical studies explicitly linking affect to multiple-goal regulation are relatively rare, one recent exception is Louro et al. (2007), who found that negative emotions can encourage increased effort toward the focal goal when it is close, whereas positive emotions facilitate effort toward distant goals.

Research on multiple goals has primarily focused on alternative tasks that fit within the same overall motivational structure (e.g., two similar tasks may both be assigned by an experimenter). In applied situations, goals related to dual tasking may involve differences at all levels of our hierarchy, including different WSCs, goals, scripts, and motor activities, each with distinct emotions (e.g., one may be text messaging a family member during a meeting or one may be talking on a cell phone while working on a computer task or driving a car). Effectively switching between such tasks may involve more than just working memory capacity, but we know little about how other levels of self-regulation are involved. Future research is needed to clarify this issue.

Knowledge and Expertise

Often, workers perform the same job for many years and possess considerable expertise in their task domains. In contrast, much of the research on self-regulation presents participants with relatively novel situations. Expertise has numerous implications for self-regulation, some of which are mentioned above. Experts can extensively rely on automatic access to structured knowledge such as scripts to generate actions, in contrast to novices for whom performance creates a greater attentional load (Anderson 1987, Kanfer & Ackerman 1989, Newell 1990). Because fewer cognitive resources are required for the execution of basic task functions, experts can devote more resources to other processes, such as more strategic, meta-cognitive considerations.

Using a cognitively complex air-traffic controller task, Kanfer & Ackerman (1989) found that active monitoring of one's performance during task engagement can impair performance by consuming attentional resources that might otherwise be devoted to the task itself, a phenomenon that is particularly debilitating for novices and individuals with low cognitive ability. They explain such effects in terms of the competing attentional demands created by self-regulation and the complex task, but based on our perspective, performance goals assigned early in learning a task may also make the wrong information available because the links between goals and useful information have not yet been refined. Following this logic, experts are likely to experience less goal conflict and greater expectancy when faced with multiple tasks, particularly if they possess expertise on all tasks, both because attentional demands are reduced and because needed information is more efficiently accessed. Through experience, experts may be better able to make decisions that strategically balance competing goals in situations where one goal must be sacrificed for the sake of the other, as well as to better anticipate and prevent such situations from arising.

Multiperson Processes

The increasing prominence of teams in the workplace elevates the importance of understanding motivational processes within workgroups. Researchers have sought to extend basic principles of individual motivation to the group level. For example, studies on team goal setting have found that difficult, specific team goals often foster better team effort, planning, and strategy development, resulting in better team performance in comparison with easy or "do your best" goals (e.g., O'Leary-Kelly et al. 1994). Feedback is also an important factor in team performance (e.g., DeShon et al. 2004). Because feedback can direct attention to particular aspects of a task, it can influence the tradeoffs that team members make between maximizing their individual attainments and contributing to the team. Provision of individual feedback produces greater emphasis on individual than on team performance and vice versa, whereas provision of both types of feedback encourages tradeoffs between individual and team orientations (DeShon et al. 2004).

Self-efficacy has also been extended to the team level in the form of team efficacy and group potency. Team efficacy refers to a shared belief that the team can effectively perform a specific task (e.g., Lindsley et al. 1995), whereas group potency is a more generalized belief in the team's capabilities across a range of tasks or situations (Guzzo et al. 1993). Similar to the typical finding regarding self-efficacy, team efficacy and potency have been found to be positively related to team performance (e.g., Gully et al. 2002). However, it is worth noting that these studies have typically utilized cross-sectional designs, leaving open the possibility of divergent effects analogous to those observed for the self-efficacy of individuals when examined longitudinally across time (e.g., Vancouver et al. 2001).

An important aspect of self-regulation is the adaptation of effort and strategies to maintain desired states despite changing external demands, ideas that have also been extended to the team domain. Similar to phase models of self-regulation discussed above (e.g., Gollwitzer 1990), Marks et al. (2001) distinguish between action phases, which are characterized by task engagement, and transition phases, which are characterized by task preparation and post-task reflection. Processes in the transition phase—such as careful mission analysis, goal clarification, strategy formulation, and contingency planning—as well as those during the action phase—such as careful monitoring of goal progress, team resources, environmental conditions, communication, and coordination—help promote adaptation to changing circumstances. LePine (2005) found that transition processes promoted adaptation during an unexpected disruption, whereas action processes facilitated adaptation after the disruption had ceased.

METHODOLOGICAL AND ANALYTIC CONSIDERATIONS

As models of motivation and self-regulation become more dynamic and complex, there is a parallel need for changes in research designs and analytic tools. In particular, repeated measures or longitudinal research designs that capture within-person data from multiple assessments are required to model or test propositions regarding cycles of self-regulation as described in previous sections of this review. Experimental designs using laboratory tasks in which multiple performance trials are performed are ideally suited for collecting such information. Additionally, experience-sampling methodology, involving the intensive collection of measures of motivational processes in daily life and natural environments, holds a great deal of promise for testing within-person motivational theories. Fortunately, this need for more sophisticated methodological approaches coincides with the recent development and refinement of a variety of statistical techniques and software designed for longitudinal data (see Collins 2006).

Repeated-measures analysis of variance and multivariate analysis of variance approaches still prove useful for the analysis of data from some research designs, but other procedures such as random coefficients modeling (e.g., hierarchical linear modeling and related techniques) provide very powerful and flexible tools for the specification of multilevel effects and linear or nonlinear patterns of change over time. For example, with such approaches one can model data in which individuals who experience different manipulations or who have different pre-existing characteristics are expected to show different patterns of within-person change over time (Singer & Willett 2003). Random coefficient modeling approaches are used increasingly (e.g., DeShon et al. 2004, Ilies & Judge 2005).

Wider application, however, could be made of some other recently developed longitudinal analysis techniques. For example, hazard/survival models (see Singer & Willett 2003) were developed to model the likelihood of occurrence and timing of events such as graduation from high school, relapse after an alcohol treatment program, or employee turnover (which may alternatively be thought of as length of stay). Perhaps because many of the events that have been traditionally modeled using this approach tend to unfold over relatively long periods of time, it has seen little application in research on self-regulation. However, hazard modeling may prove quite useful for examining phenomena such as persistance at a goal or maintenance of a regulatory focus (i.e., promotion or prevention; Shah & Higgins 2001). In such models, motivational predictors such as self-efficacy, GPDs, commitment, and other time-invariant (e.g., personality) or time-varying (e.g., affect) covariates can be linked to the likelihood of an event (e.g., abandoning a goal) occurring at a particular point in time.

In addition, more use could be made of special applications of structural equation modeling designed to estimate change over time. Particularly interesting are McArdle's (2009) latent change score models, which potentially avoid the classic issue of the unreliability of change scores created from measured variables. Some variations of latent change score models have other advantages such as allowing the decoupling of the time referent of the change score from the specific timing of measurements in the study, allowing for the specification of nonlinear (exponential) growth trajectories and determining the effect of a construct at one point in time on the change in a second construct at a later point in time. These models might be profitably applied to the within-person study of self-regulation in order to investigate issues such as the impact of GPDs experienced early in a performance cycle on potentially nonlinear changes in the allocation of resources later in the performance cycle.

An interesting possibility is to further explore issues of intraperson variability (as opposed to intraperson change) related to the functioning of self-regulatory cycles. Boker & Nesselroade (2002) build on earlier work by Boker to describe the damped linear oscillator model and demonstrate its potential

usefulness in studying self-regulatory systems. The damped linear oscillator describes a pattern of change over time that may be compared to the motion of a pendulum swinging back and forth when friction is present. The side-to-side distance covered by the pendulum gradually lessens as friction diminishes the arc that the pendulum traverses. In a similar manner, one's self-regulatory processes may adjust around a trend or baseline, with deviations above or below this baseline lessening (or in some cases, amplifying) over time.

Several potential applications of oscillator systems to the study of self-regulatory processes occur to us. For example, positive and negative variability in effort expenditure may dampen around a finely tuned baseline level as an individual develops increasing experience with a task. Similarly, affect may oscillate more widely directly after a potent event, with variability decreasing around a trend toward neutral affect as the event recedes into the past [see Bisconti et al.'s (2004) study of fluctuations in the emotional well-being of recent widows modeled by an oscillator system]. Finally, variability in self-efficacy beliefs as one pursues a goal may reveal oscillation that dampens as goal completion nears.

Graphic depictions of processes that oscillate look rather different to many researchers because they describe cyclic rather than strictly linear patterns. However, they can be estimated using linear modeling approaches (i.e., within a regression framework). This is accomplished by estimating local approximations to the first derivative (change over time) and second derivative (velocity, or rate of change over time) of the variable being modeled. These approximations are then used as weighted predictors of the third derivative (acceleration). The coefficient for the first derivative estimates a frequency parameter, and the coefficient for the second derivative estimates a damping parameter. Once data points are fit to these models for each individual in the dataset, higher-level models that predict the individual damping and frequency parameters from other situational or individual difference variables can be tested, much like is done in level-2 analyses in random coefficients modeling. Incorporating individual differences such as personality, attitudes, or values as predictors of damping or frequency parameters might help link between-person approaches to motivation and self-regulation with longitudinal, within-person processes.

Oscillator and related models may aid in more precise estimates of cycle times for specific individuals engaged in specific processes. They may also help in distinguishing data that reflect self-regulatory processes that are homogeneous within a population from those in which observed variability is simply due to normally distributed measurement error. Interestingly, other standard methods for analyzing longitudinal data, even those such as random coefficients models, cannot distinguish between these two types of data if phase length is unknown (Boker & Nesselroade 2002).

One challenge posed by the overarching self-regulatory framework described in this review is the potential that a large number of internal and external factors act as constraints on self-regulatory processes. Simulation techniques may be useful for modeling the effects of many variables that may cumulate or interact in complex manners. For instance, Lord et al. (2003) illustrates the use of simulation to investigate the internal logic of a complex model that recasts what was originally a conscious, symbolic-level approach to valence-instrumentality-expectancy theory into a subconscious neural network processing system. Similarly, Vancouver (2008) uses computational modeling to create mathematical representations of mechanisms involved in acting,

thinking, learning, and feeling, which are then compared with results from earlier studies of actual research participant responses (also see Vancouver et al. 2008).

CONCLUSION

Self-regulation is important for success in modern work organizations. The increasing emphasis on personal initiative, empowerment, and self-management places a greater burden on individual workers to control their own goal-directed activities. Yet this increased demand to self-regulate may also yield benefits, including enhanced individual growth and development, greater well-being, and the realization of desired possible selves. We have reviewed recent thought about the operation of within-person self-regulatory processes over time and at different levels of consciousness. Although there will surely be debate about the particulars, we believe a multidimensional and interdisciplinary approach to thinking about self-regulation provides a necessarily complex and nuanced view of how individuals pursue goals. Importantly, workers often pursue multiple goals simultaneously and increasingly do so in socially interdependent contexts. Accompanying this greater complexity in theory is the development of methodological tools that can model self-regulation as a multivariate and longitudinal process. We call on researchers to take advantage of these recent advances to achieve a science of motivation at work that is both accurate in its depiction of self-regulatory processes and useful in its application to daily organizational life.

SUMMARY POINTS

1. Self-regulatory processes occur at different levels of abstraction with accompanying differences in cycle time and relevant variables and processes.

2. A mechanism common across levels is the negative feedback loop, which operates by comparing the current state with a desired standard.

3. Different levels of self-regulation can be linked both through supervisory control of lower-level processes by higher levels and by the imposition of constraints from one level to another (constraints may originate at either higher or lower levels).

4. Self-identities and the working self-concept (which may be influenced by organizational factors such as leadership) create cognitive, affective, and motivational constraints that direct lower-level task-focused activities.

5. Goals and goal-performance discrepancies drive self-regulation at the intermediate level, through both conscious and automatic processes, including biasing effects of affect, and are influenced by selective attention processes.

6. Lower-level self-regulation is often dependent on the relatively automatic application of scripts.

7. Important functions such as goal shielding occur at the very fast micro level of self-regulation, which is more directly dependent on neurological and neurochemical processes than are higher-level cycles of self-regulation.

8. When expertise is high, work performance may depend as much on effective knowledge management, which reflects functions at lower hierarchical levels and thus frees more attentional resources, as it does on effort regulation, which is more dependent on higher-level processes and may require greater allocation of attentional resources.

DISCLOSURE STATEMENT

The authors are not aware of any biases that might be perceived as affecting the objectivity of this review.

ACKNOWLEDGMENT

We would like to acknowledge the helpful feedback of Dr. Robert Sternberg and Sara Shondrick in the preparation of this review.

LITERATURE CITED

Aarts H, Dijksterhuis A, Dik G. 2008. Goal contagion: inferring goals from others' actions—and what it leads to. In *Handbook of Motivation Science*, ed. JY Shah, WL Gardner, pp. 265–80. New York: Guilford

Allen P, Kaut K, Lord RG. 2008. Emotion and episodic memory. In *Handbook of Behavioral Neuroscience: Episodic Memory Research*, ed. E Dere, A Easton, L Nadel, JP Huston, 18:115–32. New York: Elsevier Sci.

Amabile TM, Hadley CN, Kramer SJ. 2002. Creativity under the gun. *Harvard Bus. Rev.* 80:52–61

Andersen SM, Chen S. 2002. The relational self: an interpersonal social-cognitive theory. *Psychol. Rev.* 109:619–45

Anderson JR. 1987. Skill acquisition: compilation of weak-method problem situations. *Psychol. Rev.* 94:192–210

Andrews FM, Farris GF. 1972. Time pressure and performance of scientists and engineers: a five-year panel study. *Organ. Behav. Hum. Perform.* 8:185–200

Aspinwall LG, Taylor SE. 1997. A stitch in time: self-regulation and proactive coping. *Psychol. Bull.* 121:417–36

Austin JT, Vancouver JB. 1996. Goal constructs in psychology: structure, process, and content. *Psychol. Bull.* 120:338–75

Bandura A, Locke EA. 2003. Negative self-efficacy and goal effects revisited. *J. Appl. Psychol.* 88:87–99

Bargh JA. 1990. Automotives: preconscious determinants of social interaction. In Higgins & Sorrentino 1990, 2:93–130

Baumeister RF, Vohs KD, De Wall CN, Zhang L. 2007. How emotions shape behavior: feedback, anticipation and reflection rather than direct causation. *Personal. Soc. Psychol. Bull.* 11:167–203

Beal DJ, Weiss HM, Barros E, MacDermid SM. 2005. An episodic process model of affective influences on performance. *J. Appl. Psychol.* 90:1054–68

Bisconti RL, Bergeman CS, Boker SM. 2004. Emotional well-being in recently bereaved widows: a dynamical systems approach. *J. Gerontol. Psychol. Sci.* 59:158–67

Boekaerts M, Corno L. 2005. Self-regulation in the classroom: a perspective on assessment and intervention. *Appl. Psychol. Intl. Rev.* 54:199–231

Boker SM, Nesselroade JR. 2002. A method for modeling the intrinsic dynamics of intraindividual variability: recovering the parameters of simulated oscillators in multi-wave panel data. *Multivar. Behav. Res.* 37:127–60

Braver TS, Cohen JD, Barch DM. 2002. The role of prefrontal cortex in normal and disordered cognitive control: a cognitive neuroscience perspective. In *Principles of Frontal Lobe Function*, ed. DT Stuss, RT Knight, pp. 428–47. New York: Oxford Univ. Press

Cacioppo JT, Gardner WL, Berntson GG. 1999. The affect system has parallel and integrative processing components: form follows function. *J. Personal. Soc. Psychol.* 76:839–55

Campion MA, Lord RG. 1982. A control systems conceptualization of the goal-setting and changing process. *Organ. Behav. Hum. Decis. Process.* 30:265–87

Carver CS, Scheier MF. 1990. Origins and functions of positive and negative affect: a control-process view. *Psychol. Rev.* 97:19–36

Carver CS, Scheier MF. 1998. *On the Self-Regulation of Behavior*. New York: Cambridge Univ. Press

Carver CS, Scheier MF. 2002. Control processes and self-organization as complementary principles underlying behavior. *Personal. Soc. Psychol. Rev.* 6:304–15

Chang CH, Johnson RE, Lord RG. 2009. *Moving beyond discrepancies: the importance of velocity as a predictor of satisfaction and motivation*. Manuscript submitted

Chartrand TL, Dalton NA, Cheng CM. 2008. The antecedents and consequences of nonconscious goal pursuit. In *Handbook of Motivation Science*, ed. JY Shah, WL Gardner, pp. 342–55. New York: Guilford

Collins LM. 2006. Analysis of longitudinal data: the integration of theoretical model, temporal design, and statistical model. *Annu. Rev. Psychol.* 57:505–28

Csikszentmihalyi M. 1990. *Flow: The Psychology of Optimal Experience*. New York: Harper & Row

Dalal RS, Hulin CL. 2008. Motivation for what? A multivariate dynamic perspective of the criterion. See Kanfer et al. 2008, pp. 63–100

Day DV, Harrison MM, Halpin SM. 2009. *An Integrative Approach to Leader Development*. New York: Routledge

De Cremer D, van Knippenberg D. 2002. How do leaders promote cooperation? The effects of charisma and procedural fairness. *J. Appl. Psychol.* 87:858–66

DeShon RP, Gillespie JZ. 2005. A motivated action theory account of goal orientation. *J. Appl. Psychol.* 90:1096–127

DeShon RP, Kozlowski SWJ, Schmidt AM, Milner KR, Wiechmann D. 2004. A multiple-goal, multilevel model of feedback effects on the regulation of individual and team performance. *J. Appl. Psychol.* 89:1035–56

Diefendorff JM, Lord RG. 2003. The volitional and strategic effects of planning on task performance and goal commitment. *Hum. Perform.* 16:365–87

Diefendorff JM, Lord RG. 2008. Self-regulation and goal striving processes. See Kanfer et al. 2008, pp. 151–96

Diefendorff JM, Lord RG, Hepburn ET, Quickle JS, Hall RJ, Sanders RE. 1998. Perceived self-regulation and individual differences in selected attention. *J. Exp. Psychol: Appl.* 4:228–47

Donovan JJ, Hafsteinsson LG. 2006. The impact of goal-performance discrepancies, self-efficacy, and goal orientation on upward goal revision. *J. Appl. Soc. Psychol.* 36:1046–69

Donovan JJ, Williams KJ. 2003. Missing the mark: effects of time and causal attributions on goal revision in response to goal-performance discrepancies. *J. Appl. Psychol.* 88:379–90

Dosenbach NUF, Fair DA, Cohen AL, Schlaggar BL, Petersen SE. 2008. A dual-network architecture of top-down control. *Trends Cogn. Sci.* 12:99–105

Dragoni L. 2005. Understanding the emergence of state goal orientation in organizational work groups: the role of leadership and multilevel climate perceptions. *J. Appl. Psychol.* 90:1084–95

Elicker JD, Lord RG, Kohari NE, Ash SR, Hruska BJ, Medvedeff ME. 2009. Velocity as a predictor of performance satisfaction, mental focus, and goal revision. *Appl. Psychol. Intl. Rev.* In press

Erez M, Gopher D, Arzi N.1990. Effects of goal difficulty, self-set goals, and monetary rewards on dual task performance. *Organ. Behav. Hum. Decis. Process.* 47:247–69

Ferguson M. 2008. On becoming ready to pursue a goal you don't know you have: effects of nonconscious goals on evaluative readiness. *J. Personal. Soc. Psychol.* 95:1268–95

Fitzsimons GM, Bargh JA. 2003. Thinking of you: nonconscious pursuit of interpersonal goals associated with relationship partners. *J. Personal. Soc. Psychol.* 84:148–64

Gioia DA, Poole PP. 1984. Scripts in organizational behavior. *Acad. Manag. Rev.* 9:449–59

Gollwitzer PM. 1990. Action phases and mind-sets. In Higgins & Sorrentino 1990, 2:53–92

Gollwitzer PM, Brandstätter V. 1997. Implementation intentions and effective goal pursuit. *J. Personal. Soc. Psychol.* 73:186–99

Gollwitzer PM, Parks-Stamm EJ, Jaudas A, Sheeran P. 2008. Flexible tenacity in goal pursuit. In *Handbook of Motivation Science*, ed. JY Shah, WL Gardner, pp. 396–411. New York: Guildford

Gollwitzer PM, Schaal B. 1998. Metacognition in action: the importance of implementation intentions. *Personal. Soc. Psychol. Rev.* 2:124–36

Gully SM, Incalcaterra KA, Joshi A, Beaubien JM. 2002. A meta-analysis of team-efficacy, potency, and performance: interdependence and level of analysis as moderators of observed relationships. *J. Appl. Psychol.* 87:819–32

Guzzo RA, Yost PR, Campbell RJ, Shea GP. 1993. Potency in groups: articulating a construct. *Br. J. Soc. Psychol.* 32:87–106

Higgins ET, Sorrentino RM, eds. 1990. *Handbook of Motivation and Cognition.* New York: Guilford

Hollenbeck JR, Klein HJ. 1987. Goal commitment and the goal-setting process: problems, prospects, and proposals for future research. *J. Appl. Psychol.* 72:212–30

Hom HL, Arbuckle B. 1986. Mood induction effects upon goal setting and performance in young children. *Motiv. Emot.* 12(2):113–22

Ibarra H. 1999. Provisional selves: experimenting with image and identity in professional adaptation. *Admin. Sci. Q.* 44:764–91

Ilies R, Judge T. 2005. Goal regulation across time: the effects of feedback and affect. *J. Appl. Psychol.* 90:453–67

Johnson RE, Chang C-H, Lord RG. 2006. Moving from cognition to behavior: what the research says. *Psychol. Bull.* 132:381–415

Kanfer R, Ackerman PL. 1989. Motivation and cognitive abilities: an integrative/aptitude treatment interaction approach to skill acquisition. *J. Appl. Psychol.* 74:657–90

Kanfer R, Chen G, Pritchard RD. 2008. *Work Motivation: Past, Present, and Future.* New York: Taylor & Francis

Karoly P. 1993. Mechanisms of self-regulation: a systems view. *Annu. Rev. Psychol.* 44:23–52

Kernan MC, Lord RG. 1990. The effects of valence, expectancies, and goal-performance discrepancies in single and multiple goal environments. *J. Appl. Psychol.* 75:194–203

Kernan MC, Lord RG. 1991. An application of control theory to understanding the relationship between performance and satisfaction. *Hum. Perform.* 4:173–86

Kihlstrom JF, Beer JS, Klein SB. 2003. Self and identity as memory. In *Handbook of Self and Identity*, ed. MR Leary, JP Tangney, pp. 68–89. New York: Guilford

Klein HJ, Austin JT, Cooper JT. 2008. Goal choice and decision processes. See Kanfer et al. 2008, pp. 101–50

Kluger AN, DeNisi A. 1996. Effects of feedback intervention on performance: a historical review, a meta-analysis, and a preliminary feedback intervention theory. *Psychol. Bull.* 119:254–84

Komives SR, Owen JE, Longerbeam SD, Mainella FC, Osteen L. 2005. Developing a leadership identity: a grounded theory. *J. Coll. Student Dev.* 46:593–611

Latham GP, Pinder CC. 2005. Work motivation theory and research at the dawn of the twenty-first century. *Annu. Rev Psychol.* 56:485–516

Lawrence JW, Carver CS, Scheier MF. 2002. Velocity toward goal attainment in immediate experience as a determinant of affect. *J. Appl. Soc. Psychol.* 32:788–802

Leary RM, Baumeister RF. 2000. The nature and function of self-esteem: sociometer theory. *Adv. Exp. Soc. Psychol.* 32:1–62

LeDoux JE. 1995. Emotion: clues from the brain. *Annu. Rev. Psychol.* 46:209–35

LePine JA. 2005. Adaptation of teams in response to unforeseen change: effects of goal difficulty and team composition in terms of cognitive ability and goal orientation. *J. Appl. Psychol.* 90:1153–67

Lind EA. 2001. Fairness heuristic theory: justice judgments as pivotal cognitions in organizational relations. In *Advances in Organizational Justice*, ed. J Greenberg, R Cropanzano, pp. 56–88. San Francisco: New Lexington Press

Lindsley DH, Brass DJ, Thomas JB. 1995. Efficacy-performance spirals: a multilevel perspective. *Acad. Manag. Rev.* 20:645–78

Locke EA, Latham GA. 1990. *A Theory of Goal Setting and Task Performance*. Englewood Cliffs, NJ: Prentice Hall

Locke EA, Latham GA. 2004. What should we do about motivation theory? Six recommendations for the twenty-first century. *Acad. Manag. Rev.* 29:388–403

Lockwood P, Kunda Z. 1997. Superstars and me: predicting the impact of role models on the self. *J. Personal. Soc. Psychol.* 73:91–103

Lord RG, Brown DJ. 2004. *Leadership Processes and Follower Self-Identity*. Mahwah, NJ: Erlbaum

Lord RG, Hanges PJ, Godfrey EG. 2003. Integrating neural networks into decision-making and motivational theory: rethinking VIE theory. *Can. Psychol.* 44:21–38

Lord RG, Levy PE. 1994. Control theory: moving from cognition to action. *Appl. Psychol.: Int. Rev.* 43:335–67

Louro MJ, Pieters R, Zeelenberg M. 2007. Dynamics of multiple-goal pursuit. *J. Personal. Soc. Psychol.* 93:174–93

Marks MA, Mathieu JE, Zaccaro SJ. 2001. A temporally based framework and taxonomy of team processes. *Acad. Manag. Rev.* 26:356–76

Markus H, Wurf E. 1987. The dynamic self-concept: a social psychological perspective. *Annu. Rev. Psychol.* 38:299–337

McArdle JJ. 2009. Latent variable modeling of differences and changes with longitudinal data. *Annu. Rev. Psychol.* 60:577–605

Navon D, Gopher D. 1979. On the economy of the human-processing system. *Psychol. Rev.* 86:214–55

Newell A. 1990. *Unified Theories of Cognition*. Cambridge, MA: Harvard Univ. Press

O'Leary-Kelly AM, Martocchio JJ, Frink DD. 1994. A review of the influence of group goals on group performance. *Acad. Manag. J.* 37:1285–301

O'Reilly RC, Braver TS, Cohen JD. 1999. A biologically based computational model of working memory. In *Models of Working Memory: Mechanisms of Active Maintenance and Executive Control*, ed. A Miyake, P Shah, pp. 375–411. Cambridge, UK: Cambridge Univ. Press

Ouellette JA, Wood W. 1998. Habit and intentions in everyday life: the multiple processes by which past behavior predicts future behavior. *Psychol. Bull.* 124:54–74

Phillips JM, Hollenbeck JR, Ilgen DR. 1996. Prevalence and prediction of a positive discrepancy creation: examining a discrepancy between two self-regulation theories. *J. Appl. Psychol.* 81:498–511

Powers WT. 1973. *Behavior: The Control of Perception*. Chicago: Aldine

Radosevich DJ, Vaidyanahan VT, Yeo S-Y, Radosevich DM. 2004. Relating goal orientation to self-regulatory processes: a longitudinal field test. *Contemp. Educ. Psychol.* 29:207–29

Raichle ME, MacLeod AM, Snyder AZ, Powers WJ, Gusnard DA, Schulman GL. 2001. A default mode of brain function. *Proc. Natl. Acad. Sci. USA* 98:676–82

Ritter BA, Lord RG. 2007. The impact of previous leaders on the evaluation of new leaders: an alternative to prototype matching. *J. Appl. Psychol.* 92:1683–95

Schank RC, Ableson RP. 1977. *Scripts, Plans, Goals, and Understanding*. Hillsdale, NJ: Erlbaum

Schmeichel BJ, Baumeister RF. 2004. Self-regulatory strength. In *Handbook of Self-Regulation: Research, Theory, and Applications*, ed. RR Baumeister, KD Vohs, pp. 84–98. New York: Guilford

Schmeichel BJ, Volokhov RN, Demaree HA. 2008. Working memory capacity and the self-regulation of emotional expression and experience. *J. Personal. Soc. Psychol.* 95:1526–40

Schmidt AM, DeShon RP. 2007. What to do? The effects of discrepancies, incentives, and time on dynamic goal prioritization. *J. Appl. Psychol.* 92:928–41

Schmidt AM, DeShon RP. 2009. Prior performance and goal progress as moderators of the relationship between self-efficacy and performance. *Hum. Perform.* In press

Schmidt AM, Dolis CM. 2009. Something's got to give: the effects of dual-goal difficulty, goal progress, and expectancies on resource allocation. *J. Appl. Psychol.* In press

Schmidt AM, Dolis CM, Tolli AP. 2009. A matter of time: individual differences, contextual dynamics, and goal progress effects on multiple-goal self-regulation. *J. Appl. Psychol.* In press

Seibt B, Neumann R, Nussinson R, S.rack F. 2008. Movement direction or change in distance? Self- and object-related approach-avoidance motions. *J. Exp. Soc. Psychol.* 44:713–20

Seo M, Feldman BL, Bartunek JM. 2004. The role of affective experience in work motivation. *Acad. Manag. Rev.* 29:423–39

Shah JY. 2003. The motivational looking glass: how significant others implicitly affect goal appraisals. *J. Personal. Soc. Psychol.* 85:424–39

Shah JY, Friedman R, Kruglanski AW. 2002. Forgetting all else: on the antecedents and consequences of goal shielding. *J. Personal. Soc. Psychol.* 83:1261–80

Shah JY, Higgins ET. 2001. Regulatory concerns and appraisal efficiency: the general impact of promotion and prevention. *J. Personal. Soc. Psychol.* 80:693–705

Shah JY, Kruglanski AW. 2003. When opportunity knocks: bottom-up priming of goals by means and its effects on self-regulation. *J. Personal. Soc. Psychol.* 84:1109–22

Shamir B, House RJ, Arthur MB. 1993. The motivational effects of charismatic leadership: a self-concept based theory. *Organ. Sci.* 4:577–94

Sherman JW, Gawronski B, Gonsalkorale K, Hugenberg K, Allen TJ, Groom CJ. 2008. The self-regulation of automatic associations and behavioral impulses. *J. Personal. Soc. Psychol.* 115:314–35

Simon HA. 1967. Motivational and emotional controls of cognition. *Psychol. Rev.* 74:29–39

Simpson JR Jr, Drevets WC, Snyder AZ, Gusnard DA, Raichle ME. 2001. Emotion-induced changes in human medial prefrontal cortex: II. During anticipated anxiety. *Proc. Natl. Acad. Sci. USA* 98:683–87

Singer JD, Willett JB. 2003. *Applied Longitudinal Data Analysis: Modeling Change and Event Occurrence.* New York: Oxford Univ. Press

Stajkovic AD, Luthans F. 1998. Self-efficacy and work-related performance: a meta-analysis. *Psychol. Bull.* 124:240–61

Steel P, Konig CJ. 2006. Integrating theories of motivation. *Acad. Manag. Rev.* 31:889–913

Steelman LA, Levy PE, Snell AF. 2004. The feedback environment scale: construct definition, measurement, and validation. *Educ. Psychol. Meas.* 64:165–84

Thomas KM, Mathieu JE. 1994. Role of causal attributions in dynamic self-regulation and goal processes. *J. Appl. Psychol.* 79:812–18

Tolli AP, Schmidt AM. 2008. The role of feedback, causal attributions, and self-efficacy in goal revision. *J. Appl. Psychol.* 93:692–701

Vallacher RR, Wegner DM. 1985. *A Theory of Action Identification.* Hillsdale, NJ: Erlbaum

Vancouver JB. 1997. The application of HLM to the analysis of the dynamic interaction of environment, person and behavior. *J. Manag.* 23:795–818

Vancouver JB. 2005. The depth of history and explanation as benefit and bane for psychological control theories. *J. Appl. Psychol.* 90:38–52

Vancouver JB. 2008. Integrating self-regulation theories of work motivation into a dynamic process theory. *Hum. Resour. Manag. Rev.* 18:1–18

Vancouver JB, Day DV. 2005. Industrial and organizational research on self-regulation: from constructs to applications. *Appl. Psychol.: Int. Rev.* 54:155–85

Vancouver JB, More JM, Yoder RJ. 2008. Self-efficacy and resource allocation: support for a nonmonotonic discontinuous model. *J. Appl. Psychol.* 93:35–47

Vancouver JB, Thompson CM, Tischner EC, Putka DJ. 2002. Two studies examining the negative effects of self-efficacy on performance. *J. Appl. Psychol.* 87:506–16

Vancouver JB, Thompson CM, Williams AA. 2001. The changing signs in the relationships among self-efficacy, personal goals, and performance. *J. Appl. Psychol.* 86:605–20

Vancouver JB, Tischner EC. 2004. The effects of feedback sign on task performance depends on self-concept discrepancies. *J. Appl. Psychol.* 89:1092–98

van Knippenberg D, van Knippenberg B, De Cremer D, Hogg MA. 2004. Leadership, self, and identity: a review and research agenda. *Leader. Q.* 15:825–56

Vohs KD, Baumeister RF, Schmeichel BJ, Twenge JM, Nelson NM, Tice DM. 2008. Making choices impairs subsequent self-control: a limited-resource account of decision making, self-regulation, and active initiative. *J. Personal. Soc. Psychol.* 94:883–98

Wakslak CJ, Nussbaum S, Liberman N, Trope Y. 2008. Representations of the self in the near and distant future. *J. Personal. Soc. Psychol.* 95:757–73

Williams KJ, Donovan JJ, Dodge TL. 2000. Self-regulation of performance: goal establishment and goal revision processes and athletes. *Hum. Perform.* 13:159–80

Wood W, Quinn JM, Kashy D. 2002. Habits in everyday life: thought, emotion and action. *J. Personal. Soc. Psychol.* 83:1281–97

Wrosch C, Miller GE, Scheier MF, Brun de Pontet SB. 2007. Giving up on unattainable goals: benefits for health? *Personal. Soc. Psychol. Bull.* 33:251–65

Creativity

Beth A. Hennessey[1] and Teresa M. Amabile[2]

[1]Department of Psychology, Wellesley College, Wellesley, Massachusetts 02481;
email: bhenness@wellesley.edu

[2]Harvard Business School, Harvard University, Boston, Massachusetts 02163;
email: tamabile@hbs.edu

Annu. Rev. Psychol. 2010. 61:569–98

First published online as a Review in Advance on
October 19, 2009

The *Annual Review of Psychology* is online at
psych.annualreviews.org

This article's doi:
10.1146/annurev.psych.093008.100416

0066-4308/10/0110-0569$20.00

Key Words

innovation, intrinsic motivation, divergent thinking

Abstract

The psychological study of creativity is essential to human progress. If
strides are to be made in the sciences, humanities, and arts, we must
arrive at a far more detailed understanding of the creative process, its
antecedents, and its inhibitors. This review, encompassing most subspecialties in the study of creativity and focusing on twenty-first-century
literature, reveals both a growing interest in creativity among psychologists and a growing fragmentation in the field. To be sure, research into
the psychology of creativity has grown theoretically and methodologically sophisticated, and researchers have made important contributions
from an ever-expanding variety of disciplines. But this expansion has not
come without a price. Investigators in one subfield often seem unaware
of advances in another. Deeper understanding requires more interdisciplinary research, based on a systems view of creativity that recognizes
a variety of interrelated forces operating at multiple levels.

Contents

INTRODUCTION

Why study creativity? Even if this mysterious phenomenon can be isolated, quantified, and dissected, why bother? Wouldn't it make more sense to revel in the mystery and wonder of it all? From a purely theoretical standpoint, researchers and scholars are anxious to learn as much as possible about the distinctively human capacity to generate new ideas, new approaches, and new solutions. We strive to understand the experiences of Picasso, da Vinci, Einstein, and the like, and we question what, if anything, we ourselves have in common with these amazing individuals. On a more practical level, educators, parents, employers, and policy makers realize all too well that it is only with creativity that we can hope to address the myriad problems facing our schools and medical facilities, our cities and towns, our economy, our nation, and the world. Creativity is one of the key factors that drive civilization forward. As he began his administration in January 2009, U.S. President Obama called for substantial increases in federal funds for basic research and efforts to boost math, science, and engineering education; he entered office with the first-ever presidential arts platform as well. But it will take more than money and rhetoric. If we are to make real strides in boosting the creativity of scientists, mathematicians, artists, and all upon whom civilization depends, we must arrive at a far more detailed understanding of the creative process, its antecedents, and its inhibitors. The study of creativity must be seen as a basic necessity.

In fact, scholarly research on creativity is proliferating; a variety of new publication outlets have emerged. When we started our own research careers, the *Journal of Creative Behavior* was the one periodical dedicated to the study of creativity. That publication was supplemented in 1988 by the *Creativity Research Journal*. The inaugural issue of *Psychology of Creativity, Aesthetics and the Arts*, a publication of APA division 10, came in 2007; in recent years, a variety of additional journals have also proven to be important outlets for creativity research. These include the *International Journal of Creativity and Problem Solving* and the *Journal of Thinking Skills and Creativity*. Add to this lineup the long list of books and general psychology journals publishing research in the area of creativity, and the prospect of reviewing the creativity literature becomes both daunting and exciting.

Our review attempts to encompass most of the subspecialties in the study of creativity, including the social psychology of creativity— our own area of specialization. We followed a two-part process. The first step involved the polling of colleagues, and the second step involved winnowing through our own search of the literature. To begin, we brainstormed a list of active researchers and theorists whom we believe have made the most significant contributions to the creativity literature and asked them to nominate up to 10 papers, published since about 2000, that they considered "must have" references. We contacted 26 colleagues and heard back from 21. Some of these suggested papers were self-nominations, but most were by others. In total, we received over 110 suggestions for specific journal articles, book

---

Creativity: the generation of products or ideas that are both novel and appropriate

chapters, books, or entire volumes of a journal devoted to a particular topic.

For our own search of the literature, we conducted a thorough electronic (EBSCO) review—searching for empirical journal articles, chapters, and entire books published between 1998 and 2008 and focused on creativity. This search yielded over 400 additional citations that we believed were interesting, relevant, and potentially important. This list too had to be significantly reduced.

Perhaps our biggest surprise, in examining the suggestions made by colleagues, was just how wide reaching their recommendations were. In fact, we came to wonder and worry about why there was so very little overlap in terms of material suggested. Of the 110 nominated papers, only seven were suggested by two colleagues, and only one was suggested by three colleagues. What did this diversity of opinion, this lack of consensus, say about the state of the field? As we compiled this review, we were consistently struck by what can only be termed a growing fragmentation of the field. For the first three decades of modern psychological research into creativity (starting circa 1950), there were a small number of "big questions" that most researchers focused on: creative personality and creative thinking techniques. Then, for many years, there was an additional focus on the social psychology of creativity. Since the 1990s, we have seen a virtual explosion of topics, perspectives, and methodologies in the creativity

literature. Yet there seem to be few, if any, "big" questions being pursued by a critical mass of creativity researchers. In many respects, scholars' understanding of the psychology of creativity has grown amazingly sophisticated, and we are excited by the contributions of researchers representing an ever-expanding variety of disciplines and backgrounds. But this expansion has not come without a price. It is our firm impression that investigators in one subfield often seem entirely unaware of advances in another. This means that research is often done at only one level of analysis—say, the individual or the group—and within only one discipline at a time. Of course, some of the work we review does cross levels of analysis. Where appropriate, we recognize and emphasize the overlap that already exists between the various subspecialties and approaches to the study of the psychology of creativity.

The underlying theme of this review is the need for a systems view of creativity. We believe that more progress will be made when more researchers recognize that creativity arises through a system of interrelated forces operating at multiple levels, often requiring interdisciplinary investigation. **Figure 1** presents a simplified schematic of the major levels at which these forces operate. The model is simplified because, as noted, existing research does cross levels. And, in fact, the "whole" of the creative process must be viewed as much more than a simple sum of its parts. Individuals are much

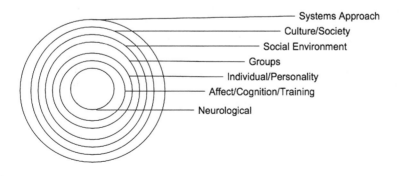

Figure 1

The increasingly large concentric circles in this simplified schematic represent the major levels at which creativity forces operate.

more than their affect, cognition, or training. And social environments or groups may be embedded within particular cultures or societies, but they also crosscut them, as when multiple cultural or religious groups live together within a society.

Figure 1 also provides the scheme we use for organizing this review. We begin with an examination of research directed at the most microscopic level—neurological activity in the brain. We then work out through ever-broadening lenses of focus and toward a review of the literature devoted to the impact of classroom or workplace environments as well as entire cultures on creative behavior. Our review ends with an overview of some of the more comprehensive theories of creativity and a call for researchers and theorists to work toward the development of entire systems perspectives.

REVIEW OF THE LITERATURE: CREATIVITY AS SEEN FROM DIFFERENT LEVELS OF ANALYSIS

Definition and Measurement

Before exploring the research being done at the various levels of our concentric circle model, it is essential to examine the current thinking and theorizing surrounding the identification of the creative person or process and the assessment of the creative product. What is it that contemporary creativity researchers claim to be investigating, and how do they operationalize this entity they call creativity? Criteria for assessing persons or products may appear to be straightforward after decades of research. But appearances deceive. Debates surrounding definition and measurement continue to loom large. Although most researchers and theorists agree that creativity involves the development of a novel product, idea, or problem solution that is of value to the individual and/or the larger social group, psychologists have had great difficulty finding consensus as to definitional components that reach beyond these two criteria of novelty and appropriateness (value).

But this doesn't mean that researchers and theorists have given up on trying to refine their definitions and measurement techniques. Plucker & Runco's seminal (1998) review rightly declared that the death of creativity measurement had been greatly exaggerated; in fact, a number of researchers are probing issues of definition. Sullivan & Ford (2005) examined the relation between assessments of product novelty and creativity in an organizational setting. And Glück et al. (2002) investigated whether artists who face strong external constraints differ in their conceptions of creativity from artists who are free in their choice of topics, materials, and time schedule. Questions of definition and the experimental paradigms employed are becoming increasingly complex, yet our ability to precisely define what we mean by creativity remains fairly stagnant. Kaufmann (2003b) argued that the concept of creativity has been too loosely defined and inappropriately driven by a bottom-up operationalist approach. Kaufmann called for a clear-cut distinction between novelty on the stimulus and novelty on the response end as well as a new taxonomy of different kinds of creativity and intelligent behavior, including proactive and reactive creativity. In a follow-up to this proposal, Beghetto & Kaufman (2007) argued that in addition to the study of "Big C" (eminent) creativity and "little c" (everyday) creativity, it is also essential to explore what might be termed "mini c" creativity, or the creative processes involved in the construction of personal knowledge and understanding. Clearly, a creativity researcher's chosen metric and methodology will largely depend on which of the concentric circles in our model is being investigated.

The Creativity of Products. The creativity of products is typically the focus of experimental paradigms that vary the conditions under which one or more individual's creativity is assessed. Here creativity is seen as a fleeting and largely situation-dependent state (rather than a relatively stable and enduring personality trait). Although Runco maintained in his 2004 *Annual Review* article that the assessment of

"Big C" (eminent) creativity: relatively rare displays of creativity that have a major impact on others

"Little c" (everyday) creativity: daily problem solving and the ability to adapt to change

product creativity is rarely used with nonem-
inent individuals, this approach was expressly
developed for and is particularly useful in the
study of everyday (little c) creativity. In the contemporary literature, the identification and assessment of creative products, be they poems,
paintings, scientific theories, or technological
breakthroughs, rests largely on a consensual assessment process. Researchers wishing to assess the creativity of tangible products have
long relied on the consensual assessment of
experts, formalized for nearly 30 years in the
Consensual Assessment Technique (Amabile
1982, Hennessey & Amabile 1999). Because
of its relative simplicity and the consistently
high levels of interrater agreements reached,
this methodology enjoys wide use and continued examination in the creativity literature (e.g.,
Baer et al. 2004, Kaufman et al. 2007). In recent
years, consensual assessment methodologies
have also been extended to far more "messy"
real-world classroom and workplace environments, including cross-cultural contexts (e.g.,
Amabile & Mueller 2008, Lee et al. 2005).

The Creativity of Persons. The creativity of
persons is typically the focus of experimental
paradigms, case studies, or questionnaire-based
investigations that operationalize creativity as a
relatively enduring and largely stable personality trait. The death of E. Paul Torrance (1915–
2003) marked the end of one of the most influential careers in creativity research of this genre.
Researchers have employed the Torrance
Tests of Creative Thinking (TTCT; Torrance
1966/1974) for more than four decades, and
these measures continue to dominate the field
when it comes to the testing of individuals.
With Torrance's passing came a proliferation
of research projects dedicated to his memory
(Fryer 2006, Kaufman & Baer 2006). Some
of this research used contemporary statistical
methods to address the underlying structure,
reliability, and validity of the TTCT (K.H. Kim
2006, Plucker 1999). In addition, Cramond
et al. (1999) and Wechsler (2006) were among
a dozen or more researchers to examine and

firmly establish the cross-cultural application
and validity of the TTCT over the past 10 years.

Despite the wide acclaim accorded to the
TTCT, many question the utility and/or psychometric properties of general tests of creative
ability. Baer (2008) concluded that creativity
is best conceptualized as domain specific and
argued that this domain specificity explains
why divergent-thinking tests have not met with
more success; research by Mumford and colleagues (1998, 2008) also questioned the validity of divergent-thinking tests. However, other
researchers have defended divergent-thinking
measures, such as those used in the Wallach-
Kogan Creativity Tests (Cheung et al. 2004, Lee
2008). A host of other researchers and psycho-
metricians have been busy with the close examination of existing creative-ability and creative-
personality measures and the development of
new ones (e.g., Epstein et al. 2008, Nassif &
Quevillon 2008, Silvia et al. 2008). Finally,
Silvia (2008) reanalyzed "old" data with the use
of advanced methodology to explore the relation of creativity and intelligence. Research
has generally shown these two constructs to be
modestly related; yet, some studies have contradicted this assumption. Silvia found that latent
originality and fluency variables significantly
predicted intelligence. The relations' magnitude ($r = 0.20$) was also consistent with previous research.

Neurological/Biological Basis

The advancement of technology, particularly
functional magnetic resonance imaging (fMRI),
coupled with increases in access to equipment
for researchers is in large part responsible for
the virtual explosion of information on the
"creative brain." How does the brain generate
creative ideas or solutions? At the neurological
level, is there only one creative process or are
there many? Is it possible to look into the brain
and find evidence of creative thinking in the
same way that modern cognitive neuroscientists
have uncovered some of the neural underpinnings of memory, emotion, and attention? Or
is creativity outside the realm of neuroscience

TTCT: Torrance
Tests of Creative
Thinking

fMRI: functional
magnetic resonance
imaging

understanding? One growing body of research attempts to uncover information about the neurological basis of creative behavior based on the study of individuals displaying aphasia or other brain abnormalities and injuries. Mell and colleagues (2003) traced the progression of aphasia symptoms associated with frontotemporal dementia in a talented artist. They observed that language is not required for, and may even inhibit, certain types of visual creativity. Miller and coworkers (2000, 2004) focused their attention on the emergence of new skills in patients with dementia and found that loss of brain function in one area may lead to facilitation of artistic or musical skills.

As early as 1998, Bowden and Jung-Beeman presented data suggesting that semantic activation in the right hemisphere may help solve insight problems. And subsequent papers by these same authors (Jung-Beeman & Bowden 2000, Bowden & Jung-Beeman 2003) built on the view that there is a strong association between semantic activation in the right hemisphere and the "Aha!" experience when people recognize solutions to insight-like problems. Using electroencephalographic topography and frequency as well as fMRI, Kounios and colleagues (2006) went on to suggest that mental preparation leading to insight involves heightened activity in medial frontal areas associated with cognitive control and in temporal areas associated with semantic processing. Noninsight preparation, in contrast, appears to involve increased occipital activity consistent with an increase in externally directed visual attention. Taken together, these investigations have offered exciting evidence of how behavioral priming and neuroimaging methods can provide information about neural activity during insight.

In addition to empirical explorations of the creative process at the neuronal level, there is theoretical work. For example, Vandervert and his coinvestigators (2007) cited the centrality of novelty and originality in creative thought and argued that, because the cerebellum increases the rapidity and efficiency of memory routines, it likely plays a central role in the creative process. However, several authors offered incisive critiques of this model (Abraham 2007, Brown 2007). In summary, although technological advances have increased exponentially, scientists interested in the neurological basis of creative behavior have a long way to go before they can hope to reach consensus. As they proceed down this groundbreaking and ever-changing investigative path, researchers must make certain that it is sound theorizing and data that drive their use of new technologies and not the technologies themselves that dictate future research questions and directions. The possibilities are promising, but we are not anywhere near the point of being able to image the creative process as it unfolds in the human brain. Even cutting-edge instruments mask the order in which various brain areas become activated in the massive parallel processing that results in high-level creativity (Miller 2007).

Affect, Cognition, and Training

Affect. Most experimental studies of affect and creativity have shown that positive affect leads to higher levels of creativity. When negative affect has an influence, it is generally negative. The bulk of this research indicates that positive affect facilitates not only intrinsic motivation (e.g., Isen & Reeve 2005) but also flexible thinking and problem solving even on especially complex and difficult tasks (see Aspinwall 1998, Isen 2000). Yet the affect-creativity association is complicated. Kaufmann (2003a) refutes the mainstream argument that positive mood reliably facilitates creativity. Some studies have shown that positive mood may facilitate productivity but not quality of ideas (e.g., Vosburg 1998). Other researchers have found that although positive affect manipulations may enhance mood and reduce state anxiety, they do not necessarily enhance divergent thinking (e.g., Clapham 2001).

Conflicting evidence comes from nonexperimental settings, as well. George & Zhou (2002) found that, under certain specific conditions within an organization, negative affect can lead to higher creativity than positive

Intrinsic motivation: the drive to engage in a task because it is interesting, enjoyable, or positively challenging

Divergent thinking: spontaneous, free-flowing thinking with the goal of generating many different ideas in a short period

affect: the work context must call for high levels of creativity, and the individual's clarity of feelings must also be high. On the other hand, another organizational study (Madjar et al. 2002) found a generally positive role for positive affect in the workplace. In this study, positive mood mediated the significant positive relationship between the support that employees received for workplace creativity and their creative performance at work. Searching for more definitive answers, Amabile and colleagues (2005) obtained multiple daily measures of affect from 222 employees in seven different companies over several weeks, as well as multiple measures of creativity. They found a positive linear relationship, with positive affect an antecedent of creativity. Another study (George & Zhou 2007) also suggested a primacy for positive affect. In this study of employees in a single company, creativity was highest when both positive and negative moods were high and the supervisory context was supportive. However, this study also found a positive main effect for positive mood.

These opposing viewpoints and the data driving them argue for more nuanced views of the impact of affect on cognitive activity. In their mood-as-input model, Martin and colleagues (1993) proposed that positive moods signal to individuals that they are safe, motivating them to seek stimulation and think expansively, making more flexible associations. Negative moods signal that there are problems at hand, motivating individuals to think precisely and analytically. Similarly, the dual-tuning model proposed by George & Zhou (2007) asserts that employees should benefit creatively by experiencing both positive and negative moods over time in a supportive context. Positive mood leads to expansive, playful, divergent thinking and the generation of new ideas. Negative mood signals that something is problematic and pushes employees to try hard to improve matters through creative ideas—careful, systematic information processing. The result of both processes is good, well-thought-out ideas that are really creative. Some recent experiments support these views of the different

supporting roles that positive and negative affect might play in the creative process (De Dreu et al. 2008, Friedman et al. 2007). Clearly, the question of the role of affect in creativity is not settled. However, it appears likely that, all else being equal, positive affect is more conducive to creativity than is negative affect.

Cognition. A review of recent work focused on the cognitive processes underlying creative performance reveals that this branch of the literature is also particularly diverse. Recently, an entire volume of the *Korean Journal of Thinking and Problem Solving* (Volume 18, 2008) offered a representative sample of the wide range of experimental and theoretical approaches being taken by researchers. The variety of investigative paths is almost as great as the variety of experimental questions being asked. For example, Kaufman & Baer (2002) employed both self-report and case-study methodologies to conclude that the cognitive mechanisms underlying creative performance are domain specific, with the likely exception of g (a general intelligence factor). Kray and colleagues (2006) explored what they termed a "relational processing style" elicited by counterfactual mind-sets. More specifically, they asked study participants to compare reality to what might have been and in so doing encouraged them to consider relationships and associations among stimuli. They found that, although such mind-sets can be detrimental to novel idea generation, they can improve performance on creative association tasks. Miller (2007) found a significant relation between field independence and creativity on a collage-making task. Necka (1999) presented experimental evidence linking creativity with impaired functioning of what he termed the "filter of attention." Groborz & Necka (2003) reported data arguing for the importance of "cognitive control" in the attentional process, and Zhengkui and colleagues (2007) provided a comprehensive review of the research on creativity and attention.

A large body of research has pointed to the importance of conceptual combination in creative thought. Ward (2001) argued for a "convergent approach" to the study of conceptual combination—incorporating both anecdotal accounts and laboratory investigations of the creative process. Treffinger & Selby (2004) presented a rubric intended to characterize individual differences in problem-solving style involving Orientation to Change, Manner of Processing, and Ways of Deciding. And Scott et al. (2005) described an elegant experiment designed to compare and contrast an analogical approach to generating combinations (involving feature search and mapping) with a case-based approach (integrating and elaborating on event models). In summary, the literature linking cognitive processes and components to creative behavior is plentiful but murky. Perhaps Mumford & Antes (2007) best summarized the state of the field when they called for caution to be applied in any attempt to account for creative achievement based on a single model of the kind of knowledge or cognitive processes involved.

Training. Armed with these new investigations of the role of affect and cognition in the creative process, are we any better equipped to *train* persons to be creative? When compared to the ongoing extensive investigative work on individual differences or affect and creativity, studies of the efficacy of creativity training have been relatively sparse. Svensson and colleagues (2002) undertook three experimental studies involving high school and university students in Sweden. In one study, the efficacy of two creativity-enhancement techniques borrowed from the work of deBono, random word input and provocation, was investigated. In a pretest/post-test design, it was found that post-training levels of fluency were lower, in fact, for the experimental group than for a no-training control group. The remaining two studies reported in this paper contrasted the effects of working individually or as a group. In both of these investigations, group work was found to produce better results on various measures of creativity (fluency, flexibility, and originality), but total fluency was higher for study participants working alone.

Interestingly, many of the more recent training investigations have focused on populations outside the United States. For example, Basadur et al. (2002) reported that training methods previously shown to be effective in helping North American and Japanese adults improve their divergent thinking skills were also applicable to Spanish-speaking South American managers. Arguing that training for divergent thinking skills often involves a large number of moderated sessions, Benedek and colleagues (2006) then set out to explore whether a computer-based divergent thinking training approach could effectively enhance the ideational fluency and originality of Austrian adults through the provision of repeated practice. A study comparing computer-based training designed to promote creativity in the verbal domain (e.g., generating nicknames and slogans) with computer training focused on creative tasks not requiring verbal creativity (e.g., coming up with unusual uses for objects) and a control (no training) group revealed significant training effects for both computer training approaches. Study participants receiving training showed significant gains in what the authors termed "intelligent-independent" aspects of ideational fluency, but no training effects were found for originality of ideas.

Focusing on insight problem solving among American adults, Dow & Mayer (2004) asked whether problem solution depends on domain-specific or domain-general problem-solving skills. Across two separate investigations, study participants who received training in spatial insight problems performed better than a verbal-insight-trained group on spatial problems. However, no other performance differences emerged between subjects receiving verbal, mathematical, spatial, or verbal-spatial training who were later asked to solve insight problems in these four category groups. Garaigordobil (2006) also explored the efficacy of training, this time with a sample of Spanish children. There was a positive effect of the intervention, with children making significant improvements in verbal creativity (originality) and graphic-figural creativity relative to a control/no-intervention group.

Is it possible to generalize about the efficacy of well-designed creativity training attempts? Scott and colleagues (2004) believe so. These researchers carried out a quantitative, meta-analytic review of 70 prior studies and found that carefully constructed creativity training programs typically result in gains in performance, with these benefits generalizing across criteria, setting, and target population. Delving deeper, these authors found that the more successful training programs tend to employ realistic exercises that focus on the development of cognitive skills and heuristics for the application of those skills.

Individual Differences/Personality

The empirical study of creativity was originally focused at the level of the individual, and many recent contributions to the literature continue to explore the question of what distinguishes highly creative persons from the rest of us. Research and theorizing in the area of creativity has much in common with studies of personality, as both fields concentrate on uniqueness. An extensive literature review focused on the personality and individual difference variables common to highly creative persons reveals that many things seem to be true of at least some creative people but not necessarily all of them. In other words, this body of work is especially difficult to decipher, although a meta-analysis carried out by Feist (1998) highlighting personality differences between scientific and artistic creators has proven helpful in this regard.

The Big Five model of personality continues to shape investigations in this area, and a good deal of research attention has also been paid to the traits labeled "openness to experience" and "latent inhibition." Low levels of latent inhibition, associated with the inability to shut out the constant stream of incoming stimuli, have been found to predict trait creativity (e.g., Carson et al. 2003). Trait creativity has also been linked to high levels of openness to experience (e.g., McCrae 1987, Perrine & Brodersen

2005), and at least two investigations have shown a negative correlation between latent inhibition and openness to experience (Peterson & Carson 2000, Peterson et al. 2002). Amabile et al. (1994) were among the first to explore a link between creativity and trait-intrinsic motivation, describing it as the drive to engage in work out of interest, enjoyment, and personal challenge. Although most of the literature linking motivational orientation with creativity has focused on intrinsic motivation as a situation-specific state, interesting recent work by Prabhu and colleagues (2008) confirmed that intrinsic motivation is also an enduring personality trait with a positive relation to creativity. There has also been ongoing interest in the developmental trajectory of a variety of other personality traits linked to creativity, with work done by Helson and colleagues continuing to dominate in this area (Helson & Pals 2000, Helson & Srivastava 2002).

Case studies published in *American Psychologist* (April 2001) revealed just how difficult the attempt to identify individual difference variables essential for creativity has proven to be. In a follow-up discussion of individual differences and creativity (*American Psychologist*, May 2002), a second set of papers argued for the central importance of a sense of curiosity (Kashdan & Fincham 2002) and self-confidence for creative behavior. Lower levels of self-confidence may actually predict higher levels of creativity (Kaufman 2002).

Individual Differences in Intelligence. Individual differences in intelligence were explored by Feist & Barron (2003) as they traced the developmental trajectories of creative persons and placed particular emphasis on the stability/instability of intelligence and intellectual giftedness. Similarly, James & Asmus (2001) examined the interface between personality and cognitive ability as they attempted to better understand sources of creativity within the individual. Although some researchers and theorists have found important parallels between the investigation of creativity and giftedness (Hennessey 2004), research tells us that these

Trait creativity: creativity viewed as a relatively stable individual-difference variable

two constructs should not be equated. Winner (2000) and Runco (1999) found that the skills and personality factors required to be a creator are very different from those typical of highly gifted children. And taking a different approach, Sternberg (2001) argued that creativity is best understood in terms of its dialectical relation to intelligence and wisdom. According to this formulation, intelligence is most often used to advance existing societal agendas, whereas creative thinking often opposes these agendas and proposes new ones. Wise people recognize the need to strike a balance between intelligence and creativity/the old and the new to achieve both stability and change within a societal context.

Gender Differences. Gender differences also continued to garner research attention, with mixed results. Ai (1999) investigated the relation between creativity and academic achievement in Spanish secondary students and showed that when operationalized by teachers' ratings, creativity was related to academic achievement for both males and females. For males, flexibility was the predominant factor. For females, elaboration and fluency played a significant role. In a related investigation again involving adolescents, Jiliang & Baoguo (2007) found no gender differences in scientific creativity on ratings of fluency or flexibility, but on originality, high school males significantly outperformed females. In addition, male scores on figural tasks were significantly higher than female scores. One possible explanation for these gender differences comes from Conti and coinvestigators (2001), who found that boys and girls react very differently to situations of extrinsic constraint. In situations involving competition, boys who had been segregated by gender reported significantly higher levels of both intrinsic and extrinsic motivation than did girls who had also been segregated by gender. Finally, Lee (2002) found that for college students completing problem-solving and problem-finding tasks, neither gender nor education exerted significant influence on creative thinking abilities in real-life situations.

Psychopathology. Psychopathology and the age-old question of whether there exists a systematic relation between creativity and mental illness continue to loom large in the literature. Becker (2001) and Sass (2001) examined how specific intellectual assumptions have, over time, transformed into a widely held belief that precludes the possibility of total mental health and sanity for the creative genius. Rothenberg (2006) also made a strong case for the fact that the literature linking creativity and mental illness is severely flawed. Despite these protestations, there is substantial research evidence of a link between psychopathology, most especially schizotypy, and creative behavior. Prentky (2001) found a greater-than-chance probability that highly creative individuals will evidence signs or symptoms of mental illness and proposed that certain biologically based cognitive styles that are peculiar to extraordinary creativity possess common biological ancestry with another group of cognitive styles that are associated with a predisposition to major mental illness. Other studies, using nonclinical populations, have found similar associations (e.g., Abraham & Windmann 2008, Cox & Leon 1999).

However, Chávez-Eakle and colleagues (2006) observed that highly creative achievers scored especially low on psychopathology and that psychopathology was more related to personality than to creativity. In another study focused on psychiatric patients, Ghadirian and colleagues (2001) reported no difference in the creative abilities of persons with bipolar illness as compared to those with other types of psychopathology. In an attempt to synthesize this work, Nettle (2006) suggested that these findings might be explained by a sort of "hybrid" model whereby schizotypal personality traits can have fitness advantages or disadvantages, with mutational load and neurodevelopmental conditions determining which outcome (promotion or hindrance of creativity) is observed.

Groups and Teams

Investigations of creative behavior and the creative process have, over time, shown a progression from attention to the individual to a focus on the creative performance of groups. In recent years, much of the theorizing and research surrounding the creative process has been targeted at this group level, and there are many important parallels between this work and the creativity training literature reviewed above. Continued and widespread interest in the question of whether creative thinking and problem solving can be trained is clearly due to the fact that in most organizational settings requiring innovative product development and problem solutions, workers are expected to become increasingly creative as they collaborate in project teams. The organizational literature is presented in a later section. Here the focus is on more general studies of creativity in groups.

Over the past decade, research on creativity within groups has undergone a significant shift—away from the simplistic conclusion that individuals can almost always be expected to outperform groups toward a far more nuanced understanding of the group process and a fine-tuning of experimental design as well as models of group interaction, motivation, and disposition. Much remains unknown about the creative process within groups, but significant progress has been made. In two separate investigations, a comparison of students working alone or in a group revealed that although group work produced better results on various measures of creativity, fluency scores were higher for individuals working alone (Svensson et al. 2002). In fact, research on creative problem solving (Osborn 1953, 1957, 1963, 1967; Parnes 1966; Treffinger & Isaksen 1992; Treffinger et al. 2006) typically shows that the performance of individuals is generally superior to that of groups. But some investigators have speculated that this pattern of results may have been driven by the specific experimental tasks, concepts, and research methods employed. Brophy (1998a,b) proposed a "tri-level matching theory" as a way of integrating and explaining contradictory experimental findings. He pointed out that creatively solvable problems vary considerably in their complexity, requisite knowledge base, and the amounts of divergent and convergent thinking that are needed. This model emphasized the fact that a complete creative problem-solving process entails both considerable convergent and divergent thought in continuing alternation, and it predicted that individuals, teams, and entire organizations with different preferences and abilities, knowledge, and work arrangements would be good matches for some problems and poor matches for others. Brophy (2006) later found empirical support for this model. In the same vein, Larey & Paulus (1999) found that brainstorming groups performed better when their members were assigned to the groups based on their preferences for working and interacting in groups. Paulus & Yang (2000) discovered two important factors that enabled idea sharing in groups to become more productive: (*a*) the extent to which group members carefully processed the ideas exchanged in the group (attention) and (*b*) the opportunity for group members to reflect on the ideas after the exchange process (incubation).

Increasingly, research, theory, and applied work on group creativity has merged with and relied on the use of computers. Brown & Paulus (2002) argued that group brainstorming can be an effective technique for generating creative ideas, based on computer simulations of an associative memory model of idea generation in groups. Also working from a cognitive/computer modeling perspective, Nijstad & Stroebe (2006) offered the SIAM model (Search for Ideas in Associative Memory), which they believe could account for various research findings on group idea generation. This model assumes that idea generation is a repeated search for ideas in associative memory, which proceeds in two stages (knowledge activation and idea production) and is controlled through negative feedback loops and cognitive failures (trials in which no idea is generated). This formulation showed that turn taking (production blocking) interfered with both stages of the process. Ideas suggested by others aided the activation of problem-relevant knowledge, and cognitive failures were important negative determinants of brainstorming persistence, satisfaction, and enjoyment. The different ways

Convergent thinking: more disciplined thinking, focused on narrowing possibilities to a workable solution

that computers can be involved in creative work were further examined in a special issue of the *International Journal of Human-Computer Studies* (2007, volume 63), where the contributing authors concluded that computers may facilitate not only communication between persons collaborating on creative projects but also the management of creative work, the use of creativity-enhancement techniques, and the creative act through integrated human-computer cooperation during idea production.

Creativity in Workplace Groups. There has been a general acknowledgment that most creative work that gets done in organizations is accomplished by two or more individuals working closely together (see Thompson & Choi 2006). Thus, although our section on organizational creativity appears later in this article, we review this part of the literature here. (As we noted in the introduction, the neatly nonoverlapping nature of the concentric circles in **Figure 1** is a convenient artifice.) One study in the comic book industry uncovered evidence that simply working in a team can, under the right circumstances, produce more creative results than working individually (Taylor & Greve 2006). On average, single creators had lower performance than did teams, and the team experience of working together increased performance. Hargadon & Bechky (2006) did a qualitative study of six professional service firms to identify behaviors leading to "moments of collective creativity." They identified four sets of interrelated behavior patterns that moved teams beyond individuals' insights: (*a*) help seeking, (*b*) help giving, (*c*) reflective reframing, and (*d*) reinforcing.

Taggar (2002) studied some facilitative team processes, examining the performance of 94 groups on 13 different open-ended tasks. At the individual-team-member level, domain knowledge and performance-relevant behavioral measures of the three components of Amabile's (1983, 1996) model of individual creativity related in predicted ways to individual differences. Support was found for new cross-level processes, labeled "team creativity-relevant processes." At the group level, these processes moderated the relationship between aggregated individual creativity and group creativity.

Work Group Diversity. Research on diversity has been one of the more active areas in organizational creativity scholarship over the past decade. Most of this work has focused on diversity in teams. Kurtzberg & Amabile (2001) suggested that the types and amount of team conflict that arise from the diversity of team members might be particularly influential in affecting outcomes. Two empirical studies exploring diversity (Kurtzberg 2005) compared and contrasted objectively measured creative fluency and subjectively perceived creativity in cognitively diverse teams. Results indicated that, although cognitive diversity may be beneficial for objective functioning, it may be detrimental to team satisfaction, affect, and members' impressions of their own creative performance.

Indeed, a recent review of the literature on this topic suggests that team diversity can just as easily lead to negative as to positive outcomes. Mannix & Neale (2005) conducted a review of 50 years of research and concluded that the preponderance of evidence yields a pessimistic view: Group diversity creates social divisions, with negative performance consequences. The authors suggest that more positive effects, such as creativity, can arise from underlying differences such as functional background, education, or personality—but only when the group process is managed carefully.

Polzer and colleagues (2002) studied one approach to managing group process that can yield creative benefits under team diversity: interpersonal congruence, the degree to which group members see others in the group as those others see themselves. This longitudinal study of 83 work groups revealed that diversity (on sex, ethnicity, and other dimensions) tended to improve creative task performance in groups with high interpersonal congruence but undermined the performance of groups with low interpersonal congruence. Surprisingly, some diverse groups were able to achieve enough interpersonal congruence during their first 10 minutes of interaction to enable better group outcomes four months later.

The Social Psychology of Creativity

Previous research has firmly established that the social environment can significantly influence an individual's motivation for doing an activity, which in turn can significantly influence creative performance. This is the intrinsic motivation principle of creativity: Intrinsic motivation, defined as the drive to do something for the sheer enjoyment, interest, and personal challenge of the task itself (rather than for some external goal), is conducive to creativity, whereas extrinsic motivation is generally detrimental. Probing further, experimentalists have determined that a variety of extrinsic constraints and extrinsic motivators can undermine intrinsic motivation and creativity, including expected reward, expected evaluation, surveillance, competition, and restricted choice. Investigators examining the social psychology of creativity have found that intrinsic motivation for a particular task can be ephemeral and, thus, quite susceptible to social-environmental influences. In fact, the undermining effect of extrinsic constraints is so robust that it has been found to occur across the entire lifespan, with preschoolers and seasoned professionals experiencing the same negative consequences of expected reward and other extrinsic motivators and constraints. (For a review of this research, see Amabile 1996; see also Hennessey 2003.)

Two recent nonexperimental studies in organizations also support the intrinsic motivation principle of creativity. Shin & Zhou (2003) found that the intrinsic motivation of Korean high-tech employees partially explained their creativity. Another study, using survey data from 165 employees and their supervisors who worked in research and development in a large U.S. organization, assessed employee intrinsic motivation and willingness to take risks, along with supervisor-rated creativity (Dewett 2007). Results showed that "one fundamental antecedent to employee creativity is intrinsic interest in one's work" (p. 204). Interestingly, willingness to take risks mediated the effect of intrinsic motivation on employee creativity.

When investigations of the effects of extrinsic constraints began about 30 years ago, it was thought that the determinants of task-motivational orientation were straightforward. Intrinsic and extrinsic motivation were believed to interact in a sort of hydraulic fashion. High levels of extrinsic motivation were thought to preclude high levels of intrinsic motivation; as extrinsic motivators and constraints were imposed, intrinsic motivation (and creativity) would necessarily decrease. Now, many years and hundreds of investigations later, most researchers taking a social-psychological approach to the study of creativity have come to appreciate the many complexities of both motivational orientation and extrinsic motivators, particularly expected reward. They have come to supplement the original hydraulic conceptualization with an additive model that recognizes that under certain specific conditions, the expectation of reward can sometimes increase levels of extrinsic motivation without having any negative impact on intrinsic motivation or performance. Specifically, rewards undermine intrinsic motivation and creativity when they lead people to feel controlled by the situation—that is, when self-determination is undermined (see Deci & Ryan 2002, Ryan & Deci 2000). However, rewards can actually enhance intrinsic motivation and creativity when they confirm competence, provide useful information in a supportive way, or enable people to do something that they were already intrinsically motivated to do. These boosting effects are most likely when initial levels of intrinsic motivation are already strong (Amabile 1993).

Some researchers trained in the behaviorist tradition have offered the strongly contrasting view that creativity can be *easily* increased by reward and is seldom undermined. These scholars, most notably Eisenberger, Cameron, and colleagues (Cameron & Pierce 1994; Eisenberger & Cameron 1996, 1998; Eisenberger & Selbst 1994), maintain that any detrimental effects of reward occur only under limited conditions that can be easily avoided. A debate over these issues surfaced in the literature in the mid 1990s, prompting researchers and theorists on both sides of the argument to publish a series of heated commentaries, critiques, and replies (see Eisenberger & Cameron 1996, 1998; Hennessey & Amabile 1998; Lepper 1998; Sansone & Harackiewicz 1998). At the core of this debate were important differences in the definitions of creativity driving investigations, the algorithmic or heuristic nature of the experimental tasks employed, and the instructions given to study participants.

Studies influenced by the behaviorist tradition have typically used dependent measures that equate creativity with novelty, and have often instructed participants to be creative (sometimes with details on the kinds of responses that would receive high creativity ratings). As Eisenberger & Shanock (2003) themselves point out, "Behaviorists have been careful to make sure the reward recipients understand that reward depends on novel performance" (p. 124). O'Hara & Sternberg (2001) specifically examined the effects of directives to "be creative." Precise instructions to be creative, practical, or analytical resulted in college students demonstrating higher levels of performance in whichever of the three areas had been targeted. These findings suggest that results of the behaviorist studies demonstrate positive effects of instructions, rather than positive effects of expected rewards, on creativity. Other experimental research also calls into question the purported ease of enhancing creativity through use of reward (Joussemet & Koestner 1999).

Despite results such as these, inconsistent with the assertion that expected rewards generally foster creativity, the debate has continued through much of the past decade. Perhaps as research programs and the theories they generate become increasingly nuanced, this rift between the two philosophical camps may narrow. In the meantime, researchers and theorists studying the social psychology of creativity have made good progress in expanding their investigative paradigms and theoretical perspectives. No longer do the variables of interest include only expected reward or other extrinsic motivators and constraints. Rather, they have expanded to include a wide range of social influences and processes. In addition, theoretical perspectives have broadened far beyond those of social and personality psychology. For example, Mouchiroud & Lubart (2002) studied the development of social creativity (original solutions to interpersonal problems) in children, and Perry-Smith (2006) studied the effects of social networks on creativity in an organizational setting.

Social Environment: Organizations

Scholars of organizations, many of whom are trained research psychologists, have increasingly turned their attention to creativity in the workplace. In the concentric circle rubric presented at the beginning of this review, the study of organizational creativity falls in the "social environment" circle. Although much research in this arena does focus on the work environment, a meaningful proportion of this literature considers more microscopic levels, including individual-difference studies and even some physiological studies. In recent years, a number of good reviews of this literature have been published, including those by prominent organizational creativity scholars Jennifer George, Christina Shalley, Jing Zhou, and Greg Oldham (George 2007, Shalley et al. 2004, Shalley & Zhou 2008). In addition, two recent edited volumes address organizational creativity (Thompson & Choi 2006, Zhou & Shalley 2008).

To some extent, the organizational creativity literature mirrors the creativity literature in general psychology. However, the greatest volume of work—and the most significant work in terms of application—concerns the social psychology of creativity. This work focuses primarily on the impact of the social environment or the work environment (generally as created by leaders or managers) on the creativity of individuals, groups, or entire organizations. Some research has even examined support for work creativity outside of the workplace.

Social Behaviors Supporting Creativity. A few studies have investigated particular behaviors of other people that support (or undermine) individuals' creativity in organizations. Team leader behavior was examined in microscopic detail in a longitudinal field study by Amabile and colleagues (2004). This study first established that perceived team leader support positively related to the peer-rated creativity of 211 individuals working on creative projects in seven companies. Qualitative analyses of the individuals' daily work diaries over several weeks revealed both positive and negative predictors of perceived leader support, in terms of specific leader behaviors. Positive predictors included showing support for the person's actions or decisions, providing constructive feedback on the work, and recognizing good performance. Negative predictors included checking on assigned work too frequently, failing to disseminate needed information, and avoiding solving problems.

The valuing of creative work is something that leaders of an organization do (or do not) communicate. Farmer and colleagues (2003) found that individuals' creativity at work was highest when they both perceived themselves as creative employees and perceived their organizations as valuing creative work. Creativity at work can even be supported by the behavior of important others outside of work. Madjar and colleagues (2002) found that the creative performance of employees was significantly related to support for creativity from both work (supervisors/coworkers) and nonwork (family/friends) sources. Positive mood mediated these relations.

Specific Aspects of the Work Environment. Of all specific aspects of the work environment, time pressure has perhaps received the most research attention recently from organizational psychologists studying creativity. Studies searching for simple linear relations have generally found no relation or weak negative relations (Amabile et al. 1996, 2002), indicating that, overall, time pressure may be detrimental to creativity at work. However, it appears that this is an oversimplification. Indeed, the influence of time pressure may be one of the most complex in the organizational creativity literature. For one thing, traits may play a role in people's response to time pressure at work, as demonstrated in an experiment by Madjar & Oldham (2006). Polychronicity is an individual-difference variable: the number of tasks with which an individual prefers to be involved at the same time. Participants exhibited higher creativity in the task condition that matched their individual preference, and perceived time pressure mediated these effects. Individuals perceived lower time pressure in conditions that matched their preference, which then contributed to higher levels of creativity.

Baer & Oldham (2006) showed that the level of time pressure matters, in a somewhat complicated person-by-situation interaction. They discovered an inverted-U relation between time pressure and creativity for employees who scored high on the personality trait of openness to experience while simultaneously receiving support for creativity. This inverted-U relation was essentially replicated by Ohly and coauthors (2006), who controlled for supervisory support for creativity but did not assess personality. Amabile and coauthors (2002) carried out a longitudinal field study suggesting that daily workplace creativity may depend on both the level and the type of time pressure. In general, the effects of time pressure on creativity were negative. However, the type of time pressure was important. Most high-time-pressure days were marked by fragmentation in the work and lack of focus on single important problems. But if individuals were protected from distractions and fragmentation under high time pressure, and if they believed in the importance of the problem they were trying to solve, creativity was enhanced. In fact, on such (relatively rare) high-time-pressure days, creativity could be as high as on low/moderate-time-pressure days.

Psychological safety, an environmental condition in which people believe that others in their group will respond positively when they speak up about concerns, report mistakes, or propose new ideas, is another work environment aspect that can be important in organizational creativity. Edmondson & Mogelof (2006) proposed that psychological safety is crucial for creativity in organizations because creativity involves so much risk-taking, experimentation, and frequent failure. In a study using data collected at three points in time from teams working on complex projects, these researchers found that individual-level and team-level variables at a particular time predicted psychological safety at a later time, but that team-level variables accounted for considerably more variance. Positive interactions within the team and with the team leader were important, as was clarity of goals for the project (particularly toward the end of the project). Another study, involving 43 new product teams composed of diverse functions (e.g., research and development, marketing, and manufacturing), found that the effect of task disagreement on team innovativeness depended on how free members felt to express task-related doubts and how collaboratively or contentiously these doubts were expressed (Lovelace et al. 2001). Gibson & Gibbs (2006) found that a psychologically safe communication climate can help mitigate several challenges faced by virtual teams attempting to produce innovative outcomes.

Autonomy in the work, leading employees to feel a degree of empowerment, has long been postulated as an important feature of the work environment for fostering creativity. The theoretical argument is that to the extent that employees feel a degree of ownership in and control over their work, they will be more intrinsically motivated and thus more likely to fully engage their cognitive processes in solving problems in the work. Alge and colleagues (2006), in two studies, found a connection between empowerment and creativity: Organizations that respect the privacy of employees' personal information enhance employee perceptions of empowerment, which in turn enhances employee creativity.

Feedback, monitoring of work, and evaluation of work are closely related and can have quite different effects on creativity depending on how they are delivered. In a chapter reviewing a great deal of empirical research, Zhou (2008) presented a summary of how feedback can affect creativity. She suggested that supervisors can affect employee creativity positively by (a) giving positive feedback whenever possible; (b) delivering both positive and negative feedback in an informational style (with the supervisor suggesting that the goal of the feedback is not to control the employee, but instead to help the employee develop creative capabilities and performance); (c) adopting a developmental orientation when giving feedback—giving employees valuable information that will enable them to learn, develop, and make improvements on the job, implying that they can constantly get better; and (d) focusing feedback on the task, not the person.

Organizational creativity scholars have also studied the environmental condition of goal setting. General studies of the work environment (e.g., Amabile et al. 1996) suggest that clear overall goals for work projects support creativity. However, Shalley has carried out a systematic research program to examine the effects of setting specific creativity goals—a topic that others have recently investigated as well. In a review chapter on supervisory goal-setting research, Shalley (2008) suggested, "if managers would like their employees to be more creative, they need to find ways to encourage employees to undertake creative activities. A major way to do this is by creating role expectations either by setting goals or making creative activity a job requirement. Further, organizations need to make sure that the work context supports these goals or job requirements..." (p. 160).

Although goal setting might be viewed as a kind of constraint on creativity, other researchers have taken up the question of constraints much more directly, by studying the effects of external demands on workplace creativity. In a review chapter, West and coauthors (2005) defined external demands on a work group as crises or severe constraints that come from the external environment within the organization or the wider society and impinge on the individual or team attempting to do creative or innovative work. These authors, like most in the field, see creativity as the generation of new and useful ideas, with innovation being the implementation of creative ideas. They suggest that because creativity requires a nonconstrained, undemanding environment, external demands have a negative impact on group creativity. However, because external demands can positively influence group processes such as cohesion, task focus, and clarity of team objectives, demands can have a positive impact on group innovation. Thus, it is important for managers to understand the stage of the creativity-innovation process in considering the imposition of demands on a team.

In summary, it appears that constraints and pressures in the work environment (except for one rare form of time pressure) are detrimental to creativity, whereas organization-wide supports, psychological safety, sufficient time, autonomy, developmental feedback, and creativity goals are facilitative.

Social Environment: Schools

In addition to the workplace, the other obvious setting for the real-world application of the social psychology of creativity literature is the classroom. Although creative performance may not be as central or universal a goal in schools as it is in the business world, the development of student creativity is crucial for economic, scientific, social, and artistic/cultural advancement. It is essential that we come to a far deeper understanding of how teaching techniques, teacher behavior, and social relationships in schools affect the motivation and creativity of students. Sternberg (2008) offered a thoughtful paper arguing for the application of psychological theories to educational practice, yet a review of the recent educational literature reveals surprisingly few direct investigations of creativity in the classroom. Plucker and colleagues (2004) reviewed the literature and concluded that a preponderance of myths and stereotypes about creativity as well as a failure to precisely define creativity has served to strangle most

research efforts on the part of educators. A recent paper by Sawyer (2006) painted a similarly bleak picture. Sawyer contended that American educational researchers have paid very little scholarly attention to the fact that the majority of the world's most developed countries, including the United States, have now made a shift from an industrial economy to an economy that is knowledge based. According to Sawyer (2006), many features of today's schools have become obsolete—to the point that the U.S. educational system needs to be entirely restructured around disciplined improvisational group processes and creative collaboration. Essential to this restructuring will be carefully controlled empirical research investigations designed to help educators determine which educational innovations actually promote student creativity and why.

How are researchers to carry out such investigations? If the results warrant it, how are they to convince policy makers that the time has come for fundamental school change? How are they to convince educators that the promotion of student creativity is a desirable goal? A study carried out by Scott (1999) investigated attitudes held by elementary school teachers and college students about creative children. Results showed that teachers were significantly more likely than college students to rate creative children as more disruptive than their more "average" peers. In fact, this bias against unique answers or problem solutions was even found in a sample of prospective teachers who had yet to head up their own classroom (Beghetto 2007). In U.S. schools, creativity is not always seen as a desirable trait. Yet at least a small body of research into the psychology of educational creativity exists.

Ruscio & Amabile (1999) explored the impact of two different instructional approaches on the creative problem solving of college students. Study participants completed a novel structure-building task after receiving algorithmic instruction, heuristic instruction, or no instruction. Type of instruction influenced students' perceptions of the task, their behavior during the task, and their final solution to the

Innovation: the successful implementation of creative ideas

structure problem. Study participants receiving algorithmic instruction showed greater confidence and speed, but they were significantly less likely than students receiving heuristic instruction to engage in exploratory behavior or to produce final products that deviated from the sample structure.

Researchers in Great Britain have recently contributed a small number of important empirical investigations of creativity in the classroom. Focusing on the creativity of young students, Cremin and collaborators (2006) reported findings of a 12-month-long investigation of children's "possibility thinking" and their teachers' pedagogical practices that foster this important component of creative behavior. In another longitudinal study, Claxton et al. (2005) followed the developmental trends in creativity from the period of the so-called fourth-grade slump through the ninth-grade year. And in a related paper, Claxton and colleagues (2006) made the argument that British schools must move from "allowing" creativity to *developing* creativity in the classroom. In support of this position, these researchers offered practical examples from action research projects designed to develop "habits of mind" conducive to creativity.

The fact that, in recent years, relatively few investigators and theorists in the industrialized nations of the West have chosen to explore creativity in the classroom stands in striking contrast to the research situation in other parts of the world. In fact, a review of the literature reveals a virtual explosion of interest in this area—especially in Asia. Consider the example of Singapore. For more than 20 years, the nation of Singapore has made the fostering of creativity in the schools a top priority (see Tan & Law 2000). In the past decade, Tan and colleagues have conducted many empirical investigations of creativity in the classrooms of Singapore. In a 2000 paper, Tan explored students' and teachers' perceptions of activities useful for fostering creativity and found that as students grow older, their views begin to more closely reflect those of their teachers; these data were then supplemented with a second paper

(Tan & Law 2002). Tan & Rasidir (2006) investigated children's views of the behaviors they believe make for a creative teacher. Also focused on students in Singapore was an empirical investigation carried out by Majid and colleagues (2003). This study contrasted the efficacy of the Internet and SCAMPER (Eberle 1997), a well-known technique based on the presentation of directed questions, in promoting the creativity of primary school children. Results revealed that students who used Internet resources targeting children's writing skills demonstrated improvement in their creative writing in terms of both fluency and elaboration. Children using SCAMPER did not show any obvious improvements.

Two studies considered Japanese educational approaches and their possible impact on creativity. DeCoker (2000) looked at U.S. education through the eyes of Japanese teachers. Twenty-four Japanese teachers visited a U.S. school for one month. Their unanimous conclusion was that schools in America were far stricter, discipline was far more punitive, and classrooms were far more rule bound, than in Japan. When it came to creativity in these schools, these visitors worried most about the strict grading policies in force at the high school level. In sum, DeCoker (2000) concluded that although the majority of Americans assume that Japanese schools are strict (and that American schools are undisciplined), in the eyes of these visitors, the American system runs the risk of being far too rigid, making student (and teacher) creativity an impossibility.

The research, theory, and applied work coming out of Mainland China and Hong Kong have been especially prolific and illuminating. Hongli (2004) asked the provocative question of why no Nobel Prize winner has ever been the product of the Chinese educational system and extracted from the literature a number of suggested strategies for nurturing the creativity of Chinese primary and middle school students. Huang and collaborators (2005) explored the implicit theories of creativity held by Chinese teachers and found that those attitudes played an important role in how teachers worked to develop and train creative behavior in their students. Similarly, Chan & Chan (1999) examined the implicit theories held by Hong Kong teachers about the characteristics of creative and uncreative students. Like the results reported in similar U.S. studies, this investigation indicated that Chinese teachers regard some characteristics of creative students as socially undesirable. A number of other researchers in the Chinese literature have examined preferred thinking styles in teaching and their links to creativity in the schools (e.g., Zhang 2006).

With their focus on 27 primary classrooms and their teachers in Hong Kong, Forrester & Hui (2007) utilized a variety of creativity measures developed in the West. These included a classroom observation form, a measure of classroom climate, an index of behaviors used by teachers to foster creative behavior, and a creative personality scale. Also employed was a creativity test for students that had been developed in China. Findings lent support to existing system and componential theories involving both flow and the impact of environmental factors on student motivation and creative behavior. Finally, Dineen & Niu (2008) explored the effectiveness of Western creative teaching methods in China. This quasi-field experiment delivered the standard Chinese undergraduate graphic design curriculum to one class of Chinese students within the framework of a creative pedagogic model developed in the United Kingdom. Another class received the standard Chinese graphic design education. Visual products produced by the students from the two classes both before and during the intervention were evaluated for overall creativity, originality, design quality, and experimental range. Levels of effort, enjoyment, motivation, and confidence in experimentation were also assessed. Both quantitative and qualitative data showed that creative methods developed in the United Kingdom were highly effective in encouraging creativity and related constructs, including intrinsic motivation, among Chinese university students.

This proliferation of school-based research in Asia and beyond raises a variety of significant questions. In particular is the issue of why more U.S. researchers and theorists do not appear to share their non-U.S. colleagues' current interest in and concerns about the promotion of student creativity. One possibility is that with America's newfound emphasis on "high-stakes testing" and other manifestations of the accountability movement has come a general de-emphasis on creative behavior in favor of the more easily quantified and assessed mastery of reading, writing, and arithmetic. Without a doubt, this change in focus has made it far more difficult for U.S. researchers to secure funding for the study of creativity in the schools. An investigation of creative behavior in schools in China (Niu & Sternberg 2003) indicated that high-stakes educational testing coupled with societal values and school pedagogic approaches has for some time impaired the creativity of students of that nation. But now, many Asian educators, policy-makers, and researchers are calling for a shift of emphasis away from testing and toward the promotion of more open-ended, creativity-boosting teaching techniques.

One concern beginning to surface in the literature involves the fact that many non-Western investigators employ Western-based measures and paradigms when investigating the creativity of persons living, working, and learning in cultures fundamentally different from those of the West. As Kim (2005) cautioned, educational systems are formed based on cultural expectations and ideologies. Of course, the same can be said of workplace environments and any other milieus where creative behavior might occur. It is questionable to expect that research approaches and tools developed in one cultural context will serve investigators in another culture.

Social Environment: Culture

Does it make sense to presume that the models, paradigms, theories, and measures constructed by scholars in the Western world can adequately explain or tap the creativity of persons living in cultures very different from those of the United

States, Canada, and Western Europe? For example, can the intrinsic motivation principle of creativity (Amabile 1996) be assumed to apply to persons in Asia? Can the Consensual Assessment Technique (Amabile 1982, Hennessey & Amabile 1999) be expected to yield reliable and valid assessments of product creativity across cultures? Baer (2003) argued convincingly that cross-cultural creativity research can teach us a great deal both about creativity and about different cultures. Yet the potential pitfalls and challenges are many. Concrete examples of some of these difficulties come from Chiu (2007) and Leung (2007), who presented thoughtful and complementary treatises on the challenges faced by those attempting to construct and promote an "Asian social psychology." And in an especially comprehensive review, Lehman et al. (2004) reminded us that psychological processes influence culture, culture influences psychological processes, individuals' thoughts and actions have the potential to influence cultural norms, and these cultural norms and practices influence the thoughts and actions of individuals.

Another important demonstration of the complexity of cross-cultural considerations came from Rudowicz (2003), who made the case that creative expression is a universally human phenomenon. Yet despite this universality, Rudowicz argued that methodological and conceptual problems loom large in cross-cultural investigations. The effects of culture on creativity are complex and highly interactive, and include historical, societal, and individual cross-cultural factors. One obvious concern faced by investigators wishing to explore creativity cross-culturally is whether definitions and operationalizations of creativity coming from one culture can be validly applied in another potentially very different culture. In studying implicit theories of creativity across cultures, Paletz & Peng (2008) found that although Japanese, Chinese, and American university students all considered novelty to be important in evaluating creativity, appropriateness was more important for the Americans and Japanese than for the Chinese. Runco and collaborators (2002)

also investigated implicit theories of creativity across cultures, examining teachers' and parents' ideas about children's creativity in the United States and India. Across cultures, significant differences emerged for intellectual and attitudinal clusters of trait adjectives. Such studies support the contention that implicit theories are influenced by cultural traditions and expectations.

Probably no cross-cultural contrast has received more research attention than the collectivist/individualistic distinction. In one investigation involving this dichotomy, Ng (2003) tested a theoretical model positing cultural individualism/collectivism as the antecedent variable, independent and interdependent self-construals as the mediating variables, and creative and conforming behaviors as the outcome variables. Survey responses of white undergraduates from Australia (individualistic orientation) and Chinese undergraduates from Singapore (collectivist orientation) were compared, and SEM results provided strong overall support for this theoretical model and the proposed relation between individualism and creativity (as well as collectivism and more conforming, less creative behavior). A subsequent paper (Ng 2005) then expanded on these findings with the demonstration of especially high indices of "fit." Zha and colleagues (2006) also explored individualism/collectivism and the impact of culture on creative potential. In this study comparing highly educated American and Chinese adults, Americans displayed significantly higher scores on a measure of creative potential. Chinese study participants showed significantly higher skill mastery in mathematics; as expected, Americans showed greater individualism, whereas the Chinese were more collectivistic.

Finally, although much of the literature in this area has been focused on cross-cultural comparisons of creative behavior, some researchers have chosen to explore directly the premise that multicultural experience fosters creativity. Leung et al. (2008) empirically demonstrated that exposure to multiple cultures can, in and of itself, enhance creative behavior. More specifically, this investigation showed that extensiveness of multicultural experience was positively related to both creative performance and thought processes considered conducive to creative behavior.

CONCLUSION: TAKING A SYSTEMS PERSPECTIVE

Clearly, the great variety of research questions and investigative approaches outlined in this review can significantly broaden our understanding of the phenomenon of creativity in many important ways. Yet no single construct, no one investigative focus, can adequately account for the emergence of creative behavior. Like many students of psychology before them, contemporary creativity researchers and theorists are faced with the daunting task of disentangling the interplay between nature and nurture. Neurological events in the brain, behavioral manifestations of mental illness, or individual differences in personality must be studied not in isolation but in conjunction with the particular environment in which an individual's physical, intellectual, and social development has taken place. More than two decades ago, Amabile (1983, 1996) offered a three-pronged Componential Model of Creativity incorporating domain skills, creativity skills, and task motivation influenced by the social environment; Sternberg's (1988) Triarchic Model of Intelligence also got us thinking in threes. The most recent decade brought few new attempts to conceptualize creativity on a broad scale.

An evolutionary approach based on the work of Charles Darwin, first conceptualized by Campbell (1960) and later modified and elaborated by Simonton (1999, 2007), has continued to garner a great deal of attention. Drawing on Campbell's blind-variation-and-selective-retention theory of creativity, Simonton made the case that the Darwinian model might actually subsume all other theories of creativity as special cases of a larger evolutionary framework. Perhaps not surprisingly, comments on Simonton's call for creativity

theorists to adopt a Darwinian perspective came swiftly. Feist (1999) argued that the application of evolutionary theory to creativity must be taken as metaphorical rather than literal. Gardner (1999) countered with the caution that true blind variation would imply that the creator, consciously or unconsciously, tries out every conceivable approach or idea in the process of finding an optimal solution or point of completion for a piece of work. Gabora (2007) and Dasgupta (2004) published particularly negative reviews of Simonton's approach and offered a number of counter examples demonstrating the essential role played by expertise. Seeking to strike a balance between these two frameworks, Weisberg & Hass (2007) suggested that "blindness" in the context of the creative process could be defined as the individual's inability to predict the outcome of his or her efforts and ended with the conclusion that although blindness may be a component of creativity, we need not assume that creative behavior must include free-association processes.

Another recent attempt at constructing a comprehensive model of creativity was also based on the application of well-established theory to the specific case of creative behavior. Over the past decade, a small group of researchers has repeatedly made the argument that the frameworks originated by Jean Piaget and Lev Vygotsky to explain cognitive development in children could also be fruitfully applied to the creative process. Ayman-Nolley (1999) challenged the assumption that Piaget failed to address the phenomenon of creativity in his exploration of the development of the mind and argued that the mechanisms of assimilation and accommodation can readily be applied to creative behavior. Vonèche (2003) applied Piaget's notions of invariance and transformations to the creative process, and J. Kim (2006) reminded researchers and theorists that Piaget had suggested reflective abstraction as the mechanism for creativity. In this same paper, Kim also explored the work of Vygotsky on the interrelation between imagination and creativity; Lindqvist (2003) argued that Vygotsky's notion of the "zone of proximal development" might help explain how creative ideas or problem solutions take shape.

J.P. Guilford's research on creativity, particularly his work on creative problem solving, also resurfaced to garner some recent attention. Guilford is perhaps best remembered for his contention that divergent thinking plays a central role in creative thought. Reviewing Guilford's (1967) structure of intellect model, Mumford (2001) argued for a return to efforts to take a broad, comprehensive approach to the study of creativity. Richards (2001) echoed this call and made a strong case for the infusion of chaos theory into interpretations of Guilford's work. More specifically, Richards argued that chaos theory can provide models and metaphors for rapid, holistic nonlinear creative processes.

Interestingly, theories of organizational creativity have tended to include more levels of analysis than creativity theories within psychology. This may be because organizational scholars converge from the disciplines of economics, sociology, organizational behavior, and others, as well as psychology. The two most frequently cited organizational creativity theories include factors in the individual and the organization (Amabile 1988, 1996) or the individual, group, and organization (Woodman et al. 1993), as well as interactions between these levels. Other,

more recent theories are similarly multilevel (Drazin et al. 1999, Ford 1996, Mumford 2000, Unsworth 2001). However, even in this realm, theories lack a truly systemic, dynamic quality.

Having seen the scholarly rigor underlying much of the contemporary literature on the psychology of creativity, we are heartened by the advances in knowledge made in recent years. However, although many theorists and researchers have broadened our perspective on creativity, their efforts do not extend far enough. Our review moves us to sound a cautionary note. The staggering array of disciplinary approaches to understanding creativity can prove to be an advantage, but only if researchers and theorists work together and understand the discoveries that are being made across creative domains and analytical levels. Otherwise, the mysteries may deepen. Only by using multiple lenses simultaneously, looking across levels, and thinking about creativity systematically, will we be able to unlock and use its secrets. What we need now are all-encompassing systems theories of creativity designed to tie together and make sense of the diversity of perspectives found in the literature—from the innermost neurological level to the outermost cultural level.

SUMMARY POINTS

1. The creativity literature has seen substantial growth in volume and scope as well as methodological and theoretical sophistication.

2. With the growth in outlets for publication has come increasing fragmentation in creativity research.

3. Researchers and theorists in one subfield often seem unaware of work being done in another.

4. The advancement of technology, especially fMRI, coupled with increases in access to equipment for researchers have contributed to a virtual explosion of information on the "creative brain."

5. Although creativity in persons has some trait-like (stable) aspects, it is also a state subject to influence by the social environment.

6. People are most creative when they are motivated primarily by the interest, enjoyment, satisfaction, and challenge of the work itself—i.e., by intrinsic motivation.

7. Scholars of organizations, many of whom are trained research psychologists, have increasingly turned their attention to creativity in the workplace.

8. We cannot presume that the models, paradigms, theories, and measures constructed by scholars in the Western world can adequately explain or tap the creativity of persons living in cultures very different from those of the United States, Canada, and Western Europe.

9. Deeper understanding of creative behavior will require more interdisciplinary research based on a systems view of creativity that recognizes a variety of interrelated forces operating at multiple levels.

DISCLOSURE STATEMENT

The authors are not aware of any biases that might be perceived as affecting the objectivity of this review.

LITERATURE CITED

Abraham A. 2007. Can a neural system geared to bring about rapid, predictive, and efficient function explain creativity? *Creat. Res. J.* 19:19–24

Abraham A, Windmann S. 2008. Selective information processing advantages in creative cognition as a function of schizotypy. *Creat. Res. J.* 20:1–6

Ai X. 1999. Creativity and academic achievement: an investigation of gender differences. *Creat. Res. J.* 12:329–37

Alge BJ, Ballinger GA, Tangirala S, Oakley JL. 2006. Information privacy in organizations: empowering creative and extrarole performance. *J. Appl. Psychol.* 91:221–32

Amabile TM. 1982. Social psychology of creativity: a consensual assessment technique. *J. Personal. Soc. Psychol.* 43:997–1013

Amabile TM. 1983. The social psychology of creativity: a componential conceptualization. *J. Personal. Soc. Psychol.* 45:357–76

Amabile TM. 1988. A model of creativity and innovation in organizations. In *Research in Organizational Behavior*, ed. BM Staw, LL Cummings, Vol. 10, pp. 123–67. Greenwich, CT: JAI

Amabile TM. 1993. Motivational synergy: toward new conceptualizations of intrinsic and extrinsic motivation in the workplace. *Hum. Resour. Manag. Rev.* 3:185–201

Amabile TM. 1996. ***Creativity in Context.*** **Boulder, CO: Westview**

Amabile TM, Barsade SG, Mueller JS, Staw BM. 2005. Affect and creativity at work. *Admin. Sci. Q.* 50:367–403

Amabile TM, Conti R, Coon H, Lazenby J, Herron M. 1996. Assessing the work environment for creativity. *Acad. Manage. J.* 39:1154–84

Amabile TM, Hadley CN, Kramer SJ. 2002. Creativity under the gun. *Harvard Bus. Rev.* 80:52–61

Amabile TM, Hill KG, Hennessey BA, Tighe EM. 1994. The Work Preference Inventory: assessing intrinsic and extrinsic motivational orientations. *J. Personal. Soc. Psychol.* 66:950–67

Amabile TM, Mueller JS. 2008. Studying creativity, its processes, and its antecedents: an exploration of the componential theory of creativity. In Zhou & Shalley 2008, pp. 33–64

Amabile TM, Schatzel E, Moneta GB, Kramer SJ. 2004. Leader behaviors and the work environment for creativity: perceived leader support. *Leadersh. Q.* 15:5–32

Aspinwall LG. 1998. Rethinking the role of positive affect in self-regulation. *Motiv. Emot.* 22:1–32

Ayman-Nolley S. 1999. A Piagetian perspective on the dialectic process of creativity. *Creat. Res. J.* 12:267–75

Baer J. 2003. Double dividends: cross-cultural creativity studies teach us about both creativity and cultures. *Inquiry: Crit. Thinking Across Discip.* 22:37–39

Presents one of the major theories of creativity and reviews social-psychological research.

Baer J. 2008. Commentary: divergent thinking tests have problems, but this is not the solution. *Psychol. Aesthet. Creat. Arts* 2:89–92

Baer J, Kaufman JC, Gentile CA. 2004. Extension of the Consensual Assessment Technique to nonparallel creative products. *Creat. Res. J.* 16:113–17

Baer M, Oldham GR. 2006. The curvilinear relation between experienced creative time pressure and creativity: moderating effects of openness to experience and support for creativity. *J. Appl. Psychol.* 91:963–70

Basadur M, Pringle P, Kirkland D. 2002. Crossing cultures: training effects on the divergent thinking attitudes of Spanish-speaking South American managers. *Creat. Res. J.* 14:395–408

Becker G. 2001. The association of creativity and psychopathology: its cultural-historical origins. *Creat. Res. J.* 13:45–53

Beghetto RA. 2007. Does creativity have a place in classroom discussions? Prospective teachers' response preferences. *Thinking Skills Creat.* 2:1–9

Beghetto RA, Kaufman JC. 2007. Toward a broader conception of creativity: a case for "mini-c" creativity. *Psychol. Aesthet. Creat. Arts* 1:73–79

Benedek M, Fink A, Neubauer AC. 2006. Enhancement of ideational fluency by means of computer-based training. *Creat. Res. J.* 18:317–28

Bowden EM, Jung-Beeman M. 1998. Getting the right idea: semantic activation in the right hemisphere may help solve insight problems. *Psychol. Sci.* 9:435–40

Bowden EM, Jung-Beeman M. 2003. Aha! Insight experience correlates with solution activation in the right hemisphere. *Psychon. Bull. Rev.* 10:730–37

Brophy DR. 1998a. Understanding, measuring, and enhancing collective creative problem-solving efforts. *Creat. Res. J.* 11:199–229

Brophy DR. 1998b. Understanding, measuring, and enhancing individual creative problem-solving efforts. *Creat. Res. J.* 11:123–50

Brophy DR. 2006. A comparison of individual and group efforts to creatively solve contrasting types of problems. *Creat. Res. J.* 18:293–315

Brown J. 2007. On Vandervert et al. "Working memory cerebellum, and creativity." *Creat. Res. J.* 19:25–29

Brown VR, Paulus PB. 2002. Making group brainstorming more effective: recommendations from an associative memory perspective. *Curr. Dir. Psychol. Sci.* 11:208–12

Cameron J, Pierce WD. 1994. Reinforcement, reward, and intrinsic motivation: a meta-analysis. *Rev. Educ. Res.* 64:363–423

Campbell DT. 1960. Blind variation and selective retentions in creative thought as in other knowledge processes. *Psychol. Rev.* 67:380–400

Carson SH, Peterson JB, Higgins DM. 2003. Decreased latent inhibition is associated with increased creative achievement in high-functioning individuals. *J. Personal. Soc. Psychol.* 85:499–506

Chan DW, Chan L-K. 1999. Implicit theories of creativity: teachers' perception of student characteristics in Hong Kong. *Creat. Res. J.* 12:185–95

Chávez-Eakle RA, del Carmen LM, Cruz-Fuentes C. 2006. Personality: a possible bridge between creativity and psychopathology? *Creat. Res. J.* 18:27–38

Cheung PC, Lau S, Chan DW, Wu WYH. 2004. Creative potential of school children in Hong Kong: norms of the Wallach-Kogan Creativity Tests and their implications. *Creat. Res. J.* 16:69–78

Chiu C. 2007. How can Asian social psychology succeed globally? *Asian J. Soc. Psychol.* 10:41–44

Clapham MM. 2001. The effects of affect manipulation and information exposure on divergent thinking. *Creat. Res. J.* 13:335–50

Claxton AF, Pannells TC, Rhoads PA. 2005. Developmental trends in the creativity of school-age children. *Creat. Res. J.* 17:327–35

Claxton G, Edwards L, Scale-Constantinou V. 2006. Cultivating creative mentalities: a framework for education. *Thinking Skills Creat.* 1:57–61

Conti R, Collins MA, Picariello ML. 2001. The impact of competition on intrinsic motivation and creativity: considering gender, gender segregation and gender role orientation. *Personal. Individ. Differ.* 31:1273–89

Cox AJ, Leon JL. 1999. Negative schizotypal traits in the relation of creativity to psychopathology. *Creat. Res. J.* 12:25–36

Cramond B, Matthews-Morgan J, Torrance EP, Zuo L. 1999. Why should the Torrance Tests of Creative Thinking be used to access creativity? *Korean J. Probl. Solv.* 9:77–101

Cremin T, Burnard P, Craft A. 2006. Pedagogy and possibility thinking in the early years. *Thinking Skills Creat.* 1:108–19

Dasgupta S. 2004. Is creativity a Darwinian process? *Creat. Res. J.* 16:403–13

De Dreu CKW, Baas M, Nijstad BA. 2008. Hedonic tone and activation level in the mood-creativity link: toward a dual pathway to creativity model. *J. Personal. Soc. Psychol.* 94:739–56

Deci EL, Ryan RM, eds. 2002. *Handbook of Self-Determination Research*. Rochester, NY: Univ. Rochester Press

DeCoker G. 2000. Looking at U.S. education through the eyes of Japanese teachers. *Phi Delta Kappan* 81:780–81

Dewett T. 2007. Linking intrinsic motivation, risk taking, and employee creativity in an R&D environment. *R&D Manag.* 37:197–208

Dineen R, Niu W. 2008. The effectiveness of western creative teaching methods in China: an action research project. *Psychol. Aesthet. Creat. Arts* 2:42–52

Dow GT, Mayer RE. 2004. Teaching students to solve insight problems: evidence for domain specificity in creativity training. *Creat. Res. J.* 16:389–402

Drazin R, Glynn MA, Kazanjian RK. 1999. Multilevel theorizing about creativity in organizations: a sense-making perspective. *Acad. Manage. Rev.* 24:286–307

Eberle B. 1997. *Scamper: Creative Games and Activities for Imagination Development*. Austin, TX: Prufrock

Edmondson AC, Mogelof JP. 2006. Explaining psychological safety in innovation teams: organizational culture, team dynamics, or personality? In *Creativity and Innovation in Organizational Teams*, ed. LL Thompson, H-S Choi, pp. 109–36. New York: Erlbaum

Eisenberger R, Cameron J. 1996. Detrimental effects of reward: reality or myth? *Am. Psychol.* **51:1153–66**

Eisenberger R, Cameron J. 1998. Reward, intrinsic interest, and creativity: new findings. *Am. Psychol.* 53:676–79

Eisenberger R, Selbst M. 1994. Does reward increase or decrease creativity? *J. Personal. Soc. Psychol.* 66:1116–27

Eisenberger R, Shanock L. 2003. Rewards, intrinsic motivation, and creativity: a case study of conceptual and methodological isolation. *Creat. Res. J.* 15:121–30

Epstein R, Schmidt SM, Warfel R. 2008. Measuring and training creativity competencies: validation of a new test. *Creat. Res. J.* 20:7–12

Farmer SM, Tierney P, Kung-McIntyre K. 2003. Employee creativity in Taiwan: an application of role identity theory. *Acad. Manage. J.* 46:618–30

Feist GJ. 1998. A meta-analysis of personality in scientific and artistic creativity. *Personal. Soc. Psychol. Rev.* 2:290–309

Feist GJ. 1999. Is the theory of evolution winning the battle of the survival of the fittest in the social sciences? *Psychol. Inq.* 10:334–38

Feist GJ, Barron FX. 2003. Predicting creativity from early to late adulthood: intellect, potential, and personality. *J. Res. Personal.* 37:62–88

Ford CM. 1996. A theory of individual creativity in multiple social domains. *Acad. Manage. Rev.* 21:1112–34

Forrester V, Hui A. 2007. Creativity in the Hong Kong classroom: what is the contextual practice? *Thinking Skills Creat.* 2:30–38

Friedman RS, Förster J, Denzler M. 2007. Interactive effects of mood and task framing on creative generation. *Creat. Res. J.* 19:141–62

Fryer M. 2006. Making a difference: a tribute to E. Paul Torrance from the United Kingdom. *Creat. Res. J.* 18:121–28

Gabora L. 2007. Why the creative process is not Darwinian: comment on "The creative process in Picasso's Guernica sketches: monotonic improvements versus nonmonotonic variants." *Creat. Res. J.* 19:361–65

Garaigordobil M. 2006. Intervention in creativity with children aged 10 and 11 years: impact of a play program on verbal and graphic-figural creativity. *Creat. Res. J.* 18:329–45

Gardner H. 1999. Was Darwin's creativity Darwinian? *Psychol. Inq.* 10:338–40

George JM. 2007. Chapter 9: creativity in organizations. *Acad. Manage. Ann.* **1:439–77**

Presents the controversial view that rewards undermine intrinsic motivation and creativity only under very limited conditions.

Reviews theory and research on organizational creativity, focusing on psychological aspects.

George JM, Zhou J. 2002. Understanding when bad moods foster creativity and good ones don't: the role of context and clarity of feelings. *J. Appl. Psychol.* 87:687–97

George JM, Zhou J. 2007. Dual tuning in a supportive context: joint contributions of positive mood, negative mood, and supervisory behaviors to employee creativity. *Acad. Manage. J.* 50:605–22

Ghadirian AM, Gregoire P, Kosmidis H. 2001. Creativity and the evolution of psychopathologies. *Creat. Res. J.* 13:145–48

Gibson CB, Gibbs JL. 2006. Unpacking the concept of virtuality: the effects of geographic dispersion, electronic dependence, dynamic structure, and national diversity on team innovation. *Admin. Sci. Q.* 51:451–95

Glück J, Ernst R, Unger F. 2002. How creatives define creativity: Definitions reflect different types of creativity. *Creat. Res. J.* 14:55–67

Groborz M, Necka E. 2003. Creativity and cognitive control: explorations of generation and evaluation skills. *Creat. Res. J.* 15:183–97

Guilford JP. 1967. *The Nature of Human Intelligence*. New York: McGraw-Hill

Hargadon AB, Bechky BA. 2006. When collections of creatives become creative collectives: a field study of problem solving at work. *Organ. Sci.* 17:484–500

Helson R, Pals JL. 2000. Creative potential, creative achievement, and personal growth. *J. Personal.* 68:1–27

Helson R, Srivastava S. 2002. Creative and wise people: similarities, differences and how they develop. *Personal. Soc. Psychol. Bull.* 28:1430–40

Hennessey BA. 2003. The social psychology of creativity. *Scand. J. Educ. Res.* 47:253–71

Hennessey BA. 2004. *Developing Creativity in Gifted Children: The Central Importance of Motivation and Classroom Climate*. Storrs, CT: Natl. Res. Cent. Gifted Talented

Hennessey BA, Amabile TM. 1998. Reality, intrinsic motivation, and creativity. *Am. Psychol.* 53:674–75

Hennessey BA, Amabile TM. 1999. Consensual assessment. In *Encyclopedia of Creativity*, ed. M Runco, S Pritzker, pp. 34–36. New York: Academic

Hongli W. 2004. On developing creativity in primary and middle school students. *Psychol. Sci. (China)* 27:383–85

Huang S, Lin C, Wang Y. 2005. A review on implicit theories of teachers' creativity. *Psychol. Sci. (China)* 28:1243–45

Isen AM. 2000. Positive affect and decision making. In *Handbook of Emotions*, ed. M Lewis, J Haviland-Jones, pp. 417–35. New York: Guildford

Isen AM, Reeve J. 2005. The influence of positive affect on intrinsic and extrinsic motivation: facilitating enjoyment of play, responsible work behavior, and self-control. *Motiv. Emot.* 29:297–325

James K, Asmus C. 2001. Personality, cognitive skills, and creativity in different life domains. *Creat. Res. J.* 13:149–59

Jiliang S, Baoguo S. 2007. Effects of gender and types of materials on creativity. *Psychol. Sci. (China)* 30:285–88

Joussemet M, Koestner R. 1999. Effect of expected rewards on children's creativity. *Creat. Res. J.* 12:231–39

Jung-Beeman MJ, Bowden EM. 2000. The right hemisphere maintains solution-related activation for yet-to-be-solved problems. *Mem. Cogn.* 28:1231–41

Kashdan TB, Fincham FD. 2002. Facilitating creativity by regulating curiosity. Comment. *Am. Psychol.* 57:373–74

Kaufman JC. 2002. Creativity and confidence: price of achievement? Comment. *Am. Psychol.* 57:375–76

Kaufman JC, Baer J. 2002. Could Steven Spielberg manage the Yankees? Creative thinking in different domains. *Korean J. Probl. Solv.* 12:5–14

Kaufman JC, Baer J. 2006. An introduction to the special issue: a tribute to E. Paul Torrance. *Creat. Res. J.* 18:1–2

Kaufman JC, Lee J, Baer J, Lee S. 2007. Captions, consistency, creativity, and the consensual assessment technique: new evidence of reliability. *Thinking Skills Creat.* 2:96–106

Kaufmann G. 2003a. Expanding the mood-creativity equation. *Creat. Res. J.* 15:131–35

Kaufmann G. 2003b. What to measure? A new look at the concept of creativity. *Scand. J. Educ. Res.* 47:235–51

Kim J. 2006. Piagetian and Vygotskian perspectives on creativity. *Korean J. Probl. Solv.* 16:25–38

Kim KH. 2005. Learning from each other: creativity in East Asian and American education. *Creat. Res. J.* 17:337–47

Refutes claims of Eisenberger and colleagues and asserts that expected rewards are typically detrimental to creativity.

Kim KH. 2006. Is creativity unidimensional or multidimensional? Analyses of the Torrance Tests of Creative Thinking. *Creat. Res. J.* 18:251–59

Kounios J, Frymiare JL, Bowden EM, Fleck JI, Subramaniam K, et al. 2006. The prepared mind: neural activity prior to problem presentation predicts subsequent solution by sudden insight. *Psychol. Sci.* 17:882–90

Kray LJ, Galinsky AD, Wong EM. 2006. Thinking within the box: the relational processing style elicited by counterfactual mind-sets. *J. Personal. Soc. Psychol.* 91:33–48

Kurtzberg TR. 2005. Feeling creative, being creative: an empirical study of diversity and creativity in teams. *Creat. Res. J.* 17:51–65

Kurtzberg TR, Amabile TM. 2001. From Guilford to creative synergy: opening the black box of team-level creativity. *Creat. Res. J.* 13:285–94

Larey TS, Paulus PB. 1999. Group preference and convergent tendencies in small groups: a content analysis of group brainstorming performance. *Creat. Res. J.* 12:175–84

Lee K-H. 2002. Creative thinking in real world situations in relation to gender and education of late adolescents. *Korean J. Probl. Solv.* 12:59–70

Lee S. 2008. Commentary: reliability and validity of uniqueness scoring in creativity assessment. *Psychol. Aesthet. Creat. Arts* 2:103–8

Lee S, Lee J, Youn C-Y. 2005. A variation of CAT for measuring creativity in business products. *Korean J. Probl. Solv.* 15:143–53

Lehman DR, Chiu C-Y, Schaller M. 2004. Psychology and culture. *Annu. Rev. Psychol.* 55:689–714

Lepper MR. 1998. A whole much less than the sum of its parts. *Am. Psychol.* 53:675–76

Leung AK-Y, Maddux WW, Galinsky AD, Chiu C-Y. 2008. Multicultural experience enhances creativity: the when and how. *Am. Psychol.* 63:169–81

Leung K. 2007. Asian social psychology: achievements, threats, and opportunities. *Asian J. Soc. Psychol.* 10:8–15

Lindqvist G. 2003. Vygotsky's theory of creativity. *Creat. Res. J.* 15:245–51

Lovelace K, Shapiro DL, Weingart LR. 2001. Maximizing crossfunctional new product teams' innovativeness and constraint adherence: a conflict communications perspective. *Acad. Manage. J.* 44:479–93

Madjar N, Oldham GR. 2006. Task rotation and polychronicity: effects on individuals' creativity. *Hum. Perform.* 19:117–31

Madjar N, Oldham GR, Pratt MG. 2002. There's no place like home? The contributions of work and nonwork creativity support to employees' creative performance. *Acad. Manage. J.* 45:757–67

Majid DA, Tan A-G, Soh K-C. 2003. Enhancing children's creativity: an exploratory study on using the Internet and SCAMPER as creative writing tools. *Korean J. Probl. Solv.* 13:67–81

Mannix E, Neale M. 2005. What differences make a difference? The promise and reality of diverse teams in organizations. *Psychol. Public Int.* 6:31–55

Martin LL, Ward DW, Achee JW, Wyer RS. 1993. Mood as input: people have to interpret the motivational implications of their moods. *J. Personal. Soc. Psychol.* 64:317–26

McCrae RR. 1987. Creativity, divergent thinking, and openness to experience. *J. Personal. Soc. Psychol.* 52:1258–65

Mell JC, Howard SM, Miller BL. 2003. Art and the brain: the influence of frontotemporal dementia on an accomplished artist. *Neurology* 60:1707–10

Miller AL. 2007. Creativity and cognitive style: the relationship between field-dependence-independence, expected evaluation, and creative performance. *Psychol. Aesthet. Creat. Arts* 1:243–46

Miller BL, Boone K, Cummings JL, Read SL, Mishkin F. 2000. Functional correlates of musical and visual ability in frontotemporal dementia. *Br. J. Psychiatry* 176:458–63

Miller BL, Hou CE. 2004. Portraits of artists: emergence of visual creativity in dementia. *Arch. Neurol.* 61:842–44

Mouchiroud C, Lubart T. 2002. Social creativity: a cross-sectional study of 6- to 11-year-old children. *Int. J. Behav. Dev.* 26:60–69

Mumford MD. 2000. Managing creative people: strategies and tactics for innovation. *Hum. Resour. Manag. Rev.* 10:313–51

Mumford MD. 2001. Something old, something new: revisiting Guilford's conception of creative problem solving. *Creat. Res. J.* 13:267–76

Provides an excellent example of the "new wave" of neuro-psychological research on creativity.

Presents empirical evidence that creativity can be enhanced by social support from various sources.

Mumford MD, Antes AL. 2007. Debates about the "general" picture: cognition and creative achievement. *Creat. Res. J.* 19:367–74

Mumford MD, Marks MA, Connelly MS, Zaccaro SJ, Johnson JF. 1998. Domain-based scoring of divergent-thinking tests: validation evidence in an occupational sample. *Creat. Res. J.* 11:151–63

Mumford MD, Vessey WB, Barrett JD. 2008. Commentary. Measuring divergent thinking: Is there really one solution to the problem? *Psychol. Aesthet. Creat. Arts* 2:86–88

Nassif C, Quevillon R. 2008. The development of a preliminary creativity scale for the MMPI-2: the C scale. *Creat. Res. J.* 20:13–20

Necka E. 1999. Creativity and attention. *Polish Psychol. Bull.* 30:85–97

Nettle D. 2006. Reconciling the mutation-selection balance model with the schizotypy-creativity connection. *Behav. Brain Sci.* 29:418

Ng AK. 2003. A cultural model of creative and conforming behavior. *Creat. Res. J.* 15:223–33

Ng AK. 2005. Creativity, learning goal and self-construal: a cross-cultural investigation. *Korean J. Probl. Solv.* 15:65–80

Nijstad BA, Stroebe W. 2006. How the group affects the mind: a cognitive model of idea generation in groups. *Personal. Soc. Psychol. Rev.* 10:186–213

Niu W, Sternberg RJ. 2003. Societal and school influences on student creativity: the case of China. *Psychol. Sch.* 40:103–14

O'Hara LA, Sternberg RJ. 2001. It doesn't hurt to ask: effects of instructions to be creative, practical, or analytical on essay-writing performance and their interaction with students' thinking styles. *Creat. Res. J.* 13:197–210

Ohly S, Sonnentag S, Pluntke F. 2006. Routinization, work characteristics and their relationships with creative and proactive behaviors. *J. Organ. Behav.* 27:257–79

Osborn AF. 1953/1957/1963/1967. *Applied Imagination: Principles and Procedures of Creative Problem Solving.* New York: Scribner's

Parnes SJ. 1966. *Manual for Institutes and Programs.* Buffalo, NY: Creative Educ. Found.

Paletz SBF, Peng K. 2008. Implicit theories of creativity across cultures: novelty and appropriateness in two product domains. *J. Cross-Cult. Psychol.* 39:286–302

Paulus PB, Yang H-C. 2000. Idea generation in groups: a basis for creativity in organizations. *Organ. Behav. Hum. Decis. Process.* 82:76–87

Perrine NE, Brodersen RM. 2005. Artistic and scientific creative behavior: openness and the mediating role of interests. *Creat. Res. J.* 39:217–36

Perry-Smith JE. 2006. Social yet creative: the role of social relationships in facilitating individual creativity. *Acad. Manage. J.* 49:85–101

Peterson JB, Carson S. 2000. Latent inhibition and openness to experience in a high-achieving student population. *Personal. Individ. Differ.* 28:323–32

Peterson JB, Smith KW, Carson S. 2002. Openness and extraversion are associated with reduced latent inhibition: replication and commentary. *Personal. Individ. Differ.* 33:1137–47

Plucker JA. 1999. Is the proof in the pudding? Reanalyses of Torrance's (1958 to present) longitudinal data. *Creat. Res. J.* 12:103–14

Plucker JA, Beghetto RA, Dow GT. 2004. Why isn't creativity more important to educational psychologists? Potentials, pitfalls, and future directions in creativity research. *Educ. Psychol.* 39:83–96

Plucker JA, Runco MA. 1998. The death of creativity measurement has been greatly exaggerated: current issues, recent advances, and future directions in creativity assessment. *Roeper Rev.* 21:36–39

Polzer J, Milton LP, Swann B. 2002. Capitalizing on diversity: interpersonal congruence in small work groups. *Adm. Sci. Q.* 47:296–324

Prabhu V, Sutton C, Sauser W. 2008. Creativity and certain personality traits: understanding the mediating effect of intrinsic motivation. *Creat. Res. J.* 20:53–66

Prentky RA. 2001. Mental illness and roots of genius. *Creat. Res. J.* 13:95–104

Richards R. 2001. Millennium as opportunity: chaos, creativity, and Guilford's structure of intellect model. *Creat. Res. J.* 13:249–65

Rothenberg A. 2006. Essay: Creativity—the healthy muse. *Lancet* 368:S8–9

Demonstrates conditions for positive or negative effects of diversity on group creative outcomes.

Rudowicz E. 2003. Creativity and culture: a two-way interaction. *Scand. J. Educ. Res.* 47:273–90

Runco MA. 1999. A longitudinal study of exceptional giftedness and creativity. *Creat. Res. J.* 12:161–64

Runco MA. 2004. Creativity. *Annu. Rev. Psychol.* 55:657–87

Runco MA, Johnson DJ, Raina MK. 2002. Parents' and teachers' implicit theories of children's creativity: a cross-cultural perspective. *Creat. Res. J.* 15:427–38

Ruscio AM, Amabile TM. 1999. Effects of instructional style on problem-solving creativity. *Creat. Res. J.* 12:251–66

Ryan RM, Deci EL. 2000. Self-determination theory and the facilitation of intrinsic motivation, social development, and well-being. *Am. Psychol.* 55:68–78

Sansone C, Harackiewicz JM. 1998. "Reality" is complicated. *Am. Psychol.* 53:673–74

Sass LA. 2001. Schizophrenia, modernism, and the "creative imagination": on creativity and psychopathology. *Creat. Res. J.* 13:55–74

Sawyer RK. 2006. Education for innovation. *Thinking Skills Creat.* 1:41–48

Scott CL. 1999. Teachers' biases toward creative children. *Creat. Res. J.* 12:321–37

Scott GM, Leritz LE, Mumford MD. 2004. The effectiveness of creativity training: a quantitative review. *Creat. Res. J.* 16:361–88

Scott GM, Lonergan DC, Mumford MD. 2005. Conceptual combination: alternative knowledge structures, alternative heuristics. *Creat. Res. J.* 17:79–98

Shalley CE. 2008. Creating roles: what managers can do to establish expectations for creative performance. In Zhou & Shalley, pp. 147–64

Shalley CE, Zhou J. 2008. Organizational creativity research: a historical overview. In Zhou & Shalley 2008, pp. 3–31

Shalley CE, Zhou J, Oldham GR. 2004. Effects of personal and contextual characteristics on creativity: Where should we go from here? *J. Manag.* 30:933–58

Shin SJ, Zhou J. 2003. Transformational leadership, conservation, and creativity: evidence from Korea. *Acad. Manage. J.* 46:703–14

Silvia PJ. 2008. Creativity and intelligence revisited: a latent variable analysis of Wallach and Kogan (1965). *Creat. Res. J.* 20:34–39

Silvia PJ, Winterstein BP, Willse JT, Barona CM, Cram JT, et al. 2008. Assessing creativity with divergent thinking tasks: exploring the reliability and validity of new subjective scoring methods. *Psychol. Aesthet. Creat. Arts* 2:68–85

Simonton DK. 1999. *Origins of Genius: Darwinian Perspectives on Creativity*. New York: Oxford Univ. Press

Simonton DK. 2007. Picasso's Guernica creativity as a Darwinian process: definitions, clarifications, misconceptions, and applications. *Creat. Res. J.* 19:381–94

Sternberg RJ. 1988. *The Triarchic Mind: A New Theory of Human Intelligence*. New York: Viking

Sternberg RJ. 2001. What is the common thread of creativity? Its dialectical relation to intelligence and wisdom. *Am. Psychol.* 56:360–62

Sternberg RJ. 2008. Applying psychological theories to educational practice. *Am. Educ. Res. J.* 45:150–65

Sullivan DM, Ford CM. 2005. The relationship between novelty and value in the assessment of organizational creativity. *Korean J. Probl. Solv.* 15:117–31

Svensson N, Norlander T, Archer T. 2002. Effects of individual performance versus group performance with and without de Bono techniques for enhancing creativity. *Korean J. Probl. Solv.* 12:15–34

Taggar S. 2002. A multi-level model of creativity in intact workgroups. *Acad. Manage. J.* 45:315–31

Tan A-G. 2000. Students' versus teachers' perceptions of activities useful for fostering creativity. *Korean J. Probl. Solv.* 10:49–59

Tan A-G, Law L-C. 2000. Teaching creativity: Singapore's experiences. *Korean J. Probl. Solv.* 10:79–96

Tan A-G, Law L-C. 2002. Activities useful for fostering creativity: Singaporean children's views. *Korean J. Probl. Solv.* 12:59–74

Tan A-G, Rasidir R. 2006. An exploratory study on children's views of a creative teacher. *Korean J. Probl. Solv.* 16:17–28

One of very few recent attempts to construct a systems theory of creativity.

Synthesizes implications of creativity theories (among others) for a crucial arena: education.

Taylor A, Greve HR. 2006. Superman or the fantastic four? Knowledge combination and experience in innovative teams. *Acad. Manage. J.* 49:723–40

Thompson L, Choi HS, eds. 2006. *Creativity and Innovation in Organizational Teams.* Mahwah, NJ: Erlbaum

Torrance EP. 1966/1974. Torrance. *Tests of Creative Thinking: Norms—Technical Manual.* Lexington, MA: Ginn

Treffinger DJ, Isaksen SG. 1992. *Creative Problem Solving: An Introduction.* Sarasota, FL: Cent. Creative Learn.

Treffinger DJ, Isaksen SG, Dorval KB. 2006. *Creative Problem Solving: An Introduction.* Waco, TX: Prufrock. 4th ed.

Treffinger DJ, Selby EC. 2004. Problem solving style: a new approach to understanding and using individual differences. *Korean J. Probl. Solv.* 14:5–10

Unsworth K. 2001. Unpacking creativity. *Acad. Manage. Rev.* 26:289–97

Vandervert LR, Schimpf PH, Liu H. 2007. How working memory and the cerebellum collaborate to produce creativity and innovation. *Creat. Res. J.* 19:1–18

Vonèche J. 2003. The changing structure of Piaget's thinking: invariance and transformations. *Creat. Res. J.* 15:3–9

Vosburg SK. 1998. Mood and the quantity and quality of ideas. *Creat. Res. J.* 11:315–31

Ward TB. 2001. Creative cognition, conceptual combination, and the creative writing of Stephen R. Donaldson. *Am. Psychol.* 56:350–54

Wechsler S. 2006. Validity of the Torrance Tests of Creative Thinking to the Brazilian culture. *Creat. Res. J.* 18:15–25

Weisberg RW, Hass R. 2007. We are all partly right: comment on Simonton. *Creat. Res. J.* 19:345–60

West MA, Sacramento CA, Fay D. 2005. Creativity and innovation in work groups: the paradoxical role of demands. In *Creativity and Innovation in Organizational Teams*, ed. L Thompson, HS Choi, pp. 137–59. Mahwah, NJ: Erlbaum

Winner E. 2000. The origins and ends of giftedness. *Am. Psychol.* 55:159–69

Woodman RW, Sawyer JE, Griffin RW. 1993. Toward a theory of organizational creativity. *Acad. Manage. Rev.* 18:293–321

Zha P, Walczyk JJ, Griffith-Ross DA, Tobacyk JJ, Walczyk DF. 2006. The impact of culture and individualism-collectivism on the creative potential and achievement of American and Chinese adults. *Creat. Res. J.* 18:355–66

Zhang L-F. 2006. Preferred teaching styles and modes of thinking among university students in mainland China. *Thinking Skills Creat.* 1:95–107

Zhengkui L, Li C, Jiannong S. 2007. A review of researches on creativity and attention. *Psychol. Sci. (China)* 30:387–90

Zhou J. 2008. Promoting creativity through feedback. In Zhou & Shalley 2008, pp. 125–45

Zhou J, Shalley CE, eds. 2008. *Handbook of Organizational Creativity.* New York: Erlbaum

The Intersection of Work and Family Life: The Role of Affect

Lillian T. Eby,[1] Charleen P. Maher,[1]
and Marcus M. Butts[2]

[1] Department of Psychology, University of Georgia, Athens, Georgia 30602;
email: leby@uga.edu, charleen@uga.edu; [2] Department of Management,
University of Texas at Arlington, Texas 76019; email: mbutts@uta.edu

Annu. Rev. Psychol. 2010. 61:599–622

First published online as a Review in Advance on
July 2, 2009

The *Annual Review of Psychology* is online at
psych.annualreviews.org

This article's doi:
10.1146/annurev.psych.093008.100422

0066-4308/10/0110-0599$20.00

Key Words

emotion, mood, work attitudes, family attitudes, nonwork experiences

Abstract

This review examines the role that trait-based and state-based affect plays in understanding the intersection of work and family life. We start with the definition of key terms and concepts. This is followed by a historical overview of the two bodies of scholarship that are the focus of this review, the work-family interface and affect. Next, we provide a review and synthesis of 79 empirical studies examining affect in relation to work-family interaction, organized around three perspectives: the dispositional perspective, the state-based specific affective reactions perspective, and the state-based global affective reactions perspective. A methodological critique of these studies follows, providing a springboard for the discussion of recommended methodologies and data analytic approaches, along with directions for future research.

Contents

INTRODUCTION

Over the past few decades, research on the intersection of work and family life has burgeoned. Once viewed as separate domains, contemporary perspectives on work and family recognize the dynamic interplay between these two major life roles. Work and family life experiences are affect laden. Both major life events (e.g., childbirth, divorce, career change, promotion) and more mundane day-to-day experiences (e.g., helping a coworker, talking to one's spouse) in both domains trigger affective reactions, which in turn influence behavior (Stanley & Burrows 2001). Likewise, affective dispositional traits such as trait-based positive and negative affect, neuroticism, and attachment style influence how individuals interpret and respond to work and family life (Ainsworth 1989, Watson & Clark 1984, Watson et al. 1988).

Based on the increasing interest in the intersection of work-family life, and the growing recognition that affective experiences are an essential component of daily life (Gray & Watson 2001, Stanley & Burrows 2001), in this article we provide a selective review of research examining affect in relation to the work-family interface. We begin by outlining conceptual and definitional issues of relevance to work, family, and affect. This is followed by a historical overview of the major perspectives used to understand the work-family interface and affect, emphasizing the study of affect in organizational settings. Then, we review empirical research on the role of affect in relation to the intersection of work and family life. Following this review, we discuss methodological issues associated with the study of affect in relation to work-family interaction and propose important directions for future research.

CONCEPTUAL AND DEFINITIONAL ISSUES

Defining the Domain of Work-Family Interaction

Broadly speaking, work-family interaction refers to experiences in the family (work) domain that impact experiences in the work (family) domain. Work is defined as instrumental activities that provide goods and services to support life (Piotrkowski et al. 1987) and generally refers to paid work (Burke & Greenglass 1987). There has been some debate in the literature regarding similarities and differences between paid work and work that occurs in the family domain (see Kanter 1977, Zedeck 1992). We agree that work occurs in the family domain, yet consistent with much of the literature on work-family, we restrict our use of the term "work" to refer to paid work. Family consists of those individuals that one is related to as a function of biological ties, marriage, or adoption (Burke & Greenglass 1987, Piotrkowski et al. 1987). Unlike contributions to the work role, the instrumental purpose of family role activities is to keep the family unit intact and enhance the well-being of all members (Edwards & Rothbard 2000).

Negative aspects of work-family interaction. Traditionally, work-family interaction has been examined in terms of the conflict that can occur between work and family roles. This perspective is based on the scarcity hypothesis, which argues that individuals have limited resources (e.g., time, energy) and by devoting resources to one role, they are by depriving either tangible or intangible resources from the other role (Goode 1960). In their seminal work on the topic, Greenhaus & Beutell (1985) defined the construct of work-family conflict as a specific form of interrole conflict where the obligations associated with work and family roles are mutually incompatible and where participation in one role is made more difficult or stressful because of participation in the other role.

Greenhaus & Beutell (1985) defined three distinct types of work-family conflict. Time-based work-family conflict is created when time spent in one role (e.g., work) reduces the time available in the other role (e.g., family) or when pressures from one role (e.g., family) create a preoccupation with that role when one is trying to meet the demands of the other role (e.g., work). For example, a parent may have to miss a child's dance recital because s/he needs to work late to meet a work-related deadline. Strain-based work-family conflict refers to role-generated strain symptoms (e.g., anxiety, fatigue, irritability) that are produced as a result of participation in one role (e.g., work) and

hinder performance in the other role (e.g., family). As an illustration, anger and frustration experienced at home after fighting with one's spouse may make it difficult to act upbeat and enthusiastic when interacting with clients at work. A final type of work-family conflict is behavior based. This occurs when behaviors that are required in one role (e.g., family) are incompatible with behaviors expected in the other role (e.g., work). For instance, a manager may be expected to act self-reliant, tough, and assertive at work, but at home family members may expect him/her to act nurturing, vulnerable, and empathetic.

Early research on the work-family interface conceptualized work-family conflict as a general phenomenon and did not differentiate the directionality of the experienced conflict. Research by Netemeyer and colleagues (1996) made an important contribution by recognizing the bidirectionality of work-family conflict. They argued that work can interfere with family (e.g., business travel may leave less time for family activities), and family can interfere with work (e.g., a sick child may cause one to miss an important meeting at work). This is an important distinction because these two aspects of work-family conflict are conceptually distinct and have some different antecedents (e.g., Mesmer-Magnus & Viswesvaran 2005, Netemeyer et al. 1996).

Positive aspects of work-family interaction. Although most research has focused on negative aspects of work-family interaction (see Eby et al. 2005 for a review), scholars also recognize that there is a positive side of the work-family interface (Greenhaus & Powell 2006). Specifically, experiences in the family (work) role have the potential to enhance or even improve experiences in the work (family) life. The recognition of positive synergy between work and family roles provides a more balanced perspective on work-family interaction. Research is increasingly examining positive relationships between experiences in the work and the family domain (e.g., Hammer et al. 2003, Kirchmeyer 1992b, Rothbard 2001, Wayne et al. 2004). As with work-family conflict, the positive side of work-family interaction is bidirectional. That is, work can have a positive impact on family just as family can have a positive impact on work (Greenhaus & Powell 2006).

Defining the Domain of Affect

Affect refers to a mental state involving evaluative feelings (Parkinson et al. 1996). It is an umbrella term that includes a wide range of dispositions, moods, emotions, and generalized affective reactions to events, objects, and daily experiences. The construct domain of affect includes both stable, trait-based individual differences that influence how one characteristically views and interprets the world as well as state-based reactions that may range from somewhat transitory and specific states (e.g., moods, emotions) to more general affectively oriented evaluative judgments (e.g., job satisfaction, life satisfaction).

Trait-based affect. Individuals differ systematically in their tendency to respond to stimuli in a particular manner. Such individual differences in emotional reactivity and emotional self-regulation are reflective of trait-based affect (Davidson & Ekman 1994, Rothbart & Ahadi 1994). Trait-based affect includes both personality traits and temperament. A wide range of specific individual differences fall into the category of trait-based affect. This includes temperaments such as positive and negative affect, global personality traits (most notably neuroticism and extraversion; see Watson 2000), and more specific individual difference variables such as attachment style, emotional intelligence, and trait-based guilt.

State-based specific affective reactions. State-based specific affect refers to subjectively experienced affective states, which reflect the current status of an individual in relation to his or her environment (Parkinson et al. 1996). This includes both moods and emotions, which are controlled by similar processes and contain similar components, yet represent distinct

affective states (Parkinson et al. 1996). Moods are generalized feelings states that are not associated with a particular object or event and are not characterized as intense enough to interrupt ongoing cognitive processes (Clark & Isen 1982, Thayer 1989). In contrast, emotions are associated with specific events or experiences and disrupt thought processes (Gray & Watson 2001). Another way to differentiate moods from emotions is in terms of their specificity and duration. Moods tend to be defined in terms of overall positivity or negativity (e.g., Watson 2000), whereas emotions are characterized by discrete affective reactions such as guilt, disgust, anger, fear, interest, rage, and joy (Plutchik 1994). Moods also tend to be of longer duration than emotions (Davidson 1994); moods can last hours or even days, whereas emotional reactions are typically intense and brief (Gray & Watson 2001, Izard 1991). Finally, moods are experienced more frequently and consistently than are emotions. Moods are almost always present since "waking consciousness is experienced as a continuous stream of affect, such that people are always experiencing some type of mood" (Watson & Clark 1994, p. 90). In contrast, emotions are high-intensity activation states that are not part of our daily life but have a major influence on us when they occur (Gray & Watson 2001). Emotions in particular are adaptive; they supply information, shift our attention, and alter our memory in ways that allow us to more effectively meet the challenges of everyday life (Clark & Watson 1994, Gray & Watson 2001).

State-based global affective reactions. State-based global affect refers to a wide range of summative evaluative constructs, which describe how one feels about objects, events, and life experiences. Life satisfaction is a general affective reaction and represents an important indicator of well-being since it captures one's overall appraisal of the quality of life as a whole (Argyle 1987). Other global affective states that are indicators of well-being include the absence of depression and psychological withdrawal, as well as higher levels of state-based positive affect and lower levels of state-based negative affect (Diener et al. 1985, Watson 2000). More distinct satisfactions represent general affective reactions to specific aspects of the work domain (e.g., job satisfaction, career satisfaction) and family domain (e.g., marital satisfaction, family satisfaction). These global affective states should not be confused with real emotions or moods, since each has unique causes and consequences. Emotions and moods also have physiological components that are not necessarily related to global evaluative reactions such as job satisfaction (Weiss 2002).

HISTORICAL OVERVIEW OF PERSPECTIVES USED TO UNDERSTAND WORK-FAMILY INTERACTION

Dominant Theoretical Perspectives

Numerous perspectives have been used to understand the intersection of work and family life. Early research presumed that these two life domains were unrelated such that experiences in the work (family) domain had little or no effect on the family (work) domain. The notion of separate life spheres was the basis of segmentation theory (Evans & Bartolomé 1984, Piotrkowski 1978), and the idea is that the physical and psychological separation of these two life domains is adaptive, allowing individuals to compartmentalize their lives. The work domain is viewed as impersonal, competitive, and instrumental, whereas the family domain is associated with affectivity, intimacy, and significant relational experiences (Piotrkowski 1978). Although some individuals may experience work-family segmentation, subsequent research finds that this is more of a specific coping strategy than a behavioral pattern for most individuals (Lambert 1990).

The recognition that work and family experiences do affect one another led to the emergence of compensation theory (Champoux 1978, Staines 1980). This perspective presumes that individuals make differential investments in work and family life and that we make up for

deficits in one domain by investing more in the other domain (Evans & Bartolomé 1984). For example, an individual in a dissatisfying job may invest more in the family role as a way to reap satisfaction that she or he is not obtaining from the work role. This perspective grew out of research on the experience of blue-collar workers who report working in unsatisfying work environments and indicate that their home life is a primary source of satisfaction that is missing from their occupational life (Piotrkowski 1979).

A third perspective on the work-family interface is spillover theory (Champoux 1978, Staines 1980). This is the dominant paradigm used to understand work-family interaction and suggests that experiences in the work (family) domain spillover and affect experiences in the family (work) domain. These spillover experiences include domain-specific affective experiences, skills, attitudes, and behaviors (Kando & Summers 1971). For example, the emotions generated at work can spillover into the family domain by influencing one's mood at home after a frustrating day at work. Although work-family spillover has been historically viewed as negative, spillover can also be positive (Hanson et al. 2006, Kirchmeyer 1993, Small & Riley 1990). For instance, feelings of satisfaction and pride in one's family can enhance job satisfaction and boost work-related self-efficacy.

Building on the notion that positive spillover can occur between work and family life, Greenhaus & Powell (2006) developed a theory of work-family enrichment, which proposes that experiences in the work (family) role improve performance and enhance affect in the family (work) role. This occurs through the transmission of positive affect and either tangible or intangible resources from one role to the other role. For instance, negotiation skills learned at work (a tangible resource) can be used in the family role to enhance marital quality or improve interactions with children. Work-family enrichment theory was informed by role enhancement theory (Marks 1977, Sieber 1974), which argues that engagement in multiple, high-quality roles provides both psychological and tangible resources for individuals, which in turn enhance experiences in other roles. Indeed, research finds that role accumulation is positively related to well-being (Barnett & Hyde 2001). Moreover, research finds that satisfaction with work and satisfaction with family have additive effects on overall life satisfaction (Rice et al. 1985, 1992).

A growing body of scholarship has examined the positive synergy associated with work-family interaction, and numerous constructs have been identified to explain this phenomenon. Indicators of this positive synergy include work-family facilitation (e.g., Grzywacz & Bass 2003, Wayne et al. 2004), work-family enrichment (e.g., Kirchmeyer 1992a, Rothbard 2001), and as mentioned previously, positive spillover (e.g., Crouter 1984, Grzywacz 2000, Grzywacz et al. 2002, Hanson et al. 2006). As this literature base continues to grow, further construct refinement and theory development will undoubtedly occur.

HISTORICAL OVERVIEW OF PERSPECTIVES USED TO UNDERSTAND AFFECT

Dominant Theoretical Perspectives

Various theories have been put forward to understand trait-based and state-based affect. These frameworks generally agree that affect has a two-dimensional structure consisting of positive affect and negative affect (Barrett & Russell 1998, Stanley & Burrows 2001, Watson & Tellegen 1985). Positive affect refers to the experience of pleasant psychological states such as cheerfulness, alertness, and confidence. Negative affect refers to the experience of unpleasant psychological states such as anger, sadness, and fear (Gray & Watson 2001). Both trait-based and state-based affect are conceptualized along these two dimensions, facilitating the integration of research on personality and temperament on one hand with moods, emotions, and satisfactions on the other hand (Gray & Watson 2001).

The circumplex model (Russell 1980, Watson & Tellegen 1985) codified the two-dimensional structure of affect. Based on a secondary analysis of eight published studies on transient self-reported affect, Watson & Tellegen (1985) consistently identified two independent higher-order dimensions of affect representing high and low levels of positive affect and negative affect, respectively. High positive affect is represented by terms such as active, elated, enthusiastic, and strong, whereas low positive affect is defined by terms such as drowsy, dull, sleepy, and sluggish. In contrast, terms such as distressed, fearful, hostile, and jittery are indicators of high negative affect, whereas low negative affect is reflected in the terms calm, at rest, placid, and relaxed. Not all the moods included on the circumplex fall neatly into the positive or negative affect dimensions; some terms reflect a combination of these two core dimensions (Watson & Tellegen 1985). For instance, terms indicating pleasantness (e.g., content, happy, satisfied) represent a mixture of high positive affect and low negative affect. In contrast, terms indicative of unpleasantness (e.g., blue, lonely, unhappy) represent a mixture of low positive affect and high negative affect.

An extension of the circumplex model focuses on the more general biobehavioral systems that underlie positive and negative affect (Watson et al. 1999). Discussed within an evolutionary perspective, two general motivational systems are believed to exist, both of which facilitate adaptive behavior (Carver & White 1994, Tomarken & Keener 1998). The behavioral facilitation system represents approach motivation, and the behavioral inhibition system represents withdrawal motivation (Watson et al. 1999). The feeling states associated with positive affect motivate goal-directed behavior. In other words, positive affect mobilizes the behavioral facilitation system. The feeling states associated with negative affect facilitate apprehensiveness and cautiousness such that negative affect drives the behavioral inhibition system.

The broaden-and-build theory (Fredrickson 1998) also argues that positive and negative affective experiences operate vis-à-vis distinct pathways, yet emphasizes the important role that positive emotions play in our everyday lives. Fredrickson (1998) argues that positive emotional experiences are not simply an indicator of "being happy" in the moment. Rather, over time the experience of positive emotions leads to psychological growth and flourishing. This is thought to occur because discrete positive emotional experiences such as pride, joy, interest, and love all have the ability to broaden individuals' momentary thought-action repertoire and build physical, social, psychological, and intellectual resources (Fredrickson 2001, 2003). This stands in contrast to the specific action tendencies associated with negative emotions where an individual's thought-action repertoire is narrowed and a very specific behavioral response is cued (e.g., flee in response to feeling threatened, attack in response to anger). The reason that positive emotions are believed to broaden and build rather than constrain individual behavior, is that positive emotions are not typically generated in adverse situations that require decisive action (Fredrickson 2001). Rather, positive emotions tend to occur as part of everyday life, and their experience encourages creativity and exploratory behavior (Csikszentmihalyi 1990, Fredrickson & Branigan 2005).

Several other perspectives focus more specifically on understanding affective experiences in the workplace. Affective events theory (Weiss & Cropanzano 1996) suggests that specific events at work (e.g., coworker interactions, promotions) create discrete emotional reactions, which in turn lead to spontaneous work behaviors and attitudes. This theory proposes that affective experiences at work have an immediate effect such that affect influences attitudes and behaviors when an individual is in a particular affective state. This emphasis on intraindividual differences in attitudes and behavior highlights the importance of studying affective events as they unfold over time.

Another perspective on the role of emotions in the workplace is Hochschild's (1979, 1983) research on the phenomenon of emotional labor. In many work contexts, there are either implicit or explicit role expectations about the expression of feelings and emotions. In early research, emotional labor was defined as the emotions that employees are expected to display during service interactions (Ashforth & Humphrey 1993). From an organizational standpoint, it is presumed that requiring employees in the service industry to express positive emotions will increase organizational profits. However, this line of research found that there are mixed or even negative results associated with requiring employees to display certain service-oriented behaviors (Rafaeli & Sutton 1989). This is because the emotions required by service interactions may not be genuinely experienced by the role occupant, and faking these emotions can be emotionally draining. Although far less developed, the construct of emotional labor has also been discussed in relation to normative expectations regarding emotional expression in the family domain and the consequences associated with emotional labor generated in one's nonwork life (Wharton & Erickson 1993, Yanchus et al. 2009).

THE ROLE OF AFFECT IN UNDERSTANDING THE INTERSECTION OF WORK AND FAMILY LIFE

Our review of empirical research on the role of affect in work-family interaction is organized around three perspectives: (a) the dispositional perspective, which examines trait-based affect in relation to work-family interaction; (b) the state-based specific affective reactions perspective, which examines mood and specific emotional reactions in relation to work and family life; and (c) the state-based global affective reactions perspective, which focuses on the association between overall summative affective evaluations (e.g., job satisfaction, family satisfaction) and work-family interaction.

The Dispositional Perspective

Three affectively oriented Big 5 personality traits have been examined in relation to the work-family interface: neuroticism, extraversion, and agreeableness. Neuroticism has received the most research attention. Individuals high on neuroticism are more likely to experience worry, apprehension, fear, sadness, and irritability. They also tend to cope less effectively with stress and tend to view events as threatening and troubling (Watson 2000). Given these characteristics, it is not surprising that neuroticism is positively related to both work-to-family conflict (Blanch & Aluja 2009, Bruck & Allen 2003, Horwitz et al. 2008, Hughes & Parkes 2007, Rantanen et al. 2008, Wayne et al. 2004) and family-to-work conflict (Blanch & Aluja 2009, Bruck & Allen 2003, Horwitz et al. 2008, Rantanen et al. 2008, Wayne et al. 2004). Furthermore, Bruck & Allen (2003) found significant positive zero-order correlations between neuroticism and all three types of work-family conflict (time-, strain-, and behavior-based), although no unique variance was explained by neuroticism when negative affect was included in the regression models. There is also evidence that neuroticism may reduce the likelihood that an individual experiences positive work-family interaction. Two studies found that as neuroticism increases, work-family facilitation decreases (Horwitz et al. 2008, Wayne et al. 2004). Another stream of research examined the moderating effect of neuroticism, arguing that emotional stability (the positive pole of neuroticism) may buffer individuals from work-family stressors. In support of this idea, the negative effects of work interfering with family on burnout (Kinnunen et al. 2003), depression (Kinnunen et al. 2003), and psychological distress (Rantanen et al. 2008, women only) were less pronounced among those with greater emotional stability.

Extraversion is also an affectively oriented disposition because higher levels of this trait are associated with positive emotionality. Individuals higher on extraversion tend to be more outgoing, energetic, lively, cheerful, confident, and assertive (Watson 2000). Research on the role of extraversion in work-family interaction is not conclusive. Some studies have found that as extraversion increases, work-family conflict decreases (Horwitz et al. 2008; Kinnunen et al. 2003, all-male sample), but other research has found no significant effects (Bruck & Allen 2003). Extraversion has also been examined as a predictor of the positive aspects of work-family interaction, with two studies supporting the notion that extraversion is positively related to work-family facilitation (Horwitz et al. 2008, Wayne et al. 2004).

A growing body of literature suggests that agreeableness can also be viewed as a temperamental trait (see Gray & Watson 2001). Individuals higher on this trait are less likely to experience irritability and jealousy. They also tend to be kind, trusting, cooperative, and mild mannered (Saucier 1994). Given these characteristics, it is presumed that as agreeableness increases, individuals should report fewer negative and more positive work-family interactions. Indeed, several studies have found that individuals higher on agreeableness (Bruck & Allen 2003, Rantanen et al. 2008, Wayne et al. 2004) or similar traits such as sociability (Blanch & Aluja 2009) reported less work-family conflict. Moreover, there is some evidence that agreeableness interacts with family-to-work conflict in predicting marital satisfaction among working fathers such that marital satisfaction was lowest when family-to-work conflict was reported to be high and agreeableness was low (Kinnunen et al. 2003).

Trait-based positive and negative affects have also been examined as predictors of work-family interaction. As discussed above, negative affect is characterized by feelings of distress, anger, contempt, nervousness, and unpleasurable engagement. In contrast, positive affect reflects feelings of enthusiasm, energy, concentration, and pleasurable engagement (Watson et al. 1988). Most studies have examined negative affect in relation to work-family conflict, typically finding a positive correlation (Bruck & Allen 2003, Carlson 1999, Karatepe & Uludag 2008, Little et al. 2007, Montgomery et al. 2006, Stoeva et al. 2002). Less research has focused on positive affect, but there is some evidence that positive affect is negatively related to both work-to-family conflict and family-to-work conflict (Karatepe & Uludag 2008, Little et al. 2007).

Other more specific affectively oriented dispositions have been examined in the work-family literature. Burke and colleagues found that wives' perceptions of their husbands' Type A personality (characterized by aggressiveness, competitiveness, hostility, and impatience; Spence et al. 1987) were negatively related to their own marital satisfaction (Burke et al. 1980). There is also evidence that Type A personality is positively related to work-family conflict, although the specific pattern of effects is not consistent across types of work-family conflict (compare Bruck & Allen 2003 to Carlson 1999). Trait-based hostility is also positively related to work-family conflict (Blanch & Aluja 2009, Judge et al. 2006) and appears to exacerbate the positive relationship between the experience of work-to-family conflict and hostile emotional reactions. Judge and colleagues (2006) further found that trait-based guilt was positively associated with work-family conflict, and the positive relationship between work-family conflict and guilt-related emotional reactions was stronger among those reporting higher trait-based guilt (Judge et al. 2006).

Several additional affectively oriented dispositional variables have been examined in relation to the work-family interface. Sumer & Knight (2001) examined positive and negative work-family spillover in relation to attachment style, arguing that an individual's working model of close relationships is likely to influence how he or she responds to work-family issues. They found that negative spillover from home to work was greater among individuals with a preoccupied attachment style (characterized by a negative image of self and positive image of other) compared with individuals with either a secure attachment style (characterized by a positive image of self and other) or dismissing attachment style (characterized by a positive image of self and negative image of other). In addition, positive spillover from home to work

(and vice versa) was most pronounced among those with a secure attachment style. There is also some initial evidence that individuals who are higher in emotional intelligence report less family-to-work conflict, ostensibly because they are better able to recognize, regulate, and appropriately respond to emotional cues in both life domains (Carmeli 2003).

A final affectively oriented trait that has been examined in relation to work-family conflict is psychological hardiness. Individuals who are higher on this trait tend to be more resistant to strain reactions because of their tendency to view stressors as challenges that can be overcome rather than as circumstances over which they have little control (Kobasa 1979). As expected, Bernas & Major (2000) found that hardiness had an indirect effect on work-family conflict; hardiness predicted lower family stress, which in turn predicted less family interfering with work. Hardiness also predicted lower work stress, which in turn was associated with less work interfering with family. In a related study, Barling (1986) examined hardiness as a moderator of the relationship between work and nonwork conflict and marital adjustment among men. He found that when both interrole conflict and hardiness were high, marital adjustment was high. However, when interrole conflict was high and hardiness was low, marital adjustment was low. This suggests that like many of the other affectively oriented dispositional traits discussed in this section, hardiness may play a stress-buffering role in work-family interaction.

In summary, the dispositional perspective illustrates that certain traits predispose individuals to experience more intense emotional reactions to work-family interactions. The evidence is particularly strong for neuroticism, agreeableness, negative affect, and other traits associated with the tendency to experience anger (e.g., Type A personality, trait-based hostility). There is also some evidence that affective dispositions may buffer individuals from the negative effects of work or family stressors on strain reactions.

The State-Based Specific Affective Reactions Perspective

A second perspective focuses on the role of mood and emotion in the work-family interface. Consistent with the research reviewed above, state-based negative affective experiences (e.g., anxiety, tension, worry, frustration, guilt, distress, irritation) are positively related to both work-family conflict (Frone et al. 1997b, Geurts et al. 2003, Livingston & Judge 2008, Matthews et al. 2006) and greater juggling of work and family responsibilities (Williams & Alliger 1994, Williams et al. 1991). Moreover, as work and family role juggling increases, the positive mood state of calmness tends to decrease (Williams & Alliger 1994). The positive correlation between work-family conflict and negative mood states also appears to be stronger among those with a more traditional gender role orientation, and the nature of this effect varies by gender. Specifically, there is a stronger positive relationship between family-to-work conflict and the emotional reaction of guilt among men with traditional gender role orientations. In contrast, the positive association between family-to-work conflict and guilt is strongest among women who report a more egalitarian gender role orientation (Livingston & Judge 2008). In a more fine-grained examination of the manner in which mood states in one domain relate to outcomes in the other domain, Judge & Ilies (2004) found that daily experiences of fatigue and distress in the family predicted family-to-work interference. Interestingly, a parallel effect was not found for daily experiences of fatigue and distress at work on work-to-family interference.

Other studies find negative mood spillover from home to work as well as positive mood spillover across domains (Ilies et al. 2007; Judge & Ilies 2004; Song et al. 2008; Williams & Alliger 1994, elation only from family to work; Williams et al. 1991). There is also some evidence that negative mood spillover may be greater for those higher in work orientation (Song et al. 2008). Workload appears to be a catalyst for this work-to-home spillover effect such that increased workload leads to negative work affect, which in turn creates a negative affective reaction in the family domain (Ilies et al. 2007). Other correlates of negative mood include dissatisfaction with the amount of time available for family based on one's work schedule (Jackson et al. 1985), lack of feedback at work, training inadequacy, and work role ambiguity (Doby & Caplan 1995). Another indication of work-family spillover is the finding that momentary satisfaction experienced in the work domain is positively associated with marital satisfaction reported later the same day (and vice versa) (Heller & Watson 2005). Mood appears to be an important explanatory mechanism here because both positive and negative mood partially mediated the relationship between momentary work satisfaction and momentary marital satisfaction (Heller & Watson 2005). Evidence for affective spillover was also found in research by Ilies and colleagues (2009). These authors found that on days where employees report high daily job satisfaction, they also tend to report higher daily marital satisfaction, greater positive affect at home, and less negative affect at home.

There is some evidence of gender differences in mood spillover across domains. Specifically, Williams & Alliger (1994) found that spillover of negative mood across domains was stronger for women than men. Schulz et al. (2004) also found gender differences in the effect of negative emotions at work on one's home life. Husbands (but not wives) were more withdrawn at night and reported fewer angry behaviors toward their wives after experiencing more negative emotional arousal at work. In contrast, wives reported more angry behaviors toward their husbands after a more negative emotionally arousing day at work. The amount of workload reported during the day also had differential effects on the emotional reactions of husbands and wives. Wives reported being more withdrawn and were perceived by their husbands as being more angry at home if they experienced a heavy workload during the day. No such effects were found for husbands. Schulz et al. (2004) further found that marital satisfaction influenced how individuals respond to emotionally taxing experiences at work. Husbands in less satisfying marriages were less likely to report angry behavior at the end of more emotionally distressing workdays. Husbands in less satisfying marriages also reported that their wives engaged in less angry behavior toward them after a difficult day at work. These findings suggest that emotional expression or venting behavior may be inhibited among individuals in less satisfying marriages. It may also reflect differences in household responsibilities and family role salience between the sexes.

Crossover mood effects between partners have also been documented. Song et al. (2008) studied marital dyads and found a significant positive relationship between both positive and negative mood states as reported by spouses. These authors also demonstrated that mood crossover only occurred when husbands and wives reported spending time together, and the mood spillover that occurred tended to decrease as time spent apart increased. Ilies et al. (2009) reported similar crossover effects. Daily job satisfaction reported by the employee was positively related to spouse ratings of the employee's positive affect at home, and this effect held only for employees who reported a high degree of work-family role integration. A similar pattern was found for the spouse's ratings of employee's negative affect. Children's perceptions of the affective work reactions of adults who play a significant role in their life suggest that there may also be crossover effects from adult to child. Specifically, children reported more positive expectations regarding their own emotional reaction to work when they believed that significant adults in their life held more favorable affective reactions toward work (Porfeli et al. 2008).

A final area of research related to state-based affect involves the emotional demands associated with one's home life. Similar to Hochschild's (1979, 1983) conceptualization of emotional labor, emotion work is a form of domestic labor that involves providing emotional support and encouragement to others in an effort to create and sustain positive emotions in the family (Minnotte et al. 2007). Several studies find that emotion work at home is associated with work-family spillover. For men (but not women), as emotion work increased, so did spouses' negative work-family spillover (Minnotte et al. 2007). Similar effects were documented by Demerouti and colleagues (2005). For both genders, job requirements (which included emotional demands) were positively related to employees' work-to-family conflict as well as partners' reports of work-to-family conflict. Furthermore, Stevens et al. (2007) found that for women, both satisfaction with emotion work at home and family cohesion (feelings of togetherness, harmony, and engagement) predicted less negative work-to-family spillover and more positive family-to-work spillover. For men, positive family-to-work spillover was predicted by satisfaction with emotion work at home and relationship satisfaction. Interestingly, satisfaction with emotion work at home was also associated with more negative work-to-family spillover for men. Other research finds that emotional cohesion within the family is positively associated with job satisfaction for women, suggesting another emotional spillover mechanism between the work and home domain (Stevens et al. 2002).

Several conclusions can be reached from research on state-based specific affective reactions. First, state-based moods and emotions are associated with the strains of balancing work and family obligations; as the demands of work and family life increase, individuals tend to experience more negative affective states and fewer positive affective states. Second, there is evidence of both positive and negative mood spillover across work and family domains, suggesting that work and family life likely have reciprocal effects on one another. Gender differences in mood spillover are also evident in research on state-based specific affective reactions, perhaps due to different gender role expectations regarding the expression of emotion in daily life. Third, there is mounting evidence of crossover effects between partners such that one individual's mood influences the other partner's mood and/or emotional reaction to work and family life.

The State-Based Global Affective Reactions Perspective

A final perspective on the role of affect in the work-family interface considers state-based global affective reactions, typically as consequences of work-family experiences. Numerous studies find that as work-family conflict increases, job satisfaction decreases (Adams et al. 1996; Allen 2001; Aryee et al. 1999a,b; Behson 2002; Burke & Greenglass 1999; Carlson & Perrewé 1999; Frone et al. 1994a,b; Grandey et al. 2005, women only; Hill 2005; Kinnunen et al. 2004, women only; Parasuraman et al. 1992; Shaffer et al. 2001; Steenbergen et al. 2007; Thomas & Ganster 1995; Wiese & Salmela-Aro 2008), life satisfaction decreases (Adams et al. 1996; Aryee et al. 1999a,b; Hill 2005), and family/home/nonwork satisfaction decreases (Carlson & Perrewé 1999; Frone et al. 1994a,b; Hill 2005; Hughes & Parkes 2007; Karatepe & Uludag 2008; Kinnunen et al. 2006; Shaffer et al. 2001; Steenbergen et al. 2007). This is consistent with research indicating that juggling work and family role responsibilities is associated with less task enjoyment, especially among those higher in extraversion (Williams et al. 1991). There is also ample evidence that work-family conflict is positively related to various indicators of psychological health such as less depression (Frone et al. 1997a,b; Major et al. 2002; Schwartzberg & Dytell 1996, fathers only; Thomas & Ganster 1995), fewer psychiatric disorders (Frone 2000), and lower psychological distress (Burke & Greenglass 1999; Frone et al. 1994a; Grandey & Cropanzano 1999; Harvey et al. 2003; Hughes & Parkes 2007; Kinnunen et al. 2004, women only; Kinnunen et al. 2006; LaPierre & Allen 2006; Mauno et al. 2005; O'Driscoll et al. 1992, 2003; Van der Zee et al. 2005). Work-family conflict is also negatively related to engagement at work (Innstrand et al. 2008, Wiese & Salmela-Aro 2008). Overall psychological adjustment to living overseas has also been linked to both job and nonwork satisfaction (Takeuchi et al. 2002). Finally, there is some evidence that well-being, job satisfaction, family satisfaction (Edwards & Rothbard 1999), and burnout (Barnett et al. 1999) are related to greater perceived fit between work and family life.

There are numerous studies examining the emotionally draining syndrome of burnout in relation to work-family interaction. This literature finds that greater work-family conflict is associated with higher levels of burnout (Bacharach et al. 1991, Burke & Greenglass 1999, Demerouti et al. 2005, Harvey et al. 2003, Innstrand et al. 2008, Kinnunen et al. 2006, Montgomery et al. 2006). There is also evidence of a reciprocal relationship such that greater burnout at time 1 predicts more work-family conflict at time 2 (Demerouti et al. 2004, Innstrand et al. 2008). Work-family interference serves as a partial explanation for why working long hours and experiencing emotional demands at work leads to burnout (Montgomery et al. 2006a,b). Burnout is also negatively related to other indicators of family functioning such as marital satisfaction and family climate (Kinnunen et al. 2003). Furthermore, Westman & Etzion (1995) found that burnout experienced by one spouse was associated with increased burnout as reported by the other spouse, suggesting crossover effects within marital dyads. Likewise, Demerouti et al. (2005) found that for women (but not men), partners' ratings of work-to-family conflict predicted target employees' burnout.

Another line of research on global affective reactions links one partner's work-family conflict to the other partner's psychological well-being. Hammer and colleagues (2005) found that husbands' work-family conflict was positively correlated with wives' reports of depression. Similar effects have been documented among expatriate families. Van der Zee et al. (2005) found that as expatriates perceived greater home-to-work interference, their spouses reported lower psychological well-being. Reciprocal crossover adjustment effects have also been documented such that one person's reported psychological comfort with the host country is positively related to the other person's cross-cultural adjustment

(Takeuchi et al. 2002). Reciprocal relationships were also found between expatriate work adjustment and spouse cross-cultural adjustment (Takeuchi et al. 2002).

Evidence is beginning to accumulate that as individuals report more positive work-family experiences (e.g., positive spillover, facilitation, enrichment), they also tend to report greater satisfaction with their work lives (Hill 2005, Steenbergen et al. 2007, Wiese & Salmela-Aro 2008) and nonwork lives (Hill 2005, Steenbergen et al. 2007). Likewise, positive work-family experiences predict greater overall psychological health (Hammer et al. 2005, Kinnunen et al. 2006, Steenbergen et al. 2007, Van der Zee et al. 2005), partner satisfaction (Wiese & Salmela-Aro 2008), engagement with one's partner (Innstrand et al. 2008, Wiese & Salmela-Aro 2008), and less burnout (Innstrand et al. 2008). Finally, a longitudinal study of dual-career couples revealed crossover effects for positive spillover such that husbands' (wives') positive spillover at time 1 was negatively related to wives' (husbands') depression at time 2 (Hammer et al. 2005).

Finally, crossover effects have been examined in relation to other work-family variables. Grandey et al. (2005) found that women's job satisfaction (but not men's job satisfaction) was predicted by their husbands' perceptions of their wives' work interfering with family. Grandey et al. speculate that when a husband perceives that his wife is violating the gender-prescribed family role by working, this creates resentment and conflict in the family. In turn, this reduces women's job satisfaction because they attribute blame to their job. Similarly, Matthews et al. (2006) found a positive correlation between an individual's perception of work-to-relationship conflict and his/her partner's perception of the target individual's work-to-relationship conflict. This suggests that if one person experiences work-to-relationship conflict, the other person is also likely to report feeling that his/her partner's work is interfering with the relationship. Gender differences were also reported by Matthews

et al. (2006). As expected, as women's reports of work-to-relationship conflict increased, so did relationship tension as reported by their partner. However, the opposite effect was found for men; as men reported greater relationship conflict, their partners tended to report feeling less annoyed and irritated with them. This seemingly counterintuitive finding awaits replication before firm conclusions can be drawn.

Research on state-based global affective reactions consistently finds that the experience of work-family conflict predicts a whole host of negative affective reactions to work and family life, as well as impaired psychological well-being among employees. Work-family conflict is also consistently related to burnout, which in turn has negative repercussions for overall family functioning. Another mechanism by which state-based global reactions influence work-family interaction involves crossover effects among relational partners. This can come in the form of crossover burnout, work-to-relationship conflict, and work-family conflict. There is also some evidence that positive work-family experiences have the potential to facilitate more favorable reactions to both work and nonwork.

METHODOLOGICAL ISSUES ASSOCIATED WITH EXAMINING AFFECT IN WORK-FAMILY RESEARCH

Methodology is an important vantage point to use in synthesizing a body of scholarship and identifying future research directions because methodological choices influence the accumulation of knowledge over time (Sackett & Larson 1990, Schriescheim et al. 1993). For example, if an area of inquiry relies almost exclusively on cross-sectional survey data collected from a single individual, then concerns arise regarding internal validity due to lack of triangulation, mono-method bias, and the inability to isolate cause-and-effect relationships among study variables. On the other hand, if laboratory experiments dominate a body of scholarship, then criticisms often focus on external validity because of the artificiality of the context and the use of samples that may not be representative of the population to whom one wants to ultimately generalize. To offset the inherent limitations of any single methodology, corroborating evidence from studies using different methodological characteristics is desirable. In this section, we summarize the methodological characteristics of the empirical studies reviewed above. This provides a platform for recommending specific methodologies and data analytic techniques that have utility for addressing critical unanswered questions about the role of affect in the work-family interface.

Typical Methodological Approaches

Seventy-nine individual studies published in 78 empirical articles were included in this review (one article presented data from two independent studies). Sixteen of these articles represented the dispositional perspective, 20 articles focused on the state-based specific affective reactions perspective, and the remaining 43 articles corresponded to the state-based global affective reactions perspective. Drawing from Casper et al.'s (2007) review, the following methodological features were examined: time horizon (cross-sectional versus longitudinal), research design (within-subjects, between-subjects, and both within- and between-subjects design), and level of analysis. This last category is conceptualized in terms of the "level of theory" (Klein et al. 1994, p. 198) and included individual, crossover (e.g., spouse burnout predicting employee work-family conflict), dyad (e.g., employee-child dyad as the unit of analysis), and both individual and crossover. For all of these methodological features, the coding was mutually exclusive such that a given study was classified into only one category. The data collection method (survey, archival, diary focus group or observation, other) was also recorded for each study, and the coding here was exhaustive since a given study could use more than one data collection method (e.g., survey and focus group). We focused on these particular methodological features because scholars have criticized work-family research in general as relying too heavily on individual-level, survey-based, cross-sectional methodologies (Casper et al. 2007). We added the methodological feature of research design because of the ephemeral nature of state-based affect and the tendency for organizational scholars to focus on differences between individuals rather than intraindividual variability.

Table 1 illustrates the methodological characteristics of the studies included in the present review, organized in terms of the three perspectives used in this review. Research adopting the dispositional perspective relies almost exclusively on cross-sectional, individual-level, survey-based methodologies and tends to focus on interindividual differences. Perhaps owing to the stable nature of dispositions, longitudinal research from the dispositional perspective is uncommon as is research examining intraindividual differences. The dispositional perspective is also the least diverse in terms of data collection methods, utilizing surveys to the virtual exclusion of other data collection methods. The state-based global affective reactions perspective also tends to rely on cross-sectional, between-subjects research designs and to focus on research questions at the individual level of analysis. These findings align with the conclusions reached about the general work-family literature. As such, the same criticisms apply to the dispositional and state-based global affective reactions perspectives.

In contrast, the state-based specific affective reactions perspective relies on both cross-sectional and longitudinal approaches and focuses attention on both intraindividual and interindividual differences in the affective experiences of work-family interaction. With the emphasis on transient affective states, this perspective frequently uses the diary method for data collection, typically in conjunction with surveys. The state-based specific affective reactions perspective is also more likely to address research questions from both the individual and crossover levels of analysis.

Table 1 Methodological characteristics of studies examining affect in relation to work-family interactions[a]

	Dispositional perspective	State-based specific affective reactions perspective	State-based global affective reactions perspective
Time horizon			
Cross-sectional	94%	45%	86%
Longitudinal	6%	55%	14%
Research design			
Within-subjects	6%	0%	2%
Between-subjects	88%	40%	91%
Both within- and between-subjects	6%	60%	7%
Level of analysis			
Individual	94%	50%	88%
Crossover	0%	5%	5%
Dyad	6%	0%	0%
Both individual and crossover	0%	45%	7%
Data collection method			
Survey	100%	100%	100%
Archival	0%	0%	0%
Diary	0%	50%	0%
Focus group	0%	0%	0%
Observation	0%	0%	0%
Other (e.g., interview)	6%	5%	14%

[a]Coding for all of methodological features except data collection method is mutually exclusive. Coding for data collection method is exhaustive.

Recommended Methodologies

As illustrated throughout this review, trait-based affect and state-based affect play a prominent role in the intersection of work and family life. Disentangling the complex interplay between affect and work-family interaction requires careful attention to research methodology and creative approaches to the design of research studies. We believe that there are a variety of underutilized methodologies and analytical techniques that hold promise in terms of broadening and deepening our understanding of the role of affect in work-family interaction. In fact, given the widespread use of cross-sectional, individual-level approaches, particularly among studies taking the dispositional and global affective reactions perspectives, our knowledge of the work-family interface in these areas may be somewhat method bound. In the sections that follow, we provide specific methodological and statistical recommendations to advance theory and research in this area.

Longitudinal research. Of particular importance for understanding the role of affect in work-family interaction is the consideration of temporal changes over time, which requires a longitudinal perspective. The call for more longitudinal research in the work-family literature is not new (Casper et al. 2007), and we recognize the many barriers to conducting such research including subject attrition over time, tenure criteria that encourages and rewards quantity of publications, and the highly competitive nature of extramural funding, which makes longitudinal research more feasible. Nonetheless, the nature of affective experiences makes longitudinal research particularly important. For example, the temporal-based additive quality of positive emotions proposed by Fredrickson's (1998) broaden-and-build theory suggests a cumulative effect of affective experiences over time. This might include additive effects associated with recurring positive emotional experiences in the work domain (e.g., successive positive job experiences), the family domain (e.g., a long-term fulfilling marriage), or a combination of the two.

Another reason that longitudinal research is so important is that family dynamics and priorities shift across the course of one's life. During the early career (age 25 to 40), individuals often make important life decisions regarding marriage, children, and career (Greenhaus et al. 2000). These decisions have the potential to engender major affective reactions that can spillover into the work (family) domain. For instance, preparing for marriage or the birth of a child is typically anxiety inducing as well as exciting. These family-generated emotional experiences may have particularly potent spillover effects into the work domain in the early career years. Similarly, accepting one's first "real job" can create feelings of pride and personal fulfillment or lead to a sense of regret and disappointment that in turn affects one's family experience. For some individuals, middle career (age 40 to 55) is associated with career stagnation due to fewer opportunities for professional growth or skill atrophy. This can engender negative emotional reactions (e.g., apathy, depressed mood, anger), which in turn creates tension at home. For others, the middle career period is associated with positive affective experiences, as individuals reflect on work accomplishments and prepare for new career challenges (Greenhaus et al. 2000). The late career (age 55 to retirement) also represents an important transition for working individuals, particularly if one's sense of self-worth is closely tied to the work role (Greenhaus et al. 2000). As retirement approaches, individuals may experience positive and/or negative emotional reactions to this life transition, and these affective experiences undoubtedly influence family life.

Multiple levels of analysis. Work-family research involves the simultaneous consideration of work and family life as well as different viewpoints (e.g., employee-spouse, employee-supervisor, employee-child). In other words, work's influence on family (and vice versa) cannot be completely understood without accounting for both life domains and the entire set of role occupants in each domain. Given these characteristics, work-family interaction can naturally be viewed from multiple levels of analysis. Consistent with general criticisms of the work-family literature (Casper et al. 2007), much of the existing research on affect and work-family has examined individual-level effects (although in this review, crossover effects were more frequently examined than in the general work-family literature) and relied on individual-level theories rather than theories that consider dyadic, familial, or system-level effects. When crossover effects have been examined, the focus has typically been on married or cohabitating partners. Absent in the literature on affect and work-family is research examining other types of crossover effects. This is somewhat surprising given the emotional contagion process whereby one individual's affective state either consciously or unconsciously influences the emotions or behaviors of another person or group (Barsade 2002). Emotional contagion seems likely among various dyads in the family unit. For instance, a child's positive mood may influence employee mood either on or off the job. Likewise, a sibling who is experiencing anxiety or depression as a result of a difficult life experience (e.g., divorce, medical problems) may engender similar negative emotional states in an employee, either at home or at work. Other possible emotional crossover effects include interactions between employee and coworker, employee and customer, and employee and supervisor.

Our review revealed that no research to date has taken a dyadic perspective in understanding the role of affect in work-family interaction. This is surprising given the considerable crossover research in this area and the consistent finding that employee (partner) affect relates to partner (employee) affect. Dyadic research examining similarity in trait-based or state-based affect among partners may provide unique insight into how individuals respond to work-family conflict or experience work-family enrichment. Likewise, shared perceptions of work-family conflict among partners may be an important predictor of family attitudes as well as work outcomes. Finally, an important variant of multilevel approaches to the study of affect and work-family is research that simultaneously examines intraindividual and interindividual variability in affective experiences. This type of research is most frequently seen in the study of state-based specific affective reactions due to the transient nature of emotions and moods. This research consistently demonstrates that there is meaningful within-person variability in affective experiences and that this variability is predictive of individual outcomes (e.g., Ilies et al. 2009).

To better understand such complex associations between affective responses in the work and family domain, Allen (2009) recently called for more multilevel work-family research. Although we agree that multilevel research is needed, such designs must take into account possible linkages through both bottom-up processes (e.g., from the employee to the employee-spouse couple) and top-down processes (e.g., from the work team to the employee). Furthermore, measures designed to capture higher-level constructs such as family affect or family emotional contagion should be developed. Moreover, multilevel designs should draw samples from multiple dyad combinations, multiple families, multiple organizations, and across multiple time horizons (short term, long term). Multiple short-term measurements, preferably in real time (i.e., experience sampling), seem particularly important to account for the aforementioned ephemeral nature of state-based affect.

Nonlinear change. Specific events (e.g., graduation, first employment, job loss, home ownership, health crises) or major role changes (e.g., getting married or divorced, becoming a parent, being promoted to a supervisory role) in either domain can have profound nonlinear effects on individuals, influencing attitudes and behaviors after that point as well as subsequent interactions with those around them. Research on these triggers, or turning points, indicates that completely new behavior systems may develop in response to the opportunities and demands resulting from turning points (Cohen 2008). As an illustration, it may be that the birth of an individual's first child has a major effect on work role identity or job satisfaction, whereas the birth of subsequent children has little or no effect. Likewise, an event in the work domain, such as receiving a scathing performance review, could set off an extreme emotional reaction that irrevocably alters one's attitudes toward work or one's employer. These represent a few of the many potential avenues for understanding affective turning points in work-family research. Finding and employing rigorous empirical methods able to address causal processes unfolding over time (turning points) are critical steps to furthering the accumulation of scientific knowledge in this area.

Recommended Data Analytic Strategies

Given the appropriate research design, there is a broad array of innovative data analytic techniques that may contribute to our understanding of the role of affect in work-family interaction. First, latent growth curve models, or random effects models, extend the common structural equation modeling (SEM) framework to provide a flexible statistical tool for testing the significance of change across time and predictors/outcomes of such change (McArdle 1988). Latent growth curve models are beneficial because in addition to incorporating the accepted benefits of SEM (i.e., accounting for measurement error, inclusion of multiple independent and dependent variables), they also can estimate linear (longitudinal) and nonlinear (turning points) effects.

Second, there is a whole set of statistical approaches dedicated to dyadic effects, some of which incorporate multiple levels of analyses simultaneously and others that only take into account the dyadic nature of the data while maintaining an individual level of analysis (see Kenny et al. 2006). Illustrating the latter, path analysis with dyadic data could be used to examine the effect of employee job satisfaction on employee work-family conflict while controlling for the correlation between spouse and employee job satisfaction as well as the nonindependence between employee and spouse work-family conflict. Examples of analytical strategies that allow for incorporation of effects at more than one level (i.e., individual-dyad, individual-group) simultaneously include hierarchical linear modeling (Raudenbush & Bryk 2002) and multilevel SEM (Heck & Thomas 2000). Finally, there are occasions where the primary research question focuses on how the similarity (dissimilarity) between dyad members on the same construct affects other variables of interest. For instance, is the similarity in job satisfaction between husband and wife a stronger predictor of marital satisfaction than their dyadic mean-level job satisfaction? Two analytical techniques that provide the ability to examine such similarity, in addition to dyadic mean-level effects, include polynomial regression (Edwards 2007) and the latent congruence model for SEM (Cheung 2009).

Unique situations also exist where examining affect in the work-family interaction may necessitate accounting for a large spectrum of relationships among group members. Two particular types of analyses that incorporate the entirety of social relationships are social network analysis and social relations models. Social network analysis (Scott 1991) identifies the breadth and quality of ties, connections, or links between persons in a group using various types of network measures. Some network measures focus on the individual (e.g., centrality), others on dyads (e.g., reciprocity), others on triads (e.g., transitivity), while others focus on the entire network as a whole (e.g., density). Those indices can then be used as predictors or outcomes of other variables of interest (e.g., positive affect as a predictor of network density at work and/or outside of work). Social relations models (Kenny 1994) also attempt to answer group-level relationship-oriented research questions and require just as intensive data collection, but they usually rely on interval-level data, whereas in social network research the data are typically at the nominal level.

CONCLUSION

Research on work-family interaction continues to accumulate, and there is increasing recognition that affective experiences in both work and family life are important to consider in work-family scholarship. This article provides a historical overview of these two bodies of scholarship, reviews the dominant paradigms adopted in these areas of inquiry, synthesizes existing empirical research on affect and work-family interaction, and provides an original methodological critique of this body of research. From this critique, important avenues for future research are identified, which should both broaden and deepen our understanding of the complex interplay between affective experiences in these two important life domains.

DISCLOSURE STATEMENT

The authors are not aware of any biases that might be perceived as affecting the objectivity of this review.

LITERATURE CITED

Adams GA, King LA, King DW. 1996. Relationships of job and family involvement, family social support, and work-family conflict with job and life satisfaction. *J. Appl. Psychol.* 81:411–20

Ainsworth MS. 1989. Attachments beyond infancy. *Am. Psychol.* 44:709–16

Allen TD. 2001. Family-supportive work environments: the role of organizational perceptions. *J. Vocat. Behav.* 58:414–35

Allen TD. 2009. The work and family interface. In *Oxford Handbook of Industrial and Organizational Psychology*, ed. S Kozlowski. Oxford Univ. Press. In press

Argyle M. 1987. *The Psychology of Happiness*. New York: Methuen. 272 pp.

Aryee S, Fields D, Luk V. 1999a. A cross-cultural test of a model of the work-family interface. *J. Manag.* 25:491–511

Aryee S, Luk V, Leung A, Lo S. 1999b. Role stressors, interrole conflict, and well-being: the moderating influence of spousal support and coping behaviors among employed parents in Hong Kong. *J. Vocat. Behav.* 54:259–78

Ashforth BE, Humphrey RH. 1993. Emotional labor in service role: the influence of identity. *Acad. Manage. Rev.* 88:88–115

Bacharach SB, Bamberger P, Conley S. 1991. Work-home conflict among nurses and engineers: the mediating impact of role stress on burnout and satisfaction at work. *J. Organ. Behav.* 12:39–53

Barling J. 1986. Interrole conflict and marital functioning among employed fathers. *J. Occup. Behav.* 7:1–8

Barnett RC, Hyde JS. 2001. Women, men, work and family. *Am. Psychol.* 56:781–96

Barnett RC, Gareis KC, Brennan RT. 1999. Fit as a mediator of the relationship between work hours and burnout. *J. Occup. Health Psychol.* 74:967–84

Barrett LF, Russell JA. 1998. Independence and bipolarity in the structure of current affect. *J. Personal. Soc. Psychol.* 74:967–84

Barsade SG. 2002. The ripple effect: emotional contagion and its influence on group behavior. *Admin. Sci. Q.* 47:644–75

Behson SJ. 2002. Which dominates? The relative importance of work-family organizational support and general organizational context on employee outcomes. *J. Vocat. Behav.* 61:53–72

Bernas KH, Major DA. 2000. Contributors to stress resistance: testing a model of women's work-family conflict. *Psychol. Women Q.* 24:170–78

Blanch A, Aluja A. 2009. Work, family and personality: a study of work-family conflict. *Personal. Individ. Differ.* 46:520–24

Bruck CS, Allen TD. 2003. The relationship between big five personality traits, negative affectivity, Type A behavior, and work-family conflict. *J. Vocat. Behav.* 63:457–72

Burke RJ, Greenglass ER. 1987. Work and family. In *International Review of Industrial and Organizational Psychology*, ed. CL Cooper, IT Robertson, pp. 273–320. New York: Wiley

Burke RJ, Greenglass ER. 1999. Work-family conflict, spouse support, and nursing staff well-being during organizational restructuring. *J. Occup. Health Psychol.* 4:327–36

Burke RJ, Weir T, DuWors RE. 1980. Perceived Type A behaviour of husbands' and wives' satisfaction and well-being. *J. Occup. Behav.* 1:139–50

Carlson DS. 1999. Personality and role variables as predictors of three forms of work-family conflict. *J. Vocat. Behav.* 55:236–53

Carlson DS, Perrewé PL. 1999. The role of social support in the stressor-strain relationship: an examination of work-family conflict. *J. Manag.* 25:513–40

Carmeli A. 2003. The relationship between emotional intelligence and work attitudes, behavior and outcomes: an examination among senior managers. *J. Manage. Psychol.* 18:788–813

Carver CS, White TL. 1994. Behavioral inhibition, behavioral activation, and affective responses to impending reward and punishment: the BIS/BAS scales. *J. Personal. Soc. Psychol.* 67:319–33

Casper WJ, Eby LT, Bordeaux C, Lockwood A, Lambert D. 2007. A review of research methods in IO/OB work-family research. *J. Appl. Psychol.* 92:28–43

Champoux JE. 1978. Perceptions of work and nonwork: re-examination of compensatory and spillover models. *Soc. Work Occup.* 5:402–22

Cheung GWH. 2009. Introducing the latent congruence model for improving the assessment of similarity, agreement, and fit in organizational research. *Organ. Res. Methods* 12:6–33

Clark LA, Watson D. 1994. Distinguishing functional from dysfunctional affective responses. See Ekman & Davidson 1994, pp. 131–36

Clark MS, Isen AM. 1982. Toward understanding the relationship between feeling states and social behavior. In *Cognitive Social Psychology*, ed. A Hastorf, AM Isen, pp. 73–108. New York: Elsevier

Cohen P. 2008. The origins of this book. In *Applied Data Analytic Techniques for Turning Points Research*, ed. P Cohen, pp. 1–16. New York: Routledge. 256 pp.

Crouter A. 1984. Spillover from family to work: the neglected side of the work-family interface. *Hum. Relat.* 37:425–42

Csikszentmihalyi M. 1990. *Flow: The Psychology of Optimal Experience*. New York: Harper Perennial. 303 pp.

Davidson RJ. 1994. On emotion, mood, and related affective constructs. See Ekman & Davidson 1994, pp. 51–55

Davidson RJ, Ekman P. 1994. Afterword: How are emotions distinguished from moods, temperament and other related affective constructs? See Ekman & Davidson 1994, pp. 94–96

Demerouti E, Bakkera AB, Butlers AJ. 2004. The loss spiral of work pressure, work–home interference and exhaustion: reciprocal relations in a three-wave study. *J. Vocat. Behav.* 64:131–49

Demerouti E, Bakker AB, Schaufeli WB. 2005. Spillover and crossover of exhaustion and life satisfaction among dual-earner parents. *J. Vocat. Behav.* 67:266–89

Diener E, Emmons RA, Larsen RJ, Griffin S. 1985. The satisfaction with life scale. *J. Personal. Assess.* 49:71–75

Doby VJ, Caplan RD. 1995. Organizational stress as threat to reputation: effects on anxiety at work and at home. *Acad. Manage. J.* 38:1105–23

Eby LT, Casper WJ, Lockwood A, Bordeaux C, Brinley A. 2005. Work and family research in IO/OB: content analysis and review of the literature (1980–2002). *J. Vocat. Behav.* 66:124–97

Edwards JR. 2007. Polynomial regression and response surface methodology. In *Perspectives on Organizational Fit*, ed. C Ostroff, TA Judge, pp. 361–72. San Francisco: Jossey-Bass. 464 pp.

Edwards JR, Rothbard NP. 1999. Work and family stress and well-being: an examination of person-environment fit in the work and family domains. *Organ. Behav. Hum. Decis. Process.* 85–129

Edwards JR, Rothbard NP. 2000. Mechanisms linking work and family: clarifying the relationship between work and family constructs. *Acad. Manage. Rev.* 25:178–99

Ekman P, Davidson RJ, eds. 1994. *The Nature of Emotions: Fundamental Questions*. New York: Oxford Univ. Press. 496 pp.

Evans P, Bartolomé F. 1984. The changing pictures of the relationship between career and family. *J. Occup. Behav.* 5:9–21

Fredrickson BL. 1998. What good are positive emotions? *Rev. Gen. Psychol.* 2:300–19

Fredrickson BL. 2001. The role of positive emotions in positive psychology. *Am. Psychol.* 56:218–26

Fredrickson BL. 2003. The value of positive emotions. *Am. Sci.* 91:330–35

Fredrickson BL, Branigan C. 2005. Positive emotions broaden the scope of attention and thought-action repertoires. *Cogn. Emot.* 19:313–32

Frone MR. 2000. Work-family conflict and employee psychiatric disorders: the National Comorbidity Survey. *J. Appl. Psychol.* 85:888–95

Frone MR, Barnes GM, Farrell MP. 1994a. Relationship of work-family conflict to substance use among employed mothers: the role of negative affect. *J. Marriage Fam.* 56:1019–30

Frone MR, Russell M, Cooper ML. 1994b. Relationship between job and family satisfaction: causal or non-causal covariation. *J. Manage.* 20:565–79

Frone MR, Russell M, Cooper ML. 1997a. Relation of work-family conflict to health outcomes: a four-year longitudinal study of employed parents. *J. Occup. Organ. Psychol.* 70:325–35

Frone MR, Yardley JK, Markel KS. 1997b. Developing and testing an integrative model of the work-family interface. *J. Vocat. Behav.* 50:145–67

Geurts SAE, Kompier MAJ, Roxburgh S, Houtman ILD. 2003. Does work-home interference mediate the relationship between workload and well-being? *J. Vocat. Behav.* 63:532–59

Goode WJ. 1960. A theory of role strain. *Am. Sociol. Rev.* 25:483–96

Grandey AA, Cordeiro BL, Crouter AC. 2005. A longitudinal and multi-source test of the work-family conflict and job satisfaction relationship. *J. Occup. Organ. Psychol.* 78:305–23

Grandey AA, Cropanzano R. 1999. The conservation of resources model applied to work-family conflict and strain. *J. Vocat. Behav.* 54:350–70

Gray EK, Watson D. 2001. Emotion, mood, and temperament: similarities, differences, and a synthesis. In *Emotions at Work: Theory, Research and Applications for Management*, ed. RL Payne, CL Cooper, pp. 21–43. Chichester, UK: Wiley-Intersci. 350 pp.

Greenhaus JH, Beutell NJ. 1985. Sources of conflict between work and family roles. *Acad. Manage. Rev.* 10:76–88

Greenhaus JH, Callanan GA, Godshalk VM. 2000. *Career Management*. Fort Worth, TX: Dryden. 491 pp.

Greenhaus JH, Powell GN. 2006. When work and family are allies: a theory of work-family enrichment. *Acad. Manage. Rev.* 31:72–92

Grzywacz JC. 2000. Work-family spillover and health during midlife: Is managing conflict everything? *Am. J. Health Promot.* 14:236–43

Grzywacz JG, Almeida DM, McDonald DA. 2002. Work-family spillover and daily reports of work and family stress in the adult labor force. *Fam. Relat.* 51:28–36

Grzywacz JG, Bass BL. 2003. Work, family, and mental health: testing different models of work-family fit. *J. Marriage Fam.* 65:248–61

Hammer LB, Bauer TN, Grandey AA. 2003. Work-family conflict and work-related withdrawal behaviors. *J. Bus. Psychol.* 17:419–36

Hammer LB, Cullen JC, Neal MB, Sinclair RR, Shafiro MV. 2005. The longitudinal effects of work-family conflict and positive spillover on depressive symptoms among dual-earner couples. *J. Occup. Health Psychol.* 10:138–54

Hanson GC, Hammer LB, Colton CL. 2006. Development and validation of a multidimensional scale of perceived work-family positive spillover. *J. Occup. Health Psychol.* 11:249–65

Harvey S, Kelloway EK, Duncan-Leiper L. 2003. Trust in management as a buffer of the relationships between overload and strain. *J. Occup. Health Psychol.* 8:306–15

Heck RH, Thomas SL. 2000. *An Introduction to Multilevel Modeling Techniques*. Mahwah, NJ: Erlbaum. 209 pp.

Heller D, Watson D. 2005. The dynamic spillover of satisfaction between work and marriage: the role of time and mood. *J. Appl. Psychol.* 90:1273–79

Hill EJ. 2005. Work-family facilitation and conflict, working fathers and mothers, work-family stressors and support. *J. Fam. Issues* 26:793–819

Hochschild AR. 1979. Emotion work, feeling rules, and social structure. *Am. J. Sociol.* 85:551–75

Hochschild AR. 1983. Social constructionist and positivist approaches to the sociology of emotions: comment. *Am. J. Sociol.* 89:432–34

Horwitz BN, Luong G, Charles ST. 2008. Neuroticism and extraversion share genetic and environmental effects with negative and positive mood spillover in a nationally representative sample. *Personal. Individ. Differ.* 45:636–42

Hughes EL, Parkes KR. 2007. Work hours and well-being: the roles of work-time control and work-family interference. *Work Stress* 21:264–78

Ilies R, Schwind KM, Wagner DT, Johnson MD, DeRue DS, Ilgen DR. 2007. When can employees have a family life? The effects of daily workload and affect on work-family conflict and social behaviors at home. *J. Appl. Psychol.* 92:1368–79

Ilies R, Wilson KS, Wagner DT. 2009. The spillover of daily job satisfaction onto employees' family lives: the facilitating role of work-family integration. *Acad. Manage. J.* 52:87–102

Innstrand ST, Langballe EM, Espnes GA, Falkum E, Aasland OG. 2008. Positive and negative work-family interaction and burnout: a longitudinal study of reciprocal relations. *Work Stress* 22:1–15

Izard CE. 1991. *The Psychology of Emotions*. New York: Plenum. 451 pp.

Jackson SE, Zedeck S, Summers E. 1985. Family life disruptions: effect of job-induced structural and emotional interference. *Acad. Manage. J.* 28:574–86

Judge TA, Ilies R. 2004. Affect and job satisfaction: a study of their relationship at work and at home. *J. Appl. Psychol.* 89:661–73

Judge TA, Ilies R, Scott BA. 2006. Work-family conflict and emotions: effects at work and at home. *Personal. Psychol.* 59:779–814

Kando TM, Summers WC. 1971. The impact of work on leisure: toward a paradigm and research strategy. *Pac. Sociol. Rev.* 14:310–27

Kanter RM. 1977. *Men and Women of the Corporation*. New York: Basic Books. 348 pp.

Karatepe OM, Uludag O. 2008. Affectivity, conflicts in the work-family interface, and hotel employee outcomes. *Int. J. Hospitality Manage.* 27:30–41

Kenny DA. 1994. *Interpersonal Perception: A Social Relations Analysis*. New York: Guilford. 270 pp.

Kenny DA, Kashy DA, Cook WL. 2006. *Dyadic Data Analysis*. New York: Guilford. 481 pp.

Kinnunen U, Feldt T, Geurts S, Pulkkinen L. 2006. Types of work-family interface: well-being correlates of negative and positive spillover between work and family. *Scand. J. Psychol.* 47:149–62

Kinnunen U, Geurts S, Mauno S. 2004. Work-to-family conflict and its relationship with satisfaction and well-being: a one-year longitudinal study on gender differences. *Work Stress* 18:1–22

Kinnunen U, Vermulst A, Gerris J, Makikangas A. 2003. Work-family conflict and its relations to well-being: the role of personality as a moderating factor. *Personal. Individ. Differ.* 35:1669–83

Kirchmeyer C. 1992a. Nonwork participation and work attitudes: a test of scarcity vs. expansion models of personal resources. *Hum. Relat.* 45:775–95

Kirchmeyer C. 1992b. Perceptions of nonwork-to-work spillover: challenging the common view of conflict-ridden domain relationships. *Basic Appl. Soc. Psychol.* 13:231–49

Kirchmeyer C. 1993. Nonwork-to-work spillover: a more balanced view of the experiences and coping of professional women and men. *Sex Roles* 28:531–52

Klein KJ, Dansereau F, Hall RJ. 1994. Levels issues in theory development, data collection, and analysis. *Acad. Manage. Rev.* 19:195–229

Kobasa SC. 1979. Stressful life events, personality, and health: inquiry into hardiness. *J. Personal. Soc. Psychol.* 37:1–11

Lambert SJ. 1990. Processes linking work and family: a critical review and research agenda. *Hum. Relat.* 43:239–57

Lapierre LM, Allen TD. 2006. Work-supportive family, family-supportive supervision, use of organizational benefits, and problem-focused coping: implications for work-family conflict and employee well-being. *J. Occup. Health Psychol.* 11:169–81

Little LM, Simmons BL, Nelson DL. 2007. Health among leaders: positive and negative affect, engagement and burnout, forgiveness and revenge. *J. Manage. Stud.* 44:243–60

Livingston BA, Judge TA. 2008. Emotional responses to work-family conflict: an examination of gender role orientation among working men and women. *J. Appl. Psychol.* 93:207–16

Major VS, Klein KJ, Ehrhart MG. 2002. Work time, work interference with family, and psychological distress. *J. Appl. Psychol.* 87:427–36

Marks SR. 1977. Multiple roles and role strain: some notes on human energy, time and commitment. *Am. Sociol. Rev.* 42:921–36

Matthews RA, Del Priore RE, Acitelli LK, Barnes-Farrell JL. 2006. Work-to-relationship conflict: crossover effects in dual-earner couples. *J. Occup. Health Psychol.* 11:228–40

Mauno S, Kinnunen U, Pyykko M. 2005. Does work-family conflict mediate the relationship between work-family culture and self-reported distress? Evidence from five Finnish organizations. *J. Occup. Organ. Psychol.* 78:509–30

McArdle JJ. 1988. Dynamic but structural equation modeling of repeated measures data. In *Handbook of Multivariate Experimental Psychology*, ed. JR Nesselroade, RB Cattell, pp. 561–614. New York: Plenum. 966 pp.

Mesmer-Magnus JR, Viswesvaran C. 2005. Convergence between measures of work-to-family and family-to-work conflict: a meta-analytic examination. *J. Vocat. Behav.* 67:215–32

Minnotte KL, Stevens DP, Minnotte MC, Kiger G. 2007. Emotion-work performance among dual-earner couples: testing four theoretical perspectives. *J. Fam. Issues* 28:773–93

Montgomery AJ, Panagopolou E, Benos A. 2006. Work-family interference as a mediator between job demands and job burnout among doctors. *Stress Health* 22:203–12

Netemeyer RG, Boles JS, McMurrian R. 1996. Development and validation of work-family conflict and family-work conflict scales. *J. Appl. Psychol.* 81:400–10

O'Driscoll MP, Ilgen DR, Hildreth K. 1992. Time devoted to job and off-job activities, interrole conflict, and affective experiences. *J. Appl. Psychol.* 77:272–79

O'Driscoll MP, Poelmans S, Spector PE, Kalliath T, Allen TD, et al. 2003. Family-responsive interventions, perceived organizational and supervisor support, work-family conflict, and psychological strain. *Int. J. Stress Manage.* 10:326–44

Parasuraman S, Greenhaus JH, Granrose CS. 1992. Role stressors, social support, and well-being among two-career couples. *J. Organ. Behav.* 13:339–56

Parkinson B, Totterdell P, Briner RB, Reynolds S. 1996. *Changing Moods: The Psychology of Mood and Mood Regulation*. London: Addison Wesley Longman. 254 pp.

Piotrkowski CS. 1978. *Work and the Family System: A Naturalistic Study of Working-Class and Lower-Middle-Class Families*. New York: Free Press. 337 pp.

Piotrkowski CS. 1979. *Work and the Family System*. New York: Free Press. 337 pp.

Piotrkowski CS, Rapoport RN, Rapoport N. 1987. Families and work. In *Handbook of Marriage and the Family*, ed. M Sussman, S Steinmetz, pp. 251–83. New York: Plenum. 915 pp.

Plutchik R. 1994. *The Psychology and Biology of Emotion*. New York: Harper Collins. 396 pp.

Porfeli E, Wang C, Hartung P. 2008. Family transmission of work affectivity and experiences to children. *J. Vocat. Behav.* 43:278–86

Rafaeli A, Sutton RI. 1989. The expression of emotion in organizational life. *Res. Organ. Behav.* 11:1–42

Rantanen J, Kinnunen U, Feldt T, Pulkkinena L. 2008. Work–family conflict and psychological well-being: stability and cross-lagged relations within one- and six-year follow-ups. *J. Vocat. Behav.* 73:37-51

Raudenbush SW, Bryk AS. 2002. *Hierarchical Linear Models: Applications and Data Analysis Methods*. Thousand Oaks, CA: Sage. 520 pp. 2nd ed.

Rice RW, Frone MR, McFarlin DB. 1992. Work-nonwork conflict and perceived quality of life. *J. Organ. Behav.* 13:155–68

Rice RW, McFarlin DB, Hunt RG, Near JP. 1985. Organizational work and the perceived quality of life: toward a conceptual model. *Acad. Manage. Rev.* 10:296–310

Rothbard NP. 2001. Enriching or depleting: the dynamics of engagement in work and family roles. *Admin. Sci. Q.* 46:655–84

Rothbart MK, Ahadi SA. 1994. Temperament and the development of personality. *J. Abnorm. Psychol.* 103:55–66

Russell JA. 1980. A circumplex model of affect. *J. Personal. Soc. Psychol.* 39:1161–78

Sackett PR, Larson JR. 1990. Research strategies and tactics in industrial and organizational psychology. In *Handbook of Industrial and Organizational Psychology*, vol. 1, ed. MD Dunnette, LM Hough, pp. 419–89. Palo Alto, CA: Consult. Psychol. Press. 755 pp.

Saucier G. 1994. Mini-Markers: a brief version of Goldberg's unipolar Big-Five markers. *J. Personal. Assess.* 63:506–16

Schriescheim CA, Powers KJ, Scandura TA, Gardiner CG, Lankau MJ. 1993. Improving construct measurement in management research: comments and a quantitative approach for assessing the theoretical content adequacy of paper-and-pencil survey type instruments. *J. Manage.* 19:385–417

Schulz MS, Cowan PA, Cowan CP, Brennan RT. 2004. Coming home upset: gender, marital satisfaction, and the daily spillover of workday experience into couple interactions. *J. Fam. Psychol.* 18:250–63

Schwartzberg NS, Dytel RS. 1996. Dual-earner families: the importance of work stress and family stress for psychological well-being. *J. Occup. Health Psychol.* 1:211–23

Scott J. 1991. *Social Network Analysis: A Handbook*. Thousand Oaks, CA: Sage. 208 pp.

Shaffer MA, Harrison DA, Gilley KM, Luk DM. 2001. Struggling for balance amid turbulence on international assignments: work-family conflict, support and commitment. *J. Manage.* 27:99–121

Sieber SD. 1974. Toward a theory of role accumulation. *Am. Sociol. Rev.* 39:567–78

Small SA, Riley D. 1990. Toward a multidimensional assessment of work spillover into family life. *J. Marriage Fam.* 52:51–61

Song ZL, Foo MD, Uy MA. 2008. Mood spillover and crossover among dual-earner couples: a cell phone event sampling study. *J. Appl. Psychol.* 93:443–52

Spence JT, Helmreich RL, Pred RS. 1987. Impatience versus achievement strivings in the type-A pattern: differential effects on students' health and academic achievement. *J. Appl. Psychol.* 72:522–28

Staines GL. 1980. Spillover versus compensation: a review of the literature on the relationship between work and nonwork. *Hum. Relat.* 33:111–29

Stanley RO, Burrows GD. 2001. Varieties and functions of human emotions. In *Emotions at Work: Theory, Research and Applications for Management*, ed. RL Payne, CL Cooper, pp. 3–19. Chichester, UK: Wiley. 350 pp.

Stevens DP, Kiger G, Riley PJ. 2002. Coming unglued? Workplace characteristics, work satisfaction, and family cohesion. *Soc. Behav. Personal.* 30:289–302

Stevens DP, Minnotte KL, Mannon SE, Kiger G. 2007. Examining the neglected side of the work-family interface: antecedents of positive and negative family-to-work spillover. *J. Fam. Issues* 28:242–62

Stoeva AZ, Chiu RK, Greenhaus JH. 2002. Negative affectivity, role stress, and work-family conflict. *J. Vocat. Behav.* 60:1–16

Sumer HC, Knight PA. 2001. How do people with different attachment styles balance work and family? A personality perspective on work-family linkage. *J. Appl. Psychol.* 86:653–63

Takeuchi R, Yun S, Tesluk PE. 2002. An examination of crossover and spillover effects of spousal and expatriate cross-cultural adjustment on expatriate outcomes. *J. Appl. Psychol.* 87:655–66

Thayer RE. 1989. *The Biopsychology of Mood and Arousal.* New York: Oxford Univ. Press. 234 pp.

Thomas LT, Ganster DC. 1995. Impact of family-supportive work variables on work-family conflict and strain: a control perspective. *J. Appl. Psychol.* 80:6–15

Tomkarten AJ, Keener SD. 1998. Frontal brain asymmetry and depression: a self-regulatory perspective. *Cogn. Emot.* 12:387–420

Van Der Zee KI, Ali AJ, Salome E. 2005. Role interference and subjective well-being among expatriate families. *Eur. J. Work Organ. Psychol.* 14:239–62

van Steenbergen EF, Ellemers N, Mooijaart A. 2007. How work and family can facilitate each other: distinct types of work-family facilitation and outcomes for women and men. *J. Occup. Organ. Psychol.* 12:279–300

Watson D. 2000. *Mood and Temperament.* New York: Guilford. 340 pp.

Watson D, Clark LA. 1984. Negative affectivity: the disposition to experience aversive emotional states. *Psychol. Bull.* 96:465–90

Watson D, Clark LA. 1994. Emotions, moods, traits and temperament: conceptual distinctions and empirical findings. See Ekman & Davidson 1994, pp. 89–93

Watson D, Clark LA, Tellegen A. 1988. Development and validation of a brief measure of positive and negative affect: the PANAS scales. *J. Personal. Soc. Psychol.* 54:1063–70

Watson D, Tellegen A. 1985. Toward a consensual structure of mood. *Psychol. Bull.* 98:219–35

Watson D, Wiese D, Vidya J, Tellegen A. 1999. The two general activation systems of affect: structural findings, evolutionary considerations, and psychobiological evidence. *J. Personal. Soc. Psychol.* 76:820–38

Wayne JH, Musisca N, Fleeson W. 2004. Considering the role of personality in the work-family experience: relationships of the Big Five to work-family conflict and facilitation. *J. Vocat. Behav.* 64:108–30

Weiss HM. 2002. Deconstructing job satisfaction: separating evaluations, beliefs, and affective experiences. *Hum. Resour. Manage. Rev.* 12:173–94

Weiss HM, Cropanzano R. 1996. Affective events theory: a theoretical discussion of the structure, causes and consequences of affective experiences at work. *Res. Organ. Behav.* 18:1–74

Westman M, Etzion D. 1995. Crossover of stress, strain, and resources from one spouse to another. *J. Organ. Behav.* 16:169–81

Wharton AS, Erickson RJ. 1993. Managing emotions on the job and at home: understanding the consequences of multiple emotional roles. *Acad. Manage. Rev.* 18:457–86

Wiese BS, Salemela-Aro K. 2008. Goal conflict and facilitation as predictors of work–family satisfaction and engagement. *J. Vocat. Behav.* 73:490–97

Williams KJ, Alliger GM. 1994. Role stressors, mood spillover, and perceptions of work-family conflict in employed parents. *Acad. Manage. J.* 37:837–68

Williams KJ, Suls J, Alliger GM, Learner SM, Wan CK. 1991. Multiple role juggling and daily mood states in working mothers: an experience sampling study. *J. Appl. Psychol.* 76:664–74

Yanchus N, Eby LT, Lance CE, Drollinger S. 2009. The impact of emotional labor on work-family balance outcomes. *J. Vocat. Behav.* In press

Zedeck S. 1992. Introduction: exploring the domain of work and family concerns. In *Work, Family and Organizations*, ed. S Zedeck, pp. 1–32. San Francisco: Jossey-Bass. 475 pp.

Cumulative Knowledge and Progress in Human Factors

Robert W. Proctor[1] and Kim-Phuong L. Vu[2]

[1] Department of Psychological Sciences, Purdue University, West Lafayette, Indiana 47907-2081; email: proctor@psych.purdue.edu

[2] Department of Psychology, California State University, Long Beach, California 90840-0901; email: kvu8@csulb.edu

Annu. Rev. Psychol. 2010. 61:623–51

First published online as a Review in Advance on June 17, 2009

The *Annual Review of Psychology* is online at psych.annualreviews.org

This article's doi: 10.1146/annurev.psych.093008.100325

Key Words

applied experimental psychology, engineering psychology, ergonomics, human-computer interaction, human information processing

Abstract

This review provides a cumulative perspective on current human factors research by first briefly acknowledging previous *Annual Review* articles. We show that several recent conceptual advances are an outgrowth of the information-processing approach adopted by the field and present several areas of current research that are built directly on prior work. Topic areas that provide fundamental tools for human factors analyses are summarized, and several current application areas are reviewed. We end by considering alternatives to the information-processing approach that have been proposed and placing those alternatives in context. We argue that the information-processing language provides the foundation that has enabled much of the growth in human factors. This growth reflects a cumulative development of concepts and methods that continues today.

Contents

INTRODUCTION

"Human factors" and "ergonomics" refer to an interdisciplinary field concerned with designing systems and products for human use. Human factors' accomplishments have been well documented in the *Annual Review of Psychology*, although this is the first review to use the term in the title. From 1958 to 1993, eight *Annual Review* articles appeared under the title "Engineering Psychology," a term used historically to identify the psychological part of this field. Division 21 of the American Psychological Association is still named Applied Experimental and Engineering Psychology, but the term "engineering psychology" is not as widely used as it once was. Indeed, in the last *Annual Review* article with that title, Howell (1993) said, "Engineering psychology may well be disappearing as an identifiable specialty" (p. 232).

In agreement with Howell's assessment, PsycINFO of February, Week 4, 2009 listed nine entries from 1994 to the present with engineering psychology in the title, compared to 79 entries from 1950 to 1993. The contributions of psychology to human factors nowadays also extend beyond those traditionally associated with applied experimental psychology. Consequently, we use the term "human factors" to include the full range of psychological research relevant to designing for human use.

Since Kuhn (1962) introduced the term "paradigm" to the vocabulary of scientists, there has been a tendency to emphasize new paradigms and paradigm shifts as central to the advancement of science. For example, a 2008 National Science Foundation program solicitation (08–604), *Cyber-Enabled Discovery and Innovation*, states that submitted research proposals

Engineering psychology: the branch of psychology involving application of principles from experimental psychology to design of systems and products for human use

should "promise radical, paradigm-changing research findings." One implication of an emphasis on paradigm shifts is that past research is of little relevance because it is from "old" paradigms. This view is reinforced within human factors because the field deals with new, increasingly sophisticated technologies.

Although the notion of paradigm shift is popular in science, most contemporary philosophies of science do not view science as operating in this manner (e.g., Laudan 1996). The theme of this review is that, to the contrary, the progress of scientific psychology in general—and human factors in particular—is cumulative. We argue that it is more constructive to view progress in science as building on past achievements and to consider new theories and data in relation to those of the past rather than to view science in terms of paradigm shifts. Our position is similar to that of Posner (1982) and Logan (2004), who made strong cases that progress of attentional theory is cumulative. As in the study of attention, we attribute much of the cumulative development in human factors to the human information-processing language. We begin with a brief review of the previous *Annual Review* articles on engineering psychology and related topics because they provide a necessary context for understanding how contemporary research in human factors builds on the knowledge developed in the past.

REVIEWS ON ENGINEERING PSYCHOLOGY

The first four reviews titled "Engineering Psychology" were published between 1958 and 1966. Fitts's (1958) review contained sections on human-machine systems and automation, but it focused on topics involving basic human performance, including perceptual-motor skill, stimulus-response (S-R) compatibility, and the core human factors areas of display and control design. Melton & Briggs (1960) added mention of space travel, effects of stress on human performance, monitoring and vigilance, and multi-operator systems. Chapanis (1963), writing soon after the inaugural human space flight,

began with a detailed treatment of human factors issues related to space travel. Poulton (1966) introduced "the additional-task method," which is the now commonplace use of a secondary task to measure attentional demands.

Alluisi & Morgan (1976) added the term "human performance" to the title because it better captured the scientific aspect of engineering psychology. Despite this rationale, the unique aspect of their review was its lengthy treatment of applications. The next two reviews reverted to the title "Engineering Psychology" but returned to the human performance emphasis of the earlier articles. Yet, there is a striking change in those reviews, with more weight given to complex task environments and higher-level cognitive processes. Wickens & Kramer (1985) explicitly emphasized "the cognitive aspects of engineering psychology" (p. 309) in general and human information-processing limits in particular. For the first time, there was a focus on attention and mental workload measurement, as well as detailed treatment of decision-making and the use of decision-making heuristics. Gopher & Kimchi (1989) discussed three major topics: displaying and interacting with complex visual information, mental workload, and training of complex skills. Howell (1993) continued the emphasis on complex task demands and introduced coverage of cognitive task analysis, naturalistic and group decision-making, and situation awareness (SA). The review also highlighted the emergence of human-computer interaction (HCI) and the topic of individual differences.

Although no review on engineering psychology has been published in the *Annual Review of Psychology* since 1993, two articles titled "Human-Computer Interaction" appeared subsequently. The first is that of Carroll (1997), who stated, "HCI is a science of design.... HCI is not merely applied psychology.... It illustrates the possibilities of psychology as a design science" (p. 62). Carroll noted that although HCI originated from cognitive, experimental psychology, "In the 1990s, new voices entered the HCI discussion, urging a stronger social

Stimulus-response (S-R) compatibility: differences in performance as a function of the relations between stimulus and response sets and the elements within those sets

Mental workload: the demands placed on information-processing capacities by tasks that a person is to perform

Situation awareness (SA): understanding of the events occurring in a task environment and their implications for actions and future events

HCI: human-computer interaction

and contextual orientation" (p. 74). This trend has continued in HCI and human factors to the present. Olson & Olson's (2003) review elaborated several themes from Carroll's article, but took a less extreme position about the centrality of HCI research. They added description of work on information foraging and included discussion of computer-supported cooperative work. Related to the latter topic, Hodgkinson & Healey's (2008) review, "Cognition in Organizations," examined group and team work from the human factors tradition.

One cannot help but be impressed with how relevant the topics covered in these reviews are to current human factors and how contemporary those from Wickens & Kramer (1985) onward read. The articles bear out our view that research in human factors has evolved and produced an ever-increasing understanding of human performance in applied settings.

HUMAN INFORMATION PROCESSING AND RELATED APPROACHES

The growth of human factors parallels that of cognitive psychology. Beginning in the 1950s, cognitive psychology embraced the human information-processing approach, which characterizes the human as a communication system consisting of several distinct processes that operate on representations, or codes, mediating between perception and action. Posner (1986) eloquently described the impact and value of this approach. After noting that a mix of ideas regarding mental processes was evident during the first half of the twentieth century, and that the languages of introspection, behaviorism, and physiology were inadequate for conveying those ideas, he stated:

This mix of ideas was ignited by the information processing language that arrived in psychology in the early 1950s. The view of the nervous system in terms of information flow provided a common language in which both conscious and unconscious events might be discussed. Computers could be programmed

to simulate exciting tasks heretofore only performed by human beings without requiring any discussion of consciousness. By analogies with computing systems, one could deal with the format (code) in which information is presented to the senses and the computations required to change code (recodings) and for storage and overt responses. These concepts brought a new unity to areas of psychology and a way of translating between psychological and physiological processes. (Posner 1986, pp. V-6–V-7)

A virtue of this approach for human factors is that the human is analyzed as a system, which allows human information processing to be characterized in much the same way as machine processing. In this regard, Posner (1986) said:

Because the language of information processing provides an objective and quantitative way of describing the basis of human performance, it has proven useful in applications... Indeed, much of the impetus for the development of this kind of empirical study stemmed from the desire to integrate description of the human within overall systems. (p. V-6)

In summary, the information-processing approach provides a language that allows consideration of human performance from the level of brain mechanisms up to that of complex sociotechnical systems consisting of people interacting with technology. Our contention is that adoption of the information-processing language by psychologists was, and continues to be, vital to the development of human factors (Proctor & Vu 2006a). It is not just happenstance that the field emerged around the same time as the human information-processing approach and that its continued progress has paralleled that of cognitive psychology. Many recent developments in human factors, several of which we describe, can be seen as outgrowths of this approach.

One recent trend in cognitive psychology is a move toward cognitive neuroscience, the goal of which is to understand the biological mechanisms that underlie human information processing. Neural activity recordings [e.g., electroencephalograms (EEGs) and event-related potentials (ERPs)] and other physiological techniques (e.g., transcranial magnetic stimulation, the activation of neurons in a brain region through electromagnetic induction) are used along with experimental methods and theories from cognitive psychology to determine the neural underpinnings. Contemporary cognitive theories are informed as well by these studies examining neural correlates of behavior, with many theories explaining a variety of behavioral and psychophysiological data. Cognitive neuroscience is also having an impact on the areas of evolutionary psychology, social cognition, and affect described later in this section (e.g., Harmon-Jones & Winkielman 2007).

The idea that human factors can benefit from incorporating knowledge about the human brain has been advocated using the term "neuroergonomics" (Parasuraman & Rizzo 2007). Neuroergonomics emphasizes neuroimaging and other psychophysiological methods, including functional magnetic resonance imaging (fMRI), EEGs, and ERPs. Recording these measures of brain activity while people perform complex tasks can enhance understanding of phenomena of concern in human factors. For example, Berka et al. (2007) identified two distinct EEG indices for engagement and workload in individuals performing a 20-minute vigilance task. As time on vigil increased, the workload index increased, but the engagement index decreased. Based on correlations of these measures with performance of other perceptual and cognitive tasks, Berka et al. concluded that the decrease in the engagement index reflects decreases in visual information processing, whereas the increase in the workload index reflects increasing demands on working memory and executive control processes. Another aspect of neuroergonomics involves the genetic basis of individual differences in cognition (Parasuraman & Rizzo 2007). As more is learned about the influences of specific genes on the efficiency of brain functions, this knowledge may prove useful in

designing new technological systems and in the training for those systems to be most suitable for subgroups of individual users with distinct patterns of cognitive capabilities.

A more immediate application of neuroergonomics is to adaptive automation, flexible allocation of tasks to automation as a function of dynamic changes in demands on an operator's information-processing capabilities (Parasuraman & Wickens 2008). Such adaptations can be based on known demands associated with various task components, measures of operator performance, models that calculate current and future operator needs, or psychophysiological measures (Scerbo 2007). Adaptation based on psychophysiological measures, often called "augmented cognition" (Schmorrow & Stanney 2008), relies on measures of neural activity to determine an individual's cognitive state in real-time and then uses that information to adapt the technology to meet current cognitive needs. Berka et al. (2007) noted that their EEG indices correlated with specific task events and could potentially be used to adapt tasks and interfaces in real-time.

Another contemporary movement is that of evolutionary psychology (Gangestad & Simpson 2007). Evolutionary psychologists argue that cognitive psychology has placed insufficient emphasis on the adaptive evolutionary function of cognitive mechanisms. Their point is that cognitive mechanisms are adaptations, and therefore it is important to consider what functions these mechanisms would have served in survival and reproductive fitness (Nairne et al. 2008). An implication of this view is that information processing is highly modular. For example, Nairne et al. showed that words within a category relating to survival were recalled better than were words in other categories. They interpreted this finding as suggesting that "human memory systems may be 'tuned' to remember information that is processed for survival" (Nairne et al. 2008, p. 176). With respect to human factors, evolutionary psychology suggests that information provided to users will be processed more

EEGs: electroencephalograms

ERPs: event-related potentials

Neuroergonomics: application of cognitive neuroscience knowledge and methods to human factors issues in performance of complex tasks

fMRI: functional magnetic resonance imaging

efficiently and remembered better when it is consistent with the functional adaptations of the information-processing system.

One approach in human factors that is linked to evolutionary views is that of information foraging. Among the evolutionary problems that the cognitive system evolved to solve are navigation in the environment and foraging for food. Pirolli (2007) has applied this perspective to adaptive information interaction involving the Internet and other sources, with the idea that people use foraging strategies to find and "consume" information in much the same way that our ancestors found and consumed food. Research on information foraging focuses on the ways in which people navigate/search through information structures and determine the information that they will attend to and use. The goal is to understand and improve human-information interaction, resulting in technology that is a better match to human capabilities and strategies.

Human factors psychologists increasingly study social factors because people perform tasks and activities in the context of others. As part of the effort to understand social factors, social psychologists have applied the information-processing approach through what is called "social cognition," which refers to "the processes by which people make sense of other people" (Fiske 2005, p. 37). Researchers in social cognition take an information-processing approach to understanding social attitudes and behaviors such as stereotypes and prejudice. Results of numerous studies have suggested that much social cognition is unconscious: People categorize input automatically, and these implicit categorizations activate a host of associations that influence judgment and choice as well as what someone will remember. In a review, Uhlmann et al. (2008) conclude that the data from several methods establish unconscious influences on judgment and behavior but are ambiguous as to whether the mental states themselves are unconscious.

A specialty called "macroergonomics," which relates to social and organizational factors, has developed within human factors.

Like the information-processing approach, macroergonomics takes a systems perspective, with an emphasis on organizational design and management. Much of the concern focuses on how to integrate information technology into organizations effectively by considering human characteristics. This specialty has had sufficient impact to warrant a special issue of *Applied Ergonomics* (Imada & Carayon 2008). One outgrowth of social cognition and macroergonomics has been increased emphasis on team cognition and performance. Of particular interest is the idea that shared cognitions, e.g., common goals and awareness of issues and status, are necessary for effective team performance (Van den Bossche et al. 2006).

Another trend within cognitive psychology and social cognition has been increased emphasis on the role of affect. According to Forgas (2008), "The emerging cognitive information processing paradigm in the 1960s initially also focused on cold, affect-less thinking. . ." (p. 95). Although affect was overlooked initially, this is no longer the case, as emphasized by Wilson et al. (2007, p. 184): "The past two decades have witnessed a remarkable growth of interest in cognitive aspects of emotional vulnerability . . . much of this research has been designed to address predictions concerning the selective processing of emotional information." It is now acknowledged both in psychology in general and in human factors (Khalid 2006) that there is close interplay between cognition and affect. As Forgas (2008) states, "Affect plays a key role in determining how mental representations about the social world are created and maintained in memory. Conversely, cognitive processes are also involved in the generation of affective responses" (p. 96).

The increased emphasis on affect has been evident in human factors through consideration of how affective reactions can be incorporated into design. This work goes under various names, including affective design, engineering aesthetics, and hedonomics (Helander & Tham 2003). The idea is that it is not enough just to satisfy human physical and cognitive needs, but that emotional needs must be satisfied as well.

One area in which affective interfaces have been developed is that of intelligent tutors (Millis et al. 2008). These tutoring systems use digital humans called avatars to provide feedback to students by incorporating emotion in their facial expressions and digital voices. The incorporation of affect into the avatars has been shown to be effective at promoting learning.

We reiterate that these contemporary topic areas within basic and applied psychology are products of the information-processing approach. That the approach continues to spawn new areas of research is testimony to the utility of the information-processing language.

PERFORMANCE OF PERCEPTUAL-MOTOR TASKS

The *Annual Review of Psychology* articles on engineering psychology up to and including that of Alluisi & Morgan (1976) focused on perceptual-motor performance from an information-processing perspective. With the exception of a general interest in attention, those topics tended to receive little coverage in the subsequent reviews. Therefore, one might conclude that the perceptual-motor topics are of little relevance to contemporary human factors and are no longer active areas of research. Yet, the situation is to the contrary. We provide descriptions of recent research conducted on four topics from the early volumes and indicate how that research has changed understanding of these topic areas.

Vigilance

Contemporary research on vigilance can be traced to Mackworth (1948), who was interested in why sonar and radar operators failed to detect many enemy submarines. Vigilance was studied during the early days of human factors research and covered in several of the engineering psychology articles in the *Annual Review of Psychology*. Though research on vigilance never ceased, its prominence decreased. However, interest in vigilance has revived recently due in part to the increasing pervasiveness of automation in human-machine systems (Warm et al. 2008). Automation changes the role of the operator from active controller to passive monitor. Operators must oversee the automation for infrequently occurring signals that require responses, which is a vigilance task.

Mackworth (1948) identified the vigilance decrement: Detection of critical events decreases over the first 15 minutes of the vigil for a variety of tasks. For many years, the vigilance decrement was attributed to decreased arousal resulting from the monotonous nature of vigilance tasks (Kass et al. 2001). However, recent evidence has converged to indicate that the vigilance decrement is due partially to high mental demands associated with maintaining a vigil.

At the time vigilance research was covered in Alluisi & Morgan's (1976) review, vigilance was characterized as highly task specific because several studies reported low intrasubject correlations of performance across different tasks. Parasuraman & Davies (1977) took a step toward reducing this emphasis on task specificity by incorporating resource theories of attention to explain why performers showed low correlations for certain tasks. They focused on the idea that successive tasks, which require a standard to be maintained in working memory against which potentially critical events must be compared, were more mentally demanding than simultaneous tasks, which do not require comparison to a standard. Many subsequent studies showed that increases in information-processing demands produced in various ways have more harmful effects on successive tasks than on simultaneous tasks.

Additional evidence in support of a resource account of the vigilance decrement comes from measures of mental workload and blood-flow velocity. Mental workload measures show not only that successive tasks are more demanding than simultaneous tasks, but also that vigilance tasks impose demands on multiple attentional resources (Finomore et al. 2006). Measurements of blood-flow velocity show a strong relation between velocity and task demands, particularly for the right hemisphere,

Vigilance decrement: a decline in detection of target events that often occurs as time on a vigil or monitoring task increases supporting a resource model (Warm & Parasuraman 2007). Thus, the picture of the vigilance decrement that has emerged recently is much different from the most widely accepted views of the past.

Stimulus-Response Compatibility

The first study of S-R compatibility, conducted by Fitts & Seeger (1953), is cited often in the human factors literature, and S-R compatibility was covered in the first three *Annual Review* articles on engineering psychology. Compatibility has continued to be a topic of interest in human factors but more so in basic human performance. Most widely studied are spatial compatibility effects in which the mapping of stimuli to responses is varied. For a variety of situations for which stimuli and responses have spatial properties, performance is better when the stimuli are mapped to their corresponding responses (Proctor & Vu 2006b). The stimuli can be physical locations, location words, arrow directions, motion directions, or any other stimulus that signifies location information. Responses can be key presses, linear movements of input devices such as a joystick, or rotations of a steering wheel or flight yoke. Recent studies have emphasized that compatibility effects also occur when the S-R alternatives differ in positive/negative affect, numerosity, duration, or precision/power grip (Proctor & Vu 2006b). In general, compatibility effects arise whenever there is overlap, or similarity, between the stimulus and response dimensions (Kornblum et al. 1990), regardless of the task relevance of the dimensions.

Most accounts of compatibility effects are based on two processes: automatic and intentional (Kornblum et al. 1990). Automatic response activation is produced through long-term associations between stimuli and their corresponding responses. The Simon effect (Simon 1990), a compatibility effect obtained when the stimulus dimension is task irrelevant, is attributed to automatic activation. Intentional processes, which operate by way of short-term S-R associations defined for a task, are presumed to be controlled and attention

demanding. Findings attributed to intention include that compatibility effects are larger for relevant S-R mappings and are influenced by task goals.

The benefit of a compatible spatial mapping over an incompatible one is reduced or eliminated when tasks with the two mappings are mixed, both when responses are key presses and when they are rotations of a flight yoke (Yamaguchi & Proctor 2006). One work environment in which mappings are mixed is that of mine shuttle cars, for which the control-response mapping is compatible when entering the mine but incompatible when leaving it. Zupanc et al. (2007) showed in a simulated mine environment that correct responses were slower and the proportion of operating errors higher when the control-response relationships alternated in this manner compared to when they were held constant.

Research has shown that it is not the location or movement of the response effector that is critical for compatibility effects but rather the location of the action goal (Hommel 1993). Kunde et al. (2007) illustrated this principle for operation of hand tools that require the hand to move in a direction opposite that of the tool tip. Response time varied as a function of compatibility of the stimulus location and direction of movement of the tool tip but not of the stimulus and direction of hand movement. The relation between the action goal and the hand movement required to achieve that goal also showed a compatibility effect. This result suggests that designers should avoid inversions of working ends of tools. When that is not possible, as in surgical instruments used for laparoscopic surgery, an augmented display should be provided that reinverts the visual feedback from the tool end to correspond with the direction of hand movement.

Multiple-Task Performance

Another area of human factors research that goes back to the earliest days is multiple-task performance. Although studies have been conducted with more than two tasks, the majority are concerned with dual-task performance. As with vigilance and compatibility effects, considerable research effort has been devoted to issues of multiple-task performance in recent years.

Much basic dual-task research has concentrated on the psychological refractory period (PRP) effect, which refers to the following: When stimuli for two tasks, each of which requires a response, occur with a short interval of a few hundred milliseconds or less between their onsets, the response to the second stimulus is delayed. The most widely accepted account of the PRP effect is that of a central-processing bottleneck (Pashler 1994). The fundamental idea is that the second stimulus can be identified as the first task is being processed, but later processes such as response selection for the second task cannot begin until that for the first task is completed. Recent years have seen debate concerning whether this central bottleneck is built in to the cognitive architecture or is a result of a strategy used to coordinate performance of the two tasks (Meyer & Kieras 1997) and whether the bottleneck can ever be completely bypassed (Ruthruff et al. 2006). These views are combined in recent capacity-sharing models, which depict the bottleneck as a limited-capacity resource that can be allocated in different amounts to central processes for the two tasks rather than having to be devoted to one task at a time (Tombu & Jolicœur 2005).

The view of attention as a limited-capacity resource is more widely accepted outside of the PRP literature. Within human factors, Wickens's multiple-resource model (Wickens & McCarley 2008) has been commonly adopted. This model distinguishes processing resources with respect to four dimensions: stages (perception, cognition, responding), perceptual modalities (auditory, visual), codes (spatial, verbal), and channels (focal vision, ambient vision). Support for the model comes from findings that dual-task performance is often better when the individual tasks differ on one or more dimension than when they do not. Executive control processes are important in dual-task performance, particularly when the two tasks cannot be carried out together (Wickens & McCarley 2008). In such situations, costs occur when switching between two tasks and as a consequence of the necessity of interleaving the tasks.

The PRP effect and many other attentional phenomena illustrate that people have difficulty processing the information for one task while they are performing another. This limitation in processing capacity has been shown to be important for the use of cell phones while driving. Strayer & Drews (2007) summarize evidence indicating that hands-free cell-phone use causes drivers to miss significant visual events occurring on the road, such as traffic signal changes. This attentional problem is more severe for cell-phone conversations than for conversations with other passengers because the shared contextual cues in the latter situation allow the driver to devote more attention to driving when warranted by the circumstances. William Howell, chair of the Human Factors and Ergonomics Society government relations committee, summarized the state of affairs regarding the problem of cell-phone use as, "We know enough about how attention works already to guide strategies for addressing the problem" (Novotney 2009, p. 35).

Aimed Movements and Fitts's Law

Factors influencing the speed and accuracy of aimed movements have been investigated for more than a century. Woodworth (1899) developed a two-process model, according to which execution of rapid aimed movements is achieved through an initial impulse phase, which is under control of the central nervous system, and a current control phase of modifications based on sensory feedback. Contemporary models incorporate this distinction and can be characterized as more fully developed variants of the two-process model (Elliott et al. 2001).

Fitts (1954) provided evidence that movement time is a logarithmic function of an index difficulty, which is positively related to movement distance and inversely related to the area of the target. This function, known as Fitts's law, has been the subject of much basic and applied research in control of aimed movements.

PRP: psychological refractory period

Meyer et al. (1988) developed a stochastic optimized-submovement model for Fitts's law that provides the most complete theoretical account of it and related movement phenomena. According to this model, an aimed movement is composed of a primary submovement and an optional corrective submovement, which are programmed to minimize movement time while maintaining high accuracy. This minimization of movement time is obtained by optimally adjusting the magnitudes and durations of neuromotor force impulses that generate the submovements. Recent research has suggested that control over the primary submovement can be exercised after it is initiated by comparing feedback about limb movement to a representation of the expected feedback (Elliott et al. 2009).

In human factors and HCI, Fitts's law has been applied to estimate performance with many pointing devices and control configurations (Seow 2005), including mobile devices, stylus keyboards, and aimed movements in a vibrating environment. Alexander et al. (2008) used Fitts's law to quantify the effect of walking speed on mobile HCI performance. The slope of the Fitts's law function was least when the user was standing without moving and increased as walking speed increased. As another example, Francis & Oxtoby (2006) demonstrated that algorithms based on Fitts's law can be applied to optimize text entry times for small computer or mobile screens that use single-finger or stylus input. The Fitts's law relation can be customized for individuals or for specialized tasks based on a text corpus that is derived for the individual or task.

The importance of Fitts's law for applied research is illustrated by a special issue of the *International Journal of Human-Computer Studies* published to celebrate the fiftieth anniversary of the Fitts (1954) study. According to the editors, "What has come to be known as Fitts' law has proven highly applicable in Human–Computer Interaction (HCI), making it possible to predict reliably the minimum time for a person in a pointing task to reach a specified target" (Guiard & Beaudouin-Lafon 2004, p. 747).

Summary

The research areas described in this section are ones in which contemporary research and theory can be seen to be built on a foundation of the findings from the past. These areas and others that have developed out of the information-processing approach continue to be essential sources of basic and applied knowledge in human factors.

AWARENESS, ATTENTIONAL CONTROL, AND AUTOMATICITY

One major principle of human information processing is that capacity is limited. Several concepts and applications have developed around issues of information overload, how this overload degrades performance, and how the problems associated with overload can be alleviated.

Mental Workload

Mental workload assessment—evaluation of the demands placed on a person's cognitive resources—is one area of application that is an outgrowth of research in human information processing. Wickens & Kramer (1985), the first to include the topic in an *Annual Review of Psychology* article, emphasized, "The metaphor of attention as a limited commodity or set of resources underlies the concept of *mental workload*" (p. 316). They pointed out that mental workload was "one of the most prolific research areas in the last decade" (p. 316). Gopher & Kimchi (1989) devoted a third of their review to mental workload, another indication of its prominence during that period.

Mental workload no longer commands the attention that it once did, but research on the topic continues. Much of this more recent work is oriented toward application in particular work domains: the transportation industry, interface design, job design, medicine, etc. One finding is that operators often can maintain performance under conditions of high workload by adopting information-processing strategies that direct attention to the primary tasks rather than to peripheral tasks (Parasuraman et al. 2008). Mental workload assessment is also used regularly as a tool to evaluate hypotheses about decrements in performance, as in the vigilance research described above.

Pickup et al. (2005) summarized the current state of affairs as follows: "The notion [of mental workload] has found widespread acceptance as of value in assessing the impact of new tasks, in comparing the effects of different or job interface designs and in understanding the consequences of different levels of automation" (p. 463). Though the concept of mental workload and its assessment are not completely settled matters, mental workload measurement has become a well-established tool in the human factors specialists' toolkit.

Situation Awareness

SA began to receive consideration within human factors beginning in the late 1980s. Salmon et al. (2008) noted, "The construct has since evolved into a core theme within system design and evaluation and continues to dominate human factors research worldwide" (p. 298). The most widely cited definition of SA is that developed by Endsley (1995): "The perception of elements in the environment within a volume of time and space, the comprehension of their meaning, and the projection of their status in the near future" (p. 36). This definition focuses on an operator's mental representation of the situation as generated by fundamental information processes. Durso et al. (2007) have argued that emphasis should be placed instead on the information-processing component of comprehension because awareness implies that only explicit information is important, whereas comprehension allows for an influence of implicit information as well.

Endsley (1995) based her approach to SA explicitly on stages of human information processing. Other perspectives include those of activity theory (Bedny & Meister 1999) and ecological psychology (Smith & Hancock 1995), described later in the article. Regarding these alternatives, Durso et al. (2007) make the following point: "Although it is possible to look at SA from perspectives other than cognitive information-processing...there is certainly reason to treat SA as a cognitive construct" (p. 164). This cognitive construct has been applied successfully to system design issues in aviation and medicine, especially related to the use of automated systems (Parasuraman et al. 2008).

Though much work on SA has focused on individual awareness and performance, within the team-performance literature there is interest in specifying team SA (Gorman et al. 2006). The idea is that team performance depends not only on the SA of individual team members but also on the members' shared awareness and the total SA for the team as a whole. Similar issues to those for measuring individual SA arise when measuring team awareness, but the issues are more complex and provide a challenge for human factors psychologists that remains to be resolved (Salmon et al. 2008).

Multimodal and Adaptive Display Design

Advances in technology have allowed large amounts of information to be made available to people for performing a variety of tasks and have provided novel ways of inputting and outputting information from interfaces. As one consequence, there has been interest in the potential of multimodal interfaces for allowing more effective human-machine interactions, as, for example, in the use of multimodal warning signals to alert drivers of possible hazards (Spence & Ho 2008). The mode distinctions involve use of not only various sensory systems in the display of information but also various response modalities in the input of information to systems.

Initial research with multimodal interfaces had the goal of alleviating demands on the visual system by reallocating some information from visual displays to auditory or tactile displays. The basic thought, consistent with multiple-resource views of attention (Wickens 2008), is that information-processing capacity can be enhanced by distributing information across modalities. Other possible benefits of multi-modal interfaces include providing redundant coding of information and synergy of information across modalities (Sarter 2006). Several guidelines for multimodal interface design exist (e.g., Reeves et al. 2004), but Sarter notes that many of them "do not seem to consider the existing knowledge base on the neurophysiology of crossmodal information processing and its performance implications" (p. 443).

Much of the research to which Sarter (2006) refers comes from studies examining how a cue in one sensory modality directs attention to influence processing of stimuli in another. Studies have shown that a detection response to a visual target is faster and more accurate following presentation of an uninformative auditory cue on the same side as the visual target (Proctor et al. 2005). A cross-modal cuing benefit is sometimes obtained as well when a spatially noninformative visual cue is located to the same side as an auditory target (Spence et al. 2004). The crossmodal cuing benefit also occurs for visual and tactile stimuli, regardless of the cue and target modality.

One way to convey information or data in a multimodal display is through sonification, which refers to nonspeech auditory displays. For effective use of sonification, it is necessary to know how to use various stimulus dimensions and properties of auditory displays to convey complex information in a way that can be easily perceived by users. For example, auditory displays can be used to convey a medical patient's vital signs. Spain & Bliss (2008) examined a sonification display consisting of a stream of auditory pulses that varied in frequency and presentation rate as an indicator of blood-pressure level and urgency. Monitoring the display was carried out as a secondary task while performing a visually demanding primary task. Of most interest were effects of the rates at which the tone pulses were presented. Subjective measures showed workload to be least for the medium pulse rate, for which users also indicated that their trust in the system was greatest.

Another application of sonification is to accessibility for visually impaired individuals.

Zhao et al. (2008) had blind users perform data extraction tasks with geographic data sets using iSonic, a tool that allows exploration of the data set using coordinated maps and tables that provide speech and nonspeech auditory output. The users were required to perform several tasks, and they generally were able to carry out the tasks by choosing an appropriate combination of interface features. Among the features of iSonic that users found helpful were the abilities to move between maps and tables and to use pitch changes to detect trends and speech output for specific values.

Multimodal interfaces also can be designed to adapt automatically in response to a user's habits or performance demands (Reeves et al. 2004). Adaptive systems have the potential benefit of improving user performance by automatically modifying the interface, as well as potential costs such as losing awareness of the system status that may offset any possible benefits. Sarter (2006) concludes that the design of multimodal systems "should be based on findings from empirical studies of multimodal information processing, both at the behavioral, psychophysical, and neurophysiological level" (p. 444). Sarter's view is in agreement with ours that studies of human information processing provide a foundation for system design.

Applications: Next Generation Air Transportation System and Networked Battlefield

Two sociotechnical systems to which knowledge of mental workload, SA, display design, and other aspects of human factors are being applied are the Next Generation Air Transportation System (NextGen) and the networked battlefield for military operations. The air transportation system in the United States is going through a transformation to increase air traffic flow by making use of modern technology in NextGen (**http://www.jpdo.gov**). Many government agencies are involved and have been supporting research related to the implementation of NextGen. Pilots and controllers will assume new roles and responsibilities as a consequence of changes in the air traffic management system brought about by the introduction of new automation technologies. These transformations will be achieved through a user-centered, system-based strategy intended to meet the demands of future air travelers while continuing to improve security, efficiency, and safety.

The most obvious impact of NextGen will be on the jobs of pilots and air traffic controllers. Future pilots operating in NextGen environments will assume expanded responsibility for flight planning, merging and spacing, and other air-traffic-management duties traditionally assigned to controllers. These extended responsibilities will demand that the flight deck perform more strategic and tactical flight planning by using enhanced traffic-information displays and automation tools. Controllers, on the other hand, will use automation tools that allow them to share responsibility safely and effectively with aircrews to maintain required separation of aircraft while being involved in managing dynamic airspace configurations and superdensity traffic-management operations. The effects of some of these NextGen management concepts and technologies (and corresponding shifts in operator roles and responsibilities) have been investigated since the concept of free flight (where pilots are not managed by controllers but are free to select their own speed and flight path) emerged in the mid 1990s (Wickens et al. 2002). However, many issues remain concerning function allocations and communications among pilots, controllers, and automated tools, along with effective selection and training of current and future operators (Durso & Manning 2008).

Similar to the transformation of the air-traffic-management system, numerous military operations will change as a function of the technological advances enabling the networked battlefield (Wallace 2005). The concept of the networked battlefield is that commanders and their subordinates will have access to an increased quantity and quality of information from virtually any location. There will be better sharing of that information among the personnel, resulting in improved individual and shared SA, which in turn will produce better decisions and more effective mission outcomes. Again, various human factors issues must be addressed satisfactorily for these potential benefits to be realized. Displays and tasks must be designed to keep personnel from being overloaded by the massive amount of information available to them, and displays must draw attention to mission-critical pieces of information. Because subordinate personnel will have increased access to information, it is important for the decisions they make to be consistent with the commander's intent. Thus, successful implementation of the networked battlefield necessitates consideration of individual and team information-processing capabilities and coordination.

An important human factors component for NextGen and the networked battlefield is the proper training of personnel, not only in how to use the technology but also in how to communicate and interact with others in the system. This component requires bringing to bear the knowledge of training principles developed from basic and applied research (Healy 2009). Incorporating these principles into computational models will allow quantitative predictions of the impact of alternative training methods and will support the development of effective training systems.

UBIQUITOUS COMPUTING AND ACCESSIBILITY

The presence of computers has become ubiquitous. Interactions with computers are a part of daily life that will only increase in the future. As in the examples of NextGen and the networked battlefield, human factors must play a central role in the design and implementation of these computing systems if they are to function as intended.

The Internet and the Web

The most dramatic technological change in recent years has been development of the Internet and World Wide Web. The Internet allows a degree of connectivity and access to information that could hardly have been envisioned a few decades ago. With a few clicks of a mouse, vast amounts of information on virtually any topic can be accessed from sources including journals, books, and data banks. Products and services can be purchased, and financial transactions with banks and companies can be performed. These are but a few of the activities in which users can engage.

Many human factors issues come to the fore with regard to use of the Internet and the Web that are of little importance for other aspects of HCI. Consequently, much human factors work in recent years has been devoted to issues in Web design (Proctor & Vu 2005), including the content a Web site should contain as well as how to organize and structure that content so that users will be able to achieve their goals easily. The area of content preparation draws on many methods used in human factors research, such as task analysis and interviews of subject-matter experts, along with interface guidelines regarding display and control configurations.

Because of the amount of information on the Web, an issue of concern is how users locate relevant information. Finding information can be characterized in terms of browsing, where there is no specific goal, and search, where the user is looking for a specific item or particular information. For browsing, it is useful for information to be organized by categories, and users are more likely to explore different sections of a Web site to find information. For Web search, users often want to find a box in which they can type one to three keywords that will locate the information for which they are looking (Fang et al. 2005). Both browsing and search have a system side and a user side. For browsing, the structure and organization of the Web site are of most importance. Issues include how to group and categorize the information, how to display the categories in terms of Web links or menus, what the navigational flow should be, and so on. For searches, the system side primarily involves the indexing of information and how to group the information based on relevance of

the search terms. On the user side, it is important to know strategies that users employ when searching for information. For example, users tend to abandon their searches after only a few trials (Fang et al. 2005).

Miniaturization and Mobile Technology

Another recent trend has been the miniaturization of computer technology. Nowadays, many people own personal data assistants or cell phones with multiple functionalities. Mobile devices have many unique characteristics, including smaller screen size, limited connectivity and computational resources, bandwidth, limitations on possible means of input and interaction, use in a variety of contexts, and greater personalization. Thus, many usability issues associated with information processing arise that are unique to mobile devices, and design guidelines developed for large-scale computer systems may not be directly applicable to mobile devices.

One example of this inapplicability relates to heuristic analysis for evaluating the usability of a product. In heuristic analysis, experts evaluate whether an interface conforms to best practices or established guidelines called heuristics. Bertini et al. (2006) identified four heuristics specific to evaluating the usability of mobile devices: ease of input, screen readability, and ability to perceive information with a glance; flexibility, efficiency of use, and personalization; aesthetic, privacy, and social conventions; and realistic error management. These heuristics target specific information-processing needs and user preferences that should be accommodated when designing for mobile devices.

Information Security and Privacy

With the rise of ubiquitous computing comes increasing concern with information security and privacy, which are essential for the functioning of e-commerce and other Web-based services. Security breaches in which a Web-based service is compromised have become regular occurrences. Breaches include Web-page defacements, identity thefts, and buffer overflow attacks (Viega 2005). Such incidents can result in disruption of the service that is offered, violation of user privacy, and financial loss for individual users and the organization.

Some human factors issues concerning information security include how to promote good security practices in organizations, design interfaces that allow easy detection of security breaches, and promote memory for secure passwords (Proctor et al. 2009). With regard to the latter, a common problem with the use of passwords to authenticate users is that people tend to select passwords that are easy to remember but also easy to guess, or "crack." More secure passwords contain random digits, letters, and characters, often generated by a computer system, which are difficult to remember and result in users writing them down. Vu et al. (2007) proposed a mnemonic technique that can be used to generate passwords satisfying security criteria that can be remembered by users. This method involves the user generating a sentence and taking the first letter of each word to create the password. Because this first-letter mnemonic technique only involves the 26 letters of the alphabet, the resulting passwords were shown to be cracked easily. However, if users were instructed to replace certain words with digits or characters, the passwords were more resistant to cracking. Factors that make the passwords memorable involve well-established memory principles: generation of the to-be-remembered items and use of a mnemonic to reconstruct the password string from a distinctive encoding.

Privacy assurance is closely related to that of security. Users need to be assured that their personal information will be used only in the intended manner and that their preferences concerning the use of this information will not be abused. One way in which organizations can assure users that their personal information will be protected is to post privacy policies that describe how personal information will be stored and used. Unfortunately, privacy policies are typically written to satisfy legal purposes, making them difficult for end users to comprehend (Jensen & Potts 2004). Consequently, protocols have been developed for standardizing Web privacy policies in machine-readable form so that application programs can help identify whether a site's policy conforms to users' privacy preferences. Human factors concerns revolve around issues of how to design the interface so that users can accurately select the items to be checked in the privacy policy and be provided with comprehensible displays for different Web sites that will support informed choices about whether to provide personal information to the sites (Cranor et al. 2006).

The primary point is that because security and privacy rely on the cooperation of end users, system administrators, and other personnel, security and privacy methods cannot achieve their goals unless interactions between all users and the systems with which they interact are simple and intuitive. Although usability problems are plentiful, there is not yet extensive research examining the relation between usability and the alternative ways of implementing security and privacy methods. Which design alternatives are given serious consideration should be guided by knowledge of human information-processing capabilities.

Individual Differences and Special Populations

People differ in their information-processing capabilities owing to hereditary and experiential factors. Consequently, designers need to take into account those differences. For example, people with low working-memory capacity do worse on a variety of tasks than do people with higher capacity. Research results suggest that there are two components of these individual differences: ability to maintain activation of information in working memory and ability to search for information in long-term memory (Unsworth & Engle 2007). Working-memory capacity correlates highly with measures of general intelligence, and fMRI analyses suggest a specific neuroanatomic basis in a parieto-frontal network (Colom et al. 2007).

Because working-memory capacity is a factor in performance of complex tasks, this research seems to have much to offer to human factors psychologists.

Differences between individuals from different cultures arise from practices and experiences unique to a culture. Cultural differences are of increasing concern in human factors because of the global economy. Many companies now have design teams working around the world to meet product release deadlines. Effective practice requires that the team members be able to communicate with each other. Also, products are often marketed worldwide and intended for use in different countries. For example, commercial aircraft designed in the United States and Europe are used throughout the world. Successful globalization requires understanding of various cultures, their customs, and how the differences between cultures influence people's individual performance and preferences as well as their cooperative activities in teams (Aykin 2005).

One area in which cultural factors have been taken into account historically is that of population stereotypes (Moray 2004, Smith 1981). This research has looked at relations between actions people take to manipulate controls for specific display or system outcomes in different cultures. A strong stereotype is said to exist when the majority of people prefer a certain action or interpretation. Population stereotypes are attributed to natural response tendencies that should generalize across cultures and learned response patterns that are culture specific (e.g., which direction to flip a switch to turn on a light).

Surprisingly little research has been conducted in which stereotypes for different cultures are directly compared. Yu & Chan (2004) compared direction-of-motion and spatial stereotypes of engineering students from mainland China to those of engineering students from Hong Kong and the United States. The stereotypes were similar across the three populations for the direction in which a rotary knob should be turned to align a rotary indicator with a specific marking. For labeling ambiguous spatial relations, such as which lane of a four-lane highway is the outside lane, and for spatial mappings such as forward-backward movement of a lever to left-right movement of an indicator, there was less agreement between the three groups. These results suggest that cultural factors contribute to compatibility relations and need to be taken into account by designers.

The emphasis on globalization has resulted in a broader interest in cultural differences, under the heading of cultural ergonomics (Kaplan 2004). Social relations between individuals in different cultures vary along several dimensions, two of the most important of which are individualism-collectivism and power distance (Hofstede 1980). The former refers to how much an individual's behavior is influenced by other persons, whereas the latter is the extent to which individuals lower in a power hierarchy defer to the decisions of those higher in the hierarchy. People from Asian cultures tend to be higher on collectivism and higher on power distance than do people from the United States (Kaplan 1995). Cultural differences such as these are important to take into account for situations involving team and organizational performance, as they imply that similarly structured teams in different cultures may lead to quite different performance. For example, Li et al. (2007) found that aviation accident records showed relatively more accidents attributable to failure to question orders in India and Taiwan, which are high on power distance, than in the United States, which is low on power distance.

Also of concern has been the aging of the general population. In the United States, the number of individuals of age 55 years or older has increased from 1990 to the present. Older adults have unique problems, some of which are physical (e.g., reduction of strength) and others of which are cognitive (e.g., reduced working memory capacity; Pennathur 2007). Because perceptual-motor and memory processing declines with age, and many products and systems used by older adults make substantial demands on this processing, designers must take into account these declines in information-processing capability if the products are to be used effectively by older adults.

Older adults constitute only one population with special needs. Medical technology has not only increased the average lifespan, but it also has enabled individuals with serious medical conditions to continue to lead active lives. Human factors researchers have devoted increasing amounts of effort to understanding the needs of these populations and to the design of products to support their special needs. Populations currently being targeted include deaf and blind persons and individuals with temporary or permanent physical disabilities.

The prevalence of computing technologies throughout the world has led to the development of the concept called "universal access." This concept refers to allowing all persons easy access to information, products, and services from any location at any time with any device (Stephanidis & Akoumianakis 2005). Designing for universal access and use will benefit both standard users and special populations of users, ensuring that the full benefits of the technologies have their maximal impact.

ALTERNATIVES TO THE INFORMATION-PROCESSING APPROACH

Although the human information-processing approach has undergirded much of the progress in cognitive psychology and human factors, critics of the approach have been vocal. For example, in a book on human error, Dekker (2005, p. 109) stated, "Information-processing theories have lost much of their appeal and credibility. Many realize how they have corrupted the spirit of the postbehaviorist cognitive revolution by losing sight of humanity and meaning making." Contrast this quote with one from Anderson and colleagues (1997, p. 19), major contributors to basic and applied cognitive psychology:

> Cognitive psychology has always been deeply concerned with meaning and the relations of

the parts of knowledge to the rest of the world. This is the most fundamental issue on which the cognitive revolution broke from behaviorism, and concern with meanings and relations permeates cognitive research and its applications.

The assessment of Anderson et al., with which we agree, implies that Dekker's claim about information-processing theories corrupting the spirit of the cognitive revolution is simply incorrect.

The criticisms of the information-processing approach have often been made in the context of advocating alternative frameworks as remedies for its perceived deficiencies. These alternative frameworks are frequently presented as paradigm shifts that will advance the field. We describe in this section several such alternatives that have a family resemblance of emphasizing physical and social context. Our view, as will be clear, is that most of the criticisms of the information-processing approach are misguided and reflect trends of research being conducted rather than fundamental faults in the approach itself. Although the perspectives offered by the alternative approaches are not bereft of value for specific purposes, the arguments for replacing the information-processing approach as the overall framework for studying basic and applied principles of human performance are erroneous.

Activity Theory

Activity theory has its origins in the work of Russian psychologists Vygotsky and Leon'tev as well as work in other European traditions. It places emphasis on human actions within a social context and is based in applications, including ones associated with ergonomics and work psychology. Bertelson & Bødker (2003) describe activity theory as focusing on the analysis and design of work environments and user activities, with the involvement of users in the design process.

In a recent paper advocating a version called "structural activity theory" as the best approach to human factors, Karwowski et al. (2008, p. 2) listed the following features that, in their view, distinguish it from the cognitive/information-processing approach:

1. Human activity is social in nature.
2. Cognition, external behavior, and motivation should be considered as components of a unitary system of activity.
3. Activity is a goal-directed, self-regulated system, which cannot be studied as a reactive behavior or computer-like information-processing system.
4. Activity should be analyzed as a system; therefore, not only parametric but also systemic methods of study are required.

Each of these allegedly differentiating features can be challenged. As noted, information processing provides the foundation for the widely accepted approach to social psychology known as social cognition. With regard to the second point, the information-processing approach is dedicated to explaining external behavior. Although motivation may not have received sufficient emphasis in the past, it is currently receiving increased interest. In a chapter titled "Motivated Thinking," Molden & Higgins (2005) stress that there has been a significant increase in the amount of research devoted to linking motivational concepts with information processing, which they see as a desirable development.

The goal-directedness of behavior has been acknowledged within the information-processing approach at least as far back as Miller et al.'s (1960) book *Plans and the Structure of Behavior*. The assertion that aspects of activity cannot be studied through using tasks in which participants react to stimuli and by analyzing the nature of the information processing involved is countered by many years of research using simple- and choice-reaction tasks (Hommel et al. 2001). Moreover, advances in self-guided robots (e.g., Bhat et al. 2006) belie the assertion that goal-directed action of an agent cannot be studied as an information-processing system. With regard to the fourth point, since the information-processing

approach is based on a systems viewpoint, there is no disagreement that analyses at different levels, including the whole system in which a person is operating, are needed.

Our view is that a perspective based on activity theory has value for studying people at work. However, as a foundation for explaining human performance, it is much more limited than the human information-processing approach.

The Ecological Approach, Cognitive Engineering, and Embodied Cognition

The ecological approach to perception, cognition, and action has been prominent in recent years. This approach, based on Gibson's (1979) ecological psychology, highlights the constraints provided by the natural environment in which a person perceives and acts. Emphasis is placed on affordances (opportunities for action) imposed by the physical environment. Affordances are considered to be perceived directly, that is, detected, with the world specifying all the available constraints for action. The ecological approach emphasizes determining environmental features that specify the affordances and downplays laboratory research conducted in restricted environments. We endorse the emphasis that the ecological approach places on a close coupling between perception and action. However, such emphasis is not unique to that approach and has been a viewpoint in human information processing from the earliest days (e.g., Fitts 1964) to the present (e.g., Hommel et al. 2001).

Within human factors, ecological interface design (EID) and cognitive engineering are closely linked to the ecological approach. Sanderson (2003, p. 237), an advocate of EID, notes this link and says, "One goal of EID is to make affordances visible," and "while the concept of direct perception has been heavily challenged from other areas, the concept underlies much of EID." Similarly, Marmaras & Nathanael (2005) state, "Cognitive engineering is *ecological*, because it studies behaviour in multidimensional, open worlds and not in artificially bounded closed ones, typical of the laboratory or engineer's desktop" (p. 109).

Few, if any, individuals would argue that it is unimportant to know the opportunities and constraints imposed by the physical environment. When a person is shown an unfamiliar tool such as a cherry pitter or corn stripper, the tool's use may not be identifiable, but its structure will constrain possible uses that the person will entertain (Bransford & McCarrell 1974). No one would consider the possibility that the cherry pitter is edible. However, some human factors specialists have made the stronger claim that the ecological approach could provide a better foundation for the field than does the information-processing approach. For example, Flach (1990) argued, "An ecological approach might offer an attractive alternative as a model for human factors research.... An ecological approach is most appropriate for the problems of human-machine systems" (p. 194). Similarly, the publisher's summary for Hancock et al.'s (1995) book on the ecological approach claims, "Much HF/E [Human Factors/ Ergonomics] research has been based on the wrong type of psychology, an information processing view of psychology that is reductionistic and context-free. Ecological psychology offers a viable alternative, presenting a richer view of human behavior that is holistic and contextualized" (**http://www.crcpress. com/product/isbn/9780805813807**). Similar opinions are expressed by the editors, though less strongly, in the preface: "There is a belief that the contribution of the human agent can be best understood in the context of the emergent properties that arise from interaction with an environment. Thus, there is a movement away from bottom-up reductionistic approaches toward more top-down holistic approaches to the problem of human performance" (Flach et al. 1995, p. xv).

Whether ecological psychology presents a richer view of human behavior than does information-processing psychology can surely be questioned. Moreover, it is also debatable whether a holistic and completely contextualized approach to psychology should be preferred over one that is not. Jens Rasmussen, from whose work EID and cognitive engineering emerged, clearly appreciated the vital role of human information processing. In the preface to his influential book, *Information Processing and Human-Machine Interaction: An Approach to Cognitive Engineering*, Rasmussen (1986) stated, "Models of human information-processing abilities and limitations are prerequisites for the basic conceptual design of such systems [modern industrial control systems]" (p. ix). He went on to say in Chapter 1, "Use of computer-based information technology to support decision making in supervisory systems control *necessarily* implies an attempt to match the information processes of the computer to the mental decision processes of an operator" (p. 2, emphasis added). The notion that a holistic and contextualized approach to human behavior is the "right type" of psychology for human factors runs counter to the fact that scientific progress in other disciplines has come about by conducting analytic investigations under controlled conditions that have led to general principles. It also seems inconsistent with the growth of knowledge during the past 60 years in cognitive psychology and human factors as a consequence of their adopting the information-processing approach. That the ultimate goal in human factors is designing for behavior in naturalistic contexts does not mean that only research conducted in those contexts is relevant.

A recent approach offered as an alternative to information processing that has yet to influence human factors but is likely to do so is that of embodied cognition. Although there is no agreed upon the definition of embodied cognition, the approach is characterized by "commitment to the idea that the mind must be understood in the context of its relationship to a physical body that interacts with the world" (Wilson 2002). An assumption of the embodied cognition approach is that cognition cannot be explained in terms of information-processing mechanisms that are independent of bodily implementation and that explanations must consider how cognition is grounded in the real-world environment in which cognition operates.

Perceptual-motor performance has played a prominent role in basic and applied research conducted from the information-processing perspective, as reflected in the *Annual Review of Psychology* articles on engineering psychology. As researchers who study perceptual-motor performance, we are in agreement that models of cognition must be "grounded" in perception and action. However, within the human performance tradition, this has been done since the 1950s from the information-processing perspective.

Situated Cognition, Situated Action, and Distributed Cognition

Situated cognition refers to the view that learning is a social act. This view emphasizes the importance of learning in social contexts similar to those in which the learned activity will need to be carried out. It has been developed primarily in the area of educational psychology and, as with activity theory, is attributed in part to the work of Vygotsky (Hung & Chen 2001). Within human factors, this approach has gone under the name of situated action (Suchman 1987), a perspective that also places emphasis on the social and physical context in which action occurs. The approach stems primarily from anthropology and sociology, with the aim being "not to produce formal models of knowledge and action, but to explore the relation of knowledge and action to the particular circumstances in which knowing and acting invariably occur" (Suchman 1987). Distributed cognition is another approach linked to Vygotsky. It takes the position that cognition is not unique to individuals but can reside "outside of the head" and is distributed between individuals and artifacts with which they interact. This approach is associated with Hutchins (1995), who advocated studying cognition "in the wild."

These closely related views place emphasis on social contexts, as does activity theory. Advocates often imply that traditional cognitive approaches such as information processing cannot accommodate the social context. Although the cognitive approach has been criticized for neglecting social context, Anderson et al. (1997) emphasized, "The cognitive approach in no way denies the importance of the social" (p. 20). In fact, "social information processing" has become a commonly used term, appearing in over 225 titles in PsycINFO, February, Week 4, 2009. Much learning and many actions occur in social contexts such as the family and work environments. So, there is no disagreement about incorporating situational aspects into accounts of cognition and action. The important point, made by Anderson et al. (1997) with respect to education, is, "The cognitive methodology has delivered real educational applications in a way that the situated methodology has not and, we believe, fundamentally cannot" (p. 19). Although this statement specifically targets educational technology, it applies as well to human factors applications in general. The information-processing approach has been the origin for most of the concepts in human factors, the performance metrics associated with those concepts, and the resulting tools for application.

Qualitative Descriptions Versus Quantitative Models

Human factors research has traditionally been oriented toward controlled experimentation with quantitative measurements and development of explanatory processing models. Models that allow quantitative predictions of response time and accuracy have been viewed as a goal because, among other purposes, they can be used to generate quantitative predictions for alternative possible designs early in the design process. The goals, operators, methods, and selection rules (GOMS) modeling approach (Card et al. 1983) is the most well known method of this type. GOMS predicts performance time from analyzing tasks in terms of goals, elementary cognitive operators, methods composed from those operators for achieving the goals, and selection rules for choosing between methods. This work spawned a whole family of models that can be applied to various task situations (Kieras 2004). In keeping with the emphasis of this review on cumulative development of knowledge in human factors, it is worth noting that GOMS analysis is part of the tradition of task analysis that goes back to the work of Frederick Taylor and Lillian and Frank Gilbreth early in the twentieth century and that continues today with work on cognitive and hierarchical task analyses.

Recent years have seen advances in the development of general cognitive architectures that allow implementation of specific computational models for the performance of simple and complex tasks, as well as the acquisition and transfer of skill at the tasks (Byrne 2008, Gray 2007). Computational models have been applied to education, manufacturing and production, and military issues. Progress in this area has been sufficiently great that Ritter, in the series foreword to Gray's book, states that computational cognitive models "have now reached a new level of maturity" (p. v).

A contrasting view is that the emphasis on quantitative methods and modeling in human factors is an unfortunate bias. For example, Dekker (2005) states, "Connected to information processing and the experimentalist approach to many human factors problems is a quantitativist bias" (p. xiv). According to this view, human factors research needs to place more emphasis on qualitative, ethnographic methods adopted from anthropology and sociology (e.g., Hignett & Wilson 2004). The goal of such ethnographic research is qualitative interpretation of the perceptions, beliefs, and attitudes of user groups of interest from interactions with the groups in their natural settings. Rather than being analytic, the approach is holistic. Rather than desiring causal explanation and prediction, the research is intended to provide a detailed description of the specific situations of interest.

Because human factors is an applied science, there is little doubt that ethnographic methods are useful for purposes such as providing insight into the environments in which particular products and systems will be used. However, advocates of qualitative methods often adopt a contextualistic approach for which the qualitative interpretation is the end goal. For example, Hignett & Wilson (2004) propose that use of qualitative, ethnographic methodology can move human factors to the level of what they call spiritual sciences, "a new paradigm for ergonomics characterised by 'holism'" (p. 478). They state, "This creates an opportunity for the next generation of ergonomics, with an accompanying paradigm shift, to build an even stronger base of practice by expanding the theoretical academic foundation to support the inclusion of qualitative methodology from social sciences" (p. 478).

Hignett & Wilson (2004, p. 477) list five ways in which qualitative research methodology purportedly differs from quantitative methodology:

1. The world is represented in terms of words or pictures through qualitative methodology and not in terms of numbers.
2. Qualitative studies focus on a few cases but many variables, in contrast to a focus on many cases but few variables in quantitative studies.
3. The sampling strategy is preassigned for projects using quantitative methodology, whereas the sampling strategy for qualitative research develops during the study.
4. The nature of data collection and analysis is iterative in qualitative methodology whereas it is linear in quantitative methodology.
5. Identifying the influence of the researcher is emphasized in qualitative methodology.

The first point does not seem to differentiate approaches, since words and figures are used to depict information-processing models. Certainly, the psychophysical research tradition, which provides quantitative metrics of information processing, focuses on few subjects using detailed measurement. The sampling issue also seems irrelevant, as decisions about sampling and design in so-called quantitative studies are often made on the basis of pilot studies or earlier work. Not much needs to be said about the distinction made for iterative versus linear approaches to methodology, since all research is iterative. Also, much of research design emphasizes ways to control or evaluate the influence of the researcher on the results. Of course, ethnographic methodology has the major limitation of being oriented toward interpretations of specific situations and providing no means for aggregating data across situations or for generalizing an interpretation from one context to another.

One of the reasons often given for qualitative inquiry is that quantitative models cannot handle different situational contexts. Moon & Fu (2008) demonstrated, though, that skill acquisition of a photocopying task could be captured by an information-processing model developed from a cognitive architecture, adaptive control of thought-rational (ACT-R), by incorporating a few contextual assumptions. For example, they assumed that which hand was used to flip the book on the copier was determined by the distance of each hand from the edge of the book at the time that other activities were completed. Their work showed "how situated assumptions can be combined with a set of general mechanisms of ACT-R to simulate the qualitative and quantitative changes at both the macro and micro levels" (Moon & Fu 2008, p. 938) that occurred as people acquired skills in a naturalistic task. Research of this type illustrates that models and analytic tools based on information-processing principles can be brought to bear effectively on specific applied problems.

CONCLUDING REMARKS

Human information processing has provided the foundation for human factors. The value of the information-processing language for unifying basic and applied research at different levels of analysis was understood by the prominent cognitive psychologist and neuroscientist, Michael Posner (1986), with whose comments we began our discussion of information processing. It was also understood by his academic advisor, Paul Fitts (1964), a pioneer in human factors, who said, "Rather than viewing

perceptual-motor behavior as a series of motor responses made to reach some goal, it is possible, and I believe considerably more profitable, to view such behavior as an information-processing activity guided by some general plan or program" (p. 248).

In contrast to assertions that the information-processing approach studies cognition separately from behavior, Fitts (1964) pointed out that the approach provides unifying explanations. He stated, "Emphasis on information-processing and coding is one reason why the dichotomy between verbal and motor processes, such as between verbal and motor learning, does not appear to be as important as it once seemed to be" (p. 248). Fitts (1964) also discussed control system models that view human performance as a feedback control system. Although he acknowledged the importance of the control system perspective, Fitts stated with respect to the information-processing perspective, "Of the two, the information system is probably the more general model, since any control task may also be viewed as a special case of an information-processing task" (p. 250). With regard to perceptual-motor learning, Fitts again favored an information-processing approach, saying, "The most promising model of an adaptive process is that provided by the stored-program data-system" (p. 251).

Fitts (1964) considered whether different theories of skilled performance and learning are needed for discrete and continuous tasks. After reviewing results from several research areas, he concluded, "It does appear that a discrete model is adequate for describing behavior in continuous as well as in discrete tasks" (p. 259). Fitts proposed a model for perceptual-motor skill based on "viewing skilled performance as in information-processing task, but making use of concepts borrowed from feedback and adaptive system theory" (p. 259). If there were any doubt that Fitts viewed discrete and continuous tasks as explainable in similar manners, he said, "After a decade of research devoted chiefly to the study of skilled performance in continuous tasks, I have recently turned to the study of information-handling behavior in serial and discrete tasks, but I believe that I am studying essentially the same basic perceptual-motor skill processes as before" (Fitts 1964, p. 261).

Fitts concluded his chapter with the following paragraph, on which we cannot improve:

> The crucial point in developing a general theory of skilled performance, and in support of the view that verbal and motor processes are highly similar, is the conclusion that skilled performance is dependent on discrete or quantized processes. Thus the study of discrete perceptual-motor responses, including the study of reaction time, movement time, and response accuracy (errors), can be viewed as contributing to an understanding of serial and continuous communication and control skills on the one hand, and to an understanding of the organization of thinking, decision making, and verbal behavior on the other hand. (Fitts 1964, p. 283)

Conceiving of the human as an information processor is the key step that allows integrated understanding of discrete and continuous behaviors, perceptual-motor and cognitive performance, skill acquisition and learning, and basic principles and their applications. Because human performance in all applied contexts boils down to actions of individual people, understanding how humans process information will necessarily continue to provide the foundation for human factors in the future.

SUMMARY POINTS

1. Progress in human factors research is cumulative. From the earliest *Annual Review* article on engineering psychology to the present, human factors research has produced an ever-increasing understanding of human performance in applied settings.

2. The human information-processing approach is responsible for much of the growth in human factors from its inception to the present.

3. Many recent research directions in cognitive psychology and human factors stem from the information-processing perspective.

4. Research on perceptual-motor performance is important to human factors historically and continues to contribute new insights.

5. Much research in human factors developed around issues of information overload, how this overload degrades performance, and how the problems associated with overload can be alleviated.

6. Issues associated with information overload and awareness are particularly important for introduction of new systems that provide large amounts of dynamic information in real time, such as the Next Generation Airspace Transportation System and the networked battlefield.

7. Miniaturization and mobilization of computers have made their presence ubiquitous. Realization of the potential power of computing devices in various contexts depends on human factors research.

8. Many criticisms of the human information-processing approach fail to acknowledge that it allows integration across (*a*) the most basic biological levels to conscious awareness; (*b*) perception, cognition, and action; (*c*) interactions among persons; (*d*) interactions between persons and machines; and (*e*) task and work environments in which people perform.

FUTURE ISSUES

1. What are the limits of neuroergonomics and augmented cognition for providing online adaptations of interfaces and tasks that will benefit operators' performance?

2. How can automation be incorporated most effectively into air traffic management and other large-scale systems to improve their effectiveness?

3. In what ways can designs of products and systems be improved to satisfy the needs of older adults and other special populations?

4. What human factors issues need to be addressed in the use of future technologies (e.g., nanotechnology)?

5. How can cognitive architectures based on general information-processing principles best accommodate situational factors?

6. In what ways can large amounts of information of varying reliability be presented to improve users' decision making?

7. How are design guidelines for universal access to be balanced with those that are culturally specific?

8. How best can biological, behavioral, and cultural approaches to human factors be integrated?

DISCLOSURE STATEMENT

The authors are not aware of any biases that might be perceived as affecting the objectivity of this review.

ACKNOWLEDGMENTS

Preparation of this review was supported in part by Grant W911NF-05-1-0153 from the Army Research Office and NASA Cooperative Agreement NNA06CN30A. We thank Frank Durso, Digby Elliott, Chris Wickens, Motonori Yamaguchi, and Leon Zeng for helpful comments on earlier versions of the review.

LITERATURE CITED

Alexander T, Schlick C, Sievert A, Leyk D. 2008. Assessing human mobile computing performance by Fitts' law. In *Handbook of Research on User Interface Design and Evaluation for Mobile Technology Vol. 2*, ed. J Lumsden, 2:830–46. Hershey, PA: Inform. Sci. Ref.

Alluisi EA, Morgan BB Jr. 1976. Engineering psychology and human performance. *Annu. Rev. Psychol.* 27:305–30

Anderson JR, Reder LM, Simon HA. 1997. Situative versus cognitive perspectives: form versus substance. *Educ. Res.* 26:18–21

Aykin N, ed. 2005. *Usability and Internationalization of Information Technology*. Mahwah, NJ: Erlbaum

Bedny G, Meister D. 1999. Theory of activity and situation awareness. *Int. J. Cogn. Ergonom.* 3:63–72

Berka C, Levendowski DJ, Lumicao MN, Yau A, Davis G, et al. 2007. EEG correlates of task engagement and mental workload in vigilance, learning, and memory tasks. *Aviat. Space Environ. Med.* 78:B231–44

Bertelson OW, Bødker S. 2003. Activity theory. In *HCI Models, Theories, and Frameworks*, ed. JM Carroll, pp. 291–324. San Francisco, CA: Morgan Kaufman

Bertini E, Gabrielli S, Kimani S. 2006. Appropriating and assessing heuristics for mobile computing. *Proc. Working Conf. Advanced Visual Interfaces*, pp. 119–26. New York: ACM

Bhat P, Kuffner J, Goldstein S, Srinivasa S. 2006. Hierarchical motion planning for self-reconfigurable modular robots. In *IEEE/RSJ Int. Conf. on Intelligent Robots and Systems*, Beijing

Bransford JD, McCarrell NS. 1974. A sketch of a cognitive approach to comprehension: some thoughts about understanding what it means to comprehend. In *Cognition and the Symbolic Processes*, ed. WB Weimer, DS Palermo, pp. 189–229. Hillsdale, NJ: Erlbaum

Byrne MD. 2008. Cognitive architecture. In *The Human-Computer Interaction Handbook: Fundamentals, Evolving Technologies, and Emerging Applications*, ed. A Sears, JA Jacko, pp. 93–113. Boca Raton, FL: CRC. 2nd ed.

Card SK, Moran TP, Newell A. 1983. *The Psychology of Human-Computer Interaction*. Hillsdale, NJ: Erlbaum

Carroll JM. 1997. Human-computer interaction: psychology as a science of design. *Annu. Rev. Psychol.* 48:61–83

Chapanis A. 1963. Engineering psychology. *Annu. Rev. Psychol.* 14:285–318

Colom R, Jung RE, Haier RJ. 2007. General intelligence and memory span: evidence for a common neuroanatomic framework. *Cogn. Neuropsychol.* 24:867–78

Cranor LF, Guduru P, Arjula M. 2006. User interfaces for privacy agents. *ACM Trans. Comput.-Hum. Interact.* 13:135–78

Dekker SWA. 2005. *Ten Questions about Human Error: A New View of Human Factors and System Safety*. Mahwah, NJ: Erlbaum

Durso FT, Manning CA. 2008. Air traffic control. In *Reviews of Human Factors and Ergonomics, Vol. 4*, ed. CM Carswell, pp. 195–244. Santa Monica, CA: Human Factors Ergon. Soc.

Durso FT, Rawson KA, Girotto S. 2007. Comprehension and situation awareness. In *Handbook of Applied Cognition*, ed. FT Durso, pp. 163–93. Hoboken, NJ: Wiley. 2nd ed.

Elliott D, Hansen S, Grierson EM. 2009. Optimising speed and energy expenditure in accurate visually directed upper limb movements. *Ergonomics* 52:438–47

Elliott D, Helsen WF, Chua R. 2001. A century later: Woodworth's (1899) two-component model of goal-directed aiming. *Psychol. Bull.* 127:342–57

Endsley MR. 1995. Toward a theory of situation awareness in dynamic systems. *Hum. Factors* 37:32–64

Fang X, Chen P, Chen B. 2005. User search strategies and search engine interface design. In *Handbook of Human Factors in Web Design*, ed. RW Proctor, K-PL Vu, pp. 193–210. Mahwah, NJ: Erlbaum

Finomore VS, Warm JS, Matthews G, Riley MA, Dember WN, et al. 2006. Measuring the workload of sustained attention. In *Human Factors and Ergonomics Society Annual Meeting Proceedings*, pp. 1614–18. Santa Monica, CA: Human Factors Ergon. Soc.

Fiske ST. 2005. Social cognition and the normality of prejudgment. In *On the Nature of Prejudice: Fifty Years After Allport*, ed. JF Dovidio, PS Glick, LA Rudman, pp. 36–53. Malden, MA: Blackwell

Fitts PM. 1954. The information capacity of the human motor system in controlling the amplitude of movement. *J. Exp. Psychol.* 47:381–91

Fitts PM. 1958. Engineering psychology. *Annu. Rev. Psychol.* 9:267–94

Fitts PM. 1964. Perceptual-motor skill learning. In *Categories of Human Learning*, ed. AW Melton, pp. 243–85. New York: Academic

Fitts PM, Seeger CM. 1953. S-R compatibility: spatial characteristics of stimulus and response codes. *J. Exp. Psychol.* 46:199–210

Flach JM. 1990. The ecology of human-machine systems I: introduction. *Ecol. Psychol.* 2:191–205

Flach J, Hancock P, Caird J, Vicente K. 1995. Preface. In *Local Applications of the Ecological Approach to Human-Machine Systems*, ed. P Hancock, J Flach, J Caird, K Vicente, pp. xiii–xv. Mahwah, NJ: Erlbaum

Forgas JP. 2008. Affect and cognition. *Persp. Psychol. Sci.* 3:94–101

Francis G, Oxtoby C. 2006. Building and testing optimized keyboards for specific text entry. *Hum. Factors* 48:279–87

Gangestad SW, Simpson JA. 2007. *The Evolution of Mind: Fundamental Questions and Controversies*. New York: Guilford

Gibson JJ. 1979. *The Ecological Approach to Visual Perception*. Boston: Houghton Mifflin

Provides a good introduction to cognitive architectures used in HCI and human factors.

Classic article on situation awareness from which the most widely cited definition is taken.

The classic study of aimed movements from which Fitts' law, which has been widely influential, was derived.

Chapter on perceptual-motor skill learning in which the author presents theoretical models and phases of skill acquisition.

Gopher D, Kimchi R. 1989. Engineering psychology. *Annu. Rev. Psychol.* 40:431–55

Gorman JC, Cooke NJ, Winner JL. 2006. Measuring team situation awareness in decentralized command and control environments. *Ergonomics* 49:1312–25

Gray W, ed. 2007. *Integrated Models of Cognitive Systems*. New York: Oxford Univ. Press

Guiard Y, Beaudouin-Lafon M. 2004. Fitts' law 50 years later: applications and contributions from human-computer interaction. *Int. J. Hum. Comput. Studies* 61:747–50

Hancock P, Flach J, Caird J, Vicente K, eds. 1995. *Local Applications of the Ecological Approach to Human-Machine Systems*. Mahwah, NJ: Erlbaum

Harmon-Jones E, Winkielman P. 2007. *Social Neuroscience. Integrating Biological and Psychological Explanations of Social Behavior.* New York: Guilford

Healy AF. 2009. Skill learning, enhancement of. In *Encyclopedia of the Mind*, ed. H Pashler. Thousand Oaks, CA: Sage. In press

Helander MG, Tham MP. 2003. Hedonomics—affective human factors design. *Ergonomics* 46:1269–72

Hignett S, Wilson JR. 2004. The role for qualitative methodology in ergonomics: a case study to explore theoretical issues. *Theoretical Issues Ergon. Sci.* 5:473–93

Hodgkinson GP, Healey MP. 2008. Cognition in organizations. *Annu. Rev. Psychol.* 59:387–417

Hofstede G. 1980. *Culture Consequences: International Differences in Work-Related Values*. Beverly Hills, CA: Sage

Hommel B. 1993. The relationship between stimulus processing and response selection in the Simon task: evidence for a temporal overlap. *Psychol. Res.* 55:280–90

Hommel B, Müsseler J, Aschersleben G, Prinz W. 2001. The theory of event-coding (TEC): a framework for perception and action planning. *Behav. Brain Sci.* 24:849–78

Howell WC. 1993. Engineering psychology in a changing world. *Annu. Rev. Psychol.* 44:231–63

Hung DWL, Chen D-T. 2001. Situated cognition, Vygotskian thought and learning from the communities of practice perspective: implications for the design of web-based e-learning. *Educ. Media Int.* 38:3–12

Hutchins E. 1995. *Cognition in the Wild*. Cambridge, MA: MIT Press

Imada AS, Carayon P. 2008. Editors' comments on this special issue devoted to macroergonomics. *Appl. Ergon.* 39:415–17

Jensen C, Potts J. 2004. Privacy policies as decision-making tools: an evaluation of online privacy notices. In *Proc. SIGCHI Conf. Human Factors Comput. Syst.*, Vienna. Vol. 6, pp. 471–78. New York: ACM

Kaplan M. 1995. The culture at work: cultural ergonomics. *Ergonomics* 38:606–15

Kaplan M, ed. 2004. *Cultural Ergonomics*. Amsterdam: Elsevier Sci.

Karwowski W, Bedny GZ, Chebykin OY. 2008. General and systemic—structural activity theory as a foundation of human work studies. In *Proc. Second Int. Conf. Appl. Hum. Factors Ergon.*, ed. W Karwoski, G Salvendy. W. Lafayette, IN: USA Publ.

Kass SJ, Vodanovich SJ, Stanny CJ, Taylor TM. 2001. Watching the clock: boredom and vigilance performance. *Percept. Motor Skills* 92:969–76

Khalid HM. 2006. Embracing diversity in user needs for affective design. *Appl. Ergon.* 37:409–18

Kieras D. 2004. GOMS models for task analysis. In *The Handbook of Task Analysis for Human-Computer Interaction*, ed. D Diaper, D Stanton, pp. 83–116. Mahwah, NJ: Erlbaum

Kornblum S, Hasbroucq T, Osman A. 1990. Dimensional overlap: cognitive basis for stimulus-response compatibility—a model and taxonomy. *Psychol. Rev.* 97:253–70

Kuhn TS. 1962. *The Structure of Scientific Revolutions*. Chicago, IL: Univ. Chicago Press

Kunde W, Müsseler J, Heuer H. 2007. Spatial compatibility effects with tool use. *Hum. Factors* 49:661–70

Laudan L. 1996. *Beyond Positivism and Relativism: Theory, Method, and Evidence*. Boulder, CO: Westview

Li W-C, Harris D, Chen A. 2007. Eastern minds in western cockpits: meta-analysis of human factors mishaps from three nations. *Aviat. Space Environ. Med.* 78:420–25

Logan GD. 2004. Cumulative progress in formal theories of attention. *Annu. Rev. Psychol.* 55:207–34

Mackworth NH. 1948. The breakdown of vigilance during prolonged visual search. *Q. J. Exp. Psychol.* 1:6–21

Marmaras N, Nathanael D. 2005. Cognitive engineering practice: melting theory into reality. *Theor. Issues Ergon. Sci.* 6:109–27

Melton AW, Briggs GE. 1960. Engineering psychology. *Annu. Rev. Psychol.* 11:71–98

Influential theory of event coding in which the authors describe a model of information processing in which perception and action rely on common codes.

Meyer DE, Abrams RA, Kornblum S, Wright CE, Smith JEK. 1988. Optimality in human motor performance: ideal control of rapid aimed movements. *Psychol. Rev.* 95:340–70

Meyer DE, Kieras DE. 1997. A computational theory of executive cognitive processes and multiple-task performance: I. Basic mechanisms. *Psychol. Rev.* 104:3–65

Miller GA, Galanter E, Pribram KH. 1960. *Plans and the Structure of Behavior*. New York: Holt, Rinehart & Winston

Millis K, Wallace P, Cai Z, Graesser A, Halpern D, Magiano J. 2008. *Using AutoTutor to Promote Scientific Inquiry Skills in Game Environments*. Presented at 38th Annu. Meet. Soc. Comput. Psychol., Chicago, IL

Molden DC, Higgins ET. 2005. Motivational thinking. In *The Cambridge Handbook of Thinking and Reasoning*, ed. KJ Holyoak, RJ Morrison, pp. 295–317. New York: Cambridge Univ. Press

Moon JM, Fu WT. 2008. A situated cognitive model of the routine evolution of skills. In *Proc. Human Factors Ergon. Soc. 52nd Annu. Meet.*, pp. 935–39. Santa Monica, CA: Human Factors Ergon. Soc.

Moray N. 2004. Culture, context, and performance. In *Cultural Ergonomics*, ed. M Kaplan, pp. 31–59. Amsterdam: Elsevier Sci.

Nairne JS, Pandeirada JNS, Thompson SR. 2008. Adaptive memory: the comparative value of survival processing. *Psychol. Sci.* 19:176–80

Novotney A. 2009. Dangerous distraction. *Monitor Psychol.* 40(2):32–36

Olson GM, Olson JS. 2003. Human-computer interaction: psychological aspects of the human use of computing. *Annu. Rev. Psychol.* 54:491–516

Parasuraman R, Davies DR. 1977. A taxonomic analysis of vigilance. In *Vigilance, Theory: Operational Performance and Physiological Correlates*, ed. RR Mackie, pp. 559–74. New York: Plenum

Parasuraman R, Rizzo M, eds. 2007. *Neuroergonomics: The Brain at Work*. New York: Oxford Univ. Press

Parasuraman R, Sheridan TB, Wickens CD. 2008. Situation awareness, mental workload, and trust in automation: viable, empirically supported cognitive engineering constructs. *J. Cogn. Eng. Decision Making* 2:140–60

Parasuraman R, Wickens CD. 2008. Humans: still vital after all these years of automation. *Hum. Factors* 50:511–20

Pashler H. 1994. Dual-task interference in simple tasks: data and theory. *Psychol. Bull.* 16:220–24

Pennathur A. 2007. Ergonomic design for older adults. In *Gerontechnology: Growing Old in a Technological Society*, ed. G Lesnoff-Caravaglia, pp. 153–81. Springfield, IL: Thomas

Pickup L, Wilson JR, Sharpies S, Norris B, Clarke T, Young MS. 2005. Fundamental examination of mental workload in the rail industry. *Theor. Issues Ergon. Sci.* 6:463–82

Pirolli P. 2007. *Information Foraging Theory*. New York: Oxford Univ. Press

Posner MI. 1982. Cumulative development of attentional theory. *Am. Psychol.* 37:168–79

Posner MI. 1986. Overview. In *Handbook of Perception and Human Performance Vol. II: Cognitive Processes and Performance*, ed. KR Boff, L Kaufman, JP Thomas, pp. V3–10. New York: Wiley

Poulton EC. 1966. Engineering psychology. *Annu. Rev. Psychol.* 17:177–200

Proctor RW, Schultz EE, Vu K-PL. 2009. Human factors in information security and privacy. In *Handbook of Research on Information Security and Assurance*, ed. JND Gupta, SK Sharma, pp. 402–14. Hershey, PA: Inform. Sci. Ref.

Proctor RW, Tan HZ, Vu K-PL, Gray R, Spence C. 2005. Implications of compatibility and cuing effects for multimodal interfaces. In *Foundations of Augmented Cognition*, ed. DD Schmorrow, pp. 3–12. Mahwah, NJ: Erlbaum

Proctor RW, Vu K-PL, eds. 2005. *Human Factors in Web Design*. Mahwah, NJ: Erlbaum

Proctor RW, Vu K-PL. 2006a. The cognitive revolution at age 50: Has the promise of the human information-processing approach been fulfilled? *Int. J. Hum. Comput. Int.* 21:253–84

Proctor RW, Vu K-PL. 2006b. *Stimulus-Response Compatibility Principles: Data, Theory, and Application*. Boca Raton, FL: CRC

Rasmussen J. 1986. *Information Processing and Human-Machine Interaction: An Approach to Cognitive Engineering*. Amsterdam: North-Holland

Reeves LM, Lai J, Larson JA, Oviatt S, Balaji TS, et al. 2004. Guidelines for multimodal user interface design. *Commun. ACM* 47:57–59

Provides a good introduction to the area of neuroergonomics.

The author's influential application of human information processing to cognitive engineering is described in this book.

Ruthruff E, Hazeltine E, Remington RW. 2006. What causes residual dual-task interference after practice? *Psychol. Res.* 70:494–503

Salmon PM, Stanton NA, Walker GH, Baber C, Jenkins DP, et al. 2008. What really is going on? Review of situation awareness models for individuals and teams. *Theor. Issues Ergon. Sci.* 9:297–323

Sanderson PM. 2003. Cognitive work analysis. In *HCI Models, Theories, and Frameworks*, ed. JM Carroll, pp. 225–64. San Francisco: Morgan Kaufmann.

Sarter NB. 2006. Multimodal information presentation: design guidance and research challenges. *Int. J. Industrial Ergonom.* 36:439–45

Scerbo MW. 2007. Adaptive automation. In *Neuroergonomics: The Brain at Work*, ed. R Parasuraman, M Rizzo, pp. 239–51. New York: Oxford Univ. Press

Schmorrow D, Stanney KM, eds. 2008. *Augmented Cognition: A Practitioner's Guide*. Santa Monica, CA: Human Factors Ergon. Soc.

Seow SC. 2005. Information theoretic models of HCI: a comparison of the Hick-Hyman law and Fitts' law. *Hum. Comput. Int.* 20:315–52

Simon JR. 1990. The effects of an irrelevant directional cue on human information processing. In *Stimulus-Response Compatibility: An Integrated Perspective*, ed. RW Proctor, TG Reeve, pp. 31–86. Amsterdam: North-Holland

Smith K, Hancock PA. 1995. Situation awareness is adaptive, externally directed consciousness. *Hum. Factors* 37:137–48

Smith SL. 1981. Exploring compatibility with words and pictures. *Hum. Factors* 23:305–15

Spain RD, Bliss JP. 2008. The effect of sonification display pulse rate and reliability on operator trust and perceived workload during a simulated patient monitoring task. *Ergonomics* 51:1320–37

Spence C, Ho C. 2008. Multisensory warning signals for event perception and safe driving. *Theor. Issues Ergonom. Sci.* 9:523–54

Spence C, McDonald J, Driver J. 2004. Exogenous spatial cuing studies of human crossmodal attention and multisensory integration. In *Crossmodal Space and Crossmodal Attention*, ed. C Spence, J Driver, pp. 277–320. Oxford, UK: Oxford Univ. Press

Stephanidis C, Akoumianakis D. 2005. A design code of practice for universal access: methods and techniques. In *Human Factors in Web Design*, ed. RW Proctor, K-PL Vu, pp. 239–50. Mahwah, NJ: Erlbaum

Strayer DL, Drews FA. 2007. Cell-phone–induced driver distraction. *Curr. Direct. Psychol. Sci.* 16:128–31

Suchman LA. 1987. *Plans and Situated Actions: The Problem of Human-Machine Communication*. New York: Cambridge Univ. Press

Tombu M, Jolicœur P. 2005. Testing the predictions of the central capacity sharing model. *J. Exp. Psychol. Hum.* 31:790–802

Uhlmann EL, Pizarro DA, Bloom P. 2008. Varieties of social cognition. *J. Theor. Soc. Behav.* 38:293–322

Unsworth N, Engle RW. 2007. The nature of individual differences in working memory capacity: active maintenance in primary memory and controlled search from secondary memory. *Psychol. Rev.* 114:104–32

Van Den Bossche P, Gijselaers WH, Segers M, Kirschner PA. 2006. Social and cognitive factors driving teamwork in collaborative learning environments. *Small Group Res.* 37:490–521

Viega J. 2005. Solutions to many of our security problems already exist, so why are we still so vulnerable? *Queue* June:40–50

Vu K-PL, Proctor RW, Bhargav-Spanzel A, Tai B-L, Cook J, Schultz EE. 2007. Improving password security and memorability to protect personal and organizational information. *Int. J. Hum. Comput. Studies* 65:744–57

Wallace WS. 2005. Network-enabled battle command. *Military Rev.*, May-June:1–5

Warm JS, Parasuraman R. 2007. Cerebral hemodynamics and vigilance. In *Neuroergonomics: The Brain at Work*, ed. R Parasuraman, M Rizzo, pp. 146–58. New York: Oxford Univ. Press

Warm JS, Parasuraman R, Matthews G. 2008. Vigilance requires hard mental work and is stressful. *Hum. Factors* 50:433–41

Wickens CD. 2008. Multiple resources and mental workload. *Hum. Factors* 50:449–55

Wickens CD, Helleberg J, Xu X. 2002. Pilot maneuver choice and workload in free flight. *Hum. Factors* 44:171–88

Wickens CD, Kramer A. 1985. Engineering psychology. *Annu. Rev. Psychol.* 36:307–48

Wickens CD, McCarley J. 2008. *Applied Attention Theory*. Boca Raton, FL: CRC

Wilson E, MacLeod C, Campbell L. 2007. The information-processing approach to emotion research. In *Handbook of Emotion Elicitation and Assessment*, ed. JA Coan, JB Allen, pp. 184–202. New York: Oxford Univ. Press

Wilson M. 2002. Six views of embodied cognition. *Psychon. B. Rev.* 9:625–36

Woodworth RS. 1899. The accuracy of voluntary movement. *Psychol. Rev.* 3(3 Suppl. 13):1–119

Yamaguchi M, Proctor RW. 2006. Stimulus-response compatibility with pure and mixed mappings in a flight task environment. *J. Exp. Psychol.: Appl.* 12:207–22

Yu R-F, Chan AHS. 2004. Comparative research on response stereotypes for daily operation tasks of Chinese and American engineering students. *Percept. Motor Skills* 98:179–91

Zhao H, Plaisant C, Schneiderman B, Lazar J. 2008. Data sonification for users with visual impairment: a case study with georeferenced data. *ACM Trans. Comput.-Hum. Interact.* 15(Article 4):1–28

Zupanc CM, Burgess-Limerick RJ, Wallis G. 2007. Performance consequences of alternating directional control-response compatibility: evidence from a coal mine shuttle car simulator. *Hum. Factors* 49:628–36

Provides good illustrations of applications of attention research to human factors problems.

The Psychology
of Academic Achievement

Philip H. Winne and John C. Nesbit

Faculty of Education, Simon Fraser University, Burnaby, BC V5A 1S6, Canada;
email: winne@sfu.ca, jcnesbit@sfu.ca

Annu. Rev. Psychol. 2010. 61:653–78

First published online as a Review in Advance on
October 19, 2009

The *Annual Review of Psychology* is online at
psych.annualreviews.org

This article's doi:
10.1146/annurev.psych.093008.100348

0066-4308/10/0110-0653$20.00

Key Words

school learning, educational psychology, motivation, metacognition,
experimental methodology, self-regulated learning

Abstract

Educational psychology has generated a prolific array of findings about
factors that influence and correlate with academic achievement. We review select findings from this voluminous literature and identify two domains of psychology: heuristics that describe generic relations between
instructional designs and learning, which we call the psychology of "the
way things are," and findings about metacognition and self-regulated
learning that demonstrate learners selectively apply and change their
use of those heuristics, which we call the psychology of "the way learners make things." Distinguishing these domains highlights a need to
marry two approaches to research methodology: the classical approach,
which we describe as snapshot, bookend, between-group experimentation; and a microgenetic approach that traces proximal cause-effect
bonds over time to validate theoretical accounts of how learning generates achievements. We argue for fusing these methods to advance a
validated psychology of academic achievement.

Contents

INTRODUCTION

"Extensive" significantly understates the scope of research relevant to a psychology of academic achievement. Not having examined all relevant books, chapters, proceedings, and articles—a task we estimate might require three decades of full-time work—we nonetheless posit it is possible to develop a unified account of why, how, and under what conditions learners succeed or fail in school. That account could lead to powerful theories about improving educational practices. Advancing toward such a model is our aim here although, necessarily, much has been omitted from our review. Like all models, our model will have limitations.

The model we sketch acknowledges two categories of psychological phenomena. The first concerns a psychology of "the way things are." By this we mean psychological phenomena that,

in principle, are universal among learners and across subject areas and are not likely under learners' control. One example is that cognition can simultaneously manage only a limited number of tasks or chunks of information. Another is that learners express biases that can be shaped by information in their environment. This is the framing effect. A third is that information studied and then immediately restudied will be recalled less completely and less accurately than if restudying is delayed.

The second category concerns a psychology of "the way learners make things." In this category we consider learners as agents. Agents choose among tasks and among psychological tools for working on tasks. An example is deciding whether to prepare for an exam by massed or spaced review. Another example is deciding whether and how long to try retrieving information when it can't be found but there is a feeling of knowing it. If learners have knowledge of several mnemonic techniques for recalling information, they can choose among those mnemonics. If a first choice fails but strengthens the feeling of knowing, learners can metacognitively monitor what they did to make an informed choice about the next mnemonic technique to try. They have the option to interpret success and failure as due to effort or ability. When these choices are made and acted on, new information is created and feeds forward. In this way, learners shape their learning environment.

Is it important to distinguish between psychologies of the way things are and the way learners make things? In his recent review of research on memory, Roediger (2008, p. 247) wrote: "The aim of this review has been to remind us of the quest for laws and the difficulty in achieving them. . . . The most fundamental principle of learning and memory, perhaps its only sort of general law, is that in making any generalization about memory one must add that 'it depends.'" We suggest Roediger's lament may derive from failing to incorporate our distinction. While one significant source of variance in the psychology of academic achievement is due to the way things are, a second significant source of variance originates in the psychology of the way learners make things. We argue that a psychology of academic achievement must account for how each psychology separately and jointly affects achievement.

Our account of the psychology of academic achievement also borrows a view presented by Borsboom et al. (2003). In brief, they argue and we agree that both kinds of psychology have been hampered, even misled, by failing to address proximal psychological processes. We consider questions about psychological processes that are shaped and constrained by how things are, and about processes that provide tools with which learners make things. In our account, we portray academic achievement as the result of self-regulated learning and argue that improving research entails rethinking constructs and the paradigm that guides experimental research.

COGNITIVE FACTORS

Since the publication of Thorndike's (1903) classic book *Educational Psychology*, the field has generated thousands of studies. Most investigated how environmental factors can be designed and how conditions within learners can be arranged to promote learning facts, principles, skills, and schemas. Recently, a consortium of approximately 35 eminent researchers (see **http://psyc.memphis.edu/learning/index.shtml**) summarized from this voluminous library 25 empirically grounded heuristics for instructional designs (see **Table 1**).

Intending no slight to the range of work contributing to each heuristic, we choose cognitive load theory to epitomize the category of a psychology describing "the way things are."

The Example of Cognitive Load

The construct of cognitive load has proven a powerful explanatory device for spanning the oft-cited gap between a science of learning and the arts of teaching and instructional design. Sweller (1988) developed cognitive load theory from models of working memory (e.g.,

Baddeley & Hitch 1974) that emphasized the limited capacity of working memory as a fundamental resource bottleneck in cognition. Vis-à-vis instruction, cognitive load is the total processing required by a learning activity. It has three components. First, intrinsic load is due to the inherent difficulty of an instructional task. It is indexed by the number of active interacting schemas needed to perform the task. Intrinsic load cannot be directly reduced by manipulating instructional factors. However, as the learner forms schemas and gains proficiency, intrinsic load decreases. Second, germane load arises from the cognitive processing that forms those schemas and boosts proficiency. Third, extrinsic cognitive load is any unnecessary processing. This load can be eliminated by manipulating instructional factors.

The three forms of cognitive load are additive; their sum cannot exceed working memory's limited capacity (Paas et al. 2003a). Intrinsic processing receives priority access to working memory. Remaining capacity is shared between germane and extrinsic processing. When total load is less than available capacity, an instructional designer, teacher, or learner can deliberately increase germane load to increase learning efficiency. Changing instructional factors may reduce extrinsic load. If working memory capacity is fully loaded, this can free resources for germane processing and ultimately produce more efficient learning. Total cognitive load has been measured by real-time recordings of performance and psychophysiological indices. It is most commonly gauged by self-report ratings collected after the task (Paas et al. 2003b).

Cognitive load is now liberally cited as an explanatory construct in research ranging over chemistry problem solving (Ngu et al. 2009), moral reasoning (Murphy et al. 2009), driver performance (Reyes & Lee 2008), and even motherhood (Purhonen et al. 2008). When cited by researchers outside the learning sciences, the tripartite nature of cognitive load is typically disregarded.

Reducing extraneous cognitive load links to several heuristics in **Table 1**. It is the primary theoretical grounding for improving learning

Table 1 Twenty-five heuristics for promoting learning[a]

Contiguity effects	Ideas that need to be associated should be presented contiguously in space and time.
Perceptual-motor grounding	Concepts benefit from being grounded in perceptual motor experiences, particularly at early stages of learning.
Dual code and multimedia effects	Materials presented in verbal, visual, and multimedia form richer representations than a single medium.
Testing effect	Testing enhances learning, particularly when the tests are aligned with important content.
Spacing effect	Spaced schedules of studying and testing produce better long-term retention than a single study session or test.
Exam expectations	Students benefit more from repeated testing when they expect a final exam.
Generation effect	Learning is enhanced when learners produce answers compared to having them recognize answers.
Organization effects	Outlining, integrating, and synthesizing information produces better learning than rereading materials or other more passive strategies.
Coherence effect	Materials and multimedia should explicitly link related ideas and minimize distracting irrelevant material.
Stories and example cases	Stories and example cases tend to be remembered better than didactic facts and abstract principles.
Multiple examples	An understanding of an abstract concept improves with multiple and varied examples.
Feedback effects	Students benefit from feedback on their performance in a learning task, but the timing of the feedback depends on the task.
Negative suggestion effects	Learning wrong information can be reduced when feedback is immediate.
Desirable difficulties	Challenges make learning and retrieval effortful and thereby have positive effects on long-term retention.
Manageable cognitive load	The information presented to the learner should not overload working memory.
Segmentation principle	A complex lesson should be broken down into manageable subparts.
Explanation effects	Students benefit more from constructing deep coherent explanations (mental models) of the material than memorizing shallow isolated facts.
Deep questions	Students benefit more from asking and answering deep questions that elicit explanations (e.g., why, why not, how, what-if) than shallow questions (e.g., who, what, when, where).
Cognitive disequilibrium	Deep reasoning and learning is stimulated by problems that create cognitive disequilibrium, such as obstacles to goals, contradictions, conflict, and anomalies.
Cognitive flexibility	Cognitive flexibility improves with multiple viewpoints that link facts, skills, procedures, and deep conceptual principles.
Goldilocks principle	Assignments should not be too hard or too easy, but at the right level of difficulty for the student's level of skill or prior knowledge.
Imperfect metacognition	Students rarely have an accurate knowledge of their cognition, so their ability to calibrate their comprehension, learning, and memory should not be trusted.
Discovery learning	Most students have trouble discovering important principles on their own, without careful guidance, scaffolding, or materials with well-crafted affordances.
Self-regulated learning	Most students need training in how to self-regulate their learning and other cognitive processes.
Anchored learning	Learning is deeper and students are more motivated when the materials and skills are anchored in real-world problems that matter to the learner.

[a] Reproduced from **http://psyc.memphis.edu/learning/whatweknow/index.shtml**. An elaborated description of each principle plus citations identifying empirical support is available as *25 Learning Principles to Guide Pedagogy and the Design of Learning Environments*. Retrieved Jan. 2, 2009 from **http://psyc.memphis.edu/learning/whatweknow/25principles.doc**.

by eliminating unnecessary information (coherence), cueing learners' attention (signaling), colocating items to be mentally integrated (spatial contiguity), and synchronizing events to be mentally integrated (temporal contiguity) (Mayer 2005).

Laboratory tasks designed to elevate cognitive load are reported by learners to feel more difficult (Paas et al. 2003b). From this, we assume the state of working memory overload is consciously experienced. Thus, it is within the purview of metacognition. Students can avoid overload by segmenting complex tasks for sequential work or using external mnemonics such as notes or diagrams. The cost of adopting learning tactics is initially experienced as added difficulty. But this investment can pay off in the long run.

METACOGNITIVE FACTORS

Flavell (1971) is credited with motivating psychologists to research the "intelligent monitoring and knowledge of storage and retrieval operations—a kind of metamemory, perhaps" (p. 277). He succeeded wildly. Since then, the broader topic of metacognition—cognition focused on the nature of one's thoughts and one's mental actions, and exercising control over one's cognitions—has generated a body of work that merits its own *Handbook of Metacognition in Education* (Hacker et al. 2009).

Metacognition is basically a two-step event with critical features. First, learners monitor features of a situation. They may monitor their knowledge, whether a peer or resource can provide information, and possible consequences if they make a particular move in solving a problem. The metacognitive account of the situation is determined by what the learner perceives, which may differ from its actual qualities. Monitoring compares those perceived features to standards set by the learner. Often, these are linked to but not necessarily identical to standards indicated by a teacher, parent, or peer. Second, based on the profile of differences between the learner's perception of the situation and standards—which differences there are

and how large they are—the learner exercises control. The learner may choose to stay the prior course at a task's midpoint, adapt slightly or significantly, or exit the task to pursue something else. Together, these steps set the stage for self-regulated learning, a potentially ubiquitous activity (Winne 1995).

Learners are considered agents. This means they choose whether and how to engage in tasks. But learners are not omnipotent. Nor are they insulated from their cerebral and the external worlds. Agency is reciprocally governed: As learners change their local environment, the environment's web of causal factors modulates affordances available to them (Martin 2004). For example, having monitored a problem's statement and classified it as solvable, inherent spreading activation in memory may render information that the problem is difficult. This may arouse anxiety. Seeking information from a peer may return a reply that warrants a positive attribution to effort. Or, it may generate a negative view that success can't be achieved without help from others. Some information the environment provides (e.g., by spreading activation) is not controllable, whereas other information (e.g., the affect associated with a peer's assessment) can be at least partially the learner's choice.

Given this account, four metacognitive achievements can be identified: (*a*) alertness to occasions to monitor, (*b*) having and choosing useful standards for monitoring, (*c*) accuracy in interpreting the profile generated by monitoring, and (*d*) having and choosing useful tactics or strategies. After setting the stage to reach subject matter achievements by developing these metacognitive skills, two further steps are required: (*e*) being motivated to act and (*f*) modifying the environment or locating oneself in an environment that affords the chosen action (Winne & Nesbit 2009).

Alertness to occasions appropriate to metacognitive monitoring has not been much researched beyond studies of readers' capabilities to detect superficial (e.g., spelling) or meaningful errors in texts. In this limited domain, detecting errors is proportional to measures of prior achievement and inversely proportional to load on working memory (Oakhill et al. 2005, Walczyk & Raska 1992). The former suggests that standards used in monitoring derive from prior knowledge, similar to what learners use to construct a situation model for new information (Kintsch 1988). The latter reflects that working memory's resources play a ubiquitous role in the economy of information processing.

Learners may struggle to assimilate useful standards and apply them in monitoring. Beyond simplistic misperceptions about what counts when assignments are graded, learners may focus on information at the wrong grain size. They may judge work at a global level when more-specific targets or items should be the standard (Dunlosky et al. 2005).

Research on learners' accuracy of metacognitive monitoring has blossomed under the rubric of judgments of learning. It is rooted in the concept of feeling of knowing (Hart 1965), a belief that information is in memory although it cannot be retrieved. There are four main findings. First, learners are poor at monitoring learning and have a bias toward overconfidence (Maki 1998). Second, engaging with information in meaningful ways, such as generating a summary of a large amount of information, can improve accuracy (see Thomas & McDaniel 2007). Third, accuracy improves by delaying monitoring so that learners experience recall (or lack of it) rather than just scan residual information in working memory (Koriat 1993, Nelson & Dunlosky 1991, Thiede et al. 2005). Fourth, after experiencing difficulty in recall, judgments shift from being overconfident to the opposite, dubbed the "underconfidence with practice effect" (Koriat et al. 2002).

Relatively much more research is available about tools learners have for exercising metacognitive control. These tools, commonly termed metacognitive skills or learning strategies, vary widely and are researched using two common experimental formats. The first trains learners to competence in a tactic and then compares pretraining performance to post-training performance. The second compares trained learners to a group not trained in the tactic. Early studies investigated very specific learning tactics, such as whether young children could verbally mediate how they learned associations when rules governing associative pairs changed (Kendler et al. 1972). At the other end of this continuum, Dansereau and colleagues (see Dansereau 1985) trained undergraduates in a typology of strategies summarized by the acronym MURDER: set mood, understand requirements of a task, recall key features of task requirements, detail (elaborating) main ideas studied, expand information into organized forms (e.g., an outline), and review. In a semester-long course, students showed statistically detectable but modest benefits when using MURDER (Dansereau et al. 1979). Other research investigated various methods for engaging learners with information and providing opportunities to monitor (see Thomas & McDaniel 2007), including deciding when to stop initial study and when to restudy (see Rohrer & Pashler 2007), self-questioning (Davey & McBride 1986), and summarizing information in keyword (Thiede et al. 2003) or prose form (Thiede & Anderson 2003).

Haller et al. (1988) meta-analyzed 20 studies on the effects of metacognitive instruction on reading comprehension. The average effect size was 0.72. Hattie and colleagues (1996) meta-analyzed 51 newer studies in reading and other subject areas. The average effect sizes due to training in cognitive or metacognitive skills were 0.57 on performance, 0.16 on study skills expertise, and 0.48 on positive affect. Because comparison groups typically represent "business as usual" conditions, two corollaries are warranted: Learners don't naturally learn metacognitive skills to an optimum level, and schooling does not sufficiently remedy this disadvantage. Findings show training has immediate benefits, but they leave unanswered a critical question: Do positive effects of training persist and transfer?

Dignath et al. (2008) meta-analyzed research investigating whether primary school children could be trained to use theoretically more effective forms of self-regulated learning than they had developed themselves and, if so, whether training benefited reading, writing, mathematics, science, other areas of academic performance, attributions, self-efficacy, and metacognitive strategies. Overall, various kinds of training in self-regulated learning produced a weighted effect size of 0.69. But there were two notable issues. First, results were quite variable. Second, the research was overly dependent on self-reports about psychological events such as metacognition and uses of learning tactics.

Metacognition is not "cold"—affect and motivationally "hot" variables interact, including attributions (Hacker et al. 2008), goal orientations (Vrugt & Oort 2008), epistemological beliefs (Pieschl et al. 2008), and self-efficacy. The picture here is complex and inconsistent, in part because learners' self-reports of motivation may not correspond to choices they make to study (Zhou 2008). A broader model of metacognition is needed.

MOTIVATIONAL FACTORS

Motivation is conceptualized as a factor that influences learning. It also is an outcome of learning sought for its own sake. As an influence, motivation divides into two broad categories: factors that direct or limit choices for engagement—choosing to study history for interest but mathematics out of necessity, and factors that affect intensity of engagement—trying hard versus barely trying. As an outcome, motivations concern satisfaction or some other inherent value.

The vast span of theories and empirical work on motivational factors and academic achievement was surveyed, in part, by Covington (2000) and Meece et al. (2006). Both reviews emphasized research on motivation arising from goal-orientation frameworks, so we briefly update that topic before turning to other issues.

Covington (2000) divided the field into two sectors grounded in Kelly's (1955) distinction between (*a*) motives as drives, "an internal state, need or condition that impels individuals toward action" (p. 173) and (*b*) motives as goals, where "actions are given meaning, direction, and purpose by the goals that individuals seek out, and... the quality and intensity of behavior will change as these goals change" (p. 174). As Covington noted, this distinction can be arbitrary because the same behavior can be conceived as reflecting both forms.

We scan three main areas of contemporary research, acknowledging that others are omitted. Our choices reflect a judgment about the intensity of recent work in educational psychology and fit our view of learners as self-regulating.

Achievement Goals

Achievement goals describe what learners orient to when learning, particularly the instrumental role of what is learned. The main research question has been whether achievement goals existing before learning is engaged correlate with levels or types of learning. The reviews by Covington (2000) and Meece et al. (2006) provide ample evidence that different goals correlate variously with outcomes.

A more interesting issue for self-regulated learning is whether achievement goals shape or constrain activities learners choose as they strive for goals. According to this view, goals play the role of standards for metacognitively monitoring situations—a task or the classroom—to classify them in terms of options for behavior. For example, students holding mastery approach goals, defined as intentions to deeply and thoroughly comprehend a subject, may judge that a situation affords opportunity to substantially extend expertise. In contrast, learners with performance approach goals may classify that same situation (as an observer determines sameness) as offering excellent chances to prove competence to others. Because of their differing classifications, these learners may exercise metacognitive control to choose very different tactics for learning (e.g., Dweck & Master 2008, Kolic-Vehovec et al. 2008, Miki & Yamauchi 2005, Pintrich & De Groot 1990).

This line of research faces several challenges. First, learners are not unidimensional in their goal orientations (Pintrich 2000), so bindings between goal orientations and learning events are correspondingly complicated. Second, self-reports have been almost the only basis for researchers to identify goal orientation(s) (cf. Zhou 2008). One-time self-reports about adopted goals have some inherent validity—learners' declarations are what they are. But goals may be unstable, and the task's context may differ from the survey's context (Dowson et al. 2006). Like goal orientations, self-reports are almost the only data gathered to reflect tactics that learners use in learning. These self-reports also are contextually sensitive (Hadwin et al. 2001) and may not be trustworthy accounts of tactics learners actually use during study (Jamieson-Noel & Winne 2003, Winne & Jamieson-Noel 2002).

Together, these challenges weaken prior accounts about how goal orientations lead to choices of learning tactics that directly raise achievement. In addition to developing performance-based measures, gaining experimental control over goal orientation is a promising strategy for advancing research in this area (Gano-Overway 2008).

Interest

Interest predicts choices that learners make about where and how intensely to focus attention; whether to engage in an activity; and the intensity of, concentration on, or persistence in that engagement. Interest also describes a psychological state of positive affect related to features a learner perceives about the environment. Following a revival of research on interest and learning in the early 1990s (Renninger et al. 1992), two main forms of interest have been differentiated. Individual interest captures the predictive quality of interest, as in "I'm interested in science." Situational interest arises either from an opportunistic interaction between a person and features of the transient environment or because a learner exercises volition to create a context that is interesting.

Krapp (2005) reviewed research supporting a model that interest arises because learners experience feedback as they work. His model echoes Dewey's (1913) notion that a fusion of productive cognition and positive affect abets interest. Specifically, when feedback about task engagement supports a view of oneself as competent, agentic, and accepted by others, the task and its method of engagement acquire a degree of interest. Future tasks can be monitored for similar qualities, and the learner accordingly regulates future perceptions as well as engagement.

Research on interest documents that when a situation is monitored to match a priori interest, learners choose that situation, persist, and report positive affect as expected. As a consequence of persistence, learners usually learn more (Ainley et al. 2002). However, interest can debilitate when it leads learners to regulate learning by allocating more or more-intense cognitive processing to less-relevant but interesting content (Lehman et al. 2007, Senko & Miles 2008).

Interest dynamically interacts in complex ways with other variables that mediate the effects of interest and interest itself. A tiny sample of the roll call of these variables follows. Prior interest (Randler & Bogner 2007), prior knowledge, and the structure of knowledge in the domain (Lawless & Kulikowich 2006) all increase achievement and correlate with higher interest. Mastery goals and values attributed to tasks regarding their future utility and enjoyment (Hulleman et al. 2008) predict higher interest but not necessarily higher achievement. Self-concept of ability (Denissen et al. 2007) positively correlates with interest and mediates achievement. Need for cognition (Dai & Wang 2007) does the same. To this list we add self-monitoring and regulation, which we theorize increase students' sense of task-specific agency and consequently interest (Goddard & Sendi 2008). Given the centrality of teachers' and parents' concerns about students' interests in school topics and tasks, this tangle of findings begs for order. Some order might be achieved by applying Occam's razor to coalesce an overabundance of currently differentiated variables.

Epistemic Beliefs

Epistemic beliefs describe views a learner holds about features that distinguish information from knowledge, how knowledge originates, and whether and how knowledge changes. Two studies sparked an explosion of research in this area. The first was Perry's (1970) longitudinal study of undergraduates' developing views of these topics. The second was Schommer's (1990) extension of Ryan's (1984) study, showing that epistemic beliefs moderated comprehension of text.

A general conclusion is that epistemic beliefs predict interactions: When information is complex and probabilistic and its application in tasks cannot be definitively prescribed—when a task is ill-structured—learners who hold less well developed and less flexible epistemic beliefs recall, learn, argue, and solve problems less well than do peers with better developed snd more flexible epistemic beliefs (e.g., Mason & Scirica 2006, Stathopoulou & Vosniadou 2007). But when tasks and information are not ill structured, holding sophisticated epistemological beliefs can interfere with recall and comprehension (Bräten et al. 2008). In short, match of aptitude to task matters.

Muis (2007) synthesized theory and research on epistemic beliefs and self-regulated learning. She offered four main conclusions. First, learners observe features of tasks that reflect epistemic qualities (Muis 2008). Second, they use these perceptions to set goals and frame plans for accomplishing work. Third, as work on a task proceeds, learners use epistemic standards to metacognitively monitor and regulate learning processes (Dahl et al. 2005). Last, engaging in successful self-regulated learning can alter epistemic beliefs, specifically, toward a more constructivist stance (Verschaffel et al. 1999).

CONTEXT FACTORS

Peer-Supported Learning

Peer-supported learning encompasses collaborative, cooperative, and small-group arrangements in dyads or groups of up to about six members. It is theorized to offer multiple social, motivational, behavioral, metacognitive, and academic benefits. O'Donnell (2006) observed that the varied models of peer-supported learning are founded on theories emphasizing sociomotivational or cognitive aspects of the collaborative process.

Sociomotivationally grounded approaches to cooperative learning highlight the role of positive interdependence among group members and individual accountability of each member. These approaches lead to forming groups that are heterogeneous in ability, gender, and ethnicity, and suggest teachers set goals that require students to work together. For example, Slavin (1996) developed types of cooperative learning in which the whole group is rewarded for each of its members' gains in performance, thus incentivizing mutual support for learning within the group. In what he called the social cohesion approach (e.g., Johnson & Johnson 1991), small groups work on developing social skills, concern for others, and giving productive feedback and encouragement. In this approach, group members take on predefined roles (e.g., note keeper), and the teacher assigns a single grade for the group's work to reduce intragroup competition and promote positive interdependence.

Moderate achievement benefits arise from types of peer-supported learning that include positive interdependence, particularly in the form of interdependent reward contingencies (Rohrbeck et al. 2003, Slavin 1996). Using structured roles, as advocated by social cohesion theorists, appears to have little or no effect on achievement (Rohrbeck et al. 2003) but may boost students' social competence and self-concept (Ginsburg-Block et al. 2006). Peer-supported learning interventions are particularly effective in boosting achievement, social competence, self-concept, and task behavior among urban, low-income, minority students (Ginsburg-Block et al. 2006, Rohrbeck et al. 2003). Cooperative tasks designed to enhance student autonomy, such as allowing students to select goals and monitor and evaluate performance, enhance social skills, self-concept, and achievement. A plausible but unresearched hypothesis is that practicing metacognitive control at the group level may help internalize metacognitive control at the individual level.

Cognitive theories of peer-supported learning claim it strengthens individual students' cognitive and metacognitive operations more than solo learning. Peer-supported learning is thought to offer more opportunities for retrieving and activating schemas, elaborating new knowledge, self-monitoring, and exercising metacognitive control (O'Donnell 2006). For example, using a method called guided reciprocal peer questioning (King 2002), a teacher might present a list of generic question stems such as "How does...affect...?" and invite students to use the question stems to generate topic-relevant questions they can pose within their small group or dyad. Students can also learn to pose metacognitive questions, such as "How do you know that?" Having pairs of elementary students generate questions from cognitive question stems can enhance learning outcomes (King 1994, King et al. 1998), but the efficacy of metacognitive prompting by peers is less certain.

A student who helps another by generating an explanation often learns more from the exchange than does the student who receives the explanation (Webb & Palincsar 1996). In research investigating why only some students who need help benefit from explanations, Webb & Mastergeorge (2003) described several qualities of successful help-seekers. They persisted in requesting help until they obtained explanations they understood. They attempted to solve problems without assistance and asked for specific explanations rather than answers to problems. These students adopted difficult but productive standards for monitoring and controlling learning. Classroom observations by Webb et al. (2008) indicate that teachers in primary grades can substantially increase the quality and quantity of explanations peers generate in collaborative groups by encouraging them to request additional explanations that extend or clarify an initial explanation. From the perspective of SRL, teachers who provide such encouragements are leading students to set higher standards for metacognitive monitoring.

In Piagetian terms, equal-status peer interactions are more likely to trigger cognitive disequilibrium, thus engendering more engaged cooperation than do adult-child interactions (De Lisi 2002). After exposure to peers' differing beliefs, dialogue can develop a new understanding that restores equilibrium. In Piaget's theory, this process is hindered if collaborators have unequal status, as in adult-child interactions, because the higher-status participant is less likely to be challenged, and the lower-status participant tends to accept the other's beliefs with little cognitive engagement. In other words, this is a form of self-handicapping metacognitive monitoring and control. In contrast, Vygotsky (1978) held that children construct knowledge primarily by internalizing interactions with a more capable participant who adjusts guidance to match the less capable participant's growing ability. This calls for sophisticated monitoring of a peer's understanding and sensitive metacognitive control that is gradually released to the developing learner. Studies of learning gains by children who collaboratively solved problems without external feedback found that among children paired with a lower-ability, similar-ability, or higher-ability partner, only those paired with a higher-ability partner tended to benefit from collaboration (Fawcett & Garton 2005, Garton & Pratt 2001, Tudge 1992). Tudge (1992) found that the members of similar-ability dyads were at risk of regressing in performance as a result of collaboration. These results favor Vygotsky's over Piaget's account of how status among collaborators stimulates knowledge construction.

How can learners of nearly equal knowledge and ability benefit from collaboration? How can more-capable children adjust help given to meet a peer's needs when they may be unable to monitor even their own abilities? Answers may lie in cognitive strategy instruction in which (*a*) the teacher guides and models group interactions and (*b*) students are assigned to roles that require metacognitive monitoring (Palincsar & Herrenkohl 2002). This approach is best reflected in research on reciprocal teaching to improve the reading comprehension of below-average readers. Here, the teacher's role gradually shifts from direct explanation and modeling to coaching group interactions. A review of quantitative studies found that reciprocal teaching is consistently more effective than are methods in which teachers lead students in reading and answering questions about text passages (Rosenshine & Meister 1994).

For social-cognitive theorists, collaboration is an academic context to which individuals bring personal efficacy and achievement goals. Surprisingly, there is a lack of social-cognitive research on peer-supported learning (Pintrich et al. 2003). This is not because social-cognitive theories have no implications for collaborative learning. As an example, students who have performance avoidance goals and low personal efficacy are less likely to seek help from teachers and are theoretically also less willing to seek help from peers (Webb & Mastergeorge 2003). These students monitor collaborations using standards that handicap learning or lack skills for interacting with peers in more productive ways. At a more fundamental level, Bandura (2000) argued human groups manifest a collective efficacy, the members' perceptions of the efficacy of the group. Because collective efficacy is interdependent with group performance and the personal efficacy of its members, it has potentially important but unexplored implications for peer-supported learning. These and other unexamined implications of sociocognitive theory are opportunities to elaborate peer-supported learning in terms of metacognitive monitoring and control.

Research has offered only weak accounts of the many opportunities for metacognitive monitoring and control in peer-supported learning, including soliciting and giving explanation, sharing appropriate schemas, and using appropriate standards for monitoring progress. Feldmann & Martinezpons (1995) found that individual self-regulation beliefs predicted collaborative verbal behavior and individual achievement. However, there is little evidence that self-regulatory ability improves

collaboration and, if so, which aspects of self-regulation affect qualities of collaboration that recursively promote academic achievement. In what is perhaps the most informative research in this area, low-achieving students were induced to approach a collaborative problem-solving activity with either learning or performance goals as standards for monitoring interactions (Gabriele 2007). Those with a learning goal demonstrated higher comprehension monitoring, more constructive collaborative engagement, and higher posttest performance. Without further research like this, the role played by metacognitive monitoring and control in peer-supported learning will remain obscure.

Classrooms and Class Size

The relationship between class size and student achievement has been widely studied. This issue is so alluring it has attracted researchers even from economics and sociology. Smith & Glass's (1980) meta-analysis established that reducing class size tends to raise students' achievement in a nonlinear relationship. Removing one student from a class of thirty tends to raise the class mean far less than removing one student from a class of two. In textbooks and thumbnail reviews, the nonlinearity of the effect is usually reduced to a simpler principle: gains in achievement are achieved when class size falls to 15 students or fewer.

Project STAR (Student Teacher Achievement Ratio), a large-scale experiment on class size, is lauded as one of the most significant educational investigations ever conducted (Mosteller 1995). The project randomly assigned approximately 12,000 Tennessee elementary school students and their teachers to small (13–17 students) and regular-sized (22–25 students) classes. The students entered the experiment in kindergarten, grade 1, grade 2, or grade 3. Although the intervention ended after grade 3, achievement data were collected until grade 9. In one analysis of the STAR data, Krueger (1999) concluded that students in their first year of small classes scored an average of

4 percentiles higher and increased that advantage in subsequent years of small classes by about 1 percentile per year. This analysis offers limited value to policy makers because the cost of reducing class sizes by one third is high, and other interventions are known to produce larger effects. Even more concerning is that the benefits of some educational interventions diminish rapidly after the intervention terminates.

Fortunately, a more-detailed picture has emerged from the STAR data. Krueger (1999) reported that low-socioeconomic-status (SES) students, African American students, and inner-city students all benefited from small class sizes more than did the general population. Evidence has also emerged that benefits obtained from small class sizes in grades K–3, including the extra gains for disadvantaged groups, persisted until at least grade 8 (Nye et al. 2004). There is an important complication: Small class sizes tend to increase variability in achievement and expand the gap between the highest- and lowest-achieving students (Konstantopoulos 2008). Still more challenging is that recent observational research reports no positive achievement effects from small class sizes in kindergarten (Milesi & Gamoran 2006).

Research relating class size and demographic variables to achievement fails to explain how learning is affected. Looking inside the black box of class size could shine light on this mystery. Blatchford and colleagues (2002, 2007) conducted a series of systematic observations in England of teaching and learning in small and regular-sized classrooms for students ages 11 and under. They found that children in small classes interacted more with their teachers, received more one-to-one instruction, and paid more attention to their teachers (Blatchford et al. 2002, 2007). Teachers and observers in small classes reported that more time was allocated to assessing individual student products and progress. Despite these impacts on teaching, Blatchford et al. (2007) concluded teachers may not take full advantage of reduced class size. They often persisted with more whole-class instruction than necessary and failed to adopt cooperative learning strategies that become more feasible in smaller classes.

This is consistent with conclusions of the STAR project. On the whole, teachers assigned to smaller classes did not strategically modify their teaching (Finn & Achilles 1999). Indeed, taking a sociological perspective, Finn et al. (2003) proposed that improved learning outcomes in small classes are strongly mediated by students' sense of belonging and their academic and social engagement. Students' choices about how they learn and teachers' choices about how they teach are manifestations of metacognitive control. These choices are shaped by standards they each use to metacognitively monitor their circumstances and themselves. In short, standards matter. How do students and teachers acquire them, search for and select them, and use them in these situations?

If resources are allocated to decreasing class sizes in the early grades, how can administrators and teachers know when students are ready to learn in larger classrooms, where they have less teacher support? We speculate that students' abilities to independently monitor and regulate their learning are crucial to successful performance in larger classes. We recommend developing performance-based tools to assess when children have self-regulating skills for learning where there is less teacher attention.

Homework

In her article "Homework is a Complicated Thing," Corno (1996) described difficulties in forming widely applicable, evidence-based homework policies. Corno's title is still the best one-line summation of what is known about the psychology of homework. This is yet another case illustrating that hundreds of investigations using a variety of methods have only weakly informed teaching practices and policy, perhaps because these studies failed to consider learners as metacognitive agents.

Teachers assign readings, problem sets, reports, and projects as homework for a variety of instructional purposes, including practicing skills demonstrated in class, preparing for class discussions, and creatively integrating and applying knowledge acquired from multiple sources (Epstein & Van Voorhis 2001). Homework also may be assigned with intentions to develop time-management and other self-regulatory skills, stimulate parental involvement, and foster parent-teacher communication.

Historically, homework has been controversial. Periodic calls to abolish it are grounded in claims that it is instructionally ineffective and pulls time away from family activities. Calls for abolishing homework interleave with calls for assigning more homework to increase children's preparation for a knowledge-based, competitive world. Homework can be misused when teachers assign too much or use it to punish (Corno 1996). In investigating links between stress and homework, Kouzma & Kennedy (2002) found Australian senior high school students reported a mean of 37 hours of homework per week. Time spent on homework correlated with self-reported mood disturbance. Advocates for educational equity have claimed that homework can increase the performance gap between high- and low-achieving students (McDermott et al. 1984).

The relationship between homework and academic achievement is most fully mapped in two landmark meta-analyses (Cooper 1989, Cooper et al. 2006). Cooper (1989) set out a detailed model of homework effects that includes (*a*) exogenous factors such as student ability and subject matter, and assignment characteristics such as amount and purpose; (*b*) classroom factors, such as the provision of materials; (*c*) home-community factors, such as activities competing for student time; and (*d*) classroom follow-up factors, such as feedback and uses of homework in class discussions. The strongest evidence for homework's efficacy comes from intervention studies, some using random assignment, in which students were or were not given homework. Cooper's meta-analyses statistically detected advantages due to homework in these studies, with weighted mean effect sizes for student test performance of $d = 0.60$ (Cooper et al. 2006) and $d = 0.21$ (Cooper

1989). In a review of studies correlating self-reported time spent on homework and achievement, Cooper et al. (2006) statistically detected a positive weighted average effect size of $r = 0.25$ for high school students but did not detect an effect for elementary students. They reported some evidence of a curvilinear relationship between amount of homework and performance. In Lam's study of grade 12 students cited by Cooper et al. (2006), the benefit from homework was strongest for students doing 7 to 12 hours of homework per week and weakest for students doing more than 20 or less than 6 hours per week.

Trautwein and colleagues (Trautwein 2007, Trautwein et al. 2009) argued that homework is a "classic example of the multi-level problem" whereby generally positive effects of homework reported in Cooper's meta-analyses mask considerable underlying complexity. Working with data from 1275 Swiss students in 70 eighth-grade classes, they distinguished three levels of analysis. At the class level, they found a positive relationship between the frequency of homework assigned by teachers and classes' achievement. At the between-individual level, achievement related positively to students' homework effort but negatively to homework time. At the intraindividual level, in which students were assessed longitudinally, the time-achievement effect flipped direction—homework time related positively to achievement.

Cooper and Trautwein and their colleagues call for better-designed and more-ambitious research on homework. As in so many areas of educational research, there is a need for large-scale experiments, longitudinal observations, hierarchical analyses, and improved methods for gathering qualitative, time-on-task, and fine-grained data that trace cognitive processes. Research also is needed on the effects of potentially moderating variables such as culture, grade level, subject area, cognitive ability, and the manifold factors identified in Cooper's model. Finally, there is a need to develop and investigate innovative homework activities and compare them with conventional forms of homework.

Alongside these macro-level relations, we theorize self-regulation is a key factor in determining the effects of homework activities. Here, there is a dearth of research. In one observational study, Zimmerman & Kitsantas (2005) found that homework experiences positively predicted secondary students' sense of personal responsibility and self-efficacy beliefs, including self-monitoring and organizing. Those beliefs predicted academic achievement. In research on the other side of the reciprocal relationship, training in homework self-monitoring was equally effective as parental monitoring in raising homework-completion rates above those of a no-intervention control group (Toney et al. 2003).

Socioeconomic Status

In educational research, SES is most commonly measured by a composite of parents' education, occupation, and income. Despite older, widespread beliefs about its overwhelming predictive power, SES is only a moderately strong predictor (relative to other known factors) of school achievement in the United States (White 1982). The most recent meta-analysis of U.S. studies found correlations between SES and achievement of 0.23 to 0.30 when measured at the student level (Sirin 2005). By comparison, this effect size is about the same as the meta-analytically derived correlation between parental involvement and achievement (Fan & Chen 2001) and considerably weaker than correlations of achievement with educational resources available in the home ($r = 0.51$) (Sirin 2005) and parental attitudes toward education ($r = 0.55$) (White 1982). Internationally, the effects of SES are pervasive and operate both within and between countries (Chiu & Xihua 2008).

Determining which factors mediate the relationship between SES and students' achievement is challenging because the relevant research is observational, and data range in levels from the student to whole countries. Using multilevel modeling of data from 25 countries, Park (2008) investigated the role of the home literacy environment (early home literacy

activities, parental attitudes toward reading, and number of books at home) in mediating the relationship between parental education and reading performance. He found the home literacy environment strongly predicted reading achievement even after statistically controlling for parental education, but it only partially mediated the relationship between parental education and reading performance.

Another factor that may account for better reading performance by higher-SES children is orally transmitted vocabulary. A U.S. study (Farkas & Beron 2004) found a gap between the oral vocabulary of high- and low-SES children by three years of age, but this did not increase after children entered kindergarten. This suggests that school helps equalize prior differences between children from different socioeconomic backgrounds. A structural equation modeling study found that parent-led home learning experiences (e.g., reading, games, and trips to the zoo or park) mediated the relationship between SES and literacy (Foster et al. 2005). We have not found research investigating the relationship between SES and metacognitive monitoring and control and whether these skills mediate the effects of SES on achievement. Thus, a full explanation of how SES affects learning is not available.

In summary, low SES appears to create significant but not insurmountable barriers to achievement in elementary school and beyond. The effects of SES are likely mediated by factors such as educational resources available in the home, parental aspirations for their children's education, home literacy activities, and parental transmission of oral vocabulary. More high-quality research is needed to investigate the most effective types of interventions for low-SES children, especially whether programs that develop metacognitive and self-regulatory skills could reduce the disadvantages they face.

PERSISTENT DEBATES

Learning and Cognitive Styles

We have never met a teacher who held that teaching is maximally successful when all learners are taught identically. The opposite view—that teaching should adapt to learners' individual differences—requires identifying one or more qualities of learners upon which to pivot features of instruction. One class of such qualities is styles.

Allport (1937) is credited with introducing the phrase "cognitive style" to describe people's preferred or customary approaches to perception and cognition. When situations involve learning, stylistic approaches are termed "learning styles" (Cassidy 2004).

In an early paper, Messick (1970) distinguished nine cognitive styles. More recently, Coffield et al. (2004) cataloged 71 different models grouped into 13 families. Kozhevnikov (2007) classified 10 major groupings. Sternberg et al. (2008) collapsed all these into two categories. Ability-based styles characterize the typical approach(es) a learner takes in achievement tasks, such as representing givens in a problem using symbolic expressions or diagrams. Personality-based styles describe a learner's preference(s) for using abilities. Typical and preferred approaches may or may not match.

A recent theoretical synthesis (Kozhevnikov 2007) described styles as "heuristics [that] can be identified at each level of information processing, from perceptual to metacognitive... [whose] main function is regulatory, controlling processes from automatic data encoding to conscious allocation of cognitive resources." Very few studies are researching this view. The vast majority of research in educational settings aligns with Messick's (1984) view that styles "are spontaneously applied without conscious consideration or choice across a wide variety of situations" (p. 61). Therefore, studies have mainly developed and contrasted self-report inventories or explored correlates of styles while attempting to show that matching styles to forms of instruction has benefits while mismatching does not. Learners often can reliably describe themselves as behaving stylistically. Their reports correlate moderately with various demographic variables, individual differences, and achievement (e.g., Watkins 2001, Zhang & Sternberg 2001). Contrary to expectations, matching instruction to style does not have reliable effects (Coffield et al. 2004).

There are challenges to using styles in psychological accounts of school performance. First, thorough and critical syntheses of the psychometric properties and validity of self-report style measures are scant. One of the few was Pittenger's (1993) review of the Myers-Briggs Type Indicator. He concluded, "...there is no convincing evidence to justify that knowledge of type is a reliable or valid predictor of important behavioral conditions" (p. 483). Second, studies investigating the match of self-reports to behaviors are also rare. Krätzig & Arbuthnott's (2006) study of visual, auditory, kinesthetic, and mixed learning styles found no correlation between self-reported preferences for styles and objective scores on cognitive tasks measuring what the style was about. The study of field dependency-independence by Miyake et al. (2001) led them to conclude that this style "should be construed more as a cognitive ability, rather than a cognitive style" (p. 456).

Discovery Learning

Discovery learning is most strongly associated with science and math education. It has roots in the Piagetian view that "each time one prematurely teaches a child something he could have discovered for himself, that child is kept from inventing it and consequently from understanding it completely" (Piaget 1970, p. 715). Bruner (1961) theorized that discovery learning fosters intrinsic motivation, leads to an understanding of and inclination toward the heuristics of inquiry, and allows for the active self-organization of new knowledge in a way that fits the specific prior knowledge of the learner. According to Hammer (1997, p. 489), discovery learning usually "refers to a form of curriculum in which students are exposed to particular questions and experiences in such a way that they 'discover' for themselves the intended concepts." In unguided and minimally guided discovery learning, the role of the teacher is constrained to providing a learning environment or problem space and perhaps posing questions. In discovery learning, teacher-posed questions should lead the student toward Piagetian disequilibrium, which is conceived as cognitive conflict between prior knowledge and new information from the environment.

Proponents of discovery learning believe it produces highly durable and transferable knowledge, a claim consistent with some observational evidence. For example, children in grades one and two who spontaneously invented and used arithmetic strategies subsequently showed greater understanding of base 10 number concepts and better performance on transfer problems than did children who initially acquired the standard arithmetic algorithms from instruction (Carpenter et al. 1998).

In a widely cited review, Mayer (2004) criticized discovery methods that emphasize unguided exploration in learning environments and problem spaces. Describing a belief in the value of pure discovery learning as "like some zombie that keeps returning from its grave" (p. 17), he reviewed investigations in three domains—problem-solving rules, conservation strategies, and Logo programming strategies. Mayer (2004) observed how in each case, accumulated evidence favored methods in which learners received guidance. He questioned the supposed connection between discovery teaching methods and constructivist theories, arguing that cognitive activity, not behavioral activity, is the essential requirement for constructivist learning. He maintained that, as a consequence, "active-learning" interventions such as hands-on work with materials and group discussions are effective only when they promote cognitive engagement directed toward educational goals.

The debate often pits discovery learning against direct instruction. Direct instruction is a broad domain of explicit teaching practices that include stating learning goals, reviewing prerequisite knowledge, presenting new information in small steps, offering clear instructions and explanations, providing opportunity for frequent practice, guiding performance, and giving customized, explanatory feedback (Rosenshine 1987). Originating as an approach to teaching primary reading, direct instruction has been successful within a wide range of general- and special-education programs at the elementary level (Swanson & Hoskyn 1998).

Discovery learning has been seen as a tool for acquiring difficult, developmentally significant knowledge, such as the control of variables strategy (CVS) used in designing experiments. However, when Klahr & Nigam (2004) randomly assigned elementary students to learn CVS by discovery or direct instruction, many more succeeded in the direct-instruction condition. Moreover, on an authentic transfer task involving evaluating science fair posters, the many students in the direct instruction condition who showed success while learning performed as well as the few students in the discovery group who also showed success while learning. Dean & Kuhn (2007) randomly assigned students learning CVS to direct instruction, discovery learning, and a combination of the two. Direct instruction was presented only during an initial session, and the discovery learning treatment extended over 12 sessions. In this study, direct instruction produced an immediate advantage, which disappeared in a posttest and a transfer task given several weeks after the termination of the discovery learning sessions. Although both of these experiments implemented direct instruction as a single session in which CVS was presented and modeled by a teacher, the experiments failed to include teacher-guided practice with feedback, which is a powerful and essential component of direct instruction.

A review by Kirschner et al. (2006) explained the evidence against minimally guided instruction in terms of cognitive load theory. They cast discovery learning as a type of problem solving that requires a cognitively demanding search in a problem space. According to cognitive load theory, such a search is extrinsic load that requires time and cognitive resources that otherwise could be used for understanding and elaborative processing of solution schemas. To support this claim, they cited evidence that novices learn to solve problems more effectively by initially studying worked solutions before starting to solve problems (Tuovinen & Sweller 1999).

Rittle-Johnson (2006) pointed out that discovery learning theorists tend to conflate the two separate cognitive processes of reasoning about solutions and inventing them. She did a 2 × 2 experiment in which elementary school children learning the concept of mathematical equivalence were assigned to either instruction or invention and either self-explanation or no self-explanation. The invention condition offered no advantages. Both instruction and self-explanation conditions produced advantages for procedural learning on a delayed posttest, and only self-explanation produced advantages for transfer. It may be that self-directed elaborative processing, in this case manifested as self-explanation, is the only way to obtain high-level transfer (Salomon & Perkins 1989). The search of the problem space entailed by unguided discovery may hinder high-level transfer by taxing cognitive resources.

Another explanation of evidence favoring guided instruction is that students lack metacognitive skills needed to learn from unguided exploration. They may be unable to manage time to explore all relevant possibilities, keep track of which conditions and cases they have already explored, accurately monitor what they know and need to know, and monitor what works over the course of learning.

There is a need for better theory and evidentiary support for principles of guided discovery. We recommend investigating multiple ways of guiding discovery so that, ideally, every child is led to the brink of invention and extensive search of the problem space is avoided. Metacognitive guidance could include suggestions to generate a hypothesis, to make a detailed action plan, and to monitor the gap between the research question and the observations. These cognitive and metacognitive activities improve learning outcomes (Veenman et al. 1994).

The timing of metacognitive guidance may be critical. Hulshof & de Jong (2006) provided "just-in-time" instructional tips in a computer-based environment for conducting simulated optics experiments. A new tip became accessible every three minutes and could be consulted at any time thereafter. Although consulting the tips was optional, and tips contained no information that was directly assessed by the posttest, students randomly assigned to a condition that provided the tips outperformed peers in a control condition on the posttest. A potential drawback to this type of optional support is that students may misjudge their need for guidance and fail to access a needed tip or make excessive use of tips to avoid genuine cognitive engagement with the problem (Aleven et al. 2003). Theories about guided learning that may emerge from such research should strive to account for the motivational, cognitive, and metacognitive factors reviewed in this article.

METHODOLOGICAL ISSUES IN MODELING A PSYCHOLOGY OF ACADEMIC ACHIEVEMENT

Paradigmatic Issues

The psychology of school achievement has been studied mainly within a paradigm that we suggest faces difficult challenges. Intending no disrespect, we call this the "snapshot, bookend, between-groups paradigm"—SBBG for short. Recall Roediger's (2008) conclusion that the "only sort of general law, is that in making any generalization about memory one must add that 'it depends'" (p. 247). We posit that his claim generalizes to most if not all findings in a psychology about the way things are because of rules for doing research according to the SBBG paradigm.

SBBG is snapshot because data that reflect the effect of a causal variable almost always are collected just once, after an intervention is over. We acknowledge some studies are longitudinal but maintain that snapshot studies overwhelmingly form the basis of today's psychology of academic achievement.

Beyond the shortcoming of insufficiently tracing events between the bookends of a learning session, there is another reason that educational psychology's snapshot-oriented research paradigm may model academic achievement incompletely. Students in classrooms and people in training learn new information and shift motivation and affect across time. A snapshot study captures just one posttest or pre-to-post segment within a longer trajectory of psychological events. The field has insufficiently attended to how segments concatenate. This is a necessary concern in modeling a trajectory of learning because the next segment may not match a researcher's predicted concatenation. But this issue is not one to validate analytically and a priori. Data are required to characterize how, at any point in the trajectory of a learning activity, a learner metacognitively monitors and exercises the metacognitive control that forms a trajectory of learning.

SBBG is a bookend paradigm because researchers rarely gather data representing proximally cognitive or motivational events between the time when learners are randomly assigned to an intervention and the time when potential effects are measured after the intervention is over. Ideally, random assignment reduces the necessity to gather data before an intervention. (But see Winne 2006 for an argument about challenges to random assignment as a panacea for erasing extraneous variance.) Otherwise, premeasures are secured to reduce "error" variance by blocking or statistically residualizing the outcome variable. (But see Winne 1983 for challenges to interpretation that arise in this case.) Random assignment and premeasures cannot identify cognitive processes that create changes in achievement. Randomness cannot help researchers interpret a systematic effect. Change in a learner's achievement can be conditioned by an aptitude that remains constant for that learner during the intervention, but that change cannot be caused unless this aptitude varies during the intervention.

An alternative that could illuminate achievement-changing processes inside an intervention is to gather data to proximally trace those processes (Borsboom et al. 2003, Winne 1982). Regrettably, data of this kind are rarely gathered because it is impractical. (But see Winne 2006 for ideas about how impracticalities might be overcome using software technologies.) Thus, in bookend experiments, psychological processes that unfold as learners experience the intervention must be inferred rather than validated using fine-grained data gathered over time between the experiment's bookends (Winne & Nesbit 2009). Traces of processing allow opening the book between a traditional experiment's bookends and viewing each "page" situated in relation to prior events and following events. This allows merging psychologies of "the way things are" with "the way learners make things." Modeling should honor the dual role of events observed at points within the intervention, first as the outcome of prior psychological process and second as a process that generates the next state. Empirically investigating a learning trajectory, therefore, entails gathering data that can more fully contribute to accounting for change over time. This stands in contrast to data that reflect only the cumulative products of multiple processes that unfold over time with an intervention.

SBBG is a between-groups paradigm because it forces interpretations about whether an intervention changes learners' achievement to be grounded in differences (variance) between the central tendencies of a treatment group versus a comparison group. Data are lacking that trace how learners make things. Therefore, variance within each group due, in part, to individuals' self-regulating learning—metacognitive monitoring and control applied "on the fly"—has to be treated as "residual" or "error." In fact, the epitome of an experiment in the between-groups tradition would zero out individual differences in the ways learners make things.

If learners are agents, this approach leaves out key parts of the story about how achievement changes. The between-groups experimental approach relieves this tension by explaining effects in terms of a psychological process that does not vary across individuals despite researchers' belief in variance in the way learners make things. Thus, without opening the book of each group member's experience, "between-subjects models do not imply, test, or support causal accounts that are valid at the individual level" (Borsboom et al. 2003, p. 214). The result is that a psychology about the way things are becomes an "it depends" science because between-groups experiments must neglect causal effects that arise from individual differences in the way learners make things.

A Revised Paradigm

We suggest that a more productive psychology of academic achievement should probe and map how learners construct and use information within boundaries set by the way things are. This entails three major paradigmatic changes. First, gather data that trace variance in learners' psychological states over time during an intervention. Supplement snapshot data. Second, conceptualize trajectories of learning as a succession of outcomes reciprocally determined by learners who choose information and modes of processing it to construct successive informational products. Read between bookends. Third, in the many situations where random assignment is not feasible and even where it is, define groups of learners a posteriori in terms of trace data that prove learners to be approximately homogenous in their information processing. Fix causes at the individual level, then explore for mediating and moderating variables post hoc. A paradigm that includes tracing agents' self-regulated processes provides raw materials that can support grounded accounts of what happens in the psychology of academic achievement at the same time it accommodates variations in instructional designs.

SHAPES FOR FUTURE RESEARCH

We judge that the field of educational psychology is in the midst of striving to integrate two streams. One stream investigates whether achievement improves by manipulating instructional conditions (e.g., class size, discovery learning) or accommodating trait-like individual differences (e.g., epistemic beliefs) or social conditions (e.g., SES). In these studies, what individual learners do inside the span of a learning session and how each learner adjusts goals, tactics, and perceptions have been of interest. But these generating variables have rarely been directly operationalized and, when acknowledged, they are mostly treated as error variance terms in analyses of data. The second stream of studies seeks to operationalize reciprocally determined relations among a learner's metacognition, broadly conceptualized, and outcomes. In these studies, bookend variables set a stage of movable props: standards for metacognitively monitoring and choices exercised in metacognitive control. Learners choose the information-processing tools they use within bounds of a psychology of the way things are.

We take as prima facie that changes in academic achievement have origins in psychological phenomena. Snapshot, bookend between-groups studies in educational psychology have not traced those phenomena, as Winne (1983) and Borsboom et al. (2003) argued. Educational psychology should turn its attention to methods that penetrate correlations among distal variables. The goal should be to develop maps of proximal psychological processes that reflect causes of learning. In doing so, we hypothesize research must concern itself with learners' metacognitive monitoring and control. These processes set into motion forms of self-regulated learning that have been demonstrated to influence achievement. Studies should be not only more intensely focused on proximal indicators of psychological processes; researchers also need to gather data inside the bookends of learning sessions to track reciprocally determined relations that shape learning trajectories. In short, we recommend that snapshot, bookend between-groups research be complemented with a microgenetic method (Siegler & Crowley 1991). This suggests several requirements. One is operationally defining traces to describe which psychological processes in the realm of "the way things are" are applied during learning. Another is determining which standards learners apply in their metacognitive monitoring that leads to metacognitive control. These data model the way learners make things.

By a mix of natural exploration and instruction, learners develop their own heuristics, reflective of a naïve psychology of the way things are, about how cognitive and external factors can be arranged to acquire and successfully use academic knowledge. As agents, they operationalize those heuristics by metacognitively monitoring and controlling mental states and by manipulating external factors. By tracking their academic achievements and side effects over time, they become informed about how to regulate engagement in learning to improve the results of subsequent engagements. In short, over time, self-regulating learners experiment with learning to improve how they learn alongside what they learn (Winne 1995).

Findings from the psychology of the way things are will become better understood as we advance the psychology of how learners make things. This will involve learning more about standards that learners use to metacognitively monitor, the nature of monitoring per se, how learners characterize a profile of features generated by monitoring, and how potential actions are searched for and matched to a profile generated by monitoring that sets a stage for metacognitive control. Metaphorically, because learners are in the driver's seat, educational psychology needs a model of how learners drive to understand more fully how they reach destinations of academic achievement. By incorporating metacognition and its larger-scale form, self-regulated learning, into data and analyses of data, rather than randomizing out these factors, we submit a psychology of academic achievement can advance theoretically and offer more powerful principles for practice.

Our hypothesis is that gluing together the two psychologies of the way things are and the way learners make things will reduce the degree of Roediger's "it depends" hedge on laws of memory (and learning). Two inherent sources of variance need examining: What do learners already know and access over the fine-grained course of a learning session? How do learners self-regulate learning across sessions to adapt in service of achieving their goals? Richer interpretations will need to be grounded on fine-grained trace data that fill in gaps about processes in learning, specifically: Which heuristics for learning do learners consider, choose, apply, and adapt? How do those processes by which learners make things and self-regulate unfold under constraints of how things are?

DISCLOSURE STATEMENT

The authors are not aware of any biases that might be perceived as affecting the objectivity of this review.

LITERATURE CITED

Ainley M, Hidi S, Berndorff D. 2002. Interest, learning, and the psychological processes that mediate their relationship. *J. Educ. Psychol.* 94:545–61

Aleven V, Stahl E, Schworm S, Fischer F, Wallace R. 2003. Help seeking and help design in interactive learning environments. *Rev. Educ. Res.* 73:277–320

Allport GW. 1937. *Personality: A Psychological Interpretation.* New York: Holt

Baddeley AD, Hitch GJ. 1974. Working memory. In *Recent Advances in Learning and Motivation* Vol. 8, ed. GA Bower, pp. 47–89. New York: Academic

Bandura A. 2000. Exercise of human agency through collective efficacy. *Curr. Dir. Psychol. Sci.* 9:75–78

Blatchford P, Moriarty V, Edmonds S, Martin C. 2002. Relationships between class size and teaching: a multimethod analysis of English infant schools. *Am. Educ. Res. J.* 39:101–32

Blatchford P, Russell A, Bassett P, Brown P, Martin C. 2007. The effect of class size on the teaching of pupils aged 7–11 years. *Sch. Eff. Sch. Improv.* 18:147–72

Borsboom D, Mellenbergh GJ, van Heerden J. 2003. The theoretical status of latent variables. *Psychol. Rev.* 110:203–19

Bräten I, Strømsöä HI, Samuelstuen MS. 2008. Are sophisticated students always better? The role of topic-specific personal epistemology in the understanding of multiple expository texts. *Contemp. Educ. Psychol.* 33:814–40

Bruner JS. 1961. The act of discovery. *Harvard Educ. Rev.* 31:21–32

Carpenter TP, Franke ML, Jacobs VR, Fennema E, Empson SB. 1998. A longitudinal study of invention and understanding in children's multidigit addition and subtraction. *J. Res. Math. Educ.* 29:3–20

Cassidy S. 2004. Learning styles: an overview of theories, models, and measures. *Educ. Psychol.* 24:419–44

Chiu MM, Xihua Z. 2008. Family and motivation effects on mathematics achievement: analyses of students in 41 countries. *Learn. Instruc.* 18:321–36

Coffield F, Moseley D, Hall E, Ecclestone K. 2004. *Learning Styles and Pedagogy in Post-16 Learning. A Systematic and Critical Review.* (Report No. 041543.) London: Learning Skills Res. Cent.

Cooper H. 1989. *Homework.* New York: Longman

Cooper H, Robinson JC, Patall EA. 2006. Does homework improve academic achievement? A synthesis of research, 1987–2003. *Rev. Educ. Res.* 76:1–62

Corno L. 1996. Homework is a complicated thing. *Educ. Researcher* 25:27–30

Covington MV. 2000. Goal theory, motivation, and school achievement: an integrative review. *Annu. Rev. Psychol.* 51:171–200

Dahl TI, Bals M, Turi AL. 2005. Are students' beliefs about knowledge and learning associated with their reported use of learning strategies? *Br. J. Educ. Psychol.* 75:257–73

Dai DY, Wang X. 2007. The role of need for cognition and reader beliefs in text comprehension and interest development. *Contemp. Educ. Psychol.* 32:332–47

Dansereau DF. 1985. Learning strategy research. In *Thinking and Learning Skills. Vol. 1: Relating Instruction to Research*, ed. JW Segal, SF Chipman, R Glaser, pp. 209–39. Hillsdale, NJ: Erlbaum

Dansereau DF, Collins KW, McDonald BA, Holley DD, Garland J, et al. 1979. Development and evaluation of a learning strategy training program. *J. Educ. Psychol.* 71:64–73

Davey B, McBride S. 1986. Effects of question-generation training on reading comprehension. *J. Educ. Psychol.* 78:256–62

Dean D, Kuhn D. 2007. Direct instruction vs discovery: the long view. *Sci. Educ.* 91:384–97

De Lisi R. 2002. From marbles to instant messenger: implications of Piaget's ideas about peer learning. *Theory Pract.* 41:5–12

Denissen JJA, Zarrett NR, Eccles JS. 2007. I like to do it, I'm able, and I know I am: longitudinal couplings between domain-specific achievement, self-concept, and interest. *Child Dev.* 78:430–47

Dewey J. 1913. *Interest and Effort in Education.* Boston: Riverside

Dignath D, Buettner G, Langfeldt H-P. 2008. How can primary school students learn self-regulated learning strategies most effectively? A meta-analysis on self-regulation training programmes. *Ed. Res. Rev.* 3:101–29

Dowson M, McInerney DM, Nelson GF. 2006. An investigation of the effects of school context and sex differences on students' motivational goal orientations. *Educ. Psychol.* 26:781–811

Dunlosky J, Rawson KA, Middleton EL. 2005. What constrains the accuracy of metacomprehension judgments? Testing the transfer-appropriate-monitoring and accessibility hypotheses. *J. Mem. Lang.* 52:551–65

Dweck CS, Master A. 2008. Self-theories motivate self-regulated learning. In *Motivation and Self-Regulated Learning: Theory, Research, and Applications*, ed. DH Schunk, BJ Zimmerman, pp. 31–51. Mahwah, NJ: Erlbaum

Epstein JL, Van Voorhis FL. 2001. More than minutes: teachers' roles in designing homework. *Educ. Psychol.* 36:181–93

Fan X, Chen M. 2001. Parental involvement and students' academic achievement: a meta-analysis. *Educ. Psychol. Rev.* 13:1–22

Farkas G, Beron K. 2004. The detailed age trajectory of oral vocabulary knowledge: differences by class and race. *Soc. Sci. Res.* 33:464–97

Fawcett LM, Garton AF. 2005. The effect of peer collaboration on children's problem-solving ability. *Br. J. Educ. Psychol.* 75:157–69

Feldmann SC, Martinez-Pons M. 1995. The relationship of self-efficacy, self-regulation, and collaborative verbal behavior with grades—preliminary findings. *Psychol. Rep.* 77:971–78

Finn JD, Achilles CM. 1999. Tennessee's class size study: findings, implications, misconceptions. *Educ. Eval. Pol. Anal.* 21:97–109

Finn JD, Pannozzo GM, Achilles CM. 2003. The "why's" of class size: student behavior in small classes. *Rev. Educ. Res.* 73:321–68

Flavell JH. 1971. First discussant's comments: What is memory development the development of? *Hum. Dev.* 14:272–78

Foster MA, Lambert R, Abbott-Shim M, McCarty F, Franze S. 2005. A model of home learning environment and social risk factors in relation to children's emergent literacy and social outcomes. *Early Childhood Res. Q.* 20:13–36

Gabriele AJ. 2007. The influence of achievement goals on the constructive activity of low achievers during collaborative problem solving. *Br. J. Educ. Psychol.* 77:121–41

Gano-Overway LA. 2008. The effect of goal involvement on self-regulatory processes. *Int. J. Sport Exerc. Psychol.* 6:132–56

Garton AF, Pratt C. 2001. Peer assistance in children's problem solving. *Br. J. Dev. Psychol.* 19:307–18

Ginsburg-Block MD, Rohrbeck CA, Fantuzzo JW. 2006. A meta-analytic review of social, self-concept, and behavioral outcomes of peer-assisted learning. *J. Educ. Psychol.* 98:732–49

Goddard YL, Sendi C. 2008. Effects of self-monitoring on the narrative and expository writing of four fourth-grade students with learning disabilities. *Read. Writ. Q.* 24:408–33

Hacker DJ, Bol L, Bahbahani K. 2008. Explaining calibration accuracy in classroom contexts: the effects of incentives, reflection, and explanatory style. *Metacogn. Learn.* 3:101–21

Hacker DJ, Dunlosky J, Graesser AC, eds. 2009. *Handbook of Metacognition in Education.* Mahwah, NJ: Erlbaum

Hadwin AF, Winne PH, Stockley DB, Nesbit JC, Woszczyna C. 2001. Context moderates students' self-reports about how they study. *J. Educ. Psychol.* 93:477–87

Haller EP, Child DA, Walberg HJ. 1988. Can comprehension be taught? *Educ. Res.* 17(9):5–8

Hammer D. 1997. Discovery learning and discovery teaching. *Cogn. Instruc.* 15:485–529

Hart JT. 1965. Memory and the feeling-of-knowing experience. *J. Educ. Psychol.* 56:208–16

Hattie J, Biggs J, Purdie N. 1996. Effects of learning skills interventions on student learning: a meta-analysis. *Rev. Educ. Res.* 66:99–136

Hulleman CS, Durik AM, Schweigert SB, Harackiewicz JM. 2008. Task values, achievement goals, and interest: an integrative analysis. *J. Educ. Psychol.* 100:398–416

Hulshof CD, de Jong T. 2006. Using just-in-time information to support scientific discovery learning in a computer-based simulation. *Interact. Learn. Environ.* 14:79–94

Jamieson-Noel D, Winne PH. 2003. Comparing self-reports to traces of studying behavior as representations of students' studying and achievement. *Z. Pädagog. Psychol./German J. Educ. Psychol.* 17:159–71

Johnson DW, Johnson RT. 1991. *Learning Together and Alone: Cooperative, Competitive, and Individualistic Learning.* Englewood Cliffs, NJ: Prentice Hall

Kelly GA. 1955. *Psychology of Personal Constructs. Vol. 1: A Theory of Personality.* New York: Norton

Kendler HH, Kendler TS, Ward JW. 1972. An ontogenetic analysis of optional intradimensional and extradimensional shifts. *J. Exp. Psychol.* 95:102–9

King A. 1994. Guiding knowledge construction in the classroom: effects of teaching children how to question and how to explain. *Am. Educ. Res. J.* 31:338–68

King A. 2002. Structuring peer interaction to promote high-level cognitive processing. *Theory Pract.* 41:33–39

King A, Staffieri A, Adelgais A. 1998. Mutual peer tutoring: effects of structuring tutorial interaction to scaffold peer learning. *J. Educ. Psychol.* 90:134–52

Kintsch W. 1988. The role of knowledge in discourse comprehension: a construction-integration model. *Psychol. Rev.* 95:163–82

Kirschner PA, Sweller J, Clark RE. 2006. Why minimal guidance during instruction does not work: an analysis of the failure of constructivist, discovery, problem-based, experiential, and inquiry-based teaching. *Educ. Psychol.* 41:75–86

Klahr D, Nigam M. 2004. The equivalence of learning paths in early science instruction: effects of direct instruction and discovery learning. *Psychol. Sci.* 15:661–67

Kolic-Vehovec S, Roncevic B, Bajšanski I. 2008. Motivational components of self-regulated learning and reading strategy use in university students: the role of goal orientation patterns. *Learn. Individ. Diff.* 18:108–13

Konstantopoulos S. 2008. Do small classes reduce the achievement gap between low and high achievers? Evidence from project STAR. *Elem. Sch. J.* 108:275–91

Koriat A. 1993. How do we know that we know? The accessibility model of the feeling of knowing. *Psychol. Rev.* 100:609–39

Koriat A, Sheffer L, Ma'ayan H. 2002. Comparing objective and subjective learning curves: judgments of learning exhibit increased underconfidence with practice. *J. Exp. Psychol.: Gen.* 131:147–62

Kouzma NM, Kennedy GA. 2002. Homework, stress and mood disturbance in senior high school students. *Psychol. Rep.* 91:193–98

Kozhevnikov M. 2007. Cognitive styles in the context of modern psychology: toward an integrated framework of cognitive style. *Psychol. Bull.* 133:464–81

Krapp A. 2005. Basic needs and the development of interest and intrinsic motivational orientations. *Learn. Instruc.* 15:381–95

Krätzig GP, Arbuthnott KD. 2006. Perceptual learning style and learning proficiency: a test of the hypothesis. *J. Educ. Psychol.* 98:238–46

Krueger AB. 1999. Experimental estimates of education production functions. *Q. J. Econ.* 114:497–532

Lawless KA, Kulikowich JM. 2006. Domain knowledge and individual interest: the effects of academic level and specialization in statistics and psychology. *Contemp. Educ. Psychol.* 31:30–43

Lehman S, Schraw G, McCrudden MT, Hartley K. 2007. Processing and recall of seductive details in scientific text. *Contemp. Educ. Psychol.* 32:569–87

Maki RH. 1998. Test predictions over text material. In *Metacognition in Educational Theory and Practice*, ed. DJ Hacker, J Dunlosky, AC Graesser, pp. 117–44. Mahwah, NJ: Erlbaum

Martin J. 2004. Self-regulated learning, social cognitive theory, and agency. *Educ. Psychol.* 39:135–45

Mason L, Scirica F. 2006. Prediction of students' argumentation skills about controversial topics by epistemological understanding. *Learn. Instruc.* 16:492–509

Mayer RE. 2004. Should there be a three-strikes rule against pure discovery learning? The case for guided methods of instruction. *Am. Psychol.* 59:14–19

Mayer RE. 2005. Principles for reducing extraneous processing in multimedia learning. In *The Cambridge Handbook of Multimedia Learning*, ed. RE Mayer, pp. 183–200. New York: Cambridge Univ. Press

McDermott RP, Goldman SV, Varenne H. 1984. When school goes home: some problems in the organization of homework. *Teach. Coll. Rec.* 85:391–409

Meece JL, Anderman EM, Anderman LH. 2006. Classroom goal structure, student motivation, and academic achievement. *Annu. Rev. Psychol.* 57:487–503

Messick S. 1970. The criterion problem in the evaluation of instruction: assessing possible, not just intended outcomes. In *The Evaluation of Instruction: Issues and Problems*, ed. MC Wittrock, DE Wiley, pp. 188–89. New York: Holt, Rinehart & Winston

Messick S. 1984. The nature of cognitive styles: problems and promise in educational practice. *Educ. Psychol.* 19:59–74

Miki K, Yamauchi H. 2005. Perceptions of classroom goal structures, personal achievement goal orientations, and learning strategies. *Jpn. J. Psychol.* 76:260–68

Milesi C, Gamoran A. 2006. Effects of class size and instruction on kindergarten achievement. *Educ. Eval. Pol. Anal.* 28:287–313

Miyake A, Witzki AH, Emerson MJ. 2001. Field dependence-independence from a working memory perspective: a dual-task investigation of the Hidden Figures Test. *Memory* 9:445–57

Mosteller F. 1995. The Tennessee study of class size in the early school grades. *Future Children* 5:113–27

Muis KR. 2007. The role of epistemic beliefs in self-regulated learning. *Educ. Psychol.* 42:173–90

Muis KR. 2008. Epistemic profiles and self-regulated learning: examining relations in the context of mathematics problem solving. *Contemp. Educ. Psychol.* 33:177–208

Murphy FC, Wilde G, Ogden N, Barnard PJ, Calder AJ. 2009. Assessing the automaticity of moral processing: efficient coding of moral information during narrative comprehension. *Q. J. Exp. Psychol.* 62:41–49

Nelson TO, Dunlosky J. 1991. When people's judgments of learning (JOLs) are extremely accurate at predicting subsequent recall: the "delayed-JOL effect." *Psychol. Sci.* 2:267–70

Ngu BH, Mit E, Shahbodin F, Tuovinen J. 2009. Chemistry problem solving instruction: a comparison of three computer-based formats for learning from hierarchical network problem representations. *Instr. Sci.* 37:21–42

Nye B, Hedges LV, Konstantopoulos S. 2004. Do minorities experience larger lasting benefits from small classes? *J. Educ. Res.* 98:94–100

Oakhill J, Hartt J, Samols D. 2005. Levels of comprehension monitoring and working memory in good and poor comprehenders. *Read. Writ.* 18:657–86

O'Donnell AM. 2006. The role of peers and group learning. In *Handbook of Educational Psychology*, ed. PA Alexander, PH Winne, pp. 781–802. Mahwah, NJ: Erlbaum

Paas F, Renkl A, Sweller J. 2003a. Cognitive load theory and instructional design: Recent developments. *Educ. Psychol.* 38:1–4

Paas F, Tuovinen JE, Tabbers H, Van Gerven PWM. 2003b. Cognitive load measurement as a means to advance cognitive load theory. *Educ. Psychol.* 38:63–71

Palincsar AS, Herrenkohl L. 2002. Designing collaborative learning contexts. *Theory Pract.* 41:26–32

Park H. 2008. Home literacy environments and children's reading performance: A comparative study of 25 countries. *Educ. Res. Eval.* 14:489–505

Perry WG Jr. 1970. *Forms of Intellectual and Ethical Development in the College Years: A Scheme*. New York: Holt, Rinehart & Winston

Piaget J. 1970. Piaget's theory. In *Carmichael's Manual of Child Psychology*, ed. P Mussen, Vol. 1, pp. 703–72. New York: Wiley

Pieschl S, Stahl E, Bromme R. 2008. Epistemological beliefs and self-regulated learning with hypertext. *Metacogn. Learn.* 3:17–27

Pintrich PR. 2000. Multiple goals, multiple pathways: the role of goal orientation in learning and achievement. *J. Educ. Psychol.* 92:544–55

Pintrich PR, Conley AM, Kempler TM. 2003. Current issues in achievement goal theory and research. *Int. J. Educ. Res.* 39:319–37

Pintrich PR, DeGroot E. 1990. Motivational and self-regulated learning components of classroom academic performance. *J. Educ. Psychol.* 82:33–40

Pittenger DJ. 1993. The utility of the Myers-Briggs type indicator. *Rev. Educ. Res.* 63:467–88

Purhonen M, Valkonen-Korhonen M, Lehtonen J. 2008. The impact of stimulus type and early motherhood on attentional processing. *Dev. Psychobiol.* 50:600–7

Randler C, Bogner FX. 2007. Pupils' interest before, during, and after a curriculum dealing with ecological topics and its relationship with achievement. *Educ. Res. Eval.* 13:463–78

Renninger KA, Hidi S, Krapp A, eds. 1992. *The Role of Interest in Learning and Development*. Hillsdale, NJ: Erlbaum

Reyes ML, Lee JD. 2008. Effects of cognitive load presence and duration on driver eye movements and event detection performance. *Transportation Res. Part F: Traffic Psychol. Behav.* 11:391–402

Rittle-Johnson B. 2006. Promoting transfer: effects of self-explanation and direct instruction. *Child Dev.* 77:1–15

Roediger HL. 2008. Relativity of remembering: why the laws of memory vanished. *Annu. Rev. Psychol.* 59:225–54

Rohrbeck CA, Ginsburg-Block MD, Fantuzzo JW, Miller TR. 2003. Peer-assisted learning interventions with elementary school students: a meta-analytic review. *J. Educ. Psychol.* 95:240–57

Rohrer D, Pashler H. 2007. Increasing retention without increasing study time. *Curr. Dir. Psychol. Sci.* 16:183–86

Rosenshine B. 1987. Explicit teaching and teacher training. *J. Teacher Educ.* 38(3):34–36

Rosenshine B, Meister C. 1994. Reciprocal teaching: a review of the research. *Rev. Educ. Res.* 64:479–530

Ryan MP. 1984. Monitoring text comprehension: individual differences in epistemological standards. *J. Educ. Psychol.* 76:248–58

Salomon G, Perkins DN. 1989. Rocky roads to transfer: rethinking mechanisms of a neglected phenomenon. *Educ. Psychol.* 24:113–42

Schommer M. 1990. Effects of beliefs about the nature of knowledge on comprehension. *J. Educ. Psychol.* 82:498–504

Senko C, Miles KM. 2008. Pursuing their own learning agenda: how mastery-oriented students jeopardize their class performance. *Contemp. Educ. Psychol.* 33:561–83

Siegler RS, Crowley K. 1991. The microgenetic method: a direct means for studying cognitive development. *Am. Psychol.* 46:606–20

Sirin SR. 2005. Socioeconomic status and academic achievement: a meta-analytic review of research. *Rev. Educ. Res.* 75:417–53

Slavin RE. 1996. Research on cooperative learning and achievement: what we know, what we need to know. *Contemp. Educ. Psychol.* 21:43–69

Smith ML, Glass GV. 1980. Meta-analysis of research on class size and its relationship to attitudes and instruction. *Am. Educ. Res. J.* 17:419–33

Stathopoulou C, Vosniadou S. 2007. Exploring the relationship between physics-related epistemological beliefs and physics understanding. *Contemp. Educ. Psychol.* 32:255–81

Sternberg RJ, Grigorenko EL, Zhang LF. 2008. Styles of learning and thinking matter in instruction and assessment. *Perspect. Psychol. Sci.* 3:486–506

Swanson HL, Hoskyn M. 1998. Experimental intervention research on students with learning disabilities: a meta-analysis of treatment outcomes. *Rev. Educ. Res.* 68:277–321

Sweller J. 1988. Cognitive load during problem solving: effects on learning. *Cogn. Sci.* 12:257–85

Thiede KW, Anderson MCM. 2003. Summarizing can improve metacomprehension accuracy. *Contemp. Educ. Psychol.* 28:129–60

Thiede KW, Anderson MCM, Therriault D. 2003. Accuracy of metacognitive monitoring affects learning of texts. *J. Educ. Psychol.* 95:66–73

Thiede KW, Dunlosky J, Griffin TD, Wiley J. 2005. Understanding the delayed-keyword effect on metacomprehension accuracy. *J. Exp. Psychol.: Learn. Mem. Cogn.* 31:1267–80

Thomas AK, McDaniel MA. 2007. Metacomprehension for educationally relevant materials: dramatic effects of encoding–retrieval interactions. *Psychon. Bull. Rev.* 14:212–18

Thorndike EL. 1903. *Educational Psychology.* New York: Lemcke & Buechner

Toney LP, Kelley ML, Lanclos NF. 2003. Self- and parental monitoring of homework in adolescents: comparative effects on parents' perceptions of homework behavior problems. *Child Fam. Behav. Ther.* 25:35–51

Trautwein U. 2007. The homework-achievement relation reconsidered: differentiating homework time, homework frequency, and homework effort. *Learn. Instruc.* 17:372–88

Trautwein U, Schnyder I, Niggli A, Neumann M, Ludtke O. 2009. Chameleon effects in homework research: the homework-achievement association depends on the measures used and the level of analysis chosen. *Contemp. Educ. Psychol.* 34:77–88

Tudge JR. 1992. Processes and consequences of peer collaboration: a Vygotskian analysis. *Child Dev.* 63:1364–79

Tuovinen JE, Sweller J. 1999. A comparison of cognitive load associated with discovery learning and worked examples. *J. Educ. Psychol.* 91:334–41

Veenman MV, Elshout JJ, Busato VV. 1994. Metacognitive mediation in learning with computer-based simulations. *Comput. Hum. Behav.* 10:93–106

Verschaffel L, de Corte E, Lasure S, Van Vaerenbergh G, Bogaerts H, Ratinckx E. 1999. Learning to solve mathematical application problems: a design experiment with fifth graders. *Math. Think. Learn.* 1:195–229

Vrugt A, Oort FJ. 2008. Metacognition, achievement goals, study strategies and academic achievement: pathways to achievement. *Metacogn. Learn.* 3:123–46

Vygotsky LS. 1978. *Mind in Society.* Cambridge, MA: Harvard Univ. Press

Walczyk JJ, Raska LJ. 1992. The relation between low- and high-level reading skills in children. *Contemp. Educ. Psychol.* 17:38–46

Watkins D. 2001. Correlates of approaches to learning: a cross-cultural meta-analysis. In *Perspectives on Thinking, Learning and Cognitive Styles*, ed. RJ Sternberg, LF Zhang, pp. 165–95. Mahwah, NJ: Erlbaum

Webb NM, Franke ML, Ing M, Chan A, De T, et al. 2008. The role of teacher instructional practices in student collaboration. *Contemp. Educ. Psychol.* 33:360–81

Webb NM, Mastergeorge AM. 2003. The development of students' helping behavior and learning in peer-directed small groups. *Cogn. Instruc.* 21:361–428

Webb NM, Palincsar AS. 1996. Group processes in the classroom. In *Handbook of Educational Psychology*, ed. DC Berliner, RC Calfee, pp. 841–73. New York: Prentice Hall

White KR. 1982. The relation between socioeconomic status and academic achievement. *Psychol. Bull.* 91:461–81

Winne PH. 1982. Minimizing the black box problem to enhance the validity of theories about instructional effects. *Instruc. Sci.* 11:13–28

Winne PH. 1983. Distortions of construct validity in multiple regression analysis. *Canadian J. Behav. Sci.* 15:187–202

Winne PH. 1995. Inherent details in self-regulated learning. *Educ. Psychol.* 30:173–87

Winne PH. 2006. How software technologies can improve research on learning and bolster school reform. *Educ. Psychol.* 41:5–17

Winne PH, Jamieson-Noel DL. 2002. Exploring students' calibration of self-reports about study tactics and achievement. *Contemp. Educ. Psychol.* 27:551–72

Winne PH, Nesbit JC. 2009. Supporting self-regulated learning with cognitive tools. In *Handbook of Metacognition in Education*, ed. DJ Hacker, J Dunlosky, AC Graesser, pp. 259–77. New York: Routledge

Zhang LF, Sternberg RJ. 2001. Thinking styles across cultures: their relationships with student learning. In *Perspectives on Thinking, Learning and Cognitive Styles*, ed. RJ Sternberg, LF Zhang, pp. 197–226. Mahwah, NJ: Erlbaum

Zhou M. 2008. *Operationalizing and Tracing Goal Orientation and Learning Strategy.* Unpubl. doctoral dissert., Simon Fraser Univ.

Zimmerman BJ, Kitsantas A. 2005. Homework practices and academic achievement: the mediating role of self-efficacy and perceived responsibility beliefs. *Contemp. Educ. Psychol.* 30:397–417

Personality and Coping

Charles S. Carver[1] and Jennifer Connor-Smith[2]

[1]Department of Psychology, University of Miami, Coral Gables, Florida 33124,
[2]Department of Psychology, Oregon State University, Corvallis, Oregon 97331;
email: ccarver@miami.edu, jconn@pdx.edu

Annu. Rev. Psychol. 2010. 61:679–704

First published online as a Review in Advance on July 2, 2009

The *Annual Review of Psychology* is online at psych.annualreviews.org

This article's doi:
10.1146/annurev.psych.093008.100352

Key Words

optimism, effortful control, stress, goal pursuit, five-factor model

Abstract

Personality psychology addresses views of human nature and individual differences. Biological and goal-based views of human nature provide an especially useful basis for construing coping; the five-factor model of traits adds a useful set of individual differences. Coping—responses to adversity and to the distress that results—is categorized in many ways. Meta-analyses link optimism, extraversion, conscientiousness, and openness to more engagement coping; neuroticism to more disengagement coping; and optimism, conscientiousness, and agreeableness to less disengagement coping. Relations of traits to specific coping responses reveal a more nuanced picture. Several moderators of these associations also emerge: age, stressor severity, and temporal proximity between the coping activity and the coping report. Personality and coping play both independent and interactive roles in influencing physical and mental health. Recommendations are presented for ways future research can expand on the growing understanding of how personality and coping shape adjustment to stress.

Contents

INTRODUCTION

This review addresses personality and coping. By strong implication, this topic also extends to the outcomes that may follow from either functional or dysfunctional coping. Taken together, the various literatures that might be brought to bear on this topic are both numerous and large.

Personality, for example, has been approached in quite different ways by many theorists (see, e.g., Carver & Scheier 2008). There are also several ways to group coping responses (e.g., Compas et al. 2001, Skinner et al. 2003). Finally, the potential effects of coping are themselves numerous, ranging from emotional distress, to physiological reactivity, to mortality. Obviously a full treatment of all the relevant literatures is beyond the scope of this review, though we do touch on many of them.

The review begins with a brief consideration of personality. Although most first associations to the word "personality" probably focus on individual differences, we also consider core processes of human functioning that inform the analysis of coping. Next the review turns to the concept of stress, the term most often applied to circumstances that elicit coping. Then comes a closer look at coping itself, differentiating coping from other responses to stress and distinguishing among categories of coping. The central constructs having been introduced, the review then turns to their interrelations. We begin with links (theoretical and empirical) between personality and coping. Following is a discussion of how stress, personality, and coping interact in predicting mental and physical well-being. The article closes with recommendations for future research.

PERSONALITY

The psychology of personality is a very broad topic, to which people have taken diverse theoretical approaches (see recent *Annual Review of Psychology* articles by Caspi et al. 2005, Cervone 2005, Funder 2001, McAdams & Olson 2010, Mischel 2004, Ryan & Deci 2001). Personality is easy to observe but hard to pin down. To paraphrase Allport (1961), personality is the dynamic organization within the person of the psychological and physical systems that underlie that person's patterns of actions, thoughts, and feelings. What dynamics are assumed, however, and what systems are proposed to underlie those dynamics vary greatly across theoretical viewpoints.

Human Nature and Individual Differences

Personality psychology is partly about what makes everyone the same and partly about what makes people differ from each other. That is, personality theories are partly statements about human nature: assertions that people are basically (for example) biological creatures, social creatures, self-protective, self-actualizing, or learning creatures. To understand the person, one has to adopt some view of the essence of human nature.

Personality also concerns individual differences. Individual differences can be found on any dimension imaginable, but the so-called five-factor model (Digman 1990, Goldberg 1981, McCrae & Costa 2003) has been widely adopted as a consensual framework. The five factors are most commonly labeled extraversion, neuroticism, agreeableness, conscientiousness, and openness to experience. In this view, these broad dimensions are key determinants of behavior, and the aggregation of information resulting from a person's placement on these dimensions gives a reasonably good snapshot of what that person is like. Each broad trait is composed of multiple facets, which provide a more nuanced picture.

Broad adoption of the five-factor model does not mean unanimity about it. There are staunch advocates of other frameworks, including two three-factor models (Eysenck 1975, 1986; Tellegen 1985), an alternative five-factor model (Zuckerman et al. 1993), and a six-factor model (Ashton et al. 2004). Indeed, some important traits do not fit smoothly into the five-factor framework. For example, optimism has overtones of both extraversion and neuroticism, but does not quite fit either construct (Marshall et al. 1992).

Both human nature and individual differences are important to the topic of this review. In thinking about the nature of coping, it is helpful to have some view of how best to construe core human functions. Whatever view of human nature is adopted channels interpretation of people's reactions to stress. It will also be useful to have a sense of some of the ways in which people differ and expectations of how those differences may play a role in coping. These issues are addressed in greater detail in the next two sections.

Functional Organization: Two Views of Human Nature

Of the great many viewpoints that have been taken on human nature, two appear particularly relevant to stress and coping.

Biological models. An increasingly influential perspective, not just in personality but in all of psychology, treats humans as biological entities. From this view, it is desirable to develop a clear understanding of the basic properties of animal self-regulation and of how those properties are manifested in human behavior. We focus here on three properties: the tendency to approach desirable objects and situations (e.g., food), the tendency to avoid dangerous objects and situations (e.g., predators), and the capacity to regulate the approach and avoidance tendencies.

Biological models assuming approach and avoidance temperaments have acquired a good deal of influence over the past decade (see Davidson 1998, Depue & Collins 1999, Caspi & Shiner 2006, Caspi et al. 2005, Elliott & Thrash 2002, Fowles 1993, Gray 1994, Rothbart & Hwang 2005). They hold that approach and avoidance systems are supported partly by distinct brain areas, and that the sensitivity of each system (which varies among persons) influences behavior in response to environmental reward and threat cues.

Developmental theorists have posited another temperament, generally termed effortful control (Kochanska & Knaack 2003; Nigg 2000, 2003, 2006; Rothbart et al. 2004; Rothbart & Rueda 2005), slower to develop (Casey et al. 2008) and superordinate to approach and avoidance temperaments. Effortful control can override impulses stemming from the approach and avoidance systems. It acts as a supervisory system, provided sufficient mental resources are available. This confers many

Effortful control: superordinate temperament that can override the impulses of approach and avoidance temperaments to take broader considerations into account

advantages, including constraining emotions and permitting the organism to plan for the future and take situational complexities into account in behavioral decisions. Effortful control is a construct from developmental psychology, but its features closely resemble those of adult self-control: the ability to override impulses to act and the ability to make oneself undertake or persist in difficult, uninteresting, or unpleasant tasks.

Approach and avoidance systems, together with a supervisory system able to reorder the priorities they pursue, form the core of a biological model of human nature. They also form the core of a conceptually distinct but complementary view of human nature grounded in the goal construct (Austin & Vancouver 1996, Carver & Scheier 1998, Elliott 2008, Higgins 1996).

Goal-based models. Some views of behavior emphasize its goal-directed quality. From this perspective, knowing a person means knowing the person's goals and values and the relations among them. In goal-based theories, it is important to distinguish between motivational processes aimed at moving toward goals and those aimed at staying away from threats (Carver & Scheier 2008, Elliott 2008, Higgins 1996). A desired goal has a positive incentive value that pulls behavior to it. Looming harm or pain has a negative incentive value that pushes behavior away from it. Sometimes only approach or avoidance is engaged. Sometimes they conflict, as when moving toward a goal also increases possibility of harm. Sometimes they work together, as when attaining a desired goal simultaneously forestalls something the person wants to avoid.

Goal-based models also typically incorporate an expectancy construct: a sense of confidence or doubt that a given outcome will be attained successfully (e.g., Bandura 1986, Carver & Scheier 1998). This forms a link to the expectancy-value tradition in motivational theory. Not every behavior produces its intended outcome; goal-directed efforts can be bogged down. Under such conditions, people's efforts are believed to be determined partly by their expectancies of succeeding or failing (e.g., Bandura 1986, Brehm & Self 1989, Carver & Scheier 1998, Eccles & Wigfield 2002, Klinger 1975, Wright 1996).

Goal-based models highlight something that is less obvious in biological models: People sometimes give up or scale back on goals they have been pursuing. It is sometimes important to relinquish goals (Miller & Wrosch 2007, Wrosch et al. 2007), though the process of doing so involves feelings of sadness and despair (Klinger 1975, Nesse 2000). An alternative to giving up is scaling back. This is disengagement in the sense that the initial goal is no longer operative. It avoids complete disengagement, however, by substituting the more restricted goal. This accommodation thus keeps the person involved in that area of life, at a level that holds the potential for successful outcomes.

Issues of goals and threats are important to understanding the structure of stressors. Issues of goal engagement and disengagement are important to understanding the structure of coping, as are issues of positive and negative expectancies for the future.

Structural Organization: Individual Differences

Five-factor model. We now return to individual differences, first in the form of the five-factor model. This model has its origins in a decades-long factor-analytic research tradition. It has not been without critics (e.g., Block 1995), partly because until relatively recently it has had little to say about how the traits function or how they map onto any picture of human nature. This has changed to a considerable extent over the past decade and a half. Not only has more information been collected on how traits operate, but several of the traits have also been linked to the process models of functioning described above.

The first of the five factors is extraversion. As is true of several traits, extraversion has different emphases in different measures. Sometimes it is based in assertiveness, sometimes in spontaneity and energy. Sometimes it is based in dominance, confidence, and agency (Depue & Collins 1999), sometimes in a tendency toward happiness. Extraversion is often thought of as implying sociability (Ashton et al. 2002). Some see a sense of agency and a sense of sociability as two facets of extraversion (Depue & Morrone-Strupinsky 2005). Others argue sociability is a by-product of other features of extraversion (Lucas et al. 2000). A connection has also been drawn between extraversion and the approach temperament; some now view extraversion as reflecting relative sensitivity of a general approach system (Depue & Collins 1999, Caspi & Shiner 2006, Caspi et al. 2005, Elliott & Thrash 2002, Evans & Rothbart 2007).

The second factor, neuroticism, concerns the ease and frequency with which a person becomes upset and distressed. Moodiness, anxiety, and depression reflect higher neuroticism. Measures often include items or facets pertaining to hostility and other negative feelings, but they are dominated by vulnerability to experiences of anxiety and general distress. Neuroticism has been linked to the avoidance temperament discussed above (Caspi & Shiner 2006, Caspi et al. 2005, Evans & Rothbart 2007), suggesting that anxiety and sensitivity to threat is indeed its emotional core.

The next factor is agreeableness. Agreeable people are friendly and helpful (John & Srivastava 1999), empathic (Graziano et al. 2007), and able to inhibit their negative feelings (Graziano & Eisenberg 1999). Agreeable people get less angry over others' transgressions than do less agreeable people (Meier & Robinson 2004), and this seems to short-circuit aggression (Meier et al. 2006). At the opposite pole is an oppositional or antagonistic quality. People low in agreeableness use displays of power to deal with social conflict (Graziano et al. 1996). Agreeableness as a dimension is often characterized as being broadly concerned with the maintaining of relationships (Jensen-Campbell & Graziano 2001).

The most commonly used label for the next factor is conscientiousness, although this label does not fully reflect the qualities of planning, persistence, and purposeful striving toward goals that are part of it (Digman & Inouye 1986). Other suggested names include constraint and responsibility, reflecting qualities of impulse control and reliability. Specific qualities included in this trait vary considerably across measures (Roberts et al. 2005).

Agreeableness and conscientiousness appear to share an important property. Both suggest breadth of perspective. Many manifestations of conscientiousness imply broad time perspective: taking future contingencies into account. Agreeableness implies a broad social perspective: taking the needs of others into account. It has been suggested that both of these traits have origins in the effortful control temperament (Ahadi & Rothbart 1994, Caspi & Shiner 2006, Jensen-Campbell et al. 2002).

The fifth factor, most often called openness to experience (Costa & McCrae 1985), is the one about which there is most disagreement on content. Some measures (and theories) imbue this factor with greater overtones of intelligence, terming it intellect (Peabody & Goldberg 1989). It involves curiosity, flexibility, imaginativeness, and willingness to immerse oneself in atypical experiences (for a review of its involvement in social experience, see McCrae 1996).

Optimism. Another individual difference that figures prominently in the coping literature is optimism (Carver et al. 2009, Scheier & Carver 1992). Optimism connects directly to the expectancy-value motivational tradition discussed above in the context of goal-based models. Optimism and pessimism reflect confidence versus doubt, not regarding a specific situation but regarding life in general. As noted above, optimism does not fit neatly into the five-factor model. Its place in the goal-based view of self-regulation, however, has made it a popular trait for examination in the coping literature.

STRESS

It is common to think of stress as being a special class of experiences. It may be, however, that stress is nothing more (and nothing less) than the experience of encountering or anticipating adversity in one's goal-related efforts. It is often said that stress exists when people confront situations that tax or exceed their ability to manage them (e.g., Lazarus 1966, 1999; Lazarus & Folkman 1984). Whenever a person is hard-pressed to deal with some obstacle or impediment or looming threat, the experience is stressful.

A somewhat different view of stress uses an economic metaphor (Hobfoll 1989, 1998), holding that people have resources that they try to protect, defend, and conserve. Resources are anything the person values. They can be physical (e.g., house, car), conditions of life (e.g., having friends and relatives, stable employment), personal qualities (e.g., a positive world view, work skills), or other assets (e.g., money or knowledge). From this view, stress occurs when resources are threatened or lost.

In translating adversity to stress, at least three terms are used, two of which are more slippery than they might seem: Threat is the impending occurrence of an event that is expected to have bad consequences, harm is the perception that the bad consequences already exist, and loss is the perception that something desired has been taken away. These adverse experiences are all stressful, but they vary in their motivational underpinnings.

Loss seems specific to approach goals: Loss precludes the continuation of a desired state of affairs. For example, the death of a spouse prevents the continuation of the relationship and its activities. Threat and harm are more ambiguous because they apply to both failures to gain incentives (approach-related events) and failures to avoid punishers (avoidance-related events). For approach-related events, threat means imminent interference with desired goals or conditions; harm implies that the interference has already occurred. For avoidance-related events, threat implies the imminent arrival of intrinsically aversive states such as pain or discomfort (Rolls 2005); harm implies that punishment has already arrived.

There appear to be differences in the negative emotions arising from problems in approach versus problems in avoidance (Carver 2004, Carver & Harmon-Jones 2009, Higgins 1996, Higgins et al. 1997). Threat in a purely approach context yields frustration and anger; threat in a purely avoidance context yields anxiety and fear. Loss yields sadness and dejection, as may harm in the context of avoidance. To the extent that stress is approach related, then, one set of negatively valenced affects will predominate. To the extent that the experience is avoidance related, other negatively valenced affects will predominate. To the extent that anger and fear differ physiologically, the grounding of the stress response in approach versus avoidance also matters physiologically.

Also sometimes invoked in the context of stress is the concept of challenge (Lazarus & Folkman 1984). Challenge is a situation in which the person's efforts are strongly engaged, thus taxing abilities, but in which the person sees opportunity for gain. Challenge might be thought of as an "optimal" obstacle—one that appears surmountable (with effort) and the removal of which will lead to a better state of affairs. Pure challenge seems to involve the approach system but not the avoidance system. Challenge also implies expectation of success. Affects linked to challenge include hope, eagerness, and excitement (Lazarus 2006). The characteristics (and consequences) of challenge appear to be different enough from those of threat and loss as to cast serious doubt on the position that challenge should be viewed as a form of stress (Blascovich 2008, Tomaka et al. 1993).

The experience of stress seems inexorably linked to the pursuit of goals and avoidance of threats. Most basically, stress occurs when a person perceives an impending punisher or the impending inability to attain a goal, or perceives the actual occurrence of a punisher or removal of access to a goal. From the goal-pursuit view, these experiences constitute the broad and very general realm of behavior-under-adversity.

COPING

People respond to perceptions of threat, harm, and loss in diverse ways, many of which receive the label "coping." Coping is often defined as efforts to prevent or diminish threat, harm, and loss, or to reduce associated distress. Some prefer to limit the concept of coping to voluntary responses (Compas et al. 2001); others include automatic and involuntary responses within the coping construct (Eisenberg et al. 1997, Skinner & Zimmer-Gembeck 2007). Of course, distinguishing between voluntary and involuntary responses to stress is not simple; indeed, responses that begin as intentional and effortful may become automatic with repetition. Here we limit ourselves only to responses that are recognized by the person engaging in them, thus removing unconscious defensive reactions from the realm of consideration (cf. Cramer 2003).

Coping Distinctions and Groupings

Coping is a very broad concept with a long and complex history (Compas et al. 2001, Folkman & Moscowitz 2004). Several distinctions have been made within the broad domain; indeed, it might even be said that a bewildering number of distinctions have been made (see Skinner et al. 2003). Some of the more important ones follow.

Problem versus emotion focus. The distinction that launched modern examination of coping was that between problem-focused and emotion-focused coping (Lazarus & Folkman 1984). Problem-focused coping is directed at the stressor itself: taking steps to remove or to evade it, or to diminish its impact if it cannot be evaded. For example, if layoffs are expected, an employee's problem-focused coping might include saving money, applying for other jobs, obtaining training to enhance hiring prospects, or working harder at the current job to reduce the likelihood of being let go. Emotion-focused coping is aimed at minimizing distress triggered by stressors. Because there are many ways to reduce distress, emotion-focused coping includes a wide range of responses, ranging from self-soothing (e.g., relaxation, seeking emotional support), to expression of negative emotion (e.g., yelling, crying), to a focus on negative thoughts (e.g., rumination), to attempts to escape stressful situations (e.g., avoidance, denial, wishful thinking).

Problem-focused and emotion-focused coping have distinct proximal goals. The proximal goal determines the response's category assignment. Some behaviors can serve either function, depending on the goal behind their use. For example, seeking support is emotion focused if the goal is to obtain emotional support and reassurance, but problem focused if the goal is to obtain advice or instrumental help.

Problem- and emotion-focused coping can also facilitate one another. Effective problem-focused coping diminishes the threat, but thereby also diminishes the distress generated by that threat. Effective emotion-focused coping diminishes negative distress, making it possible to consider the problem more calmly, perhaps yielding better problem-focused coping. This interrelatedness of problem- and emotion-focused coping makes it more useful to think of the two as complementary coping functions rather than as two fully distinct and independent coping categories (Lazarus 2006).

Engagement versus disengagement. A particularly important distinction is between engagement or approach coping, which is aimed at dealing with the stressor or related emotions, and disengagement or avoidance coping, which is aimed at escaping the threat or related emotions (e.g., Moos & Schaefer 1993, Roth & Cohen 1986, Skinner et al. 2003). Engagement coping includes problem-focused coping and some forms of emotion-focused coping: support seeking, emotion regulation, acceptance, and cognitive restructuring. Disengagement coping includes responses such as avoidance, denial, and wishful thinking. Disengagement coping is often emotion focused, because it involves an attempt to escape feelings of distress. Sometimes disengagement coping is almost literally an effort to act as though the stressor does not exist, so that it does not have to be reacted to, behaviorally or emotionally. Wishful thinking and fantasy distance the person from the stressor, at least temporarily, and denial creates a boundary between reality and the person's experience.

Despite this aim of escaping distress, disengagement coping is generally ineffective in reducing distress over the long term, as it does nothing about the threat's existence and its eventual impact. If you are experiencing a real threat in your life and you respond by going to the movies, the threat will remain when the movie is over. Eventually it must be dealt with. Indeed, for many stresses, the longer one avoids dealing with the problem, the more intractable it becomes and the less time is available to deal with it when one finally turns to it. Another problem is that avoidance and denial can promote a paradoxical increase in intrusive thoughts about the stressor and an increase in negative mood and anxiety (Najmi & Wegner 2008). Finally, some kinds of disengagement create problems of their own. Excessive use of alcohol or drugs can create social and health problems, and shopping or gambling as an escape can create financial problems.

The concept of disengagement coping has been extended to include relinquishing goals that are threatened by the stressor (Carver et al. 1989). This differs from other disengagement responses in that it addresses both the stressor's existence and its emotional impact by abandoning an investment in something else. Disengaging from the threatened goal may allow the person to avoid negative feelings associated with the threat.

Accommodative coping and meaning-focused coping. Within engagement coping, distinctions have been made between attempts to control the stressor itself, called primary-control coping, and attempts to adapt or adjust to the stressor, termed accommodative or secondary-control coping (Morling & Evered 2006, Skinner et al. 2003). We use the term "accommodative" here because it does not carry connotations either of exerting control or of being secondary to other coping efforts.

The notion of accommodative coping derives from conceptions of the process of successful aging (Brandtstädter & Renner 1990).

It refers to adjustments within the self that are made in response to constraints. In the realm of coping, accommodation applies to responses such as acceptance, cognitive restructuring, and scaling back one's goals in the face of insurmountable interference. Another kind of accommodation is self-distraction. Historically this reaction has been considered disengagement coping, but confirmatory factor analyses consistently indicate that intentionally engaging with positive activities is a means of adapting to uncontrollable events (Skinner et al. 2003).

A related concept is what Folkman (1997) called "meaning-focused coping" (see also Folkman 2008, Park & Folkman 1997), in which people draw on their beliefs and values to find, or remind themselves of, benefits in stressful experiences (Tennen & Affleck 2002). Meaning-focused coping may include reordering life priorities and infusing ordinary events with positive meaning. This construct has roots in evidence that positive as well as negative emotions are common during stressful experiences (e.g., Andrykowsky et al. 1993), that positive feelings influence outcomes, and particularly that people try to find benefit and meaning in adversity (Helgeson et al. 2006, Park et al. 2009). Although this construct emphasizes the positive changes a stressor brings to a person's life, it is noteworthy that meaning-focused coping also represents an accommodation to the constraints of one's life situation. Meaning-focused coping involves reappraisal, and appears to be most likely when stressful experiences are uncontrollable or are going badly (Folkman 2008).

Proactive coping. Although most discussions of coping emphasize responses to threat and harm, Aspinwall & Taylor (1997) have pointed out that some coping occurs proactively before the occurrence of any stressor. Proactive coping is not necessarily different in nature from other coping, but it is intended to prevent threatening or harmful situations from arising. Proactive coping is nearly always problem focused, involving accumulation of resources that will be useful if a threat arises and scanning the experiential horizon for signs that a threat may be building. If the beginning of a threat is perceived, the person can engage strategies that will prevent it from growing or that will remove the person from its path. If the anticipation of an emerging threat helps the person avoid it, the person will experience fewer stressful episodes and will experience stress of less intensity when the experiences are unavoidable.

Conclusions. This brief review (which is far from exhaustive—see Compas et al. 2001, Skinner et al. 2003) makes clear that there are many ways to group coping responses and that these distinctions do not form a neat matrix into which coping reactions can be sorted. A given response typically fits several places. For example, the seeking of emotional support is engagement, emotion-focused, and accommodative coping. Each distinction has a focus of convenience and is useful for answering different questions about responses to stress. Furthermore, no one distinction fully represents the structure of coping. Confirmatory analyses clearly support hierarchical, multidimensional models of coping (Skinner et al. 2003). The distinction that appears to have greatest importance is engagement versus disengagement, a distinction that also maps well onto the goal-based model discussed in the context of personality.

Coping dispositions and personality. One more issue should be addressed before we continue. There is some evidence that coping is stable over time in a given stress domain (e.g., Gil et al. 1997, Powers et al. 2003) and that people have habitual coping tendencies (Moos & Holahan 2003). Do these coping dispositions differ in any fundamental way from personality? If coping dispositions are trait-like, how meaningful is the topic of how coping relates to personality?

Murberg et al. (2002) argued that several conditions should be met for personality and coping to be viewed as parts of the same construct. First, they should be highly correlated. Second, because personality is quite stable,

coping should also be highly stable. Third, coping should not account for substantial unique variance in outcomes after controlling for personality. In general, these conditions do not hold. Relations between personality and coping are modest, coping is less stable than personality, and coping predicts adjustment over and above personality (Connor-Smith & Flachsbart 2007, Murberg et al. 2002). Coping styles are only modestly heritable, and the genetic bases for personality and coping do not overlap strongly (Jang et al. 2007). Although personality and coping are related, coping is not simply direct manifestation of personality under adverse conditions.

PERSONALITY AND COPING

Personality does influence coping in many ways, however, some of which occur prior to coping. Even prior to coping, personality influences the frequency of exposure to stressors, the type of stressors experienced, and appraisals (Vollrath 2001). Neuroticism predicts exposure to interpersonal stress, and tendencies to appraise events as highly threatening and coping resources as low (Bolger & Zuckerman 1995, Grant & Langan-Fox 2007, Gunthert et al. 1999, Penley & Tomaka 2002, Suls & Martin 2005). Conscientiousness predicts low stress exposure (Lee-Baggley et al. 2005, Vollrath 2001), probably because conscientious persons plan for predictable stressors and avoid impulsive actions that can lead to financial, health, or interpersonal problems. Agreeableness is linked to low interpersonal conflict and thus less social stress (Asendorpf 1998). Extraversion, conscientiousness, and openness all relate to perceiving events as challenges rather than threats and to positive appraisals of coping resources (Penley & Tomaka 2002, Vollrath 2001). Unsurprisingly, high neuroticism plus low conscientiousness predicts especially high stress exposure and threat appraisals, and low neuroticism plus high extraversion or high conscientiousness predicts especially low stress exposure and threat appraisals (Grant & Langan-Fox 2006, Vollrath & Torgersen 2000).

Theoretical Relations Between Personality and Coping

Given exposure to stressors, personality can be expected to influence coping responses in several ways. From a biological view, responses to stress presumably stem from temperament-based approach, avoidance, and attentional regulation systems (Derryberry et al. 2003, Skinner & Zimmer-Gembeck 2007). From an expectancy-value view, coping efforts presumably are influenced by expectations of future outcomes (Carver et al. 2009).

Extraversion, grounded in an approach temperament, involves sensitivity to reward, positive emotions, sociability, assertiveness, and high energy (Caspi et al. 2005, McCrae & John 1992, Rothbart & Hwang 2005). Strong approach tendencies and assertiveness should provide the energy required to initiate and persist in problem solving (Lengua et al. 1999, Vollrath 2001); positive affect should facilitate cognitive restructuring; and an orientation toward others and access to a social network should facilitate social support coping.

Neuroticism, grounded in an avoidance temperament, reflects tendencies to experience fear, sadness, distress, and physiological arousal (McCrae & John 1992, Miles & Hempel 2003, Rothbart & Hwang 2005). Given this vulnerability to distress, neuroticism should lead to emotion-focused coping and disengagement from threat. Disengagement may be reinforced through short-term relief of distress (Lengua et al. 1999); this relief may reduce motivation to return to the stressor, thus minimizing engagement coping. Furthermore, the mere presence of intense emotional arousal can interfere with the use of engagement strategies that require careful planning. Negative affect should also make positive thinking and cognitive restructuring difficult.

Conscientiousness implies persistence, self-discipline, organization, achievement orientation, and a deliberative approach (Caspi et al. 2005, McCrae & John 1992). The planful, disciplined properties of this trait should facilitate problem solving and make disengagement less likely (Lengua et al. 1999, Vollrath 2001). The strong attention-regulation capacity underpinning conscientiousness (Derryberry et al. 2003) should predict success at cognitive restructuring, which requires a capacity to disengage from powerful negative thoughts.

Agreeableness involves high levels of trust and concern for others (Caspi et al. 2005, McCrae & John 1992). Because those high in agreeableness tend to have strong social networks (Bowling et al. 2005, Tong et al. 2004), agreeableness may predict social support coping. Openness to experience involves the tendency to be imaginative, creative, curious, flexible, attuned to inner feelings, and inclined toward new activities and ideas (John & Srivastava 1999, McCrae & John 1992). These tendencies may facilitate engagement coping strategies that require considering new perspectives, such as cognitive restructuring and problem solving, but may also facilitate use of disengagement strategies such as wishful thinking.

Optimism involves the expectation of good outcomes and an engaged approach to life, apparently reflecting the belief that good outcomes require some effort. These characteristics suggest that optimism will relate positively to engagement types of coping, such as problem solving and cognitive restructuring, and inversely to avoidance or disengagement coping. Pessimism involves the expectation of bad outcomes, which should promote distress and disengagement coping.

Empirical Relations Between Personality and Coping

Evidence bearing on these predicted associations is now available from hundreds of studies of relations between personality and coping. Most report cross-sectional correlations between personality and broad measures of dispositional coping; others address coping with specific stresses. The number of studies, and the great diversity of situations investigated, makes summarizing the associations a difficult task. Two recent meta-analyses have attempted to integrate this literature. Connor-Smith &

Table 1 Mean weighted correlations between personality and measures of engagement and disengagement coping, aggregated at broad levels and separated by specific responses. Adapted from Connor-Smith & Flachsbart (2007).

	E	N	C	A	O
Broad engagement coping	0.15	0.00	0.11	0.05	0.10
Primary control engagement	0.19	−0.06	0.18	0.07	0.11
Secondary control engagement	0.15	−0.03	0.09	0.07	0.11
Specific engagement responses:					
Problem solving	0.20	−0.13	0.30	0.09	0.14
Use of social support	0.24	−0.01	0.09	0.11	0.06
Cognitive restructuring	0.22	−0.16	0.20	0.14	0.15
Acceptance	0.02	−0.10	0.07	0.08	0.07
Emotion regulation	0.03	0.00	0.08	0.01	0.06
Expression of negative emotion	−0.05	0.41	−0.14	−0.09	0.03
Broad disengagement coping	−0.04	0.27	−0.15	−0.13	−0.02
Specific disengagement responses:					
Denial	−0.02	0.18	−0.17	−0.12	−0.07
Withdrawal	−0.05	0.29	0.01	0.08	0.10
Wishful thinking	−0.03	0.35	—	—	0.11
Substance use	−0.04	0.28	−0.18	−0.18	0.04

Abbreviations: E, extraversion; N, neuroticism; C, conscientiousness; A, agreeableness; O, openness to experience. Note: Effect sizes in this table represent mean correlations, weighted for sample size. As a general rule, mean correlations of 0.10 are considered small effects, 0.30 medium effects, and 0.50 large effects (Cohen 1988). Dash in cell indicates too few studies to analyze.

Flachsbart (2007) focused on Big Five personality traits in a meta-analysis of data from 165 adult, adolescent, and middle-childhood samples. Solberg Nes & Segerstrom (2006) focused on optimism as measured by the Life Orientation Test or its revised version (LOT-R) using data from 50 samples of adults and adolescents.

Some individual studies have found strong correlations between personality and coping. Overall, however, both meta-analyses suggest that relations between personality and coping are modest (see **Tables 1** and **2**). This does not mean that the impact of personality on coping is unimportant. A small influence, multiplied by the thousands of stressors experienced over a lifetime, may result in a large impact over time. Furthermore, both meta-analyses found substantial heterogeneity in effect sizes across studies. In part, this heterogeneity reflects diversity among samples and measures. But it also illustrates the need to test specific coping strategies rather than only broad coping types, and to consider moderators of relations between personality and coping. This section first reviews overall relationships between personality and coping, then considers some important moderators.

Table 2 Mean weighted correlations between optimism and four classes of coping, separated by three classes of stressors. Adapted from Solberg Nes & Segerstrom (2006).

	Academic stressor	Trauma stressor	Health stressor
Problem approach coping	0.17[a]	0.06[b]	0.13[a]
Emotion approach coping	0.08[a]	0.13[b]	0.12[b]
Problem avoidance coping	−0.27[a]	−0.15[b]	−0.39[c]
Emotion avoidance coping	−0.21[a]	−0.05[b]	−0.32[c]

Note: Effect sizes in each row that share a superscript do not differ significantly.

Both meta-analyses presented effect sizes for broad engagement and disengagement coping responses. Connor-Smith & Flachsbart (2007) also considered specific strategies within the broad categories and (separately) examined two emotion-focused categories with varying overtones of engagement and disengagement. Solberg Nes & Segerstrom (2006) also presented effect sizes for problem-focused and emotion-focused categories, and crossed those categories with engagement and disengagement to explore four more focused coping types.

Engagement coping. Optimism was positively associated with broad measures of engagement coping, $r = 0.17$, and problem-focused coping, $r = 0.13$ (Solberg Nes & Segerstrom 2006). Optimism was also positively, and about equivalently, associated with the subsets of problem-focused engagement responses (e.g., planning, seeking instrumental support), $r = 0.17$, and emotion-focused engagement responses (e.g., cognitive restructuring, acceptance), $r = 0.13$. Thus, as expected, optimism predicts active attempts to both change and accommodate to stressful circumstances.

Results for five-factor traits are in **Table 1**. Overall, extraversion, conscientiousness, and openness to experience predicted greater use of engagement coping, with conscientiousness more strongly related to primary control coping than to accommodative coping (Connor-Smith & Flachsbart 2007). Although effect sizes for relations between five-factor traits and broad coping were relatively small, results for specific coping types were more interesting. Analyses with specific coping types revealed stronger relationships between personality and coping, with several effects in the range considered moderately strong (Cohen 1988). Analyses of specific coping types also showed that a trait can correlate positively with one type of engagement coping and negatively with another, which may partially explain the relatively small effect sizes for relations between broad personality traits and broad coping types.

Of the specific coping responses, cognitive restructuring and problem solving were the most strongly related to personality, and emotion regulation and acceptance were the least strongly related. Extraversion predicted more problem solving, use of social support, and cognitive restructuring (one kind of accommodation), but was unrelated to acceptance (another kind of accommodation) or emotion regulation. Neuroticism predicted less problem solving, cognitive restructuring, and acceptance, but more seeking of emotional support and distraction. Conscientiousness predicted greater problem solving and cognitive restructuring but was unrelated to use of social support or acceptance. Agreeableness was unrelated to most engagement coping but predicted greater use of social support and cognitive restructuring. Openness predicted more problem solving and cognitive restructuring.

Just as specific coping responses were more strongly associated with personality than were broad coping tendencies, it is likely that specific personality facets would better predict coping than do broad traits. For example, the warmth and gregariousness facets of extraversion may be the best predictors of social support coping, and the assertiveness facet may better predict problem solving. Regrettably, too few studies have explored relationships of personality facets to coping for this question to be addressed.

Disengagement coping. The pattern for disengagement coping is in some ways opposite that of engagement coping. This is particularly true for optimism. Optimism related negatively to disengagement coping, $r = -0.21$ and to specific subsets of problem-focused disengagement (e.g., behavioral disengagement) and emotion-focused disengagement (e.g., denial, wishful thinking), $r = -0.29$ and -0.21, respectively (Solberg Nes & Segerstrom 2006).

Among the five-factor traits (**Table 1**), disengagement coping related to personality less strongly than did engagement coping. Of the specific strategies, denial and substance use were most clearly linked to personality. However, many specific disengagement strategies did not have enough effect sizes for analysis, making this conclusion tentative. Neuroticism was positively related to overall disengagement and to all specific disengagement responses, particularly wishful thinking and withdrawal. In contrast, extraversion, which was positively related to most engagement responses, was unrelated to any disengagement response. Conscientiousness and agreeableness predicted less overall disengagement and less denial and substance use. Openness to experience showed a complex relationship to disengagement coping, predicting slightly more wishful thinking and withdrawal and slightly less denial.

Emotion-focused coping. Relations of personality to broad emotion-focused scales differed from relations of personality to more specific emotion-regulation scales. Optimism was largely unrelated to broad emotion-focused coping, $r = -0.08$, but related positively to emotion-focused engagement and negatively to emotion-focused disengagement, as described above (Solberg Nes & Segerstrom 2006). As expected on theoretical grounds, the relationship of optimism to coping differed far more substantially between engagement and disengagement than between problem focus and emotion focus.

Relations of five-factor traits to emotion-focused coping also suggest the importance of distinguishing between types of emotion-focused coping (Connor-Smith & Flachsbart 2007). Emotion regulation scales focused on relaxation and controlled expression of emotion were essentially unrelated to five-factor traits. However, scales assessing the expression of negative emotions related positively (and strongly) to neuroticism and negatively to conscientiousness and agreeableness.

Moderators of Relations Between Personality and Coping

A few of the most important moderators of relations between personality and coping are described here (for more complete accounts,

see Connor-Smith & Flachsbart 2007, Solberg Nes & Segerstrom 2006). Because the literature on optimism and coping is smaller than the literature on five-factor traits and coping, fewer moderators could be tested. Findings described here pertain to five-factor traits unless indicated otherwise.

Age. Many relations between personality and coping were stronger in younger than in older samples, particularly those for problem solving and cognitive restructuring. There probably are several reasons for this. Temperament may affect coping responses more strongly in children than in adults, who are likely more skilled at matching coping strategies to situational demands (Skinner & Zimmer-Gembeck 2007). Age-related declines in neuroticism and increases in agreeableness and conscientiousness (McCrae et al. 2000, Roberts & Del Vecchio 2000) may lead older adults to experience less distress and thus less variability in coping. Indeed, the fact that much of the moderation occurred for problem solving and cognitive restructuring suggests the possibility that most people acquire more skill with these responses to adversity as they age, tending to wash out individual differences.

Stressor type and severity. Relations between personality and coping were generally stronger in samples facing a high degree of stress (e.g., cancer, chronic pain, divorce) than in samples with little stress (Connor-Smith & Flachsbart 2007). Low-grade stressors promote less coping variability than do chronic stressors such as poverty, divorce, or serious illness, which affect multiple life domains. Stressors that require clear, specific responses, such as changing a flat tire or meeting a work deadline, also provide little room for individual differences to operate. Thus, chronic or high-intensity stressors may best reveal relations between personality and coping (Gomez et al. 1999, Moos & Holahan 2003, Murberg et al. 2002).

The domain of stress also moderates relations between optimism and coping.

Associations of optimism with coping differed fairly substantially across academic, trauma-related, and health-related stressors (**Table 2**). Optimism was more strongly linked to problem-focused engagement for academic and health stressors than for the less controllable trauma-related stressors. In contrast, optimism related more strongly to emotion-focused engagement for traumatic and health stressors, which are more severe and less controllable than academic stressors. These results suggest that optimism is associated with flexible coping and the capacity to match coping to the demands of the stressor.

Daily-report studies also suggest the importance of context (Lee-Baggley et al. 2005). Most simply, context can influence what personality traits matter. For example, agreeableness appears to be a stronger predictor of coping in studies involving interpersonal stressors than in studies involving stressors such as pain (DeLongis & Holtzman 2005).

Situational versus dispositional coping. Unsurprisingly, personality predicted dispositional coping better than it predicted responses to specific stressors. There are several probable reasons for this. General tendencies are likely to be more clearly revealed across an aggregation of responses (Epstein 1980, Ptacek et al. 2005), which is what a dispositional response format asks respondents to create. In contrast, responses to specific stressors may be strongly influenced by the event type, available resources, and stressor severity and controllability. Personality may also influence recall of coping, with people best recalling strategies that are familiar and personality-congruent, further strengthening relations between personality and dispositional coping.

Time lag. Another potentially important moderator is the time lag between the coping activity and the coping report. Retrospective coping reports are weakly related to daily reports, with longer recall periods and higher stress levels promoting greater discrepancies (Ptacek et al. 2008, Schwartz et al. 1999, Smith et al. 1999). Again, there are several likely reasons. Accuracy of reports is influenced by difficulty aggregating responses over time, memory errors, self-presentation biases, and the extent to which stresses were resolved (e.g., Ptacek et al. 1994, Stone et al. 1995). Indeed, personality may influence the nature of recall biases: People may be more likely to remember and report strategies that work well for them or are consistent with their traits.

Some specific results from the Connor-Smith & Flachsbart (2007) meta-analysis raise interesting questions concerning time lag. Although neuroticism was unrelated to engagement in retrospective reports, it was positively related to engagement in daily reports. Perhaps persons high in neuroticism fail to remember engagement responses because they are trait-inconsistent. Or perhaps they use engagement coping but do not persist long enough for engagement to comprise a significant portion of their overall coping or to be coded well in memory.

In contrast, conscientiousness was positively related to retrospective reports of engagement coping but negatively related to engagement coping in daily reports. To some extent, this may reflect a tendency of those high in conscientiousness to recall personality-congruent planning and problem-solving strategies. Alternatively, the negative relation in daily reports could reflect the reality that responses such as problem solving unfold over time and are not well captured in a daily report, or that conscientious individuals have lower overall levels of stress exposure and thus less need for engagement coping.

PERSONALITY, COPING, AND WELL-BEING

Our target question is how personality relates to coping. On the personality side, information on that question provides an elaborated view of how traits influence behavior. On the coping side, it provides a clearer view of who can be expected to engage in which type of coping in response to different kinds of adversities.

Another question, distinct from how personality influences coping, concerns links from personality and coping to well-being.

Personality Relations with Mental and Physical Health

Personality has been linked to both psychological and physical outcomes. Most research on this topic focuses on relations of neuroticism to anxiety and depression. Meta-analyses show that neuroticism predicts clinical symptoms and disorders, with a stronger relationship to mood and anxiety disorders than to externalizing problems (Malouff et al. 2005). Neuroticism is also linked to greater risk for suicidal ideation, attempts, and completion (Brezo et al. 2006) and to more alcohol use (Malouff et al. 2007). Pessimism is similarly related to lower levels of subjective well-being across many studies (Carver et al. 2009).

In contrast, conscientiousness has a consistent protective effect, predicting lower risk for internalizing problems, externalizing problems, and substance use problems (Malouff et al. 2005, 2007), less negative affect, greater academic achievement, and greater subjective well-being (Steel et al. 2008, Trapmann et al. 2007). Similarly, effortful control temperament has been linked to low levels of anxiety and depression (Compas et al. 2004, Muris et al. 2004). Conscientiousness also appears to buffer risks for lasting distress associated with high neuroticism (Lonigan & Phillips 2001, Muris 2006).

Extraversion is strongly associated with measures of well-being, explaining up to 19% of the variance in positive mood (Steel et al. 2008). Extraversion is negatively associated with suicidality (Brezo et al. 2006) and with clinical symptoms in general, particularly symptoms of mood, anxiety, and eating disorders. However, extraversion is associated with slightly elevated risk for conduct problems (Malouff et al. 2005).

Although less research has been conducted on relations between agreeableness and adjustment, agreeableness is associated with greater subjective well-being (Steel et al. 2008) and lower risk for clinical symptoms, particularly externalizing problems (Malouff et al. 2005) and suicide attempts (Brezo et al. 2006). Although openness to experience is largely unrelated to clinical symptoms and subjective well-being, it is associated with positive affect (Malouff et al. 2005, Steel et al. 2008). Relations between personality and adjustment appear relatively consistent across methodologies, informant, age, and sex (Malouff et al. 2005, Steel et al. 2008), but may differ slightly across cultures (Ozer & Benet-Martínez 2006).

A similar pattern is seen for relations between personality and physical health outcomes (see reviews by Caspi et al. 2005, Friedman 2008, Ozer & Benet-Martínez 2006). A meta-analysis links higher optimism to better health (Rasmussen et al. 2009). Conscientiousness also relates to better health, and a recent meta-analysis links this trait to greater longevity (Kern & Friedman 2008), perhaps because conscientiousness is associated with fewer risky health behaviors and better treatment adherence. Extraversion is also associated with better health, perhaps due in part to the link between extraversion and social engagement. Neuroticism appears related to poorer health, although it remains unclear whether the link is to actual disease or simply to greater distress over symptoms and more illness-focused behaviors (Ozer & Benet-Martínez 2006). However, a recent meta-analysis of laboratory research found that neuroticism predicts slower cardiovascular recovery from stress (Chida & Hamer 2008). Agreeableness predicts health, whereas traits linked to low agreeableness, such as hostility, are linked both to greater cardiovascular stress reactivity (Chida & Hamer 2008) and to greater risk for cardiovascular illness (Caspi et al. 2005).

Relations Between Coping and Adjustment

How do coping responses themselves influence well-being? Behind this question lie a number of further methodological issues (Carver 2007), including how often coping should be measured, what time lag should be assumed between coping and health outcomes, and whether coping should be viewed as a cluster or a sequence of responses.

In meta-analyses of relations between coping and adjustment, effect sizes are typically small to moderate, with coping more strongly linked to psychological outcomes than to physical health (Clarke 2006, Penley et al. 2002). Meta-analyses indicate that most engagement coping relates to better physical and mental health in samples coping with stressors as diverse as traumatic events, social stress, HIV, prostate cancer, and diabetes (Clarke 2006, Duangdao & Roesch 2008, Littleton et al. 2007, Moskowitz et al. 2009, Penley et al. 2002, Roesch et al. 2005). However, less-volitional responses that might be seen as reflecting engagement, including rumination, self-blame, and venting, predict poorer emotional and physical outcomes (Austenfeld & Stanton 2004, Moskowitz et al. 2009). Acceptance in the context of other accommodative strategies aimed at adapting to stress is helpful, but acceptance that reflects resignation and abandonment of incentives predicts distress (Morling & Evered 2006). Disengagement coping typically predicts poorer outcomes, such as more anxiety, depression, and disruptive behavior, less positive affect, and poorer physical health, across an array of stressors (Littleton et al. 2007, Moskowitz et al. 2009, Roesch et al. 2005), although negative effects appear less pronounced in the context of uncontrollable stressors (Clarke 2006, Penley et al. 2002).

Relations between coping and adjustment are also moderated by the nature, duration, context, and controllability of the stressor. In meta-analyses of both children and adults, matching coping to stressor controllability and available resources appears important. Active attempts to solve problems and change circumstances are helpful for controllable stressors but are potentially harmful as responses to uncontrollable stressors (Aldridge & Roesch 2007, Clarke 2006). Similarly, taking responsibility for uncontrollable stressors predicts distress, but this response is unrelated to adjustment to controllable stressors (Penley et al. 2002). In contrast, emotional approach coping (e.g., self-regulation and controlled expression of emotion) is most beneficial for uncontrollable stressors (Austenfeld & Stanton 2004). Avoidance coping is more harmful in response to acute stressors than to chronic stressors, perhaps because acute stressors are more controllable and amenable to problem solving (Penley et al. 2002).

Interplay of Personality and Coping in Predicting Adjustment

Many studies have examined links from personality and coping individually to outcomes, but far fewer have explored the intersection of personality and coping in relation to outcomes. Bolger & Zuckerman (1995) detailed several ways in which personality and coping could jointly influence adjustment. One possibility is mediation: Personality influences coping-strategy selection, which in turn influences outcomes. Another possibility is moderation: Personality influences how well a given strategy works for an individual. A combined possibility involves mediated moderation, with personality influencing both the selection and the effectiveness of coping.

There is evidence supporting coping mediation between personality and adjustment across a range of personality types and outcomes (Bolger 1990, Bolger & Zuckerman 1995, Carver et al. 1993, Holahan & Moos 1990, Knoll et al. 2005, Stanton & Snider 1993). For example, confrontive coping strategies mediate relations between neuroticism and subsequent anger (Bolger & Zuckerman 1995), problem solving mediates relations between reward sensitivity and delinquency (Hasking 2007), and avoidant coping partially explains relations between behavioral inhibition and disordered eating (Hasking 2006). However, inasmuch as direct relationships between personality and coping are modest, coping is unlikely to fully mediate the link from personality to well-being.

Mounting evidence suggests that personality and coping also interact to predict adjustment, with coping either increasing or decreasing the impact of personality-related vulnerabilities. For example, engagement coping buffers the link between vulnerability to social stress and internalizing problems, and disengagement coping amplifies the link (Connor-Smith & Compas 2002). Avoidant coping amplifies the relationship between high behavioral approach tendencies and outcomes such as delinquent behavior and disordered eating (Hasking 2006, 2007). Certain kinds of emotion-focused coping amplify the link from neuroticism to post-traumatic stress symptoms (Chung et al. 2005).

Personality may influence the effectiveness of coping strategies by facilitating or interfering with successful implementation of the strategy. For example, persons high in extraversion or agreeableness may intrinsically be especially skilled at obtaining social support (Vollrath 2001). Conscientious persons may not only do more problem solving, but also better problem solving. The distress associated with high neuroticism may interfere with successful problem solving. Indeed, persons high in neuroticism appear to experience fewer short-term benefits of engagement coping and more short-term benefits of disengagement than do those low in neuroticism (Bolger & Zuckerman 1995, Connor-Smith & Compas 2004, Dunkley et al. 2003, Gunthert et al. 1999). This may help explain why neuroticism relates to tendencies to disengage despite long-term negative effects of doing so. Neuroticism is also linked to less flexibility in coping across situations (Lee-Baggley et al. 2005), perhaps because distress interferes with selection of optimal strategies.

Differential effectiveness of coping may even have treatment implications. For example, persons low in conscientiousness may benefit from an emphasis on coping persistence. Persons high in neuroticism may benefit from improving emotion regulation (so that unregulated distress will not interfere with planful coping and disengagement will be less tempting) and from practice in matching coping to the unique needs of each situation.

RESEARCH RECOMMENDATIONS

Despite hundreds of studies, the influence of personality on coping, and of both on outcomes, is only partly understood. Impediments include problems in the measurement of personality and coping, overreliance on cross-sectional and retrospective studies, inadequate consideration of situational factors, and lack of attention to interactions between and among personality traits and coping strategies.

Assessing Coping and Personality

Several reviews have highlighted common problems with coping assessment, including a proliferation of coping measures with structures that cannot be replicated, use of overly broad categories, and reliance on self-report to the exclusion of observational and multiple-informant approaches (e.g., Compas et al. 2001, Skinner et al. 2003). Personality assessment has a long history, and there is more consensus about the structure of personality and optimal personality measures than about the structure and assessment of coping. However, the focus there is almost exclusively on broad traits, despite evidence that specific personality facets account for twice the variance in predicting well-being (Steel et al. 2008). Evidence reviewed above indicates that assessing specific coping responses provides a more nuanced understanding of coping than does assessment of broad engagement, disengagement, or emotion-focused coping. Assessment of specific personality facets should similarly provide a more complete picture of how personality relates to coping.

Attention to models of personality other than the Big Five is also merited. Optimism is a good example of a trait that does not fit neatly into the five-factor framework, but it fits well with the expectancy-value viewpoint discussed as part of the goal-based model of personality. Thus, optimism plugs nicely into the fundamental distinction between engagement and disengagement coping (Solberg Nes &

Segerstrom 2006). Consistent with the importance of that distinction, optimism has proven important in the coping literature.

Abandoning Cross-Sectional Retrospective Research Designs

Although coping is almost universally viewed as an ever-changing response to evolving situational demands, most coping research fails to reflect this view. Many studies assess only dispositional coping, or one-time retrospective reports of overall coping with some stressor. Virtually nothing is known from those studies about how the timing, order, combination, or duration of coping influences outcomes. Tennen et al. (2000) proposed that people typically use emotion-focused coping largely after they have tried problem-focused coping and found it ineffective. This suggests an approach to examining coping in which the question is whether the individual changes from one sort of coping to another across successive assessments as a function of lack of effectiveness of the first response used.

Because the impact of a coping strategy may be brief, laboratory and daily report studies are essential to understanding immediate effects of coping strategies (Bolger et al. 2003). The small number of daily report studies of personality and coping make it clear that the impact of coping changes over time, with responses that are useful one day having a negative impact on next-day mood or long-term adjustment (DeLongis & Holtzman 2005). Laboratory research also permits disentangling stressor severity from individual differences in stress appraisals by use of standardized stressors; it facilitates supplementing of self-reports with observations of coping and assessment of physiological responses.

More generally, little more can be gained from additional cross-sectional studies. Future work should focus on responses to specific stressors, using prospective designs, daily coping reports, or detailed laboratory assessments, all of which facilitate exploration of the impact of the order and timing of coping responses (Tennen et al. 2000).

Incorporating Context

Context influences situational demands, resources, coping response selection, and the costs and benefits of coping responses. Greater attention to the nature of stressors, including severity, controllability, and domain, is essential. Studies should not simply combine participant responses to a wide array of self-generated stressors.

Context may also influence the manifestation of personality, leading relations between personality and coping to differ across domains of stress (Prokopcakova 2004). For example, extraversion and agreeableness should be more relevant to social stressors, and conscientious to stressors requiring planning and persistence. The main relationship between conscientiousness and coping may lie not in the initial selection of coping strategies, but rather in the capacity to persist over time or to problem solve skillfully. Personality may influence coping flexibility and the capacity to tailor coping to situational demands (Vollrath 2001). Research should also explore responses to multiple stressors over time to assess how personality influences the capacity to match coping to problems, change strategies that are not helpful, and persist in those that are.

Although factors such as age, sex, culture, and ethnicity have not been considered in depth here, they affect relations between personality and coping (Connor-Smith & Flachsbart 2007). It seems likely that strategies such as seeking social support will be more beneficial for extraverted women from collectivistic cultures than for introverted adolescent boys from individualistic cultures. Nonetheless, more work is required to understand how age, sex, and culture interact with coping and personality to influence adaptation to stress.

Considering Multiple Traits, Strategies, and Interactions

Finally, most of our understanding is of relations between single personality traits and coping responses. This is a poor reflection of reality. Personality does not constitute one trait at a time. Similarly, stress exposure and responses to stress are influenced not by one trait at a time but by all of personality at once. Research should consider joint influences of traits on coping, whether by examining personality profiles, controlling for one trait when studying others, or looking at interactions among traits. Similarly, future research should also explore joint and interactive impacts of multiple coping responses. For example, although cognitive restructuring and positive thinking typically predict positive outcomes in controllable situations, in the absence of problem solving they predict poor outcomes (Newth & DeLongis 2004). How important and widespread such contingencies are, in the grand scheme, is relatively unknown.

SUMMARY POINTS

1. Biological (temperament) and goal-based views of human nature specify basic processes that underlie coping.

2. A fundamental distinction is between engagement coping and disengagement coping.

3. Trait optimism predicts engagement coping (positively) and disengagement coping (inversely).

4. The five-factor traits of extraversion, conscientiousness, and openness relate to more engagement coping; neuroticism to more disengagement coping; and conscientiousness and agreeableness to less disengagement coping.

5. Relations between traits and coping are often moderated by other variables (age, severity of stressor, and the time between coping and report of coping).

6. Future research must test for greater complexity in associations (e.g., interactions) among personality traits, coping, and outcomes.

FUTURE ISSUES

1. The role of personality facets, rather than overall broad traits, as predictors of coping and outcomes.

2. Variation in coping responses across a transaction and whether specific responses are more or less useful at different points.

3. Prospective, daily report, and lab-based studies of coping to expand upon cross-sectional knowledge base.

4. More explicitly incorporating the coping context into coping research.

5. Developmental and cultural differences in coping and in relations among personality, coping, and well-being.

6. How traits interact in determining coping responses and how traits and coping interact in determining outcomes.

DISCLOSURE STATEMENT

The authors are not aware of any biases that might be perceived as affecting the objectivity of this review.

ACKNOWLEDGMENTS

Preparation of this review was facilitated by grants from the National Cancer Institute (CA64710) and the National Science Foundation (BCS0544617).

LITERATURE CITED

Ahadi SA, Rothbart MK. 1994. Temperament, development and the Big Five. In *The Developing Structure of Temperament and Personality from Infancy to Adulthood*, ed. CF Halverson Jr, GA Kohnstamm, RP Martin, pp. 189–207. Hillsdale, NJ: Erlbaum

Aldridge AA, Roesch SC. 2007. Coping and adjustment in children with cancer: a meta-analytic study. *J. Behav. Med.* 30:115–29

Allport GW. 1961. *Pattern and Growth in Personality*. New York: Holt, Rinehart & Winston

Andrykowsky MA, Brady MJ, Hunt JW. 1993. Positive psychosocial adjustment in potential bone marrow transplant recipients: cancer as a psychosocial transition. *Psychol. Oncol.* 2:261–76

Asendorpf JB. 1998. Personality effects on social relationships. *J. Personal. Soc. Psychol.* 74:1531–44

Ashton MC, Lee K, Paunonen SV. 2002. What is the central feature of extraversion? Social attention versus reward sensitivity. *J. Personal. Soc. Psychol.* 83:245–52

Ashton MC, Lee K, Perugini M, Szarota P, de Vries RE, et al. 2004. A six-factor structure of personality-descriptive adjectives: solutions from psycholexical studies in seven languages. *J. Personal. Soc. Psychol.* 86:356–66

Aspinwall LG, Taylor SE. 1997. A stitch in time: self-regulation and proactive coping. *Psychol. Bull.* 121:417–36

Austenfeld JL, Stanton AL. 2004. Coping through emotional approach: a new look at emotion, coping, and health-related outcomes. *J. Personal.* 72:1335–63

Austin JT, Vancouver JB. 1996. Goal constructs in psychology: structure, process, and content. *Psychol. Bull.* 120:338–75

Bandura A. 1986. *Social Foundations of Thought and Action: A Social Cognitive Theory*. Englewood Cliffs, NJ: Prentice-Hall

Blascovich J. 2008. Challenge and threat. In *Handbook of Approach and Avoidance Motivation*, ed. AJ Elliot, pp. 431–45. New York: Psychology Press

Block J. 1995. A contrarian view of the five-factor approach to personality assessment. *Psychol. Bull.* 117:187–215

Bolger N. 1990. Coping as a personality process: a prospective study. *J. Personal. Soc. Psychol.* 59:525–37

Bolger N, Davis A, Rafaeli E. 2003. Diary methods: capturing life as it is lived. *Annu. Rev. Psychol.* 54:579–616

Bolger N, Zuckerman A. 1995. A framework for studying personality in the stress process. *J. Personal. Soc. Psychol.* 69:890–902

Bowling N, Beehr T, Swader W. 2005. Giving and receiving social support at work: the roles of personality and reciprocity. *J. Vocat. Behav.* 67:476–89

Brandtstädter J, Renner G. 1990. Tenacious goal pursuit and flexible goal adjustment: explication and age-related analysis of assimilative and accommodative strategies of coping. *Psychol. Aging* 5:58–67

Brehm JW, Self EA. 1989. The intensity of motivation. *Annu. Rev. Psychol.* 40:109–31

Brezo J, Paris J, Turecki G. 2006. Personality traits as correlates of suicidal ideation, suicide attempts, and suicide completions: a systematic review. *Acta Psychiatr. Scand.* 113:180–206

Carver CS. 2004. Negative affects deriving from the behavioral approach system. *Emotion* 4:3–22

Carver CS. 2007. Stress, coping, and health. In *Foundations of Health Psychology*, ed. HS Friedman, RC Silver, pp. 117–44. New York: Oxford Univ. Press

Carver CS, Harmon-Jones E. 2009. Anger is an approach-related affect: evidence and implications. *Psychol. Bull.* 135:183–204

Carver CS, Pozo C, Harris SD, Noriega V, Scheier MF, et al. 1993. How coping mediates the effect of optimism on distress: a study of women with early stage breast cancer. *J. Personal. Soc. Psychol.* 65:375–90

Carver CS, Scheier MF, Weintraub JK. 1989. Assessing coping strategies: a theoretically based approach. *J. Personal. Soc. Psychol.* 56:267–83

Carver CS, Scheier MF. 1998. *On the Self-Regulation of Behavior*. New York: Cambridge Univ. Press

Carver CS, Scheier MF. 2008. *Perspectives on Personality*. Boston, MA: Allyn & Bacon. 6th ed.

Carver CS, Scheier MF, Miller CJ, Fulford D. 2009. Optimism. In *Oxford Handbook of Positive Psychology*, ed. CR Snyder, SJ Lopez, pp. 303–11. New York: Oxford Univ. Press. 2nd ed.

Casey BJ, Getz S, Galvan A. 2008. The adolescent brain. *Dev. Rev.* 28:62–77

Caspi A, Roberts BW, Shiner RL. 2005. Personality development: stability and change. *Annu. Rev. Psychol.* 56:453–84

Caspi A, Shiner RL. 2006. Personality development. In *Handbook of Child Psychology, Vol. 3. Social, Emotional, and Personality Development*, series ed. W Damon, R Lerner, vol. ed. N Eisenberg, pp. 300–65. New York: Wiley. 6th ed.

Cervone D. 2005. Personality architecture: within-person structures and processes. *Annu. Rev. Psychol.* 56:423–52

Chida Y, Hamer M. 2008. Chronic psychosocial factors and acute physiological responses to laboratory-induced stress in healthy populations: a quantitative review of 30 years of investigations. *Psychol. Bull.* 134:829–85

Chung MC, Dennis I, Easthope Y, Werrett J, Farmer S. 2005. A multiple-indicator multiple-cause model for posttraumatic stress reactions: personality, coping, and maladjustment. *Psychosom. Med.* 67:251–59

Clarke AT. 2006. Coping with interpersonal stress and psychosocial health among children and adolescents: a meta-analysis. *J. Youth Adolesc.* 35:11–24

Cohen J. 1988. *Statistical Power Analysis for the Behavioral Sciences*. Mahwah, NJ: Erlbaum. 2nd ed.

Compas BE, Connor-Smith JK, Jaser SS. 2004. Temperament, stress reactivity, and coping: implications for depression in childhood and adolescence. *J. Clin. Child Adolesc. Psychol.* 33:21–31

Compas BE, Connor-Smith JK, Saltzman H, Thomsen AH, Wadsworth ME. 2001. Coping with stress during childhood and adolescence: problems, progress, and potential in theory and research. *Psychol. Bull.* 127:87–127

Connor-Smith JK, Compas BE. 2002. Vulnerability to social stress: coping as a mediator or moderator of sociotropy and symptoms of anxiety and depression. *Cogn. Ther. Res.* 26:39–55

Connor-Smith JK, Compas BE. 2004. Coping as a moderator of relations between reactivity to interpersonal stress, health status, and internalizing problems. *Cogn. Ther. Res.* 28:347–68

Connor-Smith JK, Flachsbart C. 2007. Relations between personality and coping: a meta-analysis. *J. Personal. Soc. Psychol.* 93:1080–107

Costa PT Jr, McCrae RR. 1985. *The NEO Personality Inventory Manual*. Odessa, FL: Psychol. Assess. Resourc.

Cramer P. 2003. Personality change in later adulthood is predicted by defense mechanism use in early adulthood. *J. Res. Personal.* 37:76–104

Davidson RJ. 1998. Affective style and affective disorders: perspectives from affective neuroscience. *Cogn. Emot.* 12:307–30

DeLongis A, Holtzman S. 2005. Coping in context: the role of stress, social support, and personality in coping. *J. Personal.* 73:1–24

Depue RA, Collins PF. 1999. Neurobiology of the structure of personality: dopamine, facilitation of incentive motivation, and extraversion. *Behav. Brain Sci.* 22:491–517

Depue RA, Morrone-Strupinksy JV. 2005. A neurobehavioral model of affiliative bonding: implications for conceptualizing a human trait of affiliation. *Behav. Brain Sci.* 28:313–95

Derryberry D, Reed MA, Pilkenton-Taylor C. 2003. Temperament and coping: advantages of an individual differences perspective. *Dev. Psychopathol.* 15:1049–66

Digman JM. 1990. Personality structure: emergence of the five-factor model. *Annu. Rev. Psychol.* 41:417–40

Digman JM, Inouye J. 1986. Further specification of the five robust factors of personality. *J. Personal. Soc. Psychol.* 50:116–23

Duangdao KM, Roesch SC. 2008. Coping with diabetes in adulthood: a meta-analysis. *J. Behav. Med.* 31:291–300

Dunkley DM, Zuroff DC, Blankstein KR. 2003. Self-critical perfectionism and daily affect: dispositional and situational influences on stress and coping. *J. Personal. Soc. Psychol.* 84:234–52

Eccles JS, Wigfield A. 2002. Motivational beliefs, values and goals. *Annu. Rev. Psychol.* 53:109–32

Eisenberg N, Fabes RA, Guthrie I. 1997. Coping with stress: the roles of regulation and development. In *Handbook of Children's Coping with Common Stressors: Linking Theory, Research, and Intervention*, ed. JN Sandler, SA Wolchik, pp. 41–70. New York: Plenum

Elliot AJ, ed. 2008. *Handbook of Approach and Avoidance Motivation*. New York: Psychology Press

Elliot AJ, Thrash TM. 2002. Approach-avoidance motivation in personality: approach and avoidance temperaments and goals. *J. Personal. Soc. Psychol.* 82:804–18

Epstein S. 1980. The stability of behavior: II. Implications for psychological research. *Am. Psychol.* 35:790–806

Evans DE, Rothbart MK. 2007. Developing a model for adult temperament. *J. Res. Personal.* 41:868–88

Eysenck HJ. 1975. *The Inequality of Man*. San Diego, CA: EdITS

Eysenck HJ. 1986. Models and paradigms in personality research. In *Personality Psychology in Europe, Vol. 2: Current Trends and Controversies*, ed. A Angleitner, A Furnham, G Van Heck, pp. 213–23. Lisse, Netherlands: Swets & Zeitlinger

Folkman S. 1997. Positive psychological states and coping with severe stress. *Soc. Sci. Med.* 45:1207–21

Folkman S. 2008. The case for positive emotions in the stress response. *Anx. Stress Coping* 21:3–14

Folkman S, Moskowitz JT. 2004. Coping: pitfalls and promise. *Annu. Rev. Psychol.* 55:745–74

Fowles DC. 1993. Biological variables in psychopathology: a psychobiological perspective. In *Comprehensive Handbook of Psychopathology*, ed. PB Sutker, HE Adams, pp. 57–82. New York: Plenum. 2nd ed.

Friedman HS. 2008. The multiple linkages of personality and disease. *Brain Behav. Immun.* 22:668–75

Funder DC. 2001. Personality. *Annu. Rev. Psychol.* 52:197–221

Gil KM, Wilson JJ, Edens JL. 1997. The stability of pain coping strategies in young children, adolescents, and adults with sickle cell disease over an 18-month period. *Clin. J. Pain* 13:110–15

Goldberg LR. 1981. Language and individual differences: the search for universals in personality lexicons. In *Review of Personality and Social Psychology*, ed. L Wheeler, Vol. 2, pp. 141–65. Beverly Hills, CA: Sage

Gomez R, Bounds J, Holmberg K, Fullarton C, Gomez A. 1999. Effects of neuroticism and avoidant coping style on maladjustment during early adolescence. *Personal. Individ. Diff.* 26:305–319

Grant S, Langan-Fox J. 2006. Occupational stress, coping, and strain: the combined/interactive effect of the Big Five traits. *Personal. Individ. Differ.* 41:719–32

Grant S, Langan-Fox J. 2007. Personality and the occupational stressor-strain relationship: the role of the Big Five. *J. Occup. Health Psychol.* 12:20–33

Gray JA. 1994. Personality dimensions and emotion systems. In *The Nature of Emotion: Fundamental Questions*, ed. P Ekman, RJ Davidson, pp. 329–31. New York: Oxford Univ. Press

Graziano WG, Eisenberg NH. 1999. Agreeableness as a dimension of personality. In *Handbook of Personality*, ed. R Hogan, J Johnson, S Briggs, pp. 795–825. San Diego, CA: Academic

Graziano WG, Habashi MM, Sheese BE, Tobin RM. 2007. Agreeableness, empathy, and helping: a person X situation perspective. *J. Personal. Soc. Psychol.* 93:583–99

Graziano WG, Jensen-Campbell LA, Hair EC. 1996. Perceiving interpersonal conflict and reacting to it: the case for agreeableness. *J. Personal. Soc. Psychol.* 70:820–35

Gunthert KC, Cohen LH, Armeli S. 1999. Role of neuroticism in daily stress and coping. *J. Personal. Soc. Psychol.* 77:1087–100

Hasking PA. 2006. Reinforcement sensitivity, coping, disordered eating, and drinking behavior in adolescents. *Personal. Individ. Differ.* 40:677–88

Hasking PA. 2007. Reinforcement sensitivity, coping, and delinquent behavior in adolescents. *J. Adolesc.* 30:739–49

Helgeson VS, Reynolds KA, Tomich PL. 2006. A meta-analytic approach to benefit finding and health. *J. Consult. Clin. Psychol.* 74:797–816

Higgins ET. 1996. Ideals, oughts, and regulatory focus: affect and motivation from distinct pains and pleasures. In *The Psychology of Action: Linking Cognition and Motivation to Behavior*, ed. PM Gollwitzer, JA Bargh, pp. 91–114. New York: Guilford

Higgins ET, Shah J, Friedman R. 1997. Emotional responses to goal attainment: strength of regulatory focus as moderator. *J. Personal. Soc. Psychol.* 72:515–25

Hobfoll SE. 1989. Conservation of resources: a new attempt at conceptualizing stress. *Am. Psychol.* 44:513–24

Hobfoll SE. 1998. *Stress, Culture, and Community*. New York: Plenum

Holahan CJ, Moos RH. 1990. Life stressors, resistance factors, and improved psychological functioning: an extension of the stress resistance paradigm. *J. Personal. Soc. Psychol.* 58:909–17

Jang KL, Thordarson DS, Stein MB, Cohan SL, Taylor S. 2007. Coping styles and personality: a biometric analysis. *Anx. Stress Coping* 20:17–24

Jensen-Campbell LA, Adams R, Perry DG, Workman KA, Furdella JQ, Egan SK. 2002. Agreeableness, extraversion, and peer relations in early adolescence: winning friends and deflecting aggression. *J. Res. Personal.* 36:224–51

Jensen-Campbell LA, Graziano WG. 2001. Agreeableness as a moderator of interpersonal conflict. *J. Personal.* 69:323–62

John OP, Srivastava S. 1999. The Big Five trait taxonomy: history, measurement, and theoretical perspectives. In *Handbook of Personality: Theory and Research*, ed. LA Pervin, OP John, pp. 102–38. New York: Guilford. 2nd ed.

Kern ML, Friedman HS. 2008. Do conscientious individuals live longer? A quantitative review. *Health Psychol.* 27:505–12

Klinger E. 1975. Consequences of commitment to and disengagement from incentives. *Psychol. Rev.* 82:1–25

Knoll N, Rieckmann N, Schwarzer R. 2005. Coping as a mediator between personality and stress outcomes: a longitudinal study with cataract surgery patients. *Eur. J. Personal.* 19:229–47

Kochanska G, Knaack A. 2003. Effortful control as a personality characteristic of young children: antecedents, correlates, and consequences. *J. Personal.* 71:1087–112

Lazarus RS. 1966. *Psychological Stress and the Coping Process*. New York: McGraw-Hill

Lazarus RS. 1999. *Stress and Emotion: A New Synthesis*. New York: Springer

Lazarus RS. 2006. Emotions and interpersonal relationships: toward a person-centered conceptualization of emotions and coping. *J. Personal.* 74:9–46

Lazarus RS, Folkman S. 1984. *Stress, Appraisal, and Coping*. New York: Springer

Lee-Baggley D, Preece M, DeLongis A. 2005. Coping with interpersonal stress: role of Big Five traits. *J. Personal.* 73:1141–80

Lengua LJ, Sandler IN, West SG, Wolchik SA, Curran PJ. 1999. Emotionality and self-regulation, threat appraisal, and coping in children of divorce. *Dev. Psychopathol.* 11:15–37

Littleton H, Horsley S, John S, Nelson DV. 2007. Trauma coping strategies and psychological distress: a meta-analysis. *J. Traumatic Stress* 20:977–88

Lonigan CJ, Phillips BM. 2001. Temperamental basis of anxiety disorders in children. In *The Developmental Psychopathology of Anxiety*, ed. MW Vasey, MR Dadds, pp. 60–91. New York: Oxford Univ. Press

Lucas RE, Diener E, Grob A, Suh EM, Shao L. 2000. Cross-cultural evidence for the fundamental features of extraversion. *J. Personal. Soc. Psychol.* 79:452–68

Malouff JM, Thorsteinsson EB, Rooke SE, Schutte NS. 2007. Alcohol involvement and the five-factor model of personality: a meta-analysis. *J. Drug Educ.* 37:277–94

Malouff JM, Thorsteinsson EB, Schutte NS. 2005. The relationship between the five-factor model of personality and symptoms of clinical disorders: a meta-analysis. *J. Psychopathol. Behav. Assess.* 27:101–14

Marshall GN, Wortman CB, Kusulas JW, Hervig LK, Vickers RR Jr. 1992. Distinguishing optimism from pessimism: relations to fundamental dimensions of mood and personality. *J. Personal. Soc. Psychol.* 62:1067–74

McAdams DP, Olson BD. 2010. Personality development: continuity and change. *Annu. Rev. Psychol.* 61:517–42

McCrae RR. 1996. Social consequences of experiential openness. *Psychol. Bull.* 120:323–37

McCrae RR, Costa PT Jr. 2003. *Personality in Adulthood: A Five-Factor Theory Perspective*. New York: Guilford. 2nd ed.

McCrae RR, Costa PT Jr, Ostendorf F, Angleitner A, Hrebickova M, et al. 2000. Nature over nurture: temperament, personality, and life span development. *J. Personal. Soc. Psychol.* 78:173–86

McCrae RR, John OP. 1992. Introduction to the five-factor model and its applications. *J. Personal.* 60:175–215

Meier BP, Robinson MD. 2004. Does quick to blame mean quick to anger? The role of agreeableness in dissociating blame and anger. *Personal. Soc. Psychol. Bull.* 30:856–67

Meier BP, Robinson MD, Wilkowski BM. 2006. Turning the other cheek: agreeableness and the regulation of aggression-related primes. *Psychol. Sci.* 17:136–42

Miles JNV, Hempel S. 2003. The Eysenck personality scales: the Eysenck Personality Questionnaire-Revised (EPQ-R) and the Eysenck Personality Profiler (EPP). In *Comprehensive Handbook of Psychological Assessment: Personality Assessment*, ed. M Hersen, M Hilsenroth, D Segal, Vol. 2, pp. 99–107. New York: Wiley

Miller GE, Wrosch C. 2007. You've gotta know when to fold 'em: goal disengagement and systemic inflammation in adolescence. *Psychol. Sci.* 18:773–77

Mischel W. 2004. Toward an integrative science of the person. *Annu. Rev. Psychol.* 55:1–22

Moos RH, Holahan CJ. 2003. Dispositional and contextual perspectives on coping: toward an integrative framework. *J. Clin. Psychol.* 59:1387–403

Moos RH, Schaefer JA. 1993. Coping resources and processes: current concepts and measures. In *Handbook of Stress: Theoretical and Clinical Aspects*, ed. L Goldberger, S Breznitz, pp. 234–57. New York: Free Press. 2nd ed.

Morling B, Evered S. 2006. Secondary control reviewed and defined. *Psychol. Bull.* 132:269–96

Moskowitz JT, Hult JR, Bussolari C, Acree M. 2009. What works in coping with HIV? A meta-analysis with implications for coping with serious illness. *Psychol. Bull.* 135:121–41

Murberg TA, Bru E, Stephens P. 2002. Personality and coping among congestive heart failure patients. *Personal. Individ. Differ.* 32:775–84

Muris P. 2006. Unique and interactive effects of neuroticism and effortful control on psychopathological symptoms in nonclinical adolescents. *Personal. Individ. Differ.* 40:1409–19

Muris P, de Jong PJ, Engelen S. 2004. Relationships between neuroticism, attentional control, and anxiety disorders symptoms in nonclinical children. *Personal. Individ. Differ.* 37:789–97

Najmi S, Wegner DM. 2008. Thought suppression and psychopathology. In *Handbook of Approach and Avoidance Motivation*, ed. A Elliott, pp. 447–59. Mahwah, NJ: Erlbaum

Nesse RM. 2000. Is depression an adaptation? *Arch. Gen. Psychiatry* 57:14–20

Newth S, DeLongis A. 2004. Individual differences, mood and coping with chronic pain in rheumatoid arthritis: a daily process analysis. *Psychol. Health* 19:283–305

Nigg JT. 2000. On inhibition/disinhibition in developmental psychopathology: views from cognitive and personality psychology as a working inhibition taxonomy. *Psychol. Bull.* 126:220–46

Nigg JT. 2003. Response inhibition and disruptive behaviors: toward a multiprocess conception of etiological heterogeneity for ADHD combined type and conduct disorder early-onset type. *Ann. N. Y. Acad. Sci.* 1008:170–82

Nigg JT. 2006. Temperament and developmental psychopathology. *J. Child Psychol. Psychiatry* 47:395–422

Ozer DJ, Benet-Martínez VB. 2006. Personality and the prediction of consequential outcomes. *Annu. Rev. Psychol.* 57:401–21

Park CL, Folkman S. 1997. Meaning in the context of stress and coping. *Rev. Gen. Psychol.* 1:115–44

Park CL, Lechner SC, Antoni MH, Stanton AL, eds. 2009. *Medical Illness and Positive Life Change: Can Crisis Lead to Personal Transformation?* Washington, DC: Am. Psychol. Assoc.

Peabody D, Goldberg LR. 1989. Some determinants of factor structures from personality-trait descriptors. *J. Personal. Soc. Psychol.* 57:552–67

Penley JA, Tomaka J. 2002. Associations among the Big Five, emotional responses, and coping with acute stress. *Personal. Individ. Differ.* 32:1215–28

Penley JA, Tomaka J, Wiebe JS. 2002. The association of coping to physical and psychological health outcomes: a meta-analytic review. *J. Behav. Med.* 25:551–603

Powers DV, Gallagher-Thompson D, Kraemer HC. 2003. Coping and depression in Alzheimer's caregivers: longitudinal evidence of stability. *J. Gerontol. B Psychol. Soc. Sci.* 57:205–11

Prokopcakova A. 2004. Choice of coping strategies in the interaction: anxiety and type of a demanding life situation (a research probe). *Studia Psychologica* 46:235–38

Ptacek JT, Pierce GR, Thompson EL. 2005. Finding evidence of dispositional coping. *J. Res. Personal.* 40:1137–51

Ptacek JT, Smith RE, Espe K, Raffety B. 1994. Limited correspondence between daily coping reports and retrospective coping recall. *Psychol. Assess.* 6:41–49

Ptacek JT, Smith RE, Raffety BD, Lindgren KP. 2008. Coherence and transituational generality in coping: the unity and the diversity. *Anx. Stress Coping* 21:155–72

Rasmussen HN, Scheier MF, Greenhouse JB. 2009. Optimism and physical health: a meta-analytic review. *Ann. Behav. Med.* In press

Roberts BW, DelVecchio WF. 2000. The rank-order consistency of personality traits from childhood to old age: a quantitative review of longitudinal studies. *Psychol. Bull.* 126:3–25

Roberts BW, Walton KE, Bogg T. 2005. Conscientiousness and health across the life course. *Rev. Gen. Psychol.* 9:156–68

Roesch SC, Adams L, Hines A, Palmores A, Vyas P, et al. 2005. Coping with prostate cancer: a meta-analytic review. *J. Behav. Med.* 28:281–93

Rolls ET. 2005. *Emotion Explained.* Oxford, UK: Oxford Univ. Press

Roth S, Cohen LJ. 1986. Approach, avoidance, and coping with stress. *Am. Psychol.* 41:813–19

Rothbart MK, Ellis LK, Posner MI. 2004. Temperament and self-regulation. In *Handbook of Self-Regulation: Research, Theory, and Applications*, ed. RF Baumeister, KD Vohs, pp. 357–70. New York: Guilford

Rothbart MK, Hwang J. 2005. Temperament and the development of competence and motivation. In *Handbook of Competence and Motivation*, ed. AJ Elliot, CS Dweck, pp. 167–84. New York: Guilford

Rothbart MK, Rueda MR. 2005. The development of effortful control. In *Developing Individuality in the Human Brain: A Tribute to Michael I. Posner*, ed. U Mayr, E Awh, S Keele, pp. 167–88. Washington, DC: Am. Psychol. Assoc.

Ryan RM, Deci EL. 2001. On happiness and human potentials: a review of research on hedonic and eudaimonic well-being. *Annu. Rev. Psychol.* 52:141–66

Scheier MF, Carver CS. 1992. Effects of optimism on psychological and physical well-being: theoretical overview and empirical update. *Cogn. Ther. Res.* 16:201–28

Schwartz JE, Neale JM, Marco CA, Shiffman S, Stone AA. 1999. Does trait coping exist? A momentary assessment approach to the evaluation of traits. *J. Personal. Soc. Psychol.* 77:360–69

Skinner EA, Edge K, Altman J, Sherwood H. 2003. Searching for the structure of coping: a review and critique of category systems for classifying ways of coping. *Psychol. Bull.* 129:216–69

Skinner EA, Zimmer-Gembeck MJ. 2007. The development of coping. *Annu. Rev. Psychol.* 58:119–44

Smith RE, Leffingwell TR, Ptacek JT. 1999. Can people remember how they coped? Factors associated with discordance between same-day and retrospective reports. *J. Personal. Soc. Psychol.* 76:1050–61

Solberg Nes L, Segerstrom SC. 2006. Dispositional optimism and coping: a meta-analytic review. *Personal. Soc. Psychol. Rev.* 10:235–51

Stanton AL, Snider PR. 1993. Coping with a breast cancer diagnosis: a prospective study. *Health Psychol.* 12:16–23

Steel P, Schmidt J, Shultz J. 2008. Refining the relationship between personality and subjective well-being. *Psychol. Bull.* 134:138–61

Stone AA, Kennedy-Moore E, Neale JM. 1995. Association between daily coping and end-of-day mood. *Health Psychol.* 14:341–49

Suls J, Martin R. 2005. The daily life of the garden-variety neurotic: reactivity, stressor exposure, mood spillover, and maladaptive coping. *J. Personal.* 73:1485–509

Tellegen A. 1985. Structure of mood and personality and their relevance to assessing anxiety, with an emphasis on self-report. In *Anxiety and the Anxiety Disorders*, ed. AH Tuma, JD Maser, pp. 681–706. Hillsdale, NJ: Erlbaum

Tennen H, Affleck G. 2002. Benefit-finding and benefit-reminding. In *Handbook of Positive Psychology*, ed. CR Snyder, SJ Lopez, pp. 584–97. New York: Oxford Univ. Press

Tennen H, Affleck G, Armeli S, Carney MA. 2000. A daily process approach to coping: linking theory, research, and practice. *Am. Psychol.* 55:626–36

Tomaka J, Blascovich J, Kelsey RM, Leitten CL. 1993. Subjective, physiological, and behavioral effects of threat and challenge appraisal. *J. Personal. Soc. Psychol.* 65:248–60

Tong EM, Bishop GD, Diong SM, Enkelmann HC, Why YP, et al. 2004. Social support and personality among male police officers in Singapore. *Personal. Individ. Differ.* 36:109–23

Trapmann S, Hell B, Hirn JW, Schuler H. 2007. Meta-analysis of the relationship between the Big Five and academic success at university. *J. Psychol.* 215:132–51

Vollrath M. 2001. Personality and stress. *Scand. J. Psychol.* 42:335–47

Vollrath M, Torgersen S. 2000. Personality types and coping. *Personal. Individ. Differ.* 29:367–78

Wright RA. 1996. Brehm's theory of motivation as a model of effort and cardiovascular response. In *The Psychology of Action: Linking Cognition and Motivation to Behavior*, ed. PM Gollwitzer, JA Bargh, pp. 424–53. New York: Guilford

Wrosch C, Miller GE, Scheier MF, Brun de Pontet S. 2007. Giving up on unattainable goals: benefits for health? *Personal. Soc. Psychol. Bull.* 33:251–65

Zuckerman M, Kuhlman DM, Joireman J, Teta P, Kraft M. 1993. A comparison of three structural models for personality: the Big Three, the Big Five, and the Alternative Five. *J. Personal. Soc. Psychol.* 65:757–68

Cumulative Indexes

Contributing Authors, Volumes 51–61

Clark LA, 58:227–57
Clayton NS, 60:87–113
Clifton C Jr, 52:167–96
Cloitre M, 59:301–28
Cochran SD, 58:201–25
Cohen JD, 59:647–72
Cole S, 60:501–24
Collins DW, 53:309–39
Collins LM, 57:505–28
Collins WA 60:631–52
Colombo J, 52:337–67
Conger RD, 58:175–99
Connor-Smith J, 61:679–704
Cook TD, 60:607–29
Coplan RJ, 60:141–71
Cordray DS, 51:345–75
Correa-Chávez M, 54:175–203
Corwyn RF, 53:371–99
Covington MV, 51:171–200
Crabbe JC, 53:435–62
Crano WD, 57:345–74
Crosby FJ, 57:585–611
Cudeck R, 58:615–37
Curhan JR, 51:279–314
Curry SJ, 60:229–55

D

Davidson RJ, 53:545–74
Davis A, 54:579–616
Deci EL, 52:141–66
Delicato LS, 55:181–205
Derrington AM, 55:181–205
Devescovi A, 52:369–96
de Waal FBM, 59:279–300
Dhar R, 52:249–75
Diefendorff JM, 61:543–68
Diehl RL, 55:149–79
Diener E, 54:403–25
Dijksterhuis A, 61:467–90
DiMatteo MR, 52:59–82
DiZio P, 56:115–47
Doctoroff GL, 54:517–45
Domjan M, 56:179–206
Donnellan MB, 58:175–99
Doosje B, 53:161–86
Doss AJ, 56:337–63
Doty RL, 52:423–52
Dovidio JF, 56:365–92
Drolet A, 52:249–75
Dudai Y, 55:51–86
Duffy SA, 52:167–96

Dunn EW, 55:493–518
Dupré KE, 60:671–92

E

Eby LT, 61:599–622
Eccles JS, 53:109–32
Edwards W, 52:581–606
Einarsson E, 61:141–67
Eisenberg N, 51:665–97
Ellemers N, 53:161–86
Emery NJ, 60:87–113
Emmons RA, 54:377–402
Erez M, 58:479–514
Espie CA, 53:215–43
Evans GW, 57:423–51
Evans JSBT, 59:255–78

F

Faigman DL, 56:631–59
Fairchild AJ, 58:593–614
Fanselow MS, 56:207–34
Fasolo B, 52:581–606
Fazio RH, 54:297–327
Federico CM, 60:307–37
Feng AS, 51:699–725
Fernández-Dols J-M, 54:329–49
Fingerhut AW, 58:405–24
Finniss DG, 59:565–90
Folkman S, 55:745–74
Fouad NA, 58:543–64
Fox NA, 56:235–62
French DC, 59:591–616
Friston KJ, 56:57–87
Fritz MS, 58:593–614
Fuligni A, 54:461–90
Funder DC, 52:197–221
Furman W, 60:631–52

G

Garb HN, 53:519–43
Geisler WS, 59:167–92
Gelfand MJ, 58:479–514
Gelman SA, 60:115–40
Gentner D, 52:223–47
Gerhart B, 56:571–600
Gernsbacher MA, 54:91–114
Gervain J, 61:191–218
Ghera MA, 56:235–62
Gilmore RO, 52:453–70
Glaser R, 53:83–107

Glimcher PW, 56:25–56
Goethals GR, 56:545–70
Goldsmith M, 51:481–537
Goldstein NJ, 55:591–621
Gonzalez CM, 59:329–60
Goodman GS, 61:325–51
Gordis EB, 51:445–79
Gorman-Smith D, 57:557–83
Gottesman II, 56:263–86
Gould E, 61:111–40
Graber D, 55:545–71
Graham JW, 60:549–76
Green DP, 60:339–67
Greenfield PM, 54:461–90
Gross JJ, 58:373–403
Guarnaccia PJ, 51:571–98
Gunia BC, 61:491–515
Gunnar M, 58:145–73

H

Hall RJ, 61:543–68
Hanson DR, 56:263–86
Hardt O, 61:141–67
Harring JR, 58:615–37
Hastie R, 52:653–83
Hauser M, 61:303–24
Hawkins EH, 60:197–227
Hawley KM, 56:337–63
Hayman-Abello BA, 53:309–39
Hayman-Abello SE, 53:309–39
Healey MP, 59:387–417
Heil SH, 55:431–61
Heine SJ, 60:369–94
Hen R, 57:117–37
Henderson HA, 56:235–62
Hennessey BA, 61:569–98
Henry D, 57:557–83
Herman CP, 53:187–213
Hewstone M, 53:575–604
Higgins ET, 59:361–85
Higgins ST, 55:431–61
Hochman KM, 55:401–30
Hodgkinson GP, 59:387–417
Hollenbeck JR, 56:517–43
Hollins M, 61:243–71
Hollon SD, 57:285–315
Holsboer F, 61:81–109
Holt LL, 55:149–79
Hough LM, 51:631–64
Huston AC, 61:411–37
Hwang E, 61:169–90

Olson EA, 54:277–95
Olson GM, 54:491–516
Olson JS, 54:491–516
Olson MA, 54:297–327
Orehek E, 58:291–316
Oswald FL, 51:631–64
Ozer DJ, 57:401–21

P

Paloutzian RF, 54:377–402
Paluck EL 60:339–67
Pansky A, 51:481–537
Paradise R, 54:175–203
Park DC, 60:173–96
Parke RD, 55:365–99
Parks L, 56:571–600
Pashler H, 52:629–51
Pearce JM, 52:111–39
Peissig JJ, 58:75–96
Penn DC, 58:97–118
Pennebaker JW, 54:547–77
Penner LA, 56:365–92
Pennington BF, 60:283–306
Peplau LA, 58:405–24
Peretz I, 56:89–114
Phelps EA, 57:27–53
Phillips LA, 59:477–505
Piliavin JA, 56:365–92
Pinder CC, 56:485–516
Pittman TS, 59:361–85
Pizzagalli D, 53:545–74
Plomin R, 54:205–28
Polivy J, 53:187–213
Posner MI, 58:1–23
Poulos AM, 56:207–34
Povinelli DJ, 58:97–118
Price DD, 59:565–90
Prislin R, 57:345–74
Proctor RW, 61:623–51
Putnam K, 53:545–74

Q

Quas JA, 61:325–51
Quevedo K, 58:145–73

R

Rafaeli E, 54:579–616
Ratnam R, 51:699–725
Raudenbush SW, 52:501–25

Rausch JR, 59:537–63
Recanzone GH, 59:119–42
Rensink RA, 53:245–77
Reuter-Lorenz P, 60:173–96
Revenson TA, 58:565–92
Rhodes G, 57:199–226
Rick S, 59:647–72
Roberts BW, 56:453–84
Roberts RD, 59:507–36
Robinson TE, 54:25–53
Robles TF, 53:83–107
Roediger HL III, 59:225–54
Rogoff B, 54:175–203
Rolls ET, 51:599–630
Rosenbaum DA, 52:453–70
Rosenthal R, 52:59–82
Rothbart MK, 58:1–23
Rourke BP, 53:309–39
Rubin KH, 60:141–71
Rubin M, 53:575–604
Ruble DN, 61:353–81
Runco MA, 55:657–87
Rusbult CE, 54:351–75
Russell JA, 54:329–49
Ruthruff E, 52:629–51
Rutter M, 53:463–90
Ryan RM, 52:141–66
Rynes SL, 56:571–600

S

Saab PG, 52:555–80
Sackett PR, 59:419–50
Salas E, 52:471–99
Salmon DP, 60:257–82
Sankis LM, 51:377–404
Sargis EG, 57:529–55
Saribay SA, 59:329–60
Saxe R, 55:87–124
Schall JD, 55:23–50
Schaller M, 55:689–714
Schaufeli WB, 52:397–422
Schippers MC, 58:515–41
Schmidt AC, 61:543–68
Schneiderman N, 52:555–80
Schroeder DA, 56:365–92
Schultz W, 57:87–115
Schwartz MW, 51:255–77
Seeley RJ, 51:255–77
Serbin LA, 55:333–63
Seyfarth RM, 54:145–73
Shadish WR, 60:607–29

Shafir E, 53:491–517
Shanks DR, 61:273–301
Shaywitz BA, 59:451–75
Shaywitz SE, 59:451–75
Sherry DF, 57:167–97
Shevell SK, 59:143–66
Shiffrar M, 58:47–73
Shiner RL, 56:453–84
Shinn M, 54:427–59
Shors TJ, 57:55–85
Siegel JM, 55:125–48
Silberg J, 53:463–90
Simon AF, 51:149–69
Simonson I, 52:249–75
Simonton DK, 54:617–40
Sincharoen S, 57:585–611
Skinner EA, 58:119–44
Skitka LJ, 57:529–55
Smetana JG, 57:255–84
Snyder DK, 57:317–44
Sobel N, 61:219–41
Solomon KO, 51:121–47
Spears R, 53:161–86
Sporer AK, 60:229–55
Staddon JER, 54:115–44
Stanton AL, 58:565–92
Steel GD, 51:227–53
Steinberg L, 52:83–110
Stewart AJ, 55:519–44
Stewart MO, 57:285–315
Stickgold R, 57:139–66
Strunk D, 57:285–315
Stuewig J, 58:345–72
Stuss DT, 53:401–33
Sue S, 60:525–48
Suedfeld P, 51:227–53
Suh EM, 53:133–60
Sutter ML, 59:119–42

T

Tangney JP, 58:345–72
Tarr MJ, 58:75–96
Tennen H, 58:565–92
Thau S, 60:717–41
Thompson LL, 61:491–515
Thompson RF, 56:1–23
Tindale RS, 55:623–55
Tolan P, 57:557–83
Toohey SM, 54:427–59
Tourangeau R, 55:775–801
Triandis HC, 53:133–60

Trickett EJ, 60:395–419
Tulving E, 53:1–25
Tyler TR, 57:375–400

U

Uleman JS, 59:329–60

V

Valley KL, 51:279–314
van Knippenberg D, 58:515–41
Van Lange PAM, 54:351–75
Velleman PF, 52:305–35
Volkmar F, 56:315–36
Vu KL, 61:623–51

W

Wainer H, 52:305–35
Walker BM, 58:453–77
Walker E, 55:401–30

Walker MP, 57:139–66
Walumbwa FO, 60:421–49
Wang J, 61:491–515
Wang S, 61:49–79
Warriner EM, 53:309–39
Watkins LR, 51:29–57
Weber EU, 60:53–85
Weber TJ, 60:421–49
Wegner DM, 51:59–91
Weinman J, 59:477–505
Weiss H, 53:279–307
Weisz JR, 56:337–63
Wells GL, 54:277–95
Welsh DP, 60:631–52
Wenzlaff RM, 51:59–91
Whisman MA, 57:317–44
Widiger TA, 51:377–404
Wigfield A, 53:109–32
Williams KD, 58:425–52
Willis H, 53:575–604
Wilson TD, 55:493–518
Wingate LR, 56:287–314

Winne PH, 61:653–78
Winter DA, 58:453–77
Wixted JT, 55:235–69
Wood J, 61:303–24
Wood JM, 53:519–43
Wood W, 51:539–70
Woods SC, 51:255–77
Wulfeck B, 52:369–96

Y

Yeshurun Y, 61:219–41
Yuille A, 55:271–304

Z

Zane N, 60:525–48
Zatorre RJ, 56:89–114
Zhang T, 61:439–66
Zimmer-Gembeck MJ,
    58:119–44

Chapter Titles, Volumes 51–61

Health Psychology

Health Psychology: Psychosocial and
  Biobehavioral Aspects of Chronic
  Disease Management   N Schneiderman,   52:555–80
                                                         MH Antoni,
                                                         PG Saab,
                                                         G Ironson

Adjustment to Chronic Diseases and Terminal Illness

Health Psychology: Psychological Adjustment
  to Chronic Disease   AL Stanton,   58:565–92
                                                         TA Revenson,
                                                         H Tennen

Health Promotion and Disease Prevention

The Psychological Aspects of Natural
  Language Use: Our Words, Our Selves   JW Pennebaker,   54:547–77
                                                         MR Mehl,
                                                         KG Niederhoffer

Health Psychology: The Search for Pathways
  Between Behavior and Health   H Leventhal,   59:477–505
                                                         J Weinman,
                                                         EA Leventhal,
                                                         LA Phillips

Health and Social Systems

The Case for Cultural Competency in
  Psychotherapeutic Interventions   S Sue, N Zane,   60:525–48
                                                         GC Nagayama Hall,
                                                         LK Berger

Personality and Coping Styles

Coping: Pitfalls and Promise   S Folkman,   55:745–74
                                                         JT Moskowitz
Personality and Coping   CS Carver,   61:679–704
                                                         J Connor–Smith

Psychobiological Factors

Emotions, Morbidity, and Mortality:
  New Perspectives from
  Psychoneuroimmunology   JK Kiecolt-Glaser,   53:83–107
                                                         L McGuire,
                                                         TF Robles,
                                                         R Glaser

*Psychobiological Mechanisms (Psychophysiology,
  Psychoimmunology and Hormones, Emotion, Stress)*

Health Psychology: Developing Biologically
  Plausible Models Linking the Social World
  and Physical Health   GE Miller, E Chen,   60:501–24
                                                         S Cole

Work Group Diversity	D van Knippenberg, MC Schippers	58:515–41

Leadership

Presidential Leadership	GR Goethals	56:545–70
Leadership: Current Theories, Research, and Future Directions	BJ Avolio, FO Walumbwa, TJ Weber	60:421–49

Work Attitudes (Job Satisfaction, Commitment, Identification)

The Intersection of Work and Family Life: The Role of Affect	LT Eby, CP Maher, MM Butts	61:599–622

Work Motivation

Work Motivation Theory and Research at the Dawn of the Twenty-First Century	GP Latham, CC Pinder	56:485–516
Self-Regulation at Work	RG Lord, JM Diefendorff, AC Schmidt, RJ Hall	61:543–68

Perception

Personality

Scientific and Social Significance of Assessing Individual Differences: "Sinking Shafts at a Few Critical Points"	D Lubinski	51:405–44
The Psychology of Religion	RA Emmons, RF Paloutzian	54:377–402

Cultural Influences

Consumer Research: In Search of Identity	I Simonson, Z Carmon, R Dhar, A Drolet, SM Nowlis	52:249–75
Cultural Influences on Personality	HC Triandis, EM Suh	53:133–60
Personality: The Universal and the Culturally Specific	SJ Heine, EE Buchtel	60:369–94

Individual Differences and Assessment

Personality and the Prediction of Consequential Outcomes	DJ Ozer, V Benet-Martínez	57:401–21

Sensory Processes

Olfaction	RL Doty	52:423–52

Sleep

See Biological Psychology

Social Psychology

Altruism and Aggression

Human Aggression	CA Anderson, BJ Bushman	53:27–51
Prosocial Behavior: Multilevel Perspectives	LA Penner, JF Dovidio, JA Piliavin, DA Schroeder	56:365–92

Attention, Control, and Automaticity

Eyewitness Identification	GL Wells, EA Olson	54:277–95
Social Cognitive Neuroscience: A Review of Core Processes	MD Lieberman	58:259–89

Attitude Change and Persuasion

Attitude Change: Persuasion and Social Influence	W Wood	51:539–70
Attitudes and Persuasion	WD Crano, R Prislin	57:345–74

Attitude Structure

Nature and Operation of Attitudes	I Ajzen	52:27–58
Implicit Measures in Social Cognition Research: Their Meaning and Use	RH Fazio, MA Olson	54:297–327
Political Ideology: Its Structure, Functions, and Elective Affinities	JT Jost, CM Federico, JL Napier	60:307–37

Attraction and Close Relationships

Interdependence, Interaction, and Relationships	CE Rusbult, PAM Van Lange	54:351–75
The Close Relationships of Lesbian and Gay Men	LA Peplau, AW Fingerhut	58:405–24

Bargaining, Negotiation, Conflict, Social Justice

Negotiation	MH Bazerman, JR Curhan, DA Moore, KL Valley	51:279–314

ANNUAL REVIEWS
A Nonprofit Scientific Publisher

Annual Reviews – Your Starting Point for Research Online
http://arjournals.annualreviews.org

- Over 1280 Annual Reviews volumes—more than 28,800 critical, authoritative review articles in 37 disciplines spanning the Biomedical, Life, Physical, and Social sciences—available online, including all Annual Reviews back volumes, dating to 1932

- Personal subscriptions include permanent online data rights to the volume regardless of future subscription status. Online data rights include access to full-text articles, PDFs, Reviews in Advance (as much as 6 months ahead of print publication), bibliographies, and other supplementary material

- All articles are fully supplemented, searchable, and downloadable—see http://psych.annualreviews.org

- Access links to the reviewed references (when available online)

- Site features include customized alerting services, citation tracking, and saved searches

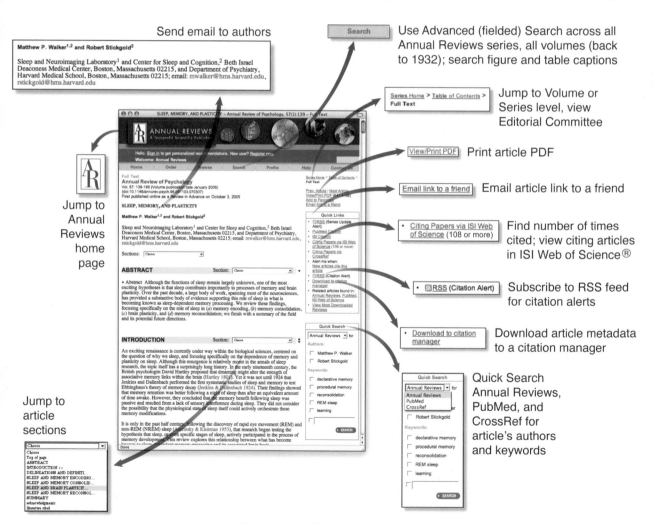

Send email to authors

Use Advanced (fielded) Search across all Annual Reviews series, all volumes (back to 1932); search figure and table captions

Jump to Volume or Series level, view Editorial Committee

Print article PDF

Email article link to a friend

Find number of times cited; view citing articles in ISI Web of Science®

Subscribe to RSS feed for citation alerts

Download article metadata to a citation manager

Quick Search Annual Reviews, PubMed, and CrossRef for article's authors and keywords

Jump to Annual Reviews home page

Jump to article sections